NEW SOCIETY

NEW SOCIETY

Fifth Edition

Robert J. Brym
University of Toronto

NELSON / EDUCATION

NELSON / E D U C A T I O N

New Society, Fifth Edition
by Robert J. Brym

Associate Vice President, Editorial Director:
Evelyn Veitch

Editor-in-Chief, Higher Education:
Anne Williams

Executive Editor:
Cara Yarzab

Director of Marketing:
Kelly Smyth

Marketing Manager:
Heather Leach

Senior Developmental Editor:
Lesley Mann

Photo Researcher:
Lisa Brant

Permissions Coordinator:
Lisa Brant

Content Production Manager:
Jamie Larson

Production Service:
Graphic World Inc.

Copy Editor:
Dawn Hunter

Proofreader:
Jody McBride

Indexer:
Gloria Tierney

Manufacturing Coordinator:
Loretta Lee

Design Director:
Ken Phipps

Interior Design:
Renata Chubb/Mighty Design Inc.

Interior Design Modifications:
Jack Steiner

Cover Design:
Johanna Liburd

Cover Image:
©Marshall Ikonography/Alamy

Compositor:
Graphic World Inc.

Printer:
Courier

Library and Archives Canada Cataloguing in Publication Data

Brym, Robert J., 1951–
New society / Robert J. Brym. — 5th ed.

Includes bibliographical references and indexes.
ISBN-13: 978-0-17-610282-1
ISBN-10: 0-17-610282-5

1. Sociology—Textbooks. I. Title.

HM586.B79 2007   301
C2006-904958-0

In memory of Jim Curtis, 1942–2005

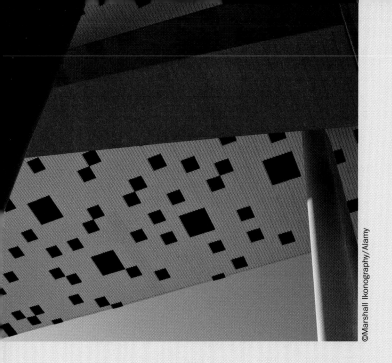
©Marshall Ikonography/Alamy

PREFACE

The job of figuring out what to do with our lives and how to act in the world is more difficult than ever. Sociology contributes to the task of clarification by analyzing the pressing social issues of the day, showing how those issues affect all of us, and setting out options for dealing with them. Moreover, as you will learn in the following pages, sociology views social issues from a unique disciplinary perspective. All in all, it is a controversial and exciting business. Social problems are typically complex. The various options for action often involve different benefits and disadvantages for various groups. Sociologists usually see things differently from other social and natural scientists. Not surprisingly, therefore, sociology, like any vibrant academic discipline, involves a lot of heated debate.

Unfortunately, most introductory sociology textbooks don't give much of a feel for the excitement of the discipline. They usually resemble encyclopedias full of definitions and presumably undeniable facts. They make sociological knowledge resemble the tablets some people say were brought down by Moses from Mount Sinai: abstract principles carved in stone, eternal truths that most people agree with but that tell us little about the way life is actually lived.

In preparing this book, I tried to overcome this deficiency in two ways. First, when I recruited authors to write chapters, I asked them to focus on social issues that are likely to be of real, everyday concern to Canadian undergraduates. Second, I asked the authors to highlight the controversies in the field, not the tired clichés. There is no sense in keeping secret what any good scientist knows: advances in knowledge usually result from intellectual conflict, not consensus.

WHAT'S NEW IN THE FIFTH EDITION

In preparing the fifth edition of *New Society*, I benefited from the recommendations that emerged from Nelson's excellent user survey. Major changes include the following:

- The fifth edition of *New Society* has been thoroughly updated to reflect the results of the latest census of Canada and the most recent sociological research findings in the various fields covered in the text.
- Three chapters have been replaced outright to better reflect the interests of users and the state of the discipline:
  - Chapter 12, Education
  - Chapter 17, Health and Aging
  - Chapter 19, Globalization
- A new online chapter has been added on Networks, Groups, Bureaucracies, and Societies (see www.newsociety5e.nelson.com).
- Four chapters have undergone major revisions:
  - Chapter 7, Gender Inequality: Economic and Political Aspects
  - Chapter 9, Inequality Among Nations: Perspectives on Development
  - Chapter 13, Religion
  - Chapter 15, Population and Urbanization
- The design has been revised to increase visual appeal, with new part- and chapter-opening design and the inclusion of more photos in every chapter.
- We welcome new authors Neena L. Chappell, Scott Davies, Josh Greenberg, Josée Johnston, John Lie, Margaret J. Penning, and Steven Rytina.
- All of the ancillaries (see p. ix) have been thoroughly revised.

ORGANIZATION OF THE TEXT

Chapter 1 sets the tone for the rest of the book and stands alone in Part 1. Instead of sermonizing on the arid question "What is sociology?" as most other textbooks do, I ask "Why sociology?"—that is, why does an undergraduate in this particular time and place need to know what sociology has to offer? My chief aim in Chapter 1 (Introducing Sociology) is to show how sociological thinking can clarify and perhaps help resolve the real-life social issues that confront all of us here and now.

The remainder of the book is divided into five parts. Part 2 could be subtitled "Becoming Human." In Chapter 2 (Culture), I make a case for the view that ours is an increasingly fragmented and globalized postmodern culture that increases our freedom to fashion identities that suit our individual tastes. I also show that, paradoxically, our increased cultural freedom develops within definite limits beyond which it is more and more difficult to move. In Chapter 3 (Socialization), William Shaffir and Michael Rosenberg thoroughly discuss the interactive mechanisms through which we learn beliefs, symbols, values, and self-identities throughout the life cycle and in various institutions. Rhonda L. Lenton then devotes Chapter 4 (Gender and Sexuality) to an in-depth analysis of what might seem to be the most intimate and biologically determined aspects of our identity—our gender and sexuality—and demonstrates that in fact they have deep roots in culture and society. In Chapter 5 (The Mass Media), Graham Knight and Josh Greenberg analyze the impact of one of the most pervasive and influential social institutions today. In sum, the analyses of Part 2 will give the reader a solid appreciation of how we become part of society and how society becomes part of us through the transmission of culture from generation to generation.

Part 3 is about how people become and remain unequal. Harvey Krahn shows in Chapter 6 (Social Stratification) that despite recent assertions of the demise of social classes, stratification persists and continues to structure our life-chances in profound ways. In Chapter 7 (Gender Inequality: Economic and Political Aspects), Monica Boyd convincingly demonstrates that gender is an equally important basis of social inequality, both in the economic and the political sphere. Vic Satzewich devotes Chapter 8 (Race and Ethnic Relations) to highlighting the deficiencies of biological and purely cultural approaches to understanding the bases of ethnic and racial inequality. Finally, in Chapter 9 (Inequality Among Nations: Perspectives on Development), Gordon Laxer incisively criticizes modernization and other theories of economic underdevelopment and global inequality, offering a compelling argument for the analytical benefits of a modified dependency approach to the problem. The reader will complete Part 3 with a firm understanding that although we are all human, we are highly differentiated and differentially rewarded, depending on our social location.

Part 4 shifts the reader's attention to some of society's fundamental institutions. A virtue of Bonnie Fox's analysis in Chapter 10 (Families) is that she usefully draws on a broad historical and anthropological literature to supplement her sociological overview, providing a clear sense of how families have developed and where they may be headed. Sandy Welsh devotes Chapter 11 (Work and Occupations) to tracing the development and future shape of work. In Chapter 12 (Education), Scott Davies dissects our educational system, demonstrating that, paradoxically, it is as much a cause of the persistence of inequality as it is an avenue for upward mobility. And in Chapter 13 (Religion), Reginald W. Bibby assesses the social origins, consequences, and future of religion, relying heavily on his own fundamentally important survey research to argue his case.

Change and conflict are the subjects of Part 5. Here the reader is introduced to the main forces of turbulence in our society. In Chapter 14 (Deviance and Crime), Rosemary Gartner and Myrna Dawson elegantly analyze one form of social conflict: deviant and criminal behaviour. They undermine several common misconceptions in the process. John Hannigan's analysis in Chapter 15 (Population and Urbanization) is a novel and revealing look at how human populations have developed in cities from preindustrial to postmodern times. He then devotes Chapter 16 (Sociology and the Environment) to one of the most pressing issues of the day—the environment—and analyzes such problems as the scope and social roots of the environmental movement and the process by which environmental issues are socially constructed. In Chapter 17 (Health and Aging), Neena L. Chappell and Margaret J. Penning discuss the aging of the Canadian population and attendant health issues. In Chapter 18 (Politics and Social Movements), I survey the evolution of politics and social movements, showing how various forms of conflict emerge, change our lives, and become institutionalized. Finally, Globalization is the title of Chapter 19, by Josée Johnston. She shows that culturally, politically, and economically, the world is becoming a single place and its inhabitants are developing a global consciousness. This does not imply that we are becoming one big happy family. To the contrary, conflict has persisted and even intensified in the early twenty-first century.

In Part 6, Chapter 20 (Research Methods) masterfully and concisely outlines how sociologists do their work. Neil Guppy's clarity, research experience, and balanced approach add much-needed lustre to a subject that first-year students often find dull. Guppy leaves the reader with the firm sense that, for all the intellectual liveliness and controversy displayed in this book, sociology can be and is disciplined by the judicious use of logic and evidence.

As a bonus feature, John Lie, Steven Rytina, and I prepared Online Chapter 21 (Networks, Groups, Bureaucracies, and Societies) that draws the connection between microlevel interactions and macrolevel social forces and institutions. We recommend that the chapter be assigned after Chapter 3 (Socialization). This chapter may be accessed at www.newsociety5e.nelson.com.

ANCILLARIES FOR INSTRUCTORS

INSTRUCTOR'S RESOURCE CD

(ISBN 0-17-610489-5) All testing and presentation software is now available in one place: the *New Society Instructor's Resource CD*. This resource contains the following invaluable materials:

- **Instructor's Manual:** This chapter-by-chapter outline helps instructors make the most of *New Society*. It summarizes each chapter in the form of lecture notes, describes how best to integrate each chapter with all of the ancillary products, and provides suggestions on how to create the most effective lectures possible.
- **Test Bank:** The test bank contains approximately 1000 multiple-choice and true-or-false questions. It is offered in Rich Text Format and can be used with Word, WordPerfect, and most other word-processing systems.
- **Computerized Test Bank in ExamView®:** Create, deliver, and customize tests (both print and online) in minutes with this easy-to-use assessment and tutorial system. *ExamView* offers both a *Quick Test Wizard* and an *Online Test Wizard* that guide you step-by-step through the process of creating tests. The test appears on screen exactly as it will print or display online. Using *ExamView's* complete word processing capabilities, you can enter an unlimited number of new questions or edit existing questions. ExamView is offered in both PC and Mac platforms.

- **PowerPoint® Slides:** More than 400 full-colour slides offer a detailed summary of each chapter of the book along with supplementary graphs, tables, and diagrams to illustrate key points. The slides can be easily output from a computer in several formats. The PowerPoint® Viewer that is packaged with the slides enables them to be (1) viewed on a computer, or (2) projected from a computer to a viewing screen in the classroom. If you have the entire Microsoft PowerPoint® package, the slides can also be (3) printed out as full-colour transparencies for use with an overhead projector, or (4) printed out as black-and-white handouts for students.
- **Instructor's Guide for Think Outside the Book: Nelson Videos for Introductory Sociology:** This guide includes a synopsis of each video, questions for critical analysis, and references to Nelson's innovative and imaginative introductory sociology titles.

THINK OUTSIDE THE BOOK: NELSON VIDEOS FOR SOCIOLOGY

Be part of something exciting! Nelson is proud to present our Think Outside the Book: Nelson Videos for Introductory Sociology. This five-volume series, which includes video segments that are each 5 to 27 minutes long, was created to stimulate discussion in your classroom. Many selections are excerpted from national and international award-winning films.

Videos were selected by leading sociologist Robert Brym. His keen eye for finding relevant, powerful, and engaging selections allows students to "think outside the book" and brings sociology concepts to life. A video guide for instructors (available on the Instructor's Resource CD) will include a synopsis of each video, questions for critical analysis, and references to Nelson's innovative and imaginative introductory sociology titles. Visit www.thinkoutsidethebook.com or ask your Thomson Nelson representative for more details.

JOININ™ ON TURNINGPOINT®

Transform your lecture into an interactive student experience with JoinIn. Combined with your choice of keypad systems, JoinIn turns your Microsoft® PowerPoint® application into audience response software. With a click on a handheld device, students can respond to multiple-choice questions, short polls, interactive exercises, and peer-review questions. You can also take attendance, check student comprehension of concepts, collect student demographics to better assess student needs, and even administer quizzes. In addition, there are interactive text-specific slide sets that you can modify and merge with any of your own PowerPoint lecture slides. This tool is available to qualified adopters at http://turningpoint.thomsonlearningconnections.com.

NEW SOCIETY ON THE WEB

http://www.newsociety5e.nelson.com/instructor

Downloadable versions of the Instructor's Manual, PowerPoint® presentations, and Instructor's Guide for Think Outside the Book: Nelson Videos for Introductory Sociology, plus Robert J. Brym's online lectures, can be accessed from the password-protected Instructor's page of the companion website.

INFOTRAC®COLLEGE EDITION

Ignite discussions or augment your lectures with the latest developments in sociology and societal change. Create your own course reader by selecting articles or by using the search keywords provided at the end of each chapter. InfoTrac College Edition (available as a free option with this text) gives you and your students four months of free access to an easy-to-use online database of reliable, full-length articles (not abstracts) from hundreds of top academic journals and popular sources. Among the journals available 24 hours a day, 7 days a week are the *Canadian Review of Sociology and Anthropology*, the *Canadian Journal of Sociology*, *Canadian Ethnic Studies*, *Public Policy*, the *American Journal of Sociology*, *Social Forces*, *Social Research*, and *Sociology*. Contact your Thomson Nelson representative for more information. InfoTrac College Edition is available only to North American college and university students. Journals are subject to change.

THOMSONNOW™

http://hed.nelson.com

An Instructor Gradebook is available to track and monitor student progress with ThomsonNOW, the online diagnostic tool customized to each student's needs. See the description below under "Ancillaries for Students."

ANCILLARIES FOR STUDENTS

STUDENT LEARNING GUIDE

(ISBN 0-17-610503-4). This concise guide helps students to check their progress with sample quizzes. Critical-thinking questions encourage them to use their imaginations to develop a richer sociological perspective.

THOMSONNOW™

http://hed.nelson.com

This online diagnostic tool identifies each student's unique needs with a Pretest that generates a personalized Study Plan for each chapter, helping students focus on concepts they have the most difficulty mastering. Students then take a Posttest to measure their under-standing of the material. An Instructor Gradebook is available to track and monitor student progress.

NEW SOCIETY ON THE WEB

http://www.newsociety5e.nelson.com

The *New Society* website contains much more than the standard features you have come to expect from Thomson Nelson Web ancillaries. In addition to chapter-by-chapter links to secondary sources, online quizzes, and other self-testing material, it boasts exciting original features, including interactive exercises, online research projects, video exercises, and a focus on Canada in a global context. Also, visit the online lecture hall to hear lectures delivered in audio by a range of prominent sociologists, including Robert Brym. These features, and others, make the *New Society* website unique and useful to Canadian instructors and students. It allows students to do sociology and better understand their place in the world.

INFOTRAC COLLEGE EDITION

http://www.infotrac-college.com

This website offers access to more than 20 million articles from nearly 6000 sources—a valuable resource when you do online research. See the description on p. x for more details.

ACKNOWLEDGMENTS

The fifth edition of *New Society* still bears the imprint of Heather McWhinney, Dan Brooks, Megan Mueller, Semareh Al-Hillal, Brad Lambertus, and Camille Isaacs. They shepherded the book through its first editions, helping to make *New Society* distinctive and highly successful.

For the past year I was privileged to work closely with publishing professionals of the highest calibre, all of whom contributed heavily to the successful completion of the fourth edition. In particular, Cara Yarzab worked diligently and with good humour on this complex project, always mindful of the need to balance the diverse needs of instructors, students, and authors. Lesley Mann's and Sandra de Ruiter's energetic and meticulous approach to the project was evident from beginning to end. Visually and linguistically, this book owes much to their exemplary skills as developmental editors. I would also like to thank Jamie Larson (content production manager), Kelly Smyth (marketing manager), Dawn Hunter (copy editor), Jody McBride (proofreader), and Lisa Brant (permissions and photo editor).

New Society could not have become what it is without the authors of each chapter. They are among the very best sociologists in Canada. I believe that, although concentrating on the exposition of their own subfields, they have conveyed to the novice a real sense of the excitement and promise of sociology. I am deeply indebted to them, as tens of thousands of introductory sociology students and their instructors inevitably have been and will be.

Finally, I would like to thank the following reviewers, whose insightful comments helped shape this edition:

Jan Clarke, Algoma University College
Gordon Drever, Northern Lakes College

Dawn Farough, Thompson Rivers University
Jaime Llambias-Wolff, York University
Chris MacKenzie, University of British Columbia
Roksana Nazneen, Concordia University
William Shaffir, McMaster University
Karen Stanbridge, Memorial University
Michelle Webber, Brock University

Thanks also to other reviewers who chose not to be acknowledged.

R.J.B.
Toronto

CONTRIBUTORS

Reginald W. Bibby, University of Lethbridge

Monica Boyd, University of Toronto

Robert J. Brym, University of Toronto

Neena L. Chappell, University of Victoria

Scott Davies, McMaster University

Myrna Dawson, University of Guelph

Bonnie Fox, University of Toronto

Rosemary Gartner, University of Toronto

Josh Greenberg, Carleton University

Neil Guppy, University of British Columbia

John Hannigan, University of Toronto

Josée Johnston, University of Toronto

Graham Knight, McMaster University

Harvey Krahn, University of Alberta

Gordon Laxer, University of Alberta

Rhonda L. Lenton, York University

John Lie, University of California at Berkeley

Margaret J. Penning, University of Victoria

Michael Rosenberg, Dawson College

Steven Rytina, McGill University

Vic Satzewich, McMaster University

William Shaffir, McMaster University

Sandy Welsh, University of Toronto

BRIEF CONTENTS

*Available online only at www.newsociety5e.nelson.com.

CONTENTS

PART THREE INEQUALITY

PART FOUR INSTITUTIONS

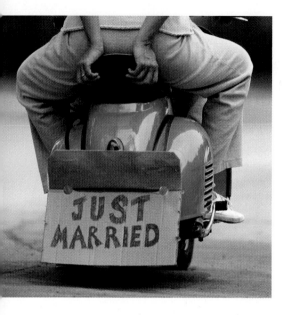

PART FIVE CHANGE AND CONFLICT

PART SIX METHODS

*Available online only at www.newsociety5e.nelson.com.

PART ONE

Introduction

CHAPTER ONE

Introducing Sociology

In this chapter you will learn that

- The causes of human behaviour lie partly in the patterns of social relations that surround and penetrate people.

- Sociologists examine the connection between personal troubles and social relations.

- Sociological research is often motivated by the desire to improve the social world. At the same time, sociologists adopt scientific methods to test their ideas.

- Sociology originated at the time of the Industrial Revolution. The founders of sociology diagnosed the massive social transformations of their day. They also suggested ways of overcoming the social problems created by the Industrial Revolution.

- Today's postindustrial revolution similarly challenges us. The chief value of sociology is that it can help clarify the scope, direction, and significance of social change. Sociology can also suggest ways of managing change.

SOURCE: Shutterstock.

Robert J. Brym
UNIVERSITY OF TORONTO

INTRODUCTION

WHY I DECIDED *NOT* TO STUDY SOCIOLOGY

When I started university at the age of 18, I was bewildered by the wide variety of courses I could choose from. Having now taught sociology for 30 years, and having met a few thousand undergraduates, I am quite sure most students today feel as I did then.

One source of confusion for me was uncertainty about why I was in university in the first place. Like you, I knew higher education could improve my chance of finding good work. But, like most students, I also had a sense that higher education is supposed to provide something more than just the training necessary to embark on a career that is interesting and pays well. Several high school teachers and guidance counsellors had told me that university was also supposed to "broaden my horizons" and teach me to "think critically." I wasn't entirely sure what they meant, but they made it sound interesting enough to make me want to know more. Thus, I decided in my first year to take mainly "practical" courses that might prepare me for a law degree (economics, political science, and psychology). I also enrolled in a couple of other courses to indulge my "intellectual" side (philosophy, drama).

One thing I knew for sure: I didn't want to study sociology. Sociology, I came to believe, was thin soup with uncertain ingredients. When I asked a second-year student what sociology is, he told me it deals mainly with why people are unequal—why some are rich and others poor, some powerful and others weak.

Life is finite, and if we want to make the most of it, we must figure out how best to live. Sociology offers a useful perspective for understanding our current predicament and seeing possible ways of dealing with it.

SOURCE: M.C. Escher's *Relativity* © 2006 The M.C. Escher Company-Holland. All rights reserved. www.mcescher.com.

Coming as I did from a poor immigrant family in the Maritimes, an economically depressed region, it appeared that sociology could teach me something about my own life. But it also seemed a lot like what I imagined economics and political science to be about. What, then, was unique about sociology? My growing sense that sociology had nothing special to offer was confirmed when another second-year student told me that sociologists try to describe the ideal society and figure out how to make the world a better place. That description appealed to my youthful sense of the world's injustice. However, it also sounded a lot like philosophy. A third-year student explained that sociology analyzes how and why people assume different roles in their lives. She made sociology appear similar to drama. Finally, one student reported that in her sociology class she was learning why people commit suicide, homicide, and other deviant acts. That seemed like abnormal psychology to me. I concluded that sociology had no distinct flavour all its own. Accordingly, I decided to forgo it for tastier courses.

A CHANGE OF MIND

Despite the opinion I'd formed, I found myself taking no fewer than four sociology courses a year after starting university. That revolution in my life was due, in part, to the pull of an extraordinary professor I happened to meet just before I began my second year. He set me thinking in an altogether new way about what I could and should do with my life. He exploded some of my deepest beliefs. He started me thinking sociologically.

Specifically, he first put Yorick's dilemma to me. Yorick is a character—sort of—in *Hamlet*. Toward the end of the play, Hamlet finds two gravediggers at work. They unearth the remains of the former court jester, Yorick, who used to amuse Hamlet and carry him around on his back when Hamlet was a child. Holding high his old friend's skull, Hamlet reflects on what we must all come to. Even the remains of Alexander the Great, he says, turn to dust.

This incident implies Yorick's dilemma and, indeed, the dilemma of all thinking people. Life is finite. If we want to make the most of it, we must figure out how best to live. That is no easy task. It requires study, reflection, and the selection of values and goals. Ideally, higher education is supposed to supply students with just that opportunity. Finally, I was beginning to understand what I could expect from university apart from job training.

The professor I met also convinced me that sociology in particular could open up a new and superior way of comprehending my world. Specifically, he said, it could clarify my place in society, how I might best manoeuvre through it, and, perhaps, even how I might contribute to improving it, however modestly. Before beginning my study of sociology, I had always taken for granted that things happen in the world—and to me—because physical and emotional forces cause them. Famine, I thought, is caused by drought, war by territorial greed, economic success by hard work, marriage by love, suicide by bottomless depression, rape by depraved lust. But now, this professor repeatedly threw evidence in my face that contradicted my easy formulas. If drought causes famine, why have so many famines occurred in perfectly normal weather conditions or involved some groups hoarding or destroying food so others would starve? If hard work causes prosperity, why are so many hard workers poor? If love causes marriage, why are so many families sites of violence against women and children? And so the questions multiplied.

As if it were not enough that the professor's sociological evidence upset many of my assumptions about the way the world worked, he also challenged me to understand sociology's unique way of explaining social life. He defined **sociology** as the systematic study of human behaviour in social context. He explained that *social* causes are distinct from physical and emotional causes. Understanding social causes can help clarify otherwise inexplicable features of famine, marriage, and so forth. In public school, my teachers had taught me that people are free to do what they want with their lives. However, my new professor taught me that the organization of the social world opens some opportunities and closes others, thus constraining our freedom and helping to make us what we are. By examining the operation of these powerful social forces, he said, sociology can help us to know ourselves, our capabilities, and our limitations. I was hooked. And so, of course, I hope you will be too.

THE GOALS OF THIS CHAPTER

In this chapter I aim to achieve three goals:

1. I first illustrate the power of sociology to dispel foggy assumptions and help us see the operation of the social world more clearly. To that end, I examine a phenomenon that at first glance appears to be solely the outcome of breakdowns in individual functioning: suicide. You will see

that, in fact, *social relations* among people powerfully influence suicide rates. This exercise introduces you to what is unique about the sociological perspective.

2. I show that, from its origins, sociological research has been motivated by a desire to improve the social world. Thus, sociology is not just a dry, academic exercise but a means of charting a better course for society. At the same time, however, sociologists adopt scientific methods to test their ideas, thus increasing the validity of the results. I illustrate these points by briefly analyzing the work of the founders of the discipline.

3. I suggest that sociology can help you come to grips with your century, just as it helped the founders of sociology deal with theirs. Today we are witnessing massive and disorienting social changes. Entire countries are breaking up. Women are demanding equality with men in all spheres of life. New religions are emerging and old ones reviving. People's wants are increasingly governed by the mass media. Computers are radically altering the way people work and entertain themselves. There are proportionately fewer good jobs to go around. Environmental ruin threatens us all. As was the case a hundred years ago, sociologists today try to understand social phenomena and suggest credible ways of improving their societies. By promising to make sociology relevant to you, this chapter should be viewed as an open invitation to participate in sociology's challenge.

But first things first. Before showing how sociology can help us comprehend and better our world, let us briefly examine the problem of suicide. That will help to illustrate how the sociological perspective can clarify and sometimes overturn commonsense beliefs.

THE SOCIOLOGICAL PERSPECTIVE

By analyzing suicide sociologically, you can put to a tough test my claim that sociology gives you a unique, surprising, and enlightening perspective on social events. After all, suicide appears to be the supremely antisocial and nonsocial act. It is condemned by nearly everyone in society. It is typically committed in private, far from the public's intrusive glare. It is rare. In recent years, there have been about 13 suicides annually for every 100 000 people in Canada (Statistics Canada, 2004a). Canada's suicide rate places us 36th among the 74 countries that publish suicide statistics; see Figure 1.1. And when you think about why people commit such acts, you are likely to focus on their individual states of mind rather than on the state of society. In other words, what usually interests us are the aspects of specific individuals' lives that caused them to become depressed or angry enough to do something as awful as killing themselves. We usually do not think about the patterns of social relations that might encourage such actions in general. If sociology can reveal the hidden social causes of such an apparently antisocial and nonsocial phenomenon, there must be something to it!

FIGURE 1.1 SUICIDE RATES, SELECTED COUNTRIES

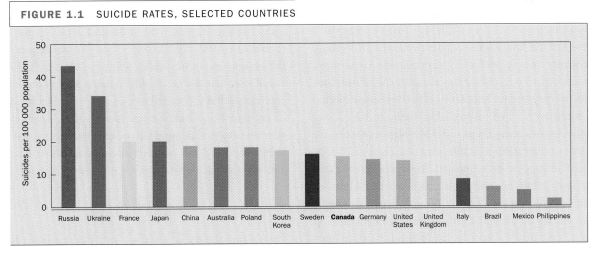

Note: These data are for the most recent year available between 1990 and 2000.
SOURCE: World Health Organization (2002). World Report on Violence and Health. Geneva, 186–87. On the World Wide Web at http://www.who.int/violence/world_report/en/full_en.pdf. Reprinted by permission of World Health Organization.

THE SOCIOLOGICAL EXPLANATION OF SUICIDE

At the end of the nineteenth century, French sociologist Émile Durkheim (1951 [1897]), one of the pioneers of the discipline, demonstrated that suicide is more than just an individual act of desperation resulting from psychological disorder, as was commonly believed at the time. Suicide rates, he showed, are strongly influenced by social forces.

Durkheim made his case by examining the association between rates of suicide and rates of psychological disorder for different groups. The idea that psychological disorder causes suicide is supported, he reasoned, only if suicide rates tend to be high where rates of psychological disorder are high, and low where rates of psychological disorder are low. But his analysis of European government statistics, hospital records, and other sources revealed nothing of the kind. He discovered there were slightly more women than men in insane asylums. Yet there were four male suicides for every female suicide. Jews had the highest rate of psychological disorder among the major religious groups in France. However, they also had the lowest suicide rate. Psychological disorders occurred most frequently when a person reached maturity. Suicide rates, though, increased steadily with age.

Clearly, suicide rates and rates of psychological disorder did not vary proportionately. What then accounts for variations in suicide rates? Durkheim argued that suicide rates vary because of differences in the degree of **social solidarity** in different groups. According to Durkheim, the more a group's members share beliefs and values, and the more frequently and intensely they interact, the more social solidarity there is in the group. In turn, the more social solidarity there is in a group, the more firmly anchored individuals are to the social world, and the less likely they are to take their own lives if adversity strikes. In other words, Durkheim expected groups with a high degree of solidarity to have lower suicide rates than groups with a low degree of solidarity did—at least up to a certain point (see Figure 1.2).

To support his argument, Durkheim showed that married adults are half as likely as unmarried adults are to commit suicide. That is because marriage usually creates social ties and a sort of moral cement that bind the individual to society. Similarly, he argued that women are less likely to commit suicide than men are. Why? Women are generally more involved in the intimate social relations of family life. Jews, Durkheim

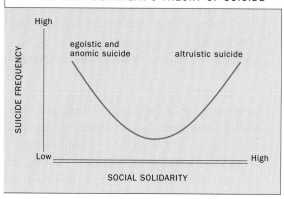

FIGURE 1.2 DURKHEIM'S THEORY OF SUICIDE

Durkheim argued that as the level of social solidarity increases, the suicide rate declines. Then, beyond a certain point, it starts to rise. Hence the U-shaped curve in this graph. Durkheim called suicides that occur in high-solidarity settings altruistic. Altruism means devotion to the interests of others. **Altruistic suicide** occurs when norms tightly govern behaviour, so individual actions are often in the group interest. For example, when soldiers knowingly give up their lives to protect members of their unit, they commit altruistic suicide out of a deep sense of comradeship. In contrast, suicide that occurs in low-solidarity settings is egoistic or anomic, said Durkheim. **Egoistic suicide** results from a lack of integration of the individual into society because of weak social ties to others. Anomie means "without order." **Anomic suicide** occurs when norms governing behaviour are vaguely defined. For example, in Durkheim's view, when people live in a society that lacks a widely shared code of morality, the rate of anomic suicide is likely to be high.

wrote, are less likely to commit suicide than Christians are. The reason? Centuries of persecution have turned them into a group that is more defensive and tightly knit. And seniors are more prone than the young and the middle-aged are to take their own lives in the face of misfortune. That is because they are most likely to live alone, to have lost a spouse, and to lack a job and a wide network of friends. In general, Durkheim wrote, "suicide varies with the degree of integration of the social groups of which the individual forms a part" (Durkheim, 1951 [1897]: 209). Note that his generalization tells us nothing about why any particular individual may take his or her life. That is a question for psychology. But it does tell us that a person's likelihood of committing suicide decreases with the degree to which he or she is anchored in society. And it says something surprising and uniquely sociological about how and why the suicide rate varies from group to group.

SUICIDE IN CANADA TODAY

Durkheim's theory is not just a historical curiosity. It sheds light on the factors that account for variations in suicide rates here and now. Consider Figure 1.3, which shows suicide rates by age and sex in Canada.

Comparing rates for men and women, we immediately see that, as in Durkheim's France, men are about four times more likely than women are to commit suicide. However, looking at differences between age groups, we see a striking difference between Durkheim's France and contemporary Canada. When Durkheim wrote, youth suicide was extremely rare and suicide among working-age people was uncommon. In Canada today, suicide among people between the ages of 15 and 64 is much more common, having increased substantially since the 1960s. Suicide rates do *not* increase steadily with age in Canada today. True, the suicide rate is highest among people over the age of 84. However, it is higher for people between the ages of 20 and 64 than it is for people between the ages of 65 and 84. Moreover, the rate of suicide for people between the ages of 15 and 19, practically zero in Durkheim's France, stands at more than 10 per 100 000 in Canada today.

Although the rate of suicide among youth was negligible in Durkheim's France, his theory of social solidarity helps us to understand why it has risen so quickly in Canada. In brief, shared moral principles and strong social ties have eroded since the early 1960s for Canada's youth. Consider the following facts:

- Church, synagogue, mosque, and temple attendance is down, particularly for young people. Thus, more than half of Canadians attended religious services weekly in the 1960s. Today the figure is less than one-third, and it is only one-sixth for people born after 1960.

- Unemployment is up, again especially for youth. Thus, the unemployment rate was around 3 percent for most of the 1960s. It rose steadily to around 10 percent for most of the 1990s and stood at about 7 percent in 2005. Moreover, the unemployment rate is more than twice as high for Canadians under the age of 20 as it is for older Canadians.

- The rate of divorce has increased sixfold since the early 1960s. Out-of-wedlock births are also much more common than they used to be. As a result, children are more often brought up in single-parent families than in the past. This suggests that they enjoy less frequent and intimate social interaction with parents and less adult supervision.

In sum, the figures cited above suggest that the level of social solidarity is now lower than it was just a few decades ago for young people. Less firmly

FIGURE 1.3 SUICIDE BY AGE AND SEX, 2002

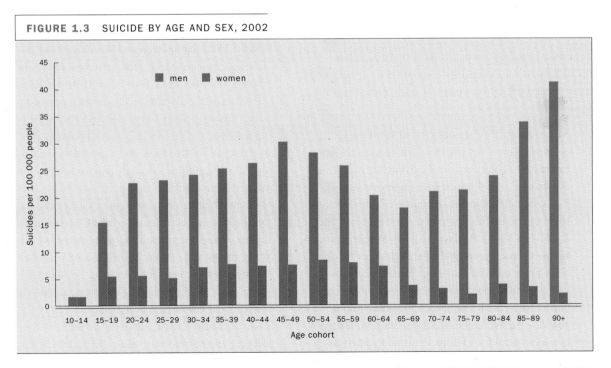

SOURCES: Adapted from the Statistics Canada publications "Age and Sex, 2001 Census (Age and Sex)," Catalogue 95F0300XIE2001004, released July 16, 2002, http://www.statcan.ca/bsolc/english/bsolc?catno=95F0300X2001004; and "Causes of Death," 2002, Catalogue 84-208-XIE, released December 6, 2004, http://www.statcan.ca/english/freepub/84-208-XIE/2002/tables/table20.pdf.

rooted in society, and less likely to share moral standards, young people in Canada today are more likely than they were 45 years ago to take their own lives if they happen to find themselves in the midst of a personal crisis.

FROM PERSONAL TROUBLES TO SOCIAL STRUCTURES

You have known for a long time that you live in a society. Yet until now, you may not have fully appreciated that society also lives in you. That is, patterns of social relations affect your innermost thoughts and feelings, influence your actions, and thus help shape who you are. As we have seen, one such pattern of social relations is the level of social solidarity characteristic of the various groups to which you belong.

Sociologists call relatively stable patterns of social relations **social structures.** One of the sociologist's main tasks is to identify and explain the connection between people's personal troubles and the social structures in which people are embedded. This work is harder than it may at first seem. In everyday life, we usually see things mainly from our own point of view. Our experiences appear unique to each of us. If we think about them at all, social structures may appear remote and impersonal. To see how social structures operate inside us, we require sociological training.

An important step in broadening our sociological awareness involves recognizing that three levels of social structure surround and penetrate us. Think of these structures as concentric circles radiating out from you:

1. **Microstructures** are patterns of intimate social relations. They are formed during face-to-face interaction. Families, friendship circles, and work associations are all examples of microstructures.

   Understanding the operation of microstructures can be useful. Let us say you are looking for a job. You might think you would do best to ask as many close friends and relatives as possible for leads and contacts. Sociological research shows, however, that people you know well are likely to know many of the same people. After asking a couple of close connections for help landing a job, you would therefore do best to ask more remote acquaintances for leads and contacts. People to whom you are weakly connected (and who are weakly connected among themselves) are more likely to know different groups of people. Therefore, they will give you more infor-

mation about job possibilities and ensure that word about your job search spreads farther. You are more likely to find a job faster if you understand "the strength of weak ties" in microstructural settings (Granovetter, 1973).

2. **Macrostructures** are patterns of social relations that lie outside and above your circle of intimates and acquaintances. Macrostructures include class relations and **patriarchy,** the traditional system of economic and political inequality between women and men in most societies.

   Understanding the operation of macrostructures can also be useful. Consider, for example, one aspect of patriarchy. Most married women who work full-time in the paid labour force do more housework, child-care, and eldercare than their husbands do. Governments and businesses support this arrangement insofar as they give little assistance to families in the form of nurseries, after-school programs for children, senior homes, and so forth. Yet the unequal division of work in the household is a major source of dissatisfaction with marriage, especially in families that cannot afford to buy these services privately. Thus, sociological research shows that when spouses share domestic responsibilities equally, they are happier with their marriages and less likely to divorce (Hochschild with Machung, 1989). When a marriage is in danger of dissolving, it is common for partners to blame themselves and each other for their troubles. However, it should now be clear that forces other than incompatible personalities often put stresses on families. Understanding how the macrostructure of patriarchy crops up in everyday life, and doing something to change that structure, can thus help people lead happier lives.

3. The third level of society that surrounds and permeates us comprises **global structures.** International organizations, patterns of worldwide travel and communication, and the economic relations between countries are examples of global structures. Global structures are increasingly important as inexpensive travel and communication allow all parts of the world to become interconnected culturally, economically, and politically.

Understanding the operation of global structures can be useful, too. For instance, many people are concerned about the world's poor. They donate money to charities to help with famine and disaster relief. Some people also approve of the Canadian government giving foreign aid to poor countries. However, many of these same people do not appreciate that charity and foreign aid alone do not seem able to end world poverty. That is because charity and foreign aid have been unable to overcome the structure of social relations among countries that have created, and now sustain, global inequality.

Let us linger on this point for a moment. As we will see in Chapter 9, Inequality among Nations: Perspectives on Development, Britain, France, and other imperial powers locked some countries into poverty when they colonized them between the seventeenth and nineteenth centuries. In the twentieth century, the poor (or "developing") countries borrowed money from these same rich countries and Western banks to pay for airports, roads, harbours, sanitation systems, basic health care, and so forth. Today, poor countries pay far more to rich countries and Western banks in interest on those loans than they receive in aid and charity. In 2002, foreign aid to the world's developing countries was only one-seventh the amount that the developing countries paid to Western banks in loan interest (United Nations, 2004: 201). It thus seems that relying exclusively on foreign aid and charity can do little to help solve the problem of world poverty. Understanding how the global structure of international relations created and helps maintain global inequality suggests new policy priorities for helping the world's poor. One such priority might involve campaigning for the cancellation of foreign debt in compensation for past injustices. Some Canadian and British government officials have been promoting this policy for the past few years.

As these examples illustrate, personal problems are connected to social structures at the micro-, macro-, and global levels. Whether the personal problem involves finding a job, keeping a marriage intact, or figuring out a way to act justly to end world poverty, social-structural considerations broaden our understanding of the problem and suggest appropriate courses of action.

THE SOCIOLOGICAL IMAGINATION

Half a century ago, the great American sociologist C. Wright Mills (1959) called the ability to see the connection between personal troubles and social structures the **sociological imagination.** He empha-

sized the difficulty of developing this quality of mind. His language is sexist by today's standards, but his argument is as true and inspiring today as it was in the 1950s:

> When a society becomes industrialized, a peasant becomes a worker; a feudal lord is liquidated or becomes a businessman. When classes rise or fall, a man is employed or unemployed; when the rate of investment goes up or down, a man takes new heart or goes broke. When war happens, an insurance salesman becomes a rocket launcher; a store clerk, a radar man; a wife lives alone; a child grows up without a father. Neither the life of an individual nor the history of a society can be understood without understanding both.
>
> Yet men do not usually define the troubles they endure in terms of historical change. . . . The well-being they enjoy, they do not usually impute to the big ups and downs of the society in which they live. Seldom aware of the intricate connection between the patterns of their own lives and the course of world history, ordinary men do not usually know what this connection means for the kind of men they are becoming and for the kind of history-making in which they might take part. They do not possess the quality of mind essential to grasp the interplay of men and society, of biography and history, of self and world. They cannot cope with their personal troubles in such a way as to control the structural transformations that usually lie behind them.
>
> What they need . . . is a quality of mind that will help them to [see] . . . what is going on in the world and . . . what may be happening within themselves. It is this quality . . . that . . . may be called the sociological imagination. (Mills, 1959: 3–4)

The sociological imagination is a recent addition to the human repertoire. It is only about two centuries old. True, in ancient and medieval times, some philosophers wrote about society. However, their thinking was not sociological. They believed God and nature controlled society. They spent much of their time sketching blueprints for the ideal society and urging people to follow those blueprints.

And they relied on speculation rather than on evidence to reach conclusions about how society works.

The sociological imagination was born when three modern revolutions pushed people to think about society in an entirely new way. First, the **Scientific Revolution** began about 1550. It encouraged the view that sound conclusions about the workings of society must be based on solid evidence, not just speculation. Second, the **Democratic Revolution** began about 1750. It suggested that people are responsible for organizing society and that human intervention can therefore solve social problems. Third, the **Industrial Revolution** began about 1780. It created a host of new and serious social problems that attracted the attention of many social thinkers. Let us briefly consider these three sources of the sociological imagination.

ORIGINS OF THE SOCIOLOGICAL IMAGINATION

The Scientific Revolution

It is said that a group of medieval monks once wanted to know how many angels could dance on the head of a pin. They consulted ancient books in Hebrew, Greek, and Latin. They thought long and hard. They employed all their intellectual skills to debate the issue. They did not, however, resolve the dispute. That is because they never considered inspecting the head of a pin and counting. Any such suggestion would have been considered heresy. We, in contrast, would call it the beginning of a scientific approach to the subject.

People often link the Scientific Revolution to specific ideas, such as Copernicus's theory that Earth revolves around the sun and Newton's laws of motion. However, science is less a collection of ideas than a method of inquiry. For instance, in 1609, Galileo pointed his newly invented telescope at the heavens, made some careful observations, and showed that his observations fit Copernicus's theory. This is the core of the scientific method: using evidence to make a case for a particular point of view. By the mid-1600s, some philosophers, such as Descartes in France and Hobbes in England, were calling for a science of society. When sociology emerged as a distinct discipline in the nineteenth century, commitment to the scientific method was one firm pillar of the sociological imagination.

The Democratic Revolution

The second pillar of the sociological imagination is the realization that people control society and can change it. Four hundred years ago, most Europeans thought otherwise. For them, God ordained the social order.

Consider the English engraving reproduced in Figure 1.4. It shows how most educated Europeans pictured the universe in Shakespeare's time. Note the cloud at the top of the circle. The Hebrew name of God is inscribed on it. God's hand extends from the cloud. It holds a chain, which is attached to a woman representing Nature. Nature also holds a chain in her hand. It is connected to "the ape of Nature," representing humankind. The symbolism is clear: God and his intermediary, Nature, control human action. Note also that the engraving arranges everything in a linked hierarchy. The hierarchy includes the mineral, vegetable, and animal kingdoms; the elements; heavenly objects; angels; and so forth. Each level of the hierarchy corresponds to and controls some aspect of the level below it. For example, people believed Archangels regulate the movements of the planet Mercury and the movements of Mercury affect human commerce. Similarly, in the medieval view, God ordained a hierarchy of people. The richest people were seen as the closest to God and therefore deserving of great privilege. Supposedly, kings and queens ruled because God wanted them to (Tillyard, 1943).

The American Revolution (1775–83) and the French Revolution (1789–99) helped to undermine these ideas. These democratic political upheavals showed that society could experience massive change in a short period. They proved that people could replace unsatisfactory rulers. And they suggested that *people* control society. The implications for social thought were profound, for if it was possible to change society by human intervention, then a science of society could play a big role. The new science could help people figure out ways of overcoming various social problems, improving the welfare of all citizens, and finding the most effective way to reach given goals. Much of the justification for sociology as a science arose out of the democratic revolutions that shook Europe and North America.

The Industrial Revolution

The third pillar of the sociological imagination was the Industrial Revolution. It began in England about 1780. Because of the growth of industry, masses of people moved from countryside to city, worked agonizingly long hours in crowded and dangerous mines and facto-

FIGURE 1.4   THE ELIZABETHAN WORLDVIEW

SOURCE: From Robert Fludd's *Utriusque Cosmi Historia* (1617–19). Photograph courtesy of Houghton Library, Harvard College Library.

ries, lost faith in their religions, confronted faceless bureaucracies, and reacted to the filth and poverty of their existence by means of strikes, crime, revolution, and war. Scholars had never seen a sociological laboratory like this. The Scientific Revolution suggested that a science of society is possible. The Democratic Revolution suggested that people *can* intervene to improve society. The Industrial Revolution now presented social thinkers with a host of pressing social problems crying out for solutions. They responded by giving birth to the sociological imagination.

SOCIOLOGICAL THEORIES

THE ORIGINS OF SOCIOLOGY

The term *sociology* was coined by the French social thinker Auguste Comte in 1838 (Thompson, 1975). Comte tried to place the study of society on scientific foundations. He wanted to understand the social world as it is, not as he or anyone else imagined it should be. This was a highly original approach to the study of society. In ancient and medieval times, philosophers from diverse civilizations had sketched blueprints for the ideal society. We see evidence of this in the work of Confucius in China, Ibn Khaldun in Tunisia, and Plato and Aristotle in Greece, to name only a few of the best-known figures. But Comte was swept up in the scientific revolution of his time. He was inspired by the astronomers and physicists of the modern era—Copernicus in Poland, Galileo in Italy, Newton in England. He wanted to test the validity of his ideas through careful observation of the real world rather than assuming that "God" or "human nature" determined the shape of society (see Box 1.1).

Despite Comte's breakthrough, there was a tension in his work, for although he was eager to adopt the scientific method in his study of society, he was a

BOX 1.1 SCIENTIFIC VERSUS COMMONSENSE KNOWLEDGE

To better understand how scientific and nonscientific knowledge differ, consider the following statements, each of which represents a commonly accepted basis for knowing that something is "true" in our everyday lives:

1. *"The proper place for women is in the home. That's the way it's always been."* This statement represents knowledge based on *tradition*. Although some traditional knowledge is valid (sugar will rot your teeth), some is not (masturbation will not blind you). Science is required to sort out valid from invalid knowledge.

2. *"Apparently, weak magnets can be used to heal many illnesses. I read all about it in the newspaper."* This statement represents knowledge based on *authority*. We often think something is true because we read it in an authoritative source or hear it from an expert. But authoritative sources and experts can be wrong. For example, nineteenth-century Western physicians commonly "bled" their patients with leeches to draw "poisons" from their bodies, often doing more harm than good. As this example suggests, scientists should always question authority to arrive at more valid knowledge.

3. *"The car that caused the accident was dark brown. I was driving my bike last night when I saw the car accident."* This statement represents knowledge based on *casual observation*. However, we are usually pretty careless observers. That is why good lawyers can often trip up eyewitnesses in courtrooms; eyewitnesses are rarely certain about what they saw. In general, uncertainty can be reduced by observing in a conscious and deliberate manner and by recording observations. That is just what scientists do.

4. *"If you work hard, you can get ahead. I know because several of my parents' friends started off poor but are now comfortably middle class."* This statement represents knowledge based on *overgeneralization*. For instance, if you know a few people who started off poor, worked hard, and became rich, you may think any poor person can become rich if he or she works hard enough. You may not know about the more numerous poor people who work hard and remain poor. Scientists, however, sample cases that are representative of entire populations. This enables them to avoid overgeneralization. They also avoid overgeneralization by repeating research. This ensures that research findings are not idiosyncratic.

5. *"I'm right because I can't think of any contrary cases."* This statement represents knowledge based on *selective observation*. Sometimes we ignore evidence that challenges our firmly held beliefs. Thus, you may know people who work hard but remain poor. To maintain your belief that hard work results in wealth, you will have to ignore those cases. The scientific requirement that evidence be drawn from representative samples of the population minimizes bias arising from selective observation.

6. *"Mr. Smith is poor even though he works hard but that's because he has a disability. People with disabilities are the only exception to the rule that if you work hard you can get ahead."* This statement represents knowledge based on *qualification*. Qualifications or "exceptions to the rule" are often made in everyday life—and they are in science too. The difference is that in everyday life qualifications are easily accepted as valid, whereas in scientific inquiry, they are typically treated as hypotheses that must be tested as rigorously as the original hypothesis.

7. *"The Toronto Blue Jays won 50 percent of their baseball games last month but 80 percent of the games they played on Thursdays. Because it happened so often before, I bet they'll win next Thursday."* This statement represents knowledge based on *illogical reasoning*. In everyday life, we may expect the recurrence of events without reasonable cause, ignoring the fact that rare sequences of events often occur just by chance. For example, it is possible to flip a coin ten times and have it come up heads each time. On average, this will happen once every 1024 times you flip a coin ten times. In the absence of any apparent reason for this happening, it is merely coincidental. It is illogical to believe otherwise. Scientists refrain from such illogical reasoning. They also use statistical techniques to distinguish between events that are probably due to chance and those that are not.

8. *"I just can't be wrong."* This statement represents knowledge based on *ego-defence*. Even scientists may be passionately committed to the conclusions they reach in their research because they have invested much time and energy in them. It is other scientists—more accurately, the whole institution of science, with its commitment to publishing research results and critically scrutinizing findings—that strictly limits ego-defence in scientific understanding.

9. *"The matter is settled once and for all."* This statement represents knowledge based on the *premature closure of inquiry*. This involves deciding that all the relevant evidence has been gathered on a particular subject. Science, however, is committed to the idea that all theories are only temporarily true. Matters are never settled.

BOX 1.1 *(continued)*

10. *"There must be supernatural forces at work here."* This statement represents knowledge based on *mystification.* When we can find no rational explanation for a phenomenon, we may attribute it to forces that cannot be observed or fully understood. Although such forces may exist, scientists remain skeptical. They are committed to discovering real, observable causes of real, observable effects.

SOURCE: From *The Practice of Social Research*, by Earl Babbie. ©1992. Reprinted with permission of Wadsworth, a division of Thomson Learning: http://www.thomsonrights.com. Fax 800-730-2215.

conservative thinker, motivated by strong opposition to rapid change in French society. His was a time not only of scientific but also of political and social revolution. Comte witnessed the democratic forces unleashed by the French Revolution, the early industrialization of society, and the rapid growth of cities. And what he saw shocked and angered him because rapid social change was destroying many of the things he valued, especially respect for authority. He therefore urged slow change and the preservation of much that was traditional in social life. Thus, at its very origin, sociological research was motivated by adherence to scientific methods of research *and* a vision of the ideal society.

The same sort of tension is evident in the work of the most important early figures in the history of sociology: Karl Marx, Émile Durkheim, and Max Weber. These three men lived in the period from 1820 to 1920. They witnessed various phases of Europe's wrenching transition to industrial capitalism, and they wanted to understand and explain it. Like Comte, they were all committed to the scientific method of research. However, they also wanted to chart a better course for their societies. The ideas they developed are therefore not just diagnostic tools from which we can still learn much but also, like many sociological ideas, prescriptions for combating social ills.

THEORY, RESEARCH, AND VALUES

To clarify the tension in sociology between analysis and ideal, diagnosis and prescription, we can usefully distinguish three terms: theory, research, and values.

Sociological ideas are generally stated in the form of theories. A **theory** is a tentative explanation of some aspect of social life that states how and why certain facts are related. For example, in his theory of suicide, Durkheim showed how facts about suicide rates are related to facts about social solidarity. This enabled him

to explain suicide as a function of social solidarity. In this broad definition, even a hunch qualifies as a theory if it suggests how and why certain facts are related.

After theories are formulated, the sociologist can conduct research. **Research** is the process of carefully observing social reality to assess the validity of a theory. It is because research can call the validity of a theory into question that theories are said to be only "tentative" explanations. The research process is discussed in detail in Chapter 20, Research Methods.

Before delving into social research, a sociologist must first develop hypotheses—testable claims about the social world. Testing hypotheses by means of research helps determine the validity of theories.

SOURCE: PhotoDisc/Getty Images

Before sociologists can formulate a theory, however, they must decide which problems are important enough to study and how the parts of society fit together. If they are going to recommend ways of improving the operation of some aspect of society, they must even have an opinion about what the ideal society ought to look like. As we will soon see, these issues are shaped in large measure by sociologists' values. **Values** are ideas about what is right and wrong, good and bad. Inevitably, values help sociologists formulate and favour certain theories over others (Edel, 1965; Kuhn, 1970). So sociological theories may be modified and even rejected due to research, but they are often motivated by sociologists' values.

Durkheim, Marx, and Weber initiated three of the major theoretical traditions in sociology: functionalism, conflict theory, and symbolic interactionism. A fourth approach, feminism, has arisen in recent decades to correct some of the deficiencies of the three long-established traditions. It will become clear as you read this book that there are many more sociological theories than just these four. However, because these four traditions have been especially influential in the development of sociology, you will find it useful to read a thumbnail sketch of each one here at the beginning.[1]

FUNCTIONALISM

Durkheim's theory of suicide is an early example of what sociologists now call **functionalism.** Functionalist theories incorporate four features:

1. They stress that human behaviour is governed by relatively stable patterns of social relations, or social structures. For example, Durkheim emphasized how suicide rates are influenced by patterns of social solidarity. Usually the social structures analyzed by functionalists are macrostructures.

2. Functionalism underlines how social structures maintain or undermine social stability. Typically, Durkheim analyzed how the growth of industries and cities in nineteenth-century Europe lowered the level of social solidarity and contributed to social instability. One aspect of instability, said Durkheim, is a higher suicide rate. Another is frequent strikes by workers.

3. Functionalist theories emphasize that social structures are based mainly on shared values. Thus, when Durkheim wrote about social solidarity, he sometimes meant the frequency and intensity of social interaction, but more often he thought of social solidarity as a sort of moral cement that binds people together.

4. Functionalism suggests that re-establishing equilibrium can best solve most social problems. Thus, Durkheim said that social stability could be restored in late-nineteenth-century Europe by creating new associations of employers and workers that would lower workers' expectations about what they could expect out of life. If, said Durkheim, more people could agree on wanting less, social solidarity would rise and there would be fewer strikes, fewer suicides, and so on. Functionalism, then, was a conservative response to widespread social unrest in nineteenth-century France. (A more radical response would have been to argue that if people are expressing discontent because they are getting less out of life than they expect, discontent can be lowered by figuring out ways for them to get more out of life.)

Although functionalist thinking influenced North American sociology at the end of the nineteenth century, it was only during the continent's greatest economic crisis ever, the Great Depression of 1929–39, that functionalism took deep root here (Russett, 1966). With 30 percent of the paid labour force unemployed and labour unrest reaching unprecedented levels, it is not surprising that sociologists with a conservative frame of mind were attracted to a theory that focused on how social equilibrium could be restored. Functionalist theory remained popular in North America for 30 years. It experienced a minor revival in the early 1990s but never regained the dominance it enjoyed from the 1930s to the early 1960s.

Sociologist Talcott Parsons was the foremost proponent of functionalism. He is best known for identifying how various institutions must work to ensure the smooth operation of society as a whole. For instance, when the family successfully raises new generations, the military successfully defends society against external threats, schools are able to teach students the skills and values they need to function as productive adults, and religions create a shared moral code among people, then, said Parsons, society is well integrated and in equilibrium (Parsons, 1951).

Parsons was criticized for exaggerating the degree to which members of society share common values and social institutions contribute to social harmony. This led North America's other leading functionalist, Robert Merton, to propose that social structures may have different consequences for different groups of people. Merton noted that some of those consequences might be disruptive or **dysfunctional** (Merton, 1968 [1949]). Moreover, said Merton, although some functions are **manifest** (visible and intended), others are **latent** (invisible and unintended). For instance, a manifest function of schools is to transmit skills from one generation to the next. A latent function of schools is to encourage the development of a separate youth culture that often conflicts with parents' values (Coleman, 1961; Hersch, 1998).

CONFLICT THEORY

The second major theoretical tradition in sociology emphasizes the centrality of conflict in social life. **Conflict theory** incorporates these four features:

1. It generally focuses on large, macrolevel structures, such as relations between or among classes.
2. Conflict theory shows how major patterns of inequality in society produce social stability in some circumstances and social change in others.
3. Conflict theory stresses how members of privileged groups try to maintain their advantages while subordinate groups struggle to increase theirs. From this point of view, social conditions at a given time are the expression of an ongoing power struggle between privileged and subordinate groups.
4. Conflict theory typically leads to the suggestion that eliminating privilege will lower the level of conflict and increase the sum total of human welfare.

The conflict paradigm originated in the work of Karl Marx. A generation before Durkheim, Marx observed the destitution and discontent produced by the Industrial Revolution and proposed a sweeping argument about the way societies develop (Marx, 1904 [1859]; Marx and Engels, 1972 [1848]). Marx's theory was radically different from Durkheim's. Class conflict lies at the centre of his ideas.

Marx argued that owners of industry are eager to improve the way work is organized and to adopt new tools, machines, and production methods. These innovations allow them to produce more efficiently, earn higher profits, and drive inefficient competitors out of business. However, the drive for profits causes capitalists to concentrate workers in larger and larger establishments, keep wages as low as possible, and invest as little as possible in improving working conditions. Thus, said Marx, in factory and in mine, a large and growing class of poor workers comes to oppose a small and shrinking class of wealthy owners.

Marx felt that workers would ultimately become aware of belonging to the same exploited class. Their sense of "class consciousness," he wrote, would encourage the growth of trade unions and labour parties. These organizations would eventually seek to put an end to private ownership of property, replacing it with a system in which everyone shared property and wealth. This was the "communist" society envisaged by Marx—a society in which there is no private property and everyone shares property and wealth.

Weber

Although some of Marx's ideas have been usefully adapted to the study of contemporary society, his predictions about the inevitable collapse of capitalism have been questioned. Max Weber, a German sociologist who wrote his major works a generation after Marx, was among the first to find flaws in Marx's argument (Weber, 1946). Weber noted the rapid growth of the "service" sector of the economy with its many nonmanual workers and professionals. He argued that many members of these occupational groups stabilize society because they enjoy higher status and income than do manual workers employed in the manufacturing sector. In addition, Weber showed that class conflict is not the only driving force of history. In his view, politics and religion are also important sources of historical change (see the following text). Other writers pointed out that Marx did not understand how investing in technology would

Max Weber wrote that the modern era is a bureaucratically organized "iron cage." Sociology promises to teach us both the dimensions of that cage and the possibilities for release.
SOURCE: Carol Waino, *Untitled* (1985). Acrylic on canvas, 33″ × 50″. Photograph courtesy of the S.L. Simpson Gallery, Toronto. Reproduced with permission of the artist.

make it possible for workers to toil fewer hours under less oppressive conditions. Nor did he foresee that higher wages, better working conditions, and welfare state benefits would pacify manual workers. Thus, we see that many of the particulars of Marx's theory were called into question by Weber and other sociologists. Nonetheless, Marx's insights about the fundamental importance of conflict in social life were influential—and still are today.

SYMBOLIC INTERACTIONISM

Above we noted that Weber criticized Marx's interpretation of the development of capitalism. Among other things, Weber argued that early capitalist development was caused not just by favourable *economic* circumstances. In addition, he said, certain *religious* beliefs facilitated robust capitalist growth. In particular, sixteenth- and seventeenth-century Protestants believed their religious doubts could be reduced, and a state of grace ensured, if they worked diligently and lived modestly. Weber called this belief the **Protestant ethic.** He believed it had an unintended effect: People who adhered to the Protestant ethic saved and invested more than others. Thus, according to Weber, capitalism developed most robustly where the Protestant ethic took hold. He concluded that capitalism did not develop due to the operation of economic forces alone, as Marx argued. Instead, it depended partly on the religious meaning individuals attached to their work (Weber, 1958 [1904–05]).

In much of his research, Weber emphasized the importance of empathetically understanding people's motives and the meanings they attach to things to gain a clear sense of the significance of their actions. He called this aspect of his approach to sociological research the method of *Verstehen* (pronounced Fer-SHTAY-en, meaning "understanding" in German).

The idea that subjective meanings must be analyzed in any complete sociological analysis was only one of Weber's contributions to early sociological theory. Weber was also an important conflict theorist, as you will learn in later chapters. At present, however, it is enough to note that his emphasis on subjective meanings found rich soil in North America, for here was an idea that resonated deeply with the individualism of North American culture. A century ago, it was widely believed that individual talent and initiative could achieve just about anything on this continent of opportunity. Small wonder, then, that much of early

North American sociology focused on the individual or, more precisely, on the connection between the individual and the larger society. For example, George Herbert Mead at the University of Chicago was the driving force behind the study of how individual identity is formed in the course of interaction with other people. We discuss his contribution in Chapter 3, Socialization. Here we note only that the work of Mead and his colleagues gave birth to symbolic interactionism, a distinctively North American theoretical tradition that continues to be a major force today.

Functionalists and conflict theorists assume that people's group memberships—whether they are young or old, male or female, rich or poor—determine their behaviour. This can sometimes make people seem like balls on a pool table: They get knocked around and cannot determine their destinations. We know from our everyday experience, however, that people are not like that. You often make choices, sometimes difficult ones. You sometimes change your mind. Moreover, two people with similar social characteristics may react differently to similar social circumstances because they may interpret those circumstances differently.

Recognizing these issues, some sociologists focus on the subjective side of social life. They work in the symbolic interactionist tradition. **Symbolic interactionism** incorporates these four features:

1. It focuses on face-to-face communication or interaction in microlevel social settings. This distinguishes it from both the functionalist and the conflict paradigms.
2. Symbolic interactionism emphasizes that an adequate explanation of social behaviour requires understanding the subjective meanings people attach to their social circumstances.
3. Symbolic interactionism stresses that people help to create their social circumstances and do not merely react to them.[2]
4. By underscoring the subjective meanings people create in small social settings, symbolic interactionists validate unpopular and nonofficial viewpoints, thus increasing our understanding and tolerance of people who may be different from us.

To understand symbolic interactionism better, let us return briefly to the problem of suicide. If a police officer discovers a dead person at the wheel of a car that has run into a tree, it may be difficult to establish with certainty whether the death was an accident or a suicide. Interviewing friends and relatives to discover the driver's state of mind just before the crash may help to rule out the possibility of suicide. But, as this example illustrates, understanding the intention or motive of the actor is critical to understanding the meaning of a social action and explaining it. Suicide, then, is not just an objective social fact but also an inferred, and therefore subjective, social fact. A state of mind must be interpreted, usually by a coroner, before the dead body becomes a suicide statistic (Douglas, 1967).

For surviving family and friends, suicide is always painful and sometimes embarrassing. Insurance policies often deny payments to beneficiaries in the case of suicide. As a result, coroners are inclined to classify deaths as accidental whenever such an interpretation is plausible. Being human, they want to minimize the family's pain after such a horrible event. Sociologists believe that, for this reason, official suicide rates are about one-third lower than actual suicide rates.

The study of the subjective side of social life reveals many such inconsistencies, helping us to go beyond the official picture, deepening our understanding of how society works, and supplementing the insights gained from macrolevel analysis. Moreover, by stressing the importance and validity of subjective meanings, symbolic interactionists also increase respect for and tolerance of minority and deviant viewpoints.

FEMINIST THEORY

Few women figured prominently in the early history of sociology, largely because the strict demands placed on women by the nineteenth-century household and the lack of opportunity outside the household prevented most of them from obtaining a higher education and finding work that could support sociological research. Not surprisingly, therefore, the women who did make their mark on the discipline in its early years had unusual social backgrounds. These exceptional people introduced into the discipline gender issues that were largely ignored by Marx, Durkheim, and Weber. Appreciation for the sociological contribution of these pioneer women has grown in recent years as concern with gender issues has come to form a substantial part of the modern sociological enterprise.

Harriet Martineau is often called the first woman sociologist. Born in England at the beginning of the nineteenth century to a prosperous family, she never married and was able to support herself comfortably from her journalistic writings. Martineau translated Comte into English. She undertook critical studies of slavery and factory laws. She also wrote about gender inequality and was a leading advocate of voting rights and higher education for women, as well as gender equality in the family. As such, Martineau was one of the first feminists (Yates, 1985).

Despite its auspicious beginnings, feminist thinking had little impact on sociology until the mid-1960s, when the rise of the modern women's movement drew attention to the many remaining inequalities between women and men. Since then, feminist theory has had such a big influence on sociology it may now fairly be regarded as sociology's fourth major tradition. There are several variants of modern feminism (see Chapter 7, Gender Inequality: Economic and Political Aspects). However, the various strands of **feminist theory** share the following four features:

1. Feminist theory focuses on various aspects of patriarchy, the system of male domination in society. Patriarchy, feminists contend, is at least as important as class inequality in determining a person's opportunities in life, and perhaps more so.
2. The feminist paradigm holds that male domination and female subordination are determined not by biological necessity but by structures of power and social convention. From their point of view, women are subordinate to men only because men enjoy more legal, economic, political, and cultural rights.
3. The feminist paradigm examines the operation of patriarchy in both micro and macro settings.
4. The feminist paradigm contends that existing patterns of gender inequality can and should be changed for the benefit of all members of society. The main sources of gender inequality include differences in the way boys and girls are brought up, barriers to equal opportunity in education, paid work, and politics, and the unequal division of domestic responsibilities between women and men.

The theoretical traditions outlined above are summarized in Table 1.1. As you will see in the following pages, sociologists in Canada and elsewhere have applied them to all branches of the discipline (see Box 1.2). They have elaborated and refined each of them. Some sociologists work exclusively within one tradition. Others conduct research that

TABLE 1.1   THE MAIN THEORETICAL TRADITIONS IN SOCIOLOGY

PARADIGM	MAIN LEVEL OF ANALYSIS	MAIN FOCUS	MAIN QUESTION	IMAGE OF IDEAL SOCIETY
functionalism	macro	values	How do the institutions of society contribute to social stability?	A state of equilibrium
conflict theory	macro	class inequality	How do privileged groups seek to maintain their advantages and subordinate groups seek to increase theirs, often causing social change in the process?	The elimination of privilege, especially class privilege
symbolic interactionism	micro	meaning	How do individuals communicate so as to make their social settings meaningful?	Respect for the validity of minority views
feminism	micro and macro	patriarchy	Which social structures and interaction processes maintain male dominance and female subordination?	The elimination of gender inequality

borrows from more than one tradition. But all sociologists are deeply indebted to the founders of the discipline.

THEIR REVOLUTION AND OURS

In the nineteenth century, the founders of the discipline devoted their lives to solving the great sociological puzzle of their time: the causes and consequences of the Industrial Revolution. But the ideas that stirred them did not spring fully grown from their minds. Rather, their social experiences helped to shape their ideas. There is an important lesson to be learned here. In general, sociological ideas are influenced by the social settings in which they emerge.

This lesson immediately suggests two important questions. First, what are the great sociological puzzles of *our* time? Second, how are today's sociologists responding to the challenges presented by the social settings in which *they* live? We devote the rest of the book to answering these questions in depth. In the remainder of this chapter, we offer an outline of what you can expect to learn. To provide a context for this outline, we first say a few words about how the Industrial Revolution of the nineteenth century was transformed into the Postindustrial Revolution of our day.

THE INDUSTRIAL REVOLUTION

The Industrial Revolution involved the application of science and technology to industrial processes, the creation of factories, and the formation of a large class of "blue-collar" workers. Within about a century, it had taken root throughout Western Europe, North America, and Japan. A century after that, industry had begun implanting itself in most of the rest of the world.

As noted in our discussion of Marx, the industrial working class protested long workdays, low pay, and dangerous working conditions. Workers went on strike, formed unions, and joined political parties. Their protests forced governments to tax citizens to provide at least minimal protection against ill health, unemployment, and poverty. Working-class protests also forced employers to limit the length of the workweek to 40 hours, improve working conditions, and raise wages. Employers were still able to increase their profits, however, by making the organization of work more efficient and introducing new technologies.

Collecting taxes, administering social services, and investing heavily in technological change required the growth of government and business offices, hospitals, schools, universities, and research laboratories.

BOX 1.2 THE FOUR PARADIGMS IN CANADA

Each of the four major sociological paradigms has influenced research in Canada. This is evident from the following portraits of some of Canada's leading sociologists.

S.D. Clark (1910–2003) received his Ph.D. from the University of Toronto. He became the first chair of the Department of Sociology at that institution. Born in Lloydminster, Alberta, he is especially well known for his studies of Canadian social development as a process of disorganization and reorganization on a series of economic frontiers (Clark, 1968). The influence of functionalism on his work is apparent in his emphasis on the way society re-establishes equilibrium after experiencing disruptions caused by economic change.

SOURCE: Photo courtesy of Ed Clark.

John Porter (1921–79) was Canada's premier sociologist in the 1960s and 1970s. Born in Vancouver, he received his Ph.D. from the London School of Economics. He spent his academic career at Carleton University in Ottawa. There he served as chair of the Department of Sociology and Anthropology, dean of Arts and Science, and vice-president. His major work, *The Vertical Mosaic* (1965), is a study of class and power in Canada. Firmly rooted in the conflict paradigm, it influenced a generation of Canadian sociologists in their studies on social inequality, elite groups, French–English relations, and Canadian–American relations.

SOURCE: Carleton University Archives.

Erving Goffman (1922–82) was born in Mannville, Alberta. He studied sociology and anthropology as an undergraduate at the University of Toronto and completed his Ph.D. at the University of Chicago. He pursued his academic career at the University of California, Berkeley, and the University of Pennsylvania. Goffman developed an international reputation for his "dramaturgical" approach to symbolic interactionism. This approach highlights the way people present themselves to others, managing their identities to create desired impressions on their "audience," in much the same way actors do on stage (Goffman, 1959).

SOURCE: American Sociological Association.

Margrit Eichler (1942–) was born in Berlin, Germany. She did her Ph.D. at Duke University in the United States before beginning her academic career in Canada. She served as chair of the Department of Sociology at the Ontario Institute for Studies in Education and head of the Women's Studies Programme at the University of Toronto. She is internationally known for her work on feminist methodology (Eichler, 1987). Her work on family policy in Canada has influenced students, professional sociologists, and policymakers for more than two decades (Eichler, 1988).

SOURCE: Margrit Eichler.

Thus, alongside the old manufacturing sector of the economy, the new "service" sector was born. Its employees came to be known as "white-collar" workers. Highly trained professionals stood at the peak of the service sector. Secretaries and clerks were positioned near its base. By 1980, more than half of all people working in Canada's paid labour force were in nonmanual occupations (Ornstein, 1983: 252). Sociologists call this most recent transformation of human society the **Postindustrial Revolution.** Specifically, the Postindustrial Revolution refers to the technology-driven shift from manufacturing to service industries and the consequences of that shift for virtually all human activities (Bell, 1976; Toffler, 1990).

Especially since the early 1980s, the Postindustrial Revolution has been sped up by **globalization—** the process by which formerly separate economies, states, and cultures become tied together and people become increasingly aware of their growing interdependence (Giddens, 1990: 64; Guillén, 2001). In recent decades, rapid increases in the volume of international trade, travel, and communication have broken down the isolation and independence of most countries and people. Also contributing to globalization is the growth of many institutions that bind corporations, companies, and cultures together. These processes have caused people to depend more than ever on people in other countries for products, services, ideas, and even a sense of identity.

The causes and consequences of postindustrialism and globalization form the great sociological puzzles of our time. Much of this book is devoted to analyzing postindustrialism, globalization, and their effects. In concluding this chapter, a review of some of the sociological issues raised by the Postindustrial Revolution and globalization is therefore in order.

POSTINDUSTRIALISM AND GLOBALIZATION: OPPORTUNITIES AND PITFALLS

Toward the end of the twentieth century, many observers were wildly optimistic about the benefits that postindustrialism and globalization were supposedly going to bring to humanity. One commentator proclaimed "the end of history," by which he meant that liberal capitalism had become the unrivalled socioeconomic system in the world and its dominance was bound to usher in a long era of peace, freedom,

and prosperity, leaving no corner of the world untouched (Fukuyama, 1992). Similarly, in a special issue of the *New York Times Magazine* devoted to technology, one staff writer gushed:

> Individuals are acquiring more control over their lives, their minds and their bodies, even their genes, thanks to the transformations in medicine, communications, transportation and industry. At the same time, these technologies are providing social benefits and undoing some of the damage of the past. Technology helps to conserve natural resources and diminish pollution. . . . The Information Revolution, besides enabling us to visit Mars at will, is fostering peaceful cooperation on Earth by decentralizing power. Political tyrants and demagogic warmongers are losing control now that their subjects have tools to communicate directly with one another. People are using the tools to do their jobs without leaving their families. They're forming new communities in cyberspace and forming new bonds with their neighbors in real space. Technology has the potential to increase individual freedom and strengthen community. (Tierney, 1997: 46–7)

This and similar outpourings of optimism were written before the stock-market crash of 2000, the terrorist attacks of September 11, 2001, the second invasion of Iraq by the United States in 2003, and heightened fears about the consequences of climate change that surrounded the 2005 hurricane season. But even before these devastating shocks changed the minds of all but the most starry-eyed observers, sociologists were more realistic about the prospects of humanity. On the whole, they agreed that postindustrialism and globalization promise many exciting opportunities to enhance the quality of life and increase human freedom. But they also saw many social-structural barriers to the realization of that promise.

The unresolved social issues that confront us in the era of postindustrialism and globalization fall under three headings. Each issue is addressed in later chapters:

1. *Autonomy versus constraint.* One of the major themes that emerges from *New Society* is that many people are freer to construct their own identities than ever before. Almost everyone used

to retain their religious, ethnic, racial, and sexual identities for a lifetime, even if they were not particularly comfortable with them. In the era of postindustrialism and globalization, however, various social developments and technological advances, ranging from international migration to the World Wide Web to greater acceptance of sexual diversity, free people from traditional constraints. The theme of increasing personal autonomy is taken up in Chapter 2, Culture; Chapter 3, Socialization; Chapter 4, Gender and Sexuality; Chapter 5, The Mass Media; and Chapter 13, Religion.

Some chapters, however, point out that we experience increased freedom only within certain limits. For example, we can choose a far wider variety of consumer products than ever before. But consumerism itself increasingly seems a compulsory way of life (Chapter 2, Culture). Moreover, it is a way of life that threatens the natural environment (Chapter 16, Sociology and the Environment). Meanwhile, new technologies, such as surveillance cameras, cause us to modify our behaviour and act in more conformist ways (Chapter 14, Deviance and Crime). As these examples show, the autonomy promised by postindustrialism is only half the story. The other half is that postindustrialism places new constraints on us.

2. *Prosperity versus inequality.* The second major theme that emerges from *New Society* is that postindustrialism opens up new economic, political, and educational opportunities. It makes work less onerous for many people. It raises the average standard of living. It enables women in particular to make rapid strides in all institutional spheres.

Again, however, we must face the less rosy aspects of postindustrialism. Tremendous economic and political inequality persists between women and men (Chapter 7, Gender Inequality: Economic and Political Aspects). So does inequality between Aboriginal and other Canadians (Chapter 8, Race and Ethnic Relations). Inequality between rich and poor in Canada has not decreased (Chapter 6, Social Stratification). It is maintained partly by the educational system (Chapter 12, Education). Inequality between rich and poor nations has increased sharply (Chapter 9, Inequality among Nations: Perspectives on Development). There

are more good jobs at the top of the occupational structure but many more bad jobs at the bottom (Chapter 11, Work and Occupations). The quality of the Canadian health-care system is threatened at precisely the moment when our population is rapidly aging and most in need of health care (Chapter 17, Health and Aging). And although elections are regularly held throughout much of the world, it is an illusion to think that democracy has conquered the planet (Chapter 18, Politics and Social Movements). Thus, economic and political inequality persist despite growing prosperity and opportunity.

3. *Diversity versus uniformity.* The third major theme that emerges from *New Society* is that postindustrial society is more tolerant of diversity than any previous form of society. Immigration

With postindustrial society more tolerant of diversity than any previous form of society, our cities are more socially heterogeneous. At the same time, the globalization of economic, political, and cultural affairs may threaten the survival of distinct national cultures. SOURCE: © Biddle, Paul/The Image Bank.

policies no longer stipulate racial, ethnic, or religious criteria for entry into the country. As a result, our cities are more socially heterogeneous than ever before (Chapter 15, Population and Urbanization). The traditional nuclear family made up of mother, father, and children has given way to a wide variety of new family forms. Dozens of radio stations, hundreds of TV channels, thousands of newspapers and magazines, hundreds of thousands of CD titles, millions of books, and tens of millions of websites are now available to us.

Yet despite growing social diversity, there is a strong push to conformity in many spheres of life. For example, most of our diverse cultural consumption is governed by the tastes and the profit motive of vast media conglomerates, most of them American-owned (Chapter 5, The Mass Media). Powerful interests are trying to shore up the traditional nuclear family despite its inappropriateness for many people in postindustrial society (Chapter 10, Families). The globalization of economic, political, and cultural affairs may be threatening the survival of distinct national cultures (Chapter 19, Globalization). The push to uniformity thus counters the trend toward growing social diversity.

WHY SOCIOLOGY?

The renowned English sociologist Anthony Giddens wrote that we live in an era "suspended between extraordinary opportunity . . . and global catastrophe" (Giddens, 1982: 166). Because of the collapse of the USSR in 1991 and the work of international terrorists, nuclear, chemical, and biological catastrophes are more likely now than they were just a few years ago. A whole range of environmental issues, profound inequalities in the wealth of nations and of classes, racial and ethnic violence, and unsolved problems in the relations between women and men continue to stare us in the face and profoundly affect the quality of our daily life.

Despair and apathy is one possible response to these complex issues. But it is not a response that humans have often favoured. If it were our nature to give up hope, we would still be sitting around half-naked in the mud outside a cave.

People are more inclined to look for ways of improving their lives, and this period of human history is full of opportunities to do so. We have, for example, advanced to the point where for the first time we have the means to feed and educate everyone in the world. Similarly, it now seems possible to erode some of the inequalities that have always been with us and have always been the major source of human conflict. Students of sociology pursue careers that further such goals (see Box 1.3).

Although sociology offers no easy solutions as to how the goal of improving society may be accomplished, it does promise a useful way of understanding our current predicament and seeing possible ways of dealing with it, of leading us a little farther away from the mud outside the cave. You sampled sociology's ability to tie personal troubles to social-structural issues when we discussed suicide. You reviewed the major theoretical perspectives that enable sociologists to connect the personal with the social-structural. When I outlined the half-fulfilled promises of postindustrialism and globalization, you saw sociology's ability to provide an understanding of where we are and where we can head.

I frankly admit that the questions raised in this book are tough to answer. Sharp controversy surrounds them all. However, I am sure that if you try to grapple with them, you will enhance your understanding of your society's, and your own, possibilities. In brief, sociology can help you figure out where you fit in to society and how you can make society fit you. That, fundamentally, is sociology's goal.

BOX 1.3 CAREERS IN SOCIOLOGY

Students often ask: "Can I get a good job with a sociology degree?" "Exactly what kind of work could I do with a major in sociology?" "Aren't all the good jobs these days in technical areas and the natural sciences?" To answer these questions—and to help you decide whether a sociology or other social science major makes sense for you—consider the following data on the employment of Canadians with degrees in sociology and related fields.

A study based on 1988 data found that a higher percentage of Canadian sociology graduates were employed full-time than were graduates in the other social sciences (Guppy and Hedley, 1993). A study based mainly on 1996 data (Allen, 1999) showed that, in Canada

- the unemployment rate among social science graduates was lower than among graduates in math, physics, engineering, agriculture, and biology
- between 1991 and 1996, there were more new jobs for people with social science degrees than for people with degrees in other fields
- although women earned less than men in all fields in 1996, the discrepancy between men's and women's income was smallest among social science graduates

On the basis of these findings it seems that sociology degrees promise more employment security for both men and women, and less income discrimination against women, than other degrees. It also seems that the postindustrial economy requires more new employees with a social science background than new employees with a background in some technical and scientific fields.

Tens of thousands of Canadians have sociology B.A.s. A sociology B.A. improves your understanding of the diverse social conditions affecting men and women, people with different sexual orientations, and people from different countries, regions, classes, races, and ethnic groups. Therefore, people with a B.A. in sociology tend to be attracted to jobs requiring good people skills and jobs involved with managing and promoting social change (see Table 1.2). Often, people with a B.A. in sociology go on to graduate and obtain professional degrees in other fields, including law, urban planning, industrial relations, social work, and public policy. You will therefore find many people with sociology B.A.s working as lawyers, urban planners, city managers, and health care and education administrators.

Most people with a graduate degree in sociology teach and conduct research in universities, with research being a more important component of the job in larger and more prestigious institutions. But many sociologists do not teach. Instead, they conduct research and give policy advice in a wide range of settings outside the system of higher education. In many federal government agencies, for example, sociologists are employed as researchers and policy consultants. Sociologists also conduct research and policy analysis in trade unions, nongovernmental organizations, and professional and public interest associations. In the private sector, you can find sociologists practising their craft in firms specializing in public opinion polling, management consulting, market research, standardized testing, and "evaluation research," which assesses the impact of particular policies and programs before or after they go into effect.

One way of seeing the benefits of a sociological education is to compile a list of some of the famous practical idealists who studied sociology in university. That list includes several former heads of state, among them President Fernando Cardoso of Brazil, President Tomas Masaryk of Czechoslovakia, Prime Minister Edward Seaga of Jamaica, and President Ronald Reagan of the United States. The former vice-president of the Liberal Party of Canada and current president and vice-chancellor of York University in Toronto, Lorna Marsden, is a sociologist. Anthony Giddens, former director of the London School of Economics and adviser to British Prime Minister Tony Blair, also holds a sociology doctorate. So do Martin Goldfarb, chairman, president, and CEO of Goldfarb Consultants International; and Donna Dasko, senior vice-president of Environics, two of Canada's leading public opinion firms with offices and affiliates around the world. Alex Himelfarb, former clerk of the Privy Council, former secretary to the Cabinet in Ottawa, and now the Canadian ambassador to Italy, holds a sociology Ph.D. too. British Columbia native Steve Nash of the Phoenix Suns is widely considered the best team player in professional basketball today. His agent claims he is "the most color-blind person I've ever known" (Robbins, 2005). Arguably, Nash's sociology degree contributes to his team-building ability and his performance on the court by helping him to better understand the importance of groups and diverse social conditions in shaping human behaviour.

BOX 1.3 CAREERS IN SOCIOLOGY *(continued)*

TABLE 1.2 JOBS COMMONLY HELD BY CANADIANS WITH DEGREES IN SOCIOLOGY

Government

community affairs officer
urban/regional planner
legislative aide
affirmative action/employment equity worker
foreign service officer
human rights officer
personnel coordinator

Research

social research specialist
consumer researcher
data analyst
market researcher
survey researcher
census officer/analyst
demographer/population analyst
system analyst

Community Affairs

occupational/career counsellor
homeless/housing worker
public health/hospital administrator
child development technician
public administration assistant
social assistance advocate
resident planning aide
group home worker
rehabilitation program worker
rural health outreach worker
housing coordinator
fundraising director/assistant
caseworker/aide
community organizer
youth outreach worker

Corrections

corrections officer
criminology assistant
police officer
rehabilitation counsellor
criminal investigator
juvenile court worker
parole officer

Teaching

college/university placement worker
public health educator
teacher
admissions counsellor

Business

market analyst
project manager
sales representative
real estate agent
journalist
public relations officer
actuary
insurance agent
human resources manager
production manager
labour relations officer
administrative assistant
quality control manager
merchandiser/purchaser
computer analyst
data entry manager
publishing officer
advertising officer
sales manager

SOURCE: Guppy and Hedley (1993).

SUMMARY

1. Durkheim showed that even apparently nonsocial and antisocial actions are influenced by social structures. Specifically, he showed how levels of social solidarity affect suicide rates.

2. Because of the rise in youth suicide, the pattern of suicide rates in Canada today is not exactly the same as in Durkheim's France. Nevertheless, Durkheim's theory explains the contemporary Canadian pattern well.

3. Sociologists analyze the connection between personal troubles and social structures.

4. Sociologists analyze the influence of three levels of social structure on human action: microstructures, macrostructures, and global structures.

5. Values suggest which sociological research questions are worth asking and how the parts of society fit together. Values underlie sociological theories. A theory is a tentative explanation of some aspect of social life. It states how and why specific facts are connected. Research is the process of carefully observing social reality to assess the validity of a theory.

6. There are four major theoretical traditions in sociology. Functionalism analyzes how social order is supported by macrostructures. Conflict theory analyzes how social inequality is maintained and challenged. Symbolic interactionism analyzes how meaning is created when people communicate in microlevel settings. Feminism focuses on the social sources of patriarchy in both macro and micro settings.

7. The rise of sociology was stimulated by the Scientific, Industrial, and Democratic Revolutions.

8. The Postindustrial Revolution is the technology-driven shift from manufacturing to service industries and the consequences of that shift for virtually all human activities. Globalization is the process by which formerly separate economies, states, and cultures become tied together and people become increasingly aware of their growing interdependence.

9. The causes and consequences of postindustrialism and globalization form the great sociological puzzle of our time. The tension between autonomy and constraint, prosperity and inequality, and diversity and uniformity are among the chief interests of sociology today.

QUESTIONS TO CONSIDER

1. Do you think the promise of autonomy, prosperity, and diversity will be realized in the twenty-first century? Why or why not?

2. In this chapter you learned how variations in the level of social solidarity affect the suicide rate. How do you think variations in social solidarity might affect other areas of social life, such as criminal behaviour and political protest?

3. Is a science of society possible? If you agree that such a science is possible, what are its advantages over common sense? What are its limitations?

GLOSSARY

Altruistic suicide occurs in settings that exhibit high levels of social solidarity, according to Durkheim. Altruistic suicide results from norms very tightly governing behaviour.

Anomic suicide occurs in settings that exhibit low levels of social solidarity, according to Durkheim. Anomic suicide results from vaguely defined norms governing behaviour.

Conflict theory generally focuses on large, macrolevel structures, such as the relations between or among classes. It shows how major patterns of inequality in society produce social stability in some circumstances and social change in others. It stresses how members of privileged groups try to maintain their advantages while subordinate groups struggle to increase theirs. And it typically leads to the suggestion that eliminating privilege will lower the level of conflict and increase the sum total of human welfare.

The **Democratic Revolution** began about 1750. It suggested that people are responsible for organizing society and that human intervention can therefore solve social problems.

Dysfunctional consequences are effects of social structures that create social instability.

Egoistic suicide results from a lack of integration of the individual into society because of weak social ties to others.

Ethnomethodology is the study of how people make sense of what others do and say in terms of norms that exist independently of individual social actors.

Feminist theory claims that patriarchy is at least as important as class inequality in determining a person's opportunities in life. It holds that male domination and female subordination are determined not by biological necessity but by structures of power and social convention. It examines the operation of patriarchy in both micro and macro settings. And it contends that existing patterns of gender inequality can and should be changed for the benefit of all members of society.

Functionalist theory stresses that human behaviour is governed by relatively stable social structures. It underlines how social structures maintain or undermine social stability. It emphasizes that social structures are based mainly on shared values or preferences. And it suggests that re-establishing equilibrium can best solve most social problems.

Global structures are patterns of social relations that lie outside and above the national level. They include international organizations, patterns of worldwide travel and communication, and the economic relations between and among countries.

Globalization is the process by which formerly separate economies, states, and cultures are becoming tied together and people are becoming increasingly aware of their growing interdependence.

The **Industrial Revolution** refers to the rapid economic transformation that began in Britain in the 1780s. It involved the large-scale application of science and technology to industrial processes, the creation of factories, and the formation of a working class.

Latent functions are invisible and unintended effects of social structures.

Macrostructures are overarching patterns of social relations that lie outside and above one's circle of intimates and acquaintances. Macrostructures include classes, bureaucracies, and power systems, such as patriarchy.

Manifest functions are visible and intended effects of social structures.

Microstructures are the patterns of relatively intimate social relations formed during face-to-face interaction. Families, friendship circles, and work associations are all microstructures.

Patriarchy is the traditional system of economic and political inequality between women and men.

The **Postindustrial Revolution** refers to the technology-driven shift from manufacturing to service industries and the consequences of that shift for virtually all human activities.

The **Protestant ethic** is the sixteenth- and seventeenth-century Protestant belief that religious doubts can be reduced, and a state of grace ensured, if people work diligently and live ascetically. According to Weber, the Protestant ethic had the unintended effect of increasing savings and investment and thus stimulating capitalist growth.

Research is the process of systematically observing reality to assess the validity of a theory.

The **Scientific Revolution** began about 1550. It encouraged the view that sound conclusions about the workings of society must be based on solid evidence, not just speculation.

Social solidarity refers to (1) the degree to which group members share beliefs and values and (2) the intensity and frequency of their interaction.

Social structures are relatively stable patterns of social relations.

The **sociological imagination** is the quality of mind that enables a person to see the connection between personal troubles and social structures.

Sociology is the systematic study of human behaviour in social context.

Symbolic interactionism focuses on face-to-face communication, or interaction in microlevel social settings. It emphasizes that an adequate explanation of social behaviour requires understanding the subjective meanings people attach to their social circumstances. It stresses that people help to create their social circumstances and do not merely react to them. And by underscoring the subjective meanings people create in small social settings, symbolic interactionism validates unpopular and nonofficial viewpoints. This increases our understanding and tolerance of people who may be different from us.

A **theory** is a tentative explanation of some aspect of social life that states how and why certain facts are related.

Values are ideas about what is right and wrong.

SUGGESTED READING

Brym, Robert J. (2007). *Sociology as a Life or Death Issue.* Toronto and New York: Penguin. A guide to the socio-logical craft for beginners, emphasizing how sociology can help people live longer and better lives. Focuses on the sociological analysis of "natural" disasters, suicide, and hip hop.

The Canadian Journal of Sociology Online will give you a taste of the practice of sociology in Canada. Go to http://www.cjsonline.ca for book reviews and online articles. Visit the website of the Canadian Sociological Association at http://www.csaa.ca for sociological news and conferences.

Stephens, W. Richard, Jr. (1998). *Careers in Sociology.* New York: Allyn & Bacon. In this book, 18 sociology graduates talk about the diverse and fascinating careers they have pursued. It is available online at http://www.abacon.com/socsite/careers.html.

NOTES

1. You will find more detailed discussion of these theories throughout the book. For example, on functionalism, see Chapters 12 and 13. On conflict theory, see Chapters 6, 10, 13, and 18. On symbolic interactionism, see Chapter 3 and 14. On feminism, see Chapters 4, 7, 10, and 18.

2. By emphasizing how social reality is constructed during interaction, symbolic interactionists downplay the importance of norms and understandings that precede any given interaction. **Ethnomethodology** tries to correct this shortcoming. Ethnomethodologists study how people make sense of what others do and say but stress that norms exist independently of individual social actors. Indeed, in the ethnomethodological view, everyday interactions could not take place without pre-existing shared norms. Say you pass an acquaintance on the street, who offers a friendly "How are you?" If you proceed to outline in detail your financial situation, your love life, interesting developments at work, and so forth, the acquaintance will quickly become annoyed. Most people expect "How are you?" to be answered with an equally brief reply. Violate the norm, and communication quickly breaks down (Garfinkel, 1967).

WEB RESOURCES

Companion Web Site for This Book

http://www.newsociety5e.nelson.com

Begin by clicking on the Student Resources section of the website. Next, select the chapter you are studying from the pull-down menu. From the Student Resources page, you have easy access to InfoTrac College Edition and other resources, such as the Glossary and Flashcards. The website also has many useful tips to aid you in your study of sociology.

InfoTrac College Edition Search Terms

Visit http://www.infotrac-college.com for access to more than 20 million articles from nearly 6000 sources when doing your online research.

ThomsonNOW™

http://hed.nelson.com

This online diagnostic tool identifies each student's unique needs with a Pretest that generates a personalized Study Plan for each chapter, helping students focus on concepts they are having the most difficulty mastering. Students then take a Posttest after reading the chapter to measure their understanding of the material. An Instructor Gradebook is available to track and monitor student progress.

PART TWO

Culture

CHAPTER TWO

Culture

In this chapter you will learn that

- Culture is the sum of ideas, practices, and material objects that people create to adapt to, and thrive in, their environments.

- Humans have been able to thrive in their environments because of their unique ability to think abstractly, cooperate with one another, and make tools.

- We can see the contours of culture most sharply if we are neither too deeply immersed in it nor too much removed from it.

- As societies become more complex, culture becomes more diversified and consensus declines in many areas of life. This increases human freedom.

- As societies become more complex, the limits within which freedom may increase become more rigid. This constrains human freedom.

- Although culture is created to solve human problems, it sometimes has negative consequences that create new problems.

SOURCE: Shutterstock.

Robert J. Brym
UNIVERSITY OF TORONTO

INTRODUCTION

CULTURE AS PROBLEM SOLVING

Canadian hockey legend Wayne Gretzky refused to get his hair cut while playing on the road because the last time he did, his team lost. He always put his equipment on in the same order: left shin pad, left stocking, right shin pad, right stocking, pants, left skate, right skate, shoulder pads, left elbow pad, right elbow pad, and finally, jersey—with only the right side tucked into his pants. During warm-up, he would always shoot his first puck far to the right of the goal. When he went back to the dressing room, he would drink a Diet Coke, a glass of ice water, a Gatorade, and another Diet Coke—and always in that order ("Mad About Hockey," 2002). He believed these routines brought him luck.

Hockey legend Wayne Gretzky would tuck only the right side of his jersey into his pants. This superstitious practice helped to put his mind at ease before and during play. It is an example of how people create culture to cope with anxiety and other concrete problems they face.

SOURCE: F. Scott Grant/CP Picture Archive.

Like soldiers going off to battle, university students about to write final exams, and other people in high-stress situations, athletes invent routines to help them stop worrying and focus on the job at hand. Some wear a lucky piece of jewellery or item of clothing. Others say special words or a quick prayer. Still others cross themselves. And then there are those who engage in more elaborate rituals. For example, sociologists Cheryl and Daniel Albas of the University of Manitoba interviewed 300 university students about their superstitious practices before final exams. One student felt she would do well only if she ate a sausage and two eggs sunny-side up on the morning of each exam. The sausage had to be arranged vertically on the left side of her plate and the eggs placed to the right of the sausage so they formed the "100" percent she was aiming for (Albas and Albas, 1989). Of course, the ritual had more direct influence on her cholesterol level than on her grade. But indirectly it may have had the desired effect. To the degree it helped to relieve her anxiety and relax her, she may have done better in exams.

When some people say culture, they refer to opera, ballet, art, and fine literature. For sociologists, however, this definition is too narrow. Sociologists define **culture** broadly as all the socially transmitted ideas, practices, and material objects that people create to deal with real-life problems. For example, when Gretzky developed his dressing habits and the university student invented the ritual of preparing for exams by eating a sausage and eggs arranged just so, they were creating culture in the sociological sense. These practices helped Gretzky and the student deal with the real-life problem of high anxiety. Similarly, tools help people solve the problem of how to plant crops and build houses. Religion helps people face the problem of death and how to give meaning to life. Tools and religion are also elements of culture because they, too, help people solve real-life problems.

Note, however, that religion, technology, and many other elements of culture differ from the superstitions of athletes and undergraduates in one important respect. Superstitions are often unique to the individuals who create them. In contrast, religion and technology are widely shared. They are even passed on from one generation to the next. How does cultural sharing take place? By means of human interaction, communication, and learning. In other words, culture becomes shared when it is socially transmitted. A **society** involves people interacting socially and sharing culture, usually in a defined geographical area.[1] Culture, then, is the sum of the *socially transmitted* ideas, practices, and material objects that enable people to adapt to, and thrive in, their environments.

THE ORIGINS OF CULTURE

You can appreciate the importance of culture for human survival by considering the predicament of early humans about 100 000 years ago. They lived in harsh natural environments. They had poor physical endowments, being slower runners and weaker fighters than many other animals. Yet, despite these disadvantages, they survived. More than that—they prospered and came to dominate nature. This was possible largely because they were the smartest creatures around. Their sophisticated brains enabled them to create cultural survival kits of enormous complexity and flexibility. These cultural survival kits contained three main tools. Each tool was a uniquely human talent. Each gave rise to a different element of culture.

The first tool in the human cultural survival kit was **abstraction,** the capacity to create ideas or ways of thinking. **Symbols,** for example, are one important type of idea. They are things that carry particular meanings. Languages, mathematical notations, and signs are all sets of symbols. Symbols allow us to classify experience and generalize from it. For example, we recognize that we can sit on many objects but that only some of those objects have four legs, a back, and space for one person. We distinguish the latter from other objects by giving them a name: "chairs." By the time a baby reaches the end of her first year, she has heard that word repeatedly and understands that it refers to a certain class of objects. True, a few chimpanzees have been taught how to make some signs with their hands. In this way, they have learned a few dozen words and how to string together some simple phrases. But even these extraordinarily intelligent animals cannot learn any rules of grammar, teach other chimps what they know, or advance much beyond the vocabulary of a human toddler (Pinker, 1994). Abstraction at anything beyond the most rudimentary level is a uniquely human capacity. The ability to abstract enables humans to learn and transmit knowledge in a way no other animal can.

Cooperation is the second main tool in the human cultural survival kit. It is the capacity to create a complex social life by establishing **norms.** Norms are standards of behaviour or generally accepted ways of doing things. When we raise children and build schools, we are cooperating to reproduce and advance the human race. When we create communities and industries, we are cooperating by pooling resources and encouraging people to acquire specialized skills, thus enabling them to accomplish things no person could possibly do alone. An enormous variety of social arrangements and institutions, ranging from health-care systems to forms of religious worship to political parties, demonstrate the advanced human capacity to cooperate and adhere to norms. Of course, there is also plenty of war, crime, and revolution in the world. However, even when people engage in conflict, they must cooperate and respect norms or fail to achieve their survival aims. The bank robber who is left stranded by his getaway man will be caught; the navy captain whose sailors mutiny will lose the battle.

Production is the third main tool in the human cultural survival kit. It involves devising and using tools and techniques that improve our ability to take what we want from nature. Such tools and techniques are known as **material culture.** Of course, all animals take from nature in order to subsist, and an ape may sometimes use a rock to break another object or use a stick to keep its balance in a fast-flowing stream. But only humans are sufficiently intelligent and dexterous to *make* tools and use them to produce everything from food to computers. Understood in this sense, production is a uniquely human activity.

Table 2.1 illustrates each of the basic human capacities and their cultural offshoots with respect to three types of human activity: medicine, law, and religion. It shows, for these three types of activity, how abstraction, cooperation, and production give rise to specific kinds of ideas, norms, and elements of material culture. In medicine, theoretical ideas about the way our bodies work are evaluated by using norms about how to test theories experimentally. Experimentation, in turn, results in the production of new medicines and therapies, which are parts of material culture. In law, values, or shared ideas about what is right and wrong, good and bad, are embodied in a legal code, or norms defining illegal behaviour and punishments for breaking the law. The application of the law requires the creation of courts and jails, which are also part of material culture. And in religion, **folklore**—traditional ideas about how the universe was created, the meaning of life, and so on—is expressed in **folkways,** or norms regarding how to worship and how to treat fellow human beings. Folklore and folkways can give rise to material culture, which includes churches, their associated art and architecture, and so forth. As these examples show, the capacity for abstraction, cooperation, and production is evident in all spheres of culture.

In concluding this discussion of the origins of culture, we must note that people are usually rewarded when they follow cultural guidelines and punished when they do not. Taken together, these rewards and punishments, aimed at ensuring conformity, are known as **sanctions** or the system of **social control.** Rewards (or positive sanctions) include everything from praise and encouragement to money and power. Punishments (or negative sanctions) range from avoidance and contempt to physical violence and arrest.

Despite efforts to control people, they often reject elements of existing culture and create new elements of culture. Reasons for this are discussed in Chapter 14 (Deviance and Crime) and Chapter 18 (Politics and Social Movements). Here, it is enough to say that, just as social control is needed to ensure stable patterns of interaction, so resistance to social control is needed to ensure cultural innovation and social renewal. Stable but vibrant societies are able to find a balance between social control and cultural innovation.

CULTURE FROM THE MARGINS

Martians can never hope to grasp the tacit knowledge of real human beings. On the other hand, they sometimes see things real human beings fail to notice.

— Michael Ignatieff (2000: x)

I was once introduced to an interesting woman at a party and began a conversation with her that started agreeably. Within ten minutes, however, I found myself on the other side of the room, my back pressed hard against the wall, trying to figure out how I could politely end our interaction. I wasn't immediately aware of the reason for my discomfort. Only after I told the woman that I had to make an important phone call and had left the room did I realize the source of the problem: She had invaded my culturally defined comfort zone. Research shows the average North American prefers to stand 75 to 90 centimetres (30 to 36 inches) away from strangers or acquaintances when they are engaged in face-to-face interaction (Hall, 1959: 158–80). But this woman had recently arrived from her home in a part of the Middle East where the culturally defined comfort zone is generally smaller. She stood only about 50 centimetres (20 inches) from me as we spoke. Without thinking, I retreated half a step. Without thinking, she advanced half a step. And soon we had waltzed across the faculty club lounge, completely unaware of what we were doing, until I had no further room to retreat and had to concoct a means of escape.

As this example shows, culture, despite its central importance in human life, is often invisible to people who are immersed in it. That is, people tend to take their own culture for granted; it usually seems so sensible and natural they rarely think about it. I was unable to understand how my culture was affecting me while I was in its grip. I understood its effect only when I removed myself from the faculty club lounge, the immediate context of its operation, and thought hard about how it was making me behave.

If people often take their own culture for granted, they are often startled when confronted by cultures other than their own. That is, the ideas,

TABLE 2.1	THE BUILDING BLOCKS OF CULTURE		
HUMAN CAPACITIES	**ABSTRACTION**	**COOPERATION**	**PRODUCTION**
	↓	↓	↓
ELEMENTS OF CULTURE	**IDEAS**	**NORMS**	**MATERIAL CULTURE**
CULTURAL ACTIVITIES			
Medicine	theories	experiments	treatments
Law	values	laws	courts, jails
Religion	religious folklore	religious customs	church art, architecture

SOURCE: Adapted from Robert Bierstedt, *The Social Order* (New York: McGraw-Hill, 1963).

Taking public transportation often forces us to abandon our culturally defined personal space. However, this abandonment of personal space is itself a cultural norm.

SOURCE: Andrew Benyei, *Commuters.*

norms, and techniques of other cultures frequently seem odd, irrational, and even inferior. Judging another culture exclusively by the standards of our own is called **ethnocentrism.** Ethnocentrism impairs the sociological understanding of culture as much as taking our own culture for granted does.

The negative effect of ethnocentrism on sociological understanding may be illustrated by a practice that seems bizarre to many Westerners: cow worship among Hindu peasants in India. Hindu peasants refuse to slaughter cattle and eat beef because, for them, the cow is a religious symbol of life. Pin-up calendars throughout rural India portray beautiful women with the bodies of fat white cows, milk jetting out of each teat. Cows are permitted to wander the streets, defecate on the sidewalks, and stop to chew their cud in busy intersections and on railroad tracks, causing traffic to come to a halt. In Madras, the police maintain fields where stray cows that have fallen ill can graze and be nursed back to health. The government even runs old age homes for cows, where dry and decrepit cattle are kept free of charge. All this seems inscrutable to most Westerners, for it takes place amid poverty and hunger that could presumably be alleviated if only the peasants would slaughter their "useless" cattle for food instead of squandering scarce resources on feeding and protecting them.

The trouble is, ethnocentrism misleads many Western observers (Harris, 1974: 3–32). Cow worship, it turns out, is an economically rational practice in rural India. For one thing, Indian peasants can't afford tractors, so cows are needed to give birth to oxen, which are in high demand for ploughing. For another, the cows produce hundreds of millions of kilograms of recoverable manure, about half of which is used as fertilizer and half as cooking fuel. With oil, coal, and wood in short supply, and with the peasants unable to afford chemical fertilizers, cow dung is, well, a godsend. What is more, cows in India don't cost much to maintain since they eat mostly food that isn't fit for human consumption. And they represent an important source of protein and a livelihood for members of low-ranking castes, who have the right to dispose of the bodies of dead cattle. These "untouchables" eat beef and form the work force of India's large leathercraft industry. Thus, the protection of cows by means of cow worship is in fact a perfectly sensible and highly efficient economic practice. It only seems irrational when judged by the standards of Western agribusiness.

We can draw much the same lesson from the case of cow worship in India as from my hurried exit from the faculty club lounge. Culture is most clearly visible from the margins, as it were. We see its contours most sharply if we are neither too deeply immersed in it (as I was during the faculty club conversation) nor too much removed from it (as most Western observers are when they analyze cow worship in India). Said differently, if you refrain from taking your own culture for granted and judging other cultures by the standards of your own, you will have taken important first steps toward developing a sociological understanding of culture.

THE TWO FACES OF CULTURE

Having defined culture, discussed its origins, and located the ideal vantage point for analyzing it, we can now turn to the chapter's main theme. You will now see that although some aspects of culture make us freer, others constrain and even endanger us.

When we develop new ideas, practices, and artifacts, we give ourselves more choices and often come closer to realizing our full human potential. For example, you will see in the following text that we are now freer than ever to draw on all cultures in all their variety. This allows us to fashion our identities to suit our individual tastes. The story is much the same whether we consider ethnic identities, religious beliefs, political affiliations, or sexual orientations. We now become who we are less because traditional authority imposes a set of cultural definitions on us, and more because we are able to choose who we want to be.

However, cultural freedom develops within definite limits. Beyond those limits it is more and more difficult to move. In particular, our lives are increasingly governed by the twin forces of rationalization and consumerism:

- **Rationalization** is the application of the most efficient means to achieve given goals and the unintended, negative consequences of doing so. Modern bureaucracies exemplify the rationaliza-

tion process (Weber, 1946 [1922]). The factory, the government office, the military, the system of higher education, and the institutions of science all seek to apply the most efficient means to achieving given goals (see Box 2.1). Yet bureaucracies are composed of unelected officials. Consequently, they concentrate power and threaten democracy. Moreover, bureaucracies discourage officeholders from considering what the goals of their organization ought to be. Bureaucrats are asked only to determine the best way of achieving the goals defined by their superiors. Officeholders thus lose their spontaneity and their inventiveness. Like other aspects of the rationalization process, the growth of bureaucracy thus constrains our freedom.

- **Consumerism** is a lifestyle that involves defining ourselves in terms of the goods we purchase. Some sociologists argue that consumerism impoverishes the self and society by drawing resources and attention away from pressing social issues and encouraging environmentally dangerous levels of consumption. From this point of

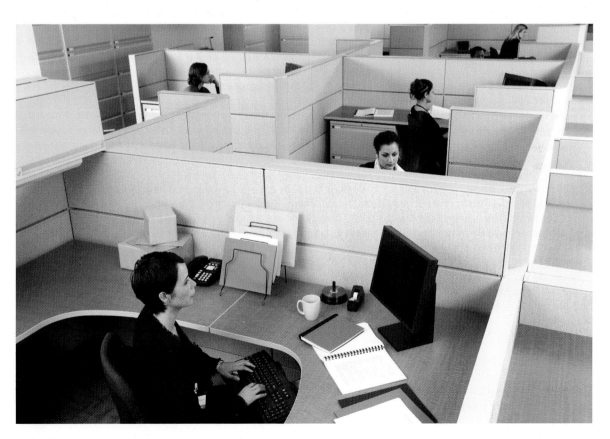

Rationalization constrains freedom.
SOURCE: Photos.com.

BOX 2.1   THE RATIONALIZATION OF SCIENCE: HOW HIGH TECH BECAME BIG TECH AND LOST ITS INNOCENCE

In the last quarter of the nineteenth century, it was already clear that turning scientific principles into technological innovations was going to require not just genius but substantial resources, especially money and organization. The first "invention factory" was established by Thomas Edison at Menlo Park, New Jersey, in the late 1870s. Historian of science Robert Pool notes:

> The most important factor in Edison's success—outside of his genius for invention—was the organization he had set up to assist him. By 1878, Edison had assembled at Menlo Park a staff of thirty scientists, metalworkers, glassblowers, draftsmen, and others working under his close direction and supervision. With such support, Edison boasted that he could turn out "a minor invention every ten days and a big thing every six months or so." (1997: 22)

The phonograph and the electric light bulb were two such "big things." Both were inspired by Edison. Both, however, were also expensive team efforts, motivated by vast commercial possibilities. (Edison founded General Electric, one of the most profitable companies in the world and one of the most valuable based on market capitalization.)

By the middle of the twentieth century, the great bulk of technological innovation was organized along industrial lines. Entire armies of experts and vast sums of capital were required to run the new invention factories. Only governments and, increasingly, giant multinational corporations could afford to sustain the research effort of the second half of the twentieth century. In the course of the century, the number of research scientists in the industrialized countries increased a hundredfold. In the United States between 1960 and 2000, research and development spending tripled after taking inflation into account, and the proportion spent by corporations increased from one-third to two-thirds of the total (Hobsbawm, 1994: 522–57; U.S. Department of Commerce, 1998: 609).

In light of these developments, it should come as no surprise that military and profit-making considerations now govern the direction of most research and development. A reporter once asked the infamous bank robber Willy Sutton why he robbed banks. Sutton answered: "Because that's where the money is." This is by no means the only motivation prompting scientists and engineers to research particular topics. Especially in theoretical (as opposed to applied) research and especially in universities (as opposed to the research institutes of governments and private industry), the direction of inquiry is strongly influenced by personal interests, individual creativity, and the state of a field's intellectual development. It would, however, be naïve to think that practicality doesn't also enter into the scientist's calculation of what he or she ought to study. Even in a more innocent era, Sir Isaac Newton studied astronomy partly because the explorers and mariners of his day needed better navigational cues, just as Michael Faraday was partly motivated to discover the relationship between electricity and magnetism by his society's search for new forms of power (Bronowski, 1965: 7–8). The connection between practicality and research is even more evident today, when many researchers—even many of those who do theoretically driven research in universities—are pulled in particular directions by large research grants, well-paying jobs, access to expensive state-of-the-art equipment, and the possibility of winning patents and achieving commercial success. For example, many of the leading molecular biologists have established genetic engineering companies, serve on their boards of directors, or receive research funding from them. In not a few cases, these companies have been bought out by major pharmaceutical and agrochemical corporations who see their vast profit potential (Rural Advancement Foundation International, 1999; Rifkin, 1998: 56).

Economic lures, increasingly provided by the military and big corporations, have generated moral and political qualms among some researchers. Some scientists and engineers wonder whether research on particular topics achieves optimum benefits for humanity, and some are even troubled by the possibility that some types of research may be harmful to humankind. A growing number of researchers, however, if they are at all preoccupied by these issues, recognize that to do cutting-edge research they must still any residual misgivings, hop on the bandwagon, and adhere to military and industrial requirements and priorities. That, after all, is where the money is.

view, culture, which started out as a means of solving real-life problems, has become the biggest real-life problem of all (Postman, 1992).

Let us begin our examination of the two faces of culture by first considering the ways in which culture makes us freer.

CULTURE AS FREEDOM

CULTURAL DIVERSIFICATION AND GLOBALIZATION

In the 1950s, the Christmas pageant was a fixture of every elementary school in the country. Today, some Canadian public schools have abolished Christmas pageants. Others have put Christmas on par with the Hindu Diwali, the Jewish Chanukah, and the seasonal festivals of other ethnic and religious groups. In some schools, an ethnically and religiously neutral "winter solstice" forms the basis of celebration in mid- to late December. The reason for this change is plain: According to the most recent census, 23 percent of Canadians do not identify with Christianity (Statistics Canada, 2005). Moreover, many Christians recognize that the use of public institutions to promote their religion is an imposition that creates discomfort for many minority students and denies the value of non-Christian cultures. Therefore, particularly in big-city schools, where students who are members of minority groups are sometimes in the numerical majority, cultural uniformity has given way to cultural diversity.

Canada used to be composed almost exclusively of northern Europeans and an Aboriginal minority. By eliminating overt racism in its immigration policies in the 1960s, Canada began to diversify culturally. In the 1970s, the Canadian government continued the trend by adopting a policy of multiculturalism, which funds the maintenance of cultural diversity (Fleras and Elliott, 2002).

Canada's growing cultural diversification is well illustrated in Table 2.2. For immigrants who arrived in Canada before 1961, nine of the top ten source countries for Canadian immigrants were in Europe and North America. For immigrants who arrived in Canada in 2002, six of the top ten source countries were in Asia. As a result of the inflow of immigrants from nontraditional sources—not just Asia but also the Caribbean, Latin America, and Africa—5.7 million people in Canada in 2001 were not white—nearly 18 percent of the population. In Montreal, Edmonton, Calgary, and Winnipeg, the figure was closer to one-quarter. In Vancouver, it was nearly 40 percent, while in Toronto non-whites made up about 45 percent of the population (Henry, Tabor, Mattis, and Rees, 2001: 145–47).

Some critics argue that our immigration and multiculturalist policies weaken Canada's social fabric. Specifically, multiculturalism supposedly encourages immigrants to cling to their past rather than to shrug off their old self-conceptions and create a distinctive *Canadian* identity (Bissoondath, 2002). This viewpoint has two problems. First, it is by no means certain that we lack a distinctive Canadian identity. In fact, as noted below, a defining element of our distinctive Canadian identity is precisely our deep respect for diversity. Second, contrary to the claims of the critics of multiculturalism, survey research shows that support for multiculturalism is *not* correlated with traditional atti-

---

TABLE 2.2   TOP TEN PLACES OF BIRTH OF CANADIAN IMMIGRANTS, BEFORE 1961 AND IN 2002

IMMIGRATED BEFORE 1961		IMMIGRATED IN 2002	
Country	**% of All Immigrants**	**Country**	**% of All Immigrants**
1. United Kingdom	25.2	1. China	14.5
2. Italy	15.3	2. India	12.6
3. Germany	10.2	3. Pakistan	6.2
4. Netherlands	8.4	4. Philippines	4.8
5. Poland	5.5	5. Iran	3.4
6. United States	4.3	6. South Korea	3.2
7. Hungary	3.1	7. Romania	2.5
8. Ukraine	2.6	8. United States	2.3
9. Greece	2.0	9. Sri Lanka	2.2
10. China	1.7	10. United Kingdom	2.1
Other	21.7	Other	46.2
Total	100.0	Total	100.0

SOURCES: Statistics Canada, "Top Ten Places of Birth for Total Immigrants, Immigrants Arriving Before 1961 and Recent Immigrants for Canada, 1996 Census—20% Sample Data," Cat. No. 93F0023XDB6003. Reprinted by permission of the Minister of Industry, 2002; Statistics Canada, "Facts and Figures 2002: Immigration Overview," on the World Wide Web at http://www.cic.gc.ca/english/pub/facts2002/immigration/immigration_5.html (29 October 2005).

Multiculturalism on the move.
SOURCE: ©Mike Randolph/Masterfile.

tudes (such as religiosity) that keep people rooted in the past. Support for multiculturalism *is* correlated with various modern trends, such as support for equality between women and men (Adams, 1997: 173).

From this point of view, Canada's multiculturalist policies are simply the latest stage in a long process of cultural evolution. In general, cultures tend to become more diverse or heterogeneous as societies become more complex, with important consequences for everyday life. Thus, in preliterate or tribal societies, cultural beliefs and practices are virtually the same for all group members. For example, many tribal societies organize puberty ceremonies to mark the end of childhood and the beginning of adulthood, fertility dances to pray for good crops and healthy babies, and other rites. These rituals involve elaborate body painting, carefully orchestrated chants and movements, and so forth. They are conducted in public. No variation from prescribed practice is allowed. Culture is homogeneous (Durkheim, 1976 [1915]).

In contrast, preindustrial Western Europe and North America were rocked by artistic, religious, scientific, and political forces that fragmented culture.

The Renaissance, the Protestant Reformation, the Scientific Revolution, the French and American Revolutions—between the fourteenth and eighteenth centuries, all these movements involved people questioning old ways of seeing and doing things. Science placed skepticism about established authority at the very heart of its method. Political revolution proved there was nothing ordained about who should rule and how they should do so. Religious dissent ensured that the Catholic Church would no longer be the supreme interpreter of God's will in the eyes of all Christians. Authority and truth became divided as never before.

Cultural fragmentation picked up steam during industrialization, as the variety of occupational roles grew and new political and intellectual movements crystallized. Its pace is quickening again today in the postindustrial era under the impact of a variety of globalizing forces.

The roots of globalization are many (see Chapter 19). International trade and investment are expanding. Members of different ethnic and racial groups are migrating and coming into sustained contact with one another. A growing number of people from these diverse groups date, court, and marry across religious, ethnic, and racial lines. Influential "transnational" organizations have been created, such as the International Monetary Fund, the European Union, Greenpeace, and Amnesty International. Inexpensive international travel and communication make contacts between people from diverse cultures routine. The mass media make Vin Diesel and *Friends* nearly as well known in Warsaw as in Winnipeg, and MTV brings rock music to the world via MTV Latino, MTV Brazil, MTV Europe, MTV Asia, MTV Japan, MTV Mandarin, MTV India, and MTV Canada (Hanke, 1998). Globalization, in short, destroys political, economic, and cultural isolation, bringing people together in what Canadian communications guru Marshall McLuhan (1964) called a "global village." As a result of globalization, people are less obliged to accept the culture into which they are born and freer to combine elements of culture from a wide variety of historical periods and geographical settings. Globalization is a Bombay schoolboy listening to Bob Marley on his CD player as he rushes to slip into his Levis, wolf down a bowl of Kellogg's Basmati Flakes, and say goodbye to his parents in Hindi because he's late for his English-language school (see Box 2.2).

THE RIGHTS REVOLUTION

Underlying cultural diversification is the **rights revolution,** the process by which socially excluded groups have struggled to win equal rights under the law and in practice. After the outburst of nationalism, racism, and genocidal behaviour among the combatants in World War II, the United Nations proclaimed the Universal Declaration of Human Rights in 1948. Its preamble reads in part:

> Whereas recognition of the inherent dignity and of the equal and inalienable rights of all members of the human family is the foundation of freedom, justice and peace in the world. . . . Now, therefore The General Assembly proclaims this Universal Declaration of Human Rights as a common standard of achievement for all peoples and all nations, to the end that every individual and every organ of society, keeping this Declaration constantly in mind, shall strive by teaching and education to promote respect for these rights and freedoms and

by progressive measures, national and international, to secure their universal and effective recognition and observance. (United Nations, 1998)

Fanned by such sentiment, the rights revolution was in full swing by the 1960s. Today, women's rights, Aboriginal rights, gay and lesbian rights, the rights of people with special needs, constitutional rights, and language rights are a key part of our political discourse. As a result of the rights revolution, democracy has been widened and deepened (see Chapter 18, Politics and Social Movements). The rights revolution is by no means finished—many categories of people are still discriminated against socially, politically, and economically—but in much of the world all categories of people now participate more fully than ever before in the life of their societies (Ignatieff, 2000).

The rights revolution raises some difficult issues. For example, groups that have suffered extraordinarily high levels of discrimination historically, such as Aboriginal Canadians, Jewish Canadians, Chinese Canadians, and Japanese Canadians, have demanded reparations in the form of money, symbolic gestures, and, in the case of Aboriginal Canadians, land and political autonomy.[2] Much controversy surrounds the extent of the obligation of current citizens to compensate past injustices.

Another problem raised by the rights revolution concerns how we can achieve an acceptable balance between the right to be equal and the right to be different. For example, most residents of Quebec expect all Quebeckers to be able to compete on an equal footing for jobs, regardless of whether they are of French, English, or other origin. This is the right to equality. But Quebeckers of French origin have also exercised their right to be different. They have, for instance, passed laws restricting the use of English on public signs. These laws are controversial. Some English Quebeckers accept them as legitimate; others do not. Controversy therefore persists regarding the balance between the right to equality and the right to be different.

These problems notwithstanding, the rights revolution is here to stay and it affects our culture profoundly. Specifically, the rights revolution fragments Canadian culture by legitimizing the grievances of groups that were formerly excluded from full social participation and renewing pride in their identity and heritage. Our history books, our literature, our music,

The spread of English is a key marker of the extent of globalization. In 1600, English was the mother tongue of between 4 million and 7 million people. Not even all people in England spoke it. Today, 750 million to 1 billion people speak English worldwide, more than half as a second language. With the exception of the many varieties of Chinese, English is the most widespread language on Earth, and it is by far the most important. More than half the world's technical and scientific periodicals are written in English. English is the official language of the Olympics, of the Miss Universe contest, of navigation in the air and on the seas, and of the World Council of Churches.

English is dominant because Britain and the United States have been the world's most powerful and influential countries—economically, militarily, and culturally—for more than two centuries. (Someone once defined *language* as a dialect backed up by an army.) In recent decades, the global spread of capitalism, the popularity of Hollywood movies and American TV shows, and widespread access to instant communication via telephone and the Internet have increased the reach of the English language. There are now more speakers of excellent English in India than in the United Kingdom, and when a construction company jointly owned by German, French, and Italian interests undertakes a building project in Spain, the language of business is English (McCrum, Cran, and MacNeil, 1992).

Even in Japan, where relatively few people speak the language, English words are commonly used and Japanese words that are badly translated into English often become popular. The result is what is commonly known as "Japlish." Sometimes the results are unintelligible to a native English speaker. "Push to my nose! I might be changing to you?" says the catchy sign in a T-shirt store in Tokyo's Ueno district. Certain computer terms are more comprehensible to a native English speaker. For example, when you learn to open a computer file's *ai-kon* (icon) you are told to *daburu-kurikku* (double-click) the *mausu* (mouse) (Kristof, 1997).

In view of the extensive use of English in Japan, *The Japanese Times*, one of Tokyo's four English daily newspapers, ran a story a few years ago noting the pressures of globalization and suggesting it might be time for Japan to switch to English. However, it met with an official backlash. To limit the Anglicization of Japanese, the Ministry of Health and Welfare banned excessive use of English in its documents a couple of years ago. The Ministry of Education is now replacing many English words in official documents—such words as *sukeemu* (scheme), *eensenchibu* (incentive), *deribatibu* (derivative), and *identyityi* (identity). Whether official pronouncements will have much effect on the way English and Japlish are used in advertising and on the streets is, however, another question entirely. As one Japanese newspaper pointed out, given the popularity of English words, it's doubtful there will be much *foro-uppu* (follow-up).

For Japanese teenagers, English and Japlish are certainly considered the very height of fashion. "Japlish words are easy to pronounce. And English sounds very cool," says 11-year-old Mai Asai (quoted in Delmos, 2002). A 15-year old girl, wearing her trademark *roozu sokusu* (loose socks), might greet a friend sporting new sunglasses with a spirited *chekaraccho* (Check it out, Joe). If she likes the shades, she might say they're *cho beri gu* (ultra-good) and invite her friend *deniru* (to go to a Denny's restaurant) or *hageru* (to go to a Häagen-Dazs ice cream outlet). Of course, the girl might also *disu* (diss, or show disrespect toward) her friend. She might come right out and inform him that the new shades look *cho beri ba* (ultra-bad) or *cho beri bu* (ultra-blue, depressing, or ultra-ugly). If so, the situation that develops could be a little *denjarasu* (dangerous). Terms of affection, such as *wonchu* (I want you), might not be exchanged. The boy might decide that he has made a *misu* (mistake) and that the girl is too *hi mentay* (high maintenance) to justify pursuing. The budding relationship might go nowhere. Nonetheless, we can be pretty sure that Japanese teenagers' use of English slang will intensify under the pressures of globalization.

Less humorously, the rise of English (as well as the influence of French, Spanish, and the languages of a few other colonizing nations) is eliminating several thousand languages around the world. These endangered languages are spoken by the tribes of Papua New Guinea; the native peoples of the Americas; the national and tribal minorities of Asia, Africa, and Oceania; and marginalized European peoples, such as the Irish and the Basques. An estimated 5000 to 6000 languages spoken in the world today will be reduced to 1000 to 3000 in a century. Much of the culture of a people—its prayers, humour, conversational styles, technical vocabulary, myths, and so on—is expressed through language. Therefore, the loss of language amounts to the disappearance of tradition and perhaps even identity. These are often replaced by the traditions and identity of the colonial power, with television playing an important role in the transformation (Woodbury, 2003).

our use of languages, our very sense of what it means to be Canadian have diversified culturally. White male heterosexual property owners of British origin are still disproportionately influential in Canada, but our culture is no longer dominated by them in the way that it was just four decades ago.

POSTMODERNISM

In part because of the rights revolution, so much cultural fragmentation and reconfiguration has taken place in the last few decades that some sociologists think a new term is needed to characterize the culture of our times: **postmodernism.**

Postmodern culture has three main features:

1. It involves *an eclectic mixing of elements from different times and places.* That is, in the postmodern era it is easier to create individualized belief systems and practices by blending facets of different cultures and historical periods. Consider religion. Surveys conducted by Reginald Bibby of the University of Lethbridge show that Canadians often supplement Judeo-Christian beliefs and practices with less conventional ideas about astrology, psychic powers, communication with the dead, and so forth (Bibby, 1987). People who attend church regularly are just as likely to hold such unconventional beliefs as nonattenders. But despite the widespread acceptance of unconventional beliefs, the overwhelming majority of Canadians still turn to established religions for **rites of passage,** or cultural ceremonies that mark the transition from one stage of life to another (e.g., baptisms, confirmations, weddings) or from life to death (funerals). Individuals thus choose their own mix of unconventional and conventional beliefs and practices. They draw on religions much like consumers shop in a mall; as Bibby says, they practise religion à la carte. Meanwhile, the churches in Canada have diversified their menus to appeal to the spiritual, leisure, and social needs of religious consumers and retain their loyalties in the competitive market for congregants and parishioners. The mix-and-match approach we see when it comes to religion is evident in virtually all spheres of culture.

2. Postmodernism involves *the erosion of authority.* Half a century ago, Canadians were more likely than they are today to defer to authority in the family, schools, politics, medicine, and religion. In fact, Canadians were often characterized as an especially deferential people, more respectful of authority than, say, their individualistic, revolutionary, violent, and entrepreneurial cousins in the United States. In the second half of the twentieth century, however, Canadians grew skeptical about authority in many institutions, especially political institutions—even more skeptical than Americans in many respects (Brym with Fox, 1989; Nevitte, 1996; see Figure 2.1 and Box 2.3). For example, voting and other forms of conventional politics are less popular than they used to be, while nonconventional political action is more popular. In 2000, 30 percent of Canadians said they had participated in nonconventional political actions (joining a boycott, taking part in an unlawful demonstration, joining an unofficial strike, or occupying a building or a factory). That was up from 24 percent in 1980. Meanwhile, just 60.5 percent of eligible voters cast a ballot in the 2004 federal election, down from 73 percent in the 1980s (see Figure 2.2).

3. Postmodernism is characterized by *the decline of consensus around core values.* Half a century ago, people's values remained quite stable over the course of their adult lives and many values were widely accepted. Today, value shifts are more rapid and consensus has broken down on many issues. For instance, half a century ago, the great majority of adults remained loyal to one political party from one election to the next. Today,

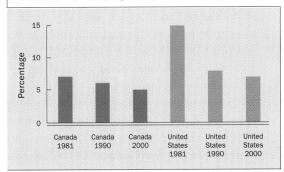

FIGURE 2.1 PERCENTAGE OF PEOPLE WITH "A GREAT DEAL OF CONFIDENCE" IN PARLIAMENT/ CONGRESS, CANADA/UNITED STATES, 1981–2000

SOURCE: *World Values Survey* (2000). Reprinted with permission.

FIGURE 2.2 PERCENTAGE OF ADULTS VOTING IN FEDERAL ELECTIONS AND PARTICIPATING IN NONCONVENTIONAL POLITICAL ACTION, SELECTED YEARS

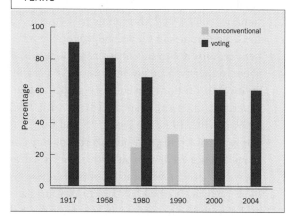

SOURCES: "Voter Turnout" (2004); *World Values Survey* (2000). Reprinted with permission.

FIGURE 2.3 PERCENTAGE WHO BELIEVE SCIENTIFIC ADVANCES WILL HELP HUMANITY, 2000

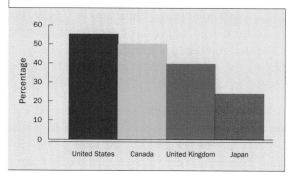

SOURCE: *World Values Survey* (2000). Reprinted with permission.

people are more likely to vote for different parties in succeeding elections (Clarke, Jenson, LeDuc, and Pammett, 1996: 139–46).

The decline of consensus can also be illustrated by considering the fate of Big Historical Projects. For most of the past 200 years, consensus throughout the world was built around Big Historical Projects. Various social movements convinced people they could take history into their own hands and create a glorious future just by signing up. German Nazism was a Big Historical Project. Its followers expected the Reich to enjoy 1000 years of power. Communism was an even bigger Big Historical Project, mobilizing hundreds of millions of people for a future that promised to end inequality and injustice for all time. However, the biggest and most successful Big Historical Project was not so much a social movement as a powerful idea—the belief that progress is inevitable, that life will always improve, mainly because of the spread of democracy and scientific innovation.

The twentieth century was unkind to Big Historical Projects. Russian communism lasted 74 years, German Nazism a mere 12. And the idea of progress fell on hard times as 100 million soldiers and civilians died in wars; the forward march of democracy took wrong turns into fascism, communism, and regimes based on religious

fanaticism; and pollution from urbanization and industrialization threatened the planet. In the postmodern era, more and more people recognize that apparent progress, including scientific advances, often has negative consequences (Scott, 1998; see Figure 2.3).

The aspects of postmodernism listed previously—the eclectic mixing of cultural elements from different times and places, the erosion of authority, and the decline of consensus around core values—have many parents, teachers, politicians, religious leaders, and not a few university professors worried. How can we make binding decisions? How can we govern? How can we teach children and adolescents the difference between right and wrong? How can we transmit accepted literary tastes and artistic standards from one generation to the next? These are the kinds of issues that plague people in positions of authority today. Although their concerns are legitimate, many of them seem not to have considered the other side of the coin: The postmodern condition, as described above, empowers ordinary people and makes them more responsible for their own fate. It renders them more tolerant and appreciative of ethnic, racial, religious, and sexual groups other than their own—no small matter in a world torn by group conflict. The postmodern attitude encourages a healthy skepticism about rosy and naïve scientific and political promises. And it frees people to adopt religious, ethnic, and other identities they are comfortable with, as opposed to identities imposed on them by others.

Until the mid-1960s, the image of Canadians among most sociologists was that of a stodgy people: peaceful, conservative, respectful of authority, and therefore quite unlike our American cousins.

According to conventional wisdom, the United States was born in open rebellion against the British motherland. Its Western frontier was lawless. Vast opportunities for striking it rich bred a spirit of individualism. Thus, American culture became an anti-authoritarian culture.

Canada developed differently according to the conventional view. It became an independent country not through a revolutionary upheaval but in a gradual, evolutionary manner. The Northwest Mounted Police and two highly hierarchical churches (Roman Catholic and Anglican) established themselves on the Western frontier *before* the era of mass settlement, allowing for the creation of an orderly society rather than a "wild West." Beginning with the Hudson's Bay Company, large corporations quickly came to dominate the Canadian economy, hampering individualism and the entrepreneurial spirit. Thus, Canadian culture became a culture of deference to authority. That, at least, was the common view until the 1960s (Lipset, 1963).

Although the contrast between deferential Canadian culture and anti-authoritarian American culture may have had some validity 40 years ago, it is an inaccurate characterization today (Adams, 1997: 62–95). As we have seen, the questioning of authority spread throughout the Western world beginning in the 1960s. Nowhere, however, did it spread as quickly and thoroughly as in Canada. Canadians used to express more confidence in big business than Americans did, but surveys now show the opposite. Canadians used to be more religious than Americans, but that is no longer the case. Fewer Canadians (in percentage terms) say they believe in God and fewer attend weekly religious services. Confidence in government has eroded more quickly in Canada than in the United States. Americans are more patriotic than Canadians, according more respect to the state. Finally, Americans are more likely than Canadians to regard the traditional nuclear family as the ideal family form and to think of deviations from tradition—same-sex couples, single-parent families, cohabitation without marriage—as the source of a whole range of social problems. Thus, whether sociologists examine attitudes toward the family, the state, government, religion, or big business, they now find that Americans are more deferential to traditional institutional authority than Canadians are.

Because Canadians are less deferential to traditional institutional authority than Americans are, some commentators say that Canadians lack a distinct culture. For example, American patriotism sparks awareness of great national accomplishments in art, war, sports, science, and, indeed, all fields of human endeavour. Anthems, rituals, myths, and celebrations celebrate these accomplishments and give Americans a keen sense of who they are and how they differ from non-Americans. Not surprisingly, therefore, a larger percentage of Americans than of Canadians think of themselves in unhyphenated terms—as "Americans" plain and simple rather than, say, Italian-Americans. In Canada, a larger percentage of the population thinks of itself in hyphenated terms; compared with the Americans, our identity is qualified, even tentative.

Does this mean that Canadians lack a distinct national culture? Hardly. It means that although American culture is characterized by a relatively high degree of deference to dominant institutions, Canadian culture is characterized by a relatively high degree of tolerance and respect for diversity. We are more likely than Americans to favour gender equality, accept gay and lesbian relationships, encourage bilingualism and multiculturalism, and accept the right of Aboriginals to political autonomy. Characteristically, a large international survey by a condom manufacturer found that Americans have sex more often than anyone else, but Canadians are most likely to say that the pleasure of their partner is very important. As public opinion pollster Michael Adams writes:

> Twenty-five years of public-opinion polling in Canada has taught me a seemingly paradoxical truth. Canadians feel *strongly* about their *weak* attachments to Canada, its political institutions and their fellow citizens. In other words, they feel strongly about the right to live in a society that allows its citizens to be detached from ideology and critical of organizations, and not to feel obliged to be jingoistic or sentimentally patriotic. Canadians *lack* of nationalism is, in many ways, a distinguishing feature of the country. (1997: 171)

In short, Canadian culture *is* distinctive, and its chief distinction may be that it qualifies us as the first thoroughly postmodern society.

Thus, the news about postmodern culture is not all bad. However, as you will now see, it's not all good either.

CULTURE AS CONSTRAINT AND AS DANGER

We noted previously that culture has two faces. One we labelled "freedom," the other "constraint." Diversity, globalization, and postmodernism are all aspects of the new freedoms that culture allows us today. We now turn to an examination of two contemporary aspects of culture that act as constraining forces on our lives: rationalization and consumerism.

RATIONALIZATION

In fourteenth-century Europe, an upsurge in demand for textiles caused loom owners to look for ways to increase productivity. To that end, they imposed longer hours on loom workers and installed the first public clocks. The clocks, known as *Werkglocken* ("work clocks") in German, signalled the beginning of the workday, the timing of meals, and quitting time.

Workers were accustomed to enjoying many holidays and a flexible and vague work schedule regulated only approximately by the seasons and the rising and setting of the sun. The regimentation imposed by the work clocks made life harder. So the workers staged uprisings to silence the clocks. But to no avail. City officials sided with the employers and imposed fines for ignoring the *Werkglocken*. Harsher penalties, including death, were imposed on anyone trying to use the clocks' bells to signal a revolt (Thompson, 1967).

Now, more than 600 years later, many people in the world's rich countries—especially big-city couples who are employed full-time in the paid labour force and have preteen children—are, in effect, slaves of the *Werkglock*. Life often seems an endless round of waking up at 6:30 a.m., getting everyone washed and dressed, preparing the kids' lunches, getting them out the door in time for the school bus or the car pool, driving to work through rush-hour traffic, facing the speed-up at work that resulted from the recent downsizing, driving back home through rush-hour traffic, preparing dinner, taking the kids to their soccer game, returning home to clean up the dishes and help with homework, getting the kids washed, brushed, and into bed, and (if you haven't brought some office work home) grabbing an hour of TV before collapsing, exhausted, for six-and-a-half hours before the story repeats itself. Life is less hectic for residents of small cities and towns, unmarried people, couples without small children, retirees, and the unemployed. But the lives of most people are so packed with activities that time must be carefully regulated, each moment precisely parcelled out so we may tick off item after item from an ever-growing list of tasks that need to be completed on schedule (Schor, 1992). In 2000, 14 percent of Canadians in the paid labour force worked for pay 50 or more hours a week, up from 11 percent in 1976. In 1999, the figure was 38 percent among senior managers, the most overworked job category. Among transport and equipment operators, the second most overworked job category, the figure was 27 percent. Among teachers and professors, the sixth most overworked job category, the figure was 18 percent (Lowe, 2001: 8, 9).

After more than 600 years of conditioning, it is unusual for people to rebel against the clock in the town square anymore. In fact, we now wear a watch on our wrist without giving it a second thought, as it were. This signifies that we have accepted and internalized the regime of the work clock. Allowing clocks to regulate our activities precisely seems the most natural thing in the world—which is a pretty good sign that the internalized *Werkglock* is, in fact, a product of culture.

Is the precise regulation of time rational? It certainly is rational as a means of ensuring efficiency, that is, maximizing how much work you get done in a day. But is it rational as an end in itself? For many people, it is not. The precise regulation of time has gotten out of hand. Life has simply become too hectic for many people to enjoy fully. In this sense, rationality of means has led to irrationality of ends.

For American sociologist George Ritzer, the McDonald's fast-food restaurant epitomizes the rationalization process. Ritzer speaks of the "McDonaldization" of the world, by which he means that the organizational principles of the fast-food restaurant are coming to dominate everywhere (Ritzer, 1993, 1996).

At McDonald's, a set list of carefully weighed food portions with identical ingredients are cooked according to a uniform and precisely timed process. But, says Ritzer, the application of assembly-line procedures to meal preparation is dehumanizing for both employees and customers. Thus, the work is done by mainly nonunionized, uniformed, teenage workers who receive minimum wage. To boost sales, they are required to smile as they recite fixed scripts ("Would you like some fries or a drink with your burger?"). Nearly half of all McDonald's employees are so dissatisfied with their work they quit after a year or less. To deal with this problem, McDonald's is field-testing self-service kiosks in which an automated machine cooks and bags French fries while a vertical grill takes patties from the freezer and grills them to your liking (Carpenter, 2003). Meanwhile, customers are expected to spend as little time as possible eating the food—hence the drive-through window, chairs designed to be comfortable for only about 20 minutes, and small express outlets in subways and department stores where customers eat standing up or on the run. In short, McDonald's executives have carefully thought through every aspect of your lunch. With the goal of making profits, they have rationalized food preparation, making it as inexpensive and as fast as possible.

Taking McDonaldization to a new extreme, one restaurant in Japan has even installed a punch-clock for its customers. The restaurant offers all you can eat for 35 yen per minute. As a result, "the diners rush in, punch the clock, load their trays from the buffet table, and concentrate intensely on efficient chewing and swallowing, trying not to waste time talking to their companions before rushing back to punch out. This version of fast food is so popular that, as the restaurant prepares to open at lunchtime, Tokyo residents *wait in line*" (Gleick, 2000: 244; emphasis in the original). Meanwhile, in New York and Los Angeles, some upscale restaurants have got in on the act. An increasingly large number of business clients are so pressed for time they feel the need to pack in *two* half-hour lunches with successive guests. The restaurants oblige, making the resetting of tables "resemble the pit-stop activity at the Indianapolis 500" (Gleick, 2000: 155).

As the examples of the *Werkglock* and fast food show, rationalization enables us to do just about everything more efficiently, but at a steep cost. In fact, because it is so widespread, rationalization is one of the most constraining aspects of culture today. In Weber's view, it makes life in the modern world akin to living inside an "iron cage."

The second constraining aspect of culture that we will examine is consumerism, the tendency to define our selves in terms of the goods we purchase.

CONSUMERISM

A few years ago, the Gap hired Hollywood talent to create a slick and highly effective series of TV ads for khaki pants. According to the promotional material for the ad campaign, the purpose of the ads was to "reinvent khakis," that is, to stimulate demand for the pants. In *Khakis rock*, "skateboarders and in-line skaters dance, glide, and fly to music by the Crystal Method." In *Khakis groove*, "hip-hop dancers throw radical moves to the funky beat of Bill Mason." In *Khakis swing*, "two couples break away from a crowd to demonstrate swing techniques to the vintage sounds of Louis Prima" (Gap.com, 1999).

About 55 seconds of each ad featured the dancers. During the last 5 seconds, the words "GAP khakis" appeared on the screen. The GAP followed a similar approach in another ad campaign a couple years later. Inspired by the 1957 musical, *West Side Story*, the 30-second spots replaced the play's warring street gangs, the Jets and the Sharks, with fashion factions of their own, the Khakis and the Jeans. Again, most of the ad was devoted to the riveting dance number. The pants were mentioned for only a few seconds at the end.

As the imbalance between stylish come-on and mere information suggests, the people who created the ads understood that it was really the appeal of the dancers that would sell the pants. They knew that to stimulate demand for their product, they had to associate the khakis with desirable properties, such as youth, good health, coolness, popularity, beauty, and sex. As an advertising executive said in the 1940s: "It's not the steak we sell. It's the sizzle."

Because advertising stimulates sales, business has a tendency to spend more on advertising over time. Because advertising is widespread, most people unquestioningly accept it as part of their lives. In fact, many people have *become* ads. Thus, when your father was a child and quickly threw on a shirt, allowing a label to hang out, your grandmother might admonish him to "tuck in that label." Today, in contrast, many people proudly display consumer labels as marks of status and identity. Advertisers teach us to associate the words "Gucci" and "Nike" with different kinds of people, and when people display these labels on their clothes they are telling us something about the kind of people they are and whom they associate with. Advertising becomes us.

Since the 1980s, there has been an explosion of advertising directed at children in particular. Here, advertisers recognized, was a vast untapped market;

children could be used to nag their parents to buy more products. The manipulation of children by advertisers soon became a sort of quasi-science. One advertising expert said there are seven basic types of nagging tactics that can be unleashed by effective child-directed advertising:

> A *pleading* nag is one accompanied by repetitions of words like "please" or "mom, mom, mom." A *persistent* nag involves constant requests for the coveted product and may include the phrase "I'm gonna ask just one more time." *Forceful* nags are extremely pushy and may include subtle threats, like "Well, then, I'll go and ask Dad." *Demonstrative* nags are the most high-risk, often characterized by full-blown tantrums in public places, breath-holding, tears, a refusal to leave the store. *Sugar-coated* nags promise affection in return for a purchase and may rely on seemingly heartfelt declarations like "You're the best dad in the world." *Threatening* nags are youthful forms of blackmail, vows of eternal hatred and of running away if something isn't bought. *Pity* nags claim the child will be heartbroken, teased, or socially stunted if the parent refuses to buy a certain product. (Schlosser, 2002: 44)

Note that getting children to nag their parents to buy more products is only one aim of child-directed advertising. In addition, advertisers recognize that ads directed at children can be used to develop brand loyalty that will, in the ideal case, last a lifetime. Executives at one large brewery must have been delighted to read the results of a consumer survey that found that the most popular ads among American children were a Taco Bell commercial featuring a talking Chihuahua and an ad for Budweiser beer.

The rationalization process enables us to produce more efficiently, to have more of just about everything than our parents did. But it is consumerism, the tendency to define our selves in terms of the goods we purchase, that ensures the goods will be bought. Of course, people living in the world's rich countries have lots of choice. We can select from dozens of styles of running shoes, cars, and all the rest. We can also choose to buy items that help to define us as members of a particular **subculture,** adherents of a set of distinctive values, norms, and practices within a larger culture. But, regardless of individual tastes and inclinations, nearly all of us have one thing in common: We tend to be good consumers. We are motivated by advertising, which is based on the accurate insight that people will likely be considered social outcasts if they fail to conform to stylish trends. By creating those trends, advertisers push us to buy. That is why North Americans' "shop-till-you-drop" lifestyle prompted French sociologist Jean Baudrillard to remark pointedly that even what is best in North America is compulsory (Baudrillard, 1988 [1986]).

FROM COUNTERCULTURE TO SUBCULTURE

In concluding my discussion of culture as a constraining force, I want to note that consumerism is remarkably effective at taming countercultures. **Countercultures** are subversive subcultures. They oppose dominant values and seek to replace them. The hippies of the 1960s formed a counterculture and so do environmentalists today.

Countercultures rarely pose a serious threat to social stability. Most often, the system of social control, of rewards and punishments, keeps countercultures at bay. In our society, consumerism acts as a social control mechanism that normally prevents countercultures from disrupting the social order. It does that by transforming deviations from mainstream culture into means of making money and by enticing rebels to become entrepreneurs (Frank and Weiland, 1997). Two examples from popular music help illustrate the point:

- Ozzy Osbourne was an important figure in the counterculture that grew up around heavy metal music beginning in the late 1960s. He and his band, Black Sabbath, inspired Metallica, Kiss, Judas Priest, Marilyn Manson, and others to play loud, nihilistic music, reject conventional morality, embrace death and violence, and spark youthful rebellion and parental panic. In 1982, Osbourne bit the head off a bat during a performance and urinated on the Alamo. He was given rabies shots for the former and arrested for the latter. Around the same time, Tipper Gore, wife of the future presidential candidate, formed the Parents' Music Resource Center to fight against violence and sex in the lyrics of popular music. Osbourne was one of the committee's principal targets. The "Prince of Darkness," as he was often called, was about as rebellious a figure as one could imagine in 1982.

Flash forward 20 years. Osbourne, now 53, has the sixth most popular show on North American television among 18- to 34-year-olds, just behind *Survivor* in the ratings. MTV placed a dozen cameras throughout his Beverly Hills mansion, and every Tuesday night viewers get to see everything going on in the Osbourne household for half an hour. According to *USA Today*, Osbourne is "a lot like anyone's adorable dad. Shuffles a bit. Forgets things. Worries about the garbage. Snores on the couch while the TV blares. Walks the dog" (Gunderson, Keveney, and Oldenburg: 1A). CNN's Greta Van Susteren says she finds the Osbournes "charming," and Rosie O'Donnell says to Ozzy's wife, Sharon, "What I love most about [your show] is not only the relationship you have with Ozzy—and you obviously adore each other—but the honesty with which you relate to your children. The love is so evident between all of you. It's heartwarming" (Gunderson, Keveney, and Oldenburg: 2A). Sharon and Ozzy Osbourne were invited to dinner at the White House in 2002, and in the same year, former Republican Vice President Dan Quayle (who in 1992 criticized the TV character Murphy Brown for deciding to have a baby out of wedlock) admitted "there are some very good lessons being transmitted" by the Osbournes (Beck, 2002). *The Osbournes*, it turns out, is a comfort to many people. The show seems to prove that heavy metal's frightening rejection of mainstream culture in the 1970s and 1980s was just a passing phase and that the nuclear family remains intact. Ozzy Osbourne has thus been transformed from the embodiment of rebellion against society to a family man, a small industry, and a conservative media icon.

- The development of hip-hop also illustrates the commercialization and taming of rebellion (Brym, 2001). Originating in the squalor of inner-city American ghettoes in the 1970s, hip-hop gave rise to a highly politicized counterculture. Early hip-hop artists glorified the mean streets of the inner city and held the police, the mass media, and other pillars of white society in utter contempt, blaming them for arbitrary arrests, the political suppression of black activists, and the spreading of lies about African Americans. However, by the time *Public Enemy* became a hit in the late 1980s, MTV had aired its first regular program devoted to the genre and much of hip-hop's audience comprised white, middle-class youth. Hip-hop artists were quick to see the potential of commercialization. Soon WU-Tang Clan had its own line of clothes, Versace was marketing clothing influenced by ghetto styles, and Puff Daddy (who later had a makeover as P. Diddy and now as Diddy) was reminding his audience: "N—— get money, that's simply the plan" (from his CD, *Forever*). No less than heavy metal and punk, most of hip-hop's radicalism gave way to the lures of commerce.

The stories of heavy metal and hip-hop are testimony to the capacity of consumerism to change countercultures into mere subcultures, thus constraining dissent and rebellion. They are compelling illustrations of culture's second face.

Diddy marketing "rebellion."
SOURCE: ©Reuters/Corbis.

SUMMARY

1. Humans have been able to adapt to their environments because they are able to create culture. In particular, the ability to create symbols, cooperate, and make tools has enabled humans to thrive.

2. Culture can be invisible if we are too deeply immersed in it. The cultures of others can seem inscrutable if we view them exclusively from the perspective of our own culture. Therefore, the best vantage point for analyzing culture is on the margins—neither too deeply immersed in it nor too much removed from it.

3. Culture becomes more diversified and consensus declines in many areas of life as societies become more complex. This increases human freedom, giving people more choice in their ethnic, religious, sexual, and other identities.

4. So much cultural diversification and reconfiguration has taken place that some sociologists characterize the culture of our times as postmodern. Postmodernism involves an eclectic mixing of cultural elements from different times and places, the erosion of authority, and the decline of consensus around core values.

5. Underlying cultural diversification is the rights revolution, the process by which socially excluded groups have struggled to win equal rights under the law and in practice.

6. Although the diversification of culture increases human freedom, the growth of complex societies also establishes definite limits within which diversification may occur. This is illustrated by the process of rationalization (the optimization of means to achieve given ends) and the growth of consumerism (which involves defining one's self in terms of the goods one purchases).

QUESTIONS TO CONSIDER

1. We imbibe culture but also create it. What elements of culture have you created? Under what conditions were you prompted to do so? Was your cultural contribution strictly personal or was it shared with others? Why?

2. Do you think of yourself in a fundamentally different way from the way your parents (or other close relatives or friends at least 20 years older than you) thought of themselves when they were your age? Are your attitudes toward authority different? Interview your parents, relatives, or friends to find out. Pay particular attention to the way in which the forces of globalization have altered ethnic, racial, and religious self-conceptions and how your attitudes to authority differ from those of your elders.

3. One of the main themes of this chapter is that rationality of means sometimes results in irrationality of ends. Select a sphere of culture (religion, education, the mass media, etc.) and illustrate the point.

GLOSSARY

Abstraction is the human capacity to create complex symbols, including languages, mathematical notations, and signs, in order to classify experience and generalize from it.

Consumerism involves defining ourselves in terms of the goods we purchase.

Cooperation is the human capacity to create a complex social life by establishing norms.

Countercultures are subversive subcultures. They oppose dominant values and seek to replace them.

Culture is the sum of socially transmitted practices, languages, symbols, beliefs, values, ideologies, and material objects that people create to deal with real-life problems. Cultures enable people to adapt to, and thrive in, their environments.

Ethnocentrism is the tendency to judge other cultures exclusively by the standards of our own.

Folklore in religion refers to traditional ideas about how the universe was created, the meaning of life, and so on.

Folkways in religion are norms about how to worship and how to treat fellow human beings.

Material culture comprises the tools and techniques that improve our ability to take what we want from nature.

Norms are standards of behaviour or generally accepted ways of doing things.

Postmodernism is characterized by an eclectic mixing of cultural elements, the erosion of authority, and the decline of consensus around core values.

Production is the human capacity to make and use tools. It improves our ability to take what we want from nature.

Rationalization is Max Weber's term for the systematic application of standardized means to predetermined ends.

The **rights revolution** is the process by which excluded groups have obtained equal rights under the law and in practice.

A **rite of passage** is a cultural ceremony that marks the transition from one stage of life to another or from life to death.

Sanctions are rewards and punishments intended to ensure conformity to cultural guidelines.

The system of **social control** is the means by which members of society ensure people conform to cultural guidelines.

A **society** involves people interacting socially and sharing culture, usually in a defined geographical area.

A **subculture** is a distinctive set of values, norms, and practices within a larger culture.

A **symbol** is anything that carries a particular meaning, including the components of language, mathematical notations, and signs. Symbols allow us to classify experience and generalize from it.

SUGGESTED READING

Adams, Michael. (1997). *Sex in the Snow: Canadian Social Values at the End of the Millennium*. Toronto: Penguin. Adams is a sociologist and one of Canada's leading public opinion pollsters. Here he identifies and analyzes the core values of Canadian culture, highlighting differences by generation, gender, and country (Canada versus the United States).

Klein, Naomi. (2000). *No Logo: Taking Aim at the Brand Bullies*. Toronto: Vintage Canada. This is the definitive work on the negative effects of marketing on our culture by the young *Globe and Mail* columnist.

Schlosser, Eric. (2002). *Fast Food Nation: The Dark Side of the All-American Meal*. New York: Perennial. You may never eat another fast-food meal after reading this insightful exposé, but you will learn much about the major forces shaping our culture.

Spillman, Lyn, ed. (2002). *Cultural Sociology*. Oxford, UK: Blackwell. This book comprehensively analyzes major issues in the sociological study of culture.

NOTES

1. New forms of society on the Internet ("virtual communities") show that physical proximity is not always a necessary part of the definition.

2. Many children of Aboriginal Canadians were put into residential schools in the twentieth century, and many of them were physically and sexually abused by the ministers, priests, and nuns who ran these schools. Many Aboriginal Canadians also claim that much land was taken from them illegally. Some 21 000 Japanese Canadians living within 160 kilometres of the Pacific Coast, three-quarters of them Canadian citizens, were forcibly moved to prisoner-of-war, internment, and work camps in 1942. They lost most of their property. Descendants of many Chinese Canadians were forced to pay an exorbitant "head tax" in the late nineteenth and early twentieth centuries, the purpose of which was to encourage them to leave the country. The Nazis enslaved and slaughtered millions of European Jews in World War II and stole their property. Survivors, a considerable number of them residing in Canada, later sought and received reparations from the German and Swiss governments.

WEB RESOURCES

Companion Web Site for This Book

http://www.newsociety5e.nelson.com

Begin by clicking on the Student Resources section of the website. Next, select the chapter you are studying from the pull-down menu. From the Student Resources page, you have easy access to InfoTrac College Edition and other resources, such as the Glossary and Flashcards. The website also has many useful tips to aid you in your study of sociology.

InfoTrac College Edition Search Terms

Visit http://www.infotrac-college.com for access to more than 20 million articles from nearly 6000 sources when doing your online research.

ThomsonNOW™

http://hed.nelson.com

This online diagnostic tool identifies each student's unique needs with a Pretest that generates a personalized Study Plan for each chapter, helping students focus on concepts they are having the most difficulty mastering. Students then take a Posttest after reading the chapter to measure their understanding of the material. An Instructor Gradebook is available to track and monitor student progress.

CHAPTER THREE

Socialization

In this chapter you will learn that

- Socialization refers to the processes that allow people to become members of society, develop a sense of self, and learn to participate in social relationships with others.

- Socialization takes place at all stages of the life cycle and in a variety of settings: families, schools, peer groups, the mass media, and occupational groups.

- Among the major contributors to socialization theory are Charles Cooley (who argued that individuals develop a sense of self as they interact with others), George Herbert Mead (who focused on the way we actively create a sense of self by taking the roles of others), and Paul Willis (who demonstrated that young people creatively participate in generating and maintaining their sense of self, both in accordance with and sometimes in opposition to their social context).

- Socialization continues into adulthood. As people work, marry, divorce, raise children, and retire, they enter new relationships with others, learn new behaviour, and adopt new roles.

- Sometimes our self-concept undergoes abrupt change as we learn new role identities and negotiate a new self-image. Such "resocialization" occurs when we replace our way of life with a radically different one. It is most evident in jails, mental hospitals, and boot camps, and in religious and political conversions.

William Shaffir
MCMASTER UNIVERSITY
Michael Rosenberg
DAWSON COLLEGE

WHAT IS SOCIALIZATION?

Anyone who has been a parent is probably more familiar than they would like to be with the "terrible twos," the stage many two-year-olds pass through and that childhood development experts call the "negativism" stage. During negativism a child will often be contrary and obstinate, refusing to cooperate even in simple tasks and saying "no" to everything and everyone. What's worse, the child may often willfully break norms, or generally accepted ways of doing things, in the household—sometimes also breaking valued objects, dishes, and almost anything else that comes to hand. Negativism can be a difficult stage to live through for both the parents and the child. Yet, childhood socialization experts insist, it is an essential stage in developing a sense of self and becoming an autonomous human being.

An anecdote will illustrate what is meant by negativism. One of the authors of this chapter used to have a large houseplant in his living room of which he and his wife were very fond. When their first child was still young, they made it clear that he was not to touch the plant. "Plants are beautiful things that we must cherish, nourish, and allow to grow," they explained. Still, there was always a gleam in their son's eyes when he looked at the plant, and they were careful never to leave him alone when he was near it.

One day, when he was about one-and-a-half, the child walked into the living room where his father was reading, approached the plant, observed it for several seconds and then muttered "no" to himself. He then looked at his father with a big smile on his face. His father, smiling back at him, said, "That's right. No." The boy left, but came back a few minutes later and repeated his actions, once again reminding himself with a smile, "No." His father, not yet sensing disaster, smiled back. The boy left, but a few minutes later returned yet again, walking up close to the plant, looking at it, and saying "No" with a big smile. But this time he grabbed the largest leaf of the plant as he spoke and, crushing it, repeated "No" yet again. The plant was given to neighbours the next day.

The truth is, of course, that young children are constantly being told "No" by the adults around them: "Don't touch that!" "Don't eat this!" "Don't go there!" If children always listened to what their parents said, they would never be able to do anything. Negativism is the way a child learns what really can or cannot be done. It is a way of testing the limits to find out which of the many No's they hear are serious and which are only a preference. It is also a form of rebellion whereby the child sets limits for the parents as well. Parents also have to learn how far they can go in restricting and controlling the child. Children are not robots who just follow instructions; they need to develop as autonomous, competent, and self-directed actors if they are to be full-fledged members of a family—and of society. The social process whereby they undergo such development through interacting with the people around them is known as **socialization.**

To be socialized means to learn how to act and interact appropriately with others, to become a competent and effective member of society. Yet, paradoxically, sociologists assert that to be socialized is also to develop a **self,** a sense of individual identity that allows us to understand ourselves and differentiate

The terrible twos.
SOURCE: Shutterstock.

ourselves from others. Each of these processes depends on and implies the other: To have a self, we must interact with others; to interact competently, we must reflect on and understand ourselves in relation to those others. That is why understanding socialization requires us to examine both people's sense of belonging and their sense of autonomy, both how people are constrained by norms and values (shared ideas about what is right and wrong) and how people are autonomous agents able to make decisions for themselves. Freedom and constraint, we will see, are not opposites but interconnected features of everyone's ordinary, everyday life.

The approach taken in this chapter is that socialization is an active process, one in which those being socialized participate and to which they contribute. It is also an interactive process in which those who are socializing, like the parents in the example above, are themselves undergoing a learning process. Of course, we may learn from others without their knowledge; we learn from role models, from stories about heroes or villains, from the example of our parents and friends, and just by observing the people around us. But the most important learning, the crucial learning that transforms us into cultural beings, proceeds through interaction with others who are important to us and—usually—to whom we are important.

The crucial learning process that occurs in childhood and makes us members of society is called **primary socialization.** Because primary socialization is so important to becoming who and what we are, it is the focus of the first part of this chapter. But because humans are creative, adaptable beings, learning and change continue throughout our lives. Learning to be a student, a husband or wife, or a parent; learning a job and how to carry it out effectively; making new friends and undertaking new commitments—all these involve socialization. This kind of learning is called **secondary socialization** because it occurs after people have already undergone primary socialization. It is not secondary in importance, however. We live in a world of constant and dramatic change, and secondary socialization is an ongoing feature of our lives.

As Chapter 2 showed, culture provides us with the tools to solve the problems of survival. Symbols, norms, values, and everyday practices are examples of such tools. Their use allows us to master nature and build orderly societies; they must, however, be learned. Indeed, insofar as human beings are cultural beings, these tools must become a part of us—inter-

nalized through socialization. In a very real sense, then, it is socialization that makes social interaction, social organization, and social order possible.

Think of all the things we do every day involving other people. When we walk along a busy sidewalk, for example, we are able to pass many pedestrians heading toward us without colliding with any of them. This is possible because of the norms that regulate sidewalk behaviour without our being aware of them. Most of the time each of us will move to the right to avoid colliding with someone walking toward us. We don't even have to think about it; we simply move to the right. If we move to our right when walking toward others and they move to their right (which is our left) when walking toward us, then we will not collide (Wolff, 1973). Such norms as these make social life orderly and allow us to deal with and interact with hundreds of anonymous strangers daily. It is not only norms that regulate behaviour, however. There are also many conventions, rituals, rules, and laws that direct our behaviour both with people whom we know well, such as co-workers, and with strangers.

How do we know to act on such norms, conventions, or rules? How do we know to move to the right to avoid colliding with a fellow pedestrian? We know through socialization. There is nothing "natural" about moving to the right to avoid a collision. In some societies, people move to the left; in others they don't particularly mind bumping into others. In our society we have learned to move to the right by watching others, and by seeing how others react when, on occasion, we have moved to the left by mistake. In this respect, norms constrain us; they channel and guide our behaviour in everyday life. Consider the alternative: Imagine what it would be like to have to decide separately as we walked along a sidewalk which way we should move to avoid colliding with each person we were walking toward. Norms make smooth and orderly interaction possible, freeing us from the need to plan every step we take and communicate in detail with everyone we meet about all the possible ways we could interact.

Because the process of becoming socialized occurs in a cultural context, the content of socialization differs greatly from one society to another. People in a particular society learn the norms, values, and lifestyles specific to their social environment. At the same time, however, within every society individuals differ in significant ways from one another. Such individual differences, too, are to some extent the product of socialization. Each person is influenced by distinctive or overlapping subcultures of family and friends, by class and gender. A subculture is a group within the larger culture that has distinctive values, norms, and practices. Our unique personal histories permit us not only to share in the larger society but also to participate in a specific part of it. The socialization process helps to explain both similarities and differences among people in a particular society.

NATURE AND NURTURE

Does that mean that everything we do and know is a product of socialization? Don't we have **instincts,** such as an instinct for survival or a maternal instinct? What about natural differences among people? Aren't there people with charismatic personalities, who have more of an impact on others than ordinary people do? Aren't some brighter than others, some more aggressive than others, some more compliant than others? Aren't there people who simply won't get out of the way when you walk toward them?

Although natural differences obviously exist among people, such differences explain very little about social behaviour or how a society is organized. It is very doubtful, for instance, that human beings have either an instinct for survival or a maternal instinct. There are countless examples of people who clearly give little thought to their own survival or who have proven to be indifferent or abusive parents. Still, we can't deny that some human behaviour is the outcome of biological factors, and the debate over whether it is nature (biological inheritance) or nurture (the social environment) that is more important in shaping our beliefs and behaviour is an old one. Most sociologists who participate in this debate emphasize the importance of society and of socialization, suggesting that someone who is aggressive in our society might well have become gentle—or at least less aggressive—had that person been born in some other society or raised in some other set of circumstances.

Sociologists are also suspicious of explanations that emphasize biological inheritance because such explanations often shift from an initial focus on individual differences to an emphasis on group differences. In this way, they often lead to racist or sexist explanations or views (Gould, 1996). An example is the longstanding debate over intelligence: Is our intelligence the outcome of hereditary and genetic

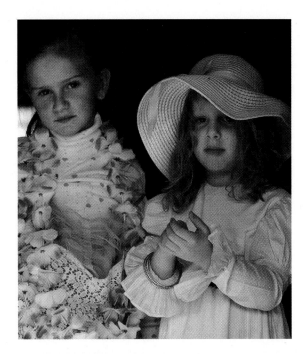

Most socialization takes place informally, with the participants unaware that they are being socialized. These little girls are unconsciously learning gender roles by playing dress-up.
SOURCE: Photo courtesy of Nurit Bodemann and Shira Brym.

factors, or is it a product of social variables, such as class and family structure? Phrased that way, the debate is about the sources of individual differences. True to many sociologists' concerns, however, this debate has shifted from a question about individual differences to one focused on the supposed connection between race and IQ test scores (Herrnstein and Murray, 1994).

It is becoming more and more apparent today that the old debate on nature versus nurture sets up a false opposition. It is clear that nature and nurture are both complementary and inseparable. The human brain provides the physiological apparatus required for interpreting experiences, but unless children have the opportunity to learn, reason, and solve problems in early life, the brain itself may not fully develop (Begley, 1995). Attempts at determining the relative importance of nature and nurture in human development are much like trying to establish whether width or height is more significant in determining area.

We are not born human. We become human through the process of social interaction. Indeed, strong evidence exists that human beings have a biologically grounded need for social interaction and intimate relations with others. Evidence suggests that human infants have both a biological and an emotional need to cling to and interact with a warm, sheltering figure. Verbal communication may not be part of this contact, but some form of communication is—whether smiles, laughs, or touch. Without this contact, socialization is impaired, the individual is but a shell of a human being, and irreversible damage may be done to the person's sense of self.

Convincing evidence comes from studies of children raised in isolation by their families. The case of Anna is the best-known instance of the long-term social isolation of an infant. Anna was an illegitimate child hidden away in a room until she was nearly six years old. Her mother gave her only enough care to keep her alive. When she was discovered, her clothing and bedding were filthy, she was emaciated, and she was unable to walk, talk, feed herself, or respond to others. As she was cared for and began to interact with others, Anna made slow yet steady progress, but years of social isolation left her with permanent disabilities. By the age of eight, Anna's mental and social development was still less than that of a two-year-old. Not until she was ten did she show the first signs of using language (Davis, 1947).

The importance of social contact in the development of human infants was also demonstrated when one research compared infants raised in an orphanage with those raised in a women's prison nursery (Spitz, 1945). The infants in the prison nursery interacted with their own mothers for the first year of their lives, whereas infants raised in the orphanage were attended only by nurses and spent their days lying on their backs, seeing and hearing very few people, and lacking social stimulation. Although in the beginning the orphan children were as healthy as those in the nursery, after two years the development of some of children in the orphanage was retarded, and all were psychologically and socially underdeveloped for their age. More shockingly, by age four a third of them had died! No such problems were observed among the prison nursery infants.

These examples show that socialization is essential both to the physical well-being and to the social competence of an infant. Even when, as in the case of Anna, infants survive lack of interaction and caring in early childhood, they are incapable of becoming fully competent, active members of society. This is not just a matter of "intelligence." Rather, the children have not had the opportunity to develop a self; they have no sense of social identity in terms of which they understand themselves and others around them. We can view the self as the point of reference for planning and orientation, for sorting and assessing life's situations in terms of their relative importance. As noted earlier, the self refers to our awareness of ideas and attitudes about our own personal and social identity. It is through interaction that such a sense of self emerges, and the development of the self is a crucial part of socialization.

THE SELF AND SOCIALIZATION

Where does our sense of self come from? Sociologists and psychologists alike have sought to answer that question. They have examined how individuals develop and modify a sense of who they are—their sense of self—and found that self-image greatly depends on social interaction. For instance, the newborn does not differentiate itself from its mother (Piaget, 1950). Such differentiation occurs gradually as the newborn learns to see its mother as a separate person. Through interaction the infant acquires the ability to see himself or herself reflected in the eyes of others and to sense his or her own identity. It is precisely this ability that children who have been reared in isolation lack.

Though sociologists typically focus on the development of the social self, it is important to recognize the connections between the physical and the social selves. Research demonstrates the importance of the body for constructing self and identity. One sociologist recently examined women's experiences following weight-loss surgery, reporting on how it influenced their sense of embodiment and self during the transition from presurgery to postsurgery. Her study confirms that non-normative bodies can profoundly influence a person's self and identity. The women in the surgical group maintained that they were "new" people, both in terms of body and self. Although the women did not feel they were fundamentally different since their surgery, "they thought the surgery removed the layers of fat to reveal the 'real' body and its corresponding 'real' self" (Joanisse, 2005). This study illustrates that the self is not fixed. A person can modify the self, when necessary radically altering it in response to interactions with others.

Socialization, then, involves not only learning about others but also developing a sense of self. To understand the process of self-growth, we will examine the theories of two early scholars—Charles Horton Cooley (1864–1929) and George Herbert

Mead (1863–1931). We will then see how their ideas were used and modified by a more recent sociologist, Paul Willis.

TWO EARLY THEORISTS

CHARLES HORTON COOLEY

In the early 1900s, few sociologists or psychologists paid much attention to the role of interaction in socialization. In this respect, Cooley's work was groundbreaking. Cooley (1902) introduced the idea of the **looking-glass self,** suggesting that the gestures and reactions of others are a mirror or "looking glass" in which we see ourselves. Just as we look in a mirror to see a reflection of our physical body, we look to others to see a reflection of our psychological and social self. Cooley's emphasis was less on the actual responses of others than on our imagination, or interpretation, of those responses. And just as we may be pleased or displeased with what we see when we look at ourselves in a mirror, depending on our expectations about ourselves physically, so too are our conceptions about ourselves socially—our feelings about who and what we are—organized around our evaluation of how we believe ourselves to be judged by others.

This means that without the social mirror, there can be no sense of self. For Cooley, self-image emerges as a product of involvement in groups and communication with others. The first images of the self are received from **significant others**—those people, such as parents, who are of central importance to the individual in the development of the self. Later, other images both complement and supplant those first images, especially as the child's interaction network expands. Particularly important in this regard is the role played by the **primary group,** the small group (especially the family) that is characterized by intimate, face-to-face association and cooperation. Through repeated processes of imagination and identification, the self-concept is built and organized. In this way, Cooley suggested, the structure and content of the self are derived from society, which is represented by the groups and significant others surrounding the individual.

GEORGE HERBERT MEAD

Mead followed Cooley's lead, concentrating his analysis on the importance of the interplay between society and the individual. His major contribution was a theory of the relationship among mind, self, and society that became the foundation of symbolic interactionism (see Chapter 1) and influenced many sociologists who use a wide variety of other perspectives.

Unlike Cooley, Mead did not assume that socialization consists largely of learning to conform to the rest of society. Rather, he saw socialization as an active process in which individuals play a crucial role in their own development.

Key to that process, Mead (1934) suggested, is the ability to communicate, especially to make use of symbolic communication. Symbols are gestures, objects, or sounds that stand for something else and whose meaning depends on shared understandings. A dove, for example, is a bird, but when we see a picture of a dove on a poster, we know that it is supposed to represent—or be a symbol of—peace. Like other animals, human infants first communicate through nonverbal gestures. Unlike animal communication, however, even at this rudimentary level, most human

George Herbert Mead (1863–1931) was the driving force behind the study of how individual identity is formed in the course of interaction with other people. The work of Mead and his colleagues gave birth to symbolic interactionism, a distinctively North American theoretical tradition that continues to be a major force in sociology today.
SOURCE: Granger Collection.

communication is symbolic, as infants and the others around them develop shared understandings about the meaning of the gestures. This process lays the foundation for the development of language, which makes possible the replacement of gestures with ideas. The use of symbols enables the child to think of itself in relation to others and is at the core of all stages of the socialization process.

Suppose that you are not sure how another person understands the meaning of an action, an object, or a word. Because you share a language, you can ask the other person what he or she means and determine whether your understanding and the other person's are the same. Of course, that is not always possible or desirable. If you are attending a job interview, you would not wear a pair of dirty jeans and then ask the interviewer whether he or she considers your clothing to be appropriate. Instead you would try to anticipate in advance how others will see and react to you. You will "take the role of the other," that is, attempt to determine or appreciate someone else's perspective in a particular situation.

What is true for us only sometimes is always true for infants. Infants do not know how others understand and react to the world and especially to the infants themselves. **Taking the role of the other,** then, is an essential skill children must develop to be effective members of society. Children are not born with the ability to understand other people. As Mead showed, children, through their interaction with others, develop an ability to take the role of the other. This ability is central to children's understanding of others and to the internalization of the values, attitudes, and beliefs of the society in which they live. Mead, though, went even further. He suggested that it is through taking the role of the other that children also develop a sense of self. That is, conformity and individuality are interconnected; mind, self, and society are the product of interaction.

Three Stages in Taking the Role of the Other

The ability to take the role of the other, Mead suggested, is acquired in three stages. First is the **imitative stage.** Children two years old and under do not interact effectively with others because they cannot take the role of the other. They lack the verbal and other skills needed to communicate effectively. Much of their behaviour is imitative make-believe. At this stage of development, children have no real concep-

tion of themselves as separate social beings or understanding of what it is like to be a mother, father, or doctor. When they play, they may act out the behaviour associated with these roles, but what they are doing is not true role-playing, only imitation.

The second developmental stage described by Mead is the **play stage** in which children begin to adopt the roles of significant others—a parent, a sports celebrity, a storybook hero—and their play shifts from imitative to imaginative. Through play they learn to imagine how people will respond without actually having to act out the situation. Though language, children can now manipulate the various roles without physical action. At this stage, the role need not be firmly rooted in reality but can be defined according to the children's own wishes or their desire to please significant others. Children do not yet see role-playing as a social necessity—they merely play at the social roles of life.

Still, children at the play stage have difficulty coordinating their actions with others. Look at a group of four- or five-year-olds playing a game like soccer, for example. Typically, such children will pay no attention to the team they are supposed to be part of, caring only that they get to the ball and have the opportunity to kick it. They have no concept of playing a particular position. Almost all of them will be wherever the ball is. Often they shove and push others to get at the ball—including those who are supposed to be their own teammates. The idea that there are rules, positions to be played, and actions to take in cooperation with others is difficult for children at this stage to grasp.

The third and final stage in the development of the self is the **game stage.** In this stage children have developed a generalized impression of the behaviour people expect as well as awareness of their own importance to the group and vice-versa. Mead used the metaphor of a game to describe the complex behaviour that is required at this stage. In an organized game, such as baseball, a player must continually adjust behaviour to the needs of the team as a whole and to the specific situations that arise in the game. If the batter is running to first base, the outfielder does not throw the ball to the second baseman because she likes him better than the first baseman. Instead, her actions are oriented to the general rules and practices that make up the game. At this point, Mead held, children are responding to what he called the **generalized other,** a conception of how people in general—not someone specific in particular—will respond in a situation. This generalized other is internalized. It comprises the values, attitudes, and beliefs that the individual understands to be a part of the society and in terms of which the individual assumes others will react. In effect, taking the role of the generalized other means that we respond to our idea of the organized group or community of which we are a part.

Suppose you are among a group of strangers when you do something embarrassing, such as tripping and falling. Chances are you will feel embarrassed even though you know none of the people around you. You may look to see how they are reacting to what you have done or you may studiously avoid looking at anyone else, but in either case your response is not really to the particular people present but to your own idea of how people in general will respond to what you have done. You have, in effect, internalized the attitudes, values, and beliefs that are a part of the society in which you live. Internalization means that the attitudes, values, and beliefs that were at one time imposed on you by others, such as parents, come to be a part of you; you are the one who reacts with shame when you do something embarrassing.

Socialization in this sense is an active process because it proceeds through interaction with others. Our ability to communicate allows us not only to interact with others but also to communicate with ourselves. As we observe the conduct and reactions of other people, learning their expectations and point of view, we anticipate how *we* should react in a particular situation and then plan, rehearse, modify, and perfect our own behaviour. We may debate alternative courses of action, impress ourselves with our own wit, or cringe in remembered embarrassment at some ancient gaffe. In these and many other ways, we engage in what Mead called an internal conversation, and it is through such internal conversations that we come to develop an integrated sense of self. To the degree that we experience the generalized other as a unity, our sense of self, too, will be unitary.

The "Me" and the "I"

In a way, then, we are not only subjects—thinking, knowing, and feeling beings—but also objects to ourselves—social and cultural beings who we can evaluate, respond to, have feelings about, and try to modify. Because we first imagine ourselves from the perspectives of other people, Mead suggested that we are first aware of ourselves as social objects. He called this objective element of the self the **me.** Accompanying

the me is the subjective or active part of the self, which Mead called the **I.** It is this subjective component of the self that allows us to react to and assess ourselves, to engage in what Mead described as an "internal conversation." Have you ever done something and then asked yourself, "Why did I do that?" Asking such a question implies that we can question ourselves, wonder at our motives, analyze our feelings, and respond to ourselves as we would respond to someone else. But who is it we are responding to? Mead's answer is that all social experience involves an interaction of the I and the me, with the I initiating action and the me reflectively taking the role of the other. In other words, the self is both spontaneous (the I) and conformist (the me), both active (the I) and reflective (the me), both experiencing (the I) and experienced (the me). Throughout our life, our sense of self continues to develop, Mead suggested, because our experiences involve a continuing conversation between the me and the I. Changing contexts and contacts produce new opportunities for learning. But Mead also believed that our decisions and choices about action affect others. In other words, human beings shape their own circumstances and lives, and those of the people around them.

Mead's discussion of childhood socialization remained rather general. Yet, precisely because we are creative participants in the socialization process, we do not all respond in the same way to the same circumstances; that is, we do not all share a "generalized other." The generalized other is not society; it is not even a set of rules, norms, or guidelines imposed by society. Rather, the generalized other is our particular set of ideas about how others will respond (or should respond) to what we do. That means that not everyone is socialized in the same way. The self we develop is not purely the result of our own intentions, preferences, and interactions. There are constraints, such as class, ethnic, religious, and geographic differences, that have a profound impact on how a person is socialized, on his or her sense of self and self-worth, and on that person's understanding of others. We are not free to become whomever or whatever we want to be.

WILLIS'S APPLICATION AND EXTENSION OF MEAD'S THEORY

The recognition that socialization implies both conformity and creativity and that the individual must both deal with constraints and take advantage of opportunities underlies the work of British sociologist Paul Willis. Willis uses a theoretical approach similar to that of Mead but extends it by looking at youths rather than at children and, more importantly, by recognizing the institutional and social contexts within which the self is forged, maintained, and transformed.

Typically, sociologists have assumed that the most fundamental forms of socialization occur in childhood and that after children start school, most socialization consists of little more than learning institutional roles. Willis (1990) disagreed with this assumption, arguing instead that teens and young adults are still engaged in a process of developing their identity and sense of self.

As children we may take the role of the other, but as young people we tend to be more concerned with our own identity and with announcing ourselves to others. What becomes evident when we look at youths, rather than at children, is the significance of social location, that is, class, race, ethnicity, gender, and the other institutional and social collectivities of which people may be members. Membership makes a difference, if only in the kind of symbolic resources available to people to express themselves and to have an impact on how others see them. Commercialization also makes a difference, as cultural industries try to profit from the desire of young people to have fun, express themselves, and be up-to-date. Understanding socialization, Willis asserts, requires that we recognize "the materiality of context as well as the symbolism of self" (1990). As Willis explains, "Memberships of race, class, gender, age and region are not only learned, they are lived and experimented with. This is so even if only by pushing up against the oppressive limits of established order and power" (1990: 12).

Willis's argument is that we are all creative individuals trying to transform the world in ways that allow us to express and control our selves. Take the e-mail usernames that young people adopt. An e-mail user name can be boring and to the point—like the usernames of most professors. The addresses invented by students, conversely, tend to be communicative in their own right. They provide students with the opportunity to name themselves in a way that tells others something distinctive about them. We do not believe our students are in any sense unusual, despite having such usernames as I_hate_being, partyguy109, malaprohibita_oyvey, mymyopicview, crazygirl378, filthylummox, and the like. As stuffy adults, the authors of this chapter would never think of employing such evocative usernames, but the people who chose them were expressing something they consider important about themselves and saying (sometimes ironically), "This is who I am." The username has a meaning that goes beyond a simple identifier. Even if we don't get it, we understand that the name means something and we may be curious what that meaning is. The username is a creative way of generating interest; it attempts to control how others respond to the user. In fact, the Internet as a whole is an explosion of opportunities for creativity. People can design their own websites; communicate with others at any time by using chat programs, e-mail, and blogs; share art work, photos, music, poems, and stories; write fan fiction, contribute to online journals; and play games. In all these ways they communicate creatively, indicating to others by symbolic means what matters to them and who they really are.

In stressing the link among creativity, identity, and social context, Willis does not mean to imply that all young people are "artists" but that they take advantage of every opportunity to make the everyday world around them meaningful, as we see in the example of e-mail usernames. Another example centres on the way young people use musical taste as a means of signifying identity. The teenage daughter of one of this chapter's authors recently announced that she "could never date someone with different musical taste from mine." Music, in this case, is seen less as a means of entertainment than as a sign of group membership. Music can also serve as a set of markers indicating change and development. Reflection on changing musical taste, from pop to rock to jazz, for example, can indicate to the individual that he or she has "grown up" and is no longer a teeny-bopper, an immature adolescent, or a rebellious teen (Jackson and Rosenberg, 2004).

Like Mead, Willis reminds us that the human being is a creative and strategic social actor, rather than a social dope or the pawn of vast, impersonal forces. Still, Willis acknowledges, social categories do make a difference. Socialization is not a unitary process. Different categories of people will participate in socialization in different ways. One of the most important of those differences is gender. In many societies it makes an enormous difference whether a person is socialized male or female, a difference that determines the course of life.

GENDER SOCIALIZATION

What about our own society? What does it mean to be male or female here and now? How are we socialized to be male or female? Are gender definitions changing? Are socialization processes with respect to gender changing as well? Let us examine these questions in detail.

Gender socialization is the "process through which individuals learn to become feminine and masculine according to expectations current in their society" (Mackie, 1991: 75). As discussed in detail in Chapter 4, gender identity is learned. Still, gender appears as so much a natural part of everyday life that we typically take it for granted. We assume that people are either male or female and we quickly learn how each sex is expected to behave. Sometimes, though, we find ourselves in situations where someone's behaviour deviates from expectations. In such a situation, we are unsure how to relate to that person. Although gender identity, or identification of oneself as male or female, ordinarily emerges early in life and remains unchanged, the experiences of transvestites and transsexuals suggest that moderate to radical changes are possible.

To the extent that a culture defines male and female roles as distinctly different, parents raise boys and girls so that they *will* be different. Moreover, boys and girls grow up *wanting* to be different, believing that gender role differences are normal and necessary. Patterns of gender role socialization reveal that, from the first days of life, an infant is not simply a child but a boy or a girl. Infant boys are usually addressed differently from infant girls, the blankets in which they are covered are usually different colours, and the rooms in which they sleep are usually decorated to show their gender. One of the first things that a child learns is whether he or she is a "he" or a "she." From an early age, children show marked gender-specific preferences for certain toys and activities (Huston, 1983). These preferences are reinforced in later years. For example, among preteens femininity is constructed partly by means of shopping. Specialty stores and specialized departments in large department stories define (and, every season, redefine) certain clothing, hair styling products, cosmetics, and accessories as appropriate and fashionable for girls. In this way, the meaning of becoming a woman is tied to various aspects of consumer culture (Russell and Tyler, 2002).

Parents are usually the first source of children's gender learning, and indications are that parents hold and communicate different expectations for males and females. An early study compared two groups of first-time parents: those who had daughters and those who had sons (Rubin, Provenzano, and Luria, 1974). Within 24 hours of their child's birth, the parents of daughters tended to describe their child as soft, fine-featured, and delicate, while parents of sons tended to describe their child as firm, strong, well coordinated, hardy, and alert. Similarly, a study of children's assigned household tasks found a clear gender division of labour (White and Brinkerhoff, 1981): Boys were expected to mow the lawn, shovel snow, take out the garbage, and do yard work, while the girls were expected to clean house, wash dishes, cook, and babysit younger children. Although couples today enter parenthood with a stronger commitment to sharing household responsibilities than couples did in the past, most nevertheless develop a gendered division of labour (Fox, 1998, 2001).

The mass media, too, present idealized images and stereotypes of appropriate masculine and feminine characteristics (Goffman, 1979). To the degree that females were portrayed in a narrow and biased way by the media for years, the impact of gender-role stereotypes negatively affected how children perceived themselves (Narahara, 1998). Oversimplified gender-role stereotypes affected children's self-concept and interaction with peers and adults (Kortenhaus and Demarest, 1993). More recently, researchers examined 83 leading children's books in terms of the gender of the main character, illustrations, and title (Gooden and Gooden, 2001). They found that although gender stereotyping has decreased since the 1970s, it is still prevalent.

Stereotyping contributes to the streaming of males and females into traditional "male" and "female" jobs. More often than not, teachers and guidance counsellors unwittingly encourage boys and girls to pursue occupational goals that are perceived as appropriate to their gender. This becomes a self-fulfilling prophecy: Girls develop a self-image consistent with others' perceptions of them. Thus, one study of 150 Canadian teenagers found a tendency for girls to make traditionally feminine occupational choices and to express less confidence than boys that they would realize their occupational goals (Baker, 1985). About three-quarters of the girls planned to hold paying jobs as adults. However, they tended to see the responsibility for the household and for child-care as primarily theirs and to assume that paid work must fit in with these other duties. This expectation about the future fits with the actual division of household tasks (Barber and Allen, 1992; Blau and Ferber, 1992; South and Spitze, 1994). Although more and more women are choosing careers that are not traditionally feminine, women still do not have the range of choice that is available to men. Even today there are many careers that most of the public does not see as "appropriate" for women.

The study of gender shows us that children and adults are socialized to respond to their social world by developing certain potentials and inhibiting others. It is less their innate differences than it is differences in the socialization of males and females that affect the assumption of "masculine" and "feminine" characteristics.

The prevailing importance of gender socialization, especially as men and women cross gender lines in work and leisure and participate more fully in previously gender-segregated activities, is examined in a recent study of how traditional gender roles are reproduced in modern wedding showers (Montemurro, 2005). Showers are ideal areas of social life in which to investigate shifts in gender socialization because they involve well-defined gender "scripts" and rituals that tend to celebrate heterosexuality. Based on in-depth interviews with 51 young women, along with participant observation conducted at five bridal showers, the author concludes that men's presence at wedding showers does not reflect gender convergence or alterations in traditional marriage roles: "Rather, the fact that the co-ed shower was a supplement, that women still had traditional bridal showers, and that jokes were often made that reinforced traditional notions of husband and wife roles during the gift opening at co-ed showers all suggest a lack of change" (Montemurro, 2005: 33). Hence, the author concludes that bridal and co-ed showers perpetuate traditional gender roles in marriage.

SOCIALIZATION THROUGH THE LIFE COURSE

Childhood socialization is referred to as primary socialization because it lays a foundation that influences our self-concept and involvement in social life for as long as we live. But socialization continues throughout life, as we now show.

ADOLESCENCE AND YOUTH

As Willis noted, during adolescence and youth, dramatic transformations of identity, **status,** and social relationships tend to occur. (Although in everyday speech *status* means "prestige," in sociology it refers to the culturally and socially defined position a person occupies in an interaction.) We enter adolescence as children and are somehow transformed by the end of that period into young adults.

Adolescence, the period between childhood and adulthood, is a crucial period of life in which people undergo new experiences, deal with new demands and responsibilities, and strive to develop an identity that is distinctively their own. Even more than in childhood, socialization during adolescence requires that we find a balance between autonomy and conformity, between freedom and constraint. Unlike children, however, most adolescents are acutely aware of the demands being placed on them by others and of the demands they place on themselves. This makes adolescence a difficult time of life, not only for adolescents but also for parents, friends, and teachers.

Because adolescence is such a difficult time for many people, we generally associate it with emotional and social turmoil. Young people experience conflict with their parents and other adults as they attempt to develop their own identity, act on their own preferences, and form their own relationships. Though much of the social turmoil at this stage is often attributed to physiological changes linked to the onset of puberty, a more sociological way of thinking focuses on inconsistencies in the socialization process. Adolescents, for example, are repeatedly told by adults to "grow up" but are treated as if they are still children. Sexuality is a case in point. Adolescents receive messages of encouragement from the mass media and restraint from parents. Although adolescents associate adulthood with freedom, they get the confusing message from adults that in order to "act like an adult" they must not decide for themselves but rather do exactly what adults tell them to do.

This would not be such a problem if most adolescents did not live at home under the authority of adults. But that has not always been so. In premodern societies, adolescence did not exist as a separate and prolonged stage of life. Young people would often marry by the age of 16 or 17, sometimes even

It is during adolescence that the most dramatic transformations of identity, status, and social relationships tend to occur.
SOURCE: Jeremy Weiss/Nonstock/Firstlight.ca.

younger. If they did live at home, they had large responsibilities of their own and ways to demonstrate competence and maturity.

Adolescence as a distinct period of life is a product of industrialization and the extension of education that it introduced. Mass education and compulsory school attendance altered the role of the family and helped give rise to adolescence. Because young people were required to remain in school, they were not expected to assume economic responsibility as soon as they reached sexual maturity. Instead they continued to live at home. Burgess and Richardson (1984) traced the distinctiveness of adolescence to the modern high school, where students became educated in skills and knowledge that the family was not equipped to impart. Paradoxically, although high school may provide skills that eventually allow the adolescent to become independent of the family, it does so in a context where students have little autonomy.

Although many families subscribe to the ideal of democracy, the reality is otherwise (Solomon, Warin, Lewis, and Langford, 2002). Parents and teenagers often claim that openness is the route to intimacy and democracy, but in practice young people experience rules imposed by parents who are often unwilling to compromise. Parents, seeking to preserve their own identity, exercise control and seek to monitor the adolescent's behaviour. This is a source of resentment among adolescents who realize that reciprocity in communication is often lacking in parent-teenager relationships. As parents demand more and more information, the relationship moves further away from friendship.

We should not exaggerate adults' impact on adolescents. Although, on average, the family exerts more of an influence than peer groups do regarding such fundamental matters as religious orientation, political preferences, and career aspirations, occasions also arise when young people are less influenced by their families or teachers than by their peers, and this peer influence promotes youthful autonomy. It is not that adults give young people freedom but that the conflicting and confusing messages they receive from adults, peers, the media, and their own experience require them to make up their own minds. For those who are unable to reconcile the demands of the new and the old, adolescence may be a time of considerable confusion and turmoil (Hogan and Astone, 1986). Yet for all the turbulence and rebellion generally associated with adolescence, evidence suggests that most teenagers have good experiences of adolescence and believe they have positive relationships with their parents (Coleman and Hendry, 1990).

Why is this so? Adolescents may experience adolescence positively because much of it is exciting and fun. Friendships, for example, take on a different character in adolescence than in childhood. They often become very intense, and people come to feel very close to their friends, developing attachments that often last a lifetime. Many new interests arise in music, art, and fashion that are used by adolescents as symbols of group membership and indicators of personal taste and status. This allows for the development of passionate commitments and a sense of satisfaction and achievement when, for example, a favourite musical group has a number one song on the charts. Then, of course, there is the excitement of dating, the thrill of romance and sex, and the intense involvement in all of the accompanying activities, such as gossiping with friends, showing off a boyfriend or girlfriend, and going places together.

Finally, adolescence is also a period of **anticipatory socialization,** "the process by which aspirants to a particular social role begin to discern what it will be like to function in that position" (Stebbins, 1990: 99). Through interaction with people who act out various roles, and by observing how roles are portrayed in the mass media, adolescents learn to incorporate the perspectives and expectations of the larger society and imagine what it would be like to enact the roles to which they aspire (Stryker, 1980: 63). Again, many young people experience this kind of anticipatory socialization as fun. Ahead of them, though, lies an uncertain future and the responsibilities of adulthood.

ADULT SOCIALIZATION

Adult socialization is the process by which adults take on new statuses and acquire new and different social identities. Adults frequently find themselves in new situations at work or in private life, meeting new people and taking on new responsibilities. To participate effectively in their society, adults must continue to undergo socialization (Clausen, 1986; Hogan and Astone, 1986).

Adult socialization differs from adolescent socialization in several important respects (Brim, 1968). Whereas adolescents seek to achieve autonomy, adults generally have control over the content and direction of their socialization. Although adolescents often have little choice but to participate in various activities, adults usually engage in socializing activities voluntarily, such as enrolling in evening courses or joining a church. Because adults can often choose roles of their own free will, they can better understand and articulate their motives for new undertakings.

When we assume new statuses as adults, we need to become familiar with the expectations associated with them, learning how the statuses are best performed. Frequently such learning occurs over a considerable period as individuals interact with others in a similar situation.

The status of university student is a case in point. New students discover an institutional and social scene unlike any they have encountered and whose demands and requirements are initially unclear. In high school, young people have little autonomy and are continually being told what to do. In university, they find themselves in a very different milieu. University students vary widely in age, are in a better

position to follow their interests, and are usually expected by their professors to be autonomous, mature adults.

Research by University of Manitoba sociologists Cheryl and Dan Albas focuses on how university students learn to perform a seemingly natural activity: studying. Based on data derived from their own observations, interviews, and logs obtained from students in their classes, the researchers demonstrate that students must learn to approach, accomplish, and maintain their study practices. As they assert: "While they build on the stock of knowledge required in high school, they also find themselves subjected to a potentially conflicting set of definitions which predate their presence, but characterize the university subculture" (Albas and Albas, 1994: 288).

Concentrating their analysis on the drama surrounding exam preparation, Albas and Albas (1994) distinguished three types of students:

1. The diligently planning, high-achieving "Aces" recognize the importance of keeping their nose to the grindstone, are never satisfied with a grade lower than A, and plan their schedule to allow for adequate exam preparation.
2. The procrastinating, low-achieving "Bombers" make use of "wise nostrums, self-lulling mantras, and numerous convenient distractions, all of which are directed toward delaying serious study until the very last moment when guilt and fright force them into it" (Albas and Albas, 1994: 281).
3. The "Moderates" form the largest category of students. They are most likely to have to juggle multiple roles (student, parent, spouse, caregiver, and so forth) so they have to ration their time and energy among roles.

These three categories, according to the Albases, are roles that students learn to play. In the process of learning them, they become aware of the significance of demonstrating competence or coolness in their everyday experiences in the university setting. Moreover, once students are categorized or categorize themselves as Aces, Moderates, or Bombers, their identity plays an important role in structuring action. For example, students who view themselves as Aces and discover their grades are faltering typically study more or consult with the professor. In contrast, Bombers conclude they have little to lose by weak performance. "Give me a C and let me be free" is their motto. The Albases observe that students who share similar identities tend to be attracted to one another. They find that studying is easier if they interact with others like themselves.

Marriage constitutes one of the most important changes in anyone's life and is therefore perhaps the most important example of adult socialization. Although many of the traditional role expectations of marriage are no longer accepted uncritically, most people still choose to get married. In contrast to an earlier period when tradition largely determined the choices new couples would make, newlyweds and live-in partners now chart their own course. This independence is highly valued by most people, but it can lead to stress and strain in relationships with friends, family, and partners. There are no courses on how to adapt to married life. Most socialization consists of a couple learning, through trial and error, how to get along with others (such as in-laws) as a couple and how to get along with each other.

A significant decision during adulthood is whether to become parents. Becoming a parent also involves acquiring new skills and statuses. Although the statuses are conferred automatically, the roles and expectations accompanying them must be learned. As parents inevitably discover, relationships with children require active negotiation and adjustment. Moreover, children grow and change. This means that adults cannot simply adjust to their new role as parents and then relax. They must continuously adapt and accommodate to changing circumstances. No wonder many parents try to take control in rigid ways; they are simply trying to achieve some measure of stability in their lives and that of their family.

Socialization during adulthood also may involve the development of a career. As many postsecondary graduates discover, the difficulty of meeting this challenge successfully is increased by an economy in which employment prospects are uncertain. A set of "R words" serve as signposts of the changes taking place in the workplace—restructuring, reorganization, rationalizing, and re-engineering—that strike fear into the hearts of employees and postsecondary students (Lawson, 1996). As well, the type of employment offered to graduates is in flux. Many positions are now contractual, making employment less secure and stable (see Chapter 11). People can now expect to undergo career changes, with accompanying retraining, several times in their lives.

SOCIALIZATION AMONG SENIORS

Some of the most difficult changes in adult attitudes and behaviour occur in the later years of life (Erikson, 1982). It is during this period that the individual is most directly confronted by lowered prestige, decreased physical ability, and the prospect of chronic illness and death. Our society extends little dignity to aging. Although medical advances have prolonged lives, they have given little dignity and esteem to older people. The mass media present seniors in stereotypical terms. Consequently, many of us see old age as a period of increasing helplessness and dependence. Most of what we see is that achieving the status of "senior" is often accompanied by the loss of useful roles and valued statuses, such as those of worker and spouse.

Although many people spend a good part of their working life looking forward to retirement from the paid labour force, the realities of retirement may create identity problems for the retiree. Although most Canadians retire at age 65, they have made little preparation for retired life. Cut off from work at an arbitrary age, retirees are forced to assume what has been called a "roleless status" (Hooyman and Kiyak, 1993; Shanas, Townsend, Wedderburn, Friis, Milhøj, and Stehouwer, 1972). The transition from work to retirement typically carries negative consequences:

> If the older worker incorporates the negative societal stereotypes, a gradual shift in self-image will occur. . . . When the negative appraisal summarized in "We see you as a bumbling fool" becomes internalized to "I am a bumbling fool," a downward spiral is set in motion that is difficult to break. (Hendricks and Hendricks, 1986: 332)

Many older people, particularly women, must also face the loss of a spouse. Widowhood, like retirement, is a roleless status for which society offers little preparation and little guidance. Few defined norms govern when "normal" functioning should be resumed or how this should come about. This period also involves stress as the widow seeks to accommodate a new status, a new identity, and a new set of problems.

Finally, socialization in old age also involves facing death and dying. Western society attempts to deny death and to remove all reference to it in everyday life (Ariès, 1981). We are taught not to talk about death, particularly to the dying. Relatives often attempt to keep the dying person from knowing his or her condition, and dying people sometimes keep their own prognosis secret (Atchley, 1994; Glaser and Strauss, 1967; Leming and Dickinson, 1990). As one sociologist comments, "The status of a dying person is, like retirement and widowhood, a status almost devoid of roles" (Shepard, 1993: 153).

AGENTS OF SOCIALIZATION

Whatever stage of the life course we may be in, socialization, as we have continually stressed, is a *social* process in which we interact with others, are changed by others, and in turn may have an impact on them. Who are these others? They can be almost anyone, but as we have already noted certain categories of people are especially likely to influence us, such as family members or peers. They serve as **agents of socialization**—individuals, groups, and institutions that impart, and from which we acquire, the range of information required to interact effectively and participate in society. In addition to parents and peers are social institutions, such as schools and the mass media, which have a significant impact on us and socialize us. We cannot interact with such institutions directly, although we do interact with people, such as classmates, with whom we participate in these institutions. Since they provide a context within which we come to take on new ideas and, sometimes, new roles, institutions too can serve as agents of socialization.

You may note that some agents of socialization, such as the family and the school, receive a mandate from society to "train" the next generation of members. In contrast, the peer group and the mass media do much of their "teaching" less formally or directly. Nonetheless, they can profoundly influence how individuals perceive and respond to the people and the world around them.

FAMILIES

For young children in most societies, the family is virtually their entire world for the first few years of life. Parents are in a powerful position to influence their child. After all, the newborn is helpless, and his or her survival, physical and emotional, depends on the parents, who are the source of all rewards: security, love, affection, food, and approval. Through close interaction with parents and a small number of other people,

the child learns to think and speak; internalizes norms, beliefs, and values; forms basic attitudes; develops a capacity for intimate and personal relationships; and begins to develop a self-image (Handel, 1990). Later experiences may lead to a modification of what is learned in the family, but it is not unusual for people to bring into adult life habits and expectations that characterized their childhood. Often, young people who rebelled against their parents' way of life and values as adolescents adopt the very same way of life and values when they become parents.

We discussed socialization into gender roles earlier. Although various institutions, including schools, the mass media, the church, and sports, may contribute substantially to the child's socialization into feminine and masculine norms and activities, the family's role is critical (Fox, 2001). Parents may not deliberately teach boys to be aggressive or girls to be submissive and dependent (Lytton and Romney, 1991), but in the family gender-typing prevails. This is evident in how children play, which toys are chosen for them, and how household chores are assigned. It is also in the family that children observe and model their parents' gender roles (Stockard and Johnson, 1992; Weitzman, 1979).

Family life also teaches about affection, anger management, financial responsibilities, and respect for others (Benokraitis, 1997). Such socialization occurs informally, often offering a tentative model of marriage and parenthood.

In some ways, the family is well suited to the task of socialization. It is a small group in which all members can have constant face-to-face contact with one another. As a result, children's progress can be closely observed and adjustments made as necessary. Also, parents are usually well motivated. They have a strong emotional tie to their children, and the most meaningful and effective kind of social interaction for the purpose of socialization is that that is fused with emotion.

However, the family is not always an effective or efficient agent of socialization. Parents may be negative role models too. For instance, highly career-oriented parents may be surprised when their son opts to drop out of university to enjoy life, rejecting a way of life that requires enormous sacrifices be made for career success. Some parents have little understanding of parenting. They may be unprepared for it emotionally and their dedication and commitment to the task may be offset by competing considerations

FIGURE 3.1 TOP 12 CONCERNS OF CANADIANS (PERCENTAGE CONCERNED "A GREAT DEAL" OR "QUITE A BIT")

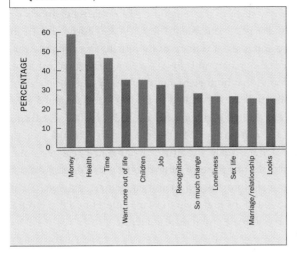

Source: Adapted from Reginald W. Bibby, *Social Trends Canadian Style* (Toronto: Stoddart, 1992), p. 82. Used with the permission of the author.

(see Figure 3.1). Some parents neglect, abuse, or even abandon their children. As well, much evidence indicates that parents may reproduce in their children the negative modelling they experienced in their own upbringing.

At the same time, however, families bestow statuses on us—such as class statuses—that may significantly affect our lives and sense of self. Class status will very likely place constraints on the opportunities that we are afforded. Research suggests that middle-class parents tend to rear their children differently from working-class parents (Kohn, Naoi, Schooler, and Slomczynski, 1990). Middle-class families are likely to instill such values as achievement and independent thinking in their children, encouraging their curiosity and initiative. Working-class and poor families, by contrast, stress obedience and authority, punishing their children's transgressions by withholding privileges.

Kohn and his colleagues (1990) explained their findings by looking at the different work situations of the two groups. Whereas middle-class parents often work at jobs that reward autonomy and creativity, the jobs of working-class parents often involve the repetitive performance of tasks under close supervision. Parents, they concluded, socialize their children in ways that reflect their experiences of autonomy and conformity on the job. However, such differences in

socialization patterns have narrowed as families of different social class backgrounds have tuned to similar media sources, including books, television talk shows, and magazines, for advice on rearing children (Luster, Rhoades, and Haas, 1989).

The impact parents have on their children's educational aspirations and occupational success has occupied an important place in the sociological literature. Here again, research suggests that class differences exist in parents' attitudes toward education, which have a significant effect on their children's educational aspirations. For example, in line with conflict theorists' claims that socialization reproduces the class structure in successive generations, Ballantine (1997) has shown that children in poor and low-income families are socialized to believe that aspiring to lofty ambitions and acquiring an education may be unrealistic in light of existing economic conditions in the family. Middle- and upper-income families emphasize and instill ideas of social success in their children. A culture of professionalism drives the attitudes of middle-class parents toward education. In contrast, working-class people see their chances of upward mobility as slim. For that reason, they resist the advice of the educational establishment (Lareau, 1987).

Three macrosocial changes over the past century have strained the institution of the family (Skolnick, 1991). First, the shift from an industrial to an information and service economy drew women into the labour force and set the stage for both a feminist revival and an adolescent rebellion. Second, demographic change shortened the active parenting stage and extended old age and living alone as expected parts of the life course. Third, people are increasingly preoccupied with the quality of intimate relationships, which has contributed to rising divorce rates. Other social changes have also contributed to the reversal of past family trends, including increasing age at marriage, lower rates of marriage, increasing rates of cohabitation outside of marriage, and more single-parent households with "latch-key" children who return home from school before their parents return home from work (Baker, 1989).

Finally, we should mention the ever-increasing diversity of forms taken by the family. It is becoming less and less reasonable to use such terms as the "middle-class" family or the "working-class" family as we did above. Families come in all shapes and sizes and the socialization of children and young people in the family can be very different from one household to the next. Will the child of two gay men be brought up in the same way as a child living in a blended family with half-brothers and half-sisters? How relevant is it that in both cases the parents are "middle-class?"

Dependence on parents shifts as the child interacts with other adults and peers. The latter also offer approval and emotional support, and they may offer alternative views of reality. This sets up additional challenges in the socialization process, as we will now see.

SCHOOLS

Traditionally, schools have been seen as settings within which social learning is just as important as learning such skills as reading, writing, and arithmetic. One of the authors of this chapter used to drive past a high school that had carved out in large letters above its main entrance the phrase, "To Build Character." Building character is what most teachers, school administrators, and parents expect the school system to do. Parents send their children to school to be socialized, and schools are deliberately organized to achieve that goal.

School is also usually the first setting in which children are supervised by adults who are not relatives or friends of the family. Moving from an environment of personal and intimate relationships to one that is impersonal is difficult for many children and something of a shock to almost all of them. Whereas parents may praise their children regardless of the talent they display, teachers typically seek to evaluate all students by a common set of standards. As a place where children are taught indirectly to be less emotionally dependent, the school serves as a model of much of the adult world. Although some interpersonal relationships may be based on love and affection, others are impersonal and defined by society with little regard for the particular individuals who enter them. Of all the functions of the school, adjusting children to its social order—which offers a preview of what will be expected of them as they negotiate their way among the institutions of adult society—may be the most important (Oakes, 1985).

Building character takes time. Accompanying the formal curriculum of the school is a "hidden curriculum"—the informal teaching that helps ensure students' integration into society (Richer, 1988). Students are exposed to, and rewarded for, the acquisition and display of such desired qualities as discipline, conformity, respect for authority, and cooperation. Gender socialization messages, for example, are imparted by teachers who may ask girls to perform "feminine" tasks, such as cleaning the board or tidying a shelf, while delegating more "masculine" tasks to boys, such as rearranging desks or carrying sports or audiovisual equipment (Best, 1983; Thorne, 1993). In research on the effects of the teacher's gender, the student's gender, and the classroom subject, researchers found that both elementary and high school classroom interactions are related to teachers' and students' genders (Duffy, Warren, and Walsh, 2001–2002; Hopf and Hatzichristou, 1999). Specifically, female math teachers, male literature or language teachers, and female literature or language teachers directed more interactions toward male than female students. Such interactions may help to shape emerging self-concepts among male and female students.

PEER GROUPS

Although the family is the most important socializing agent in the early years, peers often begin to influence even young children. Children eventually disengage from the family as their cast of significant others begin to shift to those of similar age and interests. A **peer group** comprises individuals who are usually of the same age and enjoy approximately equal status. The earliest peer contacts often occur under the watchful eye of parents or adults, such as teachers in a nursery school or daycare centre, who are supervising the children's activities. In time, however, the influence of the peer group may totally supersede, and even conflict with, parents and familial expectations.

In childhood, peer groups are formed largely by the accident of association. Members of the same peer group are not necessarily friends. For instance, all children in a given classroom may constitute a peer group, but they are not necessarily all friends. Later in life, however, we *choose* peer groups on the basis of such criteria as common interests and activities and similar income level or occupation.

Significantly, the peer group is the only agent of socialization in childhood and youth that is not controlled mainly by adults (Corsaro, 1992). Although parents typically play the initial leading roles in the inculcation of basic values, peers seem to have the greatest influence in lifestyle issues, such as appearance, social activities, and dating (Sebald, 1992). Research indicates that, especially during adolescence, peers can strongly shape the individual's aspirations and behaviour with respect to both acceptable and criminal behaviour (Giordano, Cernkovich, and DeMaris, 1986). Certainly, the peer group contributes to socialization by enabling children to engage in experiences that may not be provided in the family. Here they can interact in give-and-take relationships—relationships involving conflict, competition, and cooperation—that are not always possible at home. In this manner, children are provided with opportunities for self-direction and self-expression (Adler and Adler, 1998). Peer groups allow young people to examine feelings, beliefs, and ideas that are unacceptable to the family. Friends share a vision of the world. They discuss sexual and emotional relationships and developments within their school and friendship circle.

Often, peer group socialization is not very subtle. Peers may pressure one another to conform to a standard deemed appropriate by the group. Little deviation may be tolerated from group norms concerning speech, attitudes, and dress. Adolescents, preoccupied with gaining autonomy from their parents, and anxious about gaining acceptance from others like themselves, may find such pressures difficult to resist (Thorne, 1993). In fact, by the teenage years, the peer group may demand behaviour that conflicts sharply with the norms and values of the parental generation. In this regard, it is understandable that parents often express concern about their children's friends, particularly during the teenage years.

If peer groups often reject the norms and values of their parents, from where does the group get its norms and values? Chances are, from the mass media. Peer groups are fascinated by the media and look to media heroes as symbols of identity. Taste in music, movies, television shows, and fashion express not only common preferences but also a common style that sets the group apart, both from parents and from other sets of peers (Hebdige, 1979).

MEDIA AND TECHNOLOGY

Sociologists agree that the mass media are powerful socializing influences but it is difficult to measure their effects. Most forms of mass media, such as

The student's values are strongly influenced by his or her peer group, which consists of people of similar age and status, regardless of whether they are friends.

SOURCE: © Stockbyte Platinum/Alamy

television, radio, newspapers, videos, magazines, movies, CDs, DVDs, and books, are impersonal; information is transmitted in just one direction. This creates an audience conditioned to passively receive what is sometimes called mass culture, consisting of whatever news, messages, programs, or events that are brought to them. About 15 years ago, a new mass medium was introduced. Allowing information to be communicated to a global audience, the World Wide Web gives children relatively unfettered access to pornography and groups propagating racial strife and violence. Music videos and films, also available on the Internet, contain controversial content that alarms some people concerned about their impact on youth.

Television has attracted considerable critical attention in light of its portrayal of violence, both on the news and in TV dramas. Some analysts argue that pervasive violence on television fosters violent behaviour on the part of some viewers while at the same time making the majority of people more indifferent to, and thus more accepting of, a violent society. The killings at Columbine High School in Colorado and W.R. Myers High School in Alberta—and the suspected linkage between the two—are examples of incidents sometimes blamed at least in part on television violence (Garbarino, 1999). The American Academy of Pediatrics holds that television viewing can affect the mental, social, and physical health of young people. In studies by the American Medical Association, the American Psychiatric Association, and other agencies, violence in movies and television is linked to violent behaviour in young people.

Sociological research on violence in the mass media and the real world suggests a weaker connection between the two. As you will read in Chapter 5, the consensus is that violence in the mass media may push some people who may already be predisposed to aggression to engage in more violent acts. But it is doubtful that most viewers are similarly incited.

In contrast to television violence, which is passively experienced, video and computer games promote acting out violent scenarios. The player not only watches violence but also initiates it and is then rewarded for using it effectively. An example is *Grand Theft Auto: Vice City*, one of the best-selling video games at the time of this writing, described by one reviewer as "a lush and wild adrenaline-fuelled, shoot-'em-up role-playing game that is surely the most ambitious piece of interactive entertainment ever made" (Fussel, 2003: D16). The player can kill police officers by blowing up their cars, commit drive-by shootings, blow people's heads off with a sniper rifle and watch blood spew from their necks, distribute pornography, and traffic cocaine for organized crime.

Critics of the game have sounded an alarm because it rewards players for criminal behaviour. Whether the game influences anyone to actually commit a crime, the critics suggest, misses the point. Violent video games increase aggressive thoughts and behaviour, thus increasing the likelihood that children will get into fights in school. Such games, critics say, increasingly desensitize successive generations to violence.

Apart from the issue of violence, there is no denying that the mass media have a profound impact on the public. By selecting and emphasizing certain topics, stressing particular views and interpretations, and concentrating on specific themes, the media create, manage, and control impressions of what is important and real. The Web and video games have enabled outside influences to help shape the direction of socialization, frequently in opposition to values and beliefs conveyed in the family. By displaying role models that the young imitate, the media may inadvertently perpetuate stereotypes. For example, some parents work against the transmission of gender stereotypes to their children but video games often characterize women as subservient to men in the family and the workplace. As well, media influences are not always apparent, as when they teach individuals to become obedient consumers, for example.

OTHER SOCIALIZING AGENTS

The family, school, peer group, and mass media are the main socializing agents, but other agents of socialization are important too. Religious institutions, for example, may deeply affect the moral outlook of young people even in highly secular societies, such as Canada's. Athletic teams may teach young people to compete, cooperate with others, follow rules, and make friends. Youth groups may be instrumental in teaching young people about group rules and expectations about conformity, and even about deviance. In such complex societies as ours, conflict among the agencies of socialization is virtually inevitable. Moreover, conflict may also occur within a single socializing agency. For instance, soccer coaches may extol the virtues of cooperation but also insist on and emphasize the importance of winning at all costs.

Some socialization takes place in so-called people-processing institutions, "whose primary goal is the shaping, reshaping, removing, overhauling, retooling, reassembling, and recording the physical, psychological, legal, and moral aspects of human subjects" (Goffman, 1961; Kitsuse, 1970: 163). Such institutions carefully direct their charges to behave, think, and feel as prescribed by the institutions.

A classic illustration of socialization in a people-processing institution is a study of the socialization of the blind (Scott, 1969). Rather than identifying the attitudes and behaviour patterns of blind people as inevitable and natural, the sociologist who conducted the study maintained that they are learned. Thus, new students in schools for the blind are typically admonished by others, including medical and welfare specialists, friends, and family, to "face the facts." Even students who were previously treated as sighted people experiencing difficulty seeing are now redefined as blind people with residual vision. Consequently, "many of the basic techniques that were originally devised for people who are completely blind may be taught to the [legally] blind person who has [some] vision. Such persons may be expected to learn Braille, even though special lenses would enable them to read ordinary or enlarged ink print. . . . They may also be trained for jobs that were originally devised for totally blind persons, even though their remaining vision would enable them to continue doing the jobs they have always done" (Scott, 1969: 74). In this manner, people with vision impairments come under strong pressure to define themselves as blind and as requiring extensive social services: "The visually impaired person's readiness for the offered service is measured by his willingness to admit to himself the fact of his blindness and to show that he is resigned to the alleged permanence of his condition" (Scott, 1969: 74).

Other sociologists have investigated socialization into the world of the deaf. The claim that the deaf must be socialized may appear strange. A person does not, after all, learn to be deaf. Children who are deaf do, however, learn the behaviours and attitudes associated with being deaf, not so much at home as in institutions devoted to their education. Specifically, in schools for the deaf, the hearing world typically serves as the yardstick for what is considered normative. Thus, chewing gum may be forbidden because the sound of smacking lips, which children who are deaf cannot hear, may offend people who can hear: "The message is always the same: hearing people must not be offended or intruded upon by the noises of the deaf" (Evans and Falk, 1986: 157). It is in this sense that people who are deaf learn how to act like normative people who are deaf in institutions devoted to their education.

IDENTITY AND SOCIAL CHANGE

Are we free to become whomever we want, however we want? Of course not. Socialization is an active process in which we transform our identity as we take on new roles, but we do not always do so in conditions of our own choosing. It is important to remember that the social circumstances of life powerfully influence identity. Premodern societies formed relatively cohesive communities in which most people could find solidarity and meaning in primary groups, such as the family. Although primary groups limit the range of personal experience, they confer a strong sense of identity and purpose. Modernity expanded the range of personal choice and permitted a greater diversity of beliefs. Still, although modernization has emancipated people from the tyranny of tradition, it leaves people without the comfort and security of heritage and roots. Modern societies, in general, offer more autonomy but less sense of purpose and fewer enduring social ties than past societies. Not surprisingly, many people have difficulty establishing a stable and coherent sense of who they are in modern and postmodern societies.

The result is that some people shuttle from one identity to another, changing their lifestyle in search of an elusive "true self." They may join various social groups in search of purpose and belonging, and even experiment with various religions in the hope of finding a system of beliefs that "fits" them (Wuthnow, 1998). In sociological terms, the difficulty in developing a stable and coherent identity is rooted in the individual's social surroundings. The problem of answering the question "Who am I?" reflects not only a personal crisis but also the complexity and instability of modern and postmodern societies (Berger, 1970).

Understanding the connection between personal development and social conditions calls for a malleable view of human development, one in which there is the constant possibility of change—even radical change. In fact, as many of us are only too aware, we have not only changed but we also know others who have experienced substantial transformations, either forcibly or voluntarily. Some changes are minor or inconsequential, such as developing a new taste in clothes or dieting for a brief period. But there are also more profound life-altering experiences over which we may exercise relatively little control. A life-threatening illness, imprisonment, and severe depres-sion that requires institutionalization are examples. In each instance, people must learn to adapt to funda-mental alterations in daily routines. Although these changes may be temporary, they nevertheless strongly influence the individual's identity (Box 3.1).

BOX 3.1   THE CLOAK OF COMPETENCE

Medical students during clerkship believe they are expected to act as if they are in the know, not in ways that might put their developing competence into question. The pressure to be seen as competent by faculty, fellow students, hospital personnel, and patients narrows the range of alternative roles students can assume. Students recognize their low status in the hospital hierarchy and on hospital rotations. They realize that the extent of their medical knowledge can easily be called into question by fellow students, tutors, interns, residents, and faculty. To reduce the possibility of embarrassment and humiliation, which, at this stage in their medical career, is easily their fate, students attempt to reduce the unpredictability of their situation by manipulating an impression of themselves as enthusiastic, interested, and eager to learn. At the same time, students seize opportunities which allow them to impress others, particularly faculty and fellow students, with their growing competence and confidence.

A strategy shared by students to manage an appearance of competence is to limit their initiatives to those situations which will be convincing demonstrations of their competence. Some students decide, for example, to ask questions in areas with which they are already familiar, to cultivate an impression of competence.

The general strategy that the students adopt is to mask their uncertainty and anxiety with an image of self-confidence. Image making becomes recognized as being as important as technical competence. As one student remarks: "We have to be good actors, put across the image of self-confidence, that you know it all." Referring to the importance of creating the right impression, another student said:

> Dr. Jones, who was my adviser or boss for medicine, he always came and did rounds on Wednesday morn-ings. Well, he didn't have very many patients on the service, but we always knew that his interest was in endocrinology, and . . . if he had an endocrine patient . . . we knew . . . that he was going to pick that endocrine patient to talk about. And so, of course, . . . any dummy can read up Tuesday night like hell on the new American Diabetic Association standards for diabetes or hyperglycemia . . . and you can handle general medicine. So the next day you seem fairly knowledgeable. . . . That afternoon you forget about it because you figure Thursday morning hematology people make their rounds and, of course, you have to read up on hematology.

Students realize that to be a good student-physician is either to be or appear to be competent. They observe that others react to their role-playing. A student describes the self-fulfilling nature of this process when he says:

> To be a good GP, you've got to be a good actor, you've got to respond to a situation. You have to be quick, pick up the dynamics of what is going on at the time and try to make the person leave the office thinking that you know something. And a lot of people, the way they handle that is by letting the patient know that they know it all, and only letting out a little bit at a time, and as little as possible. I think that they eventu-ally reach a plateau where they start thinking themselves they are really great and they know it all, because they have these people who are worshipping at their feet.

The process of adopting the cloak of competence is justified by students as helpful to the patient. A stu-dent summarizes the relationship between acting competently and patients responding to such a performance by getting well when he says:

> You know the patients put pressure on you to act as if you are in the know. If you know anything about the placebo effect, you know that a lot of the healing and curing of patients does not involve doing anything that will really help them, but rather creating confidence in the patient that things are being done and will be done. We know that the placebo effect for example has even cured cancer patients. If they have the confidence in the doctor . . . and what treatment they are undergoing, they are much more likely to get well, irrespective of the objective effects of the treatment.

SOURCE: Excerpted from J. Haas and W. Shaffir, "The Cloak of Competence," *Symbolic Interaction*, Vol. 1, No. 1, Fall 1977, pp. 71–88. Copyright © 1991 by Society for the Study of Symbolic Interaction. Reprinted by permission.

RESOCIALIZATION

A significant change in how we live, in the kinds of people with whom we interact, or in the ways we understand others or ourselves often requires a process of **resocialization.** As part of a transformation in life, resocialization is an attempt to correct or instill particular values and behaviours. Sociologists, however, generally restrict the idea of resocialization to those contexts in which *deliberate* efforts are made to change the individual or group.

The classic example is Erving Goffman's (1961) research on total institutions. Goffman examined how people may be socialized against their will. This is the special world of **total institutions,** settings, such as the military, convents, prisons, boarding schools, and

mental hospitals, within which people are isolated from the rest of society for a set period and where all aspects of a person's life are regulated under one authority. According to Goffman, total institutions impose regimented routines with the goal of resocialization into a new identity. The total institution attempts to achieve this objective by completely controlling and manipulating the environment, thus depriving its inmates of contradictory forms of social experience. Total institutions, in Goffman's words, are "the forcing houses for changing persons; each is a natural experiment in what can be done to the self" (1961: 11–12).

Resocialization in total institutions is a two-part process. First, the staff attempts to strip away the new inmate's established identity. This is accompanied by

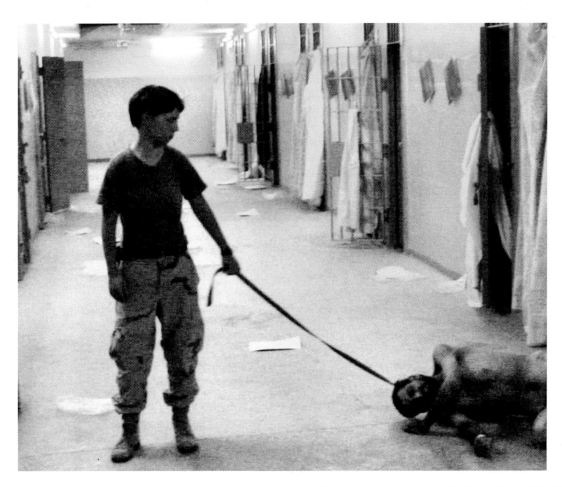

Private Lynndie England became infamous when photographs were made public showing her and other American soldiers abusing Iraqi prisoners at Abu Ghraib prison in obvious contravention of international law. "She's never been in trouble. She's not the person that the photographs point her out to be," said her childhood friend, Destiny Gloin (quoted in "Woman Soldier," 2004). Ms. Gloin was undoubtedly right. Private England at Abu Ghraib was not the Lynndie England from high school. She was transformed by a total institution, a structure of power, and a culture of intimidation that made the prisoners seem subhuman.

SOURCE: ©Exclusive to *The Washington Post*/epa/Corbis.

a series of experiences that include humiliations, degradations, and "mortification rituals," which may include physical pain. Second, efforts are made to reconstitute the inmate's sense of self by imposing a new identity and a new way of life on him or her. In a childlike condition of heightened ambiguity and stress created by degradation and humiliation, the person is ripe for conversion to the expectations of the more powerful group. The desire for security and acceptance often leads to imitation or adoption of the behaviour of authority figures (Light, 1980). The resocialized person often undergoes a symbolic ritual death and rebirth, shedding the old identity and taking on a new one.

An example of resocialization is basic training in the military. Here the primary goal is to modify the recruit's civilian self-image and replace it with a military identity. Recruits are removed from their civilian environment and confined to a military base, where they are required to submit to a vast range of stresses, disciplinary measures, and indoctrination to a new set of role expectations. The well-known example in which the new recruit is issued a uniform that does not fit is often presented on television or in the movies as a comic moment, but it has a symbolic significance as well. New recruits are expected to understand that the military is not concerned about them as individuals, only as soldiers. Soldiers follow commands and adapt to the needs of the military, not the other way around.

Identity change in total institutions is often dramatic. Yet even in total institutions, Goffman showed, people interact with, adapt to, and resist others with whom they are in personal contact. Much less dramatic but often anxiety-provoking resocialization occurs outside total institutions when newcomers are inducted into prestigious professions, such as law, the ministry, and medicine. The transformative experience of medical students en route to becoming professional is a case in point. Professionalization involves the moral and symbolic transformation of a layperson into an individual who can assume the special role and status claimed by a professional (Davis, 1961; Haas and Shaffir, 1987). The would-be professional must undergo public initiations involving testing and ritual ordeal before being elevated to the special status and role afforded by the profession.

The image of society Goffman presents in his research on total institutions is one in which large, impersonal institutions are gaining more and more control over people—over their actions, experience of the world, and sense of self. Resistance is possible in Goffman's view, and it is often successful, but only in the small events of everyday life, such as forming personal relationships with others or exchanging gifts and services. Yet today, with the advent of new forms of communication and technology, we find that new forms of autonomy and new sources of freedom and creativity have also emerged. Active, malleable, and innovative, human beings are not content to accept the world as they find it. They look for ways to transform the world and adapt it to their social needs and personal desires. Nothing better exemplifies this creative aspect of social life than the process of socialization.

SUMMARY

1. Socialization is an active process through which human beings become members of society, develop a sense of self, and learn to participate in social relationships with others. Through socialization we acquire knowledge, skills, and motivations for participation in society.

2. Each of us is born with a set of human potentials. Nature and nurture interact in contributing to human development.

3. Socialization is lifelong, typically involving relationships with family, school, peer groups, mass media, and occupational groups. Ours is an age-graded society as well, and early childhood, adolescence, adulthood, and old age or retirement are significant stages; different roles and responsibilities are associated with each stage.

4. Because of its importance, many scholars have focused on examining socialization as an active, interactional process. Charles Horton Cooley was noteworthy for his concept of the "looking-glass self," which stressed that we view ourselves as we think others view us. George Herbert Mead emphasized how people assume roles by imagining themselves in the roles of others. Paul Willis, looking at the ways in which young people do not merely accept the world around them but transform into a symbolic expression of their particular identity and their meaningful culture, has shown the intimate links connecting the acting individual and the broader social context.

5. Gender socialization is the learning of masculine and feminine behaviour and roles. From birth, and in every area of social life, the socialization of the sexes in terms of content and expectations makes the socially constructed gender role more significant than the biological role of male or female. Assumptions about appropriate male and female attributes limit the range of acceptable behaviour and options for both sexes.

6. The most important agent of socialization is the family. As the examples of orphanages and child neglect demonstrate, initial warmth and nurturing are essential to healthy development. The self-concept formed during childhood has lasting consequences.

7. The central function of schools in industrial society is the teaching of skills and knowledge, but they also transmit society's central cultural values and ideologies. Schools expose children to situations in which the same rules, regulations, and authority patterns apply to everyone.

8. Peer groups provide young people with a looking glass unclouded by love or duty, and an opportunity to learn roles and values that adults do not teach.

9. The traditional mass media are impersonal and large-scale socializers. New forms of media are more interactive and allow people to play with and try out different identities.

10. During adulthood, individuals are socialized as they get jobs, marry, divorce, raise children, retire, and prepare for death. These many roles involve new and different relationships with others and guidelines for behaviour.

11. Sometimes there are abrupt changes in our self-concept, and we must learn new role identities and negotiate a new self-image. Resocialization occurs when we abandon or are forced to abandon our way of life and self-concept for a radically different one. This is most efficiently done in total institutions—for example, jails, mental hospitals, and boot camps—or in religious or political conversions.

QUESTIONS TO CONSIDER

1. Consider the significant others in your life. Have they always been important to you? How have they shaped and influenced your sense of self?

2. Goffman's dramaturgical approach implies that "all the world's a stage" and all of us are merely "players." Do you agree with Goffman? Cite examples of impression management that you rely on and encounter in your life.

3. Prisons and mental hospitals are socialization institutions organized to change, test, or "correct" people. How effective are these institutions and why are they not more successful in meeting their goals?

4. Think of any job you have had and consider the socialization that was required. Distinguish the formal and informal components of the socialization process.

5. What, if any, are the possible effects on personal identity of the use of the Internet? Could the consequences be greater separation and alienation from reality, others, and ourselves, or might the outcome for the user be a heightened sense of belonging, integration, and shared understanding? Are both extremes possible?

GLOSSARY

Adolescence is the period between childhood and adulthood.

Adult socialization is the process by which adults take on new statuses and acquire new and different social identities.

Agents of socialization are the individuals, groups, and institutions that impart, and from which we acquire, the range of information required to interact effectively and participate in society.

Anticipatory socialization involves beginning to take on the norms and behaviours of a role you aspire to but do not yet occupy.

In the **game stage** of development, children have developed a generalized impression of the behaviour people expect as well as awareness of their own importance to the group and vice-versa. This is the third and final developmental stage described by Mead.

The **generalized other** is a conception of how people in general will respond in a situation. It is internalized.

The **I** is the subjective or active part of the self, according to Mead.

In the **imitative stage** of development, children two years old and under do not interact effectively with others because they cannot take the role of the other. They merely imitate the behaviour of others. This is the first developmental stage described by Mead.

Instincts are inborn patterns of behaviour that are often responses to specific stimuli.

The idea of the **looking-glass self** suggests that the gestures and reactions of others are a mirror in which we see ourselves.

The **me** is the objective element of the self, according to Mead.

A **peer group** comprises individuals who are usually of the same age and enjoy approximately equal status.

In the **play stage,** children begin to adopt the roles of significant others—a parent, a sports celebrity, a storybook hero—and their play shifts from imitative to imaginative. This is the second developmental stage described by Mead.

A **primary group** is a small group (especially the family) that is characterized by intimate, face-to-face association and cooperation.

Primary socialization is the crucial learning process that occurs in childhood and makes us members of society.

Resocialization is the deliberate attempt to correct or instill particular values and behaviours in an individual or group.

Secondary socialization is learning that occurs after people have undergone primary socialization.

The **self,** a sense of individual identity, allows us to understand ourselves and differentiate ourselves from others.

Significant others are people, such as parents, who are of central importance in the development of the self.

Socialization is the social process whereby people undergo development by interacting with the people around them.

Status refers to the culturally and socially defined position a person occupies in an interaction.

Taking the role of the other involves anticipating in advance how others will see and react to you. It is an essential skill that children must develop to be effective members of society.

Total institutions are settings in which people are isolated from the rest of society for a set period and where all aspects of a person's life are regulated under one authority.

SUGGESTED READING

Adler, Patricia A., and Peter Adler. (1998). *Peer Power: Preadolescent Culture and Identity.* New Brunswick, NJ: Rutgers University Press. Based on eight years of observation research, this is a first-rate sociological study of the role of peer groups in preadolescent socialization.

Becker, Howard S., Blanche Geer, Everett C. Hughes, and Anselm L. Strauss. (1961). *Boys in White: Student Culture in Medical School.* This is arguably *the* classic study of professional socialization. It examines how medical students negotiate their transition into the medical profession and are transformed into physicians.

Ebaugh, Helen Rose Fuchs. (1988). *Becoming an Ex: The Process of Role Exit.* Chicago: University of Chicago Press. This excellent study examines the process whereby people learn to disengage themselves from previous roles and claims to identity.

Goffman, Erving. (1961). *Asylums: Essays on the Social Situation of Mental Patients and Other Inmates.* Garden City, NY: Anchor Books. This account analyzes life in total institutions and describes what such institutions make of inmates and how the latter organize their life inside them.

WEB RESOURCES

Companion Web Site for This Book

http://www.newsociety5e.nelson.com

Begin by clicking on the Student Resources section of the website. Next, select the chapter you are studying from the pull-down menu. From the Student Resources page, you have easy access to InfoTrac College Edition and other resources, such as the Glossary and Flashcards. The website also has many useful tips to aid you in your study of sociology.

InfoTrac College Edition Search Terms

Visit http://www.infotrac-college.com for access to more than 20 million articles from nearly 6000 sources when doing your online research.

ThomsonNOW™

http://hed.nelson.com

This online diagnostic tool identifies each student's unique needs with a Pretest that generates a personalized Study Plan for each chapter, helping students focus on concepts they are having the most difficulty mastering. Students then take a Posttest after reading the chapter to measure their understanding of the material. An Instructor Gradebook is available to track and monitor student progress.

CHAPTER **FOUR**

Gender and Sexuality

In this chapter you will learn that

- Sex refers to biological differences between males and females, while gender refers to the attitudes, beliefs, and behaviours we associate with masculinity and femininity.

- Individuals form a "gender identity" or a sense of biological, psychological, and social belonging to a particular sex. Individuals also learn to play a "gender role," that is, to act in accordance with expectations about how members of their gender are supposed to behave.

- Sexuality refers to activities intended to lead to erotic arousal and produce a genital response. Sexuality is guided by a set of social "scripts" that tell us whom we should find attractive, when and where it is appropriate to be aroused, when it is permissible to have sex, and so forth.

- There are two major perspectives on the relationship among sex, gender, and sexuality. One ("essentialism") holds that gender roles and sexual scripts develop naturally from biological differences between the sexes. The other ("social constructionism") holds that gender roles and sexual scripts emerge in response to the different social positions women and men occupy.

- Because of the way gender and sexuality are structured in our society, intolerance for sexual minorities is widespread and male sexual aggression against women is common.

- A substantial decrease in gender inequality is now possible. The redefinition of sexuality is an important step in that process.

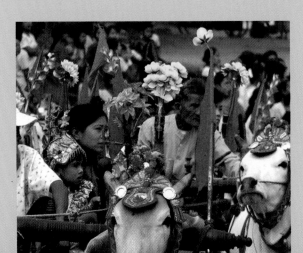

Rhonda L. Lenton
YORK UNIVERSITY

INTRODUCTION

GENDER, SEX, AND THE CASE OF DAVID/BRENDA

In April 1966, identical eight-month-old twin boys were brought to St. Boniface hospital in Winnipeg to be circumcised. They had developed a condition called phimosis, or closing of the foreskin. However, because of mechanical malfunction or doctor error, the electric cauterizing needle used for the procedure released a surge of heat. It burnt off the entire penis of one baby.

The parents sought expert medical advice but were given little hope. One psychiatrist summarized the baby's future as follows: "[H]e will be unable to consummate marriage or have normal heterosexual relations . . . he will have to recognize that he is incomplete, physically defective, and that he must live apart" (quoted in Colapinto, 2001: 16). The baby's name was David Reimer.

Seven months later, now deeply depressed, David Reimer's parents happened to be watching a CBC television program featuring Dr. John Money of Johns Hopkins University in Baltimore. He was discussing how he had successfully assigned a male or female identity to children whose external sex organs and internal reproductive system were not clearly male or female. The main criterion he used for deciding the child's sex was expected "erotic functioning" as an adult. He recommended boys born with a penis shorter than 2.5 centimetres and girls born with a clitoris longer than 1 centimetre for sex reassignment, preferably within weeks of birth. According to Money, it was imperative, once the child's sex was decided, that doctors and parents never waver in their decision and never tell the child about his or her condition at birth.

Until David Reimer, Dr. Money had never had the opportunity to test his idea on a child born unequivocally a boy or girl. Therefore, when David's mother wrote to Dr. Money shortly after the television show, he urged her to bring the baby to his office in Baltimore. He considered it a bonus that David was a twin. This would allow him to compare the development of the two siblings. Dr. Money was eager to proceed. He believed that the "gender identity gate"—the time after which a child is "locked" into an identity as a male or a female—closes at two years of age. The parents nevertheless took several months to deliberate and consult with family and friends before giving the go-ahead. On July 3, 1967, David, now 22 months old, underwent surgical castration and reconstructive surgery. He became Brenda Reimer.

As the years passed, the parents tried their best to follow Dr. Money's instructions. Brenda was given dresses to wear, skipping ropes and dolls for presents, and regular doses of the female hormone estrogen at puberty.

In 1972, at a meeting of the American Association for the Advancement of Science in Washington, DC, Dr. Money unveiled the story of David/Brenda Reimer. He claimed that the experiment was an unqualified success. In *Sexual Signatures*, a co-authored book intended for the general public, he described David's sex reassignment as "dramatic proof that the gender-identity option is open at birth for normal infants." Money was equally optimistic in a 1978 journal article, where he reported that "[n]ow prepubertal in age, [Brenda Reimer] has . . . a feminine gender identity and role, distinctly different from that of her brother" (quoted in Colapinto, 1997: 72).

Then, in March 1997, a bombshell: Dr. Money, it emerged, had doctored his reports. A biologist from the University of Hawaii and a psychiatrist from the Canadian Ministry of Health started a scientific scandal when they published an article in the *Archives of Adolescent and Pediatric Medicine* showing that David/Brenda had, in fact, struggled against his/her

David Reimer, February 2001
SOURCE: ©Reuters New Media Inc./Corbis.

imposed girlhood from the start. In December, a long and moving exposé of the case in *Rolling Stone* magazine gave further details.

The authors documented Brenda's resistance to being a girl, including everything from tearing off her first dress to insisting on standing to urinate. According to her brother, Kevin, there was "nothing feminine about Brenda. . . . She walked like a guy. Sat with her legs apart. She talked about guy things, didn't give a crap about cleaning house, getting married, wearing makeup. We both wanted to play with guys, build forts and have snowball fights and play army" (quoted in Colapinto, 2001: 57).

By the age of seven, Brenda announced she wanted to be a boy, and she refused to have further vaginal surgery because it would make her look more like a girl. She took estrogen only after being told that failure to do so would result in her limbs being disproportionate to her body. She refused to see Dr. Money after 1978. In 1979, Brenda made the decision to stop living as a girl.

In 1980, her father finally told Brenda what had happened to her. Brenda's first reaction was relief. She then resolved to become David again. By the age of 16, she started taking male hormone treatments and had her breasts removed and a penis surgically constructed. Subsequent surgeries allowed David to have sex with a woman at the age of 23. He married the woman two years later, in 1990, and adopted her three children. That did not, however, end his ordeal. In May 2004, at the age of 38, David Reimer committed suicide.

The story of David/Brenda introduces many of the issues raised in this chapter. How do we define *female* and *male*? What is the relationship between biological sex and the attitudes and behaviours that we associate with being male or female? What are the implications of this relationship for our sexual identity and sexual relations? I will touch on all these questions here. The answers, it will emerge, are not as obvious as they may at first appear.

DEFINING MALE AND FEMALE: SEX AND GENDER

While preparing to write this chapter, I asked my then six-year-old the difference between boys and girls. She answered: "Boys have a penis, girls have a vagina." Like most people, she distinguished men and women on the basis of biological **sex.** Your sex depends on whether you were born with distinct male or female genitalia and a genetic program that released either male or female hormones to stimulate the development of your reproductive system. Table 4.1 gives a more complete version of this common view by summarizing four key sex differences.

At the point of conception, a newly formed zygote has 46 chromosomes. If the last chromosome has an XX pattern, the zygote becomes a female. If it has an XY pattern, it becomes a male. About 1 in 400 children is born with an unusual 46th chromosome pattern caused by the failure of the sperm to divide properly (Berch and Bender, 1987). Most of these combinations are never diagnosed.

Around the sixth or seventh week of gestation, the gonads or sex glands begin to develop—testes in the case of a male, ovaries in the case of a female. The testes and ovaries subsequently produce various hormones in varying amounts. These hormones contribute to the development of the sex organs.

TABLE 4.1   SUMMARY OF BIOLOGICAL SEX DIFFERENCES DURING TYPICAL FETAL DEVELOPMENT

VARIABLE	FEMALE	MALE
Chromosomal pattern	XX	XY
Gonadal	ovaries	testes
Hormonal	more estrogens than androgens	more androgens than estrogens + MIH
Sex organs	uterus, fallopian tubes, vagina, clitoris, labia	epididymis, vas deferens, seminal vesicles, prostate, penis, scrotum

SOURCE: Adapted from E.D. Nelson and Barrie W. Robinson, *Gender in Canada* (Scarborough, ON: Prentice Hall Allyn and Bacon, 1999), p. 48. Reprinted with permission of Pearson Education Canada.

Differences between the sex organs are noticeable by the 14th week after conception. The scientific community appears to agree about only one sex difference in the brain (Blum, 1997): The part of the brain known as the hypothalamus makes the female brain sensitive to estrogen and is responsible for creating menstrual cycles in women.

Being male or female is more than just biological sex differences, however, as the case of David/Brenda shows. Recalling his life as Brenda, David said: "[E]veryone is telling you that you're a girl. But you say to yourself, 'I don't *feel* like a girl.' You think girls are supposed to be delicate and *like* girl things—tea parties, things like that. But I like to *do* guy stuff. It doesn't match" (quoted in Colapinto, 1997: 66; my emphasis). As this quotation shows, being male or female involves not just biology but also certain "masculine" and "feminine" feelings, attitudes, and behaviours. Accordingly, biological sex must be distinguished from sociological **gender.** Gender comprises the feelings, attitudes, and behaviours associated with being male or female. Furthermore, identification with, or sense of belonging to, a particular sex—biologically, psychologically, and socially—is known as **gender identity.** When people behave according to widely shared expectations about how males or females are supposed to act, they adopt a **gender role.**

Research shows that North Americans' expectations about how men and women are supposed to act have changed only somewhat over the last 40 years (Bergen and Williams, 1991; Broverman, Vogel, Broverman, Clarkson, and Rosenkratz, 1972; Rosenkrantz, Vogel, Bee, Broverman, and Broverman, 1968; Williams and Bennett, 1975; Williams and Best, 1982). This is true despite significant changes in women's lives in particular. For example, in the 1960s and 1970s, males were generally expected to act tough and hide their emotions. This is still true today, albeit to a lesser extent. Boys still tend to learn at a young age that crying or displaying their feelings in public is likely to result in taunts and accusations of being a "sissy." As a result, they curb their nurturing abilities, thus fulfilling gender expectations.

Great pressure can be brought to bear on individuals who do not conform to gender expectations. Brenda is a case in point. She was ostracized and tormented by her peers for not acting feminine. **Transgendered people** report similar experiences of

Being male or female involves not just biology but also certain "masculine" or "feminine" feelings, attitudes, and behaviours.
SOURCE: Susan G. Scott, *The Princess*.

rejection (see Box 4.1). Transgendered people are individuals who want to alter their gender by changing their appearance or resorting to medical intervention. According to Dr. Diane Watson, a psychiatrist who heads the gender-identity clinic at Vancouver Hospital, 1 in every 5000 to 10 000 Canadians is transgendered (quoted in Nolen, 1999: D1). Moreover, says Dr. Watson, 1 in 30 000 Canadians is fully **transsexual.** Transsexuals are people who believe they were born with the "wrong" body—that is, they identify with, and want to live fully as, a member of the "opposite" sex. They often take the lengthy and painful path to a sex-change operation. The apparent contradiction between biological sex and gender experienced by these individuals brings us back to the question of how we define males and females.

We typically accept "masculine men" and "feminine women" as normal. That is, we expect individuals to possess unambiguous sex organs and to adopt the gender role that is consistent with their biological sex. In fact, the World Health Organization classifies transgendered individuals as suffering from a psychiatric disorder. As Canadian sociologist Margrit Eichler points out, however, if our notions of masculinity and femininity were less rigid, sex-change operations would be unnecessary since someone with a "gender identity problem" would not be defined as "sick." From Eichler's point of view, transgendered individuals represent a "problem" for most people only because our society does not recognize the validity of intermediate sexes (Eichler, 1980: 31).

In the case of David/Brenda, the rigidity of gender roles probably contributed to the failure of the sex-change operation. David had, after all, been raised as a boy for nearly two years. He had seen boys treated differently from girls on television and in storybooks. He had played only with stereotypical boys' toys. After the sex reassignment, however, he got new clothes and new toys. He was also expected to behave differently. The contrast must have been all

---

BOX 4.1   THE THIRD WAY: REFUSING TO GENDER IDENTIFY

It's not that Matt Lundie wants to be a man, particularly. He just doesn't want to be a woman.

"Just enough so people won't pick me out as being a freak"—that's his goal for the next year.

He has done two years of engineering at Carleton University in Ottawa, and he is taking the next year off to start another project. Next week, he moves to Winnipeg. In six months, he will begin to take male hormones and, a few months after that, he will have a mastectomy: both of his 38C breasts will be removed and his chest reshaped in a male contour. That will be it for the scalpel, though: "I don't have any need to modify my genitals."

He's having just enough surgery to get him what he wants: not a facsimile of a male body, just a less female one.

Matt was born Fiona, in a small southwestern Ontario town. For 21 years, he lived confused. "Even as a child I knew the expectations placed on me weren't realistic," he says, calm and resolute. "Until puberty, I thought I was a boy. The social messages of my whole childhood, of being told the boy's washroom was down the hall, was that I didn't fit, not in either mould."

Then he arrived at university and began to encounter variations on gender identity in the gay community. Last year, he tried something new: "I didn't gender identify."

He was still Fiona, but offered no other clues. That felt better, better than being a woman, anyway, but it wasn't great. When people couldn't figure him out, they reacted with confusion, awkwardness and often hostility. He got sick of dealing with that every day. So now, at 23, he's starting a new life as Matt.

"I don't believe gender is concrete, and people shouldn't be limited by their biological sex. But I can't really live in between."

Yet if he feels neither concretely male nor female, then why Matt over Fiona? "I like male clothes," he says with a small chuckle, then turns serious. "And the box you put men into has a bit more room."

He tried life in the other box. "Around Grade 11, I made an honest effort to be a traditionally gendered girl. I grew my hair; if you saw my prom picture, you'd think I was my sister or something." It didn't work. "I knew I didn't fit the mould of a woman, but I didn't know I had options. Now I know that neither of those two options fit who I am, so I'm going to stake out a third."

SOURCE: Excerpted from Stephanie Nolen, "The Third Way," *The Globe and Mail*, September 25, 1999, p. D1. Reprinted with permission of *The Globe and Mail*.

the more evident because the constant presence of his twin brother reinforced David's early understanding of how boys ought to behave. Evidence suggests that if gender reassignment takes place before the age of 18 months, it tends to be "successful" (Creighton and Minto, 2001; Lightfoot-Klein, Chase, Hammond, and Goldman, 2000).

The rigidity just described fosters the view that gender roles are entirely natural and spring fully formed from human physiology. But no one-to-one relationship exists between sex and gender. The two may be in discord, as transgendered individuals and transsexuals demonstrate. The picture becomes still more complicated when we consider sexual behaviour. Expectations about sexual behaviour are arguably among the most rigid of our gender norms, yet sexual behaviour often departs widely from biological sex and sociological gender.

SEXUALITY

Sexuality refers to activities that are intended "to lead to erotic arousal and produce genital response" (Reiss, 1986: 20). Some people think such activities are idiosyncratic. In fact, sexual behaviour is guided by a set of **sexual scripts** that tell us whom we should find attractive, when and where it is appropriate to be aroused, what is permissible, and how to behave sexually. These scripts are linked to gender roles. Men are usually expected to be the sexual aggressors, typically more experienced and promiscuous than women are. Women are expected to desire love before intimacy. They are assumed to be sexually passive, giving only subtle cues to indicate their interest in male overtures. Lacking the urgent sex drive that preoccupies males, women are therefore often held accountable for moral standards and contraception (Jensen, 1984).

For a long time, sexuality was assumed to be heterosexuality. The term *heterosexuality* was coined about 30 years after the term *homosexuality* made its appearance in the 1860s. Apparently, before then nobody felt much need to describe what was felt to be entirely natural. In contrast, homosexuality was considered a serious psychiatric disorder from the mid-nineteenth century until 1974, when it was finally dropped from the *Diagnostic and Statistical Manual of Mental Disorders*, the standard diagnostic tool used by North American psychiatrists (Shorter, 1997: 304). Even today, many people assume that

individuals should desire only members of the opposite sex. Sociologists call this assumption **compulsory heterosexuality.**

The assumption of heterosexuality has negative implications for both lesbians and gays. They face discrimination, are denied basic civil rights in most countries (such as access to spousal benefits), and risk abuse, including "gay-bashing." In addition, some feminists say that heterosexuality puts *all* women at a disadvantage, because heterosexuality is based on unequal economic, political, legal, and social relations between women and men. Adrienne Rich (1996: 132–33) thus defines compulsory heterosexuality as "the ideologically and materially enforced insistence that women see themselves entirely as the complements of men and live under male control or risk severe sanctions ranging from social stigma to death." Rich says that the institutionalization of heterosexuality in marriage and the family is a way of ensuring males' rights to physical, economic, and emotional access to women. Some feminists even take the extreme position that women should reject heterosexuality altogether since all such relationships are based on inequality. Below, I present an opposing view—that it is not individual women's heterosexual practices and identities that need to be criticized but rather the institution of heterosexuality *insofar as it is as a system of male domination*. First, however, let us examine some research on sexual behaviour.

SEXUAL ATTITUDES AND BEHAVIOUR

Traditional sexual scripts expect each of us to meet a member of the opposite sex, fall in love, get married, and then have intercourse with our spouse. However, surveys reveal some departure from tradition and considerable diversity in sexual attitudes and behaviour. For example, premarital sex is widely accepted by the Canadian public. In 1975, 32 percent of Canadians disapproved of premarital sex. The figure fell to 20 percent in 1990. Sociologist Reginald Bibby (1995: 70) predicts that by about 2010, only a "durable core of some 15 percent will continue to be opposed to such behaviour." The great majority of Canadians also approve of an unmarried couple living together (Bibby, 1995: 65–66).

Acceptance of premarital sex extends even to young people. Ninety-four percent of Canadians agree that "birth control information should be available to teenagers who want it" (Bibby, 1995: 65). About 55 percent of 15- to 19-year-olds say they have had sexual intercourse (62 percent of males and 49 percent of females), as do about 75 percent of those of university age, both males and females (Hobart, 1996: 150). However, according to one study, men are more willing than women to participate in unconventional sexual activities (Hatfield, 1995).

A 2005 survey of 317 000 people provides recent information on sexual behaviour in 41 countries, including Canada (Durex, 2005). The average annual frequency of sexual intercourse in all 41 countries is 103 (see Figure 4.1). Greeks have sexual intercourse most often—138 times per year on average. Japanese have sexual intercourse least often—45 times per year on average. Canadians rank 17th out of 41 at 108 times per year. On average, Canadians become sexually active at the relatively early age of 17.0. Residents of 15 countries get started earlier, with Iceland topping the list at age 15.6. Residents of 25 countries become sexually active later, with India in last place at 19.8 years

on average. Canadians also tend to have had many sexual partners—10.7 on average, placing us 12th on the list of 41 countries in the survey. Turks lead the list at 14.5 partners. At the other extreme are Indians (3.0). In terms of number of minutes spent having sexual intercourse, Canadians are at the high end, according to a comparable 1998 survey of 15 countries. On average we spend 23 minutes having sexual intercourse. Only Americans (at 28 minutes) and Brazilians (at 30 minutes) surpass us. At the low end, Russians spend 12 minutes on average having sexual intercourse (Durex, 2001: 12; Mackay, 2000: 20–21).

Table 4.2 shows the frequency of sexual activity by gender and age in Canada. Not surprisingly, sexual activity declines with age. However, a considerable number of people over the age of 70 say they engage in sexual activity at least once a week. This finding challenges the myth that the elderly are asexual.

Also of interest are male-female differences. For nearly all age groups, men report more frequent intercourse than women, while women more often

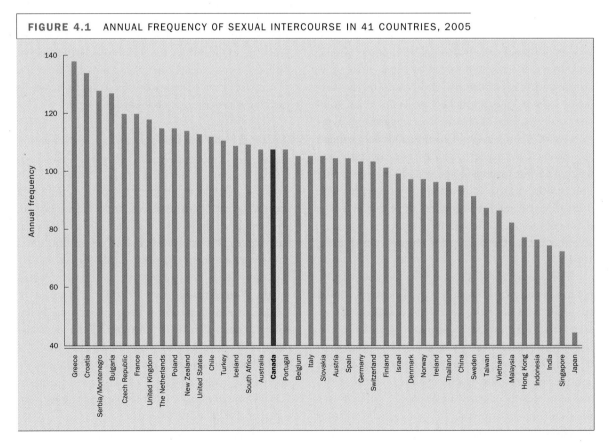

FIGURE 4.1   ANNUAL FREQUENCY OF SEXUAL INTERCOURSE IN 41 COUNTRIES, 2005

SOURCE: Durex (2005).

TABLE 4.2 FREQUENCY OF SEXUAL INTERCOURSE AMONG CANADIANS BY AGE AND SEX

AGE		NEVER	SOMETIMES, BUT LESS OFTEN THAN ONCE A WEEK	ONCE A WEEK OR MORE	TOTAL
18–29	men	4	38	58	100
	women	5	29	66	100
30–39	men	2	20	78	100
	women	4	29	67	100
40–49	men	3	37	60	100
	women	7	35	58	100
50–59	men	1	47	52	100
	women	13	40	47	100
60–69	men	5	65	30	100
	women	41	34	25	100
70+	men	25	53	22	100
	women	58	35	7	100

SOURCE: Adapted from Reginald W. Bibby, *The Bibby Report: Social Trends Canadian Style* (Toronto: Stoddart Publishing Co., Ltd., 1995), p. 67. Reprinted with permission of the author.
NOTE: Data are from a 1995 survey.

report abstention than men. For instance, in the 50–59 age group, 13 percent of women say they never have sex compared with only 1 percent of men. And in the 70+ age group, 22 percent of men say they have sex once a week or more, compared with only 7 percent of women. These figures probably reflect a tendency on the part of men to exaggerate their virility to conform to gender stereotypes.

Men and women differ in terms of the standards they use to justify sexual activity. Hobart (1996: 148) distinguishes the "love standard," according to which sexual activity is acceptable as long as the partners are in love, from the "fun standard," according to which sexual activity is acceptable as long as both partners want it. He shows that, in Canada, men and francophones are more likely than women and anglophones to endorse the fun standard. For example, almost 52 percent of Canadian francophone men and more than 37 percent of francophone women believe it is appropriate to engage in heterosexual involvement for casual, recreational reasons. The comparable figures for anglophone men and anglophone women are 36 percent and 20 percent, respectively. Hatfield (1995) similarly reports that men are somewhat more concerned than women with sex. Women

Research shows that while men are somewhat more concerned with sex than women, women are somewhat more concerned with love.
SOURCE: Shutterstock.

are somewhat more concerned than men with love. American research shows that women are more likely to cite "affection for partner" as the major reason for their first intercourse experience (48 percent) followed by "curiosity/readiness for sex" (24 percent). Men most often mention "curiosity" (51 percent), followed by "affection" (25 percent). A small percentage of women (3 percent) report having their first sexual experience for physical pleasure. In contrast, 12 percent of men cite this reason (Michael, Gagnon, Laumann, and Kolata, 1994: 93–94).

Canadians are also becoming more tolerant of homosexuality and same-sex marriage (see Box 4.2). It is sometimes asserted that one in ten North Americans is homosexual. American research shows

that this is certainly an oversimplification and probably an exaggeration. In the most comprehensive survey on sexuality to date, a group of American sociologists showed that just more than 10 percent of men and 8.6 percent of women report *some* same-sex experience *or* desire (Laumann, Gagnon, Michael, and Michaels, 1994: 299). However, only 5.5 percent of women said they find the thought of sexual activity with another woman appealing, 4 percent reported being sexually attracted to women, and less than 2 percent reported having a sexual encounter with another woman in the past year. Just more than 4 percent said they had had a sexual experience with another woman at some point in their lives. Only 1.4 percent identified themselves as bisexual or

BOX 4.2 SAME-SEX MARRIAGE AND CIVIL UNION

In July 2005, Canada became the third country (after the Netherlands and Belgium) to legalize same-sex marriage. At about the same time, Spain became the fourth country to pass such a law. The major world religions officially disapprove of homosexuality for the most part (see Table 4.3), so it is not surprising that several Canadian church leaders spoke out strongly against the new law. In the 2006 federal election campaign, Stephen Harper, leader of the Conservative Party, promised to revisit the law in Parliament if his party formed the government. Meanwhile, Canadian public opinion is divided. In February 2005, a nationwide poll showed that 42 percent of Canadians favoured same-sex marriage, 17 percent were indifferent, and 40 percent were opposed. Younger Canadians, women, and people living outside Alberta and Ontario were more likely to support same-sex marriage than were older Canadians, men, and people living in Alberta and Ontario ("Same-Sex Marriage," 2005).

Many governments have dealt with such splits in public opinion by distinguishing between marriage and "civil union." A civil union grants *some* of the rights and privileges of marriage to a same-sex couple. At least some jurisdictions in 17 countries (Argentina, Australia, Brazil, Denmark, Finland, France, Germany, Greenland, Hungary, Iceland, Liechtenstein, New Zealand, Norway, Sweden, Switzerland, the United Kingdom, and the United States) allow homosexual couples to enter civil unions. The new Canadian law goes one step further by making no distinction between heterosexual and same-sex marriage. At the same time, Canadian law respects the right of religious organizations to discriminate against homosexuals who want to marry. No religious organization is required by law to marry a homosexual couple.

Canadians are becoming more tolerant of homosexuality.
SOURCE: Shutterstock.

TABLE 4.3 THE OFFICIAL POSITION OF THE MAJOR WORLD RELIGIONS ON SEXUAL ISSUES, 2001 (NUMBER OF ADHERENTS IN PARENTHESES)

RELIGION	MASTURBATION	PREMARITAL SEX	EXTRAMARITAL SEX	HOMOSEXUAL SEX
Buddhism (354 million)	acceptable	mostly acceptable	unacceptable	mostly acceptable
Christianity (1.9 billion)	generally unacceptable (but no clear position for some Protestant denominations)	unacceptable	unacceptable	unacceptable (but generally tolerated in the United Church of Canada)
Hinduism (762 million)	mostly acceptable	unacceptable	unacceptable	unacceptable
Islam (1.4 billion)	unacceptable	unacceptable	unacceptable	unacceptable
Judaism (14 million)	no clear position	mostly acceptable	unacceptable	generally unacceptable (but generally tolerated in the Reform and Reconstructionist denominations)

SOURCES: Adherents.com (2001); Mackay (2000: 73).

homosexual. Among men, about 6 percent said they are sexually attracted to other men, 4.5 percent said they find the idea of sex with another man appealing, and 2 percent reported a sexual encounter with another man in the previous year. Nine percent of men reported a sexual experience with another man at least once since puberty, and 2.8 percent of men identified themselves as homosexual or bisexual. Unfortunately, we do not have comparable Canadian data. However, in a 2000 survey, about 6 percent of Torontonians identified themselves as homosexual or bisexual. This is roughly comparable to the percentage for major American cities, such as New York ("Homosexuality and Bisexuality," 2000).

These findings suggest that estimates of the prevalence of homosexuality depend on how homosexuality is measured. An estimate based on sexual identity results in a lower percentage than does an estimate focusing on **sexual orientation.** (Sexual orientation refers to the way a person derives sexual pleasure, including whether desirable partners are of the same or a different sex.) I conclude that it is inaccurate to think about sexuality in terms of a strict dichotomy between heterosexuality and homosexu-

ality. It is more appropriate to conceptualize sexuality as comprising four continua: sexual attraction, sexual desire, sexual behaviour, and sexual identity (Michael et al., 1994: 174–79).

Attitudes about extramarital affairs are more conservative than those about homosexuality, and they are becoming more so. In 1975, 28 percent of Canadian adults felt that sex with someone other than the marriage partner was "almost always wrong" and 50 percent felt it was "always wrong." By 1995, those figures were 25 percent and 60 percent, respectively, suggesting movement in a more conservative direction (Bibby, 1995: 75). As far as actual behaviour is concerned, in a 1998 survey of 13 countries, 30 percent–39 percent of Canadians between the ages of 16 and 45 admitted to sexual infidelity. This puts Canadians in the same league as South Africans, Australians, French, Italians, and Thais. By comparison, 40 percent or more of Americans, Russians, British, and Germans between the ages of 16 and 45 admitted to sexual infidelity. For Spaniards, Poles, and residents of Hong Kong, the comparable figure was in the 20 percent–29 percent range (Mackay, 2000: 36–37).

Changing attitudes toward extramarital affairs are part of a more general tendency for people to want and have fewer sexual partners. Although there are undoubtedly several reasons for this tendency, one of the most important is the spread of sexually transmitted diseases, HIV/AIDS in particular, since about 1980. Sexual attitudes were relatively liberal in the 1960s and 1970s. During those decades, contraception and abortion were legalized. The youth counterculture successfully promoted the idea of "free love." Thus, the culture of the times encouraged people to have multiple sexual partners, while changes in the law minimized the reproductive consequences of doing so. In contrast, once the dangers of HIV/AIDS and other sexually transmitted diseases became widely known in the early 1980s, many people became more cautious in their sexual relations. Of those Canadians who took precautions against sexually transmitted infections in 2003, the most common method was to use a condom with a new partner. Still, 49 percent of Canadians had unprotected sex without knowing their partner's sexual history in 2005 (Durex, 2005; see Figure 4.2).

As the foregoing discussion shows, surveys provide evidence of wide variation in attitudes toward sex and sexual conduct over time and place. Therefore, they help to dispel myths about sexuality as natural or "fixed." However, they do not answer questions about the *origins* of sexual scripts or why inconsistencies exist between norms and behaviour. The next section addresses these issues by looking at the relationships among sex, gender, and sexuality.

DOES SEX DETERMINE DESTINY?

ESSENTIALISM

Most arguments about the origins of gender differences in human behaviour adopt one of two perspectives. Some analysts see gender as a reflection of naturally evolved dispositions. Others see gender as a reflection of the different social positions occupied by women and men. Sociologists call these two perspectives, respectively, essentialism and social constructionism. I now summarize and criticize essentialism. I then turn to social constructionism.

Essentialists first observe male-female differences in sexual scripts, the division of labour at home and in the workplace, mate selection, sexual aggression, jealousy, promiscuity, fidelity, and so forth. They then interpret these differences as natural and uni-

FIGURE 4.2   PREVENTATIVE MEASURES TAKEN BY CANADIANS AGAINST SEXUALLY TRANSMITTED INFECTIONS, 2003 (IN PERCENTAGE)

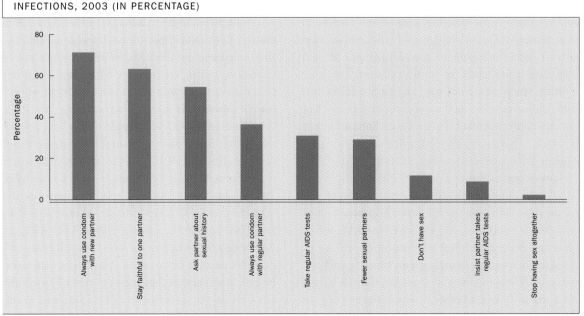

Source: Durex (2003).

versal. According to essentialists, childrearing may exaggerate differences between men and women but nature is the ultimate force at work in shaping them.

Essentialism has many variants, most of which originate in biology and psychology. Here we briefly consider three of the most popular variants: brain studies, sociobiology, and Freudian theory.

Brain Studies

Male-female differences in brain structure are sometimes said to account for male-female differences in behaviour and achievement. The brain comprises two hemispheres of about equal size, connected by a bundle of fibres. The left hemisphere is generally associated with language abilities, the right with nonverbal perception and visual and spatial skills. About this little controversy exists in the scientific community. However, some brain researchers argue that the two hemispheres develop differently in boys and girls, as do the fibres connecting the hemispheres. Specifically, they claim that when the male fetus starts to secrete testosterone (the hormone responsible for furthering the sexual development of the male), it washes over the brain and briefly inhibits the growth of the left hemisphere. As a result, use of the *right* hemisphere becomes dominant in men. This supposedly allows men to excel in mathematical, artistic, musical, and visual-spatial abilities. Meanwhile (the theory continues), the bundle of fibres connecting the left and right hemispheres is bigger in women. This supposedly allows women to use the hemispheres more symmetrically, giving them an edge in feelings, intuition, language skills, and quick judgments (Bleier, 1984: 92; Blum, 1997: 36–63; Tavris, 1992: 45–46).

Such presumably innate differences in brain structure allegedly give rise to male-female differences in behaviour and achievement. For example, some proponents of this line of thought claim that men are best at jobs requiring logic and visual-spatial manipulation. Hence the disproportionately large number of men who work as scientists, mechanics, pilots, and so forth. For their part, women are presumably best at jobs requiring empathy, intuition, and language skills. Hence the disproportionately large number of women who stay home to raise children and who work outside the home as teachers, secretaries, social workers, and nurses. It follows from this line of reasoning that the gender division of labour is perfectly natural, structured by our brains rather than by society.

Sociobiology

Sociobiology is a second variant of essentialism, and E.O. Wilson (1975) is its leading exponent. Wilson argues that all human beings instinctually want to ensure that their genes get passed on to future generations. However, the different reproductive status of men and women means they have had to overcome different adaptive problems and develop different adaptive strategies. This gave rise to patterns of behaviour we now call "masculine" and "feminine." Individuals who possessed the characteristics that best resolved these problems—the most feminine women and the most masculine men—had a better chance of surviving and passing their genes to their offspring. Thus, over time, masculine and feminine behaviours became genetically encoded. According to sociobiology, genetic factors also trigger biochemical processes that further enhance sex differences through varying levels of hormone production in women and men.

David Buss, a well-known evolutionary psychologist, argues that four adaptive strategies or "universal features of our evolved selves" govern the relations between the sexes and contribute to the preservation of the human species (Buss, 1994: 211; see also Buss, 1995a, 1995b, 1998; Dawkins, 1976; Wilson, 1978). First, men want casual sex with women. Second, men treat women's bodies as men's property. Third, men beat or kill women who incite male sexual jealousy. And fourth, women are greedy for money.

Buss bases his argument on the claim that a woman has a bigger investment than a man in ensuring the survival of their offspring. That is because the woman produces only a small number of eggs during her reproductive life. Specifically, she releases fewer than 400 eggs during her reproductive years. At most, she can give birth to about 20 children. Men, however, typically release between 200 million and 500 million sperm every time they ejaculate. This number of sperm can be produced every 24 to 48 hours (Saxton, 1990: 94–95). It is thus adaptive in an evolutionary sense for a man to be promiscuous yet jealously possessive of his partners (Wilson and Daly, 1998), for a promiscuous yet jealous man maximizes the chance that his, and only his, offspring will be produced. Moreover, since men compete with other men for sexual access to women, men evolve competitive and aggressive dispositions that include physical violence. In contrast, Buss says, it is in a woman's best interest to maintain primary responsibility for her genetic child and to look around for the best mate with whom to intermix her genes. He is the man who can best help support the child after birth. Hence women's alleged greed for money in contemporary society.

Research certainly supports the view that men and women emphasize different characteristics in selecting a mate. Simon Davis, for example, conducted a content analysis of personal advertisements in the *Vancouver Sun*. He discovered that attractive physical features were the most frequently mentioned desirable characteristic in a partner for both men and women. However, women were more likely than men to list professional status, employment status, financial considerations, intelligence, commitment, and emotion. Men, conversely, were more likely to list attractiveness, physique, and sexiness, and to require a picture (Davis, 1990: 43–50). These results do not, however, establish that sex-typed mating preferences are *genetically* determined. As we will see, the results are also consistent with differences in how we assign status to masculine and feminine gender roles.

Freud

Freud (1977 [1905]) offered a third influential essentialist explanation of male–female differences. He believed that sexuality is the main human instinct. In his view, it motivates human behaviour and accounts for the development of distinct masculine and feminine gender roles.

According to Freud, children around the age of three to five begin to pay attention to their genitals. As a young boy becomes preoccupied with his penis, he unconsciously develops a fantasy of sexually possessing his mother. He begins to resent his father because only his father is allowed to sexually possess the mother. But because he has seen his mother or another girl naked, the boy also develops anxiety that he will be castrated by his father for desiring his mother.[1] To resolve this fear, the boy represses his feelings for his mother. That is, he stores them in the unconscious part of his personality. In due course, this repression allows him to begin identifying with his father. This leads to the development of a strong, masculine personality.

In contrast, the young girl begins to develop a feminine personality when she realizes she lacks a penis. According to Freud:

> [girls] notice the penis of a brother or play-mate, strikingly visible and of large proportions, at once recognize it as the superior

counterpart of their own small and inconspicuous organ, and from that time forward fall a victim to envy for the penis. . . . She has seen it and knows that she is without it and wants to have it. (Quoted in Steinem, 1994: 50)

Because of her "penis envy," the young girl soon develops a sense of inferiority, according to Freud. She also grows angry with her mother, who, she naïvely thinks, is responsible for cutting off the penis the girl must have once had. She rejects her mother and develops an unconscious sexual desire for her father. Eventually, however, realizing she will never have a penis, the girl comes to identify with her mother. This is a way of vicariously acquiring her father's penis in Freud's view. In the "normal" development of a mature woman, the girl's wish to have a penis is transformed into a desire to have children. However, says Freud, since women are never able to completely resolve their penis envy, the feminine gender identity is normally immature and dependent on men. This dependence is evident from the "fact" that women can be fully sexually satisfied only by vaginally induced orgasm. Thus, a host of gender differences in personality and behaviour follow from the anatomical sex differences that children first observe around the age of three.[2]

A Critique of Essentialism

Essentialist arguments, such as those described above, have six main problems:

1. *Essentialists ignore the historical and cultural variability of gender and sexuality.* In some cultures, men are socialized to be nurturing and sensitive. Rape is incomprehensible. For example, anthropologist Margaret Mead reports that the Arapesh, a preliterate people in New Guinea, "know nothing of rape beyond the fact that it is the unpleasant custom of the Nugum people to the southeast of them" (Mead, 1935: 110). More generally, rates of rape vary widely across cultures (Sanday, 1981). This variability deflates the idea that biological constants account for innate behavioural differences between women and men, such as male aggressiveness and violence. Moreover, societies and cultures often change rapidly without any apparent genetic change taking place. Essentialist arguments have a difficult time explaining, for example, recent changes in child-care arrangements, women's participa-

tion in the labour force, and other aspects of women's lives, given the absence of any documented shift in male or female genetic structure that might account for this change.

2. *Essentialists ignore the fact that gender differences are declining rapidly and in some cases have already disappeared* (Caplan and Caplan, 1999). Hundreds of studies have shown that women are developing traits that were traditionally considered masculine. For example, psychological research shows that women have become more assertive, competitive, independent, and analytical since the early 1970s. They play more aggressive sports, choose more mathematics and science courses, perform better in standardized tests, take more nontraditional jobs, and earn more money than they used to (Twenge, 1997). In what must be considered a serious blow to brain research on alleged male-female differences, a review of 165 studies of verbal ability representing tests of more than 1.4 million people found no gender differences in verbal skills. A review of 100 studies of mathematics performance representing tests of nearly 4 million students showed small differences favouring *females* in the general population. (Larger differences favouring males were, however, found in samples of precocious individuals.) A review of dozens of studies on spatial ability reported that some studies found no gender differences, while other studies found only small differences in favour of men (Tavris, 1992: 52). Taken as a whole, this body of research suggests that few gender differences in ability remain to be explained, the few remaining differences are small, and those few small differences are disappearing.

3. *The research evidence employed by essentialists is often deeply flawed.* Consider the sociobiologists' observation that men are more independent than women. Research shows that, in fact, girls are more dependent than boys *only at certain ages*. Thus, although infant girls seem to behave in a more dependent fashion than infant boys, girls at the age of two are more independent than boys (Feiring and Lewis, 1979; Goldberg and Lewis, 1969). Evidence from studies purporting to find a genetic cause of homosexuality is also problematic. Hamer and Copeland (1996), for example, claim to have found a possible genetic marker for homosexuality in 33 of 40 brothers who were both gay. As Peele and De Grandpre (1995) point out, however, the study did not check for the frequency of the supposed marker in *heterosexual* brothers. Nor has anyone been able to replicate the findings. More generally, sociobiologists and evolutionary psychologists have not been able to identify *any* of the genes that, they claim, cause male jealousy, female nurturance, or the unequal division of labour between men and women. Meanwhile, brain researchers have had great difficulty showing how observed physical differences between male and female brains might be related to (nonexistent, small, and shrinking) differences in male and female abilities. That is one reason several brain theories make contradictory arguments. For example, the theory reviewed previously says that men have greater right hemisphere specialization. However, a second theory holds that men have greater *left* hemisphere specialization, which gives them an intellectual advantage over women. Meanwhile, a third theory agrees that men have greater right brain specialization but insists that this gives men superior artistic and musical abilities; yet this contradicts the first theory, which says that women have the edge in musical and artistic skills, which rely on intuition and empathy (Tavris, 1992: 45–49). Lack of hard evidence encourages such unsubstantiated speculation.

4. *Essentialists tend to generalize from the average, ignoring variations within gender groups.* On average, women and men do, of course, differ in some respects. For example, one of the best-documented average differences between women and men concerns aggressiveness. Men are on average more verbally and physically aggressive than women. However, when sociobiologists say men are *inherently* more aggressive than women, they make it seem as if this is true of all men and all women. As Figure 4.3 shows, however, it is not. When verbal or physical aggressiveness is measured by trained researchers, scores vary widely within gender groups. Aggressiveness is distributed so that considerable overlap occurs between men and women. Thus, many women are more aggressive than the average man, and many men are less aggressive than the average woman.

5. *Essentialists exaggerate the degree to which gender differences are unchangeable.* For example, evolutionary psychologist David Buss and colleagues

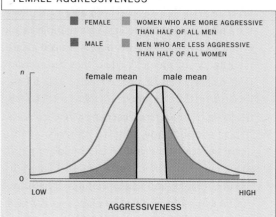

FIGURE 4.3   THE DISTRIBUTION OF MALE AND FEMALE AGGRESSIVENESS

(1990) used data from 37 cultures to show that women consistently prefer older men with high earning capacity as partners. In contrast, men prefer women with good domestic capabilities. Buss claims that this demonstrates a genetic basis for mate selection. But Eagley and Wood (1999) re-examined Buss's data. They show that women's tendency to stress the "good provider" role in selecting male partners and men's tendency to stress women's domestic skills decrease in societies that have more gender equality. Similarly, women express less preference for older men, and men less preference for younger women, in more gender-egalitarian societies. As this example shows, gender differences vary with social conditions, a fact that essentialists ignore. Another example of how social conditions affect gender differences: The "male" hormone testosterone is associated with greater aggressiveness. However, Pulitzer-prize-winning science writer Deborah Blum (1997: 158–88) notes that social situations involving competition and threat stimulate production of testosterone in *women* and cause them to act more aggressively (compare Caplan and Caplan, 1999). For example, when women take jobs that maximize competition and threat— when they become, say, corporate lawyers or police officers—they undergo hormonal and behavioural changes, thus decreasing behavioural differences between men and women.

6. *Essentialists offer explanations for gender differences that ignore the role of power.* Sociobiologists assume that existing behaviour patterns help ensure the survival of the species because they are the patterns that endured as humans evolved. However, their assumption overlooks the fact that some groups (such as men) are in a position of greater power and authority than are other groups (such as women). Behavioural differences between men and women may, therefore, result not from any biological imperative but from men's ability to establish their preferences over the interests of women. Indeed, from this point of view, sociobiology may be seen as an example of the exercise of male power, that is, a rationalization for male domination and sexual aggression. The same may be said of Freud's interpretation. *Must* young girls define themselves in relation to young boys by focusing on their lack of a penis? *Do* they define themselves that way? Freud offers no evidence to support his case. There is no reason why young girls' sexual self-definitions cannot focus positively on their own reproductive organs, including their unique ability to bear children. Freud simply assumes that men are superior to women and then creates a speculative theory that justifies gender differences.

SOCIAL CONSTRUCTIONISM

Social constructionism is the main alternative to essentialism. Social constructionists argue that gender differences are not the product of biological properties, whether chromosomal, gonadal, or hormonal. Instead, gender and sexuality are products of social structure and culture. *Culture* is composed of shared systems of meaning. It incorporates people's values and beliefs. Although many systems of meaning coexist and compete at any one time, patriarchy, or male domination and belief in its validity, is widely accepted in nearly all societies today. *Social structure* refers to the way major institutions, such as families, the economy, and the political system, are organized. Social structures in most societies today are patriarchal in that they reinforce inequalities between women and men.

Social constructionists stress three main sociohistorical changes that led to the development of gender inequality:

1. *Long-distance warfare and conquest.* Anthropologists have shown that a high level of gender equality existed in foraging or hunting-and-gathering soci-

eties, the dominant form of society for 90 percent of human history. Rough equality between women and men was based on the fact that women produced a substantial amount of the band's food, up to 80 percent in some cases (see Chapter 10, Families). Archaeological evidence from "Old Europe" tells a similar story. Old Europe is a region stretching roughly from Poland in the north to the Mediterranean island of Crete in the south, and from Switzerland in the west to Bulgaria in the east (see Figure 4.4). Between 7000 and 3500 B.C.E., men and women enjoyed rough equality throughout the region. The religions of the region gave primacy to fertility and creator goddesses. Kinship was traced through the mother's side of the family. Then, sometime between 4300 and 4200 B.C.E., all this began to change. Old Europe was invaded by successive waves of warring peoples from the Asiatic and European northeast (the Kurgans) and the deserts to the south (the Semites). Both the Kurgan and Semitic civilizations were based on a steeply hierarchical and patriarchal social structure. Their religions gave primacy to male warrior gods. They acquired property and slaves by conquering other

peoples and imposed their religions on the vanquished. They eliminated, or at least downgraded, goddesses as divine powers. God became a male who willed that women should be ruled by men. Laws reinforced women's sexual, economic, and political subjugation to men. Traditional Judaism, Christianity, and Islam all embody ideas of male dominance and they all derive from the tribes who conquered Old Europe in the fifth millennium B.C.E. (Eisler, 1987).

2. *Plow agriculture.* Long-distance warfare and conquest catered to men's strengths and so greatly enhanced male power and authority. Large-scale farming with plows harnessed to animals had much the same effect. Plow agriculture originated in the Middle East around 5000 years ago. It required that strong adults remain in the fields all day for much of the year. It also reinforced the principle of private ownership of land. Since men were on average stronger than women, and since women were restricted in their activities by pregnancy, nursing, and childbirth, plow agriculture made men more powerful socially. Thus, land was owned by men and ownership was typically passed from father to son (Coontz and Henderson, 1986).

3. *The separation of public and private spheres.* In the agricultural era, economic production was organized around the household. Men may have worked apart from women in the fields, but the fields were still part of the *family* farm. In contrast, during the early phase of industrialization, men's work was moved out of the household and into the factory and the office. Most men became wage or salary workers. Some assumed decision-making roles in economic and political institutions. But while men went public, most women remained in the domestic or private sphere. The idea soon developed that this was a "natural" division of labour. This idea persisted until the second half of the twentieth century, when a variety of social circumstances, ranging from the introduction of the birth control pill to women's demands for entry into university, finally allowed women to enter the public sphere in large numbers.

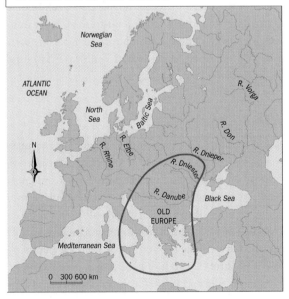

FIGURE 4.4 APPROXIMATE AREA FOR EARLY CIVILIZATION OF OLD EUROPE

SOURCE: Adapted from Marija Gimbutas, *Goddesses and Gods of Old Europe: 6500–3500 B.C. Myths and Cult Images* (Berkeley and Los Angeles: University of California Press, 1982), p. 16.

So we see that, according to social constructionists, gender inequality derives historically from three main circumstances: the advent of long-distance warfare and conquest, the development of plow agriculture, and the assignment of women to the domestic sphere and men to the public sphere during the early industrial era.

Although gender inequality is decreasing somewhat in many societies today, it still persists. It is supported by a variety of economic and political arrangements discussed elsewhere in this book (see especially Chapter 7). In what follows, I fill out the social constructionist perspective by outlining just two dimensions of contemporary gender inequality. First, I show how socialization still pushes girls to act in stereotypically feminine ways and boys to act in stereotypically masculine ways. I then discuss eating disorders and male violence against women to show that the social construction of gender has far-reaching implications for women, men, and the relations between them.

CONSTRUCTING GENDER THROUGH SOCIALIZATION

PRIMARY SOCIALIZATION

Research shows that, from the moment of birth, infant boys and girls are treated differently by parents, particularly fathers. Girls are more likely to be characterized as delicate, weak, beautiful, and cute; boys as strong, alert, and well coordinated (Rubin, Provenzano, and Lurra, 1974). Interpretations of behaviour vary by sex. For example, when viewing a videotape of a nine-month-old infant, experimental subjects tend to label startled reactions to a stimulus as "anger" if the baby has been previously identified as a boy, and as "fear" if the baby is identified as a girl, *regardless of the baby's actual sex* (Condry and Condry, 1976). Parents also tend to encourage their sons to engage in boisterous behaviour and competitive play. They tend to encourage their daughters to engage in cooperative play (MacDonald and Parke, 1986). Boys are more likely than girls are to be praised for assertiveness, and girls are more likely than boys are to be rewarded for compliance (Kerig, Cowan, and Cowan, 1993). Parents reinforce gender-specific behaviour by the design of the child's room, the clothes they buy, and the toys they provide. Boys' toys, for example, are more likely to emphasize aggressive competition and spatial manipulation. Girls' toys tend to be more passive and oriented toward the home (e.g., dolls, kitchen sets, washers and dryers) (Hughes, 1995). Most parents encourage their children to play with gender-stereotyped toys.

Preschool boys are just as likely to play with a dish set as a tool set if given a choice—unless they are told that the dish set is a girl's toy and they think their fathers will view playing with it as "bad" (Raag and Rackliff, 1998).

SECONDARY SOCIALIZATION

The process of channelling girls into roles culturally defined as appropriately feminine and boys into roles culturally defined as appropriately masculine continues in school. In most schools, teachers still tend to assume that boys will do better in the sciences and mathematics, girls in languages. Parents reinforce these expectations at home (Eccles, Jacobs, and Harold, 1990). Teachers also praise boys more than they praise girls and give boys more help. They are more likely to agree with boys' comments during class and give boys instructions on how to complete a task rather than do the task for them. This reinforces gender stereotypes and results in a less effective learning experience for girls.

By the age of about 14, interaction with peers becomes an important factor in reinforcing gender-typed attitudes and behaviours. That is because the subcultures of male and female peer groups emphasize gender-stereotypical values. Boys tend to establish less intimate friendships than girls do. Moreover, boys' friendships tend to be based on such activities as team sports, which focus on independence, emotional control, and conquest. Girls tend to form less extensive friendship networks than boys and focus on sociability, popularity, and attractiveness (Elkin and Handel, 1989; Udry, 1971: 76, 82).

THE MASS MEDIA

The symbolic representation of gender in the mass media also creates and reinforces gender stereotypes. The social construction of gender in the mass media begins when small children learn that only a kiss from Snow White's Prince Charming will save her from eternal sleep. It continues in magazines, romance novels, advertisements, and music, and on television and the Internet. It is big business. For example, Harlequin Enterprises of Toronto dominates the production and sale of romance novels worldwide. The company sells more than 175 million books a year in 23 languages in more than 100 national markets. The average romance reader spends $1200 a year on the

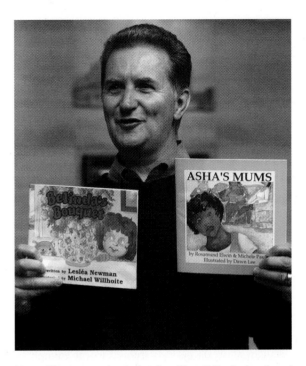

Murray Warren, a teacher in Port Coquitlam, B.C., displays two of three children's books featuring children with same-gender parents at the Supreme Court of Canada in Ottawa, June 2002. The books were banned by the Surrey School Board in which Warren teaches. What gender stereotypes do these kinds of books seek to offset?

SOURCE: Fred Chartrand/CP Picture Archive.

genre. Most readers of Harlequin romances consume between 3 and 20 books a month. A central theme in these romances is the transformation of women's bodies into objects for men's pleasure (Grescoe, 1996). As such, romance novels may be seen as a less extreme form of the pornography industry for men.

GENDER SOCIALIZATION AND SEXUALITY

In our society, we receive little formal socialization—that is, systematic instruction—regarding sexuality. That is probably because of our rather prudish history and the popular assumption that sexuality is a natural instinct that does not have to be taught. By default, therefore, as adults we tend to express our sexuality in a framework defined by our early, informal gender socialization.

Boys and girls do not always accept informal gender socialization passively; they sometimes resist it. For the most part, however, boys and girls try to develop the skills that will help them perform conven-

tional gender roles (Eagley and Wood, 1999: 412–13). Of course, conventions change. It is important to note in this regard that what children learn about femininity and masculinity today is less sexist than what they learned just a few generations ago. For example, comparing *Cinderella* and *Snow White* with *Mulan*, we see immediately that girls going to Disney movies today are sometimes presented with assertive and heroic female role models rather than the passive and, by today's standards, quite pathetic heroines of the 1930s and 1940s. However, the amount of change in gender socialization should not be exaggerated, nor its effects on sexuality. *Cinderella* and *Snow White* are still popular movies for girls. Moreover, for every *Mulan* there is a *Little Mermaid*, a movie that simply modernizes old themes about female passivity and male conquest. As we saw in our discussion of sexual behaviour, survey research shows that men are still more likely than women are to adhere to sexual scripts emphasizing fun, conquest, and orgasm rather than love, tenderness, and emotionality. The fact that girls learn that sexuality is something they must fear—think of unwanted pregnancy and sexual assault—also serves to perpetuate passive sexual scripts for women today (Nelson and Robinson, 1999: 351).

The social construction of gender and sexuality has far-reaching implications for men and women. As we have just seen, the social construction of gender during childhood socialization influences the way men and women express their sexuality. You will learn in detail later in this book how the social construction of gender also helps determine the kind of formal education men and women pursue, the kinds of jobs they get, and the way domestic work is divided between men and women. As you will now see, the standards of physical attractiveness that are internalized through gender socialization and sexual scripts have contributed to dieting and eating disorders.

BODY IMAGE AND EATING DISORDERS

The social construction of gender involves defining standards of physical attractiveness for women and men. These standards are reinforced by the mass media.

Physical attractiveness is especially important for women. That is because they are judged on the basis of appearance more often than men are. Moreover, unattractive women are described in more negative terms than equally unattractive men are (Wolf, 1991). Masculinity is more likely to be assessed in terms of status and power than in terms of physical attractiveness.

Weight has become an increasingly important dimension of body image over the past 40 years. Thus, research shows that *Playboy* centrefold models and Miss America contestants have grown substantially thinner since 1959. A 1997 survey shows that 89 percent of North American women want to lose weight (Garner, 1997). Canadian women list "being overweight" as one of their major health problems (Walters, 1992). Many men are concerned about their body image, too, but among women the emphasis on being thin is especially common. The "cult of thinness" has spawned major industries, including diet and self-help, cosmetic surgery, diet foods, and fitness (Hesse-Biber, 1996).

Standards of breast size pose a special problem for women. Although thin is in, large breasts have been popular since the 1960s (Koff and Benavage, 1998). Breasts, however, are composed mainly of fat;

Canadian women list "being overweight" as one of their major health problems.
SOURCE: Shutterstock.

and the amount of breast fat is associated with total body fat. Thus, it is virtually impossible for most women to achieve the ideal standard of beauty.

Many women and men resent the thin models they see in the mass media. Nonetheless, fear of being fat and dieting to lose weight are common in girls as young as nine. One study found that half of all teenage girls are on diets (Pipher, 1994: 184–85).

Body image is associated with self-esteem and behaviour. People who are dissatisfied with their bodies are less likely to desire and engage in sexual activity. Conversely, bad sexual experiences contribute to a poor body image. For example, sexual abuse is an important cause of body dissatisfaction. In the 1997 survey cited previously, 23 percent of women and 10 percent of men viewed sexual abuse as having been moderately to very important in shaping their body image in childhood or adolescence (Garner, 1997).

At the extreme, concern with body image may result in anorexia nervosa (refusal to eat enough to remain healthy) or bulimia (regular, self-induced vomiting). Estimates of the percentage of young women with such eating disorders range from 2 percent to 20 percent. For young men, estimates are in the 1 percent to 3 percent range (Averett and Korenman, 1996: 305; Garner, 1997; Lips, 1993: 254; Pipher, 1994: 184–85). Some women and men have changed their body shape by means of surgical procedures, such as liposuction and cosmetic surgery. More than 90 percent of cosmetic surgery patients are women (Hesse-Biber, 1996: 51, 53).

There are cultural variations in standards of beauty. For instance, in the United States, black women are more likely to be above the recommended body weight than non-black women. At the same time, they are less likely to see themselves as overweight. Obesity also results in fewer social penalties in the case of black women. Thus, obese white women have smaller family incomes than non-obese white women because they are less likely to be married and more likely to face job discrimination. This is not the case for obese black women compared with non-obese black women (Averett and Korenman, 1996).

MALE VIOLENCE AGAINST WOMEN

The way in which gender and sexual scripts are socially constructed also affects the frequency with which men sexually assault and harass women. Let us now consider this issue in detail.

SEXUAL ASSAULT

The sexual assault of women is common. Thus, surveys suggest that one in eight girls growing up in Canada today will be a victim of serious sexual abuse before the age of 16 (Bagley and King, 1990; Gadd, 1997). Perpetrators of child sexual assault are typically male, known to the victim, and in a position of authority over the child. Research demonstrates that, in general, victims of sexual assault are selected less because of sexual desirability than because of their availability and powerlessness (Duffy, 1998). One survey found that 60 percent of high school boys approve of forcing sexual activities on a girl, at least in some circumstances (Davis, Peck, and Stormant, 1993).

A survey of Canadian college and university students asked a series of questions about male violence against women during elementary school, during high school, since high school, and in the year preceding the survey (DeKeseredy and Schwartz, 1998). The researchers found that psychological or emotional abuse of women is most common, followed by sexual and then physical abuse. Males consistently reported lower levels of sexual, psychological, and physical violence against women than women reported. However, even the percentages reported by males are disturbingly high. Moreover, the percentages grow as boys turn into men and advance from high school to postsecondary education. For example, 1.5 percent of boys said they forced girls to engage in sexual activities with them in elementary school and 2.3 percent said they forced girls to engage in sexual activities with them in high school. For the year preceding the survey, the percentage was 11 percent. Fully 19.5 percent of men in Canadian colleges and universities said they had forced a woman to engage in sexual activities with them at least once since high school (see also Table 4.4).

Of course, men are the victims of violence too. Like women, they are far more likely to be assaulted by men than by women. Some studies show that female partners are as likely as male partners to participate in abusive acts—with the exception of sexual assault, which is almost exclusively a male domain (Straus, 1995). Note, however, that women are more likely to use violence as a response to their own powerlessness, attacking partners out of self-defence or

---

TABLE 4.4   VIOLENCE AGAINST WOMEN IN CANADA

TYPE OF ASSAULT	NUMBER OF WOMEN (MILLIONS)	PERCENTAGE OF ALL WOMEN
Total women harassed	9.4	87
Harassed by a stranger	9.2	85
Harassed by someone known to victim	5.5	51
Total women assaulted by a stranger	2.5	23
Sexual assault	2.0	19
Unwanted sexual touching	1.6	15
Violent sexual attack	0.7	7
Physical assault	0.8	8
Total women assaulted by a date or boyfriend	1.7	16
Sexual assault	1.3	12
Physical assault	0.8	7
Total women assaulted by a married or common-law partner	2.7	29
Total women forced into sexual activity against their will	0.7	8

SOURCE: Compiled from Statistics Canada, Violence against Women Survey, Microdata File, Ottawa, 1994a.
NOTE: Data are based on a 1993 survey of 12 000 women.

lashing out at their children following abuse by their husbands. Men, conversely, are more likely to use force to retain control and power over their partners and children. Moreover, abusive men are far more likely to cause serious physical injuries than are abusive women, and abused men are therefore far less likely than abused women are to report their partners' violent acts to the police (Fitzgerald, 1993; Koss et al., 1994; see Figure 4.5).

The most severe form of sexual assault involves rape. Research shows that some rapists are men who were physically or sexually abused in their youth. They develop a deep-seated need to feel powerful as psychological compensation for their early powerlessness. Other rapists are men who, as children, saw their mothers as potentially hostile figures who needed to be controlled, or as mere objects available for male gratification, and saw their fathers as emotionally cold and distant. Raised in such a family atmosphere, rapists learn not to empathize with women. Instead, they learn to want to dominate them (Lisak, 1992). Significantly, rates of rape are highest in war situations, when many conquering male soldiers feel justified in wanting to humiliate the vanquished, who are powerless to stop them (Human Rights Watch, 1995). This suggests that, in general, rape involves using sex to establish dominance. The incidence of rape is highest in situations where early socialization experiences predispose men to want to control women, where norms justify the domination of women, and where a large power imbalance between men and women exists.

SEXUAL HARASSMENT

Two types of sexual harassment occur in the workplace. **Quid pro quo sexual harassment** takes place when sexual threats or bribery are made a condition of employment decisions. **Hostile environment sexual harassment** involves sexual jokes, comments, and touching that interferes with work or creates an unfriendly work setting. Surveys show that between 23 percent and 51 percent of women have been sexually harassed in the workplace (Gruber, 1997; Welsh and Nierobisz, 1997). When semi-public and public settings are included, up to 87 percent of women report being sexually harassed (see Table 4.4; Lenton Smith, Fox, and Morra, 1999). On the basis of available research, it seems clear that relatively powerless women are the most likely to be sexually harassed. Moreover, sexual harassment is most common in work settings that exhibit high levels of gender inequality and a culture justifying male domination of women. Specifically, women who are young, unmarried, and employed in nonprofessional jobs are most likely to become objects of sexual harassment. They are particularly likely to be sexually harassed if they are temporary workers, the ratio of women to men in the workplace is low, and the organizational culture of the workplace tolerates sexual harassment (Welsh, 1999).

As the foregoing discussion makes clear, large power imbalances between men and women and a culture that supports patriarchy are associated with high rates of sexual assault and harassment. Where men are much more powerful than women, and where gender inequality is justified culturally, gender is socially constructed to permit and even encourage violence against women. The research literature is clear on this point. It shows, for example, that men who most enjoy sexist jokes are most likely to report engaging in acts of sexual aggression against women (Ryan and Kanjorski, 1998). Men who link sexuality with social dominance are more likely to sexually harass women (Pryor, Giedd, and Williams, 1995). And both men and women who abuse their intimate partners value control and dominance more than harmony in interpersonal relationships (Thompson, 1991).

FIGURE 4.5   SPOUSAL VIOLENCE BY SEX OF VICTIM, 1995–1999

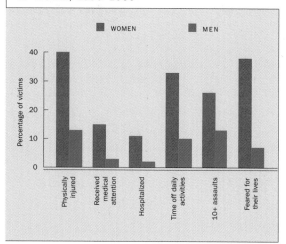

NOTE: Data are from a 1999 survey.
SOURCE: Data are adapted from the Statistics Canada, General Social Survey on Victimization (GSS) (1999), Cycle 13.

LOOKING AHEAD: TOWARD A NEW SEXUAL ETHIC

For the past 40 years, most sociologists of gender have criticized the essentialist view that sexual scripts are part of "human nature." Rather than seeing sexuality as natural, they have examined how it is socially constructed. They do not deny the biological basis of sexuality. They simply appreciate that the form sexual expression takes is not inevitable and immutable. In the preceding pages, I illustrated the social constructionist case by examining the historical factors that shaped the emergence of sexual scripts, the relationship between gender socialization and sexuality, the ways in which sexual relations reflect and reinforce power differentials, the privileging of heterosexuality, the marginalization of other sexual identities, and the implications of gender roles for the sexual assault and harassment of women by men.

SEXUAL PLURALISM

Social constructionism has overturned many ideas about sexuality. As a result, more and more people accept that sexuality does not have to be expressed in traditionally feminine or masculine ways. An attitude of **sexual pluralism** is growing (Weeks, 1986). For most people, sexual pluralism does *not* mean "anything goes." Most sexual pluralists recognize that there will always be a need to regulate sexual behaviour. For example, they oppose the abuse of power in sexual relations and see the need for the state to punish, and help prevent, incest, rape, and other forms of sexual abuse. Sexual pluralism *does* mean judging sexual acts only by their meaning for the participants. Are power relations at play? If so, are they harmful to the participants? These are the sorts of questions that sexual pluralists use in evaluating the validity of sexual acts. They do not automatically condemn a sexual practice because it is, say, "homosexual" or "heterosexual."

Some feminists are not sexual pluralists. They reject all forms of heterosexuality because, they say, it perpetuates male dominance (Dworkin, 1981; Jeffreys, 1990; Kitzinger and Wilkinson, 1994). From a sexual-pluralist perspective, however, heterosexuality is not *inherently* about men dominating women any more than it is inherently about strict adherence to traditional masculine and feminine sexual scripts. The sexual expression of heterosexuality may involve the perpetuation of harmful relations of domination or it may not. Sexual pluralists would judge only the former negatively.

Sexual pluralism, then, fosters a view of sexuality as something more than a form of victimization because of unequal power relations. It also encourages people to see sexuality positively, as a means of achieving greater pleasure, freedom of expression, and self-realization. Consider pornography. From the 1960s to the 1980s, some feminists fought to ban pornography on the grounds that it presents women as powerless sex objects and encourages men to sexually assault women (Dworkin, 1981; MacKinnon, 1987). Most pornography does indeed have that effect. However, must it? Recently, sexual pluralists have argued that pornography does not have to reinforce the domination and degradation of women by men. For example, pornography can be a means for women to create and disseminate their own sexual scripts based on female sexual fantasies, both heterosexual and lesbian. Pornographic art, literature, and movies of this type are now being produced (Matrix, 1996). From the sexual-pluralist point of view, seeing pornography as *necessarily* harmful to women is little more than a new form of essentialism.

Riane Eisler (1987) convincingly argues that, for the first time in 7000 years, social conditions now make it possible for humanity to return to the state of rough gender equality that existed before the invasion of Old Europe by conquering hordes from the north, east, and south. At least in the world's rich countries, nothing prevents us from adopting social policies that would create gender equality in the workplace, the home, and other spheres of life (see Chapter 9). As this chapter demonstrates, the examination and redefinition of sexuality is an important step in the process of achieving gender equality.

SUMMARY

1. Sex refers to biological differences between males and females while gender refers to the attitudes, beliefs, and behaviours that we commonly associate with each sex.

2. Although it is popular to trace the origins of masculine and feminine gender roles to biological differences between the sexes, most sociologists focus on the ways in which gender is socially constructed.

3. Three major sociohistorical changes have led to the development of gender inequality: long-distance warfare and conquest, plow agriculture, and the separation of public and private spheres during early industrialization.

4. Conscious sexual learning begins around adolescence in the context of firmly established gender identities.

5. Although we receive little formal socialization regarding sexuality, sexual relationships tend to be male-dominated as a result of the character of gender socialization and men's continuing dominant position in society.

6. The social construction of gender and sexual scripts has defined standards of beauty that are nearly impossible for most women to achieve. This contributes to widespread anxiety about body image, leading in some cases to eating disorders.

7. Gender inequality and a sociocultural context that justifies and eroticizes male sexual aggression contribute to the widespread problem of male sexual aggression in our society.

8. The mass media reflect and reinforce the relationship between heterosexuality and male domination.

9. Social constructionism encourages sexual pluralism, which assesses the validity of sexual activities in terms of the meanings of the acts to the participants.

QUESTIONS TO CONSIDER

1. Do you think sexual orientation is genetically programmed or a function of social and psychological experience? On what do you base your opinion? What type of evidence would persuade you one way or the other?

2. Design a study to test whether gender roles are inherent or socially constructed.

3. What policy recommendations would you make to lower the level of sexual assault and sexual harassment? Why do you think these policies would be effective?

GLOSSARY

Compulsory heterosexuality is the assumption that individuals should desire only members of the "opposite" sex.

Essentialists observe male–female differences in sexual scripts, the division of labour at home and in the workplace, mate selection, sexual aggression, jealousy, promiscuity, fidelity, and so forth. They then interpret these differences as natural and universal.

Gender encompasses the feelings, attitudes, and behaviours that are associated with being male or female as conventionally understood.

Gender identity refers to identification with, or a sense of belonging to, a particular sex, biologically, psychologically, and socially.

Gender roles comprise the repertoire of behaviours that match widely shared expectations about how males and females are supposed to act.

Hostile environment sexual harassment involves sexual jokes, comments, and touching that interfere with work or create an unfriendly work setting.

Quid pro quo sexual harassment involves sexual threats or bribery used to extract sexual favours as a condition of employment decisions.

Sex refers to being born with distinct male or female genitalia and a genetic program that releases either male or female hormones to stimulate the development of one's reproductive system.

Sexual orientation refers to the way a person derives sexual pleasure, including whether desirable partners are of the same or a different sex.

Sexual pluralism assesses sexual acts only by their meaning for the participants.

Sexual scripts are assumptions that guide sexual behaviour by telling us whom we should find attractive, when and where it is appropriate to be aroused, what is sexually permissible, and so on.

Sexuality involves actions that are intended to produce erotic arousal and genital response.

Social constructionism is the main alternative to essentialism. Social constructionists argue that gender differences are not the product of biological properties, whether chromosomal, gonadal, or hormonal. Instead, gender and sexuality are products of social structure and culture.

Sociobiology is the best-known variant of essentialism. It holds that all human beings instinctually want to ensure that their genes get passed on to future generations. However, the different reproductive status of men and women means that they have had to develop different adaptive strategies. This gave rise to "masculine" and "feminine" patterns of behaviour that presumably became genetically encoded because of their adaptive value.

Transgendered people defy society's gender norms and blur widely accepted gender roles by, for example, cross-dressing. About 1 in every 5,000 to 10,000 people in North America is transgendered.

Transsexuals are people who want to alter their gender by changing their appearance or resorting to medical intervention. About 1 in every 30,000 people in North America is a transsexual.

SUGGESTED READING

1. Do you think that sexual orientation is genetically programmed or a function of social and psychological experience? On what do you base your opinion? What type of evidence would persuade you one way or the other?

2. Design a study to test whether gender roles are inherent or socially constructed.

3. What policy recommendations would you make to lower the level of sexual assault and sexual harassment? Why do you think these policies would be effective?

NOTES

1. Freud called this set of emotions the "Oedipus complex" after the ancient Greek legend of Oedipus. Oedipus was abandoned as a child. When he became an adult he accidentally killed his father and unwittingly married his mother. Discovering his true relationship to his mother, he blinded himself and died in exile.

2. Freud called this set of emotions the "Electra complex" after the ancient Greek legend of Electra. Electra persuaded her brother to kill their mother and their mother's lover in order to avenge their father's murder. Incidentally, some sexologists call into question the existence of vaginal orgasm and stress the importance of clitoral stimulation (Masters and Johnson, 1966). This viewpoint emerged around the same time as the modern feminist movement and as more and more people came to view sexuality not just as a means of reproduction but also as a means of erotic enjoyment, including orgasm.

WEB RESOURCES

Companion Web Site for This Book

http://www.newsociety5e.nelson.com

Begin by clicking on the Student Resources section of the website. Next, select the chapter you are studying from the pull-down menu. From the Student Resources page, you have easy access to InfoTrac College Edition and other resources, such as the Glossary and Flashcards. The website also has many useful tips to aid you in your study of sociology.

InfoTrac College Edition Search Terms

Visit http://www.infotrac-college.com for access to more than 20 million articles from nearly 6000 sources when doing your online research.

ThomsonNOW™

http://hed.nelson.com

This online diagnostic tool identifies each student's unique needs with a Pretest that generates a personalized Study Plan for each chapter, helping students focus on concepts they are having the most difficulty mastering. Students then take a Posttest after reading the chapter to measure their understanding of the material. An Instructor Gradebook is available to track and monitor student progress.

CHAPTER FIVE

The Mass Media

In this chapter you will learn that

- The mass media may be examined in terms of their economic and political organization, their representation of ideas, and their effects on people.

- Newspapers are local monopolies with high levels of ownership concentration; their dependency on advertising has an impact on news content because it limits the survival prospects of newspapers with radical views.

- English-speaking Canadians watch mostly American television programming, especially prime-time drama and comedies. Although some analysts view this as a "sellout" of Canadian culture, others regard it as an effect of globalization and argue that it does not undermine the institutional structure of society.

- Some analysts claim that news coverage has a left-Liberal political bias, while other analysts argue that news coverage is ideologically conservative.

- Many analysts believe that a causal link exists between media violence and violent behaviour, but studies that demonstrate this alleged connection have been criticized on the grounds of flawed methodology. Even those who believe that media violence causes aggressive behaviour disagree about how it does so.

- Studies on the viewing habits of TV audiences indicate that men tend to use TV in a more planned way than women do and watch more intently, whereas women are more likely to use TV as a focus for social interaction.

- Access to and use of the Internet reflect broader patterns of social inequality, though this appears to be in decline as the technology becomes less costly and more widely available. Use of the Internet for social interaction creates virtual communities that act as sources of identity and social support.

Graham Knight
MCMASTER UNIVERSITY
Josh Greenberg
CARLETON UNIVERSITY

INTRODUCTION

In 2003, the average Canadian spent just less than 20 hours a week listening to radio and 21.7 hours a week watching television (Statistics Canada, 2005a). These amounts vary by social factors, such as region, sex, and age, particularly for television. Quebeckers and Maritimers watch more TV than other Canadians do, women watch more TV than men do, and seniors watch more TV than younger adults, adolescents, and children do (Statistics Canada, 2005a). These facts may come as a surprise, since we tend to associate high levels of radio and television consumption and its effects with teens, not senior women.

Traditional television watching has been declining, while radio listening has remained fairly stable. This points to a number of changes in media technology and use. Since the early 1990s, Internet use has grown rapidly, especially home-based use. By 2003, 64 percent of the 12.3 million Canadian households had at least one member who used the Internet regularly, whether at home, work, school, a public library, or some other location (Statistics Canada, 2004). To some extent television viewing has suffered because of this. Despite the decline in television

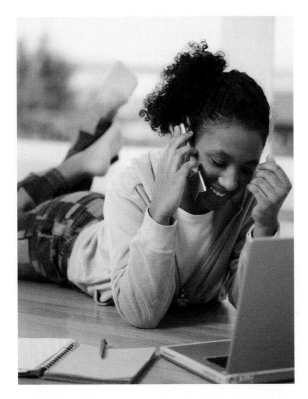

Between 1997 and 2000, regular home-based use of the Internet grew from 16 percent to 40 percent of Canadian households.
SOURCE: PhotoDisc/Getty Images.

viewing, the overall picture of media use remains fairly stable. Add movie viewing and newspaper and magazine reading to radio, television, and the Internet, and it becomes clear that we spend more time interacting with the media than doing anything else, including working.

The term media is the plural of "medium," or middle—hence the idea of media as the means for connecting two or more points. Although the term is sometimes used to refer to any instrument or tool, it is more commonly found in association with the process of communication. **Communication** means to bring together or unify by establishing shared meanings and understandings between groups and individuals. This unification occurs through the transmission of information, knowledge, or beliefs by means of language, visual images, and other sign systems, such as music. It used to be common to make a distinction between **mass media** and **interactive media.** With mass media, communication flows are essentially unidirectional, going from a transmission point, such as a television or radio station, to an audience whose members remain anonymous and isolated from one another. With interactive media, like the telephone, conversely, communications flow back and forth, and people exchange roles with one another in the transmission and reception of communication. This distinction is breaking down, however, with the impact of new media, like the Internet, MP3 players, and other forms of computer-mediated communication that combine aspects of both mass and interactive media.

In this chapter, we focus primarily on three media: newspapers, television, and the Internet. The chapter will address two main questions about the media. First, how do the media affect us—how do they influence individuals, groups, and institutions? The second question is the reverse: how do we affect the media—how does society influence and shape the media? To address these questions, the chapter is organized into four main sections that deal with political economy, representation and ideology, media effects and audiences, and computer-mediated communication.

We begin by considering the basic theoretical perspectives in media studies. Theories of the media fall into two main types, technological and critical. The principal difference between them concerns the ways in which the structure and role of the media are determined. Technological theories emphasize that different media technologies (e.g., print versus audiovisual media) determine social perceptions, interactions, and institutional arrangements. Critical theorists, conversely, argue for the importance of social values, interests, and conflicts in shaping the technological development, use, and impact of the media.

THE TECHNOLOGICAL PERSPECTIVE

The technological perspective derives primarily from the work of two Canadian scholars, Harold Innis and Marshall McLuhan. From his survey of the history of human communication, Innis (1951) made the distinction between time-biased and space-biased media. **Time-biased media** are modes of communication that endure over time but are not very mobile across space, such as writing on stone or clay tablets. **Space-biased media** can cover much greater areas of space but are much less durable over time—for example, writing on paper or sounds transmitted over the airwaves.

The two types of media foster different arrangements of institutions and cultural values. Time-biased media, for example, are conducive to a strong sense of tradition and custom, and these promote religious forms of power and belief. Space-biased media lead to territorial expansion, empire building, and more secular forms of power and culture as manifested in the dominance of military institutions and the growth of the state. These different forms of power, in turn, create different types of social division and conflict. The elite that controls the means of communication tries to use it to preserve its own privilege and interests. Those excluded from power struggle against elite control and in the process stimulate the development of new, alternative forms of communication. Historically, such a struggle over the means of communication resulted in the shift from time- to space-biased media.

McLuhan (1964) was influenced by Innis's ideas about the effect of communication on institutions and culture and how this effect changes over time. He argued, however, that the relationship was mediated by the way that forms of communication change our sense perceptions and cognitive processes. The invention of printing, for example, undermined oral communication and its emphasis on hearing, and ushered in a more visually oriented culture. Because

print consists of visually separated words strung together in a linear sequence, it encourages us to see the world as comprising separate objects and to interpret that world in a linear, cause-and-effect way. Print removes communication from face-to-face interaction, and so it makes information more abstract. The abstracting effect of print, in turn, fosters individualism, privacy, rationality, and social differentiation. Historically, these further effects of print coincided with the rise of nationalism and the weakening of social ties. Print then served to standardize national languages and became a principal mechanism of social identity.

For McLuhan, the spread of electronic media, particularly television, is spelling an end to the era of print dominance. The impact of TV is crucial for two reasons. First, unlike print, TV does not rely exclusively on one sense (i.e., sight)—it integrates sight and sound and achieves a better *sensory balance*. In fact, for McLuhan the effect of this balance is to make TV a kind of tactile medium in the sense that it "touches" its audience more easily than print. Second, TV allows communication to be *instantaneous*—there is no significant delay between transmission and reception of the message. These differences make TV more socially inclusive than print is. This observation has led some of McLuhan's adherents to claim that TV is also more accessible and less hierarchical than print (Znaimer, 1996) and that the electronic media have the capacity to usher in a new era of global democracy. McLuhan described this new era as a "global village" in which the expansive information-gathering and transmission capacities of modern societies could make us more aware of and familiar with the goings on of people in other parts of the world. It is incredible to think that McLuhan's argument that electronic media would create a "global village" predated the arrival of the Internet and other new communications technologies!

McLuhan's views, however, have proven controversial because he was somewhat naïve about the ability of media to enhance social change. Indeed, this controversy stems from a tendency in McLuhan's work to see media technologies as something of an autonomous force that operates outside social control (and therefore beyond human agency). Although he famously stated that "we shape our tools, thereafter our tools shape us," McLuhan has been dismissed as a *technological determinist* for encouraging us to think that social change is not determined in the first instance by conscious human action, but by the nature and function of technology. Those who subscribe to the critical perspective have developed this criticism most forcefully.

THE CRITICAL PERSPECTIVE

According to the **critical perspective,** institutions, such as the media, and processes, such as socialization and social control, cannot be understood from the viewpoint of society as a whole, but only from that of unequal and conflicting groups and classes. In fact, the critical perspective has two variants, one that emphasizes the relationship between media and inequality, and one that emphasizes the relationship between media and social conflict.

The first variant of the critical perspective is derived from the orthodox interpretation of Marxism. In this perspective, the role of the media is defined in terms of how the media serve the economic interests and political power of the dominant class, those who own and control the means of material production. To maintain and consolidate its power and interests, the dominant class also exercises control over the means of cultural and moral production—that is, the production of ideas, beliefs, values, and norms that constitute a society's **dominant ideology.** The

The invention of the printing press reduced the influence of oral communication as it lessened face-to-face interaction and made information more abstract.

SOURCE: P.J. Crook. *May 2.* Courtesy of Nancy Poole's Studio.

media, by disseminating this dominant ideology, are used to create acceptance and legitimization of the status quo.

This view was initially developed by Max Horkheimer and Theodor Adorno (1972 [1947]), who saw the media as part of a broader "culture industry" that functions to create "mass deception" about the exploitative and oppressive character of capitalist society. In their view, the role of the media is to distract and pacify people by feeding them standardized images and messages that stifle the capacity for independent, critical thought.

Similar to this view of the culture industry is the "propaganda model" of the news media put forward by Edward Herman and Noam Chomsky (1988). They argue that the media serve the interests of the leading political and economic class by "filtering" information to reduce or eliminate radical or subversive views. Herman and Chomsky identify five main filters: (1) the media's orientation to profit-making, (2) its dependency on advertising for revenue and profit, (3) its reliance on powerful institutions and individuals as sources of information, (4) negative reaction—what they call *flak*—if the media deviate from promoting elite interests and values, and (5) adherence to anti-communism as an overarching belief system. With the decline of communism, the "war on terrorism" seems to have become the fifth filter.

The second variant of the critical perspective also acknowledges that the capitalist class and other powerful groups use dominant ideology to reinforce their position and maintain the status quo. They do this through the establishment of **hegemony**—the use of the media and other cultural institutions (e.g., school system) to represent their interests, values, and understandings as natural and universal. But dominant ideology is not the only ideology. Inequality can also engender resistance and struggle, which result in other, more critical perspectives from which social reality and the dominant ideology can be interpreted. A distinction should be made between **alternative** and **oppositional viewpoints.** Oppositional viewpoints represent the experiences of subordinated groups against those of the powerful; alternative viewpoints occupy an intermediate position, reflecting compromise or "negotiated" understandings, which blend elements of dominant and oppositional viewpoints (Hall, 1980). Although the media usually promote understandings that conform to the dominant ideology, their messages are always at least partially open

to the challenge of alternative and oppositional interpretations. To be successful, hegemony has to be flexible enough to accommodate and incorporate a range of different viewpoints (Knight, 1998).

POLITICAL ECONOMY OF THE MEDIA

One strength of the critical perspective is that it draws attention to the ways that the social and cultural roles of the media depend on their role as agents of political and economic power and interests. The principal approach that sociologists take to analyzing this relationship empirically is *political economy*. Political economy focuses on the ownership and control of economic resources, and on the effect of technology and economic power on cultural values, social structure, and political decision making. Media are organizations that usually are owned and controlled by large corporations or the state and that function like other bureaucracies. They have to sustain themselves economically through commercial revenue, government funding, subscriber fees and donations, or some mixture of these. What, then, are the primary goals of media organizations—to inform and entertain or to capture market share and make money? And in whose interests do they operate—owners, advertisers, or audiences? These questions are especially pertinent in democratic societies where values, such as freedom, diversity of opinion, and the promotion of both minority and national cultural identities, are strong.

Ownership and control of the media are generally becoming more concentrated in a smaller number of giant corporate hands. This trend is part of the

What are the primary goals of media organizations: to inform and entertain or to capture market share and make money?
SOURCE: Photos.com.

wider process of economic globalization, and it is leading to the creation of large **multimedia chains.** These are corporations that own a diversified array of media operations and outlets in different fields, such as radio, TV, and publishing, and operate worldwide. One of the world's best-known multimedia corporations is the Walt Disney Company (see Figure 5.1), whose total revenues in 2005 stood at US$31.9 billion. The world's dominant media corporations are primarily American-based. Only two of the top six media giants are headquartered outside the United States—Bertelsmann and Vivendi—and these are located in Western Europe (Rupert Murdoch's News Corporation is considered a joint American-Australian company). Two Canadian companies make it into the global top 50: Rogers and CanWest Global.

To secure and enhance their market position, multimedia chains practise both horizontal consolidation and vertical integration. **Horizontal consolidation** refers to the sharing of facilities and resources between different plants and outlets. **Vertical integration** is the controlling of resources and assets at different stages of production, such as ownership of a major league sports team along with the stations and cable channels on which the games are televised. The recent development of digital technology has enhanced both horizontal consolidation and vertical integration, and has led to a series of corporate mergers, such as AOL Time Warner, that have strengthened the position of multimedia chains as the dominant form of organization. These mergers comprise the union of delivery conduits (cable, satellite, telephony) and content (news, information, and entertainment).

The effects of these mergers are mixed. Critics argue that consolidation of media properties into fewer hands, and the convergence of media platforms, reduces the range of voices and perspectives that can be represented in the so-called marketplace of ideas. Although the names of the top owners may

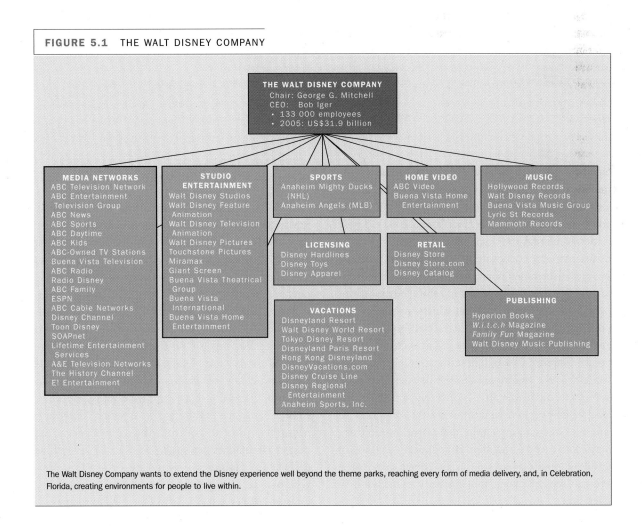

FIGURE 5.1 THE WALT DISNEY COMPANY

The Walt Disney Company wants to extend the Disney experience well beyond the theme parks, reaching every form of media delivery, and, in Celebration, Florida, creating environments for people to live within.

TABLE 5.1 GLOBAL ENTERTAINMENT MEDIA CORPORATIONS

"About six players now own virtually everything, all aspects of the media experience."

— *Drew Marcus, Deutsche Bank*
media sector analyst

RANK	REVENUE (US$ BILLION)	
Top Six (2005)		
1. AOL Time Warner (U.S.)	42.1	
2. Disney (U.S.)	31.9	
3. Vivendi Universal* (France)	25.7	
4. News Corp. (U.S./Australia)	22.7†	
5. Viacom (U.S.)	22.5	
6. Bertelsmann (Germany)	20.9‡	
Canadian Companies (2001, 2004§)		
27. Rogers	2.4 (2001)	4.9 (2004)
43. CanWest	1.4 (2001)	2.2 (2004)

NOTES

* Media and communications holdings only

† Estimated US$ equivalent; original financial data given in AUD$

‡ Estimated US$ equivalent; original financial data given in Euros

§ Canadian rankings reflect 2001 data reported in *Variety* (26 August–1 Sep, 2002, p. 52). More recent rankings are unavailable; however, updated annual revenues (obtained from financial data contained in annual reports on corporate websites) are indicated for the year ending 2004. Values reported are converted from Canadian to U.S. dollars by using exchange rates (1 CAD = 0.877 USD) in force at time of writing.

SOURCES: Top six data taken from Annual Reports or other financial data for each corporation. Downloaded from http://ir.timewarner.com/downloads/4Q04earnings.pdf; http://corporate.disney.go.com/investors/annual_reports/2005/introduction/financial_highlights/fh.html; http://www.vivendiuniversal.com/vu/en/files/20050629_Annual_Report_20-F.cfm; http://www.cbccorporation.com/media/pdf/qr4q04.pdf; http://investor/bertelsmann.de/bertelsmann_corp/wms41/bm/index.php?ci=255&language=2; and http://www.newscorp.com/Report2004/2004_annual_report.pdf.

change from year to year, "the domination of the media by entertainment conglomerates exerts a consistently corrosive effect . . . , undermining debate when we need it most" (*The Nation*, 2002). These critics argue that the dominant economic imperative of mainstream corporate media (i.e., the focus on profits) also impedes progressive social change by favouring "management over labor, corporations over corporate critics, affluent whites over inner-city poor, officialdom over protesters [and] privatization and free market 'reforms' over public sector development" (Parenti, 2004). These mergers also demonstrate that the traditional distinctions between print and electronic media are disappearing, at least at the level of corporate organization. At the same time, it is important to acknowledge that variations do exist, particularly in the way that the political economy of different media creates different effects and issues. We can see this when we compare newspapers and television.

NEWSPAPERS: CONCENTRATION, MONOPOLY, AND ADVERTISING

In Canada, corporate ownership and control of daily newspapers has undergone rapid change since the 1970s and has become highly concentrated. CanWest Global, Quebecor Media Inc., and Torstar dominate the field today. CanWest Global owns daily newspapers in major metropolitan areas, such as Vancouver, Calgary, Edmonton, Saskatoon, Ottawa, Montreal, and Halifax, and has control of the Toronto-based *National Post*, one of only two English-language national newspapers. Quebecor Media Inc. controls the *Sun* chain of English-language tabloids in Toronto, Ottawa, Calgary, and Edmonton, as well as French-language tabloids in Quebec City and Montreal. Torstar controls the *Toronto Star*, the largest circulation newspaper in Canada, as well as dailies in Hamilton, Kitchener-Waterloo, and Guelph. It also recently purchased a minority interest (20 percent) in Bell Globemedia, the parent company of *The Globe and Mail*. CanWest Global, Quebecor Media, and now Torstar also have significant interests in other media, such as radio, television, the Internet, and cable, which, in the case of CanWest Global, reach as far as Australia, New Zealand, and Ireland.

The concentration of ownership in the hands of a few multimedia chains has raised serious questions about freedom of the press and the diversity of opinion, both of which are widely regarded as necessary for a democratic society. These concerns came to a head in June 2002 when CanWest Global fired Russell Mills, the long-time publisher of *The Ottawa Citizen*, for running an editorial calling for the resignation of then Prime Minister Jean Chrétien, without first gaining the approval of corporate head office. Mills's firing came on the heels of a number of changes made by CanWest Global that tightened corporate control over the editorial content of its Southam newspapers. Although considerable outcry was raised over CanWest Global's actions—more than 3000 people reportedly cancelled their subscriptions to *The Ottawa Citizen*—the ability of newspaper proprietors to dictate news content continues to depend on the need to make a profit. This, in turn, depends on the ability to attract advertisers. In 2004, daily newspapers earned $2.6 billion in advertising revenues (Statistics Canada, 2005b). Advertising is by far the largest source of revenue for newspaper publishers. In 2004, advertising accounted for 72 percent of total operating revenues for daily and community newspapers combined (Statistics Canada, 2005b). But to attract advertisers, newspapers must also appeal to readers and subscribers, as these compose the market that advertisers are trying to reach and persuade.

As newspapers have become more advertising dependent, the scale and costs of operation have also grown. The major effect of this change has been to reduce competition and create local newspaper monopolies in all but the larger urban areas. Even in large cities like Toronto, where several daily newspapers exist, papers have to specialize and appeal to particular market segments to survive. The critical perspective sees multimedia chain ownership, local monopolies, and advertising dependency as resulting in the homogenization of news coverage and the decline of diversity in news topics and viewpoints. However, the evidence supporting the link is inconclusive. Studies of the 1980 closure of competing papers in Winnipeg and Ottawa, for example, found

that monopolization led to a decline in the volume and length of news stories, especially national and international coverage (Candussi and Winters, 1988; Trim, with Pizante and Yaraskavitch, 1983). In contrast, McCombs (1988), in a comparison of Winnipeg and Montreal, claims that monopolization brought about no significant change. If anything, he argues that the quality of news coverage actually improved somewhat after the closure of competing papers.

TELEVISION: ECONOMY, CULTURE, AND IDENTITY

For television as for newspapers, commercialization and advertising dependency have had the greatest impact on the content and role of the medium. Primarily the profit motive, rather than cultural goals, such as promoting Canadian content and national identity, drives private television. Income and profits come largely from advertising, and this means having to cater to large audiences with programming that will be primarily pleasurable and noncontentious. To attract audiences and advertisers, private Canadian broadcasters, particularly English-language broadcasters, rely heavily on imported, mainly American, programming. Even though the cost of licensing American programming has been increasing, it is still less expensive to purchase than it is to produce comparable Canadian programming.

The issue of Canadian content pertains largely to entertainment programming, particularly English-Canadian drama. Audiences have long shown a strong preference for American dramatic programming and, as a result, the audience for domestic programs is not large enough in economic terms to make Canadian drama attractive, particularly for private broadcasters. Indeed, roughly 70 percent of all English-language viewing in Canada is devoted to American television, and this number climbs to 90 percent during prime time (Attallah and Foster, 2006). Reaction to this situation is split. Cultural nationalists argue that broadcasting should be an instrument of Canadian culture and identity, meaning that it should actively promote Canadian content (Collins, 1990). They single out drama because of its popularity and capacity to promote and reinforce cultural myths and values that solidify a distinct national identity. Support for the argument that TV drama enforces cultural identity can be found in Quebec, where there is a strong commitment to francophone drama and other entertainment programming on the part of both public and private TV. Strong national and cultural identity on the part of francophone Quebeckers match this commitment. Francophones not only watch more Canadian programming overall but also watch proportionately more television drama than anglophones do (see Table 5.2).

The federal government has attempted to address the issue of television drama production by establishing content requirements, offering financial inducements, such as production subsidies, sheltering the national broadcaster (CBC/Radio-Canada) from market pressures and priorities, and erecting regulatory barriers preventing foreign companies from owning too many pieces of the Canadian media pie. Although production has been increasing, economic pressure means creating the kind of programming that will attract advertisers and foreign buyers, and this often means that the programming itself lacks a distinctly Canadian character. Canadian television production is increasingly part of a market that is global in scale but still dominated by the American television industry. For critical theorists in particular, this dominance amounts to **cultural imperialism,** in which one society's media exert an overwhelming and unilateral influence over another society's culture (see Tomlinson, 1997).

As evidence of cultural imperialism, critical theorists point to the uneven flow of television and other cultural products between countries. Canada, for example, is one of the world's largest importers of cultural products—in 2004, Canada's cultural trade deficit was pegged at $2 billion (Statistics Canada, 2005d; see Table 5.3). The bulk of our cultural imports come from the United States.

The view that Canadian culture and identity are threatened or undermined by the consumption of American television programs or other cultural products has not gone unchallenged, however. First, critics of the cultural nationalist position argue that although dramatic television is important, Canadians also develop a sense of collective national identity through their overwhelming preferences for domestic news and public affairs programming. *Desperate Housewives* and *American Idol* may attract a larger Canadian audience than *DaVinci's City Hall* or *This is Wonderland*, but Canadians also overwhelmingly prefer to get their news and public affairs information from the CBC and CTV than they do from Fox or CBS. It would be wrong to conclude that collective identity is fashioned in dramatic television only and not tempered by the promotion of nationalist values in public affairs and news programming.

TABLE 5.2   PERCENTAGE DISTRIBUTION OF TV VIEWING TIME, FALL 2003

| | ANGLOPHONE | | FRANCOPHONE | |
PROGRAM TYPE	CANADIAN	FOREIGN	CANADIAN	FOREIGN
News and public affairs	15.6	8.1	29.6	1.9
Documentaries	1.2	2.6	3.2	1.2
Academic	1.1	2.3	2.8	0.4
Social/recreational	0.4	0.9	0.7	0.1
Religious	0.1	0.1	0.3	—
Sports	5.4	3.9	4.3	1.2
Variety and games	1.5	10.7	13.3	2.3
Music and dance	0.7	0.4	1.6	0.2
Comedy	0.5	11.4	3.6	5.1
Drama	3.4	22.6	9.4	14.3
Other	—	7.1	—	3.5
Total	**29.9**	**70.1**	**68.8**	**30.2**

SOURCE: Adapted from the Statistics Canada publication "The Daily," Catalogue 11-001, Television viewing, Fall 2003, Thursday, March 31, 2005.

Second, the concern that Canadian culture is under siege by American-style programming operates on the assumption that Canadian values are qualitatively different from American ones and can, in fact, be reflected in our cultural products. But what are Canadian values? Are they determined by what policymakers decide is uniquely "Canadian," or are they simply the common beliefs citizens espouse, which tend to change over time? Third, we assume that Canadians are at risk of becoming Americanized by overexposure to American celebrity newmagazines *(US Weekly)*, comedy programs *(South Park)*, and popular music (Britney Spears)—but what about the impact of Canada on the Americans? If exposure has a determining effect on identity, would the popularity of films like *The History of Violence* (directed by Canadian David Cronenberg), *Crash* (directed and co-written by Canadian Paul Haggis), and *Brokeback Mountain* (filmed in Alberta); the popularity of Emmy-winning programs like *24* (starring Canadians Kiefer Sutherland and Elisha Cuthbert); or the huge impact of Canadian comedy talent on Hollywood (Mike Myers, Ivan Reitman, Jim Carrey, Dan Akroyd, Martin Short, Lorne Michaels, etc.) suggest the Canadianization of the United States?

Another reason to question the "problem" of television and Canadian culture and identity is offered by Collins (1990), who argues that Canada is quickly becoming a "postnational" society. This condition is becoming increasingly common among Western societies generally, as the association of the nation-state with particular economic, political, and cultural institutions breaks down under the effects of globalization. Canada is a pluralistic society linguistically, ethnically, and subculturally, and so it may not have a strong culture in the sense of a single, unified system of symbols, representations, and identities. It does, nevertheless, have a strong culture in the anthropological sense of shared institutions and practices. And this culture, Collins argues, is undiminished by the fact that English Canadians can't get enough of *Law & Order* or *The O.C.*

Collins's argument suggests that Western societies are now becoming postmodern. In this view, as the social structure becomes increasingly differentiated, social roles, identities, and experiences become increasingly fragmented and dissociated from one another. Postmodernists believe that fragmentation allows groups and individuals greater scope to play with and reconstruct their identities and understandings. It can foster new forms of consciousness, particularly in terms of the popular culture that is associated with the mass media (Fiske, 1987).

Fragmentation is also occurring at the level of political economy with the proliferation of new TV services, such as specialty channels, superstations, pay-per-view channels, and home-shopping channels, in addition to more conventional broadcast TV stations and networks (Ellis, 1992). As television becomes more differentiated, audiences become more

TABLE 5.3   VALUE OF INTERNATIONAL TRADE IN CULTURAL GOODS, 2004 (THOUSANDS OF DOLLARS)

Imports		Exports	
Written and published works	2 822 821	Written and published works	862 730
Film and video	867 480	Film and video	644 945
Sound recording/music publishing	151 711	Sound recording/music publishing	145 072
Visual art	255 491	Visual art	79 722
Architecture	2 580	Architecture	1 320
Advertising	175 534	Advertising	417 915
Heritage	34 359	Heritage	24 103
Photography	124 748	Photography	228 878
TOTAL	4 434 724	TOTAL	2 404 685

SOURCE: Adapted from the Statistics Canada publication "Culture Goods Trade 2004; Culture Trade-Goods: Data Tables, 1996 to 2005," Catalogue 87-007. Released October 17, 2005.

fragmented, a process that is captured by the term *narrowcasting* (as opposed to broadcasting). With this development, the role of TV as an agent of common culture is being questioned.

Concomitant with audience fragmentation, a contrary process, **technological convergence,** is also at work. The term refers to the merging and integration of previously separate communications technologies, such as print, telephony, computers, television, and radio (Ellis, 1992). Convergence has been given a boost by the development of digital technology. Technological convergence is reflected in the growing popularity of the term *home entertainment,* which includes a whole array of social activities, such as shopping, banking, and even working (telecommuting) at home. The implication is that everyday life will become privatized in the household as people find they have less and less need for face-to-face interaction. Some evidence to support such a trend can be found in a study of the consequences of the introduction of TV reception to a community in British Columbia (Williams, 1986). The researchers found that the introduction of TV led to the displacement of other activities, such as participation in the community's social and recreational life, as people stayed at home more to watch TV.

REPRESENTATION AND IDEOLOGY: THE MEANING OF THE MESSAGE

Analysis of the media from the perspective of political economy alone is limited, because it takes for granted the nature of the messages that the media communicate. The emphasis here is on the plural—*messages.* The media communicate on different levels—the pleasurable as well as the meaningful, the entertaining as well as the informative. Such communication entails the process of **representation**—that is, the use of language, visual images, and other symbolic tools to create messages people can understand and find satisfying or enjoyable. Representation, however, is a selective process. It involves countless decisions— only some of which are conscious—about what is to be included and what is to be left out, what is to be emphasized and what is to be downplayed, and about the sequence in which the elements are to be connected into a coherent message. Sociologists use the term **framing** to denote the selective, organized nature of representation (Gitlin, 1980; Goffman,

1974). To frame something (such as a picture or photograph) is to set up boundaries that define where the representation begins and ends, and to organize the contents in a way that distinguishes what is being emphasized (the foreground) from what is treated as secondary (the context or background). The framing of any representation—a news report, an advertisement, or a TV drama—has ideological effects inasmuch as it entails a particular inflection or bias. Every frame is only one of several different ways of seeing and interpreting something.

NEWS AND IDEOLOGY

Outside our immediate experience, the news media are one of our principal sources of information about social reality. Conservative and critical writers disagree on how news is framed and the ideological effects of news framing. Conservatives argue that the news media have a "left-liberal" bias that runs counter to the views and interests of the mainstream of society. They believe that cultural critics, writing from a Marxist perspective, "have oversimplified the role of journalists in liberal societies [in addition to] the nature of liberal societies as well" (Miljan and Cooper, 2003: 47). According to these conservative writers, bias operates in three related ways. First, the media have an anti-corporate bias (see Box 5.1) and are critical of market-oriented solutions to social problems. Second, journalists give greater or more favourable attention to the views of interest groups and constituencies that share their *personal* liberal or left-wing political views—for example, unions, environmentalists, social welfare organizations, and, in the case of foreign news, left-wing regimes or political movements (Miljan and Cooper, 2003). Third, the media concentrate on negative events, issues, and news angles, ignoring the positive aspects of social life (National Media Archive, 1993).

In contrast to the conservative perspective, those who employ a critical perspective believe that the news media function chiefly to reproduce the values, interests, and perspectives of dominant social groups. Critical media scholars maintain that the news is ideological because corporate media organizations must make money, thus they depend heavily on elite sources (such as politicians, police, and corporations) for the news. This is seen not as a conscious conspiracy but as the unconscious effect of the values and

CANADIAN MEDIA UNCRITICALLY ACCEPT ADVOCACY GROUPS' ASSERTION THAT 1.5 MILLION CANADIAN CHILDREN LIVE IN POVERTY

During the last week in November 1993, Campaign 2000, a 45-group coalition, reported an increase in the number of children living in poverty in Canada. This finding was widely reported in most major Canadian daily newspapers as well as on the national newscasts of the networks.

Each of the reports faithfully conveyed the coalition's findings. All had given the following information as was reported by CTV's Ken Ernhofer: "The child poverty numbers are staggering. A watchdog group, Campaign 2000, says that between 1989 and 1991, an additional 250 000 Canadian children joined the ranks of the impoverished, an increase of 30 percent. In all, 1.2 million children lived in poverty, one child in every five."

Most troubling about the way in which the media reported these stories was that there was no incredulity or question that that many Canadian children were poor. The reporters covered the story in almost exactly the same way, all repeating the information provided to them by the coalition. Despite the unanimity among the reporters, a number of facts presented could have been challenged.

All reporters covering the child poverty story mentioned the statement that Canadian children were poor or were living under the poverty line. Adrienne Tanner of the *Edmonton Journal,* Alison Bray of the *Winnipeg Free Press,* the Canadian Press report in the *Regina Leader-Post,* Rosemary Spiers of the *Toronto Star* and Carol Goar of the *St. John's Telegram* all provided the definition of the poverty line as being Statistics Canada's Low Income Cutoff (LICO). However, none of the reporters indicated that Statistics Canada does not endorse this as a measurement of poverty: "although LICO are commonly referred to as official poverty lines, they have no officially recognized status nor does Statistics Canada promote their use as poverty lines."*

Only one reporter questioned the measurement in a story: Canadian Press journalist Helen Branswell. In an article printed in the *Winnipeg Free Press,* Branswell writes: "Some contend the low-income cutoffs aren't a good measure of poverty, because they don't assess whether people who live below them can meet their basic needs. Instead the cutoffs assess how those people fared in comparison to those who are better off." While most of the story was also printed in the *Regina Leader-Post,* that section was excluded.

The Globe and Mail also noted the LICO figures but referred to them as "the poverty threshold." And while the *Globe and Mail* indicated that former Progressive Conservative MP Barbara Greene had tried to examine a real measure of poverty, her efforts were dismissed by the man who came up with the numbers for Campaign 2000, Clarence Lougheed: "When we talk about poor families there are very few poor families who live at the cutoff, or even close to that level." Contrast this attention to that given to Barbara Greene when she chaired the parliamentary committee on poverty and actually argued that the way in which we count the poor may inflate their numbers. She was vilified in the press and her motives were impugned. For example, Debra O'Connor from the National Anti-poverty Organization said on CTV News on 8 June 1993: "And when Barbara Greene gets up and says 40 to 60 percent of the poor aren't really poor, that just reinforces people's idea that life on welfare is easy and it's too soft, and that couldn't be further from the truth. There's real suffering out there, and Barbara Greene is doing her bit to make that suffering worse."

*Statistics Canada Low Income Cut-offs, 1986, Technical Paper, 1987, p. 1.
SOURCE: National Media Archive, "Canadian Media Uncritically Accept Advocacy Groups' Assertion That 1.5 Million Canadian Children Live in Poverty," *On Balance,* 6(10) (1993), p. 2. Reprinted by permission.

practices that journalists employ when they define and gather news. Let us consider the critical perspective in greater detail.

Defining the News

How is news framed? To answer this question we must begin by asking what are the criteria, or **news values,** that the media use to determine what is newsworthy. They have three major criteria: immediacy, personalization, and extraordinariness.

Immediacy By definition, news is about what is new or immediate. Although the media are often unable to capture events as they actually happen, the aim is to report them as quickly as possible after they occur. Immediacy has always been a major element in the competition among different media, and the history of media technology is dominated by the goal of making communication faster. Whenever possible, news is written in the present tense to convey the sense that events are still ongoing.

The emphasis on immediacy, however, goes beyond the present to the future. To generate interest and curiosity on the part of the audience, news stories often create some sense of uncertainty about what will happen next. The effect of this approach is that news tends to be concerned with the consequences of events and issues at the expense of their causes and development (Knight, 1982). Causes belong in the past, and news generally lacks a strong sense of historical perspective and context.

Personalization   When news does deal with causes and explanations, it often reduces them to the level of individual motives and psychology. This is an effect of personalization. To communicate with an anonymous audience, news has to enable the reader or viewer to identify with news events that are often remote from everyday experience by making them more concrete and familiar. This emphasis on personalities has been intensified by the growth of TV news, where the need to be visual makes it more difficult to deal in abstract issues, such as unemployment, and easier to deal with people, such as the unemployed. Personalization is especially strong in political news coverage, as the media focus on party leaders and other prominent politicians and their respective popularity in the opinion polls. Critics often charge that this detracts from a fuller understanding of the political system and the more substantive aspects of political policy (Taras, 1990).

Extraordinariness   Above all else, news concerns events and issues that are out of the ordinary, and that entail conflict, confrontation, deviance, or disorder (Knight, 1982). The implication of this, as conservative critics also point out, is that news is normally about the negative. For critical theorists, however, the negative emphasis of news does not undermine mainstream values and beliefs, but in fact reinforces dominant ideology in at least two ways. First, by dwelling on the negative, news invokes and reproduces dominant definitions of what is socially normal and desirable. It identifies events and actors that deviate from this definition—events and actors that are already viewed as dangerous, bizarre, or disruptive—and represents them as a threat to what is socially desirable (Knight, 1982) (see Figure 5.2). Second, news coverage of deviance and conflict tends to focus on the actions of the appropriate social control authorities— the government, the police, the experts—to restore order. The threat of bad news is offset by reassurance that someone with authority is responding to the problem.

Gathering the News

Initially, newsworthy events come to the attention of the media via news releases, tipoffs, and the routine monitoring of institutional communications, like emergency services radio. Further information is then gathered from key sources, usually by means of interviewing. In choosing their sources, news media also

---

FIGURE 5.2   TORONTO'S "DAYS OF ACTION" HEADLINES: DISRUPTION-RELATED THEMES IN A LOCAL NEWSPAPER, 1996

These headlines illustrate the way the media emphasize the disruptive or confrontational effects of new events rather than their causes or effects on social solidarity. They also highlight the way labour and other social movements are often portrayed as the source of social disruption and conflict.

October 24:   "Brace yourself for tough tomorrow"
October 25:   "Don't be intimidated by protesters: Harris"
            "Ambulances, police go on high alert" (continuation of previous report)
            "No mail, trash but beer's on. TTC in doubt as protest affects many services"
            "Days of action hits many services" (continuation of previous report)
            "Parade, rallies expected to jam city tomorrow"
October 26:   "Days of Disruption"
            "Day of frustration, frayed nerves" (continuation of previous report)
            "Shut out: pickets block mayor from city hall"
            "Protest a pain for many StarPhone callers"
            "TTC workers didn't ask for help: police chief says heavy police presence kept trouble to a minimum"
            "Barely a blip. The labour protest pretty much failed to disrupt Bay Street. The TSE hummed along nicely."
            "Protestors failed to tarnish Metro's image"
            "Employers cope with disruptions"

take account of a fourth news value: objectivity or fairness (Knight, 1982). In practice, objectivity translates into an attempt to achieve a balance of sources representing the different, often antagonistic, viewpoints that are involved in the event or issue being reported. These sources include not only authority figures (such as police, politicians, and experts) but also eyewitnesses, victims, and the representatives of groups and organizations ranging from big business to social activist groups that may have a stake in the event or issue.

However, just as news framing tends to focus on the activities of certain social actors, so too does it tend to rely on certain sources of information over others. Objectivity does not mean absolute equality or neutrality. A hierarchy of access exists to and for the media, and this has important ideological implications, as it reflects the general distribution of power in society. The media have easier access to certain sources, and certain sources have easier access to the media. For example, public representatives, such as elected politicians, have a much greater obligation to speak to the media than do private sector officials, such as corporate executives, who can invoke the values of private property as a way to justify their own and their organization's privacy. At the same time, because of their power and status, corporate officials can easily gain access to the news media when they choose to do so.

This hierarchy of access is reflected in the division of labour among three broad types of news source—official, ordinary, and alternative (Knight, 1998). **Official news sources** are representatives of dominant institutions—for example, politicians, police officers, professionals, experts, and corporate spokespeople. They appear more frequently and prominently than other sources and are usually treated by the media as authoritative and credible. Official sources normally speak rationally and objectively about an event, an issue, or a problem, providing information about what is happening and what steps are being taken to respond to the situation. Official sources are offset by **ordinary news sources.** These play a double role in the news as either eyewitnesses or, more important, as victims of newsworthy events or problems. As victims, ordinary sources personalize the harmful effects (actual and potential) of bad news. They are the ones adversely affected by deviance, conflict, and disruption. They speak more subjectively of personal experiences, feelings, and

emotions—anger at what has happened to them and fear of what may happen next. **Alternative news sources** are the representatives of social movements and of social advocacy and activism groups. They stand between official and ordinary voices. Alternative sources address the social problems that underlie the harm that ordinary victims suffer. In this respect, they compete with official sources over the definition of victimhood: who is a victim, who is responsible, who should act, and what should be done. Alternative sources attempt to reframe the experiences and emotions of victims into a critical, normative, and political perspective of injustice and inequity. These sources attempt to use the media as a way to publicize their cause, gain legitimacy and social recognition, and pressure dominant institutions to take steps to rectify what is wrong (Carroll and Ratner, 1999).

The three types of source appear in the media to varying degrees. Although official sources represent the interests and values of particular institutions or organizations, they are often used to speak on behalf of society as a whole. This gives them an advantage in defining the news frame and establishing what the terms of the event, issue, or problem are. Deviance and disorder thus tend to be framed from a police perspective as a series of discrete events that are explained in terms of individual motives, rather than as social phenomena caused by social forces. Ordinary and particularly alternative sources, conversely, are used to represent specific points of view. These may often contradict what official sources are saying, but they normally do so on grounds that have already been determined by the news frame. In the case of news about mental illness, for example, the media tend to rely on representatives from the legal and medical establishments (such as criminal prosecutors and psychiatrists) rather than on mental health advocacy groups, case workers, or people with mental illness as their primary source of information and interpretation. When the latter groups are included in the coverage, their views are usually framed in response to the arguments of those in positions of authority (e.g., police, courts, medical professionals) restoring order by protecting the normal from the sick. This typically helps to construct a dominant interpretation of mental illness as a threatening condition associated with violence and other forms of unpredictable or dangerous behaviour. Media coverage tends to emphasize the risks and threats people with mental illnesses pose to themselves, their families, and their communities by constructing a boundary between "us" (normal and at risk) and "them" (sick and risky) (Greenberg, 2006).

Alternative sources are often faced with a dilemma in their relationship with the media. On the one hand, they are used simply as a reaction to official sources. In this case, their voice is a negative one of grievances and complaints, rather than a constructive one of analysis and proposals. On the other hand, they can attempt to draw the media's attention to their own framing of an issue or a problem. However, to do this, they may have to engage in the kind of activity, such as public protests, that associates their views with disruptive behaviour and undermines their legitimacy (Hackett, 1991).

Despite the advantage official sources have in defining particular news frames, alternative voices can nonetheless influence and reshape the framing process over the longer term. For example, popular opinion has gradually become more amenable to the views of the environmental movement and more skeptical and critical of governments and big business. In their study of the controversy over logging practices in old-growth forests in British Columbia, Doyle, Elliott, and Tindall (1997) show how the forest industry has attempted to control the framing process through publicity campaigns, the use of the world's largest public relations firm (Burson-Marsteller), and sponsorship of the B.C. Forest Alliance, a supposedly independent, nonprofit organization with representatives from the wider community. The strategy of the B.C. Forest Alliance is to try to occupy the middle ground between the industry and the environmental movement by being critical of both. However, it has achieved only "limited success in convincing the media" (Doyle et al., 1997: 263). That is because it continues to frame the issue as a dichotomy—"trees versus jobs"—in which the goals of environmentalists are seen as harmful to the interests of workers. The media has reacted skeptically, labelling the Alliance as pro-business and criticizing the "trees versus jobs" frame by noting that job loss in forestry was the result of industry rationalization and downsizing, not environmentalism.

Although critical theorists see the media as generally representative of dominant ideology, they also recognize that relations between journalists and their sources involve an ongoing struggle for control on both sides (Ericson, Baranek, and Chan, 1989). The outcome depends chiefly on the status of the sources and the power they can exercise over the flow of information. In the case of crime news, the police enjoy an effective monopoly over the supply of information because there is no alternative or competing source on which the media can rely for credible, timely information. With politics, however, journalists have more leverage over sources by virtue of the adversarial structure of the political process, at least in democratic societies. This does not, however, alter the fact that the government exercises the greatest control over the flow of information because of its political authority and control over policy. What the government does or says is intrinsically newsworthy, and governments attempt to use this fact to manage the media and mobilize popular consent and support for their actions. Governments employ various tactics to maximize favourable news coverage and minimize unfavourable coverage, such as providing news releases, freezing out hostile media by limiting access to information, staging events to attract media attention, timing the release of information to improve positive and limit negative coverage, and leaking information as a way of testing the waters or manipulating public expectations (Taras, 1990).

MEDIA EFFECTS AND AUDIENCES

What is most striking about research in the area of media effects is that the predominant focus has been on the socially problematic aspects of the media's relationship with its audiences. There has been little research on the "pro-social" effects of the media. Even in the area of child socialization, research has tended to focus on the way the media reproduce and disseminate negative stereotypes of, for example, gender roles, the elderly, or racial and ethnic minority groups (Buckingham, 1998: 135–36). Research suggests, however, that television does not have a direct effect on gender socialization. Children's social context and relationships, as well as the existing dispositions they bring to television viewing, mediate the relationship. When television images diverge from the information about gender roles that children have from other sources, the effect of those images is often undercut (Gunter, 1995: 79–93).

Similar findings have been reported with respect to the supposed influence of television food advertising on the eating behaviours and health of children. Many scholars, politicians, activists, teachers, and parents have argued that television advertising is to blame for the growing problem of childhood obesity in North America. The food industry is certainly a key player in the field of advertising, dominating television airtime with promotions for everything from breakfast cereals to soft drinks, fast-food restaurants, and other "fun" foods. According to the Center for Science in the Public Interest, food marketers have more than doubled their marketing spending in the past 10 years to US$15 billion in 2004. Every day, children see about 58 commercial messages on television alone, and about half of those are for food products (Mayer, 2005). However, research suggests that children's food knowledge, preferences, and behaviours are "multiply determined, requiring the simultaneous investigation of the effects of multiple interacting factors" (Livingstone, 2005: 292). In other words, aside from repeated exposure to advertising, children's food knowledge, preferences, and eating behaviours likely are also influenced by their class, gender, age, and race, as well as their viewing strategies and the other ways they negotiate their way through the modern food- and media-scapes.

In the next section, we examine two approaches to the study of media effects. The first is the study of *media violence*, and it deals most directly with the negative aspects of the media's influence. The second focuses on *audience interpretation*, the way viewers make sense of what they see and hear on television.

MEDIA VIOLENCE

The effects of portrayals of crime and violence in the media have been a longstanding matter of social concern and have become a major topic of public policy and debate. This concern illustrates the widespread assumption that media violence is a social problem that should be understood primarily in terms of its harmful effects. This point is worth emphasizing because it raises the question of how, why, and when particular social phenomena become defined as problems. It also highlights the fact that concerns about the effects of media violence overshadow concerns about its causes. Focusing on effects suggests the need for social control to resolve the problem by limiting or eliminating the supply of violent imagery and overlooks the need to understand what creates the demand for it.

Early research on the psychological and behavioural effects of the media swung between two poles of opinion. In the 1930s and 1940s, the effects of the media were generally thought to be harmful, direct, and strong. The metaphor of a "bullet" or "hypodermic needle" was commonly used to describe how the media functioned. By the early 1960s, however, the prevailing view had been revised and media influence came to be seen as more innocuous. Media effects were thought to be minimal, to be mediated by a diversity of intervening social and psychological factors, and to be confined largely to reinforcing existing beliefs and habits (Klapper, 1960). This shift in views demonstrates that the issue of media effects is a complex one, and this is especially true in the case of media violence. More recent research on the effects of media violence, particularly on TV and in films, but, increasingly, in video games marketed to youth, has generated much controversy. There has been extensive debate about what constitutes violence (on TV, in video games, and in real life), how to measure its extent and intensity, and how to account for possible intervening factors, such as personality differences and social environment.

Most researchers believe that media violence has some real-life effects. Current research can be broken down into two main approaches. The first examines the effect of media violence on attitudes. The principal perspective here is known as **cultivation analysis.** It stems from research on television effects by George Gerbner and his associates. Gerbner argues that long-term exposure to television tends to cultivate perceptions that are often at odds with objective reality (Gerbner, Gross, Morgan, and Signorielli, 1994). One of the main arguments of the cultivation perspective is that people who watch a lot of television (or play a lot of video games) will be more exposed to violent imagery and more likely to perceive society as more violent and dangerous than it really is. This tendency is what Gerbner and his colleagues call the "'mean world' syndrome."

This argument has stimulated considerable research. Some of it disputes the view that a causal relationship exists between the amount of time people spend watching television or playing video games and their beliefs and emotions. Other research provides qualified support but argues that the relationship is affected by intervening factors, such as the type of programming people watch (Wober, 1998). A Canadian study suggests that what may be the central issue in cultivation analysis is the fundamental relationship between perceptions of violence and danger on the one hand, and fear on the other. Gosselin,

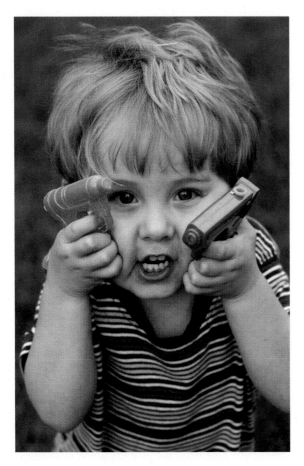

Most researchers believe that media violence has some real-life effects.

SOURCE: Shutterstock.

DeGuise, Pacquette, and Benoit (1997) found evidence to support the view that people who watch TV a lot believe the world is more dangerous than other viewers do, regardless of age and sex. However, although they found that women who thought the world was dangerous were also more likely to be fearful, they did not find this to be true for men. Moreover, even for women the relationship between perception and fear of danger could not be explained empirically by the influence of television. They concluded that "the influence of television viewing seems restricted to beliefs" and does not extend to the emotions we feel about reality (1997: 155).

The second approach focuses on the effects of television on behaviour, and the predominant view is that television does play some limited role in generating real-life violence (Friedrich-Cofer and Huston, 1986; Geen and Thomas, 1986; Huesmann and Malamuth, 1986; Perse, 2001). Those who accept the majority view claim that the evidence is consistent for a link between TV and real-life violence or aggressiveness, though the strength of the evidence varies according to the methodology used. The strongest support for a causal link comes from laboratory experiments (Friedrich-Coffer and Huston, 1986). They usually compare the responses of two randomly chosen groups who watch TV under the same controlled conditions, with the exception that one group watches violent programming and the other, nonviolent. Various measures of aggressiveness have been used to assess the responses, among them physical and verbal aggressiveness, aggressiveness toward both people and objects, actual and fantasized aggressiveness, and reduced self-discipline (lack of patience and perseverance in trying to accomplish tasks or dealing with others). The lab experiments have shown that television violence has an effect on real-life violence *independent* of the intervening factors that have been shown to affect overall levels of aggressiveness (such as personality, age, gender, and social background).

Studies of the effects of television on behaviour have been subject to a variety of criticisms, ranging from the ideological bias of researchers to imprecise concepts to a misplaced focus on individual psychology at the expense of social processes (Gauntlett, 1997). The most significant criticisms, however, have been methodological. Laboratory experiments have been strongly criticized for their inability to replicate the normal social conditions under which people, particularly children, watch TV (McCormack, 1994). Children, like adults, normally watch a mixture of violent and nonviolent programming that blends together in an ongoing flow (Freedman, 1984). Younger children watch more television than older children and they also watch it more intermittently because of their shorter attention spans and because their social setting provides an easy distraction. As a result, although the TV set may be on for long periods, the children are not paying attention to it a large part of the time. The question of what exactly counts as an "act of violence" is also poorly defined and could include a whole host of examples, from Bugs Bunny dropping an anvil on Wile E. Coyote to repeated broadcasts of the terrorist attacks on the World Trade Center in 2001. It is questionable that the effects of cartoon violence will be as hard-hitting and forceful as the effects of watching real acts of terrorism repeatedly play out on the evening news.

Laboratory experiments have also been criticized for providing research subjects with an artificial social environment. At home, if children act aggressively their parents may punish them, or their siblings or friends may retaliate; in most cases, the possibility of such a response is eliminated in the laboratory. Freedman (1984) also points out that many experimental studies entail some intervention on the experimenter's part to provoke aggressive behaviour after the groups have finished watching TV. Research subjects may come to feel the experimenter is expecting or condoning aggressive behaviour simply by showing violent images (Felson, 1996). In addition, Freedman points out that laboratory experiments, primarily for ethical reasons, often measure aggressiveness expressed against surrogate objects, such as dolls. Since children generally start to recognize the difference between reality and make-believe at about the age of five (McCormack, 1994), the use of surrogate aggression measures casts some doubt on the results. The evidence from experimental studies is confined to demonstrating only the short-term link between TV violence and aggressiveness; the evidence for a long-term relationship is weaker and less consistent (Freedman, 1984).

Despite these criticisms, the belief that a link exists between media images and aggressive behaviour has generated several theories about how the relationship functions. One of the most important findings of studies examining TV viewing in natural social settings is that the relationship between TV and real violence is bidirectional (Friedrich-Cofer and Huston, 1986). In other words, watching violent TV fosters aggressiveness, but those who prefer to watch violent TV already have more aggressive tendencies. Consequently, a self-reinforcing cycle is established. Most of the theories, however, have focused on explaining the process whereby viewing violent TV generates aggressive behaviour. Two theories are particularly important because they make opposite assumptions about the relationship between the individual and society.

Disinhibition and Desensitization

Disinhibition refers to the possibility that continued exposure to violent imagery may weaken the mechanisms of self-control that an individual acquires through socialization and that discourage or inhibit the use of violence. Related to this notion is the theory of **desensitization,** which suggests that extended exposure to violent imagery has an emotionally numbing effect that leads to increased tolerance and acceptance of violence by others.

Social Learning

In contrast to disinhibition theory, the social learning perspective does not assume that individuals are intrinsically aggressive but argues that aggression, like any other form of behaviour, is learned through identification with role models. Aggression is the product of socialization, not of the lack of it. TV acts as a socializing agent by providing children with "scripts" for violence. Scripts for violence are packages of information about how, when, and why to use violence. The extent to which a child will learn such scripts and reproduce them in real behaviour depends on the child's overall cognitive development and varies with age. The learning and activation of scripts is also influenced by intervening psychological, social, and cultural factors, such as personality, social environment, family situation, and the broader cultural values to which the child is exposed. The effect of TV on aggressiveness is therefore not uniform but selective and variable, and it is cumulative over time (Huesmann and Malamuth, 1986).

Whatever the link between images of violence and real-life violence, the relationship remains complex. TV is a heterogeneous medium, and its imagery is usually open to some interpretative variation. The degree of variation depends partly on the extent to which imagery approximates real life. Animated cartoons, fictional drama, and news lie along a continuum in this regard. By the end of primary socialization, children have normally learned to distinguish levels of realism and understand the narrative meaning of violence. The paradox of television violence may be that the most realisitc images have the most disturbing effect (Fiske, 1987), since children can recognize and experience images of violence in news and current affairs programming as representations of real-life aggression and suffering. Yet it is unrealistic programs, especially cartoons and crime shows, that have been the main targets of concern about the effects of violence.

AUDIENCE RESEARCH: INTERPRETATION AND MEDIA USE

Theories of disinhibition and cognitive learning focus chiefly on the *unconscious* ways in which children are influenced by the media they watch. What this overlooks is the way in which individuals also process *con-sciously* and *actively* what they see and hear. What may appear as simply the unwitting effect of learning violent scripts may be a more complex interaction between the unconscious influences and conscious uses of media (Hodge and Tripp, 1986).

The effects of TV and other media depend on how they are used, as well as on how they are related to the other activities and interests of people in their everyday lives. We use the media to make sense of our social world. Audiences filter, interpret, and often challenge and resist what they see and hear according to their social context, experiences, and beliefs. But these contexts, experiences, and beliefs are themselves influenced by media use. This is the argument of recent audience research that has grown out of dissatisfaction with the behaviourist focus of media violence research.

Since the 1980s, a growing number of researchers have shifted their approach from treating audience members as isolated individuals and begun to study television use in its "natural" social settings, especially the home. Much of this research has focused on the ways that gender relations structure the use and interpretation of television. Research in Britain by Morley (1986), for example, found that men and women differed in the way they watched television and what they preferred to watch. Men were more likely to use TV in a planned way, selecting programs beforehand and watching attentively, whereas women had a "much more take-it-or-leave-it attitude" to program choice and a generally less attentive way of viewing (1986: 153). Men enjoyed sport and information programming, whereas women found little they liked except soap operas. Women were also much less reluctant than men to admit that they talked about TV with their friends and co-workers, which suggests that television plays a greater role in women's patterns of sociability than men's. Morley attributed this to the fact that women felt guilty about watching TV while "surrounded by their domestic obligations" (1986: 155). Making it a topic of conversation gave it greater legitimacy. The idea of television as a guilty pleasure also surfaced in research by Hobson (1982), who found that women justified watching TV by engaging in domestic tasks like ironing at the same time.

Television has been the primary focus of audience research because it has played a central role in the definition of the private sphere in modern society—family, domesticity, gender relations, consumption,

British research suggests that television plays a greater role in women's patterns of sociability than in men's.
SOURCE: Dick Hemingway

and suburban living—since World War II. During the 1950s and 1960s, the TV set became a virtual family hearth, the central point of the household around which family members gathered to share a common experience. Television helped define the household's social boundaries, while making those boundaries porous by delivering images from the outside world into the heart of the primary social group (Morley, 2000). This symbolic role has since declined for a number of reasons (see Box 5.2). TV has spread to other social settings, such as bars, malls, classrooms, and sports stadiums. TV has also become more dispersed within the household (in the kitchen, bedroom, and even bathroom), not only because it is more affordable but also because having more than one set reduces conflict by allowing household members more autonomy and privacy. Personalized watching has also been encouraged by the proliferation of specialty channels and services catering to particular tastes and interests. And new interactive technologies, such as mobile phones, personal computers, and third-screens (e.g., iPods and other portable media devices), have also become more accessible, creating a more complex communications environment that mediates the role and tempers the impact that any single medium can have at home, work, or school.

These changes have shifted the focus of audience research toward the ways television fits into in this broader media culture and its place in everyday social

BOX 5.2   NEW TECHNOLOGY CHANGES HOW WE WATCH TV

After Alexis Yamamoto became a belated fan of *The O.C.,* she was desperate to learn about the frothy show's first season.

The teenager turned to the Internet, but not for chat-room descriptions of past twists and turns in Ryan and Marissa's stormy relationship. Instead, like so many members of her generation, she watched downloads of the television program on a computer.

In a trend that is increasingly seizing the attention of advertisers and broadcasters, more teens are watching television without ever laying eyes on a TV set. In yet another blow to appointment television and the notion of captive audiences, tech-savvy young people are abandoning the system by using file-sharing programs such as BitTorrent to download unauthorized, commercial-free episodes of their favourite shows.

"You don't have time to come home and watch *Desperate Housewives* if you're at the library. If it's on your computer, you can watch it any time," said Ms. Gavloski, a 20-year-old marketing student at the University of Guelph.

The unrelenting migration of teens from traditional television to the Internet creates challenges for companies that see young people—with their high levels of disposable income and slavish trend-worshipping—as a prized, though difficult to reach, demographic. As a result, firms are continuing to shift marketing dollars into on-line advertising. Last year, Canadian businesses spent about $500-million on Internet advertising, up more than 40 percent from 2004, according to the Interactive Advertising Bureau of Canada.

And while television executives have long cried foul—unauthorized downloads are not included in TV ratings and steal eyeballs from revenue-generating advertising—many are also trying to adapt. Some American networks have struck deals to sell TV episodes on iTunes or through video-on-demand services. Others allow free downloads of clips, and many broadcasters, including in Canada, offer streaming video of programs on their websites. Some also have deals to provide content to telecommunications companies, which sell access to cellphone subscribers.

Observers predict an increase in product placement, as seen in the companies that parade their wares on *The Apprentice* and the Kia dealership that is featured in CBC's hockey mockumentary *The Tournament*. They also expect to see more branded entertainment, such as Home Depot's role as the supplier of the do-it-yourself home renovation show *Trading Spaces*.

The prevalence of downloading is changing family dynamics, Prof. Pacom argues. The notion of the whole brood crowding around the television set for a full hour at 8 p.m. sharp to watch the latest installment of *Lost* seems old fashioned when the show can be downloaded at the click of a mouse and watched commercial free, say at noon two days later.

However, Prof. Attallah sees an inherent tension in downloading TV shows. While computer users evade the traditional control of broadcasters, they still consume their products in an involved process that often includes monitoring on-line buzz, planning downloads and watching episodes repeatedly. Perhaps ironically, the result is often more loyal fans.

"One of the things that happens when you download programs from the Internet is that far from spending less time with TV, I think that you actually spend more time with TV."

SOURCE: Jill Mahoney, "Teens watching TV without going near a set," *The Globe and Mail*, January 7, 2006, p. A3. Reprinted with permission of *The Globe and Mail*.

life. The shift is illustrated by Gillespie's (1995) study of media use by adolescents of Punjabi background in England. The study demonstrates how television is used both to preserve a distinct sense of religious and ethnic customs, identity, and community, and to negotiate individual difference and autonomy in the face of pressures to conform to family expectations. For example, viewing Hindi films on video was a common family practice and was seen as an important way of reinforcing linguistic and cultural identification with India, especially for females, who took on the role of preserving and transmitting cultural tradi-

tions more than males did. The young women in Gillespie's study were subject to stronger social control by their families than their brothers were, and this meant that they were expected to spend more time at home and be more involved in household activities. At the same time, television also exposed these adolescents to the pressures of the wider culture with its emphasis on individualism and consumption. The marketing of products aimed at young consumers, particularly products associated with an American lifestyle, such as soft drinks and fast foods, is becoming increasingly globalized. Gillespie found, for example, that TV ads for McDonald's and Coca-Cola as well as the products themselves were consumed as a way of negotiating and accommodating the various identity demands—Punjabi, English, Asian, European, even Anglo-American—these adolescents faced.

THE INTERNET: COMPUTER-MEDIATED COMMUNICATION

The shift in audience research toward an interest in the wider media culture is partly due to the rapid growth and use of the Internet since the early 1990s. The Internet is a term that is now used generically to refer to a variety of different forms of **computer-mediated communication (CMC),** such as e-mail, the World Wide Web, newsgroups, instant messaging, chat forums, MUDs (multi-user dungeons or domains), and MOOs (multi-user domains, object-oriented). The fact that these have given rise to a host of new terms, like *cyberspace, life online, virtual reality, digital culture,* the *electronic highway,* and so on, suggests that the primary definition of CMC is uncertain and under continuous development. This uncertainty is compounded by the fact that the medium continues to change technologically and socially, and that research on its structure, use, and effects also continues to produce divergent findings and interpretations.

Early research and commentary on the Internet tended to polarize optimists and critics. For optimists, CMC was seen positively as a vehicle for greater democracy, globalism, and identity experimentation. The growth of the Internet in the 1990s revitalized the democratic imagination by promising to revive the public sphere through providing broad, diverse forums for discussions. The Internet, it was argued, was going to revolutionize civil society by enabling citizen-to-citizen interaction through online debate, deliberation, consultation, decision making, administration, and scrutiny, as well as facilitating online mobilizing, organizing, petitioning, and protesting. Optimists believed the voice of "the people" could be expressed regularly and loudly, through the Internet making polling, plebiscites, and elections relatively cheap and accessible, expanding popular decision making, and closing the gap between citizens and their representatives.

Critics focused on such negative effects as disengagement from "real" social relations and the spread of offensive images and ideas, such as pornography and racism—the ease with which a website could be established and the potentially infinite reach of the Internet enabled hate groups to more easily expand their recruitment initiatives by propagating anti-Semitic or racist speech. Critics also point to the massive growth of the pornography industry as an effect of the expansion and increased use of the Internet.

As the Internet has developed research has tended to paint a more complex picture of its role and how this role may be changing. Macrolevel research has focused mainly on inequalities in Internet access, differences in overall usage, and the challenges of bringing the seemingly borderless nature of the Internet into a bordered world of national public policies governing Internet use. Microlevel research has been concerned with the relationship of reciprocal effects between real and virtual social interaction. These studies have addressed issues of individual and collective identity, community, and social action in situations where people are no longer required to be together in either time or space.

THE DIGITAL DIVIDE: CMC AND SOCIAL INEQUALITY

The *digital divide* is a term that is commonly used to explain how access to and use of CMC mirrors the broader system of social stratification. Access to the Internet has grown rapidly since the early 1990s not only in developed nations but also in developing countries. At the same time, there continues to be considerable inequality in access and use.

Inequalities of Access

In 1995 about 45 million people were estimated to be online; by 2000 this number increased to 420 million and in 2005 the numbers of people online across the world surpassed 1 billion (or 15.7 percent of the world's population). The vast majority of people online are located in the affluent, developed nations of the world, such as Canada, the United States, and Japan, where approximately 70 percent of the total population has access to the Internet (Tekrati, 2006). By contrast, in more populous but less economically developed countries, such as India and China, Internet user numbers are in the range of 10 percent to 20 percent of the population (Tekrati, 2006). Statistics on PC ownership are also suggestive of a digital divide. Such countries as Canada, the Netherlands, the United States, and Sweden have more than 60 personal computers for every 100 citizens. By contrast, such countries as Iraq, Algeria, Laos, and Somalia (indeed, much of Africa, the

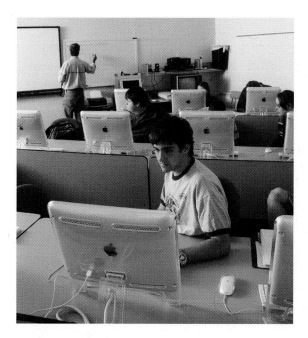

In Canadian universities, students use the latest electronic technologies in classrooms, dorms, and campus pubs.
SOURCE: Shutterstock.

Middle East, and Asia) have less than 1 personal computer for every 100 citizens (International Telecommunication Union [ITU], 2004).

The development of online access and use mirrors that of earlier media, such as television, originating in developed countries and then spreading to the developing world as the technology becomes more readily available. In this process a software gap also tends to develop. Just as global television content continues to be dominated by programming produced in the developed world, so the Internet is dominated by content produced in the developed world. In 2004 the top five countries—Canada, the United States, Japan, Germany, and the United Kingdom—owned 83 percent of all Internet hosts worldwide (ITU, 2004).

Social class also tends to be a strong predictor of who is online. In Canada, between 1997 and 1999, Internet access grew for all income levels, but it grew fastest for the top 25 percent, from 53.7 percent to 71.2 percent of households. For the poorest 25 percent of households, access grew much more slowly, from 12.4 percent to 18.8 percent (Dickinson and Ellison, 2000: 7). Unequal access reflects several factors. The most obvious is cost of access, which acts as an obstacle for poor Canadians. Occupation is also relevant. Rich households are likely to contain adult members who are familiar with CMC because of their

work, and this makes home use easier in terms of operating skill. Education also plays an important role. People with higher levels of education are more likely to be online, a pattern that holds independently of income and occupation. (Dickinson and Ellison, 2000). In 2003, the percentage of Canadian households with Internet access whose head had a university degree increased to 88 percent. In households whose head had less than high school education, Internet access stood at 32 percent (Statistics Canada, 2004).

Early access to the Internet was marked by strong gender bias, with males outnumbering females online by a considerable margin. In 1995, for example, 93 percent of Europeans and 82 percent of Americans online were men (Cuneo, 2002: 24). As access and use grew, the margin of difference declined. In the United States in 2003, for example, women slightly outnumbered men online (U.S. Department of Commerce, 2004). Similarly, access is also related to race and ethnicity. In the United States, Internet access is highest in white households (65 percent), followed closely by households of Asian and Pacific Island background (63 percent). Internet access is available in only 45 percent of African-American households and in 37 percent of Hispanic households (U.S. Department of Commerce, 2004).

Differences of Use

E-mail is the most commonly used form of CMC among Canadians, but overall use of the Internet is becoming more varied and increasing for educational, financial, and consumption purposes in particular (see Table 5.4). Like access, use varies by social status and identity. Marketing research, for example, has found that men are more likely to visit "personals" sites than women are. Women are more likely than men to visit retail and electronic greeting card sites (Jupiter Media Metrix, 2001). Research on racial and ethnic differences in Internet use in the United States shows that African and Hispanic Americans are less likely to research or purchase goods online than is the general population; they are, however, more likely to use the Internet for purposes of career advancement, family and health information, education, and community and social activities, such as participation in chat rooms. Hispanic Americans are also more likely to use the Internet to access news and are less inclined to use it for recreational purpose (Cultural Access Group, 2001: 18–24).

TABLE 5.4   HOUSEHOLD INTERNET USE AT HOME BY INTERNET ACTIVITY, 2003

	PERCENTAGE OF ALL HOUSEHOLDS		PERCENTAGE OF ALL HOUSEHOLDS
E-mail	52.1	Other Internet services	23.5
Electronic banking	30.8	Obtain and save music	20.6
Purchasing goods and services	18.6	Listen to the radio	13.1
Medical or health information	35.6	Find sports related information	24.6
Formal education/training	24.9	Financial information	25.0
Government information	32.2	View the news	30.2
General browsing	48.5	Travel information/arrangements	33.6
Playing games	27.9	Search for a job	19.6
Chat groups	14.4		

SOURCES: Adapted from the Statistics Canada publication "Internet Use in Canada," 2003, Catalogue 56F0003XIE, September 23, 2004; and from the Statistics Canada CANSIM database, http://cansim2.statcan.ca, Table 358-0006.

To a large extent, variations in Internet use tend to represent social differences in the real world. The fact that women are more likely to visit retail-oriented websites reflects the ways that everyday consumption continues to be a greater part of women's family role than it is of men's. A higher proportion of women use the Internet for health and religious information, compared with men, who go online mostly for news about sports, politics, and finance (Madden, 2003). Similarly, the greater than average use of the Internet for news by Hispanic Americans can be attributed partly to the fact that a large proportion of the Hispanic population was born outside the United States. The Internet provides a convenient way to access Spanish-language news from and about "home"—in other words, the Internet becomes a key component in the construction and maintenance of ethnocultural identities. Social ties, especially those based on kinship or friendship, are being globalized by CMC. A major reason for the rapid growth of Internet use in Trinidad, for example, is that it has enabled people to keep in frequent and regular contact with family members who have moved abroad (Miller and Slater, 2000). E-mail and instant messaging provide ways in which families can re-create primary social ties in a virtual form. Although differences in Internet use cannot be as easily quantified as variations in access, some researchers believe that they nonetheless represent another dimension of social inequality in CMC—a "second digital divide" (Attewell, 2001). When, for example, working-class

children use the Internet primarily for pleasure, such as playing games, rather than for educational purposes, external class inequalities are reproduced and reinforced. Differences become inequalities inasmuch as they can translate into uneven benefits or advantages in terms of their offline consequences.

VIRTUAL COMMUNITY: THE INTERNET'S IMPACT

As was the case with other media, such as radio and TV, the rapid growth of the Internet has created concern that its aggregate social effect is primarily negative. Research, however, has painted a more mixed picture. The negative view was partly borne out by one of the first longitudinal studies of Internet use undertaken in the U.S. between 1995 and 1996 (Kraut et. al., 1998). The study discovered that higher Internet use was associated with lower levels of social interaction with family members, a reduction in social ties, and greater feelings of loneliness and depression. The authors dubbed their findings the "Internet Paradox" because they ran counter to expectations. Other studies at that time also arrived at findings that suggest Internet use leads to greater anomie and social disengagement (DiMaggio, Hargittai, Neuman, and Robinson, 2001).

In a subsequent study, however, Kraut and colleagues (2002) found that the negative consequences of online use had disappeared. Their follow-up study determined that Internet use in general was positively correlated with social involvement and psychological well-being. However, they also found that heavy use continued to be associated with higher levels of personal stress and lowered commitment to the local community. Though the study was not designed to account for these changes, the authors suggest that growing familiarity with CMC and changes in the Internet itself are the likeliest explanation for these changes. The growing number of people online, and the continued use of e-mail as the primary online activity of both Canadians (Statistics Canada, 2004) and Americans (Madden, 2003), suggests that people are using the Internet to maintain connections and ties with their friends, family, and other close acquaintances. Indeed, other research has found that Internet use can enhance rather than erode social involvement. Canadian researchers Wellman and Gulia (1999) argue that **virtual communities** are part of a broader shift in modern and postmodern societies toward social ties and relationships based on shared interests and aspirations rather than shared locality (neighbourhood) or ancestry (kinship). As such, virtual communities can be as socially and emotionally supportive for their members as are communities based on face-to-face interaction. Even online forums, such as newsgroups, that are designed primarily to provide factual or practical information can have socially supportive side effects, as they act as forums in which participants exchange views and feelings about common concerns. Although virtual communities lack the kind of interpersonal cues available in face-to-face social relationships, this lack can actually *promote* interaction by removing risks and status or identity barriers that might normally inhibit the successful development of real world ties.

The structure of virtual communities has been a topic of particular interest in Internet research. Real communities differ fundamentally from virtual communities inasmuch as people cannot simply log off and walk away from real ones (Postman, 1992; Watson, 1997). Nonetheless, much of the research has shown similarities and parallels between the two, as studies of social control and activism on the Internet have shown.

Social Control

Because online interaction is more anonymous and almost entirely based on discursive interaction alone, many of the mechanisms of social control that function in offline communities are weak or absent. It was

partly for this reason that the Internet acquired an early reputation for individualistic attitudes and verbal aggression or "flaming." This reputation was especially connected with fantasy- or game-oriented forms of CMC, such as adventure MUDs, where participants adopt imaginary identities and act out fictitious narratives in which aggression toward others may be considered more acceptable than in real life. Despite the emphasis on imagination and fantasy, however, MUDs are usually structured through a hierarchy of positions with unequal capacities, skills, and knowledge. This gives rise to a virtual "power elite" that can control the domain's programming and the terms on which other users can be involved (Cherny, 1999; Reid, 1999).

Large MUDs usually have a more elaborate, formal system of rules and controls, but in small MUDs, informal social controls can function effectively when conflict or other disruptions arise. In her study of a MUD community, Cherny (1999), for example, found that gossip distributed through private online conversations acted as a common form of social control by building networks of solidarity, reaffirming shared values and goals, and excluding and ostracizing those seen as a threat to the community.

Social Activism

Virtual communities resemble real communities inasmuch as they entail not only shared values and a sense of belonging but also a common project or purpose (Baym, 2000). However, the shared interests these projects derive from originate mainly in the offline world—even if, as in the case of Baym's soap opera fans, they are situated in media culture more generally. People bring their offline interests, needs, and aspirations to CMC, just as they do to other communications media. By the same token, relationships and knowledge acquired through CMC can spill over into the world of face-to-face reality. The exchanges that occur between the real and virtual worlds are mediated by structures of social relevance, that is, how well experiences in one sphere pertain to interests and concerns in the other (Schutz, 1970). This means that virtuality and reality are not so much worlds apart as, to borrow McLuhan's (1964) term, *extensions* of each other. Thus, research on cyberactivism shows how the borderless nature of the Internet has the potential to enable political activists to integrate the social and political experiences from one locale with struggles in another.

The example of the global social movement against Nike and other transnational corporations that take advantage of cheap labour in developing countries illustrates the power and potential of the Internet to invigorate democratic debate and improve the human condition (Knight and Greenberg, 2002). Nike has emerged as arguably the most successful corporation in the global footwear and apparel industry. Its success has stemmed from a combination of effective logistics and persuasive promotions. Nike's strategy of farming out the most capital intensive stages of production (i.e., labour) to the poorest regions of the world, combined with cutting-edge strategies in marketing, advertising, and public relations, has made it the most visible brand in its industry. But Nike's very success has made it a salient target of activist criticism (Knight and Greenberg, 2002). The network of student anti-sweatshop groups that emerged around the world, but especially in the United States, in the mid-1990s were able to make use of the Internet to share information about protest strategies, disseminate factory monitoring reports that were embarrassing to the corporation, and coordinate collective action. In addition to its online activism, Nike protesters also made use of other forms of communication to press their case, such as street protest, consumer boycotts, and the lobbying of university administrators to turn down contracts with Nike and other companies engaged in dubious labour practices. As Knight and Greenberg argue, "although the Internet has something of a democratizing effect on the capacity to communicate, it functions primarily as a tool to inform and motivate those who are already aware of and sympathetic" to the cause of a particular social movement (2002: 566).

Despite the potential of the Internet and other CMC technologies to enhance democracy, we would do well to heed U.S. media critic Robert McChesney's note of caution. McChesney reminds us that historically the development of new communications technologies—from electricity to the telegraph and television—always met with an enthusiasm that was later tempered by processes of commodification: "once the technologies proved profitable . . . they were turned over to private interests" (1996: 8). However, despite the attempts of corporate powers to control the Internet and other new avenues of communication, struggles by oppositional groups to elude or puncture the dominant informational infrastructure will always remain.

SUMMARY

1. Canadian newspapers exhibit high levels of ownership concentration, are usually part of large multimedia chains, and function largely as local monopolies. The factor that has the greatest impact on news content, however, is dependency on advertising.

2. In the case of television, advertising dependency, the high costs of production, and audience preferences mean that much of the programming Canadians watch is primarily American. This is especially so for drama and sitcoms, and particularly among anglophones. Nationalists view the situation as a sellout of Canadian culture, whereas postmodernists see it as part of the general effect of globalization and do not believe that it undermines the institutional structure of Canadian society.

3. Conservatives claim that news coverage has a left-Liberal political bias that is unrepresentative of society's mainstream. Critical theorists argue that news coverage is ideologically conservative, in that it defines reality from the perspective of dominant ideology and views events and issues through the lens of social control. At the same time, some critical theorists argue that the media are not completely closed to alternative voices and viewpoints, and that these can challenge, to some extent, the hegemony of dominant social groups and interests.

4. Many observers believe that a causal link exists between television and violent behaviour, but the studies that support this view have been criticized on the grounds of flawed methodology. Moreover, the majority view is split on the issue of how television causes aggression. Some argue that watching TV counteracts the effects of socialization by weakening self-control; others believe that it socializes children in the use of violence.

5. Studies of audiences indicate that TV viewing and the responses to it vary according to gender. Men and women tend to prefer different types of programming. Men are more likely to watch attentively and privately, whereas women watch in a more interactive, social way. Women also tend to be more open about their TV viewing and use TV as a topic of casual social interaction and conversation.

6. Although early views about the development of computer-mediated communication and the Internet tended to polarize between optimists and pessimists, recent research has yielded a more complex, balanced view. Inequalities of access (especially globally) and differences of use persist; however, the former show signs of declining as the technology becomes less costly. Research on the impact of the Internet shows that virtual communities develop normative structures like real communities, and function as sources of identity and social solidarity. For the most part, however, life online supplements and complements real-world social interaction and involvement rather than replacing it.

QUESTIONS TO CONSIDER

1. Despite the lack of strong, consistent, and unequivocal evidence to confirm a direct link between violence in the media and in real life, why are many people convinced that such a link does exist?

2. Critics of media imperialism often point to Canada as an example of a country overwhelmed by American popular culture—movies, magazines, music, and television. What is so appealing about American popular culture, not only in Canada but in other countries as well? Are Canadians vulnerable to becoming Americanized by the gross imbalance between the amount of domestic and U.S. dramatic programming we watch?

GLOSSARY

Alternative news sources are representatives of social movements and of social advocacy groups whose viewpoints often diverge from those of dominant social groups and their representatives.

Alternative viewpoints are interpretations that differ from the meanings contained in society's dominant ideology, representing compromises between the latter and the meanings promoted by oppositional viewpoints. See also *oppositional viewpoints.*

Communication derives from the Latin, meaning "to bring together or unify." The term is now used to denote the transmission of knowledge, ideas, meanings, and understandings.

Computer-mediated communication (CMC) refers to social interaction or information gathering through the use of computer technology. It's now commonly referred to as the Internet.

The **critical perspective** takes the view that the media reinforce dominant ideology and the position of the dominant class and other powerful groups. The theory has two variants. One sees dominance as more open to challenge and resistance than does the other.

Cultivation analysis examines the long-term effects of television viewing on beliefs about social reality. People who watch TV a lot tend to see the world as more violent and dangerous than it really is, and tend to be more fearful.

Cultural imperialism is a situation in which one society's media exert an overwhelming and unilateral influence over another society's culture.

Desensitization refers to the effect of prolonged exposure to television violence that supposedly makes people indifferent toward, or tolerant of, real violence by others.

Disinhibition refers to the effect of prolonged exposure to television violence that weakens the mechanisms of self-control acquired through socialization and thereby contributes to aggressive behaviour.

The **dominant ideology** comprises the interests, perspectives, viewpoints, and understandings of the dominant class and other powerful groups.

Framing is the process of defining the boundaries of a representation and the organization of its contents. Framing pertains to the selection of what is included and excluded, what is accentuated, and what is played down.

Hegemony is the exercise by the dominant class of cultural leadership by using the media to naturalize and universalize dominant ideology and to absorb the challenge of alternative and oppositional points of view.

Horizontal consolidation is the ownership of different outlets in a media chain for purposes of sharing resources.

Interactive media are technologically mediated means of communication in which the flow of messages is two-way—between actors who transmit and receive messages (e.g., the telephone).

Mass media are technologically mediated means of communication in which the flow of messages is largely one-way, from a single point of transmission to a large, anonymous, dispersed audience of receivers (e.g., television).

Multimedia chains are corporations that own and control a string of media operations or outlets in different fields of mass communication, such as television, radio, and magazines.

News values include such criteria as immediacy, personalization, and extraordinariness, in terms of which news media define and represent events and issues.

Official news sources are authoritative voices—for example, politicians, police officers, and professional experts—that the media use to define the meaning of an event or issue.

Oppositional viewpoints are used to interpret reality in terms that contradict the dominant ideology, representing the experiences of subordinated groups against those of the powerful.

Ordinary news sources are news sources that do not derive from organizations or groups, such as eyewitnesses or victims of news events and issues.

Representation is the use of language, visual images, or other means of communication to portray something in a coherent and meaningful way that others can understand.

Space-biased media are media that enable communication over extended distances, such as print, radio, or television. The messages, however, are not long lasting. Space-biased media promote territorial expansion together with secular beliefs and military-political forms of power.

Technological convergence is the integration of different communications technologies, such as television and telephony, into a single system that obliterates the distinction between mass communication and telecommunication.

Time-biased media are media that are durable (the messages endure), but are relatively immobile, such as stone carvings or inscriptions on clay tablets. Time-biased media promote a sense of tradition as well as religious forms of belief and power.

Vertical integration refers to a media corporation's ownership and control of the means of production at all stages of the production process—for example, from producing newsprint to delivering newspapers.

Virtual communities are long-term forms of social association and interaction based on computer-mediated communication.

SUGGESTED READING

Atton, C. (2004). *An Alternative Internet: Radical Media, Politics and Creativity*. Edinburgh: Edinburgh University Press. Explores how new communications technology provides alternative ways of organizing social and political change.

Collins, R. (1990). *Culture, Communication and National Identity: The Case of Canadian Television.* Toronto: University of Toronto Press. Examines the effect of the Americanization of Canadian television (especially drama), from the perspective of increasing globalization, and argues that the effects are not as harmful to national identity as nationalists assume.

Miljan, L., and B. Cooper. (2003). *Hidden Agendas: How Journalists Influence the News*. Vancouver: UBC Press. The authors challenge the conventional thesis that structures of media ownership and a conservative bias lead to news coverage that is favourable to the dominant ideology. Drawing on interview data with more than 250 journalists, general population surveys, and content analyses of news, the authors argue "that coverage of public policy issues in the Canadian media reflects journalists' opinions to a far greater extent than the views that cultural critics presume to be held by managers or owners" (p. 167).

Taras, D. (1999). *Power and Betrayal in the Canadian Media*. Peterborough, ON: Broadview Press. Presents an analysis of the Canadian media in light of the impact of such factors as corporate concentration, audience fragmentation, and technological convergence. The author sounds a critical note, warning that these changes, together with "the growing international commercial culture," are making the media "less open and diverse" despite their continuing expansion (pp. 219, 221).

WEB RESOURCES

Companion Web Site for This Book

http://www.newsociety5e.nelson.com

Begin by clicking on the Student Resources section of the website. Next, select the chapter you are studying from the pull-down menu. From the Student Resources page, you have easy access to InfoTrac College Edition and other resources, such as the Glossary and Flashcards. The website also has many useful tips to aid you in your study of sociology.

InfoTrac College Edition Search Terms

Visit http://www.infotrac-college.com for access to more than 20 million articles from nearly 6000 sources when doing your online research.

ThomsonNOW™

http://hed.nelson.com

This online diagnostic tool identifies each student's unique needs with a Pretest that generates a personalized Study Plan for each chapter, helping students focus on concepts they are having the most difficulty mastering. Students then take a Posttest after reading the chapter to measure their understanding of the material. An Instructor Gradebook is available to track and monitor student progress.

PART THREE

Inequality

CHAPTER SIX

Social Stratification

In this chapter you will learn that

- Persistent patterns of social inequality are based on statuses assigned to individuals at birth and on how well individuals perform certain roles. Societies vary in the degree to which mobility up and down the stratification system occurs.

- Explanations of the origins and impact of social stratification include the theory of Karl Marx, which emphasizes the exploitation of the working class by owners of land and industry as the main source of inequality and change; the theory of Max Weber, which emphasizes the power that derives from property ownership, prestige, and politics; structural-functionalist theory, which holds that stratification is both inevitable and necessary; and several revisions of Marx's and Weber's ideas that render them more relevant to today's society.

- Although there has been considerable opportunity for upward occupational mobility in Canada, wealth and property are concentrated in relatively few hands, and one in seven Canadians lives in poverty. Because of labour-market changes, income and wealth inequality have been increasing. Thus, the stratification structure of the future will probably not resemble the pattern that emerged in the affluent middle of the twentieth century.

- A person's position in society's stratification system has important consequences, both for lifestyle and for the quality of life. Those who are situated higher in the economic hierarchy tend to live better and live longer.

Harvey Krahn
UNIVERSITY OF ALBERTA

INTRODUCTION

While bundling up old newspapers for recycling, I flip through them quickly. Although the news writers don't use the term, I find myself reading about **social stratification**—that is, persistent patterns of social inequality within society. A photograph of a large painting of the sombre faces of several black men catches my attention. The artist, a refugee from the civil war in Sudan, is also in the photograph. In his home country, he was an award-winning actor and painter. In Canada, he works the evening shift as a cleaning person at my university. Because of his low pay, he cannot afford the canvas on which he would love to paint. Instead, he paints on manila file folders, glued together, that he has salvaged from the garbage tossed out of university offices (Simons, 2006).

Another news item a few days later reports that the City of Edmonton has approved a new program that will provide residents who live below Statistics Canada's low-income line free admission to the city's recreation facilities, leisure centres, and the zoo, as well as 25 percent off the regular registration fee for recreation programs, sports lessons, and summer camps ("Swimming, golf, zoo," 2006). Knowing that the unemployment rate has been very low in Edmonton for several years, I wonder whether many people will benefit from this new program. I learn that the city is expecting at least 16 000 people to take advantage of it each year.

This reminds me that not all poor Canadians are out of work. Many are better described as being among the "working poor." Reinforcing this point, a headline in a national newspaper states that "[l]ow-paying jobs [lie] behind employment boom" (Scoffield, 2006). The economics reporter describes a new study showing that, despite unemployment rates in the country being at their lowest point in three decades, "the quality of Canadian employment has been declining." Better-paying, full-time, permanent jobs

Canadian fishers have a history of making do on low incomes. Quotas on certain stocks of fish have made the situation worse.
SOURCE: Lois Dierlam OSA.

are not being generated at nearly the same rate as lower-paying, part-time, and temporary jobs. As a result, although corporate earnings are up, Canadian families are falling behind. A news item published a few weeks later describes another report showing that, after taking inflation into account, the average Canadian family was earning only about 1 percent more in 2005 than in 1990. In contrast, over the same period, average household debt increased by 40 percent (Beauchesne, 2006).

Although the very poor, whether unemployed or in low-paying jobs, catch our attention, so do the very rich. An article in the business section of a national newspaper reports that the former chief executive officer (CEO) of the Canadian Imperial Bank of Commerce (CIBC) was paid $3.75 million dollars for the nine months he led the bank during 2005. This was a significant drop in income, since in 2004 he earned about $9 million (Stewart, 2006). Although the article does not say so directly, there appears to be a connection between the reduced earnings of the CEO (and his departure from the job) and the fact that the CIBC lost a lot of money in 2005, specifically the US$2.4 billion it had to pay because of CIBC's involvement in previous years with the Enron investor fraud case. The article makes me wonder why some people are paid so much more than others are, even if they are not doing a good job. But the next news item I spot simply makes me laugh. Donald Trump, the self-proclaimed billionaire, is suing an American author who wrote that Trump is worth only $250 million ("Trump suing author," 2006). If Trump is not a billionaire, he will be if he wins the lawsuit, since he is asking for $5 billion in damages!

Back in Canada, in British Columbia, Aboriginal leaders have signed a groundbreaking agreement with the provincial government that will allow them to take control of schools on Indian reserves, certify their own teachers, and develop their own curriculum (Steffenhagen, 2006). Given the generally low level of educational attainment within Canadian Indian, Inuit, and Métis communities, and the historically high levels of unemployment and poverty within these communities, this step toward achieving educational autonomy is welcomed by Aboriginal leaders as movement toward the long-term goal of economic and social equality within Canadian society. I wonder just how long this might take.

The common theme in these quite different stories is the existence of groups—the unemployed, the working poor, refugees and other immigrants, Aboriginal Canadians—that are ranked lower than others in the social stratification system. A low position in this ranking typically means having little power, little wealth, and little prestige, whereas a higher position generally implies the opposite. In this chapter, I begin by discussing some of the ways in which sociologists study social stratification. I then examine a variety of theories of social stratification that attempt to explain its origins and impacts. The last section of the chapter focuses on occupational and class structures and material inequality in Canada, and concludes by asking whether inequality has been increasing.

STRATIFICATION: A CORNERSTONE OF SOCIOLOGY

Standing back and looking at the whole discipline of sociology, we see four basic areas of inquiry. Sociologists study *social structure*, or the way in which society is organized, both formally and informally. We also ask questions about *social order*. What is it that holds together a society comprising individuals with different interests, and when and why does social order break down? Inquiries about *social change* form a third key area within the discipline. How and why do societies, the institutions and power structures within them, and the values and beliefs held by individual members change? Finally, sociologists spend a lot of time studying *social stratification*, the manner in which valued resources—that is, wealth, power, and prestige—are distributed, and the way in which advantages of wealth, power, and prestige are passed from generation to generation.

It could easily be argued that social stratification is the cornerstone of sociology. Descriptions of social structure that ignore the stratification system are clearly inadequate. For example, imagine describing Canadian society to someone from another country without referring to some features of stratification. Would the listener really have an adequate understanding of our society if she or he did not know that most large corporations are run by men, that the working poor continue to struggle to make ends meet even though the economy has been booming for some time, that Aboriginal Canadians are much more likely than most others to be living in poverty, and that immigrants are doing less well today than they were several decades ago, even though they are better educated?

Furthermore, inequalities in wealth can threaten social stability (the poor resenting the wealthy, for example, and demanding more equality), and inequalities in power can be used to maintain social order. For example, powerful corporations might lobby provincial or territorial governments for changes in the labour laws that would make it more difficult for unions to organize company employees. In less democratic countries, direct control of the police and military by a powerful minority can lead to the quick and violent suppression of unrest among the masses.

An understanding of social stratification is also essential for studying social change, since, frequently, it is the stratification system that is undergoing change. For example, changing gender roles and the slow movement of women into positions of power and authority in North America in the past few decades are really features of a changing stratification system. The massive social, economic, and political changes that began in the former Soviet Union in the late 1980s and that continue today are, among other things, changes in stratification systems, as the main source of power shifts from control of the political system to include control of the emerging free-market economy.

SOCIAL HIERARCHIES IN STRATIFIED SOCIETIES

Imagine a society in which stratification did not exist, in which all things of value were distributed equally. Even if you picture a very small group, perhaps a preindustrial society with only a few hundred members, living on some isolated island where the necessities of life are easily obtained, it is still difficult to imagine a nonstratified society. A social hierarchy might emerge as a result of skill differences in fishing, in nursing the ill back to health, or in communicating with the spirits, for example. Inequalities in wealth might develop simply because some families were fortunate enough to have a larger number of children, providing more of the labour needed to accumulate valued possessions. And once accumulations of wealth began to be passed from generation to generation, a structured and relatively permanent pattern of inequality would emerge.

Perhaps you imagined some contemporary society comprising adults who, believing strongly in equality, decided to live and work together in some kind of urban or rural commune, sharing all their pos-

sessions. Again, it is easy to imagine how a social hierarchy could emerge, as those with more useful skills found themselves playing a more central role in this small-scale society. No doubt, when important decisions needed to be made, these individuals would be more likely to influence the outcome.

We do not need to repeat this mental exercise too many times before we see that social stratification in one form or another exists in all societies. But our hypothetical examples are far from typical. In most societies, stratification is much more pronounced, and basic skills are seldom the foundation of primary social hierarchies. Nevertheless, cross-cultural variations exist in the criteria by which individuals and groups are ranked, the degree to which they can move from one position to another within the hierarchy, and the extent of inequality in wealth and power that exists within the hierarchy.

ASCRIBED AND ACHIEVED STATUS

Let's begin by defining the rank or position that a person has within a social hierarchy as that person's **status.** We can further distinguish between an **ascribed status** and an **achieved status.** The former is assigned to individuals, typically at birth. An ascribed status can be a function of race, gender, age, and other factors that are not chosen or earned and that cannot be changed (a few people do choose their gender status, but they are rare exceptions). In contrast, an achieved status is precisely that—a position in a hierarchy that has been achieved by virtue of how well someone performs in some role. The most obvious example is that of occupational status—for instance, individuals who have performed well in law school are entitled to become lawyers, and high-performance athletes strive to achieve the status of "professional athlete." By the same logic, someone could achieve the status of "bum" by performing poorly in educational, employment, family, and other social roles.

Although we may accept that a completely nonstratified society is impossible, most of us would probably agree that a stratification system in which higher positions were achieved, not ascribed, would be preferable. In a **meritocracy,** everyone would have equal chances to compete for higher-status positions and, presumably, those most capable would be awarded the highest rank. Such a society would exhibit a considerable degree of **social mobility,** as those who were more qualified moved up the social hierarchy to replace those who were less competent and who were consequently compelled to move down.

OPEN AND CLOSED STRATIFICATION SYSTEMS

When we compare Canada with other societies, or look back at our history, we find that this country has had what appears to be a fairly **open stratification system,** in which merit, rather than inheritance (or ascribed characteristics), determines social rank and in which social change is therefore possible. For example, dramatic changes in the status of various groups have occurred in this country over time. Although the practice was not nearly as widespread in Canada as in the United States, slaves (most of them black people from Africa but also some Aboriginal people) were bought and sold in Canada from the 1630s till the 1830s (Derreck, 2003). Chinese labourers, brought into the country to help build the railways, were kept out of most "white" jobs by law until well into the twentieth century (Li, 1982). Similarly, it was not until the 1960s that black Canadians were allowed to compete for much more than the lowest-level positions in the Canadian railway industry (Calliste, 1987). However, by the 1830s, slavery had disappeared in Canada, and we now have laws against racial discrimination.

Comparing ourselves with other contemporary societies, we note that Canada does not have an aristocracy such as the one that exists in Britain, where children of wealthy and powerful families of long standing inherit positions and titles. The degree to which Canadians compete for higher-status occupations (in the education system and, later, within the workplace) stands in clear contrast to the situation in India, for example, where the caste into which an individual is born largely determines the type of work that he or she will be allowed to do. Although discrimination on the basis of caste membership has been illegal in India for many decades, the **caste system** continues to underpin a relatively **closed stratification system.** Compared with India, Canada offers many more chances for upward social mobility, an indication of a more open stratification system.

It is all too easy, however, to overlook the extent to which ascribed statuses continue to limit opportunities for many Canadians as well. Discrimination against members of Aboriginal and visible-minority groups continues to occur in Canada today. So too does discrimination against members of the gay community, against people with disabilities and seniors, and against women. These people are in lower-status positions not because they competed poorly for some higher ranking in the social hierarchy, but because they are gay, have disabilities, are old, or are female.

These are fairly obvious examples of the ways in which ascribed statuses continue to play a prominent role in Canada's social stratification system. But what about the child from a wealthy family who graduates from an excellent high school in a wealthy neighbourhood, completes a degree or two in a prestigious and costly university, and then begins a career in a high-status, well-paying profession? Is this simply an example of someone achieving a deserved high-status position, or did the advantages of birth (ascribed status) play some part in this success story? Similarly, when we hear of large companies laying off hundreds or thousands of workers, does their sudden downward mobility reflect their failure to compete in an open, merit-based stratification system, or were they simply unfortunate enough to be employed in a corporation that was being downsized?

As these examples illustrate, the social stratification system consists of a number of different hierarchies, some based on ascribed characteristics, others on achievement. As you make your way through this book, you will read chapters devoted to dimensions of stratification and inequality, such as gender, race, and ethnicity. Other chapters address activities (e.g., work) and institutions (e.g., education) in which stratification processes are extremely important, and still others focus on inequalities between regions and countries. Once you have read all these chapters, you will, I expect, be convinced of the central importance of social stratification in the discipline of sociology.

CLASS AND CLASS STRUCTURE

You will also notice that, even though studies of gender, race, ethnicity, and work take you in quite different directions, all frequently share an emphasis on inequalities in income, wealth, or property, and on resulting inequalities in power. On average, women earn about 70 percent of what men earn. Older women are much more likely than older men to be living in poverty. Members of visible minority groups and, particularly, Aboriginal Canadians are more likely to be unemployed and if they are employed, to be in low-paying jobs. Owners of large workplaces (employers, in other words) are wealthier than most other members of society, and employees in professional and managerial occupations typically earn a great deal more than lower-level employees. Owners, self-employed professionals, and managers typically have more job security than do nonmanagerial employees who are either paid by the hour or are salaried. Recognizing, then, the extent to which such material inequality (i.e., differences in income and wealth or property) parallels and overlaps other social hierarchies, the rest of this chapter will focus primarily on material inequality or, after we define the terms, on *class* and *class structure*.

Although the concept of **class** is seldom absent from discussions of social stratification, the definitions attached to it vary considerably. I will examine some of these definitions in the next section, which outlines several different theories of stratification. My own preference is to use the term in a fairly general sense,

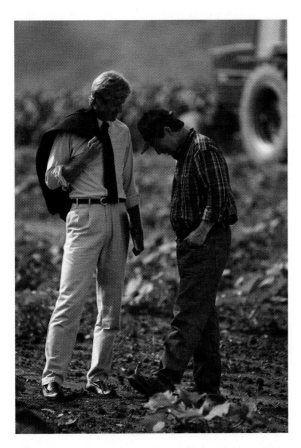

Employees in professional and managerial occupations typically earn a great deal more than lower-level employees do.
SOURCE: Photos.com.

to indicate the position of an individual or a family within an economic hierarchy, along with others who have roughly the same amount of control over or access to economic or material resources. Thus, an individual can be said to be a member of a particular class, whether this is a class of large landowners, a class of wage-labourers and salaried workers (i.e., the "working class"), or a "professional/managerial class." It is their similar economic situation and opportunities, a result of their shared position within a society's system of economic production, that makes these individuals members of the same class. In turn, we can use the term **class structure** to refer to the overall economic hierarchy comprising all such classes, choosing the word *structure* deliberately to indicate the relative stability and prominence of this social ranking.

Do you think of yourself as a member of a specific social class? Probably not very often, if at all. Like most North Americans, you probably have a reasonably good idea of how well off you are compared with others in your community. You probably have some sense of where your education, occupation, and income, or the education, occupation, and income of your parents, fit in some general hierarchy of **socioeconomic status,** or position in an economic hierarchy, based on income, education, and occupation. "Class," however, is unlikely to be part of your everyday vocabulary. Nor is it typically part of the media's vocabulary. The newspaper stories I examined earlier, for example, identified a number of different dimensions of stratification, but social class was not among them.

Does this make "class" a useless concept? I argue the opposite. As I have already suggested, and as you will see in this and other chapters, pronounced patterns of material inequality exist in our society and overlap with most other dimensions of social stratification. The economic hierarchy is obviously not completely closed, but it is relatively stable and permanent, and it comprises some fairly distinct categories of individuals with similar amounts of control over material resources. Hence, it is useful to try to identify the "classes" that make up the stratification system (or class structure), to seek to understand their origin, and to examine the effects of membership in them on individuals and families. Rather than discarding the concept of "class" because few people think in these terms, we can ask why few people think about classes despite their prominence. In fact, you will see that some of the major theories of social stratification address this issue directly, inquiring about the conditions under which members of an economic class begin to recognize their shared interests and, perhaps, begin to act accordingly as a group.

In the following section, I begin with a detailed look at the ideas of the nineteenth-century social and political philosopher Karl Marx, who put social class at the very centre of his discussions of social structure and his theory of social change. In turn, some of the theories of social stratification developed in the twentieth century downplay the role of class or even ignore it completely, because the theorists believe that material inequalities are decreasing. Summing up this line of reasoning, Terry Nichols Clark and Seymour Martin Lipset (1991: 397) wrote that

> class is an increasingly outmoded concept, although it is sometimes appropriate to earlier historical periods. . . . Class analysis has grown increasingly inadequate in recent decades as traditional hierarchies have declined and new social differences have emerged. The cumulative impact of these changes is fundamentally altering the nature of social stratification—placing past theories in need of substantial modification.

As you read about the various theories of social stratification in the next section, and as you examine the data on material inequalities in Canada in the section after that, keep in mind Clark and Lipset's question: "Are social classes dying?"

EXPLANATIONS OF SOCIAL STRATIFICATION

So far, you have considered some examples of social stratification and its effects, and you have added to your vocabulary a number of useful concepts that allow you to discuss the phenomenon and to compare this society with others. But I have not really tried to explain social stratification, to account for its origins and its impacts. In this section, I will briefly examine the theories (or explanations) of social stratification elaborated by a number of important social theorists, including some who were analyzing society many decades ago and others who have written about it more recently. As you will see, it is important to take into account the time and place in which a social theory was developed, since theorists construct their social explanations on the basis of what they see around them and expect to see in the future.

KARL MARX: CAPITALISM, EXPLOITATION, AND CLASS CONFLICT

Karl Marx had an immense impact on how we think about social stratification. He was born in Germany in 1818 but lived in England from 1849 until he died in 1883. His writings about the social and economic forces that brought about economic change look back over history but focus particularly on the rapidly changing European world that he observed during his lifetime. This was a time when industrial capitalism was transforming the economy and society. Large, mechanized, factory-based systems of production were emerging; cities were growing rapidly as rural peasants were being forced off the land or attracted to the city by the possibility of jobs in factories; and material inequality was extreme, as factory owners and merchants made huge profits while labourers lived in poverty. Trade unions, labour laws, and other arrangements that offer some protection to workers did not yet exist. Thus, as Marx observed, the Industrial Revolution was a time when both the level of economic production and the degree of inequality in society increased tremendously.

Modes of Production and Social Classes

Marx called the overall system of economic activity in a society its **mode of production.** In turn, its major components were the **means of production** (technology, capital investments, and raw materials) and the **social relations of production** (the relationships between the main classes involved in production). Slavery had been the primary mode of production in some societies in earlier times, and feudalism, an economic system in which peasants worked for landowners, not for a wage but for some share of the produce, was the mode of production that gave way to industrial capitalism in Europe.

Within industrial capitalism, Marx identified two major classes: the capitalist class, or **bourgeoisie,** which owned the means of production; and the **proletariat,** or working class, which exchanged its labour for wages. He also described a middle class—the **petite bourgeoisie**—comprising independent owners/producers (farmers, for example) and small-business owners. Marx expected this middle class largely to disappear as capitalism matured and drew some of its members up into the bourgeoisie but pushed most down into the proletariat. Of much greater importance in his theory of class inequality and social change was the relationship between workers and owners.

Marx reasoned that the value of a product sold was directly proportional to the average amount of labour needed to produce it. Thus, for example, an elegant piece of furniture was more valuable than its component pieces mainly because of the labour invested in it by the worker(s) who built it. Marx argued that the value of goods produced by wage-labourers far exceeded the amount needed to pay their wages and the cost of raw materials, technology, and other components of the means of production. Marx referred to this excess as **surplus value.** According to Marx, when commodities were sold, their surplus value was turned into profits for the owner. Marx viewed this as an exploitive relationship, but one that differed from the exploitive relationships that characterized slavery or feudalism. After all, factory workers were paid a wage for their labour and were not legally forced to stay with the job. However, because most workers had few other options for making a living, and because owners controlled all aspects of the work, the legal freedom of wage-labourers to change jobs was, in practical terms, an illusion.

Class Conflict and Class Consciousness

The idea of **class conflict** between the major classes in a society was the driving force behind Marx's theory of social change. Marx noted that previous modes of production had collapsed and been replaced because of class conflict. Feudalism in Europe, for example, had given way to capitalism as a result of the growing power of the merchant class relative to the traditional alliance of landowners and the aristocracy, and the deteriorating relationship between landowners and peasants. Furthermore, Marx argued, capitalism would eventually be replaced by a socialist mode of production, in which private ownership of property would disappear, along with the exploitation and inequality it produced. The impetus for this massive change would again be widespread class conflict, this time between wage-labourers and the owners of the means of production, as inequality between these two classes became more pronounced.

Marx held that this revolution would take place only when members of the working class began to recognize that they were being exploited. In other words, Marx did not take it for granted that members of a class would see how their interests were similar. Whereas capitalists might be conscious of their group interests, wage-labourers needed to become aware of their common enemy. They needed to be transformed from a "class in itself" to a "class for itself." Thus, **class consciousness** was an important social-psychological component of Marx's theory of social inequality and social change. His vision of the future was that of a revolutionary upheaval in which the oppressed working class would recognize its enemy, destroy the institutions of capitalism, and replace them with a classless socialist society based on collective ownership of the means of production.

Responses to Marx

Over the years, many critics of Marx's ideas pointed to the communist countries, with their apparently socialist system of government and absence of private property, and noted that inequality had not disappeared there. Instead, a new hierarchy had emerged, in which control of the political and bureaucratic apparatus was the main basis of power. These observations were largely correct. As a Russian joke from the 1970s noted, under capitalism man exploits man, but under communism it is the other way around.

In fact, I wonder just how critical Marx himself would have been of the Soviet communist system, given the degree to which individual citizens were exploited and harshly treated by a powerful minority. However, it is slowly becoming apparent that the emergence of a capitalist economy in Eastern Europe is not eliminating material inequalities so much as changing their source. Today, individuals with control over some form of production or access to some marketing system are accumulating wealth while the majority of citizens appear to be no better off than before—indeed, many are worse off. The same pattern of growing social inequality has been observed in China where, despite the continued control of the economy by the Communist Party, some forms of free enterprise have been encouraged (Wu and Xie, 2002). In other words, while Marx's predictions about the inevitable emergence of a classless society have not been borne out, his type of class analysis still has considerable relevance for understanding the changing stratification system in North America, Eastern Europe, and even communist China.

Most theories of social stratification developed after Marx's were essentially a "debate with Marx's ghost" (Zeitlin with Brym, 1991: 117). Some social philosophers and sociologists elaborated on Marx's ideas, while others attempted to refute them. Among the critics, some focused on the absence of widespread class conflict, the growth of the middle class, and the relative decline in material inequality in Western Europe and North America in the twentieth century. I will examine some of these theories below, along with others that tried to develop more complex models of the contemporary class structure while basically following Marx's form of class-based analysis.

MAX WEBER: CLASS AND OTHER DIMENSIONS OF INEQUALITY

Max Weber was born in Germany half a century later than Marx—in 1864. Like Marx, he built his analysis of social stratification on a careful reading of history as well as a thorough analysis of the economic and political events of his day. But because he was only beginning his university studies about the time Marx died, Weber had the advantage of seeing the direction in which a more mature industrial capitalism was taking European society. He continued to write about many aspects of social stratification and social change until his death in 1920.

Class, Status, and Party

Weber shared with Marx a belief that economic inequalities were central to the social stratification system and that the ownership of property was a primary determinant of **power,** or the ability to impose your wishes on others, to get them to do what you want them to do. However, he argued that power could lie in controlling other types of resources as well (Weber, 1948 [1922]). Specifically, he proposed that structures of social stratification could be better understood by looking at economic inequalities, hierarchies of prestige (or social honour), and political inequalities (control of power blocs, such as political parties or other organizations)—or, in his words, at "class, status, and party." Although these different hierarchies often overlap, they need not. For example, suddenly wealthy individuals might not receive the prestige they desire, being rejected in "high society" by those with "old money." Similarly, a politician might have considerable power through control of government resources but might not be very wealthy or, for that matter, have much prestige.

Since Weber lived to see the emergence of white-collar workers, the growth of large private- and public-sector bureaucracies, and the growing power of trade unions, he was able to write about these alternative sources of power in a stratified capitalist society. He provided an insightful analysis of how power resided in the control of top positions in large bureaucratic organizations, even if the officeholder was not an owner of the organization. He recognized that well-educated wage-labourers might not be as powerless as were the factory workers of an earlier era. He also saw that a new class of middle-level, educated workers might not necessarily align themselves with blue-collar workers, and he was less inclined to conclude, as had Marx, that the middle class would disappear (Zeitlin with Brym, 1991: 118–19). In fact, he expected that the number of educated technical and professional workers in bureaucratic capitalist society would increase.

What Weber saw, compared with what Marx saw, was considerably more complexity in the social stratification system because of the growing diversity of the occupational structure and of capitalist enterprises. And although Weber was sometimes pessimistic in his writings about the future of democracy in a bureaucratic capitalist society, he did not link inequality and class conflict to the ultimate demise of capitalism itself, as did Marx. Similarly, although Weber, like Marx, commented on how members of a class might or might not recognize their shared interests, he did not conclude that it was the inevitable destiny of the working class to become a "class for itself."

Social Class and Life-Chances

Despite these divergences in their thinking, Weber, like Marx, placed primary emphasis on the economic underpinnings of social stratification. However, he defined "class" more broadly. Rather than insisting that a limited number of class positions were based on an individual's relationship to the means of production, Weber saw a larger variety of class positions based both on ownership of property and on other labour-market statuses, such as occupation and education. Furthermore, he tended to emphasize the **life-chances** that class position offered. In other words, a higher position in the economic hierarchy, however obtained, provided more power and allowed an individual and his or her family to enjoy more of the good things in life.

It should be apparent, then, that the general approach to studying stratification that I outlined earlier, one that recognizes the central importance of class while acknowledging that gender, race, and other dimensions of social inequality can also be very important, is in the Weberian tradition. Similarly, my general definition of "class" as a relatively stable position within an economic hierarchy held by an individual or family, along with others with roughly the same amount of control over or access to material resources, follows Weber's use of the term.

DAVIS AND MOORE: A FUNCTIONAL THEORY OF STRATIFICATION

Twentieth-Century Affluence and Structural-Functionalist Theory

Although a number of other social theorists in Europe and North America wrote about social stratification in the early decades of the twentieth century, I will skip ahead to 1945, when Kingsley Davis and Wilbert Moore published their short but much-debated "principles of social stratification." In other chapters in this text, you will read about the **structural-functionalist theory** in sociology, an approach that emphasizes consensus over conflict and that seeks to explain the function, for society as a whole, of social institutions and various aspects of social structure. Davis and Moore were part of this intellectual tradition, which arose in reaction to the conflict-oriented and socially radical theories of Marx (and, to a lesser extent, of Weber).

The emergence of structural-functionalism as an alternative theoretical approach can be better understood if we view it as reflecting the optimistic view in postwar North America that affluence was increasing, social conflict was decreasing, and a harmonious future for society was dawning. For example, Arthur Schlesinger, Jr., an American historian writing in 1956, suggested that Americans should start thinking about the "miseries of an age of abundance." Rather than worrying about economic growth, employment, and improving the standard of living, it was time to concentrate on "the bettering of our mass media and the elevation of our popular culture, in short, with the quality of civilization to which our nation aspires in an age of ever-increasing abundance and leisure" (as quoted in Longman, 1985: 75). Thus, during the several decades following World War II, many social scientists were attracted to theories that downplayed conflict and emphasized the benefits, to all, of an apparently ever-expanding economy.

The Functional Necessity of Stratification

Davis and Moore (1945) argued that, because inequality exists in all societies, it must be a necessary part of society. All societies, they noted, have a variety of occupational roles that need to be filled, some requiring more training than others, some having more functional importance, and some being less pleasant and more difficult to perform. To get people to fill important roles and to perform these critical tasks well, and to spend time training for high-skill occupations, societies must ensure that the rewards for performance (money, prestige, and other intangibles) are greater. Thus, for example, doctors and schoolteachers need to be paid more than factory workers and truck drivers, and also must rank higher than the latter in terms of social honour and prestige.

In short, according to Davis and Moore, social inequality is both inevitable and functionally necessary for society. But theirs was not a class-based and conflict-prone stratification system. Rather, Davis and Moore described a much more fluid socioeconomic hierarchy, with many different occupational statuses into which individuals are slotted on the basis of their effort and ability. The system is held together by consensus and shared values (not torn apart by conflict, as Marx theorized), because members of society generally agree that the hierarchy is fair and just. It follows from this line of reasoning that efforts to reduce social inequality will be ineffective and might even be harmful to society.

Criticisms of Davis and Moore

Various criticisms have been levelled against Davis and Moore's theory. For example, although some differences in pay might be justified to reimburse those who spend more years in school preparing for an occupation, are the huge income and wealth inequalities we see in our society really necessary? (See Box 6.1.) Why do women often earn less than men, even if they are doing the same type of work? Are movie stars, professional athletes, and chief executive officers with million-dollar-plus annual incomes really so much more important to society than nurses, daycare workers, prison guards, and most other low-paid

According to calculations by McMaster University economist Michael Veall, the top-earning 1 percent of Canadians have almost doubled their share of the national income—from 7.6 percent in 1980 to 13.6 percent in 2000. . . . But mere statistics about inequality can suck the real-life drama out of the story. . . . So Dutch statistician Jan Pen came up with a more vivid way to illustrate inequality, by presenting the national distribution of income as a one-hour parade in which everyone in the country marches and everyone's size is determined by his or her income. . . . Here's what Canada's parade looks like.

For the first six minutes, the marchers are so small, it's hard to see them. With average family incomes of about $10 000, they stand only about one foot tall. The marchers get gradually taller. When we reach the midpoint of the parade, they measure about 5 foot, 6 inches, with an income of $55 000—the median Canadian family income.

After that, the marchers continue to increase gradually in height until the last few minutes, when they shoot up dramatically to heights of 16, 17, 18 feet and more. By the last few seconds, we see some extraordinary giants, such as John Hunkin, chairman of CIBC, with an income of $13.8 million, measuring almost 1380 feet high, and auto parts magnate Frank Stronach, father of Belinda, with an income of $53.5 million, measuring just over a mile high!

But this parade only measures inequality of income. The more meaningful measure is inequality of wealth—that is, financial assets. So here's the same parade of Canadians, but this time with their height measured in wealth, not income. This time, the parade has been going for about 10 minutes before we even realize it's begun—because those at the front aren't just tiny, they're actually underground. (They own nothing of value and are net debtors).

At about 20 minutes, we see people the size of dwarfs, until the midpoint of the parade, where marchers stand 5 foot 6 inches, with net wealth of $81 000. . . . With less than one-tenth of a second to go, some of Canada's wealthiest men stride past. There's Ted Rogers, with assets of $1.7 billion, standing 21 miles high, and Galen Weston, with assets of $9.7 billion, stretching up a full 121 miles. Finally, bringing up the rear, [was] Canada's richest man, Ken Thomson, with $21.6 billion—towering a breathtaking 272 miles above us.

SOURCE: Excerpted from Linda McQuaig, "Rich walk ever taller in Canada," *The Toronto Star,* 12 December, 2004. p. A17. Reprinted by permission of Linda McQuaig.

workers? And how does a theory like this account for inherited wealth, for the fact that wealth leads to power and the ability to accumulate more wealth?

Given these criticisms, what accounts for the appeal of this theory? Perhaps it is the kernel of truth at its core that is so attractive—namely, the recognition that, *to some extent*, differences in income and prestige are based on different amounts of effort and ability. After all, we can easily think of examples of better-paying occupations that require long years of education and training. Nevertheless, this is far from the complete story about inequality in our society, which is much more pronounced than what such differences in effort and ability might lead us to expect. In fact, the theory's appeal probably lies more in its apparent justification of these large inequalities. You might test this hypothesis by explaining the theory, first to someone with a high income or inherited wealth, and then to someone who is unemployed or earning very little. The odds are that the functionalist explanation of stratification would sound much more plausible to the wealthier person.

GERHARD LENSKI: TECHNOLOGY AND STRATIFICATION SYSTEMS

Writing in the 1960s, a time of economic expansion and growing prosperity in North America, Gerhard Lenski (1966) developed a theory of "power and privilege" that attempted to explain the extent of material inequality in both contemporary and past societies. Lenski's explanation recognized power and conflict much more explicitly than had the Davis and Moore functionalist explanation of stratification. And, like Weber, he identified a number of different dimensions of social stratification, such as education and ethnicity, while emphasizing the centrality of economic inequalities. Although he used the term *class*, Lenski did not define it precisely, choosing instead to talk about the ruling elites in society in general terms and about how they managed to maintain their wealth and power at the expense of the masses.

Lenski reasoned that a society's *technological base* largely determines the degree of inequality within it. In simple hunting-and-gathering societies, he argued, the few resources of the society were distributed primarily on the basis of need. But as societies became more technologically complex, resources in excess of those required to fulfill basic needs were produced. Control of those surplus resources, or privilege, came to be based on power, allowing ruling elites to take a much larger share of these resources for themselves. Thus, the more complex agricultural societies, such as that of pre-colonial India, developed highly structured governing and tax-collecting systems, through which the privileged ruling elites accumulated immense amounts of wealth, while the masses lived in poverty.

As a result of industrialization and the complexity of modern technology, this "age-old evolutionary trend toward ever-increasing inequality" (Lenski, 1966: 308) was reversed. Owners of the means of production could no longer control the production process directly and had to rely instead on well-educated managerial and technical workers to keep the complex system operating. Education broadened the horizons of these middle-level employees, introducing them to ideas of democracy, encouraging them to demand a larger share of the profits they were helping to produce, and making them more articulate in their demands for equality.

Thus, Lenski's theory proposed a causal link between complex industrial technology, the higher education of workers, and workers' insistence on sharing the growing wealth of an industrial society. But why would employers give in to such demands? Because, argued Lenski, the industrial elite needed educated workers—they could not produce wealth without them. Equally important, the much greater productivity of industrial societies compared with preindustrial societies meant that the elite could "make economic concessions in relative terms without necessarily suffering any loss in absolute terms" (Lenski, 1966: 314). Because the economic pie was so much bigger, everyone could have a larger slice.

In one obvious sense, Lenski's theory resembled the functionalist theory of stratification—both noted that better-educated and more highly skilled workers are paid more. However, unlike the functionalist approach, Lenski's theory clearly took power differences into account, emphasizing how the extent of accumulation of wealth by elites, or the degree of material inequality, depends on the power and bargaining ability of middle-level workers. In fact, Lenski placed material inequality at the centre of his theory of stratification. But in contrast to Marx's

Although high technology has created many new jobs, it has also eliminated many. For the chronically unemployed, the closest they may get to high technology is a computer at the local unemployment office.
SOURCE: Dick Hemingway.

nineteenth-century predictions of growing inequality as industrial capitalism matured, Lenski, writing in the middle of the twentieth century, saw a movement toward a more equal distribution of society's wealth.

ERIK OLIN WRIGHT: A NEO-MARXIST APPROACH

In reaction against functionalism, Lenski brought power and conflict back into his explanation of social inequality. He placed material inequalities resulting from one group's domination of another at the centre of his model, thus coming closer to the approach taken by Marx and Weber. But he did not carry through with a traditional Marxist analysis built around the relationships of different classes to the means of production. In contrast, a number of neo-Marxist scholars, writing in the 1970s and 1980s, attempted to update the original Marxist model so that it could be applied to the late-twentieth century. We will discuss only one theorist from the neo-Marxist camp, Erik Olin Wright.

Although Marx acknowledged the existence of a middle class comprising several distinct groups, including independent producers and small-business owners, he predicted that this middle class would disappear and so spent much more time writing about the relationship between the two primary classes (capitalists and workers). Wright's contribution lies in recognizing that as industrial capitalism matured, the middle class had grown and become more diverse, and in trying to understand the class dynamics of our more complex capitalist system of production. Of particular importance in Wright's theory is the emphasis on **contradictory class locations**—that is, on occupational groupings that have divided loyalties within a class structure. For example, although managers work for capitalists, supervising lower-level employees and trying to get them to produce as much as possible, managers are themselves employees, potentially exploited by owners. Considering the substantial numbers of people in such contradictory locations, you can begin to understand why the widespread class conflict envisioned by Marx has seldom emerged.

In a later reformulation of his ideas, Wright (1985) argued that exploitation of one class by another can occur through control of property or the means of production (as Marx had insisted), as well as through ownership of skill or credential assets and control of high positions within organizations. Thus, he identified three classes of owners (the bourgeoisie, small employers, and the petite bourgeoisie with no employees), and nine classes of wage-labourers (nonowners), differentiated on two dimensions, the possession of organizational assets and of skill/credential assets (Wright, 1985: 88). For example, "expert managers" (e.g., engineers or lawyers in senior management positions within large companies) fill a class location characterized by extensive organizational assets and high skill/credential assets, in contrast to basic "proletarians," who have no specific skill/credential assets and no management or supervisory responsibilities (see Figure 6.1).

Despite his intention of developing a neo-Marxist theoretical model updated to the late twentieth century, Wright's theory is similar to Weber's view of class structure in some ways (Grabb, 2002).

FIGURE 6.1   ERIC OLIN WRIGHT'S TYPOLOGY OF CLASS LOCATION IN CAPITALIST SOCIETY

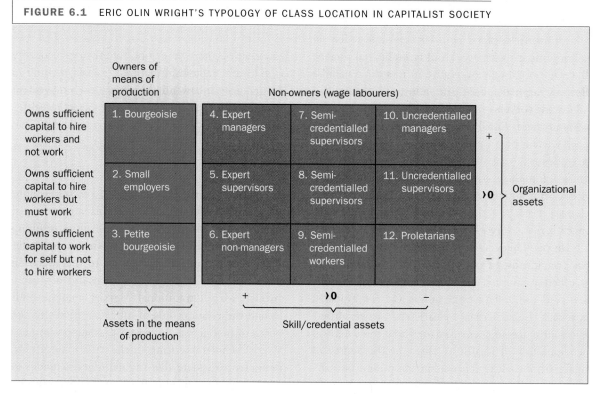

SOURCE: Erik Olin Wright. *Classes* (London: Verso, 1985), p. 88.

Specifically, the different class locations created by the intersection of organizational and skill/credential assets remind us of the different classes Weber described as he commented on how similar educational and occupational statuses resulted in similar control over and access to material resources. Even so, Wright's theory of class structure and his observations about contradictory locations within it are useful, because he deliberately attempts to incorporate the complexities of modern capitalist society into his explanation of social inequality.

FRANK PARKIN: A NEO-WEBERIAN APPROACH

Wright attempted to bring Marx's class analysis back into the discussion of contemporary forms of social stratification. Frank Parkin (1972, 1979) was equally explicit in stating his intellectual debts to Max Weber's discussions of power, class, and social stratification (Grabb, 2002). In fact, Parkin went so far as to argue that neo-Marxist scholars, espousing what he calls "professorial Marxism" (1979: x), were merely putting forth dressed-up Weberian arguments. As a neo-Weberian, Parkin criticized traditional Marxist and contemporary neo-Marxist analyses for failing to take into account gender, race, religious, and other forms of social stratification that do not grow out of the relations of production in capitalist society but clearly have an origin and permanency all of their own (1979: 4–5). Nevertheless, like both Weber and Marx before him, Parkin continued to emphasize the importance of property relations in contemporary stratification systems (Grabb, 2002).

Among Parkin's most useful contributions to stratification theory is his explanation of how patterns of structured inequality, whether based on class, gender, race, or some other ascribed or achieved status, are maintained or changed. To do so, Parkin returned to a concept introduced by Weber, that of **social closure.** Parkin defines this term as "the process by which social collectivities seek to maximize rewards by restricting access to resources and opportunities to a limited circle of eligibles" (1979: 44). He then goes on to elaborate two types of closure strategies that help us understand how patterns of social inequality are maintained but also sometimes altered.

Exclusion refers to the organized efforts of privileged, more powerful groups to maintain their advantaged position. Processes of exclusion can range from centuries-old caste systems in closed societies to the use, in contemporary open societies, of educational credentials to maintain power and privilege. For example, lawyers and other professional groups have managed to ensure, via legal restrictions, that only they can perform certain types of work in our society. By excluding others from engaging in such work, it is possible to maintain high incomes, enjoy a high standard of living, and exercise a great deal of power. Similarly, members of trade unions can also use legal sanctions to keep nonmembers, who might have the same skills, from taking on some well-paying jobs.

In contrast, **usurpation** refers to the efforts of excluded groups within a stratification system to gain advantages and power. As Parkin put it, all usurpation actions have as their goal "biting into the resources and benefits accruing to dominant groups in society" (1979: 74). As with exclusionary practices, usurpation efforts range across a continuum, from lobbying and voting for social change to outright revolt against groups in power. Thus, over the past several decades, we have seen successful efforts by women's groups, Aboriginal groups, and other disadvantaged groups to change the balance of power and privilege in Canada. Going back further, labour unions took even stronger, sometimes illegal, actions to gain new powers and a more equitable distribution of resources for their members.

Thus, like Lenski, Parkin took a keen interest in the power struggles within society between groups with more and less power (Grabb, 2002). However, Parkin's neo-Weberian theory does not contain a premise of inevitability, either one of increased inequality and eventual social revolution as Marx predicted, or one of reduced inequality resulting from technological change and economic growth, as Lenski predicted. But Parkin did see a clear trend with respect to processes of social closure. With the growing emphasis on education in modern society, the use of educational credentials to maintain power and privilege has become more widespread. As a result, well-educated professionals have become a powerful class grouping, sometimes almost as powerful as wealthy capitalists who control the means of production (Grabb, 2002). Beneath these two powerful groups are a range of other groups with varying amounts of power, trying, when possible, to usurp more power from those above.

EXPLANATIONS OF SOCIAL STRATIFICATION: SUMMING UP

There are other theories of social inequality in addition to those reviewed previously (Grabb, 2002). However, having been introduced to Marx and Weber, the functionalist theory of stratification, and a number of more recent approaches, you will now have some sense of the range of existing explanations. Davis and Moore's functionalist approach stressed that inequality was inevitable and useful, and it downplayed social conflict resulting from inequality. In contrast to this *consensus* approach to stratification, a variety of *conflict* approaches highlighted differences in power resulting from and contributing to material inequality, the exploitation of some groups by others, and the social conflict that could result. Marx was the most explicit in this regard, arguing that class conflict would eventually transform capitalist society itself.

The theories we have reviewed differ in the assumptions they make and the conclusions they draw about the future of material inequality. Marx clearly saw inequality and exploitation of the working class increasing, and he predicted that class conflict would lead to the death of capitalism. Although Weber was not convinced that a socialist society would eventually emerge, neither did he argue that inequalities would gradually decrease (Grabb, 2002). As a neo-Weberian, Parkin takes a similar stance. Wright's emphasis on the growing number of middle-class locations also does not suggest an increasing level of material inequality, but neither does it imply the opposite. However, the functionalists and Lenski, writing in an era of economic growth and widespread optimism about the ability of capitalism to raise the overall standard of living, clearly felt that material inequalities were shrinking in Western industrial societies.

The various explanations also differ in the degree to which they emphasize class differences in access to and control of material resources. For Marx, class was the primary determining factor in this regard. Weber, using the term *class* somewhat more broadly, emphasized its central role but recognized other important dimensions of social stratification. So, too, did Parkin, who explicitly discussed the independent effects of gender, race, and religion. Davis and Moore basically ignored the concept of class. Although Lenski again focused more directly on economic inequality, he did not really describe society in terms of distinct classes, as Wright, in his neo-Marxist approach, did. Thus, if you view these theories in chronological order, it appears that class, at least as defined in the Weberian sense, has made a comeback as an explanatory concept.

Furthermore, those who felt that the level of material inequality was remaining high or increasing viewed society from a class-based perspective. In other words, they focused on the distinctly different life-chances of individuals and families with similar amounts of access to and control over material resources. In contrast, theorists who thought economic inequalities were declining preferred a model of society composed of many different overlapping strata that reflected a variety of equally important dimensions of social stratification.

Clark and Lipset, whose question "Are social classes dying?" introduced this section, make the latter point explicitly when they state that "one simple, powerful change has affected the economy: growth. And economic growth undermines hierarchical class stratification" (1991: 405). As you turn to the next section of the chapter—an overview of statistics on occupational and class structures and material inequality in Canada today—keep this argument in mind, because the statistics allow you to assess its validity.

OCCUPATIONS, SOCIAL CLASS, AND INEQUALITY IN CANADA

OCCUPATIONAL SHIFTS OVER TIME

As noted above, explanations of social stratification differ in the extent to which they emphasize social class compared with other bases of social inequality. Some theories focus more on how occupational patterns have changed as industrial capitalism matured. But even such theorists as Erik Olin Wright, who place social class at the centre of their explanations, rely to a considerable extent on occupational data. So it would be useful to begin this section by examining occupational shifts in Canada over the past century.

Table 6.1 displays the types of occupations most common at the beginning (1911) and in the middle (1951) of the last century, and at the very beginning of the twenty-first century (2001). The most prominent occupational shift over the course of the century is the decline in agricultural occupations, from 34 percent of all labour force participants in 1911 to only 3 percent in 2001. We also observe a decline, albeit not as

TABLE 6.1 OCCUPATIONAL DISTRIBUTION OF LABOUR FORCE PARTICIPANTS,* CANADA, 1911, 1951, 2001

OCCUPATION TYPE	1911	1951	2001
Managerial/administrative	5%	8%	14%
Professional/technical	4	7	20
Clerical	4	11	12
Sales	5	7	11
Service	8	10	14
Manufacturing	14	17	9
Transportation	6	8	8
Construction	5	6	6
Agriculture	34	16	3
Forestry/fishing/mining	5	4	2
Other occupations	10	6	1
Total	**100**	**100**	**100**

SOURCE: 1911 and 1951 data: adapted from 1911 and 1951 Census results, presented by Jeff O'Neill, "Changing Occupational Structure," *Canadian Social Trends*, Winter 1991, p. 10; 2001 data: adapted from 2001 Census results, Table 97F0012XCB2001024, http://www12.statcan.ca/english/census01/home/index.cfm.

*Labour force participants include both the employed (paid employees and the self-employed) and the unemployed (those who want a paid job but who are unable to find one); based on the population aged 15 and older.

steep, in other natural resource–based occupations (forestry, fishing, mining). Manufacturing occupations increased in relative terms (from 14 percent to 17 percent) between the beginning and middle of the last century, but by 2001 had dropped to only 9 percent of the total labour force.

Manufacturing, construction, transportation, and resource-based occupations are typically called *blue-collar occupations*, in contrast to *white-collar occupations* in the managerial, professional, clerical (office jobs), sales, and service categories. It is apparent from Table 6.1 that white-collar occupations have come to greatly outnumber blue-collar occupations as industrial capitalism has matured. In 2001, 14 percent of Canadian labour force participants were identified as having managerial/administrative occupations, up from only 5 percent in 1911. Professional/technical occupations had multiplied by five times in relative terms, from 4 percent to 20 percent. Clerical, sales, and service occupations also had become much more common, from a total of only 17 percent in 1911 to 37 percent of all occupations in 2001.

What do these occupational changes tell you, with respect to my previous discussions of the bases of social stratification? First, as various theories have indicated, the proportion of occupations requiring higher education has increased, while the proportion of traditional blue-collar, "working-class" occupations has declined. With the expansion in white-collar occupations, average incomes rose, at least until the early 1980s. Thus, to the extent that occupational data can inform about class structure in the Weberian sense, occupational shifts over the past 90 years suggest greater class diversity, rather than a polarization of classes, as a strict reading of Marx's theory would predict, and a rising standard of living for Canadian workers, rather than increasing poverty and exploitation.

And what do the numbers in Table 6.1 fail to tell you? First, they do not distinguish between the occupations typically held by women and those typically held by men. Since the middle of the last century, a rising proportion of women have been entering the labour force. But, as we will see (Chapter 7, "Gender Inequality: Economic and Political Aspects"), women have been more likely to find employment in the clerical, sales, and service occupations (what might be called a "pink-collar sector") than in blue-collar occupations or in higher-status and better-paying managerial and professional occupations, even though there has been some movement by women into higher-level white-collar occupations in the past decades (Krahn, Lowe, and Hughes, 2006: ch. 2). Thus, gender-based labour market stratification continues to exist, intersecting with class-based stratification.

Second, even though you might draw some conclusions about social class from the occupational data in Table 6.1, the data do not directly describe workers' relationships to the means of production, in Marx's terms. Statistics Canada has never collected and categorized national data along these lines, but a series of Ontario-wide surveys have, by using Erik Olin Wright's approach to class analysis to profile the class composition of that province since the early 1980s (Livingstone, 1999: 158). In 1996, the Ontario employed labour force was described as comprising corporate capitalists (1 percent), small employers (8 percent), the own-account self-employed or *petite bourgeoisie* (14 percent), managers (8 percent), supervisors (4 percent), professional/semi-professional employees (19 percent), and service and industrial workers (46 percent). The small sample size in this study (about 600 respondents) means that these estimates are not precise, and the single province focus does not allow for generalizations to all of Canada. Even so, this study clearly shows that the large class of paid workers contains several distinct types with varying amounts of decision-making authority and substantial differences in income, status, and occupational power.

Third, neither Table 6.1 (which displays occupational change over time) nor the 1996 Ontario study (which uses class data from only one point in time) can give a sense of how the Canadian class structure might be changing. But you can get one indication of change from other data on self-employment. Over the course of the century, particularly with the decline in the number of people employed in agriculture, the proportion of self-employed Canadians dropped dramatically. By 1971, only 11 percent of the Canadian labour force was self-employed. However, beginning in the 1980s, a slow reversal of the trend began in Canada, the United States, and other Western industrialized countries. By 2004, 10 percent of employed Canadians were own-account self-employed (without any employees) and 5 percent employed others (Krahn, Lowe, and Hughes, 2006: ch. 2). Researchers still have not determined whether more Canadians are voluntarily choosing self-employment or are being pushed into it as a result of higher levels of unemployment and growing corporate and public-sector "downsizing." Nevertheless, the reversal of the decline in self-employment—the increase in the size of the petite bourgeoisie—is something that theorists are trying to explain as they attempt to further update Marx's ideas of class-based stratification (Breen and Rottman, 1995: 87–88; Myles and Turegun, 1994).

Finally, the data in Table 6.1 do not reflect some of the dramatic changes in employment opportunities and outcomes that have been occurring in the past three decades. I will return to this topic later, but for now I will simply note that unemployment rates have risen, part-time and temporary work have become much more common, and income growth appears to have stopped, while income and wealth inequality have increased. Consequently, the higher standard of living that accompanied occupational changes in the second half of the twentieth century is no longer guaranteed for all those in middle-status occupations. Thus, it is essential that we look carefully at the distributional side of the occupation and class structures, at "who gets what" in return for their employment, as well as at the occupational and class positions that

Many women were able to make important inroads into the labour force during World War II, as this painting illustrates. To this day, women are more likely to find work in the pink-collar sector than in higher-status, better-paying occupations.

SOURCE: Paraskeva Clark, *Parachute Riggers*. Courtesy Canadian War Museum. Reproduced with permission of Clive and Ben Clark, Toronto.

people hold (Westergaard, 1995). But before beginning to examine changing patterns of material inequality in Canada, I will first discuss another important feature of stratification systems in modern societies—opportunities for occupational mobility and status attainment.

OCCUPATIONAL MOBILITY AND STATUS ATTAINMENT

Many people move up the occupational and income ladders during their careers, frequently after investing in higher education of some kind. And some move down, often because of economic circumstances beyond their control. Sociologists have conducted a great deal of research on such **intragenerational occupational mobility** (mobility within an individual's lifetime) and on **intergenerational occupational mobility,** the process of reaching an occupational location higher or lower than the location your parents held. Research of this type is interesting in itself, since we all like to compare how well we have done relative to others. However, such research is also theoretically important, since it tests hypotheses derived from theories of inequality (the functionalist perspective, for example) that propose that higher positions in society are generally filled by those most qualified, not by those who inherit them.

If the only intergenerational occupational mobility we observed was a result of better-qualified people moving up to replace those who were less qualified, we should also see an equivalent amount of downward mobility. Such a scenario of "musical jobs" or, to use the technical term, **circulatory mobility** does not really describe the Canadian situation over the past half-century, however, because of the pronounced parallel process of **structural mobility** resulting from a significant change in the shape of Canada's overall occupational structure. As noted earlier, over the past half-century, industrial societies, including Canada, experienced a great deal of growth in white-collar occupations (clerical, managerial, and professional positions) as traditional agricultural and blue-collar industrial jobs declined in relative importance. Hence, with an increase in the number of higher-status jobs, each generation had more chances than the preceding one to improve the status of their jobs.

Even so, Canadian studies conducted over the past several decades indicate that Canada, like the United States, has a relatively open stratification system, more so than countries like Sweden, the United Kingdom, France, the Netherlands, and Australia (Wanner, 2004). In other words, in Canada relatively more people have been able to move up the occupational ladder relative to their parents. During the second half of the last century, the Canadian occupational structure opened up for women and men in different ways. The steep decline in agricultural employment meant that many men moved out of the agricultural occupations held by their fathers. For women, the major shift was away from the housework that had been the main female occupation for their mothers' generation. For both sexes, expansion of postsecondary educational opportunities, leading to higher status occupations, played an important role (Wanner, 2004). However, most of this opening of the stratification system occurred between 1973 and 1986. Little changed in terms of mobility opportunities in the following decade, with the exception of continued slow movement of women into managerial positions.

Thus, overall, Canadian mobility studies find only a limited amount of direct occupational inheritance across generations and conclude that the occupational stratification system became somewhat more open during the 1970s and 1980s. Yet those at or near the top of the occupational hierarchy are still more likely to pass their advantages on to their children. As Richard Wanner (2004: 144) concludes: "Canada is still a stratified society characterized by a considerable amount of inheritance of privilege" (Wanner, 2004: 144). This intergenerational transfer of advantage takes place primarily through different levels of access to the postsecondary education system.

Research in Canada and other Western countries examining the process of **occupational status attainment** has shown, not surprisingly, that the most important influence on the status of an individual's current job is the status of that person's first job. Individuals who enter the labour market as articling lawyers, for example, typically make their way higher up the occupational ladder than do those who began as unskilled labourers. In turn, the status of that first job is heavily influenced by the amount of education completed. Such findings obviously lend some support to theories that suggest that more qualified people, as indicated by higher education, end up in higher-status and better-paying occupations.

However, many studies have also traced education-job linkages back to the previous generation, showing that those who obtain more education and hence better jobs are more likely to come from families with better-educated parents. For example, a 14-year longitudinal study of high school graduates in Edmonton, Alberta, showed that young people from families in which one or both parents had completed universities were almost three times more likely to complete university themselves (Krahn, 2004). For a variety of reasons (e.g., more money for higher education, more well-educated role models), children from more advantaged backgrounds can build on their initial advantages.

THE DISTRIBUTION OF WEALTH

Evidence from various sources demonstrates that a limited number of people continue to own or control a very large portion of the wealth in Canada. For example, in 2000, one-quarter of the companies listed on the Toronto Stock Exchange 300 Index were each controlled by a single owner holding more than 50 percent of the voting shares (Yakabuski, 2001). Such statistics highlight the immense wealth held by families, such as the Thomsons, the Westons, and the Irvings, with business holdings spread around the globe as well as in Canada. Together with highly paid chief executive officers and corporate directors, these wealthy families clearly form a distinct upper class, the haute (or high) bourgeoisie in Marx's terms.

By way of example, in 2004, the CEOs of the top 160 companies listed on the Toronto Stock Exchange received a median compensation package (earnings, bonuses, and stock options) of $1.8 million (Church, 2005). Several CEOs were exceptionally well paid. Robert Gratton of Power Financial Corporation led the pack, with $173.2 million (including $169 million from stock options). Gerry Schwartz of Onex Corporation and Frank Stronach of Magna International were probably envious, taking home only $76.4 million and $52.5 million, respectively. It would take the average Canadian worker, with annual earnings of about $32 000 in 2000, almost 2400 years to accumulate as much money as Schwartz and more than 5400 years to earn what Gratton received in one year.

At the other end of the wealth scale are the 11 percent of Canadian families who reported no *net worth* in 1999, net worth being defined as the difference between total assets (shares, bonds, savings, property, businesses, and possessions, but excluding future pension income) and total debt (Morissette, 2002). Almost one in five families (19 percent) reported no *net wealth*, defined as net worth minus the value of property that could not be disposed of quickly if necessary (i.e., a home and furnishings or a business). In fact, the poorest 10 percent of Canadian families in 1999 reported an average net worth of –$6700, indicating that, on average, their debts outstripped the value of all their assets (Chawla, 2004). In contrast, the wealthiest 10 percent of families, with an average net worth of $1 320 900, held almost half (49.4 percent) of all wealth in Canada.

Over the long term, the economic growth experienced in Western industrialized countries, along with some income redistribution efforts by governments, has had an equalizing effect on the distribution of household wealth. Wolff (1991), for example, showed that inequality in household wealth decreased between 1920 and the 1970s in Sweden, Britain, and the United States. Although comparable data are not available for Canada for the same period, it is likely that a similar decline occurred here as well. However, Wolff also noted that, in the mid-1970s, wealth inequality began to increase again in the United States and Sweden (it remained constant in Britain). What about in Canada?

A recent study shows that, between 1984 and 1999, median wealth for the total Canadian population grew by about 10 percent in real terms (i.e., adjusted for inflation). But this growth in wealth was distributed unequally. Over the 15-year period ending in 1999, real median wealth declined for the poorest 30 percent of Canadian families while increasing substantially for the richest 30 percent (Morissette, Zhang, and Drolet, 2002). In other words, wealth inequality has been slowly increasing over the past two decades in Canada.

INCOME DISTRIBUTION

High-Paying and Low-Paying Occupations

Although most people have virtually no contact with the wealthiest families in Canada, we are much more aware of, or perhaps are even members of, a larger, not quite as wealthy, but still very affluent group of households containing one or more individuals in high-paying occupations. By way of example, 2001 census data revealed Canadian dentists earning an average of $108 034 (in 2000), while medical specialists earned even more ($134 581). Judges earned almost as much ($134 143) while lawyers had to be content with average yearly earnings of $94 731 (Statistics Canada, 2001). In contrast, cashiers, many employed part-time, earned only a fraction of this ($10 051), as did hotel clerks ($15 937), hair stylists and barbers ($17 390), security guards ($18 843) and workers in fish-processing plants ($10 483).

Using the term *class* in the Weberian sense, you would be justified in labelling individuals in well-paid managerial and professional occupations as members of an upper-middle class, given their high incomes and their access to and control of material resources through their employment positions. In contrast, retail workers and those employed in some service occupations (e.g., food and beverage services, child-care and home support services) work in the low-paying, insecure occupations that we might describe as the lower working class.

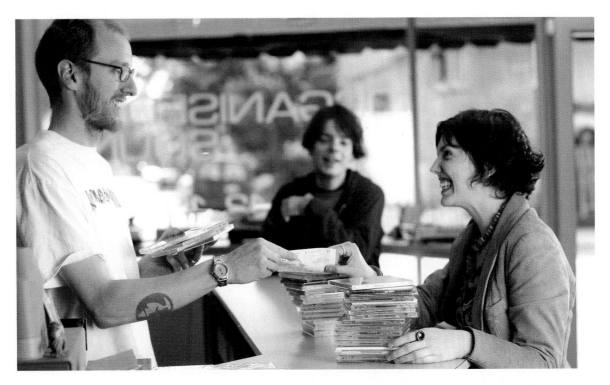

According to 2001 Canadian census data, cashiers earned about $10 000 per year.

SOURCE: Photos.com.

These occupational earning patterns hide large gender differences. Thus, among people working full-time and full-year, women's earnings were 71 percent of men's in 2000. More specifically, female dentists earned, on average, 64 percent of what their male counterparts earned. Among senior managers, women earned 61 percent of what men earned (averages of $69 993 and $114 519, respectively). Female university professors, however, reported 2000 earnings of $63 746, 80 percent of the earnings of male professors ($79 993). Among the lower-paid occupations, male grocery clerks reported annual 2000 earnings of $25 905, considerably higher than the earnings of their female counterparts ($20 691). Similar gender differences are observed in all occupational groupings but, as these examples demonstrate, the female–male earnings ratio does vary considerably by occupation (see Box 6.2 and Chapter 7, "Gender Inequality: Economic and Political Aspects").

Income Inequality

The census data discussed above give some indication of the distribution of employment earnings, the largest component of total income. If you were to look back to the middle of the last century, you would see that the distribution of total income (from employment,

BOX 6.2   WILL THE GENDER WAGE GAP DISAPPEAR?

Census data from 2001 show that, for full-time, full-year employed Canadians, women earn 71 percent of what men earn. This statistic is based on earnings comparisons for workers of all ages and with a wide range of formal education. However, when looking at only young (age 25 to 29), university-educated workers, we generally see a much higher female-male earnings ratio or, in other words, a smaller gender wage gap. For example, in the computer and information systems occupational category (the most commonly held job in 2001 among 25- to 29-year-olds with a university degree), the female-male earnings ratio was 85 percent (Figure 6.2). In the second most commonly held occupation (elementary schoolteacher), the ratio was 98 percent. In other words, in this occupation, women earned almost the same amount as men.

Does the smaller gender wage gap among young, university-educated Canadians signify that gender-based stratification in the workplace has almost disappeared, at least for well-educated workers? As these young women and men move further into their careers and, for some, into parenthood, will a gender wage gap once again appear? For that matter, why is the gender wage gap already larger in some of these occupations?

FIGURE 6.2 AVERAGE EARNINGS IN SIX
OCCUPATIONS MOST COMMONLY HELD BY
25- TO 29-YEAR-OLDS WITH A UNIVERSITY
DEGREE AND WORKING FULL-YEAR, FULL–TIME,
BY SEX, CANADA, 2001

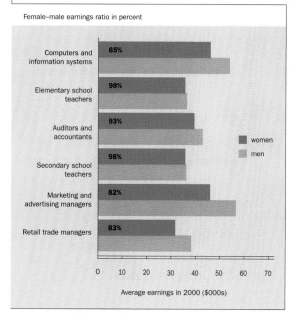

SOURCE: Adapted from the Statistics Canada website http://www12.statcan.ca/english/census01/products/Analytic/companion/earn/Canada.cfm.

investments, government assistance, and all other sources) across households (families and individuals living alone) in Canada has changed relatively little. In 1951, the most advantaged 20 percent of households (the top quintile) received 43 percent of total Canadian income, whereas the bottom quintile (the 20 percent with the lowest incomes) received only 4 percent of all income (Statistics Canada, 1984: 6). In 2003, the distribution looked similar, at least at the bottom, where the poorest 20 percent were still taking home only 4 percent of all income.

However, a closer examination reveals that income inequality has increased—in 2003 the top quintile was receiving 46 percent of all income (Statistics Canada, 2005: 109). Thus, the share of total income received by the three middle quintiles has declined, and income inequality has been slowly increasing. The three middle quintiles largely comprise working Canadians (in other words, not the unemployed or seniors) who would be most affected by a changing labour market in which some well-paying jobs have slowly been replaced by others that pay less and are less secure (Vosko, Zukewich, and Crawford, 2003; Yalnizyan, 1998).

In addition, the lowest-income quintiles have increasingly come to be filled by recent immigrants, despite the fact that most immigrants to Canada today are typically young, well educated, and well trained (see Chapter 8, "Race and Ethnic Relations"). As Picot and Myles (2005: 19) observe: "Low income trends among the population as a whole tend to mask an underlying divide that has opened up between the Canadian-born and immigrants to Canada." In short, over the past several decades, immigrants have come to be significantly overrepresented among Canada's working poor, and they are finding it increasingly difficult to catch up with equivalently well-educated Canadian-born workers (Galarneau and Morissette, 2004).

Although the proportion of total income received by each population quintile shows how equally or unequally income is being distributed, it tells little about the standard of living of individuals and families within each quintile. For example, if total income doubled but the percentage received by each quintile stayed the same, the bottom 20 percent with their 4 percent of total income would now have twice as much income as before (of course, the same would apply to the top quintile, who would also have twice as much). In fact, when looking back over the past six decades, you find that average family income has increased by more than 150 percent, after taking inflation into account. In other words, the Canadian standard of living increased substantially in the decades following World War II. But most of this increase took place in the 1950s, 1960s, and 1970s. By the 1980s, inflation was typically as high as, or higher than, the income gains of Canadian families (Love and Poulin, 1991). In the 1990s, inflation declined but incomes did not really increase. Unemployment rates remained high, and deficit-cutting efforts by the provincial, territorial, and federal governments led to reductions in income-support payments to both the poorly paid employed and the unemployed.

During the first decade of the twenty-first century, unemployment rates have been relatively low, and government transfer payments have generally not been cut back further, but incomes have stagnated. In fact, a recent report by the Vanier Institute observed that, in constant dollars (in other words, taking inflation into account), average Canadian family incomes were no higher in 2005 than in 2000 and only about 1 percent higher than in 1990 (Sauvé, 2006). At the same time, average family debt had increased by

40 percent since 1990. In other words, despite Canada's strong economy in the early 2000s, Canadian families are less well off than they were 15 years ago.

Finally, how does income inequality in Canada compare with the situation in other countries? At the end of the last century, the highest earning 10 percent of Canadian families had incomes four times as high as the lowest earning 10 percent. Inequality was higher in the United Kingdom and the United States, where the comparable ratios were 4.5 and 5.4, respectively (Picot and Myles, 2005). But before we compliment ourselves too much for being a more egalitarian society, note that the highest to lowest income ratios were only 3.2 in Germany and Belgium and even lower in Sweden (3.0) and Finland (2.9).

THE POOR

Defining and Measuring Poverty

Poverty can be defined in different ways. We could talk about **absolute poverty,** arguing that the poor are those who have barely enough to stay alive, like many of the inhabitants of developing countries. Or we could concede, as most Canadians do, that **relative poverty** is really what matters. If your neighbours own their homes, drive cars, eat out at nice restaurants, put money into pension plans, and take vacations outside the country, while you rent a small apartment, ride the bus, look forward to a meal at McDonald's, have no savings, and read about foreign countries in the public library, you probably consider yourself poor. According to this definition, Canada does have a considerable number of poor people.

Most discussions of poverty in Canada rely on the **low-income cutoff** or **LICO** (commonly, though unofficially, known as the "poverty line"), estimated by Statistics Canada on the basis of data obtained from its ongoing Survey of Labour and Income Dynamics. According to this survey, the average Canadian spends about 35 percent of (pretax) income on the basic necessities (food, shelter, and clothing); to establish the LICO, Statistics Canada adds 20 percent to this figure. Hence, anyone spending more than 55 percent of gross income on the basic necessities is considered poor (see Box 6.3). Obviously, some people budget better than others, so these are average cost estimates. However, there is no denying that the cost of living is higher in larger urban centres and that it takes more money to feed and clothe additional

people, so different LICOs are calculated for communities of various sizes and for families of various sizes within those communities (National Council of Welfare, 2005). For example, based on 2004 income data, Statistics Canada set the (pretax) LICO for a single person living in a city with more than half a million residents at $20 337, compared with $14 000 for a single person living in a rural area. The low-income line for a family of three in a large city was $31 126, substantially higher than that for a similar-sized family in a rural area ($21 426).

Who Are the Poor?

Rising unemployment causes the number and proportion of people living below the poverty line to increase. In 1980, for example, 16 percent of all Canadians were below the poverty line but, with the recession of the early 1980s, that figure climbed to 18.7 percent by 1984. As the economy recovered, the proportion of poor Canadians dropped to 14.0 percent in 1989 but then rose again to 18.0 percent in 1993. Four years later, in 1997, little had changed—18.2 percent of all Canadians were still living below

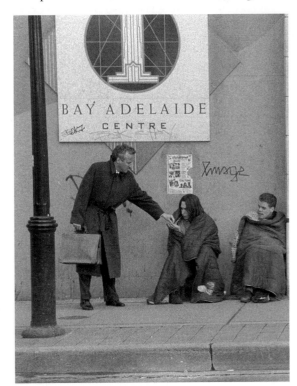

In 2001, Statistics Canada estimated that 14.4 percent of all Canadians were living below the LICO. Living on the streets is a dangerous alternative to a more socially acceptable struggle for survival.
SOURCE: Dick Hemingway.

Whenever a Canadian news outlet uses Statistics Canada numbers to say a certain percentage of Canadians are "below the poverty line," Statistics Canada makes it clear that its numbers say no such thing. The agency sends off letters stating that its low-income cut-off (LICO) figures are not a measure of poverty, but of income inequality. Despite this, many media companies and poverty activists use Statistics Canada's LICOs as Canada's "unofficial" poverty line.

The LICO counts the number of Canadians who spend 20 percent more of their gross income on food, shelter and clothing than the average Canadian. So, if a family spends more than 55 percent of its gross income on these necessities, it's below the LICO. About 17 percent of Canadians [14 percent in 2001] were below the low-income cut-off.

Critics of the use of the LICO as a benchmark for poverty say the 55 percent level is arbitrary and doesn't translate to a state of destitute poverty. A 2000 *National Post* editorial put it this way: "Say 54 percent of a family's income goes to food, shelter and clothing, it still has 46 percent to spend elsewhere. That's not poverty."

[A] feature of the LICO that causes controversy is that it's a relative measure of poverty. That is, as the economy grows and people make more money on average, the LICO moves up with it. "Using the LICO to measure the poor means poverty can never be eliminated since there will always be a range of incomes in Canada—unless we adopt a Soviet-style command economy," the *National Post* said in 2000.

Poverty activists argue that it's possible to reduce relative poverty without moving to a completely communist system. "In reality, relative poverty will not be reduced by economic growth unless there is redistribution to the poor," [Richard] Shillington wrote.

Another way to measure poverty is in absolute terms: how many people make less than what is needed to survive or lead a decent life? Human Resources and Development Canada is developing such a measurement, called the Market Basket Measure, based on the costs of goods and services needed for people to eat a nutritious diet, buy clothing for work and social occasions, house themselves in their community and pay for necessary expenditures, such as furniture, public transportation and entertainment. By that measure, most of the country's poverty is in Ontario and British Columbia, where the living costs are highest.

Nipissing University economics professor Christopher Sarlo developed another absolute measure of poverty for the 1992 study "Poverty in Canada." Sarlo defines poverty as lacking the means for the basic necessities of life, such as food, shelter and clothing. The first version of his Basic Needs Index put the poverty rate at just four percent. It was criticized for its frugality, though: Sarlo's weekly food budget for an elderly woman was $25. A revised version of the index was released in 2001, including such things as out-of-pocket medical expenses. That study put the poverty rate at eight percent.

SOURCE: "How Do We Measure Poverty" by Martin O'Malley and John Bowman, CBC News Online, 7 May, 2002. Updated 4 November, 2002 (http://cbc.ca/news/features/poverty_line.html).

the LICO. But by 2001, the proportion of poor Canadians had again dropped to 14.4 percent (National Council of Welfare, 2004).

Although poverty rates tend to follow unemployment rates, only a minority of Canada's poor are unemployed or out of the labour force. In 2001, for example, among low-income families whose major earners were under 65 years old, 50 percent of these families relied solely on earnings for their livelihood. Another 14 percent combined earnings and employment insurance, while the same proportion relied on earnings and social assistance. Only 22 percent did not work at all during the year, and many of these people were seniors or individuals with disabilities that kept them from finding jobs (National Council of

Welfare 2004). In short, the **working poor,** those employed in low-wage jobs, make up a very large proportion of the poor in Canada. Hence, not only rising unemployment but also any decline in real wages will lead to an increase in the number of people below the poverty line.

Aboriginal Canadians living on reserves and in other rural and urban centres are among the poorest citizens of our country (see Box 6.4). Unemployment rates among Aboriginal Canadians are more than twice as high as among non-Aboriginals (19 percent versus 7 percent, respectively, in 2001). Consequently, Aboriginal Canadians are also more than twice as likely to be living in low-income households (Statistics Canada, 2001).

[Provincial] government authorities began an emergency airlift [October 26, 2005] to move more than 1000 residents from an impoverished Indian reserve where drinking water was contaminated by raw sewage. . . . The evacuation was being carried out at Kashechewan, a Cree Indian reserve on the western shore of James Bay, about 600 miles north of Toronto. The water intake of the reserve, a riverbank community of about 1900, is downstream from a sewage outlet. Local Cree leaders have long complained about the water quality, but various federal agencies have argued over how to deal with it.

Lindsay MacMillan, a visiting physician in the town of Moose Factory, which has the closest hospital, went to the reserve by helicopter with another doctor on Saturday after hearing complaints of a spike in deadly *E. coli* bacteria followed by overchlorination of the water. "I was shocked," she said by telephone Wednesday from Moose Factory. "It was like a developing country. It was appalling to me that we were in Canada." . . . MacMillan said she found families crowded into homes and living in "extreme poverty."

SOURCE: ©2005, *The Washington Post*, reprinted with permission.

Single-parent families headed by a female are more than four times as likely as two-adult families with children to be living below the poverty line. In 2001, the poverty rates for these two groups were 42 percent and 10 percent, respectively (see Figure 6.3). The incidence of low income has really not changed since 1980 for two-adult families with children, while the equivalent statistic has dropped somewhat for female-headed single-parent families. Even so, four out of ten of the latter family units are living below the poverty line. Many are completely dependent on social assistance, since it is almost impossible for a single young mother to both look after children and hold down a job.

In 2001, 42 percent of senior Canadians (65 and older) living alone had incomes below the LICO, compared with only 6 percent of senior couples. It is clear that shared incomes among seniors (or anyone else, for that matter) typically keep people above the poverty line, whereas losing a spouse and her or his income can push many seniors below the poverty line. Also, because women are less likely to be employed outside the home, and since women typically earn less than men, older women living alone are less likely to have the pensions and savings that men in a similar position might have. Hence, in 2001, 46 percent of

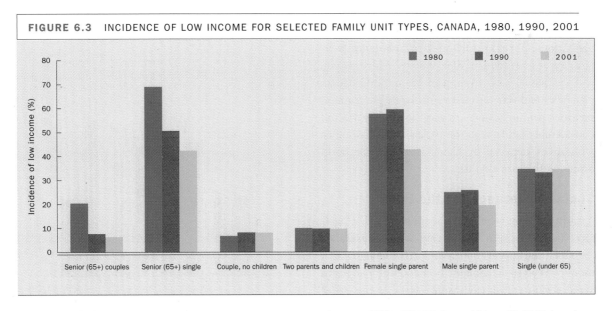

FIGURE 6.3 INCIDENCE OF LOW INCOME FOR SELECTED FAMILY UNIT TYPES, CANADA, 1980, 1990, 2001

SOURCE: National Council of Welfare, 2004, Poverty Profile 2001. Tables 1-6 to 1-12. Cat. no. SD25-1/2001-PEF. (Ottawa: Minister of Public Works and Government Services Canada).

single older women were in the low-income category, compared with only 33 percent of single older men (National Council of Welfare, 2004).

Figure 6.3 demonstrates that relative poverty among seniors has declined since 1980. Increased government transfer payments to older Canadians and an increase in the number of people retiring with personal pension plans and RRSPs form a large part of the explanation. In contrast, the poverty rate has not changed much for childless couples (under age 65), two-parent families with children, and non-senior (under 65) single individuals. In short, over the past decades, as labour market conditions have deteriorated and as governments have cut back on transfer payments, the working poor and the unemployed have come to make up a larger proportion of Canada's poor (Yalnizyan, 1998; Sauvé, 2006).

Although the low-income cutoff is a useful measurement tool, it can create an oversimplified picture of poverty in Canada, one that separates those who are poor and needy from those who are well off, without recognizing the large variations within each group. For example, in 2001, the depth of poverty for single women and men under age 65 who were living below the poverty line was much greater than for single men and women over age 65 (National Council of Welfare, 2004). Specifically, the average income for poor nonsenior singles was about 50 percent of the poverty line, compared with an average income of about 80 percent of the poverty line for poor senior singles. Why the difference? Because many nonsenior poor rely on social assistance (welfare) for at least some of their income, which, as you will see below, is far from generous in all Canadian provinces and territories. Even though government pensions paid to seniors are very small, they are still considerably larger than the typical social-assistance allowances received by Canada's nonsenior poor, assuming they are eligible.

Social Assistance for the Poor

A fairly common belief exists in our society that "welfare" (social assistance) and employment insurance are much too easy to obtain and that the amount of money received is enough to encourage people to avoid seeking work (Swanson, 2001). Is this true? Because welfare regulations vary across provinces and territories, we will examine data from Ontario, the largest province and among the provinces with the highest welfare incomes in 2004.

Figure 6.4 shows that a single "employable" adult (i.e., an adult who did not have a disability, was not a senior, and was not considered unable to seek work because of family responsibilities) who was eligible for Ontario social assistance received $6753 in 2004, an amount only one-third (34 percent) of the poverty line and less than one-third (31 percent) of the median income for single adults in the province (National Council of Welfare, 2005). Welfare recipients who had disabilities received a larger total annual transfer payment ($11 686), putting them at 59 percent of the LICO and at 53 percent of the median income for single adults with disabilities. Welfare rates for single parents were lower than those for people with disabilities ($10 784), an income level that placed them at 56 percent of the poverty line and at only 42 percent of the median income for all single parents in the province in 2004. Although welfare rates for couples with two children were the highest ($13 044), this amount was also intended to support more people. Consequently, even if receiving the maximum amount of social assistance, the income of these Ontario families would only have been half of the amount required to get above the poverty line, and only one-quarter (28 percent) of the median income for all couples with children in Ontario in 2004.

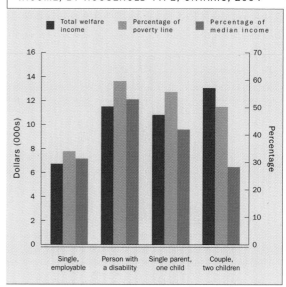

FIGURE 6.4 TOTAL WELFARE INCOME AS PERCENTAGE OF POVERTY LINE AND OF MEDIAN INCOME, BY HOUSEHOLD TYPE, ONTARIO, 2004

SOURCE: National Council of Welfare, 2005, Welfare Incomes, 2004. Tables 4.1, 5.1, and Appendix G. Cat. no. SD25-2/2004E. (Ottawa: Minister of Public Works and Government Services Canada).

In short, in Ontario and across Canada, the amount of welfare assistance provided is very low. In fact, welfare rates have been cut dramatically in every province and territory since the early 1980s (National Council of Welfare, 2005). In Ontario, for example, taking inflation into account, welfare rates were cut by about 50 percent for single employable adults, by about 20 percent for adults with disabilities, by about 70 percent for single parents, and by about 85 percent for couples with children. Consequently, it is difficult to accept the argument that overly generous welfare systems discourage people from looking for work. Many of those who receive assistance cannot work outside the home, and the money provided seldom pushes the poor who receive it anywhere even close to the poverty line.

Moving in to and out of Poverty

Discussions of poverty, such as this one, can leave the impression that the poor and the nonpoor are basically separate groups and that there is little mobility from one status to the other. In fact, Statistics Canada data show that, between 1993 and 1998, one in four Canadians (24 percent) lived in a low-income ("poor") family for at least one year (Morissette and Zhang, 2001). A similar but more recent analysis shows that, even with a strong economy, this picture had not changed: Between 1996 and 2001, 25 percent of all Canadians were living below the poverty line for at least one year (Statistics Canada, 2005: 122).

The earlier study provided a somewhat more detailed analysis, showing that just more than 8 percent of the total population experienced poverty (were in the low-income group) for four or more years out of a possible six. However, among Canadians living in lone-parent families, 38 percent had experienced poverty for at least four years between 1993 and 1998. Thus, poverty is not a static status. A sizable number of Canadians move into and out of poverty each year. Nevertheless, a small minority remain stuck in poverty year after year. As we noted above, losing a job, having to take a lower-paying job, becoming a single parent, or being widowed can drastically increase the chance of falling into, and remaining stuck, in poverty.

MATERIAL INEQUALITY IN CANADA: SUMMING UP

Is Inequality Increasing in Canada?

Compared with some other countries, and compared with the situation in Canada a century ago, the level of material inequality in this country today is relatively low. Even so, you have seen evidence of a great deal of inequality in wealth and income. Furthermore, there are indications that, for at least a decade and perhaps two, the level of inequality has been slowly rising. Corporate concentration has been increasing as a small number of huge business enterprises, many of them family-owned or family-run, have gained control over a larger share of the assets of Canada's biggest corporations. Wealth inequality in general appears to be increasing, income inequality has risen, and the number of working poor in Canada has increased.

Looking more closely at the labour market, we see that unemployment rates have been rising steadily for several decades. Although these rates have gone up and down a number of times, and are lower now than they were a decade ago, the long-term trend since the mid-twentieth century has been upward. Hence, in 2004, the average annual unemployment rate was 7.2 percent, representing 1.2 million unemployed Canadians, a number larger than the populations (children included) of Nova Scotia and Prince Edward Island combined. Similarly, the part-time employment rate has been rising. Forty years ago, fewer than 4 percent of employed Canadians worked part-time. Today, almost one in five (18 percent in 2004) has a part-time job. Since the 1980s, the number of temporary jobs has significantly increased, as employers have begun to cut long-term wage costs by offering more limited-term contract positions (Vosko, Zukewich, and Crawford, 2003). By 2004, one in eight (13 percent) working Canadians had a job with a specific end date (Krahn, Lowe, and Hughes, 2006). Real wages are no longer increasing, and inequality in earnings has risen as a result of polarization in hours worked (Hall, 1999).

A More Polarized Society?

It is difficult to avoid the conclusion that, in Canada, the gap between the advantaged (those with full-time, permanent jobs) and the disadvantaged (those with part-time, temporary, or no jobs) is slowly increasing (Vosko, Zukewich and Crawford, 2003; Yalnizyan, 1998). A similar pattern has been observed in Britain (Westergaard, 1995) and in the United States (Ryscavage, 1995). This is not to suggest that a new era of massive inequalities is dawning. However, the evidence is clear enough that material inequalities are rising, not declining, and that society is becoming more polarized in terms of access to and control over economic resources (Picot and Myles, 2005). Using

Weber's definition of class, I conclude that class differences in Canada and the United States (and in other countries like Britain) are becoming more pronounced.

Obviously, many interrelated factors are contributing to growth in material inequality (Krahn, Lowe, and Hughes, 2006). Although some new high-skill and well-paying jobs have emerged with the introduction of automated production technologies, the overall outcome still appears to have been a reduction in employment opportunities. Globalization, the process whereby goods and services are produced by business enterprises operating in many different countries, has led to a much more competitive economic environment. Business enterprises have responded by shifting some of their activities to countries in which lower wages and less rigorous environmental and labour laws allow higher profits to be made. In North America, layoffs and downsizing have been a frequent response, along with the replacement of full-time permanent jobs with part-time and temporary positions. Labour unions, which traditionally resisted attempts to cut wages and jobs, have lost some of their power. At the political level, a belief system or ideology emphasizing that "the market knows best" and that people need less rather than more government intervention in the economy and labour market has led to fewer government efforts to reduce material inequalities.

I will leave it to other authors in this text to examine associated economic, labour-market, political, and ideological trends in more detail, since this is a chapter on social stratification. Early in this chapter, I invited you to examine the evidence on changing patterns of social stratification in Canada and, while doing so, to keep in mind Clark and Lipset's (1991) question: "Are social classes dying?" Clark and Lipset answered yes, but given the evidence reviewed in this chapter, it would appear that they were wrong.

CONSEQUENCES OF MATERIAL INEQUALITY

Other chapters in this textbook will go into more detail about some of the many consequences of material inequality for individuals and families. You will see that position in the class structure has an effect on belief systems, behaviours, and lifestyles, and that the poor, the middle classes, and the very wealthy frequently

hold different opinions on various subjects, may vote differently, and certainly enjoy different lifestyles. But, much more important, people in different positions in society's economic hierarchy experience different life-chances, to use the term introduced by Weber.

Consequences for Individuals and Families

Children from poorer families typically do not do as well as more affluent children do in school, are more likely to drop out before completing high school (Tanner, Krahn, and Hartnagel, 1995), and are less likely to go on to higher education (Krahn, 2004). As noted above in the discussion of occupational mobility, such effects of poverty are largely responsible for the perpetuation of class inequalities from one generation to the next.

For a variety of reasons, including better nutrition, access to better health care, and less hazardous working conditions, those who are situated higher in the economic hierarchy are typically healthier than the poor (Raphael, 2004). On average, the poor do not live as long as those who are better off (Wilkinson, 1992). Similarly, when dealing with the criminal justice system, those with greater access to and control over economic resources tend to fare better (National Council of Welfare, 2001–02). The poor are consequently overrepresented in jails. I could go on, but these examples are probably sufficient to make the point that life-chances are a function of position in the class structure and that those higher up in the economic hierarchy enjoy a better quality of life.

Consequences for Society

In addition to these substantial consequences of material inequality for individuals and families, can material inequality have other social outcomes? Specifically, given the relatively high and increasing level of inequality in Canada, can we expect more social unrest? Will conflict between the "haves" and the "have-nots" increase? Those committed to a classical Marxist theory of social change might welcome such conflict; for them, it would indicate that capitalism was finally beginning to give way to a socialist society. Others might view such conflict much more negatively. Whatever the response to such a possibility, it is clear that values and beliefs directly influence the way the people respond to evidence of inequality and its consequences.

But returning to the question, can we expect an increase in social unrest and conflict as a result of higher levels of inequality? During the early 1980s, for example, the solidarity movement in British Columbia brought together members of trade unions, social-welfare organizations, and various community-based groups in opposition to the Social Credit government's cutbacks in government programs and attempts to change labour legislation. Bryan Palmer (1986) described the protests and rallies that took place as evidence of growing class conflict. However, these events were exceptional. Much more often, the poor and the near-poor put up with their less advantaged position because they have few of the resources (e.g., money, education, organizations) that make it possible to fight for social change (Brym, 1979). In fact, in the past few years, we have seen more opposition from a better-organized middle class, in response to government cutbacks in health and education, than from the poor in response to welfare cutbacks. And we have seen intensified negative stereotyping of the poor and those on welfare, a process that Jean Swanson (2001) calls "poor-bashing."

Thus, it is by no means clear that a higher level of inequality and fewer opportunities for upward mobility will translate into greater social unrest in Canada. Nevertheless, greater inequality means greater hardship and more limited life-chances for more Canadians. Although this chapter has documented growing social inequality in Canada, other chapters in this text describe similar processes globally. The long-term consequences for global peace and security as a result of a growing gap between rich and poor countries are difficult to predict. Even so, as Paul Krugman, the influential American economist, has noted: "The ultimate effects of growing economic disparities on our social and political health may be hard to predict, but they are unlikely to be pleasant" (Krugman, 1994: F9).

RESPONDING TO INEQUALITY

Some people believe that more equal distribution of society's resources would be preferable to the current level of inequality. They believe that the existing differences in life-chances are unjust and look for ways in which social institutions, laws, and tax systems might be changed to reduce material inequality. Others, equally offended by inequality and its consequences, reject this reformist approach in favour of a more radical position, advocating the replacement of capitalist society by some kind of socialist alternative. Still others respond to evidence of extensive inequality with little ambition to change it, believing, simply, that this is "the way things are." Although perhaps bothered by its consequences, members of this group might still conclude that the existing level of inequality is inevitable and that well-intentioned efforts to reduce it will, in the long run, have little effect. They might even conclude that inequality is functional, as Davis and Moore (1945) argued more than half a century ago, and that efforts to reduce it will be counterproductive. In short, reactions to the fact of inequality, and recommendations about what, if anything, should be done about it, directly reflect personal values and political orientation.

Assuming that a lower level of inequality *is* a goal worth striving for, it is clear that the government has a role to play in trying to reach that goal. The Canadian state has an impact on the distribution of wealth and income through tax systems that redistribute wealth from the rich to the poor; through minimum-wage and other types of legislation; and through transfer payments, such as pensions for seniors and those with disabilities, social assistance for low-income individuals and families, and employment insurance. Even so, compared with a number of other industrialized countries, Canada spends considerably less on attempts to reduce poverty (Yalnizyan, 1998).

Canada's "liberal" welfare policies place much more faith in the power of a free market, unregulated by government legislation and policies, to produce wealth and jobs that should, it is expected, trickle down to the poor (Esping-Andersen, 1990). Unfortunately, as the review of labour-market trends indicates, there is little evidence that the free market has performed successfully in this regard. Instead, unemployment rates have risen, precarious employment has become more common, and social inequality has increased. Furthermore, during the past several decades, the political mood has changed, and concerns about reducing government deficits, streamlining government, and making Canada more competitive in the global marketplace appear to have been influencing government policy much more than concerns about reducing inequality. In fact, some deficit-reducing initiatives (e.g., reductions in social-assistance payments) have led to increases in material inequality in Canada. But other approaches to government spending do not necessarily involve this tradeoff. For example, job-creation strategies may be as useful in the long run, and tax alternatives that would raise corporate income taxes or eliminate some of the tax write-offs enjoyed by the upper and middle classes (such as tax deductions for pension plans and RRSPs) might also be appropriate.

A large part of the problem lies, of course, in the fact that any serious effort to redistribute the wealth and income from the well-off to the poor would probably be opposed by the former. If we really want to do something about material inequality in Canada, and globally, if we want a different kind of society and a different kind of world, many of us have to be willing to accept less so that others can have more.

SUMMARY

1. Persistent patterns of social inequality within a society are referred to as a structure of social stratification. Some social hierarchies within a society are based on ascribed statuses, such as gender, race, or age, which are typically assigned to an individual at birth. Other social hierarchies are based on achieved statuses, which index how well an individual has performed in some role. A society in which considerable social mobility between statuses is possible is said to have an open stratification system.

2. Social theorists have proposed a variety of different explanations of the origins and effects of social-stratification systems. In his class-based theory of social stratification, Karl Marx emphasized the exploitation of the working class by the owners of the means of production and the capacity of class conflict to generate social change. Max Weber also put considerable emphasis on the power that resides in ownership of property but argued that hierarchies of prestige and political power are influential as well.

3. The structural-functionalist theory of social stratification suggests that inequality is both inevitable and functionally necessary for a society, ensuring that the most qualified individuals are selected to fill the most important (and most rewarding) roles. Power differences are downplayed in this theory, as is conflict between different social classes. A number of more recent theories of social stratification, including those put forward by Gerhard Lenski, Frank Parkin, and Erik Olin Wright, have placed more emphasis on power and conflict. Although Wright developed a class-based theory of stratification that adapts many of Marx's ideas to contemporary circumstances, Parkin's approach follows in the footsteps of Weber.

4. Examination of occupational shifts in Canada over the past century reveals some of the changing features of Canada's stratification system. Studies of occupational mobility reveal that Canada is a relatively open society. Even so, considerable evidence suggests that class-based advantages are often passed from one generation to the next.

5. A detailed analysis of material inequality in Canada reveals that ownership of wealth and property is highly concentrated and that income inequality is relatively high. By using a relative measure of poverty, we observe that about one in seven Canadians is living below the "poverty line." Considerable evidence shows that the poor and others near the bottom of the social hierarchies in our society enjoy fewer life-chances than do the well-off. For example, they are less likely to do well in school and to continue on to higher education, they are less healthy and have a shorter life expectancy, and they do not fare as well when dealing with the criminal justice system. Because of their limited access to social and material resources, the poor have seldom become an active force for social change.

6. Some theories of social stratification developed in the middle of the twentieth century suggested that material inequality was declining as the North American economy expanded. However, the period of rapid economic growth and relative affluence that characterized the middle decades of the century appears to have ended. And, as unemployment rates rise, as part-time and temporary work becomes more common, and as governments cut back on social-assistance programs, evidence accumulates that material inequality is also slowly increasing in Canada.

QUESTIONS TO CONSIDER

1. Does social class play a more or less significant role than do ascribed statuses (such as race and gender) in determining patterns of inequality within Canadian society?

2. How are social and material advantages passed from one generation to the next, resulting in persistent patterns of social inequality?

3. What role, if any, should governments play in addressing persistent patterns of social inequality? How successful have such attempts been in the past?

4. What does "poverty" really mean, and how should we measure it? Does Christopher Sarlo's "absolute poverty" approach (see Box 6.3 on page 162) make more sense than the "relative poverty" approach underlying Statistics Canada's low-income cutoffs?

5. As Canada becomes a more culturally diverse country, what are the implications of high levels of poverty among immigrants and Aboriginal peoples?

GLOSSARY

Absolute poverty is the state of existence of those who have so little income that they can barely stay alive.

Achieved status is a changeable status that is acquired on the basis of how well an individual performs in a particular role.

Ascribed status is a status, such as age, gender, or race, that is assigned to an individual, typically at birth, not chosen by the individual.

The **bourgeoisie,** according to Marx, is one of the two main classes in the capitalist mode of production. It comprises the owners of the means of production.

A **caste system** is a closed stratification system, most common in India, with strict rules regarding the type of work that members of different castes (the strata of society into which people are born) can do.

Circulatory mobility is the occupational mobility that occurs within a society when better-qualified individuals move upward to replace those who are less qualified and who must consequently move downward.

Class is a position in an economic hierarchy occupied by individuals or families with similar access to, or control over, material resources.

Class conflict, according to Marx, is conflict between major classes within a mode of production. It eventually leads to the evolution of a new mode of production.

Class consciousness, according to Marx, is the recognition by members of a class of their shared interests in opposition to members of another class.

Class structure is the relatively permanent economic hierarchy comprising different social classes.

A **closed stratification system** is a stratification system in which little or no social mobility occurs, because most or all statuses are ascribed.

Contradictory class locations, according to Erik Olin Wright, are the locations within a class structure populated by occupational groupings with divided loyalties (e.g., managers who both supervise others and report to owners).

Exclusion, according to Frank Parkin, is the organized effort of privileged, more powerful groups to maintain their advantaged position.

Intergenerational occupational mobility refers to an individual's occupational mobility, either upward or downward, in relation to her or his parents' occupational status.

Intragenerational occupational mobility refers to an individual's occupational mobility, either upward or downward, within his or her own lifetime.

Life-chances, according to Weber, are the opportunities (or lack thereof) for a higher standard of living and a better quality of life that are available to members of a given class.

The **low-income cutoff (LICO),** also known unofficially as the "poverty line," is an estimate of the income level below which one might be considered to be living in relative poverty. It is defined by Statistics Canada as the level of income at which more than 55 percent of income is spent on basic necessities.

The **means of production,** according to Marx, is one of the main components of a mode of production, consisting of the technology, capital investments, and raw materials used in production.

A **meritocracy** is a society in which most or all statuses are achieved on the basis of merit (how well a person performs in a given role).

The **mode of production,** according to Marx, is the overall system of economic activity within a society, comprising the means of production and the social relations of production.

Occupational status attainment refers to the process whereby an individual obtains a particular occupational status, and the factors that influence this process.

An **open stratification system** is a stratification system in which merit, rather than inheritance (or ascribed characteristics), determines social rank.

The **petite bourgeoisie,** according to Marx, is a secondary class within the capitalist mode of production, including independent owners/producers (e.g., farmers) and small-business owners.

Power is the ability to impose one's wishes on others.

The **proletariat,** according to Marx, is one of the two main classes within a capitalist mode of production, comprising workers who exchange their labour for a wage.

Relative poverty is a state of existence in which individuals have significantly less income than most others in their society, causing their lifestyle to be much more restricted and their life-chances substantially curtailed.

Social closure, according to Max Weber and Frank Parkin, refers to the methods used by more powerful groups to maintain their unequal access to status and resources and to exclude others from such access.

Social mobility is the process whereby individuals, families, or other groups move up or down a status hierarchy.

Social relations of production, according to Marx, are one of the main components of a given mode of production—specifically, the relationships between the main classes involved in production.

Social stratification refers to persistent patterns of social inequality perpetuated by the way wealth, power, and prestige are distributed and passed on from one generation to the next.

Socioeconomic status refers to a person's general status within an economic hierarchy, based on income, education, and occupation.

Status is a culturally and socially defined position that a person occupies in a group.

Structural-functionalist theory is a school of thought that views social organization as analogous to a biological organism or system, in which the parts (or organs) exist because of the functions they perform in maintaining the whole. Thus, stratification exists because of vital functions it performs in maintaining social equilibrium.

Structural mobility refers to the occupational mobility within a society resulting from changes in the occupational structure (e.g., the upward mobility of many individuals resulting from the creation of more middle- and upper-level jobs in the economy).

Surplus value, according to Marx, is the value added to a product by labour (i.e., the profit taken by the owners when the product is sold).

Usurpation, according to Frank Parkin, is the effort of excluded groups within a stratification system to gain advantages and power at the expense of more powerful groups.

The **working poor** are individuals who work but whose income leaves them below a designated low-income, or poverty, line.

SUGGESTED READING

Curtis, James E., Edward Grabb, and Neil Guppy, eds. (2004). *Social Inequality in Canada: Patterns, Problems, and Policies,* 4th ed. Toronto: Pearson/Prentice Hall. A comprehensive collection of readings on the various dimensions of stratification in Canada.

Grabb, Edward G. (2002). *Theories of Social Inequality,* 4th ed. Toronto: Harcourt Canada. This advanced but readable book discusses various theories of social inequality, some of which were summarized in this chapter.

McMullin, Julie. (2004). *Understanding Social Inequality: Intersections of Class, Age, Gender, Ethnicity, and Race in Canada.* Toronto: Oxford University Press. An insightful advanced undergraduate discussion of the bases of social stratification in Canada.

Swanson, Jean. (2001). *Poor-Bashing: The Politics of Exclusion.* Toronto: Between the Lines. A social activist takes a critical look at how the poor and welfare recipients in Canada are stereotyped and mistreated by the media and government, and offers some useful suggestions for social change.

WEB RESOURCES

Companion Web Site for This Book

http://www.newsociety5e.nelson.com

Begin by clicking on the Student Resources section of the website. Next, select the chapter you are studying from the pull-down menu. From the Student Resources page, you have easy access to InfoTrac College Edition® and other resources, such as the Glossary and Flashcards. The website also has many useful tips to aid you in your study of sociology.

InfoTrac College Edition Search Terms

Visit http://www.infotrac-college.com for access to more than 20 million articles from nearly 6000 sources when doing your online research.

ThomsonNOW™

http://hed.nelson.com

This online diagnostic tool identifies each student's unique needs with a Pretest that generates a personalized Study Plan for each chapter, helping students focus on concepts they are having the most difficulty mastering. Students then take a Posttest after reading the chapter to measure their understanding of the material. An Instructor Gradebook is available to track and monitor student progress.

CHAPTER SEVEN

Gender Inequality: Economic and Political Aspects

In this chapter you will learn that

- A major source of inequality between women and men is the greater exclusion of women from public economic and political activity. The persistent tendency of many women to be relegated to domestic affairs leads to less income, prestige, and power.

- Although women have entered politics and the paid labour force in increasing numbers over the past century, they still tend to be chiefly responsible for meal preparation, cleaning, laundry, and child-care.

- In the paid labour force, women and men still tend to be segregated in different kinds of jobs; "women's jobs" typically pay less, carry less prestige, offer less security, and bestow less authority.

- Although women make up more than half the Canadian population, only one in five members of Parliament is a woman.

- In recent years, employment equity policies and policies requiring equal pay for work of equal value have been implemented to help lessen gender inequalities, but much research and political action are still required before gender equality is achieved.

Monica Boyd
UNIVERSITY OF TORONTO

INTRODUCTION

As we look back on the twentieth century, we see enormous change in the attitudes, expectations, and behaviours of women and men. Compare the lifestyle of typical men and women born in 1925, 1950, and 1975. The pair born in 1925 would have been 25 years old in 1950. During the 1950s, they would almost certainly have married and had children. In the 1950s, most women were expected to work exclusively in the home and take complete responsibility for domestic affairs. **Social roles** are the behaviours that are expected of people occupying particular social positions. In the 1950s, women's roles were those of wives and mothers. In contrast, men were expected to have paying jobs, and their responsibilities were to meet their family's needs for food, clothing, and shelter. Their roles were those captured by the terms "provider" and "head of household."

In contrast, by the time the pair born in 1950 turned 25, the belief that women should marry and work exclusively in the home was rapidly eroding. The average age at marriage had increased, indicating that many women and men were postponing marriage. After divorce laws were revised in 1969, divorce rates rose, signalling that fewer women and men would have a single spouse for the duration of their adult lives. Other changes were blurring the line between work in the home and work in the labour force. Men were starting to become more involved in household maintenance and childrearing, and more women were joining the paid labour force.

The scenario for the pair born in 1975 and turning 25 in 2000 is different again. Most people born during the mid-1970s still see themselves as eventually having spouses or partners and raising children. Unlike the generation born in the 1920s, however, they probably also see themselves as sharing domestic responsibilities with their spouse or partner and as both holding paid jobs.

A changed world does not, however, mean an equal world. Although we often hear about the "revolution" in gender equality that has taken place in recent decades, the revolution is not finished. As I show in this chapter, gender inequality still exists: In your lifetime, you have probably seen and are likely yet to see at least some of the gender inequalities discussed here. At the same time, you are also likely to witness a variety of interventions aimed at reducing those inequalities.

I begin with a definition of gender inequality and then explore its major aspects and the three main arenas in Canadian society in which gender inequality is evident: the home, the labour force, and politics. I end with a review of the actions, policies, and laws that could reduce gender inequality in the future.

UNDERSTANDING GENDER INEQUALITY

GENDER INEQUALITY DEFINED

Social scientists usually refer to inequalities between men and women as "gender inequalities" rather than "sex inequalities." They favour *gender* because it refers to the *social* meanings associated with being a man or a woman, whereas *sex* refers to the *biological* characteristics of men and women. Gender is found in social roles, in daily interactions, and in institutions (Andersen, 2005; Martin, 2003; Wharton, 2000).

Gender Stereotypes

To better understand the gendered nature of roles, think about such words as "provider" and "caregiver." They do more than describe the expected behaviour associated with being a partner in a

Through parental behaviour and the media, children learn to define certain social behaviours as inherently male or female. A male child is likely to receive stuffed animals, trucks, and play toolkits, while a girl more often receives dolls, play dishes, and play makeup. SOURCE: Photos.com.

marriage; they also cause people to evaluate types of behaviour as "masculine" or "feminine." Once in place, these images of masculinity and femininity influence how people see themselves and how they experience the world. The observation that "it's a boy" often causes Canadian parents to decorate the child's room in bold colours, or at least in pale blue as opposed to pink. A male child is likely to receive stuffed animals, trucks, and play toolkits rather than the dolls, play dishes, and play makeup that are likely to be given a girl. Through parental behaviour, television, movies, and print media (including schoolbooks), children learn to define certain social behaviours as inherent in being chromosomally male or female, even when such traits are largely learned. By the time children have grown into adults, they have adopted and identified with many "masculine" or "feminine" personality traits and behaviours. In turn, they are likely to treat others around them through the lenses of their own identities and understandings of masculinity and femininity. In many instances, these conceptualizations are **gender stereotypes**—that is, oversimplified beliefs about how men and women, by virtue of their physical sex, possess different personality traits and, as a result, may behave differently and experience the world in different ways.

The cartoon below illustrates a gender stereotype. Of course, no shopping or hunting gene exists. Gender-related identities and behaviours are largely socially constructed. They are outcomes of the way we interact with others and encounter taken-for-granted rules and ways of doing things in families, schools, the legal system, politics, and the paid workplace (West and Fenstermaker, 1993).

The fact that gender is largely learned and that its content is continually renewed and altered through social interaction has three implications:

1. Gender identities and behaviours are not stable and fixed (see Chapter 4). What people take to be masculine or feminine varies from one society to the next and, within any given society, over time.
2. Gender identities—the internalized sense of being a man or a woman—and gender-specific behaviours need not be congruent with the sex assigned to individuals at birth.
3. Just like sexuality and sex, gender identities and behaviours are not polar opposites (Gagne and Tewksbury, 1998; Segal, 1998). Images of masculinity and femininity often emphasize opposites but there are in fact *degrees* of masculinity and femininity.

A fixation on the allegedly opposed characteristics of men and women is evident in such phrases as the "opposite sex" and *"vive la différence."* Psychological studies of gender stereotypes also lead us to conclude that most people think of men and women as opposites. In one famous study, psychologists asked respondents to indicate which traits, from a checklist of 122 adjectives, characterized average men and women. They found that men were described as very aggressive, very independent, very active, very competitive, very logical, able to make decisions easily, and almost always acting as leaders. Women were described as not at all aggressive, not at all independent, very emotional, very passive, not at all competitive, very illogical, able to make decisions only with difficulty, and almost never acting as leaders (Broverman, Vogel, Broverman, Clarkson, and Rosenkranz, 1972).

SOURCE: ©KING FEATURES SYNDICATE.

These results were obtained from respondents in the late 1960s; a study today would almost certainly have some different results. However, a Canadian sociologist, Marlene Mackie (1980), still found evidence of polarized gender stereotypes in research conducted about a decade later. The persistence of stereotypical thinking about feminine and masculine characteristics as polar opposites should sensitize you to two things. First, the idea of difference is apparently a powerful one and hard to dispel even when it is contradicted by research. Second, in these polarized depictions, feminine traits are viewed as less desirable than masculine ones.

Dimensions of Inequality

Gender stereotypes shape our attitudes about girls and boys, men and women, and they are often important factors in determining the ideologies that perpetuate gender inequalities. Sociologists usually define **gender inequalities** as hierarchical asymmetries between men and women with respect to the distribution of power, material well-being, and prestige (as recognized through deference or honour). This definition does not imply that men as individuals always have greater prestige, wealth, and power than do individual women. It does imply that, *on average*, compared with women, men have more wealth, greater power, and positions that are accorded higher prestige.

Power is the capacity to impose your will on others, regardless of any resistance they might offer. It thus refers to the capacity to influence, manipulate, and control others. Power is exercised not only in the overt imposition of the will of one individual on others but also in the control or support by groups or organizations of agendas that either uphold or challenge existing conditions (Duffy, 1986). For example, professorial power over students not only reflects professors' capacity to assign grades but also the authority that the university gives them in the classroom.

Material well-being involves access to the economic resources necessary to pay for food, clothing, housing, and other possessions and advantages. Two important sources of material well-being are work-related earnings and accumulated wealth.

Prestige is the average evaluation of occupational activities and positions that are arranged in a hierarchy. It reflects the degree of respect, honour, or deference generally accorded to a person occupying a given position. Commonly, two or more differently evaluated positions are described as having higher or lower prestige. How would you rank someone who works as a physician and someone who works as a cashier at a fast-food outlet? In general, people rank the former above the latter.

The three dimensions of inequality just defined—power, material well-being, and prestige—are found in discussions of social stratification, the unequal ranking of groups in society in terms of prestige, material possessions, and power (see Chapter 6). Stratification is the result, achieved over time, of routine and frequently recurring practices and often unstated rules. Gender inequality is social stratification based on gender.

What explains gender inequalities in prestige, material well-being, and power? What form do these inequalities take? I will now examine these issues in turn.

EXPLAINING GENDER INEQUALITY

As sociology developed during the twentieth century, the earlier neglect of gender by the fathers of sociology ceased. New theories emerged that explained gender inequality and its persistence. It was mainly women who developed these theories, and they frequently included insights taken not just from sociology but also from other disciplines (Chafetz, 1999; Lengermann and Niebrugge-Brantley, 1996; Lorber, 1998). **Feminism** refers to the body of thought on the cause and nature of women's disadvantages and subordinate position in society and to efforts to minimize or eliminate that subordination. Because many different perspectives exist on the sources of gender inequality, we can discuss a variety of feminist theories.

Of the many feminist theories that exist, liberal, Marxist, and socialist feminism are three popular explanations for gender inequalities in Canada's economy and polity. Liberal feminism is rooted in the liberalism of the 1700s. It assumes that human beings are rational and will correct inequalities when they know about them. Liberalism assumes that a good society is one in which men and women enjoy equal rights and opportunities. According to liberal feminism, gender inequalities are caused and perpetuated by gender stereotyping and the division of work into "women's" and "men's" jobs. Accordingly, the two main ways to achieve gender equality are by (1) removing gender stereotyping and discrimination in education and paid work and

(2) changing laws so that men and women have equal opportunities in the labour force and in politics (Lorber, 1998).

A different perspective on gender inequality derives from the writings of Karl Marx. According to Marxist feminists, women's unpaid work in the home maintains and reproduces the labour force. Capitalists benefit because they obtain refreshed workers at the beginning of each day and mothers raise children who will become future labourers. They also benefit from women's paid work because women in the paid labour force, like men, help capitalists earn profit and because they act as a "reserve army of labour" that can be hired and fired as labour demands change. Marxist feminists believe that gender equality is possible once socialism replaces capitalism.

Socialist feminists build on Marxist feminism. They agree that gender inequality is caused by the gendered division of labour and its exploitation by capitalism. However, they argue that classes constitute only one set of social relations that oppress women. The second set of social relations that performs this function is that of patriarchy, the system of male domination over women. Patriarchy predates capitalism. The forms it takes vary across time and within societies. But generally, childbearing and the sexual activities of women are the foundation of gender inequality. Moreover, because domestic and public spheres intersect, inequalities in one sphere can create disadvantages for women in the other sphere. (The "public sphere" refers to government and the world of paid work.) For socialist feminists, the steps required to decrease gender inequality include government-subsidized maternal benefits and child-care, and the payment of equal wages and salaries to people who do equally valued work. Removing inequality altogether requires the eradication of male dominance as expressed in the legal system, the educational system, the family, and the economy (Chafetz, 1999; Jaggar, 1983; Lorber, 1998).

Many other feminist theories also exist. Multiracial feminism emphasizes the importance of race in understanding gender inequality. This approach modifies the socialist feminist perspective by observing that hierarchical systems of domination incorporate race. For sociologist Patricia Hill Collins (1990), race, class, and gender combine to form a "matrix of domination." All three intersect, so the way that people experience gender inequality depends on their location within class and racially defined structures (Chafetz, 1999; Lorber, 1999; Zinn with Dill, 1997). Multiracial feminism contributes to our understanding of gender inequality in three ways. First, it highlights differences among women in terms of gender inequality. Second, it points out that women of specific races and in certain class locations are in positions of power and domination over other groups of women. Third, it emphasizes that solutions to gender inequality vary according to the location of groups of women in the matrix of domination.

EXERCISING POWER

Since the ability to control and influence others—to use power—indicates the twin processes of domination and subordination, most sociologists describe the power relations between men and women as those of male domination and female subordination.

Male influence and control over women is broadly defined. It does not, for example, refer just to the predominance of men rather than women in political positions or in the military. Instead, power pervades all social relations, routine behaviours, and commonly accepted practices. For example, denying women the right to vote clearly denied them a voice in choosing who would govern them and, equally important, denied them direct input into the formulation of laws that affect them, bestowing that right on men instead. Similarly, a workplace regulation that encouraged or compelled women to quit work upon marriage, such as the one that existed in the federal civil service until 1955, made it difficult for married women to earn income and forced many of them to depend on their husbands for money. Power is also evident in day-to-day situations, such as when a young woman becomes the object of sexual innuendo or leering by her male classmates, co-workers, or strangers. In our society, such behaviour on the part of males is often considered "normal"; it draws on conceptualizations of femininity and masculinity that define women as "sexy" or "available" and men as sexual aggressors. If she protests such attention, a woman may discover that she is the object of further derision and that no rules or formal appeal mechanisms exist to stop or penalize the offenders. In short, she cannot prevent or protest unwanted attention that arises from the social meanings attached to her biological sex.

Sexual harassment is essentially a display of power in which one person attempts to control, and often succeeds in controlling, another through sexual overtures. Although isolated cases of women harassing men have received attention from the press, in most cases of sexual harassment, it is the man who makes the sexual overtures. When the capacity or incapacity to control and influence becomes routine and patterned, we can speak of power as a *system* of dominance and exploitation.

Sexual harassment is the result of the general belief that men are superior to women and may impose their will on them. It is also the outcome of patterned ways of behaving that are based on this belief and that serve to reinforce it. For example, because of our society's higher evaluation of men (and its corresponding devaluation of women), men are more likely to be employed in positions in which they are the bosses and women are supervised by them. The harassment potential that is associated with this imbalance of power is evident in such situations as a female secretary working for a senior-level male manager or a female assembly worker supervised by a male foreman.

Gender inequalities in power also combine with racial inequalities. As a result, minority women experience the most harassment because they are both women and members of a minority group (Berdahl and Moore, 2006). For these women, the experience of harassment is doubly problematic since it includes not only sexual harassment but racial harassment as well. It also is problematic for immigrant women who, as recent arrivals, are uncertain of their rights and may have had different understandings in their home country as to what constitutes sexual harassment (Welsh, Carr, MacQuarrie, and Huntley, 2006).

SEPARATE SPHERES

Power relations are important for understanding inequality because power, prestige, and material well-being are often interrelated. For example, although the ability to control others does not necessarily depend on having a higher income or being wealthy, wealth and high income normally bestow power, just as power normally enhances the capacity to be wealthy and earn high income. In seeking to understand gender inequalities, researchers point out that, historically, women have been excluded from certain types of activities that create opportunities for acquiring power, prestige, and wealth. During the late 1800s and for much of the 1900s, the "proper place" of Canadian women was thought to be in the home,

where they would be responsible for producing and raising the next generation (Ursel, 1992). They were not expected to participate in politics, to enact legislation, or to be employed. The denial of voting rights for women until the end of World War I and the existence of legislation that limited the hours and times when women could be employed limited their participation in the public sphere. The public sphere was viewed as the domain of men, who were expected to be the breadwinners and heads of households.

What have been the consequences of the separation of the public sphere for men and the private sphere for women? To answer this question, consider what is implied by work in the home. For family members, work in the home, including child-care, is unpaid, and, all too frequently, the amount of skill, effort, and energy expended is not widely noticed because most housework is not done in the presence of husbands. Adding to the devaluation of work in the home is the tendency to view nurturing and care-giving activities as biologically determined traits rather than acquired skills.

Restricting women to the home reduces their access to power, prestige, and material well-being. Although a woman who works only in the home may receive part of the income of another household member, she is dependent on the person who hands over the money. Economic dependency, in turn, is likely to produce asymmetries in power between the woman and the income earner, who, after all, can withhold money for the purposes of control or influence. Similarly, if all her activities are limited to the private sphere, a woman cannot obtain direct access to power through political representation, political office, or favourable laws.

Finally, because material well-being and power are so closely connected to deference and respect, the societal evaluation of work done in the home is not high. One classic indication of the devaluation of housework is the phrase "just a housewife." Sociological research shows that many activities done in the home, such as cooking, cleaning, and babysitting, are not high in prestige (Armstrong and Armstrong, 1994: Table 16). The low regard for housework is also evident from interviews conducted with 1200 17-year-olds in Hamilton, Halifax, and rural Nova Scotia. Sociologists Dianne Looker and Victor Thiessen found that young people view housework as women's work. They consider it tiring since it involves long hours, high pressure, and much boredom. It generates few financial rewards. It is unimportant for the community. And young men consider housework—especially if it is full-time—to be a job at the bottom of the occupational hierarchy (Looker and Thiessen, 1999).

In short, the belief that a woman's place is in the home disadvantages women relative to men in the distribution of prestige, power, and economic resources. Recognition of these disadvantages has elicited two main responses. First, some people have tried to eliminate the devaluation of domestic labour by having women's unpaid work recognized officially and having a dollar value assigned to it. In Canada, women's unpaid work was recognized officially in the 1996 census. After intense lobbying, questions on unpaid child-care, unpaid home maintenance, and unpaid eldercare were included in the census (Luxton and Vosko, 1998). Assigning a dollar value to women's unpaid work was raised in feminist discussions in the 1970s and there is still interest in measuring the value of unpaid work today. One Statistics Canada economist estimated that unpaid domestic work, if done in the market for wages, would be worth about one-third of the gross national product (the total value of market-produced goods and services produced in the country over a year). He also found that women do about two-thirds of all unpaid domestic work (Jackson, 1996).

The second response to the recognition of women's disadvantages emphasizes the entry of women into the public sphere. Women's growing labour-force participation and their political activities are often viewed optimistically because many people think these developments generate more money and power for women. Liberal feminists are especially likely to hold this view. Yet the fact that women are now part of the public sphere of paid work and politics does not mean that gender equality exists. Women's **labour-force participation rate** is still lower than men's. (The labour-force participation rate is the proportion of women of working age who work full-time for money, expressed as a percentage.) Women are still less likely to become elected politicians than men. Paid work does not mean liberation from unpaid work, as you have seen. And substantial gender inequality remains in the labour force and in the political sphere. In the remainder of this chapter, I examine the movement of women into the public sphere, their continuing disproportionate involvement in unpaid work in the home, and the inequalities that still exist today in the public sphere.

SITES OF WORK

FEMALE LABOUR-FORCE PARTICIPATION

In the past, most work done by women was unpaid domestic labour. In the early days of Canadian settlement by Europeans, women processed food, wove fabric, sewed clothing, tended the sick, and produced the next generation of labourers. Women also took in boarders, did laundry, and prepared meals for others in their homes (Phillips and Phillips, 1983).

Canadian women continue to work in the home, but in the past 50 years, they have increasingly done work that is paid and usually performed outside the home. At the beginning of the twentieth century, only 14 percent of women were economically active in the paid labour force compared with 78 percent of men (Leacy, 1983). By 2005, slightly more than 60 percent of women were in the paid labour force, compared to just over 70 percent of men (Statistics Canada, 2006a).

The marital status of the female labour force participants also changed dramatically during the twentieth century. Until the 1960s, the typical female worker in the paid labour force was a never-married woman, but today married women constitute the majority. The labour-force participation rate of women with young children has also increased substantially. By 2004, almost two-thirds of women with their youngest child under the age of three were employed in the paid labour force, more than double the proportion in the mid-1970s (Statistics Canada, 2006b: Table 5.5).

Explaining the Increase

Three factors caused these changes in the women's labour-force participation rate: changes in Canada's economy that increased the demand for workers in service jobs, decreases in the number of children born, and increases in the financial pressures on families. These factors altered attitudes toward the paid employment of women and helped remove barriers to such employment. I'll review each of them in turn.

Canada's Changing Economy In the early 1900s, most Canadian jobs were in agriculture or manufacturing. Starting in the 1920s, more and more jobs became available in firms that provided services:

telephone communication, financial assistance, medical care, educational instruction, and so forth. Women were often considered suitable employees for the newly emerging service jobs. By the early twentieth century, women—albeit mainly young and single women, in accordance with the prevailing belief that married women belonged in the home—had already supplanted men as office workers (Lowe, 1987) and teachers (Prentice, 1977). With respect to office work, this development was made possible by the introduction of the typewriter, which was thought to lower the skill requirements of secretarial work. Hiring women as teachers and secretaries was also appealing because they could be paid lower wages than men on the strength of the belief that women were economically supported by the men in their household anyway.

Fertility Decline and Labour Supply Declining fertility also facilitated women's entry into the paid labour force, since it created an imbalance between the labour demands of the expanding service economy after World War II and the available labour supply. Canada's fertility rates dropped substantially during the 1930s and early 1940s as a result of the Depression and World War II. Consequently, the supply of new workers was relatively small when the postwar Canadian economy boomed. There were too few men and young single women—the traditionally preferred source of labour—to meet the growing demands for labour in Canada's new service-based economy. In response to labour scarcity and the desire to minimize wage costs (Connelly, 1978), employers began loosening restrictions against the hiring of married women. The fact that married women were not averse to working for wages—indeed, that they were eager to do so—had been proved by the experience of their employment during World War II (Pierson, 1977). As a result, female labour-force participation rates increased rapidly in the postwar years.

Family Finances Family finances also influenced the rise in female labour-force participation. Despite the idea that a woman's proper place was in the home, women's employment had always been an important source of income for low-income families. To meet economic needs, many working-class women were employed as domestics and in factories during the late 1800s and early 1900s. After World War II, women's paid employment became an important source of

family income for single-parent and two-adult families alike. Today, one in five families is headed by women who are single parents, most of whom work in the paid labour force (Statistics Canada, 2006b: Table 2.6 and Chart 5.3). Census data show that when single-parent mothers are employed, average family income is more than 2.5 times higher than that reported by families without earnings from the mother. In husband-wife families, wives' earnings not only increase family incomes but also help to keep many families out of poverty, particularly when the husbands earn little or nothing (Statistics Canada, 1998: 15).

DOMESTIC LABOUR

"Though she may toil from sun to sun, a woman's work is never done." The exclusion of women from the public sphere was part of a more general predicament in which women were almost solely responsible for

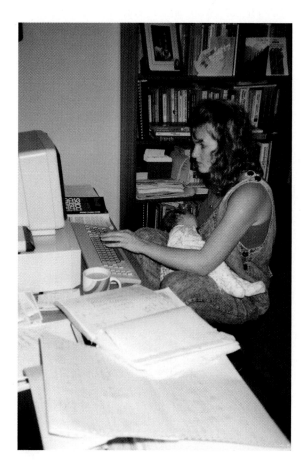

Women normally shoulder the burden of dual responsibility—for child-care as well as for wage earning. Women also spend more time than their male counterparts on housework and child-care.
SOURCE: Photo courtesy of Rhonda Lenton and Talia Lenton-Brym.

unpaid domestic production and for work associated with reproduction (bearing and rearing children). Canadian women cooked, cleaned, and took care of children, and men provided the money necessary to sustain the family. Has this structure changed with the rising labour-force participation of women?

If you think that the answer is "no," you are correct. My analysis of 2001 census data shows that women are still more likely than men to do unpaid work involving home maintenance and child-care. Women also spend more hours than men do on these activities. Both women and men are less likely to be caring for seniors than to be doing home maintenance or child-care, although women are more often caregivers for seniors than men are.

Even when they are in the paid labour force, married women continue to spend more time than married men do on housework and child-care. Figure 7.1 shows that, compared with married men, higher percentages of married women spend 15 hours or more on housework and on child-care among those who have at least one child under age 15 in the household (see Chapter 10 for more on housework).

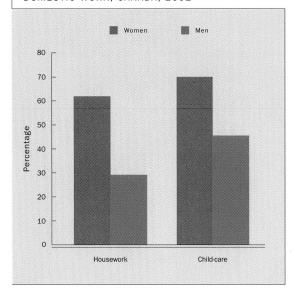

FIGURE 7.1 PERCENTAGE OF MEN AND WOMEN DOING 15 OR MORE HOURS PER WEEK OF DOMESTIC WORK, CANADA, 2001

Note: The graph refers to unpaid housework and child-care by employed married women and men with at least one child under the age of 15 in the household.
SOURCE: Adapted from the Statistics Canada product "Individuals File (Flat ASCII File), 2001 Census (Public Use Microdata Files)," Catalogue 95M0016XCB, released April 26, 2006.

Not surprisingly, women report spending less time than men do watching television, pursuing hobbies, and playing sports and games (Devereaux, 1993). Also, women are more likely than men to report feeling stressed because of lack of time. This is especially true for women who are working full-time and who have young children (Statistics Canada, 1999: 2).

The greater amount of time spent by women on unpaid work illustrates the phrase "the double day." Entering the labour force may mean fewer hours spent on work in the home, but it increases the hours of total work, paid and unpaid, performed by women. In fact, the demands on women to provide unpaid care likely will increase, because the number of senior Canadians in need of care will increase substantially. Past caregiving patterns suggest future providers of care are most likely to be women (Frederick and Fast, 1999).

In addition to increasing hours of unpaid work, caregiving responsibilities alter the way women and men lead their lives. Consider Grace, who is in her early fifties, has teenage children, and also has an 80-year-old ailing parent living nearby. She represents what is called the "sandwich" generation—individuals caught between the demands of caring for children and older relatives. As she cares for her children and parent, Grace is likely to cut back on her social activities, move closer to her parent, report that her own health is affected, and experience altered sleep patterns. The strongest impact, however, is on paid work. Grace is likely to find that caregiving activities cause her to arrive late at work, leave work early, or miss work occasionally (Cranswick, 1997; Williams, 2004). Clearly, the domestic sphere and the public spheres intersect. What people do (or don't do) in one sphere affects their activities in the other.

LABOUR-FORCE INEQUALITIES

OCCUPATIONAL SEGREGATION AND SEX TYPING

Liberal feminists explain the fact that unpaid caregivers tend to be women by referring to gender stereotypes and gender roles. Gender stereotypes imply women are generally thought to be more caring and therefore better caregivers. Gender roles emphasize that "good" daughters, wives, and mothers are women who care for their parents, partners, and offspring. Socialist feminists note that caregiving is consistent with other activities that maintain male wage workers and benefit men.

The equation of women and caregiving is also found in paid work. Although more and more Canadian women are now paid workers, they are frequently in jobs that involve caregiving, nurturing, and the sort of management functions typically found in the home. Women tend to be secretaries (the "office wife"), nurses, social workers, teachers, seamstresses, and wait staff. In contrast, men tend to be managers, doctors, professors, and factory and construction workers. This concentration of men in some occupations and women in others is often called the **sex segregation of occupations,** and the notion that a given occupation is appropriate for one sex versus the other is referred to as the **sex typing (or sex labelling) of occupations.**

Occupational Segregation

Men and women can be compared across occupations in a given place (a firm, a city, or a country). If men and women are concentrated in different occupations, the occupational structure is considered sex-segregated. Figures 7.2 and 7.3 show that, according to the 2001 census, sex segregation does exist in Canada. For women, the ten most frequent jobs include secretary, registered nurse, elementary schoolteacher, babysitter, and receptionist. For men, the ten most frequent jobs include truck driver, jan-

itor, retail trade manager, farmer, carpenter, and so on. The only occupation that both men and women occupy in large numbers is retail salesperson.

The figures show only the top ten occupations. The census collects information on more than 500 different occupational titles. These longer lists confirm that women and men often are concentrated in different occupations. The degree of occupational segregation by gender has, however, declined somewhat since the 1960s. This decline is attributable mainly to the movement of women into previously male-dominated occupations rather than that of men into female-dominated occupations.

Sex labelling of occupations usually accompanies occupational segregation. Certain occupations are seen as jobs that are more appropriate for women. Other occupations are seen as jobs that are more appropriate for men. Often these views are so ingrained in our thinking that we recognize sex labelling (or "sex typing") only when unstated expectations are contradicted. Consider the terms *woman doctor* and *male babysitter.* We frequently use these terms to indicate a departure from the implied norm—that men are physicians and women are babysitters. We rarely say "female babysitter" Or "male doctor." Or consider the list of the ten most frequent occupations for men and women. What

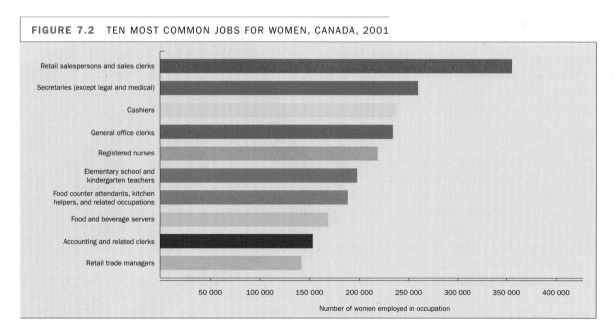

FIGURE 7.2   TEN MOST COMMON JOBS FOR WOMEN, CANADA, 2001

SOURCE: Adapted from the Statistics Canada publication "Canda's Workforce: Paid Work, 2001, Census," Catalogue 97F0012XIE2001021, released Februrary 11, 2003.

FIGURE 7.3   TEN MOST COMMON JOBS FOR MEN, CANADA, 2001

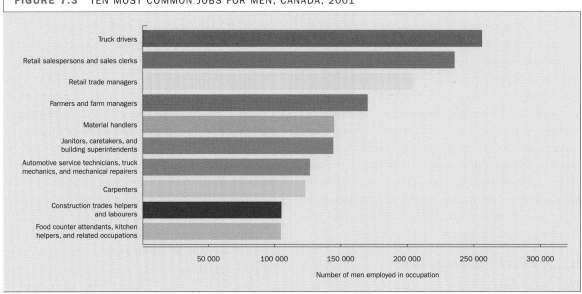

Truck drivers
Retail salespersons and sales clerks
Retail trade managers
Farmers and farm managers
Material handlers
Janitors, caretakers, and building superintendents
Automotive service technicians, truck mechanics, and mechanical repairers
Carpenters
Construction trades helpers and labourers
Food counter attendants, kitchen helpers, and related occupations

50 000   100 000   150 000   200 000   250 000   300 000

Number of men employed in occupation

SOURCE: Adapted from the Statistics Canada publication "Canada's Workforce: Paid Work, 2001 Census," Catalogue 97F0012XIE2001021, released Februrary 11, 2003.

gender comes to mind for *secretary, nurse,* or *receptionist* or for *truck driver, farmer,* or *carpenter?* These occupations are strongly sex-typed both in imagery and in reality.

The fact that women are now about 47 percent of the labour force is a yardstick by which occupations are female sex-typed or male sex-typed. In such occupations as actor, cook, dispatcher and radio operator, journalist, optometrist, school principal or administrator, and veterinarian, 45 percent to 50 percent of workers are women. These occupations are not sex-typed (Statistics Canada, 2001b).

Why Care?

Why should you be concerned about sex typing and sex segregation? Because the occupations in which women are concentrated are often lower than those held predominantly by men in terms of authority, responsibility, skill requirements, mobility opportunities, and earnings. I will discuss many of these inequalities later. The important point for now is that these inequalities indicate male advantages in the labour force. Furthermore, the nature of sex typing in our society implies that the work traditionally performed by women in the home has created sex stereotypes about the work that women should do in the paid labour force.

POWER AT WORK

You have seen that substantial occupational segregation exists, but to document gender asymmetry in the ability to influence and control others you need to know whether men are indeed able to make more

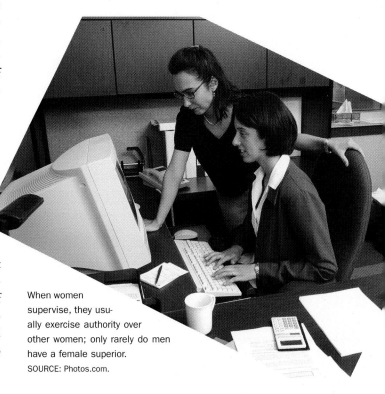

When women supervise, they usually exercise authority over other women; only rarely do men have a female superior.
SOURCE: Photos.com.

decisions and exercise authority over women. In analyzing the 1994 Statistics Canada General Social Survey, my colleagues and I found that men were more likely than women to describe their jobs as managerial or as supervising others. Specifically, 25 percent of women and 40 percent of men described themselves as supervisors. Male supervisors managed more employees than did female supervisors. Male managers were more likely than female managers to hold top positions and plan the activities of all parts of the business (Boyd, Hughes, and Miller, 1997). This pattern illustrates the **glass ceiling** effect: Women face invisible barriers that prevent them from penetrating the highest levels of organizations where power is concentrated and exercised (see Box 7.1). Finally, men often supervise women; when women supervise, they usually exercise authority over other women. Only rarely do men have a female superior (Boyd, Mulvihill, and Myles, 1991: 424).

GENDER AND SKILL

Jobs typically held by women have lower skill requirements than jobs typically held by men (Boyd, 1990; Myles and Fawcett, 1990). Since higher-skilled jobs usually pay more and offer more security, employment in lower-skilled jobs implies economic and quality-of-work inequalities between men and women.

Why are women less likely than men to be employed in high-skilled jobs? One possible answer is that gender bias exists in the definition of **skill.** Sex typing and a general devaluation of work done by women influence commonsense evaluations of what is or is not "skilled" work. For example, nursing occupations may require high levels of interpersonal skill in dealing with relatives of dying patients but because the ability to handle distraught people is considered "natural" in a woman, it is not recognized as a professional skill in a nursing occupation. In contrast, plumbing jobs, usually performed by men, require knowledge of toilets and sinks, soldering, and pipe fitting—so-called technical skills. Bias in the evaluation of skills occurs when such technical knowledge is considered more valuable than knowledge about personal interactions and caregiving.

This example indicates that our definitions of skill are socially constructed. What we define as skill reflects other social evaluations and hierarchies—in this case, hierarchies based on gender (Gaskell, 1986; Steinberg, 1990). If people think of women as being worth less than men, they are inclined to let their attitude influence how they define the skill requirements of jobs held primarily by women or primarily by men. Jane Gaskell (1986) suggests that women are disadvantaged in the skill definitions assigned to jobs sex-typed as female because, historically, women have not been represented by strong

---

BOX 7.1   CORPORATE CANADA MAINTAINS THE GLASS CEILING

It's lonely for women who have managed to slip through a crack in the almost impervious glass ceiling.

Of the 500 highest-paid executives in Canada's 100 largest public companies, only 23 are females.

A study of the 2005 executive compensation filings of those companies, with revenues ranging from $2.2 billion to $30 billion a year, found fewer than two dozen of the 497 chief executive officers, chief financial officers and other top executives are women. That's 4.6 percent. . . .

"We've heard a lot of talk over the past decade or so about women breaking through the glass ceiling," said Jay Rosenzweig, managing partner of Toronto executive search firm Rosenzweig & Company, which conducted the study.

"But clearly these numbers speak volumes as to how much action—or inaction—has occurred in filling the highest executive positions with women. There remains great hesitancy to give women the key to the top five executive officer jobs."

. . . This is the first time Canada's top five executives at the top 100 public companies have been scrutinized. But a study last year by Catalyst found more than 14 percent of all executives are women and it will take 20 years to reach even 25 percent.

Critics point out women have been in the workforce in droves for several decades and now make up 46.6 percent of workers. Yet the pace of change at the uppermost levels has been evolutionary rather than revolutionary.

SOURCE: "Too few female execs: survey" by Meredith Macleod. *Hamilton Spectator,* January 19, 2006. Reprinted by permission.

unions that have lobbied in their interest. Furthermore, women are less likely to be trained on the shop floor as apprentices. Instead, the training required for "female" jobs is often incorporated into high-school curricula, with the result that the skill-training component is less visible than it is in occupations in which training is provided on the job.

Skill undervaluation of female sex-typed occupations is a concern for two reasons. First, wage levels are associated with skill requirements. Thus, if the skill requirements of jobs in which women predominate are undervalued, the pay rates in those jobs are likely to be lower. Second, current pay equity policies often ask whether men and women are receiving equal pay for performing jobs of comparable worth. The "worth" of a job, however, includes its skill requirements. If the skill requirements of jobs employing predominantly women are already devalued, then fair comparisons between appropriate sets of jobs may not be made (Gaskell, 1991; Steinberg, 1990).

NONSTANDARD WORK

Another example of gender inequality may be seen in **standard** and **nonstandard work.** If asked to describe a typical job in the labour market, you would probably mention full-time, full-year employment with job-related benefits. This is usually what we mean by standard work. In contrast, nonstandard work includes **part-time work,** part-year employment, limited-term contract employment, employment through temporary-help agencies, self-employment, and multiple job-holding (Economic Council of Canada, 1991: 71; Krahn, 1995). Nonstandard work, also called precarious employment, is more common for women than for men (Cooke-Reynolds and Zukewich, 2004; Cranford, Vosko, and Zukewich, 2004).

Women and Part-Time Work

Compared with men at every age, women in the labour force are much more likely to be part-time workers—nearly three times more likely than men in 2000 (Statistics Canada, 2001b: Table 7). This is significant because part-time work has been increasing as a share of all employment. Many workers now take part-time employment because they cannot find full-time employment.

Nurses may be required to deal with dying patients and their relatives, but because the ability to handle distraught people is considered "natural" in a woman, this high level of interpersonal skill is not recognized as a professional skill in a nursing occupation. SOURCE: Photos.com.

Women and Nonstandard Work

Since 1980, women have made up around 70 percent of the part-time labour force. Part-time work can thus be seen as an employment ghetto for women. Women are also overrepresented in nonstandard work defined more broadly. Using a definition of nonstandard employment that includes self-employment, temporary work, part-time work, part-year work, and multiple job-holding, a 1994 Canadian study found that 40 percent of all currently employed women, compared with 27 percent of men, were working in nonstandard employment (Krahn, 1995). These levels of nonstandard work remained stable through the 1990s and early 2000s (Vosko, Zukewich, and Cranford, 2003: Chart A).

Concerns about Nonstandard Work

Employment in nonstandard work is of concern for two reasons. First, it is becoming more common, especially among young people. Second, compared with full-year, full-time jobs, nonstandard jobs generally provide less job security, lower pay, and fewer fringe benefits, such as pension plans (Duffy and Pupo, 1992). Thus, nonstandard employment in general and part-time work in particular imply a marginal work force—marginal in terms of earnings, benefits, and job security.

EARNINGS

In addition to gender inequalities in occupations, power, skill, and type of work, women in Canada earn less than men on average—70.5 cents for every dollar earned by men in 2003 for full-time, full-year workers (Statistics Canada, 2006b: Table 6.9). As we can see from Figure 7.4, this ratio represents gradual improvement from earlier times.

Explanations of Women's Lower Pay

Observers have explained the pay gap between women and men by focusing on four factors:

1. gender differences in the characteristics that influence pay rates
2. gender differences in the type of work performed
3. discrimination
4. societal devaluation of women's work

Explanations that focus on gender differences in the characteristics that influence pay rates usually assume that earnings reflect the productivity of workers and that productivity is increased by more education, labour-force experience, and length of time on the job. Advocates of this explanation argue

that the lower wages of women are caused by lower productivity resulting from women's lower educational achievements and labour-force interruptions because of women's family responsibilities.

Explanations that focus on gender differences in the type of work performed assume that the gender gap in pay reflects the concentration of women in certain occupations and industries characterized by low wages, including nonstandard (particularly part-time) work.

Explanations that focus on discrimination argue that women are paid less than men because of their gender. Such discrimination can be personal and deliberate, but it is often impersonal, produced by standard, unquestioned practices, such as assigning women to certain jobs and men to other jobs, and paying men and women different wages even when they hold the same job. Much of this impersonal discrimination is called **statistical discrimination,** the process whereby employers make decisions about whether to hire and how much to pay any given woman on the basis of the employers' perceptions of the average characteristics of *all* women. For example, if an employer believes that women typically leave the labour force for long periods to raise children, or will not travel extensively or work overtime because of family responsibilities, the employer may impose those generalized beliefs on particular women. Thus, a single woman with no children might find herself being paid less than a man because of the employer's belief that women in general are less productive than men. Alternatively, she might find herself denied opportunities for job training or advancement because of her employer's belief that women in general will leave their jobs to have families or will not perform certain tasks, such as long-distance travelling, because of family obligations.

Finally, explanations of the gender earnings gap that focus on the societal devaluation of women's work hold that the lower earnings of women reflect a general devaluation of "women's work"—that is, of tasks initially performed in the home—and the incorporation of that devaluation into pay practices. As we have seen, the work women perform in the home can be invisible and often is not viewed as work. Accordingly, people who do domestic work for money receive low wages. The devaluation of women's labour is rooted in the historical image of every woman having a male breadwinner to provide for her and not "needing" to be paid the same wage as a man who, after all, has a family to support! Once in place, pay practices persist

FIGURE 7.4 RATIO OF WOMEN'S TO MEN'S EARNINGS, CANADA, 1967 TO 2003

Note: Earnings are expressed in constant 2003 dollars
SOURCE: Statistics Canada, 2006 Table 6.9.

and fuel a faulty logic that not only sustains pay differences between men and women in the same jobs but also provides a rationale for the lower wage rates paid in sex-typed occupations and jobs. Wages in occupations fall as the percentage of women in those occupations rises (England, 1993: ch. 3).

Assessing the Explanations

Most sociologists emphasize discrimination and the devaluation of work performed by women (explanations 3 and 4) as the main reasons for gender inequality in earnings. They point to the absence of proof that women are less productive than men or that they expend less effort (England, 1993: 27). They also observe that earnings gaps persist even when women and men have comparable levels of education, are in full-time, full-year jobs, and are in the same occupations (Best, 1995; see Box 7.2).

BOX 7.2   MORE WOMEN THAN MEN CALLED TO BAR, BUT MALES STILL EARN MORE ON AVERAGE

After centuries of being outnumbered by men, women aren't simply making inroads into the legal profession. In sheer numbers, they're starting to dominate.

The majority of law graduates admitted into the profession in Ontario yesterday and today—53 percent to be precise—are women. The Law Society of Upper Canada hasn't seen anything like it in its 205 years.

Until 1999, there were still more men being called to the bar than women. In 2000, the sexes tied. [In 2001], women inched ahead for the first time and made up 51 percent of new lawyers. Overall, they now account for about a third of the profession.

In some cases men still have the upper hand when it comes to partnerships and pay. At the beginning of their careers, male and female lawyers earn about the same, but between ages 30 and 34, men earn about $7,900 per year more on average. That rises to $16,000 more for male lawyers between 35 and 39, according to a report prepared for the law society last year.

Between ages 40 and 49 men make about $35,000 more a year on average, about $65,000 more between 50 and 54.

SOURCE: Tracey Tyler, "More women than men called to bar. But males still earn more than average." Reprinted with permission of Torstar Syndication Services. Excerpted from an article originally appearing in *The Toronto Star* February 22, 2002, p. A18.

BIRTHPLACE AND COLOUR MATTER

So far, my discussion of gender inequality in work has proceeded as if all women were alike and all men were alike. This is of course not the case. Some women and men are young and others are older. Some are married or living with a partner, others are not. Some women are born in Canada, others are born elsewhere. In addition, women differ in their colour and ancestral origins, as do men.

The intersection of gender inequality with inequalities stemming from birthplace and colour is of interest to many Canadians. That interest is fuelled by the changing ethnic and colour composition of Canada's population, initiated by changes in Canada's immigration policies starting in 1962. It has become evident since then that foreign-born women and women of colour experience not only gender inequality but also the inequalities that arise in a society that allocates privileges to certain groups and not to others on the basis of colour, ethnicity, birthplace, and class.

In popular and official usage, members of a **visible minority** are Canadian residents who are not of white European and U.S. origin and who may consequently experience discrimination. However, the term is an umbrella label for diverse groups.

Government statistics lead us to four conclusions about the earnings of women who are members of visible minorities:

1. Women who are members of Aboriginal or visible-minority groups are more likely than white women to be employed in low-skill occupations. Such occupations include cleaning hotel rooms and offices and working in manufacturing jobs in food-processing plants and the textile industry. Many workers in Canada's garment firms are immigrant women of colour, and their jobs are often characterized by irregular employment, deadlines, bad lighting, poor ventilation, and low pay (Das Gupta, 1996; Yanz, Ladd, Atlin, and Maquila Solidarity Network, 1999).

2. Foreign-born women who are permanent residents of Canada and who are members of visible minorities earn less on average than their Canadian-born counterparts. My research shows that the earnings gap increases between Canadian-born and foreign-born women when foreign-born women of colour have no knowledge of English or French (Boyd, 1999).

3. Overall, women who are members of Aboriginal or visible-minority groups earn less per week than women who are not members of visible-minority groups. My own research and that of others show that earnings differentials persist between women who are and women who are not members of visible-minority groups, even when we account for the fact that differences between groups can exist with respect to age, education, and other factors that influence the levels of earnings (Pendakur and Pendakur, 1998). This means we cannot rule out discrimination as a factor and that at least part of the lower earnings of women who are members of visible-minority groups and Aboriginal women may be caused by employers not hiring these women for certain jobs, promoting them slowly, or paying them less.

4. Considerable diversity exists among women in their labour-force characteristics. Thus, we should not think of women as a homogeneous group.

These findings reaffirm the criticisms voiced by women who are members of minority groups and foreign-born women—namely, that, for them, inequality issues are not restricted to gender but also include race and immigrant status, and that each group is unique in the kinds of disadvantages and subordinations it experiences. These criticisms are consistent with multiracial feminism.

WOMEN'S GROUPS: ORGANIZING FOR CHANGE

So far, I have discussed the increasing movement of women out of the home and into the labour force. The economy, however, is only one of several arenas in the public sphere from which women have historically been excluded and in which their participation remains very limited. Politics is another important arena that initially excluded women and that women have now begun to penetrate. The political arena includes more than voting or running for political office. It can be broadly defined to include any activity that mobilizes people to make their views known, to press for change, and to achieve objectives.

Collective actions aimed at such change are called **social movements.** The **women's movement** is a social movement that takes action to improve the status of women. Feminism is an important part of the women's movement. However, as I observed ear-

lier, many different forms of feminism exist, each with a different understanding of the causes of gender inequality and subordination and of the actions required to improve the situation.

Over time, changes have occurred in feminist thought and in the nature of the women's movement. Both before and immediately after women were granted the right to vote, early efforts focused on improving the quality of life in the home for women and their families (Brodie, 1996). The large-scale entry of women into the paid labour force during the 1960s and 1970s elicited a different set of concerns. Based on a model of equal rights between women and men, women pressed for gender equality in employment opportunities and earnings.

Beginning in the 1960s, advocacy groups, some closely affiliated with the federal government, such as the Advisory Council for the Status of Women, and others receiving substantial government funding, presented agendas for change to parliamentarians, ministers, and key civil servants in government departments. Such direct interaction with the formal agencies and members of the state achieved some successes, depending on the party in power and how robust the economy was. For example, through the lobbying efforts of various groups, women's rights are now enshrined in the 1982 Canadian Charter of Rights and Freedoms, and legislative changes ensure a fairer division of assets in divorce cases. However, the efforts of women's groups have been limited by at least three factors (Burt, 1993). First, because many women's groups rely on governments for funding, their roles as critics of government policy can be easily compromised. They may change their agendas or adopt a conciliatory style. The consensus-building approach found in many women's organizations constitutes a second constraint on their effectiveness. This decision-making style can be time-consuming and it can place groups at a disadvantage given that political interventions often require quick reactions. The heterogeneity of women's groups is a third factor limiting their impact. There are many different women's groups, and not all of them agree on what should be done for women. For example, diverse opinions exist among women's associations on child-care issues and on access to abortion; it is often impossible to create a coalition to lobby for one clear policy.

Women's groups still lobby governments for change, but during the 1980s and 1990s three factors changed the interaction between women's groups and governments: the electoral success of more conservative parties; the federal government's calls for economic restraint and increased provincial/territorial and private-sector responsibility; and the dissatisfaction within women's advocacy groups on agendas reflecting the concerns of white, largely middle-class women (Tremblay and Andrew, 1998). By the mid-1990s, political representatives and departments of federal and provincial governments (which in the case of Quebec and Ontario had also taken leadership on certain issues, such as pay equity) were no longer as responsive to lobby efforts by women's groups. They reduced funding. In 1995 the federal government reorganized their units dealing with women's issues and disbanded the Canadian Advisory Council on the Status of Women, which had been mandated to inform the public and the Canadian federal government on issues of concern to women. Alongside all these changes, a different model of advocacy emerged in which women's groups operated in coalition with other social-movement-based groups, often rejecting networking and direct contact with political parties (Erickson, 1998; Young, 1998).

Recently, associations that represent the interests of women of colour, immigrant women, and lesbians have added much to the landscape of women's associations in Canada. The attention they have directed to issues of racism, sexual identity, and class inequality has forced mainstream groups representing primarily white, heterosexual, and often middle-class women to become more inclusive in their membership base and their agendas. Women of colour have argued that these groups fail to acknowledge concerns other than those of white middle-class women. The mainstream argument that gender subordination reflects the restriction of women to the private sphere fails to recognize that many women of colour have always engaged in paid work and that issues of racism in employment are of equal importance for them. Furthermore, to the extent that women of colour work as domestics, it is white women who have power over them as their employers; women of colour tend to see both gender oppression and racial oppression as important issues. Immigrant women have their own concerns, including language training, job-skill training, culturally sensitive child-care, and culturally sensitive assistance in situations of domestic violence. For lesbians, areas of interest include gay rights and related issues,

such as the inclusion of sexual orientation in human rights codes and the prohibition of employment discrimination on the basis of sexual orientation.

GENDER IN POLITICS

> The voice of government, as the [1971] Royal Commission on the Status of Women observed. . ., is still a man's voice. Women remain governed rather than governors, legislated rather than legislators. (Brodie, 1991: 9)

Formal politics is an important area of gender inequality because that is where laws determining rights and entitlements are formulated and public policies set. Politics and political representation are the mechanisms that translate the interests of groups into political demands and actions (Brodie, 1991: 9). If some groups are politically disenfranchised or face barriers to the representation of their interests, their needs may not be met and the premise that democratic governments represent all the people is falsified. For the first 50 years after Confederation, the notion that the private sphere was the appropriate place for women went hand in hand with the exclusion of women from politics. During the twentieth century, however, women moved into the political arena. They obtained and exercised the right to vote. They participated in political parties and were elected to political office. And they created associations to represent the interests of women, including access to abortion and child-care; equality in the labour force and pensions; the prevention of family violence (including spousal violence and child abuse), prostitution, and rape; and participation in politics.

VOTING RIGHTS

Before 1915, Canadian women did not have the right to vote. Without that right, they could not elect candidates to represent their interests in government. Between 1916 and 1925, however, all provinces and territories except Quebec and the Northwest Territories enfranchised women. Quebec granted women the vote in 1940, and the Northwest Territories did in 1951. The federal government granted voting rights in 1917 to women who were British subjects and who had served with the military or had a close relative in the military. It extended those rights to women not connected to the military in 1918. But voting rights were not given to women or men of Chinese, East Indian, or Japanese ancestry until the late 1940s, to male and female Inuit until 1950, or to registered Indians living on reserves until 1960 (Maille, 1990: 1).

The suffrage movement in English Canada was a factor in winning the vote for women (Bashevkin, 1993: ch. 1). However, the vote was granted on the premise that women would use it only to improve the quality of home life and that enfranchisement would not divert women from their "natural and sacred" duties in the domestic sphere (Burt, 1993: 216).

Such sex stereotyping of women also led to the expectation that women would not be interested in politics. Men believed that women would not vote at the same rate as men. Men also believed that women would vote in a politically naïve and parochial way as a result of being isolated at home. These stereotypes proved false. In Canada today, the percentage of eligible voters who cast a ballot is about the same for women and men. The political agendas of men and women differ but not because women's views are parochial. Research shows that women are more likely than men to oppose free markets and military spending and to be more concerned with social-welfare policies (Bashevkin, 1993: ch. 2). Gender differences in voting interests may be due to the fact that women and men operate in different political cultures (which have been moulded by gender differences in political socialization) and have different opportunities to participate in politics. Again and again, women hear that "politics is a man's world." Excluded from political life, women are more likely to be concerned with moral and community-based political issues than with issues pertaining to the acquisition and exercise of power (McCormack, 1975: 25–26). However, women do not act as a cohesive voting bloc on any issue (Brodie, 1991).

PARTICIPATING IN THE WORLD OF POLITICS

In the mid-1970s, women composed fewer than 4 percent of Canada's members of Parliament (MPs). After the January 2006 federal election, 21 percent of MPs were women, as were 35 percent of all senators (Table 7.1). However, enthusiasm over such progress should be tempered by the recognition that women represent more than half of Canada's electorate. Table 7.1 shows variations by party in the percentages of federal MPs who are women, with the highest per-

centage (41 percent) in the New Democratic Party (NDP). These differences reflect such factors as the recruiting strategies of parties and barriers to women in politics, both of which are discussed later in this chapter. Other variations exist. My analysis of women who were sitting in the House of Commons in late 2002 shows that 9 of the 63 women were foreign-born, which is below the percentage in the female Canadian population as a whole. Also, visible minorities in general, and visible-minority women in particular, are underrepresented in politics (Black, 2000; Ship, 1998; Trimble and Arscott, 2003).

When elected, women are seldom found in the upper ranks of political parties. Kim Campbell served briefly as prime minister of Canada in 1993. However, the presence of women in the upper echelons of power is rare enough to be newsworthy. If gender made no difference, why would the cover of *Maclean's* run a photo of Kim Campbell over the caption "When the

TABLE 7.1 FEMALE FEDERAL POLITICAL REPRESENTATIVES, CANADA, JUNE 2006

	TOTAL	WOMEN	PERCENTAGE WOMEN
House of Commons			
Conservative	125	14	11
Liberal	102	21	21
Bloc Québécois	50	17	34
Independent	1	0	—
NDP	29	12	41
Vacant seats	1	—	—
Total	308	64	21
Senate			
Liberal	65	22	34
Conservative	23	8	35
Progressive Conservative	3	1	33
NDP	1	1	100
Independent	5	2	40
Vacant seats	8	—	—
Total	105	34	35*

SOURCE: www.parl.gc.ca (March 29, 2006).
*Excludes the eight vacant Senate seats.

Canadian Governor General Michaëlle Jean and U.S. Secretary of State Condoleezza Rice are exceptions to the scarcity of women, particularly women who are members of visible-minority groups, in the top echelons of power.

SOURCE: Tom Hanson/CP Picture Archive.

Boss Is a Woman" (October 4, 1993) and why would newspaper articles describe what MP Brenda Stronach was wearing? Governor General Michaëlle Jean and U.S. Secretary of State Condoleezza Rice are also exceptions who demonstrate the scarcity of women, particularly women who are members of visible minorities, in the top echelons of power.

Table 7.1 illustrates the truth of the saying "the higher, the fewer" with respect to the participation of women in Canadian political parties. Sylvia Bashevkin (1993: ch. 3) found that women are more likely to be local riding secretaries (as opposed to presidents) and that they do the necessary clerical work, paralleling the "pink ghetto" of female-typed clerical work found in the labour force. In the 90 years since most women gained the vote federally, only three women have been elected as party leaders, all within the last two decades. Audrey McLaughlin served as leader of the NDP between 1989 and 1995; Kim Campbell was leader of the Progressive Conservatives (PCs) between June and December 1993; and Alexa McDonough was leader of the NDP from 1995 to 2003 (Young, 1997: 82).

EXPLAINING THE POLITICAL PARTICIPATION OF WOMEN

Five major explanations exist for the underrepresentation of women in Canadian politics. The first focuses on sex-role stereotypes. It argues that certain characteristics of women keep them from participating in politics. According to this argument, women are less assertive than men, more oriented to family than to politics, and conditioned through childhood socialization to view politics as an inappropriate activity (Brodie, 1991). This explanation is less popular than it once was because it stereotypes all women, failing to acknowledge that the traits of men and women often overlap and that women have diverse traits. Moreover, this explanation invokes the behaviour of men as the standard, implying that women are "deficient," and that the problem is to be found in women rather than in the characteristics of political life.

The second explanation for the underrepresentation of women in Canadian politics reverses the emphasis by arguing that the culture of politics is "male" and therefore hostile to the participation of women. Descriptions of political life as "gladiatorial" create the image of a blood sport in which the stakes are the acquisition and display of power (Bashevkin, 1991). Such an environment creates a chilly climate for women, who may have interests beyond domination and who may prefer to resolve conflicts in non-confrontational ways. Thus, in their research on the media coverage of women politicians, Gertrude Robinson, Armande Saint-Jean, and Christine Rioux (1991) found that, before the 1970s, the portrayal of women MPs emphasized such themes as that of the spinster or the club woman, or focused on the politician's relationship to significant family members, including her husband, as the reason for her political success. All these themes emphasized a woman's gender and looks or affiliation rather than her competence. Between the 1970s and 1990s, new labels and stereotypes came to be used, but they still failed to evaluate women's political competence. Robinson, Saint-Jean, and Rioux (1991: 142–46) describe these new labels and stereotypes as follows:

- *Superwoman:* A young, intelligent, active, and ambitious woman who succeeds on all levels and has it all
- *Champion:* Similar to "superwoman" but tends to be used in reference to older women politicians who have led a more traditional life

- *One of the boys:* A female politician who "adopts a masculine stance, which means either that she does not resort to what are called feminine wiles to achieve her goals (charm, coquetry, wheedling) or that she accepts and operates by the conventional rules of the game"
- *Wife of . . . :* Invoked whenever the interests and activities of the female politician are linked by the media to those of her spouse

Robinson and her co-authors conclude that the media continue to emphasize the personal characteristics (e.g., looks, hair, and dress) of female politicians. Writing some ten years later, political scientists Linda Trimble and Jane Arscott (2003) report similar findings. Robinson and co-authors also note three additional characteristics of media descriptions of female politicians: (1) they fail to recognize the prior political activities of female politicians, with the result that the women's histories of acquiring competency remain unknown; (2) they suggest that female politicians are responsible for women's issues, when, in fact, gender interests may not be on the agenda of any politician, male or female; and (3) they use the term *feminism* or *feminist* to denote negative personal characteristics.

The third reason for women's underrepresentation in politics is gate-keeping. By controlling the nomination of candidates for elected office, political parties influence the gender composition of their electoral slate and the ridings that nominees represent. In the past, women candidates were often "sacrificial lambs," allowed to run mainly in ridings in which the chances of winning were small. In today's climate of striving for gender equality, few parties can afford to provide a slate of candidates with few or no women. But parties can and still do assign women to ridings in which their chances of winning are poor. Many of the representational gains that women have made are attributable to a volatile electorate and last-minute voter shifts that carry ridings in which female candidates were not expected to win (Brodie, 1991: 6).

Insufficient resources are the fourth reason for the lack of gender parity in Canadian politics. Money is an important resource for winning nominations and mounting publicity campaigns. Even 20 years ago, it cost $50 000 to contest a nomination in a winnable urban riding (Brodie, 1991: 40). Women may be at a disadvantage to the extent that they earn less than male candidates and consequently have less to put into a campaign. Whereas men who enter politics tend to come from law and business, women candidates tend to come from social work, journalism, and education, where earnings are lower (Bashevkin, 1991). Social networks are also an important resource needed for contesting nominations and elections. They are useful for obtaining financial contributions and recruiting volunteers to lobby voters. Yet, to the extent that politics is "an old boys' club," women may not have access to insider or "old boy" networks.

Finally, the clash between political and family life influences the participation of some women in politics. The culture that emphasizes politics as a man's world fails to recognize that politicians also have personal lives and family responsibilities. Indeed, the lifestyle that is part of this culture is almost anti-family. Ignoring the family needs and responsibilities of politicians affects both men and women. However, because women more than men are designated as the primary child-care providers, their participation in politics can require greater personal and child-care costs.

REPRESENTATION BY WOMEN, REPRESENTATION FOR WOMEN

Until recently, most research on women in politics focused on the question of how many women held party positions or were elected legislators. However, representation *by* women is not the same as representation *for* women. Although both men and women may use their legislative roles to place women's issues on the political agenda and to support party policies and legislation that reflect women's situations and concerns, they may not.

Jane Arscott and Linda Trimble (1997) summarize the views of numerous social scientists and women's groups when they call for "representation by women as if women mattered"—that is, the election of women who will act in the interests of women. They raise a second issue too: How are differences of class and race among women to be represented? Specifically, can women legislators and party officers understand and speak for women who are different from them and who may have different experiences and concerns? The great majority of Canadian female legislators are white, middle-class, publicly heterosexual, and well educated.

Do they understand, stand for, and speak for other women, including Aboriginal women, women of colour, immigrant women, senior women, poor women, homeless women, lesbians, and women who are victims of spousal abuse (Vickers, 1997: 28)? Furthermore, if mainstream women cannot speak for all women, then should targets or quotas be set for women of colour, poor women, lesbians, and so on? These questions are now being debated but Canadian governments at all levels appear unwilling to exercise the political will, spend the money, and change the electoral laws and party practices that would accommodate such differences.

ELIMINATING GENDER INEQUALITY

In this section, I consider the mechanisms that can be used to lessen the degree of gender inequality, starting with a review of general approaches and then looking at specific interventions designed to reduce inequality in the labour force and political representation.

MODELS OF CHANGE

One's choice of mechanism for bringing about change depends on how one explains gender inequality. If we see gender inequality as arising out of personality differences between men and women, we are likely to prefer a mechanism that influences personality traits—for example, we may seek ways of altering the messages that people receive about masculinity and femininity in schools and through the mass media. If we see inequalities as resulting from organizational rules and practices governing recruitment and promotion, we are likely to emphasize the need to change those rules and practices.

Starting in the 1970s, North American research on inequality began to shift away from perspectives that attributed unequal outcomes to individual differences in talent, educational achievement, and opportunity. That viewpoint resulted in social programs and public policies oriented to individuals, such as efforts to increase access to education and training for members of less privileged groups (Agocs and Boyd, 1993).

By the 1980s, people were becoming more aware of power relations and the influence of workplace cultures and practices as sources of gender inequality. This awareness was partly fuelled by feminism, with its twin emphases on the undervaluation of women and men's domination of women in diverse areas of social life. Accompanying such changing perspectives was growing impatience with organizations slow to change their practices voluntarily. Increased pressure was put on governments to develop public policies that lessened or eliminated gender inequalities.

Public policy refers to the statements made and the actions taken—or not taken—by governments with respect to a given problem or set of problems (Pal, 1989: 4). State intervention influences the magnitude of gender inequality and sustains or minimizes male domination of women in reproduction, family, and the labour force. In the category of reproduction are government actions pertaining to medical care, new reproductive technologies (such as in vitro fertilization), contraception, and abortion. In the category of the family are government policies regarding family law (including regulations governing divorce and property division) and child-care. Government intervention in the labour force affects gender inequality through employment insurance policies, maternity- and parental-leave policies, job-training programs, employment policies, and pay policies. So far, no government policy targets gender inequality in politics.

PUBLIC POLICY AND GENDER INEQUALITY IN THE LABOUR FORCE

Two areas of policy development that bear on gender inequality in the labour force are **employment equity,** including **affirmative action,** and pay equity, as expressed in the principle of **equal pay for work of equal value** (or "work of comparable worth"). Policies in both areas seek to correct inequalities in paid work by removing barriers that handicap certain groups, including women. Many of these barriers are seen as systemic. Rather than reflecting deliberate and conscious decisions to discriminate, systemic barriers refer to organizational practices, such as informal methods of recruitment or weight and height requirements for designated jobs. These practices often privilege members of one group while handicapping others. They differ in the populations they cover, the mechanisms they employ to determine and eliminate inequalities, and the aspects of labour-force inequality that they address.

Assessing the Impact

Many publications outline the specifics of Canadian employment-equity and equal-pay policies (Agocs, Burr, and Somerset, 1992; Weiner and Gunderson,

1990). Do such policies work? Have related programs succeeded in moving women into jobs from which they were previously excluded? Is the real monetary worth of women's work in female job ghettos being acknowledged?

In answering these questions, there is good news and bad news. The good news is that legal action has been taken against some cases of inequality. In the mid-1980s, for example, litigation forced CN Rail to hire women in the St. Lawrence region. At the time of the complaint, women held less than 1 percent of blue-collar jobs in the company, and a pattern of discriminatory hiring practices was revealed (Agocs, Burr, and Somerset, 1992: 104). The company was ordered to discontinue a number of these practices and to adopt new recruiting and hiring practices. Similarly, equal-pay-for-work-of-equal-value legislation has resulted in pay adjustments in a number of cases. For example, nurses' pay has been raised to match that of orderlies and the federal court upheld the right of pay equity for federally employed women in selected female-dominated occupations. In the fall of 2005, Canada Post was ordered to pay an estimated $150 million in back wages to clerical workers who were in a mostly female bargaining unit and who were paid substantially less than workers, most of them men, performing equivalent tasks sorting mail.

A few isolated victories do not, however, amount to winning the war. Critics of employment-equity policies note three types of "bad news." First, the legislation is limited in its jurisdiction and does not apply to a large part of the population. For example, the federal Employment Equity Act of 1995, which replaced the Employment Equity Act of 1986, covers only the public service, federally regulated employers, and portions of the public sector specified by orders in council, such as contractors who have 100 or more employees and who are doing business with the government. Second, failure to comply with the legislation is penalized only lightly. Although the federal Employment Equity Act of 1995 imposes fines on employers who do not report the required data or who knowingly provide false or misleading information, the amount cannot exceed $10 000 for a single violation and $50 000 for repeated or continued violations (Canada, 1995: s. 36[2]).

Numerous criticisms have been voiced about equal-pay-for-work-of-equal-value policies. First, many of the policies exclude small firms. Second, they compare men and women within the same firms, so they do not apply to women employed in firms in which the labour force is all female. Third, the method of establishing the comparable worth of two jobs is based on existing job descriptions. Jobs that are considered similar by virtue of pay or classification are evaluated on the basis of knowledge and skills, effort, responsibility, and working conditions (England, 1993; Steinberg, 1990). But such evaluation does not correct for the *a priori* undervaluation of certain skills, as discussed earlier.

For many feminists, these and other criticisms suggest that limited change can be expected from employment-equity and pay-equity policies in their current forms. Supporters are likely to press for stronger policies and broader coverage in the decades to come. However, government and business support for such changes is not assured. Business owners may argue that such equity is unaffordable in times of economic downturn. In Quebec, protests by business leaders caused amendments to the provincial bill on pay equity in the private sector, effective January 1, 1997. As a result of these changes, Quebec pay-equity legislation will not be fully implemented until 2006 (Séguin, 1996).

CORRECTING THE BALANCE: WOMEN IN POLITICS

No federal policy is aimed at reducing gender inequality among elected politicians. But numerous actions could increase the percentage of women in Canadian politics in the future. All have to do with reducing barriers erected by social roles and changing organizational aspects of political recruitment and elections:

- Displaying good intentions. Commonly taking the form of party statements indicating commitment to the principle of gender parity, such displays have little impact.
- Reducing the economic barriers to winning nominations and running for office. Reducing the financial burden facing women and some men can be achieved by introducing legislation that would allow candidates the right to take unpaid leave from employment to contest party nominations and elections; setting spending limits for nomination contests and party leadership campaigns; making contributions for nomination contests tax-deductible; reimbursing money spent on

nomination contests if the candidate gets a minimum level of support (say, 15 percent of the vote); using centralized party funds for nomination battles; and treating child-care and housekeeping costs as part of the overall campaign costs, thereby making them subject to reimbursement (Brodie, 1991: 49–50; Erickson, 1991).

- Recognizing family needs and responsibilities and the social roles of women. Lynda Erickson (1991) suggests that a fixed term for governments would increase the predictability of politicians' lives rather than leaving them at the mercy of a vote of non-confidence or a leader's prerogative to call an election. Changing the rules of elections might indirectly help politicians to anticipate their futures, taking into account the needs of their families.

- Weakening or eliminating the gate-keeping tradition. This reform could be accomplished by basing the amount of the government subsidy paid to political parties for their campaign expenses on an upward sliding scale according to the proportion of their elected candidates who are women (Brodie, 1991: 50). Under this system, the amount of the subsidy would vary with the number of women elected.

- Engaging in affirmative action. Affirmative action measures include setting quotas to ensure that a certain percentage of women are on riding nomination lists and establishing guarantees that a certain percentage of women are nominated for and are present in the party organization.

- Centralizing decision-making in political parties. Research suggests that affirmative action measures can be difficult to implement in a single-member electoral system. Under the single-member system in Canada, a person running for office in a riding wins by getting the most votes. This approach is conducive to the control of nominations by local party organizations. However, attempts to increase the numbers of women holding office are most effective in electoral systems that place decision making about nominations and party representation at levels higher than the local ridings. A more centralized decision-making structure gives party elites more control over the representation of women and other minority groups. Modifying Canada's single-member system is another area in which action could be taken to increase the percentage of women politicians (Erickson, 1991).

Which, if any, of these reforms will be adopted remains to be seen. It is highly likely, however, that debate over gender inequalities in politics and the economy will remain an important issue in Canadian social life for a long time.

SUMMARY

1. Many sociologists view the segregation of women and men in the private and public spheres as an important source of gender inequality. Exclusion from the economic and political arenas of Canadian life can mean disadvantages in access to income, economic well-being, prestige, and power. Restricted in the past to the domestic sphere, women have been economically disadvantaged and have had little or no opportunity to influence legislation directly. In addition, their unpaid work in the home has been considered low in prestige, or at least lower in value than their spouses' paid work.

2. During the twentieth century, women have entered the labour force and the political arena in ever-increasing numbers. Today, more than half of all women are in the labour force. Politically enfranchised, women have also entered the political arena, either as politicians or in connection with groups associated with the women's movement. Many of these changes have occurred—or, at least, have accelerated—in recent decades. Between the 1970s and the early 1990s, the labour-force participation rate of women more than doubled, and the number of elected women MPs quadrupled.

3. Although they do paid work, many women are still responsible for most of the meal preparation, cleaning, and laundry needs of their families. Women still tend to be considered the primary caregivers of children and of seniors. In short, women are more likely than men to work a double or triple "shift" every day.

4. In the labour force, women and men are occupationally segregated, with women concentrated in jobs stereotyped as "women's jobs." Women are more likely than men to be employed in jobs that are part-time or otherwise nonstandard. They earn less than men, on average, and their skills tend not to be fully recognized or fairly evaluated. These issues affect women to varying degrees, depending on their birthplace, race, and ethnicity. Nevertheless, the overall picture is one of gender inequality in the labour force, with women disadvantaged relative to men.

5. There is evidence of a gender gap in politics as well. Women represent more than half of Canada's adult population, but only 21 percent of federally elected legislators. This imbalance notwithstanding, substantial gains have been made in recent elections. And, as agents pressing for improvements in their own status, Canadian women have left a considerable legacy of influence and change.

6. Future generations will have to combat not only gender-role stereotypes, but also ideologies and structures that privilege men and handicap women. In recent years, employment-equity and equal-pay-for-work-of-equal-value policies have been developed to remedy some of the inequalities in the paid labour force. Analysts have also documented the various ways in which women's participation and influence in the political arena can be enhanced.

QUESTIONS TO CONSIDER

1. If you grew up in a two-parent household, describe the types of activities that each parent did around the house. Were they different? Did the amount of time each spent on activities in the home vary? Why?

2. Think back to jobs you have held in the past three years that involved working with other people. Reflecting on the type of work you did compared with the work of others, would you say that sex segregation or sex typing existed? Why or why not?

3. In some of the occupational skill assessments that have been conducted in recent years, the job of dog-catcher was deemed more skilled than the job of child-care worker. Why do you think such an evaluation was made? Do you agree with the ranking? Why or why not?

4. This chapter discussed the principles of political "representation by women," "representation for women," and "representation of difference." Should women legislators be elected only if they champion women's causes? Should electoral rules be changed to allow for the proportionate or even disproportionate election of women of colour and other disadvantaged women in order to represent their interests and experiences?

GLOSSARY

Affirmative action comprises the policies and programs designed to create opportunities for, and to further the achievements of, historically disadvantaged groups in the labour force. One form of action to correct past inequalities involves setting targets and quotas for the hiring and promotion of members of groups that have faced barriers and discrimination in the past. The term is often used interchangeably with employment equity; strictly speaking, it is one aspect of employment equity.

Employment equity is the principle of equal treatment of all groups in the labour force. Employment-equity policies and programs seek to dismantle barriers and alter workplace cultures to create opportunities for and to further the advancement of historically disadvantaged groups.

Equal pay for work of equal value, also known as "equal pay for work of comparable worth," is a principle supported by policies and programs that seek to equalize the wage rates offered for different jobs that are of comparable worth or value in terms of such factors as knowledge, complexity, responsibility, and skill.

Feminism refers both to the body of knowledge about the causes and nature of women's subordination to men in society, and the various agendas, often involving political action, for removing that subordination.

Gender inequalities are inequalities between men and women in the distribution of prestige, material well-being, and power. They are also inequalities in relations of male domination and female subordination.

Gender stereotypes are a set of prejudicial generalizations about men and women based on the oversimplified belief that sex determines distinct personality traits and, as a result, causes men and women to experience the world and behave in different ways.

The **glass ceiling** is the level in an organization above which women and members of minorities are seldom found.

The **labour-force participation rate** is the percentage of the population, age 15 and older, that is in the paid labour force.

Material well-being refers to having access to the economic resources necessary to pay for adequate food, clothing, housing, and possessions.

Nonstandard work refers to one or a combination of the following types of employment: part-week employment (reduced hours per week), part-year employment, limited-term contract employment, employment through temporary-help agencies, self-employment, and multiple job-holding.

Part-time work refers to jobs with reduced hours of work.

Power is the capacity to influence and control others, regardless of any resistance they might offer.

Prestige is the social evaluation or ranking, by general consensus, of occupational activities and positions in a hierarchical order that reflects the degree of respect, honour, or deference the person engaged in the activity or occupying the position is to be accorded.

Public policy refers to the government's stance on issues and problems, as expressed through its statements and actions, or its inaction.

Sex segregation of occupations refers to the concentration of women and men in different occupations.

Sex typing (or sex labelling) of occupations is the designation of an occupation as "female" or "male," depending on the sex for whom it is considered appropriate.

Skill is ability or expertise in performing a given technique or task. Researchers describe tasks as requiring more or less skill on the basis of their complexity and the degree of autonomy required to perform them. Existing rankings, incomes, and levels of education associated with various occupations are often accepted by researchers as proxy measures of skill.

A **social movement** is an enduring collective attempt to change part or all of society by means of rioting, petitioning, striking, demonstrating, or establishing pressure groups, unions, and political parties.

Social roles are the expectations and behaviours associated with particular positions in society.

Standard work is full-time, full-year employment, usually accompanied by job-related benefits, such as vacation leave, sick leave, and parental leave, as well as by health and pension benefits.

Statistical discrimination is the discrimination that occurs when negative decisions concerning the hiring or promotion of a given individual are made on the basis of the average characteristics of the group to which the individual belongs. Thus, an employer may not hire a particular woman because of a belief that women, in general, are likely to take time off work to have children, even though the woman in question may intend not to have children.

A **visible minority** is a category of people (other than Aboriginal people) who are nonwhite and who, because of their race, may face discrimination in hiring and promotion.

The **women's movement** is a social movement that takes action to improve the conditions of women.

SUGGESTED READING

Das Gupta, Tania. (1996). *Racism and Paid Work.* Toronto: Garamond Press. Examines discrimination in paid employment as it affects immigrant women and women of colour.

Statistics Canada. (2006). *Women in Canada: A Gender Based Statistical Report* (5th ed.). Ottawa: Minister of Industry (Catalogue No. 89-503-XPE). This report contains textual overviews and data on women, covering such topics as their family status, health, educational patterns, paid and unpaid work characteristics, and treatment by the criminal justice system. Separate chapters deal with Aboriginal, visible minority, and immigrant women.

Tremblay, Manon, and Caroline Andrew. (1998). *Women and Political Representation in Canada.* Women's Studies Series. Ottawa: University of Ottawa Press. An excellent collection of essays on various aspects of the women's movement in Canada and women's involvement in politics. A chapter by Julia O'Conner looks at women in paid employment.

Trimble, Linda, and Jane Arscott. (2003). *Still Counting: Women in Politics across Canada.* Peterborough, ON: Broadview Press. This highly readable book reviews the absence of women among elected politicians, provides reasons and suggests remedies.

WEB RESOURCES

Companion Web Site for This Book

http://www.newsociety5e.nelson.com

Begin by clicking on the Student Resources section of the website. Next, select the chapter you are studying from the pull-down menu. From the Student Resources page, you have easy access to InfoTrac College Edition® and other resources, such as the Glossary and Flashcards. The website also has many useful tips to aid you in your study of sociology.

InfoTrac College Edition Search Terms

Visit http://www.infotrac-college.com for access to more than 20 million articles from nearly 6000 sources when doing your online research.

ThomsonNOW™

http://hed.nelson.com

This online diagnostic tool identifies each student's unique needs with a Pretest that generates a personalized Study Plan for each chapter, helping students focus on concepts they are having the most difficulty mastering. Students then take a Posttest after reading the chapter to measure their understanding of the material. An Instructor Gradebook is available to track and monitor student progress.

CHAPTER **EIGHT**

Race and Ethnic Relations

In this chapter you will learn that

· The study of race and ethnic relations involves the analysis of the unequal distribution of power and resources, and it involves a number of sociological approaches. Among the most important are the frustration-aggression, sociobiology, socialization, and power-conflict approaches.

· *Ethnicity* and *race* are terms used to categorize groups on the basis of cultural and physical criteria. Although the concept of race has no basis in biology, and although ethnic identities and boundaries are situational, variable, and flexible, race and ethnicity are important parts of social reality.

· Aboriginal people in Canada are Indians, Métis, and Inuit. There are two main sociological interpretations of Aboriginal people's socioeconomic status in Canada, the culture of poverty thesis and the internal colonial model.

· The nationalist movement in Quebec has deep historical roots. The contemporary nationalist movement is united around the goal of maintaining the French character of Quebec. One of the main problems facing the nationalist movement in Quebec is exactly how to define the boundaries of the nation.

· Immigration played a central role in both the early and later phases of Canadian capitalist development. Canada accepts refugees, family class, and independent immigrants, each of whom is subject to different selection criteria.

· John Porter's description of Canadian society as a vertical mosaic is not as accurate as it once was.

Vic Satzewich
MCMASTER UNIVERSITY

INTRODUCTION

It started as a peaceful protest aimed at grabbing the government's attention over a dispute about an old burial ground. It ended with what journalist Peter Edwards (2001) referred to as "one dead Indian." On September 5, 1995, just after the Labour Day long-weekend campers had gone home, about 30 Kettle Point and Stoney Point band members from the Kettle Point Reserve near Sarnia occupied Ipperwash Provincial Park. Some band members believed that an ancient burial ground in the park was being desecrated and they wanted to protect their ancestors' resting place. A few weeks earlier, a group of reserve members had reclaimed land that was part of a nearby military base. That land had been lent temporarily to the federal government during World War II for military training purposes. Various provincial and federal governments had dragged their feet over the return of the land that was part of the military base for nearly 50 years, and the occupants of Ipperwash did not feel like waiting another 50 years for their concerns about the graves in the park to be dealt with.

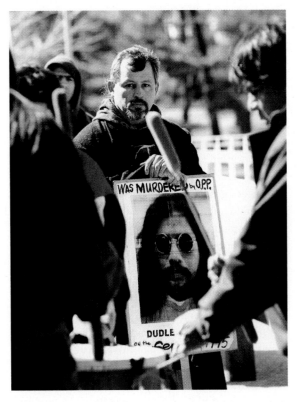

Native protester Dudley George was shot and killed by an Ontario Provincial Police officer during the occupation of Ipperwash Provincial Park (near Sarnia) in 1995.

SOURCE: Nora Penhale/CP Picture Archive.

Dudley George was shot and killed by an Ontario Provincial Police officer in a chaotic altercation the day after the occupation of Ipperwash started. The officer who shot George was eventually convicted of criminal negligence causing death, and the larger circumstances surrounding the incident were investigated at a public inquiry in late 2005 and early 2006. Both the trial of the OPP officer and the public inquiry turned up unpleasant facts about racism within the OPP and within the provincial Conservative government of the day. For instance, the day before George was shot, two OPP officers were posing as a television crew. The lens of their camera was covered, but the audio was turned on. One officer, responding to his colleague's question about whether any members of the media were in the area, said, "No, there's no one down there. Just a big fat-fuck Indian." After a few minutes, another voice is heard: "We had this plan, you know. We thought if we could get five or six cases of Labatt's 50, we could bait them. And we would have this big net and a pit." People are heard laughing in the background. The officer calls the plan "creative thinking" and adds that it "works in the South with watermelons" (Gray, 2004: A7).

According to Murray Klippenstein, the lawyer for the George family, "the reference to baiting Indians with alcohol and the reference to the South and the watermelon are the kind of poisonous, racist talk I thought we had put behind us in Ontario. . . . The reference to blacks in the South is the kind of talk you would hear when people are dehumanizing someone, and that attitude makes it easy to lynch or shoot them" (Gray, 2004).

In November 2005, the Ipperwash inquiry into the death of Dudley George turned up some equally ugly racist views expressed by provincial government officials. Former provincial Attorney General Charles Harnick told the inquiry that at a top-level meeting to discuss how the provincial government ought to handle the occupation of the park, then Premier Mike Harris, in a moment of anger, shouted, "I want those fucking Indians out of the park" (Harries, 2005: A1). Although Mr. Harris has denied saying this, Mr. Harnick insists that "I heard what I heard" (Appleby, 2006: A7).

We may never know with certainty whether racism played a central role in why Dudley George died. Some say that although the expression of racism by some OPP officers was regrettable, it was incidental to the way the events surrounding George's death unfolded. Others say that the police do not take their marching orders from politicians, so whatever the premier might have said at the meeting was irrelevant to how the police eventually dealt with the situation.

Ethnic and racial tensions in Canada do not often end in physical violence or violent death. And, in comparison to many other countries, ethnic and racial relations seem peaceful here. But other kinds of ethnic and racial problems exist. In Ontario, the 2001 Safe Schools Act, which mandates a policy of "zero tolerance" for violent and disruptive behaviour in schools, is alleged by some to work to the disadvantage of black students (Henry and Tator, 2006: 211). Some parents and educational researchers call for the establishment of black-focused schools in Ontario. Others argue that this is racism in reverse. In 2001, 1071 land claims had been filed against the federal government by First Nations; only 251 had been successfully resolved (Frideres and Gadacz, 2005: 220). Former Toronto Mayor Mel Lastman's 2001 racist jest that he was reluctant to travel to Kenya because he feared being put in a pot of boiling water by "dancing natives" probably did not help Toronto's unsuccessful bid to host the 2008 Summer Olympic Games (Walcott, 2003). Arab Canadians complain that they have faced increased stereotyping and discrimination in Canada and at the Canada-U.S. border since September 11, 2001 (Li, 2003). Just over ten years ago, the country was on the verge of collapse after nearly half the voters in Quebec voted in favour of separation. And some observers claim that the federal government's policy of multiculturalism undermines the unity of our country (Bissondath, 1994), causing "more overt hostility in Canada to those of European ancestry . . . than to the non-white minority" (Stoffman, 2002: 126).

These examples all touch in some way on the issue of what different ethnic and racial groups are allowed, and able, to do in our society, and how they are treated. In other words, they all say something about the distribution of power and resources in Canada. The sociology of ethnic and racial relations concerns primarily the study of how power and resources are unequally distributed among ethnic and racial groups. Sociologists who are interested in race and ethnic relations ask a number of interrelated questions: What are the conditions under which ethnic and racial groups come into contact? Which ethnic and racial groups hold power in a society? How

do they exercise power? Are there social and economic advantages associated with having a particular ethnic or racial background? What are the social consequences of the unequal distribution of power and resources? How have ethnic and racial groups challenged inequality and power imbalances? How have governments tried to manage and contain ethnic and racial conflict?

My aim in this chapter is to provide some sociological answers to these questions. I begin by examining what sociologists mean by the terms *ethnicity*, *race*, and *racism*, and then discuss various theoretical approaches to the study of ethnic and racial relations. Next, I examine the three main forms of ethnic and racial relations in Canada: Aboriginal and non-Aboriginal relations, French and English relations, and immigrant and non-immigrant relations. In each case, you will see how power and resource imbalances play important roles in structuring relationships among groups.

ETHNICITY AND RACE: THE SOCIAL CONSTRUCTION OF DIFFERENCE

We use the terms *race*, *racial*, *ethnic*, and *ethnicity* in a variety of ways in our everyday lives. Some students in my classes talk about how they are under pressure from their parents to marry someone of the same "race" or "ethnicity." Others are concerned that "race relations" in Canada seem to be getting worse. Yet others describe the joys of living in a "multiethnic" country, of eating meals in a variety of "ethnic" restaurants, and of observing and participating in the rituals and festivals of "ethnic" groups from around the world.

The assumption underlying our commonsense understandings of these terms is that race and ethnicity are *ascribed* characteristics. That is, we assume that we are born with a certain race or ethnicity that cannot be changed. Sociologists, however, recognize that, although we cannot change our birth parents, and generally cannot change our skin colour, we do not necessarily have fixed and unalterable ethnic and racial characteristics or identities. Instead, sociologists believe it is more useful to see race and ethnicity as certain kinds of *achieved* statuses—statuses that are acquired by virtue of social definition. In contrast, Box 8.1 shows how Statistics Canada used ascribed characteristics for its measurement of ethnicity and race in the 2001 census.

BOX 8.1 THE ETHNICITY AND "RACE" QUESTIONS IN THE 2001 CENSUS

ETHNIC ORIGIN

Although most people in Canada view themselves as Canadians, information on their ancestral origins has been collected since the 1901 census to capture the changing composition of Canada's diverse population. Therefore, this question refers to the **origins of the person's ancestors.**

17. To which ethnic or cultural group(s) did this person's **ancestors** belong?

   For example, Canadian, French, English, Chinese, Italian, German, Scottish, Irish, Cree, Micmac, Métis, Inuit (Eskimo), East Indian, Ukrainian, Dutch, Polish, Portuguese, Filipino, Jewish, Greek, Jamaican, Vietnamese, Lebanese, Chilean, Somali, etc.

RACIAL ORIGIN

19. Is this person:

   Mark "x" more than one or specify, if applicable
   White
   Chinese
   South Asian (e.g., East Indian, Pakistani, Sri Lankan, etc.)
   Black
   Filipino
   Latin American
   Southeast Asian (e.g., Cambodian, Indonesian, Laotian, Vietnamese, etc.)
   Arab
   West Asian (e.g., Afghan, Iranian, etc.)
   Japanese
   Korean
   Other—specify

This information is collected to support programs that promote equal opportunity for everyone to share in the social, cultural, and economic life of Canada.

SOURCE: Adapted from the Statistics Canada website http://www12.statcan.ca/english/census01/home/questionnaire.cfm.

ETHNICITY AND RACE

Ethnicity

Sociologists do not agree on how to define and measure ethnicity. *Objective definitions of ethnicity* assume that ethnic groups exist because of people's social attachments (Isajiw, 1999). From this point of view, ethnicity is something that people possess because of differences in language, culture, customs, national origin, and ancestry. *Subjective approaches to ethnicity* focus on the process of ethnic identification. Sociologists who emphasize the socially constructed nature of perceived reality insist that ethnicity is a "transactional" process. Ethnic groups are made up of people who identify themselves, or who are identified by others, as belonging to the same ancestral or cultural group. Whether they display any of the cultural

characteristics of the group with which they identify, or whether they are merely born into that group, is largely irrelevant. When subjective definitions are used, then, "ethnicity" is self-defined and reflects "a shared 'we-feeling' within a collectivity (groupness) whose symbolic components can vary [over] time and place" (Fleras and Elliot, 1996). From this perspective, ethnic identities and boundaries are situational, variable, and flexible.

Most of the ethnic categories that we take for granted are actually recent historical creations. The ethnic category "English" would have been unthinkable to the person who lived in the British Isles 800 years ago. People defined themselves, and were defined by others, as Celts, Saxons, Normans, and so on. Only some of those people came to be known as "the English" (Lieberson, 1991). Similarly, the people whom we now think of as "Germans" did not exist 150 years ago. As these examples suggest, the way in which people define themselves, and are defined by others, is in constant flux (Lieberson, 1991: 444). If we take a long view, it is common for ethnic categories and identities to be recast and created anew.

This is what seems to be happening in Canada now. A feeling of commonality has crystallized that is the basis for a common ethnic identification. In preparing for the 1991 census, Statistics Canada held meetings, organized focus groups, and tested different ways of posing questions that tried to measure the ethnicity of our population. One thing that Statistics Canada found "was a strong tendency [for respondents] to report Canadian as their ethnic origin and as their ethnic identity" (White, 1992: 166). Largely because of political pressure, "Canadian" was included as a response category in the ethnicity question for the next census. "Canadians" are now the numerically largest ethnic group in Canada (see Table 8.1).

TABLE 8.1   TOP 25 ETHNIC ORIGINS IN CANADA, 2001

Ethnic Origin	SINGLE AND MULTIPLE RESPONSES	SINGLE RESPONSES	MULTIPLE RESPONSES	INDEX OF ASSIMILATION[1]
CANADIAN	11 682 680	6 748 135	4 934 550	NA
English	5 978 875	1 479 520	4 499 355	75.2
French	4 668 410	1 060 755	3 607 655	77.2
Scottish	4 157 210	607 235	3 549 975	85.4
Irish	3 822 660	496 865	3 325 800	87.0
German	2 742 765	705 595	2 037 170	74.3
Italian	1 270 370	726 275	544 090	42.8
Chinese	1 094 700	936 210	158 490	14.5
Ukrainian	1 071 060	326 200	744 860	69.5
North American Indian	1 000 890	455 805	545 085	54.5
Dutch	923 310	316 220	607 090	65.8
Polish	817 085	260 415	556 670	68.1
East Indian	713 330	581 665	131 665	18.5
Norwegian	363 760	47 230	316 530	87.0
Portuguese	357 690	252 835	104 855	29.3
Welsh	350 365	28445	321 925	91.9
Jewish	348 605	186 475	162 130	46.5
Russian	337 960	70 890	267 070	79.0
Filipino	327 545	266 140	61 410	18.7
Métis	307 845	72 210	235 635	76.5
Swedish	282 760	30 440	252 320	89.2
Hungarian	267 255	91 795	175 460	62.4
American	250 010	25 200	224 805	89.9
Greek	215 105	143 780	71 320	33.2
Spanish	213 100	66 545	146 555	68.8

SOURCE: Adapted from the Statistics Canada website http://www12.statcan.ca/english/census01/products/highlights/ETO/Table1.cfm.
[1]Multiple responses expressed as a percentage of single plus multiple responses.

Why do some of us define our ethnic roots or ethnic identity as "Canadian"? Some of us may simply be unaware of or uninterested in our so-called roots and, hence, by default define ourselves as Canadian. For others, defining ourselves as Canadian is a political act used to express our dissatisfaction with the government's policy of multiculturalism (White, 1992: 168–69). At the same time, though, many of us insist that we are Canadian because that is simply the group with whom we identify and with whom we share a sense of belonging (Angus Reid Group, 1991; Howard, 1998). According to Rhoda Howard-Hassmann (1999: 528), the emergence of this sense of community means that "the ethnic English-Canadian is a new social creation."

Race

For much of the twentieth century, there was little difference between commonsense understandings of **race** and the way that race was analyzed in the social and natural sciences. Most scientists believed that races were real and objective subdivisions of *Homo sapiens*. These divisions were supposedly based on a combination of unalterable physical and genetic characteristics. Features, such as skin colour, hair texture, body and facial shape, genetic diseases, metabolic rates, and distribution of blood groups, were used to construct various racial typologies. The most common typology was the division of humanity into "Caucasoid," "mongoloid," and "negroid" races (Montagu, 1972).

During the 1930s, scientists began to raise doubts about the scientific validity of the concept of race (Barkan, 1992). Since the 1950s, the scientific consensus is that racial classifications of humanity are arbitrary, that genetic differences between groups are small, and that genetic differences are behaviourally insignificant (Montagu, 1972). Racial classifications based on a characteristic such as skin colour are as illogical as racial classifications based on the length of index fingers (Miles, 1982). Moreover, only about 0.2 percent of all human genes are necessarily shared by members of the same race, genetically defined. Thus, from a strictly genetic point of view, Jean Chrétien may have much more in common with Oscar Peterson than with Jean Charest.

In sum, differences between races are arbitrary, extremely small, and without behavioural consequences. Ethnic boundaries and identities are flexible, negotiated, and historically variable. We should not conclude, however, that race and ethnicity are unimportant aspects of modern society. According to W.I. Thomas's famous sociological dictum, if people define situations as real, they are real in their consequences (Thomas and Znaniecki, 1918: 79). Even though race is a hollow biological concept, and even though ethnic identities and boundaries are neither fixed nor unchanging, many people believe in the existence of ethnicity and race and organize their relationships with others on the basis of those beliefs. Therefore, race and ethnicity are important parts of our social reality.

Racism

If race is a biological myth, what is racism? Is a school racist if it puts on hot dog days but not chow mein days? Are black people in Toronto subject to racist policing? Is Don Cherry a racist because he denigrates European hockey players who compete in the National Hockey League? Is Professor Philippe Rushton of the University of Western Ontario a racist because he believes that black people have smaller brains than whites and Asians? Is a black woman racist if she wants to marry only a black man? Is a white man racist if he wants to marry only a white woman? Is the Bush administration in the United States racist for the way that it managed the aftermath of Hurricane Katrina in New Orleans in September 2005?

Before we can begin to answer these kinds of questions, we need to define racism. Sociologists define racism as both a certain kind of idea and a certain kind of institutional practice. I will consider each of these definitions in turn.

Traditionally, sociologists defined racism as "the belief that humans are subdivided into distinct hereditary groups that are innately different in their social behaviour and mental capacities and that can therefore be ranked as superior or inferior" (Marger, 1997: 27). By this definition, only a small minority of Canadians could be called racist. A survey conducted in 1990 by Decima Research Ltd. (cited in Reitz and Breton, 1994: 68) showed that 90 percent of Canadians agreed with the statement, "All races are created equal." It might be argued, then, that the 10 percent who either disagreed or did not know are racist. How can we reconcile the fact that so few Canadians believe in the inherent superiority of some races over others with the fact that people and institutions are so often called racist?

One answer is that, because ideas about the inherent superiority and inferiority of groups have been so thoroughly discredited, racism has taken new forms (Omi and Winant, 1986). Biological versions of racism may very well be dead, but researchers have developed the concept of **new racism** as a way of analyzing its changing manifestations.

The concept of new racism was developed by Martin Barker (1981) to analyze the way that racist ideas were being expressed in the 1970s by British members of Parliament (MPs) when they were speaking out against British immigration policy. That policy permitted people from former British colonies in Asia, Africa, and the Caribbean unrestricted entry to the country. In their speeches, the MPs did not make references to British *biological* superiority or to Indian, African, or Caribbean *biological* inferiority. Instead, they regarded immigrants from these areas as *culturally* different from British people and alleged that the ability of British people to advance the moral level of humanity was being undermined by immigration policy. The MPs' statements could not be considered "racist" by the traditional definition of racism. However, the statements had the real consequence of helping to stop almost all nonwhite immigration from those countries.

These events suggested that the definition of racism had to be broadened. Accordingly, Barker (1981: 21) argued that the new racism involves the beliefs that, although races of people cannot be ranked biologically, they are different from each other and that social problems are created when different groups try to live together. These beliefs should be considered racist because of their underlying intent: to socially exclude, marginalize, and denigrate certain groups of people, but to do so without reference to unalterable biology. People may even believe in abstract virtues, such as equality, justice, and fairness, yet still hold negative attitudes, and engage in discriminatory behaviour, toward minority group members (Henry and Tator, 2006: 19).

How widespread is racism? A 2003 survey conducted by the Centre for Research and Information about Canada (CRIC) and *The Globe and Mail* found that

- 10 percent of Canadians agreed that "non-whites living here should not push themselves where they are not wanted."
- 10 percent agreed that "it is a bad idea for people of different races to marry."

- 11 percent said they would be "uncomfortable" if a close relative, such as a sister or daughter, were to marry a person who was black.
- 31 percent said they would be "uncomfortable" if a close relative married a Muslim (Parkin and Mendelsohn, 2003: 3).

However, Canada fares well in international comparisons. Although 18 percent of Canadians who were polled in a 2002 international survey felt that immigrants have a bad influence on the country, 43 percent of Americans and 50 percent of respondents in the United Kingdom said that immigrants had a bad influence on their respective countries (Parkin and Mendelsohn, 2003: 5).

A different indicator of the scope of racism in Canada is given in Table 8.2, which focuses on *perceived* discrimination. Table 8.2 shows the results of the Ethnic Diversity Survey conducted by Statistics Canada in 2002. Among other things, the survey asked Canadians whether they had experienced discrimination or unfair treatment during the past five years. The survey found that 64 percent of visible minority Canadians reported that they "did not" experience discrimination or unfair treatment because of their ethnocultural characteristics in the past five years. Another 15 percent reported that they "rarely" experienced discrimination and 20 percent of respondents reported that they had "sometimes" or "often" experienced discrimination. In contrast, just 5 percent of nonvisible minorities reported experiencing discrimination or unfair treatment because of their ethnocultural characteristics during the past five years.

Institutional racism refers to "discriminatory racial practices built into such prominent structures as the political, economic and education systems" (Doob, 1996: 6). Institutional racism can take three forms. First, some institutional practices are based on explicitly racist ideas. Canadian history has plenty of examples of this form of institutional racism (Bolaria and Li, 1988). Chinese people were excluded from certain jobs and were denied the right to vote in federal elections until 1947. Japanese Canadians were denied their basic civil rights, were forcibly expelled from the west coast of British Columbia, and had their property confiscated during World War II (Bolaria and Li, 1988). Status Indians were denied the right to vote in federal elections until 1960. Residential segregation was widespread for black people living in Canada. Restrictive covenants in

TABLE 8.2 PERCEPTIONS OF DISCRIMINATION BY GENERATION AND VISIBLE MINORITY STATUS, CANADA, 2002

DISCRIMINATION	TOTAL POPULATION	FREQUENCY OF DISCRIMINATION		
		SOMETIMES OR OFTEN	RARELY	DID NOT EXPERIENCE
	000s	%	%	%
Total Population	22 444	7	6	86
Not a Visible Minority	19 252	5	5	90
Visible Minority	3000	20	15	64
First Generation	5272	13	10	77
Not a Visible Minority	2674	5	6	89
Visible Minority	2516	21	14	65
Second Generation or More	16 929	6	5	89
Not a Visible Minority	16 349	5	5	90
Visible Minority	480	18	23	59

Source: Adapted from the Statistics Canada Publication "Ethnic Diversity Survey: Portrait of a Multicultural Society," 2002, Catalogue 89-593, released September 29, 2003.

wills, deeds, and leases were used to ensure that property could not be sold or leased to blacks and Jews. Blacks were frequently refused service in restaurants, theatres, and recreational facilities (Henry and Tator, 2006: 69). Canada had the worst record of all Allied countries in allowing Jewish immigration during World War II, when millions of Jews were being gassed in Europe (Abella and Troper, 1982). In each case, ideas about the alleged inferiority of certain groups underpinned institutional practices.

Second, some institutional practices arose from, but are no longer sustained by, racist ideas (Miles and Brown, 2003). For example, in 1966, the federal government admitted a small number of black workers from the Caribbean to work on Canadian farms. Now, more than 16 000 migrant workers from the Caribbean and Mexico enter Canada each year to harvest fruits, vegetables, and tobacco in southern Ontario and other agricultural areas in Canada during the summer months. Canadian government officials originally justified this practice partly by arguing that black workers are racially suited to back-breaking labour under the hot sun but racially unsuited to the cold Canadian winters (Satzewich, 1991). The present migrant-labour policy had its origins in racist thinking, but racist ideas are no longer used to justify this migration stream.

Originally, racist thinking was used to justify allowing Caribbean and Mexican agricultural workers into Canada during the hot summer months but not the cold Canadian winters.
SOURCE: Shutterstock.

Third, institutions sometimes unintentionally restrict the life-chances of certain groups through a variety of seemingly neutral rules, regulations, and procedures. This is sometimes referred to as *systemic discrimination*. For example, height and weight requirements for jobs with police forces and fire departments did not necessarily originate in racist ideas, but these requirements meant that for many years certain Asian groups could not get jobs as police officers or firefighters. Word-of-mouth recruiting in organizations and inflated educational requirements for nontechnical jobs are also forms of systemic discrimination because they unintentionally put minority groups at a disadvantage in the distribution of scarce resources like jobs (Special Committee on the Participation of Visible Minorities in Canadian Society, 1984).

The debate about racial profiling in policing is also about this kind of institutional racism. According to a study conducted by University of Toronto criminologist Scott Wortley (2005), black people in Kingston, Ontario, are nearly four times more likely to be pulled over by police than white people are. Aboriginal people are 1.4 times more likely to be pulled over than white people are. When the study results were announced, the chief of the Kingston Police Force tearfully apologized, saying "especially to the black community and the aboriginal community where there are disparities, we apologize. I apologize. I'm not asking any police officer to apologize. . . . My police officers have the right to . . . walk tall with pride. What we're doing wrong, if we're doing anything wrong, is systemic and that's my problem. So I apologize to the black community, the aboriginal community and we'll do better" (Farmer, 2005).

THEORIES OF RACE AND ETHNIC RELATIONS

There are a number of sociological approaches to the interpretation of race and ethnic relations (Rex and Mason, 1986). In this section, I discuss four approaches that seek to explain various forms of ethnic and racial hostility. Such hostility is multifaceted and, depending on the circumstances, is described as racism, prejudice, ethnocentrism, or xenophobia.

Social Psychology

Social-psychological approaches to the interpretation of race and ethnic relations focus on how **prejudice**—an unfavourable, generalized, and rigid belief applied to all members of a group—and racism satisfy the psychic needs of certain people. *Frustration-aggression* is a popular variant of social-psychological theory. It explains prejudice and racism as forms of hostility that arise from frustration. The theory suggests that people who are frustrated in their efforts to achieve a desired goal—a better-paying job, for example, or entry to a university—respond with aggression (Marger, 1997). Since the real source of frustration is usually too powerful to confront directly, or may not be known, people take out their frustrations on the less powerful. From this perspective, minority ethnic and racial groups are convenient and safe targets of displaced aggression. This displacement is also referred to as scapegoating. The concept of scapegoating is sometimes used to explain anti-Semitism—negative attitudes and everyday discrimination directed against Jews (Brym and Lenton, 1993).

This kind of explanation has a seductive, almost commonsense, appeal. We all have bad days at work or at school, and when we get home, we sometimes lash out at the people close to us. However, the theory has limitations. First, people respond to frustrating circumstances in a variety of ways. Displaced aggression does not always follow frustration. We sometimes internalize our frustrations and end up giving ourselves an ulcer, or we may direct our frustrations at the real source of our problems. The theory does not say why we respond to frustrating circumstances in different ways. Second, the theory does not explain why some groups, and not others, are chosen as scapegoats.

Primordialism

The **primordialist thesis** suggests that ethnic and racial attachments reflect an innate tendency for people to seek out, and associate with, others who are similar in terms of language, culture, beliefs, ancestry, and appearance (Scott, 1990). From this point of view, ethnic prejudice and racism are ways of maintaining social boundaries. Sociobiologists offer a popular form of primordial theory. They suggest that prejudice and **discrimination**—practices that deny members of particular groups equal access to societal rewards—stem from our supposedly biologically grounded tendency to be nepotistic. Sociobiologists argue that the process of natural selection does not operate at the level of individuals, but rather at the level of kin-related groups. Clusters of genes are assumed to be passed on through kin selection (Wilson, 1978). Ethnic and racial groups are seen to be nothing more than large extended families. Since people have a "natural" tendency to want to pass on their genes, they favour their own "families." Thus, people are inherently both altruistic (prepared to sacrifice their own individual interests for the sake of the group) and ethnocentric because they want to pass on their genes to their own group. Humans, therefore, naturally favour members of their own ethnic or racial group—their "relatives"—and have a natural distrust and dislike of "nonfamily" members (van den Berghe, 1986: 255).

Are racism, prejudice, and discrimination programmed by our genes? It seems unlikely. The first problem with sociobiology is that shared ethnicity or race does not prevent conflict from erupting. In the history of the United States, white workers have struck against white-owned factories, and Americans have killed members of their own ethnic or racial group without concern for common ethnicity or race (Bonacich, 1980). Second, sociobiology is not able to explain how and why we frequently break out of our supposed genetically programmed nepotism. For example, Canadians of diverse ethnic and racial origins participate together in various kinds of anti-racist social movements (Henry and Tator, 2006). Ethnic and racial relations, therefore, are not necessarily zero-sum games in which one group wins at the expense of another.

Normative Theories

Normative theories of ethnic and racial prejudices concentrate on the way in which prejudices are transmitted through socialization and the social circumstances that compel discriminatory behaviour (Marger, 1997). For example, the *socialization approach* focuses on how we are taught ethnic and racial stereotypes, prejudices, and attitudes by our families, peer groups, and the mass media. For instance, as a teenager in Saskatchewan in the 1970s, I remember watching the TV show *All in the Family*. People in Saskatchewan at the time held many prejudicial attitudes, particularly toward Aboriginal people. However, the television program *All in the Family* exposed my generation to a repertoire of ethnic and racial slang and stereotypes that we had not heard before. Archie Bunker, the show's central character, was supposed to be a caricature of an American "bigot," but he also taught us terms like "wop," "dago," "spic," and "nigger," and the corresponding stereotypes. Similarly, as Box 8.2 shows, the English language places different values on the colours black and white in subtle ways. Our language, in turn, shapes how we perceive and socially evaluate different racial groups.

BOX 8.2 LANGUAGE, COLOUR OF RACE

Language is an integral part of our culture. Language not only expresses ideas but shapes our thought. Our childhood socialization involves, in part, the ability to use language. In the following "Short Play on 'Black' and 'White' Words," Robert Moore shows how aspects of our language help unwittingly to reproduce both negative and positive racial imagery:

"Some may blackly (angrily) accuse me of trying to blacken (defame) the English language, to give it a black eye (a mark of shame) by writing such black words (hostile). They may denigrate (to cast aspersions; to darken) me by accusing me of being blackhearted (malevolent), of having a black outlook (pessimistic, dismal) on life, of being a blackguard (scoundrel)—which would certainly be a black mark (detrimental fact) against me. Some may black-brow (scowl at) me and hope that a black cat crosses in front of me because of this black deed. I may become a black sheep (one who causes shame or embarrassment because of deviation from the accepted standards), who will be blackballed (ostracized) by being placed on a blacklist (list of undesirables) in an attempt to blackmail (to force or coerce into a particular action) me to retract my words. But attempts to blackjack (to compel by threat) me will have a Chinaman's chance of success, for I am not a yellow-bellied Indian-giver of words, who will whitewash (cover up or gloss over vices or crimes) a black lie (harmful, inexcusable). I challenge the purity and innocence (white) of the English language. I don't see things in black and white (entirely bad or entirely good) terms, for I am a white man (marked by upright firmness) if there ever was one. However, it would be a black day when I would not "call a spade a spade," even though some will suggest a white man calling the English language racist is like the pot calling the kettle black. While many may be niggardly (grudging, scanty) in their support, others will be honest and decent—and to them I say, that's very white of you (honest, decent).

"The preceding is of course a white lie (not intended to cause harm), meant only to illustrate some examples of racist terminology in the English language."

SOURCE: "Racist stereotyping in the English Language" by Robert B. Moore (pp. 269–297). Reprinted from *Racism in the English Language* by Robert B. Moore, Council on Interracial Books for Children, 1976.

Socialization theories are superior to social-psychological and primordialist approaches because they emphasize the way in which ethnic and racial prejudices and attitudes are learned through social interaction. The limitation of socialization theories is that they are unable to explain how prejudicial ideas, attitudes, and practices arise in the first place. This is where power-conflict theories come into play.

Power-Conflict Theories

Karl Marx (1967 [1867]: 751) wrote that "the turning of Africa into a warren for the commercial hunting of black-skins signaled the rosy dawn of the era of capitalist production." Marx did not take his analysis of slavery and racism much farther than this. Later generations of Marxist scholars, however, have sought to link racism to the overall structure of capitalist societies.

Orthodox Marxists argue that racism is an *ideology*—a set of statements shaped by economic interests about the way the social world "really works." Racism is ideological insofar as it is used by capitalists to mystify social reality and justify the exploitation and the unequal treatment of groups of people.

This justification can take many forms. For example, in the seventeenth century, American and Caribbean plantation owners justified the use of Africans as slaves by denying the humanity of Africans (Williams, 1964). In Marxist terms, the existence of racist ideas did not cause slavery; rather, slavery was a particular system of labour control that was justified by racist ideology.

In the case of advanced capitalism, racism is viewed by Marxists as an ideology that justifies the especially intense exploitation of racial minority and immigrant workers (Bolaria and Li, 1988; Castles and Kosack, 1984). From this point of view, racist ideas are used by employers as a means of creating artificial divisions in the working class so as to prevent the formation of a class consciousness that would threaten the social and economic order (Bolaria and Li, 1988; Castles and Kosack, 1984; Nikolinakos, 1973). Also, racist ideas help to justify the allocation of certain groups to low-wage, socially marginal jobs.

Race and the Split Labour Market Split labour-market theory was developed by Edna Bonacich (1972, 1979) because of the limitations of orthodox Marxism in analyzing racism. She argues that orthodox Marxism tends to assume that the capitalist class is all-powerful and that other classes play no

role in the development of racist thinking. This is inaccurate; racism is found in all classes to varying degrees. Second, orthodox Marxism portrays racism in overly conspiratorial terms. Little evidence demonstrates that capitalists sit around plotting new and devious ways of using racism to stop workers from developing class consciousness. Third, orthodox Marxism has trouble explaining why racialized conflict so often results in *exclusionary practices*—practices that deny employers access to cheaper, more exploitable labour. In 1885, for example, the Canadian government instituted a "head tax" on new immigrants from China. Chinese immigrants had to pay $50 to the federal government. In 1900, the tax was raised to $100, and in 1903 to $500. The Chinese Immigration Act of 1923 completely barred Chinese immigration until 1947 (Li, 1988: 30). If racism is developed by capitalists to justify exploitation, then why does it so often result in efforts to *block* the entry of new immigrants and limit the job opportunities of those already in the country? Bonacich feels that more attention has to be paid to the way in which the competition for jobs and other scarce resources among the working class creates and sustains racism.

Split labour-market theory suggests that racial and ethnic conflict is rooted in differences in the price of labour. For historical reasons—mainly involving military conquest—nonwhite workers have often received low wages and white workers high wages. Employers try to replace high-paid white workers with low-paid nonwhite workers. Meanwhile, high-paid workers, faced with displacement or the threat of displacement, try to protect their own interests by limiting capitalists' access to cheaper nonwhite workers. Thus, cheaper nonwhite workers are the victims of a complicated process of class struggle between expensive labour, cheap labour, and capitalists.

The theory applies well to Canada. During the late nineteenth and early twentieth centuries, the presence of Chinese workers and merchants in British Columbia provoked a negative response on the part of various segments of the white working class and shop owners. As split labour-market theory predicts, the hostility of whites was rooted in differences in the price of labour. According to evidence presented at the Royal Commission on Chinese and Japanese Immigration in 1903, Chinese workers earned about one-half of the wages that white workers earned in the same jobs (Li, 1988: 44). A number of racist organizations emerged whose aim was to limit the number of places where Chinese people could work, which helped stop additional Chinese immigration (Roy, 1989).

Split labour-market theory makes three other points that are relevant to the analysis of ethnic and race relations in general. First, it argues that individual racism, ethnic prejudice, and institutional racism emerge from intergroup conflict. Second, the theory maintains that prejudicial ideas and discriminatory behaviour are ways of socially marginalizing minority groups that the dominant group sees as threats to their position of power and privilege. Third, the theory suggests that to understand ethnic and racial relations, we need to look beyond individual personalities and sociobiological processes and analyze processes of economic, social, and political competition among groups (Marger, 1997: 98).

Keeping these three observations in mind will help you understand the three main patterns of ethnic and racial relations in Canada: Aboriginal and non-Aboriginal relations, French and English relations, and immigrant and non-immigrant relations. These are the topics that we turn to next.

ABORIGINAL PEOPLES

Have you ever fumbled trying to find the right way to refer to someone who is ethnically or racially different from you? Are we supposed to say that a person is a "Native," an "Indian," an "Aboriginal," or a member of the "First Nations"? Are you sensitive about how you want others to refer to your own ethnic or racial origins? You may think that this sensitivity is an indication that political correctness has run amok. In either case, you should not dismiss the issue of labels and names easily.

Ethnic and racial labels are about power. Take the term *Indian*. A hopelessly lost Christopher Columbus thought he had found a sea route to India when he was discovered in 1492 by people indigenous to this part of the world. He mislabelled the people he met as "Indians." Britain's military, political, and economic domination of North America in the 1700s meant that it had the power to ignore the linguistic and cultural differences between indigenous groups and define them in any way they saw fit. They chose the term *Indian*.

As indigenous people have acquired more power, they have begun to challenge externally imposed labels. In the 1980s, for example, the National Indian

Brotherhood renamed itself the Assembly of First Nations, and people in Alberta who were called Sarcee Indians by Europeans for most of the twentieth century now refer to themselves as Tsuu T'ina, which means "Earth People" in English (Steckley, 2003: 7). Groups have rejected externally imposed labels as part of a search for forms of consciousness, identity, and culture that are untainted by the colonizing power's definition of the situation (Jenson, 1993).

One, albeit imperfect, way to make our way through the complex issue of naming is to use the definition of "Aboriginal peoples" that is contained in the 1982 Canadian Charter of Rights and Freedoms. In the Charter, the "Aboriginal peoples" of Canada include Indians, Inuit, and Métis. In 2001, there were 675 499 Indians, 307 845 Métis, and 56 330 Inuit in Canada, who made up about 3 percent of the total population.

At its simplest level, the term *Indian* (or *status* or *registered Indian*) refers to people who are recognized as "Indians" by virtue of the federal government's Indian Act. Many people now use the term "First Nations" to refer to Indians. But deciding who is an Indian under the Indian Act is a much more complicated question. Until 1985, Indian women who married non-Indian men, along with their children, lost their federally recognized Indian status; they became *non-status Indians*. In 1985, Bill C-31 was passed. It allowed these women and their dependent children to regain their Indian status. Indian bands, however, now have the power to develop their own membership codes. This means that not all individuals who have had their Indian status reinstated are members of an Indian band (Frideres and Gadacz, 2005: 35).

There are two definitions of *Métis*. Métis organizations in Western Canada tend to focus on a person's objective "roots" as the condition for being considered Métis. Thus, the Métis National Council defines the Métis as "descendants of the historic Métis who evolved in what is now Western Canada as a people with a common political will" (Métis National Council, 1983). Métis organizations in Eastern Canada, such as the Native Council of Canada, argue that the Métis should include descendants of the historic Métis in Western Canada *and* anyone of mixed European-Indian ancestry who defines himself or herself as Métis and is accepted by other Métis people as such. Thus, subjective definitions of ethnic group membership are more important for groups like the Native Council of Canada.

Finally, *Inuit* are part of a diverse group of people who have lived for many centuries north of the tree line. In Canada, the name *Inuit* has replaced the earlier name *Eskimo*. The language of the Inuit is Inuktitut (McMillan, 1988: 240).

EXPLANATIONS OF ABORIGINAL CONDITIONS

The socioeconomic conditions of Canada's Aboriginal people are a national tragedy (Royal Commission on Aboriginal Peoples, 1996). Canada has made admirable efforts to condemn social inequality and the denial of human rights in other countries, such as South Africa when apartheid—the policy of legalized ethnic separation and inequality—was still in force. Ironically, though, the commitment to social justice for Aboriginal peoples in our own country has not been as strong. In the 1980s, the South African government routinely defended itself against our criticisms of apartheid by saying that we should first clean up our own backyard (Bourgeault, 1988; York, 1989). Statistical evidence shows that Aboriginal peoples are the most socially and economically disadvantaged groups in the country. In 2002–03, 46.8 percent of housing units on reserves in Canada needed to be replaced or were in need of major or minor repairs (Department of Indian Affairs and Northern Development [DIAND], 2004: 62). Though DIAND statistics indicate that 98 percent of houses on reserves have adequate water supplies (DIAND, 2004: 63), the October 2005 mass evacuation of the Kashechewan reserve in northern Ontario because of water supply problems shows that decent water supplies are not available to all reserve communities; indeed, 98 other reserve communities were also under boil water advisories at the same time (Curry, 2005).

On average, Aboriginal people have much lower family incomes, lower rates of labour-force participation, and higher rates of unemployment than non-Aboriginal Canadians do (Frideres and Gadacz, 2005: 98–107). The crude death rate for Aboriginal people in Canada was 8.0 per 1000 in 2001, compared with a rate of 5.3 per 1000 for Canada as a whole (Frideres and Gadacz, 2005: 72). In 2005, the life expectancy of status Indian men was 71.1 years, 6 years lower than the Canadian average. Life expectancy for status Indian women was higher than

that for Indian men but still below life expectancy for other Canadian women: 76.3 compared with 82.4 years. In 2000, the infant mortality rate (the number of deaths of children under one year old per 1000 people) for status Indians was 6.4, which was 14 percent higher than the national rate of 5.5 (DIAND, 2004: 28).

For many years, Canadian politicians, bureaucrats, and social scientists have puzzled over where these differences and inequalities come from, how and why they persist, and what can be done about them. Indeed, when the federal government announced in 1991 the establishment of the Royal Commission on Aboriginal Peoples, Ovide Mercredi, the chief of the Assembly of First Nations, caustically commented that "Indians have been studied to death." I want first to consider the federal government's historical explanation of these conditions and then examine two sociological accounts of them: the culture of poverty thesis and the conflict theory.

The Government's View

Throughout the first half of the twentieth century, government Indian policy was premised on the belief that Aboriginal culture was both different from and inferior to European culture. Armed with this ethnocentric attitude, the federal government sought to assimilate Aboriginal people into mainstream Canadian society (Gibbins and Ponting, 1986). In 1920, this approach was summed up in the following terms by Duncan Campbell Scott, the deputy minister of the federal government's Department of Indian Affairs: "[O]ur object is to continue until there is not a single Indian . . . that has not been absorbed into the body politic and there is no [longer an] Indian question" (quoted in Titley, 1986).

The government, therefore, forcibly tried to Europeanize Aboriginal people and culture. Traditional cultural practices like the potlatch, a winter exchange of gifts and property on the British Columbia coast, and the sun dance, a summer solstice religious ceremony on the Prairies, were outlawed. Such practices were regarded as pagan, anti-capitalist rituals that inhibited the development of both Christianity and a capitalistic work ethic (Cole and Chaikin, 1990; Pettipas, 1995). The federal government also tried to assimilate and Christianize Aboriginal children by establishing a series of residential schools. These boarding schools were located far from the children's families and home communities. While in school, the children were forbidden to speak in their mother tongue and to speak with siblings of the opposite sex and had their hair shorn. Boys were given extensive training in manual labour and girls were taught domestic labour skills. The goal of this schooling was to resocialize Aboriginal children and to instill in them a new European identity (Titley, 1986). The government's legislative, regulatory, and educational approach to Aboriginal people reflected the view that inequality, poverty, and poor social conditions were rooted in Aboriginal cultural and racial inferiority.

The Culture of Poverty Thesis

In the 1960s and 1970s, many sociologists also saw Aboriginal culture as the source of the "Indian problem." To account for the origins and persistence of the problem, some sociologists proposed a variant of the **culture of poverty thesis.** The concept of a culture of poverty was first developed by Oscar Lewis (1961), an American anthropologist interested in explaining the slow pace at which Mexican Americans and Puerto Ricans were being assimilated into U.S. society. He suggested that some ethnic groups do not readily assimilate, and hence are poor, because their culture does not value economic success, hard work, and achievement.

Kazemipur and Halli (2000) have applied Lewis's framework to the issue of ethnic poverty in Canada, and Nagler (1972) has applied it to the conditions of Aboriginal people. In his view, Indian culture displayed the following characteristics: a present rather than a future time-orientation, a high value on mutual aid without the expectation of return, a lack of emphasis on the possession of material goods, a lack of appreciation for the monetary value of time, and the absence of a capitalist work ethic. These cultural characteristics meant that "a large segment of the Indian population refuse or find themselves unable to partake in full time economic pursuits" (Nagler, 1972: 131).

Sociologists like Steven Steinberg (1981) criticize culture of poverty explanations by arguing that groups generally do not get ahead or lag behind because of their cultural values. Instead, they are born into certain stations in life and adopt the values and attitudes that are consistent with their life-chances. If Aboriginal people have low aspirations, it is likely the result of a realistic assessment of their dismal job prospects and a resignation born out of bitter personal experience. For Steinberg, the *culture* of poverty is the consequence, not the cause, of poverty.

Conflict Theory

Since the 1970s, sociologists have focused on blocked opportunities rather than culture as the explanation for inequalities between Aboriginal and non-Aboriginal people. The *internal colonial model* is the most popular variant of the conflict approach (Frideres and Gadacz, 2005). The internal colonial model analyzes the problem of inequality in terms of power imbalances and the exploitation of Aboriginal people and lands by white society.

Theorists of internal colonialism argue that the Indian Act, which outlines the federal government's policies and procedures for dealing with Indian issues, is a paternalistic document that disempowers Indian people (Frideres and Gadacz, 2005). It places real limits on the actions of both individual Indians and their band councils. When Indians from Brantford, Ontario, wanted to sue the federal government over unfulfilled treaty promises in the 1920s, the government passed a law making it illegal for them to use band funds to hire lawyers to pursue their claims (Titley, 1986). Indians did not get much help from federal or provincial/territorial politicians either. Since Indians could not vote in either federal or provincial/territorial elections until the 1960s, politicians had no need to stand up for the interests of Indians who lived in their constituency. Chiefs who failed to cooperate with the government's designs were routinely removed from their positions (Satzewich and Mahood, 1994). Band councils are still required to have their decisions approved by the federal minister of Indian Affairs. Thus, rather than helping to create the social conditions that would afford Indian people greater autonomy over their lives, government policy has fostered social marginality and dependence. This is why many Indian leaders have called for the abolition of the Indian Act.

Furthermore, most of the present-day conflicts between Aboriginal people and various levels of government originated in the past misuse of power by government officials. Present-day land-claim disputes sometimes go back 100 years, when government officials could arbitrarily lop off chunks of Indian reserve land and sell it to whites (Frideres and Gadacz, 2005). The Canadian government and private business have derived tremendous economic benefits from the exploitation of land appropriated from Aboriginal communities. According to internal colonial theorists, the time has come for Canadians to pay the rent. In Alberta, Aboriginal people are suing the federal government for $1.5 billion over the nonpayment of royalties on the extraction of resources from their land. As Frideres and Gadacz (2005: 5) note, with long-term profits estimated at $1 billion to $2 billion, the government and private enterprise "are not about to give up easily."

CLASS AND GENDER DIVERSITY

Criticisms of the internal colonial model have focused on its tendency to overgeneralize about the conditions of Aboriginal people in Canada. As significant as the inequalities between Aboriginal and non-Aboriginal people are, conflict and feminist sociologists argue that it is worth remembering that socioeconomic diversity also exists within Aboriginal communities. These sociologists analyze class and gender differentiation within Aboriginal communities and the implications of such differences for both individual life-chances and wider community life (Satzewich and Wotherspoon, 2001).

Feminist sociologists have been interested in the role of gender in recent debates about the inclusion of the right to self-government in the Canadian Constitution. During the debate over the Charlottetown Accord in 1992, many Aboriginal women were concerned that the proposal for self-government, which was advanced by the predominantly male leadership of Aboriginal organizations, did not contain any guarantees of sexual equality between Aboriginal women and men (Fiske, 1996; Krosenbrink-Gelissen, 1994: 357–60). The Native Women's Association of Canada, therefore, fought against the accord in the months leading up to the referendum.

Other conflict theorists are interested in the political and economic implications of socioeconomic differentiation within Aboriginal communities. Researchers challenge the stereotype that all Aboriginal people are either poor, unemployed, living on welfare, or working in low-skill, dead-end jobs. In fact, a small but nevertheless significant proportion of Aboriginal men and women work in skilled professional and technical occupations, and others are owners or managers of small and large businesses

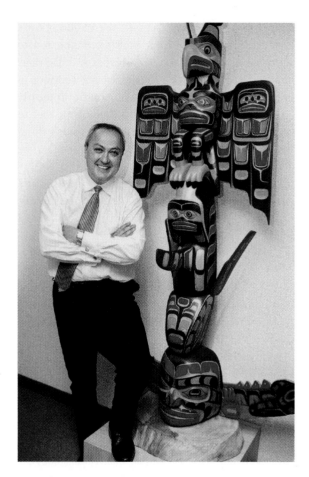

A significant proportion of Aboriginal men and women are owners and managers of both small and large businesses. John Kim Bell, for example, put his musical career on hold to set up the Canadian Native Arts Foundation.
SOURCE: Colin McConnell/CP Picture Archive.

(Gerber, 1990). Menno Boldt (1993: 124; Alfred, 1999) argues that most Indian reserves are characterized by a two-class social order. The first class consists of "a small, virtually closed élite class comprising influential landowners, politicians, bureaucrats, and a few entrepreneurs," while the second consists of "a large lower class comprising destitute, dependent, powerless [and wage-earning] people" (Boldt, 1993: 124). Boldt argues (1993: 125) that this two-class structure has important consequences for community life and community politics:

> With the élite class controlling the political agenda, lower-class interests get neglected. Elite class interests tend to be primarily "power" not "problem" oriented; that is, such interests are related to expanding their jurisdiction and control over band/tribal

political and administrative structures. . . . [These] are given preference over the problems that afflict the Indian lower class: high unemployment; excessive rates of family disintegration; alcohol and substance abuse; extraordinary levels of violence, suicide, incarceration, and so on.

Researchers are also studying the formation of a capitalist class within Aboriginal communities. Land-claim settlements, although ostensibly earmarked for the benefit of all community members, are frequently controlled by small ruling elites. In the case of the Inuit, Marybelle Mitchell (1996: 449) argues,

The state's acknowledgment in 1973 of its responsibility to negotiate land settlements with Native people led to the formation of an Inuit ruling class. Created by the state to facilitate access by the multinationals to the Arctic's natural resources, these leaders, a wholly new kind of talking chief, are signing away the land and aboriginal rights of their fellow Inuit in return for limited entitlement to land, some managerial powers and varying amounts of cash channeled through development corporations.

The members of this new capitalist class are different from other Canadian capitalists, in that they do not personally own all the wealth and capital that is at their disposal. They do, however, control the compensation that communities receive from land-claims settlements. They establish development corporations, hire and fire employees, make capital-planning and investment decisions, and decide what and how much to produce. The unanswered sociological question is whether this capitalist class will make decisions about the future that are in their own material interests or in the interests of the community as a whole.

QUEBEC: NATIONALISM AND IDENTITY

On the evening of October 30, 1995, many adult Canadians were tuned to TV or radio coverage of the Quebec referendum on separation. I followed the results that night with mixed emotions. On the one hand, as a second-generation Canadian with no ethnic roots in the old British Empire, I could empathize with people in Quebec. On the other hand,

as a child of the Trudeau years, I was socialized to believe in a vision of Canadian unity. Many on the "no" side believed that a lot of Quebeckers were just bluffing in the pre-referendum rhetoric; when it came to the crunch, they would vote in favour of staying in Canada. Then the results came in. In some parts of Quebec, 90 percent of voters were in favour of separation. As the results from around Montreal were tabulated, the "no" side gained ground. When the final count was tallied, 49.6 percent of Quebeckers voted for separation. Across Canada, people were both exhilarated and downcast because Canada had "won."

Will the issue of separation go away? Despite the ebb and flow in support for separation, the answer is clearly "no." As with other areas of ethnic relations in Canada, an understanding of the contemporary scene must begin with an appreciation of history and of power relations. In this section, I examine three main sociological questions: (1) What is the historical basis for the emergence of Québécois nationalism? (2) Who is a Québécois? (3) What does the close 1995 vote mean for ethnic relations in Quebec and the country?

THE SOCIAL BASIS OF QUÉBÉCOIS NATIONALISM

Even though the 1867 British North America Act asserted that there were two founding peoples of Canada, the English and the French, and that they had equal places in Canadian Confederation, *les Québécois* are one of the oldest colonized peoples in the world (Milner and Milner, 1973). The French government controlled the colony of New France from the early 1600s to 1763. The inhabitants of New France were expected to serve the interests of France. The colony was established in part to pursue the fur trade and to transfer economic resources to the mother country. Much of the French commercial and political elite left the colony following the British victory over France in 1763. When New France was transferred to British control—what the Québécois refer to as "The Conquest"—a new colonizing power came to dominate the society.

An anglophone—unilingual, English-speaking—elite gradually took over the economic and political affairs of the province. Most French-Canadian peasants (*habitants*) remained subsistence farmers. During the nineteenth century, some of them immigrated to the northeastern United States to work in the expanding cotton and linen mills; others moved to other provinces in Canada; and still others became part of the urban industrial working class in the province (Ramirez, 1991). By the late nineteenth century, Quebec was a province where "capital speaks English and labour speaks French" (Whitaker, 1993: 22)—a telling description of the way in which linguistic and class structures overlapped. The French Canadians in Quebec, who formed a numerical majority, were worse off than the anglophone minority in virtually every material way (Whitaker, 1993: 22).

The Catholic Church occupied a unique position as a social, political, and religious intermediary between the two groups. In addition to attending to the religious needs of its French-speaking parishioners, the Catholic Church acted as an agent of social control over French-Canadian workers and farmers. The church promoted social ideologies that were conservative and anti-modern. It devalued the importance of formal education for the masses, discouraged workers from forming and joining secular trade unions, encouraged married couples to have large families, and vigorously discouraged French Canadians from taking up professions or establishing businesses of their own. These ideas were not in the best material interests of French-Canadian workers and farmers, but they helped ensure the survival of French-Canadian culture (Latouche, 1993).

This social structure began to change significantly during the rapid industrialization stimulated by World War I, as the industrial working class became a significant player on the political scene. One of the biggest changes in the 1940s and 1950s was the rise of a new francophone middle class of technical workers and professionals. The upper echelons of the corporate world, still under the control of anglophones, remained hostile to the advancement of francophones, even if they were bilingual. The new francophone middle class, therefore, faced a situation of blocked social mobility, which was partly responsible for the Quiet Revolution in Quebec.

The term **Quiet Revolution** describes the social, political, and cultural changes that occurred in Quebec in the 1960s, in part because of the initiatives of this new middle class. These changes included the secularization of the educational system, reform of the civil service, growth in the provincially controlled public sector, greater involvement of the Quebec provincial government in the economic affairs of the province, and questioning of the Catholic Church's authority in all areas of life. Facing blocked mobility in the corporate world, francophones created their own economic opportunities by expanding the power of the provincial government.

Social scientists and political pundits have pored over referendum and federal and provincial election results over the past 30 years in an effort to determine which social forces are responsible for sustaining the push for sovereignty. Some see the present-day sovereignty movement as an expression of *middle-class nationalism* that is a continuation of the Quiet Revolution. From this perspective, separation is being promoted by middle-class professionals as a way of furthering their own material interests. Emboldened by the success at expanding the activities of the provincial government during the Quiet Revolution, they desire even more control over their affairs (Whitaker, 1993).

However, likening the sovereignty movement to a massive job-creation project is too simplistic. First, francophone professionals are no longer shut out of the corporate sector in Quebec. Over the past 30 years, middle-class francophones have achieved upward mobility in both the private and the public sectors. Second, a diversity of class interests exists within the sovereignty movement. Many francophone professionals support sovereignty, but there is also a social democratic tradition within the movement that is trying to mobilize working people against foreign (anglophone and U.S.) capitalist domination. Their vision of a sovereign Quebec involves a reorganization of power relations between francophones and nonfrancophones, and between workers and capitalists. Some francophone capitalists also support the sovereignty movement (Whitaker, 1993).

Clearly, the contemporary sovereignty movement is not based on the support of only one social class. According to Fleras and Elliot (1996), the nationalist movement is sustained by a broadly based desire among most francophone Quebeckers to achieve a common goal—to create the conditions that will allow them to preserve their French language and culture and to "*voler de ses propres ailes* (fly on her own wings) by acquiring the freedom to make their own decisions on everything from cultural policy to social development" (Turp, 2005: A25). Fleras and Elliot argue that, rather than defining support for the sovereignty movement in class terms, it is more useful to conceptualize the movement as made up of groups who have differing views about how best to maintain their language and culture. Thus, the present-day sovereignty movement consists in part of moderates who want to strengthen Quebec's position within the federal system. This involves a new constitutional division of powers that has yet to be settled. Radical supporters, however, argue that the best way for the French language and culture to survive is for the people of Quebec to have their own state. They argue that they will always be a minority if they stay in Canada and that they will always be subject to the tyranny of the majority. As Louise Beaudoin of the Parti Québécois put it, "I want to be a majority in my own country" (Fleras and Elliot, 1996: 270).

WHO IS QUÉBÉCOIS?

The population of Quebec is ethnically heterogeneous—19.4 percent of the population of Quebec is made up of people whose mother tongue is not French: Jews, anglophones, allophones (people whose mother tongue is neither French nor English),

visible-minority immigrants, and Aboriginal people (Fournier, Rosenberg, and White, 1997: 282). One of the central issues facing the nationalist movement in Quebec is the definition of a Québécois. This question cuts to the heart of ethnic relations in the province.

Benedict Anderson (1983) regards nations as "imagined communities." They are imagined in the sense that, even though members of the smallest nation can never know everyone in the community, there is still a common feeling of fellowship with others in the nation. People in Shawinigan do not personally know all other Quebeckers. Nevertheless, they have a comradeship that extends beyond personal relationships. Nations also possess physical and symbolic boundaries that define who is a member and who is not. Sociologists interested in nationalism want to identify the symbolic boundaries of the nation. In the case of the nationalist movement in Quebec, this issue is translated into the question of who is "in" and who is "outside" the imagined community. And if some groups are "out," will they ever be accepted as Québécois?

With 19.4 percent of Quebec's population made up of people whose mother tongue is not French, one of the central issues facing the nationalist movement in Quebec is the definition of a Québécois.
SOURCE: Megapress/Alamy.

A majority of nationalists define the imagined community as all those people who now live in the province of Quebec. For them, the social and symbolic boundaries of the nation correspond to present-day provincial boundaries. Sociologists call this a form of **civic nationalism** (Balthazar, 1993).

A minority of nationalists reject civic nationalism in favour of cultural and linguistic criteria for membership in the nation. *Ethnic nationalists* define the Québécois as people who share a common history, culture, ancestry, or language. This is where the concept of *pure laine* ("pure wool") Québécois becomes important. Some nationalists regard the true Québécois as only those who are the direct descendants of the French people who settled in the colony of New France before the conquest of 1763. Other groups in the province are regarded as "cultural communities" (GRES, 1997: 107). According to the province's policy of interculturalism, these cultural communities must learn to accommodate themselves to the dominant francophone culture and language.

The debate about how to define a nation is not academic hairsplitting. Premier Jacques Parizeau commented on referendum night in 1995 that the pro-sovereignty forces were defeated by "money and the ethnic vote." After his resignation, Parizeau commented further that it was the first time in Canadian history that the majority (60 percent) of francophone Quebeckers voted in favour of sovereignty. These statements implied that ethnic minorities were not really part of the nation and that *pure laine* votes should be worth more than the votes of others. At the time, Parizeau's remarks also confirmed the worst fears of ethnic minorities—namely, that sovereigntists are not civic nationalists but rather ethnic nationalists at heart and that ethnic minorities will never be considered full and equal citizens in a sovereign Quebec (Ha, 1995).

Many people in the sovereignty movement distanced themselves from Parizeau's comments, and the movement has sought to repair the damage that they caused to ethnic relations. Yet polls conducted in 2005 indicated that just more than half of Quebeckers would vote in favour of sovereignty in a new referendum (*The Economist*, 2005: 8). One of the reasons for the resurgence in support for sovereignty is that the "children of Bill 101" are coming of age. Bill 101 was enacted in 1977 and requires that the children of immigrants attend francophone schools. Immigrant children educated in francophone schools are now entering the political arena and many believe that their interests would be better served in an indepen-dent Quebec (Laforest, 2005: A25; Turp, 2005: A25). Clearly, the definition of the Québécois imagined community is changing.

IMMIGRATION: STATE FORMATION AND ECONOMIC DEVELOPMENT

The third aspect of ethnic and racial relations in Canada that I consider is immigrant and non-immigrant relations. In 2001, 5.5 million immigrants were living in Canada, representing 18.4 percent of our population. In large cities, the impact of immigration is even greater. In 2001, immigrants made up 23.6 percent of the population of Hamilton, 37.5 percent of the population of Vancouver, and 43.7 percent of the population of Toronto (Statistics Canada, 2004). Canada accepts more immigrants and refugees in proportion to our population than virtually any other country in the world (Li, 2003).

Migration has been a feature of our history for more than 300 years. However, the nature, sources, determinants, and consequences of immigration have varied through history. In the nineteenth century, immigrants contributed to the processes of capitalist state formation—the process of creating a capitalist system of production and governance. They did this in a number of ways. The early working class in Canada was made up largely of immigrants (Avery, 1995; Pentland, 1981). Immigrant workers helped build the canals, railways, and roads that became part of our economic infrastructure. Many nineteenth-century immigrants were farmers. Their crops were used to feed Canadian workers and, as productivity increased, were exported to feed people in other countries. Those same farmers, in turn, helped stimulate capitalist industry through their roles as consumers of goods. A significant proportion of the corporate elite in nineteenth-century Canada were made up of immigrants (Clement, 1975; Macmillan, 1985), as was a large segment of the early political elite. Canada's first prime minister, Sir John A. Macdonald, was an immigrant from Glasgow, Scotland.

Immigrants continue to make important contributions to the social reproduction of Canadian society. Demographers predict that, in the absence of new immigrants, the population of Canada would begin to decline by 2015. Without new immigrants to replenish our population, the next generation of taxpayers would have to pay far more in taxes and Canada Pension Plan contributions. Retiring at the age of 55, or even 65, would become a pipe dream for many older workers, as employers and governments would need to take steps to retain enough workers. Employers would face serious shortages of workers, and manufacturers would face a much smaller consumer market in which to sell their goods (Economic Council of Canada, 1991).

FACTORS THAT SHAPE CANADIAN IMMIGRATION

No single variable can explain the complex pattern of immigration to Canada. Over the past 100 years, six main variables have influenced which groups of people have been let into the country as immigrants.

The first variable is social class. Most immigrants are admitted to Canada because they fill jobs in the Canadian economy, have certain skills that are in demand, or because they create jobs for other Canadians. As such, the flow of immigrants to Canada has been very closely linked to the overall structure of the Canadian economy. Between 1947 and the early 1960s, for example, immigrants were regarded by the Canadian government as what Australian economist Jock Collins (1988) calls "factory fodder." Immigrants were recruited to fill unskilled and semiskilled manual jobs in agriculture, construction, mining, logging, the garment industry, and heavy manufacturing. During this time, it was common for individual employers to demand that the government recruit as many as 300 immigrant workers at a time to fill job openings (Avery, 1995).

In the early 1960s, immigration policy began to place more emphasis on the recruitment of highly skilled professional and technical workers, and on immigrants with large amounts of investment capital. As a result, by 2001, immigrants made up 18.4 percent of the population and 19.9 percent of the total Canadian labour force, but 21.7 percent of people in managerial occupations and 21.4 percent of people in professional and technical occupations (Statistics Canada, 2001b).

The second determinant of immigration is ethnic and racial **stereotypes**—exaggerated, oversimplified images of the characteristics of social groups. Before 1962, Canadian immigration policy had a racialized hierarchy of desirability. Immigration policy was based on the assumption that European immigrants were racially and culturally superior to all other potential immigrants. Non-Europeans were stereotyped as racially and culturally inferior and, therefore, were not welcome. In the 1950s, for example, immigration officials could bar groups from entering Canada on the grounds that the groups were "unsuited to climatic and economic conditions" or that they were "unable to assimilate" (Bolaria and Li, 1988). These phrases were thinly veiled masks for racial preferences in the selection of immigrants.

Since 1962, ethnic and racial stereotyping in selecting new immigrants has become less important. Canadian immigration policy is now more open in terms of the ethnic and racial origins of immigrants

TABLE 8.3 TOP 10 SOURCE COUNTRIES OF IMMIGRANTS (PRINCIPAL APPLICANTS AND DEPENDANTS) TO CANADA, 1968, 2004

1968		2004	
COUNTRY OF ORIGIN	NUMBER	COUNTRY OF ORIGIN	NUMBER
United Kingdom	63 291	China	36 411
Italy	31 625	India	25 569
United States	17 514	Philippines	13 301
Germany	9263	Pakistan	12 796
Portugal	7930	United States	7494
France	7872	Iran	6063
Greece	7174	United Kingdom	6058
The Netherlands	3749	Romania	5655
Australia	3329	Korea, Republic of	5337
Switzerland	2982	France	5026

SOURCE: Manpower and Immigration, Immigration Statistics, 1966, Ottawa: Queen's Printer, 1967, p. 5; Citizenship and Immigration Canada, Facts and Figures 2004: Immigration Overview, http://www.cic.gc.ca/English/pub/facts2004/permanent/12.html.

(see Table 8.3). Before 1961, Europeans made up more than 90 percent of total immigrants to Canada. Now, immigrants from Europe make up about 17 percent of the yearly flow of immigrants to Canada.

The third variable that shapes immigrant selection consists of a variety of geopolitical considerations stemming from Canada's relationships with other countries. Racist selection criteria were taken out of immigration regulations in the 1960s, in part because they interfered with Canadian international diplomacy. In the early 1960s, Canada began to assert itself as a middle power in world politics that could mediate social conflicts in and between other countries. Outside of Europe, though, our diplomats did not have much credibility because our immigration policy implied that certain groups were inferior and therefore not suited to life in Canada (Hawkins, 1989).

In the 1980s, the Cold War also played a role in shaping who was let in. According to Whitaker (1987), a double standard was at work in the admittance of refugees. People who managed to escape from the Soviet Union or other Eastern Bloc coun-tries were routinely granted refugee status in Canada. In 1985, for example, it took a day for the brother of a Czech hockey star who played for the Toronto Maple Leafs to be granted refugee status in Canada. Canadian immigration bureaucrats were much more cautious, however, about admitting "socialist" refugees who were fleeing right-wing dictatorships in various Central American countries.

The fourth variable affecting immigrant selection is humanitarianism. Canada accepts immigrants and refugees partly on humanitarian and compassionate grounds. In 1986, Canada was the first country ever to be awarded the Nansen Medal by the United Nations for its generosity and commitment to international refugee programs (Fleras and Elliot, 1996).

The influence of the fifth variable, public opinion, is more difficult to determine, in part because Canadians do not speak with one voice regarding immigration. A 1991 poll found five distinct segments of opinion regarding immigration. Twenty-three percent were "protagonists" who supported increased levels of immigration and believed that immigrants

After the terrorist attack on the United States of September 11, 2001, Canada introduced a new Permanent Resident Card and a number of new measures to increase security at Canadian borders.

SOURCE: Shutterstock.

made important contributions to the betterment of Canadian society; 22 percent were "concerned supporters" who approved of current levels of immigration but who were concerned that immigration had certain negative effects on Canadian institutions; 21 percent were "indifferent" in their attitudes toward immigration and ambivalent about the contributions that immigrants make; 19 percent were "reactionaries" who felt that the government has lost control over immigration and that immigration was largely negative for Canada. The size of this segment seems to rise when cases of people who appear to be abusing the immigration system come to light. This happened during the summer of 1999, when four boatloads of what appeared to be economic migrants from China were dumped on the Vancouver Island coastline. The remaining 15 percent of Canadians in the poll had no opinion on immigration (Holton and Lanphier, 1994). Holton and Lanphier (1994; see also Zong, 1994) suggest that these findings point to a hardening of Canadian attitudes toward immigration.

The sixth variable, security considerations, has become more important since the terrorist attacks on the United States on September 11, 2001. In the aftermath of the attacks, Canada introduced a new Permanent Resident Card and a number of new measures to increase security at Canadian borders. In addition, Canada and the United States are increasingly discussing the harmonization of immigration policies, particularly in the area of security screening of immigrants and refugees. Some commentators refer to this harmonization as a move toward a "Fortress North America" (Satzewich and Wong, 2003).

THE CONTEMPORARY IMMIGRATION CATEGORIES

Immigrants in Canada fit one of three main categories: refugees, family class, and independent immigrants. Altogether, 235 824 immigrants entered Canada in 2004.

Refugees

Nearly 33 000 refugees and their dependants were admitted to Canada in 2004. There are three categories of refugees that Canada accepts through its immigration program. *Convention refugees* are people who are defined as refugees by the 1951 Geneva Convention Relating to the Status of Refugees and its 1967 protocol. They are people who, by reason of their

race, religion, nationality, membership in a particular social group, or political opinion, live outside of their country of nationality or their country of habitual residence and who are unable or unwilling, because of fear of persecution, to return to their country of origin (Citizenship and Immigration Canada, 1996: 28).

Country of asylum class refugees are people who are outside their country of citizenship or residence who are seriously and personally affected by civil war, armed conflict, or massive violations of human rights. Finally, *source country class* refugees include people who would meet the definition of a Convention refugee but who are still in their country of citizenship or residence. This category also includes people who have been detained or imprisoned and are suffering serious deprivations of the right of freedom of expression, the right of dissent, or the right to engage in trade union activity.

Family Class Immigrants

About 62 000 *family class immigrants* arrived in Canada in 2004. Family class immigrants have close family members already living in Canada who are willing and able to support them. A sponsor must be a Canadian citizen or a permanent resident who is over 18 years of age and who is living in Canada. Depending on the specific circumstances, a sponsor must be able to provide for the lodging, care, maintenance, and normal settlement needs of the family member(s) for between three and ten years (Citizenship and Immigration Canada, 2002).

Economic/Independent Immigrants

Economic immigrants numbered about 134 000 in 2004. The federal government has increased the size of this category in total immigration flows and has decreased the number of family class immigrants, because it believes that the former are of greater economic benefit to Canada. There are four subcategories of independent immigrants. *Skilled workers* are selected by the federal government on the basis of their ability to meet certain minimum work experience requirements, to prove that they have enough funds to support themselves and their family members in Canada, and merit as measured by the **points system.** As Table 8.4 shows, applicants are awarded points for various attributes that the Canadian government deems important in determining an immigrant's economic and settlement prospects. An applicant has to earn a minimum of 67 out of 100 points to "pass" and potentially gain admission to Canada as a skilled worker. The amount of money immigrants need to have when they arrive in

TABLE 8.4 THE POINTS SYSTEM FOR THE SELECTION OF INDEPENDENT IMMIGRANTS, CANADA, 2005

CRITERIA	UNITS OF ASSESSMENT (MAXIMUM)
Education	25 points
Knowledge of French and/or English	24 points
Experience	21 points
Age	10 points
Arranged employment in Canada	10 points
Adaptability	10 points
Pass Mark	**67 points**

SOURCE: Citizenship and Immigration Canada, Skilled Workers: Will You Qualify as a Skilled Worker? http://www.cic.gc.ca/English/skilled/qual-5.html, pp. 1–4. Reproduced with the permission of the Minister of Public Works and Government Services Canada, 2006.

Canada depends on the number of family members they have. For example, an immigrant who brings four family members to Canada needs to have $17 286.

Immigrant entrepreneurs are people who will own and actively manage a business that will contribute to the economy and create jobs. They must have business experience and a minimum net worth of $300 000. *Immigrant investors* are capitalists who have a personal net worth of at least $800 000 and who plan to invest at least $400 000 in a business in Canada. *Self-employed immigrants* must have the intention and ability to create their own employment. They are expected to contribute to the cultural or artistic life of the country. They can also qualify under this program if they purchase and manage a farm in Canada. The 890 immigrant entrepreneurs admitted to Canada in 2002 invested more than $122 000 000 and created 1100 jobs after just one year in Canada (Citizenship and Immigration Canada, 2004).

ETHNIC INEQUALITY AND THE CANADIAN LABOUR MARKET

JOHN PORTER AND THE VERTICAL MOSAIC

What happens to immigrants after they come to Canada? How are they sorted and placed in the socioeconomic structure? John Porter's answers to these questions in *The Vertical Mosaic* have had a profound impact on Canadian sociology. Since its publication in 1965, Canadian sociologists have been interested in whether ethnicity and race affect the operation of the labour market, social mobility, and the composition of elites.

Porter argued that Canada is a **vertical mosaic,** a society in which ethnic groups tend to occupy different and unequal positions in the stratification system. He suggested that the first ethnic group to take control of a previously unoccupied or newly conquered territory is the *charter group* of that society. One prerogative that goes to a charter group is the ability to decide "what other groups are to be let in and what they will be permitted to do" (Porter, 1965: 62). Canada has two charter groups, the English and the French. Although their power was, and is, unequal, Porter argued that the two charter groups have been able to set the terms by which other immigrants are admitted to Canada. These charter groups reserved for themselves the top positions in the occupational hierarchy. They also made up the upper ranks of the labour, political, bureaucratic, religious, and media elites.

Immigrants who arrived after these charter groups were assigned to less preferred positions. Non-English and non-French immigrants were assigned an *entrance status* that was linked in part to the social evaluation of their cultural and racial capacities. Groups from Northern and Western Europe were considered more racially and culturally like the English and French, and were accorded a higher entrance status than Southern and Eastern European immigrants. The latter were regarded as culturally, if not racially, inferior to the charter groups and were therefore placed in lower levels of the occupational hierarchy and excluded from elite positions. Non-Europeans were defined as inassimilable and were virtually barred from entry (Woodsworth, 1972).

Porter argued that once the vertical mosaic was established, it took on a life of its own. Immigrants and their descendants who were initially allocated a subordinate entrance status faced limited prospects for upward social mobility. He thought two factors accounted for the rigidity of the vertical mosaic. One was blatant prejudice and discrimination by charter groups. The other was the retention by ethnic groups of cultural practices that were incompatible with economic success in modern, industrialized societies. In other words, certain immigrants and their descendants were caught in an *ethnic mobility trap* because of their continued identification with a subordinated and marginalized ethnic group (Wiley, 1967).

In the context of its time, Porter's analysis was both powerful and insightful. As we have seen, before 1962, the selection of new immigrants was based on ethnic and racial stereotypes. These stereotypes also shaped charter group perceptions of what kinds of jobs immigrants were fit to do. In the 1950s, for example, Italian immigrant men were regarded by immigration bureaucrats and members of the economic elite as culturally willing and able to "tolerate irregular employment, low wages and physically demanding work." They were recruited specifically for work in agriculture, mining, domestic service, the metal trades, and logging (Iacovetta, 1992: 28). Black women from the Caribbean were recruited specifically as housekeepers and nannies for middle-class families in the 1950s and 1960s, in part because they were believed to be nurturing and passive (Daenzer, 1993).

THE DECLINING SIGNIFICANCE OF THE VERTICAL MOSAIC

Does the vertical mosaic still exist? Is the distribution of economic rewards still based on ethnicity? Over the past two decades, debates have raged among Canadian sociologists about whether race and ethnicity continue to shape our stratification system (Brym with Fox, 1989). Gordon Darroch (1979) and Edward Herberg (1990) argue that the vertical mosaic is no longer a useful way of describing our society. Later in his life, John Porter also had doubts about its continued existence (Pineo and Porter, 1985). Others argue that, although we may be moving in the direc-

tion of greater equality, the vertical mosaic is still a useful metaphor for describing our society. They suggest that the vertical mosaic has been recast along racial lines (Fleras and Elliot, 1996).

What is the evidence for the view that "race," or visible minority status, constitutes a fundamental dividing line in Canadian society? To answer this question, it is important to compare like with like. Sociologists need to statistically match people from different visible minority groups in terms of occupation, age, gender, language abilities, experience, education, region of work, and number of weeks worked per year before they can see whether visible minority status affects people's life-chances. It is only when these sources of variation in earnings are controlled that we can sketch an accurate picture of earnings differences because of visible-minority status. Table 8.5 provides information on some of the important recent patterns of earnings inequality:

- Earnings for different groups vary by the size of the community they live in.
- Canadian-born men earn more than immigrant men, and Canadian-born women earn more than immigrant women.
- Among men born in Canada, white men have average yearly earnings that are higher than those for men from visible minorities.
- Among women born in Canada, women who are members of visible minority groups have average yearly earnings that are higher than those of white women.

The storefront of a downtown Toronto street reflects the ethnic diversity of most large Canadian cities.
SOURCE: Dick Hemingway.

TABLE 8.5 NET EARNINGS OF IMMIGRANTS AND NATIVE-BORN CANADIANS AS DEVIATIONS FROM NATIONAL MEAN EARNINGS ($26 521) FOR FOUR CENSUS METROPOLITAN AREA (CMA) LEVELS, 1996 CENSUS (IN DOLLARS)

		NET EARNINGS AFTER ADJUSTING FOR INDIVIDUAL AND MARKET CHARACTERISTICS*	
		Native-Born Canadian	**Immigrant**
Not CMA			
White	Male	5136	1258
	Female	−2901	−8645
Visible Minority	Male	4801	1686
	Female	336	−5768
Small CMA (<500 000)			
White	Male	6044	2432
	Female	−3238	−9578
Visible Minority	Male	4764	−2151
	Female	−1517	−8250
Medium CMA (500 000–999 999)			
White	Male	5136	1349
	Female	−3813	−10 578
Visible Minority	Male	61	−6372
	Female	−1588	−9823
Large CMA (1 000 000+)			
White	Male	5392	−314
	Female	−3508	−10 188
Visible Minority	Male	479	−6654
	Female	−2722	−10 372

SOURCE: From Destination Canada: Immigration Debates and Issues by P. Li. Copyright © 2003 Oxford University Press Canada. Reprinted by permission of the publisher.

*Net earnings are adjusted for differences in individual characteristics and differences in market characteristics. Individual characteristics include industry of work, occupation, full-time or part-time work, years of schooling, years of work experience, experience, number of weeks worked, official languages ability, and number of years since immigrated to Canada for immigrants. Market characteristics include the level of unemployment in the person's region of residence, and the size of immigrants' population as a percent of the region's total population.

- Among immigrant men, white immigrants generally have average yearly earnings that are higher than those for men in visible minorities.
- For both immigrant and Canadian-born men, the differences in average yearly earnings are more pronounced in census metropolitan areas than in rural areas.
- Women who are members of visible minority groups and born outside Canada, and white women born outside Canada are about equally disadvantaged, having the lowest average yearly earnings of all.

These findings should lead us to be cautious about concluding that "race" constitutes a fundamental socioeconomic dividing line in Canadian society. Canada does not have a single, clear-cut pattern of ethnic or racial economic disadvantage, and significant differences exist in the relative positions of visible minority men and women.

Note that the categories "visible minority" and "white" are made up of diverse groups of people. "Visible minority" Canadians have different immigration histories, histories of settlement, and times of arrival in Canada, so some do better economically in

Canada than others. Similarly, "white" individuals of Portuguese background tend to do significantly less well in Canada than individuals of other European origins and visible minorities. Table 8.6 shows, for example, that in 2001, Portuguese men had the lowest socioeconomic status for all men (tied with Aboriginal men) and that Chinese men had the second-highest occupational skill level.

Notwithstanding these cautions, at the very least the vertical mosaic metaphor seems to describe accurately the position of male immigrants in Canada. Differences between male immigrants who are members of visible minorities and white immigrants have

been explained by the devaluation of immigrant credentials. Some suggest that education credentials of immigrants from visible minorities are devalued in the labour market and by certification authorities. In one celebrated case, an evaluation officer of the Ontario Ministry of Education wrote to a Jamaican immigrant that his honours degree from Harvard University and his Ph.D. from Stanford were equivalent to "at least Grade Thirteen in the Ontario school system" (Special Committee on the Participation of Visible Minorities in Canadian Society, 1984). Although this may have been a bureaucratic error, evidence shows that many immigrant teachers,

TABLE 8.6 NET DIFFERENCE[a] IN OCCUPATIONAL STATUS (1971) AND OCCUPATIONAL SKILL GROUP (2001) BETWEEN SELECTED ETHNIC GROUPS AND THE REST OF THE LABOUR FORCE, BY SEX, CANADA

Ethnic Group	MALE 1971	MALE 2001	FEMALE 1971	FEMALE 2001
British	0.13	0.06	0.14	0.05
French	−0.06	0.04	−0.02	0.06
German	−0.08	0.04	−0.09	0.01
Dutch	−0.09	0.05	−0.10	0.04
Scandinavian	−0.08	0.07	−0.01	0.05
Ukrainian	−0.09	0.06	−0.13	0.03
Polish	−0.08	0.03	−0.12	−0.02
Hungarian	−0.06	0.07	−0.13	0.02
Italian	−0.22	0.01	−0.35	0.00
Portuguese	−0.38	−0.15	−0.62	−0.16
Greek	−0.27	0.02	−0.48	−0.04
Yugoslav	−0.12	0.03	−0.29	−0.03
Jewish	0.36	0.34	0.24	0.24
Chinese	−0.04	0.19	−0.20	0.00
South Asian	0.26	−0.05	0.19	−0.12
Aboriginal	−0.35[b]	−0.15	−0.23[b]	−0.08
Black	NI	−0.10	NI	−0.09
Mean	0.17	0.09	0.21	0.06
Number of Occupational Ranks/Skill Groups	(498)	(4)	(464)	(4)

SOURCE: From *Society in Question* 5/E by Brym. © 2008. Reprinted with permission of Nelson, a division of Thomson Learning: www.thomsonrights.com. Fax: 800-730-2215.

[a]A negative figure indicates a relatively low occupational status/skill group; a positive figure indicates a relatively high status/skill group. Zero indicates equality of occupational status/skill group. The greater the absolute size of the index, the greater the inequality.

[b]Does not include Inuit.

NI: Not included.

doctors, nurses, and engineers find that their non-Western university degrees and diplomas are of little value in Canada (Basran and Zong, 1998; Henry and Tator, 2006). Some say that this devaluation of credentials is a reflection of racism in Canadian society.

Other research on employers' hiring practices has documented the influence of racial discrimination in employment. Henry and Ginsberg (1985) conducted a study in Toronto in which they sent two groups of actors with virtually identical résumés to apply for various jobs. The only difference between members of the two was the colour of their skin or their accent: One group consisted of actors who were white and who had Anglo-Canadian accents, and the other group consisted of visible minority group members, some of whom had non-Anglo-Canadian accents. The researchers found that, in both face-to-face interviews and approaches over the telephone, whites received three job offers for every job offered to applicants from visible minority groups. Applicants from visible-minority groups were five times more likely to be told that the job had been filled when a subsequent white applicant was invited for an interview (Henry and Ginsberg, 1985).

A follow-up study conducted in 1989 showed no racial discrimination in job offers following face-to-face contacts between applicants and employers. Blacks and whites received equal numbers of job offers. When it came to approaches over the telephone, however, callers with foreign accents were less likely to be invited for an interview and more likely to be told that the job was filled when in fact it was not (Henry, 1989). Without more recent research, it is difficult to know whether outright discrimination helps explain patterns of earnings inequality today.

SUMMARY

1. Ethnic categories and identities are not fixed and unchanging; they evolve socially and historically. Canadians may now be considered an ethnic group, as they display a strong desire to define their ethnicity as "Canadian."

2. Racism refers to ideas and institutional practices that discriminate against members of groups that are perceived as racially distinct. Institutional racism refers to circumstances in which social institutions operate, or once operated, on the basis of racist ideas.

3. Racism, prejudice, and discrimination have been analyzed from different sociological perspectives. Social-psychological theories, primordialism, normative theories, and power-conflict theories each offer different interpretations of ethnic and racial hostility.

4. The term "Aboriginal people" includes people who are defined in the Constitution as "Indian," "Métis," and "Inuit." The terms used to describe Aboriginal people are socially negotiated and change because of shifts in power relations among groups.

5. The culture of poverty thesis was used in the 1970s as a way of explaining the poor socioeconomic conditions of Aboriginal people. Problems with the culture of poverty thesis led to the development of the internal colonial model, a variant of conflict theory. Conflict and feminist sociologists are beginning to be more interested in class and gender diversity within the Aboriginal population.

6. Material inequalities between French and English in Quebec provided the historical basis for the emergence of nationalism in Quebec. The contemporary nationalist movement has a diverse class base.

7. Debates exist in the nationalist movement about who is Québécois. Tensions exist between ethnic and civic nationalists.

8. Immigration has played different roles in Canadian history. During the nineteenth century, immigrants contributed to capitalist state formation. Now, immigrants contribute to the social and economic reproduction of Canadian society.

9. There are six main variables that have shaped immigrant selection in Canada: social class, ethnic and racial stereotypes, geopolitical considerations, humanitarianism, public opinion, and security considerations. Immigrants are categorized as refugees, family class, or independents. Independent immigrants are selected on the basis of the points system.

10. John Porter argued that Canada was a vertical mosaic, a social structure in which ethnic groups occupy different and unequal positions within the stratification system. Evidence suggests that the vertical mosaic is declining in importance, at least for European immigrants and people born in Canada. Discrimination against immigrants from visible-minority groups is still a problem.

QUESTIONS TO CONSIDER

1. What are the strengths and weaknesses of different sociological approaches to the study of the social significance of race and ethnicity?

2. To what extent do racist attitudes and behaviour affect the life-chances of people in Canada?

3. How would you account for the apparent growth in support for sovereignty in Quebec?

4. Do you think that the importance of class and gender diversity within Aboriginal communities will increase or decrease in the future?

5. Are Canadians an ethnic group? Why or why not?

GLOSSARY

Civic nationalism is a form of nationalism in which the social boundaries of the nation are defined in territorial and geographic terms.

The **culture of poverty thesis** is the theory that some ethnic groups do not readily assimilate, and hence are poor, because their culture does not value economic success, hard work, and achievement.

Discrimination refers to practices that deny members of particular groups equal access to societal rewards.

Institutional racism refers to discriminatory racial practices built into such prominent structures as the political, economic, and education systems.

New racism is a theory of human nature that suggests that it is natural for groups to form bounded communities. One group is neither better nor worse than another, but feelings of antagonism will be aroused if outsiders are admitted.

The **points system** is a system used by the Canadian government to select independent immigrants. Applicants are awarded "points" for various attributes that the Canadian government deems important in determining an immigrant's economic contribution to Canada.

Prejudice is an unfavourable, generalized, and rigid belief applied to all members of a group.

The **primordialist thesis** is the theory that ethnic attachments reflect a basic tendency of people to seek out, and associate with, their "own kind."

The **Quiet Revolution** refers to the social, political, and cultural changes that occurred in Quebec in the 1960s, in part because of the emergence of a francophone middle class.

Race is a socially constructed label that has been used to describe certain kinds of physical differences between people.

The **split labour-market theory** is the theory that racial and ethnic conflicts are rooted in differences in the price of labour.

Stereotypes are exaggerated, oversimplified images of the characteristics of social categories.

The **vertical mosaic** is a social structure in which ethnic groups occupy different, and unequal, positions within the stratification system.

SUGGESTED READING

Fleras, Augie, and Jean Leonard Elliott. (2003). *Unequal Relations: An Introduction to Race and Ethnic Dynamics in Canada* (4th ed.). Toronto: Prentice Hall. Deals with a wide range of issues surrounding diversity in Canada, focusing on themes of power, politics, group dynamics, and macro-processes.

Frideres, James, and René Gadacz. (2005). *Aboriginal People in Canada: Contemporary Conflicts* (7th ed.). Toronto: Pearson Prentice Hall. Presents a thorough historical and contemporary overview of Aboriginal and non-Aboriginal relations in Canada.

Henry, Francis, and Carol Tator. (2006). *The Colour of Democracy: Racism in Canadian Society* (3rd ed.). Toronto: Thomson Nelson. Argues that Canadians continue to harbour deeply held racist beliefs and engage in racist practices.

Li, Peter. (2003). *Destination Canada: Immigration Debates and Issues.* Toronto: Oxford University Press. A well-argued and critical analysis of a number of contemporary immigration issues.

Miles, Robert, and Malcolm Brown. (2003). *Racism* (2nd ed.). London: Routledge. One of the best theoretical discussions of the meaning of race and racism in modern Western societies. The authors argue for a critical, social constructionist approach to race and racism.

WEB RESOURCES

Companion Web Site for This Book

http://www.newsociety5e.nelson.com

Begin by clicking on the Student Resources section of the website. Next, select the chapter you are studying from the pull-down menu. From the Student Resources page, you have easy access to InfoTrac College Edition® and other resources, such as the Glossary and Flashcards. The website also has many useful tips to aid you in your study of sociology.

InfoTrac College Edition Search Terms

Visit http://www.infotrac-college.com for access to more than 20 million articles from nearly 6000 sources when doing your online research.

ThomsonNOW™

http://hed.nelson.com

This online diagnostic tool identifies each student's unique needs with a Pretest that generates a personalized Study Plan for each chapter, helping students focus on concepts they are having the most difficulty mastering. Students then take a Posttest after reading the chapter to measure their understanding of the material. An Instructor Gradebook is available to track and monitor student progress.

CHAPTER NINE

Inequality Among Nations: Perspectives on Development

In this chapter you will learn that

- Transnational corporations are prepared to shift worksites to maximize profits. This undermines the employment and well-being of many people.

- Two hundred and fifty years ago there were small gaps in living standards and levels of productivity between countries. Now the gaps are huge.

- The poor countries today are mainly those that were colonized by the West.

- Liberal development theory argues that if markets are allowed to function without state interference, prosperity follows. Although liberal theory has been adopted by some countries, it has not led to improvements in the well-being of most citizens of less developed countries.

- Dependency theory suggests that underdevelopment results from foreign economic and political control. The development breakthroughs of some countries suggest that domestic control of corporations and activist governments can be the keys to economic success.

Gordon Laxer
UNIVERSITY OF ALBERTA

INTRODUCTION

These days, most toys come from China but workers are not having much fun making them. Many workers are forced to toil 15 to 19.5 hours a day, seven days a week, completing one operation every three seconds, repeating the same furious motion 10 000 times daily, literally wearing the skin off their hands. More than 15 000 people were killed in industrial accidents in 2004 alone. Chinese workers receive US60¢ for every pair of Timberland boots they make. The boots retail for US$100. Many workers are injured, suffering broken or severed fingers. Few receive insurance. They can do little about it because unions are illegal; dozens of labour activists are in jail. Nonetheless, the number of labour disputes in the country approaches 200 000 a year (Workers' Voice @ WTO, 2006). China is rising. It is now the world's factory floor. But it is questionable how much ordinary workers benefit from China's progress (see Box 9.1).

Globalization, or world integration of investment, production, and economic policies, has brought working such conditions as those just described to many areas of the southern hemisphere. Much of the southern hemisphere comprises less developed countries, most of which were colonies of the rich countries of Western Europe. In the less developed countries, hundreds of millions of destitute tenant farm families are forced off the land by policies that

SOURCE: Ajit Ninan/India. Reprinted with permission from IPS—Inter Press Service.

open their countries' markets to subsidized farm exports from rich countries. The workers are often segregated in special "export processing zones" that have been set up for **transnational corporations,** companies with subsidiaries in more than one country. They are privately owned and most are controlled by investors in the rich countries.

In 1996, Lawrence Summers, former U.S. Secretary of the Treasury, argued that "capitalism is in ascendance everywhere. . . . Globalist economic policy . . . is the forward defense of America's deepest security interest." Anyone critical of the "globalist Washington consensus" is a "separatist," he said (Summers, 1996: 3). After the attacks against the United States on September 11, 2001, Summers's argument was transformed into the so-called Bush doctrine. The United States National Security Strategy asserts that the United States has the right to "pre-emptively strike" countries that pose immediate threats or potential risks to the United States (United States, 2002, 2006). Among the demands of the United States is that other countries allow U.S. transnationals to do business wherever they want. Critics argue that the pre-emptive war doctrine sweeps away diplomacy, self-determination, and the democratic sovereignty of other countries, especially weak ones. In effect, it declares the United States an empire.

The globalist "Washington consensus" mandates every country to remove domestic control over its own economy and adopt **neoliberal economic policies.** In exchange for loans and financial aid, such policies require that countries

- Dismantle laws against foreign ownership and control
- Privatize public enterprises (e.g., Crown corporations)
- Reduce government regulation of businesses, such as electrical power generation and transmission
- Cut public expenditures on health care, education, and the like
- Reduce corporate taxes
- Balance government budgets
- Set currencies at low levels to encourage exports (Williamson, 1994: 18)

Do neoliberal policies promote economic progress? Or are they a new way for corporations in rich countries to exploit people in poor countries? Whose interests are best served by neoliberal policies—citizens or transnational corporations? These are the

BOX 9.1   FLAWS IN CHINA'S ECONOMIC MIRACLE

China is rapidly becoming the world's dominant manufacturing country. It makes more clothes, shoes, toys, TVs, DVD players, and cell phones than any other country in the world. China makes parts for Boeing 757s and explores space in domestically built satellites. Its telephone system is more wireless than wired, and China will soon have the world's most advanced rapid transit system. Astonishing economic growth has accompanied China's quick climb up the technological ladder. China set a world record when it doubled per capita income in just nine years between 1978 and 1987. Then it repeated the record performance between 1987 and 1996. Since 1978, China has sustained an unprecedented annual growth rate of 9.3 percent (Fishman, 2005). The number of poor people in rural areas dropped from 250 million in 1978 to 26 million in 2005. In that same period, life expectancy rose from 63 to 71 years. Primary school enrolment and youth literacy are now almost universal. Housing space per person has more than tripled since 1978 (China Development Research Foundation, 2005: 8).

Yet productivity remains low and hundreds of millions of people have paid dearly for China's growth. Exploitation of labour is rampant. Seven hundred million Chinese people live on less than US$2 a day; 200 million earn less than US$1. A generation ago, China was one of the world's most egalitarian societies. Today, it ranks 90th of 131 countries in degree of equality. More than 300 million peasants are expected to lose their livelihood because China has joined the World Trade Organization, throwing peasants open to world competition in agriculture. Meanwhile, hundreds of millions of urban poor have lost jobs in state-owned companies because of massive privatization.

Such inequities have led to widespread perceptions of injustices. The view that "corrupt officials and the privileged few . . . have enriched themselves through exploitation and at the expense of the masses" is growing (Jiang, 2006: 3). Polls show that more than 80 percent of China's population decry the country's unequal income distribution. Such perceptions have led to many protest actions, with 87 000 "public order disturbances" recorded in 2005. According to one expert, "China today is at a crossroads of unprecedented prosperity, high, unmet expectations, and growing frustrations with perceived social injustice" (Jiang, 2006: 1–3).

Democracy, human rights, security of the person, increased leisure time to spend with family and friends, and supplies of basic food for all are missing from China's economic miracle. China remains one of the world's worst dictatorships and human rights abusers and it is unclear when China will become democratic.

main questions I address in this chapter. To answer them, I explore competing perspectives on why some countries are rich and others poor in the first place and what can be done to enable people in all countries to fully develop their unique capacities.

WHY ARE SOME COUNTRIES RICH AND OTHERS POOR?

Why are some countries rich and others poor? Will the global reach of transnational corporations reduce or increase gaps in economic, social, and political development? If neoliberal policies dominate, are the benefits likely to reach everyone in the less developed countries?

Experts disagree about the answers to these questions. We may first distinguish two broad approaches to answering them: neoliberal and "anti-imperialist." Neoliberalism is the dominant approach in Canada and other Western countries. We repeatedly hear its assumptions: Most countries are poor because Western capitalist institutions and values have not

penetrated them deeply enough. Poor countries can better themselves by becoming like "us," by adopting capitalism, elections, schooling, secularism, science, transparency, and the work ethic. Poor countries remain poor because of ignorance, laziness, and corrupt elites, who deny "civilization's" benefits to their people. Neoliberal arguments ease the conscience of affluent people in rich countries, who are disturbed by images of hunger in less developed countries. We are not to blame. It's their fault they are poor, neoliberalism says.

Anti-imperialist perspectives are the mirror image of neoliberal views. Proponents argue that most countries are poor because Western capitalism and imperialism have penetrated them too deeply. Rich countries are rich because they exploit poor countries. Poor countries cannot follow the neoliberal route because obstacles now block that path—the biggest obstacle being the entrenched position of the largest transnational corporations, almost all of which are controlled by people in rich countries (United Nations Conference on Trade and Development [UNCTAD],

2005). The world's 70 000 transnationals account for US$19 trillion in annual sales (UNCTAD, 2005). Their right to do business anywhere they please is backed by the rich countries. Accordingly, power differentials and the advantages of being ahead explain most of the disparities among countries.

Rich countries and dominant corporations have an interest, the argument continues, in keeping poor countries underdeveloped so they will remain sources of cheap labour and resources. Elites in rich countries fear that real democracy and independence would serve the interests of most citizens rather than transnational corporations. By allying with local capitalists, and often with military leaders, transnational corporations help maintain exploitation and underdevelopment. Adherents of anti-imperialist approaches thus blame underdevelopment on external forces and internal elites, who would lose power if external support was withdrawn. In their view, poor countries can develop only by reducing ties to rich countries, abandoning capitalism, and developing their own economic, political, and cultural resources.

In what follows I assess the competing perspectives just outlined by examining the historical record. I offer a more balanced approach than either perspective provides alone. First, though, I discuss how most people's well-being can still deteriorate while the economy grows. Understanding this point will prove important to the later discussion.

UNEQUAL DEVELOPMENT AND UNEQUAL BENEFITS

We often hear reports of economic growth. It is assumed that more is better, that everyone benefits when the economy grows. But what exactly is growing and who gains? Economists often measure growth and living standards by using **gross national product (GNP)** or gross domestic product (GDP) data. (The distinction between the two is unimportant for our purposes so I use the terms interchangeably.) GNP is the value of all goods and services produced in a country in one year as measured officially by money transactions.

Simon Kuznets, who invented the GNP concept in the 1930s, stressed its limitations: "The welfare of the nation can scarcely be inferred from a measurement of national income. . . . Distinctions must be kept in mind between quantity and quality . . . returns and costs . . . the short and long run" (quoted in Cobb, Halstead, and Rowe, 1995: 67). Despite Kuznets's cautions, the mass media accept GNP as a credible measure of growth and well-being.

The GNP counts all monetary activity whether positive or destructive. As one critic notes, it's like a calculating machine that can only add and not subtract. Disasters lead to growth. Earthquakes, tsunamis, ice storms, hurricanes, industrial pollution, divorces, traffic accidents, and disease all add to GNP. Similarly, economic growth can coexist with widespread poverty, exploitation, long working hours, lack of democratic control, discrimination, polluted environments, and poor education. Focusing on growth can hide economic injustices.

Who benefits from growth? If average incomes rise, do most people benefit? Not necessarily. National averages hide poverty by lumping together incomes of rich and poor people. For example, Canadian billionaire Kenneth Thomson was the world's ninth richest person, with assets of US$17.9 billion, before his death in June 2006 (*Forbes*, 2006). If he earned 8 percent on his assets in a year, his annual income would have been US$1.432 billion. If we average his income with Joan Owens, a $12 000-a-year Wal-Mart cashier, their average income is more than US$716 million per year. Averaging leaves Joan just as poor, but it sounds good. When Emilio Medici, a former Brazilian president, was told Brazil's GNP grew quickly, he said: "Brazil is doing well but the people are not" (Barnet and Muller, 1974: 141). Similarly, world GNP rises annually, yet

- The assets of the world's six richest people are more than the combined GDP of the 49 least developed countries with a combined population of 700 million (UNCTAD, 2004).
- The assets of the world's 200 richest people are more than the combined income of 2.4 billion people, 41 percent of humanity (*Forbes*, 2002; World Bank, 2000).
- The richest fifth of humanity has on average 50 times the market income of the poorest fifth (United Nations, 2005: 36).

HUMAN DEVELOPMENT: A BETTER MEASURE

The United Nations measures well-being with the concept of human development rather than GNP. **Human development** involves improving per capita income, education, health, environmental quality, democracy, equality, and freedom. The United Nations combines some of these factors into a single human development index (HDI). By using this index, United Nations analysts have shown that poverty in East Asia has been cut dramatically in recent decades, but poverty levels are rising sharply in South Asia, sub-Saharan Africa, and most of Eastern Europe. Disparities between rich and poor countries are enormous. Life expectancy is 60 years in the less developed southern hemisphere compared with 79 years in rich capitalist countries (United Nations, 2005). Almost 800 million people in the less developed countries go to sleep hungry, equal to the combined populations of Western Europe and North America (Food and Agriculture Organization of the United Nations [FAO], 2006; World Hunger Education Service Associates, 2006). More than 10 million children under the age of five die needlessly every year. Some 800 million adults are illiterate, two-thirds of them women (United Nations, 2005: 20, 24). Most poor people live in ecologically vulnerable areas.

CLASS AND INEQUALITY

Although inequalities among countries are enormous, most people in rich countries are, of course, not rich. Moreover, some rich people live in poor countries (Table 9.1). The gap between rich and poor is generally greater in poor countries than in rich countries. But big class differences exist almost everywhere.

WOMEN AND DEVELOPMENT

Gender profoundly affects a person's life-chances everywhere and especially in less developed countries. Here is a typical scene in Kenya:

> Bent double under fifty pounds or more of stout fuel-wood branches, a woman staggers along a dirt road in Kenya. . . . By her side, her husband strolls erect, a furled brolly [umbrella] his only load. . . . In Kenya, as in many other parts of the world, women are the beasts of burden. (Harrison, 1993: 328)

Circumstances vary, but the lives of all women but rich ones in the South are usually hard. They are the poorest of the poor. In most areas, women do much of the farm work, but most are landless labourers, tenant farmers, or their husbands'

TABLE 9.1 RICHEST AND POOREST 20 PERCENT OF INCOME BY REGION OF RESIDENCE, 2003

The richest 20% of income earners in the world reside in	
High-income countries	69.0
Eastern and Central Europe and the former Soviet Union	9.5
Latin America and the Caribbean	9.5
East Asia and the Pacific	9.5
South Asia	9.5
Sub-Saharan Africa	2.4
Total	100.4*
The poorest 20% of income earners in the world reside in	
High-income countries	0
Eastern and Central Europe and the former Soviet Union	1.1
Latin America and the Caribbean	2.4
East Asia and the Pacific	32.1
South Asia	28.6
Sub-Saharan Africa	35.7
Total	99.9*

SOURCE: United Nations (2005: 37). By permission of Oxford University Press, Inc.
*Percentages do not equal 100 percent because they were estimated from a graph.

employees. Men own the land. Typically, women work a double day—one domestic, the other in the fields—and both shifts are more onerous than most work in rich countries. Fetching water and firewood and hand-milling flour can consume up to eight hours a day. While doing much of the productive labour and increasingly heading single-parent families, women bear and raise children and run households. They are subject to the "near universal male curses of intoxication, violence, and unilateral infidelity" (Harrison, 1993: 329).

Poor pregnant women face enormous health risks. Poor women's risk of dying during pregnancy and birth is up to 600 times higher than in developed countries. "One woman dies every minute, over half a million women a year. A woman's lifetime risk of dying due to maternal causes ranges from one in 18 in Nigeria, to one in 8700 in Canada" (United Nations,

Women born in developing nations face much hardship. From birth, girls are often fed less and are less likely to receive costly medical care. They tend to receive less schooling and are paid less for their labour. Here, Sri Lankan women pick tea.
SOURCE: Hugh Sitton/Stone/Getty Images.

2005: 32). Educational opportunities are unequal too. Girls receive on average two fewer years of education than boys in South Asia and one fewer year in African and Arab states (United Nations, 2005: 25). In South Asia, a third of men are illiterate, compared with nearly 60 percent of women. Happily, between 1990 and 2000, literacy rates for women rose from 41 percent to 54 percent in sub-Saharan Africa and from 37 percent to 50 percent in Arab states (United Nations Educational, Scientific and Cultural Organization [UNESCO], 2000: 19).

HOW THE WEST CREATED RICH AND POOR COUNTRIES

When we think of human development, we should think in historical time. Not that much has changed in development rankings since I was born in 1944. The "developed" countries more than 60 years ago are largely the ones that are more developed now. Only a few countries rose or fell spectacularly. Only Hong Kong and Singapore, two city-states, broke through to advanced levels. South Korea, Taiwan, and Israel shifted from low to middle levels. A few countries, such as Argentina and most of formerly communist Eastern Europe, dropped from middle to somewhat lower levels. During World War II, Japan already had the world's sixth-largest industrial economy. Economic growth has been spectacular in China and solid in India in the past 25 years, but many people in both countries receive few benefits.

Development is usually portrayed as involving anonymous processes and inevitable movements. Other terms were used in the past to describe economic development, but globalization is now the term of choice. It implies unstoppable, nonhuman processes. Yet the concept of globalization hides the major actors of the past two centuries: corporations pursuing profits, powerful states, and citizens' movements. Since 1945, **supranational institutions** have emerged as important players on the world scene. All supranational institutions assume some of the sovereign rights of nation states, and the most powerful supranational institutions support corporate rights. The latter include the International Monetary Fund (IMF), the World Bank, the G7 countries (the United States, Japan, Germany, France, Italy, the United Kingdom, and Canada), the European Union (an organization of 25 European states), and signatories to the North American Free Trade Agreement (the United States, Canada, and Mexico).

As technologies evolve, corporations move and communicate with greater ease. In contrast, states are tied to political territories and maintain legitimacy in the eyes of their citizens, most of whom live and die in their native countries. But the most powerful states extend influence over weaker states. **Colonialism**— direct political rule without consent—was the old means of control. New ways involve dominant states exercising influence over supranational agencies and promoting the interests of "their" transnationals. Diplomacy, trade and investment sanctions, and military are other means of coercing weaker states. The United States, the world's only superpower, exercises considerable influence over other countries, largely by the newer means, but it partly reverted to old-style colonialism in 2002 when it adopted the doctrine of pre-emptive war.

Much of the corporate motivation to change the world's economy derives from periodic profitability crises. Such crises affect the location of jobs and production. In the early phases of industrialization (1760–1960), modern industry emerged in the few advanced capitalist economies. Increasingly, profits were made by continually expanding production and consumption in those countries. Leading businesses, and the states where they were located, viewed the rest of the world as sources of cheap raw materials and markets for their products. Colonization ensured that businesses in the advanced countries held monopoly positions over resources and markets in the colonies. Generally, there was little interest in locating manufacturing or services in the colonies. Early capitalists reaped high profits by following this strategy.

Capitalist strategy changed in the late 1960s. In the rich countries, wage earners gained more economic and political power. Voters demanded generous public services and the regulation of businesses to serve the common good. Gains for most citizens contributed to one of capitalism's profitability crises. In response, the new corporate strategy was to escape the "pay explosion" in rich countries and restore profit rates by shifting production to poor countries (Arrighi, 1993).

Leading transnationals, such as Nike, General Electric, and McDonald's, reverted to the strategy of hiring low-wage workers to reap high profits. In ex-colonies, a few resources, especially oil, commanded much higher prices beginning in the 1970s, giving oil-exporting states greater bargaining strength. That development, combined with the shift of some low-skilled mass-production jobs to poor countries, helped reduce income gaps between more and less developed countries (Arrighi, 1993).

However, the 1980s and 1990s saw a reversal of these trends. To make high profits in the less developed countries, transnational companies no longer needed to expand production and consumption. Higher profits were earned by reducing wages, firing workers ("downsizing"), shifting to part-time work, and hiring nonunion labour. As well, corporations used the threat of moving jobs abroad to bargain down what they saw as excessive public services and wages in the rich countries. Investment in poor countries declined while poor countries continued to pay billions in debt charges to banks in rich countries.

What accounts for these shifting patterns? I answer this question by examining why some countries are rich and others are poor and what is meant by "development." I also discuss the origins of the divergence between rich and poor countries and competing perspectives on development.

BEFORE THERE WERE RICH AND POOR COUNTRIES: THE WORLD IN 1750

Most of us view the world from the vantage point of the present. In the 1970s, many observers believed in the inevitability of expanding socialism. Then came neoliberalism and the fall of communism. Perceptions shifted regarding the "inevitable" direction of history, and few observers could foresee any alternative to capitalism's spread everywhere. How will people view the inevitable direction of history in ten years? We don't know. Predominant opinion may shift again.

To escape present-minded fads, I take the long view. The relative position of countries shifts slowly. To understand current inequalities between countries, we must go back to 1750 to look at relative income and productivity levels. Doing so will help us decide which perspective best explains why some countries today are developed and many more are underdeveloped. The year 1750 is a good place to start. It was just before capitalism and industrialization transformed England and then the rest of the world.

England was probably the world's richest country in 1750, but its output per capita (that is, per person) was only about 50 percent greater than the world average, and only 25 percent more than China's (Bairoch, 1982: 294). As one economic historian notes, Britain "was poor, though not without some economic surplus; it was relatively stagnant, though not completely static; it was based on agriculture as its main activity. . . . The mass of people lived close to economic disaster and . . . they had little prospect of enjoying an appreciably higher standard of living" (Deane, 1979: 18).

As in all preindustrial societies, there existed in Britain a rigid limit to attainable output per person. Most people had few possessions and very basic, overcrowded shelter, and they spent most of their income on food. Famine and epidemics were ever-present dangers. Most children in London died before their fifth birthday (Delage, 1993: 250). Britons did not have the future orientation of modernists, who expect life to improve with each generation. No one was aware of the tumultuous and revolutionary changes that lay just a few decades ahead.

Paul Bairoch (1982) challenged the standard interpretation of development, which starts with Britain's Industrial Revolution and ignores anything not made by modern machines as irrelevant to industry's later progress. Handicrafts are ignored, as if people did not make clothes, mill flour, or construct buildings before the Industrial Revolution. Bairoch argues that if something is made, it should be counted as production, no matter how it is produced. Handicrafts still accounted for half of world industrial output in 1900. In 1750, with huge populations and output per capita comparable to that of Western countries, China and India produced more than half the world's total output of finished goods (Bairoch, 1982). Their output per capita was double that of the rural Thirteen Colonies (soon to become the United States), where people imported most of the finished goods they consumed.

In 1750, the countries that we today call less developed accounted for 73 percent of global industrial production. By 1913, they accounted for just 7.5 percent. Conversely, in 1913, a dozen or so countries with fewer than 20 percent of the world's people made close to 90 percent of the world's finished products (by using modern and handicraft methods). The decline of the less developed countries was due to rapid gains in a few countries, whose per capita output rose sevenfold, and a decline in production of catastrophic proportions among the rest (Bairoch, 1982: 295).

By 1913, today's less developed countries made less than a third as much per capita as their ancestors did in 1750 (Bairoch, 1982: 278). Modern manufacturing was introduced to less developed countries in the 1880s and became significant only in the 1920s. Thus, the less developed countries started development at a much lower level than what prevailed in 1750, and now they faced competition from modern Western industries, Western monopolies over-patented technologies and strategic resources, and Western military might. Capitalist industrialization and empires brought the less developed countries to levels of destitution not experienced for centuries.

The era of Western empire stretched from 1750 to the end of World War II (1945). Imperial centres and a few independent countries developed, while colonies deteriorated economically. Most of the less developed world was colonized or semi-colonized by the West. Only predominantly "white-settler" colonies, such as Canada and Australia, managed to develop and prosper.

Japan is the exception. Japan was the remotest of the three fabled rich countries of Asia coveted by Westerners. India's subcontinent (present-day India, Pakistan, and Bangladesh), the nearest to the West, was colonized earliest. China, never fully colonized, was carved into zones of Western influence. (My mother was born to Canadian missionary parents in one of these zones in 1914. Her birth was registered in London, not China. She attended a Canadian school in China.) Although Japan was forced to trade with the West on unfavourable terms for 50 years after U.S. gunboats entered Tokyo harbour in 1853, Japan alone escaped colonization or semi-colonization. It is no coincidence that of the three rich countries of Asia, only Japan developed an advanced economy.

Latin America appears to contradict the thesis that Western colonization had deindustrializing effects. Although most Latin American colonies won independence from Spain and Portugal between 1809 and 1839, at a fairly early time in the spread of industrialization in Europe, none generated independent, fully developed industrial economies. However, European conquest had made conditions unfavourable to capitalist industrialization there.

Spanish and Portuguese colonization was ruthless, led not by self-sufficient settlers but by people who came to rule and live off others' toil. Conquest led to the decimation of local peoples, the looting of the Aztec and Inca civilizations, the cruel servitude of Aboriginal peoples, the enslavement of Africans, and peasant exploitation (Harrison, 1993: 105–08). The resulting extreme inequalities created societies inhospitable to capitalist industrialization. Why would Latin American upper classes switch to modern industry when they lived so well through precapitalist exploitation?

After contact with Europeans, Aboriginal people suffered population declines probably unequalled in history. These were not the empty lands of pioneering legend. When Columbus arrived in America, it was inhabited by an estimated 70 million to 100 million Aboriginal people (compared with 60 million to 65 million Europeans in Europe). A century later, Aboriginal people numbered just 12 million to 15 million (Delage, 1993: 43). Aboriginals' deaths enhanced standards of living for European settlers, especially in North America, because the latter took over unspoiled environments in which humans were rare and resources abundant. With vast expanses of fertile land, Europeans in North America could escape full-fledged feudal oppression and demand unprecedentedly high wages (Delage, 1993: 250). From the days of first settlement, Europeans in North America had the highest living standard and longest life expectancy in the world. They were "born" rich. It was a unique head start.

THE INDUSTRIAL REVOLUTION IN BRITAIN

The Industrial Revolution had its roots in cotton. Cotton's success depended on raw cotton picked by slaves in colonies. Moreover, Britain's cotton industry would not have succeeded without the destruction of India's better-established industry.

It was in cotton textiles that machines first showed their vast superiority to human energy and skill. Gains in output per person and declines in prices were astonishing. From 1760 to the late 1830s, British cotton consumption rose about 150 times, while the price of cotton yarn fell 95 percent (Landes, 1969: 41–42). Handicraft cotton makers were doomed. This pattern was repeated in industry after industry, slowly and unevenly over many decades around the world. Whenever an item could be produced more profitably by machine than by hand, businesses quickly adopted the new method. Over several generations, machine production supplanted one handicraft industry after another.

If industry had spread evenly around the world, the Industrial Revolution would have displaced traditional handicrafts and led to new industries and

Capitalism in the early twentieth century was unbridled, West-dominated, and internationally expansive. Many people saw it as an overwhelmingly progressive force. The exploitation of foreign markets and the destruction of foreign cultures were not contentious issues.

SOURCE: Max Beckmann, *The Iron Bridge* (1922). © Estate of Max Beckmann/ VG Bildkunst (Bonn)/SODRAC (Montreal) 2003.

new work everywhere. That did not happen. Instead, capitalist industrialization began in Britain and was copied in stages over the next century in Western Europe and North America. The success of these countries led not to sharing the benefits of the new technologies, but to greater power for these states and their corporations to exploit people and resources elsewhere. To aid their national businesses, dominant states imposed capitalism, through empire and unequal trade, on less developed countries.

Colonial handicraft industries were destroyed and their markets forced to absorb modern products from imperial mother countries. Colonies were not usually allowed to develop modern industries to replace destroyed handicrafts. Colonies did not determine their destinies, nor were they controlled for the benefit of the colonized. The case of India, the "jewel" of the British Empire, illustrates these points.

THE DEINDUSTRIALIZATION OF INDIA

Two thousand years ago, Indian silk had such a high reputation that the wealthiest Roman ladies would accept no other. Seventeen centuries later, wealthy European ladies had a similar passion for Indian cotton goods. They disdained domestically made imitations.

What could the Romans and later the British sell to India in return for buying Indian cotton fabrics? Only gold, for they produced nothing fine enough or inexpensive enough to sell in India. Even in the 1700s, when Britain was the world's great naval power, India built ships that were cheaper and more durable than British ships.

The British East India Company was established in 1600 to bring Indian goods to Britain. The effort was so successful that, a century later, Britain's clothing industry was near collapse. To survive, the latter used political influence to prohibit imported Indian textiles. According to Daniel Defoe (author of *Robinson Crusoe*), this prohibition "averted the ruin of our manufactures, and revived their prosperity" (quoted in Gupta, 1979: 8). The Industrial Revolution got its start in cotton textiles in Britain only because of protectionism against India's vastly superior industry.

In 1813, 50 years after the Industrial Revolution began, Britain finally exported cotton goods to India

under a one-way "free-trade" arrangement that turned India into a captive market. While India had to remove barriers to British textiles, Britain applied high duties on Indian textiles. Despite modern production techniques, British textiles were still unable to compete (Gupta, 1979: 32). By the late 1800s, however, Britain's policy of building up its own industry and destroying India's finally bore fruit. Textiles became Britain's leading industry and India received almost half of Britain's textile exports (Hobsbawm, 1968: 147). The famed Indian industry that had dominated world commerce for 3000 years was ruined, destroying many jobs and impoverishing India. Ironically, Britain got much of the capital needed to start modern industry by looting India's vast holdings of gold, silver, and jewels, and taking over land to grow opium and cotton (Wolf, 1982: 244–9).

In this section, I considered the world of ten generations ago to discover the origin of current gaps between developed and less developed countries. I showed that today's inequalities did not exist in 1750 and conclude that capitalist industrialization and imperialism contributed strongly to inequality among nations today.

PERSPECTIVES ON DEVELOPMENT

To understand why a few countries are rich and many more are poor, observers make assumptions about development. There is no consensus. Some theories justify the position of the privileged. Others challenge it. Moreover, competing development theories have at times inspired both the privileged and the masses to act. The development perspectives outlined in this section are thus not just abstract academic debates. They lie at the heart of contests for power and justice. Indeed, the triumph of one idea over another is not determined only in the court of public opinion or by debates in universities; the most important courts are the political, diplomatic, economic, and military arenas. Ideas connected to power have material force.

In this section I assess the adequacy of competing development perspectives that purport to explain why a few countries are rich and many more are poor. I also assess whether any perspective proposes solutions that are likely to lead to development that will benefit most people in the world.

THE NEOLIBERAL/WESTERNIZATION PERSPECTIVE

Liberal means "generous" or "generally mind-broadening." It also is the name of political parties standing for moderate progress and reform. I am not using liberal in those senses. For this discussion, **liberalism** is the classical doctrine that equates capitalism with freedom and distrusts the power of governments. Economic liberalism has long been the doctrine of ruling economic elites, especially in Britain, the United States, and Canada, and it is propounded by transnational corporations. Liberalism fell into disfavour during the Great Depression, World War II, and the boom years of the 1960s and early 1970s, when increased government involvement in running Western economies was popular. It re-emerged as an important theory in the late 1970s and people began referring to it as "neoconservatism" and "the Washington consensus." It is associated with free markets and minimal government involvement in the operation of the economy. Liberalism is paraded as new, but is an old doctrine, going back to the 1700s and Adam Smith, the father of liberal economics. Most economists are classical liberals.

Liberalism makes six assumptions, all contested by other perspectives:

1. The most basic human characteristic is individual self-interest, which, when left unchecked, unconsciously promotes the common good. Likening a free market to the work of God, Adam Smith (1976 [1776]: vol. 1, 447) argued that "an invisible hand" turns individual greed into society's gain.

2. Profits are the best incentive for innovation and business efficiency. There should be no limits to capital accumulation and the extent to which a single individual or corporation controls a country's economy.

3. Market freedom maximizes human freedom, while government power threatens freedom.

4. Free markets for capital, labour, and resources separate productive from unproductive firms more efficiently than governments. Government strategies for national economic development cannot pick winners and losers as well as competition does. Markets work best when left alone.

5. For global markets to work efficiently, there should be "no place for the nation, or any collectivity larger than the firm" (Hobsbawm, 1990: 26). As many state functions as possible should be

removed and placed under supranational liberal institutions (Block, 1977: 212).

6. Underdeveloped countries will reach the level of advanced countries if economic factors (e.g., capital) are allowed to flow freely around the world.

Liberalism is a doctrine that removed the power of kings and aristocrats in the 1700s and now justifies the power of the few families and foreign corporations that dominate Canada's economy. Liberal doctrine justified India's deindustrialization and is now promoted by the United States and its allies, transnationals, banks, the International Monetary Fund (IMF), and the World Bank.

The IMF was set up in 1944 to facilitate international trade and corporate investment by making national currencies readily convertible into the currencies of other member countries. The IMF provides credit to states that buy more than they sell abroad (and so have "balance of payments" problems) and pay more charges on international debt than they borrow anew (and so have international debt problems). Since the debt crisis of the less developed countries in the early 1980s threatened to ruin the rich countries' major banks and creditors, the IMF has taken an activist approach to defending rich bankers. The IMF uses the power of credit to police debtor countries' internal policies, often overturning citizens' democratic choices. Countries requiring international financial assistance need the IMF's stamp of approval. IMF policies practise the neoliberal doctrine of its dominant members: the United States, the European Union (EU), and Japan. The IMF represents the interests of the creditors (the rich), not the debtors (poor countries) (see Figure 9.1).

The World Bank provides commercial and low-interest loans for projects, such as telecommunications and education in the South. The World Bank is also controlled by major capitalist states and uses its power to persuade underdeveloped countries to follow liberal principles (see Box 9.2).

The Foreign Debt of Less Developed Countries

Less developed countries receive liberal doctrine not as textbook ideas, but as policies they must follow to resolve debt and balance-of-payments crises. Many developing countries, especially in Africa and Latin America, have faced debt problems since the early 1980s. Debts were usually incurred by corrupt local officials, military dictators, and wealthy businessmen.

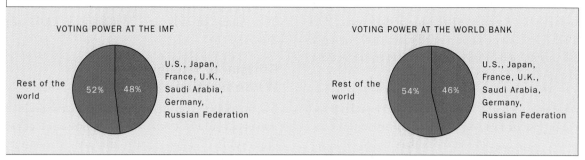

FIGURE 9.1   WHOSE VOICE COUNTS AT THE IMF AND WORLD BANK?

BOX 9.2   WORLD BANK FIRES ITS CHIEF ECONOMIST

In 1999 the World Bank fired Joseph Stiglitz, its chief economist, because he expressed doubts about the World Bank's and the IMF's neoliberal policies.

The World Bank and the IMF, though separate institutions, are linked by "triggers." For example, taking a World Bank loan to build a school triggers a requirement to accept every neoliberal condition—on average, 111 per country—laid down by the IMF and World Bank. Loans and assistance to countries in economic trouble are, says the World Bank, designed after careful in-country investigation. Stiglitz disagrees. The "investigation" consists of close inspection of a country's five-star hotels, he says. Stiglitz claims that World Bank officials analyze each country's economy and then hand each government the same four-step program:

1. *Privatization,* which Stiglitz calls "briberization." National leaders, he says, happily flogged state-owned electricity and water companies to private interests. "You could see their eyes widen" at the prospect of 10 percent commissions paid to Swiss bank accounts for shaving a few billion off the price of national assets.
2. *Capital market liberalization,* which deregulates financial markets. In theory, this allows capital to flow in and out, but often the money just flows out. Predictably, this resulted in financial crises in Asia and Latin America in the 1990s.
3. a) *Market-based pricing,* which means removing subsidies on basics, including food, cooking fuel, and water. Predictably, this leads to the next sub-step.
   b) *The IMF riot.* Eliminating subsidies on basic needs hits the poor hard. In 1998, riots exploded in Indonesia over the elimination of food and fuel subsidies; Bolivians protested in 2002 over higher water prices. In 2003, the rise in cooking gas prices in Ecuador—imposed by the World Bank—led to widespread demonstrations, met by bullets, tanks, and tear gas.
4. *Free trade.* Countries must remove tariffs and barriers to the entry of foreign corporations and play by the rules of the World Trade Organization. Stiglitz is particularly concerned about the WTO's intellectual property rights treaty (TRIPS), which "condemns people to death" by imposing tariffs and tributes to pay pharmaceutical companies for branded medicines. "They don't care if people live or die."

The World Bank's and IMF's policies are driven by an ideology that is designed in secret and not open to discussion or dissent. That, says the World Bank's former chief economist, is the greatest concern.

SOURCE: Based on Palast, Greg. 2002. "The Globalizer Who Came in from the Cold: The IMF's Four Steps to Economic Damnation." Pp. 50–4 in *The Best Democracy Money Can Buy*. London: Pluto Press. Reprinted by permission.

This raises questions: Should citizens be held responsible for debts incurred by undemocratic elites? Did the loans help the national economy and most citizens? Have the economic programs imposed by dominant countries and agencies helped resolve these crises?

In the period 1970–82, two major oil price hikes, the internationalization of banking, and slower growth in the rich countries spurred much lending to the less developed countries. Poor countries were thus able to import more. For their part, banks acted out of self-interest in making loans. About US$15 billion per year flowed into Latin America alone between 1978 and 1981 (Pastor and Dymski, 1991: 203). The lending boom ended when world oil prices fell in 1982 and Mexico, a major oil exporter, declared it could no longer pay debt charges.

After Mexico's debt crisis, little new foreign capital came to Latin America or other less developed countries. In fact, capital flows reversed direction. Latin America paid out more than the total debt in interest, shelling out US$730 billion from 1982 to 1996 without reducing its debt. At US$720 billion, Latin America's foreign debt is 38 percent of the continent's GDP. Payments on debt servicing can consume more than half the annual expenditures of Latin American governments (Asper, 2005). To export this much capital, most Latin American countries have had to cut imports, and thus living standards, and raise exports. This postpones economic diversification.

The debt crisis led the IMF and World Bank to impose **structural adjustment programs** (recently renamed poverty reduction programs) on indebted countries. Liberal doctrine assumed that debt results from the "excessive demand" of less developed countries. They supposedly live beyond their means, importing too much and exporting too little. This presumably created imbalances in international transactions. The IMF's solution was simple: follow liberal principles—privatize state-owned industry, cut state budgets and subsidies, open up the economy to foreign investment, export more, and so on—and the difficulties will self-correct.

By and large, structural adjustment programs have not worked. Typically, they have not reduced poverty but they have increased inequality (Killick, 1999). UNICEF (United Nations International Children's Emergency Fund) estimates that at least half a million young children died in 1990 as a result of structural adjustment programs slowing down development (Adams, 1991: 160). Structural adjustment programs sparked hunger riots in Zambia in 1987 and in Venezuela in 1989, and neoliberal policies led to an uprising of indigenous people dispossessed from their land in the state of Chiapas in Mexico in 1994 (Johnston and Laxer, 2003: 41). Hugo Chávez was elected Venezuela's president in the aftermath of the brutal repression of the 1989 hunger riots. Since Chávez's election (1998), several Latin American governments that oppose neoliberalism have been elected. They are currently working together to gain greater independence from American influence (McCaughan, 2005) (see Box 9.3).

Critique of Neoliberalism/ Westernization

Neoliberalism is an elegant doctrine that appeals to universalism and impartiality. It promises equal opportunity for all. Does the record support its claims? Not well. Countries adopting neoliberalism have entrenched the power of economic elites, whose rise to the top usually owed more to inheritance than to merit. By not limiting capital accumulation and by dispossessing the many, neoliberalism has difficulty fulfilling promises of equality.

Neoliberalism has trouble explaining why today's 20 or so advanced countries are virtually the same ones as those of a century ago. A few countries have moved from less developed to highly developed over the past hundred years but they did not follow liberal doctrine. Venezuela and Middle Eastern oil-producing countries limited production and drove up oil prices in the 1970s and again since 2002. By using a cartel to change markets, these countries made major economic gains. Nor did Britain or the United States, during their early development, follow liberal free trade policies. As you saw earlier in this chapter, Britain's cotton industry grew behind protectionist barriers. The United States maintained high tariffs from the 1830s, when it began industrializing, until 1945, when it became a world superpower.

Neoliberalism is blind to power inequalities and how they affect equality of opportunity for ordinary people. Its principles are drawn from idealized models of perfect markets. The model of equal buyers and sellers may occur in a farmers' market, but it does not apply to corporate power and its relation to the state. In the real world, United Brands Company (formerly United Fruit) had a reputation for calling in the U.S. Marines or the CIA when its monopoly in several Central American countries was challenged (Barnet and Muller, 1974: 57). By embracing the world of economic models and ignoring the real world of vastly unequal power, neoliberalism justifies the privileges of the already powerful. And most less developed countries are not powerful.

BOX 9.3 "WASHINGTON CONSENSUS" GIVEN LAST RITES IN LATIN AMERICA

After promises that capitalism, transnationals, and free trade would spread prosperity to the people, the South American economies are in trouble again, and voters are turning against Washington's policy advice. Argentina, once South America's most developed country, fell into shambles in 2001–02. Two governments fell in ten days, not in military coups but as a result of massive public protests. Argentina had been the International Monetary Fund's model student. It did it all in the 1990s: flung open its economy, massively privatized state enterprises, and adopted the American dollar. The result was economic disaster, with more than half of Argentineans falling into poverty. Tens of thousands of citizens have been meeting in neighbourhood assemblies, discussing how to restart local industries and renationalize Argentina's recently privatized assets.

South American voters elected to government the critics of Washington consensus policies. New government leaders advocated for and began addressing deep problems of poverty, inequality, lack of sovereignty, and poor health and education services. Hugo Chávez was elected and re-elected as president of oil-rich Venezuela on a "patriotic-nationalist" platform supporting the poor—land reform, increased education, health and housing spending, basic food for the poor, and higher taxes for the rich. Chávez survived a coup in April 2002 and a two-month bosses' lockout led by upper-income Venezuelans in 2002–03, and he won a recall referendum decisively in 2004.

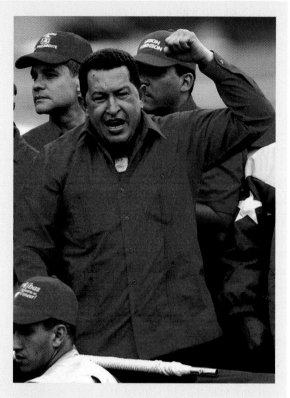

Venezuelan president Hugo Chávez was elected on a "patriotic-nationalist" platform supporting the poor.
SOURCE: ©Chico Sanchez/epa/Corbis.

Venezuela, Bolivia, Uruguay, and to a lesser extent Argentina are charting new, more independent economic and political paths. Their policies combine several elements, including direct aid for the poor rather than hoping a bit of money trickles down to them from a fast-growing GNP, emphasis on cooperatives and self-organizing among the poor, and greater South American cooperation and integration along social justice lines, rather than neoliberal ones.

SOURCES: Naomi Klein, "Revolt of the Wronged," *Guardian Weekly*, April 4–10, 2002, p. 11; Kevin G. Hall, "Consensus' given last rites," *Edmonton Journal*, Nov. 30, 2002, p. A17; Larry Rohter, "Brazil set to get its first working-class president," *Edmonton Journal*, Oct. 10, 2002, p. A17; Julian Borger and Alex Bellos, "US 'gave the nod' to Venezuelan coup," *Guardian Unlimited* (http://www.guardian.co.uk/international story/0,3604,685531.oohtml).

THE MODERNIZATION APPROACH

In October 1981, 22 heads of state met at Cancun, Mexico, to discuss North-South development. U.S. President Ronald Reagan advised the leaders of less developed countries not to talk about altering power structures in the World Bank or the IMF, or reallocating resources from North to South. Setting aside his text, Reagan offered the leaders homespun advice: If you want to develop, copy the example of American pioneers. They were poor, worked hard, saved their money, and believed in private ownership. You can achieve what they did if you change your attitudes and

values and become like Americans, he said. This was a folksy version of the modernization approach to development, a second variant of Western-centrism.

By the 1960s, the world's less developed countries had emerged from European colonialism and adopted economists' liberal prescriptions. However, rosy predictions of growth failed to materialize in most cases. Some scholars felt that liberalism was an inadequate theory because it focused too narrowly on economic factors. They attempted to rescue liberal explanations and prescriptions by grafting noneconomic factors onto liberalism. Several prominent sociologists and economic historians developed what came to be called **modernization theory.** They argued that, although liberal institutions are *necessary* for the development of the world's poor countries, they are not *sufficient;* the less developed countries must adopt "modern"—that is, Western—values before people can take advantage of capitalism.

Modernization theorists described sociocultural changes in Western Europe from the 1300s and isolated those they believed necessary for capitalism to succeed. As one economic historian put it, "with a slight twist of the pen, all basic traits of a modern economy [were] declared to be 'prerequisites' of industrial development" (Gerschenkron, 1962: 32–33). Less developed countries were urged to Westernize and become more economically differentiated and rational. Private property, individual rights, urbanization, universal literacy, modern health care, secularization, bureaucratization, and the shift to nuclear families were considered necessary for progress. So, too, was liberal democracy: a large unified territory, political participation, elections, an independent mass media, and a merit-based civil service. Culturally, people were encouraged to value choice, objectivity, future-orientation, and achievement over ascription. People had to believe that individual action is effective and reject fatalism. With all these elements present, the stage would be set for the emergence of capital investment, technological knowledge, and an entrepreneurial group willing to innovate (Armer and Katsillis, 1992; Gerschenkron, 1962: 32; Goldthorpe, 1984: 4–12).

Modernization theory was so influential in the 1950s and 1960s that the World Bank told the governments of less developed countries that, to qualify for aid, they had to follow the theory's prescriptions (Hoogvelt, 1982: 118). In the 1970s, however, the approach fell into disfavour when it became apparent that a few countries were advancing but most were not. Economic success was apparently not dependent on modernization.

The Critique of Modernization

Modernization theory was an advance over classical liberalism. First, it acknowledged that development occurs in cultural, social, and historical contexts and is not automatic. Second, mass education was seen as crucial for development. Where modernization theory failed was in its ethnocentric, evolutionary assumption that all countries must develop in exactly the same way as Western countries. It was naïve and incorrect to explain economic stagnation as a result of failing to become Westernized. The case of Japan, for example, discredits modernization theory. Lifetime employment, loyalty to the collective, pronounced status differences, and extended kinship ties—characteristics retained from Japan's precapitalist days—did not fit modernization theorists' vision of necessary development conditions. Clearly, not all the characteristics of Western societies were necessary for the emergence of advanced capitalism.

The chief weakness of the liberal and modernization approaches, however, is that they ignore the power and motivation of the advanced states and leading transnationals to maintain the advantages they already possess, even if this means keeping down the majority of countries. In contrast, dependency theory places unequal power at the centre of its vision.

DEPENDENCY THEORY

Dependency theory was formulated in the 1940s and 1950s when the less developed countries failed to meet the expectations of liberals, modernization theorists, and some classical Marxists. (The latter expected that capitalist growth would cause world proletarian revolution and lead to socialist industrialization everywhere.) Dependency theory was the intellectual response to that failure. Its initial focus was Latin America, which had been free of formal empires since the 1800s but had yet to experience extensive development.

The dependency school had two major sources. The first derived from the work of Raúl Prebisch and the United Nations Economic Commission for Latin America (ECLA). The second derived from the work of Paul Baran (1957), an American Marxist who reassessed the classical Marxist proposition that capitalism would spread everywhere, if unevenly. Together, these two streams of thought shaped the dependency approach, which became influential in the less developed countries, at the United Nations, and in several academic disciplines during the 1960s and 1970s. Although the popularity of this approach declined in the 1980s because it was too deterministic, it has been modified to good effect by some scholars (Evans, 1987: 321).

The United Nations Economic Commission for Latin America (ECLA)

The perspective of the United Nations Economic Commission for Latin America (ECLA) on development was the opposite of the modernization approach. Instead of assuming that underdeveloped countries are similar to developed countries in an earlier period, ECLA argued that the economies of less developed countries were fundamentally different. Because of these differences, the liberal assumptions that emerged from the industrial **core** (developed) **countries** did not apply well to the agrarian **peripheral** (less developed) **countries** (Love, 1980).

ECLA economists analyzed global conditions that prevailed from 1940 to 1980 and argued that core economies were *homogeneous and diversified*, whereas those in the periphery were *heterogeneous and specialized* (Palma, 1981: 51). "Unequal exchange" between core and periphery led to "unequal development."

The homogeneity of the core countries refers to the presence of high levels of productivity in all sectors: industry, agriculture, and services. It accounts for the overall high standard of living in these countries. In contrast, peripheral economies show no such consistency in performance from sector to sector; they are heterogeneous. Their only high-productivity sector is in modern export enclaves, whose products are sent to core countries. These enclaves are dominated by foreign-owned transnationals. Peripheral countries' exports consist almost entirely of raw materials.

Contrary to liberal assumptions, continued Prebisch, modern export enclaves do not benefit peripheral economies. Their effects do not spread to the local economy. The enclaves are tied largely to the core economies. The transnationals purchase their machinery and do their planning, research, and marketing in core countries. In addition, they process and transform the periphery's resources into finished products in the core (Palma, 1981: 51–52). It might be expected that tax and resource revenues from export enclaves would enable peripheral countries to develop modern education and communications systems. However, revenues are usually very low. For most primary commodities, transnationals have many sources of supply and they demand relief from taxes and resource rents in what are now called "free-trade" or "export-processing zones." If peripheral country A raises taxes, transnationals can usually move to country B.

The major benefit of export enclaves, ECLA argued, is jobs for local labour. Wages are usually higher there than elsewhere in the periphery, although they do not rise to core levels because surplus workers are continually generated by the country's low-productivity sectors, particularly subsistence agriculture. Because they lack alternatives, such workers accept low wages. Thus, the heterogeneity of productivity in modern and traditional sectors of peripheral economies impedes development and the creation of a mass market for local goods.

Peripheral economies are structurally different from core economies. They are "specialized," not "diversified." Whole countries or regions are dependent on the export of one or two resources, such as coffee, sugar, copper, oil, beef, or wheat. If there is a world glut of these products, their price falls, sometimes catastrophically. Because the economy is not diversified, it must continue to import most of what it consumes, even when export prices collapse. When that happens, the country no longer earns the revenue to import what it needs. In contrast, core economies are diversified, industrialized, and monopolistic. If demand declines, their monopoly corporations allow them to cut production and maintain price levels. This cannot usually be done in agriculture, because the producers lack economic and political coordination. As well, the nature of farming often precludes shutting down output to meet falling demand (Love, 1980: 52). Small farmers usually put in years of work and care before reaping benefits. A coffee bush takes five years to mature, rubber trees and coconut palms eight years, and cocoa fifteen years (Harrison, 1993: 353–54). They cannot reduce production the way transnationals do to maintain world prices. Thus, prices fall for all farmers.

The differences between core and periphery, ECLA argued, lead to "unequal exchange," in which the "terms of trade" between the periphery's resources and the core's finished goods worsen. This means that, over time, peripheral countries must export more and more resources to import a given number of finished products, such as cars or computers. Unequal exchange thus stacks the deck against industrialization in less developed countries. Peripheral countries have to run faster to stay in the same place. If they falter because of falling commodity prices or natural disasters, they have to incur debt to import necessities. Subsequent debt-servicing charges put them further behind.

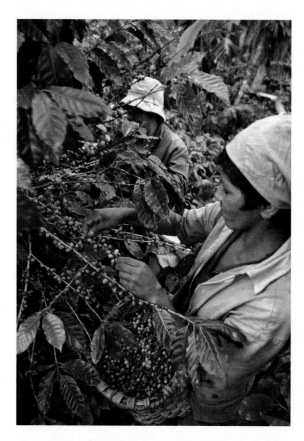

Some crops require years of work and care before farmers can reap the benefits—for example, a coffee bush takes five years to mature.
SOURCE: ©James Quine/Alamy.

Can the disadvantages of the periphery be surmounted? Prebisch and ECLA believed they could, calling the means to do so "inwardly directed development." To overcome having to import so much from the core under worsening terms of trade, peripheral economies must produce domestically as many goods as possible. Tariffs must be erected and control wrested from the transnationals. This import substitution strategy was followed by many governments in Latin America and elsewhere in the 1960s and 1970s. But by the 1980s and 1990s, it was attacked relentlessly on neoliberal grounds by the United States, transnationals, and agencies responsible for the structural adjustment programs. In the end, "free-trade" agreements undermined the import substitution approach in Latin America. That is why many consider neoliberalism a vehicle for neo-imperialism.

Marxism and Dependency Theory

A Marxist stream added a rich body of insight to dependency theory. For Marx, capitalism contains "the seeds of its own destruction." As capitalism replaces less efficient modes of production, such as feudalism, and destroys entire classes, such as serfs, it creates larger and larger communities of wage earners who have to sell their labour power to survive. Marx thought workers would eventually take control of society, first in the most highly advanced capitalist countries (Marx and Engels, 1986 [1848]).

Confronted by evidence that capitalism was developing slowly in the less developed countries and that communism was more successful in some of them (notably the Soviet Union and China), Marx's followers also contributed to dependency theory. Paul Baran (1957), for example, argued that major capitalist powers oppose industrialization in less developed countries, especially those countries in which governments oppose the domination of foreign transnationals. In Baran's view, the states and corporations of advanced countries form alliances with traditional, precapitalist elites in the less developed countries. These elites of wealthy landowners, army officers, corrupt state officials and their allies oppose the spread of capitalism to their countries because their power and wealth are based on precapitalist modes of exploitation and domination. Much of these countries' wealth is squandered on luxuries for the elites or is removed in the form of corporate profit. Baran concluded that it is in the interests of Western and domestic elites to keep less developed countries unindustrialized (Palma, 1981: 43). Accordingly, the only way out of this trap is to break close ties with the core capitalist countries.

Many historical cases substantiate dependency theory. Since 1945, the United States consistently has supported dictatorships based on traditional oligarchies and opposed governments democratically elected to take control of their own economies by nationalizing U.S.-based transnationals (Herman and Chomsky, 1988). An example is the 1973 overthrow of the democratically elected socialist government of Salvador Allende in Chile. The military dictatorship that overthrew Allende was aided by the United States and American corporations, such as ITT (O'Brien, 1976: 229; Sampson, 1973: 259). Chile went on to become the first country in the world to experiment with "free-market" neoliberalism.

Critique of Dependency Theory

Dependency theory was a great advance over the liberal and modernization approaches. Unfortunately, its pessimism about development prospects for less developed countries has been largely confirmed. Only a few poor countries have become rich. Development has been hampered by economies in which large populations are involved in traditional sectors. These conditions keep wages down, hinder the creation of mass markets, and remove much of the incentive for technological advance. Authoritarian regimes are frequently supported by landed elites and tiny classes of the super-rich, who hold power against the demands of the masses by armed force in alliance with the IMF, transnationals, and the United States.

However, like the liberal and modernization approaches, dependency theory is too deterministic. Just as it is misleading to argue that nothing prevents any less-developed country from developing like the United States or Japan, it is untrue that less developed countries can never develop under capitalism. Some countries (South Korea, for example) have done so. Furthermore, the less developed countries are becoming more differentiated. On the one hand are declining economies, most of which are in Africa and Latin America, that rely on exporting primary products or low-wage mass-production. On the other hand are developing economies that are branching into new products, including computers and telecommunications equipment. Of the 30 top high-tech exporters, 11 are in developing countries, including Korea, Malaysia, and Mexico (United Nations, 2001: 42).

The worst of the dependency literature simply turned the simplistic liberal and modernization propositions on their heads. They contained too much theory and not enough history (Evans, 1985; Seers, 1981). To develop a more nuanced approach to understanding economic development, let us now examine some countries that succeeded in transforming themselves from poor to rich.

DOMESTIC CONTROL: THE KEY TO ECONOMIC BREAKTHROUGH

The countries that developed most spectacularly in the past century did not follow simple models. South Korea and Sweden are global exporters of highly sophisticated products, but they were once very poor, agricultural countries. Their transformations were complex, contradictory, and somewhat idiosyncratic. The processes occurred over several generations.

Despite their different histories, South Korea and Sweden shared several characteristics. Breaking orthodox liberal rules, they emphasized national rather than foreign corporate control, an activist economic role for the state, and strong national identities.

SWEDEN

We briefly review the Swedish case because, like Canada, Sweden began the industrial era as a resource-exporting country with a small population and little domestic capital. But Sweden developed a more diverse and independent economy than Canada did. Sweden's development strategy emphasized economic independence, exporting sophisticated manufactured goods, and violating several liberal principles while remaining an exemplar of democracy and equality.

In the mid–nineteenth century, Sweden was poor, overwhelmingly rural, and subject to famines and epidemics. While industrialization progressed in much of Europe, Sweden remained a backwater. Widespread rural poverty was eased only by massive emigration to America. In 1870, Sweden, like Canada, was an exporter of natural resources to more advanced countries. Today, it exports sophisticated manufactured goods—precision ball bearings, telephones, electrical equipment, precision machines, cars, trucks, and aircraft—composing about half of Sweden's total exports (Central Intelligence Agency, 2006). Raw materials now compose only a small percentage of Sweden's exports and the country now has one of the world's highest living standards and most egalitarian income distributions.

How did Sweden transform itself? A strong national identity led to a desire to develop independently. Swedes found export niches and prohibited majority foreign ownership without government permission from 1916 to 1982 (Nordlund, 1989: 298). The prohibition ensured the dominance of domestic corporations. Also, Swedish investment banks made risky investments in innovative firms early in Sweden's development.

Powerful unions, local communities, and businesses played a big role in Sweden's economic development, as did the Swedish state, with its long tradition of bureaucratic competence, independence, and integrity. Widespread agreement existed on the goals of equality and jobs for all. The state, usually controlled by social democratic governments, encouraged investment, especially during recessions, and ran a labour-market policy that retrained and quickly re-employed people who were laid off. Influential unions supported rapid technological change through policies of reinvestment, "wage solidarity" (relative wage equality), and workers' code-termination of corporate decision making (Esping-Andersen, 1985). In the 1990s, Sweden lost some of its distinctiveness as some Swedish corporations emigrated and governments adopted neoliberal policies to join the European Union. But Sweden remains one of the world's most egalitarian societies.

The Swedish case suggests that divergence from liberalism can lead to successful development. Sweden combined an active state role in developing the economy with equity and aggressive exporting. It managed to retain considerable domestic control over its economy. It is useful to bear these attributes in mind as we turn to our next task: surveying divergence among less developed countries in recent decades. As we will see, the countries that have developed most successfully have been able to follow policies similar to those adopted by Sweden (and, before it, Japan).

EAST ASIA: DEVELOPMENTAL STATES

Singapore, Hong Kong, South Korea, and Taiwan, the four Asian "Tigers," have gone from underdeveloped to developed status since 1960. Hong Kong and Singapore reached rich country income levels, while Taiwan and South Korea have nearly done so. Why have the Tigers develop while most countries in the southern hemisphere have not? Some attribute the Tigers' success to "Confucian" cultures of ethical-moral legitimation, obedience, meritocracy, and harmony. But the more compelling explanation is that these states followed variants of Japan's model of earlier development: state capitalism, export-led growth, and domestic economic control. To stop the spread of communism beyond China and showcase capitalism's superiority, the United States poured US$13 billion into South Korea and US$5.6 billion into Taiwan from 1945 to 1979 (Hoogvelt, 2001: 224). Hong Kong found a niche as Communist China's gateway to the capitalist world. Singapore profited from supplying oil and repairing U.S. ships during the Vietnam war. Because of their geopolitical value, the United States tolerated the Tigers' deviance from neoliberalism, whereas they suppressed deviance in other less developed countries, often by military means. After communism fell, the United States, the World Bank, and the IMF insisted the Tigers follow neoliberalism (Bello, 2002: 44–50).

Several southeast Asian countries have tried, so far fruitlessly, to copy the Tigers' success (see Figure 9.2). But rather than follow the Tigers' economic nationalist model, Indonesia and Thailand invited in foreign transnationals and adopted financial liberalization. Huge capital inflows led to feverish growth in the mid-1990s, followed by even more rapid capital flight when currencies were about to fall. Socioeconomic devastation was the result (MacLean, Bowles, and Croci, 1998: 24–25). Meanwhile, China and Taiwan, which defied neoliberal principles and controlled capital flows, avoided Asia's 1997–98 financial crisis.

AFRICA: EXCLUSION

In the sharpest possible contrast to the Asian Tigers, sub-Saharan Africa has been deteriorating for a generation. Resource exports collapsed from 7 percent of the world's total in the mid-1970s to less than 0.5 percent in the 1990s. Food consumption per capita declined and life expectancy dropped to 49 years. Foreign debt has tripled since 1982 (Hoogvelt, 2001: 173–75). Structural adjustment programs have not worked. They have "undermined investment and employment. . . . The poor and most vulnerable sections of society have all too often been undermined by the deregulation of labour markets and erosion of social welfare provisions. . . . Women have suffered in extreme form" (Watkins in Hoogvelt, 2001: 183).

As elsewhere, structural adjustment programs more effectively extracted African economic surpluses for rich bankers (Hoogvelt, 2001: 184–85). Worsening economies accentuated existing social cohesion problems in countries whose borders made sense only to the Western empires that created them. With 10 percent of the world's people, Africa suffers more than 40 percent of the world's conflicts (see Figure 9.3), including the slaughter in the Darfur region of Sudan and civil wars in Algeria, the Democratic Republic of Congo, and elsewhere (United Nations, 2005: 153–54).

LATIN AMERICA

Latin America used to be home to dependency theory, inwardly directed development, and economic nationalism. Immediately after the 1980s debt crisis, it turned to neoliberal experiments, economic devastation for many, but not economic breakthroughs, as in East Asia. More recently, popular democratic

FIGURE 9.2 GLOBAL DISPARITIES IN INCOME: ARE REGIONS CLOSING THE GAP?

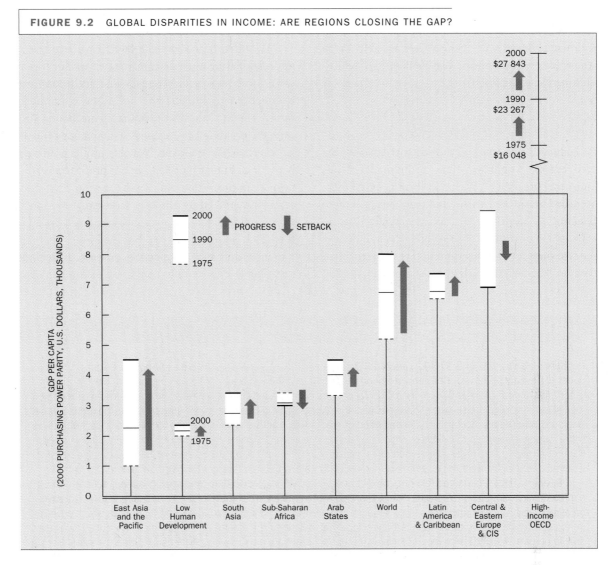

SOURCE: From *Human Development Report 2002* by United Nations Development Programme. Copyright © United Nations Development Programme, 2002. Used by permission of Oxford University Press, Inc.

movements have succeeded in most Latin American countries and voters used their new-found voices to elect left-wing governments, partly as a reaction to neoliberalism's failures.

In the 1970s, Latin American dictators had ran up huge debts to benefit themselves and their corporate allies: "Spectacular waste and corruption fed a spiral of inflation and a frenzy of capital flight in which much of the money being borrowed from abroad was funnelled straight out again" (Hoogvelt, 1997: 227). Bankers from developed countries lent eagerly. When the debt crisis struck in 1982, dictators and their cronies could not repay them. How could the bankers recover their money?

The World Bank, the IMF, and U.S. bankers knew that popular legitimacy was necessary to get everyone to sacrifice to pay off the debts. Thus, human rights and electoral democracy suddenly appeared on the American agenda. Ironically, however, in many cases voters used democracy to elect socialist governments that rejected neoliberalism. Some of those governments followed through on their radical promises. Others, burdened by huge debts and pressured by domestic capitalists and outside forces, continued to advocate neoliberal policies. The latter is what happened in Brazil, Latin America's most populous and unequal country. Other countries, led by Hugo Chávez in

Venezuela, adopted more radical, pro-poor policies. Whether most of Latin America will end up following Brazil's or Venezuela's model, Latin America now represents a big challenge to neoliberalism. (See Box 9.4.)

THE CHALLENGE AHEAD

Something is fundamentally wrong with a world that can create wondrous new technologies, life-enhancing breakthroughs, and brilliant works of literature and music but hasn't found ways to spread these benefits to most people. War, hunger, disease, exploitation of workers, forced child labour, illiteracy, homelessness, and ecological disasters are very much with us. Their burden is borne disproportionately by the poor everywhere, who outnumber the rich many times over.

We often hear about the benefits of free trade, international investment agreements, private enterprise, and new technologies. The profit motive is supposed to provide the spark for continuous improvement. But who benefits? Consider health care. Pharmaceutical companies spend billions of dollars on research if they anticipate big profits protected by patents. But corporations do not profit from environmental protection and wiping out poverty, illiteracy, and infectious disease. Consequently, more than 6 million children a year die needlessly because they lack simple low-cost interventions, such as immunization against infectious disease. Providing such simple interventions could save 2.3 million lives

---

BOX 9.4   LEASING THE RAIN (OR "LET THEM SIP CHAMPAGNE")

Cochabamba is a city of 800 000 situated high in the Andes Mountains in Bolivia, the poorest South American country. Seventy percent of Bolivians are poor and the local minimum wage is US$60 per month. Nearly one child in ten dies before the age of five. In 2000, Cochabamba erupted in riots; hundreds were injured and a teenager was killed. The issue was water. The IMF and the World Bank dictated that the city privatize its water supply. Behind closed doors, Bechtel, a U.S. engineering giant, was granted a 40-year lease to take over Cochabamba's water supply through a subsidiary. Bechtel was guaranteed a 16 percent annual rate of profit. Within weeks, Bechtel imposed huge rate hikes, increasing water bills to as much as 25 percent of minimum wage earners' incomes. Four months of mass protests followed. Protesters blamed Bechtel for trying to "lease the rain."

Deeply in debt, Bolivia had followed the dictates of the IMF and World Bank and sold its airline, railroad, mining, and electricity companies to private, mostly foreign, corporations. The strategy tamed inflation but led to severe recession and massive unemployment. Although the World Bank claims it advised Bolivia against water privatization and rate increases, the evidence contradicts that position. The Bank had written that "no public subsidies should be given to ameliorate increases in water tariffs in Cochabamba." James Wolfensohn, then the World Bank's president, responded to the protests by saying that Bolivians would just waste water unless there was a "proper system of charging." In Cochabamba, water is available in most people's homes for an hour every day or two.

Cochabamba residents claimed victory in April 2000, when they reached an agreement with their government that guaranteed the withdrawal of Bechtel's subsidiary and control over water was granted to a grassroots coalition. The coalition vowed to run the water system as a human right, not as a commodity. But without new investment they have been unable to improve or expand service. The government and World Bank were unwilling to help. Bechtel filed legal action against Bolivia, claiming US$50 million in damages for lost future profits.

Bechtel's action and that of several other transnationals led to a change in Bolivian politics. Evo Morales, leader of the Movement toward Socialism (MAS) won a majority of the vote in the 2005 presidential election. The next month, Bechtel settled, receiving 2 Bolivianos, 30 cents. In 2006, at the Fourth World Water Forum in Mexico City, the delegation representing the new socialist Bolivian government proposed to withdraw water from all free trade agreements and firmly opposed agreements that failed to acknowledge water as a human right.

Addressing 60 000 people in Cochabamba in December 2005, President-elect Morales declared: "We're very close . . . to nationalizing all of the natural resources. The natural resources can't be given away, can't be privatized, they belong in the hands of the Bolivian state!"

SOURCE: William Finnegan, June 2002, PBS, Frontline/NOW (wysiwig://8/http://www.pbs.org/frontlingworld/stories/bolivia/thestory.htm and wysiwig://6/http://www.pbs.org/frontlineworld/stories/bolivia/timeline.htm); Earth Justice, August 2002, "Solidarity with Cochabamba Water Uprising: Call for Transparency in ICSID Case Aguas del Tunari vs. Bolivia" (http://www.xs4all.nl/~arenaria/water/petition0802.htm); Democracy Centre, June 2000, "Water Privatization in Bolivia" (http://www.democracyctr.org/water/html).

FIGURE 9.3 THE POOREST HAVE SUFFERED THE MOST FROM CONFLICT

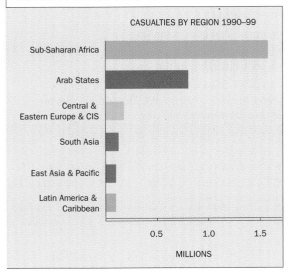

CASUALTIES BY REGION 1990–99

SOURCE: From *Human Development Report 2002* by United Nations Development Programme. Copyright © United Nations Development Programme, 2002. Used by permission of Oxford University Press, Inc.

annually at a cost of just US$4 billion, equivalent to two days of military spending in developed countries (United Nations, 2005: 33). But it doesn't happen because there is no profit to be made from it.

Transnationals want freedom to roam the world in search of the lowest wages, the laxest environmental protections, and the lowest corporate taxes. Their right to do so is encoded in international free trade agreements. But most people do not want to follow the transnationals from country to country in search of a job. Most prefer to stay put and build families and communities. For most, "home" is a definite place. Transnationals, however, have no location commitment or sense of responsibility to the communities where they make profits.

The Western capitalist model is not sustainable in the long run. A child born in the United States or Canada will consume, on average, 10 times the resources and produce 10 times the pollution of a child born in Bangladesh or Bolivia (Stern, Dietz, Ruttan, Socolow, and Sweeney, 1997: vii). "We need to recognize," writes Stuart Walker (1993: 46), "that the pattern of excessive consumption epitomized in North America—and envied around the world—is fundamentally unsustainable and unachievable for most of the world's population."

Markets, international cooperation, and new technologies are good if they serve humanity and the environment. However, if their control remains in the hands of a few transnationals that are guided by greed, even at the expense of the many, humanity is not served. The challenge is to ensure that development spreads to all people, conforms to human values, and sustains the environment. Democracy and sovereignty, equality, respect for all, and the spirit of community support must be the core of development policies.

A child born in Canada or the United States will consume, on average, 10 times the resources and produce 10 times the pollution of a child born in Bangladesh or Bolivia.
SOURCE: Shutterstock.

SUMMARY

1. The search for profits leads transnational corporations to move work sites to places where labour costs are low. This has negative implications for the well-being of many people.

2. Great disparities exist in the well-being of people residing in rich and poor countries.

3. In 1750, substantial gaps in living standards and levels of productivity among countries did not exist. For the most part, today's poor countries are those that were once colonized by the West.

4. The assumptions of liberalism about free markets and capitalist development have been adopted by the International Monetary Fund, transnational corporations, and the U.S. government. They do not live up to their promise to improve the well-being of most people in less developed countries.

5. Anti-imperialist theories emphasize the importance of domestic economic control and democracy in the development of the less developed countries.

6. Domestic control of corporations and activist governments were keys to the historical success and spectacular development breakthrough of Japan and Sweden, and they are likely to benefit less developed countries today.

QUESTIONS TO CONSIDER

1. What are the major obstacles to development in less developed countries today? How can these obstacles be overcome?

2. Can development be made more democratic and more equal across countries, classes, genders, and races? If so, how?

3. What are the consequences for development of capital moving wherever conditions are most favourable but people (labour) being unable to do so? How do the differing constraints on the mobility of capital and labour affect democracy?

GLOSSARY

Colonialism involves one country taking over another by force and ruling it without consent. In informal colonialism, a country gains control over another country through diplomacy, economic threats and incentives, and, in the last resort, threatening or carrying out regime change militarily.

Core countries are the world's most economically developed countries, including the United States, Japan, and Germany.

Gross national product (GNP) is the value of all goods and services produced in a country in a year as measured officially by money transactions.

Human development incorporates income growth with nonmaterial aspects of well-being, such as education, modern health care, access to employment, democracy, civil rights, and a healthy environment.

Liberalism is a political-economic doctrine that equates capitalism with freedom and distrusts the power of governments.

Modernization theory argues that, although liberal institutions are *necessary* for development, they are not *sufficient*. Less developed countries must also adopt "modern"—that is, Western—values before they can take advantage of capitalism.

Neoliberal economic policies require that, in exchange for loans and financial aid, countries dismantle laws against foreign ownership and control; privatize public enterprises (e.g., Crown corporations); reduce government regulation of businesses, such as electrical power generation and transmission; cut public expenditures on health care, education, and the like; reduce corporate taxes; balance government budgets; and set currencies at low levels to encourage exports.

Peripheral countries are less developed countries.

Structural adjustment programs were initiated by the IMF and the World Bank. In exchange for debt relief, they require that less developed countries adopt liberal principles—privatize state-owned industry, cut state budgets and subsidies, open up the economy to foreign investment, export more, and so on.

Supranational institutions extend beyond country borders and assume some of the sovereign rights of nation states. The most powerful supranational institutions support corporate rights. Supranational institutions include the International Monetary Fund, the World Bank, the G7 countries, the European Union, and the North American Free Trade Agreement.

Transnational corporations are corporations that own subsidiaries in more than one country. Most of the biggest transnational corporations are owned and controlled in the United States, Japan, Britain, Germany, France, and Italy.

SUGGESTED READING

Ali, Tariq. (2005). *Speaking of Empire and Resistance.* New York: The New Press.

Bello, Walden. (2002). *Deglobalization: Ideas for a New World Economy.* London: Zed Books.

Chang, Ha-Joon, and Ilene Grabel. (2004). *Reclaiming Development: An Alternative Economic Policy Manual.* London: Zed Books.

Hoogvelt, Ankie. (2001). *Globalization and the Postcolonial World. The New Political Economy of Development.* Baltimore: Johns Hopkins University Press.

WEB RESOURCES

Companion Web Site for This Book

http://www.newsociety5e.nelson.com

Begin by clicking on the Student Resources section of the website. Next, select the chapter you are studying from the pull-down menu. From the Student Resources page, you have easy access to InfoTrac College Edition® and other resources, such as the Glossary and Flashcards. The website also has many useful tips to aid you in your study of sociology.

InfoTrac College Edition Search Terms

Visit http://www.infotrac-college.com for access to more than 20 million articles from nearly 6000 sources when doing your online research.

ThomsonNOW™

http://hed.nelson.com

This online diagnostic tool identifies each student's unique needs with a Pretest that generates a personalized Study Plan for each chapter, helping students focus on concepts they are having the most difficulty mastering. Students then take a Posttest after reading the chapter to measure their understanding of the material. An Instructor Gradebook is available to track and monitor student progress.

PART FOUR

Institutions

CHAPTER
TEN

Families

In this chapter you will learn that

· Although common sense suggests that current dilemmas in family life are private problems, sociology helps uncover their public sources and solutions.

· The family does not have a universal form and its structure is therefore not a product of some biological imperative: Families vary widely in the way they are organized across different cultures and through history, and family organization is loosely related to the way material production is organized.

· Our society is organized around a gendered division of labour and the heterosexual nuclear family; this is the main reason that families that assume a different form—especially lone-parent families—have a particularly hard time meeting the needs of their members.

· Although women have increasingly assumed part of the financial support of their families, men do not share equally the work that must be done in the home, nor has society changed in ways that accommodate this changed reality for families.

· The gendered division of labour that makes it possible for nuclear families to care for young children involves sizable liabilities for women and children. The social isolation of full-time mothers and the stress attached to their high-demand, low-control situation reduces the quality of child-care.

· The chief negative effect of divorce for women and children is the loss of income that follows. The most effective solution to this problem—government support of all children—has not been adopted by the Canadian government, although most advanced industrial societies do have such a policy objective.

Bonnie Fox
UNIVERSITY OF TORONTO

INTRODUCTION

Contemporary life presents difficult choices for those of us who live in or plan to live in families. The constraints on these choices affect our lives profoundly. I begin this chapter by reviewing dilemmas in family life in the light of popular myths. Because family life is so familiar to us, we all too easily accept commonsense understandings that portray family problems as personal, private, and attributable to "human nature." Commonsense solutions prescribe individual change and ignore the social context. In contrast, sociology uncovers the social origins of family patterns and the problems they entail.

As a way of challenging the commonsense perspective, the second section of this chapter examines two patterns of family life that are different from our own. In these cases, it is clear that the family patterns people have created are a response to the problems posed by the needs of daily survival. Next, I review the history that produced our own family arrangements.

In the chapter's fourth section, I explore some of the main features of family life today: sexuality, marriage, parenthood, housework, and the **gendered division of labour** (i.e., the difference in the work that men and women do). My aim is to analyze how these activities are organized so as to give you an idea of the sources of problems that often plague modern families. I then discuss divorce and its aftermath and lone-parent and reconstituted families. I finish with a brief discussion of government policies to support families.

EXPLORING THE FAMILIAR: FAMILIES IN WESTERN SOCIETY TODAY

DILEMMAS OF CONTEMPORARY FAMILY LIFE

When you imagine yourself at age 39, you probably think of yourself as married, with a child or two. You probably also assume—or at least hope—that your children will enjoy full-time mothering for their early years. You are not unusual if you envision your adulthood in family terms. Moreover, when you think of family, you likely think of the conventional

nuclear family, in which the man is the main breadwinner and the woman has primary responsibility for the children. Alternatively, your dream may be to have occupational success and a loving, committed relationship without children. And the relationship you imagine may be with a same-sex partner. Or perhaps you hope to raise a child without any long-term partner. Whether or not you already anticipate parenthood, and whatever the gender of the partner you dream of, you likely envision a relationship in which the work and the responsibility, as well as the intimacy and joy, are shared.

Along with your dreams, you probably also have nagging concerns about your future. Full-time mothering seems a luxury few women can afford these days. Most married women—even those with young children—now have to assume some of the responsibility of breadwinning. Indeed, women attending university anticipate building a career, which involves far more commitment and time than does simply holding a job. Building a career makes it difficult to take time out for children, because the necessary time commitment is at odds with the demands of motherhood. These realities lead to obvious questions: Women wonder when they will have time to have children and how they will care for them once they arrive.

Whereas women's concerns about family tend to focus on the difficulties of combining employment and child-care, men's concerns probably centre on the growing elusiveness of occupational success in this uncertain economy. At the same time, men are increasingly pressured by the women they live with to change in ways for which they are unprepared. Manhood was once equated with occupational success, but such success is now both harder to achieve and insufficient for a happy marriage. Today, many women expect men to be emotionally open in ways that women tend to find easy, in addition to aggressively pursuing occupational success *and* sharing the housework.

Lesbians and gays face even greater challenges creating families in a society organized around heterosexuality and gender divisions. Parenthood without a partner is also particularly difficult: while two-earner couples find juggling income earning and child-care stressful, the task increases exponentially for a lone parent. Most obviously, the threat of poverty is far greater for a lone mother than for a

Full-time mothering is a luxury most women cannot afford. Combining employment and child-care is an act that requires women to wear two masks.

SOURCE: Mimi Matte, *Family Outing*. Photo courtesy Bau-Xi Gallery, Toronto. Collection of Granite Club, Toronto.

couple. Indeed, inequalities based on social class and the disadvantages women and racial minorities face in the labour force provide the inhospitable context in which all Canadians build their families.

Although conventional family patterns are in decline, our society still seems to be organized around nuclear families and the assumption that children are a private responsibility. Houses are designed for nuclear families and not extended families; social policies often assume family membership and men sharing their earnings with their wives; and, except in Quebec, governments refuse to provide adequate child-care facilities for the families needing them. The limitations of nuclear-family living and private responsibility for children are, however, clear when couples become parents. Parents (usually mothers) with infants typically face round-the-clock demands and anxieties about their

new responsibilities on their own. Whatever support grandparents want to offer is inhibited by the fact that they may live in another house, if not another city, as well as by the demands of their employment. Aside from the gift giving and visiting that occurs when a baby is born, friends are unlikely to help a mother with her child-care responsibilities. Meanwhile, when mothers return to their paid work, their earnings will likely be insufficient to support them and their children—so parenthood also reinforces nuclear families.

Conventional gender roles also seem central to the organization of our society. It is difficult to keep a family going with no one at home to buy groceries, plan and make meals, organize doctors' appointments, and meet repair people. In English-speaking Canada, the dearth of good, affordable daycare means that having children is difficult unless the mother becomes a full-time homemaker. And men have depended on the emotional support and caring work provided by their wives to keep them happy and productive. Thus, a gendered division of labour has sustained families in an economy in which employers bear no direct responsibility for the welfare of their employees' families.

Clearly, the future poses dilemmas. How will we earn enough money to support a family and raise our children? How will we sustain loving relationships with our partners while coping with the problems outlined above? Indeed, are our ideals about family sustainable? And if the conventional nuclear family is an unlikely prospect for most of us, how will we live in a society that assumes it is an essential part of life?

MYTHS ABOUT FAMILY

Thinking through these dilemmas is especially difficult because myths about family pervade our culture. Measured against the idealized image of family life that emerged during the 1950s and was beamed into homes across the country by television, the problems in family life today assume crisis proportions. "The family" seems to be disintegrating. Actually, real families in the 1950s bore little resemblance to those depicted in *Leave It to Beaver* and *Father Knows Best*. Nevertheless, the 1950s was an unusually "familistic" decade: People married earlier, had more children, and were less likely to divorce than the generations that preceded and followed them (E. May, 1988). The 1950s are thus an odd benchmark. Moreover, researchers find that women who combine motherhood with labour-force involvement are mentally and physically healthier than those who stay home (Coontz, 1992); women who are home full time with young children often find the situation stressful and isolating. And there is little scientific evidence to support the belief that babies and toddlers need full-time mothers at home.

Also mythical is the popular view that the traditional European family consisted of three generations of family living harmoniously under one roof, caring for all its members. In fact, **extended-family households**—consisting of three generations—were rare in preindustrial Europe. Moreover, children spent much of their childhood in the care of people other than their parents; and the elderly did not expect to be cared for lovingly by their children. Where large extended families were common—for instance, among the wealthy in ancient China—the lives of all but the male patriarch were wholly circumscribed by his authority.

Myths about family easily play into the hands of politicians who aim to reinforce individual responsibility for the welfare of children and other dependants and to avoid providing the social services necessary to support them in carrying out those responsibilities. Calls for a return to "family values" evoke an undefined past, free of today's social problems, a time when the values we associate with family—community, decency, and morality—were dominant. Such political rhetoric uses "the family" to symbolize all that is good and decent—the bedrock on which society rests. Of course, the family in question is the heterosexual breadwinner/homemaker family, and deviations from this ideal are held responsible for myriad social problems. Moreover, the assumption is that this kind of family is "natural," and not the product of the daily efforts of women and men living in particular circumstances.

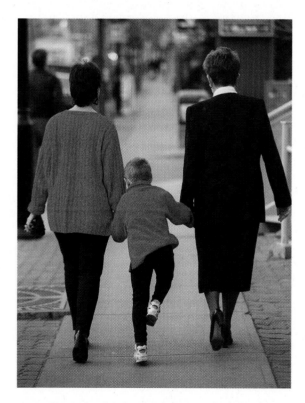

The decline of the nuclear family has been accompanied by the rise of other family forms.
SOURCE: Jim Wells/CP Picture Archive.

THE MYTH OF THE NATURAL FAMILY

One reason for the popular fixation on the heterosexual nuclear family is that it seems to derive from the biology of reproduction. Common sense suggests that biology produces the family. Heralded by the news media, arguments based on **biological determinism** are immensely popular these days. One common variant of this approach, known as **evolutionary psychology,** or sociobiology, attempts to apply the laws of biological evolution to social behaviour. Sociobiologists hold that, as with physical traits, social behaviour is inherited biologically—in other words, that behaviour can be linked to specific genetic configurations. Typically, sociobiologists construct a story about the history of human evolution that assumes genetic encoding of behaviour—a problematic assumption since there is no evidence to support it (Lewontin, Rose, and Kamin, 1984).

The sociobiological argument about family is that, over the course of human history, certain behaviours were adaptive because they contributed to "reproductive success." Specifically, males who were more aggressive and females who were more nurturant had more offspring. Thus, these behaviours were "naturally selected," and turned up in more and more individuals over the generations. According to this perspective, today's behaviour is the product of human evolution—and thus inevitable. Yet research by psychologists shows that women are no more empathic or sensitive to others than men are. Nor is there a natural maternal instinct that tells mothers how to care for their newborn baby.

The family, consisting of the biological mother and father and their offspring, is also a product of evolution, according to sociobiologists. Because children represent people's genetic investment, they argue, evolutionary forces have selected a pattern that is most likely to ensure the survival of offspring—namely, the union of two biological parents in a lasting relationship.

Although sociobiology accords with common sense, its claims do not accord with observable evidence. Evidence on family patterns across various cultures indicates that, although the nuclear family is common in many cultures, it is often embedded in a larger household that constitutes the unit of production, consumption, and child-care. For example, in Europe in the Middle Ages, the wealthier a married couple was, the larger the household. Spouses and their children lived amid an array of additional, unrelated people—from children and teens sent "into service" by their parents to adults providing necessary labour to the household (Mitterauer and Sieder, 1982). Preindustrial European households also provide evidence that mothers do not always raise, or even live with, their biological children. In many parts of Europe until the twentieth century, the babies of women who could afford it were given to "wet nurses," who were paid to nurse and care for them, and young teens were sent into service or apprenticeship in other households.

According to ethnographic evidence, in many non-Western cultures, mothers are the primary caregivers for babies but not for older children. Siblings often take on the bulk of the care of children, although in some cultures (like Tahiti or parts of the Caribbean) the children of a young woman are given to her parents or close kin to be raised, and in others (throughout Melanesia and Polynesia) they are adopted after weaning (Edholm, 1982). Moreover, because the biology of reproduction—which we take as "given"—is interpreted in different ways across different cultures, the role of the father in conception is not always recognized. Often the social father is different from the biological father. Finally, incest rules, which we take to reflect a kind of natural avoidance of inbreeding, have sometimes allowed brother-sister marriage to ensure the "purity" of the royal line (e.g., in Egypt and Hawaii). Many of the things we often assume to be natural and universal are neither. There is a diversity of family patterns across history and cultures.

CONCEPTUALIZING AND DEFINING FAMILY

Structural Functionalism

It is widely believed that the best unit in which to raise children is the nuclear family. This common-sense notion was promoted by Talcott Parsons (Parsons and Bales, 1955), whose writings on family constituted the dominant perspective in post–World War II sociology. In arguing that an institution (in this case, the heterosexual nuclear family) exists because of the useful functions it performs for the larger society, Parsons was making an argument reflecting the school of thought called structural functionalism.

Although structural functionalism dominated the study of families until recently, this perspective has obvious problems. First, just because an institution performs a social function, there is no reason to assume that some other institution might not perform that function equally well. Whether exclusive care by the biological mother and father is best for children is an empirical question.

Another problem with the functionalist perspective is its focus on how institutions create social *order*, and its consequent failure to analyze the tensions in family life that can generate social *change*. Moreover, the functions that are emphasized allegedly meet the needs of society, not necessarily of the individuals in it. So, for instance, although Parsons recognized the problems faced by full-time homemakers, it was not until feminists analyzed family life that the power dynamics and conflicts common to heterosexual nuclear families were highlighted.

Definitions

How *family* is defined has practical, as well as methodological, consequences. Rights and responsibilities follow from definitions. For instance, state-regulated institutions, such as schools and hospitals, often use legal definitions of marriage and family to determine which people will be informed and consulted about the status of someone in the institution. Accordingly, critically ill patients may find that family members with whom they have had little recent contact are admitted to their rooms and entitled to make important medical decisions on their behalf, whereas the friends who have been constant companions and who know them best are excluded. Government entitlements, such as widows' pensions and tax deductions for the support of dependants, apply only to family relations as defined by the government. A wife of a few years may be entitled to a widow's pension, whereas a same-sex lover of 20 years is not. A woman supporting a friend who is a senior and has disabilities cannot take the same tax deduction as a father supporting a child.

Similarly, when social scientists define *family*, some of them still assume the nuclear unit. This tendency has often resulted in a focus on the frequency with which nuclear-family patterns appear across history and cultures. Conceptualizing family in a way that focuses on common properties does not serve the interests of good empirical inquiry, however. Focusing on diversity in social patterns can, in contrast, help us acquire a better understanding of the nature of families. By studying diversity and noting the social circumstances that vary with family patterns, we can derive some idea of the social forces and factors that influence those patterns.

Accordingly, I define **family** as the sets of relationships people create to share resources daily in order to ensure their own and any dependants' welfare. What this definition offers is a focus on what is of critical importance to both individual survival and generational reproduction across many cultures. At the same time, it does not exclude groupings of people who are in essence functioning as family, though they may lack formal recognition as such (e.g., female relatives who live in separate households but cooperate daily to care for their children).

This definition holds family to be the unit of **social reproduction.** As opposed to biological reproduction, social reproduction refers to a wide range of activities that "maintain existing life and . . . [in most cases] reproduce the next generation" (Laslett and Brenner, 1989: 381–403). In other words, social reproduction refers to feeding, clothing, and otherwise looking after people's subsistence needs, as well as emotionally supporting adults and usually nurturing and socializing children. A "family" is thus a set of social relationships that work to reproduce life on a daily and a generational basis.

A LOOK AT OTHER FAMILY PATTERNS

To gain some perspective on family life, it is useful to examine family patterns that are significantly different from our own. When we do, one of the things we notice is that family patterns vary with the way people organize themselves to acquire their subsistence. To illustrate this point, I describe two interesting configurations: the communal households that are characteristic of many foraging (or hunting-and-gathering) societies, and the household economies typical of agricultural societies in preindustrial Europe.

FORAGING SOCIETIES: THE COMMUNAL HOUSEHOLD

In **foraging societies,** people acquire subsistence by gathering edibles and hunting live game. Foragers live in fairly small camps, or bands, comprising people who are compatible and not necessarily related by marriage or blood. Because they live off the resources available to them in the local area, foragers are nomadic. Their ability to move when necessary is critical to survival, so they cannot accumulate many possessions and they must keep the ratio of dependants (children and seniors) to productive foragers low (Lee, 1979).

Although foragers meet their subsistence needs by doing relatively little work, their inability to accumulate any surplus means that survival depends on reciprocity and cooperation among the people living together. For example, successful hunters distribute game to all members of the camp. Doing so is economically rational for an individual living in an economy based on reciprocity because giving establishes reciprocal obligations. Hunting is an especially uncertain occupation, so sharing the product is a sort of personal insurance. For the group, sharing ensures that a valuable source of protein is distributed widely.

In addition to sharing, a division of labour by gender and age organizes the acquisition of subsistence in foraging societies. Women typically gather and men typically hunt, although men also gather after an unsuccessful day of hunting and women hunt in some societies. Among the !Kung San of the Kalahari Desert in Botswana, as among many foragers, the food that women gather provides the bulk of subsistence—about 60 percent to 80 percent (Lee, 1979). In foraging societies, children and older adults typically do not forage for food.

The reciprocity that is the basis of foragers' daily subsistence no doubt generally influences the organization of their societies. Living has a communal character. Responsibilities that are assumed by families in our society—that is, responsibilities that are private—are held collectively in foraging societies. Thus, although marriage establishes the mother/father/child (i.e., nuclear) unit, the group of cooperating adults that is crucial for survival—the unit of social reproduction—is the camp. That is, all the members of the camp decide together when and where to move, and they share food and the responsibility for children. Moreover, perhaps because individual coopera-

tion is central to daily living, and because these societies are without authority figures who might enforce such cooperation, individuals are allowed considerable freedom.

Just as subsistence is shared, so too is responsibility for children (Leacock, 1981; Turnbull, 1961). Although women do most of the child-care—which is considerable, when children are carried constantly, as they are among the !Kung San—they do not bear the burden alone. Women care for one another's children; they even breastfeed one another's babies. Men also often tend babies and children.

Life in foraging societies seems to produce an absence of possessiveness toward children and spouses. This attitude is clear in the comment of a seventeenth-century Montagnais-Naskapi (Innu) man in response to a Jesuit missionary's attempt to shame him for not practising monogamy: "Thou hast no sense. You French people love only your own children; but we all love all the children of our tribe" (Leacock, 1981: 50). With respect to spouses, anthropologist Colin Turnbull (1961: 125) writes of the Pygmies of Congo:

> They think of responsibility as communal. If you ask a father, or a husband, why he allows his son to flirt with a married girl, or his wife to flirt with other men, he will answer, "It is not my affair," and he is right. It is their affair and the affair of the other men and women, and of their brothers and sisters. He will try to settle it himself . . . but if this fails he brings everyone else into the dispute.

In addition to a minimized sense of personal life as private, another consequence of communal living is that quarrelling and especially violence between spouses are seen, and treated, as community problems rather than private problems. Whatever disrupts the peace of the community is likely to be stopped—whether it is a beating or an extramarital relationship that takes an adult away from his or her responsibilities.

At the same time, the members of these communal societies have considerable autonomy. On consideration, the reasons are clear: Every adult has access to what is necessary for subsistence, so no person is in a position of dependency on another person. Moreover, because individual cooperation is essential for the survival of the collective, every person's happiness matters. For these and other reasons, relations between women and men are egalitarian: men have no more power or privilege than women do (Leacock, 1981).

Individual autonomy is evident in many aspects of family life. Although a girl's first marriage may be arranged by her parents, a divorce is fairly easy to obtain (Lee, 1979). Similarly, although women typically have babies only about every four years (largely because they breastfeed each infant for several years and because they have low body fat), they can also decide not to keep every child. Women can choose infanticide if a child is born before other children are able to fend for themselves (thereby overburdening the mother), or if a child is born who requires too much special care (thereby jeopardizing the lives of others). Sexuality is also quite unconstrained. Although monogamy is usually expected in marriage, women and men are typically able to enter into extramarital sexual relations as long as they do not interfere with the performance of their duties.

As this brief sketch demonstrates, the unit of social reproduction among foragers is larger than the nuclear family. Because foragers' survival depends on cooperation and reciprocity, the larger community assumes responsibilities that belong to nuclear families in our society. In turn, the communal basis of life and the absence of private households in foraging societies have far-reaching implications, including collective responsibility for people's welfare, individual autonomy, and gender egalitarianism.

PREINDUSTRIAL AGRICULTURAL SOCIETIES: HOUSEHOLD ECONOMIES

Our family patterns developed out of the patterns that were typical of precapitalist agricultural societies. In those societies, the household itself was the productive unit; producing subsistence was its main objective. This was true of craftsmen's households as well as those of the peasants and nobility who lived directly off the land. Thus, the social relations of family life in precapitalist households—that is, relations between spouses, between parents and children, and among residents of the same household—were also the relations of production. The chief economic relationship was that between husband and wife. Wives did necessary work that was complementary to that of their husbands, so an able-bodied wife was indispensable to the survival of the household (Tilly and Scott, 1978).

Land, which was the key means of production, was privately owned in preindustrial Europe. That meant that marriage—and thus adulthood—was predicated on acquiring land or some other means of livelihood. Consequently, people often married late—and chose their mates according to practical considerations as well as feelings (Mitterauer and Sieder, 1982). Typically, one son waited to inherit the land, his brothers were apprenticed to learn a skilled trade, and his sisters were given dowries. In the interim, children's dependence on their father to set them up for adulthood gave him considerable authority over them (Greven, 1973).

Land scarcity, and the fact that landlords extracted a substantial portion of the year's produce from the peasantry, meant that the struggle to survive was the chief household dynamic in these societies. It was constantly necessary to balance the number of productive adults against the number of dependants and the available economic resources (Tilly and Scott, 1978). Accordingly, household composition varied with changing economic requirements, especially labour requirements. In fact, much of the nature of household and family life was governed by economic considerations. So, in contrast with foragers, the interests of individuals in precapitalist agricultural societies were subordinated to those of the larger kin group and of the land from which they derived subsistence.

Labour requirements dictated household membership. Various types of labourers were taken into households as they were needed. Wives who died were quickly replaced. In peasant households, children were kept home only if their labour was needed. Otherwise, they were sent to wealthier households to be raised or into neighbouring households that could use extra labour. For this reason, and because of extra adult workers, wealthy households were often huge, consisting of 15 to 30 people (Flandrin, 1979).

It was not only poor children who were sent away, however; few children from any economic background were raised exclusively at home by their mothers. Raising a child usually involved several households. Babies were often sent to "wet nurses," peasant women who were paid to care for them. About one in two children survived and returned home after several years, to be looked after, in most cases, by an older sibling. In their early teens, children were then sent off to be trained for adulthood in yet another household. They were either apprenticed to learn a skilled trade or simply sent to another household to learn basic skills essential to adulthood (Mitterauer and Sieder, 1982). Women's critical economic role precluded their spending much time on child-care or being distracted by the needs of loved ones.

Although parents no doubt loved their children and missed those who were living in other households, in many marriages sentiment and emotional connection probably took a distant back seat to practical imperatives (Mitterauer and Sieder, 1982). Similarly, the privacy that we take for granted at home was absent in preindustrial households. Because the household was a place of work, business and family life were not distinguished. Moreover, rooms were not reserved for special purposes, like sleeping. In peasant hovels, entire families often slept in the same bed (Flandrin, 1979). In wealthier households, servants often slept with members of the family. Even sexuality was not entirely a private matter. This is clear from evidence of the community's intervention to regulate behaviour—whether to humiliate newlyweds it deemed inappropriate matches, to punish women suspected of adultery, or to force men to stop beating their wives. The interests of the collective—whether the household or the peasant community—seems to have taken precedence over individual autonomy.

These were truly patriarchal households: Married women owed their husbands absolute obedience and, according to British common law, could not hold property, enter into contractual arrangements, or, in the rare event of divorce, get custody of the children. Many historians conclude that most married women were entirely subordinate to their husbands.

Nevertheless, women's work was vital to the ongoing survival of the household. The married couple was the chief labour force in every household. Whereas men did the heavy farm work (or supervised those who did), women were typically in charge of the dairy, the poultry, and the garden, as well as household management—mostly supervising the full range of household chores (Tilly and Scott, 1978).

Women's and children's interests were generally subordinated to the needs of the household far more than were men's. For example, women had little control over their sexual and reproductive lives; at a time when childbirth was life threatening, they were subject to pressure to have children, given the value of child labour in an agricultural context.

It is a myth that preindustrial agricultural households involved extended families, with three generations living under the same roof (Gottlieb, 1993). Short life spans tended to preclude the co-residence of three generations of family. Equally, however, the establishment of the next generation's family was often delayed because male property owners avoided turning the land over to their sons—on whom they would then become dependent—for as long as possible (Mitterauer and Sieder, 1982). In fact, older men typically retired only after carefully specifying in writing how they were to be provided for by their heirs; feelings between the generations were ambivalent enough that seniors had to protect themselves against possible neglect by their children.

In sum, the nuclear unit was embedded in a larger household in preindustrial Europe. Unlike today, families were not sustained by sentimental or romantic feelings. Family and household relations were primarily relations of work, and individual needs were subordinated to those of the household to ensure its survival. Whereas the absence of private family life empowered individuals in foraging societies, private ownership of the means of production and a considerable struggle to survive meant that all individuals in agricultural societies were subordinated to the household enterprise, women were subordinated to men, and children were subordinated to parents.

THE ORIGINS OF CONTEMPORARY FAMILY PATTERNS IN WESTERN SOCIETIES

Given how different family life today is from what I have just described, how did contemporary family patterns develop? Actually, it is only recently in Western history that the family characteristics we take for granted coalesced—namely, the gendered division of labour in which women are primarily responsible for child-care and housework and men for financial provision, motherhood as women's primary vocation, and emotional intensity as the foundation of family relations.

Before the nineteenth century, "family" generally referred to all the people who lived under the same roof, many of whom, as we have just seen, were not related by blood or marriage (Flandrin, 1979). Only when household economies eroded and an economy developed outside the household did our concept of family develop. As you will see, the concept of family and many of its defining features are products of the separation of public and private spheres that accompanied industrialization. As people grappled with the problems of survival in a new social order, patterns of family life changed.

THE MIDDLE CLASS

Modern ideas about family developed largely out of changes brought about by the development of an industrial capitalist economy. In both England and North America, a "cult of domesticity" developed in reaction to, and as a critique of, an unfolding capitalist economy that people experienced as cruel, immoral, and beyond human control (Cott, 1977). It was an economy in which impersonal forces of supply and demand were replacing face-to-face negotiations and customs, such as those reflected in the phrases "an honest price" and "a fair wage." It was an economy in which a person could be rich one day and penniless the next. In contrast, the domestic sphere came to be defined as a moral abode characterized by peace, virtuous behaviour, and the selfless care of loved ones—a "haven in a heartless world" (Lasch, 1977).

Domesticity as an ideology and, for those who could afford it, a practice was a way of coping with a rapidly changing social order. For the business and professional class, men's work was increasingly moving out of the household. Home and business were separating as the scale of business increased. The middle-class home became a retreat, where the concerns and evils of the world of business were banished.

Mirroring the separation of men's and women's work, a new conception of gender emerged in the nineteenth century. Probably in an attempt to make sense of the new social order, people came to believe that men and women had fundamentally different natures. Women were assumed to belong naturally in the domestic sphere, as its guardian, and to be naturally nurturing. Men were believed to be suited to the competitive world of business, although their objective there was to provide for their families. Thus, an ideology of gender difference made sense of the unfolding social order, and in the middle class an evolving gendered division of labour developed with the physical separation of public and private spheres.

More than reflecting changes in social organization, these domestic and gender ideologies were developed by the large middle class that emerged in the nineteenth century. In England, the middle class struggled to assert its social identity and establish its right to political power by claiming a moral superiority over the aristocracy and the labouring masses. Borrowing religious imagery common in the Evangelical movements to which they were drawn, members of the middle class on both sides of the Atlantic shaped a domestic ideology that juxtaposed the home and the economy just as religious imagery juxtaposed Heaven and Earth. Dissociating themselves from a world seen as devoid of morality, the middle class wore their ideology of domesticity as a social badge—a symbol of their moral distance from the business world they inhabited (Davidoff and Hall, 1987).

In practice, these ideas provided more than an identity for the middle class. They also reflected the strategy this class was devising to deal with the fact that in the new capitalist economy, fathers could no longer ensure their children's futures by passing on skills or property. That strategy involved educating children in ways that would equip them to adapt to the changing demands of the new economy. It involved instilling proper work habits and attitudes, and keeping them home through their teens so they might attend school

By the late nineteenth century, mothers and children were idealized. This image depicts a well-to-do mother and her children in 1894.
SOURCE: The Schlesinger Library, Radcliffe Institute, Harvard University.

rather than go to work. Central to this strategy was a role for mothers. And women themselves seem to have had a hand in fashioning the role of mother as socializer of her children, as they responded to the withdrawal of productive work from the household and the demise of their role as husbands' economic partners (Ryan, 1981). Of course, full-time motherhood—which was equated with womanhood for the middle class in the nineteenth century—entailed women's economic dependence on men.

Finally, the turn toward domesticity brought about a change in the emotional texture of family relations. When the need to produce subsistence was no longer the driving dynamic in daily household life, time and space became available for attending to emotional needs. By the end of the nineteenth century, children were the sentimental focus of middle-class family life (Davidoff and Hall, 1987).

Ironically, although nineteenth-century marriage entailed an ideal of love and companionship, the separation of men's and women's daily work undermined emotional closeness between them. In the increasingly gender-segregated world, women's emotional energy seems, in many cases, to have been directed largely toward other women—family and friends—in addition to children, rather than toward their husbands (Smith-Rosenberg, 1975).

THE WORKING CLASS

Although family life was becoming a sentimental focus for the middle class, it was nearly endangered for the working class. Men's wages were so low in the nineteenth century that their children were often forced to work for pay—at long shifts, in horrible factory conditions, for cruel bosses, and at risk for illness and early death. Although working-class wives attempted to feed and clothe their families in the tradition of peasant or farm wives, they lacked vital means of production, especially land. In turn, women's dependency on men—who had access to higher wages in the labour market—resulted in strained relations between men and women, marital tensions that focused on money, and probably frequent violence against women (Stansell, 1987). The ability of families to cope was so fragile that many working-class families were forced to place their children in orphanages when unemployment, illness, or death occurred (Bradbury, 1982).

As they had in preindustrial times, families developed collective survival strategies to cope with the ravages of developing capitalism. Accordingly, individual needs were often sacrificed to the imperatives of family survival. Teenagers in the labour force gave their parents most of their earnings, and young adults postponed marriage until their parents could withstand the withdrawal of their earnings (Hareven, 1982). Married women did whatever they could, over and above child-care and homemaking, to contribute to household provisions—from doing mending and laundering for neighbours to hawking goods on the street and taking in boarders (Stansell, 1987). Moreover, families doubled up to save on rent; in England, there were more extended-family households during the Industrial Revolution than before or after it (Anderson, 1971). Neighbours also helped each other out in urban environments where housing afforded few amenities and little privacy.

Meanwhile, the trade-union movement responded to the straits of working-class life with a campaign for a **family wage**—that is, a wage paid to a man sufficient to support a wife and children (M. May, 1985). Social

Forty years after the idealized mother and children photo on p. 259, we have this harrowing photo of a migrant mother and children. This striking juxtaposition illustrates the difference between middle-class and working-class lives.

SOURCE: Dorothea Lange, *Migrant Mother, Nipomo, California* (1936). The Museum of Modern Art, New York.

historians continue to debate the reasons that the goal of the labour movement was a family wage rather than simply decent wages for all. Whatever the reasons, defining the struggle in these terms undoubtedly had the effect of reinforcing a working-class conception of family that was not unlike the middle-class ideal—with women defined as mothers and homemakers, dependent on men as breadwinners.

SOCIAL RELATIONS IN FAMILIES TODAY

MAIN FEATURES

We have seen how the development of an economy characterized by competition among people led to a mistrust of the public sphere and a turn toward domesticity. The family became the location identified with caring relationships. It was some time, however, before romance became a core characteristic of marriages. Only in the twentieth century did people begin to assume that romantic love, sex for the sake of pleasure, and marriage should be intimately bound together (Rapp and Ross, 1986).

An emotionally intense relationship between a man and a woman became key to marriage in the twentieth century. In the 1950s, amid a booming postwar economy, and no doubt in reaction to years of insecurity caused by the Depression and World War II and sustained by the Cold War, adults plunged into marriage and family as never before. Social historian Stephanie Coontz (1992) argues that the 1950s represented an unusual era in which adults expected that marriage and family would meet all of their needs. Women's and men's responsibilities in marriage were, of course, different: Women assumed responsibility for household and children, while men assumed responsibility for earning money. Unfortunately, although some people who married in the 1950s found family life and gender roles to be fulfilling, many women felt constrained ("trapped" according to some writers at the time) and stressed by being home all day. Although their husbands fared better, men too often felt less than fulfilled (Coontz, 1992; E. May, 1988).

Research indicated that men benefited more from marriage than women did: Married men's mental and physical health was better than that of single men, while married women fared worse than single women (Bernard, 1972). In the worse cases,

conventional gender roles—which place women in the position of meeting husbands' needs—contributed to men's violence against women, as they do today. Women are still more likely to be seriously hurt by husbands, lovers, and especially ex-partners than by anyone else (Gartner, Dawson, and Crawford, 1998–99).

An intense mother-child relationship is also typical of modern families. As we have seen, raising children has not always been a private parental responsibility. Although capitalist employers bear no responsibility for the next generation of employees, feudal master craftsmen housed and fed their young apprentices as they trained them and used their labour. In precapitalist times, several households usually contributed to the rearing of a child. Community responsibility for children extended to more recent centuries as well: In the British colonies in North America, community leaders sometimes exercised the power to order households to take in orphans and raise them to adulthood.

In recent years, the state has avoided the assumption of responsibility for the welfare of children, except for their schooling, and instead has enforced fathers' responsibility for the financial support of their children and mothers' responsibility for childcare. When "mothers' allowances" were introduced in early twentieth century Canada, they were paid only to widows even though other types of lone mothers were equally in need of assistance (Baker, 1995). Newer forms of social assistance have involved "man-in-the-house" rules, which disqualify any woman who appears to have a man in her life. Moreover, one of the key government responses to growing concerns about child poverty is to strengthen attempts to force fathers who are separated from their wives to meet their child-support obligations. This strategy turns attention away from governmental and community responsibility for children's welfare. Similarly, aside from wartime emergencies, governments have failed to provide affordable daycare sufficient to meet the need for it. Child abuse sometimes results from the heavy responsibilities carried by parents, especially mothers.

In the 1950s, 1960s, and 1970s, when many men earned a "family wage," a majority of married women stayed home and assumed full-time domestic responsibilities. A gendered division of responsibility and labour was the way most families met the daily needs of adults and children. Because wages and salaries have eroded since the 1970s and most women (even those with preschool children) must work outside the home, the issue of who cares for the children is now a social problem. Compounding it are government cuts to education, health care, and other social services, which increase the work that must be done in the home. The assumption that child-care is a private responsibility is increasingly problematic.

Most Canadian women are faced with the need to juggle the fundamentally incompatible demands of employment and family every day. The stress of their "double day" of work generates considerable tension between women and their male partners, as men typically have failed to assume an equal share of housework, child-care, and eldercare (Marshall, 1994). In some cases, that tension contributes to divorce (Kurz, 1995). Nevertheless, men are doing more housework and child-care now than they did decades ago. And although women who are employed full-time juggle a heavy load, and lose sleep in the process, they also are significantly healthier (mentally and physically) than other women (Barnett and Rivers, 1996; Sayer, 2005).The change in women's lives, coupled with the lack of significant accommodating change in many areas of society, has prompted increased diversity in household patterns. More people live alone—and only partly because of population aging. People are marrying at a later age, and more people are never marrying. The percentage of people under 50 who never marry is increasing, as is the percentage of people who are neither married nor cohabiting (Beaujot, Gee, Rajulton, and Ravanera, 1995).

In terms of family diversity, cohabiting men and women constitute the fastest-growing type of family in Canada. They more than doubled in number between 1981 and 1991; and by 2001 almost 14 percent of families involved a common-law couple (see Table 10.1). The popularity of this kind of relationship probably reflects peoples' assessment of the personal costs involved in marriage. The sacrifices that women make after they marry, and especially when they become mothers, are emotionally and financially risky, given current rates of divorce. The interdependence that is characteristic of marriage may be less attractive to younger generations than to older ones who married when women were less able to support themselves without a man and sexual activity outside marriage was widely frowned upon. Research on how couples handle their money indicates that independence may be an objective of people who cohabit:

Common-law couples are more likely to keep their money separate than married couples, who often create joint accounts (Singh and Lindsay, 1996). These relations are also more unstable than those involving marriage; that is, people feel freer to leave them (Marcil-Gratton, 1993).

The growing number of gay and lesbian families reflects some of the same social changes that produce common-law unions—increased social acceptance of sexual expression and women's decreased economic dependence on men. The 2001 census produced our first estimate of families headed by same-sex common-law couples: 34 200 Canadians declared themselves to be living in same-sex relationships; the number represents 0.5 percent of all couples (Statistics Canada, 2002). About 15 percent of lesbian couples are raising children, and about 3 percent of gay male couples are living with children.

Same-sex couples have faced an uphill battle for acceptance as families. For decades, the courts denied child custody to lesbian mothers leaving their husbands. Same-sex partners were also denied spousal benefits and the right to adopt nonbiological children they were raising. After years of protracted court battles, gays and lesbians won the right to marry in Ontario, Quebec,

TABLE 10.1 FAMILY STRUCTURE, CANADA, 2001

	NUMBER (IN MILLIONS)	PERCENTAGE
Married couples	**5.90**	**70.5**
Without children at home	2.43	29.0
With children at home	3.47	41.4
Common-law couples	**1.16**	**13.8**
Without children at home	0.63	7.5
With children at home	0.53	6.3
Lone-parent	**1.31**	**15.7**
Male parent	0.25	2.9
Female parent	1.07	12.7
Total	**8.37**	**100.0**

Note: Some percentages do not add up precisely because of rounding.

and British Columbia. In December 2004, the Supreme Court of Canada ruled that a definition of marriage that includes same-sex partners was not unconstitutional. After much debate, the House of Commons voted in June 2005 to approve gay marriage in Canada.

In fact, same-sex couples' relationships display characteristics that approximate family ideals. Lesbian and gay relationships are as stable as those of cohabiting heterosexual couples (Stacey and Biblarz, 2001). Their stability is impressive given the higher standards of emotional intimacy they typically have relative to heterosexual couples, the weaker institutional pressures to stay together, and the fewer social supports (Stacey and Biblarz, 2001). Same-sex couples are also more likely to have egalitarian housework and child-care

This poster was produced by the Queer Parenting Initiative (Toronto) to "celebrate the diversity of family structures within which children live and thrive." It reflects how concepts of social relations in families have changed from just a few decades ago.

SOURCE: The Queer Parenting Initiative is a joint project of the LGBT Parenting Network, FSA Toronto; Centre for Addiction and Mental Health; Gay Fathers of Toronto; Chinese Family Services, TGStation.com, and community members. For more information: www.queerparent.ca.

arrangements than heterosexual married and cohabiting couples (Dunne, 2000; Nelson, 1996). Moreover, given the obstacles they face, the families of same-sex couples can be seen to be the products of choice to a greater degree than other families (Weston, 1991). Certainly, although women married to men often allow "fate" to decide whether or not they have children, lesbians must choose to get pregnant. In turn, the children they raise, despite the stigma they may face, show levels of well-being similar to children who grow up in other families (Stacey and Biblarz, 2001).

Still more family diversity is indicated by the growing incidence of lone-parent families. In 2001, 15.7 percent of families consisted of one parent—usually a mother—and her dependent children (see Table 10.1). Early in the twentieth century, when they were as common as today, such families typically involved a widow and her children. Since the early 1990s more than half of them have involved separated or divorced women, and in 1991 about 20 percent involved never-married women (Statistics Canada, 1992: 5). In 2001, 19 percent of Canadian children lived with only one parent (Statistics Canada, 2002) (see Figure 10.1). More than half of these families were poor in the late 1990s (National Council of Welfare, 1998). The changes many governments are making to social assistance ("welfare") programs, which tie assistance to employment ("workfare") and thus require that one adult both support the household financially and take care of children, increases the problems faced by lone-parent families.

Other trends indicate the increasing diversity of families. Decades of fairly high rates of divorce have produced large numbers of "reconstituted" families. It is estimated that in 2001 almost 12 percent of couples with children involved a stepparent, compared with 10 percent in 1995 (Statistics Canada, 2002). Children whose parents have remarried after divorce have a fairly complicated network of family relations. In addition, more young adults are continuing to live with their parents or returning to their parents' home after leaving it. In 2001, 41 percent of adults 20 to 29 years of age lived with their parents, compared with 27.5 percent in 1981 (Statistics Canada, 2002).

Family patterns in Canada show racial, ethnic, and class differences as well, although our knowledge of them is limited. Approximately 18 percent of black women and 15 percent of Aboriginal women in Canada were lone parents in 1991, compared with 7 percent of non-Aboriginal women (Statistics Canada, 1992: 14,

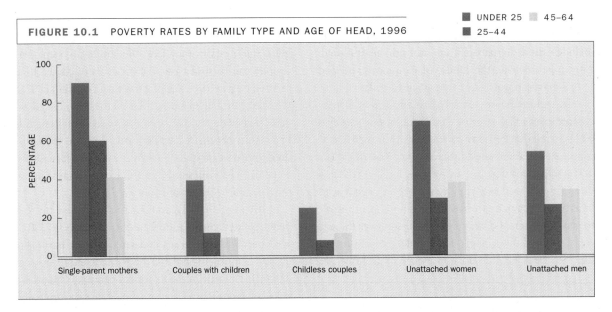

FIGURE 10.1   POVERTY RATES BY FAMILY TYPE AND AGE OF HEAD, 1996

SOURCE: Human Resources Development Canada, National Council Of Welfare, *Poverty Profile 1996* (Ottawa: Minister Of Public Works And Government Services, 1998), p. 36. Reprinted with permission of the Minister of Public Works and Government Services, 2000.

19). The fact that black families in Canada are less likely to contain a married or common-law couple is related to the lower likelihood that black men can earn a stable, sizable income. Rates of marriage increase significantly with income among black Canadians (Calliste, 2001). We do not know if black lone mothers regularly compensate for low incomes and absence of a partner by relying on personal support networks of relatives and friends. In the early 1970s, poor African Americans were found to create women-centred networks whose members shared scarce resources and cooperated in child-care (Stack, 1974). Certainly, a pattern of cooperation among kin, across nuclear families—including living together in extended-family households—has been typical of many working-class and immigrant Canadians and Americans (Iacovetta, 1992; Kibria, 1993).

I next discuss the practices and social relationships that are central to family life. Emotional intimacy and sexual expression are so important to the creation of committed relations that I examine them first. Because family life is typically organized around a gendered division of labour, I next discuss the sources of gender differences. Then I review changes in marriage. Parenthood, child-care, and housework "make family," and I discuss them before considering both divorce and social policies.

SEXUALITY AND FAMILIES

Although historically families were largely arrangements for perpetuating wealth or ensuring economic survival, now it is love and the promise of ongoing intimacy and caring that propel people into long-term commitment. Increasingly, we have come to expect lasting sexual, emotional, and social happiness in a relationship. This is an ambitious expectation in a society where we also expect to grow and change as we mature, and where, for many job categories, hours of paid work have risen since the mid-twentieth century.

We also live in a society where images of sexuality surround us, and specifically where noncommitted, or recreational, sex is eroticized. Although we think of sexuality as very personal matter, our desires are clearly subject to the influence of film, TV, and advertising. Even governments historically have attempted to exert control over their citizens' sexuality. The most obvious reason sexuality has been the object of state control is that the family is the unit of social reproduction. Society depends on families to produce and care for the next generation. Accordingly, with the aim of tying sexuality to reproduction, most Western governments in the nineteenth century passed laws banning the use of all forms of contraception. In Canada, section 179c of the 1892 Criminal Code made the selling or advertising of any contraceptive or device for performing abortion an indictable offence. This legislation was not only a form of **pronatalism** (a policy aimed at increasing the population) but also the product of the fear that white, middle-class Canadians of northern European descent were not reproducing in large enough numbers, while other immigrants were doing just that. Not until 1969 was the Criminal Code amended to make contraceptives legal. Abortion remained a criminal offence until 1988, after Dr. Henry Morgentaler's repeated challenges of the law.

Since the "sexual revolution" of the 1960s, women and men typically have become sexually active before they marry or begin to cohabit (see Chapter 4). In other words, people enter committed relationships with more knowledge of each other and a better sense of their compatibility on a number of important dimensions. At the same time, sexuality is affected by the social context in which it occurs—and the fact that it occurs between people who are products of gender socialization. Consequently, certain social patterns are common over the course of relationships, which present couples with challenges for ensuring the vitality and endurance of long-term relationships.

The first challenge to couples who love each other and commit to a lasting relationship has to do with the fact that social context, or situation, strongly affects people's sexual behaviour. Because opportunity is a major determinant of the frequency of intercourse, people who live together are on average more active sexually (despite TV images of the singles lifestyle). Married and cohabiting men and women have sex more often than men and women who are single (Schwartz and Rutter, 1998). However, people who are married are significantly less active sexually than people who are cohabiting (comparing people of the same age, who are together the same length of time) (Schwartz and Rutter, 1998). Moreover, for all types of relationship—married, common-law, gay, and lesbian—sexual activity decreases considerably over the course of a relationship, dropping especially after the first two years or so (Schwartz and Rutter, 1998). The decline over time is due not only to the reduced excitement attached to familiarity but also to the effects of having children and growing responsibilities. With an infant or a toddler in the house, sleep often becomes more valuable than sexuality. Long

hours of employment, worries over money, anxieties about children, and other issues common to long-term relationships also inhibit sexual desire.

Gender differences also affect sexuality, as well as intimacy. The "sexual revolution" was limited in a number of ways. For instance, there remain different norms for men and women with respect to sexuality. Men are still expected to initiate sexual activity. Women can still cross a line—they can be too aggressive. Couples have to continually negotiate around this set of expectations.

Aside from sexuality, intimacy must also be negotiated amidst gender differences. While men typically experience sex as the route to intimacy, women typically need intimacy—and expressions of it—before sex (Rubin 1990). Intimacy is also made more difficult by gender differences in the expression of love and caring. Women typically seem to be better at discussing their feelings (as well as accessing them)—something central to our culture's definition of intimacy—while men may be more likely to express intimacy through caring activities, which may not be recognized as such. These gender differences are probably due to gendered experiences and family responsibilities; most obviously, women need to learn to nurture, given the responsibilities for children's well-being that they take on with motherhood (Tavris, 1992).

Sexual behaviour in same-sex couples also reflects gender differences. Typically, gay male couples have more frequent sex, and lesbian couples have less sex, than heterosexual couples (Schwartz and Rutter, 1998). That men find recreational sex appealing, and that women are socialized not to initiate sex, presents a variety of issues for same-sex couples. Ongoing social stigma attached to these relationships compounds the obstacles to lasting relationships—making their durability all the more impressive.

Certainly, there are obstacles to long-term heterosexual and homosexual relationships. Yet the majority of Canadians who marry stay together, so we can only assume that they find their relationships satisfying in a number of respects.

GENDER AND FAMILIES

Most nuclear families built around a heterosexual couple are organized around a division of work and responsibility between men and women. It is not surprising, then, that surveys of Canadian high-school students consistently find that girls plan to take time out of their adult employment to devote to family while boys do not. There is evidence that girls and boys are socialized differently as they are growing up, probably in part because of a pervasive conviction that boys and girls are naturally different. Yet, research that examines the choices that adults make in their lives about whether to prioritize work or family shows that childhood socialization has less effect on such choices than adult experiences in paid work and intimate relations (Gerson, 1985). Thus, a better explanation of girls' tendency to focus on domesticity emphasizes that they make decisions in light of the opportunities and constraints they face. American sociologist Arlie Hochschild (1989) has argued that an adult faces life with a gender strategy that involves, for example, a prioritization of either career/job or family relationships. That prioritization then guides their life decisions. According to Hochschild, people's gender strategies result from a combination of ideas about gender in the culture, emotionally charged reactions to childhood (especially parents' gender roles), and the opportunities and constraints that they faced as they became adults.

A good illustration of gender strategy can be found in Jane Gaskell's study of the expectations of young people graduating from three high schools in working-class areas of Vancouver (1983). Most of the girls judged paid work to be more satisfying than the domestic roles of mother, wife, and homemaker: Their socialization had not produced a desire for domestic roles. At the same time, they overwhelmingly agreed that they would eventually assume primary responsibility for housework and child-care. They saw their futures as bound up with domesticity for a number of reasons. First, they assumed that they would have a male partner and that he would be unwilling and unable to share the household work. Second, they predicted that their future earnings, relative to their spouse's, would be low and that it would therefore make economic sense for them to assume household responsibility rather than paid employment. Third, they felt that babies were better off at home with their mothers. The boys in the study concurred with the girls about who should take on housework and child-care duties (Gaskell, 1983). Gaskell's findings indicate that girls prioritize domestic responsibilities largely because of the lack of opportunities

facing them, from good jobs to good daycare to egalitarian men.

Similarly, an American study of the decisions that women make about whether to prioritize family or paid work found that women who ended up prioritizing family and the care of loved ones often did so as a result of either a negative experience of paid work or a very fulfilling intimate relationship, coupled with a dawning realization that the responsibilities of family life and paid work were incompatible (Gerson, 1985). Thus, gender inequality in the labour force promotes the gendered division of labour in the home. It also pushes women toward marriage. Women's relatively weaker market position and the growing need for two incomes when there are dependants to support means that if women want children and a decent standard of living, marriage is still a wise choice.

Labour-market inequality forces women to make difficult choices. Employers still define jobs, especially professional jobs, in terms of employees who are unencumbered by family responsibilities and are able to work after 5 p.m., at night, on weekends, and so on. Job sharing, part-time work with good benefits, workplace daycare facilities, and paid leave for tending sick children are still uncommon in Canadian workplaces. Careers and family responsibilities are still incompatible for women. Thus, many successful career women are single. In the face of little change in the workplace, dual-earner couples with children are left to design their own ways to balance conflicting responsibilities. One person—usually the woman—cuts back on paid work, works nonstandard hours, and so forth.

MARRIAGE AND DIVORCE

Today, because relatively few men earn enough to support a family, and women need to do paid work, the conventional gendered division of work and responsibility is no longer viable. Old patterns die hard, however. And the contradictory nature of old family patterns existing in new circumstances has generated an increase in divorce, pressures on men to assume new family roles, and a need for new social policies.

Family law has changed to reflect the new circumstances. Before the late 1970s, the marriage contract stipulated a simple but unequal exchange between a woman and a man: He was responsible for his and her maintenance, and she owed him domestic and sexual services. Meg Luxton (1980) explored the personal consequences of the conventional gendered division of labour in her study of working-class, breadwinner/homemaker families living in Flin Flon, Manitoba, in the late 1970s. Her clearest finding was that breadwinning translated into privilege. Because men's families depended on them, their needs assumed priority—meals prepared according to their taste, children kept quiet for the sake of their need for peace, and so on. Conversely, homemakers' economic dependence typically meant an inability to get their own needs met in the relationship.

That these inequalities were typical in a conventional marriage is suggested by statistics on physical and mental health. Comparisons of men's and women's physical and mental health in the 1960s and 1970s show that men benefited from the care they received in marriage, while the work of personal care took a toll on women. Married men were significantly better off physically and mentally than single men, whereas the opposite was true for women (Bernard, 1972).

Divorce became more common over the last century and especially since 1968, when federal law was liberalized. Recently, the divorce rate has levelled off. According to popular opinion (and some sociologists), the rise in the divorce rate testifies to increased selfishness, unwillingness to make the compromises required by a relationship, and laziness when it comes to "working out" interpersonal problems. This explanation denies the rights of individuals to happiness and emphasizes instead the importance of maintaining the institution of marriage. It ignores the fact that there have tended to be two experiences of marriage—"his" and "hers"—and that women are typically the ones called on to overcome selfishness, make compromises, and work to create happy homes. In the worst marriages, women are the ones subject to severe violence (Gartner et al., 1998–99). Thus, women are more likely than men to initiate separation and divorce—and do so for reasons often having to do with gender inequities in their marriage (Kurz, 1995).

In view of the fact that women have entered the labour market in increasing numbers—and thus gained the possibility of self-support—and have been exposed to the climate of change brought about by the women's liberation movement, it is not surprising that divorce rates have risen. It is estimated that about 30 percent of marriages in Canada will end in divorce, which is considerably below rates in the United States and Sweden, but high when the consequences for children are considered. (The aftermath of divorce is considered below.) Although most adults who divorce later remarry, marriage is now no longer the only basis of family formation. By the late 1980s, 20 percent of Canadian babies were born out of wedlock; in 1990, 38 percent of parents of newborns in Quebec were not married, though most were cohabiting (Marcil-Gratton, 1993).

Meanwhile, marriage as an institution has changed. In the late 1970s, with the aim of recognizing the work that women do in the home, provinces and territories across Canada reformed their family laws to omit any mention of gender-specific obligations and exchanges. Replacing the old model of a "community" of interdependent men and women was one assuming the spousal relationship to be a partnership of equal individuals, both of whom contribute to the marriage and are responsible for themselves. Under the old laws, a woman had no right to "family assets," including property that resulted from her own work over the years (because she owed her husband her labour). Now, "family assets," which include some of the fruits of advanced degrees and pensions, are to be divided equally on divorce (Morton, 1988). The new laws encourage people leaving a marriage to become independent as quickly as possible; women are not entitled to continued support, as they were under the old laws.

Ironically, because the new laws treat women and men equally, the results are inequitable. The assumption that women can support themselves as men do is incorrect given the gender inequality that continues to characterize the labour market. For many working-class women, there is the additional problem that sharing "family assets" means sharing the poverty. Not surprisingly, the chief result of divorce is a significantly lowered standard of living for women and the children who usually live with them (Finnie, 1993).

HOUSEWORK AND MOTHERWORK

Although the new family laws stipulate equality, a gendered division of labour still predominates in households. Women may have assumed part of the responsibility of breadwinning but they remain largely responsible for the housework (Marshall,

1994; Presser, 1994). Men do more when their partners are employed, and more housework than they used to, but women continue to bear most of the responsibility and do more of the necessary daily chores. Consequently, employed women generally work longer hours than their partners every week and have less time for sleep, leisure, friends, and children than do full-time homemakers and men (Sayer, 2005). As Chapter 7 argues, this gender difference is both a manifestation and a cause of the inequality between women and men in Canada today.

Why does this gender inequity persist? Some men translate higher earnings into privilege at home. Marriage involves negotiation—if not daily, then at least periodically and especially early in the relationship. Women's bargaining power in those negotiations is undermined by the following factors: women's disadvantage in the labour market; women's perceived disadvantage on the remarriage market (which weakens their courage to push for change in the relationship); a cultural devaluation of caring work; and cultural definitions of gender, especially of masculinity (Hochschild, 1989).

Meanwhile, surveys show that couples who share housework are significantly happier than others. Among couples who do not share housework, the resulting tension in the relationship affects the men and the children as well as the women (Hochschild, 1989). Research also shows that equality in the labour market and at home goes hand in hand: Couples who do similar work, especially dual-career couples, seem to be more likely to share household work (Hertz, 1986). Given that gender inequality exists in the labour market, the unequal division of housework is likely to persist for some time.

Having children also contributes to the division of labour between women and men: When heterosexual couples become parents, their lives typically become more conventional. With motherhood, women tend to take on the bulk of the caring for their babies and a greater proportion of the housework than before they were mothers; with fatherhood, men tend to concentrate more on financial providing and also become their babies' playmates and their wives' helpers (Fox, 1997). The added financial responsibility that parenthood entails, coupled with the absence of change in employment practices to accommodate family obligations, binds men to long workdays, inhibits their sharing of baby care and

housework, and thus promotes the development of a pattern of gender divisions. More than the organization of paid work induces gender divisions with parenthood, however. Gender is also at issue: Same-sex parents do not feel driven to adopt specialized roles (Dunne, 2000; Nelson, 1996).

The conviction is growing that full-time mothering is bad for women and, consequently, for their children and that men's physical absence from the home also can be detrimental to the social development of children. For women, the private nature of parenting causes problems. Because full-time mothers are home alone much of the day, many suffer from social isolation. Alone with the responsibility, most women find the full-time care of young children stressful because it combines high demands and low control over time (Rosenberg, 1987). A Canadian study likened the work of full-time mothers with young children to that of "front-line" workers servicing people with pressing needs, workers among whom "burnout" is a common problem. At work and on call 24 hours a day, full-time mothers have no "downtime" and often only minimal sleep (Rosenberg, 1987). For single mothers, of course, all these problems are intensified.

These problems are the result of the way child-care is organized in our society. The responsibility for child-care is private, which means that it rests with the parents alone. Neither the health-care system nor the educational system provide many services for the early years of children's lives. Neighbourhood drop-in facilities, frequent home visiting, and good-quality daycare have yet to be considered a basic part of our social infrastructure.

At the same time, most of us are certain it is best for babies and toddlers to be at home with their mothers. On dispassionate and careful consideration, however, the more logical conclusion is that toddlers and even infants fare better when they are cared for by several adults and when they spend at least part of the time outside the home. A single, isolated caregiver inevitably loses some inspiration, enthusiasm, and even warmth over the course of a 24-hour-a-day, seven-day-a-week schedule. Moreover, the home is not designed for toddlers; it is typically more dangerous and less stimulating than it should be. Indeed, adult needs for order compete with toddler needs to explore and manipulate their environment: Housework and child-care conflict. Moreover, evidence shows that children who are in good-quality daycare from an early age are significantly advantaged in terms of cognitive and social development over those who stay at home (Clarke-Stewart, 1982).

Most mothers of young children today work outside the home, unable to afford full-time motherhood even if they prefer it. The problem they confront is in having to handle a stressful balancing act (juggling responsibilities at home and the workplace) every weekday. Although attention to this problem has typically focused on increasing men's contribution, perhaps there is just not enough time in the day to do the work that many couples face. Solutions require a collective response. However, the Canadian government's main response to the problem has been to recruit foreign domestic workers, obliging them to provide domestic service for several years before they can obtain permanent-resident status. The use of nannies to solve the child-care problem involves the continued **privatization** of domestic labour, which, in effect, allows the community to avoid solving the problem. It allows wealthy professionals, who might otherwise combine forces to put political pressure on the government for a solution that would help everyone, to solve the problem privately. This solution also means having child-care and housework done by workers who are highly vulnerable to exploitation, given their long hours of work, low pay, social isolation, lack of citizenship rights, and the private nature of their relationship with the employer (Arat-Koc, 1993). The arrangement puts women from less developed countries in the position of subsidizing the dual careers and comfortable lifestyles of middle-class Canadians.

BECOMING PARENTS

Aside from the work it entails, parenthood changes people's lives profoundly. We have already discussed the difficulties that the private responsibilities of motherhood pose for women. Even medicalized childbirth offers women limited assistance—aimed at relieving pain, minimizing physical danger, and delivering the baby.

In the past, women giving birth were assisted by other women, who continued to care for them and instruct them about mothering in the weeks following the birth. Because women giving birth in hospital today are usually without this kind of support, most experience at least one bout of postpartum depression and many begin motherhood upset or angry because of

their experience of childbirth (Fox and Worts, 1999). Many new mothers are also overwhelmed by the responsibility they have taken on; most find themselves totally unprepared to care for a new baby. It is hoped that the licensing and public funding of midwives in Ontario, Quebec, British Columbia, and Manitoba means that women have a good alternative to medically managed birth. Midwives provide assistance and support from before the birth to months afterward, for births in hospital as well as at home.[1]

Following a baby's birth, parents go through a challenging time of adjustment, which leads to significant changes in their lives. As we saw, the division of work and responsibility usually becomes more conventional for heterosexual couples, though usually not for same-sex couples (Fox, 1997; Patterson, 1995). Ties with friends also tend to weaken, as new parents typically spend more time with extended kin (Fox, 1997). These changes obviously are not inevitable. Couples negotiate them, and some resist the various forces moving them in this direction.

Having children entails other changes in most parents' lives. Women typically feel that motherhood completely changes their lives. Men who become involved in the care of their children seem to have the same reaction. Most research has found that having children brings profound meaning to people's lives. One study suggested that becoming a mother was not only to "fall in love" with a child but also to experience a transformation in the sense of self. Women tend to feel more loving and caring, and thus more closely identified with femininity, when they care for their children (McMahon, 1995).

DIVORCE AND ITS AFTERMATH

When people live together as a couple and a family, the dissolution of that unit brings turmoil for some time. People divorce largely because at least one spouse feels that something central to the marriage no longer exists—such as a sharing of responsibility or mutual caring. One of the chief reasons women initiate divorce is men's violence against them. Women are more likely than men to initiate divorce (Kurz, 1995).

Research indicates that serious violence committed against a woman is likely to involve a pattern of control by a man (Gartner et al., 1998–99). That some men need to be in control is a product of social forces as well as of psychological characteristics. In this culture, ideals of masculinity hold men to an expectation of some kind of dominance over women—an ideal often achieved through superior earnings. Poverty and unemployment can, then, be factors in men's violence against women, since they pose threats to men's identity. Moreover, conventional gender roles place women living with men in the position of meeting their needs—whether that involves meeting emotional needs or ensuring that meals are prepared. A woman's failure to do so may trigger violence from a man who feels entitled to her services. Given how central men's control is to violence against women, the process of separating from a man makes a woman especially vulnerable to violence (Gartner et al., 1998–99).

When intimate relationships break up, people face considerable adjustment. Probably the most important consequence of divorce for women and the children who live with them is a significant decline in family income. This decline is often so great that many fall out of the middle class, lose their family home, move, and change schools (Finnie, 1993). Most single-parent mothers with dependent children live in poverty (National Council of Welfare, 1998: 18). Low income is especially significant because it reduces the mother's ability to provide what researchers find to be most important for children's adjustment after divorce—additional emotional support and a predictable daily schedule (Furstenberg and Cherlin, 1991).

The conflict between spouses that precedes and accompanies divorce (and persists for some couples who do not divorce) is certainly damaging for children. Yet, in the vast majority of cases, children return to normal development about two years after divorce. Nevertheless, some research indicates that women whose parents divorced are more likely to marry and have children early, give birth before marriage, and have their own marriages break up (McLanahan and Bumpass, 1988: 147). The reasons are not clear, but it is possible that the children of divorce carry emotional baggage from their childhood. As for the adults who divorce, the vast majority feel after a while that their divorce improved their lives. Even women struggling with poverty can feel relieved to be in control of the money (Graham, 1987).

Lone Parents

In the last two decades, in addition to an increase in the divorce rate, there has been an increase in the proportion of mothers who are unmarried. In 2001, 15.7 percent of all Canadian families were lone-parent families, and 19 percent of children lived in one-parent families (Statistics Canada, 2002). There are also racial and ethnic differences in the likelihood that children will be raised by one parent. Nearly one-quarter of Aboriginal families living off reserves are headed by one parent, almost twice the rate for all Canadians (McKie, 1993: 59).

The chief problem facing lone-parent families is poverty. The reasons for the poverty are clear. A woman—someone already disadvantaged in the labour market—is expected both to earn money and to care for children, since support from the former spouse (if there is one) and the state is generally meagre. Thus, the tension between employment and family is acute in these families. Evidence shows that children who grow up in female-headed families are less likely to complete high school than those living in two-parent families because of the financial stress that lone parents face, not because of the absence of a father figure (McLanahan, 1985).

Reconstituted Families

Adults who divorce usually remarry, so they and their children establish new families. Although reconstituted families find themselves in a better financial situation than lone-parent families, they face their own problems. Stepparents are in a difficult position with respect to their spouses' children; stepmothers especially face considerable challenges. According to the research, the outcomes of these new situations are uncertain. In many reconstituted families, both stepparents and stepchildren establish close relationships. In a sizable number of such families, though, the tensions continue (Furstenberg and Cherlin, 1991). Many reconstituted families do not survive the early years of adjustment: Divorce rates are higher for second marriages, especially if children are present. Children in reconstituted families—like those in lone-parent families—face a heightened risk of experiencing developmental and social problems.

POLICIES TO SUPPORT FAMILIES

The chief problem for families today seems to be the difficulty of caring for children while earning enough money to support a family. The problem assumes

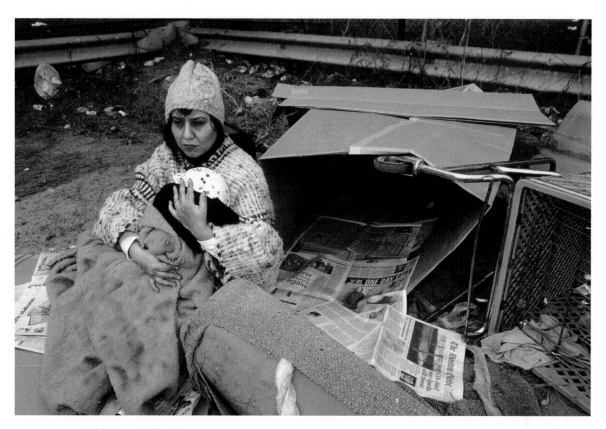

A homeless mother holds her sleeping baby.
SOURCE: Copyright © David Urbina/PhotoEdit.

crisis proportions for many lone-parent families, but is also of major importance in dual-earner families. The policies that most industrial countries have developed to address this problem include direct family subsidies, significant paid parental leave following birth, and high-quality, subsidized child-care facilities—especially preschool for children over two-and-a-half years of age (Eyer, 1996). Such policies are predicated both on the assumption of the community's responsibility for all its children and on state actions to support women as mothers *and* wage earners. In some cases, they are based on goals of universality and equity. In Canada, in contrast, children are assumed to be a private responsibility, as is the problem women face in juggling family and employment (see Box 10.1).

Although most European countries provide more generous state support of families than Canada, Sweden has especially good policies. There, it is assumed that children are a collective responsibility, and it is an official policy objective to promote gender equality in the home and the labour force. Behind this, the state in Sweden directly acts to control the effects of market forces in order to pursue the goals of social equity and meeting human needs.

The Swedish government effectively redistributes income from families with high incomes and without children to those with lower incomes and children. Its universal family allowances were four-and-a-half times the amount paid in Canada in 1991. Lone parents receive supplemental child support. Consequently, fewer than 5 percent of lone-parent families in Sweden are poor (Baker, 1995: 72, 126–27).

In Sweden, all new parents can take 18 months of parental leave (i.e., for either a mother or father)—12 months at 80 percent of their previous wage or salary, the next 3 months at a low flat rate, and the last 3 months without pay (Eyer, 1996). Most families take 12 months of maternity leave. In addition to parental leave, new parents can reduce their working hours to 30 per week and retain their job until their child is eight years old. All employees are entitled to leave from employment to care for a sick child at 90 percent of their wage or salary (Eyer, 1996).

BOX 10.1   IT'S TIME TO ACT ON CHILD-CARE

You can park your children in front of *Sesame Street* and they will learn. But there is not nearly the same impact as if you stay with them and watch.

— Dr. Fraser Mustard, quoted in *Maclean's* magazine, March 1, 1999

A nice mental prod, those words, to thinking about what today's Speech from the Throne is going to say about the long-awaited, much-trumpeted national children's agenda. Are we going to get something real or are we going to get suckered?

Like a lot of quotes from Dr. Mustard, the famed student of child-brain development, this one is layered and rather enigmatic. At one level, his words will guilt-out working parents across the country. At another level, they will be ammunition for advocates of quality child care and early childhood education.

At still a third level, they'll assault all those of us who do not make it home from work until 7 at night; who are too busy working weekends; who have jobs that provide miserly parental leave and time off for family needs; who are under financial pressure to take jobs that mean leaving the children with a neighbour or an untrained teenager down the hall.

Most important, Dr. Mustard's words generically disturb us. For just a moment, a day or two, they focus our minds on how important the children are to our society.

Those who argue that a national children's agenda should be just about tax measures and fiscal transfers to the provinces or just about a national child-care program or just about peripheral nips and tucks to existing programs and a lot of warm statements for the future about federal-provincial co-operation—those people are missing the point.

Here is the point:

By conservative estimate—from a number of scholars and research institutions—the physical health, mental health, competence and future productivity of at least one in four Canadian children is being compromised by psychiatric disorders, school failure and antisocial and violent behaviour.

We know that what aggravates those phenomena are poverty, parental depression and other mental illnesses and financial and workplace stresses on the family. A national children's agenda means addressing the issues of family stress, of what happens to the family when it conflicts with the demands of the workplace.

Here is the point:

McMaster University's System Linked Research Unit studied what happened to 100 mothers on social assistance who were offered a complete range of medical and social services for themselves over two years, along with free access to high-quality child care for the youngsters who required it and well-supervised recreation programs for all children from birth to age 18.

Twenty-five percent of those mothers left social assistance. In comparison, only 10 percent of mothers offered no extra services—and, specifically, no licensed quality child care—and only 10 percent of mothers on the province's workfare program left social assistance in the same time period.

The savings to government calculated by the McMaster researchers was $500 000 over and above the cost of providing the comprehensive services. The McMaster researchers estimated that if the full-service model were to be adopted throughout Ontario, the savings would be $12 million over two years.

The point is this:

A national children's agenda means addressing the requirements of the whole child.

It means a new national standard of longer work-leaves for parents of newborns.

It means firmly cemented national standards on health determinants for children and youth.

It means more federally funded research and demonstration projects on child abuse, on innovative school-based programs for troubled children, on physical and mental-health programs for poor children and immigrant and refugee children. It means addressing homelessness.

The point is this:

A national children's agenda means that the dividend of budget balancing is high-quality, affordable, accessible child care available to Canadian parents who need it. There can't be any more political blather on whether this is necessary.

SOURCE: Michael Valpy, "It's time to act on child care," *The Globe and Mail,* October 12, 1999. Reprinted with permission of *The Globe and Mail.*

Although Swedish babies are cared for at home by their parents, from age six months to seven years (when they enter school) all Swedish children are eligible for daycare services. Since 1988, more than 70 percent of children under six years of age have been enrolled in daycare, usually in a daycare centre, but also in family daycare (where a woman takes up to four children in her home and is regularly supervised) (Baker, 1995). Before-school and after-school care is also available for children up to the age of 12. Because of such support, about 90 percent of Swedish women are employed.

English Canada stands in sharp contrast to the situation in Sweden. In a political climate that prioritizes fiscal restraint, both Conservative and Liberal governments have avoided commitment to universal child-care, focusing instead on assistance targeted at low-income families and social-assistance recipients. The Canada Child Tax Benefit applies only to families with incomes up to just slightly above the low-income cutoff. Although the federal government under Paul Martin was pressed by the NDP to commit substantial funding for new daycare spaces across Canada, the Conservative Party came into office promising instead to provide a small subsidy to women who stay home with their children. So, Canadians will likely continue to scramble to find care for their children, often without the resources to pay for good child-care when both parents are in the labour force. About half of Canadian children under the age of 12 and with parents in paid work or full-time studies are in some form of nonparental care, and most are in unregulated care, provided by unlicensed caregivers outside the home, or nannies (Beach Bertrand, and Cleveland, 1998). Spaces for babies and toddlers in daycare centres are limited and usually expensive. The legacy of the Liberal government is parents' right to 52 weeks of parental leave following childbirth (with considerable limits on earnings and eligibility). This policy reinforces parents' responsibility to care for their children full-time and reduces demand for child-care services.

Since the late 1990s, Quebec has moved in the opposite direction—toward creating a broad set of family policies that feature universal, affordable child-care (Jenson, 2002). After eliminating a longstanding tax deduction for child-care of all kinds, the Parti Québécois used the savings to support and create child-care facilities featuring programs with an educational emphasis, run by professionals (Jenson, 2002). Parents pay $5 a day for child-care, which is expected to be available to every child who needs it in the near future. Additionally, the Quebec government pays family allowances that are targeted to low-income parents, with additional money going to lone-parent families. So, at present, two very different policy approaches coexist in Canada.

CONCLUSION

Nuclear families centred on the emotional fulfillment of adults and the nurturing of children are relatively new in human history. Fundamental to their existence is women's assumption of domestic responsibilities and men's assumption of financial responsibilities. The fact that most men no longer earn enough to support their families and that most women are essential breadwinners has created strains in nuclear families. The stress is greatest for women, who must daily juggle the conflicting demands of family and paid work. In turn, divorce rates are high, and the number of lone-parent families is increasing.

Because the Canadian government provides little support to people raising children, families without two adult income earners are especially likely to struggle financially. Thus, family diversity exacerbates income inequality. Government cutbacks of social services have meant a greater burden on most Canadian families, however they are organized.

Because women deal with the strain between family and employment every day, pressure on governments to provide family support, such as good-quality, affordable daycare, is likely to grow. There is also likely to be increasing pressure on employers to build flexibility into the workweek and career structures. Thus, just as recent economic change has promoted change in family patterns, we may expect people's family concerns to cause a variety of other social changes.

SUMMARY

1. Commonsense arguments hold that current dilemmas in family life, such as how women can balance the responsibilities of family and paid work and how men can succeed at breadwinning and also do their share of the housework, are private, individual problems. Similarly, family-values advocates argue that change by individuals is the solution to family problems. In the absence of a sociological analysis, the public sources of these problems—and of their potential solutions—remain unclear and unrecognized.

2. Biology does not produce the family, which varies in its organization considerably across different cultures and through history. Although the nuclear family unit is common, it is not always responsible for child-care; often, the family is embedded in a larger household or community that collectively assumes responsibility for all the children of the group.

3. Family organization can be seen as loosely related to the organization of production, especially if family is defined as the set of relationships that people create to meet the daily needs of adults and children.

4. In foraging societies, the nuclear family is embedded in a larger group that cooperates with respect to subsistence, consumption, and child-care. Paradoxically, the communal nature of these societies grants considerable autonomy to the individuals living in them.

5. In the agricultural societies of preindustrial Europe, households were primarily units of production in which the need to survive took precedence over all else. Household composition, even the texture of emotional life, reflected economic pressures.

6. Contemporary family patterns are the product of a particular history. Our history is marked by the development of an economy outside the household, in which the relations of paid employment are separated from the relations that provide for daily personal needs and the needs of children. A gendered division of labour corresponds to this separation.

7. As women have increasingly come to share the burden of family financial support, men have not proportionally increased the work they do in the home. That jobs are usually geared to people who lack family responsibilities is partly what prevents men from taking on more housework—their time is too limited. However, ideas about gender also make men reluctant to do "women's work."

8. The gendered division of labour that makes it possible for nuclear families to care for young children involves significant liabilities for women and even for children. The social isolation that full-time mothers experience, combined with the stress attached to their high-demand, low-control situation, reduces the quality of child-care they are able to provide. Now that so many mothers are working outside the home, however, the problems associated with privatized responsibility for child-care may prove too burdensome, and government support is likely to provide the only viable solution.

9. Because of fairly high rates of divorce and an increasing incidence of births to unmarried women, many Canadian children will spend some part of their lives in lone-parent families. The most problematic thing about this type of family is its typically low income and the attendant stress on the parent.

10. The policies of the Canadian state pertaining to families are premised on the assumption that the welfare of family members—even children—is not the responsibility of the government or of the community. Accordingly, family law in Canada now views marriage as the union of two individuals who are responsible for their own support, even in the case of a divorcing woman who was a full-time homemaker.

QUESTIONS TO CONSIDER

1. Common sense holds that, if everyone embraced "family values," problems in family life today would disappear. Explain why this perspective is naïve, and describe some of the barriers in the way of solving problems, such as child-care, the difficult balance between the responsibilities of family and paid employment, and the unequal allocation of housework.

2. Explain how family patterns are related to the ways that people acquire their subsistence in foraging societies. Do the same for our society.

3. Explain how the development of capitalism influenced family ideals in the nineteenth century. Then sketch how the marketplace today influences family life—even aspects of it as basic as conceiving and having children.

4. Describe some of the "crises" typical of family life today, and speculate on possible solutions.

GLOSSARY

Biological determinism is the argument that individual behaviour or social organization is directly caused by biology or biological processes.

Evolutionary psychology, or sociobiology, is a type of biological determinism that views human behaviour as the product of human evolution.

Extended-family households are residential units of people who are blood relatives but consist of more than the members of a nuclear family (e.g., an extended family may consist of children, their parents, and a set of grandparents living together).

The **family** is the set of relationships people create to share resources daily in order to ensure their own and any dependants' welfare.

A **family wage** is an ideal of the trade-union movement in the nineteenth century; it refers to a wage that is paid to a man and is sufficient to support him, his wife, and his children.

Foraging societies, also known as hunting-and-gathering societies, are societies in which people acquire their subsistence from the resources around them, without cultivating the earth.

Gendered division of labour refers to the separation of the tasks men and women regularly do.

The **nuclear family** comprises a man who is the main breadwinner, a woman who is the main caregiver, and one or more children.

Privatization is the assumption of responsibility by the individual, the household, or the family; it is the opposite of collectivization.

Pronatalism refers to inducements by government to encourage women to have children.

Social reproduction, as opposed to biological reproduction, refers to all that is necessary to meet the needs of adults and children, from feeding them and clothing them to meeting their emotional needs and socializing them. It is "the activities and attitudes, behaviors and emotions, responsibilities and relations directly involved in the maintenance of life on a daily basis, and intergenerationally" (Laslett and Brenner, 1989: 382).

SUGGESTED READING

Carrington, Christopher. (1999). *No Place Like Home: Relationships and Family Life Lesbians and Gay Men.* Chicago: The University of Chicago Press. With great attention to detail, Carrington documents the extensive work gay and lesbian couples undertake when they "make family." Many of his findings apply to heterosexual couples as well.

Coontz, Stephanie. (1992). *The Way We Never Were: American Families and the Nostalgia Trap.* New York: Basic Books. Fascinating, provocative, and well researched, this book reviews and criticizes "family-values" arguments by analyzing family life, past and present.

Hansen, Karen H. (2005). *Not-So-Nuclear Families: Class, Gender, and Networks of Care.* New Jersey: Rutgers University Press. An interesting study of the networks that provide care for children whose parents are juggling paid work and household responsibilities, this book explores the impact of social class and challenges our assumptions about the independence of nuclear families.

Hochschild, Arlie. (1989). *The Second Shift: Working Parents and the Revolution at Home.* New York: Viking. This unsettling study addresses the question of why men are so slow to take on household responsibilities as their wives take over some of the responsibilities of breadwinning.

Luxton, Meg. (1980). *More Than a Labour of Love: Three Generations of Women's Work in the Home.* Toronto: Women's Press. Now a Canadian classic, this study of three generations of homemakers in Flin Flon, Manitoba, shows the changes that have occurred in women's household work over time and also how the capitalist economy shapes women's work and gender relations.

McMahon, Martha. (1995). *Engendering Motherhood: Identity and Self-Transformation in Women's Lives.* Toronto: Guilford Press. This award-winning book by a Canadian sociologist is an insightful look at the transformation many women experience when they become mothers.

NOTE

1. Based on personal communication with Ivy Bourgeault, one of Canada's leading experts on midwifery.

The second industrial revolution started in the early twentieth century. Henry Ford's assembly line and other mass-production technologies transformed the workplace.

SOURCE: Ellen Griesedieck, Rouge Assembly Line. Courtesy Gallery Henoch.

WORK IN THE SERVICE ECONOMY

Many researchers argue that, in the years since World War II, Canadians have been witnessing—and living through—a third industrial revolution (Toffler, 1980). Our economy has shifted from its early industrial base of primary production (mining and logging) and secondary production (manufacturing) to tertiary production (service industries). As Table 11.1 shows, from 1980 to 2004, the portion of Canadians employed in service industries grew from 67 percent to 75 percent. Increased global competitiveness contributed to the lowering of labour costs as companies tried to maintain their market position. Global markets also facilitated the movement of some goods production to low-wage areas. These factors have helped push many manufacturing jobs out of Canada. Free-trade agreements with the United States and Mexico and the drive to reduce labour costs have also played a role in the decline of the goods sector (Canadian Labour Congress, 1993). Fewer jobs in the goods sector means that most new jobs are in the service sector.

Much debate has ensued about the rise of the service, or "postindustrial," economy. Writing in the early 1970s, Daniel Bell (1973) presented an optimistic picture of the rise of the postindustrial economy. In his view, work would be transformed from repetitive, low-skilled production work to highly skilled, knowledge-based work. Today, however, more pessimistic analyses of the postindustrial economy are prevalent. We are witnessing an increase in low-skilled, low-paying service jobs and a rise in

TABLE 11.1   CANADIAN LABOUR-FORCE CHARACTERISTICS, 1980 AND 2004

LABOUR-FORCE CHARACTERISTICS	1980	2004
Total number employed (thousands)	10 708	15 950
Percentage in goods sector	33	25
Percentage in service sector	67	75
Unionization rate (out of all paid workers) (percentage)	32	31

SOURCES: Compiled from Statistics Canada, "Social Indicators," Canadian Social Trends, Cat. No. 11-008, Winter 1988, p. 31; Statistics Canada, "Table 282-0088, Labour force survey estimates, employment by North American Industry Classification System, May 2004;" Statistics Canada, "Social Indicators," Canadian Social Trends, Cat. No. 11-008, Summer 2005, p. 31; Statistics Canada, "Diverging Trends in Unionization," The Daily, Friday, April 22, 2005. Used by authority of the Minister of Industry, 2000.

the level of unemployment. It may be too early to tell whether the optimistic or pessimistic scenario will eventually prevail. As sociologist John Myles notes (1991: 128), "the issue for the future is not whether we will have a service economy but what kind of service economy" we will have.

GOOD JOBS OR BAD JOBS?

One way to discover what kind of service economy we will have in Canada is to look at the mix of good and bad jobs available for workers. At minimum, good jobs are those that provide **extrinsic rewards,** such as good wages, benefits, employment security, and opportunities for advancement. Good jobs should also provide **intrinsic rewards,** such as decision-making opportunities; challenging, nonrepetitive work; and autonomy that allows for self-direction and responsibility over tasks.

A misconception about the service economy is that the service sector creates only bad jobs and that the goods sector is the source of good jobs. This scenario assumes that all service jobs are alike and ignores important divisions within the service sector. Instead, we should think of the service sector as having a lower tier made up of traditional services, such as retail trade, food, and personal services, and an upper tier consisting of other services, such as finance and business, utilities, health, education, and public administration. Whether you find yourself in a lower- or upper-tier service job has implications for your wages, job security, and the skill content of your work (Economic Council of Canada, 1991; Krahn, 1992).

Debates also revolve around changes in the skill level of jobs in the service economy. Conventional wisdom suggests that skill requirements are increasing as a result of technology (Spenner, 1983). As Daniel Bell and other postindustrialists propose, we should experience an upgrading of jobs in the economy as skill requirements increase within specific occupations. This group also predicts that job growth will occur in the higher-skilled occupations. In contrast, Harry Braverman (1974) and other postindustrial critics believe that skill levels are being downgraded. In this view, although some highly skilled professional and technical jobs will be created, most jobs will be lower-skilled industrial and service jobs.

So which is it? Are we moving to the postindustrial world of Bell or the downgraded world of Braverman? When we examine the shifts in the Canadian occupational structure, a more complex picture than the ones sketched by Bell and Braverman emerges: Blue-collar jobs in the middle are declining and job growth is occurring at the top and the bottom of the occupational structure (Economic Council of Canada, 1991; Myles, 1988). Thus, we see an increasing polarization of jobs in the service sector—higher-skilled knowledge jobs on the one hand and lower-skilled "hamburger" jobs on the other (Myles, 1988).

What do recent statistics tell us about these trends? Figure 11.1 shows that between 1987 and 2003, service industries experienced the greatest growth in employment. Goods-producing occupations in manufacturing experienced only small amounts of employment growth. Resource-based industries of forestry, fishing, oil and gas production, and agriculture experienced declines in the percentage of people employed. Some of the upper-tier service industries grew (e.g., health and educational services) as did lower-tier services such as accommodation, food, and beverage services. Thus, we see a mixed picture with growth in some higher-skilled and lower-skilled jobs.

However, these statistics are partly misleading. Statistics Canada points out that driving the growth in business services is an increase in part-time work and self-employment. So although business service has the potential to create good jobs, some of those jobs may not be full-time. We'll explore the issue of part-time work in the following section.

Finally, let's take a quick look at the ten most common jobs for women and men. The 2001 census

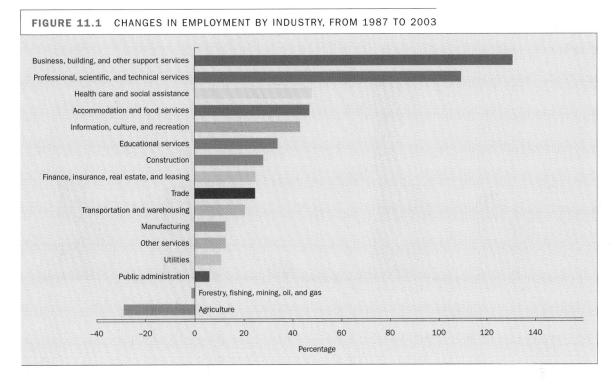

FIGURE 11.1   CHANGES IN EMPLOYMENT BY INDUSTRY, FROM 1987 TO 2003

SOURCE: Adapted from the Statistics Canada publication "The Canadian Labour Market at a Glance," 2003, Catalogue 71-222, released November 17, 2004, URL: http://www.statcan.ca/english/freepub/71-222-XIE/2004000/chart-e.28.htm.

shows that retail service jobs dominate for both sexes (see Chapter 7, Figures 7.2 and 7.3). Missing from the list for women are any non-service-industry jobs. For the men, we see a mix of lower-tier service jobs (retail salesperson, janitor) and blue-collar jobs (truck driver, material handler, carpenter, and construction trade helper). Missing from the male list are any of the higher-skilled "knowledge" jobs.

As the service industry grows, we should be concerned about those who minimize the significance of the goods or manufacturing sector for our economic well-being. Such a view is shortsighted: It is increasingly clear that the goods and services sectors are interdependent and that manufacturing is important for the creation of good jobs (Economic Council of Canada, 1991). For example, the production of telecommunications technology drives the development of telecommunications services in Canada (Myles, 1991). We need both sectors to fuel our economic growth. This is why trade agreements that threaten Canadian manufacturing may be detrimental to our overall economy. The movement of goods-producing industries to other countries could ultimately hurt the ability of the service economy to generate good jobs.

NONSTANDARD JOBS

One crucial outcome of the shift to a service-based global economy is the rise of **nonstandard jobs.** These are jobs that provide part-time, temporary or seasonal (part-year) employment. For employers, nonstandard jobs can reduce labour costs since part-time and temporary workers receive less in pay and benefits (Krahn, 1992; Morissette and Johnson, 2005). Some sociologists call these jobs "precarious" because they do not provide stable and long-term employment or adequate pay (Cranford, Vosko, and Zukewich, 2003). In most industrial countries, including Canada, one-quarter to one-third of all jobs are now nonstandard (Economic Council of Canada, 1991).

To understand nonstandard work, it is useful to look at part-time and temporary employment separately. In 2003, almost 20 percent of Canadians worked in part-time jobs. Figure 11.2 shows that part-time employment is highest for workers between the age of 15 and 24. Since 1976 the part-time rate has grown for older workers, those over the age of 55. This may be due to older workers opting for part-time work as a stepping stone to retirement (Pold,

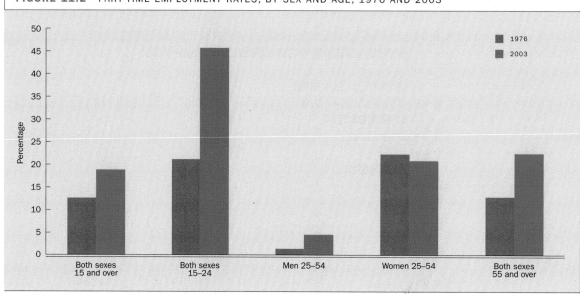

FIGURE 11.2 PART-TIME EMPLOYMENT RATES, BY SEX AND AGE, 1976 AND 2003

SOURCE: Adapted from the Statistics Canada website http://www.statcan.ca/english/freepub/71-222-XIE/2004000/chart-g42.htm.

2004). Alternatively, it could signal older workers not being able to find full-time work to replace a full-time job they lost because of downsizing or corporate restructuring. Some employees, particularly women and young workers between the ages of 15 and 24, prefer the flexibility of part-time work. They voluntarily choose part-time work because it allows time for school attendance and family responsibilities or because they do not want to work full-time. Most disturbing, though, is the growing number of involuntary part-time workers—part-time workers who would prefer full-time work (Noreau, 1994). In 2003, one in four part-time workers in Canada stated they would prefer to be working full-time (Statistics Canada, 2004a). There are also regional differences, with involuntary part-time jobs being more common in the Atlantic provinces and British Columbia (Statistics Canada, 2004a).

To respond to changes in demand for their products and services, some employers now rely on temporary workers, ranging from clerical help to computer programmers, hired through temporary-employment agencies. In 2003, almost 13 percent of Canadian workers were employed in temporary or contract positions (Statistics Canada, 2004a). Like part-time workers, temporaries tend to be young and female (Economic Council of Canada, 1991). Figure 11.3 shows that youth (between the ages of 15 and 24) are more than twice as likely as others to be temporary workers. We've also seen a sharp increase in the number of newly hired workers holding temporary jobs. In 1989, 11 percent of newly hired employees were in temporary jobs. By 2004, this increased to 21 percent (Morissette and Johnson, 2005). These temporary workers are usually hired for short-term contracts to fill in for absent full-time workers or as part of a "just-in-time" labour force called in to fill production or service demands. Although some workers are drawn to temporary work for its perceived flexibility in scheduling, the reality for most workers is that such jobs are often inflexible. As a result of work shortages, many temporary workers find themselves taking whatever work is available, even if it means putting up with inappropriate work, such as cleaning offices while on a clerical assignment (Henson, 1996). As these jobs become more common, workers may enjoy fewer opportunities for full-time jobs.

The movement to a service economy, or the third industrial revolution, has affected the type of jobs available in Canada. Some good jobs are created in financial services and health services, while bad jobs with nonstandard hours are also created, primarily in sales and service. In the following section on labour-market segmentation, I'll continue to explore Canadians' access to good and bad jobs.

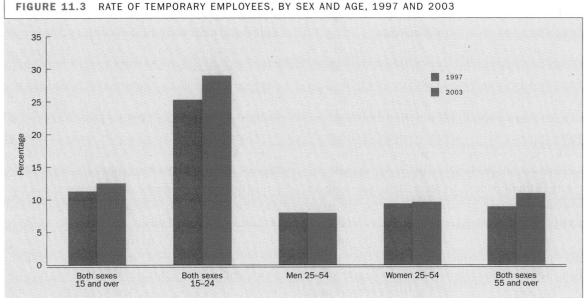

FIGURE 11.3 RATE OF TEMPORARY EMPLOYEES, BY SEX AND AGE, 1997 AND 2003

SOURCE: Adapted from the Statistics Canada website http://www.statcan.ca/english/freepub/71-222-XIE/2004000/chart-i50.htm.

LABOUR-MARKET SEGMENTATION

All of us hope to have an equal chance of getting a good job. But do we really have an equal chance, especially given polarization in the service sector? As you know from your study of stratification and inequality (see Chapter 6), some groups of workers, such as individuals from upper-class families and more educated workers, are more likely than less-advantaged workers to end up in good jobs. Another factor that affects your chances is the structure of the labour market. Although some economists, especially human-capital theorists, conceive of the labour market as a single and open competition in which people are rewarded in proportion to their education and skills (Becker, 1975), **labour-market segmentation** theory offers a different perspective. Instead of assuming that we all have an equal chance of getting good jobs, labour-market segmentation theory shows that *where* you enter the labour market may limit your chances of getting a different, better job.

Labour-market segmentation theory emphasizes that jobs are divided according to their location in the "core" or "periphery" of the economy. A core industry is a group of companies in a relatively non-competitive market, such as the automobile industry. Core industries tend to be capital-intensive, large, and unionized, and they tend to exert control over

their environment (e.g., by influencing governments to limit foreign competition). For a variety of reasons, such as the need to maintain skilled workers who can operate expensive capital equipment, and in response to the presence of unions, jobs in core industries tend to be stable and to offer good wages and access to benefits (Morissette, 1991).

The periphery, in contrast, is characterized by lower-tier service jobs and jobs in highly competitive markets. Firms in this sector tend to be smaller, labour-intensive, and nonunionized, and the employment they offer lacks security and pays low wages. Work is also characterized by high turnover rates, owing to product-demand fluctuations and seasonal work cycles, such as in the fisheries on the east and west coasts of Canada.

Your chance of finding a good job is determined not only by the sector of the economy you enter but also by the existence of **primary labour markets,** both external and internal to firms. Internal labour markets provide opportunities for advancement by providing the chance to climb up the job ladder as you gain skills and knowledge (Althauser, 1989). Secondary labour-market jobs do not offer much of a job ladder. These jobs are sometimes referred to as "dead-end jobs" because of their lack of upward mobility. Workers at McDonald's may be able to move from being on the crew to assistant manager, but unless they buy their own franchise (which is rare), that is the extent of their mobility.

Employers often create primary labour markets for some employees but not for others. In a single firm, managers can have access to mobility through an internal labour market while their clerical, production, and maintenance staff may have little room to move up. In today's service economy, employers' increasing use of temporary and part-time workers is another way in which secondary labour markets are created within companies. Increasingly, these types of secondary markets are found outside the lower-tier service industries. At the university where I work, and in all other Canadian universities, departments have full-time professors to do research and teach. In addition, "sessional" instructors are hired to teach one or two classes each. Substantial differences exist between these two groups in terms of pay, job security, and mobility opportunities. As a full-time professor, I have a multiyear contract and may be promoted if I fulfill my job duties. My colleague, who is a part-time

instructor, has no access to promotions or job security. Instead, she receives year-to-year contracts only if the department needs her to teach a specific course. Although having secondary labour-market positions gives organizations the "flexibility" to unload employees when they are not needed, it increases the insecurity of these employees and decreases their chances of getting ahead, both in their jobs and in life.

Geography also plays a role in the chances of ending up in the primary or secondary labour market. Regions like the Atlantic provinces that have a high proportion of seasonal jobs, such as fishing and logging, have higher unemployment rates than the rest of Canada (Statistics Canada, 2004a; see Figure 11.4). Even if you are a highly skilled and motivated worker, you will have trouble finding a good job in Newfoundland and Labrador, where the cod fisheries have fallen on hard times (Krahn and Lowe, 1998: 135). Those of us who live in the major urban and industrial areas of Canada are more likely to end up in a better job simply because there are more such jobs in our regional labour markets.

FIGURE 11.4   UNEMPLOYMENT RATE BY PROVINCE, JULY 2006

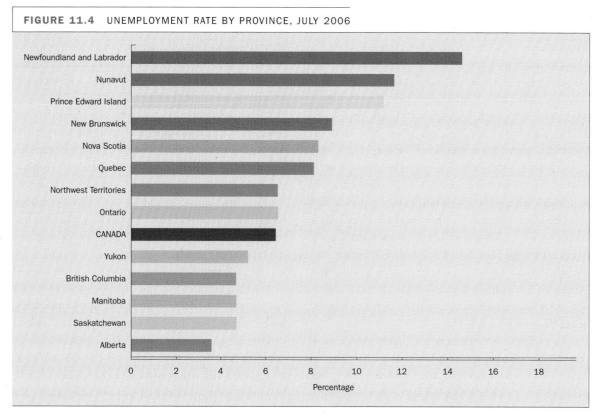

SOURCE: Adapted from the Statistics Canada website http://www.statcan.ca/english/freepub/71-222-XIE/2004000/chart-c12.htm.

Geography affects a person's chance of finding work. For example, it is more difficult to find a good job in Atlantic Canada than in Alberta.

SOURCE: David Blackwood, *For Edgar Glover: The Splitting Table Etching,* 1999. Courtesy The Edward Day Gallery.

Ethnic job ghettos are a pervasive component of past and current labour markets throughout the world. In Canada, between 1860 and 1960, black railway workers were restricted to sleeping-car porter jobs and were not allowed to compete for the higher-paid jobs of sleeping-car conductor and dining-car steward (Calliste, 1993). Today, employer prejudice can keep qualified minorities from being hired. Since many visible minorities are also recent immigrants, their ability to move into better jobs is constrained by this dual status, unless they are entrepreneurs. Often, employers will request "Canadian work experience" before hiring white-collar

We may conclude that whether you end up in a good job or a bad job is the result of more than your individual characteristics or the occupation you choose. Your chances of landing a rewarding job depend on what sector of the economy your job is in and whether your job has an internal labour market associated with it. In the next section, I develop this idea by showing how some groups of workers find themselves stuck in job ghettos.

JOB GHETTOS AND DISADVANTAGED GROUPS

Job ghettos are parts of the labour market that prevent certain groups of workers from experiencing upward mobility. Structural barriers based on stereotypes work to keep some individuals from entering the primary labour market and the best jobs. The labelling of occupations as "female" or "male" jobs is one such example. In the health-care industry, women are still more likely to become nurses than doctors, and, as doctors, women are more likely to be found in pediatric and family medicine than the higher-paying specialties of neurology and cardiology. Chapter 7 discusses how female job ghettos are formed through occupational sex segregation, sex typing, and other forms of discrimination.

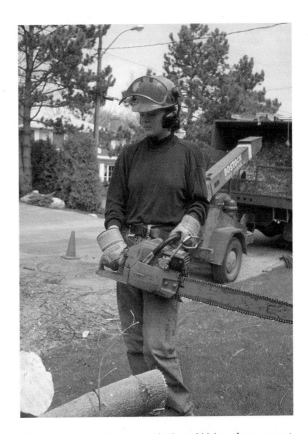

Although most Canadian women in the paid labour force are segregated in jobs traditionally dominated by women, they are making advances in traditionally male-dominated jobs.

SOURCE: Dick Hemingway.

workers. And some professional occupations, like doctor and veterinarian, require additional training for professionals emigrating from certain countries. Highly educated members of visible minorities in these situations may find themselves forced to take low-level service jobs, such as taxi driver or restaurant worker. For more on this topic, see Chapter 8.

People with disabilities face barriers to good jobs because of the inaccessibility of education and workplaces. In 2000, only 45 percent of men and 39 percent of women with disabilities were employed, compared with 79 percent of men and 69 percent of women without disabilities (Statistics Canada, 2004b). Lack of financial resources to attend school, inflexible workplace schedules, and lack of employers' commitment to hiring workers with disabilities are some of the reasons people with disabilities have trouble getting good jobs. Jamie Hunter, a 29-year-old with minimal control over his limbs as a result of a diving accident, experiences these barriers firsthand. Speaking about looking for work, he states (quoted in McKay, 1993: 170):

> I recall one fellow, from the personnel department of a major corporation, who was so uncomfortable he couldn't even bring himself to take me to his office. So we sat in the lobby and he read me back my resume. "You're Jamie Hunter? You graduated from York University? You worked for a summer at Ontario Hydro?" Then he said thanks and left. That was it. The interview was over and I never heard from him again.

Hiring workers who have disabilities is not as costly as some employers believe. Recent studies show that only 20 percent of people with disabilities require changes to the physical accommodations of workplaces (Shain, 1995). Until more employers make the effort to hire people with disabilities, these workers will continue to face barriers to good jobs.

Aboriginal people face formidable barriers in their search for employment. Living in remote areas limits both their job opportunities and their access to education and work training. Even when Aboriginals move to areas where jobs are more readily available, they often lack crucial work experience. Aboriginal workers are especially vulnerable to the "bad-work syndrome" (Krahn and Lowe, 1998). Having access only to low-skill and part-time work gives individuals a spotty work history. They are then caught in a cycle where one low-skill job leads to another. For many, the "bad-work syndrome" makes it impossible to get better jobs.

Finally, the *youngest and oldest workers* may find themselves trapped in job ghettos that are based on age. Some employers view younger workers as less serious and less interested in full-time jobs. In many ways, trying to improve the jobs in the teenage-student job ghetto was the motivation behind Debora De Angelis's union drive at Suzy Shier in Toronto. Older workers, who are defined as those over 45, also face employment limitations. As a result of downsizing and early retirement incentives, older workers may find themselves out of a job before they are ready to stop working. Access to better jobs is also limited by the prejudices of employers, who tend to view older workers as less productive and more resistant to new work methods. As the population of older Canadians grows, it is increasingly difficult to ignore the effects of age discrimination.

Labour-market segmentation creates areas of better and worse jobs in the labour market. Although we would like to think that we all have an equal chance of getting the better jobs, the research on job ghettos shows that some groups of workers may be trapped in the worse jobs. And, as I show in the next sections, some workers are able to protect their good jobs through the labour-market shelters of professional occupations and unions.

PROFESSIONS

The occupations of doctor, lawyer, and other professions are some of the most desirable jobs in the labour market. High pay, autonomy, and respect from the outside community are some of the advantages bestowed on members of professional occupations. Many of us consider these occupations to be different from other occupations. This special status has caught the attention of sociologists.

Early studies of professions attempted to delineate their general characteristics or hallmarks. First, all professional occupations control a special body of abstract knowledge, held only by members of that profession. Second, professional occupations are autonomous. Third, professionals generally have authority over their clients and subordinates because of the special knowledge they possess. Finally, professional occupations are supposed to be altruistic because of their focus on helping clients.

But are these four characteristics all there are to professions? Many sociologists believe that the hall-mark model is really an "idealized model that imperfectly describes reality" (Hodson and Sullivan, 1990: 266) and that it provides only a checklist for determining which occupations are more or less a profession. Overlooked by this approach is how these occupations became "professions" in the first place. To address this issue, we need to consider power and the contested nature of professions. Doing this will uncover how professions act as **labour-market shelters,** protecting their members' access to good jobs.

Were doctors, dentists, and lawyers always considered professional occupations? The answer to this is no because professions are not static categories. Which occupations are viewed as legitimate professions changes over time and is part of a historical process. For example, in Ontario in the nineteenth century, there were few dentists as we know them today. Instead many different occupations provided dental services. Most people were served by itinerant "tramp dentists" who travelled from town to town. If citizens needed teeth pulled or false teeth constructed, they could go to their local blacksmith and gunsmith. In terms of the dental services provided, when a patient came to visit, the blacksmith would "leave the forge, wipe his hands on his apron, get the old turnkey wrench, and his brawny arm would soon draw not only the sufferer's tooth, but often the screaming patient himself from the old kitchen chair" (Wood, 1989: 266, quoted in Adams, 2000: 22). This example is far removed from our twenty-first century understanding of dentists.

To get to where they are today, dentists, like people in other occupations, engaged in a professionalization process. This process includes the establishment of "professional dominance" and securing legitimacy from the public (Friedson, 1970; Pescosolido, Tuch, and Martin, 2001: 3). Professional dominance occurs when the government acknowledges an occupation's knowledge claims and expertise, and then grants an occupation the right to be the only (or one of a few) practitioners of this knowledge. Professions, though, also need the public's approval to be fully professionalized. This is where securing legitimacy comes into the picture. If the public will not follow the directions of members of the profession or views the members as not being legitimate experts (or the sole legitimate experts), then professions will have difficulty establishing their authority. You can see

these issues more clearly when you think about the relationships or "battles" between professional occupations over who can claim expertise in a certain body of professional knowledge (e.g., Friedson, 1970). For example, until recently, only doctors had the authority to deliver babies in Ontario. Doctors maintained their authority because of their monopoly over the relevant knowledge and used their national associations to lobby provincial and federal governments to deny others the right to practise. This is how professional dominance helped doctors maintain their position. Yet, doctors' legitimacy as the only deliverers of babies was called into question by the public and other health-care practitioners. As a result of current public demands for access to midwives and the development of professional midwifery schools, doctors have lost some control over the birthing process and have lost their monopoly over this body of professional knowledge.

Some occupations are continually striving for professional status. Semi-professions are occupations that have some professional characteristics but to a lesser degree than full-fledged professions (Hodson and Sullivan, 1990). Examples of semi-professions are nurses, engineers, accountants, pharmacists, and teachers. Although we may call these occupations "professions" in our everyday use of the term, the sociological definition of professions requires us to view these occupations as "not quite" or "semi" professions. Often semi-professions do not have full control over their body of knowledge, or their autonomy may be constrained by a more powerful profession, as is the case with nurses. Furthermore, female-dominated semi-professions, such as teachers and librarians, face additional barriers to professionalization because of occupational sex segregation.

Third parties, such as the government, can threaten professional power by intervening in the decisions of professional organizations. We become most aware of this when the government pays for part or all of the services received by clients, as is the case for the Canadian health-care system. During the summer and fall of 1996, doctors in Ontario fought the provincial government over who has the right to decide where doctors work. Doctors wanted to maintain their professional autonomy to work and live where they choose, while the Ministry of Health believed it had the right to force doctors to work in underserviced areas. Some doctors did not accept new patients to protest what they saw as government interference with their autonomy. As it stands now, these protests appear to have helped the cause of the doctors. They made some gains in terms of their salaries and partially satisfied the government's demand for more doctors to work in northern areas of the province. How this "battle" continues to play out will determine who is the legitimate authority over doctors—their own profession or the provincial government of Ontario.

UNIONS

Unions, like professions and their associations, also attempt to attain or maintain good jobs for their members. Workers have organized unions to gain respect, increase wages, reduce working hours, and gain more control over their working day. In fact, the presence of unions has helped all of us. Without union efforts, we would not have such things as the eight-hour workday, child-labour laws, and occupational health and safety standards. I return to the state of unions in Canada and the role they play in the Canadian labour market when I discuss alienation later in this chapter.

In sum, unions and professional associations, like the Canadian Medical Association, are alike in a number of respects. They both act as labour-market shelters from loss of jobs, pay cuts, and other employment-related risks. Legislation that mandates the hiring of union workers, such as may be found on some construction sites, protects the jobs of union members. Likewise, when the professional association of lawyers restricts access to law school and the number of new lawyers, they too are protecting the jobs and incomes of existing members. Groups of workers who organize—whether it is a local union for flight attendants or a national association of doctors—may increase their ability to maintain their position in good jobs.

TECHNOLOGY AND THE SERVICE INDUSTRY

The use of technology has long been a part of the relationship between employees and employers. One of the most famous technologies, the assembly line, was used to control the pace of work (Edwards, 1979). In today's service economy, managers are more likely to invest in computers and information technology than in other forms of work reorganization to improve their firms' productivity and efficiency

(Osterman, 1995). Computerizing office systems can reduce the time-consuming work of filing. In some instances, robots can be used to do heavy and dangerous work. Technological changes, such as advanced telecommunications systems, make the globalization of work possible. Today, it is not surprising to find companies, such as Nike, with factories in Asia and product-development labs in the United States. Technology brings added flexibility to companies. No longer does geography limit the search for inexpensive labour or market expansion.

Even though technology is changing the face of work, it does not mean that we have no control over what happens. Although some technological determinists might have us believe that the implementation of technology in our workplaces is an inevitable process, most sociologists (e.g., Wallace, 1989) view the effects of technology as contingent on various social and technological factors. We now understand that whether technology will have positive or negative effects on work depends on such factors as the outcomes desired by management, the type of technology that companies can afford, and whether workers have a say in technological change.

According to Shoshana Zuboff (1988), management can design computer-based jobs to either increase or decrease the need for workers to use knowledge and judgment on the job. She provides examples of jobs being enhanced, on the one hand, when workers were given the opportunity to use computers in complex ways. On the other hand, she also found that if management is interested only in productivity and efficiency, technology can have detrimental effects on the quality of work. For example, one office used computers to automate and speed up the work of clerks. Any decisions that clerks formerly made about their work were now programmed into the computer. Box 11.1 describes some of the experiences of these workers. The stick-figure drawings represent the drastic change in workers' views of their jobs. What makes these pictures compelling is knowing that a consultant recommended further automation of the clerks' jobs. But management held back. As one manager acknowledged, the company realized it couldn't remove all variety from tasks because "there's a limit to how boring you can make a job if you want even reasonably capable people" (Zuboff, 1988: 134). This example shows us, then, that management can choose to implement technology in a way that either enhances work or downgrades it.

BOX 11.1   HOW TECHNOLOGY CAN CHANGE THE WORKPLACE

What can computer technology do to the quality of work life? In her study of technological change, Shoshana Zuboff (1988) asked office workers to draw pictures that "represented their 'felt sense' about their job experience before and after the conversion to the new computer system" that automated and standardized work. Below are two workers' views of how their work experience changed. Note the shifts in facial expressions and the loss of mobility. Even the flower on the benefit analyst's desk has wilted. As one office manager said about work after the conversion, "The system controls the transfer assistants in some ways because it ties them to the desk. It forces them to do the input and to really be tied to the machine. It forces control in terms of physically having to just be there."

TRANSFER ASSISTANT

Before

After

"Before, I was able to get up and hand things to people without having someone say, what are you doing? Now, I feel like I am with my head down, doing my work."

BENEFIT ANALYST

Before

After

"My supervisor is frowning because we shouldn't be talking. I have on the stripes of a convict. It's all true. It feels like a prison in here."

SOURCE: Adapted from *In the Age of the Smart Machine: The Future of Work and Power* by Shoshana Zuboff. Copyright © 1988 by Basic Books, Inc. Reprinted by permission of Basic Books, a member of Perseus Books, L.L.C.

From video cameras to computer programs, workers are finding themselves increasingly monitored by technology. In one high-tech firm, management used scanners to detect motion in rooms that were not supposed to be used (Wallace, 1989). Air Canada uses electronic surveillance to make the job of telephone airline reservation agents more visible and easily controlled (Robertson and Wareham, 1990). Detailed information can be collected about how many phone calls an agent handles, the duration of each phone call, and how long each agent is "out of the system" or unavailable for calls. This information is then used to determine who is working up to speed. Reservation agents complain that these computer measures do not adequately capture all components of their job, such as providing friendly and useful service to customers. As the use of computers and high-technology systems becomes more common, more of us may find ourselves monitored electronically. How far monitoring will go in the name of increasing employee productivity will hinge on the ability of workers and unions to participate in decisions about the implementation of technology.

Computers also affect unemployment and job creation. At Dofasco in Hamilton, computer technology is partly responsible for reducing the work force from 12 500 to 7000 over the past ten years (Campbell, 1996). Automated banking machines have reduced the number of teller positions in banks (McLaughlin, 1983) while creating a small number of jobs for those who repair and maintain these machines. These examples show technology's initial effect on employment. Although some skilled jobs directly connected to the technology are created, a greater number of lower-skilled jobs are lost. And, more often now, workers facing technological unemployment can find only lower-tier service jobs to replace their previous jobs (Wallace, 1989).

COMPUTERS AND PRODUCTIVITY

Since the 1970s, companies' investment in computers has grown. This increased investment is motivated by the expectation that computers will increase workers' productivity. Yet, if we look at official figures, since 1973 there has been a slowdown in productivity (Triplett, 1999). Therefore, it appears that computers have not made the economy more productive or efficient (David, 1990; "Productivity," 1997). Some social scientists believe we are experiencing a "productivity paradox." It's called a paradox because the introduction

of computers and new technology has not led to the expected boost in productivity. As Robert Solow, a Nobel-prize-winning economist stated, "You can see computers everywhere but in the productivity statistics" (1987). And as an old Dilbert cartoon once mentioned, the "total time that humans have waited for Web pages to load . . . cancels out all the productivity gains of the information age" (quoted in Triplett, 1999).

Much speculation exists as to why the productivity paradox is occurring. The first and most pessimistic view is that the supposed computer revolution is not in the same league as earlier technological advances. In other words, the computer revolution has only a marginal effect on the average person's life. For example, Paul Krugman, an economist at MIT, states that "computerised ticketing is a great thing, but a cross-country flight still takes five hours; bar codes and laser scanners are nifty, but a shopper still has to queue at the checkout" ("Paradox Lost," 1996: 13).

A second explanation of the productivity paradox looks to history for the answer. Looking at past relationships between technological implementation and productivity, we see that it often takes several decades before technological breakthroughs increase productivity. The classic example of this is the electric dynamo, which made the commercial use of electricity possible (David, 1990). It took 40 years for the electric dynamo to yield significant productivity gains. Factories slowly adopted electricity, and even then it took time to learn how to organize factories around electric power. Before this, machines had to be located near waterwheels or steam engines. But electric power allowed for the placement of machines along production lines, which maximized the efficiency of the work process. Considering that computers didn't start making their way into offices until the 1970s, we may still be a decade or more away from realizing productivity gains. It is not the *invention* of new technology that increases productivity, but the *identification* of the most efficient uses of technology.

Third, some economists believe the productivity paradox is the result of "measurement error" or problems in how we assess productivity. When we look at national or industry-wide statistics on productivity, we don't see any increase in productivity. But when we look at productivity for individual firms, there is some increase in productivity in the 1973–97 period (Lehr and Lichtenberg, 1999). Complicating matters is the fact that computers are used most extensively in

New technologies require job retraining, even for middle-aged and older workers.

SOURCE: David Pollack/First Light.

the service industry—and it's harder to measure productivity in the service industry than in the goods-producing industry.

The fourth explanation for the productivity paradox brings in the social or human element (Martinsons and Chong, 1999). The choices that managers make about how to implement technology are part of the equation. Also, some scholars say there is a relatively short "window of opportunity" in which organizations can adopt technology in its most productive and useful form (Tyre and Orlikowski, 1994). When a company brings in computers or a new computer program, employees may circumvent some of the new features that may increase productivity but are difficult to learn. For example, when I first used WordPerfect for Windows, I changed all the commands back to DOS commands because that was what I knew. In the short term it saved time, but in the long term I could not take advantage of any of the new features that could help speed up my work. So do we have a productivity paradox? The answer at this stage is yes and no. It depends on how you measure productivity and whether you look at national or firm-level productivity statistics. As social scientists develop a better understanding of what productivity means in

the service industry, we may find that the paradox disappears.

BUREAUCRACIES AND WORK ORGANIZATION

We live and work in a bureaucratic society. According to Max Weber, bureaucracies are the most efficient and rational organizational form for reaching the goals of capitalism. In bureaucracies, written rules provide guidelines for handling routine situations. A complex division of labour ensures that workers know what is required of them and helps to identify who is responsible when something goes wrong. Weber also saw bureaucracies as a way to overcome arbitrary decisions and corruption in nonbureaucratic organizations. For example, by having written rules about how decisions must be made and having a hierarchy of authority that clarifies who makes decisions, it is less likely that organizational decision makers can decide to hire someone out of loyalty or obligation. Yet Weber was the first to admit that bureaucracies are not without their problems. Referring to bureaucracies as "the iron cage of the future," Weber was concerned about the potential for bureaucracies to limit creativity and initiative (Hodson and Sullivan, 1990: 184). Bureaucracies also can be rigid, full of "red tape," and lead to communication problems between managers and workers (Jones, 1996).

Weber believed that increased bureaucratization was the fate of modern society. Building on Weber, sociologist George Ritzer (1993) argues that society is now undergoing a new kind of rationalization process that he calls "McDonaldization." Today, writes, Ritzer, the fast-food restaurant has surpassed bureaucracy as the organizational ideal. This means that our workplace, as well as schools, leisure activities and culture are taking on the characteristics of a fast-food restaurant.

There are four components to McDonaldization:

1. Creating the most *efficient* way to accomplish a task
2. Emphasizing things that can be *calculated* or counted, such as a large amount of food ("Biggie" fries) that can be bought with a seemingly small amount of money
3. Creating a *predictable* product and experience, so that a Big Mac in Calgary tastes the same as one in Taipei
4. Setting up systems of *control* to standardize the work of employees (Ritzer, 1993: 9–12).

What Ritzer says is different about McDonald-ization is how extreme it is in its attempt to rationalize and how it is "sweeping through society."

Consider Ritzer's discussion of the McDonaldization of universities. Ritzer would criticize the textbook that you are reading as part of the drive for increased efficiency, predictability, and standardization. Chapters are written by experts in each area. Instead of one author taking years to learn all of sociology, the book can be produced quicker because, presumably, each expert knows his or her area inside and out (Ritzer, 1993: 57). On the other side, you could also argue that chapters are actually better because they are written by experts. And, if you are like my students at the University of Toronto, your introductory sociology class is probably a large class that uses multiple-choice exams. Gone are the days of inefficient and unpredictable one-on-one examinations of students and, in many places, essay exams (Ritzer, 1993: 55). Multiple-choice exams take less time to mark compared with other ways of testing student's knowledge. I would be doing my colleagues who are teaching you a disservice if I said that the only value of multiple-choice exams is their efficiency over other testing methods; evidence also shows that a well-written multiple-choice exam does a good job of capturing student's knowledge. Still, Ritzer's thesis is correct in that as universities have increased in size, faculty have been pushed to look for ways to increase the efficiency and the predictability of what they produce. This mimics some of the trends in the fast-food industry. Standardizing textbooks and exams are just two examples. If you look at other aspects of society, you will see other examples, such as vacationers who travel to other countries and stay at places like Sandals and ClubMed, which offer a standard resort experience with little regard for the local culture.

If you look around at the organizations that touch your life, you will see evidence that Weber and Ritzer are correct. But bureaucratic structure alone is not enough to ensure that the work of organizations is done. As the following section discusses, management has also been developing strategies to organize how work is done by their employees.

MANAGERIAL STRATEGIES FOR ORGANIZING WORK

In the past 100 years, several approaches to organizing work in bureaucracies have come and gone. Some have endured the test of time (Braverman, 1974). As I'll discuss, many of these strategies emerged in earlier revolutions but are now integral parts of the service economy. Although early strategies were geared toward removing the need for workers to think on the job, more recent strategies have paid more attention to the ability and desire of workers to participate in workplace decisions. Whether these strategies offer real participation is a question to keep in mind as you read the following sections.

Taylorism

Frederick Taylor, an American industrial engineer, was the founder of scientific management or **Taylorism.** Originating in the 1890s, scientific management was an attempt by management to regain direct control of the labour process. Based on his own experience in factories, Taylor discovered that workers knew more than their managers about the work processes. As long as this was the case, workers could control how fast they worked and how much they produced. To shift control back to management, Taylor recommended a detailed division of labour that broke complex tasks into several subtasks. To do this, management needed to learn how workers did their jobs and then convert this knowledge into formal procedures. Using time and motion studies, managers documented the exact movements of workers and the length of time required to complete the task. Taylor also believed that conceptual work should be separated from the execution of tasks. It was management's job to design work procedures and the workers' job to follow those procedures. By breaking jobs into their smallest components and removing the need for workers to think, Taylorism opened the door for management to reduce its reliance on skilled labour. Cheaper, unskilled workers could now be hired to perform simplified tasks. Managers and intellectuals worldwide, including the Russian communist leader Lenin, hailed Taylor as a pioneer in the rationalization of work.

Fordism is often discussed in relation to Taylorism. **Fordism** refers to the bureaucratically organized mass production of standardized goods by assembly-line methods. Although Henry Ford was not the first to use assembly-line technology, he was one of the most successful at using it to change the way things were made. Ford used assembly-line technology to implement many of the principles of Taylorism. This allowed him to create a division of labour in which workers stood in one place on the assembly line to do their assigned job and produce large numbers of standardized products.

Taylorism is not limited to factory work. Lowe (1987) shows how Taylorist principles rationalized office work in early twentieth-century Canada. And Taylorism is still around in many service industry jobs. Making hamburgers in a fast-food restaurant is broken down into minute tasks, and telephone reservation agents for airlines are given scripts to follow when dealing with clients. But today, as in the past, workers complain about the limited opportunities for creativity and self-fulfilment when working under scientific management.

Human Relations

One shortcoming of Taylorism is its assumption that workers are motivated only by desire for their paycheques (Bendix, 1974; Jones, 1996). In reaction to this simplistic view, the **human relations school of management** pushed management to rethink the Taylorist image of workers by showing the importance of the social aspects of work. Based on a series of experiments at the Western Electric Company's Hawthorne plant in Chicago, Elton Mayo and others found that friendly supervision and attention to the social environment increased workers' cooperation and productivity. The "Hawthorne studies" started the movement to consider how employers can fulfill employees' social needs, increase their satisfaction, and make them feel better about their jobs.

Although the validity of the Hawthorne studies has been called into question (Carey, 1967), most researchers agree that management strategies today still incorporate and build on elements of the human relations school. From suggestion boxes to workplace participation programs, organizations are trying to find the right "human touch" to decrease worker resistance and increase productivity.

Recent "Humanization" of Work and Worker Participation

During the 1970s, management efforts to "humanize" workplaces gave rise to quality-control circles, quality-of-work-life programs, and other forms of workplace participation. At minimum, management introduced some of these newer strategies to diminish worker resistance and boost profits (Rinehart, 1996). Unlike worker cooperatives and worker ownership, though, participation schemes implemented by management are not true examples of workplace democracy.

As their name implies, quality-control (QC) circles emphasize the need to improve production quality. QC circles involve a small number of employees working with a team leader or supervisor. Together, these labour-management teams brainstorm about how to solve production problems. Quality-of-work-life (QWL) programs are broader in scope than QC circles. Management promotes QWL programs as democratizing the workplace, by giving workers more responsibility and control over their work through self-regulating work teams and by providing more complex jobs for workers. Although both QC circles and QWL programs make reference to worker participation, the decision-making authority of workers is usually limited to improving individual work tasks or improving the atmosphere at work. Workers are left out of decisions about "what is to be produced, investments, distribution of profits, technology, size of the work force or plant closings" (Rinehart, 1996: 169).

Recently, concepts such as total quality management (TQM), Japanese management, lean production, and "just-in-time" production have been promoted as the panacea for the productivity and quality "problems" of management. These programs emphasize quality control through communication and teamwork between management and workers. The rhetoric surrounding these programs continues to promote the potential for democratizing workplaces and increasing the participation of workers. Because of the attention it has received in North America, I now consider the trend toward Japanese management and lean production in North American plants.

Japanese Management: Lean or Mean Production?

You may have seen the television commercial about the Saturn automobile employee and "the day he stopped the line." While doing his job, this worker noticed a problem with the cars going past him, so he reached up, pulled the cord that stopped the line, and received the help he needed to solve the problem. As part of their marketing campaign, Saturn used this commercial to show how the commitment to quality production runs throughout the plant. When I first saw this commercial, I remember thinking that this looked like a change from the old forms of production, where workers were told to leave their brains at the door, to a new form of production, where workers were encouraged to use their mental skills. And, to confirm my initial impression, I found out at the end of the commercial that Saturn is a "different kind of company" producing "a different kind of car."

What is Saturn promoting with this commercial? What does this commercial signify about potential changes to the way work is organized? Saturn, like CAMI in Ingersoll, Ontario, and Subaru-Isuzu in Lafayette, Indiana, is part of the movement to **Japanese production techniques (JPT).** Initial reactions to these Japanese transplants and joint operations were positive. "Just-in-time" production cut costs as companies reduced their parts inventories and the need for warehouses. And the use of participatory work teams led some academics and industry experts to consider JPT a new way of organizing work (Womack, Jones, and Roos, 1990). They see Japanese production as an alternative to Taylorism and Fordism. JPT is seen as enhancing workers' skills and participation at work and, in general, promoting the use of workers' mental capacities in conjunction with their physical labour. Many observers believe that companies using JPT represent a new era in labour–management relations.

But does the Saturn dream of a different kind of company really hold true? A growing body of research from both the United States and Canada suggests that JPT is really a direct extension of Taylorism and assembly-line production (Dassbach, 1996; Robertson et al., 1993). Even though work is subdivided into teams, scientific management is apparent insofar as jobs are still broken down into small tasks. For example, instructions for the first few tasks of a welding shop job at the CAMI plant read as follows: "A) Press the cycle stop button to release the locking pin from the tray; B) Remove empty parts tray and roll over to parts bin; C) Load parts from bin into tray, using 2 hands, lifting approximately 10 parts at a time" (Robertson et al., 1993). This is followed by six or seven more detailed instructions. When the list is completed, another car has moved in front of the worker and the cycle starts all over again. Although JPT does involve some job rotation, it is usually between two similar jobs or it is instituted simply to reduce repetitive strain injuries. Also, as in traditional plants, managers and the computerized assembly-line technology, not the workers, set the speed of the line and the pace of work.

Just as the service industry incorporated Taylorism (e.g., how McDonald's makes hamburgers), we are now seeing the use of JPT and total quality management in service industries. Hotel chains, grocery stores, and airlines now utilize JPT strategies. Often these programs come with names like "service excellence." Most of these programs focus on improving customer service and may allow employees some discretion in dealing with customer complaints. For example, as part of a program to increase sensitivity to individual customers, one grocery store in England encourages staff to accompany customers to products rather than just give directions and to send flowers to customers in the event of a service lapse (Rosenthal, Hill, and Peccei, 1997). Employees are given greater discretion in the hope that this will lead to improved service. How successful these programs are for improving service and increasing employee empowerment remains to be seen.

Workers are beginning to question whether lean production represents a new type of worker participation. A statement by a local union official at the Ingersoll, Ontario, CAMI plant sums things up nicely (quoted in Rinehart, Robertson, Huxley, and Wareham, 1994: 166): "This empowerment, when it's cost saving or quality problem, okay, but when it's human problems, a comfort issue, whatever, there's no empowerment. It's one sided. That's the bottom line."

Results from the service industry are mixed. Some new evidence shows that employee empowerment schemes can increase the development of workers' interpersonal and problem-solving skills because employees have to deal with customers' problems and requests (Smith, 2001). As one employee of a copier service states, "[before the employee involvement program] I used to say [to customers] 'Here's your copies, now get out of here.' Now I have to make sure I'm communicating, *to understand their needs.* . . . I'm trying to have more sensitivity to their needs" (Smith, 2001: 44). Whether or not these strategies will lead to increased empowerment on the part of workers depends on management's attitude. As we saw in the section on technology, how management implements these strategies affects their outcomes. As long as these programs continue to be linked solely to management's desire for productivity increases and "the bottom line," their participatory potential will be limited. Alternatives, such as worker-owned companies, like Algoma Steel in Sault Ste. Marie,

Ontario, may bring us closer to real worker participation (Livingstone, 1993).

DIVERSITY IN ORGANIZATIONS

We previously discussed problems of race, ethnicity, disability, and age in the section on job ghettos. Recently, sociologists have started to focus on issues of diversity in organizations. Organizations now talk about **managing diversity** within their boundaries. This is the catchphrase for programs designed to reduce barriers for women, members of visible minorities, Aboriginal people, and people with disabilities. Managing diversity can include providing sexual harassment awareness seminars, actively hiring and promoting visible minority groups, and establishing mentorship relationships. Most of these diversity programs aim to make the formal structures of organizations discrimination-free and tolerable for all members. Some argue that the term *managing diversity* is problematic (Prasad and Mills, 1997). It places the focus on managing rather than understanding diversity. In this section, I discuss some of the ways we can understand the effect of diversity on organizational life. To begin, we need to understand why women, members of ethnic and racial minorities, people with disabilities, and others may have trouble adjusting to life in organizations.

A complicating factor in the potential of these programs is the informal structure or *organizational culture* of organizations. Members have shared meanings about what life is like in their organizations. Organizational culture comprises, among other things, implicit understandings of how to complete work and shared assumptions about how to interact with and treat co-workers. Some sociologists show the image of organizations as one in which race, gender, sexuality, and age are absent or reflect the dominant white heterosexual culture (e.g., Mills and Simmons, 1999; see Chapter 8 for a more detailed discussion of ethnicity and race). In Canada, immigrant women who are members of visible minorities speak of experiencing "triple jeopardy" and of having difficulties fitting into organizational life (Mighty, 1997). When the majority of workers are white and heterosexual, the organizational culture may implicitly discount the experiences of other employees. One lesbian employee was distressed by her own self-betrayal as she attempted to fit into her organizational culture: "I'd just come back from a gay rights

march . . . and yet in that situation with those people I worked with, I couldn't say anything . . . it was extremely upsetting" (quoted in Hall, 1993: 133). To understand diversity, we must do more than change the formal structures of organizations. We must also look at how the informal culture of organizations constrains members of minority groups.

WOMEN IN MANAGEMENT

Much research concerning women working in organizations has focused on the movement of women into management. In Canada between 1971 and 2001, the number of women managers increased from 6 percent to 35 percent of all managers. However, since only 25 percent of senior managers in Canada are women and only 12 percent of the top 500 companies in Canada have women board members (Catalyst, 2005), the "glass ceiling" for women has by no means disappeared. Research suggests that it is not easy for women to move into the male-dominated world of management.

Do Women and Men Manage Differently?

One barrier that women have to overcome in moving up the managerial ladder is the perception that they are ineffective managers. One stereotype is that of the bossy and overly controlling female manager. Yet research points to an image of women as more effective and participatory managers than men. So what are we to conclude? Are female managers authoritarian or consensus-oriented? Are they different from male managers?

In her classic study of a large, white-collar organization she called "Indsco," Rosabeth Moss Kanter (1977) demonstrates that whether female managers are participatory or authoritarian often depends on their position in the organization. Kanter found that female managers at Indsco tend to be in relatively powerless positions in the lower managerial ranks. These positions offer little room for risk taking and limited authority over organizational decisions. They also breed rule-mindedness and territoriality on the part of managers. Knowing the rules and being able to force subordinates to follow the rules represents one of the few areas of power for "powerless" managers. Kanter concludes that, regardless of gender, if managers find themselves in a relatively powerless position, they will likely be narrow-minded and overly controlling. So we now have a partial answer to our question. To understand why some managers—male or female—are authoritarian, we need to know whether they are in relatively powerful or powerless positions.

Judy Rosener (1990) offers a different perspective by arguing that some female managers are more interactive and people-oriented than male managers. The women interviewed by Rosener see themselves as encouraging participation, sharing power and information, enhancing the self-worth of others, and energizing co-workers and subordinates. Indicative of this style is the decision-making approach of one female CEO, who stated: "When I face a tough decision, I always ask my employees, 'What would you do if you were me?' This approach generates good ideas and introduces my employees to the complexity of management decisions" (quoted in Rosener, 1990: 122).

At first glance, Rosener seems to be supporting the view that women and men make essentially different managers. This would lead us to believe that there is something about women—biology, socialization, or life experiences—that turns them into interactive, participatory managers. Yet Rosener also acknowledges that management style is determined by organizational context, such as the location of managers in the organization hierarchy, the degree of bureaucratization and rigidity in the organizational structure, and the presence—or absence—of a culture that allows for innovation. In addition, the way in which a woman's managerial style is perceived may lead to the development of different styles. In her study of Canadian managers, Sheppard (1993) found that although both male and female managers made "gut-level" decisions, men's quick decision making was viewed as more credible than women's. Sheppard argues that the way in which male and female decision makers are perceived may lead women to develop a slower, more participatory style of management.

The answer to the question about gender differences in managerial style, then, is not entirely clear. In some instances, we see differences, but just as often we do not. The consensus that seems to be growing among researchers, however, is that no real differences exist between male and female managerial behaviour and effectiveness (Powell, 1990). This body of research suggests that, rather than defining certain managerial styles as male and female, we should develop a contextualized understanding of managerial styles.

"WILL I LIKE MY JOB?" JOB SATISFACTION AND ALIENATION

The service revolution has changed the structure of work in Canada and across the world. There are more part-time jobs and increased use of computer surveillance, as well as some increases in knowledge-based jobs. Given these changes, how do Canadians feel about their jobs? According to a 2001 survey, 93 percent of Canadians reported they were satisfied with their jobs (McKenzie, 2001). Surveys show that getting respect from their bosses and feeling in control of their job mattered most to Canadian workers. Less important was the amount of money they made (see Figure 11.5). This reflects much of what we know about job satisfaction. To be satisfied at work, intrinsic rewards, such as autonomy and challenging work, are at least as important as extrinsic or material rewards (see Box 11.2).

Are 93 percent of Canadians *really* satisfied with their jobs? What do sociologists mean by **job satisfaction?** These are important questions. Job satisfaction is usually determined by a survey question, such as "How satisfied are you with your job?" In many ways the responses to job satisfaction questions are similar to replies to the question "How are you today?" (Krahn and Lowe, 1998: 408). Most of us would answer "fine" to such a general question. Similarly, many workers respond that they like their jobs when asked how satisfied they are. Some analysts believe, however, that most workers do not want to admit that they do not like their jobs.

One solution to this problem is to use more specific job satisfaction measures, especially measures that refer to behaviours or behavioural intentions (e.g., Hodson, 1991; Rinehart, 1978). For example, the 2001 survey found that 22 percent of Canadians interviewed said they planned to change their job in the near future (Canadian Press/Leger Marketing 2001). When we discuss alienation, we will look more closely at workers' behaviours to understand workers' negative reactions to their job. For now, we'll spend a bit more time on job satisfaction. Even though it is a problematic measure, it is still used by management to gauge how happy and productive their workers are.

FIGURE 11.5   WHAT CANADIANS SAY IS VERY IMPORTANT IN A JOB

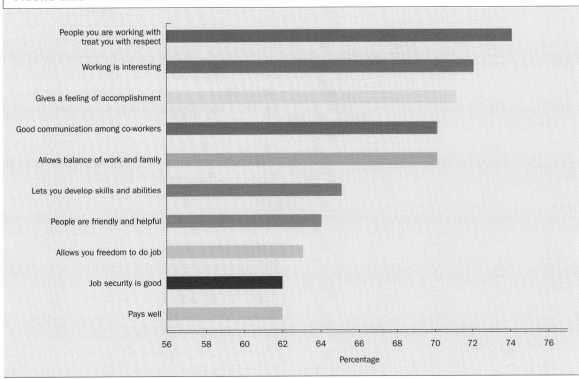

SOURCE: Canadian Policy Research Networks, 2006, "It's More than the Money—What Canadians Want in a Job." On the World Wide Web at http://www.jobquality.ca/indicator_e/rew001.stm (March 9, 2006). Reprinted by permission of Canadian Policy Research Network.

BOX 11.2   WHY EXECUTIVES QUIT: CHALLENGE, NOT MONEY

Executives are much more likely to leave a job for a greater challenge than for a bigger salary, an international survey . . . found. Lack of challenges or career growth was the reason that 33 percent of respondents changed jobs, according to the study by recruiter Korn/Ferry International, which included answers from 2000 people in 80 countries.

Ineffective leadership drove another 20 percent from their jobs, and 17 percent moved to a better job in the same field. Just 5 percent said the reason for leaving was inadequate or inconsistent compensation. Of the rest, 15 percent left involuntarily, 7 percent moved to a completely different field and 4 percent cited lack of recognition for their contributions.

The findings show that companies looking to retain top talent can get the biggest results from placing more emphasis on identifying and developing top performers, said Jack MacPhail, managing director for leadership development solutions at Korn/Ferry.

SOURCE: Wallace Immen, *Globe and Mail*, March 3, 2006. On the World Wide Web at http://globecareers.workopolis.com (March 9, 2006). Reprinted with permission from *The Globe and Mail*.

WHAT DETERMINES JOB SATISFACTION?

A multitude of factors affect how we feel about our jobs, ranging from our individual characteristics to the size of the firm we work in. To give you an idea of this range, I'll discuss some of the major predictors of job satisfaction.

Individual Characteristics

Based on what we know about job ghettos, it might be a safe bet to predict that women, older workers, and younger workers will be some of the least satisfied groups of workers. Although it is true that younger workers are some of the most dissatisfied workers (see

TABLE 11.2   JOB SATISFACTION OF CANADIANS, 2000

EMPLOYEE CHARACTERISTICS	PERCENTAGE WHO ARE "VERY SATISFIED" WITH THEIR JOB
All Canadians	28
Size of company	
Very small	30
Small	23
Medium	18
Large	26
Age	
18–25	22
26–45	26
45+	33
Gender	
Women	29
Men	27
Employment status	
Full-time	25
Self-employed	43

SOURCE: Canadian Policy Research Networks, 2006, "Job Satisfaction." On the World Wide Web at http://www.jobquality.ca/indicator_e/rew002.stm (March 9, 2006). Reprinted by permission of Canadian Policy Network.

Table 11.2), older workers—at least those who have stable jobs—are actually a relatively happy group (Krahn, 1992). The higher job satisfaction reported by older employed workers may be the result of reduced expectations about work, more meaningful lives outside of work, or past advancement in jobs (Krahn and Lowe, 1998).

When you consider occupational sex segregation and the differences in jobs held by women and men, you might expect women to be less satisfied than men. In most studies, though, women and men report similar levels of job satisfaction (see Table 11.2 and Krahn, 1992). However, when evaluating their feelings about their work, women tend to compare themselves with other women (Hodson and Sullivan, 1990). If women compared themselves with men, their reported level of satisfaction might be lower.

Job and Organizational Characteristics

Opportunities for autonomous and complex work are important predictors of job satisfaction: Satisfaction increases with autonomy and decreases with repeti-

tive or automated work. For example, fast-food workers who repeat the same phrases every day and autoworkers who must do the same task repeatedly are less likely to be satisfied than people who do more creative work. Opportunities for participation and decision-making can increase satisfaction. Workers at the CAMI plant in Ingersoll, Ontario, were initially excited about Japanese management. But when the promise of participation faded, workers' negative feelings increased (Robertson et al., 1993). What occupation we are in also affects job satisfaction. Figure 11.6 shows that people employed in social science, government, education, and religion occupations are the most satisfied.

Organizational structure, such as technology and firm size, affect how happy we are at work. Blauner's (1964) classic study *Alienation and Freedom* shows how workers' alienation increased as technology shifted from craftwork to machine tending and assembly-line work. In contrast, technology that requires the use of conceptual skills increases job satisfaction. Employees in small companies experience higher levels of satisfaction. In 2000, 30 percent of Canadians who worked in very small companies were very satisfied, compared with 18 percent who worked in medium-sized companies and 26 percent in large companies (see Table 11.2). As company size increases, so do workers' feelings of isolation and powerlessness. Thus, workers in small, locally owned companies are more likely to be satisfied than those working in regional and national corporations (Hodson and Sullivan, 1985).

When I consider all the individual, job, and organizational factors that influence job satisfaction, I am struck by the realization that much of our satisfaction at work is determined by things over which we have little or no control. Our employers determine how much we are paid and how challenging and autonomous our jobs will be. And the chance to work in a small, locally owned company has much to do with the employment opportunities where we live.

ALIENATION

If job satisfaction focuses on the individual worker's feelings about his or her job, alienation is linked to the lack of control or powerlessness an individual experiences in relation to his or her job. Originating in the work of Karl Marx, the concept of **alienation** examines how the structural conditions of work lead

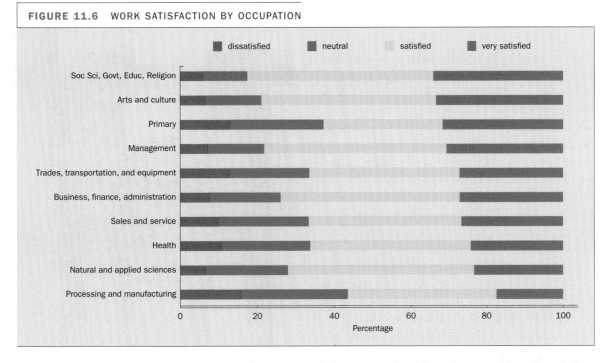

FIGURE 11.6   WORK SATISFACTION BY OCCUPATION

SOURCE: Canadian Policy Research Networks, 2006, "Satisfaction Most Common in Social Sciences, Arts/Culture and Management Occupations." On the World Wide Web at http://www.jobquality.ca/indicator_e/rew002_1.stm#2 (March 9, 2006).

to workers' lack of power over their work and lives (Rinehart, 1996). For Marx, alienation is an "objective condition" that stems from capitalism. Marx argued that capitalism robs workers of control over the means of production and the products of their labour and puts control in the hands of owners.

According to Marx, alienation of workers under capitalism has four sources:

1. Workers are alienated from the product that they produce. They do not own the products they are producing, and they have no say over how the product will be used. Rather, under capitalism, work is a means to an end—work provides a paycheque so workers can buy things they need, but workers no longer directly produce what they need.

2. Workers do not have control over the process of production. The advanced division of labour is indicative of this condition. Decisions about how fast to work, the order in which to complete tasks, and the use of equipment are made by someone other than workers. Workers lose control over their daily work activity.

3. Workers are alienated from engaging in creative activity and thus from themselves.

4. Workers are alienated from others as they have fewer opportunities to talk and connect with co-workers. Also, work is not a collective process that can help the whole community. Overall, the division of labour under capitalism physically and emotionally isolates workers from one another.

Recently, some sociologists have conceptualized alienation as a way to think about how workers' psychological and emotional states are linked to the organization of work (Rogers, 1995). For example, when work is repetitive and does not allow for interaction between co-workers, workers may experience a high level of alienation. Some sociologists conceptualize alienation as a subjective state that arises from the reality of capitalist working conditions. Here the emphasis is on workers' feelings of powerlessness and lack of control or connection to their work and fellow employees.

Fighting Alienation: Individual and Collective Responses to Work

To understand alienation, we also need to look at how workers resist it (Schmitt and Moody, 1994). This can shed light on their negative feelings toward work.

When a worker engages in sabotage or repeatedly skips work, management may define the worker as destructive or lazy. Yet, in the minds of workers, these seemingly insubordinate behaviours may be an attempt to gain control over their job or reduce the amount of alienation they experience. To overcome a boring job where she was not assigned enough work, one temporary clerical worker stated, "I used to sleep there. Yes there's nothing to do. I always bring my book. When I get sick and tired of reading, I sleep. Sometimes, OK, you're not supposed to make phone calls, but what am I going to do with 8 hours?" (Rogers, 1995: 157). If management had provided enough work, this temporary worker might have exhibited good work habits.

When viewed as potential resistance to alienating conditions, the "misbehaviour" of workers appears in a different light. Some researchers argue that the alienating conditions of work lead some workers to "fight back" or react to these conditions (Edwards and Scullion, 1982; Rinehart, 1996). You may have had similar reactions to work, such as slacking off if you believed your supervisor required you to work too hard, or turning your work into a game to make the time go faster. Engaging in these behaviours does not mean you are lazy or incompetent. Rather, they are typical reactions to alienating work.

To cope with poor working conditions, some workers quit their jobs. Those who cannot quit may respond passively by socializing with co-workers, playing games, or reducing their productivity (Burawoy, 1979). Management often devises strategies to prevent these types of behaviours. For example, Taylorism was motivated in part by management's desire to reduce opportunities for workers to restrict their output.

For management, theft and destruction of company property is a particularly bothersome behaviour. But these criminal acts may be motivated by poor working conditions. A few years ago, an undergraduate student in my class confessed that, while working in a small T-shirt design factory, she purposely poked holes in some shirts. Because management had a policy of giving damaged T-shirts to employees, you might think she did this only to take advantage of her situation. As it turns out, though, employees were paid low wages and worked under conditions of extreme heat. This student saw her behaviour as a protest against the inadequate pay and difficult working conditions. Other workers engage in sabotage to gain

Workers often resist alienating work conditions. Forms of resistance include striking, being absent, quitting, slacking off, and committing industrial sabotage.
SOURCE: Juan Manuel Sanchez. Courtesy Simon Patrich Gallery.

concessions from management or to gain control over the work process. Factory workers may damage the assembly line to slow down the pace of work, or clerical workers may hide files to reduce their workload (Hodson and Sullivan, 1990; Rinehart, 1996).

Do these individual acts of resistance change the amount of alienation workers experience? The answer to this question is complex. Many sociologists, beginning with Marx, illustrate how alienation is a condition of objective powerlessness that exists regardless of whether workers themselves consciously recognize it. Some workers become aware or conscious of the alienating conditions they experience at work. As predicted by Marx, these workers may respond to these conditions by forming unions, going on strike, or engaging in revolutionary behaviour focused on overthrowing capitalism. However, many workers do not develop "class-consciousness." Sociologists Harvey Krahn and Graham Lowe state, "In the absence of a well-defined alternative to the current economic system, we would not expect most workers to be able to clearly articulate their alienation and act on it. Apathy, or an attempt to forget about work as soon as one leaves it behind, are the common responses of many workers to a situation in which there is no viable alternative" (1998: 419).

This means that hiding files or poking holes in a shirt may make the worker feel better and thus make it possible to get through the day. These types of activities may reduce the subjective feeling of alienation: Workers may feel less powerless or may feel they have more control over their working conditions. But these types of individual strategies do not change the structural conditions of work. Collective responses to workplace conditions are more likely to lead to lasting changes in how work is organized. These collective responses, such as forming a union, may not "overthrow" the economic system, but they can improve working conditions. Debora De Angelis's co-workers who voted to form a union put themselves in a position to bargain collectively for improved pay, job security, and working conditions. Although playing games and stealing may momentarily increase workers' feelings of control over their jobs, most researchers agree that, for lasting change to occur, collective responses are needed. Chapter 18 provides more details about the role of strikes in the Canadian labour movement's struggle for economic and social rights.

Unions play an important role in facilitating collective action by workers. Today, 31 percent of the nonagricultural paid labour force are in unions (see Table 11.1). Compared with the experience in some other countries, such as the United States and Australia, *union density*, or the percentage of paid workers who are unionized, has not significantly declined in Canada over the past 30 years (Krahn and Lowe, 1998: 246). Over the past 150 years, the characteristics of unionized workers have shifted however. During the late nineteenth century, craft workers organized; during the 1930s and 1940s, workers in the goods-producing sectors followed suit. Public-sector workers began to organize in the 1960s and 1970s. In 2003, public-sector industries had the highest rates of unionization (Statistics Canada, 2004a). Some union supporters warn that union density will stagnate if union organizing does not expand to cover new groups of workers, particularly young workers in service industries (White, 1993).

From McDonald's workers in Newfoundland and Labrador to Starbucks employees in British Columbia, we should expect to see more union drives in the service industries.

Service workers are not the only area of potential growth for unions. Over the past 30 years, the number of women in unions has increased. In 1977, women accounted for 12 percent of all union membership. In 2003, women made up 48 percent of union membership (Statistics Canada 2004b). Part of this increase is due to the movement of women into the increasingly unionized public-service sector and some unionized male-dominated work, such as construction. Unions also have worked hard to show that they are relevant to women's working issues, including daycare, family leave, and sexual harassment.

Whether the number of unionized workers in Canada will grow or decline depends on how unions deal with changes in the labour market and the economy. The rise of nonstandard work and the ease with which companies can move their businesses to other countries raise serious challenges to unions. Box 11.3 provides a young union organizer's views about why youth should be more involved with unions. His views highlight how unions are one of the few ways to bring about real and lasting change to the conditions of work.

THE FUTURE OF WORK

Good and bad jobs, nonstandard jobs, alienating work—what will the future of work hold? Although sociologists don't usually try to predict the future, we can look at some of the current trends to see where we are going.

In the immediate future, we can expect employers to continue looking for ways to reduce operating costs. As in the past, one focus will be on reducing the cost of labour. Employers continue to move factories to countries with the lowest labour costs. Along with labour-reducing uses of technology, this tendency may further the trend toward downsizing and company restructuring. As a result, fewer employees will spend their lifetime with the same employer. As the head of production for the PowerPC microchip said in 1994, "I'm here for the duration, five years or so" (quoted in Osterman, 1995: 72).

The rise of self-employment is related to attempts to reduce the cost of labour. Although only

BOX 11.3 YOUNG PEOPLE AND UNIONS: MAKING THE CONNECTION

I'm 21, and I live in Calgary. I work at Garden Market IGA, which is organized by UFCW Canada Local 401. An average day in my life usually involves getting up, going to work, coming home from work, and going out. I also do some volunteer organizing for the union. . . . I think the biggest challenge facing workers today, in Canada, is the right-wing, corporate agenda, which focuses solely on the bottom line. It's all about money, money, money, and not about the people. For instance, right now they're closing a Catelli pasta-production plant that Local 401 represents in Lethbridge. An American company wanted to eliminate the competition, so they just came in, bought the company, and closed it. Now there are 71 unionized, well-paid workers out of work.

Another big challenge is people's lack of education about their rights. People don't know their rights because the governments don't want them to know. Our system pretty much brainwashes kids at a young age that, "Hey, you can make it on your own, everybody can do it themselves, you don't need any help from anybody." Which is just a lie. Everybody needs a hand up.

I think educating young people has got to be priority number one for unions, because we're the new people coming into the workforce. Plus, labour itself has started to age. You go to a convention now and you hear people saying, "I've seen that same guy at the convention for the last 20 years." That's a problem. If you don't bring in new people and new ideas, you'll never change—and change has to happen. It has to occur for unions to move forward, become more productive, and represent their members better.

I think the best thing unions do is look after the concerns of working people. The worst thing we do is we don't blow our own horn or pat ourselves on the back. We don't let people—even our own members—know what we do. Say we go out and we settle a grievance about pay that our members should have received. Like, we just settled one—I think it was for $34 000. But nobody knows about it because we didn't publicize it. We didn't go running around saying, "Look what we did! Look what we did!" I believe we have to do a lot more of that, so people see the good that we actually do, and they don't just believe what they read in the papers.

Unions need to get young workers involved. We have to organize new workplaces, and we have to make unions a stronger force in the country. Right now, we don't have the power to walk up to government and say, "Change the laws."

We have to educate people about why unions are important, and why labour laws are important: to stop the exploitation by big business, and to stop the growing gap between the rich and poor. The country will fall apart if the rich keep getting richer and the poor keep getting poorer. With more workers unionized, we'll have more power.

The unions have to go into the high schools and talk to kids who are just joining the workforce. You've got to point out things like, in Alberta—depending on how much money you make—it's illegal to be charged for a uniform, but companies are doing it because the people don't know. The government hasn't provided the information to them. Nobody's been there to tell them. I think telling people how the companies are stealing from them would help them realize the need for unions, and to organize and stand up for their rights. It would help them stop being exploited just because they're young.

I think we have to move into more non-traditional union settings, like the fast food industry, and try non-traditional ways of organizing. You can't just walk into a place and say, "Hey, join the union. Look what we've done." You have to give people a reason. Young workers, older workers, and people of ethnic minorities all have different reasons for joining the union. They all have different beliefs and different ideas which we have to take into account. A young person's going to have a completely different idea of what they want at work than somebody who's 45 and married, with two kids. Somebody who's 17 is liable to want a raise more than anything else, while somebody older is liable to want a benefit plan. So, we have to look at the workplaces we're organizing, and go in the direction the members want, not just do what we've traditionally done in the past.

We also have to get governments to change the laws so we can organize temporary workers. There's a huge new Wal-Mart warehouse in Calgary, and every person working there is hired through a temp agency, so we can't organize them. You walk in there and try to apply for a job, and they send you to a temp agency. Every employee is charged by the temp agency, they're all getting barely over minimum wage, and the working conditions are disgusting. . . .

Some say young people don't care about unionizing. It's not that they don't care. It's that young people don't care about the same things as somebody who's older than them. Somebody who's 45 doesn't have the same outlook as a 17-year-old person: their lives are completely different. So, we have to change the way we organize and represent young people.

Young people can no longer look forward to getting a good job working in a plant someplace, and providing for their family. Now you have to work two part-time jobs. You can't get a full-time job because companies sit

BOX 11.3   YOUNG PEOPLE AND UNIONS: MAKING THE CONNECTION *(continued)*

there and go, "Well, if I make you full-time, I have to give you benefits. I don't want to do that." So everybody ends up in a dead-end, part-time job.

We have to get into using young people to organize young people. In my store, the younger people mostly talk to me, and the older people mostly talk to the older shop steward. You're more comfortable talking to somebody your own age, they'll have the same experiences and the same ideas as you. It's why we use Spanish-speaking people to organize Spanish-speaking people. It's somebody they can understand and relate to, someone who has faced the same discrimination.

How can workers in different countries develop solidarity with each other? That's the million dollar question. Globalization and free trade are the most destructive forces out there right now. Look at the Catelli plant in Lethbridge. It's being closed because they can produce pasta cheaper in a right-to-work state in the United States. I think globalization has made us stand up and see that the rich are getting richer and the poor are getting poorer no matter where you are, whether you're in India, Brazil, or Canada. I think globalization opened our eyes in North America to the plight of everybody else, and that it's not just them, it's us, too, who are being affected. . . .

I think there are two things unions have to do. We have to educate the members we already have: show them why it is we do stuff, so we don't have members out there who look at unions as simply a deduction off their paycheque. And we have to also organize new members. As companies get bigger, they're going to downsize to make more money, and if we don't keep organizing new members, we aren't going to be able to fight the fight as well as we can now. We're not going to be able to move forward and pressure governments and companies to treat people fairly.

Chris O'Halloran is vice-president of the Alberta Federation of Labour, representing youth and youth issues. He is a member of UFCW Canada Local 401.

SOURCE: Chris O'Halloran, 2001. "Young People and Unions: Making the Connection." *Our Times* 20(5): 19–23.

15 percent of Canadian workers were self-employed in 2003, the growth rate of self-employment since the 1970s has outpaced that for workers in the public and private sector (Statistics Canada, 2004a). Increased self-employment is due to both push and pull factors. Workers who lose jobs because of corporate restructuring may be pushed into self-employment as their only employment option. Other workers may be drawn to self-employment because of a desire to have more control over their work. Regardless of why people become self-employed, the future appears to involve an increase in self-employment.

Some researchers and futurists debate what jobs will look like. The debate divides along pessimistic and optimistic lines. Optimists emphasize the "end of the job" as we know it (Bridges, 1994) and the rise of self-employed, autonomous entrepreneurs. Part of the optimistic scenario is based on the hope that the service industry will continue to create good jobs, such as in finance and medicine. Pessimists like Jeremy Rifkin (1995) predict the "end of work." Based on an analysis of jobs in the United States, Rifkin believes that as many as three out of four white-collar and blue-collar jobs could be automated. This will push people out of work, with no jobs to replace the ones lost to automation. In Rifkin's view, unemployment levels will continue to rise and more of us will scramble for the few remaining jobs. By the middle of the twenty-first century, millions of workers could be left permanently idle. These optimistic and pessimistic scenarios are linked to trends we've discussed in this chapter: Will technology increase or decrease productivity? Will the service industry create more good jobs than bad jobs? Will the number of workers in job ghettos increase or decrease? Both optimists and pessimists agree, however, that the days of work in large corporations may be coming to an end. But it's too early to tell which scenario, if either, will emerge.

As you've learned in this chapter, employers and employees do have some control over whether technology creates good jobs or bad jobs or reduces alienating conditions. An important issue for the future of work is whether employers or employees will set the terms by which such changes will be judged. It is clear that the century-old battle between workers and management will probably continue. And it is workers like Debora De Angelis who will attempt to organize their co-workers, so that employees improve their chances of having a say in what work will look like in the future.

SUMMARY

1. In the first industrial revolution, large segments of the population moved from being peasant farmers to being wage-earning factory workers living in urban areas. During the second revolution, companies increased in size and developed administrative offices with a complex division of labour.

2. The rise of the service economy is changing the types of jobs available in the labour market. The types of jobs available in the service economy are being polarized into good jobs in upper-tier industries and bad jobs in lower-tier industries.

3. The proportion of Canadians employed in nonstandard jobs is growing. Much of this job growth is fuelled by the expansion of the lower-tier service sector.

4. The labour market comprises different segments. Good jobs are located in core industries and firms with primary labour markets, while bad jobs may be found in peripheral industries and firms with secondary labour markets. Job ghettos are areas of the labour market that trap disadvantaged groups of workers. Labour-market shelters, such as professional associations and unions, help their members maintain access to good jobs.

5. From Taylorism to Japanese production techniques, various management strategies are used to control workers and increase their productivity. Most strategies fall short on their claim to be participatory.

6. Research does not show a difference in men's and women's management styles. Differences are due to the position of managers and their organizational context.

7. Work and organizational characteristics are the primary predictors of job satisfaction.

8. Alienation is a structural condition of powerlessness that arises from the organization of work in the capitalist economy. Workers respond to alienating conditions in various ways, such as engaging in sabotage and quitting their jobs. Strikes and other collective forms of resistance may have some success in changing the conditions of work.

QUESTIONS TO CONSIDER

1. Thinking about your own work experience, do you see evidence of the service economy creating good jobs or bad jobs?

2. Do Japanese production techniques (JPT) represent a different way of organizing work from Taylorism? If yes, how is JPT different? Does JPT offer new forms of participation for workers?

3. How is technology changing the world of work? Do you believe that we are experiencing a productivity paradox? What supports your argument?

4. What is the difference between the concepts of job satisfaction and alienation? Is Marx's concept of alienation relevant for understanding work today? Why or why not? Have you ever engaged in workplace behaviour that could be interpreted as a reaction to alienating conditions? Did this behaviour change the alienating conditions? Why or why not?

GLOSSARY

In Marxist theory, **alienation** is a structural condition of "objective powerlessness." Workers do not have power or control over their work situation and are separated from the means of production. This situation is indicative of work in a capitalist economy.

Extrinsic rewards are the material benefits of working. Adequate pay, benefits, and opportunities for advancement are examples.

Fordism refers to the bureaucratically organized mass production of standardized goods by assembly-line methods.

The **human relations school of management** emphasizes the importance of the social aspects of work. Proponents argue that more satisfied workers are more productive workers.

Intrinsic rewards are the social-psychological benefits of working. They are derived from challenging work, non-repetitive work, autonomy, and decision-making opportunities.

Japanese production techniques (JPT) form a management strategy that combines teamwork with assembly-line work to improve the productivity of workers.

Job ghettos are parts of the labour market that prevent groups of workers from experiencing upward mobility.

Job satisfaction is determined by asking workers in a survey "How satisfied are you with your job as a whole?"

Labour-market segmentation involves the separation of the labour market into sectors of good and bad jobs.

Labour-market shelters are organizations that protect the jobs of certain groups of workers. Professional associations and unions are examples.

Managing diversity is a management strategy aimed at helping women and members of visible minorities succeed in the workplace. It consists of anti-racism policies, policies against sexual harassment, and awareness classes, mentorship programs, and so forth.

Nonstandard jobs include part-week employment (reduced hours per week), part-year employment, limited-term contract employment, employment through temporary-help agencies, self-employment, and multiple-job holding.

Primary labour markets are where most good jobs may be found. They have an internal labour market that provides a job ladder and the opportunity for upward mobility.

Taylorism, also known as scientific management, is named after its developer, Frederick Taylor. This style of management breaks job tasks into their smallest components. Work is also separated into conceptual and manual tasks, removing the need for workers to make decisions about their work.

SUGGESTED READING

Betcherman, Gordon, Kathryn McMullen, Norm Leckie, and Christina Caron. (1994). *The Canadian Workplace in Transition.* Kingston, ON: Industrial Relations Centre Press. Using current survey information, this book provides an overview of changes occurring in Canadian work organizations.

Duffy, Ann, Daniel Glenday, and Norene Pupo. (1997). *Good Jobs, Bad Jobs, No Jobs: The Transformation of Work in the 21st Century.* Toronto: Harcourt Brace. Chapters deal with contemporary labour force issues in Canada, including technology, restructuring, work and family, unemployment, and training.

Krahn, Harvey J., and Graham S. Lowe. (1998). *Work, Industry and Canadian Society,* 3rd ed. Scarborough, ON: Nelson. Provides an overview of major topics and research in the study of work and occupations in Canada.

Myles, John. (1988). "The Expanding Middle: Some Canadian Evidence on the Deskilling Debate." *Canadian Review of Sociology and Anthropology, 25* (3), 335–64. Assesses the polarization of the Canadian labour market into good and bad jobs.

Rinehart, James W. (2006). *The Tyranny of Work: Alienation and the Labour Process,* 5th ed. Toronto: Thomson Nelson. A compelling look at the history and sociology of alienation and work.

WEB RESOURCES

Companion Web Site for This Book

http://www.newsociety5e.nelson.com

Begin by clicking on the Student Resources section of the website. Next, select the chapter you are studying from the pull-down menu. From the Student Resources page, you have easy access to InfoTrac College Edition® and other resources, such as the Glossary and Flashcards. The website also has many useful tips to aid you in your study of sociology.

InfoTrac College Edition Search Terms

Visit http://www.infotrac-college.com for access to more than 20 million articles from nearly 6000 sources when doing your online research.

ThomsonNOW™

http://hed.nelson.com

This online diagnostic tool identifies each student's unique needs with a Pretest that generates a personalized Study Plan for each chapter, helping students focus on concepts they are having the most difficulty mastering. Students then take a Posttest after reading the chapter to measure their understanding of the material. An Instructor Gradebook is available to track and monitor student progress.

CHAPTER TWELVE

Education

In this chapter you will learn that

- Sociologists study links between schools and society, focusing on inequality, socialization, and social organization. Theoretical approaches include structural functionalism, Marxism, human capital theory, feminism, credentialism, and institutional theory.

- Canadian schooling has been marked by three broad trends. First, to fulfill a mandate to retain the vast bulk of students in secondary levels, schools have *expanded*. Second, this expansion has necessitated a greater variety of *accommodations*, as educators attempt to address a range of student abilities and exceptionalities. Third, demands for postsecondary credentials are generating a simultaneous trend toward more intense forms of *competition*.

- Canadian school-level attainment shows a pattern of inequality, in that it varies by class, gender, and race.

- Socialization through education has become less religious and now lacks the hard-edged prescriptive tone it had in the past. Reflecting trends in pedagogical philosophy, today's schools have a more indulgent quality, with teachers using less punitive tactics to elicit compliance from students.

- Canadian schools have changed from wielding traditional authority to wielding legal-rational authority and in the process have become more bureaucratic. Today, schools are being pressured to become more "accountable" and "market-like."

Scott Davies
MCMASTER UNIVERSITY

INTRODUCTION

Go to the education section in any bookstore and what do you see? Dozens of titles declare schools to be in some sort of crisis. *The Catastrophe in Public Education, Public Education: An Autopsy, Failing Our Kids: How We Are Ruining Our Public Schools, The University in Ruins,* and so on. Newspapers decry the quality of schooling with headlines like "Johnny Can't Read and He's in University." Such drama! Is it really that bad?

Not if you consider several facts about schools. Until quite recently higher education was deemed to be a waste for common people. Early in the twentieth century, most people did not complete high school. But the past half-century has brought a change in ideologies. In Canada and elsewhere, advanced levels of education are seen to be not only suitable but also necessary for many people. Over 50 years, high-school attendance has become almost universal, and attaining a secondary-school diploma the norm. University enrolments have never been higher. Further, public opinion surveys show that most Canadians rate our public schools favourably and believe that teachers and principals do a very good job (Guppy, Crocker, Davies, LaPointe, and Sackney, 2005).

This highlights a key paradox. Modern schooling has been a success story in many respects, having grown immensely, reshaped the lives of most Canadians, and received billions in government funds. Yet, as schools become more central to society, they attract more and more criticism. This chapter will illuminate this paradox by exploring the transformation and changing connections between schools and Canadian society over the past century.

HOW SCHOOLS CONNECT TO SOCIETY: CLASSICAL AND CONTEMPORARY APPROACHES

Sociologists examine three major ways that schools connect to society. First, schools shape society by **selection.** Education systems have long channelled students into different types of schools and programs. This process creates stratification when programs are designated to be "higher level" or "lower level" and link to better or worse job opportunities. The endless grading, judging, marking, and testing in schools sorts and certifies students with different "badges of ability." This may seem self-evident, since we have all written hundreds of tests in our lives. But

Schools socialize students by fostering the development of attitudes, knowledge, and skills that are necessary in adult society.
SOURCE: ©Network Productions/Index Stock Imagery.

a sociological approach sets this process within a bigger picture: Schooling connects to societal-level inequality. In a society marked by disparities in wealth and income, and where more people go to school for longer periods, never before has the pursuit of educational credentials been as consequential for income, occupational success, and other life chances. Sociologists ask *who* is selected for *what*, and *why?*

These kinds of questions can be traced back to the ideas of Karl Marx and the structural functionalists. Although Marx wrote little on schooling, his twentieth-century followers have examined the role of schooling in patterns of economic inequality. They have argued that schools are stratified in ways that reflect workplace hierarchies, with basic forms of schooling teaching youth to be punctual and compliant, and with higher levels encouraging students to internalize orders and the expectations of authority figures. In contrast, structural functionalists see school selection as an increasingly meritorious process in which the brightest and hardest working are identified, rewarded, and selected for training in professional work and high-level management.

Second, schools shape society as they *socialize* people. They help prepare new adults for the next generation, passing along values and knowledge. This too may seem glaringly obvious, but decisions on *which* values and knowledge are passed on can be contentious. When Émile Durkheim (1961 [1925]) was writing, industrialization and the rise of democracy were promoting individualism, and people felt freer to develop their talents to their fullest extent. As individualism flourished, Durkheim sought to understand how modern societies could replace the binding and authoritative voice of religion, which had traditionally prescribed norms to guide people's thoughts and actions. What would now keep individuals from being self-centred and acting only in their own interest? Durkheim cared deeply about "moral education," the normative element of schooling that he hoped would become society's prime tool to combat the rising culture of individualism.

When Canada was more religious, schools imparted old-fashioned virtues and moral codes. But society has changed, so contemporary sociologists now ask these questions: Do schools still impart a clear set of values? Is socialization better understood as a series of unintended consequences that are beyond anyone's control? Just how successful are

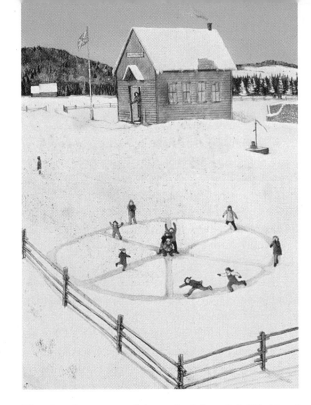

When Canada was more religious, schools imparted old-fashioned virtues and moral codes.

SOURCE: William Kurelek, *One-Room School at Kaszuby*. Art Gallery of Hamilton, Gift of the Polish Alliance of Canada and Wintario, 1978. Courtesy of the Estate of William Kurelek and the Isaacs Gallery, Toronto.

schools at socializing students? Do they treat everyone the same, or does school socialization differ by class, gender, and race?

Third, education shapes society through *social organization*. Schools affect how we learn and help define different types of occupations. This was a core interest of another classical theorist, Max Weber, who was fascinated by "rationalization," supposedly the main "logic" of modern societies, embodied in bureaucratic organizations. For him, modern schooling was changing society by teaching knowledge in a systematic fashion and creating credentials to forge more formal pathways to labour markets.

Why do employers seek and hire employees with school credentials? The conventional wisdom is that schools teach skills, employers hire the most skilled, and school credentials are signals of skills. But Weber's contemporary followers have questioned whether the school-labour market connection is so simple. They contend that most school content is only loosely connected to what is demanded in most jobs. They see schools as largely serving to distribute legitimate access to jobs.

Let us now examine in depth each of the three roles of education: selection, socialization, and social organization.

SELECTION

When Canada was an agricultural society, land was a prime economic resource, and affluent families strove to pass their property to their children. When manufacturing and commerce become the key economic activities, upper-middle-class children could inherit business fortunes. But today, most youth earn their living through employment and need credentials. "Class reproduction," the passing of advantage from one generation to the next, does not operate through direct inheritance in education. No one can legally inherit his or her parents' law degree, medical license, MBA, or teaching certificate. These things must be earned. Now that most positions of power and status require some sort of school credentials, how do the affluent pass on their advantages?

School selection occurs in two ways. First, schooling itself is structured in a stratified manner, though this structuring takes different forms across countries and over time. Second, within that structure students from different backgrounds have unequal rates of success. Families navigate their way through this structure, searching for ways to boost their children's educational success for the most prized credentials. Most parents expect their children to receive a postsecondary education (see Figure 12.1).

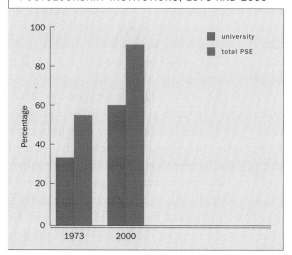

FIGURE 12.1 PERCENTAGE OF CANADIAN PARENTS EXPECTING THEIR CHILDREN TO ATTEND POSTSECONDARY INSTITUTIONS, 1973 AND 2000

SOURCES: Anisef, 1974; Davies, 2005.

CHANGING SCHOOL STRUCTURE

In Canada, the traditional form of educational selection is known as "streaming." Streaming consists of splitting students into curricular groupings, one typically bound for postsecondary schooling, one headed for general training. Students in the upper tier are exposed to advanced mathematics and works of literature, while those in the lower tiers focus on the rudiments of literacy, numeracy, and practical workplace skills. Although Canada ranks near the top of the world in reading literacy (see Figure 12.2), Canadian sociologists have long condemned streaming for limiting educational opportunity, particularly for students from working-class backgrounds. Streaming is seen to dampen their aspirations, manage their ambitions, and discourage them from moving on (Curtis, Livingstone, and Smaller, 1992). To understand Canada's form of educational stratification, we need to set streaming in an international context.

Compared with many European countries, Canadian education has actually been relatively open and flexible. For decades, schools in Britain, France, and Germany sorted students into entirely academic or entirely vocational schools at relatively young ages (Kerckhoff, 2002). European academic secondary schools were oriented to prepare elites and preserve a heritage of classic literature, philosophy, and rigorous exams. "Excellence" was equated with high culture. Until recently it was inconceivable for French secondary-school students to study "practical" electives, such as business or accounting, for instance. Stratification was rigid; once students entered a type of school, few moved out. If a student failed an examination at age 15 or 16, they were effectively eliminated from further higher education.

To understand national differences, sociologists distinguish **sponsored mobility,** which takes place in educational systems that select relatively few youth early in their lives to enter elite universities, from **contest mobility,** which takes place in educational systems that group the bulk of youth into the same school, expose them to the same curriculum, and send larger numbers to higher education (Turner, 1960). Sponsored mobility uses highly structured streaming to restrict access to higher education, while contest mobility promotes more competition within a unitary structure. Canada is an example of a contest system, while many European countries have had sponsored systems. For most of the twentieth century, Canadian

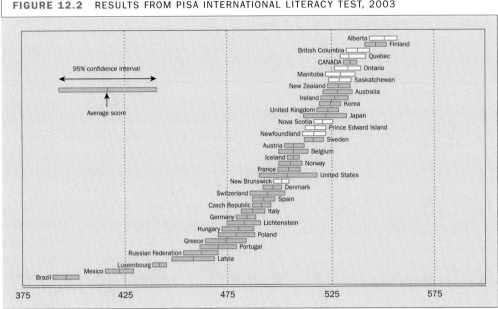

FIGURE 12.2   RESULTS FROM PISA INTERNATIONAL LITERACY TEST, 2003

SOURCE: Results from PISA International Literacy Test, 2003, Program for International Student Assessment, http://www.pisa.gc.ca/pisa/brochure_e.shtml. Reproduced with the permission of the Minister of Public Works and Government Services Canada, 2006.

schooling did not sharply separate a "gifted" minority from the rest by creating separate schools. Academic curricula were instead given to almost everyone. From the 1960s until recently, proportionately more Canadian youth flowed into Canadian universities than European youth flowed into European universities, and even lower streams were not strongly vocational; little high-school content has been directly job-related in any stream. As a result, the high-school diploma lacks vocational meaning, and it does not guarantee any particular skill for any specific occupation. Canadian high schools channel many students to postsecondary levels and prepare few for any particular job.

This distinction may be changing, however, as nations expand their universities and colleges to take in more students (Wolf, 2002). As in Canada, European policymakers want more youth to study in university, claiming that more graduates will generate wealth and improve their nation's economic competitiveness. Most European nations are removing barriers, creating more alternative channels for youth, and moving toward an ever-more streamlined contest model. As such, the form that inequality takes in education is changing.

As more youth enter higher education, competition shifts to higher levels, and stratification *within* universities and colleges becomes increasingly important.

Higher education can be seen as stratified along two main dimensions: selectivity of institution and field of study (Davies and Guppy, 1997). Universities and colleges with the best reputations offer their graduates access to elite jobs, higher wages, contacts, and other advantages. In some countries, higher education institutions differ greatly in prestige. In Europe, ancient universities, such as Oxford, Cambridge, and the Sorbonne, have much more exclusive student bodies, and they more readily provide their students with access to elite positions. In Canada, universities are generally more selective and academically intensive than are community colleges, whose vocational mandates give them a subordinate position within higher education (Dennison, 1995).

Fields of study also differ in their prestige, selectivity, access to resources, and payoffs for their graduates. High prestige was once attached to humanistic fields (such as philosophy and English) that enjoyed elite patrons, but in recent decades this has changed. Fields linked to powerful professions or commercial markets, such as medicine, law, engineering, and business, have now gained the upper hand. These fields offer students pathways to lucrative job markets (Walters, 2004).

As colleges and universities are flooded with an unprecedented number of applicants, school selection

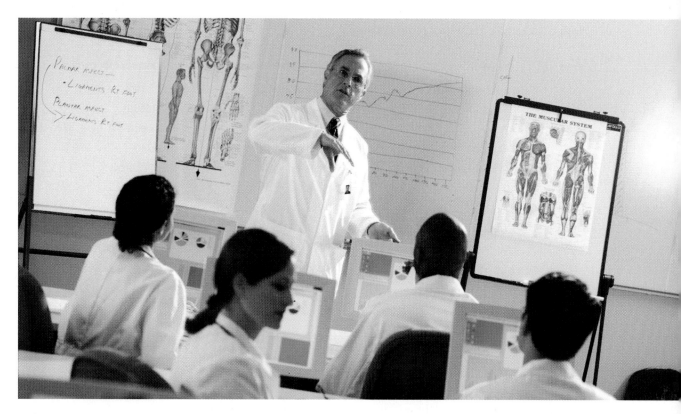

Fields linked to powerful professions or commercial markets, such as medicine, law, engineering, and business, offer students pathways to lucrative job markets.
SOURCE: ©Comstock Images/Alamy.

moves upward to higher education. Students in different institutions and fields face unequal prospects. Universities and colleges sort these larger masses for vastly different occupational and social opportunities. Since there are simply not enough high-paying jobs for all graduates, entry into the most advantageous slots in higher education is becoming increasingly valuable. Required high-school grades—the prime currency for entrance to universities—have steadily risen over the past decade. Many universities are boosting their entrance standards and tuition fees, gaining repute not only by admitting top students but also by rejecting large numbers of qualified students. Institutions that were already highly exclusive are increasingly selective, while the less discriminating are expanding their enrolments.

The degree of stratification in higher education differs across nations. For instance, the American system is a mix of private-sector and public institutions that are arrayed on a steep prestige hierarchy. American higher education has famous Ivy League universities, elite liberal arts colleges, and flagship public universities that greatly overshadow less renowned entities. This steep, entrenched system makes the name of elite institutions important to employers. Canadian higher education, in comparison, not only lacks a private sector but also lacks a steep institutional hierarchy (Davies and Hammack, 2005). Until recently, Canadian governments have allowed only publicly funded universities. The resources allocated to these institutions have been fairly equal, while their American counterparts are much more unequal. Although the top American colleges and universities select from a national and international pool of applicants, only small numbers of Canadian undergraduates cross provincial or territorial borders, and most commute to their local institution. Canada has a relatively small national market for undergraduate credentials. Although degrees from top-ranked colleges in the United States can offer great opportunities there, few employers in Canada value the name of any one Canadian university over others.

Accordingly, Americans have long ranked their universities, but the practice is relatively new in Canada. The best-known Canadian rankings are compiled by *Maclean's* magazine. The magazine gives

TABLE 12.1   THE 2005 *MACLEAN'S* RANKINGS

RANK	PRIMARILY UNDERGRADUATE	COMPREHENSIVE	MEDICAL/DOCTORAL
1.	St. Francis Xavier	Waterloo	Toronto
2.	Mount Allison	Guelph	McGill
3.	Acadia	Victoria	Western
4.	Bishops	Simon Fraser	UBC
5.	Wilfrid Laurier	Memorial	Queen's
6.	Trent	Regina	Alberta
7.	UNBC	New Brunswick	Montreal
8.	UPEI	York	Sherbrooke (tied for 8th)
9.	St Mary's	Concordia (tied for 9th)	McMaster (tied for 8th)
10.	St. Thomas	Carleton (tied for 9th)	Saskatchewan
11.	Winnipeg	Windsor	Laval
12.	Lethbridge		Ottawa
13.	Brock		Dalhousie
14.	Brandon		Calgary
15.	Mount St. Vincent		Manitoba
16.	Ryerson		
17.	Lakehead (tied for 17th)		
18.	Moncton (tied for 17th)		
19.	Laurentian		
20.	Nipissing		
21.	Cape Breton (UCCB)		

SOURCE: Reprinted by permission of *Maclean's*.

high scores to institutions with such attributes as large libraries, incoming students with top high-school grades and from other provinces and territories, faculty with research awards, and small classes. Although popular, this practice has been criticized for using questionable measures and for creating an artificial image of hierarchy and competition among our universities. But university administrators take them seriously and strive to improve their relative position. Table 12.1 shows the results from 2005.

Canada may be developing a more pronounced hierarchy in higher education. As our universities and colleges increasingly generate more of their own revenue, whether via large external research grants, corporate funds, alumni donations, or steeper tuition, some universities and colleges will likely enjoy advantages. If wealthier institutions are perceived by students and employers to offer a superior education, it may bring an intensified pecking order to Canadian higher education.

INEQUALITY AMONG STUDENTS

Within sociology, a debate has raged for 50 years over whether schools create equal opportunity for all. Functionalists believed that schools were increasingly rewarding the best, allowing any bright students, regardless of their social backgrounds, to enter high-paying professional and managerial positions. In contrast, Neo-Marxists contended that the very design of mass public schooling ensures that people who are born disadvantaged remain disadvantaged. In recent years, this claim has been extended to race and gender, with many analysts arguing that female students and those who are members of minority groups are treated poorly in school and are given little choice but to enter low-paying jobs in female and minority-group "job ghettoes." The claim here is that schools actually worsen existing inequalities by stereotyping disadvantaged youth, devaluing their cultures and skills, and steering them into lower streams. Sociologists have conducted research on this topic for several decades. The early research focused mostly on social class, but it has since broadened to include gender and race. This research has consistently uncovered the following patterns.

First, educational attainment for youth from all class backgrounds has steadily risen over the past half century. As Table 12.2 shows, more Canadians from all walks of life attend school for more years than did their fathers. Second, despite this expansion, student success has been found to be consistently related to socioeconomic background. This has been true not only across time but also across the world, and, indeed, it is one of the "iron laws" in the sociology of education. Youth from less advantaged backgrounds are repeatedly over-represented in lower streams, get lower grades, drop out of school at higher rates, and are underrepresented in higher education. Inequalities along socioeconomic lines were evident when such data were first collected and they have persisted ever since, not only in Canada but also in other Western nations (Anisef, 1974; Blossfeld and Shavit, 1993; De Broucker and Lavallee, 1998; Gamoran, 2001; Guppy and Arai, 1994;

Knighton, 2002; Krahn, 2004; Porter, Porter, and Blishen, 1982; Ryan and Adams, 1999; Wanner, 2000).

To illustrate these inequalities, Neil Guppy has examined data from Canada's 2003 General Social Survey (Davies and Guppy, 2006; see Table 12.2). These data reveal the likelihood of women and men in different age groups graduating from university who have fathers with different levels of schooling. If absolute certainty is equal to a probability of 100 percent, then for Canadians 30 years of age or older in 2003, the probability of having a university degree was 23 percent. However, this probability is different for different levels of father's schooling. For example, the likelihood of a woman between the ages of 30 and 39 attaining a university degree was 20 percent if her father had not graduated from high school; but if her father was a high-school graduate, it rose to 26 percent, and if he attended a postsecondary institution, it rose to 47 percent. We can see a clear socioeconomic effect in Table 12.2. The likelihood at least doubles, and often almost triples across each row. If equality of educational opportunity were improving, the socioeconomic effect would be smaller among younger cohorts (the 30–39-year-olds) but the table shows no evidence of this. These findings are typical of dozens of studies on this topic.

However, a different picture emerges when we compare the school success of males and females. Males

TABLE 12.2 PROBABILITY OF HAVING A UNIVERSITY DEGREE IN 2003 BY SEX, AGE GROUP, AND HIGHEST LEVEL OF FATHER'S EDUCATION

	LESS THAN HIGH SCHOOL	HIGH SCHOOL EDUCATION	POSTSECONDARY EDUCATION	NUMBER OF RESPONDENTS
Women				
Aged 30–39	.20	.26	.47	1449
Aged 40–49	.19	.26	.44	1587
Aged 50–59	.18	.29	.42	1139
Aged 60+	.11	.24	.29	1290
Men				
Aged 30–39	.17	.29	.42	1454
Aged 40–49	.14	.28	.45	1565
Aged 50–59	.23	.41	.49	1129
Aged 60+	.16	.34	.40	1086

SOURCE: Neil Guppy's calculations from 2003 General Social Survey, Statistics Canada.
Notes: Includes only Canadian born; sample weighted to represent Canadian population.

once had a virtual monopoly on higher education, but this imbalance began to change in the late 1950s. By the 1980s, more women than men were attending university. Females now drop out of high school in fewer numbers, graduate more often, enter universities in greater numbers, and score higher on many standardized tests (Statistics Canada, 2005a). Today, women have surpassed men on most measures of education attainment.

What explains this reversal? It partly reflects the success of the women's movement, partly the entry of women into traditionally male-dominated professions, such as law and medicine, and partly how some "female-dominated" occupations like teaching, nursing, and social work, not only grew but also demanded higher-level educational certificates. Men's attainment has not kept pace, partly because substantial numbers of men continue to work in blue-collar jobs, such as mining and construction, which rarely require postsecondary schooling (Guppy and Arai, 1994).

Although higher numbers of women are going to university, they often enter different fields from their male counterparts. Table 12.3 shows the distribution of university graduates among selected fields of study in 2003–04. It shows that almost 58 percent of all students in Canadian universities are female and that women form the majority in all fields except math, computer science, architecture, and engineering. These numbers are *very* different from those of previous eras. For instance, in the early 1960s, about 25 percent of university graduates were women; in some fields, such as forestry, *no* women graduated, and several others, such as law, had only a handful of female graduates (Statistics Canada, 2001). But this pattern has certainly changed. Today, most fields have seen dramatic change, including business, law, and medicine. Nonetheless, women continue to be underrepresented in dynamic and well-paying fields like engineering and computer science.

Racial and ethnic patterns of educational attainment reveal a more mixed picture. Figure 12.3 shows that on average, young members of visible minorities exceed young whites in the attainment of university degrees: 29.6 percent versus 23.7 percent. But what needs emphasis is the *variation* in the attainment in the visible minority group. Although more than 40 percent of Asians have a university degree, only 6.2 percent of Aboriginals have a degree, while about 18 percent of blacks and Hispanics have degrees. What accounts for these variations? An explanation must take three legacies into account: differences in socioeconomic status, colonization, and immigration policy.

The large variation among minority groups is partly a product of Canada's changed immigration policy. Whereas recruitment in previous eras targeted Europeans with relatively low levels of schooling,

---

TABLE 12.3   UNIVERSITY ENROLMENT BY SELECTED FIELDS OF STUDY AND SEX, 2003–2004

FIELD	TOTAL ENROLMENT	% FEMALE
Education	76 300	75.8
Humanities	148 800	63.1
Social sciences, law	162 300	65.4
Business and public administration	170 900	55.1
Physical and life sciences	92 900	55.6
Math and computer sciences	43 700	26.8
Architecture and engineering	86 900	22.8
Agriculture, natural resources	14 400	55.6
Total university enrolments	990 400	57.7

SOURCE: Adapted from the Statistics Canada publication *The Daily*, Catalogue 11-001, University Enrolment, 2003–04, Tuesday, October 11, 2005.

FIGURE 12.3   PERCENTAGE OF CANADIANS AGED 25–34 WITH A UNIVERSITY DEGREE BY VISIBLE MINORITY STATUS, 2001

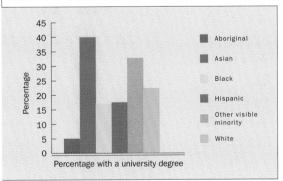

Note: "Asian" includes East, Southeast, and South Asians.
SOURCE: Davies and Guppy (2006:118).

since the late 1960s Canada has targeted Asians with advanced educational credentials. As a result, living conditions for immigrants vary widely. Some of them enter the country with profiles that typically promote educational success—high levels of parental education, comfortable incomes, urban residence—while others do not. Thus, Canada's educational rankings partly reflect the "inputs" from the immigration system as well as its own internal processes. Meanwhile, Aboriginal Canadians are products of colonialism, segregation, and discrimination, which rendered them the most impoverished ethnic group in Canada.

Given these patterns of attainment, a question arises: Do schools ameliorate inequalities in society, maintain them, or make them worse? This question is difficult to settle empirically because almost *everyone* goes to school. If there were some groups or regions where youth didn't go to school, then researchers could see whether the presence of education worsens or improves rates of inequality. For something that resembles these conditions, sociologists have looked to the time of the year in which few students are in school: summer. Although such research is scant in Canada, a large American literature is available (Burkam, Ready, Lee, and LoGerfo, 2004; Downey, von Hippel, and Broh, 2004; Entwistle and Alexander, 1992). Its basic logic runs like this: If schools gave superior treatment to middle class children, then student learning gaps (as measured by standardized test scores) would grow over the school year and would either stagnate or shrink during the summer months. Alternatively, if such gaps grow in the summer and narrow during the school year, then schools probably do not disadvantage youth of lower socioeconomic standing and may even mitigate the effects of home and neighbourhood. This research is almost unanimous in its basic conclusion: Schooling *reduces* learning gaps along socioeconomic lines, while these gaps widen in the summer when students are not in school. Researchers conclude that schools indeed function as equalizers, at least in terms of measured learning.

The near-mountain of empirical research on school inequalities thus lends support to a more nuanced position. Schools can be seen as progressive institutions that offer opportunities for all youth but are limited in their power to eliminate inequalities. Contemporary schools have enjoyed some success in reducing inequality, but they have not come close to totally eliminating such disparities. Affluent children have many more advantages and fare better in school because of their advantaged home environments.

SOCIALIZATION

Contemporary sociologists offer different depictions of how schools socialize their students. According to structural-functionalist theory (Dreeben, 1967), schools teach modern values. As societies industrialize, urbanize, and become more cosmopolitan, schools provide a common culture to compensate for the declining influence of religion. Schools are said to transmit values like universalism (which involves treating everyone as equal, rights-bearing individuals) and meritocracy (a system in which social rewards go to people with talent who exert effort in open competitions). But rather than teaching these new values overtly, the functionalists contend that schools teach them in a **hidden curriculum.** Teachers do not repeatedly lecture students on universalism and meritocracy but instead teach these values by running schools in a universalistic and meritocratic fashion—students learn by doing. By treating all students equally before common rules, schools are seen to embody the values of universalism, and by rewarding deserving students, they are seen to teach the value of meritocracy. Thus, modern schools teach core values by virtue of their very structure.

Other sociologists see a darker side to school socialization. For instance, Marxists also claim that schools impose a hidden curriculum that promotes obedience to authority, not cheery modern values (e.g., Bowles and Gintis, 1976; see Box 12.1). They contend that public education is structured to support capitalism by creating a disciplined labour force. By organizing student learning in a competitive manner and having students vie for grades and rewards, schools are said to mirror capitalist competition and individualism. Likewise, feminists and many students of race claim that schools impose subordinate identities on their students (this argument is elaborated further below).

To assess these theories, it is useful to think of school socialization as a continuum. At one extreme are boarding schools, where the institution regulates virtually all facets of life—not only lessons but also how and when students sleep, eat, dress, and play. The school

BOX 12.1   WILLIS'S *LEARNING TO LABOUR*

One of the most famous books in sociology is Paul Willis's *Learning to Labour* (1977). Willis observed a working-class school in England's industrial north in the mid-1970s, when many working-class boys dropped out of school at age 16 and took jobs in factories. He set out to explain why they would enthusiastically accept factory jobs that other youth would reject as inferior, degrading, and low-paying. Willis reasoned that it was too easy to say that these boys simply had no choice, since they experienced no physical coercion and actually exercised a degree of self-direction. To get his answer, Willis probed the cultural life of the school.

In his study, Willis found two male peer groups. One, nicknamed "the lads," was antagonistic toward teachers, lessons, school rules, and students who were diligent, deferent, and obedient. The second subculture, the "ear'oles," accepted school authority and strove to be upwardly mobile. The lads called them "ear'oles" because they saw these boys as overly passive, like a human ear, never *doing* anything, and always on the receiving side of orders. Crucially, the lads felt *superior* to the ear'oles because the lads made their own fun and excitement in school.

Although *Learning to Labour*'s description of classroom antics is rich and entertaining, the book became famous as an account of how school "resistance" helps "reproduce" the class structure. That is, when youth reject what schools have to offer, their only remaining options are bottom-level jobs. The book was also controversial for its contention that the lads embodied the culture of the working class. Since most school rebels were from working-class backgrounds, Willis saw their conflict with school as a form of *class* conflict, full of unarticulated ideological meanings. For Willis, the lads' belief that school activities were useless in the workplace was an insight into the deskilled nature of work in capitalism. Their constant denigrating of teachers' advice, he felt, signalled a recognition of the capitalist hidden curriculum. Subsequent research has questioned whether Willis's ideas can be generalized to contemporary Canada, but many remain fascinated by his depiction of male peer groups' bravado and aggression.

Marxists claim that schools impose a hidden curriculum that promotes obedience to authority.

SOURCE: PhotoDisc.

becomes the student's entire social universe, resembling what sociologists call a *total institution*, an all-controlling organization that remakes people's entire identities, where people are isolated from the larger society and are strictly controlled by a specialized staff.

In boarding schools, teachers become powerful socializing agents, forging identities and having an almost singular impact on how pupils speak, look, and act. At the other extreme of the continuum is online education. If a person's education consists solely of online courses taken at home, the school's position in that person's life can be marginal, something that merely appears on a computer screen, to be ignored at whim. School becomes just one socializing force among many, like a television program that can be turned on or off. Most Canadian students experience school socialization somewhere between these extremes. Few attend boarding schools or take only online courses from home. Most attend public schools full-time, Monday to Friday. Bearing this reality in mind, we next explore how schools socialize students, contrasting the ways socialization in schools has changed over the past 150 years. We then consider the ways in which schools treat different groups of students differently.

CHANGING FORMS OF MORAL EDUCATION

The history of Canadian schools is one of declining religious influence and altered moral content. Canadian public schools were originally organized by churches, with Roman Catholics being granted separate schools in Ontario, and Protestants being granted schools in Quebec. Similar denomination-based arrangements were made in all provinces. In the mid-nineteenth century, few people questioned the proclaimed need for public schools to provide Christian teaching. The earliest schools were nominally secular, but their religious character was overt.

Egerton Ryerson, the father of public schooling in what is now Ontario, wanted schools to create literate, religious, and devoted citizens. He and other school promoters believed that religious schooling could curb an array of perceived problems, such as the rising incidence of youth crime and general ignorance (Prentice, 1977: 128). Christianity occupied a central place in public school missions for a century. Even in the 1950s, public authorities still called for strong religious influence in public schooling, with some calling for public schools to teach "cardinal virtues" and "Christian ideals" (Government of Ontario, 1950: 36–37). By the late 1960s, educators had very different ideas. Fewer educators saw their role as passing on religiously inspired wisdom, time-honoured truths, and a sense of moral duty. Instead, school socialization was to become much more individualistic. Educators increasingly sought new ways of teaching for a new age. Consider this quotation from a 1968 provincial committee report:

> Learning by its very nature is a personal matter. There is virtually a metabolism of learning which is as unique to the individual as the metabolism of digestion. Parents and teachers may create conditions with learning in mind, but the actual learning experience is intimate and subjective, for each human being reaches out to the world in his own idiosyncratic way. (Ontario Department of Education, 1968: 49)

After the late 1960s, schools saw their role less as providing moral guidance and more as creating forums for thinking about moral issues. This created a different type of moral education, at least in emerging theories of pedagogy. Students were to be exposed to a fuller range of contemporary controversies, beliefs, and ideals than before. Teachers aimed to enable students to make informed choices, rather than have them accept moral edicts. Ideals from Christianity were replaced by ideals of critical thinking, science, and multiculturalism. Educators

wanted less to tell students what was unambiguously true or false and more to nurture a deeper understanding of various subject matters, based on discovery rather than repetition. More educators saw their mission as taking a critical stance toward society, exposing injustices, and questioning established interpretations of history (Hurn, 1993: 191).

What has been the impact of these changing ideals? Although both functionalist and Marxist theories can be compelling, what do empirical studies tell us about *actual* socialization in current schools?

In partial support of functionalist theory, schooling does appear to make people more "progressive," in the sense of supporting civil liberties, tolerating minorities, appreciating social justice and ethnic diversity, and embracing nontraditional roles for women (Kingston, Hubbard, Lapp, Schroeder, and Wilson, 2003; Pallas, 2000). However, schools do so in a relatively neutral and individualized manner, and they offer rather ambiguous moral messages. That is, although students are encouraged to identify with various progressive causes, such as protecting the environment, helping the homeless, fighting racism, and fundraising for overseas children, schools do this by having students relate their own experience and venture their own opinions. Classrooms increasingly have "feel-good" posters that exhort children to read and stay in school, a form of "bumper-sticker morality" containing catch-phrases for quick consumption rather than deep discussion and reflection. Yet, in support of Marxist theory, schools spend most of their time on mundane matters of personal conduct, striving to get students to be orderly and task-oriented. Much of teachers' time is spent on urging students to be respectful of one another, to participate in class, and to be cooperative (e.g., Brint, Contreras, and Matthews, 2001; Jackson, Boostrom, and Hansen, 1998).

Although studies tend to support elements of both functionalist and Marxist theory, they also suggest that modes of shaping students are changing. Teachers now treat students in a more indulgent fashion than in previous eras. They see self-esteem as essential for learning and control their classes with a lighter touch than in the past. They increasingly rely on "token economies," giving small rewards to get children to comply, rather than using overt authority. They use group projects, not just individual assignments, and especially in elementary schools, students work in rotating activity centres, freely moving

The diversification of Canadian society has influenced the way morality is taught in school.
SOURCE: Thomson Nelson Collection.

around the classroom and choosing their tasks. Today's schools are making less use of classic styles of enforcing obedience. Further, teachers try to inspire *all* students. Whereas schools in the past would give up on those students deemed hopeless, whether too poor, too troubled, or too slow, today's schools work hard to engage the entire student body, even the least able performers. Indeed, the law demands that schools do so.

To summarize, the morality taught in public schools has shifted from religious indoctrination to a more individualized and indulgent approach that encourages students to learn by reflecting, not reciting. This change reflects the diversification of Canadian society, where moral reference points are numerous, not singular, and where there is a sentiment that schools should address social problems but should not preach a monolithic doctrine. Within this secular and individualized form of education, do schools treat everyone the same? That is the question to which we now turn.

CREATING IDENTITIES? GENDER AND RACE

Historically, Canadian education prepared girls and boys for different roles in adult society. Traditional school systems were premised on the notion that most young women should be homemakers or schooled for a narrow range of "nurturing" occupations like nursing and elementary-school teaching. Though boys and girls were mostly grouped together at lower ages, they were often segregated at older ages, with the expectation that a select few boys would move to advanced studies (Prentice, 1977: 111–12). Although both sexes attended school, their experiences were dissimilar. Few people challenged gender traditionalism until the 1960s.

Women's educational attainment has changed since then, matching and even outpacing male attainment in many areas. But despite this apparent change, critics continue to accuse schools of continuing to reinforce traditional gender roles (American Association of University Women Educational Foundation, 1992; Bennett DeMarrais and LeCompte, 1995; Kelly and Nihlen, 1982). They detect a hidden curriculum that quietly subordinates women, prepares them for a gendered division of labour, and sends messages about their inferiority. The explicit gender stereotyping of the late nineteenth century has only been masked, they argue, and they support their argument by pointing to several indicators beyond standard measures of school attainment.

First, feminist critics examine school staffing, noting that despite some change, most positions of power remain in the hands of men. Some observers have even called schools "academic harems." For instance, an elementary school can be staffed almost entirely by women, save for the most powerful position—the principal—who is often a man. While teaching positions in lower grades are held almost entirely by women, higher-level teaching and administrative positions are held by men. A second indicator of gender bias pertains to curriculum. For several decades, feminists have charged school textbooks with being loaded with sexist language, illustrations that depict most active characters as male, and stories that depict women in nurturing occupations and as stay-at-home moms. They also contend that high-school literature courses ignore female authors and that history textbooks disregard the contributions of women. Here there has been change, especially as most provincial governments have curriculum guidelines that monitor gender representation in most course material.

A third indicator of gender inequity is the fact that schools tolerate the conduct of male students that, in the adult world, would be considered sexual harassment. Feminist critics decry schools' "hostile hallways" in which sexual comments, touching, jokes, and leers are deemed "normal" and "natural" and are therefore tacitly permitted. Schools are said to accept such behaviour when they rationalize such acts as "boys being boys." Such rationalizations are linked to inequities in extracurricular programs. Schools continue to be accused of considering it natural that men's sports teams should receive higher priority and more funding than women's teams, an imbalance said to send a message of female inferiority. Finally, teachers stand accused of treating female students unfairly, directing girls toward stereotypical nurturing fields like teaching, nursing, and administrative studies. Others claim that girls' self-esteem is damaged in the classroom when teachers ignore them in favour of boys (this particular accusation has been controversial, since research suggests teachers only give males more attention for disciplinary reasons). The sum total of these inequities, it is argued, is a gendered "hidden curriculum" that alienates females from course material, dampens their aspirations, and ultimately reinforces gender inequality.

Similarly, some analysts argue that Canadian schools sometimes socialize minority students into racial identities. The historical episode of residential schools for Aboriginal children is the most blatant. In the twentieth century, the Canadian government set out to mould Aboriginal identities by sending up to half of all Aboriginal children to these schools with the intent of making them "modern Indians" who would speak English or French, convert to Christianity, and learn skills for menial jobs. The residential school was a total institution that separated Aboriginal children from their families and communities, interrupted the rhythms of their home lives, and implanted more regimented cultural norms. The legacy of this racism is felt in Aboriginal communities to this day. Likewise, young black children in some cases were singled for discriminatory treatment in the nineteenth and early twentieth century, labelled as "coloured," and segregated in black-only schools (Axelrod, 1997: 79).

Although all overt segregation laws have been long removed, some sociologists continue to charge Canadian schools with being insensitive to the needs of youth from minority groups (Dei, 2005). Schools, they contend, "racialize" children from minority groups by making them assume racial identities and experience themselves as "different" (Lewis, 2003). In

this view, schools actively reinforce racial identities and inequalities. Students who are members of minority groups are seen to be ill-treated by school practices, particularly "colour-blind" policies that ignore the disadvantages of children from these groups. School multiculturalism, it is held, only superficially addresses historical legacies of racism, while white teachers are seen to be blind to experiences that are actually colour-coded and unwilling to challenge dominant understandings of race. For instance, a commissioned report recently accused the Ontario government's Safe Schools Act and "zero tolerance" policy of being culturally insensitive and of singling out black males for punishment (Ontario Human Rights Commission, 2003).

THE LIMITS OF SCHOOL SOCIALIZATION

Although claims that schools mould gender and racial identities are very popular, one difficulty is that they assume that schools have a great deal of socializing power, rather than provide convincing evidence of their effects. It is conceivable that some educational institutions, such as residential boarding schools, may wield great socializing power, but the average public school today is far more limited in its reach. We need to recognize other socializing influences. Students clearly are influenced by forces well beyond the school—their families, neighbourhoods, workplaces, and of course, peer groups (Looker and Thiessen, 1999).

Sociologists have long examined high-school peer groups, believing they set limits on schools' socializing sway, and how varying degrees of student autonomy may *hinder* school goals. Sociologists in the 1950s and 1960s became interested in peer cultures when they found that student populations were less deferential than in previous decades. Although most school deviance was mild, consisting of minor rule-breaking, irreverence, apathy, or truancy, it still subverted educational goals by disrupting classrooms and interrupting learning. James Coleman (1961) argued that, among adolescent peers, learning and achievement mattered less than popularity and looking good. Moreover, in the peer group, being a top student did little for a person's reputation. Coleman's ideas have since spawned a large body of research on the formation of student subcultures. This research has examined how the very structure of schooling encourages youth to respond in ways that can frustrate the socializing efforts of educators (Coleman, 1961; Tanner, 2001).

Specifically, over the decades, sociologists have interpreted youth's obsession with physical appearance, hairstyles, clothing brands, and cliques as no mere byproduct of their relative immaturity. Instead, sociologists see them as responses to particular *social* conditions. Schools segregate youth by age, give youth little power, and require their attendance by law. Yet students do have *some* degree of autonomy. High school is not overly challenging for most youth. Most students have some disposable income. These conditions, sociologists argue, encourage youth to be status-conscious. Status groups emerge when social structures offer few alternative avenues for social mobility. Students become a status group because they lack power and authority but have enough autonomy to invent their own social realm within schools. By this logic, Murray Milner (2004) has likened high-school cliques to Indian castes. Castes emerged in traditional India when there was little democracy or economic mobility for people of low social rank. Upper castes obsessed about appearance, social ranking, and maintaining social distance from inferiors. They created elaborate rituals and pressures for conformity, especially for intimacies such as eating and romantic relationships.

So how are high-school cliques like castes? According to Milner, teens risk social demotion if they are seen eating or dating someone with low status. They use small cruelties and put-downs to uphold their dominance. A jock pesters a nerd to maintain his own status at the nerd's expense. Status also explains why some teens are so concerned with conforming to brand-name clothing fashions. The isolated world of high school creates pressures for cliques to display their status through consumer commodities. Since teens are largely excluded from "producer" roles in prestigious workplaces but are freely granted "consumer" roles, the latter become their main source of reputation.

Sociologists have also traced a second, more antagonistic element of student subcultures to schools' very own selection function (Cohen, 1955; Stinchcombe, 1964). In this view, since schools reward only some students and deem others to be academically unfit, they create disincentives for unsuccessful students. Low-ranked students suffer an inglorious status and get labelled as "underachievers" and channelled into streams that lead neither to postsecondary education nor to useful job-training programs. These students suffer emotional injury in schools and hunger for a more positive self-image. Accordingly, low-achieving students form anti-school subcultures as an alternative source of social recognition. These subcultures invert the values that schools try to promote, rejecting students who are rule-abiding, obedient, and hardworking, and celebrating the rule-breaker, the insolent, and the hedonist. Among males, this rebellion is epitomized by confrontations with teachers, fighting, smoking, drinking, and sexual bravado. Among females, it is marked by a flaunting of their sexuality and a preoccupation with dating. In both cases, subcultures are seen to be a youthful expression of frustration with school selection processes that thwart upward mobility.

Since the 1980s, sociologists have argued that oppositional subcultures can also take racialized forms. Fordham and Ogbu (1986) claim that African Americans denigrate their high-achieving peers for "acting white," that is, for adopting the culture and language of white America and being disloyal to their own community. Such pressures are said to discourage black students from identifying with schooling. The "acting white" thesis has become very influential, but is it true? Several American sociologists have put it to the test, but most cast doubt on it. Some suggest that only a small portion of black students take oppositional stances to schools (Downey and Ainsworth-Darnell, 2002). Others argue that generic peer pressures are felt by *all* high-achieving students, regardless of race, and those who earn top grades are similarly labelled *geeks*, *nerds*, or *brainiacs*. Only in schools where student achievement is starkly unequal by race, they speculate, will this pressure take a racialized form (Tyson, Darity, and Castellino, 2005).

Does the "acting white" phenomenon exist in Canadian schools? Far less systematic research on the topic exists here, but some researchers claim that black Canadians sometimes form oppositional subcultures. In a field study of a Toronto high school, Patrick Solomon (1992) claimed that black males were increasingly drawn towards sports, and saw academics as a "white activity." Other sociologists, such as George Dei and Carl James, similarly contend that black youth are increasingly alienated from the mainstream curriculum and require alternative "black focus" schools to nurture a more positive cultural identity (Dei, 2005).

Studies of peer groups suggest that school selection provokes at least a mild form of antagonism from lower-achieving students and that this can frustrate the efforts of educators. But the very existence of oppositional subcultures similarly suggests that some theories may exaggerate the extent to which schools can actually mould gender and race identities. Students learn roles in their neighbourhoods, families, media, and places of employment (which can be highly segregated), and these are competing sources of socialization that may actually be partly *counteracted* by schools.

For instance, some feminists (Holland and Eisenhart, 1990; Weis, 1990) contend that peer groups, not school officials, divert female students toward established gender roles and discourage educational advancement. Some suggest that embracing a student role may actually *erode* gender traditionalism. In a field study of an English secondary school, Lynn Davies (1984) found that youth in university-bound streams were relatively more "androgynous" and less conforming to gender stereotypes. In contrast, girls who were about to drop out looked forward to motherhood rather than to careers, and would-be male dropout were more traditionally masculine. A similar pattern was found in a Canadian study that employed survey research. In a large sample of Ontario high-school students and dropouts, I found that both girls and boys in academic streams were less traditional than those in nonacademic streams, and those differences widened in later grades (Davies, 1992). Since new career opportunities for academically oriented males and females may weaken traditional conceptions of gender, it is not clear that schools continue to actively enforce gendered and racial identities. Though schools certainly treated females and minority students differently in the past, contemporary research shows that public schools promote more liberal and progressive views about gender and race and that schools have long been among the few places in society where boys and girls are grouped together to perform the same role.

These findings force us to think more about the *limits* of schools' socializing role. Paradoxically, as more people go to school for more years, the socializing impact of schooling may become *weaker*. More than in any previous era, schools now compete with other socializing agents. More youth are employed part-time, popular culture is everywhere, and today's parents are spending more time on developmental activities, hiring more tutors, and purchasing more extracurricular lessons for their children (Adler and Adler, 1994; Aurini, 2004; Daly, 2004, Davies, 2004; Quirke, 2003; Sayer, Bianchi, and Robinson, 2004; Box 12.2). Schools are losing their monopoly on structured lessons and developmental activities, at least among the middle class. The upshot is that their unique impact on students may be on the wane. Rather than being a total institution, schools are moving toward the weaker end of the socializing continuum, no longer imparting a cohesive ideology and now competing with more socializing agents than before.

SOCIAL ORGANIZATION

For Weber, modern schooling reflected the emergence of a rationalized worldview in the organizational form of bureaucracy. With schools now being one of Canada's largest expenditures, costing at least $60 billion per year, they need to be seen as legitimate organizations that generate useful skills in a relatively efficient manner. Contemporary theorists offer widely differing accounts of whether schools are indeed efficiency-seeking organizations. Some see schools as converging quite closely with Weber's ideal type of bureaucracy, others do not.

THEORIES OF SCHOOL ORGANIZATION

The most straightforward account is offered by economists. **Human capital theory** asserts that the school's role is primarily economic: to generate needed job skills. The theory assumes that both individuals and governments "invest" their time and dollars in schools because they believe it will lead to financial prosperity. The costs of schooling—books, buildings, teacher salaries—are "inputs," and student learning is the "output" or product. Human capital theorists see schools as organized to maximize student skills. If the value of the output exceeds its cost, schooling becomes a worthwhile investment, such as when an individual's expenditures in schooling early in their life eventually raises their earnings or improves their health. Schooling is thus seen as a form of capital—*human* capital—since people cannot be separated from their knowledge and skills in the same way that they can be distinguished from their financial and physical assets (Becker, 1964).

Indeed, research consistently shows that education *does* pay. On average, people with more years of

---

BOX 12.2   THE GROWING NICHE FOR TUTORING CHAINS: PREKINDERGARTENERS' ACADEMIC PREP

Merrick is 5. On this crisp October afternoon, he'd just finished a flashcard drill of simple words, and the children next to him were following suit. "Cap. Lap. Map. Trap," they recited. "Cat. Fat. Rat." Academic tutoring has dropped down to the sandbox-and-nap-time set. In recent years, early-childhood education experts and industry analysts say, more parents have started sending their 3- to 5-year-old children to for-profit tutoring centers to give them an academic edge in elementary school.

Tutoring for tots, some say, has been spurred by increased academic accountability in schools, heightened competition to get into top-ranked colleges, and new research that links early exposure to books, music, and language to better academic performance in later years. And the convenience and recognizable brand names of some established tutoring companies seem to attract parents, some industry-watchers say. While pre-K tutoring is now just a tiny segment of the $2.5 billion K–12 tutoring industry—about 1 percent—that share is likely to grow as more parents and policymakers emphasize early-childhood education. There is an annual growth rate of roughly 15 percent in the K–12 tutoring industry overall in the past few years.

Yet while some companies wax enthusiastic about pre-K tutoring, many early-childhood experts decry the trend. Tutoring 3- to 5-year-olds in a classroom setting with flashcards and workbooks can be overly prescriptive, dampen enthusiasm for learning, and even spur developmental problems, some scholars say.

"Parents have the idea that education is a race, but it is not," said David Elkind, the author of the 1981 book *The Hurried Child* and a child-development professor at Tufts University in Medford, Mass. "However well-intentioned, [pre-K tutoring] is a moneymaking thing that builds on parental anxieties, with no research or support."

"Are [parents] damaging their kids for life? Hardly," said Barbara A. Willer, a deputy executive director of the Washington-based NAEYC. "But there's a larger issue. As a society, do we make sure that tutoring is available just to those who can afford it, or do we ensure that there are high-quality pre-K programs for all?"

Merrick's mother, Mary Jansen, would agree. She says the program encourages her son to achieve beyond his grade level. And that, she says, is necessary for Merrick to succeed in school. "Kids can't only be little kids anymore," she said, after her son finished his half-hour tutoring session here. "I want him to go to the college he wants. As long as it's Ivy League."

SOURCE: Reprinted with permission from *Education Week*, October 19, 2005, Vol. 25, Issue 08, p. 10.

---

schooling earn higher wages and have better employment rates (Walters, 2004). School pays, but why? Although some analysts point directly to the skills that are generated through education, many sociologists question the extent to which schooling improves useful job-related skills and whether jobs utilize what school teach.

"Credentialists" like Randall Collins (1979) are generally skeptical of human capital theory for at least two reasons. First, usually far fewer high-skilled jobs are available than there are graduates from high schools, colleges, and universities. Employees are often overqualified; available jobs often do not require their learned skills (Livingstone, 1998). Second, Collins sees strong connections between school content and the workplace. Much schooling—hours of essay writing, studying quadratic equations and periodic tables, practising the tuba—has precious little to do with most job realities. School curricula develop according to their own dynamics, he argues, and seldom in response to employers' demands. Further, employers rarely bother to look at student grades when hiring. With the exception of a few professions, merely possessing a diploma, certificate, or degree will suffice. If school content was really connected tightly to the job market, Collins reasons, employers would surely use grades as vital indicators of a candidate's suitability. So why do employers seek graduates with credentials if indeed little of their learning actually connects to job demands? Collins offers several answers.

One is **credential inflation.** Just as monetary inflation devalues money, modern education devalues credentials. Just as a dollar cannot purchase the same goods it could 30 years ago, a high-school diploma does not lead to the same job it did 30 years ago. Inflation results from intense competition in the labour market. When hiring, managers in large corporations and in government are often flooded with job applicants. The sheer number of candidates makes careful and personal consideration of each one impossible. Hence, managers need a bureaucratic screening device, a procedure to reduce the applicant pool that is seen to be fair and efficient. Over the past few decades, employers have increasingly used credentials for this purpose, even for jobs that are not complex or demanding. Hiring someone with credentials may not reflect a need for specific skills. Seeking a leg up on competitors, people comply by obtaining an educational credential. This inflation creates a growing gap between the competencies required in jobs and the level of education possessed by job occupants.

Another reason that employers seek graduates with credentials concerns **professionalization.** Professional associations, such as the Canadian Medical Association, control occupational standards by setting the educational requirements for their profession. By demanding higher levels of education, these occupations can limit the number of eligible competitors. Over the decades, many occupations have raised entry requirements—school teachers, nurses, accountants, and social workers, to name a few. For sociologists, this is part of a process of professionalization in which an occupation tries to raise its standing and command higher wages. Think of all the requirements that didn't exist 40 years ago: M.S.W., M.B.A., B.N., and so on. What fascinates Collins is that teaching, nursing, social work, and business easily survived in past generations without demanding these credentials, and little evidence suggests that these occupations have become so much more complex as to necessitate these higher levels of schooling.

Collins also contends that some employers prefer to hire employees with advanced credentials just because they are prestigious. According to Collins, many employers hire university graduates for jobs to gain trust from clients and customers. Firms want to appear serious, businesslike, and trustworthy and not "fly-by-night." For Collins, well-educated employees are the human equivalent of a nice piece of office furniture: They signal that the firm is indeed honourable. Advertising a work force with many letters trailing their names (B.A., B.Sc., L.L.B., M.B.A, M.A., Ph.D., etc.) can be a mark of status in a world where business transactions can be highly uncertain and in which clients seek signals of repute.

SCHOOL AUTHORITY: FROM TRADITION TO RATIONALITY TO MARKETS?

Premodern schools were typically small and informal, and educational authority was decentralized. Canada had thousands of school boards, most of which con-

trolled only a few small schools. Each teacher had little formal training and enjoyed wide discretion over his or her classroom. Lessons were taught without many formal guidelines. There was little large-scale planning and there were few educational laws. Teachers had parental-like authority over students. They could discipline largely as they pleased, often resorting to corporal punishment, with little fear of reprisal. Curricula were justified in terms of passing on time-honoured doctrine and cultural traditions. Teachers were proclaimed to be moral trustees of society.

All this changed during the twentieth century. In Weber's terms, modern institutions like schools were *rationalized.* Public education was justified less in moral terms and more by its societal utility. Canadian schools cut "irrelevant" subjects like ancient languages and adopted new ones, usually justified in terms of their necessity for daily living. Teachers were seen less as trustees of the common good and more as semi-professionals with skills and responsibilities.

Rationalization was accompanied by a change in organizational form. Schools grew and looked less like little red houses and more like office buildings. They were increasingly governed by general rules. Lines of control were formalized from top to bottom, with hierarchical chains of command and clearly defined responsibilities. Regulations delegated authority to credentialed officials in a more specialized division of labour, particularly at upper grade levels. Personnel were selected for their advanced training rather than for personal ties to highly ranked officials. Public schools hired certified teachers with university diplomas. Curricula were standardized, approved by higher-ranking bodies, and arranged in uniform age-graded levels. Modern schools thus became bureaucracies.

After World War II, governments across Canada saw education as increasingly necessary for economic prosperity and the development of individual citizens. Consequently, they gave public high schools a new mandate: to retain as many youth for as many years as possible. Seeing only a few students as suitable for advanced education became passé. A new norm emerged: Virtually everyone ought to complete high school. Those who did not were to be deemed either deviant or proof of a failing system. The big challenge for schools, then, was how to translate these new ideals into new realities.

The expanded mission for schooling transformed secondary schools within a generation. School officials interpreted their mandate as delivering a broadly comparable education to all students. They further standardized schooling, from physical plant, to teacher training, to curricula. Authority and power were increasingly wielded in distant hierarchies rather than in local communities, an approach that has been dubbed, somewhat derisively, as the "one best system" (Tyack, 1974), faulted for being indifferent to the needs of individual pupils. Critics commonly portrayed schools as resembling nineteenth-century industrial factories, a "one-size-fits-all" institution.

But with a new mandate, schools needed to devise ways to motivate an increasingly wide range of students. That was not easy. In earlier times, high schools could simply steer students who were disinterested in academic work into jobs. But now schools were expected to retain the vast bulk of youth, including those with learning disabilities or little academic ambition. Since teachers encountered many youths who found academic work neither appealing nor absorbing, the big challenge for modern secondary schools was to accommodate a wide range of student aptitude, preparedness, abilities, and motivation than any high school had ever faced before. Again, that was not easy. Unlike the monetary incentives that some organizations offer their employees, the incentives that schools offer their students can be weak. Their most obvious reward is a grade—the prime currency for higher-education admissions. But for the "forgotten half"—youth who do not seek studies beyond high school—grades can be nearly useless. Schools have other organizational constraints too. Teachers would love to have students who enroll on a fully voluntary basis, but with truancy laws, many students attend school only through compulsion. Many teachers want to deal individually with students, but current funding levels force most classes to consist of 20 to 30 students. As it stands, teachers face large classes of captive students with greatly varying abilities and levels of motivation.

This has been the core challenge for reformers. **Progressive pedagogy,** rooted in the ideas of John Dewey in the early twentieth century, has been a force in Canadian schools since the 1960s. Progressives do not want students to be merely instrumental toward their schooling but aim instead to nurture intrinsic forms of motivation, to engage students and have them work voluntarily. Modern teachers want to entice students to do their work not just for grades or to evade sanction, but out of true curiosity. Dewey called for schools that catered to the interests of the learner. By having students direct their own learning, schools could unleash students' intrinsic motivation, he reasoned. Over the decades, many reforms have attempted to engage students within the parameters of schools' organizational constraints (Tyack and Cuban, 1995).

Progressives reformed schools by destructuring classrooms, creating curricula with fewer rote and memory-based exercises, and relaxing discipline. Traditional classrooms strictly regulated student talk and movement by arraying student desks in straight rows. But in the 1970s, progressives saw such regimentation as stifling student imaginations. They encouraged more interaction and tolerated some chatting and freer movement in the classroom. They also decorated classrooms, adorning walls with student art work and colourful posters, often next to traditional emblems like the flag. Corporal punishment was largely abandoned in favour of notions of student rights. The binding idea was that departures from traditional schooling were needed to motivate students (see Box 12.3).

After witnessing these changes, sociologists in the 1980s offered a different take on bureaucratic schools (Powell, Farrar, and Cohen, 1985). In their eyes, decades of reform had made schools more like "shopping malls" than factories. They were struck by the transformation of schools into human service organizations that strove to accommodate their students. Schools became mall-like, they argued, by differentiating courses by degree of difficulty and creating electives to cater to student choice. They created "specialty shops" for students with different abilities, whether "gifted," ESL, or specially-able. Schools bolstered extracurricular activities and devised services to address a wide variety of social, physical, and emotional problems. Educators became sensitized to different kinds of learning styles, as proclaimed by theories of "multiple intelligences," which claim that student ability in, say, dance, should be valued as much as student ability in math (Gardiner, 1999; see Table 12.4).

The theory of multiple intelligence was developed by Dr. Howard Gardner, who contends that the

BOX 12.3   FREE SCHOOLS

"Free schools" took the experimental attitude of the progressives much further by de-structuring *all* aspects of schooling. Inspired by Summerhill, an English private school founded in the 1920s, free schools rocketed to prominence in the 1960s and early 1970s, when hundreds of them were opened across North America. These schools were founded on the belief that only self-motivated, self-regulated, and self-evaluated education could nurture true learning. In many free schools, daily activities were chosen by students. There was no mandatory attendance. Most school exercises were optional. Standard methods of evaluating students with grades or report cards were condemned, since true learning was thought to be too personal to be measured, and since grading could create power inequities between staff and students.

Free schools were to be pressure-free places for students to develop their own interests and talents, without any compulsion to compete with others or to comply with some external standard. Yet despite generating an incredible amount of excitement, most free schools closed in a few short years. Without the benefit of clear and enforceable rules for student conduct, many became unmanageable, and teachers quickly became disillusioned and fatigued. Lacking the bureaucratic trappings of education, such as standardized curricula, certified teachers, timetables, or formal courses, the public grew skeptical of whether they were "schools" at all, and therefore free schools appeared to be illegitimate in the eyes of politicians. Some survived in the form of "alternative schools." Operated by public boards of education, these schools are less structured than regular schools but still use mandatory rules of attendance and approved curricula.

"Free schools," popular in the 1960s and 1970s, were so unstructured that many people questioned whether they were schools at all.
SOURCE: ©Roger Hutchings/Alamy.

traditional notion of intelligence based on I.Q. testing is an overly narrow model of human potential. Gardner instead proposes that there are eight different kinds of intelligence. Some Canadian schools have embraced this theory and are designing curricula to match each type of intelligence. By doing so they illustrate how schools are attempting to accommodate a wide range of student needs.

Although secondary schools in the past had openly promoted academic achievement, the shopping-mall high school eased expectations. Mastery of core subjects was no longer expected from all students.

TABLE 12.4   THE THEORY OF MULTIPLE INTELLIGENCES

INTELLIGENCE	END-STATES	CORE COMPONENTS
Logical mathematical	Scientist, mathematician	Sensitivity to, and capacity to discern, logical or numerical patterns; ability to handle long chains of reasoning
Linguistic	Poet, journalist	Sensitivity to sounds, rhythms, and meanings of words; sensitivity to the different functions of language
Musical	Composer, violinist	Abilities to produce and appreciate rhythm, pitch, and timbre; appreciation of the forms of musical expressiveness
Spatial	Navigator, sculptor	Capacities to perceive the visual-spatial world accurately and to perform transformations on one's initial perceptions
Bodily kinesthetic	Dancer, athlete	Abilities to control one's body movements and to handle objects skillfully
Interpersonal	Therapist, salesperson	Capacities to discern and respond appropriately to the moods, temperaments, motivations, and desires of other people
Intrapersonal	Person with detailed, accurate self-knowledge	Access to one's own feelings and the ability to discriminate among them and draw upon them to guide behavior, knowledge of one's own strengths, weaknesses, desires, and intelligences
Naturalist	Biologist, naturalist	Abilities to recognize and categorize objects and processes in nature

SOURCE: Adapted from Gardner, H. and Hatch, T., 1989, "Multiple intelligences go to school: Educational implications of the theory of multiple intelligences," *Educational Researcher*, 18(8), 4–10, American Educational Research Association.

Students who desired a more enriched curricula could still find it, and lower-achieving students could pass from grade to grade in return for little more than orderly attendance. High schools had evolved unwritten rules about how tough certain courses should be. These informal rules unofficially designated elective courses to be easier than required math and science courses. Teachers in the latter subjects could legitimately demand much effort and time, but other teachers could face rebellion from students, parents, and even administrators if they dared to expect anything comparable.

The idea of the shopping-mall high school was introduced in the mid 1980s and it accurately depicted how schools were then striving to accommodate students. This effort has since sparked controversy, however. Over the past decade, educators have been stung by emerging demands to raise standards and become "accountable." Canadian policymakers are promoting higher standards as they understand them, usually in the guise of standardized performance indicators.

Today, critics are claiming that public schools are too bureaucratic. For instance, Chubb and Moe (1990) see public bureaucracies as aloof and slow to change, and requiring a mechanism to inject quality-orienting dynamics. These reformers condemn public education as an inefficient monopoly that is unresponsive to its clients, and they hail "market" reforms for their potential to create competitive pressures, similar to those faced by for-profit businesses. Under the banner of "school choice," these reformers want to force schools to survive only by collecting funds directly from fee-paying clients. The imperative to attract clients, they contend, has many advantages. It can match the tastes of parents and educators. It can encourage new providers to enter the educational field, bringing innovation to schooling, and devising customized programs for their clients. And it can boost school performance in the form of standardized test scores, since market-based schools will be presumably motivated to raise their quality to attract customers (Ouchi, 2003).

School choice is indeed growing in Canada in at least two forms. One creates more choice within the public school system, expanding the menu of programs beyond standard school offerings. For instance, the City of Edmonton has largely reinvented its school system by offering a smorgasbord of pedagogical choice and offering a variety of special-theme schools, including those that specialize in sports, science, language, arts, intensive academics, alternative pedagogy, and multiple intelligences (Taylor and Woollard, 2003). Another Alberta initiative has been to create "charter schools," independently run but government funded, each pursuing a special theme, whether ESL, traditional academics, Suzuki music and philosophy, science and math, or programs aimed at gifted, Aboriginal, female, or at-risk students (Bosetti, 2001).

The second type of choice is private schooling. The proportion of Canadian students enrolled in private schools is growing, particularly in affluent locales. For instance, in Toronto, 10 percent of all students are enrolled in private schools, a rate higher than the 7 percent national average (Davies and Quirke, 2005). More than 60 nonreligious private schools have opened in the city in the past 15 years. These schools attempt to appeal to their customers by developing specialty programs and small classes. Almost all offer some sort of specialty, creating an astonishing array of programs and philosophies of teaching, each seeking a "niche" in a competitive marketplace. Similarly, homeschooling is growing in Canada, as more parents are turning to themselves to provide educational options for their children (Arai, 2000; Aurini and Davies, 2005).

Are Canadian families embracing more competitive educational strategies? Traditionally, private education has been reserved either for elites or for members of religious minorities. But various forms of private education are now expanding. The proportion of Canadian students enrolled in private schools grew from 5 percent to 7 percent over the past decade. The number of Montessori schools is growing (Aurini, 2002). The tutoring industry has also undergone a staggering transformation over the past 30 years, with the number of tutoring businesses growing between 200 percent and 500 percent in major Canadian cities (Aurini and Davies, 2004). In 2003, a quarter of Ontario parents reported that they had hired tutors for their children sometime in the previous three years (Livingstone, Hart, and Davie, 2003).

Although these private alternatives certainly create more variety in education, there is still no evidence that they offer higher-quality schooling than regular public schools do, controlling for the socioeconomic advantages of their students. Indeed, rather than being more academically intensive, many of these schools have strong "shopping-mall" and "progressive" elements, like those that have inspired public educators for decades. Proud of their customized offerings, they prize pedagogical freedom and intimate relations above all. Yet, as tuition-charging schools, they lack any mandate to ensure equal access. Despite good intentions, only wealthier families can afford them. These schools illustrate the tension between satisfying yearnings for choice and providing equity.

Indeed, a flip side of market reasoning is that the customer should pay. Such thinking has permitted Canadian universities to deregulate tuition fees for their professional schools, such as dentistry, law, medicine, and M.B.A. programs. Administrators of these professional programs believe student demand will not be deterred by soaring costs, since professional degrees often lead to high incomes, so they have raised fees well above the Canadian average of approximately $4000, sometimes charging in excess of $20 000 for a year's tuition. Although these fee hikes may not have discouraged student demand, they do appear to be influencing the composition of students in these programs. A recent study suggests that when programs deregulate their fees, they become more likely to accept students who have highly educated parents and to have students from poorer backgrounds who are eligible for bursaries and scholarships. The losers in the process appear to be middle-class students, who lack advantageous family backgrounds, yet are often ineligible for income-contingent loans and bursaries (Frenette, 2005).

CONCLUSION

The enterprise of Canadian schooling has grown immensely. We all attend high school, most of us graduate, half now go on to postsecondary school, and many will return to some sort of educational institution later in life, as ideologies of "lifelong education" become reality. But what has been the impact of this monumental expansion? Schools partially compensate for great pre-existing inequalities in student preparedness, but their selection role ensures that expansion does not bring greater equity, at least along socioeconomic lines. Further, the singular socializing impact of school in our lives actually shrinks. School becomes a weaker socializing agent as it integrates into our lives, competing with many other agents. Some forms of schooling have become more competitive. Prestigious programs that offer the most recognition and best rewards are increasingly exclusive. Other programs are more accommodating, treating students in more progressive ways and offering more choice than ever before.

These trends remind us of the paradox discussed at the outset of this chapter. Canadian schools now serve unprecedented numbers of students for longer periods of their lives, yet they are a lightning rod for more and more criticism. This is a prime instance of "disenchantment" in Max Weber's definition: As schooling becomes ever more central to society in the modern era, it loses its "magical" quality to command deference. As all citizens attend school for most of their youth, more are familiar with schooling and have higher expectations for what schools should do for them. Education has become a "motherhood" issue that everyone supports in the abstract, yet in the process it loses its overtones of elite rituals, aristocratic cultures, and time-honoured pageantry. The caps and gowns, the great halls, and Latin-inscribed coats of arms have largely disappeared, replaced by rationalized bureaucracies that merely promise access to labour markets.

This disenchantment shouldn't cloud a sunnier accomplishment: School systems now offer unparalleled opportunities for individuals. Schooling helps extend human rights and literacy to even the poorest segments of society. Who today reminisces for bygone eras in which schooling was a privilege for the few? Such ideas now provoke a sense of outrage and are rightfully seen to deny basic rights. Schooling may be demystified, yet we cannot manage without it.

SUMMARY

1. The selection function of school systems is being transferred from secondary to postsecondary levels. In past decades, secondary-level streaming played an important gate-keeping role, so an adolescent's life-chances were shaped largely by his or her performance in high school. However, as higher education expands, life-chances are determined increasingly by where a person graduates in a stratified structure of higher education.

2. As more Canadians attain advanced levels of education, formerly valuable credentials like the high-school diploma have become devalued. Devaluation generates demand for more schooling, leading to a spiral of educational expansion as groups jockey for advantages in the labour market.

3. A pattern of inequality exists in Canadian school attainment. Along social class lines, students from more affluent backgrounds continue to enjoy considerable advantages. In terms of gender, women now outpace men on many indicators, though considerable gender segregation remains in certain fields of study. The legacy of conquest for Aboriginals and their history of discrimination and segregation continue to be manifest in schools, while changing immigration selection policies have created a partial reversal in patterns of attainment for other racial groups.

4. Today's moral education is less religious and explicit than before. Schools now mostly aim to have students understand key issues, rather than having a hard-edged prescriptive tone. The hidden curriculum continues to emphasize the orderly completion of tasks, punctuality, and neatness. But today's schools have a more indulgent quality than they did in the past, trying to shore up students' self-esteem and capture rather than command their interests.

5. Canadian schools have changed from informal institutions that wielded traditional authority to legal-rational bureaucracies. In the latter form, progressive educators have pursued strategies to spark intrinsic learning and cater to students in ever-more accommodating ways. In the 1970s, this involved lessening teacher power in favour of students. Today, it sometimes involves the use of market-like mechanisms to treat students as if they are "customers."

QUESTIONS TO CONSIDER

1. Compare your schooling experience so far with that of one your grandparents by using the themes of selection, accommodation, competition, and sponsored and contest mobility.

2. From what you've experienced in school, how would you motivate students to be effective learners? What organizational reforms might best inspire students? Be honest and give examples.

3. Observe a classroom. Do you see socializing messages in operation? Cite examples. Try to sort out the socializing influences of schools from those of families, neighbourhoods, labour markets, and peer groups.

GLOSSARY

Contest mobility is a form of educational competition in which most youths are grouped into the same school and exposed to the same curriculum, and in which relatively large numbers are directed to higher education.

Credential inflation takes place when labour-market competition encourages individuals to acquire schooling and employers raise required credential levels for reasons that are not connected to their needs for skilled employees.

The **hidden curriculum** comprises elements of school content, such as rules, procedures, structures and norms, that can shape students in covert ways.

Human capital theory emphasizes how schooling can enhance productive skills and thereby generate wealth for both individuals and society.

Professionalization is the process by which an occupation attempts to raise its social standing, often including the creation of formal educational credentials.

Progressive pedagogy is an educational movement that emphasizes student-directed learning, less structured curricula, and an emphasis on inspiring students to be intrinsically motivated in their studies.

Selection is the process by which the structure of schooling feeds into broader patterns of social stratification.

Sponsored mobility is a form of educational competition in which relatively few youths are selected early in life to enter elite universities.

SUGGESTED READING

Baker, David, and Gerald LeTendre. (2005). *National Differences, Global Similarities: World Culture and the Future of Schooling.* Stanford: Stanford University Press. An international examination of schooling trends, focusing on the curriculum and student achievement.

Livingstone, David W. (2004). *The Education-Jobs Gap: Underemployment or Economic Democracy*, 2nd ed. Toronto: Garamond Press. In response to current claims about our knowledge economy and its skill shortages, this book argues that many people's skills are unrecognized and underused in today's economy.

Tyack, David, and Larry Cuban. (1995). *Tinkering toward Utopia: A Century of Public School Reform*. Cambridge, Mass.: Harvard University Press. This book presents a history of the past century of education reform and was the first recipient of the annual Harvard University Press prize for a book on education and society.

WEB RESOURCES

Companion Web Site for This Book

http://www.newsociety5e.nelson.com

Begin by clicking on the Student Resources section of the website. Next, select the chapter you are studying from the pull-down menu. From the Student Resources page, you have easy access to InfoTrac College Edition® and other resources, such as the Glossary and Flashcards. The website also has many useful tips to aid you in your study of sociology.

InfoTrac College Edition Search Terms

Visit http://www.infotrac-college.com for access to more than 20 million articles from nearly 6000 sources when doing your online research.

ThomsonNOW™

http://hed.nelson.com

This online diagnostic tool identifies each student's unique needs with a Pretest that generates a personalized Study Plan for each chapter, helping students focus on concepts they are having the most difficulty mastering. Students then take a Posttest after reading the chapter to measure their understanding of the material. An Instructor Gradebook is available to track and monitor student progress.

CHAPTER THIRTEEN

Religion

In this chapter you will learn that

· Religion has been studied by sociologists since the beginnings of sociology.

· Religion has both individual and social components—people display a wide range of levels of commitment, but groups play a major role in instilling and sustaining personal religiosity.

· Since religious groups are organizations, they can best be understood by using organizational concepts and frameworks.

· For the vast majority of people, religious commitment and involvement are rooted in social institutions, particularly the family.

· Religion's influence on individuals tends to be noteworthy but not unique, while its broader role in most societies is to support social structure and culture.

· Despite the problems of some groups, religion's future in Canada and elsewhere is secure, grounded in ongoing spiritual interests and needs.

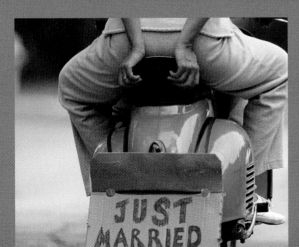

Reginald W. Bibby
UNIVERSITY OF LETHBRIDGE

INTRODUCTION

Religion is very much alive today. In recent years, religion has received worldwide attention in such varied developments as the death of Pope John Paul II and the phenomenal sales of Dan Brown's *The Da Vinci Code*. Religion's presence and importance is blatant in the conflict, terrorism, and peacemaking efforts in the Middle East. In 2006 it was centre-stage in the clash of values and perhaps even civilizations as European countries and their leaders experienced the protests and threats of Muslims for allowing their newspapers to publish cartoon depictions of Muhammad (Ghafour, 2006). Even more daunting in the light of September 11, 2001, has been the 1998 directive of "fundamentalist"/"extremist" Osama bin Laden that "in compliance with God's order . . . every Muslim who believes in God and wishes to be rewarded" is to "kill the Americans and plunder their money wherever and whenever they find it"—thinking that in turn has been widely condemned by most Muslim leaders.

In North America, religion's presence is also readily evident in the God-laced responses to such militancy on the part of American presidents, such as George W. Bush, whose supporters frequently include large numbers of the so-called "Christian Right." Apart from its links to global issues, religion in America is pervasive. Attendance at services is extremely high and the majority of people say that religion is very important to them. The organizational health of American religion can be seen in the emergence of a growing number of very large and influential "megachurches" that function as religious multinational corporations—spreading the message of "how to do ministry" to other parts of the world, including Canada. Spirituality has joined religion in going public and become part of so-called pop culture, read about in *The Celestine Prophecy*, talked about on *Oprah*, and brought to life in television programs, such as *Touched by an Angel*, and films ranging from John Travolta's *Michael* to Mel Gibson's *The Passion of the Christ*.

In Canada, beyond such media offerings, the reality of religion is readily apparent in the tendency of the vast majority of people to continue to identify with a religious tradition; in the growing numbers of individuals identifying with faiths that include Islam, Hinduism, Sikhism, and Buddhism; in the widespread interest in spirituality; in debates about same-sex marriage; in the efforts of Catholics and mainline

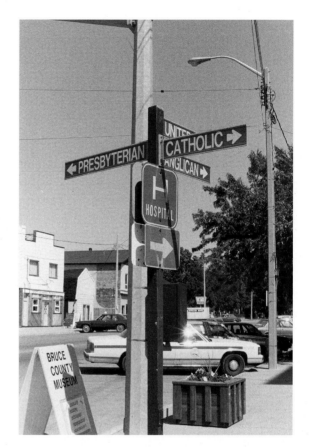

Contrary to the opinion of some people, religious belief is not disappearing in Canada. In fact, in urban areas most people have many options for worship.
SOURCE: Dick Hemingway.

Protestants to resolve problems relating to the legacy of residential schools; and in a newly elected national leader ending his 2006 victory speech with the words "God bless Canada."

Many early social scientists were convinced that religion's days were numbered, that it would be just a short time before it was discarded in favour of science. Through the 1990s, the widespread consensus was that religion's influence was declining and that Canadians and people in most other technologically advanced countries were leaving religion behind—although the United States stood out as a puzzling anomaly.

We now know that such observers were wrong. In the early years of the twenty-first century, religion lives on, embraced by large numbers of people in virtually all cultures, however "advanced" or "nonadvanced." Moreover, interest in religion and spirituality is actually on the upswing in many parts of the world, including North America, Russia, and Asia.

In many Islamic countries, it is not clear that the importance of religion has ever been in doubt. Today, religion is frequently associated with conflict and division. But it also continues to bring meaning, sustenance, and hope to billions of people.

I begin the chapter by taking a brief look at what some of the early and influential social scientists had to say about religion, and then discuss how sociologists go about studying religion in both its individual and group forms. After clarifying what sociologists mean by religion, I look at "how much of it" we have in Canada and proceed to examine its sources and consequences—what kinds of factors contribute to people being religious and the influence that religion has on both individuals and societies. In concluding the chapter, I reflect on the kinds of religious developments we can expect in the foreseeable future.

I'll be giving particular attention to Canada, in large part because I have spent much of my life examining religious developments here and have some fairly unique research findings I can tell you about. However, while focusing on Canada, I will keep my eyes on the rest of the world, starting with the United States.

SOCIOLOGY AND RELIGION

A number of years ago, an American evangelist who was holding services in Edmonton was asked by a fairly strident television interviewer, "How do you know there is a God?" The evangelist immediately responded, "Because I talked to Him five minutes ago." It was an interesting claim but one that a sociologist is not in a position to verify. A basic rule of science is that "what counts" as real is what we can detect through our senses—what we refer to as "empirical" knowledge. In contrast, proponents of religion have traditionally asserted that the world we know through the senses is only part of a greater reality that, because of the limitations of sense perception, can only be known through faith.

In principle, science and religion are compatible. Science limits itself to what is perceivable, and religion maintains that reality includes the nonperceivable. Conflict between the two should only arise when one oversteps its boundaries and invades the other's territory.

Still, for the most part, science is in the driver's seat. As Émile Durkheim (1965 [1912]: 479) pointed out many years ago, religion "can affirm nothing that [science] denies, deny nothing that it affirms." Try though it might, religion cannot overrule science in refuting basic evolutionary claims or dismissing sound medical diagnoses. At the same time, since science is limited to conclusions about the observable, it too can only go so far. Sociologists cannot address the evangelist's claim that he had actually spoken to God, anymore than it can evaluate the claim that a person whose cancer has gone into remission was healed by God.

Sociology consequently suffers from one serious methodological limitation in studying religion: It cannot probe the supernatural claims that religion so often is about. Sociologists nonetheless can offer considerable insight into "the observable part" of religion. For example, they can examine

- Who tends to think they have experienced God
- Who believes in life after death and what individuals think will happen when they die
- The extent to which people have spiritual needs, and what they mean by "spirituality"
- How many and what kinds of people are involved in religious groups
- The impact that religious involvement has on individuals and societies

In short, sociologists cannot address everything when it comes to religion; but they can address much, without getting caught up in the issue of religion's ultimate truth or falsity. Max Weber summed up the focus of sociological explorations into religion this way: "The essence of religion," he wrote, is not the concern of sociologists, since "we make it our task to study the conditions and effects of a particular type of social behaviour" (1963 [1922]: 1). For our purposes, whether or not religious ideas are true is not as important as the fact they are *believed* to be true. As W.I. Thomas and Dorothy Swaine Thomas noted in their classic theorem, if we define things as real, they are real in their consequences (Thomas and Znaniecki, 1918: 79). The very fact that religious ideas are held means they potentially can have an important impact on individuals and social life.

THEORETICAL TRADITIONS

Three early theorists have had a strong influence on the sociology of religion: Karl Marx, Émile Durkheim, and Max Weber.

MARX AND CONFLICT

Karl Marx grew up in a Jewish environment but came to believe that religion is a human creation. Using the language of the day, Marx (1970 [1843]: 131) wrote: "Man makes religion; religion does not make man." He argued that man has "found only his own reflection in the fantastic reality of heaven, where he sought a supernatural being," and that being religious characterized "the self-consciousness and self-esteem of a man who has either not yet gained himself or has lost himself again."

It has been argued that we can resolve undesirable conditions by either changing them or reinterpreting them. Peasants, slaves, and the marginalized in our day theoretically can rise up and revolt; they also can minimize the importance of "this world" by looking heavenward, singing spirituals, and dreaming of walking streets of gold after they die. According to Marx, religion constitutes the latter response, resulting in people who are economically and politically deprived redefining reality, rather than changing their oppressive conditions. Religion, Marx wrote, soothes the disadvantaged like a narcotic—functioning as "the opium of the people" (Marx, 1970 [1843]: 131), in the process blinding them to the inequalities at hand and bottling up their creative energies. So it is that some observers today would argue that many socially and financially deprived individuals who are unable or unwilling to play an active role in altering social conditions or even their own lives substitute religious status for social status. A taxi driver by day is the head of a temple committee by night; the housekeeper in the hotel during the week is the star soloist in the church choir on the weekend. Religious status supplants social status; the next world supplants this world.

But Marx did not see such a redefining of reality as a chance happening. On the contrary, he maintained that those who hold power encourage religious belief among the masses as a subtle tool in the process of exploiting and subjugating them. Aligned with the interests of the dominant few, religion serves to hold in check the potentially explosive tensions of a society. Consistent with his thinking, respected social historian H. Richard Niebuhr (1957 [1929]: 51) has been among those who have claimed, for example, that a widely held belief among nineteenth-century American slave owners was that religion helped African Americans to become "better" slaves. He cites one advocate of "negro missions" who asserted that "slaves well-instructed in the Christian faith were less likely to develop revolutionary inclinations than the half-educated, such as [revolt leader] Nat Turner."

Historically, said Marx, society and religion were so intertwined that attacks on feudalism, for example, were attacks on the church, while revolutionary social and political doctrines were simultaneously viewed as theological heresies (Marx and Engels, 1963: 132). We might argue that we see similar fusion between politics and religion today, not only in theocracies such as Iran but also in such a country as the United States, where the dominant religion, according to some observers, is "the American Way of Life," supported by the country's primary religious groups. We'll return to this issue shortly.

For Marx (1970 [1843]: 131), religion was an inadequate salve for a sick society—"the sigh of the oppressed creature, the heart of a heartless world and the soul of soulless conditions." When the sickness was remedied, there would be no need for the salve. Using another metaphor, Marx (1970 [1843]: 132) wrote that his criticism of religion was an attempt to remove "the imaginary flowers from the chain, not so that man shall bear the chain without fantasy or consultation, but so that he shall cast off the chain and gather the living flowers." Freed from the panacea of religion, individuals would be able "to think, act, and fashion their reality with illusions lost and reason regained" (Marx, 1970 [1843]: 132).

If you are someone who is personally religious, you understandably are not particularly excited to have Marx suggest that you may well be disadvantaged in some way and need to open your eyes and give your energies to changing your current situation. But before you reject his thinking altogether, it is worth noting that, at minimum, Marx seems to offer considerable insight, even today, into why some people join extreme religious groups that downplay the importance of this life—encouraging them to give up what possessions they have and, in some instances, give up their lives as well.

DURKHEIM AND COLLECTIVITY

Émile Durkheim was the son of a rabbi but was raised in a Catholic educational tradition. He himself was an atheist and an anti-cleric, who believed that a scientific understanding of society has the potential to raise the quality of social life.

In his classic work *The Elementary Forms of the Religious Life* (1965 [1915]), Durkheim argued that religion's origin is social. People who live in a community come to share common sentiments, and as a result a **collective conscience** is formed. When they gather together, they have a feeling of being in the presence of something beyond themselves that is experienced by each member, yet is greater than the sum of their individual consciences. The feeling is not unlike "the electricity in the air" we experience at an exciting playoff hockey game or a big rock concert, where that feeling "out there" seems to transcend the sum of individual emotions. Durkheim maintained that the experience is so vivid that people have felt the need to label it. In reality, Durkheim asserted, "God" is the group experiencing itself. The experience *is* real, he argues; it's just that it isn't what those involved think it is.

Once people experience such an alleged supernatural reality, they proceed to designate some related objects as **sacred** and others as **profane.** Christians have accorded special status to the cross, the Bible, and holy water, in contrast to almost everything else.

Symbols of the sacred are many and diverse: Jews have accorded sacred status to the Torah and Star of David, Muslims to the Qur'an and the Saudi Arabian city of Mecca, Hindus to the Vedas and the sacred syllable "Aum"(or "Om"). In Durkheim's view, religious beliefs articulate the nature of the sacred and its symbols, and religious rites provide guidelines as to how people should act in the presence of the sacred. So it is that Muslims, for example, are expected to pray at specific times five times a day, facing Mecca, and to make a pilgrimage to Mecca at least once in their lifetime; Hindus offer daily devotional prayers in the morning and evening, sometimes accompanied by ritual bathing. Sikhs, when they enter their temples, must cover their heads and remove their shoes, and, where the opportunity is provided, wash their hands and feet.

Because all groups feel the need to uphold and reaffirm their collective sentiments, people come together as what he refers to as a "church." According to Durkheim (1965 [1912]: 62–63), "the idea of religion is inseparable from that of the Church," since it is "an eminently collective thing." Even when religion

In Durkheim's view, religious rites provide guidelines as to how people should act in the presence of the sacred. Muslims, for example, are expected to pray at specific times five times a day, facing Mecca, and to make a pilgrimage to Mecca at least once in their lifetime.
SOURCE: Shutterstock.

seems to be entirely a matter of individual conscience, it still is nourished by social sources. Besides meeting needs at the individual level, he claimed, religion creates and reinforces social solidarity. Collective life is consequently both *the source* and *the product* of religion. Accordingly, Durkheim (1965 [1912]: 62) defined religion as "a unified system of beliefs and practices relative to sacred things . . . which unite into one single moral community called a Church, all those who adhere to them."

Durkheim (1965 [1912]: 475–76) observed that "we are going through a stage of transition and moral mediocrity. The great things of the past which filled our fathers with enthusiasm do not excite the same ardour in us." He added poetically, "The gods are growing old or are already dead, and others are not yet born." But despite the problems of traditional Catholicism in particular, Durkheim didn't believe that religion would disappear: "There are no gospels which are immortal, but neither is there any reason for believing that humanity is incapable of inventing new ones." The dominant groups and forms of expression might change, but the social sources that give rise to religion obviously will remain and, with them, religion. Durkheim also contended that there will always be a place for religious explanations. The reason? Science is fragmentary and incomplete, advancing too slowly—life cannot wait. Religion will therefore continue to have an important "gap-filling" role.

Durkheim's legacy has been important. You don't have to agree with his assertion that the gods are socially created to realize that God and ethical conceptions, for example, frequently reflect social and individual characteristics. In fact, an age-old concern among people valuing faith has been the inclination of humans to create the gods in their own images. What's more, Durkheim's acknowledgment that science moves too slowly for many of us anticipated the ongoing "market" for alternative explanations on the part of religious leaders and just about anyone else, including—to use just one illustration—psychics. The vast market for explanations of the unknown is suggested by the fact that, as of 2006, the Yahoo website was listing some 7 million entries for "Psychics"!

WEBER AND IDEAS

Max Weber was born in Germany. His grandparents were Protestants who had been refugees from Catholic persecution and eventually became suc-

cessful in business. He was interested in religion from an early age but never shared the deep commitment of his Calvinist mother. His background was to be reflected in one of his most important works.

Weber's interest in the origin and nature of modern capitalism led him into extensive debate with Marx's ideas and stimulated much of his work in the sociology of religion. Unlike Marx and Durkheim, Weber had little interest in the question of whether religion is ultimately true or false. Rather, he maintained that religion, in addition to having a supernatural component, is largely oriented toward this world. As a result, religious ideas and behaviour should frequently be evident in everyday conduct. In *The Protestant Ethic and the Spirit of Capitalism* (1958 [1904–05]), for example, Weber examined the possibility that the moral tone that characterizes capitalism in the Western world—the *Protestant ethic*—can be traced back to the influence of the Protestant Reformation. His hope was that his work would contribute "to the understanding of the manner in which ideas become effective forces in history" (Weber, 1958 [1904–05]: 90).

Weber took the position that ideas, regardless of whether they are objectively true or false, represent a person's definition of reality and therefore have the potential to influence behaviour. Accordingly, he emphasized the need to interpret action by understanding the motives of the actor (a method he called *Verstehen*, or understanding). To achieve such awareness, he said, researchers should place themselves in the roles of those being studied.

Weber understood the need to study diverse societies, present and past, in order to examine culture's influence on religion. He therefore embarked on comparative and historical studies of religion and its relationship to social and economic life in China, India, and ancient Israel. A compilation of his writings, *Sociology of Religion* (1963 [1922]), illustrates the way that Weber approached religion. He noted that god-conceptions are strongly related to the economic, social, and political conditions in which people live. The gods of light and warmth and of rain and Earth have been closely related to practical economic needs; heavenly gods that rule the celestial order have been related to the more abstract problems of death and fate. In political conquest, the gods of the conquered are fused with the gods of the conqueror and reappear with revised characteristics. Furthermore, the growth of **monotheism** (belief in one god) is related to goals of political unification.

Beyond the social sources of the gods, Weber dealt with such major themes as the relationship between religion and social class and the nature of religious organizations. He reflected on religious leadership and the important process whereby a personal following is transformed into a permanent congregation, which he referred to as "routinization." He noted that different groups in society vary in their inclination to be religious: Peasants are religious when they are threatened; the nobility find religion beneath their honour; the middle class sees religion largely in ethical terms; the working class supplants religion with other ideologies.

Over the years I have found that students, whether religious or otherwise, appreciate the way in which Weber attempted to take religion seriously and not become embroiled in attacking it or dismissing it. His approach has become fairly typical in the contemporary study of religion. Still, along with Weber, some of the insights of Marx and Durkheim have remained appealing.

THE NATURE OF RELIGION

Are you religious? If you are like many Canadians, you may promptly say, "Yes" or "No, I'm not," perhaps adding, "I'm not religious but I am spiritual." The term "religion" is widely used, but obviously people have different ideas in mind when they use it. Up to now, I have been assuming that we have a consensual understanding of what we mean by "religion." But before we go much further, and particularly before we look at research into religion, we need to clarify what we actually mean by the term.

"Religion" can be a blurry concept. Many people use it in a functional sense: What people value most becomes their religion—money, career, family, sports. A lame story has a young boy telling a religious doorknocker, "My mother is RC; my dad is NHL." The problem with such functional definitions of religion, Peter Berger (1974: 129) once observed, is that they become like grey cats on a dark night. If religion is everything, then it is nothing.

In a pioneering work published more than four decades ago, Charles Glock and Rodney Stark (1965) offered some thoughts that continue to be helpful. They pointed out that, in defining religion for social scientific purposes, we should begin by recognizing that humans develop systems of meaning to interpret the world. Some systems—commonly referred to as "religions," including Christianity, Judaism, and Islam—have a supernatural referent. Others, such as a science-based system (scientism) or political "isms" (communism, fascism), do not. The latter systems, they suggested, might be viewed as human-centred or **humanist perspectives,** in contrast to *religious perspectives*, which are succinctly referred to here as **religions.**

The two types of perspectives differ on one critical point: Religion is concerned with discovering life's meaning, and humanist perspectives are concerned with making life meaningful. Humanist Bertrand Russell stated the difference well: "I do not think that life in general has any purpose. It just happened. But individual human beings have purposes" (in Cogley, 1968: 171). Religious perspectives suggest that our existence has meaning, preceding that which we, as humans, decide to give it. In contrast, humanist perspectives assume that life has no "ultimate meaning" and therefore focus on giving it meaning.

The dichotomy is not perfect; some would say that such criteria might lead us to see Buddhism, for example, as a humanist perspective. Here I would simply defer to commonly understood thinking and place Buddhism in its familiar religion category for the sake of communication. However, for the most part, I think the religious perspectives/humanist perspectives approach is helpful.

PERSONAL RELIGIOSITY

Now that I've clarified things a bit, let's go back to the pointed question: How religious are you? And to be less pointed, how religious are Canadians as a whole? Sociologists have not believed that the answers are arbitrary or simply subjective. They have given much effort to finding ways of defining and measuring what they have called **personal religiosity.**

Much of the early research used one of three basic indicators to determine the religiosity of a person. All three assumed group involvement: identification, membership, and attendance. In surveys, people were asked questions, such as "What is your religious preference?" "Do you belong to a congregation?" and "How often do you attend religious services?" People who indicated that they had a religious preference, belonged to a local group, or attended services with regularity were viewed as religious.

However, as you know well, simply knowing that someone is "Protestant" or "Hindu," "Jewish" or

"Mennonite," tells us very little about a person's actual commitment to his or her faith. Similarly, people might be group members, but members may be may be active or inactive, committed or uncommitted. And service attendance, although measuring participation in a group, excludes people who could be very committed yet, for such reasons as age, health, work schedule, and geographical location, are not overly active in a religious organization.

Since the 1960s, social scientists have responded to the limitations of these three measures by viewing religious commitment as having a variety of dimensions. In one of the more helpful frameworks devised, Stark and Glock (1968) suggested that the religions of the world typically expect their most devoted followers to hold key beliefs, engage in certain practices, have supernatural experiences, and be aware of the central tenets of their faiths. Stark and Glock refer to

these belief, practice, experience, and knowledge components of commitment as **dimensions of religiosity.** It is not enough to believe *or* practise *or* experience *or* know; all four traits are expected of the committed.

My ongoing Project Canada national surveys, which were launched in 1975 and have been carried out every five years since then, provide comprehensive data on personal religiosity in this country. The surveys have found that Canadians exhibit relatively high levels of religious belief, practice, experience, and knowledge (see Table 13.1). Indeed, some eight in ten Canadians say they believe in God, close to seven in ten maintain there is life after death, six in ten acknowledge that they pray privately at least once a month, and about five in ten think they have experienced the presence of God. Almost half also exhibit some basic knowledge of Islam, Judaism, and

TABLE 13.1   RELIGIOUS COMMITMENT ALONG FOUR DIMENSIONS, CANADA, 2005 (IN PERCENTAGE)

DIMENSION	RESPONSE	PERCENTAGE
Believe in God	Yes, I definitely do	49
	Yes, I think so	33
	No, I don't think so	11
	No, I definitely do not	7
Believe in life after death	Yes, I definitely do	36
	Yes, I think so	31
	No, I don't think so	21
	No, I definitely do not	12
Practise private prayer	Daily	27
	Several times a week	11
	About once a week	7
	Once or more times a month	8
	Hardly ever/never	47
Experience God	Yes, I definitely have	26
	Yes, I think so	23
	No, I don't think I have	30
	No, I definitely have not	21
Knowledge	The name of the sacred book of Islam (Qur'an)	53
	The first book in the Old Testament (Genesis)	47
	Who denied Jesus three times? (Peter)	41

SOURCE: Derived from Reginald W. Bibby, *Project Canada 2005 National Survey.*

Christianity. On the surface, then, early twenty-first century Canadians seem to be a fairly religious people.

However, the surveys have also found that although around 50 percent claim to be committed to Christianity or another religion, less than half of the committed demonstrate the belief, practice, experience, and knowledge characteristics that Stark and Glock (1968) saw as central to commitment. Among the other 50 percent of Canadians, about three in ten indicate that they are interested in but not committed to any religion, and the remaining two in ten simply say that they are not religious (Bibby, 1993, 2004a). According to the 2005 Project Canada survey, 25 percent of Canadians say that religion is "very important" to them, with most having fairly conventional ideas of religion in mind. Regional variations are striking, with the levels ranging from a high of about 40 percent in the Atlantic region, through around 30 percent to 35 percent in Ontario and the three Prairie provinces, to lows of 15 percent in British Columbia and 10 percent in Quebec.

An interesting footnote is worth pondering: Pollsters are continually reminding us that Americans are more religious than Canadians (Kiefer, 2004; Ray, 2003; Winseman, 2004). But New Brunswick sociologist Samuel Reimer (1995, 2003) has been arguing recently that we must not overlook an important qualitative difference in religious belief and commitment in the two countries. Reimer maintains that it is easier to be highly committed in the American religious environment than it is in Canada since, in his words, higher levels of religiosity in the United States have "more to do with cultural supports for religiosity than with deeper religious conviction." Since it is more difficult to be religiously committed in Canada, religious devotion, among Canadians, he argues, "is more likely to be based on conviction."

COLLECTIVE RELIGIOSITY

How many times have you heard people say, "I don't have to go to church to be religious"? Increasingly the generalization has been expanded to include temples and synagogues as well. It may be a common argument, but it doesn't have much sociological support.

Most social scientists, beginning officially with Durkheim, have maintained that personal religiosity is highly dependent on **collective religiosity,** or group support of some kind. Such dependence is not unique to religion. It stems from a basic fact of life: The ideas we hold tend to come from our interaction with other people. However creative we might like to think we are, the fact is that most of the ideas we have in our heads right now can be traced back to the people with whom we have been in contact—family, friends, teachers, authors, journalists, and any number of other so-called experts. Moreover, if we are to retain those ideas, they have to be continuously endorsed by at least a few other people whose opinions we value. Ideas are sustained by relationships.

It consequently is not surprising that researchers find that evangelicals, for example, one of the most numerically vibrant "religious families" in the country, have learned that they need to "grow their own and keep their own." They have more children than members of most other groups do, provide them with positive church-life experiences from the time they hit the church nursery, make sure they have youth-friendly programs when they are teens, and encourage them to marry each other—or if worst comes to worst, marry an outsider and bring the partner into the group—and then continue to be part of young adult and adult activities. To fail at any of those three crucial points in the biography of their daughters and sons is to run the risk of seeing them abandon evangelical faith. People cannot hold ideas or commitment for long without a measure of social support.

Seem like a strong claim? Try it on your own biography.

The Church-Sect Typology

Those who have examined religious groups in predominantly Christian settings have recognized two major kinds of organizations. First, there are numerically dominant groupings—the Roman Catholic Church in medieval Europe, the Church of England, the so-called mainline denominations in Canada and the United States (Anglican, United, Presbyterian, Lutheran), and so on. Second, smaller groups have broken away from the dominant bodies. For example, in the sixteenth century, protestant groups, including the Church of England, broke away from the Roman Catholic Church; but Methodists in turn broke away from the Church of England, and the Salvation Army emerged as a breakaway group from the Methodists. Today, additional emerging groups include an array of Baptist and Pentecostal denominations and nondenominational, "grassroots" congregations that are found in virtually every North American city.

From this pattern of dominant groups and breakaway groups, sociologists who try to make sense of religious groups developed an analytical scheme known as the **church-sect typology.** This framework attempted to describe the central characteristics of these two types of organizations, as well as account for the origin and development of sects.

In perhaps its earliest formulation, Max Weber distinguished between church and sect primarily on the basis of theology (churches emphasize works, sects stress faith) and relationship to society (for churches, accommodation; for sects, separation). Weber noted the irony in the sect's development: Initially a spinoff from an established church, the sect gradually evolves into a church itself (Gerth and Mills, 1958). The sect at first is characterized by spontaneity and enthusiasm. In time, however, these traits give way to routinization and institutionalization.

Although the church-sect typology has been used extensively, alternative ways of understanding religious groups have become increasingly popular.

Organizational Approaches

In sociological terms, religious organizations are no different from other social organizations. Therefore, there has been a growing tendency to analyze religious groups by making use of the same frameworks we use in studying social organizations in general.

Led by the work of respected American sociologist Rodney Stark and his associates (Finke and Stark, 1992; Stark and Bainbridge, 1985; Stark and Finke, 2000), a market model for understanding religion has become prominent in recent years. Religious groups are seen as "firms" or "companies" competing for "market share."

- Seen through such eyes, the Roman Catholic, Anglican, and Eastern Orthodox churches are part of multinational corporations; so is the Salvation Army.
- A number of groups, including the United Church and the Pentecostal Assemblies of Canada, are companies that are "Canadian-owned and operated."
- Many smaller evangelical Protestant denominations have been "branch plant" operations of American groups—not unlike "Ford Canada" or

"Wal-Mart Canada"—that, over the years, have become increasingly autonomous. Some other groups, including Presbyterians and some Lutherans and Baptists, have similarly evolved from overseas operations.

- Despite the fact that Jews, Muslims, Hindus, Sikhs, and Buddhists all have worldwide roots and ongoing ties with those roots, none have developed official international or national structures that oversee their Canadian businesses. They have lobby groups and other organizations that address some common interests. But their "business outlets" are typically highly autonomous, with their synagogues, mosques, and temples owned and operated by their local congregations.
- Similarly, large numbers of other religious firms operate as privately owned companies. They are started by religious entrepreneurs who are convinced that a market exists for their particular product. The early days are often modest, with operations launched in homes, schools, and warehouses. Some are successful; many are not.

Apart from provocative marketing language and corporate analogies, a general organizational approach to religious groups sheds new light on basic features of religious groups, including (1) the nature and the sources of their members, (2) their formal and informal goals, (3) the norms and roles that are established to accomplish their purposes, (4) the sanctions that are used to ensure that norms are followed and roles are played, and (5) the degree of success that groups experience in pursuing their goals. Let me briefly illustrate.

Membership When studying the membership of religious groups, it readily becomes apparent that the vast majority of those involved are following in parental footsteps. Canadian census data show that when two parents have the same faith, 95 percent of their children are also raised in that faith. As a result, new additions to almost any given congregation are primarily active members who are on the move geographically. These include people coming to Canada from other countries. For example, during the 1980s and 1990s immigrants contributed most of the growth to Hindu, Sikh, Muslim, and Buddhist groups.

Congregations frequently compete with one another for members and staff, especially in urban

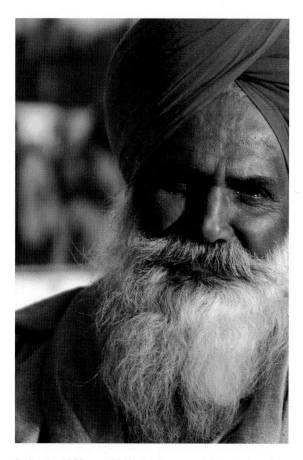

During the 1980s and 1990s immigrants contributed most of the growth to Hindu, Sikh, Muslim, and Buddhist groups in Canada.
SOURCE: Shutterstock.

areas where some "outlets" are larger and more affluent than others. The more attractive congregations typically have the resources to search farther for their leaders and hold them longer.

They also have better physical facilities. It's not just a Protestant or Catholic phenomenon: Muslims, Hindus, Sikhs, Buddhists, and Jews typically define their meeting places as important centres for social activity. Consequently groups tend to build structures as lavish as their resources will permit. In recent years, a number of Protestant "megachurches" have come into being in both Canada and the United States. They typically have seating for 1000 to 4000 people, are serviced by many full-time staff members, and have annual budgets in the millions of dollars. They are found in major cities, such as Toronto, Montreal, Winnipeg, Edmonton, Calgary, and Vancouver. But they also are appearing in smaller communities, such as Abbotsford, Red Deer, and St. Catharines. These megachurches make it difficult for other congregations to compete. Catholics are

showing signs of following suit, recognizing that one way of dealing with the priest shortage is to have larger, regional parishes.

Congregations, like secular businesses, also expand their services and personnel in keeping with their economic means. Some of the megachurches, for example, offer many of the typical worship and educational opportunities of more traditional, older groups. But they also have extensive programs aimed at children, teenagers, young adults, and seniors. The programs range from small but sophisticated groups studying in homes ("cell groups"), through well-developed music and drama programs, to multimedia education, entertainment, and elaborate Internet sites. A room in one well-known British Columbia megachurch resembles a 1950s diner—complete with a car front, jukeboxes, booths, and stools. As the church's head youth minister told me, "The young people love this room; but, I have to admit, the seniors love it too."

An obvious point of tension involves maintaining integrity while providing products that attract customers.

Goals   The conscious and unconscious goals of local religious groups vary by congregation and members. Like the goals of other social groupings, these conscious and unconscious goals commonly appear to be in conflict. For years observers have noted that the formal goals derived from religious doctrine, such as spiritual growth, frequently exist in tension with "survival goals" relating to numerical growth that translate into necessary human and financial resources (Metz, 1967).

Similarly, congregations frequently have difficulty in reconciling their pastoral or "comfort" function with their prophetical or "challenge" function (Glock, Ringer, and Babbie, 1967). For example, the national leadership of the United Church of Canada viewed itself as prophetic in its call during the mid-1980s to allow homosexuals to be eligible for ordination as ministers. In taking such a controversial position the denomination lost a sizable number of dissenting members and, in some cases, entire congregations (O'Toole, Campbell, Hannigan, Beyer, and Simpson, 1993). Prophecy has its organizational price.

There is an additional point of tension: how to satisfy the needs of the existing clientele while reaching out to new people who are not involved, yet have important needs themselves. It is a dilemma that congregations of virtually all religious stripes are not particularly adept at resolving (Bibby, 2004b), with obvious negative implications for growth.

Norms, Roles, and Sanctions If groups, like companies, are to achieve their official and unofficial goals, they have to be able to establish norms for what has to be done, and assign roles for their members to play. An examination of congregational roles reveals that most groups in Canada—led by Catholics, evangelicals, Muslims, Hindus, and Sikhs—often have a human resource problem for two main reasons. The first is that they are top-heavy with men and often inadequately tap the resources of women, a reality that has been variously met with acquiescence, resistance, and a measure of change (Nason-Clark, 1993; Nesbitt, 1997; Speaker-Yuan, 2005; Stackhouse, 2005). The second problem is that groups typically rely on volunteers to carry out key roles. These are the same people who congregational leaders have to work hard to recruit and retain—people on whom they depend for involvement and financial support. They are not hired and they can't exactly be fired. It adds up to a situation in which religious groups are frequently fragile and inefficient companies (Bibby, 1993; Brannon, 1971; Monahan, 1999).

Success In their studies of religion in Canada, researchers have tended to emphasize "the numerical bottom lines" of religious groups and to focus on such indicators of success as attendance, membership, and finances.

Through the early 1990s, the research news was not particularly good for organized religion. Overall, attendance and membership were down, with some groups feeling great hardship as a result of inadequate finances. The mainline Protestant groups—the United, Anglican, Presbyterian, and Lutheran churches—were the most severely hit, along with Roman Catholics in Quebec. Despite some attendance and membership losses, the Roman Catholic Church outside of Quebec appeared to be relatively healthy. And although their numbers were not as large as many people think, conservative Protestant groups were at least able to hold their own and grow modestly—a significant accomplishment, given that they have represented only about 8 percent of the population since 1871 and could have readily been absorbed by larger competitors. Other faith groups, such as Hindus, Muslims, Sikhs, Jews, and Buddhists, were having a difficult time growing, primarily because they were having considerable difficulty holding on to their offspring, who all too frequently were marrying Catholics and Protestants.

The size of a group is largely a function of birth and mortality factors. What was disconcerting for religious leaders in Canada through the early 1990s was that most groups were top-heavy with older people, and many did not seem able to replace them with comparable numbers of younger people. As a result, it was estimated that, by 2015, weekly attendance would drop dramatically for mainline Protestants and Quebec Catholics, decline slightly for "Other World Faith" groups, and remaining fairly stable for conservative Protestants and Roman Catholics elsewhere in Canada. The result? There was a very real possibility that the dominant players on the Canadian religious scene would soon be Roman Catholics and evangelical Protestants.

However, as we will see shortly, there is good reason to believe that this "old story" is being replaced by a "new story." There are signs that Canada's well-established religious groups are beginning to make something of a comeback. This embryonic renaissance has not taken place by chance but appears to reflect the explicit efforts of groups to be more effective in addressing the needs and interests of children, teenagers, and young adults.

The Canadian Situation

Affiliation with religious groups has been widespread in Canada since the founding of this country. Close ties have always been apparent between Canadians of British descent and the Church of England, Methodism, and Presbyterianism; between the French and the Roman Catholic Church; and between other ethnic groups and the churches of their homelands. As noted earlier, Islam, Hindu, Sikh, and Buddhist growth in recent years has been directly related to immigration from Asia.

In the 2001 census, 84 percent of Canadians indicated that they have a religious preference. Nationally, Catholics compose 45 percent of the population; Protestants, 29 percent; and unspecified Christians 3 percent. Seven percent consist of those with other religious preferences, and 16 percent have no specified religion (Table 13.2).

Such data suggest that it is an exaggeration to think of Canada as a highly diversified religious

TABLE 13.2   RELIGIOUS IDENTIFICATION, CANADA AND THE PROVINCES AND TERRITORIES, 2001 (IN PERCENTAGE)

	CANADA	BC	AB	SK	MB	ON	QC	NB	NS	PE	NL	YT	NT	NU
Catholic	**45**	**19**	**28**	**33**	**29**	**37**	**84**	**54**	**37**	**48**	**37**	**22**	**46**	**24**
Roman	43	18	26	31	27	34	83	54	37	47	37	22	46	23
Eastern Orthodox	2	1	2	2	2	2	1	<1	<1	<1	<1	<1	<1	<1
Protestant	**29**	**32**	**39**	**48**	**45**	**35**	**5**	**37**	**49**	**43**	**60**	**34**	**31**	**67**
United	10	9	14	20	16	12	<1	10	16	20	17	9	6	1
Anglican	7	8	6	7	8	9	1	8	13	5	26	15	15	58
Presbyterian	1	1	1	<1	<1	3	<1	1	3	6	<1	1	1	<1
Lutheran	2	3	5	8	5	2	<1	<1	1	<1	<1	2	1	<1
Baptist	3	3	3	2	2	3	<1	11	11	5	<1	4	2	<1
Pentecostal	1	1	1	2	2	1	<1	3	1	1	7	2	3	4
Other	8	7	9	9	12	5	3	4	4	6	10	1	3	4
Christian: Other	**3**	**5**	**4**	**3**	**4**	**3**	**1**	**1**	**1**	**2**	**1**	**4**	**3**	**3**
Other faiths	**7**	**8**	**6**	**<1**	**3**	**9**	**4**	**<1**	**<1**	**<1**	**<1**	**1**	**2**	**<1**
Jewish	1	<1	<1	<1	1	2	1	<1	<1	<1	<1	<1	<1	<1
Muslim	2	2	2	<1	<1	3	2	<1	<1	<1	<1	<1	<1	<1
Hindu	1	<1	<1	<1	<1	2	<1	<1	<1	<1	<1	<1	<1	<1
Buddhist	1	2	1	<1	<1	1	1	<1	<1	<1	<1	<1	<1	<1
Sikh	<1	4	<1	<1	<1	<1	<1	<1	<1	<1	<1	<1	<1	<1
Other	<1	<1	<1	<1	<1	<1	<1	<1	<1	<1	<1	<1	<1	<1
No religion	**16**	**36**	**23**	**16**	**19**	**16**	**6**	**8**	**12**	**6**	**2**	**39**	**18**	**6**

SOURCE: Adapted from the Statistics Canada publication "Religions in Canada," Analysis Series, 2001 Census, Catalogue 96F0030XIE2002015, released May 13, 2003.

mosaic. As Statistics Canada (2003: 5) noted in releasing the census findings, Canada is "still predominantly Roman Catholic and Protestant." It's true that Muslims, Hindus, Sikhs, and Buddhists all doubled in size between 1991 and 2001, and they have added diversity and vitality to the Canadian religious scene. Yet, measured against the Canadian population, their numbers are still relatively small. It is also premature to assume that their numbers will continue to grow, given the tendency of many of their offspring to socialize with and marry people outside their groups—a reality and challenge well known, for example, to Canada's Jewish community. Christian groups not only continue to hold a large monopoly; they frequently are the primary beneficiaries of such intermarital "religious defection." Time will fill out the story.

The Christian faith also continues to be pervasive in the United States, where surveys show that close to nine in ten Americans identify with Christian groups (Gallup, 2006). However, the numerically dominant groups in the United States are not the same as those in Canada. Whereas one in two Canadians is Catholic, the same is true of only one in four Americans. Furthermore, just one in ten Canadians identifies with conservative Protestant (evangelical) groups, in contrast to more than three in ten Americans. A tipoff on the difference is that slightly more than 40 percent of Americans claim that they are "born again" (Winseman, 2005); the term itself is not even particularly common in Canadian religious group circles, even among many of today's evangelicals. In fact, 31 percent of Canadians in our 2005 survey told us that if they were in the presence of someone they didn't know who was "born again," their immediate reaction would be to feel uncomfortable. They'd better not wander too far into the United States.

When Canadians are asked about actual *membership* in religious groups, as opposed to mere affiliation or identification, more people—about 30 percent—claim to belong to churches than to any other single voluntary group. About one in four attends services approximately once a week, and roughly the same proportion of parents with school-age children expose their children to Sunday schools or similar kinds of religious instruction on a fairly frequent basis.

However, between approximately the 1940s and 2000, church attendance in Canada declined sharply, documented by Gallup poll findings summarized in Figure 13.1. Gallup had been asking Canadians if they attended a service "in the last seven days"—the phrasing of the inquiry adds sporadic attenders to those who claim they attend every week. Using such a measure, Gallup found that Protestant attendance dropped from around 60 percent to about 30 percent between the 1940s and mid-1970s, rebounding to around 40 percent by the mid-1990s. The decline in

Roman Catholic attendance appears to have started around 1965, dropping from roughly 85 percent to 40 percent by the mid-1990s—led by low church-going in Quebec. No such dramatic decline in attendance has taken place in the United States: Weekly attendance has remained remarkably steady at just more than 40 percent dating back to the late 1930s when polling began.

To the surprise of almost everyone, evidence suggests that an attendance reversal may have started to take place in Canada. In 1984, 23 percent of the country's 15- to 19-year-olds were attending services weekly; by 1992 the figure had dropped to 18 percent. However, by 2000 the weekly figure for this age group rebounded to 22 percent, seemingly reflecting accelerated emphases on youth ministry by a wide array of Protestant, Catholic, and other faith groups. In addition, for the first time in decades, the 1990s saw the proportion of weekly attending 18- to 34-year-olds level off and in some group instances increase, rather than decline. The only notable exception? Quebec. There, regular attendance has continued to decline among people young and old.

Nonetheless, overall, there are signs of a possible renaissance of religion in Canada (Bibby, 2004a, 2004b). After declining steadily for four decades, national weekly service attendance increased from 21 percent to 25 percent between 2000 and 2005. Monthly-plus attendance, probably a more reasonable measure of involvement, has returned to levels of the late 1980s and early 1990s (Figure 13.2). What we are seeing may turn out to be just a temporary blip. But maybe not.

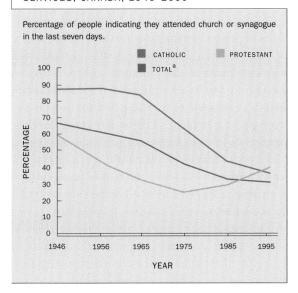

FIGURE 13.1 ATTENDANCE AT RELIGIOUS SERVICES, CANADA, 1946–2000

Percentage of people indicating they attended church or synagogue in the last seven days.

[a]Total refers to all Canadians, regardless of faith.
SOURCE: Gallup Canada, Inc., surveys, 1946–1995.

FIGURE 13.2 MONTHLY-PLUS ATTENDANCE IN CANADA, 1975–2005

SOURCE: Reginald W. Bibby, *Project Canada Survey* Series.

THE SOURCES OF RELIGION

More than a few religious leaders over the years who have seen their best efforts to involve people come up empty have murmured, "There is only so much we can do." It's an insightful lament. The best programs and ministries in the world will not hit a responsive chord with everybody. Personal and societal factors also play critically important roles in determining who embraces religion and religious groups and who does not.

Much of the early work in the scientific study of religion by people like Durkheim focused on preliterate cultures in which religion was highly pervasive. Everyone was religious, or so it seemed. Consequently, it's not surprising that observers gave considerable attention to the origin of religion itself, rather than examining variations in religious commitment.

However, individual differences in religion's importance in contemporary societies have called for explanations as to why some people are religious and others are not. The explanations tend to focus either on individuals or on social structure.

INDIVIDUAL-CENTRED EXPLANATIONS

At least three dominant "person-centred" explanations of religious commitment have emerged. See to what extent you see yourself and others in what the experts have had to say.

Reflection

The desire to comprehend reality is widespread among humans. In the course of reflecting on the meaning of existence, people have commonly concluded that life has a supernatural, "transempirical" dimension. As Weber (1963 [1922]: 117) put it, religion is the product of an "inner compulsion to understand the world as a meaningful cosmos and take up a position toward it."

There is little doubt that Canadians, like people elsewhere, reflect on life's so-called big questions. Some 80 percent say they think about such issues as the origin and purpose of life, the meaning of suffering, and what happens after we die. Such questions take on particular urgency when people have to come to grips with such events as the attacks on September 11 or a devastating tsunami—or have to deal with the suicide of a friend or the loss of a parent. Still, although such times of reflection may provide religious groups with an opportunity to respond, reflec-

tion in itself does not usually lead to religious commitment and involvement. Fewer than one in three Canadians who often raise these meaning questions give evidence of being religiously committed.

Socialization

A second person-centred explanation sees religious commitment as the product of learning—socialization factors that were the focus of Chapter 3. Freud (1962 [1928]) went so far as to say that religion is learned pretty much like the multiplication table. He may not have been exaggerating. I have never forgotten a high-school teacher who played for the Edmonton Eskimos telling us that if we had grown up in India, we would all be Hindus. As Durkheim emphasized, personal religiosity has social origins and, consequently, will strongly reflect the social environments from which we come, beginning with our family.

Why is an Iraqi a Muslim, a Londoner Church of England, a Ute (as in Utah) a Mormon, a Quebecker a Catholic? The answers are obvious. What is less clear is why some of those four people take their religion more seriously than the others. To address the question, we probably would start by looking at the commitment level of their parents. Beyond family, we would expect that individuals who are devout have been exposed to additional social sources that are positive toward religion—friends, an ethnic group, an institution, a community or region, perhaps an entire society. Religion is very much a learned phenomenon.

Accommodation to social pressures, notably those of primary groups, seems to be a related source of religious group involvement. For example, one marriage partner may become more active in response to the hopes and expectations of the other, friends in response to friends, parents in response to having young children, children in response to their parents. As John McEnroe of tennis fame once put it, "I can go to church once in a while, just for mom." In small communities where religion is pervasive and normative, accommodation would be expected to be an important source of religious involvement.

It's important to keep in mind that socialization appears to be a *necessary* but not a *sufficient* cause of religiosity. That is to say, to the extent that Canadians are currently involved in religious groups, most had parents who also were involved. However, the fact that Canadians had parents who were involved does not ensure that their sons and daughters will follow suit. Although about eight in ten of today's weekly attenders had parents who attended weekly, only about three in ten Canadians whose fathers or mothers attended weekly have followed their example.

With a decreasing number of parents actively involved in religious groups in recent decades, fewer have been passing the experience of organized religion on to their children. For example, in 1975, some 35 percent of Canadians with school-age children claimed that they and their children were attending services on a regular basis. By 2000, that figure had dropped to around 20 percent. Such a pattern, if it had continued, obviously would have had devastating numerical consequences for organized religion. But as of 2005, it had increased to 23 percent. The fact that the decline appears to have been halted provides another signal that a shift in participation patterns could be taking place.

If religious involvement and commitment are to last a lifetime, they need to receive ongoing social support. Our surveys have found that the commitment level of a partner is strongly related both to personal involvement and the importance placed on religion. In more than seven in ten cases, if one partner is a weekly attender, so is the other. In fewer than three in ten cases does a person attend weekly or view religion as "very important" if the partner does not.

Deprivation

A third person-centred explanation of religious commitment is that the devout are drawn primarily from the ranks of society's deprived or disadvantaged. Religion provides them with compensation, sometimes now, sometimes later. The roots of such thinking, of course, are found in the work of Marx and Freud.

The deprivation argument was developed more fully by Glock and Stark (1965), whose work was disseminated widely and consequently has been very influential. They maintained that five types of deprivation are predominant in the rise and development of religious and secular movements: economic, social, organismic (that is, physical or mental), psychic, and ethical. The first three types of deprivation are self-explanatory. Psychic deprivation refers to the lack of a meaningful system of values, and ethical deprivation refers to having values that are in conflict with those dominant in a society.

Some research attempts to evaluate the deprivation thesis in the 1970s and 1980s by using objective indicators, such as income, health, and social relationships, did not find deprivation to be a particularly

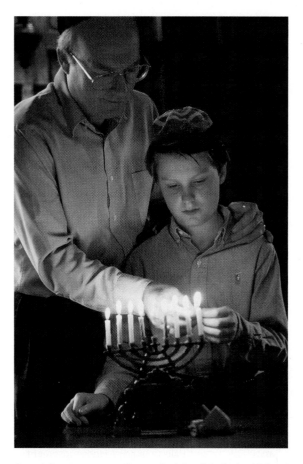

One of the strongest predictors of adult religiosity is childhood religious practice. When parents participate in religious observance with their children, the early socialization experience is often imprinted for life.
SOURCE: Bushl Soifer/Stone/Getty.

good predictor of broad religious participation in either the United States (Roof and Hoge, 1980) or Canada (Hobart, 1974). The learning perspective has far more applicability.

The world's attention has been fixed on suicide bombing since 2001. Because such attacks are often religiously inspired, and because they are so violent, you might expect the attackers to be driven by extreme deprivation. And, in fact, some observers initially hypothesized that suicide bombers must be poor, unemployed, uneducated, unmarried, socially marginal young adults with little to lose. Analysts assumed that people with such characteristics could be relatively easily convinced to exchange their lives of suffering in the here-and-now for promises of glory and martyrdom in the hereafter.

Research has demonstrated, however, that the deprivation argument does not hold in the case of suicide bombers. As Canadian sociologists Robert Brym and Bader Araj note in their study of suicide bombings in Israel, the West Bank, and Gaza from 2000 to 2005, suicide bombers typically come from working-class and middle-class backgrounds and they are generally better educated than the populations from which they are drawn. For example, the suicide bombers who were responsible for the attacks of September 11, 2001, were all well educated, middle-class men (Brym and Araj, 2006). Studies of extreme forms of religious participation thus lead us to the same conclusion as studies of general populations: Deprivation does not appear to be systematically associated with religious commitment. This leads us to additional explanations of religious commitment.

STRUCTURE-CENTRED EXPLANATIONS

Suicide bombers hardly exist in isolation. On the contrary, they typically are members of political and military groups found in the Middle East and, in the case of the Tamil Tigers, Sri Lanka. The groups to which they belong in turn are committed to getting rid of occupying forces, overthrowing existing regimes in their own countries or, in the case of a group like Hamas—the largest Palestinian resistance movement—obliterating Israel and creating an Islamic theocracy. Structural conditions clearly play an important role in such "religio-political" organizations coming into being and in individuals being recruited as members.

Such realities remind us that, in addition to personal characteristics of the reflection, socialization, and deprivation variety, religious commitment is strongly influenced by the broader national, regional, and group contexts in which people find themselves. You might immediately think of a theocracy, such as Iran, where the president and legislature are subject to clerical supervision. But in virtually every society, Canada included, history and culture combine to create milieus that, to varying degrees, do or do not support religion.

Those proclivities often vary not only along national lines but also by the region in which people live and the groups of which they are a part. Historically, Canada's "Bible Belt" has been viewed as Alberta, when by every conceivable measure it probably has actually been the Atlantic region. Regardless, growing up in either of these two regions results in being exposed to environments that are far more "pro-religious" than people experience in a province like British Columbia.

Social environments are important determinants of religious commitment and involvement.

Two early prominent Canadian sociologists, S.D. Clark (1948) and W.E. Mann (1962) argued that, historically, the emergence of sect-like groups, such as indigenous Baptists and Pentecostals, in Canada was tied to the existence of unstable conditions, which were produced by such factors as immigration and economic depression. With industrialization and increased prosperity and stability, some of these smaller, independent evangelical groups evolved into denominations—a process referred to as **denominationalism.** A further example of the impact of societal factors on religion can be found in Quebec. Much of the dropoff in Roman Catholic attendance between 1965 and 1980 was related to the accelerated modernization of Quebec, including the Church's relinquishing of much of its important role in education and social services to the provincial government (Beyer, 1993, 1997; Rouleau, 1977).

The climate that present-day societies provide for religion is the subject of considerable debate. Some observers maintain that increasing industrialization and postindustrialization contribute to a decline in the pervasiveness and importance of religion. This widely held **secularization thesis** has been prominent in the social sciences, largely because of the influence of Durkheim, Marx, and Freud. It's a framework that seems particularly appropriate to developments in much of Protestant Europe. It also is the dominant explanatory framework the media and Statistics Canada use in making sense of religious developments in Canada (Catto, 2003; Shackleton, 2005; Statistics Canada 2004a, 2004b; Valpy, 2004).

But there is also another take on religious developments—what we might call the **persistence thesis.** Proponents of this position, among them Daniel Bell (1977) and Rodney Stark and William Bainbridge (1985ff), claim that religion—traditional or otherwise—persists in industrial and postindustrial or postmodern societies, continuing to address questions of meaning and purpose, and responding to widespread interest in spirituality. Stark maintains that some religious groups or companies will fail, but because of ongoing market demand, new ones will emerge to pick up the slack. What is in doubt is not the persistence of religion, only the identity of the key players.

In Canada, we can readily explore the relationship between religious involvement and commitment and some of the correlates of social and cultural change—such as age, urbanization, education, and employment status. If the secularization thesis is correct, we would expect religiosity to be pretty low for everyone by this point in our history, particularly so for Canadians who are younger, are living in larger communities, are well-educated, and are part of the paid work force. Conversely, if the persistence thesis is correct, we would expect some variations in these anticipated patterns.

Here are the main findings:

- Differences in religious participation and commitment exist for older Canadians versus those 35 to 54. But younger adults (18 to 34) break with the pattern, attending services more often and

placing more importance on religion than 35- to 54-year-olds do (Table 13.3).

- There are no significant differences by community size. Regionally, there is some support for the idea that secularization is most advanced in those parts of Canada that were first to experience extensive economic development—central Canada and the west coast.

- Obtaining a university education is not related to a drop in religiosity.

Full-time employment, however, is associated with a noticeable decline in both attendance and the

TABLE 13.3 SERVICE ATTENDANCE, COMMITMENT, AND SPIRITUAL NEEDS BY SOCIAL CHANGE CORRELATES, CANADA, 2005 (IN PERCENTAGE)

	WEEKLY ATTENDERS	RELIGION "VERY IMPORTANT"	SEE SELF AS HAVING SPIRITUAL NEEDS
Nationally	**25**	**25**	**72**
Age			
55 and over	32	30	72
35–54	17	18	70
18–34	27	31	74
Community Size			
Under 30 000	25	26	72
30 000–400 000	25	27	73
Over 400 000	25	25	72
Region			
Atlantic	39	41	82
Prairies	31	34	77
Ontario	28	31	71
British Columbia	17	16	67
Quebec	15	9	69
Education			
High school or less	25	29	68
Some postsecondary	19	21	72
Degree or more	28	25	75
Paid labour-force participation (65 & under)			
Not employed outside the home	29	31	74
Employed outside the home	17	18	70
Women	*14*	*18*	*77*
Men	*19*	*18*	*66*

SOURCE: Derived from Reginald W. Bibby, *Project Canada 2005 National Survey.*

Canadians of every social and demographic stripe tend to acknowledge that they have spiritual needs.
SOURCE: Shutterstock.

importance given to religion. In large measure, the key issue here seems to be time pressures experienced by parents with young children and particularly by women. In my mind, this is an extremely important finding. The post-1950s rise of families with two parents in the paid labour force and the implications of the rise of this family form for the highly selective use of time may be largely responsible for the decline in mainline Protestant and Catholic attendance in Canada after the 1950s. Religious groups needed to adapt by providing "ministries" that responded to changing family life. Few did (Bibby, 2005; Brown, 2001).

Of considerable importance, despite the variations in their inclination to be involved in religious groups and to place a high value on religion, Canadians of every social and demographic stripe tend to acknowledge that they have spiritual needs. Such an admission is consistent with what observers from Durkheim to Stark have expected. It also points to the fact that an extensive market for religion and spirituality persists in Canada.

THE CONSEQUENCES OF RELIGION

In today's increasingly pragmatic world, Canadians face what seem like unlimited choices and limited resources. We need to sort out what is worth our time and what is not. Religion gets no exemption from such selective consumption.

Gone is the day when religious leaders could expect people to become involved in their groups because it's "their duty." Our 2005 national survey found that 61 percent of Canadians believed that their parents "felt they were supposed to go to church." Eighty-seven percent of respondents maintain that, today, "people who attend religious services should not go because they feel they have to but because they find it to be worthwhile."

Is religion "worthwhile"? On balance, does it enhance personal and social life?

PERSONAL CONSEQUENCES

Research findings on religion and what we might refer to generally as "mental health" are contradictory. Important early work carried out by highly respected social psychologist Milton Rokeach (1965: 2) led him to conclude: "We have found that people with formal religious affiliation are more anxious [than others]. Believers, compared with non-believers, complain more often of working under great tension, sleeping fitfully, and similar symptoms." Yet research dating back to the 1970s has consistently found a negative relationship between religious commitment and *anomie*—valuelessness and rootlessness (Lee and Clyde, 1974). Over the years a number of researchers have argued that involvement in groups, such as sects and cults, has contributed to upward mobility, providing an improved self-image and hope in the face of economic and social deprivation (e.g., Johnson, 1961; Whyte, 1966). During the 1970s and 1980s, considerable literature emerged warning against the psychological and emotional damage that could be inflicted by the alleged "brainwashing" of cults (Dawson, 2006: 95ff).

Gale Frankel and W.E. Hewitt (1994) of the University of Western Ontario have been among the researchers who have found a positive relationship between religious group involvement and good mental health. Research into the "Toronto Blessing" congregation has even maintained that physical healing sometimes occurs (Poloma, 1997; Poloma and Hoelter, 1998). National denominational surveys that I have carried out for the United Church of Canada and the evangelical Christian and Missionary Alliance document a fairly predictable conclusion: People who are highly involved in established religious groups claim that their involvement significantly enriches their lives (Bibby, 1994, 1999).

What seems apparent from all this is that some forms of religiosity are connected with well-being, while others are not.

My own analyses of our survey data dating back to 2000 suggest that, overall, Canadians who exhibit religious commitment are slightly more inclined than others to claim a high level of happiness, to find life exciting, to express a high level of satisfaction with family, friends, and leisure activities, and to view death with hope rather than with mystery or even fear (Bibby, 2004a: 128–29; Figure 13.3). However, when the impact of other factors, such as age, education, community size, and region, is taken into account, the apparent modest influence of commitment typically disappears or at least has to be qualified. For example, Gee and Veevers (1990) found that religious involvement and life satisfaction were positively related nationally, but not in British Columbia.

In short, religious commitment by itself appears to have a fairly limited influence on valued personal characteristics. Moreover, it is often less important than such variables as age, education, or employment in predicting personal well-being.

An important word of caution: this "no-difference" finding does not mean that faith is not adding something to the lives of people who value faith. Rather, in light of the high levels of happiness and contentment reported by Canadians generally, it suggests that large numbers of other people are finding alternative pathways to personal well-being. Religion is having an impact but not necessarily a unique impact.

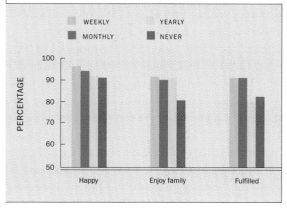

FIGURE 13.3 PERSONAL WELL-BEING AND RELIGIOUS SERVICE ATTENDANCE, 2005

SOURCE: Reginald W. Bibby, *Project Canada 2005.*

INTERPERSONAL CONSEQUENCES

One of the first attempts to examine the relationship between religious commitment and compassion was carried out by Clifford Kirkpatrick in Minnesota in 1949. He found that religiously committed people were somewhat less humanitarian in their outlook than others.

Some 20 years later, Rokeach (1969), drawing on American national data, observed that religious commitment was *negatively* related to social compassion; in the case of Roman Catholics, no relationship—positive or negative—existed. Rokeach concluded that "the results seem compatible with the hypothesis that religious values serve more as standards for condemning others . . . than as standards to judge oneself by or to guide one's own conduct" (Rokeach, 1969: 35).

These findings, however, have not gone unchallenged. Research conducted on specific religious groups and in certain locales has found a positive relationship between commitment and compassion. In a more immediate relational sense, Wilcox (1998) has found that, although conservative Protestant parents are more likely than others to use corporal punishment in disciplining their children, they also are more likely than other parents to praise and hug their children. Extensive research on religion and racial prejudice, such as Smith's (1999) look at anti-Semitism and "the Religious Right," has yielded contradictory results.

However, some three decades ago, Richard Gorsuch and Daniel Aleshire claimed to have found the key reason for the discrepancies. Church members often appear to be more prejudiced than those who have never joined a church. But, they say, it is not because of religious involvement. On the contrary, when involvement level is taken into account, the people who turn out to be the most prejudiced are the "marginally involved" members. Gorsuch and Aleshire concluded: "The highly committed religious person is—along with the nonreligious person—one of the least prejudiced members of our society" (Gorsuch and Aleshire, 1974: 287). If this is the case, then, as with personal characteristics, religion may be making a difference interpersonally—but it is not a unique difference.

Ongoing analyses of Project Canada data have found that religiously committed people in this country do not differ significantly from others with

Among other questions, the sociology of religion asks: Does religion influence the way individuals live? Does religion contribute to individual and societal well-being?

SOURCE: William Kurelek, *Kaszuby Funeral Procession*. Art Gallery of Hamilton, Gift of the Polish Alliance of Canada and Wintario, 1978.

respect to their interpersonal relationship attitudes (Bibby, 1987, 1995, 2004a). They hold a similar view of people, claim a comparable level of compassion, and appear to be no more or less tolerant of deviants, members of minority groups, and people of other religious faiths than are other Canadians. Furthermore, in contrast to the findings of Rokeach and Stark and Glock, no noteworthy differences appear in the interpersonal attitudes held by Roman Catholics and Protestants.

There is, however, one area where religion still appears to speak with a fairly loud if not unique voice—the area of personal morality, notably sexuality. With few exceptions and with varying degrees of explicitness, religious groups tend to oppose "moral innovation." Examples include opposition to changing sexual standards, legal abortion, and distribution of pornographic materials.

That said, there is considerable variation in the position that religious groups take on many sex-related issues, as well as in the inclination of average people who identify with those groups to "follow the party line." Generally speaking, evangelical Protestants are the most likely to be opposed to changes in the sexual realm, Quebec Catholics—despite the official position of their Church—the most receptive, with their open-

ness exceeded only by Canadians with no religion (see Table 13.4).

SOCIETAL CONSEQUENCES

I've looked at some personal and interpersonal consequences of religious involvement and commitment. But what about the net consequences for societies more generally? On balance, is religion a plus or a minus—or simply irrelevant?

A cursory look at the historical evidence in Canada provides mixed reviews. Many would argue that religion has played and continues to play an important role in helping immigrants adjust to life in Canada, providing resources in the form of both personal faith and social support. Others would quickly add that many religious groups, notably the United, Anglican, and Roman Catholic churches, along with the Jewish community, have played important roles in helping to establish a just society, where diversity and inclusiveness today are valued on a level matched by few countries anywhere in the world. In addition, the claim can be made that religious groups are among the few organizations in Canada that explicitly attempt to instill morality, ethics, and compassion, thereby making an important contribution to civility.

TABLE 13.4   PERCENTAGE OF CANADIANS OPPOSED TO SELECTED ISSUES BY SERVICE ATTENDANCE AND GROUP IDENTIFICATION, 2005 (IN PERCENTAGE)

	PRE-MARITAL SEX	EXTRA-MARITAL SEX	HOMO-SEXUALITY	SAME-SEX MARRIAGE	ABORTION: RAPE	ABORTION: CHILD UNWANTED	DISTRIBUTION OF PORNOGRAPHY
Attendance							
Weekly	60	96	75	62	45	79	69
Less than weekly	7	82	25	20	4	36	31
Religious Group Identification							
Conservative Protestants	64	98	74	64	41	82	69
Christian Unspecified	30	92	45	44	28	65	44
RC: Outside Quebec	25	91	47	37	25	62	47
Other World Faiths	21	86	38	33	12	46	39
Mainline Protestants	13	89	35	28	6	40	43
RC: Quebec	10	78	33	22	6	40	35
No Religion	3	73	10	7	1	19	17

SOURCE: Derived from Reginald W. Bibby, *Project Canada 2005 National Survey*.

Those things said, you hardly need me to remind you that other views of religious groups are not so charitable. For example:

- In the course of taking their place in the country, a number of Christian groups were anything but just and compassionate in their treatment of Aboriginal peoples.
- The "Quiet Revolution" in Quebec in the 1960s that saw the province take over many services from the Catholic Church was not accompanied by an overt revolt. But, covertly, large numbers of Catholics had found the Church to be highly oppressive and began to stay away (Graham, 1990: 114ff).
- A variety of highly publicized sexual abuse cases that spanned the country—from the Mount Cashel orphanage in Newfoundland and Labrador, through the "Orphans of Duplessis" in Quebec and the Christian Brothers in Ontario, to the Catholic Diocese in Prince Rupert, B.C.—left many Canadians stunned and disenchanted with organized religion (see Bibby, 1993: 68ff).
- Catholics, Jews, and Muslims, along with smaller religious bodies, including Mennonites, Hutterites, Jehovah's Witnesses, Scientologists,

and Doukhobors, have been on the receiving end of hostility and discrimination at various points in our nation's history.

Clearly the evidence to date is mixed. Religion adds to the quality of life in the country and sometimes subtracts. What does seem to contribute to a fairly unique religious situation in Canada is the entrenchment of pluralism. Religious groups here have to play by the rules of diversity, being respectful of one another—not making excessive claims of uniqueness, not being overly aggressive in raiding each other's ranks, not being exploitive of vulnerable categories, such as immigrants, children, and seniors. And they have to respect individual rights, in keeping with the Charter of Rights.

So contained, religious organizations that might otherwise have a detrimental effect on collective life in Canada are kept in check. We have no effective "Moral Majority," like the United States does. The same-sex marriage issue was not allowed to become an unrestrained and uncivil debate, and if someone tested the boundaries—as one Alberta bishop was tempted to do on occasion—public opinion tended to result in public relations retreats. This is not a country where Christians can call

BOX 13.1 WHY THE GLOBAL RAGE HASN'T ENGULFED CANADA: MULTICULTURALISM AND MEDIA LIKELY MUTED PROTESTS

Why haven't Muslims in Canada taken to the streets in large numbers to protest against cartoons of the Prophet Mohammed? It's not because everyone in Canada is so nice to each other, say Canadian Muslim leaders and Islamic scholars. It's because Canada's multiculturalism is complex.

They say Muslim immigration into Canada has been different. So has Muslim integration into Canadian society. And so has the political action of Canadian Muslim organizations around the highly sensitive issue of Islamic religious fundamentalism.

The difference is illustrated by events in France in 2004 and Canada in 2005, said Tarek Fatah, a leader of the Muslim Canadian Congress.

In France, few if any representative voices within the French Muslim community were heard in the news media speaking in favour of a law banning conspicuous religious symbols, such as the traditional Muslim head scarf, in public schools.

This was the case even though a significant percentage of French Muslims had no problem accepting the law within the cultural context of French secular society.

The powerful Muslim opposition that was heard, Mr. Fatah said, came from "the mosque structure" but "the mobilization of moderate Muslim voices never happened."

In contrast, in Canada in 2005, the news media pointedly reported that the most vociferous opposition to an Ontario law permitting Islamic religious tribunals to arbitrate family and marital disputes came from Muslim organizations themselves.

In Mr. Fatah's view, the mainstream Muslim community in Canada has recognized the need to take what he calls "ownership of the word Muslim." It has become actively involved in Canadian political life and not marginalized as is the case in many Western countries.

"It's a shift, for Canadian Muslims, that has not happened anywhere else."

Mohamed Elmasry, president of the Canadian Islamic Congress, said violent demonstrations simply aren't a fit with the Canadian Muslim community—which, because of Canada's immigration requirements, he said, is the most highly educated Muslim community in the world.

"They would find legal and peaceful means of protest far more productive," said the imam and professor at the University of Waterloo. "With demonstrations, you cannot have full control over who does what."

His organization, the largest Muslim umbrella group in Canada, has actively discouraged demonstrations over the cartoons and has spoken publicly against the violent protests—as has the Muslim Canadian Congress.

Earle Waugh, a University of Alberta Islamic scholar, said most Muslim immigrants to Canada do not feel sidelined, a factor significantly fuelling the protests in European countries.

"There is no sympathy within the Canadian Muslim community for a radical approach," he said. "No sympathy for the fundamentalists."

Canada has had no legacy of Muslim colonies like that of the British and French, and no history of migrant Muslim guest workers like that of Germany.

SOURCE: *The Globe and Mail*, 8 February 2006, p. A14. Reprinted with permission from *The Globe and Mail*.

other people "heathen," but they also cannot be ridiculed as "bigoted Bible-thumpers." This is not a country where Muslims can call for the heads and hands of artists who draw caricatures of Mohammed, but it also is not a place where artists can insult and incite Muslims. Some groups don't always like the rules; but that's the way the religion game is played in Canada. So contained and so retrained, religion—it seems to me—is positioned to contribute positively to our individual and collective life (Box 13.1).

Peter Berger (1961) has observed that Durkheim's assertion that religion functions primarily to integrate societies seems to offer a good description of religion in the United States. Religion, or at least the mainline segment of organized Christianity that historically has embraced the largest number of members, has tended to endorse American culture rather than to challenge it, to endorse the status quo rather than call for social transformation. So intense has been the bond between religion and American life that a number of years ago Robert Bellah (1967) and others described the phenomenon as American **civil religion.** In his influential book *Protestant, Catholic, Jew*, Will Herberg (1960: 75) put it this way:

> Americans, by and large, do have their "common religion" and that "religion" is the system familiarly known as the American Way of Life. . . . By every realistic criterion the American Way of Life is the operative faith of the American people. . . . To be a Protestant, a Catholic, or a Jew are today the alternative ways of being an American.

Canada, committed as it is to diversity and a downplaying of overt nationalism—except for the occasional international hockey championship—has no such civil religion. As Stahl (1986: 16) colourfully puts it, "Other than a few bands and firecrackers, Confederation was not attended by much emotional outpouring." And religious groups have done little to add fervour to our rather lifeless expressions of nationalism. Still, Harold Fallding (1978) reminds us that, historically, "Canadian Protestant churches have reflected the British position of legitimizing authority through supporting government, offering prayers, for example, for its success in securing order and justice." The fusion of Catholicism with life in Quebec, Anglicanism with the status quo in southern Ontario, and conservative Protestantism with political and social life in Alberta are obvious examples.

On occasion, of course, religion has challenged North American culture. The civil rights movement in the United States received much of its leadership and impetus from African-American evangelical churches. American Catholic bishops and the National Council of Churches have frequently spoken out against perceived injustices, including poverty, racism, and war. Jerry Falwell's "Moral Majority," which peaked in the 1980s, contributed to a very vocal "Christian Right," committed to altering the nature of American life by influencing the country's major institutions.

In Canada, religious groups have had and continue to have the freedom to address governments. To varying degrees they have availed themselves of the opportunity—and responsibility. Protestant churches, for example, have received mixed reviews for their concern about the plight of Jews during World War II; some churches and individuals were silent, while others were not (Davies and Nefsky, 1997). In the 1940s, a radical effort was made by the Roman

Catholic Church to support striking workers, a preview of the ongoing inclination of the Canadian Conference of Catholic Bishops to support average Canadians and to be vocal in criticizing the profit orientation of the nation's economy. Protestant groups, usually led by the United Church, along with a growing number of ecumenical consortia and initiatives, and, more recently, evangelical churches, have been making concerted efforts to bring about social change (Crysdale, 1961; Stiller, 1997). In recent years, religious coalitions have been among those criticizing the cutbacks to social programs in general and in Ontario in particular. They also are being increasingly outspoken on Aboriginal issues (Lewis, 1993).

It is important to note that locally, nationally, and globally religion clearly has the potential both to bring people together and to tear them apart. Religion's role in contributing to conflict, past and present, is well known. Globally, what seems like never-ending conflict in the Middle East and elsewhere provides further contemporary examples of religion playing a role in contributing to divisiveness. At times I wonder about the long-term outcome of what seems to be a deepening chasm between the West and the Muslim world.

Yet, in the aftermath of both the September 11, 2001, attacks and the fury over the publishing of the Mohammed caricatures in 2006, significant numbers of Muslim leaders were among the first to decry violence and bloodshed, and to call on people worldwide to find peaceful means of resolving their differences. Therein lies the paradox of religion: It can both enrich and destroy social life.

THE FUTURE OF RELIGION

One thing is certain: Religion is not going to disappear. Proponents of the secularization thesis expected religion to be replaced by science and reason as societies evolved. Opponents of the secularization thesis countered that humans have needs, notably the need to come to grips with death, that only religion can satisfy. Consequently, even if secularization leads to the demise of some religious groups, new providers are bound to appear. Ironically, rather than signalling the death of religion, secularization stimulates innovation (Stark and Bainbridge, 1985).

Emerging religious forms will include sects—groups that break away from established religions, and new religious movements **(cults)** with origins outside of older religions. From this point of view, shifts in the overall "religious economy" over time involve "the rising and falling fortunes of religious firms, not the rise and fall of religion per se" (Finke and Stark, 1992: 275).

As we glance around the globe, there is no need to spend time debating religion's future with the wise social scientists of old. Religion is simply everywhere.

In Canada, there are signs that a modest rise in religious involvement is taking place that will continue in the immediate future. However, it is due not so much to the arrival of new religions as it is to the rejuvenation of the older, well-established ones.

Census and survey data reveal that fairly small numbers of Canadians have opted for new religious groups in recent decades. The proportion of Canadians who identified with such groups as Jehovah's Witnesses and Mormons has never been more than one-half of 1 percent. In a country of more than 32 million people, newer, sect-like groups remain on the margins of the Canadian religious scene.

Further, we now know that relatively few people have been switching from one group to another—apart from a fair amount of movement *within* conservative Protestantism, where people who are Pentecostal move to a Baptist church, for example. The amount of "inter-family" switching—such as Roman Catholics becoming Protestants, or Jews or Muslims opting for Catholicism—has been grossly exaggerated.

A big surprise? Despite the fact that the proportion of Canadians who say they have "no religion" increased from 4 percent in 1971 to 16 percent in 2001, most people haven't really been dropping out permanently. The majority of people in this category are young and single. About one-third have come from mainline Protestant homes, another one-third from Catholic homes; only about one in three have parents who also have no religion. As they get a bit older, marry, have children, and want religious weddings, baptisms, and the like, lo and behold, many proceed to tell pollsters that they are "Catholic" or "United" or "Jewish"—again. Using the panel component of our national surveys, we have found that, within five years, one in three people who said he or she had "no religion" proceeds to have one; within ten years that figure jumps to two in three. The "no religion" category is a temporary residence for most people—sort of like living in an apartment before moving into a house (Bibby, 2004b: 29–51).

We consequently have a situation in which Canada's established religious groups find themselves with lots of "affiliates" who identify with the group and aren't about to turn elsewhere. I'm not talking only about adults. Our national surveys of teenagers between the ages of 15 and 19 have found that the country's "emerging generation" differs negligibly from adults when it comes to religion. About 90 percent of teens claim the same group affiliation as their parents, and only about 2 percent indicate any strong interest in new religions. Their belief, practice, experience, and knowledge levels are similar to those of adults. Their interest in other supernatural phenomena is also high, as is their acknowledgment of spiritual needs (see Table 13.5). Some 50 percent say that religion is "very important" to them and just over one in five attends religious services regularly—with one in five saying that he or she receives a high level of enjoyment from congregational life, the same proportion as adults (Bibby, 2001: 114–125).

TABLE 13.5 A PROFILE OF RELIGION AND SPIRITUALITY IN CANADA: TEENAGERS AND ADULTS (IN PERCENTAGE)

	ADULTS	TEENAGERS
Beliefs		
God	81	73
Divinity of Jesus	72	65
Life after death	68	78
Spirit world contact	45	43
Practice (weekly)		
Pray privately	47	33
Attend religious services	21	22
Read the Bible/ other scriptures	16	13
Experience		
Have experienced God	47	36
Salience		
High religious commitment	55	48
Spirituality		
Have spiritual needs	73	48

SOURCE: Reginald W. Bibby, *Canada's Teens*, 2001:252–4.

So let's add all this up: Canadians are not doing much switching or dropping out. The overwhelming majority continue to hold beliefs, engage in practices, experience the gods, and express spiritual needs. But maybe they just aren't interested in organized religion. Not so. Our surveys over the past ten years have been documenting a consistent finding: More than one in two people who attends services less than once a month says he or she is receptive to greater involvement if it is worthwhile for him or her or his or her family (Figure 13.4). And what do these people see as "worthwhile"? Such things as having their spiritual needs met, getting some insight into how they might have better relationships with partners and children and friends, and maybe finding some emotional resources to help them cope with the needs they face in living everyday life.

In short, many people in Canada haven't given up on religion—and haven't even given up on religious groups. But in the midst of living lives that are full, where time and other resources are often being severely stretched, they have to find significance in religious participation. Otherwise, why bother?

Research suggests that, to the extent that groups literally find "their affiliates" and succeed in touching their lives in significant ways, many will become involved. As I have been noting throughout, there are signs that something of a participation shift may be

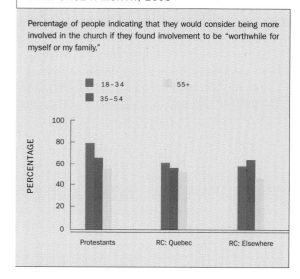

FIGURE 13.4 RECEPTIVITY TO GREATER INVOLVEMENT IN THE CHURCH BY AGE, AMONG PROTESTANTS AND CATHOLICS ATTENDING LESS THAN ONCE A MONTH, 2003

Percentage of people indicating that they would consider being more involved in the church if they found involvement to be "worthwhile for myself or my family."

SOURCE: Bibby, 2004:51.

occurring, as groups attempt to be more responsive, starting with improved ministries to children, teenagers, and young adults. To the extent such efforts continue, we may well continue to see something of a renaissance of religion in Canada.

SUMMARY

1. Sociology uses the scientific method to study religion, in contrast to religion, which explores reality beyond what can be known empirically.

2. The sociology of religion has been strongly influenced by the theoretical contributions of Marx, who stressed the compensatory role of religion in the face of economic deprivation; Durkheim, who emphasized both the social origin of religion and its important social cohesive function; and Weber, who gave considerable attention to the relationship between ideas and behaviour.

3. Religion can be defined as a system of meaning with a supernatural referent used to interpret the world. Humanist perspectives make no such use of the supernatural realm, attempting instead to make life meaningful.

4. Personal religious commitment increasingly has come to be seen as having many facets or dimensions. Four such dimensions are commonly noted: belief, practice, experience, and knowledge. Personal commitment is created and sustained by collective religiosity. In Canada, organized religion has experienced a considerable decline in participation in recent years, a trend that has had critical implications for commitment at the individual level.

5. Variations in the levels of individual commitment that characterize complex societies have led to explanations that emphasize individual and structural factors. Reflection, socialization, and deprivation have been prominent among the individual explanations, while the dominant structural assertion has been the secularization thesis.

6. At the individual level, religion appears to be, at best, one of many paths leading to valued characteristics, such as personal happiness and compassion. Although religion can be socially disruptive, Canada's emphasis on social cultural diversity functions to put limits on how religion can be expressed, thereby optimizing the possibility of religions contributing positively to social and collective life.

7. Although proponents of secularization saw religion as being replaced by science and reason, it is now apparent that religion continues to be important throughout the world, including Canada. Its future is not in doubt.

8. The search for alleged religious switchers and dropouts in Canada reveals that few have turned elsewhere or permanently opted for "no religion." Most still identify with the country's established groups.

9. Canadians young and old, in very large numbers, continue to hold religious beliefs, claim religious experiences, and express spiritual needs. Many also say they are receptive to greater involvement with religious groups.

10. To the extent that groups can locate and respond to their "affiliates"—as it appears they have been doing in recent years—there is good reason to believe that the embryonic "renaissance of religion" in Canada will continue.

QUESTIONS TO CONSIDER

1. Which of the three key theorists do you find to be the most helpful in understanding religion: Durkheim, Marx, or Freud?

2. What does it mean to be religious?

3. To what extent are people in Canada today interested in (a) spirituality and (b) organized religion? What do you mean by the term *spirituality*?

4. What kinds of people do you find are interested in (a) spirituality and (b) organized religion? Do you see any signs of increased interest on the part of young people?

5. Does religion make any difference in the lives of the people you know? Would Canadian society be any different if organized religion disappeared next weekend?

6. Are Canadians interested in the supernatural? What is the evidence?

7. Do you think it is true that secularization stimulates religious innovation—that the decline of old groups provides the opportunity for new groups to surface and prosper?

8. Imagine that you are serving as a consultant to a major Canadian religious group. What might you suggest it consider doing in order to (a) keep the young people it has and (b) gain the interest of Canadians who are not actively involved?

GLOSSARY

The **church-sect typology** is a framework, originating with Weber, in which religious organizations are studied in terms of ideal-type, church, and sect characteristics.

Civil religion refers to the tendency for nationalistic emphases to be nurtured by a society's religions, so that a culture takes on many religious-like characteristics. The term is most often used with respect to the United States.

Collective conscience is Durkheim's term that refers to the awareness of the group being more than the sum of its individual members and the belief that what is being experienced is the supernatural.

Collective religiosity is religious commitment as manifested in and through religious groups; it is key to the creation and sustenance of personal religiosity.

Cults are religious groups that have their origins outside older religions; sects, in contrast, are groups that have broken away from established religions.

Denominationalism refers to the tendency for a wide variety of Protestant religious groups to come into being, seemingly reflecting variations not only in theology but also—and perhaps primarily—in social characteristics.

Dimensions of religiosity are the various facets of religious commitment; Glock and Stark (1965), for example, identify four: belief, experience, practice, and knowledge.

Humanist perspectives are systems of meaning used to interpret the world that do not have a supernatural referent (e.g., communism, scientism).

Monotheism refers to belief in one god.

The **persistence thesis** is the assertion that religion will continue to have a significant place in the modern world, because it never has actually declined or because people continue to have interests and needs that only religion can satisfy.

Personal religiosity refers to the level of religious commitment characterizing an individual.

Profane See *sacred and profane.*

Religions are systems of meaning for interpreting the world that have a supernatural referent (e.g., Christianity, Hinduism).

Sacred and **profane** are the two categories by which Durkheim claimed all things are classified; the sacred represents those things that are deemed to warrant profound respect, and the profane encompasses essentially everything else.

The **secularization thesis** is the assertion that religion as it has been traditionally known is continually declining, resulting in a loss of religious authority, societally and individually, as well as changes in religious organizations themselves.

SUGGESTED READING

Berger, Peter L., ed. (1999). *The Desecularization of the World: Resurgent Religion and World Politics.* Washington: Ethics and Public Policy Center. This brief and readable book features Berger and six contributions from prominent observers who maintain new life is evident in Roman Catholicism, Evangelical Protestantism, Judaism, and Islam. Two additional articles deal with developments in Europe and China.

Bibby, Reginald W. (2004). *Restless Gods: The Renaissance of Religion in Canada.* Ottawa: Novalis. This book draws on the extensive national adult and youth surveys of the author and the work of others in examining religious trends in Canada since the mid-twentieth century, giving attention to developments both inside and outside religious groups that suggest a religious renaissance may be taking place in Canada.

Christiano, Kevin J., William H. Swatos, Jr., and Peter Kivisto. (2002). *Sociology of Religion: Contemporary Developments.* Walnut Creek, CA: AltaMira Press. This is an excellent introduction to the field that provides a thorough overview of theory, methods, and up-to-date findings on religion and society.

Clark, S.D. (1948). *Church and Sect in Canada.* Toronto: University of Toronto Press. This Canadian classic that examines the social factors contributing to the rise of different types of religious groups in this country.

Dawson, Lorne L. (2006). *Comprehending Cults: The Sociology of New Religious Movements,* 2nd ed. Toronto: Oxford University Press. This is a succinct overview of cults that have emerged from the 1970s onward, dealing with such issues as why cults emerge, who joins, and their social significance.

Hewitt, W.E., ed. (1993). *Sociology of Religion: A Canadian Focus.* Toronto: Harcourt Brace. Leading Canadian social scientists provide students with a good introduction both to the work being carried out in the country and to some of the scholars who are most active in this area of research. This is one of few such works available.

Niebuhr, H. Richard. (1957 [1929]). *The Social Sources of Denominationalism.* New York: Henry Holt and Company. This is a classic attempt to probe the role social factors (e.g., economics, nationality, race, and region) had in creating denominationalism in Europe and America. In the process, the author sensitizes students to the social sources of religion more generally.

WEB RESOURCES

Companion Web Site for This Book

http://www.newsociety5e.nelson.com

Begin by clicking on the Student Resources section of the website. Next, select the chapter you are studying from the pull-down menu. From the Student Resources page, you have easy access to InfoTrac College Edition® and other resources, such as the Glossary and Flashcards. The website also has many useful tips to aid you in your study of sociology.

InfoTrac College Edition Search Terms

Visit http://www.infotrac-college.com for access to more than 20 million articles from nearly 6000 sources when doing your online research.

ThomsonNOW™

http://hed.nelson.com

This online diagnostic tool identifies each student's unique needs with a Pretest that generates a personalized Study Plan for each chapter, helping students focus on concepts they are having the most difficulty mastering. Students then take a Posttest after reading the chapter to measure their understanding of the material. An Instructor Gradebook is available to track and monitor student progress.

PART FIVE

Change and Conflict

CHAPTER FOURTEEN

Deviance and Crime

In this chapter you will learn that

- What becomes defined as deviant or criminal depends on the circumstances of time and place because definitions of deviance and crime are subject to conflict and change. These definitions are the outcome of political processes and power relations in which different groups compete to define right and wrong.

- Reacting to deviance can increase a group's social solidarity and clarify its moral boundaries. But these reactions are also an important source of deviance and may lead to more serious and organized forms of deviance.

- Sociological explanations of deviance can be grouped into two types: Those that emphasize the social factors that motivate or allow people to engage in deviance, and those that emphasize the political processes and power relations that result in some individuals and behaviours being defined and treated as deviant while others are not.

- Crime rates have been declining in Canada during the past decade. However, rates of serious crime are still higher in Canada than in many other industrialized countries and are distributed unequally among various groups.

- Legal reactions to crime in Canada balance two goals: protecting society and protecting the rights of those accused of crime. Traditionally, the protection of society has received greater emphasis in the legal process. Canada incarcerates more people per capita than most industrialized countries but is increasingly relying on alternatives to incarceration for less serious criminal offences.

SOURCE: Moe Doiron/CP Picture Archive.

Rosemary Gartner
UNIVERSITY OF TORONTO
Myrna Dawson
UNIVERSITY OF GUELPH

INTRODUCTION

If Thomas Haythe had been born 25 years earlier, he would probably still have his job, his reputation, and his name on the law firm. Tory Haythe was the eighth-largest law firm in Canada. It was created in October 1999 by the merger of Haythe's New York firm and the Toronto-based firm of Tory, Tory, DesLauriers, and Binnington. However, during a November celebration of the merger at a Toronto bar, Haythe apparently got drunk and groped several female lawyers and bar employees. Within four days, the new firm put Haythe on permanent medical leave and arranged to have his name removed from its masthead. At the age of 60, Haythe, a graduate of Harvard Law School and one of North America's most successful lawyers, had run up against a corporate culture and legal climate different from that of a generation ago when such behaviour would certainly not have had public repercussions. A generation ago, employers could not be held liable for sexual harassment in the workplace as they can be today.

If Harold Samuel Fine had been born 25 years later, he would not have ended up with a criminal record for violating section 207 of the Canadian Criminal Code, which prohibited dissemination of information about birth control. In April 1961, Fine, president of Prestige Drug Products, was convicted of advertising and selling condoms through the mail. In his testimony to the court, Fine argued that he mailed his products only to married couples with children and that he was serving the public by providing them with family-planning information. Noting that the facts of the case were not in dispute, Toronto magistrate Thomas Wolfe imposed a fine of $100 or one month in jail on the charges against Fine. It was not until 1969 that the Criminal Code was amended to allow Canadians unregulated access to contraceptive information and birth control technology.

Both of these cases attracted widespread controversy, though for very different reasons. Some observers of the Haythe case, including several lawyers, expressed both surprise and disapproval over his dismissal. A corporate lawyer from Manhattan said that "taking his name off is a pretty Draconian thing to do," and another likened the move to capital punishment (Fine and Milner, 1999). Others wondered whether Haythe's behaviour would have received the same censure had he not made his unwanted advances to relatively powerful female lawyers.

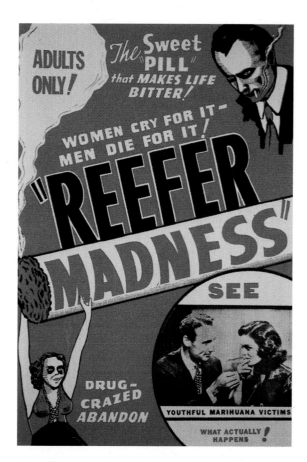

This 1936 movie poster illustrates how relative deviance is. The movie suggests that people go insane from smoking marijuana.
SOURCE: *Reefer Madness*, 1936. Directed by Louis Gasnier.

Fine's conviction also generated public debate and an organized effort to change the law. Two days after his trial, *The Globe and Mail* ran an editorial that criticized those who had informed on Fine as well as the "archaic law which compelled a magistrate" to convict him. Later the same year, a Toronto couple founded the Planned Parenthood Association of Toronto and launched what would become a nationwide campaign to legalize the dissemination of birth control information and technology.

What makes these cases interesting to a sociologist studying deviance is not whether the decisions to publicly label and punish Haythe and Fine as deviant were right or wrong, misplaced, or appropriate. They are sociologically interesting because they illustrate how definitions and perceptions of deviance change over time and how disagreements often arise over those definitions. Common sense may tell us that deviance involves breaking rules. However, sociologists who study deviance remind us that rules change and that people often disagree with the rules. Moreover, breaking rules does not always get a person labelled as deviant, and sometimes people are labelled deviant without breaking any rules. So understanding deviant behaviour requires that we look at the people and the organizations that define and react to deviance—the rule makers and the rule enforcers—as well as at those who break the rules.

In this chapter, we discuss the different ways in which sociologists have thought about deviance. Some are interested primarily in where rules about deviance come from, how and why these rules change, and the consequences of labelling people or behaviours as deviant. Others focus on why some people become rule-breakers. We also look at crime trends in Canada and at changes in crime and social control around the world. A central theme of this chapter is that deviance is not simply about marginal people and odd behaviours. Studying how deviance is defined and how people react to it tells us about how a society is organized; how power, privilege, and resources are distributed; and how social order is achieved. Deviance and crime, then, are at the heart of the struggles every society goes through to organize its social life.

DEVIANCE AND CRIME AS OUTCOMES OF SOCIAL CONTROL

Deviance does not always mean nonconformity; nor is deviance synonymous with rule violation. All of us are nonconformists at one time or another in our lives, but few of us are labelled deviant or formally punished. Nonconformity becomes deviance when it produces a negative social reaction and when concerted public efforts are made to change the behaviour or punish the person. These efforts are what sociologists call **social control** and they take many forms. *Informal* social control occurs through interactions among individuals and includes expressions of disapproval, avoidance, and the many other ways that we try to communicate and enforce what we feel are standards of appropriate behaviour in our everyday lives. All of us have been stopped from doing something by an internal voice asking, "What would others think?" This voice represents self-control—one type of informal social control and the most effective at preventing rule violations.

Formal social control is practised by the state through official organizations and agents, primarily within the criminal justice system. In contrast to informal social control, formal social control relies largely on the external control of people after they have been defined as deviants. Between informal, interpersonal control and the more punitive controls of the criminal justice system lies a network of social controls based in different organizations, agencies, and institutions, such as social welfare organizations, psychiatric agencies, public health clinics, and so on. These "softer" forms of control—some of them the focus of the work of Michel Foucault (1979)—seek to regulate behaviour through reason, persuasion, and scientific authority, but they can also be repressive and coercive. Many organizations and agents of social control do much more than react to deviance, however. We will see that they are also actively involved in influencing which people and what types of behaviours are classified as deviant and how different types of deviance are dealt with. As some sociologists point out, these decisions may depend more on the interests of those seeking to shape definitions of deviance than they do on the particular acts that are targeted for control.

Although deviance is defined by negative social reactions, it can have positive consequences for some social groups. This notion was an important theme of Émile Durkheim's work. Since deviance and crime occur in all societies, Durkheim (1938) reasoned, they must serve some positive social function. One benefit a group can gain from rule breaking by its members is increased social solidarity or integration. Serious violations of a group's rules typically bring people together in collective expressions of outrage and loss, reminding them of their common values. For instance, the killing of 14 female engineering students at the University of Montreal in 1989 was a tragedy felt throughout Canada. Both the immediate response and the continuing commemoration of the killings have brought together Canadians of all sorts in a common condemnation of violence against women.

Another potential benefit of deviance, according to Durkheim, is the clarification of a group's moral boundaries. In defining and confronting deviance, a group highlights its standards of right and wrong to its members. The "No Means No" campaign sent a message to both women and men that sex without consent is rape. As in other cases of defining deviance, this campaign drew a distinction between acceptable and unacceptable behaviour in an area of conduct that was prone to interpretational disagreement. When, as is inevitable, someone ignores the message that "no means no" and is charged with sexual assault, the public definition of his or her behaviour as deviant serves another function. It allows those who follow the rules to feel virtuous and reinforces their conformity by reminding them of the costs of rule breaking.

Durkheim stressed another social benefit of deviance. Societies need deviance, he said, to keep them flexible and to allow them to adapt to a changing world. When people test society's rules by challenging them, they provide an opportunity to consider whether the rules should be changed. For example, in the 1980s, Dr. Henry Morgentaler regularly performed abortions in Quebec abortion clinics, not hospitals, and performed them on demand—without the approval of a therapeutic abortion committee, as required by law. He was prosecuted for doing so but twice acquitted by juries, even though he admitted breaking the law and no legal defence was available to him. After the second acquittal, the government gave up prosecuting him. This effectively permitted abortion on demand at specialized clinics.

With these functions of deviance in mind, you can see why Durkheim and others have argued that deviance and crime are not only inevitable but may also be integral and useful for social order. Yet deviance has clear costs or dysfunctions for society. Too much of it, as Durkheim argued, can lead to chaos and conflict, undermining the stability of society. No society can afford to spend too much of its time, energy, and resources on defining and punishing deviance. Efforts to define and punish deviance have other costs as well. In his examination of the ironies of social control, Gary Marx (1981) identifies a number of ways in which these efforts actually produce more deviance. For example, high-speed chases by police have resulted in serious injuries and deaths of bystanders, often leading to manslaughter charges against people who otherwise would have faced less serious charges. Stepped-up enforcement actions, such as those aimed at traffickers in illegal drugs or illegal immigration, drive away amateur criminals and encourage the development of more sophisticated organized crime groups that open new markets, drive up prices, and are more adept at avoiding prosecution. Efforts to control deviance, then, can have unintended and harmful consequences for individuals and for society as a whole, as we discuss in more depth below.

Deviance is created through social control—in other words, through reactions to behaviours—and is not simply a characteristic of behaviours. The same act—adultery, for example—can be treated as merely an indiscretion in some societies and as a capital crime in others. Being gossiped about and shunned by friends signals that adultery is considered by many Canadians to be somewhere between improper and immoral behaviour. But, in other times and other places, adultery is a crime. For example, in August 2002, a woman in Nigeria received a sentence of death by stoning, a punishment prescribed for adultery under some versions of Islamic law. (The sentence, which was to be carried out after she had finished weaning the baby used as proof of her adultery at trial, was ultimately commuted as a result of international pressure.) Deviance, then, is not simply a characteristic of behaviours but exists in the territory between behaviours and reactions to them.

Crime is a special case of deviance. It is defined by social norms that are formalized in criminal law. There is often—but not always—greater consensus about the wrongfulness of crimes than about other forms of behaviour defined as deviant. For example, people consistently rate criminal acts as more deserving of harsh punishment than noncriminal acts that violate norms (Wolfgang, Figlio, Tracy, and Singer, 1985). On the surface, the consensus surrounding such crimes as murder may seem obvious and natural. But, as with other forms of deviance, crime—even in its most serious forms—is also relative. Virtually all Canadians would say that the intentional killing of one person by another should be treated as a serious crime. But how many would say that euthanasia, the death penalty, killing by soldiers during times of war, or fatal shootings by police—all of them instances of intentional killing—should be treated as serious crimes? Conversely, many people feel that the criminal law on homicide should apply to a wider array of acts, such as abortion or deaths caused by the negligence of corporations. The controversy over Saskatchewan farmer Robert Latimer's second-degree murder conviction and life sentence illustrates the debates that can take place over what types of killings should be punished (see Box 14.1).

Acts ranging from adultery to intentional killing, then, are subject to conflicting opinions and dramatically different social reactions. Because social reactions and social controls define deviance, many sociologists contend that understanding the political processes and power relations that create definitions

BOX 14.1   THE MERCY-KILLING DEBATE

More than 60,000 people have signed a petition seeking clemency for Robert Latimer, a Saskatchewan farmer serving a life sentence for killing his severely disabled daughter. He says he did it to ease her suffering; critics say murder is murder. Latimer, 48, has been locked up since Jan. 18 [2001], when the Supreme Court of Canada ruled he could not be exempt from the mandatory minimum punishment for second-degree murder—a life sentence with no chance of parole for 10 years. Latimer's only hope to avoid or reduce his sentence is under the Royal Prerogative of Mercy, which can only be granted by the Governor General or cabinet.

Groups for the disabled have fought to see that Latimer serves his full term. Anything less would devalue the lives of society's most vulnerable and signal that they deserve lesser justice, said Diane Richler of the Canadian Association of Community Living. Richler attributed the strong levels of public support for Latimer to the fact that most people don't have close contact with someone with a severe disability.

Latimer killed Tracy, 12, in 1993 by putting her in the cab of his pickup truck and pumping in exhaust. He has always said he did it to spare her further torture from chronic pain brought on by surgeries to ease her cerebral palsy. She could not walk, talk, or feed herself. The Supreme Court ruled that Latimer could have opted for medically supervised pain management but he decided against it. He is eligible for day parole on Dec. 8, 2007.

SOURCE: Excerpted from Lisa Schmidt, "Latimer Petition Draws 60,000 Signatures," Canadian Press, Dec. 13, 2001.

of deviance and determine to whom those definitions are applied is the key to explaining deviance. These sociologists, called **conflict theorists,** analyze the relationships among (1) power struggles over defining deviance, (2) the organization of social control, and (3) people defined as deviant. As such, critical theorists study deviance as a socially constructed phenomenon.

THE SOCIAL CONSTRUCTION OF DEVIANCE AND ITS CONSEQUENCES

Understanding where definitions of deviance come from, and why they are often fluid and subject to conflict, requires that we look at the processes through which they are created—or what is called the social construction of deviance. These processes involve different groups and institutions, sometimes cooperating and sometimes competing to articulate norms and expectations for behaviour for the rest of society. Some efforts to define deviance—called **moral crusades**—are initiated by individuals or grassroots organizations acting as moral crusaders or claims makers. In this role, they push for the creation of deviance definitions by making claims that certain behaviours or conditions violate fundamental moral standards and, therefore, require formal recognition as wrong, and perhaps criminal, as well as appropriate intervention.

One example of a moral crusade is the campaign by Mothers Against Drunk Driving (MADD) to educate the public about the costs of drunk driving, to stigmatize those who drink and drive, and to increase criminal penalties for drunk driving. The success of MADD's campaign, like that of many other moral crusades, reflects the group's ability to gain the support of the media and various politicians, through which both legal and popular definitions of drunk driving were changed. More recently, various groups have come together to educate the public about the health and social costs of cigarette smoking, emphasizing the consequences of secondhand smoke. This has resulted in the implementation of no-smoking bylaws in many municipalities and cities throughout North America. These bylaws prohibit people from lighting up in public places, such as restaurants and bars and, in some cities, on sidewalk space directly outside business entrances. Moral crusades are not always successful, however. Anti-abortion groups, for example, have failed to garner sufficient support to have abortion redefined as a crime. The success of a moral crusade depends on the extent to which claims makers can enlist the support of groups with substantial political and economic power, especially the state's official rule makers (e.g., legislatures) and rule enforcers (e.g., courts).

Some moral crusades are launched by groups holding or vying for political power. For example, in their 1999 campaign for re-election, the Ontario Tories publicized their determination to criminalize any "behaviour that jeopardizes the safe use of the streets" (Ontario Legislature, 1999), arguing that squeegee people and beggars had made Toronto unsafe and unattractive for tourists, commuters, and city dwellers. True to their word, in January 2000 the Tory government passed the Safe Streets Act, "the first time a modern provincial government [had] enacted a provincial statute against begging conduct in public space" (Hermer and Mosher, 2002: 12). The act and the first criminal charges laid under it were the topic of considerable debate; lawyers for 13 defendants charged under the act—called "squeegee workers" by opponents of the act and "squeegee kids" by its supporters—questioned the act's constitutionality and argued that it both infringed on the right to freedom of expression and criminalized subsistence activities of the poor. Nevertheless, in August 2001 the 13 were convicted, affirming the Ontario government's claim that the act was a legitimate response to concerns over public safety and security.

Why do such moral crusades occur? A commonsense response is that claims makers recognize the harm in the behaviours or conditions they seek to define as deviant and take it upon themselves to educate the rest of society. However, this answer fails to recognize that some behaviours defined as deviant are of questionable or limited harm (e.g., begging) and that some harmful behaviours are not widely viewed as deviant (e.g., unsafe sex). The commonsense response is also not very good at explaining why

moral crusades often meet with resistance and why the process of defining deviance is, therefore, often fraught with conflict. What explains the conflict?

STATUS CONFLICT AND THE SOCIAL CONSTRUCTION OF DEVIANCE

A number of sociological perspectives on deviance see conflict at the root of the process of defining deviance. For Marxist theorists, conflict between different classes and the desire of the capitalist class to control the working class results in some behaviours (such as burglary) being targeted for control more than other behaviours (such as corporate crime). For conflict perspectives based on Foucault's work, fundamental but often-disguised conflicts in modern society emerge over knowledge and the ways it is produced and legitimized through the media, technology, and scientific expertise. Knowledge and the languages that express it are intimately linked to power, especially the power to construct definitions of right and wrong, good and evil.

A related answer to the question of why defining deviance is often characterized by conflict can be found in the **status-conflict perspective** that has its roots in the work of Max Weber and was further developed by Vold (1958), Turk (1969), and Quinney (1970). According to this perspective, the various social, economic, political, ethnic, religious, and professional groups that characterize modern societies continually compete with one another for status and influence. Among the outcomes they compete for is control over definitions of right and wrong— deviance and conformity. The law, especially the criminal law, is an important target of these struggles because of its power to define and punish deviance. The rewards of being a winner in these struggles are many. Winning groups can advance their interests over losing groups, gaining greater access to power, resources, and authority. By controlling definitions of deviance, winning groups accomplish at least two goals. First, they legitimate their moral standards and, hence, their claims to moral authority over losing groups. Second, they can determine the types of social controls applied to deviance—and, in turn, affect the demand for different professions

Should squeegee kids' actions be considered criminal, a nuisance, or a form of subsistence work?
SOURCE: Fred Thornhill/CP Picture Archive.

and occupations, such as social workers, physicians, or criminologists, and for different social control bureaucracies. These struggles over defining deviance and social control are ultimately about symbolic politics and the social construction of perceived reality.

The central themes of the status-conflict perspective can be seen in Erickson's (1996) analysis of the criminalization of psychoactive drugs in Canada during the last century. At the beginning of the twentieth century, psychoactive drugs, such as opium, heroin, and cocaine, were widely available in Canada and commonly used, most often in the form of patent medicines. Users were rarely stigmatized, perhaps not surprisingly since many were middle-class women and men. However, within two decades, use of many psychoactive drugs was criminalized and subject to severe penalties, including long prison terms with hard labour and whipping. This dramatic change was the result of a concerted campaign by various interest groups and politicians, especially Prime Minister William Lyon Mackenzie King. To justify the crackdown on some psychoactive drugs, moral crusaders cited the dangers they posed to physical health. But, as Erickson notes, these definitions of dangerousness were socially constructed by the moral crusaders, rather than based on scientific evidence. The true motivations behind the campaign included cultural and economic antagonism toward Asian immigrants, *some* of whom brought a new form of drug use—opium smoking—to Canada. Because these immigrants were willing to work for lower wages than whites were, they were strongly resented by white workers. In addition, certain occupational groups supported the campaign, partly out of a desire to strengthen the power base of government bureaucrats. The ultimate consequences of the campaign were the control and criminalization of less powerful cultural groups in the interests of more powerful groups.

Organized interest groups also engage in similar kinds of campaigns in order to *challenge* existing definitions of deviance. The gay and lesbian rights movement in Canada is an example of such a "deviance-defying" campaign. In the mid-1960s, sodomy was a crime in Canada and RCMP investigations into the background of federal employees led to the dismissal of gays from the civil service, the CBC, and the National Film Board. By 1970, however, gay rights' groups were actively challenging legal and

Same-sex marriage became legal in Canada in 2003 but only after decades of political and legal battles.
SOURCE: Paul Chiasson/CP Picture Archive.

medical definitions of homosexuality as deviance and pushing for an end to discrimination against gays in immigration, employment, housing, family policy, and the military. However, as Adam's (1995) history of the gay and lesbian movement recounts, conservative groups mobilized a counter-campaign in the late 1970s that encouraged police raids on gay bars and bathhouses in Montreal and Toronto. The effort to get human rights coverage extended to gay men and lesbians was first successful in Quebec in 1977. Active opposition meant that almost 20 years passed before the federal government added sexual orientation to the list of protected categories in its human rights legislation in 1996. Same-sex marriage became legal in Canada in 2003 but only after decades of political and legal battles.

THE CONSEQUENCES OF DEVIANCE DEFINING

An important contribution of conflict perspectives on deviance is their focus on the consequences for the people and the groups who are targets of the deviance defining process. The **labelling perspective** is organized around the idea that societal reactions to deviance are an important *cause* of deviance. Rather than looking at the events and conditions in people's lives before they are defined as deviants, the labelling perspective directs attention to what happens after someone has been singled out and labelled deviant (Becker, 1973; Lemert, 1967). It is the people who react to deviance and the character and consequences of their reactions that are the focus of the labelling perspective. The reactors include agents of social control (such as police or psychiatrists), significant others in the labelled person's life (such as family members and friends), and members of society at large, whose disapproval of the deviant act is typically known to the labelled person.

As we already noted, all of us engage in behaviour that others strongly disapprove of at one time or another in our lives, sometimes behaviours serious enough to get us in trouble with the law. Typically, these acts—which are caused by accident, by pressure or encouragement from others, by lapses in conscience or judgment, and so on—are hidden or occasional so they can be ignored, explained away, or justified by ourselves and others. This **primary deviance** (Lemert, 1967), however, can turn into **secondary deviance** if it becomes public and the person becomes the target of a strong and enduring negative reaction by others. Public disapproval can take many forms. Family and friends may avoid you, your employer may fire you, and social control agents may treat you as if your deviance is key to who you really are—eventually becoming your **master status.** In other words, your status as a university student, a son, a brother, and a musician will matter little in comparison with your status, for example, as a regular heroin user. When, as a consequence of the social reaction, you come to define yourself as essentially and indelibly a drug addict, secondary deviance has occurred. In the final stage of this process, you have become what you were defined as: Your commitment to your deviance increases as your claims to conventionality are lost or denied. As "Ken," a young man convicted of passing a bad cheque, said: "What the hell—if I'm going to be named a criminal I might as well be one" (Frazier, 1976: 136). This is the self-fulfilling prophecy of the labelling process and it demonstrates how reactions to deviance are one of its important causes.

The process by which reactions to deviance can stabilize and reinforce such behaviours has been described in recent studies of young black males and in earlier studies of people with mental illnesses and homosexuals "outed" in the early 1960s, adolescent "troublemakers," and people with physical disabilities (Anderson, 1990; Becker, 1964; Chambliss, 1973; Scott, 1969). But, as some of these studies show, it would be a mistake to see people defined as deviants as simply passive, compliant subjects. Faced with the stigma and rejection caused by a deviant label, some fight back by denying the deviance of their actions or questioning the motivations of reactors. In 2002, Mark Hall, an Ontario high-school student, a Roman Catholic, and a homosexual, won the right to take his boyfriend to the school prom by challenging the Durham District Catholic School Board. The school board had banned the gay couple from the dance, but a Superior Court found that this violated Hall's rights to freedom from discrimination on the basis of sexual orientation.

The shared experience of being labelled deviant can also bring people together in collective responses. Sometimes these responses are efforts to resist the labels and change the definition of deviance, as we saw earlier in our discussion of the activities of gay rights groups. Other groups of stigmatized people have formed voluntary organizations to provide support and positive recognition for their nonconformity, to educate the public, and to challenge discriminatory policies. For example, organizations like the National Association to Advance Fat Acceptance, the Living Large Club, and the Ample Opportunity Group urge their members and the public to question the social intolerance of obesity (Findlay, 1996). Similarly, in response to their increasingly deviant identity, some smokers are aggressively contesting their stigmatization. For instance, they have set up a Smokers' Home Page on the World Wide Web that includes a series of articles denouncing smoking restrictions and urging block voting by smokers, who have more numerical clout than many other lobbying groups.

At other times, collective responses may lead to the development of a *subculture*, in which those labelled deviant embrace their identity and reject their labellers or express disdain for the values of conventional society. Outlaw biker gangs, skinheads, and cyberpunks can be considered deviant subcultures. Their members typically share an argot (or insider language), distinctive clothing and body language, networks of mutual support, and a set of beliefs and norms, some of which contrast with those of mainstream society. These attributes are also characteristic of many youth subcultures, of course. Whether these subcultures are *deviant* is often a

Whether certain subcultures are deviant is a source of much debate.

SOURCE: Photos.com.

source of much debate, particularly among parents, educators, police, and the youths involved. The Straight Edge subculture, for example, is highly critical of many aspects of mainstream society—especially the use of animals for food and clothing—and is opposed to tobacco, alcohol, and drug use, but its adherents disavow the label of deviant (Irwin, 1999). Similarly, youths who identify with the rave culture object to how it has been portrayed by the media and politicians.

Collective responses by those labelled deviant can have positive consequences. For instance, the recognition of shared experiences of rejection can bring otherwise isolated, and perhaps self-blaming, people together. Whether or not such groups are able to alter how the wider public perceives their members, they at least can counter some of the more damaging consequences of social condemnation. As with other moral crusades to define deviance, campaigns by groups to eliminate deviant definitions will succeed to the extent that they marshal political support and favourable media attention. Both constructing and repudiating definitions of deviance, then, involve power struggles and symbolic politics, and these struggles have been the focus of research by many sociologists.

For other sociologists, however, understanding deviance and crime requires more than understanding conflicts over definitions. Arguing that some behaviours—particularly many criminal acts—have serious individual and social costs, these sociologists have devoted considerable attention to the question of why people engage in such acts.

WHY DO PEOPLE ENGAGE IN CRIMINAL BEHAVIOUR?

On April 20, 1999, two teenage friends in Littleton, Colorado, walked into their high school during lunch break carrying an assault rifle, a semi-automatic pistol, two sawed-off shotguns, and about three-dozen homemade bombs. Over the next 90 minutes, they wandered through the school laughing and shooting teachers and students who cowered behind desks or dashed through hallways. After killing 13 people and wounding 23 others, they shot and killed themselves in the school library. Eight days later, a 14-year-old boy in Taber, Alberta, entered W.R. Myers High School with a .22-calibre semi-automatic rifle and shot two students on their way to class after lunch break. He then pointed the gun at several others before a Grade 9 student convinced him to put down the weapon. One of the wounded students, Jason Lang, died shortly after he was taken to hospital. And in September 2006, a 25-year-old gunman entered the cafeteria at Dawson College in Montreal and started shooting. He wounded 19 people and killed 1 young woman, Anastasia DeSousa, before killing himself.

How can we explain these and other types of serious criminal acts? Dozens of sociological explanations of crime have been proposed, but they can be distinguished by the different assumptions they make about the sources of human behaviour. One set of explanations asks, "Why do people engage in crime?" and answers by identifying social factors that motivate or push people toward crime. These are **motivational theories.** The other set of explanations asks, "Why doesn't everyone engage in crime?" and answers by identifying social factors that control or prevent people's criminal behaviour. These are **control theories** and **opportunity theories.** Let's consider how these theories account for criminal behaviour and what they might tell us about high school shootings.

MOTIVATIONAL THEORIES

Strain Theories

Motivational theories argue that most criminal behaviour occurs because a social context exists that encourages or pushes a person toward crime. One of the best-known examples is Robert Merton's **strain theory** (Merton, 1938). For Merton, the motivation to crime lies in society, not in individuals: "Social structures exert a definite pressure upon certain persons in the society to engage in non-conforming rather than conforming conduct" (Merton, 1957: 32). Some societies have higher rates of crime than others because their cultures value certain achievements, but their social structures fail to provide many people with legitimate ways to attain these valued goals. For example, in North America, children learn at home, at school, and from the media to value economic achievement and the status that comes with it. From an early age, we see others evaluated on the basis of what they own and what they can buy. At the same time, the structure of North American society limits available opportunities for economic success. Therefore, a university education and a high-paying job may not be realistic nor attainable goals for many people.

The lack of fit between cultural goals and social structural opportunities—or what Merton, following Durkheim, called **anomie**—means that many people feel strained because they are not able to achieve what they have been taught to value or desire. In response to this strain, people react in a variety of ways. Most continue to conform to societal norms despite the strain they feel. Others choose deviance. They may drop out of conventional society and withdraw from the competition over cultural goals. They may abandon the goal of success but follow other cultural goals in a ritualistic manner. They may rebel against convention and support alternative goals and means. Or, finally, they may find alternative but illegitimate ways to achieve cultural goals. This last deviant adaptation—Merton called it **innovation**—is the one that will most likely lead people to commit economic crimes, such as burglary, forgery, or selling drugs. For Merton, each of these adaptations is a normal reaction to the lack of fit between cultural goals and approved means. Criminals, then, are not sick, evil, or stupid. They are simply responding unconventionally to a contradiction that exists in conventional society.

But how can strain theory help us understand what happened in Littleton or Taber or Montreal? There is no evidence that the young killers lacked legitimate opportunities or were economically deprived. Indeed, the Littleton killers came from comfortable middle-class families. They usually drove to school together in a used BMW that one of them owned. But commentators on the killers noted that they felt like outcasts, were sometimes the target of ridicule, and resented the student hierarchy that valued athletic and other "preppie" accomplishments

(Bergman, 1999; Phillips, 1999). Thus, the killers may have experienced a different type of strain—status frustration—because they were unable or unwilling to achieve goals within the dominant student culture (Cohen, 1955). They may have expressed this frustration by dramatizing their strong rejection of that culture through the shootings.

This account, while plausible, illustrates some of the shortcomings of strain theory. Many teenagers feel rejected by their peers or their teachers, yet they do not react by killing them. So strain may be a necessary, but not a sufficient, condition for many types of criminal behaviour. Strain theory also does not tell us whether someone experiencing strain will choose to drop out, rebel, innovate, or conform. Another motivational theory, however, provides some insights into how strain might give rise to particular types of deviant actions.

Learning Theories

A second variant of motivational theories contends that, just as we learn to play hockey or appreciate hip-hop, we learn to engage in criminal behaviour. Like strain theory, **learning theories** see crime as a socially formed response to an environment. Like strain theory, learning theories also assert that a person's environment provides the motivation to engage in crime. The best-known version of learning theory is Edwin Sutherland's theory of **differential association** (Sutherland, 1939). Sutherland pointed out that Merton's strain theory could not predict with any precision how people under strain would respond. Would they conform or deviate? And if they deviated, would they become wife beaters, crack users, or terrorists? To understand how and why people choose any particular criminal activity, Sutherland directed his attention to people's learning histories and environments.

Throughout our lives, we all interact with people whose attitudes, values, and behaviour patterns sometimes encourage, and sometimes discourage, crime. Whether you engage in any particular type of crime depends on the mix of pro-criminal and anti-criminal influences in your environment. Crime occurs, said Sutherland, when people have experienced more pro-criminal influences. If you choose to become a car thief, then it is because you have learned from others that it is acceptable to steal cars, and you have learned which cars are easiest to steal, how to break into them, how to avoid the police, and how to justify your activities to others.

Although white-collar criminals (like Ken Lay and Jeff Skilling, pictured here) often express contempt for the law, share an organizational or business culture that rewards rule breaking, and associate with others from whom they can learn both the skills and the rationalizations needed to carry out their crimes, sociologists have continued to focus on street crime more than "suite" crime.

SOURCE: Tim Jonson/Reuters/Landov.

A distinctive feature of differential association theory is its ability to account for crime at all levels of society. Thus, Sutherland (1949) applied the theory in his landmark study of **white-collar crime.** White-collar criminals, according to Sutherland, are like street criminals in that they often express contempt for the law, share an organizational or business culture that rewards rule breaking, and associate with others from whom they can learn both the skills and the rationalizations needed to carry out their crimes. Despite Sutherland's early, path-breaking work, sociologists have continued to focus on street crime more than "suite" crime, although a recent rash of well-publicized corporate misdeeds has attracted the attention of scholars, as well as the criminal justice system, as we discuss below.

What can learning theories tell us about the school shootings? There are at least three ways in which learning theories can be applied to these events. The Littleton killers were said to be avid con-sumers of death-cult music, the movie *Natural Born Killers,* and violent video games. The Montreal gunman played video games so violent that their sale is illegal in Canada; he ordered them over the Internet. Some learning theories argue that long exposure to violent images desensitizes young people to violence and conveys the message that violence is an acceptable way to respond to frustration (Eron, 1986). Other evidence suggests that the Littleton killers learned how to make the bombs they took to school from various websites. As Sutherland's differential association theory notes, many types of crime require opportunities to learn specific techniques and procedures. Finally, the copycat nature of the Taber shootings suggests that, as some learning theories argue, much crime is imitation or modelling of others' behaviours.

A common theme uniting strain and learning theories is that for crime to occur, some kind of motivating influence must be present. Motivational theories assume that, in the absence of such influences, people will rarely misbehave. Hence, their question, "Why do people engage in crime?" Moreover, both strain and learning theories assume an underlying consensus over definitions of crime, an assumption shared by control and opportunity theories, as discussed next. Here the similarity ends, however, as the next group of theories assumes that all people are capable of crime if the rewards are sufficient; given the lack of controls or increased opportunities, these theories argue, most of us would break the law.

CONTROL AND OPPORTUNITY THEORIES

Control and opportunity theories find it easy to explain crime: It's rewarding. Stealing is a fast way to make money. Getting high on drugs can be an easy way to feel good. Trashing a subway platform is risky fun. The question then, for control and opportunity theorists, is not "Why do people commit crime?" but "Why do most of us play by the rules most of the time?" In answering this question, control and opportunity theories look to somewhat different processes.

Control Theories

For control theories, crime occurs because of the absence of controls. In one of the most influential versions of control theory, Hirschi (1969) argued that juvenile delinquency results from the lack of strong bonds to conventional social institutions. Adolescents with few attachments to their parents, teachers, or other conventional role models; with little commitment to family, school, or other conventional institutions; with weak beliefs in conventional values; and with little involvement in conventional activities are free to act on their deviant impulses. Adolescents with strong bonds to conventionality, conversely, will not want to risk breaking the rules. Ask yourself, have you ever stopped short of cheating, stealing, or driving under the influence because you did not want to hurt your parents or your chances of getting into university or college? If so, your deviant impulses were controlled or contained by your social bonds.

In a later version of control theory, Gottfredson and Hirschi (1990) identify self-control as the key to conformity. People with low self-control will try to get what they want quickly, easily, and without thinking about others, and if doing so involves excitement and risk, so much the better. As you might expect, behaving in this way often means breaking rules or failing to fulfill conventional responsibilities—in other words, being deviant. Weak self-control, then, frees people to gamble, drink and drive, bribe officials, or do anything else that provides quick and relatively effortless gratification.

Hagan, Simpson, and Gillis (1987) have used control theory to explain gender differences in delinquency. Families exert greater control over girls than over boys by socializing girls to avoid risks and by supervising them more closely. In contrast, boys are encouraged by their families to take risks and be independent. As a result, boys are freer to engage in delinquent acts. Families, then, are the major source of controls that prevent deviance, according to control theories. Early childhood socialization—the ways in which parents reward and discipline children and the extent to which they develop affectionate bonds with them—is critical to all control theories. If those controls are developed early in life, children will not be as susceptible to the deviant influences of peers, nor will they respond to strain with deviant actions.

Several observers of the school shootings described earlier saw evidence of control theory's predictions at work. The Littleton teens spent many hours alone together, unsupervised by their parents, who claimed not to know that their children had acquired several guns, built dozens of explosive devices, and developed a website that advertised their violent inclinations. In diaries and other writing, the teens indicated their disdain for school and other conventional institutions and pursuits. A Canadian researcher on teen violence, Alan Leschied of the University of Western Ontario, characterized the boys in the language of control theory when he said they had "a lessening of ties to conventional supports" (Chisholm, 1999: 22). But control theories, like strain theories, do not tell us what *type* of deviance the person who lacks bonds to conventional others will turn to, or why some people who lack bonds to society do not engage in deviance. Opportunity theories have tried to answer these questions.

Opportunity Theories

Proponents of opportunity theories, like control theorists, assume that in the absence of inner controls, such as a conscience, or external controls, such as a police officer on the corner or a lock on the door, most of us would engage in crime. The type of crime we choose, according to these theories, would depend on the opportunities available to us. Opportunities are structured by everything from other people's routine daily activities (is the house down the street empty during the day?), to access to the tools to carry out the crime (do you have a computer, a car, a gun?), to the availability of easy and attractive targets (CDs are easy to steal, big-screen televisions less so).

According to one version of opportunity theory, the large increase in property and violent crimes that occurred in North America beginning in the late 1960s can be explained, in part, by the fact that people were spending less time at home and many consumer goods were becoming more durable and more portable (Cohen and Felson, 1979). With more women in the work force, more people living in single-family homes, and more people spending evening hours at the movies and in bars, empty houses became more attractive targets for burglars during the day and entertainment seekers became more available as targets for muggers at night. As televisions, radios, and music systems became smaller, more lightweight, and more durable, they became more attractive targets for shoplifters and snatch-and-grab artists.

Opportunity theories do not try to explain why people decide to commit crime. They simply assume that many people lack the controls to stop themselves. When these people encounter criminal opportunities, they will act, but the type of crimes they commit will depend on the opportunities they encounter. Opportunity theories thus connect the potential offender described by control theories to particular offences.

The school shootings described earlier occurred, according to opportunity theories, not only because the teens lacked bonds to society but also because they had access to the tools necessary to kill people easily—that is, guns. The widespread availability of guns in North America, and especially in the United States, is linked not only to its high homicide rates but also to its high suicide rates, especially rates of suicide by teens. Canadian males aged 15 to 24 kill themselves three times more often than 15- to 24-year-old males in Italy, England, or Hong Kong (World Health Organization, 1998); and 85 percent of these suicides in Canada are committed with guns. As Dr. Katherine Leonard, an expert in adolescent depression, points out: "Teenagers who don't have a firearm available are less likely to kill themselves. You might think 'Oh, they'll just jump off a bridge or something.' That's simply not the case" (Phillips, 1999: 24). Where lethal weapons are more available, then, the opportunities for lethal violence are much greater.

Table 14.1 summarizes the major sociological theories of crime and deviance.

PATTERNS OF DEVIANCE AND CRIME

MEASURING DEVIANCE AND CRIME

Our discussion of where definitions of deviance and crime come from and why people behave in ways that get them defined as criminal suggests that rates of deviance and crime should vary among social groups as well as among societies. Documenting such variation with any accuracy is not easy, however, because of the hidden nature of much deviance and the political nature of defining it. If deviance becomes the target of formal control, it can be documented through statistics produced by official social control agents and organizations. However, these statistics are affected by more than just deviant behaviour. Control agents and the wider public make decisions about which deviant acts or persons to report and which to ignore. So, for example, if public intolerance of young "troublemakers" increases—think of the expansion of zero-tolerance policies in schools in the last few years—official statistics on youth crime may indicate an increase, not because there is more of it, but because more of it is reported to police (Tanner, 1996).

Sociologists of crime and deviance, aware of the limitations of official statistics, often rely on other information sources. Surveys that ask people to report

---

TABLE 14.1 SOCIOLOGICAL THEORIES OF CRIME AND DEVIANCE

THEORY	KEY SOCIOLOGISTS	CENTRAL FOCUS
Status conflict	Weber; Vold; Turk; Quinney	Focuses on how groups compete to control definitions of right and wrong
Labelling	Becker; Lemert	Focuses on how societal reactions to crime and deviance are an important cause of such behaviour
Strain	Merton; Cohen	Focuses on the motivations for crime and deviance that arise as a result of disjuncture between culturally prescribed goals and culturally approved means to achieve those goals
Differential association	Sutherland	Emphasizes the way in which individual learning histories and environments may contribute more pro-criminal than pro-conformity influences
Control	Hirschi; Gottfredson and Hirschi; Hagan, Simpson, and Gillis	Explains crime and deviance by focusing on the absence of controls (i.e., lack of strong bonds, lack of self-control, differential controls)
Opportunity	Cohen and Felson	Focuses on the role played by available opportunities in the production of crime

on their own involvement in deviance or on their victimization experiences produce results closer to actual behaviours and so avoid many of the problems associated with official statistics. However, survey data, like official statistics, are affected by people's willingness and ability to reveal their own or others' deviance. Indirect measures of deviance can avoid many of these problems. Examples include statistics on deaths from cirrhosis of the liver as a measure of alcohol abuse or statistics on sales of medical syringes as a measure of intravenous drug use.

How we count deviance and what we know about it is the outcome of social and political processes. Although it is important to keep in mind that all sources of information on deviance are imperfect, combining information from many sources permits greater confidence in our depiction of deviance. This means that we have a better idea of the extent and nature of some kinds of deviance than of others, because some kinds of deviance can be documented through a variety of sources. Let's turn to what we know about one of the most well documented types of deviant behaviour: crime.

CRIMINAL BEHAVIOUR IN CANADA

Recent Crime Trends

Contrary to what many Canadians believe, the crime rate in 2004 was about the same level as in 1979 (Sauvé, 2005), and the homicide rate was 36 percent lower than in 1975 (see Figure 14.1). Paralleling these declines in crime is an increasing number of Canadians who indicate that they feel safe in their neighbourhoods. In 2004, 90 percent of Canadians who walk alone after dark indicated that they felt safe doing so (Gannon, 2005). Nevertheless, close to 30 percent of the population said they thought crime levels had increased in their area during the past five years and another 58 percent believed crime had remained stable.

Why do so many Canadians think crime has increased when the evidence suggests otherwise? To answer this question, we need to know about the factors that shape people's perceptions about crime. One of the most important factors is the media. Most people get the bulk of their information about crime from watching television and reading newspapers and, in recent years, media coverage of crime has increased greatly (Committee of Concerned Journalists, 1998). Crime stories lead the nightly news and appear "above the fold" in the daily newspapers

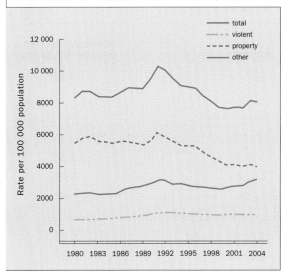

FIGURE 14.1   CRIME RATES IN CANADA, 1980–2004

SOURCE: Adapted from the Statistics Canada publication "Juristat," Catalogue 85-002, Crime statistics in Canada, 2004, Vol. 25, No. 5, released July 21, 2005.

more often now than in the past. As we hear more about crime, we perceive it to be more prevalent. People's fears about crime also increase as they age, and the Canadian population is aging (see Chapter 17). In the late 1990s, crime also became a popular topic in many Canadian political campaigns in which the need for increased law and order was emphasized. Like increased media coverage, this reflects and reinforces people's fears about crime.

Another question raised by the crime statistics cited above is "Why did crime decrease during the 1990s in Canada?" Politicians, criminal justice officials, and sociologists have all offered views on the decline in crime. Some claim it is a consequence of more effective forms of community policing. Others argue that "get tough" crime policies are working, and still others point to the recent upswing of the economy. None of these explanations is sufficient, however, because crime rates decreased not only in Canada but also in the United States and England, in cities without community policing; in provinces that have reduced their incarceration rates, and in regions with bleak economic conditions. A trend common across all these settings can help explain some of the decline in crime: A decrease in the proportion of the population in the most crime-prone age group— people between 15 and 24 years of age. So, just as the aging of the population may be associated with rising

TABLE 14.2 HOMICIDE RATES FOR SELECTED COUNTRIES, 2003

COUNTRY	HOMICIDE RATE PER 100 000 POPULATION
South Africa	44.10
Russia	19.82
United States	5.70
Hungary	2.22
Finland	1.98
Canada	**1.95**
France	1.65
England and Wales	1.62
Northern Ireland	1.53
Australia	1.51
Germany	0.99
Japan	0.51

SOURCE: Adapted from the Statistics Canada publication "Juristat," Catalogue 85-002, Homicide in Canada, 2004, Vol. 25, No. 6, released October 6, 2005.

TABLE 14.3 CRIME RATES (PER 100 000 POPULATION) FOR CANADA AND THE UNITED STATES, 2004

	CANADA	UNITED STATES
Murder and non-negligent manslaughter	1.95	5.5
Robbery	86	137
Aggravated assault	145	291
Burglary	860	730
Larceny	2131	2366
Motor vehicle theft	531	421

SOURCES: Compiled from Julie Sauve, "Crime Statistics in Canada, 2004," Juristat, Vol. 25, No. 5, Ottawa: Statistics Canada, Canadian Centre for Justice Statistics; and Federal Bureau of Investigation, Uniform Crime Reports, 2004, http://www.fbi.gov/ucr/00cius.htm.

concerns about crime, it is also associated with reduced crime rates. Demographics cannot fully explain the drop in crime, however, because the crime rate is dropping faster than the population is aging. Improved employment opportunities and changes in collective values also may have played a role in the falling crime rate (Ouimet, 2002).

Although Canadians do not appear to be at greater risk of criminal victimization now than they were in the 1970s or 1980s, they continue to be at greater risk than are citizens of some other industrialized nations. Victimization surveys indicate that rates of violent offences, theft, and burglary are higher in Canada than in several European countries (Canadian Centre for Justice Statistics, 1996). The risk of being a victim of homicide is also greater in Canada than in several other developed nations, although it's substantially less than the risk in South Africa, Russia, and the United States (see Table 14.2). In addition, crime in Canada remains distinct from crime in the United States in an important respect. Although Canadians are more likely than Americans to be the victims of burglaries and car thefts, they are much less likely than Americans to be the victims of serious violent crime, such as aggravated assault, robbery, and homicide (see Table 14.3).

The Risks of Victimization and Offending: Sex, Age, and Ethnicity

Crime is unequally distributed within and among societies. In Canada, crime rates have historically been lower in the Atlantic provinces and Quebec than in the Western provinces and highest in the territories (see Figure 14.2). Urban dwellers, young Canadians, those who are single, and those with lower household incomes report higher rates of personal victimization than do rural dwellers, older Canadians, married couples, and those with higher household incomes (Gannon and Mihorean, 2005). There is little difference in the overall risk of personal victimization for women and men. Males, however, commit a disproportionate number of violent and property offences. Criminal offenders also tend to be younger than the general population. Contrary to public perceptions about youth violence, however, the average age of those accused of homicide has *increased* in Canada since the 1970s and is currently 31 years (Dauvergne, 2005).

Some types of criminal victimization and offending also appear to be more prevalent in some ethnic and cultural groups than others. For example, Aboriginal people (including Inuit and Métis) constitute about 3 percent of the Canadian population, but about 17 percent of all homicide victims (Dauvergne, 2005). Because most homicides are intra-racial (about 85 percent of Aboriginal victims are killed by Aboriginal offenders), a disproportionate number of

FIGURE 14.2   CRIME RATES, 2004

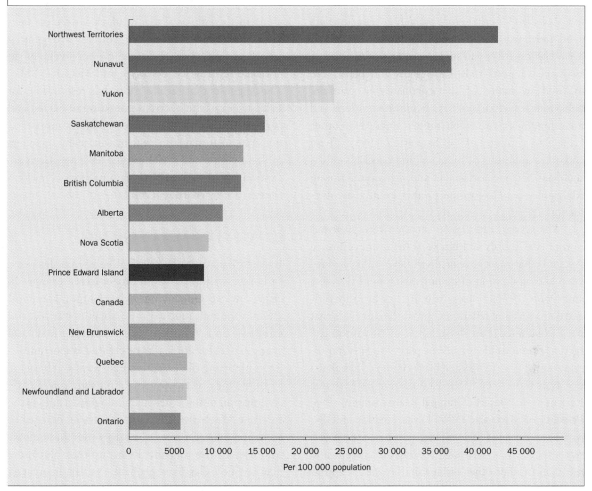

SOURCE: Uniform Crime Reporting Survey, Canadian Centre for Justice Statistics, Statistics Canada. Reproduced with the permission of the Minister of Public Works and Government Services Canada, 2006.

homicide suspects are Aboriginal as well. Aboriginal people account for about 22 percent of all people arrested for homicide in Canada, according to statistics compiled by the Canadian Centre for Justice Statistics.

Police agencies in Canada do not publish or analyze data on the ethnic and cultural backgrounds of those arrested, and so it has been difficult for researchers to determine whether other groups are overrepresented among arrestees. However, because of public concern over black-on-black violence in Toronto, the *Toronto Star* newspaper compiled information on arrestees from police reports for the period 1996 through early 2002. It found that blacks accounted for about 27 percent of all arrests for violent crimes in Toronto whereas they constitute only about 8 percent of Toronto's population (Rankin, Quinn, Shephard, Simmie, and Duncanson, 2002).

Black and Aboriginal people are also overrepresented among those serving time in Canada's jails and prisons. In 2003–04, Aboriginal people accounted for 21 percent of people admitted to provincial, territorial, and federal institutions (Beattie, 2005). Their admissions to provincial and territorial institutions have remained relatively stable during the past two decades, whereas their representation among those sentenced to federal institutions has increased steadily, from 8 percent to 18 percent. Blacks make up about 2 percent of the Canadian population, but they represent 6 percent of prisoners under federal jurisdiction; and their incarceration rate is about five times greater than that of whites (Wortley and McCalla, 2003).

There are at least two ways to explain these patterns. First, Aboriginals and blacks may be at higher risk of incarceration because they engage in the kinds of behaviours that put them in conflict with the law. Although official crime statistics by race are currently not published for crimes other than homicide, the data cited above lend some support to this explanation, at least with regard to violent crimes. In addition, other evidence suggests that Aboriginals and blacks are exposed to many of the correlates of criminal behaviour—such as poverty, family disruption, and unemployment—at much higher rates than other Canadians (Frideres, 1996; Satzewich, 1998). These and other indicators of strain and weak social bonds—such as high rates of suicide and depression among Aboriginal people—would predict greater involvement in crime.

The second explanation for the overrepresentation of Aboriginals and blacks in the criminal justice system is that there may be discrimination in the creation and application of criminal definitions (Roberts and Doob, 1997). This possibility has been investigated in a series of federal and provincial inquiries that have concluded that "systemic" or "institutional" racism is responsible for at least part of the overrepresentation of Aboriginals and blacks in the criminal justice system (Cawsey, 1991; Commission on Systemic Racism in the Ontario Criminal Justice System, 1995; Province of Manitoba, 1991). Discrimination and disparity can occur at various stages in the criminal justice process. For example, Aboriginal people and members of some other visible minority groups appear to be policed more closely than whites, and relations between these groups and the police are often hostile and distrustful, which can lead to a higher likelihood of arrest. Once arrested, blacks and Aboriginals also are significantly more likely than members of other ethnic groups to be denied pretrial release on bail and to spend longer periods in pretrial detention, both of which increase their likelihood of conviction and incarceration (Hamilton and Sinclair, 1991; Roberts and Doob, 1997).

The possibility that "racial profiling" by police could lead to an overrepresentation of certain ethnic and cultural groups in the criminal justice system has recently become a topic of considerable controversy. In Canada, police forces are not required to record the race or ethnicity of those they stop and search, and so police statistics cannot be used to determine whether racial profiling exists. Recent surveys in Toronto, however, have found that black people—especially young, black males—report having had involuntary contact with the police more often than

whites or Asians do, and these higher rates of police contact are not explained away by greater involvement in deviant activity by black youth. In fact, racial differences in police contact are *greatest* among youth with little or no involvement in deviance or drug use (Wortley and McCalla, 2003). This suggests that racial profiling is responsible for at least part of the overrepresentation of blacks, and perhaps Aboriginal Canadians, in the criminal justice system. It may also explain why many members of these ethnic and racial groups have negative perceptions of the Canadian criminal justice system (Foster, 1996; Wortley, 1996).

CRIME AND SOCIAL CHANGE

If the explanations for criminal behaviour discussed earlier are valid, we would expect to see changes in crime rates accompanying social changes that might affect criminal motivations, social control, and criminal opportunities. For example, new and changing technologies have created opportunities for committing old crimes in new ways and have led to new types of crime. An important tool in the commission of these new technological crimes is the Internet. Much media attention has been devoted to teenage "cybercriminals" or to other individuals who use the Internet for illicit purposes. But these new technologies have probably had their greatest impact on corporate and organized criminal activities and their control, because the global and decentralized nature of this technology and the almost instantaneous movement of data over national boundaries create profound problems for law enforcement.

Corporate Crime, Organized Crime, and Globalization

Globalization is affecting all arenas of human behaviour, including criminal behaviour (see Chapter 19). As the economies of nation-states become more integrated and interdependent—a move encouraged by the proliferation of electronic technology—both the motivations and the opportunities for global economic crime have increased enormously, as have the difficulties in controlling it. As a result, corporate crime and organized crime are moving beyond national boundaries, just like the pursuit of profit through legitimate activities (Findlay, 1999).

A large portion of global crime is corporate crime, that is, crime committed by legitimate business organizations. It includes violations of antitrust, environmental, food and drug, tax, health and safety, and corruption laws. The economic costs of these crimes have been estimated at 50 times those associated with street crimes (Rosoff, Pontell, and Tillman, 1998). Although the profits of global corporate crime are impossible to estimate precisely, some sense of them is suggested by the kinds of fines that have been levied against corporations that have been successfully prosecuted. For example, in the spring of 1999, the Swiss pharmaceutical giant F. Hoffmann–La-Roche Ltd., pled guilty in a U.S. court and agreed to pay a US$500 million criminal fine for its role in a ten-year, worldwide conspiracy to raise and fix prices of vitamins. Archer-Daniels-Midland, on whose board of directors former prime minister Brian Mulroney served, paid a fine of US$140 million in the United States in 1996 and a fine of $16 million in Canada in 1997 for its role in a global price-fixing conspiracy. More recently, multibillion-dollar scandals involving energy giant Enron, cable TV company Adelphia, the Tyco conglomerate, and WorldCom (owner of the second-biggest long-distance phone company in the United States and headed by Canadian-born Bernie Ebbers) have led to convictions of corporate executives on charges of conspiracy and securities fraud, and there are been several major lawsuits involving Canadian corporations. In 2002 the Canadian Imperial Bank of Commerce, for example, was named in a class-action suit filed against several top Enron executives and its lenders, including the CIBC.

Controlling corporate crime that spans national boundaries remains exceedingly difficult, in part because of the limited resources controllers have to work with and also because of national differences in how corporate misconduct is defined. Globalization has made it easier for corporations to move their factories to countries with lax occupational health and safety laws. It has also made it easier for corporations to sell products that developed countries have banned as health hazards to countries with less restrictive food and drug laws. Because of massive foreign debts and other economic pressures, less developed countries have become the largest, but not sole, market for these corporate activities. In the 1980s, the United States exported most of its hazardous wastes to Canada because Canadian laws regulating the disposal of these wastes were less stringent than U.S. laws (Rosoff, Pontell, and Tillman, 1998).

Criminal organizations are also benefiting from new opportunities for crime spawned by globalization. Previously local or nationally based criminal organizations, such as the American Mafia, the Chinese Triads, the Japanese Yakuza, the Russian Mafia, and the Colombian drug cartels, have formed global alliances to gain access to new markets and take advantage of one another's special skills. These alliances have been fostered by a number of events, including the creation of free-trade blocs, such as the European Union; the development of the World Wide Web; the collapse of the Soviet Union; and the commercialization of China (Richards, 1999). The illegal activities engaged in by global organized crime are highly diverse and include trafficking in drugs, arms, and human beings; contraband smuggling; money laundering; telecommunications piracy; and the sexual exploitation of children. A recent UN report on worldwide organized crime groups notes that as a result of their increasingly sophisticated strategies and diverse modes of operation "they are able to infiltrate the financial, economic and political systems of countries all over the world" (United Nations, 1999: 4).

Money laundering—the process by which proceeds from criminal activities are disguised as legitimate income—is key to the health of global organized crime groups. The Financial Crimes Enforcement Network estimates that money laundering could now be the world's third-largest business, with more than US$750 billion a year in illicit funds being laundered worldwide (Richards, 1999). Canada has become an increasingly popular site for money-laundering rings because of its proximity to the United States, its stable economy and sophisticated financial sector, and its lack of both mandatory reporting requirements and controls on currency crossing the Canada–U.S. border. An estimated $15 billion is laundered in or through Canada and Canadian financial institutions each year (Criminal Intelligence Service Canada, 1996).

Crime and Changing Gender Stratification

As noted in Chapter 7, one of the most influential social changes of the last generation has been the growing awareness and abatement of many forms of gender inequality. In the 1970s, some criminologists expected this change to reduce the longstanding gender gap in crime: Men have historically been much more likely than women to engage in criminal acts. This expectation was rekindled in the 1990s by some high-profile cases of violent crime by teenage girls, such as the killing of 14-year-old Rena Virk in Victoria in 1997. Put simply, some analysts believed that decreasing gender stratification might mean that females would catch up to males in their criminal behaviour as their access to less traditional roles expanded, the stresses associated with new roles increased, and controls over their activities decreased. The evidence has not backed up this expectation, however. A large gender gap persists in most crimes, especially the kinds of serious violent crimes traditionally dominated by men. In Canada, for example, consistent with previous years, almost nine in ten persons accused of homicide in 2004 were male (Dauvergne, 2005). And the homicide rate among teenage girls was lower in 2004 than it was in 1991 (see Figure 14.3).

Changes in gender stratification are, however, related to one aspect of women's involvement in crime—as victims, not offenders. In developed nations since World War II, as women have moved into the labour force in unprecedented numbers, they have also taken on less traditional domestic roles by having more children out of wedlock, marrying later, and divorcing more often. This shift toward less traditional gender roles for women has affected their risks of homicide victimization in complex ways (Gartner, Baker, and Pampel, 1990). In countries where women's status is relatively low, women's risks of being homicide victims have increased with these

changes. However, in countries where women's status is relatively high—such as Canada—women's risks have not increased relative to men's risks as women have assumed less traditional roles. In fact, in Canada, the gender gap in homicide victimization has grown substantially since the early 1970s. Males are currently twice as likely as females to be victims of homicide (Dauvergne, 2005).

Major social, economic, and political transformations can have profound and complex effects on patterns of crime and deviance, as we have seen. It is not surprising, then, that these transformations also affect patterns of social control.

PATTERNS OF SOCIAL CONTROL

For most of human history, families, communities, and the church were the major sources of social control. The punishment for serious rule breaking was physical and, to our eyes, often horrific. Before the seventeenth century, centralized states either did not exist or were not strong enough to sponsor the institutions of formal social control that predominate in modern societies. With the growth of market-based economies and industrialization—and the accompanying growth of a working class—state-based formal social controls emerged. The most obvious example of these formal controls is the confinement institution—prisons, asylums, poorhouses, and so forth—that emerged in the seventeenth century. These were places of residence and work where people who were unable or unwilling to work or conform to other rules were isolated from the outside world, closely watched, and continuously regimented by impersonal agents of control. Punishment based on physical pain shifted to punishment based on deprivation and discipline.

Confinement institutions remain one of the favoured responses to deviance and crime in Canada today and in most other industrialized nations. But throughout the twentieth century, these institutions were criticized for their inefficiency, costliness, repressiveness, and failure to rehabilitate. The 1960s and 1970s saw growing support for alternative methods of control through decentralization, deinstitutionalization, and decriminalization. The goal was to shift control to local governments and community agencies, close down large-scale institutions, and eliminate criminal sanctions for victimless crimes, such as sodomy and public drunkenness. This move reflected the growing popularity of the **medical**

FIGURE 14.3   YOUTH ACCUSED OF HOMICIDES, 1974–2004

SOURCE: Adapted from the Statistics Canada publication "Juristat," Catalogue 85-002, Homicide in Canada, 2004, Vol. 25, No. 6, released October 6, 2005.

model of deviance and a therapeutic approach to social control. During the twentieth century, many forms of deviance and crime were medicalized—in other words, defined as illnesses in need of treatment rather than sins in need of punishment. Professional groups—psychiatrists, social workers, and psychologists—urged this redefinition of deviance and its solution through psychological adjustment and community-based care, rather than through physical discipline and confinement. Whether therapeutic social controls are less coercive and repressive, as their advocates claim, has been the subject of much debate. In addition, some analysts argue that therapeutic controls have not so much replaced older, more punitive forms of social control as they have added to them, widening the social control net to capture people who might otherwise have avoided formal social controls (Cohen, 1985).

RECENT TRENDS IN CRIMINAL JUSTICE IN CANADA

The kind of deviance that the public worries most about—criminal behaviour—continues to be dealt with primarily by legal forms of social control through the criminal justice system. Two competing perspectives influence the Canadian criminal justice system—the **crime-control model** and the **due-process model**. Although the primary goal of the crime-control model is to reduce crime and protect society by granting legal officials broad powers, the due-process model emphasizes the protection of the legal rights of the accused to ensure justice. Historically, Canada has favoured the crime-control model, but with the introduction of the Canadian Charter of Rights and Freedoms in 1982, this emphasis has shifted. During the 1980s and 1990s, courts and legislatures expanded the due-process rights of those accused of crime—for example, by prohibiting unreasonable searches and seizures and by guaranteeing the right to legal counsel (Roach, 1999).

This does not mean that the concerns of the crime-control model have been overshadowed. Rather, it has been quite the opposite. At the same time that due-process rights were expanding, more people were ending up in jail. Between 1981 and 1994, the number of adults serving sentences in federal and provincial jails and prisons grew by 50 percent and the number of juvenile offenders in custody grew by 26 percent. After a decade of growth, however, prison admissions began to decline in the mid-1990s, in part because of decreasing crime rates and the introduction of legislation designed to encourage the use of alternatives to incarceration. In 2003–04, about 32 000 adults were imprisoned in federal or provincial institutions (Beattie, 2005). Despite this decline, Canada remains a leader in imprisonment among Western nations with an overall incarceration rate of 108 per 100 000 population in 2003 (see Figure 14.4).

Why, until recently, was imprisonment growing when due-process concerns were on the rise? One important reason is the emergence of the victims' rights movement, which "enabled and legitimated the criminal sanction" (Roach, 1999: 4). Increased reliance on imprisonment may also reflect public attitudes toward criminal offenders, which appear to have hardened over time—at least at first glance. In the 1970s, for example, public opinion polls found that almost two-thirds of Canadians felt sentences were not harsh enough. In the mid-1990s, similar polls found that close to 85 percent of Canadians believed the justice system was "too soft" on those convicted of crime (Roberts, 2000). If we look in more depth at people's views about criminal justice, however, we see that they are more complex than these polls suggest. For example, according to the 1999 General Social Survey, Canadians support the use of community-based, noncustodial sanctions in certain situations (Tufts, 2001). Specifically, probation, fines, and community work are preferred for first-time offenders convicted of break-and-enter or minor assault and for young, repeat offenders. And in a 1997 survey of Ontario residents, fewer than a third of respondents thought that lengthening prison sentences was the best way of preventing crime (Doob, Sprott, Marinos, and Varma, 1998).

So, although many Canadians appear to lean toward being "tough on crime," they also seem willing to consider alternatives to traditional punitive responses for some types of crimes and criminals. Both of these views are reflected in the Youth Criminal Justice Act, which came into force in 2003, replacing the Young Offenders Act. The new act allows an adult sentence for any youth 14 and older convicted of a serious crime, increases the scope of cases for which youths can presumptively receive an adult sentence, lowers the age (from 16 to 14) at which youths found guilty of certain serious offences will presumptively be sentenced as adults, and permits

FIGURE 14.4 INCARCERATION RATES IN CANADA, THE UNITED STATES, AND SELECTED WESTERN EUROPEAN COUNTRIES, 2003

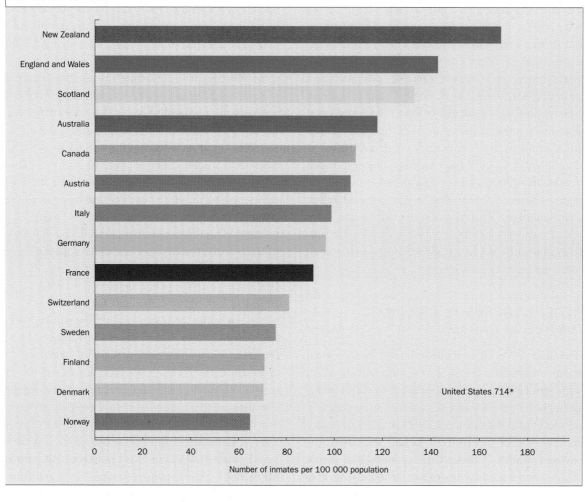

SOURCE: Canadian Centre for Justice Statistics, Statistics Canada; World Prison Population Lit (sixth edition), International Centre for Prison Studies. Reproduced with the permission of the Minister of Public Works and Government Services Canada, 2006.

judges to consider allowing the publication of names of some youths found guilty of serious violent offences even if they were not given an adult sentence (Doob and Sprott, 2004).

At the same time, unlike the Young Offenders Act, the new legislation also explicitly encourages the use of community-based alternatives and forbids the use of custodial sentences in the majority of less serious cases that come before the courts. Efforts to develop alternatives to incarceration, in part, reflect the fact that, contrary to public perceptions, the incarceration rate for young offenders in Canada is among the highest of any developed nation, higher even than in the United States for many types of offences.

A willingness to consider alternatives to prison-based sanctions can also be seen in the innovative approaches to criminal justice that have gained popularity in recent years, for both adult and young offenders. For instance, conditional sentences are now available to some convicted offenders who, traditionally subject to provincial jail terms of two years less a day, may now serve their sentences in the community under certain conditions. In addition, several provincial correctional systems have begun using electronic monitoring programs that involve placing an offender under house arrest rather than in an institution, using electronic equipment to ensure that the conditions of confinement are fulfilled. Probably the approach that has garnered the most attention in recent years, however, is the **restorative justice** movement. Restorative justice is based on a social rather than a legal view that criminal acts not only injure a victim but also affect

Contrary to the belief of many people, crime rates in Canada are declining. Nonetheless, Canada has one of the highest incarceration rates in the Western world.
SOURCE: Photodisc.

communities and offenders; thus, solutions need to involve all three parties (Griffiths and Cunningham, 2000). The most common types of restorative justice are victim-offender reconciliation, circle sentencing, and family group conferencing. In circle sentencing, for example, Aboriginal offenders, after having been found guilty in the courts, meet respected community members, elders, peers, their own family members, and victims and their families to discuss the impact of their crimes and decide what they must do to restore justice. Another recent criminal justice initiative has been the development and implementation of specialized courts to deal with chronic social and legal problems that appear to defy conventional criminal justice responses or solutions. Specialized drug courts, mental health courts, and domestic violence courts are expanding at a rapid rate throughout North America. One component of these courts is the diversion of some types of cases out of the criminal justice system into treatment programs that target what are perceived to be the broader social needs of both victims and offenders.

Why the concern with finding alternatives to confinement? Those who work in the criminal justice system as well as those who study it recognize that imprisonment is not an effective way of either rehabilitating people or deterring them from subsequent offending (Doob, Marinos, and Varma, 1995). In addition, the public is becoming more aware of the high cost of imprisonment. Canada spends more than $2 billion on adult and youth corrections. For example, in 2003–04, it cost $240.18 per day or more than $87 000 a year to keep one person in federal prison in Canada (Beattie, 2005). As governments search for ways to cut public spending, they are likely to rely more on less costly modes of social control, such as electronic monitoring of convicted criminals, and to experiment with privately run prisons and other types of correctional facilities. The privatization of jails and prisons has been growing in popularity in the United States, Britain, and Australia (Griffiths and Cunningham, 2000). For example, several thousand prisoners in the United States are held in jails and prisons operated by private companies, and some states now administer capital punishment through private contractors. In contrast, in Canada, no federal facilities have been privatized. However, Nova Scotia has privatized at least one of its provincial jails and Ontario has contracted with private industry to operate a strict-discipline program in one of its facilities for young offenders. The increasing reliance on privatization for social control is apparent at other stages of formal social control, however. The amount of policing done through private security may now be as much as or more than the amount done through public law enforcement in many countries, including Canada.

Some observers see private entrepreneurs joining with the state to extend social control through new, technically sophisticated, and more discreet techniques. Gary Marx (1995), for example, describes a **maximum-security society** characterized by "softer" social control processes where the role of human agents is reduced and control is achieved at a distance. In this maximum-security society, the goal will be to engineer away deviance and crime by controlling the physical environment, rather than people. Think of subways with graffiti-resistant metals, malls playing classical music to discourage congregations of teenagers, remote surveillance cameras, and anti-carjacking mannequins that drivers can place in the passenger seats of their cars.

Whether these new techniques of control will replace or merely add another layer to existing formal controls is unclear. Some fear that the new strategies will create an Orwellian future of more powerful and intrusive state control over our lives, whereas others see technological advances as providing control that is less discriminatory, more effective, and more accountable.

In the wake of the September 11, 2001, attacks on the World Trade Center in New York City and the Pentagon in Washington, concerns over expanding governmental controls and legal powers have taken on new meaning in and outside of Canada. The passage in January 2002 of Bill C-36, Canada's anti-terrorism legislation, which gives law enforcement authorities new powers of detection, investigation, and surveillance, was accompanied by debates over how to balance needs for safety and security against protection of civil rights and citizen privacy (see Box 14.2). International debates over the very definition of the attacks—were they crimes or acts of war?—and how persons accused of terrorist activities ought to be dealt with highlight, once again, how struggles over defining deviance and deviants are inevitable and critical elements of life in a global age.

BOX 14.2 HIGH-PRICED SECURITY

Faced with a new terrorism threat, Canada's government has enacted a far-reaching law that gives authorities extraordinary power to curtail the civil rights of Canadian citizens. Under the law, police are able to: arrest people who have committed no crime but are suspected of planning to do so; keep evidence secret, even from the accused; deny the right to remain silent and not give testimony that might lead to one's own conviction. The bill also allows for the freezing and seizure of the assets of terrorists and their supporters, as well as the establishment of a list of terrorist organizations and individuals.

The Canadian Bar Association (CBA), which represents 37 000 lawyers across the country, thought the bill should expire in three years unless it is specifically extended by a vote of Parliament. "When governments seek to impose such restraints on fundamental rights and freedoms, particularly with limited time available for study and debate, those restraints must be limited in durations," said a CBA brief presented to a government justice committee. The association also raised concerns about possible discrimination against minority groups who, under the provision for preventive arrests, could be unjustly detained as suspected terrorists for up to 72 hours without a warrant. Others expressed concern about the criminalization of peaceful protests. This was an issue long before the anti-terrorism bill, looking back to the treatment of even peaceful protesters at the Summit of the Americas in Quebec City in April 2001 and the APEC summit in Vancouver in 1997.

Alan Gold, president of the Ontario Criminal Lawyers Association, was also critical of the bill, saying it violates fundamental freedoms with no real increase in security. "It strikes me as bizarre to defend liberty by giving up liberty," he said, commenting that the new measures threaten to turn Canada into a police state. Doesn't placing such curbs on our civil liberties mean that the terrorists have already won? The government doesn't think so: it takes the view that Canada is not a free and democratic society if its citizens live in fear, and maintains that the bill respects the Charter of Rights and Freedoms.

SOURCE: "High-priced Security: Bill C-36, Canada's New Anti-Terrorism Legislation." *Canada and the World Backgrounder,* v. 67(4), Jan. 2002, pp. 24–27.

SUMMARY

1. Deviance and crime are defined by the social reactions to them. Both what is defined as deviance and the way people react to deviance depend on social circumstances. Even what you may consider to be serious deviance is subject to conflicting opinions and changing social reactions.

2. Crime is a special case of deviance and is defined by social norms that are formalized in criminal law. The response to crime is through formal social control—such as the criminal justice and correctional systems—whereas the response to noncriminal deviance is through informal social control—such as gossip, avoidance, and other forms of disapproval. There tends to be wide—though certainly not complete—agreement that crime is wrong but much less agreement that noncriminal forms of deviance are wrong.

3. Deviance is defined through a political process that typically involves struggles between competing groups over status, resources, knowledge, and power. Although a relationship often exists between the harm that a behaviour causes and the likelihood that the behaviour is defined as deviance, many harmful behaviours are not defined as deviant and some behaviours defined as deviant are not harmful.

4. Sociological explanations of deviant behaviour can be grouped into two types: those that emphasize the social factors that motivate or allow people to engage in deviance, and those that emphasize the political processes and power relations that result in some people and behaviours being defined and treated as deviant while others are not.

5. Rates of crimes have decreased in Canada in recent years. Canadians are less likely to be victims of serious violent crime than people in the United States, but Canadians face higher risks of homicide than citizens of other developed democracies. Aboriginal Canadians are at particularly high risk of involvement in criminal homicide—both as victims and as offenders. They are also overrepresented among those incarcerated in Canadian prisons and jails. This has been attributed in part to systemic racism in the criminal justice system.

6. Crime rates are often affected by major social changes. For example, rapidly changing technologies have created new opportunities for both personal and property crime and the globalization of the world's economy has been accompanied by the globalization of corporate and organized crime. Changes in gender inequalities, however, have not reduced the gender gap in criminal offences. Men still greatly outnumber women among offenders.

7. Canada has traditionally favoured the crime-control model of the criminal process and, consistent with that model, relies heavily on incarceration. More recently, however, this emphasis has shifted. With the introduction of the Charter of Rights and Freedoms, the due-process model has gained ground. And although Canada continues to incarcerate offenders at a higher rate than most other Western democracies, the Canadian incarceration rate has declined in recent years as the criminal justice system explores alternatives to imprisonment.

QUESTIONS TO CONSIDER

1. Think of a behaviour that, during your lifetime, has gone from being considered deviant to nondeviant, or vice versa. What explains this changing definition? Have any individuals, lobby groups, or professions been involved in changing the definition of the behaviour?

2. Many people engage in actions that violate the law at some time in their lives. How would the different explanations of deviance discussed in this chapter explain your rule-violating behaviour? Which explanation appears most consistent with your experience and why?

3. Where do you get your information about crime? How do you think these sources of information shape your view of what crime is and what should be done about it?

GLOSSARY

Anomie, according to Merton, is a social condition in which there is a gap between the cultural goals people are taught to aspire to and the social structural means available to achieve those goals.

Conflict theorists of deviance and crime analyze the relationships among (1) power struggles over defining deviance, (2) the organization of social control, and (3) people defined as deviant.

Control theories of deviance are explanations that emphasize the factors that prevent people from acting on deviant impulses.

The **crime-control model** is a model of the criminal process that emphasizes reducing crime and protecting society by granting legal officials broad powers.

Differential association is the process by which people learn deviance through exposure to more definitions favourable to deviance than definitions unfavourable to deviance.

The **due-process model** is a model of the criminal process that emphasizes the protection of the legal rights of the accused to ensure that justice is done.

Innovation is Merton's term for the type of adaptation to strain that involves seeking illegitimate means to achieve legitimate goals; it encompasses most types of moneymaking crimes.

The **labelling perspective** is a perspective on deviance that argues that rule making and rule enforcement—in other words, the definitions of and reactions to deviance—are often important causes of deviance.

Learning theories of deviance are explanations that emphasize that deviance is learned in the same fashion that conformity is learned—that is, by exposure to values, norms, and beliefs that, in the case of deviance, support unconventional behaviour.

Master status is a status that stands out above all others. Deviance is often a master status, overshadowing other statuses in the eyes of people who interact with the deviant.

A **maximum-security society** is a society characterized by growing importance of softer processes of social control that control at a distance, with technology, and with less human contact.

The **medical model of deviance** is the view that many forms of deviance are indications of physical or mental illness and therefore deserve treatment rather than punishment.

A **moral crusade** is an organized campaign to discredit an activity or group of people so that it becomes viewed as deviant and deserving of stigma.

Motivational theories of deviance are explanations that emphasize the factors that push or encourage people toward deviant behaviour.

Opportunity theories of deviance are theories that argue that, in the absence of social control, people's choices of deviant or criminal acts will depend on the deviant opportunities available to them.

Primary deviance is deviance that occurs for any of a variety of reasons but that does not lead to be labelled a deviant or to see yourself as a deviant.

Restorative justice is a response to crime that views it as not just injurious to a victim but also as affecting communities and offenders and therefore involves all three parties in dealing with a crime.

Secondary deviance is deviance that occurs after people have been labelled as deviant and start to view themselves as deviant.

Social control involves efforts to change the behavior of, and punish, people defined as deviant. Informal social control is exercised in the course of face-to-face interaction and may involve expressions of disapproval, avoidance, and so on. Formal social control is practised mainly through the criminal justice system and involves fines, incarceration, and so on.

The **status-conflict perspective** is a perspective that argues that definitions of deviance emerge from struggles between different interest groups that compete for status, influence, and moral authority.

Strain theory is a theory that argues that people are pressured to deviate by the incompatible demands of cultural goals and social structural opportunities.

White-collar crime, a term coined by Edwin Sutherland in 1939, refers to acts committed for personal profit or gain during everyday business life by people in positions of authority, with professional status, or in possession of specialized skills.

SUGGESTED READING

Garland, David. (2001). *The Culture of Control: Crime and Social Order in Contemporary Society.* Chicago: University of Chicago Press. Responses to crime and criminal justice have changed dramatically in the last 30 years: more gated communities, zero-tolerance policies, racial profiling, community policing. Garland explains how the character of modern life—not just crime—is responsible for these changes.

Goode, Erich, and Nachman Ben-Yehuda. (1995). *Moral Panics: The Social Construction of Deviance.* Oxford: Blackwell Publishers Limited. To illustrate the ways in which deviance is created through social reactions, the authors focus on moral panics and discuss how this concept applies to the Renaissance witch craze as well as to drug panics in the United States and Israel in the 1980s.

Hagan, John, and Bill McCarthy. (1998). *Mean Streets: Youth Crime and Homelessness.* Cambridge: Cambridge University Press. Based on interviews and surveys from more than 400 young people living on the streets of Toronto and Vancouver, this field study looks at why youth take to the streets, how they survive once there, their experiences of victimization and offending, and their efforts to leave the street.

Roberts, Julian V., ed. (2000). *Criminal Justice in Canada: A Reader.* Toronto: Harcourt Brace. This collection presents readings on policing, the courts, corrections, and youth justice, as well as such timely topics as discrimination in the criminal justice system, gun control, and criminal justice responses to wife battering.

Sacco, Vincent F., and Leslie W. Kennedy. (2002). *The Criminal Event: An Introduction to Criminology in Canada* (4th ed.). Toronto: Nelson. Using the criminal event as the unifying theme, the authors discuss conventional topics in the field, including the definition of crime, research methods, and social reactions to crime. Focusing on three contexts (family, leisure, and work), they discuss what motivates individuals to commit crimes, who the victims are that suffer, and how and what we should do about the problem of crime.

WEB RESOURCES

Companion Web Site for This Book

http://www.newsociety5e.nelson.com

Begin by clicking on the Student Resources section of the website. Next, select the chapter you are studying from the pull-down menu. From the Student Resources page, you have easy access to InfoTrac College Edition® and other resources, such as the Glossary and Flashcards. The website also has many useful tips to aid you in your study of sociology.

InfoTrac College Edition Search Terms

Visit http://www.infotrac-college.com for access to more than 20 million articles from nearly 6000 sources when doing your online research.

ThomsonNOW™

http://hed.nelson.com

This online diagnostic tool identifies each student's unique needs with a Pretest that generates a personalized Study Plan for each chapter, helping students focus on concepts they are having the most difficulty mastering. Students then take a Posttest after reading the chapter to measure their understanding of the material. An Instructor Gradebook is available to track and monitor student progress.

CHAPTER FIFTEEN

Population and Urbanization

In this chapter you will learn that

- The choice of opportunities, experiences, and lifestyles available to urban residents is shaped and constrained by three sets of factors: those related to the physical environment; those associated with population size, distribution, and composition; and those dictated by the changing structure of the wider economy.

- Contrary to the theory that the core of Canadian cities is hollowing out, recent evidence suggests that city centres are remaining relatively stable economically and demographically. In contrast, the rings of older suburbs around city cores are stagnating, losing jobs and population to constellations of edge cities in the surrounding regions.

- The fastest-growing middle-class neighbourhoods are private communities, where control over local government, public services, and security rests in the hands of non-elected, professional managers. One popular form of such neighbourhoods is the gated community, where nonresidents are considered intruders and are monitored and kept out by guards, alarm systems, and surveillance cameras.

- Cities are becoming multiethnic, with many neighbourhoods in the largest cities becoming home to members of visible minorities. This is generating racial and ethnic residential and commercial patterns that stand in marked contrast to the ecology of the older, industrial city.

John Hannigan
UNIVERSITY OF TORONTO

INTRODUCTION

A decade ago, *The Globe and Mail* published an opinion piece by Elinor Florence, a British Columbia woman who, with her husband and three teenage children, had moved from Richmond, a rapidly developing suburb on the southern boundary of Vancouver, to Invermere, an alpine town of 3000 near the Alberta border. Leaving behind a mushrooming population, the stresses of urban driving, and "a junk culture that undeniably rears its head everywhere but snarls louder in cities" (Florence, 1997), the Florence family appears to have found happiness in the shadow of the Rockies. Among the benefits that she cites are a slower pace of life, more leisure time, a greater sense of personal security, no fast-food restaurants, and the ability to walk everywhere.

Elinor Florence's profile of small-town life highlights a theme that has resounded through the discipline of sociology since its founding in the nineteenth century. Urban life, it is said, is qualitatively different from a rural or small-town existence: meaner, more stressful, more alienating. Obsessed as they are with efficiency and making money, urbanites are said to have no time for relating to others in a more holistic

and humane way. Increasing population size and density, such as that beginning to plague Richmond, bring with them a host of urban problems, from traffic gridlock and pollution to family breakdown and crime.

The tale of the Florences illustrates one of the most influential ways of looking at residential settings. Termed **environmental-opportunity theory** (Michelson, 1973), it posits that people actively choose where they want to live depending on the extent to which a particular place either meshes with or constrains their preferred lifestyle. Not all of us, of course, get to choose our community freely, but people will always strive to match their choices with their needs. This is well illustrated in the case of "Prairie Edge," a small Alberta municipality where residents perceived the "rural advantage" as being directly linked to the reduced parental anxiety that comes from a "safe" everyday environment (see Box 15.1).

A second lens through which urban life can be viewed is that of *demography*—the study of populations: their size, distribution, and composition. As you will learn later in this chapter, in the preindustrial city significant growth was constrained by a high birth

Is urban life meaner, more stressful, more alienating than small-town life? Richmond, B.C., proved too stressful for one family.
SOURCE: Al Harvey/The Slide Farm.

BOX 15.1   PRAIRIE EDGE: A "RURBAN" COMMUNITY

"Prairie Edge" is a pseudonym for Camrose, Alberta, a community of 14 000 about 100 kilometres from Edmonton. In the early 1990s, a survey research firm, John Yerxa Research Inc., asked residents of Prairie Edge (and three other "rural communities") to compare their place of residence with that of Edmonton. Just more than 80 percent reported that they believed a rural setting was a better place to raise a family. Residents particularly appreciated a quieter and smaller setting for its easy social interaction and perceived high level of personal safety. However, they recognized that their community lacked the wide choice of shopping and entertainment opportunities that were more readily available in Edmonton.

Sociologist Kieran Bonner resided in Prairie Edge around the time of the survey and independently carried out his own study among the middle-class parents who were his neighbours. Benner found that they stressed three interrelated themes—safety, convenience, and reduced parental anxiety as the key benefits of the "life world" of a smaller centre. Each of these, in turn, flowed out of the high visibility and familiarity that resulted from smallness. However, some of his informants, especially those who had moved from a larger city, indicated that the familiarity resulting from high visibility (it was difficult to be a "stranger" in Prairie Edge) led to an ethic of helping and politeness but not to sociability and friendliness. In other words, people trusted their local environment more, especially with regard to potential dangers to children, but they did not necessarily share a strong sense of "community." Prairie Edge, Bonner concluded, possessed both rural and urban characteristics and thus could be described as being "rurban."

SOURCE: Adapted from Kieran Bonner, "A Great Place to Raise Kids: Interpretation, Science, and the Urban-Rural Debate," Montreal and Kingston: McGill-Queen's University Press, 1997. Used with permission..

rate and a high death rate. Only when the death rate began to fall because of advances in hygiene, nutrition, medical knowledge, and public health did the industrial city thrive, bringing with it a distinctive spatial organization and way of life. Today, the social organization and character of cities are being powerfully influenced by flows of highly diverse groups of immigrants between countries. This has resulted in the re-urbanization of the central city, the growth of the multiethnic city, and other urban changes.

A third approach asserts that the urban experience is constrained not just by the nature of the physical environment or by demographic forces but also by the changing configuration of international, national, and local economic arrangements. In recent years, the emergence of a globalized economy has had profound implications for North American cities, changing both their physical form and their social-class patterns. In particular, it has resulted in an increasing polarization between rich and poor, affecting the homeless person sleeping in the park, the highly paid professional eating in the chic urban restaurant, and the suburban homeowner shopping in a "big-box" megastore on the fringes of the city (Kleniewski, 1997: 135).

Similarly, resource towns and farming communities have been hard hit by international trade agreements and a harsher rural-urban division of labour in the global economy. In this changing climate, the countryside comes to serve two new and very different purposes: vacation playground and toxic dumping ground. Thus, while towns in the British Columbia interior and the Alberta foothills are transformed into ski and golfing resorts linked to global tourism, other communities are forced to "grasp at environmentally dubious schemes like hazardous waste treatment, strawboard manufacture, tire incineration and mega-hog barns" (Epp and Whitson, 2001: xv).

In this chapter, I will look at this three-pronged influence of environment and structure on city life over the twentieth century. In the course of the discussion, you will encounter three main types of cities: the industrial city, the corporate city, and the **postmodern city.** The industrial city originated in the nineteenth century and reached its zenith in the 1920s and 1930s, the corporate city arose after World War II and dominated during the 1950s and 1960s, and the postmodern city dates from the 1970s up to the present.

EARLY CITIES

Cities are "relatively large, dense, permanent settlements in which the majority of the residents do not produce their own food" (McGahan, 1995: 1). By most accounts, the city as a distinct form dates back five or six thousand years to 3000–4000 B.C.E., when it first appeared in Mesopotamia (now southern Iraq) and Egypt. Initially, ancient cities were established largely as centres of religious worship and were not much larger than most single-industry towns in Canada today. For example, Memphis, at the head of the Nile River delta, had an estimated population of 40 000 in 3000 B.C.E. Cities later swelled: Babylon had a population of 200 000 during the reign of Nebuchadnezzar in the seventh century B.C.E.; Alexandria, Egypt, surpassed 300 000 three centuries later; and Rome reached 800 000 at its peak in the second century C.E. (Chandler and Fox, 1974).

Three elements of prime importance characterized these preindustrial cities: the existence of a food surplus in fertile valleys, which permitted the specialization of labour in zones of dense settlement; the achievement of literacy among scribes, priests, and other elite members of society, which allowed for the keeping of financial and other records; and technological innovations, notably metallurgy, agricultural irrigation, and the harnessing of wind and water power for sailing and grain milling.

After the fall of Rome to Germanic tribes in the fifth century C.E., cities stagnated and declined over large parts of Europe. They continued to flourish, though, in the rising Islamic empire, which, at its zenith, stretched from Spain to India. More decentralized than the Roman world, the Islamic empire contained a number of cities that reached impressive levels of size and sophistication. For example, more than 500 000 people lived in Cairo in the fourteenth century, when Egypt held a trade monopoly on the east-west spice route (Abu-Lughod, 1991: 38).

From the eleventh century on, a number of city-states along the Mediterranean—Florence, Genoa, Venice, Pisa—succeeded in re-establishing trade routes to Asia and the Middle East by means of the Crusades. The commercial revival that followed was felt even in the merchant towns of the North Sea and the Baltic, which themselves had begun to develop a brisk trade in wool and cloth. From this renaissance developed a distinct class of professional merchants who established their own municipal laws and institutions distinct from those in the surrounding feudal society, and there also emerged a market for housing and a variety of other goods and services, which generated further urban growth (Golden, 1981: 120–22).

Although preindustrial cities were important as centres of commerce, knowledge, and art, they never contained much more than a small fraction of the overall population. Even at their height, ancient and medieval cities were incapable of supporting urban populations of more than 5 percent or 10 percent of society, primarily because they could not generate a sufficiently large agricultural surplus to feed a huge urban populace. When the cities did begin to swell, periodic outbreaks of the bubonic plague (the notorious "Black Death"), spread by fleas from infected rats, killed as many as half the people in Europe's cities. Thus, by 1800, of the roughly 900 million people in the world, only about 3 percent lived in urban places of 5000 or more inhabitants (Hauser, 1965: 7). And, despite significant changes in architectural styles and building materials, the physical layout of the communities in which they lived had not changed all that much from antiquity to the eighteenth century—they were still built up within protective walls and organized around a central market square and places of worship, such as cathedrals, temples, or mosques (Abu-Lughod, 1991: 49–50).

POPULATION ISSUES AND URBAN GROWTH

Urban growth is a product not only of technological progress and social invention but also of the broader patterns of population growth that shape a society. These demographic forces operate in conjunction with other social and economic factors to create a slow-moving but powerful current that relentlessly moves us in certain directions (McQuillan, 1994: 229).

THE DEMOGRAPHIC TRANSITION

For much of human history, societies hovered in a steady state in which both birth rates and death rates were high. As a result, the overall size of the population remained more or less uniform from decade to decade.

In the absence of any effective form of birth control, women in preindustrial societies were destined to bear a large number of children. This was deemed necessary for several reasons. Infant and childhood mortality rates were high; routinely, only about half of the children born survived to adulthood. Thus, it was necessary to have large families in the hope that some would escape the grim reaper. Furthermore, in traditional societies offspring were viewed as having considerable economic value, especially in the poorer classes where children were expected to help with the farm work or were sent off to work as servants in the homes of the rich. In the absence of pension plans or retirement funds, parents fortunate enough to reach old age depended on their children to care for them.

The human life span was much shorter than it is today. For example, in 1867, the year Canada officially became a country, the average life expectancy was 42 years as compared with 77.4 years (for men) and 82.4 years (for women) in 2003 (Beaujot, 2004: 446; Statistics Canada, 2005: 27). Even the most learned medical authorities did not understand the causes of and proper treatments for illnesses, attributing them to intangibles, such as "vapours" and the like. Those who fell ill were "bled" by leeches and subjected to other such treatments.

Beginning in the eighteenth century, this pattern began to change dramatically with breakthroughs in hygiene, public health, nutrition, and medical knowledge. Once it was understood that often-fatal maladies, such as cholera, were preventable by establishing a pure water supply, the death rate declined significantly. Now the causes of death were more likely to be degenerative diseases, such as cancer and heart disease. Especially important strides were made in reducing infant mortality. Note, for example, the declining infant mortality rate in Canada: in 1831, 1 in 6 children did not survive his or her first year; in 1931 it was 1 in 14, and by 1999 this dropped to 1 in 190 (Beaujot, 2004: 446).

While death rates plunged, birth rates, at first, remained relatively high. Deeply ingrained cultural traditions and beliefs remained stubbornly embedded. Large families remained the norm and the use of birth control was outlawed. The result was a period of rapid population growth, especially in urban areas.

Eventually, however, birth rates also began to fall. Contributing to this was a series of changes associated with increasing modernization, industrialization, and urbanization. One crucial factor was the offloading of responsibilities formerly attached to the family onto the state. Children now were required to remain in school until they were adolescents; consequently, childrearing became more costly. Primary care for seniors began to shift from adult children to government-operated programs and institutions. This change from high to low birth and death rates is known as the **demographic transition** (see Figure 15.1). Initially, this change was most characteristic of cities in Western Europe and North America, but

FIGURE 15.1   THE DEMOGRAPHIC TRANSITION

ultimately it spread to rural districts as new health technologies and medical treatments expanded beyond the city limits.

From the mid-1960s onward, wealthier nations in the developed world entered a new demographic era that differs in several ways from that associated with the demographic processes outlined above. First, fertility plunged below 2.1 births per woman—the **replacement level** at which births and deaths balance and the population level remains stationery, ignoring population inflows from other countries (immigration) and population outflows to other countries (emigration). This reflects a fundamental shift in contemporary values, especially among the middle class. Whereas previously the pressure to raise a family was paramount, now the emphasis shifted to equality of opportunity and freedom of choice. Increasingly, women entered the paid labour force on a full-time basis, not just out of economic necessity but in pursuit of self-fulfillment. With declining fertility rates, the population as a whole is becoming older, especially in countries where immigration has concurrently slowed down. Some analysts have described this as the "second demographic transition" (Champion, 1993; Van de Kaa, 1987).

Malthus versus Marx

As the initial demographic transition loomed, fears arose over the possibility of overpopulation. Alarm was first sounded by the British clergyman and political economist Thomas Malthus.

Under normal conditions, Malthus (1798) believed, there exists a natural "urge to reproduce" that flows from the attraction between the sexes. The resulting population growth is potentially limited by two checks. "Positive checks" are related to mortality:

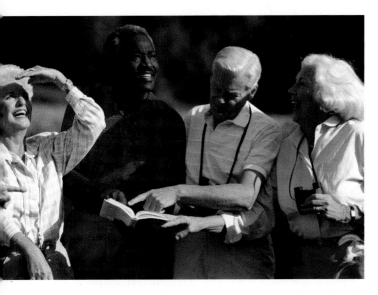

With declining fertility rates, the population as a whole is becoming older.
SOURCE: Photos.com.

famine, epidemics, wars, and plagues, such as the Black Death. Positive checks are generally beyond human control. In contrast, "preventive checks" are related to fertility. Since Malthus condemned the use of contraception as immoral, the only remaining remedy was for couples to exercise "moral constraint." For all practical purposes, this meant postponing marriages as long as possible.

Of greater interest today are Malthus's comments about the relationship between population growth and resource (especially food) depletion. Malthus argued that population, if left unchecked, would increase geometrically or exponentially (as in the series 2, 4, 8, 16). Meanwhile, food supply would increase only arithmetically (as in the series 2, 4, 6, 8). Eventually, population would outstrip the food supply, resulting in widespread poverty, hunger, and misery. Malthus concluded that only grinding poverty would ultimately succeed in discouraging people from marrying early and raising large, healthy families.

Karl Marx was one of Malthus's most outspoken critics. According to Marx, Malthus was blind to the real cause of excess population: the capitalist economic system. Capitalism, Marx insisted, is organized to keep the working class in a perpetual state of poverty and unemployment. That is because it is to the financial advantage of capitalists to have more workers than jobs. The excess supply of workers allowed factory and mill owners to keep wages low and easily replace workers who created trouble.

Furthermore, it facilitated the maintenance of a "reserve army of labour" that could be expanded or shrunk depending on whether the economy was expanding or in recession. Rapid population growth, then, was less a result of a mismatch between population and resources and more a case of deeply flawed social and economic arrangements.

The contrasting views of Malthus and Marx have reappeared in today's environmental debate. In the 1960s, several authors became widely known for their doomsday scenarios concerning overpopulation and dwindling resources. In the spirit of Malthus, conservation biologist Paul Ehrlich warns in his provocatively titled *The Population Bomb* (1968) that world population is expanding out of control, especially in Asia and Africa. At the same time, he holds, the unchecked consumption habits of people in the world's rich countries are depleting supplies of food, oil, and water. The result will be catastrophic, Ehrlich predicts. One notable critic of this viewpoint is economist Julian Simon, who argues that Ehrlich is wrong in identifying a pending population crisis. Simon notes that the price of most resources has been dropping, cities are becoming less polluted, and humans can be counted on to cope with population pressures through their technological ingenuity (Simon and Kahn, 1984).

THE INDUSTRIAL CITY

By the end of the eighteenth century, a new type of city had begun to emerge, first in England and later in continental Europe and America. This *industrial city* was larger, more complex, and more dynamic than any urban settlement that had preceded it. At century's end, more than 50 percent of the population of England and Wales lived in places with 20 000 or more people, compared with only 17 percent a century earlier (Weber, 1963 [1899]: 47). Global urbanization trends from 1800 to 2000 are shown in Figure 15.2.

What contributed to the growth of industrial cities? One popular theory emphasizes advances in transportation and agricultural technology, inasmuch as these factors contributed to the production and movement of agricultural surpluses from farm to city. Among the innovations were better methods of land drainage, the use of fertilizers, methods of seed selection, techniques of animal breeding, toll-road building, and the application of steam power to farm machinery and rail transport. Other scholars emphasize a boom in trade and commerce, which provided a powerful inducement

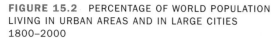

FIGURE 15.2   PERCENTAGE OF WORLD POPULATION LIVING IN URBAN AREAS AND IN LARGE CITIES 1800–2000

SOURCE: Adapted from Kingsley Davis, "The Origin and Growth of Urbanization in the World," *American Journal of Sociology*, 60(1995) p. 430.

to greater investment, technological improvements, and, ultimately, increased agricultural productivity.

Another key factor appears to have been a shift in the sources of capital accumulation—that is, how factory owners raised the investment money needed to build and improve their manufacturing facilities. In England after 1850, capital investment was facilitated by the creation of the joint stock company, a business structure that pooled the capital of many investors and that had limited liability (i.e., the shareholders could not be held personally responsible for enterprises that failed).

Finally, urban growth has been linked to the invention of the factory. Previously, under the "putting-out" system, piecework was done in village or rural cottages and collected at regular intervals by the agents of merchant entrepreneurs. With the advent of the factory system, workers were required to work in a central location. Initially, factories had to be located next to rivers, in order to run directly on water power. Then, as steam-powered machines became the standard, factories concentrated in cities because steam power could not be distributed economically over a wide grid, as electrical systems can be today.

THE DEVELOPMENT OF AN URBAN-INDUSTRIAL ECONOMY IN CANADA

At the time of Confederation in 1867, Canada lagged significantly behind both Britain and the United States in the development of an urban-industrial economy.

The British North American colonies, both inside and outside the new political union, traded very little with one another, looking instead to the United States or Great Britain. According to the first manufacturing census in 1870, such localized activities as sawmilling, flour milling, shoemaking, and clothing manufacture accounted for almost half the value of the manufactured goods produced in Canada (Nader, 1975: 207). At the same time, only a tiny minority of Canadians lived in urban areas. In 1871, fewer than 1 in 5 (18 percent) lived in a town or a city (Stone, 1967: 29).

As the twentieth century dawned, Canada had a population of just more than 5 million, with two-thirds of these people living in rural areas and dependent for their livelihood on farming and the farm economy (Kremarik, 2000: 19). Soon however, industrial cities finally began to emerge. Although Toronto and Montreal were the largest industrial centres, factory towns also grew up elsewhere in Ontario, chief among them Windsor, because of its proximity to industry and markets in Detroit, and Hamilton, because of its port and strategic location on the Great Lakes. In addition to strategic location, the availability of investment capital played a significant role in directing where industry was established. The Canada Bank Act of 1871 was instrumental in concentrating economic power in a few national metropolitan centres, notably Toronto and Montreal. The act adopted the British model of a branch-banking system wherein a handful of major banks each established a network of branches. In contrast, under the U.S. unit-banking system, many more banks are independent. Investment capital was thus concentrated in a handful of urban centres rather than being widely dispersed across the country (Nader, 1975: 215).

Through various interventions by the federal government—the building of the transcontinental railroad, the imposition of a protective tariff system to encourage domestic manufacturing, a vigorous immigration policy that encouraged agriculture on the Prairies—a system of national economic markets was eventually established. In particular, at the turn of the twentieth century, these interventions found form in the expansion of wheat production for export. With cash from wheat sales jingling in their pockets, Prairie grain farmers were able to purchase manufactured goods from the factories of Ontario and Quebec, thus stimulating a marked upsurge in Canadian urbanization from 1891 to 1911 (Stone, 1967: 20–21). By 1911, four cities had populations exceeding 100 000: Montreal (470 480), Toronto (376 538), Winnipeg

TABLE 15.1 URBAN-RURAL POPULATION, CANADA, 1931–2001

	1931	1951	1991	1996	2001
Rural farm	31%	11%	3%	3%	2%
Rural nonfarm	15	19	20	19	18
Urban	54	70	77	78	80
Total	100	100	100	100	100

SOURCES: Adapted from Statistics Canada, "Urban vs. Rural Population," http://www.statcan.ca (September 20, 1996). Used by authority of the Minister of Industry, 2000; Lance W. Roberts, Rodney A. Clifton, Barry Ferguson, Karen Kampen and Simon Langlois, "Recent Social Trends in Canada," Montreal and Kingston: McGill-Queen's University Press, 2005, p. 33.

(136 035), and Vancouver (100 401). However, the formation of a national market led to the deindustrialization of the Maritime provinces (Brym, 1986).

As the twentieth century progressed, the proportion of the Canadian population classified as "urban" increased dramatically, crossing the 50 percent mark before 1931 and reaching 70 percent in 1951. By 1991, 77 percent of the Canadian population was living in towns and cities (see Table 15.1). Toronto, Montreal, and Vancouver continued to hold the largest number of Canadians, although, the sharpest growth rates after 1951 were in the Western cities of Calgary and Edmonton.

Over the last decade of the twentieth century, Toronto and Vancouver (together with Calgary) made a major comeback as growth centres. As can be seen in Box 15.2, these three Canadian cities added new residents in different ways. Immigration has bolstered Vancouver and Toronto, but this growth has been partially offset by the loss of residents to other parts of their respective provinces. While migrants from other provinces flocked to Calgary and Vancouver, few were attracted to Toronto. Natural increase has been more of a factor in Calgary and Toronto than in Vancouver (Little, 1999). Nevertheless, with just fewer than 32 million people inhabiting 9 million square kilometers of land, Canada remains one of the most sparsely populated nations.

BOX 15.2   THREE CANADIAN CITIES: WHAT MAKES THEM GROW SO BIG

In a decade of modest population growth, three of Canada's big cities—Toronto, Vancouver, and Calgary—stand out. Not only has their performance been sizzling, they have been adding people in very different ways.

Between 1991 and 1998, the national population grew 8.1 percent, which is moderate by historical standards. But in the three hottest-growth cities, the rates of expansion were much faster—21.2 percent in Vancouver, 18.4 percent in Calgary, and 14 percent in Toronto. [In 1998, 24.7 percent of Canadians lived in those three centres, compared with 23 percent in 1991.] By size they are Canada's first-, third- and fifth-largest centres. The Toronto CMA (Census Metropolitan Area), which goes well beyond the boundaries of the city proper, had 4.6 million people in 1998, Vancouver had two million, and Calgary 907 000.

What is most striking about the fast-growth cities is the way they grew.

From 1991 to 1997, Vancouver added about 53 000 people a year. Its single biggest source—about 68 percent of the total—was net international immigration [immigrants minus emigrants]. Those were the years when immigration from Asia was especially strong, particularly from Hong Kong, where many residents were worried about the 1997 handover of the British colony to China. Migrants from the rest of Canada accounted for another 29 percent.

Now move east to Calgary, which added almost 18 000 people a year on average. Here the newcomers were largely home-grown. Natural increase [births minus deaths] was responsible for 43 percent of the growth [as against 20 percent for Vancouver]. Other countries accounted for 31 percent and other provinces 22 percent. Calgary, in effect, was firing on all cylinders, adding people by every way possible.

In Toronto, the population grew by an average of 79 000 people a year from 1991 to 1997. Net international immigration was an even bigger source of growth—85 percent of the total—than it was in Vancouver. And natural increase supplied another 45 percent, roughly the same as Calgary. But unlike its western counterparts, Toronto lost people to other provinces (2 percent of the total). And like Vancouver, but not Calgary, it lost people to the rest of its own province—a number equal to 24 percent of its population growth.

So, while the three hot cities all have a rapidly growing population, when it comes to what's making them grow, they part company.

SOURCE: Excerpted from Bruce Little, "Tale of Three Cities: What Makes Them Grow So Big," *The Globe and Mail,* September 20, 1999, p. A2. Reprinted with permission from *The Globe and Mail.*

RESEARCHING THE INDUSTRIAL CITY: THE CHICAGO SCHOOL

By the final quarter of the nineteenth century, U.S. cities were seeing jumps in population that rivalled and even surpassed those in Britain. Nowhere was this more dramatic than in Chicago, which mushroomed from 122 000 people in 1860 to 1.7 million in 1900 and 3.4 million in 1930. Such rapid growth left in its wake social dislocation and human misery. Among those who sought to address these problems was the chairman of the sociology department of the University of Chicago, Robert E. Park.

Park and his colleagues believed that they could improve conditions for the disadvantaged by discovering what made the city "tick" and then using this knowledge to help solve its "social pathologies": crime, juvenile delinquency, family breakdown, and mental illness. To carry out this task, they employed an assortment of methods and models. On the one hand, Park argued that researchers should consider themselves urban anthropologists who would venture out into the field and study the natives, and their customs, beliefs, and practices. This inspired a rich ethnographic tradition of urban research in which Park's colleagues and students rendered richly detailed, first-hand accounts of such things as homeless men, gangs, and "taxi-dance" halls. At the same time, Park also urged his students to consider the city of Chicago as a kind of social laboratory in which various natural processes took place. One way of documenting these processes was through the development of urban-growth models (discussed in the next section) by which the changing social and spatial structure of the city could be depicted visually. Another was to use "ecological spot maps" in which differences in the rate of various deviant behaviours, such as juvenile delinquency and schizophrenia, could be plotted geographically in order to discover underlying patterns. Some of the most memorable work to come out of the Chicago School tradition drew upon personal documents and other biographical materials (Zorbaugh, 1929).

To put this mountain of data into some kind of theoretical order, Park and his colleagues used several approaches. First, they tapped into a long tradition of exploring the contrast between rural and urban life. In the latter part of the nineteenth century, the German social philosopher Ferdinand Tönnies (1957 [1887]) had attempted to depict the difference

German philosopher Ferdinand Tönnies contrasted the community of feeling that exists in villages and small communities with the commercialism and individualism of the city.
SOURCE: Sheila Maloney, *Zephyr Ontario*. Courtesy Nancy Poole's Studio.

between traditional and modern societies by introducing a distinction between a *Gemeinschaft*—the "community of feeling" that exists in villages, tribes, and small communities—and *Gesellschaft*—the characteristic feature of social relations in the city. Tönnies favoured *Gemeinschaft* and saw its decline as a loss of all that is natural and satisfying about small-town life. In contrast, he wrote, *Gesellschaft* denotes a lifestyle based on money, commercial contracts, individual interest, and class antagonism. Although he was more positive about the possibilities for individual freedom in modern urban life, the German sociologist Georg Simmel (1950) used the same rural-urban contrast as a central method of dealing with the meaning of the shift to an urban society.

This rural-urban dichotomy runs through much of Chicago School theorizing. Thomas and Znaniecki (1918–20), for example, depict the city as being responsible for destroying the traditional institutions of Polish peasant life—family, neighbourhood, church—and substituting nothing but an empty well of social disorganization. Freed from the ties that formerly bound the community together, marriages dissolve, teenagers run wild, and even murder is not uncommon. In his modification of Simmel's social-psychological profile of urban life, Louis Wirth (1938) proposed that the city is characterized by the concurrent trends of increasing size, density, and heterogeneity. In his view, the city creates a distinct way of life—**urbanism**—that is economically efficient but socially destructive. Wirth's list of urban characteristics includes the decline of the family, the disappearance of the neighbourhood, and the undermining of traditional bases of social solidarity. Urbanites are said to be superficial, unable to step outside their narrow occupational roles to relate to people in a holistic and meaningful way, and guided by an all-consuming drive for success and money.

ECOLOGY OF THE INDUSTRIAL CITY

Industrial cities were also unique in their ecology—that is, their spatial layout, physical structure, and distribution of population. To depict the spatial or ecological patterns of the city, a group of sociologists and geographers from the University of Chicago devised a set of urban-growth models in the 1920s and 1930s.

Burgess's **concentric-zone model** conceptualized the expansion of cities as a succession of concentric rings, each of which contained a distinct resident population and type of land use (Burgess, 1961). This concentric model of urban growth identified five zones (see Figure 15.3).

Zone 1, the central business district (CBD), is the commercial pulse of the city. It is the site of the major department stores, live theatres, hotels, banks, and office space. The land is the most valuable in the city, which means that residential and low-rent commercial uses are inevitably displaced in favour of big-money commercial enterprises.

Zone 2 is called the zone in transition. In the 1920s, large parcels of land in Chicago's transitional zone were being held by speculators who fully expected that the CBD would push outward, making them millionaires. In the meantime, Zone 2 stood as an area of cheap housing that became the initial resting point for each new wave of immigrants who took jobs in the nearby factories. Also located here were a variety of marginal businesses—pawn shops, tattoo parlours, second-hand stores—that could not afford the high rents of the city centre. The transitional zone also attracted a raft of illegal commercial activities—gambling, prostitution, drug dealing—that needed to be accessible to clientele in the CBD but that were considered socially unacceptable in the high-profile heart of the downtown area.

Zone 3, the zone of working-class homes, denotes the area settled by second-generation immigrants and rural migrants. In Burgess's time, Zone 3 was a neighbourhood of semidetached, two-family homes where

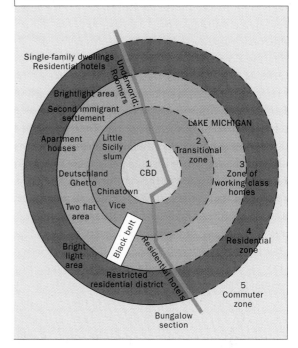

FIGURE 15.3 BURGESS'S CONCENTRIC ZONE MODEL APPLIED TO CHICAGO

SOURCE: Redrawn from Ernest W. Burgess, "The Growth of the City: An Introduction to a Research Project," in George A. Theodorson, ed., *Studies in Human Ecology*, Evanston, IL: Row, Peterson, 1961, p. 41.

fathers still worked in inner-city factories but from which the upwardly mobile children aspired to escape, into the middle-class suburban zones.

Zone 4, the zone of better residences, was where the bulk of the middle class could be found: small-business people, professionals, sales personnel, and office employees. Initially, it was an area of single-family detached houses, but by the mid-1920s, it was increasingly characterized by apartment buildings and residential hotels.

Finally, Zone 5, the commuter zone, was an area beyond the political boundaries of the city composed of satellite towns and suburbs. With the growth of commuter railroads and automobile travel, Zone 5 was a precursor of the suburbs that boomed after World War II.

Burgess's concentric-zone model made three interrelated assumptions. First, all commercial growth was said to emanate from the dominant city-centre nucleus and proceed outward in an orderly and predictable manner. Second, residential growth took place at the periphery, where it was easier and cheaper to obtain open land for development purchases. New housing was added here, but it was intended primarily for the middle and upper classes, who were increasingly able to take advantage of newly constructed commuter rail lines and, later, expressways. Third, the model was dynamic in that it assumed a sort of filtering-down process. As housing aged, it deteriorated, became less desirable, and was abandoned by better-off citizens, who moved into newer housing farther away from the city centre. The homes they left behind, some of them mansions, were subdivided into rooming houses, flats, and dormitories for artists and students. In recent years, many of these have been restored to a measure of their former glory, either by residential "gentrifiers" or by commercial users, such as restaurateurs or hair stylists. Furthermore, Burgess assumed that, as immigrant newcomers to the industrial city found their balance and began to prosper, they would want to upgrade their housing. For example, the second generation of "white ethnics"—the acculturated sons and daughters of those who had come as part of the Polish, Italian, German, and other European immigration around the turn of the century—could be expected to settle in the zone of working-class homes, which possessed superior housing to that occupied by their parents in the transitional zone.

Burgess's urban-growth model appears to have fitted Chicago in the 1920s reasonably well, but, as a scheme for understanding all cities in different places and times, it does not do as well. First, the notion of a single growth nucleus has not held up very firmly. Such cities as Calgary and Edmonton, which developed later in the century and which were shaped largely by the automobile, are more likely to possess more than one nucleus or growth centre. Similarly, Los Angeles is widely known as "the city without a downtown." This was first recognized in the 1940s by geographers Chauncey Harris and Edward Ullman (1945), who proposed a **multiple-nuclei model** of urban growth in which were located a series of growth centres—retail, wholesale, residential—each representing the concentration of a specific function or activity within the urban economy.

Second, Burgess seems to have underestimated the importance of transportation corridors as magnets for urban growth. Geographer Homer Hoyt (1939) developed a **sector model** of urban growth after studying 142 U.S. cities during the Depression years. He argued that cities grew not in concentric circles but in sectors or wedges along major transportation arteries, extending like the tentacles of an octopus from the CBD. Within each sector, the social character of the residential housing would remain constant. For example, upper-income groups would follow a northward progression, and working-class groups a southward path, thereby producing a distinct sectoral pattern to the developing city. Montreal and Vancouver seem to fit this sector model, because their populations tended to spread out along the natural shorelines of the bodies of water on which they are located (Driedger, 1991: 90).

Third, Burgess failed to appreciate that some resident groups would develop strong residential attachments to their neighbourhoods and refuse to move on, even in the face of an aging housing stock. This was first pointed out by Walter Firey (1947) in his study of Boston. Firey gives several examples that span the socioeconomic spectrum, from Beacon Hill, an elite area near the city centre, to the North End, a blue-collar Italian area where the residents chose to remain in their old neighbourhoods because the places were cherished as symbols of the residents' family connections, traditions, and culture.

URBANIZATION OF THE DEVELOPING WORLD

A century ago, most urban growth was concentrated in the rapidly industrializing countries of Europe and North America. Today, nearly two-thirds of the world's urban population resides in the less developed regions of Asia, Oceania, Africa, Latin America, and the Caribbean (Gugler, 1996: vii). In the Southern hemisphere, the demographic transition is moving faster and with far greater numbers than those experienced in the past (Ness and Law, 2000). Over the next three decades, cities in the global south are expected to double in size to about 4 billion people, with 19 cities reaching a population of more than 10 million by 2015 (see Figure 15.4).

Although urbanization in the Southern hemisphere has followed sundry paths, it has displayed some common features. To a greater extent than with Northern cities, cities of the South are characterized by a high degree of **urban primacy.** This describes a situation in which one metropolitan centre, usually the capital city, is considerably larger and more dominant than any of the others. In Mexico, for example, this primacy is indicated by roadside markers throughout the country that indicate the distance to

FIGURE 15.4 MEGA-CITY GROWTH

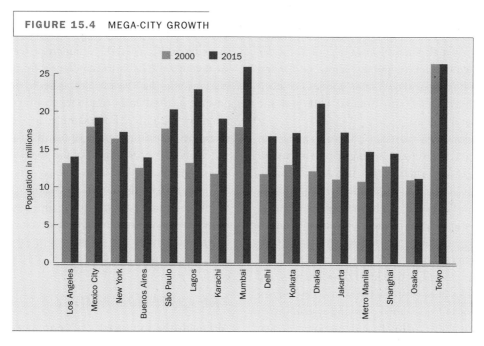

SOURCE: Reprinted by kind permission of the New Internationalist. Copyright New Internationalist, www.newint.org.

Mexico City, which is six times the size of its nearest rival, Guadalajara (Flanagan, 1995: 154). Primacy is most evident on the African continent, where 11 out of the 20 most extreme examples of primacy systems occur (Clark, 1996: 27). In many cases, they are located along the sea coast, a legacy of colonial times when they operated as shipping points for raw materials on their way to Spain, France, England, and other imperial powers. Much the same pattern exists in present times; resource-producing regions funnel export commodities to big coastal cities, where the goods are subsequently shipped overseas. This is said to contribute to the underdevelopment of the interior, where provincial towns and cities tend to stagnate, unable to sustain a robust local industrial and commercial base.

In recent years, however, cities with populations between 100 000 and 500 000 have experienced remarkable growth, especially in some Latin American countries. In Argentina, for example, intermediate cities have grown faster than Buenos Aires, while in Mexico, interior cities that have plugged into the international economy have outstripped the growth rate of Mexico City (De Oliveira and Roberts, 1996).

Cities of the South are often described as victims of **overurbanization.** This means that the population of urban areas is growing faster than the urban economy, services, and resources can absorb it. This creates an underclass of residents who live in illegal squatter settlements and employ themselves in marginal trades, such as selling food and lottery tickets on street corners (Flanagan, 1995: 153). Canadian cities have recently had a taste of this in the form of growing numbers of panhandlers, "squeegee kids," and other homeless urban people, but the numbers in Southern cities are much larger. With public housing scarce, "squatter settlements" are common. In such settlements, people occupy urban land without legal title, frequently organizing "invasions" at set times and places. Once they have staked out their plots, the squatters put up makeshift shelters and establish basic public services, such as water supply and sewage disposal. Some squatter settlements remain poor, but others significantly upgrade their housing and eventually persuade municipal governments to extend utilities and health and sanitation services into the area.

The concept of overurbanization has provoked debate among social scientists. Some claim that overurbanization is the single most important factor leading to the generation and intensification of serious social problems in southern cities: grinding poverty, mass unemployment, inadequate services, social unrest, increasing crime, and political instability (D. Smith, 1996: 148). Others claim that it is misleading to isolate the mismatch between demographic growth and employment opportunities, arguing that it makes more sense to look to larger structural factors, such as undue reliance on foreign multinational corporations and continued deep inequality between an urban-based elite and the urban and rural masses.

Some countries in Asia, Africa, and Latin America have exhibited distinctive patterns of **peri-urbanization** whereby the rural and the urban have become blurred in unplanned settlements on the outskirts of large cities. The motivation for this is mostly economic: Land in these peri-urban zones is cheaper and more easily obtained; shelter can be constructed economically by using locally available materials; and families can keep farm animals and cultivate subsistence crops without violating any of the restrictions of the formal planning system (Stren and Halfani, 2001: 478). In contemporary Asian cities, for example, urbanization is increasingly characterized by the *desakota* (from the Indonesian words for village and city). Here, most people continue to live in village settings and almost all the land is under cultivation, but most family income comes from nonagricultural sources. Some family members may even commute to work in the city, or live in the city and remit portions of their salaries to their families (Ginsburg, Koppel, and McGee, 1991). The linked processes of peri-urbanization and *desakota* challenge the conventional paradigm of the urban transition derived from the case of Western Europe and North America in the nineteenth and early twentieth centuries. Rather than remain strictly separated, the rural and the urban coexist in densely populated areas on the fringe of large mega-urban regions (McGee, 1991: 4–5).

Finally, sociologists who study urbanization in the South have been much concerned with urban bias, that is, uneven investment and development that favour urban over rural areas. Despite the problems generated by overurbanization, landless migrants continue to flow into cities, which they see as their best chance to improve their lot in life. Economic growth strategies focus primarily on these rapidly growing cities, while the rural hinterland is overlooked. Thus, for the two decades following independence (the 1960s and 1970s) many of Africa's first-generation political leaders penalized agriculture through their monetary and tax policies in order to obtain resources to finance industrial development in the cities. In addition, public services were concentrated in the large cities, especially national capitals (Lofchie, 1997: 24–25). Although poverty statistics are not always reliable, recent figures from the United Nations and the World Bank suggest that absolute poverty in rural areas continues to overshadow that found in the cities. For example, in Brazil, where there are notoriously poor slums in Rio de Janeiro and São Paulo, 65.9 percent of the population in rural areas continues to live below the poverty line versus 37.7 percent in the cities. In Mexico, the figures follow the same pattern. Much the same holds for most African nations. India, by contrast, shows more or less comparable levels of poverty in urban and rural areas (Drakakis-Smith, 1988).

THE CORPORATE CITY

Although the industrial city continued to exist in North America into the 1970s, it began to lose ground after 1945 to a new urban form. Simply defined, the **corporate city** denotes the perception and organization of the city as a vehicle for capital accumulation—that is, as a money-making machine.

The corporate city comprises five major elements (Lorimer, 1978; Reid, 1991): (1) the corporate suburb, (2) the shopping centre, (3) the suburban industrial park, (4) the downtown office tower, and (5) the high-rise apartment building.

Each of these five elements of the corporate city has evolved over the years. Some of their central features have recently changed. Facing the spectre of shopper boredom and increased competition from both revitalized downtown retail districts and exurban big-box stores (e.g., Home Depot, Costco, Wal-Mart), shopping centres have been undergoing a redesign that includes a more diverse mix of retail tenants. In the face of changing demographics, suburban developments have also been forced to include a greater variety of housing types, including more townhouses and row houses and such innovations as "granny flats" (separate quarters for aged parents). After years of being half-empty, some downtown office buildings have begun to convert to condominiums. Nevertheless, the process by which the corporate city has been assembled and maintained remains much the same and stands in marked contrast to that which undergirds the building of the industrial city. Nowhere has this been more evident than in the case of the corporate suburb.

THE CORPORATE SUBURB

Before World War II, North American cities, such as Toronto, were configured in a grid system, with residential avenues crossing long commercial streets at right angles. Since most urban residents lived within a few blocks of neighbourhood stores and services, pedestrian traffic constantly moved up and down the streets. This spawned a lively "front-yard culture" in which passers-by regularly interacted with porch sitters, since front yards and families faced the street rather than the house itself (Fowler, 1992: 205).

When cities expanded, they did so incrementally, often a dozen houses at a time. The cost of extending sewers, water lines, and other city services was assumed by the municipality and paid for over 20 or 30 years through tax increases or special bonds. Lots were narrow and houses two or three storeys high. Parking space was mostly on the street and, as auto ownership spread rapidly, increasingly scarce.

In the early 1950s, all this changed with the building of Don Mills, Canada's first mass suburb, on the northern fringe of Toronto. Don Mills emphasized a system of short curving roads in the form of circles and crescents. Initially, this layout was probably meant to convey a sense of privileged exclusivity, although over time it also came to reflect a desire to shield children from the perceived danger of through-traffic. In any case, it made public transit difficult, consigning buses to main arterial roads on the perimeter of the housing subdivision. Don Mills houses were placed on wider lots with larger setbacks from the streets. With no sidewalks, small front porches, and minimal pedestrian traffic (most residents drove to the nearby Don Mills Plaza to shop), the social action shifted to the fenced-in backyards, which were, in any case, favoured by parents, who appreciated being able to keep an eye on their toddlers from the kitchen window. Don Mills was one of the first residential areas in Canada to be planned completely from scratch and built all at once. In contrast to the development pattern in the central city, almost all the servicing costs, including that of a sewage treatment plant along the Don River, were assumed by the developer, E.P. Taylor. By doing so, Taylor changed the rules of urban development, relegating the municipality to a more passive role and introducing corporate success as a major planning consideration (Sewell, 1993: 95).

With the triumph of Don Mills, the corporate suburb spread rapidly across Canada and the United States. (The United States had already introduced its own early prototype of a planned, mass-produced suburb in Levittown, Long Island, 32 kilometres, or 20 miles, from New York City.) Although there were local differences, these first-generation postwar suburbs shared five main characteristics: a peripheral location, relatively low population densities, architectural similarity, a relatively low purchase price for houses, and a fairly high degree of economic and racial homogeneity (Jackson, 1985: 238–43).

Suburbanism as a Way of Life

In the 1950s, the suburbs were routinely disparaged as being sterile social and cultural wastelands where conformity ruled and individual taste and thought were stifled. This notion was given wide exposure in the 1956 best-seller *The Organization Man*, a study of Park Forest, Illinois, 48 kilometers (30 miles) south of Chicago, by *Fortune* magazine writer William H. Whyte (1956). Suburban dwellers were invariably depicted as living in mass-produced housing that was uniform in design and decoration. This image is bitingly evoked in folk singer Malvina Reynolds's 1950s ditty "Little Boxes" (Reynolds, 1964: 28):

> Little Boxes on the hillside
> Little Boxes made of ticky tacky,
> Little Boxes on the hillside,
> Little Boxes all the same.

Not only was the physical appearance of suburban areas said to be homogeneous, but life there was also said to revolve around a "dry-martini culture." During the workweek, fathers commuted in car pools or by rail to jobs at IBM, General Motors, and other corporate giants, while mothers ferried the children around in the family station wagon and socialized at coffee parties. On the weekend, the husbands washed the cars and tended well-manicured lawns, while the wives shopped for groceries at nearby plazas. At night, couples socialized in one another's homes, around the pool or the barbecue.

For sociological researchers, **suburbanism** represented an important trend. In a much-quoted 1956 article, "Suburbanism as a Way of Life," Sylvia Fava did a take on Louis Wirth's classic 1938 essay. Fava claimed that suburbanites were far more likely than their counterparts in the central city to be both sociable and socially active. Similarly, in a much-cited before-and-after study of middle-class couples in Toronto who chose to relocate during the early 1970s,

Michelson (1973) found that suburban movers increased their involvement with neighbours, while city relocators increased interactions with friends and relatives.

Another key feature of the suburban lifestyle was its emphasis on children and the family. Perhaps the most influential study with regard to the importance of children in suburban communities was that by Seeley and Loosley (1956) in *Crestwood Heights*, a profile of the affluent community of Forest Hill Village in 1950s Toronto. Although Crestwood Heights was more a neighbourhood on the northern edge of the city, its organization around the needs of its children (schools, camps, counselling) was said to be typical of the developing suburbs of the time.

Suburbanism was further depicted as a lifestyle choice rather than strictly as an economic decision. City dwellers who packed up and left the central city were said to be embracing a new, family-oriented way of life, seduced by advertisements in the real-estate section of the Saturday newspaper promising "bourgeois utopias" (Fishman, 1987). Not all residents, however, embraced this lifestyle with equal enthusiasm. Women in the suburbs frequently felt cut off from the social and cultural stimulation of the central city with its theatres, art galleries, restaurants, and shopping streets. Sociability in the corporate suburb was restricted to private gatherings in the home or the backyard with neighbours. Not surprisingly, a number of researchers found that women were less satisfied than their husbands with their choice of residence, often having a sense of stagnation and isolation despite relatively frequent visiting and entertaining (Michelson, 1973).

Significantly, this lifestyle did not appear to be replicated in working-class suburbs, where people's values and social behaviours remained firmly anchored in blue-collar culture. Berger (1960) refers to the myth of suburbia, by which he means a standardized and stereotyped view of the suburbs as uniformly middle-class, homogeneous, conformist, child-centred, female-dominated, and hotbeds of sociability.

It is possible to discern three alternative interpretations of the relationship between suburban residence and lifestyle patterns (McGahan, 1995: 232–36). According to the *structural* interpretation, the environmental and demographic characteristics of the suburb encourage a distinct style of life. For example, by excluding stores and services, such as restaurants, bars, and movie theatres, from residential neighbourhoods and by discouraging public transit, the Don Mills model promoted a greater reliance on private sociability, as evidenced by the weekday morning coffee klatches and weekend pool parties that came to be identified with suburban life in the 1950s and 1960s.

In contrast, the *selective migration* interpretation denies that the suburban environment exercises any independent effect on behaviour patterns. Rather, it is suggested that those who chose to move to the corporate suburbs after World War II were already primed to embrace **familism**—a lifestyle that places a high value on family living, marriage at a young age, a brief period of childlessness after marriage, and child-centredness of the type that Seeley and his colleagues observed in Crestwood Heights (Bell, 1968: 147).

Finally, the *class and life-cycle* interpretation proposes that what Berger had branded the "suburban myth" was nothing more than a snapshot of middle-class life at mid-century. Today, many of the same characteristics—child-centredness, commuting, backyard culture—can be observed in the second wave of gentrification in the central city. As the corporate suburb matured, it changed appreciably, with a new set of social activities replacing those that had prevailed at an earlier stage in the life cycle of both the suburb and the families who settled there.

Whether it was the Don Mills–style suburb or downtown office towers, the corporate city did not just happen: It was the deliberate product of an alliance between government and business interests. Logan and Molotch (1987) have termed this alliance an **urban-growth machine**, a loosely structured coalition of local economic and political interest groups with a commitment to sustained growth and development. Urban-growth machines can include an extensive cast of players: businesses, property owners, investors and developers, politicians and planners, the media, utilities, cultural institutions (museums, theatres), professional sports teams, labour unions, and even universities. Growth machines pursue a narrow band of interests, sacrificing the sentimental and symbolic value of places—which is associated with jobs, neighbourhood, home town, and community—in favour of a strict emphasis on land use as an investment and commodity to be bought and sold (Palen, 1995: 20). Although government and business may honestly believe that local communities thrive only if they continue to expand economically, it could also be said that the structure that growth machines impose on urban living gives people a minimum of freedom to live their lives in the corporate city as they choose (Lorimer, 1978: 220).

THE POSTMODERN CITY

In recent years, a new kind of urban form has appeared on the global landscape: the postmodern city. Although there is some debate over what exactly is meant by this term, several aspects do seem clear.

First, the postmodern city is the product of the simultaneous operation of the forces of re-urbanization and counter-urbanization.

Counter-urbanization occurs when people move from central cities and inner suburbs into the surrounding rural hinterland (Berry and Gillard, 1987). Writing a quarter century ago, the respected Canadian urban planner Hans Blumenfeld (1982, 1983) ventured that, if sustained, counter-urbanization might well result in a new urban form—the exurb. A decade later, exurbs in Canada and the United States were already home to nearly 60 million people, making them the fastest-growing component of the continental landscape (Davis, Nelson, and Dueher, 1994). Initially entirely residential, exurbs today are increasingly likely to take the form of edge cities that include significant commercial, leisure, and entertainment components.

At the same time, the central city has been staging a comeback from the dismal days of the 1960s and 1970s, en era in which it was effectively abandoned by middle-class families who moved in large numbers to the corporate suburbs. In part this re-urbanization of inner city districts reflects the continuing gentrification of older neighbourhoods. Additionally, however, it has been powered by the global migration of immigrants from around the world, a process that Fishman (2005) has called the "fifth great migration" to affect North America.

Second, cities are becoming multiethnic, with many ethnic neighbourhoods in the largest cities becoming home to visible minority groups. This is generating racial and ethnic residential and commercial patterns that stand in marked contrast to the ecology of the industrial city that I discussed in an earlier section of this chapter. These new urban settlers can be found both in suburban subdivisions and inner-city precincts.

The postmodern city is characterized by the privatization of public space, as shown in this mall scene.
SOURCE: PhotoDisc.

Third, the postmodern city is characteristically fragmented, even chaotic. Elizabeth Wilson (1991: 136) describes it as resembling "a split screen flickering with competing beliefs, cultures and 'stories.'" Geographically and socially split, the postmodern city does not have a single "way of life" of the sort identified by Wirth for the industrial city and Fava for the corporate suburb.

Finally, the postmodern city is characterized by the privatization of public space. Privatization occurs across a wide spectrum of settings, from downtown malls and festival marketplaces to private, "gated" communities on the fringes of the city. Although suburban dwellers have always put a premium on private space, from the enclosed backyard to the drive-in theatre, this value is now washing over the city as a whole and, in the process, drastically reducing the number of public places where people can come together to shop or socialize (Goldberger, 1996: 139).

I next examine three overlapping components of the postmodern city: the edge city, the multiethnic city, and the dual city. Although each component has real-life spatial and demographic components, none exists in pure form. Instead, they are constructions, formulated by academic researchers or journalists, that help us visualize an important dimension of the globalized, privatized, and fragmented postmodern city.

THE EDGE CITY

Although they differed significantly in their patterns of housing, transportation, and shopping, the industrial city and the corporate city displayed more or less the same spatial configuration: an urban core containing the bulk of the office space, cultural institutions, factories, and a ring of suburbs where much of the more affluent middle class resided. Even with the growth of shopping centres and industrial parks in the 1950s and 1960s, the lion's share of jobs and services remained within the city itself, and suburbanites were daily commuters.

During the past quarter-century, however, this traditional pattern has been turned inside out with the rapid growth of **edge cities** (Garreau, 1991). Situated in exurbia—the rural residential area around the suburbs within commuting range of the city—edge cities

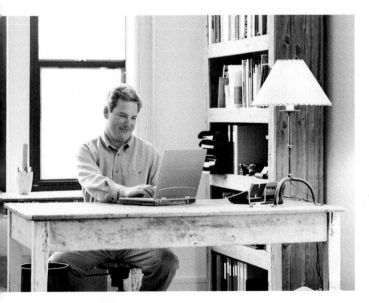

The tremendous growth of technology, such as fax machines, cellular phones, and e-mail, has geographically freed many employees whose linkages to the workplace are now activated on the road or from home offices.
SOURCE: Photos.com.

have no dominant single core or definable set of boundaries; they are typically "clusters of malls, office developments and entertainment complexes that rise where major highways cross or converge" (Fishman, 1990: 18). Some edge cities are expansions of existing satellite cities, but others sprout up in unincorporated townships, lacking clearly definable borders and legal status as places (Palen, 1995: 187).

What has led to the growth of edge cities? Leinberger and Lockwood (1986) offer five reasons for edge cities' recent emergence. First, there has been a major shift in North American economies from manufacturing to a service and knowledge base. One result of this shift is that middle-class employees are now more willing to live near where they work than they used to be when jobs were located in factories that were dirty, noisy, and unattractive. An example of the older pattern can be found in Ontario's steel industry, where the managers and executives at Stelco and Dofasco traditionally settled on the other side of the Skyway Bridge in Burlington, while the mill workers remained in Hamilton. In contrast, Kanata, the outer suburban location of Ottawa's microchip computer industry, is solidly middle class.

Second, there have been significant changes in transportation patterns that favour trucks and cars over subways, streetcars, and trains. As a result, urban facilities have scattered over the exurban landscape, unfettered by the requirement of locating along established transportation corridors.

Third, recent advances in telecommunications technology have reduced the necessity for offices to locate downtown in close physical proximity. Some types of businesses—stock brokerages, banks—still prefer to be close to one another and to central city services. But the tremendous growth of technology, such as fax machines, cellular phones, and e-mail, has geographically freed many employees whose linkages to the workplace are now activated on the road or from home offices.

Fourth, as it has become increasingly expensive to operate in the city, offices, industries, and professional practitioners (lawyers, accountants, etc.) have pulled up their roots and moved to cheaper locations in exurbia. Among other things, parking is more plentiful and less expensive out of the city.

Fifth, the coming of age of dual-income, baby-boom families with one or two children has meant that people's lives are increasingly governed by considerations of time, convenience, and efficiency. The clustering of offices, shopping centres, and recreational facilities at the juncture of exurban highways meets the needs of this subpopulation, the members of which have little time left in their lives to commute downtown to shop, eat, or be entertained.

These changes have shown up in the form of new patterns of commuting to work in large urban areas. In Canada, census data from 1996 and 2001 point to several significant trends (Heisz and LaRochelle-Coté, 2005: 16). First, the number of workers who commute within a suburb or across the city from suburb to suburb has risen appreciably. Second, the growth of "reverse commuters" (those who travel from the city centre to the suburbs) has uniformly outstripped that of traditional commuters (those who travel from outside to inside the city centre).

Edge cities have been of particular interest to urban sociologists because they are neither suburbs nor centralized cities but a hybrid that incorporates elements of each. Unlike the typical suburb, which is primarily residential, edge cities contain many of the functions of the traditional city: shopping, office space, housing, entertainment facilities. Also, in contrast to suburbanites, who commute to work in the central city by rail or car, edge-city residents are inclined to live and work in the same geographic area. Commuting now means driving to an adjoining suburb or exurb, rather than heading downtown. This can be seen in the "905 belt" surrounding Metro Toronto, where a number of areas now function as "magnets." That is, more people travel to jobs there each day than journey out of the community to jobs elsewhere in the Greater Toronto Area. Finally, in contrast to the typical suburb, which lacks a well-developed infrastructure of sports, entertainment, and cultural facilities, the edge city is increasingly the site of a burgeoning number of performing arts centres, sports palaces, and entertainment complexes.

Nevertheless, it would be wrong to think that there are no real differences between edge cities and the older cities. Unlike the industrial city, the edge city lacks a single centre. In the former, it was always possible to start downtown and eventually reach the outer boundaries of the city. In contrast, the spatial logic of the edge city dictates that centres and boundaries are not needed. Instead, the edge city is made up of three overlapping types of socioeconomic networks: household networks, networks of consumption, and networks of production. Each of these runs on the guiding principle of convenience. Two-income families with children, who make up the largest demographic segment of the edge-city population, are increasingly pressed for time and, as a result, frequently create their own "personal cities" out of the destinations they can reach within a manageable time (Fishman, 1990).

THE MULTIETHNIC CITY

According to Statistics Canada's most recent population projections, by the year 2017 nearly one Canadian in five (21 percent) is likely to be a member of a visible minority group. This contrasts with 13 percent in 2001 and less than 5 percent in 1981. (Bélanger and Malenfant, 2005). Nearly 75 percent of members of visible minorities are expected to reside in the census metropolitan areas (CMAs) of Montreal, Toronto, and Vancouver; about half the population of the latter two cities will comprise members of visible minority groups (see Table 15.2). This new demographic makeup has important implications for our understanding of contemporary urban structures and processes (Fong and Shibuya, 2005).

In particular, we are likely to witness the growth of a new generation of residentially segregated neighbourhoods (Fong, 1996; Fong and Wilkes, 1999). Whereas newcomers from Northern and Western European nations tended to blend in residentially with Canadians from the charter groups (British and French), members of most Asian ethnic groups are likely to cluster together apart from other groups. The evidence so far indicates that these visible minority neighbourhoods are formed when nonvisible minority residents move out as large numbers of a visible minority group move into the neighbourhood (Hou and Picot, 2004).

Contrary to the classic urban-growth model proposed by the Chicago School's human ecologists, the postmodern city doesn't exhibit a simple pattern of first-generation immigrant settlement (i.e., in the zone of transition adjacent to the commercial core). Using data from New York and Los Angeles, Logan, Alba, and Zhang (2002) distinguish between two very different types of ethnic communities: the traditional immigrant enclave with dense concentrations of immigrants and high levels of poverty and other urban problems; and the more desirable ethnic neighbourhood whose residents are much better endowed both financially and socially. This dual pattern is

TABLE 15.2   VISIBLE MINORITY PERSONS IN SELECTED CANADIAN CMAS, 2001–2017 (PROJECTED)

	NUMBER OF VISIBLE MINORITY PERSONS (000S)		PERCENTAGE OF TOTAL POPULATION	
	2001	**2017**	**2001**	**2017**
Canada	4038	7121	13	21
Census metropolitan area				
Toronto	1753	3194	37	51
Vancouver	741	1261	36	49
Montreal	454	749	13	19
Ottawa–Gatineau	139	316	17	28
Calgary	166	295	17	24
Edmonton	136	211	14	18
Hamilton	64	125	9	15
Winnipeg	84	115	12	16
Windsor	40	97	13	23
Kitchener	45	79	10	15
Rest of Canada	418	679	3	4

SOURCE: Adapted from the Statistics Canada publication "Canadian Social Trends," Catalogue 11-008, Ethnocultural Diversity in Canada: Prospects for 2017, Winter 2005, No. 79, p. 21.

especially evident in suburban neighbourhoods in major Canadian cities. Whereas some groups, notably the Chinese, settle here to take advantage of a more plentiful supply of new owner-occupied housing, others with fewer resources come for affordable subsidized social housing (Bourne, 1996).

What is less well understood is the nature of social relations among multiple minority groups in a multiethnic context and how these relationships shape urban structures and processes between minority groups and members of charter groups (Fong and Shibuya, 2005). One thing that we do know is that relatively little overlap exists in the minority neighbourhoods of different groups. In 2001, for example, among the 135 visible minority neighbourhoods in Toronto, only in three did both Chinese and South Asians combined represent at least 30 percent of the neighbourhood population (Hou and Picot, 2004: 11).

THE DUAL CITY

With the edge city increasingly becoming the occupational, residential, and commercial centre for the middle classes, what has become of urban downtowns? The central city, some analysts suggest, has become polarized between two starkly different realities that are spatially discrete and that have only the name of the city and some public places in common. Situated just blocks or streets away from one another, the "city of despair and squalor" and the "city of hope and splendour" are light years apart. This split reality has been called the "dual city."

The term **dual city** has come to refer to the urban expression of two increasingly divergent streams in the global economy. On the one hand, there is an information-based, formal economy rooted in financial services, telecommunications, and the microchip. Typically, those who are part of this upper-tier informational city live in a world of computer software, fax machines, cell phones, and Internet surfing. Residentially, they can be found in "gentrified" niches of the inner city (gentrification is discussed below) or in exclusive suburbs, where they isolate themselves both socially and geographically from the rest of the city. In Castells's (1989) description, these spaces constitute a microsociety with their own separate circuit of leisure, lifestyle, and services.

On the other hand, juxtaposed to the informational city is an "informal economy" that has been excluded from the main loop. Residents here rely not

TABLE 15.3 COMPARISON OF SUBURBAN AND POSTMODERN URBAN LIFESTYLES

	SUBURBAN	POSTMODERN GENTRIFIED URBAN
Neighbourhood social involvement	Deliberate and sustained	Incidental
Lifestyle focus	Family	Consumerism
Typical activities	Home activities (gardening, entertaining)	Dining out, shopping
Typical occupation of resident	Middle manager	Architect, corporate lawyer, etc.
Housing type	Split-level, detached	Victorian, semidetached
Social composition	Class-exclusive	Socially and culturally diverse
Ideology	Anti-urban	Pro-urban

SOURCE: John A. Hannigan, "The Postmodern City: A New Urbanization?" *Current Sociology,* 43(1) (1995), p. 180.

on high-technology communications, but on face-to-face social networks, usually established on the basis of shared race and ethnicity. People are engaged in a wide range of activities, from labouring in immigrant sweatshops in the clothing trade to offering such services as furniture making, home renovation, and auto repairs (Gordon and Sassen, 1992). Although this informal economy cannot be equated with urban poverty per se, its participants stand relatively little chance of ever penetrating the upper-tier information economy.

Gentrification

In the 1970s and 1980s, considerable attention was paid by urban researchers to the phenomenon of **gentrification** in the dual city. By gentrification, I mean the transformation of working-class housing into fashionable downtown neighbourhoods by middle- and upper-income newcomers. Gentrification is neither anticipated nor accounted for by the ecological growth models discussed above. Similarly, it runs counter to predictions about the mass flight to the suburbs that dominated urban sociology in the 1950s and 1960s. A comparison of the suburban lifestyle and the postmodern urban lifestyle as typified by gentrification is set out in Table 15.3.

Four primary explanations for gentrification have been advanced (Ley, 1991: 182–85). First, demographic changes led to gentrification in the 1970s and 1980s. At this time, the baby boomers who were born and raised in the suburbs began to look for housing of their own. Facing high demand levels and a shortage of supply, they turned to inner-city housing, which was cheap but in dire need of rehabilitation. They opposed demolition, favoured by urban-renewal advocates. Unlike suburban settlers in the previous period, many of these urban migrants were childless and career-oriented. This meant that schools, playgrounds, and parks were not their major concerns and they were happy with smaller housing units without the big backyards and basement recreation rooms that were characteristic of Don Mills–type housing. Since many of these young professionals worked downtown, they were willing to trade space for proximity to their places of employment and to downtown cultural and entertainment facilities.

Second, gentrification may be accounted for by economic changes related to the flow of capital in and out of the housing market. In this view, gentrification functions as a "back to the city movement by capital, not people" (N. Smith, 1979). As you have seen, in the 1950s and 1960s, financial capital flowed into the building of the suburbs under the guidance of governments that viewed the construction of large-scale projects by development companies as the fastest, most efficient way of coping with the pressures created by the baby boom. Developers were encouraged by an array of incentives: tax breaks, government-backed mortgages, guarantees, and insurance with low premiums. By the 1970s, the profit levels in suburban building had begun to shrink, and capital flow switched back to the urban centre to take advantage of the rent gap—that is, the difference between the current value of land in its "depressed" state and the value that could be charged given a higher or better land use (Smith and LeFaivre, 1984).

Third, middle-class newcomers to the central city arrived in search of a lifestyle that was more distinctive and cosmopolitan than that available within the constraints of suburban conformity. In the central city, they could express a distinctive aesthetic and style of consumption, characterized by a dislike of mass-produced goods and a penchant for objects and buildings from a bygone era, notably the Victorian age (Filion, 1991: 554). This new lifestyle also extended to the surrounding neighbourhood, which filled up with wine bars, California-style restaurants, franchise coffee outlets, and trendy boutiques.

A fourth explanation of gentrification looks to the kind of changes in the urban economy that were described at the beginning of the section on the dual city. With the tremendous boom in jobs in advanced service industries, such as those connected to the "globalized information economy," there has been a dramatic increase in the number of well-paying occupations located downtown. This growth has, in turn, produced a pool of middle-class workers interested in trying the experience of inner-city living.

It should be emphasized that the image of gentrifiers as returning from the suburbs is false; gentrification is, in fact, a "stay in the city" rather than a "back to the city" movement (Wittberg, 1992: 27). Ley (1991: 186) cites data from Canadian cities that indicate that only 2 percent to 3 percent of a sample of households moving into Toronto's Don Vale neighbourhood between 1966 and 1976 originated in the suburbs. Similarly, a high percentage of those in Ottawa's Centretown (55 percent); Vancouver's False Creek (78 percent); and Montreal's Milton-Parc, Plateau Mont-Royal, and Papineau (79 percent) neighbourhoods had previous addresses in the central city. This research suggests that gentrifiers are devoted to an inner-city lifestyle, even when they have reached a stage in the life cycle where they might have predictably moved to the suburbs.

Among those most likely to settle in gentrified areas of the inner city are women. Summarizing the empirical evidence available from these studies, Warde (1991: 228) lists the following as typical of gentrified enclaves:

a female population increasing faster than the male population; an unusually high proportion of young and single women; very high proportions of women in professional and technical occupations; high levels of academic credentials; a high proportion of dual-earner households, but few families; presence of young professional women; and the postponement of marriage and childbearing.

Why do gentrified neighbourhoods appeal to the women described by Warde? One explanation is that inner-city communities help relieve some of the pressures of women's dual roles as both members of the paid labour force and as mothers of young children. The advantages include relatively cheap housing, public transit, and readily available childcare and social-support systems. Travel time is an especially important consideration. Female gentrifiers tend to have jobs in downtown office buildings, so inner-city housing allows them to lead their lives on a tight schedule, with such services as shopping, schools, daycare, and medical clinics located nearby. In contrast, suburban residence requires long daily commutes, especially when the weather is bad, as well as the devotion of a good share of leisure time to travelling to widely scattered stores and services. Gentrification thus represents an environmental solution to a potential set of social problems (Rose, 1984: 66).

Private Communities

In recent years, another phenomenon—the rise of private communities—has been embraced by an even greater number of middle-class homeowners than has gentrification. Located in the newer suburbs and in edge cities, private communities compete with central cities for residents, offering as incentives a homogeneous middle-class population, physical security, stable housing values, local control, and freedom from exposure to the social problems of the inner city.

In the United States, nearly 4 million residents are estimated to live in access-controlled developments (Sanchez, Lang, and Dhavale, 2005) and another 28 million in areas governed by private community associations. In Canada, although there are some gated communities around Toronto and cities in British Columbia's Okanagan Valley, the majority can be found in rural areas, usually in vacation, resort, or retirement sites. As can be seen in Table 15.4, only a small percentage of these are equipped with the

TABLE 15.4 DOCUMENTED GATED PROJECTS IN CANADA, MARCH 2004

PROVINCE	TOTAL GATED PROJECTS	PROJECTS WITH 500 UNITS OR MORE	PROJECTS WITH GUARDS	VIDEO SURVEILLANCE	ADULT PROJECTS	SENIOR PROJECTS
British Columbia	228	3	5	5	44	36
Alberta	21	3	1	2	2	2
Saskatchewan	8	–	–	–	–	–
Manitoba	1	–	–	–	–	1
Ontario	49	8	9	5	10	7
Nova Scotia	7	–	–	2	1	1
Canada	314	14	15	15	57	47

SOURE: Grant, Jill (2005), "The Function of the Gates: The Social Construction of Security in Gated Developments." Town Planning Review 76, 291–313. Reprinted by permission of Town Planning Review, Liverpool University Press.

Note: Adult communities discourage children—some suggest 19+ years, other say 25+ years. Those that use the word senior or have age limits over 40 are classified as seniors' projects.

guards and video surveillance that are more standard in gated projects in the United States.

In her detailed case studies of ten gated communities in British Columbia, Ontario, and Nova Scotia, Grant (2005) found that the residents were less likely than their equivalents in other countries, such as the United States and Brazil, to cite security concerns as the major reason for moving there. Rather, they were in search of a privileged enclave where they could separate themselves from younger generations (many were seniors and empty nesters) and those who are less well off. The gates, Grant concludes, "function to secure homogeneity within a wider context of urban diversity" (p. 309).

The Fortress City

At the same time as middle-class homeowners are barricading themselves in private gated communities, the public-private partnerships that increasingly dictate what happens to postmodern cities are said to be systematically privatizing and militarizing public space in order to secure it against the homeless and the poor. Emerging from such alliances is the "fortress city" in which the urban disadvantaged are isolated socially and spatially from office workers, tourists, and suburban day trippers.

The fortress city has been described in *City of Quartz*, Mike Davis's (1990) sweeping examination of present-day Los Angeles. LA, Davis notes, is a city obsessed with urban security. What passes for a downtown, a series of billion-dollar, block-square

megastructures around Bunker Hill, has been insulated by removing almost all pedestrian linkages to the poor immigrant neighbourhoods that surround it on every side. To make public facilities and spaces as unlivable as possible for the homeless and the poor, the city is engaged in a virtual war against them. Tactics and defences include the establishment of barrel-shaped, "bum-proof" bus benches that make sleep impossible, the random deployment of outdoor overhead sprinklers in Skid Row Park to discourage overnight camping, and the removal of public toilets and washrooms in areas patronized by vagrants. To secure its garbage, one popular seafood restaurant has spent $12 000 to build a "bag-lady-proof trash cage" out of three-quarter-inch steel rods with alloy locks and vicious curved spikes. To cope with a burgeoning inmate population, law-enforcement agencies are building downtown jails and prisons designed by celebrity architects to look like hotels, convention centres, or office buildings, thus camouflaging their real purpose.

Nor is the fortress city restricted to Los Angeles. In the late 1970s, Henry Ford II persuaded the heads of 50 large corporations in Detroit to put equity capital into the Renaissance Center, a $357 million megaproject along the Detroit River opposite Windsor, Ontario. Poorly planned, the hotel-office venture resembles a castle with virtually invisible pedestrian entrances. It is cut off from downtown Detroit by a wide road and railroad tracks. It stands as a "symbol of isolation: an extreme case of a self-contained, inward-facing complex, surrounded by fortress-like two-story walls covering the heating and ventilating equipment" (Frieden and Sagalyn, 1989: 222).

The clash between the guardians of the fortress city and the urban poor was recently highlighted in the "Tent City Eviction" in Toronto. Tent City was a two-hectare (five-acre) plot of polluted, abandoned industrial land near the shore of Lake Ontario. For five years, as many as 110 residents had been squatting on the waterfront property owned by big-box building supplies store Home Depot, making it Canada's largest homeless community. After a high profile story in the *New York Times* described the site, which seemed to be increasingly hosting prostitution and drug-dealing activities, Home Depot abandoned any further pursuit of plans to erect, safe affordable housing and sent in private security guards accompanied by police to evict the squatters. Guards were posted and the former residents given 72 hours to retrieve their belongings.

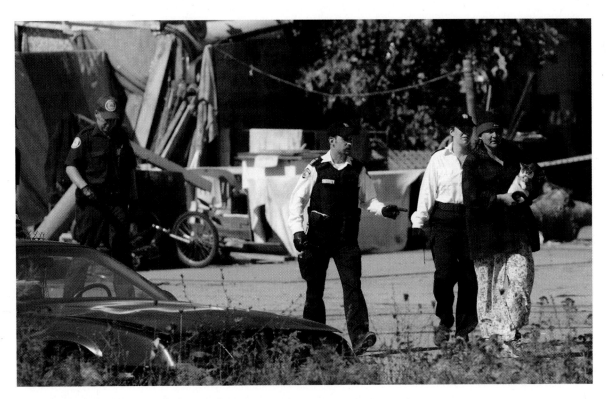

A homeless person carrying her cat is evicted from her dwelling in the shantytown on Toronto's waterfront on September 24, 2002. Home Depot, the company that owns the land, requested that police remove the squatters.
SOURCE: Frank Gunn/CP Picture Archive.

SUMMARY

1. Cities are relatively large, dense, permanent settlements in which the majority of the residents do not produce their own food.

2. Until the Industrial Revolution, cities were incapable of supporting more than about 5 percent of the total societal population, largely because of the absence of agricultural surpluses large enough to feed a big urban population. In addition, high mortality rates, especially among children under ten years of age, dictated that, even with high birth rates, urban population growth was limited.

3. Demographic transition theory holds that the main factors underlying population dynamics are industrialization and the growth of modern cultural values. In the preindustrial era, both birth rates and death rates were high, and population growth was therefore slow. In the first stages of industrialization, death rates fell, so population growth was rapid. As industrialization progressed and people's values about having children changed, the birth rate fell, resulting in slow growth again.

4. Malthus argued that while food supplies increase slowly, populations grow quickly. Because of this presumed natural law, only war, pestilence, and famine can keep human population growth in check. In contrast, Marx argued that overpopulation is not a problem of too many people. Instead, it is a problem of too much poverty. Marx said that if the exploitation of workers under capitalism is ended, then poverty will disappear along with the overpopulation problem.

5. The best-known urban-growth model in the social sciences is Ernest Burgess's concentric-zone scheme in which the expansion of cities is conceptualized as a successive series of rings, each of which segregates a distinct resident population and type of land use. Other, more recent models favour patterns of urban growth resembling pie-shaped wedges that develop along transportation routes or multiple nodes of economic activity, each with its own nucleus.

6. In contrast to the rise of the city in Western Europe and North America, cities of the South have grown at a much faster rate than the industrial economy. The resulting "overurbanization" has accelerated problems of poverty and unemployment, which are rooted in basic structural inequalities and uneven development.

7. The corporate city of the 1950s and 1960s was the product of an urban-growth machine in which a coalition of politicians, planners, real-estate developers, business people, and other interest groups joined forces to engineer economic development and progress. The main products of this alliance were (a) the corporate suburbs, (b) shopping centres, (c) suburban industrial parks, (d) downtown office towers, and (e) high-rise apartment buildings.

8. Three theories—structural, selective migration, and class and life-cycle stage—have been proposed to explain the relationship between suburban residence and lifestyle patterns. Although all three have merit, the suburban way of life observed by many researchers in the 1950s and 1960s appears to have been a unique product of a particular time and place.

9. In recent decades, the contemporary city has mirrored and incorporated a split global economy. On the one hand, the members of the upper-tier informational city work in jobs related to financial services, telecommunications, and high technology, and live either in gentrified downtown neighbourhoods or in private communities on the edge of the city. On the other hand, the members of the informal economy are excluded from the information city and live in ethnic or racial ghettos that are often, but not necessarily, located in the inner city. Together, the information city and the informal economy constitute the dual city whose residents have little in common with each other.

10. Cities are becoming multiethnic, with many ethnic neighbourhoods in the largest cities becoming home to visible minority groups. This is generating racial and ethnic residential and commercial patterns that stand in marked contrast to the ecology of the industrial city.

11. One of the defining characteristics of the postmodern city is the increasing privatization of public spaces. Privatization is manifested in the booming growth of gated communities and other private residential enclaves where outsiders are not welcome and in the construction of fortress cities where tourists and other affluent consumers are kept in while the homeless and the urban poor are kept out.

QUESTIONS TO CONSIDER

1. Are edge cities real cities? Support your answer by including examples from both Canadian and U.S. urban areas.

2. Map out your own "personal city" by keeping a record for a full week of all the trips you take to work, school, shopping, medical and dental appointments, friends' houses, restaurants and night clubs, and so on. What proportion of these trips occurs within your neighbourhood? Within the community in which you live? Across the wider metropolitan area?

3. To what extent does the big city in which you live or that you live closest to constitute a dual city?

4. How has suburban life been depicted in the mass media? Think, for example, of popular television series, such as *Desperate Housewives* and *The Simpsons*. To what extent do these depictions support the "myth of suburbia"?

5. Visit Statistics Canada's website (http://www.statcan.ca). What kinds of questions about cities could you answer by using this data source?

GLOSSARY

A **city** is a relatively large, dense, permanent settlement in which most of the residents do not produce their own food.

The **concentric-zone model** is the classic urban-growth model proposed by Ernest Burgess in which the expansion of cities is visualized as a successive series of concentric rings, each of which contains a distinct resident population and type of land use. As social groups become more established and prosperous, they move farther away from the city centre.

The perception and organization of the city as a vehicle for capital accumulation create a **corporate city.** The corporate city contains five major elements: the corporate suburb, high-rise apartments, suburban industrial parks, downtown office towers, and shopping malls.

The **demographic transition** is the change from high to low birth and death rates that characterized modernization, industrialization, and urbanization.

The juxtaposition and mutual isolation of an upper-tier information city and a lower-tier city creates a **dual city.** Members of the upper tier work in jobs related to financial services, telecommunications, and high technology, and live in gentrified neighbourhoods and private communities on the edge of the city. A lower tier of people work in informal and low-technology jobs and live in ethnic or racial ghettos.

Edge cities include self-contained entertainment, shopping, and office areas and have emerged in formerly suburban areas or just beyond the fringe of suburbia.

The **environmental-opportunity theory** proposes the idea that people choose where they want to live depending on the extent to which a particular place either meshes with or constrains their preferred lifestyle.

Familism is a lifestyle that places a high value on family living, marriage at a young age, a brief period of childlessness after marriage, and child-centredness.

In **gentrification,** working-class houses are transformed into fashionable downtown neighbourhoods by middle- and upper-income migrants.

The **multiple-nuclei model** is a model of urban growth characterized by a series of growth centres—retail, wholesale, residential—each representing the concentration of a specific function or activity within the urban economy.

Overurbanization is the process whereby the population of urban areas is growing faster than the urban economy, services, and resources can absorb. It is especially evident in large cities in the southern hemisphere.

Peri-urbanization is a process of urbanization observed in Asia, Africa, and Latin America whereby the rural and the urban have become blurred in unplanned settlements on the outskirts of large cities. One instance of this is the *desakota* in Indonesia.

The **postmodern city** is a new urban form that is more privatized and more socially and culturally fragmented and globalized than the corporate city.

The **replacement level** is the number of children that each woman must have on average to sustain the size of a population, ignoring immigration and emigration. The replacement level is 2.1 children.

The **sector model** of urban growth proposes that the city expands outward from the centre in a series of sectors or wedges along major transportation arteries, such as highways and railroad lines.

Suburbanism is a way of life outside city centres that is organized mainly around the needs of children and involves higher levels of conformity and sociability than life in the central city.

The **urban-growth machine** is a loosely structured coalition of local economic and political interest groups that hold in common a commitment to sustained growth and development.

Urbanism is a way of life that involves increased tolerance but also emotional withdrawal and specialized, impersonal, and self-interested interaction.

Urban primacy is a situation in which one metropolitan centre in a country, usually the capital city, is considerably larger and more economically dominant than any other city in the country.

SUGGESTED READING

Bishop-Stall, Shaughnessy. (2004). *Down to This: Squalor and Splendor in a Big-City Shantytown.* Toronto: Random House. This is an engaging but disturbing first-person account by a journalist of a year spent residing in Tent City, located on a marginal property along Toronto's waterfront.

Hannigan, John. (1998). *Fantasy City: Pleasure and Profit in the Postmodern City.* London and New York: Routledge. In this thoroughly researched and comprehensive account of the rise of the city as theme park in the 1980s and 1990s, Hannigan argues that megaplex cinemas, themed restaurants, casinos, and other large-scale entertainment spaces allow leisure and conviviality without real social interaction.

Hiller, Harry H. (ed.) (2005). *Urban Canada: Sociological Perspectives.* Toronto: Oxford University Press. The first new text in the field published in Canada in over a decade, this collection of 14 articles explores a broad range of topics in Canadian urban sociology, historical and contemporary.

Palen, John J. (1995). *The Suburbs.* New York: McGraw Hill. A concise, information-packed, and up-to-date overview of the suburban experience. It includes a useful discussion of edge cities and private communities.

Sewell, John. (1993). *The Shape of the City: Toronto Struggles with Modern Planning.* Toronto: University of Toronto Press. A generously illustrated history of urban growth and planning in Canada's largest city, by a well-known activist, author, and former mayor of Toronto.

WEB RESOURCES

Companion Web Site for This Book

http://www.newsociety5e.nelson.com

Begin by clicking on the Student Resources section of the website. Next, select the chapter you are studying from the pull-down menu. From the Student Resources page, you have easy access to InfoTrac College Edition® and other resources, such as the Glossary and Flashcards. The website also has many useful tips to aid you in your study of sociology.

InfoTrac College Edition Search Terms

Visit http://www.infotrac-college.com for access to more than 20 million articles from nearly 6000 sources when doing your online research.

ThomsonNOW™

http://hed.nelson.com

This online diagnostic tool identifies each student's unique needs with a Pretest that generates a personalized Study Plan for each chapter, helping students focus on concepts they are having the most difficulty mastering. Students then take a Posttest after reading the chapter to measure their understanding of the material. An Instructor Gradebook is available to track and monitor student progress.

CHAPTER SIXTEEN

Sociology and the Environment

In this chapter you will learn that

- A major focus of the sociology of the environment is the conflict between environmentalists and their opponents in industry and science.

- Support for environmentalism has remained constant for nearly three decades, with most people generally supportive of environmental values and a young, well-educated, urban, liberal group leading the movement for environmental change.

- To mobilize the reluctant majority, organizers of the environmental movement develop and spread interpretations of events that play up the possibility of environmental crises.

- The goals of conserving resources, reducing pollution, and restricting population increase are especially difficult to achieve in the developing world.

- At the community level, willingness to act on environmental problems rises as trust in authority figures declines.

- Environmental problems are often contested on the basis of acceptable risk; the definition of what is acceptable risk is strongly influenced by the distribution of power in society, with more powerful individuals and groups better able to determine what is and what is not risky.

John Hannigan
UNIVERSITY OF TORONTO

INTRODUCTION

When the March break arrives, thousands of harried Canadian parents and their children will head for the airport en route to sun-soaked holidays in Florida, the Caribbean, and Mexico. For many, getting there will most certainly not be half the fun. Crowded airports, flight delays and cancellations, and border security problems will all contribute to the stress. A handful of vacationers will choose not to fly at all, on the grounds that air travel is a highly polluting activity that releases significant amounts of carbon dioxide at an altitude where its effect on global climate change is double that on the ground. In Britain, the environmental case against flying has found a voice in the launch of "Flight Pledge," a campaign whose website offers conscientious objectors a choice between a "gold" pledge—a promise to take no flights in the coming year and a "silver" pledge, representing a maximum of two short-travel or one long-haul flight per year, except in case of emergency (Robbins, 2006).

In this chapter, I examine how sociology has dealt with the rising global crescendo of environmental awareness, signified by the movement to limit air travel voluntarily on ecological grounds. After briefly discussing the traditional lack of concern with the environment in sociology, I outline the basic value conflict in contemporary societies between those who favour unlimited economic expansion and technological solutions to human problems and those who embrace a new "ecological" view of the world, in which nature is accorded a central place. Next, I review theory and research in the four principal areas of sociological inquiry relating to the environment (Buttel, 1987): (1) environmental attitudes, concern, and behaviour; (2) the environmental movement; (3) the political economy of the environment; and (4) environmental risk and risk assessment. I conclude by arguing that it is important to deal with the environment from a "social-constructionist" perspective in order to bring more sociology into the sociological study of the environment.

TOWARD ENVIRONMENTAL SOCIOLOGY

In contrast to some other social sciences, notably anthropology and geography, sociology's interest in the environment is of relatively recent vintage, stretching back only about three decades. There are several reasons for this neglect (Dunlap and Catton, 1983).

One focus of environmental sociology is the conflict between environmentalist and mainstream views. According to the mainstream view, people have the unalienable right to dominate nature, even if that involves polluting the environment, as this McDonnell Douglas plant does.
SOURCE: Dick Hemingway.

First, for the early-twentieth-century pioneers of sociology, the term *environment* came to mean something quite different from our physical surroundings. To carve out a distinctive place for sociology as a new academic discipline, Émile Durkheim and the other founders of the field downplayed the role of biological and physical factors in influencing human affairs while at the same time elevating the importance of "social facts," such as norms, groups, and institutions. In accounting for the emergence of a wide range of behaviours, from juvenile delinquency to racism, sociologists opted for explanations that framed these behaviours in terms of "nurture" rather than "nature."

A second explanation for sociology's reluctance to embrace the study of the environment concerns sociologists' own view of technology, natural resources, and human progress. In the past, most sociologists shared the assumption of the general public that the world would see steady gains in material progress, fuelled by an apparently unlimited availability of natural resources, such as coal, lumber, and water. From this perspective, technology functioned as the linchpin of economic development, allowing humans to overcome the challenges presented by hostile habitats, such as jungles, swamps, and deserts. This **human-exceptionalism paradigm** featured the ideals of steadily evolving social progress, increasing prosperity and material comfort, and class mobility for all segments of society. This worldview had little room for sociological attention to the environmental costs of growth—pollution, health hazards in the workplace, and the loss of diversity in plant and animal species. Nor was much consideration given to the constraints that might be imposed on further economic expansion because of declining resources, the exhaustion of nutrients in the soil, and the destruction of natural ecosystems.

By the early 1970s, stimulated by increased societal attention to urban decay, pollution, overpopulation, resource shortages, and so on, a number of sociologists began at last to study environmental issues. In the first comprehensive review of the emergence of environmental sociology as a distinct area of inquiry, Dunlap and Catton (1979) distinguished between a "sociology of environmental issues" and "environmental sociology." The former, they observed, was concerned primarily with environmentally related phenomena, such as resource-management problems in wildland recreation areas or the origins, membership, and beliefs of the environmental movement. The latter focused on "the physical environment as a factor that may influence (or be influenced by) social behavior" (Dunlap and Catton, 1979: 255). This suggests that the environment can function as a contextual, an independent, or a dependent variable—that is, as background, cause, or effect.

Today, "environmental sociology" has become a catchall for the study of all social aspects of the environment. This has both advantages and disadvantages. On the plus side, it has propelled sociological inquiry into a number of important new areas—for example, studying public opposition to, and mobilization against, toxic wastes. At the same time, the very breadth of the field has made it difficult to assemble a cohesive body of work built on strong theoretical foundations. Rather than emerging from a central core, the sociological study of the environment has developed from multiple nuclei, each reflecting a different philosophical position and a corresponding research agenda. This tendency has been exacerbated by the decision of some authors, journals, and organizations to consider both the natural and the human-built environments under the same umbrella. Furthermore, some terms—notably, social ecology—have come to acquire several very different meanings, depending on the branch of environmental sociology to which the researcher claims allegiance. One unifying element, however, is the widely shared recognition of the existence of a key value conflict in contemporary society between those who hold an "environmentalist" view of the world and those who do not.

ENVIRONMENTAL VALUE CONFLICT

Values are guideposts that help us to sort out the choices we make in life. Although the vast majority of the Canadian population may be in agreement on some values (freedom, humanitarianism), other values are more controversial.

A central focus for many sociologists interested in the environment is the value cleavage between environmentalists and their opponents. At the core of this disagreement is the long-accepted notion that the environment is something to be actively used and exploited. Many of the key values that have governed North American life—activism, achievement, progress, pursuit of the good life, materialism—permit this orientation toward the environment (Turner, 1981: 87). Environmentalists, in contrast, support a different value orientation, one that advocates a more passive, less manipulative approach to nature.

How environmentalists differ from the mainstream population has been most explicitly set out by British sociologist Stephen Cotgrove (1982). Cotgrove lays out two conflicting paradigms (a *paradigm* is a type of social lens through which we view the world)—the **dominant paradigm** and the **alternative environmental paradigm** (see Table 16.1).

The dominant paradigm is anchored by two core values: the moral imperative of material-wealth creation and the moral conviction that humans have the inalienable right to dominate nature and harness the environment to that end. All major institutions reflect the widespread acceptance of this paradigm. Governments at all levels operate ministries, consulates, and trade offices that have a mandate to promote commerce and attract foreign investment. University business schools run programs in entrepreneurship. The media act as cheerleaders, linking political competence and achievement with an expanding economy and job creation. Economic growth carries with it a number of supplementary values: the view that society is best organized on a large-scale, centralized basis; respect for authority; the ascendancy of law and order; and confidence in science and technology.

TABLE 16.1   COUNTER-PARADIGMS OF THE ENVIRONMENT

	DOMINANT PARADIGM	ALTERNATIVE ENVIRONMENTAL PARADIGM
Core Values	Economic growth	Self-actualization
	Natural environment valued as resource	Domination over nature
	Natural environment intrinsically valued	Harmony with nature
Economy	Market forces	Public interest
	Risk and reward	Safety
	Rewards for achievement	Income related to need
	Inequality	Equality
	Individual self-help	Collective/social provision
Polity	Authoritative structure (experts influential)	Participative structure (citizen/worker involvement)
	Hierarchical	Nonhierarchical
	Law and order	Liberation
Society	Centralized	Decentralized
	Large scale	Small scale
	Associational	Communal
	Ordered	Flexible
Nature	Ample reserves	Earth's resources limited
	Nature hostile/neutral	Nature benign
	Environment controllable	Nature delicately balanced
Knowledge	Confidence in science and technology	Limits to science
	Rationality of means	Rationality of ends
	Separation of fact/value, thought/feeling	Integration of fact/value, thought/feeling

SOURCE: S.F. Cotgrove, "Catastrophe or Cornucopia: The Environment, Politics, and the Future," Chichester, UK: John Wiley & Sons, 1982. Copyright John Wiley & Sons Limited. Reproduced with permission.

Allied with the moral imperative of material wealth is the conviction that humans have a right and even a responsibility to dominate nature. Progress is interpreted as the increasing encroachment of civilization on jungles, deserts, frozen tundra, and other "wild" geographic environments. History, as it has been taught in our schools, is an account of how the explorers, missionaries, traders, and industrialists rolled back the frontier, "tamed" nature, and brought prosperity to "virgin" lands. Typically, one popular Hollywood epic of the 1960s was titled *How the West Was Won*. The great achievements of the last two centuries, including the opening of the Panama Canal, the completion of the Canadian transcontinental railway, and the landing of astronauts on the moon, all represent a triumph by science and industry over natural hazards and barriers.

In the dominant paradigm of our society, progress is interpreted as the increasing encroachment of civilization on jungles, deserts, frozen tundra, and other "wild" geographic environments.
SOURCE: Shutterstock.

The alternative environmental paradigm categorically rejects both of the pillars of enterprise culture (Cotgrove, 1982: 28–29):

> Not only do [environmentalists] challenge the importance attached to material and economic goals, they by contrast give much higher priority to the realization of non-material values—to social relationships and community, to the exercise of human skills and capacities and to increased participation in decisions that affect our daily lives. . . . They have little confidence in science and technology to come up with a technological fix to solve the problems of material and energy shortages. And this is in part rooted in a different view of nature, which stresses the delicate balance of ecological systems and possible irreversible damage which may result from the interventions of high technology.

Adherents of the alternative environmental paradigm value the natural environment for its own sake, thus questioning the human right to domination. Earth's resources, they claim, are limited and must therefore be conserved. Drawing on the insights of the economist E.F. Schumacher (1973), they believe that "small is beautiful." In this view, society should adopt small-scale, decentralized economic and political structures that are in harmony with nature.

The value conflict just described arches over a wide spectrum of issues and problems related to sociology and the environment. It is, for example, at the core of the dispute over commercial logging of the old-growth forests of Vancouver Island and of the Temagami region of northern Ontario. It infuses the continuing debate over world population growth as a primary factor contributing to environmental degradation. It helps account for the rise of the "Greens" in Western Europe and of other political ecology parties whose vision closely parallels the alternative environmental paradigm.

A major attempt to bridge the differences between the dominant and alternative environmental outlooks can be found in the idea of **sustainable development.** This concept achieved global currency in 1987 as a result of its use in the report of the United Nations World Commission on Environment and Development, more commonly known as the Brundtland report (after the chair of the commission, Norwegian Prime Minister Gro Harlem Brundtland).

The Brundtland report defined sustainable development as "development that meets the needs of the present without compromising the ability of future generations to meet their own needs" (World Commission on Environment and Development, 1987: 43). It foresaw a new form of economic growth, especially for developing nations, that would be both environmentally aware and egalitarian, integrating objectives for social development with the demands of science. In short, the Brundtland report suggested that it is possible to have the best of both worlds: continued economic growth but not at the expense of the environment.

However, many environmentalists have been critical of the concept of sustainable development. They argue that, in real life, it is not very easy to balance economic growth and natural-resource use with environmental protection. For example, they would argue that situating a jetport in the middle of an environmentally sensitive natural area would be ecologically destructive no matter what measures were taken to reduce noise pollution or catch the run-off of aviation fuel. In fact, environmentalists such as David Suzuki insist that the environmental dangers we face today are so extensive that we can survive as a species only by totally dismantling the "buzz saw of progress" in the industrial nations of the North and by halting its advance in the less developed countries.

Furthermore, critics of the Brundtland report point out that sustainable development requires an extraordinary degree of cooperation and a deep commitment to reform. This is difficult to achieve, especially in the nations of the Southern Hemisphere, where rural economies are often still controlled by wealthy landowners, and the poor are forced to engage in ecologically damaging practices, such as stripping the rapidly dwindling forests for cooking fuel, in order to survive.

ENVIRONMENTAL ATTITUDES, CONCERNS, AND BEHAVIOURS

The existence of a distinct set of environmental attitudes and concerns in our society has been documented by a large number of polls conducted over the last 30 years. One of the first and most important efforts to develop a research tool with which to measure an environmental view of the world was Dunlap and Van Liere's (1978) new environmental paradigm (NEP) scale. Using survey data from two samples of

TABLE 16.2 AVERAGE SCORES ON THE NEW ENVIRONMENTAL PARADIGM (NEP) SCALE BY THE GENERAL PUBLIC SAMPLE (GPS) AND THE ENVIRONMENTAL ORGANIZATION SAMPLE (EOS)[a]

		GPS	EOS
1.	We are approaching the limit of the number of people the earth can support.	3.00	3.63
2.	The balance of nature is very delicate and easily upset.	3.18	3.68
3.	Humans have the right to modify the natural environment to suit their needs.	2.76	3.30
4.	Humankind was created to rule over the rest of nature.	2.63	3.67
5.	When humans interfere with nature, it often produces disastrous consequences.	3.03	3.49
6.	Plants and animals exist primarily to be used by humans.	2.81	3.61
7.	To maintain a healthy economy, we will have to develop a "steady-state" economy in which industrial growth is controlled.	2.85	3.48
8.	Humans must live in harmony with nature in order to survive.	3.52	3.86
9.	The earth is like a spaceship with only limited room and resources.	3.21	3.85
10.	Humans need not adapt to the natural environment, because they can remake it to suit their own needs.	3.25	3.74
11.	There are limits to growth beyond which our industrialized society cannot expand.	2.94	3.64
12.	Humankind is severely abusing the environment.	3.11	3.81

SOURCE: Adapted from Riley E. Dunlap and Kenneth D. Van Liere, "The New Environmental Paradigm: A Proposed Measuring Instrument and Preliminary Results," *Journal of Environmental Education,* 9(1978), pp. 10–19.
[a]High scores indicate strong agreement with the pro-NEP position. Range = 1.0–4.0. Eight of the items are worded such that agreement reflects acceptance of the NEP, while for the other four (3, 4, 6, 10) disagreement reflects acceptance of the NEP. Respondents were assigned scores of 4 for "strongly agree," 3 for "mildly agree," 2 for "mildly disagree," and 1 for "strongly disagree" for the eight non-NEP items; scoring for the four anti-NEP items was reversed.

Washington state residents and from the membership of a statewide environmental organization, Dunlap and Van Liere developed a 12-item scale that measures the extent of agreement with such statements as "the balance of nature is very delicate and easily upset" and "humans need not adapt to the natural environment, because they can remake it to suit their own needs" (see Table 16.2). The researchers found that the general public moderately accepted the content of the emerging environmental paradigm, whereas environmentalists strongly endorsed it.

Two other techniques have been used to measure environmental concern. One simple and straightforward approach is to ask people how worried or upset they are about a series of environmental problems. A second strategy, which strives for greater concreteness, is to ask respondents to weigh tradeoffs between, for example, environmental protection and jobs (Freudenburg, 1991).

Has public concern with environmental quality changed since the first survey results were carried out in the early 1970s? Two complementary hypotheses address this question (Jones and Dunlap, 1992).

Grossman and Potter (1977) formulated the **broadening-base hypothesis,** which predicts that environmental concern will eventually diffuse throughout all groups. Buttel (1975) promoted the **economic-contingency hypothesis,** which suggests that the broadening of the social bases of environmental concern depends on prevailing economic conditions. Buttel argued that when economic conditions worsen or are perceived to be getting worse, those who are least well off will be the first to shift their focus from the environment to the economy. However, other researchers, using U.S. data for the years 1973–90, found little support for either hypothesis (Jones and Dunlap, 1992); they found instead that the level and social location of support for environmental protection have remained remarkably stable for nearly 20 years.

What are the social bases of environmental concern? It was originally thought that support for environmentalism was limited to the affluent. However, most surveys in the 1970s and 1980s found that income and occupational prestige were only weakly related to environmental concern (Buttel, 1987; Van Liere and Dunlap, 1980). Instead, higher levels of education, youth, political liberalism, and urban residence were found to be the best predictors of concern with environmental quality (Dunlap and Catton, 1979). The social bases of environmental concern have remained more or less the same from 1973 to 1990, as have levels of support (Jones and Dunlap, 1992). Greenbaum (1995) has characterized the social bases of environmental concern as "complex and subtle." That is because environmental concern spans a wide variety of subject matters, from species extinction and the thinning of the ozone layer to the contamination of local drinking waters by toxic chemicals. Although it may be possible to isolate general clusters of environmental concern, as have Dunlap and Van Liere (1978) in their NEP scale (see Table 16.2), people may not be very consistent across various issues. Part of the reason for inconsistency is that individual environmental problems may affect us in very different ways. How concerned we will be about a particular environmental problem, or whether we even perceive it as a "problem," will depend on how the activity in question affects our "interests"—that is, how we will be affected by its benefits, costs, and risks (Greenbaum, 1995: 127; and see Box 16.1).

BOX 16.1   WISE ADVICE FROM FOUR "ECO-PATHFINDERS"

COLLEEN MCCRORY: NEVER GIVE UP

Colleen McCrory, executive director of the Valhalla Wilderness Society, can claim numerous victories. Her tenacity helped bring a stop to clear-cutting on British Columbia's South Moresby Island and establish the Valhalla Wilderness Park. "Not everyone has to join an organization," she says. "It's more important that the environment is an important part of your everyday life. If you're working on an issue, never give up and never let go. Even if you lose, what you've done will help the next person continue the battle."

BRUCE WALKER: DON'T SACRIFICE CREDIBILITY

In the fall of 1972, Bruce Walker was a 20-year-old college dropout living in Montreal. Now, 27 years later, Walker is research director for the Society to Overcome Pollution. The organization has played a large role in introducing curbside blue box recycling to the Montreal region, getting an island-wide sewage-treatment system installed, and establishing air-quality monitoring, as well as educating the public. . . .

If you want to make an impact, [Walker] advises, don't wait for an issue to hit you over the head. . . . [And] never assume every issue is being taken care of by other organizations. "You'll need loads of patience, persistence, and a sense of humour," he says. "Be vigilant, and use your five senses, plus a sixth—common sense—to detect environmental threats. And lastly, never sacrifice credibility for visibility; state the facts without exaggeration."

LINDA MANZER: FOCUS YOUR ANGER

For Linda Manzer, Toronto-based guitar maker for the stars, the journey down the activist road began with a chance television viewing of an elephant hunt. She was among the first guitar artisans to stop using ivory, and soon others followed suit. "I started asking questions about where products came from," she says. "Some suppliers had good answers, others squirmed." She then focused her attention on the old-growth spruce required to make top-grade instruments. She now ensures that only trees downed by the wind serve as her medium. . . .

Manzer urges people to volunteer. "It's easier than you think," she says. "Jump in where your heart tells you. Focus your anger; use it as a tailwind and a positive force."

SHEILA WATT CLOUTIER: RESPECT THE CIRCLE

A head of the Inuit Circumpolar Conference, Sheila Watt Cloutier spends much of her time convincing southern Canadians of the importance of traditional foods. Caribou, whale, and seal have sustained her people for thousands of years, and the suggestion that Inuit should switch to imported beef, pork, and chicken angers her.

Cloutier advises those who want to make the world a better place to remember the connectedness of all living things. "I can't imagine, with all the challenges we face as a people, that we now have to worry about breast-feeding our children," she says, referring to the presence of persistent organic pollutants in arctic wildlife. "People must realize that a poisoned Inuk child is a poisoned Arctic is a poisoned planet."

SOURCE: Martin Silverstone and Kendra Toby, "Pathfinder Talk," *Equinox*, August/September, 1998, p. 90.

Do these pro-environmental attitudes convert directly into environmentally friendly behaviour? Most studies have failed to confirm such a linkage. As Maloney and Ward (1973: 585) have noted, "most people say they are willing to do a great deal to help curb pollution problems and are fairly emotional about it, but in fact they actually do very little and know even less." In a study carried out in Pennsylvania in the 1990s, Theodori and Luloff (2002) found that those who indicated in a survey that they were "proactive" in their positions on environmental issues (5.5 percent of the total) were significantly more likely to report engaging in pro-environmental behaviours than were those who described themselves as being "sympathetic" (62.2 percent). In particular, they were more inclined to attend a public hearing and meeting about the environment and to contact a government agency to get information or complain about an environmental problem. For the most part, however, those who score positively in environmental-concern polls do not show any particular willingness to go beyond low-cost, personal actions (recycling, buying "green" products) to make deep-cutting sacrifices for the environment. Uusitalo (1990), for example, found that support for measures to help the environment declined when they required any change of personal habits.

From this evidence, it appears that most people are willing to pay lip service to protecting the environment and will behave responsibly as long as it is not appreciably more expensive or inconvenient to do so. After studying recycling behaviour across Alberta, Derksen and Gartrell (1993) concluded that the key factor accounting for participation in recycling programs was the easy availability of curbside pickups rather than positive attitudes toward the environment. In fact, those who were environmentally concerned were no more likely to recycle than those who were unconcerned.

THE ENVIRONMENTAL MOVEMENT

Although environmental concern exists across a wide cross-section of the population, it has been most intensely concentrated in the environmental movement. One study from the 1990s of 733 residents of Cornwall, Ontario, found that only one in ten could be labelled an "activist" willing to invest time and energy in behaviours aimed at preserving or improving the quality of the environment. And even here, there was a big difference between easy-to-perform actions, such as voting for a government proposing environmentally conscious policies, and more demanding behaviours, such as participating in protests against current environmental conditions and writing letters to firms that manufacture harmful products (Séguin, Pelletier, and Hunsley, 1998). Movement activists have waged environmental battles with loggers, utility companies, whalers, agricultural corporations, developers, and other defenders of the dominant paradigm. Although the environmental movement has not always represented a "vanguard for a new society" (Milbrath, 1984), it does directly incorporate many of the elements of the alternative environmental paradigm in its philosophies and actions.

SOCIAL BASE AND COMPOSITION

In its early manifestations in the nineteenth century, the environmental movement was largely the creation of an elite. For example, the leadership and much of the membership of American wildlife-preservation organizations, such as the Sierra Club, the Save the Redwoods League, and the Boone and Crockett Club were drawn almost exclusively from a tightly knit network of lawyers, educators, and wealthy businessmen. Similarly, in England, preservationist causes were pursued primarily by members of the clergy and the aristocracy. Occasionally, these elite organizations would enlist the support of the general public in specific campaigns. In the fight to save Niagara Falls (1906–10), for example, a national publicity campaign waged in the pages of American popular magazines, such as *Ladies' Home Journal*, resulted in more than 6500 letters written in support of the preservation of the falls (Cylke, 1993: 22).

In Canada, the conservation movement developed in a different fashion. Environmental initiatives, such as the establishment of national parks and the protection of wildlife, were more likely to be developed by small groups of dedicated civil servants who were able to convince the federal government to take action (Foster, 1978). Two of the most significant events in early Canadian conservation history, the establishment of the first national park in Banff in 1887 and the signing of the Canada–U.S. Migratory Bird Convention in 1917, followed this pattern.

When the modern environmental movement emerged in the late 1960s and early 1970s, it was

The environmental movement has grown tremendously since the 1960s. Some members of the middle class in particular are now more personally involved in the environmental movement and raise environmentally conscious children.

SOURCE: Dick Hemingway.

largely a creature of the upper middle classes. The dominant social groups in environmental organizations were well-educated professionals from urban and suburban backgrounds and college students from white-collar backgrounds (Gale, 1983). Mainstream EMOs (environmental movement organizations) consequently favoured issues related to "saving" nature over those relating to urban environments. For example, few EMOs in the 1970s showed much interest in pursuing problems related to high concentrations of lead in the soil of inner-city properties, despite the fact that lead levels detected in the blood of local children were way above normal. These organizations only took up the issue when it became evident that lead emissions from motor vehicles were unacceptably high.

More recently, environmentalists have been identified as members of a "new middle class" drawn primarily from social and cultural specialists—teachers, social workers, journalists, artists, and professors—who work in creative or public-service-oriented jobs. This new middle class is on the firing line in the day-to-day conflicts between the engineers and technocrats who tend to ignore the human costs of progress and the ordinary citizens who are victimized by them.

There are two kinds of explanations for why members of the new middle class tend to be more radical as a group than the population as a whole. On the one hand, they are more likely to seek out jobs in the public sector, away from the pressures of a business environment that is often hostile to their values. At the same time, they tend to become personally involved in the problems faced by their clients, even to the point of becoming advocates for their interests (Kriesi, 1989: 1084). For example, a doctor working in a community health centre whose patients suffer an unusually high incidence of asthma might recognize that the source of the illness is a local incinerator and may campaign to have the polluting facility closed.

Evidence for the new middle class theory of social movements comes from different countries. Cotgrove and Duff (1981) found that 43.4 percent of their sample of environmentalists in England (compared with only about 12 percent of the general public) were employed in service, welfare, and creative occupations. Kriesi (1989) found that 23 percent of those who reported having participated in the Dutch ecology movement (compared with 12 percent of the population as a whole) were social and cultural specialists. And Tindall (1994) showed that people who had higher levels of income and education or were employed in the public sector were more likely to join the Vancouver Island wilderness-preservation movement, although these factors did not affect their level of participation after joining.

ENVIRONMENTAL MOBILIZATION

In addition to researching the social composition of the environmental movement, sociologists have also been interested in learning how environmentalists mobilize people to their cause.

Much of the research on this topic has focused on community-based, grassroots environmental organizations. Formed in opposition to the pollution problems caused by local industries and utilities, these citizens' groups differ somewhat from the rest of the environmental movement insofar as they draw their members from blue-collar as well as white-collar neighbourhoods. The prototype of the grassroots, locally based environmental group is the Love Canal Homeowners Association, formed in the 1970s by some Niagara Falls, New York, homeowners whose properties had been contaminated by toxic waste buried 30 years earlier by a local chemical company.

It is by no means a simple matter to mobilize neighbours in the face of an environmental threat. In fact, most people want to avoid trouble and must be actively convinced that their present situation is both unjust and intolerable before they will consider taking action. Capek (1993: 11) describes the initial reluctance of homeowners in Carver Terrace, a contaminated residential subdivision in the U.S. South, to recognize the dangers facing them:

> Residents knew at some level about bad-smelling air, mysterious illness or deaths among people with no prior history of medical problems, plants that would not grow or grew strangely, animals becoming ill or [being] born deformed, and a variety of other experiences that lacked explanation. The amorphous and invisible nature of chemical exposure, however, and the difficulty of diagnosing its consequences either at a popular or professional level worked against the integration of this knowledge.

Caught up in the demands of everyday life, respectful of the voices of authority who downplay the problem, and blinded by the pride of home ownership, people tend to accept the status quo and must be persuaded to redefine their situation in such a way that they can see it as a violation of their basic rights. This is easier to do when citizens are ideologically primed to question the image of progress as continual economic development (Ladd and Laska, 1991), but even those who lack this attitudinal underpinning can be brought around.

Local communities pass through four stages in the process of challenging polluters (Cable and Benson, 1993). In the first phase, residents come to see themselves as "victims" of corporate environmental crime. In phase two, they make individual appeals to government regulatory agencies to take action to force an end to the toxic dumping or other problem situation. In the third phase, the complainants become disillusioned with the slow pace or absence of official action and begin to seek environmental justice. In the final phase, increased democratic pressure has either convinced government regulators to enforce environmental standards or proven insufficient, in which case the problem continues unchecked.

Like other social movements, the environmental movement aims to convince as wide a segment of the public as possible that its interpretation of the world is correct and should, therefore, be acted on. To that end, members of the movement develop **frames**—that is, interpretations of events and their meanings. Successful framing involves three elements: diagnostic, prognostic, and motivational. Diagnostic framing involves identifying a problem and fixing the blame for it. Prognostic framing offers a proposed solution to the diagnosed problem. Motivational framing is a call to arms to potential recruits to take specific corrective action. The better these three frames are integrated, the greater their capacity for mobilizing people (Gerhards and Rucht, 1992: 583).

Contemporary environmental frames are frequently constructed around the image of an impending global collapse. In the early 1970s, this approach was typified by the best-selling book *The Limits to Growth* (Meadows, Meadows, Randers, and Behrens, 1972), in which the authors forecast that Earth's **carrying capacity**—that is, the optimum population size that the planet can support under present environmental conditions—would eventually be exceeded. With the aid of a computer model, they estimated how five interrelated factors—population growth, industrial output, food production, pollution, and nonrenewable natural resources—would interact over time. They predicted that, within a century, we would face a major crisis brought on by uncontrolled population growth and rising levels of pollution.

In the 1980s, the threat shifted to that of "biosphere crisis," generated by global climatic changes resulting from increased emissions of "greenhouse" gases, such as carbon dioxide, chlorofluorocarbons, methane, and nitrous oxide, into the atmosphere. Such changes in global weather patterns have the potential to trigger major environmental changes, including rising sea levels, hotter summers, more frequent and more severe droughts, dust storms, forest fires, and the rapid extinction of thousands of species of plants and animals.

The solution, environmentalists claim, is to embrace wholeheartedly the alternative environmental paradigm. In *Beyond the Limits* (1992), the sequel to *The Limits to Growth*, Meadows, Meadows, and Randers caution that we must draw back and ease down: conserve resources, reduce pollution, and adopt deliberate social constraints on population and industrial growth. In the less developed nations, this means both controlling family size and finding new, more sustainable avenues of economic expansion. In the industrialized world, a new value system is said to be necessary so that people will stop trying to use material growth to satisfy what are in fact nonmaterial needs for acceptance, self-importance, and community identity (Fields, 1993: 40).

More research is needed on the relationship between grassroots mobilizations protesting toxic dumps, incinerators, nuclear power plants, and other pollution sources and these wider ecological worldviews. Although we might assume that environmentalists, in accordance with the popular slogan "think globally, act locally," first become imbued with the alternative environmental paradigm and then put it to practical use in their own neighbourhoods and communities, another possibility is that ecological values arise directly out of firsthand experience. In the latter view, it is the process of dealing with recalcitrant polluters, bureaucratic cover-ups, and overly cautious scientists that eventually causes the penny to drop for local environmentalists who previously had not given much thought to broad environmental philosophies. Members of community-based, grassroots environmental organizations thus engage in a form of social learning as they go about researching their case against polluters. This social learning is further facilitated by the assembly of a widening net of environmental contacts. Irene Paparo-Stein, a Winnipeg woman who formed a citizens' lobby group to fight chemical spraying in her city, describes the environmental networking process this way (Stein, 1988: 52):

> One thing I had discovered, there was quite a network in the U.S. And the Americans, once I explained the situation and the need for information, were ready with their help. They understood the enormity of the problem, of the laypersons up against the governments, bureaucracy, and industry, and knew what to do. They were generous with their aid. We had soon compiled a list of contacts from all over the U.S.

Inevitably, someone in the network introduces the community activist to an "ecological" perspective.

IDEOLOGICAL DIVISIONS

Although we often speak of the environmental movement as a single entity, there has, in fact, long been a basic philosophical split between "value-oriented environmentalists," whose main concern is to change the way we view the world, and "success-oriented environmentalists," whose chief goal is to stop pollution and other activities that damage the physical environment (Eyerman and Jamison, 1989). These two factions differ significantly in their perceptions of the root causes of environmental problems, their preferences among strategies for coping, and their visions of an ecologically sound society (Cylke, 1993: 69).

This division became evident at the beginning of the twentieth century in the differing ideological approaches to the environment taken by the two main wings of the U.S. conservation movement—the "resource conservationists" and the "preservationists." The former wanted to "manage" natural resources by applying modern engineering and administrative techniques, whereas the latter, guided by aesthetic and even spiritual ideals, believed it was necessary for the government to intervene in order to preserve areas of natural beauty and scientific importance. For example, in a difference of opinion that has carried over to the present day, resource conservationists wanted to "harvest" public forests in a "scientific" manner, whereas preservationists advocated setting these lands aside as natural parks in which logging would be prohibited.

On Canada's West coast, where logging is still a major industry and source of employment, the heirs to the resource conservation wing of the early twentieth century are the 300 organizations who belong to the Forest Alliance of British Columbia. An industry-sponsored coalition of corporations, community associations, and municipalities, the Forest Alliance "aims to find ways to balance environmental, social and economic values in forest-use decisions" ("End War in Woods," 2000: 5). In recent years, much of the strategic action undertaken by this coalition has centred on efforts to counter claims of environmental opponents and establish public confidence in the industry's environmental performance through "certification" schemes. Operated through such organizations as the Canadian Standards Association and the Forest Stewardship Council, forest certification is a voluntary tool directed toward lumber retailers, homebuilders, and other big customers designed to reassure them (and their customers) that their purchases are derived from "well-managed" forests. The Forest Alliance's promotional literature especially favours the notion of "sustainable development" (the title of its newsletter is *Sustainability Update*).

Furthermore, value differences over the true meaning of environmentalism have become the basis for the emergence of various alternative ecophilosophies, the best known of which are "deep ecology" and "ecofeminism." Whereas success-oriented environmentalists are primarily concerned with the direct effects of industrial pollution on individuals and communities, value-oriented environmentalists stress the survival of all living and nonliving things as components of healthy ecosystems. In doing so, they come closest to any segment of the environmental movement to popularizing the alternative environmental paradigm.

Deep Ecology

The **deep-ecology** argument was set out in the early 1970s by Norwegian philosopher Arne Naess (1973) and was elaborated by U.S. ecological thinkers Bill Devall and George Sessions (1985). In contrast to the **anthropocentrism** that characterizes much of the environmental movement, deep ecologists believe in a "biocentric" approach, which emphasizes that humans are one species among many on Earth and have no special rights or privileges. This **biocentric egalitarianism** states that all things on Earth have an equal right to live and blossom and reach their own forms of self-realization.

Although the intellectual roots of this principle are varied, it owes much to the thinking of John Muir, the leading preservationist in the early American conservation movement. A second touchstone for deep ecology is the "land ethic" of Aldo Leopold, an American naturalist. Formulated in 1949, Leopold's land ethic affirms the right of soils, waters, plants, and animals to coexist in their natural state with humans, whose role is viewed not as conqueror of the land but as member and citizen of it.

The biocentric egalitarianism of deep ecology states that all things on Earth have an equal right to live and blossom and reach their own forms of self-realization.
SOURCE: Shutterstock.

Deep ecologists believe that the relation of the individual to nature cannot be fully grasped intellectually but must ultimately be experienced directly. This quite clearly sets deep ecology in opposition to mainstream environmentalism, which is primarily concerned with gathering "facts" about nature and our despoiling of it. Indeed, deep ecologists regard science and scientists with a fair degree of suspicion, depicting them as being a part of the problem as much as a part of its solution. An exception to this is the **Gaia hypothesis,** formulated in the late 1960s by British scientist James Lovelock (1987) and American microbiologist Lynn Margulis, which holds that Earth is a living superorganism with its own internal system of regulation. From this perspective, it is possible to see ourselves as having a moral obligation not just to plants, animals, and other human beings but also to the planet itself (Yearley, 1991: 145).

Ecofeminism

A second alternative ecophilosophy is **ecofeminism.** The term was first coined in 1974 by the French writer Françoise d'Eaubonne, who believes that the oppression and exploitation of women and the domination of the natural environment are part of the same phenomenon. Ecofeminists identify a distinctly "feminine" way of thinking and being that is more nurturing, cooperative, and communal than the mainstream, paternalistic culture. *Mother Nature*, a long-accepted term in the English language, is given a new meaning and significance by the ecofeminists, who celebrate the ancient pagan tradition of Goddess worship and nature cults; the Goddess is seen as the symbol of ecological wisdom.

Both deep ecologists and ecofeminists express the need for developing a new human consciousness and vision. However, a certain degree of tension exists between these two ecophilosophies, centred on differing conceptions of the main cause of the current environmental crisis: Deep ecologists point to a gender-neutral anthropocentrism, whereas ecofeminists claim that "androcentrism" (male-centredness) is the real culprit. Furthermore, deep ecologists have trouble accepting the ecofeminist claims that women are innately and more sensitively attuned to nature than men are and, therefore, have the unique capacity to construct a new, more enlightened approach to the environment (Warren, 1990).

In a recent transnational study, Perron, Vaillancourt, and Durand (2001) identified three

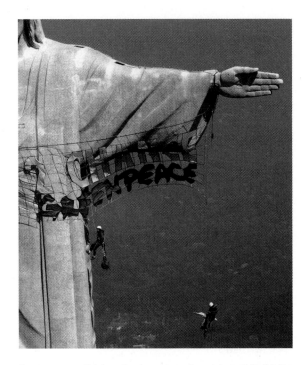

Greenpeace activists put a banner on the statue of Christ the Redeemer in Rio De Janeiro, Brazil, September 5, 2002. The protest was held to draw attention to lack of focus on renewable energy at the World Summit on Sustainable Development. The banner read, "Rio + 10 = A SECOND CHANCE, Greenpeace."
SOURCE: © Reuters New Media Inc./Corbis.

types of "green" orientations among leaders of environmental NGOs that they surveyed in Quebec and Costa Rica: ecologists ($n = 30$), mainstream environmentalists ($n = 107$), and market environmentalists ($n = 83$). Mainstream and market environmentalists perceived science and technology more positively than did ecologists; however, market environmentalists were less likely to accept economic sacrifices for the sake of the environment than were mainstreamers. This typology, Perron and his colleagues (2001: 849) claim, is "consistent with studies using the NEP scale of Dunlap and Van Liere (1978), but, instead of differentiating between those who support the NEP and those who do not, it reveals differences within the NEP."

POLITICAL ECONOMY OF THE ENVIRONMENT

A third major area of inquiry within environmental sociology is the study of the political economy of the environment. A starting point for many studies undertaken from a political-economy perspective is

Alan Schnaiberg's *The Environment: From Surplus to Scarcity* (1980). Schnaiberg distinguishes between production and consumption activities in society and blames the environmental crisis on production activities. Rather than looking to irresponsible consumers who insist on embracing an extravagant, wasteful lifestyle despite its harmful environmental effects, Schnaiberg identifies the real villain as the relentless process of economic development that is controlled by industrial capitalists and buttressed by the state.

According to Schnaiberg, the political economy of environmental problems and policies is shaped by modern industrial society's **treadmill of production.** This term refers to the inherent need of our economic system to continually yield profits by creating consumer demand for new products, even where this means expanding the ecosystem to its furthest limits. Corporate producers create demand primarily through the medium of advertising. For example, in a recent issue of a leading Canadian urban-living magazine, readers are advised that a Porsche will stir the "power of passion" in its owner, a Jenn-Air stove system is "the sign of a great cook," and a Kohler spray-and-brush attachment will "turn your shower into a personal luxury spa." Consumers are thus persuaded from early childhood to become part of a dominant materialistic culture in which personal identity depends on material possessions.

The state is said to buttress this treadmill of production by providing a variety of economic incentives to new industries, from tax breaks to worker-training programs. Traditionally, the state has also encouraged untrammelled economic growth by ensuring a continual flow of natural resources to industrial producers. For example, in the latter years of the nineteenth century, the "gospel of efficiency" (Hays, 1959) in U.S. politics dictated that the growing power of the federal government be used to regulate competition and ensure a steady supply of lumber and other resources to industry. The idea was that only government measures could ensure that resources be set aside and, then, be exploited in a controlled fashion, rather than squandered in the cutthroat competition of the unregulated marketplace (Koppes, 1988: 234). In Canada, the prevailing view has been that nature can be privately requisitioned virtually without limit (Williams, 1992), as evidenced by our export of oil, natural gas, minerals, lumber, and, more recently, water, to industrial centres in the United States, often despite negative environmental consequences.

One far-reaching example of this approach to natural resources is the Great Whale hydroelectric project, initiated by former Quebec Premier Robert Bourassa and Hydro Quebec. Great Whale is the second phase of the massive James Bay hydroelectric project, which calls for the diversion or alteration of 20 northern rivers through the construction of 36 dams and more than 1000 dikes. The project is now on hold because of Cree objections and expert opinion, but if it is ever completed, the development will flood "23 000 square kilometres of land the size of Newfoundland island and Labrador combined and [shatter] two cultures that have flourished there— surviving both natural disaster and foreign intrusion— for 5000 years" (Dwyer, 1992: 30).

Of course, the despoiling of the environment is not limited to countries that have functioned under a capitalist system: Soviet-style societies devastated the environment to an even greater degree. Two of the most memorable photographic images to come out of Eastern Europe in the early 1990s were of the Romanian town of Copsa Mica totally blackened by carbon dust from the local carbosin plant and of schoolchildren from the Czechoslovakian town of Most who had to wear face masks on "sulphur dioxide alert" days to filter the pollution-laden air. There are also indications that recent economic expansion in China has produced its own environmental nightmares. In 1988, for example, Benxi, a city covering 43 square kilometres, vanished from satellite photographs beneath a cloud of smog (Silvertown, 1989: 550). In 2005, an explosion at a PetroChina chemical plant in the northeastern province of Jilin severely damaged the Sanghua River, one of the country's largest, and the main source of drinking water for more than 3 million residents of the city of Harbin. The blast released an estimated 100 tonnes of cancer-causing benzene compounds into the river, resulting in contamination that reached levels that initially were 108 times above national safety standards (Saiget, 2005). Thus, the accusing finger should be pointed not at the capitalist system but at unbridled industrialism, with its accompanying lack of environmental responsibility.

Schnaiberg has described a pervasive conflict in advanced industrial societies between the treadmill of production and the rising public demand for protecting the environment. That is, governments are increasingly torn between a commitment to promote economic development and job creation and the goal of environmental preservation. The bitter conflict over the future of old-growth forests on Vancouver Island is a dramatic illustration of the conflict.

Environmentalists argue that the temperate rain forests of Clayoquot Sound and other parts of the province have nearly disappeared and must be declared out of bounds to further logging, particularly if it employs "clear-cutting" methods. The forestry industry replies that this solution would cripple one of British Columbia's major industries, throwing tens of thousands of loggers out of work.

In such situations, governments search for a viable compromise. In British Columbia, such a compromise was recently announced with reference to the Great Bear Rainforest, one of the world's largest remaining temperate rainforests. The proposed land-use agreement, the product of a decade of negotiations among the forestry companies, the B.C. provincial government and a handful of major environmental organizations (Greenpeace, Sierra Club, Rainforest Action Network, ForestEthics), opens Great Bear to provincially subsidized logging for the first time. In return, portions of the cedar old-growth forests, salmon rivers, the Kermode bear and most sensitive ecosystems will be protected from logging and mining.

One approach to resolving the contradictions noted by Schnaiberg involves the adoption of "environmental-management" techniques. **Environmental management** refers to moderate government intervention that affords limited protection to the environment without seriously curtailing economic development. The agreement on the Great Bear Rainforest, for example, is the product of a much heralded new enviro-industrial concept called "Environment-Based Management" that bases decisions on a combination of environmental factors and the social and economic needs of resource-dependent communities (Solomon, 2006). In this case, the extent of the protection provided by the rainforest agreement has been contested by some critics, notably members of the David Suzuki Foundation, who contend that the protected areas of Great Bear are unacceptably small.

Politicians and bureaucrats also engage in environmental management through co-opting and controlling dominant policy discourses (a discourse is a narrative or storyline). This allows them to appear to be undertaking environmental reform without actually having to do so. As Davidson and MacKendrick (2004) have shown, the Province of Alberta has successfully manipulated policy discourse associated with "integrated resource management," a policy that purports to manage conflicts between users across a range of natural resource sectors in a manner that is flexible, consultative, and fair. Beginning in the late 1990s, integrated resource management policy was increasingly expressed in terms that tapped into the discourse of "sustainable development" or "ecological modernization." This allowed the Alberta government to appear to be progressive and visionary in its approach to resource development, even as it was engaged in expanding oil and gas production and logging.

The treadmill of production exerts a major influence on the developing nations as well, where many people want access to the consumer culture that we enjoy. The unsustainable development that some industrializing countries have consequently espoused has led to considerable friction with environmentalists from northern countries, who fear that it will lead to serious worldwide environmental problems (e.g., increased destruction of tropical rain forests can lead to accelerated global warming). Leaders of the developing world reply that, having enjoyed the benefits of a century of industrial growth, environmental activists from Europe and America cannot in fairness now deny developing countries the fruits of economic expansion on ecological grounds. (For an attempt to reconcile development with environmental integrity in the developing nations, see Adams, 1990.) At the same time, planners and politicians in developing countries have not always learned from the mistakes of their counterparts in the North. In the southern Indian state of Kerala, for example, unchecked economic growth has resulted in widespread marine and atmospheric pollution, seriously threatening the future of a region famous for its lakes and canals that support a wealth of marine and bird life (see Box 16.2).

BOX 16.2 POLLUTION RAVAGES KERALA

Immortalized in Arundhati Roy's novel *The God of Small Things,* the southern Indian state of Kerala is visited by tens of thousands of vacationers each year. But an environmental crisis is threatening the heart of this beautiful corner of the Indian subcontinent.

Kerala lies on a narrow strip of land between the Western Ghats mountain chain and the Arabian Sea, buffered from the open waters by lakes and canals supporting a wealth of marine and bird life. The foremost of these natural barriers is Vembanad Lake. Over the past decade it has been reduced to a third of its previous expanse. Elsewhere, only 33 percent of the canals remain from the early 1900s. Kerala's backwaters are disappearing.

"The steady reduction of water levels because of construction and the increase in chemical discharges into the marine environment from factories over the past decade has left Kerala on the verge of an environmental catastrophe," warns Dr. Bijoy Nandan, head of the state's Central Inland Fisheries Institute. "Local crops are suffering. Fish stocks are depleted, rare birds are at risk, and the numbers of freshwater turtles are falling.

"The massive reclamation of backwaters for agriculture, urbanization, housing, aquaculture, and port construction has drastically affected the area's fauna and flora. Unbridled economic growth, a population explosion, and increased human activities along coastlines are the most serious problems facing India's fragile ecosystems today, and the backwaters are no exception to this."

One traditional occupation, involving the production of coir fibre—coconut husks woven into rope, matting, and filters for air-conditioning—has been singled out by environmentalists as a key threat to the ecosystem. The husks are immersed in shallow backwaters for up to nine months, releasing toxic compounds that kill fauna and flora. But more than 70 percent of India's coir comes from Kerala, where thousands of jobs depend on it.

The harbour in Kochi, the economic capital of Kerala and India's second most important port, is so badly polluted that local people rarely swim or fish in it. Atmospheric pollution is so bad that Kochi is nicknamed Asthma City.

Madhusoodana Kurup, professor of fisheries at Cochin University of Science and Technology, said, "For centuries these canals have sustained Keralans, but today these people have no pure air to breathe. The disaster graph is peaking."

SOURCE: Adapted from Dan McDougall, "Pollution Ravages Kerala," *The Observer* (UK), August 26–September 1, 2005, p. 29. Copyright Guardian Newspapers Limited 2005.

A second source of environmental degradation in the low-income countries is that associated with "unsustainable impoverishment." In other words, the poor engage in ecologically damaging practices just to survive from day to day (Gallopin, Gutman, and Maletta, 1989). For example, rural dwellers are often forced to strip the rapidly dwindling forests to obtain fuel for cooking. As the Brundtland commission recognized, it is futile to attempt to deal with environmental problems in the developing world without addressing broader issues of poverty and inequality. These problems in turn are rooted in a variety of social arrangements, from the continuing dominance of wealthy elites in the developing nations to economic dependency on the industrialized countries, associated with massive debt.

Nevertheless, it is important to note that environmental violations in the high-income countries of the North are directly tied to potential ecological catastrophes in the poorer nations of the South. Roberts (2001) has shown how global warming, which is linked to emissions of greenhouse gases in rich nations (20 percent of the world's population is responsible for 60 percent of current emissions of greenhouse gases), threatens poor nations with devastating disasters: draughts, floods, heat waves, and so on. At the same time, global warming contributes to the "pollution of poverty," whereby the world's poor are forced to use renewable energy sources for their basic fuel needs. As Roberts (2001: 508) stresses, "equity and ecology must be dealt with together" through aggressive efforts to support national advancement in the South, if a healthy planet is to be maintained.

RISK AND RISK ASSESSMENT

Risk refers to the probability that a particular hazard will actually occur. Everyday life is full of risks, from slipping on the ice on our front steps to being hit by a bolt of lightning on the golf course. Normally, we base our decision on whether to take a particular course of action that carries with it a degree of risk on a series of individual factors: past experience, confidence in our own abilities, and our assessment of the apparent safety of a situation. In the present-day world, however, it is increasingly difficult to make such judgments, especially with regard to new technologies and environmental conditions. For example, a summer afternoon spent sunning on the beach may

seem innocent, but it may, in fact, contribute to the onset of skin cancer unless a sun-block lotion is applied to counteract the ultraviolet rays coming through the thinned-out ozone layer. Many of today's environmental hazards are invisible to the naked eye.

To cope with such risks, we have increasingly come to rely on the judgment of medical and scientific experts, who appear to be best qualified to decide what is safe. We avoid high-fat foods, buckle our seat belts, and buy bottled spring water because risk professionals tell us that it may be risky not to do so.

Each week seems to bring some newly discovered risk to our attention. Increasingly, such risks are environmentally related—from dioxins and heavy metals in our drinking water through radiation leaks from nuclear power plants to urban smog that can cause respiratory problems. Toxic hazards are particularly devastating because they render many of the seemingly innocuous or even beneficial things that we depend on—the air we breathe, the water we drink, the sea and soil that nourish the food we eat—dangerous (Clarke and Short, 1993).

Sociologists have taken a particular interest in three aspects of risk and risk assessment: the organizational basis of risk, the community perception of risk, and the social distribution of risk.

ORGANIZATIONAL BASIS OF RISK

One consequence of the increasing size and complexity of modern industrial systems is that the source of risk has shifted to large-scale organizations that are all but beyond individual control. When environmentally threatening accidents happen, they are attributable to more than human error; they reflect a set of structural arrangements that make breakdowns inevitable. For example, the gigantic 1989 oil spill that occurred after the supertanker *Exxon Valdez* ran aground in Prince Edward Sound, Alaska, was attributable to cutbacks in maritime safety standards as much as to personal lapses by the captain (Smith, 1992). Similarly, a recent report by a review group of the American Society of Civil Engineers concluded that the levee breaches that left more than 75 percent of New Orleans flooded after Hurricane Katrina did not result from construction-related flaws. Rather, they indicated a massive and catastrophic organizational failure wherein all the agencies tasked with levee upkeep—local levee boards, parish governments, state agencies, bureaucracies within the Army Corps of Engineers—operated independently and sometimes in conflict with one another (Schwartz, 2006).

Indeed, **normal accidents**—the inevitable failures in nuclear power facilities, petrochemical plants, air-traffic control nets, and other high-risk technologies—are common. Sometimes these flaws are identified during the construction process, but on other occasions, design flaws manifest themselves only years later, in the form of disasters, such as the Three Mile Island nuclear accident. Rather than being anomalies, such technological accidents are the normal consequences of profit-driven, high-risk systems (Perrow, 1984).

Organizations are not only the source of accidents but also the groups responsible for responding to them. The ways in which they do so often amplify the risk (Clarke and Short, 1993: 392). For example, in the wake of the 1984 gas leak at a Union Carbide pesticide plant in Bhopal, India, in which 8000 people were killed and an estimated 300 000 were injured, neither the company, which lacked the necessary support structure and contingency plans for dealing with major accidents, nor the immense government bureaucracy, which took a long time to mobilize, was able to move quickly enough to cope with the catastrophe (Shrivastava, 1987).

COMMUNITY PERCEPTION OF RISK

Contrary to expectations, it is not possible to predict the public perception of risk accurately on the basis of the standard set of demographic and sociological variables (age, gender, political affiliation, etc.). Instead, the best predictor of whether people are likely to perceive risk is the degree to which they trust the ability of expert institutions, including local industries themselves, to manage danger (Freudenburg, 1993; Wynne, 1992). For example, during the Windscale inquiry into the establishment of a nuclear reprocessing facility on the east coast of England, the nuclear experts and the judge who chaired the inquiry approached the issue from a completely different vantage point from local citizens. Whereas the former restricted the scope of the inquiry to technical risk considerations, the latter wanted to deal with larger questions, such as how adequate the past performance of the nuclear plant had been and what the future of nuclear power should be. As a result, public trust in both the project and the inquiry was undermined and the perception of risk magnified (Wynne, 1992).

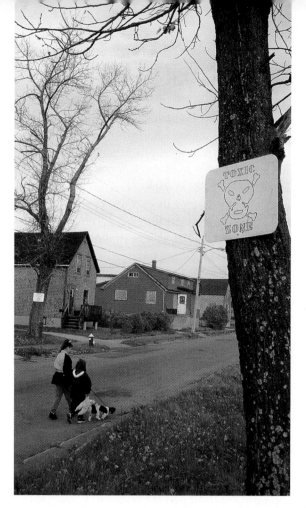

Frederick Street in Sydney, Nova Scotia, runs alongside the Sydney tar ponds, the worst toxic waste site in Canada and arguably the worst in North America. With a legacy of 100 years of steelmaking, the tar ponds contain 35 times more toxic sludge than New York's infamous Love Canal. As a result, Sydney has the highest cancer rate in Canada—19 percent for men and 14 percent for women, more than double the national averages. After 12 years of trying to clean up the mess, the clean-up project was declared a failure and the residents of Frederick Street were relocated in 1999. The toxic waste remains.
SOURCE: Warren Gordon/*Frederick Street: Life and Death on Canada's Love Canal.*

Trust in institutions varies among the members of a community. Those who trust institutions least are most likely to define environmental conditions as risky and therefore actionable. In the Love Canal case, the residents of the neighbourhood that was affected by toxic seepage could be divided into two types: *minimalists,* who denied that there was a problem at all or acknowledged a problem of only minor significance, and *maximalists,* who believed that the risks were substantial and that the chemical contamination might be more widespread than officially acknowledged. Minimalists were generally found to be social isolates in their neighbourhoods, without children at home, with occupational links to the chemical industry, and with strong attachments to their homes, which they viewed as their principal economic resource in old age. In contrast, the maximalists were typically young parents who shared common interests, placed greater emphasis on health than on property issues, and were active in seeking risk information, especially from nonofficial sources (Fowlkes and Miller, 1987). In other cases, too, researchers have confirmed that a major motivation for families to become involved in neighbourhood action against toxic wastes is concern about the quality of the community for raising children (Hallman and Wandersman, 1992). Environmental-risk perception, then, is not only a product of how much trust citizens put in the explanations and assurances offered by those in authority positions but is also linked to people's participation in family life, neighbourhood social networks, and community affairs.

SOCIAL DISTRIBUTION OF RISK

Finally, recent research in the sociology of environmental risk has documented how marginal groups in society bear a disproportionate burden of the risk associated with oil refineries, chemical plants, toxic dumps, garbage and sewage incinerators, and other sources of hazardous exposure. Racial and ethnic minorities, women, low-income urban dwellers, and residents of poor, isolated rural regions are particularly affected. After analyzing the distribution of toxic "Superfund" hazardous waste site locations in Texas and Louisiana, Denq, Constance, and Joung (2000) concluded that the three dimensions of class, status, and power are all important in explaining why toxic dumps are disproportionately located in communities with higher percentages of minorities and poor people. Rather than "environmental racism," they argue that the environmental justice issues involved here are better conceptualized as "environmental classism." Disadvantaged communities are overrepresented as risk sites because corporate polluters view them as constituting the path of least resistance, since their inhabitants are generally both economically poor and politically powerless. In many cases, existing patterns of discrimination are closely linked with inequalities in the distribution of environmental hazards.

Disadvantaged people are the primary victims of pollution (most of it generated by or on behalf of the middle and upper classes) because they live closest to the sources of pollution: power plants, industrial installations, and, in central cities, heavy vehicle traffic. Usually, they have no choice as to where they live. Discrimination created the situation, and those with wealth and influence have the political power needed to keep polluting facilities away from their homes. Living in a poor area is bad enough; high levels of pollution make it worse (Bullard, 1990).

Although the scale of environmental-risk inequality is smaller in Canada than in the United States, some striking parallels exist. For example, in July 1993, a Mi'kmaq band in Pictou Landing, Nova Scotia, was reported to have accepted a federal government package worth an estimated $35 million as compensation for the pollution of Boat Harbour, the body of water adjoining the band's reserve. At one time, Boat Harbour had clear beaches and was a source of fish and lobster for the Mi'kmaq, but in the mid-1960s, almost half the harbour was purchased for $60 000 to treat wastewater from a kraft mill operated by Scott Maritimes, a subsidiary of Scott Paper Company. The harbour subsequently became one of the most polluted spots in the province, with 87 million litres of a coffee-coloured effluent processed each day by the provincial treatment lagoon.

A similar case occurred two decades earlier in northern Ontario, when the Reed pulp-and-paper plant at Dryden was found to be responsible for dumping nine tonnes of mercury into the English Wabigoon river system between 1962 and 1970 (Macdonald, 1991: 106). The Ojibwa who lived in the area suffered serious health and economic problems. Not only were they penalized by a commercial fishing ban, but they also were found to be suffering from "Minimata disease"—mercury poisoning from fish— a toxic syndrome named after a fishing village in Japan, where victims took court action against Chisso Corporation, a large chemical firm.

Environmentally risky activities are also more likely to be located in peripheral communities, areas that are out of the mainstream by virtue of their relative geographic remoteness, their economic marginality, their political powerlessness, or their social isolation. For example, Sellafield, a town in northwest England on the Irish Sea, became a major repository for nuclear waste reprocessing. Sellafield was the archetype of a peripheral community, accessible only by twisting road and branch railway, situated in an area of high unemployment, and economically dependent on the local nuclear power plant (Blowers, Lowry, and Solomon, 1991). Such cases as these are often found in regions that Gidengil (1990) has termed the "vulnerable periphery" and the "depressed periphery," regions with chronic economic problems and dependencies and a high susceptibility to boom-and-bust industries.

Research on the social distribution of risk is not only important for humanitarian reasons, but also influences how we think about power, decision making, and institutional analyses of environmental risk (Clarke and Short, 1993: 394). Among other things, it suggests that risk decisions are not based entirely on "objective" technical and scientific criteria but are influenced by sociological factors related to inequality and power. This represents an important addition to public-policy debates on the dynamics of risk, which have tended to treat risk allocation as something that takes place outside the normal workings of society.

SOCIAL CONSTRUCTION OF ENVIRONMENTAL PROBLEMS

Among the most promising areas of research in environmental sociology today is the social-constructionist approach. According to this perspective, environmental issues rarely arise spontaneously; rather, they must be discovered, presented, promoted, and kept alive. Furthermore, environmental problems, like social problems in general, are not free-floating but are owned and managed by policy entrepreneurs in science, environmental-movement organizations, and the media. These "environmental claims-makers" invest considerable time and resources in attempting to elevate such problems as acid rain, global warming, and ozone depletion onto national and international agendas for action.

Consider, for example, the issue of indoor air pollution from radon gas. In the United States, policy entrepreneurs in Congress aggressively pressed the Environmental Protection Agency to take action to publicize the problem. Citizen groups were influential in making the public aware of the dangers of radon, especially when they were first discovered in the state of Pennsylvania. In contrast, a lack of comparable environmental claims-makers in Canada meant that the problem never really "caught on" here beyond a few investigative stories in *The Globe and Mail* (Harrison and Hoberg, 1991).

Hannigan (1995) notes that there are three central tasks in the construction of environmental claims—assembling, presenting, and contesting—each of which involves its own activities, opportunities, and pitfalls. To secure public attention and support, prospective problems must surmount a series of hurdles: They have to be considered newsworthy, they must acquire a measure of scientific credibility, and they have to be skillfully navigated across the shoals of political interest and policy relevance. Finding a way around these roadblocks is more likely if several conditions are met. First, it helps to have onside one or more scientific "popularizers" like David Suzuki who can bridge the gap between environmentalism and science, packaging claims so that they appeal to editors, journalists, political leaders, and other opinion-makers. Second, success is more likely if there are positive incentives for taking action. Moral appeals can effectively direct attention toward an environmental problem, but unless there are stakeholders in undertaking a concerted program of action, the issue may fizzle out. Protecting endangered species and conserving biodiversity in the tropical rain forest, for example, are made more attractive by the possibility that failure to do so would mean losing a wealth of as-yet-undiscovered pharmaceuticals that may be hidden there. Finally, it is crucial to recruit the support of institutional sponsors, such as the Rockefeller Foundation and the United Nations, to ensure both continuity and legitimacy, as well as financial support.

Social constructionists depict environmental problems as passing through a series of stages, from initial discovery to the waning of public interest. Earlier work in political science characterized environmental concern as inevitably proceeding through the five stages of a fixed **issue-attention cycle** (Downs, 1972). In the pre-problem stage, some highly undesirable social or environmental condition exists but has not yet captured much public attention, even though experts or interest groups may have identified it. In the second stage—"alarmed discovery and euphoric enthusiasm"—the public becomes aware of, and frightened by, the problem and is convinced that it can be solved if action is taken immediately. By the third stage, the public begins to realize the cost of significant progress and to perceive that solving the problem will not be as easy as it seemed; solutions require money, sacrifice, and loss of benefits for some. In the fourth stage, intense public interest gradually declines as the growing realization of how difficult any solutions will be sinks in. In the final, post-problem stage, the issue moves off the public-policy agenda, although it may recapture public interest at some point in the future.

More recent research has suggested that environmental issues rise and fall in the public eye in response to a number of different factors, including the clarity and viability of scientific evidence, the ability of environmental claims-makers to sustain a sense of dramatic crisis, and the rise of competing new environmental problems (Ungar, 1992).

A basic assumption of the social-constructionist perspective is that neither the appearance of collective values, such as those described by the alternative environmental paradigm, nor the documented existence of an actual environmental threat is sufficient, by itself, to create an environmental problem that ranks on the public agenda. For example, although tropical rain forest destruction in Malaysia is every bit as serious as its counterpart in Brazil, the latter has received extensive worldwide publicity whereas the former is rarely discussed. Rather, what is significant is the process through which environmental claims-makers pressure those who hold the reins of power to recognize definitions of environmental problems, to implement them, and to accept responsibility for solving them.

It is important to note that the social construction of environmental problems does not occur in isolation. Rather, just as socioeconomic structures influence the social distribution of risk, so the powerful in society have the ability to determine what is and what is not relevant with respect to the environment. It is this synergy between social definition and power inequality that makes social constructionism a distinctively sociological route to studying environmentalism and the environment.

SUMMARY

1. Sociological interest in the natural environment first developed in the early 1970s. Sociology's reluctance to embrace the study of the environment reflects its heritage, wherein biology and nature were banished from the discipline in favour of socially based theories of behaviour.

2. A central focus for much of the sociological examination of the environment has been the deep-seated value cleavage between environmentalists and their opponents in industry and science. The latter support a dominant social paradigm that stresses materialism, economic growth, and the human right to dominate nature. In contrast, environmentalists propose an alternative environmental paradigm that emphasizes the need to adopt small-scale, decentralized economic and political structures that are in harmony with nature. This value-oriented environmentalism has found its fullest expression in a number of "ecophilosophies"—deep ecology and ecofeminism—that have recently flourished on the margins of the environmental movement.

3. Support for environmentalism has remained remarkably constant for nearly 20 years. Although the majority of the population is generally supportive of environmental values, a young, well-educated, urban, liberal core has taken the lead in working for environmental change. Most other Canadians will recycle, purchase "green" products, and act positively toward the environment, but only to the extent that such action does not require any real sacrifice in terms of time and money.

4. To mobilize the reluctant majority, environmental-movement organizers develop frames (interpretations of events) that play up the possibility of an impending global collapse as a result of uncontrolled population growth and continued industrial growth. Global warming, expanding holes in the ozone layer, and the world-wide loss of biodiversity are the most recently identified symptoms of the impending crisis. The only solution, it is claimed, is to draw back and ease down, conserving resources, reducing pollution, and restricting population increase. However, these goals are especially difficult to achieve in the expanding economies of the developing world, where the environment is threatened by both unsustainable development and unsustainable impoverishment.

5. At the level of the local community, willingness to act on environmental problems rises as trust in expert institutions declines. This loss of trust is characteristic of neighbourhood-based environmental conflicts, in which citizens typically find the explanations and assurances offered by scientists and other authority figures to be faulty. Environmental-risk perception and action are also linked to people's participation in local social networks and community affairs.

6. The role of environmental entrepreneurs or claims-makers is vital in moving environmental issues from free-floating concerns to problems that are recognized and acted on by those in power. These promoters, situated in science, environmental organizations, and the media, define such problems as acid rain, global warming, and ozone depletion; package them; and elevate them to action agendas.

7. The social construction of environmental problems does not occur in a vacuum but is shaped by political and economic factors, to the extent that the powerful in society have the ability to act as gatekeepers, determining what is relevant with respect to the environment. Environmental problems, then, are actively contested, often on the basis of acceptable or unacceptable risk. Social constructionism in the context of power inequality represents a promising sociological route to understanding the environment-society relationship.

QUESTIONS TO CONSIDER

1. What types of environmental hazards do you and members of your community routinely face? Who do you think determines what is an acceptable level of risk in these situations? Scientists? The government? The media?

2. Analyze the environmental content of your local newspapers or television news programs for several weeks. Is environmental coverage balanced or does it favour a specific point of view? What types of media frames (interpretations of events) are used to organize information relating to environmental issues?

3. Keep a diary of all your consumer activities (shopping, transportation, leisure) for a week. Which of the products you buy and services you use are most likely to contribute to the deterioration of the environment? Which show signs of a "green" attitude among manufacturers, merchants, and service providers?

4. In the 1970s, Downs (1972) estimated that concern over the environment was about midway through the issue-attention cycle. Where in the cycle do you think it is now? What factors do you think have influenced its progression over the last three decades?

5. What is meant by the term *environmental management?* Think of some specific examples from Canadian political life in which governments have sought to use this strategy to distance themselves from environmental controversies.

GLOSSARY

The **alternative environmental paradigm** comprises a set of beliefs that challenge the centrality of economic growth, technological progress, and the human domination of nature as pillars of society. This paradigm stresses the need to adopt small-scale, decentralized economic and political structures that are in harmony with nature.

Anthropocentrism refers to human-centredness. It is an ideology that assumes that humans are separate from and superior to all other natural things and that judges human actions in the natural environment accordingly.

Biocentric egalitarianism is the principle, held by deep ecologists, that all things on Earth have an equal right to exist. In this view, humans have no special rights or privileges that allow them to subdue and destroy their natural surroundings.

The **broadening-base hypothesis** holds that environmental concern will eventually spread beyond its present social base—that is, of young, well-educated, urban, politically liberal citizens—to all of society.

Carrying capacity refers to the optimum population size that the planet can support under present environmental conditions.

Deep ecology is an environmental ethic emphasizing that all species in nature are of equal value. Our experience of nature, deep ecologists claim, should be the foundation for an energetic environmentalism that opposes the present domination by rational science.

The **dominant paradigm** is a widely accepted view of the world that emphasizes the moral imperative of material-wealth creation and the moral conviction that humans have the inalienable right to dominate nature and harness the environment to that end.

Ecofeminism is an environmental ethic that sees androcentrism (male-centredness) as the root of ecological destruction. Ecofeminists identify a distinctly feminine way of thinking and acting that is nurturing, cooperative, communal, and sensitive to nature.

The **economic-contingency hypothesis** says that the broadening of the social base of environmental concern is contingent on prevailing economic conditions. When economic conditions worsen or are perceived as worsening, those who are least well off will be the first to shift their focus away from the environment to the economy.

Environmental management refers to moderate government intervention in environmental conflicts that accords limited protection to the environment without seriously curtailing economic development.

Frames are interpretations of events and their meanings. Successful framing involves diagnostic, prognostic, and motivational elements.

The **Gaia hypothesis** is a controversial idea that proposes that Earth is a living organism that adjusts and regulates itself in the same manner as does the human body.

The **human-exceptionalism paradigm** is a worldview that features the ideals of steadily evolving social progress, increasing prosperity and material comfort, and class mobility for all segments of society, while ignoring the environmental costs of economic growth.

The **issue-attention cycle** is a five-stage sequence through which the "career" of most social problems is said to pass.

Normal accidents are inevitable failures in nuclear power stations, petrochemical plants, air-traffic control nets, and other high-risk technological systems. Such accidents are regarded by corporate organizations as an inevitable consequence of operating a hazardous facility.

Risk refers to the probability that a particular hazard will occur.

Sustainable development is economic development that meets the needs of the present without compromising the ability of future generations to meet their own needs.

The **treadmill of production** is the inherent need of our economic system to continually yield profits by creating consumer demand for new products, even when this means expanding the ecosystem to its furthest limits.

SUGGESTED READING

Barlow, Maude, and Elizabeth May. (2000). *Frederick Street: Life and Death on Canada's Love Canal.* Toronto: HarperCollins. This compelling dramatic account by two well-known social activists details the struggle by residents of a Cape Breton neighbourhood to force politicians and bureaucrats to clean up what could be Canada's single worst toxic site. The final chapter provides a useful survey of other toxic hot spots across the country.

Bullard, Robert D. (1990). *Dumping in Dixie: Race, Class and Environmental Quality.* Boulder, CO: Westview Press. This pioneering study looks at the environmental impact on poor black communities in the U.S. South of locating petrochemical factories, oil refineries, hazardous waste facilities, and other sources of industrial pollution in their neighbourhoods.

Hannigan, John (2006). *Environmental Sociology* (2nd ed.). London and New York: Routledge. The essential ingredients of environmental sociology, Hannigan contends, are questions of risk, media, science, nature, emergence, and social movements. In this highly readable overview of the field, students are provided with a social-constructionist model for analyzing environmental issues that can form the basis for their own research projects.

Harrison, Kathryn, and George Hoberg. (1994). *Risk, Science and Politics: Regulating Toxic Substances in Canada and the United States.* Montreal and Kingston, ON: McGill-Queen's University Press. This is a comparative study of government regulation of toxic substances in two neighbouring countries. The authors present case studies of six controversial substances suspected of causing cancer in humans: the pesticides Alar and alachlor, urea-formaldehyde foam insulation, radon gas, saccharin, and asbestos.

WEB RESOURCES

Companion Web Site for This Book

http://www.newsociety5e.nelson.com

Begin by clicking on the Student Resources section of the website. Next, select the chapter you are studying from the pull-down menu. From the Student Resources page, you have easy access to InfoTrac College Edition® and other resources, such as the Glossary and Flashcards. The website also has many useful tips to aid you in your study of sociology.

InfoTrac College Edition Search Terms

Visit http://www.infotrac-college.com for access to more than 20 million articles from nearly 6000 sources when doing your online research.

ThomsonNOW™

http://hed.nelson.com

This online diagnostic tool identifies each student's unique needs with a Pretest that generates a personalized Study Plan for each chapter, helping students focus on concepts they are having the most difficulty mastering. Students then take a Posttest after reading the chapter to measure their understanding of the material. An Instructor Gradebook is available to track and monitor student progress.

CHAPTER SEVENTEEN

Health and Aging

In this chapter you will learn that

- People are living longer and healthier lives than they did in the past. Even though this is a triumph over the alternative, the increasing size of the older population tends to be considered a social problem, one that has negative implications for demands on the nation's resources.

- Health is about more than the presence or absence of disease and, in contrast to generally accepted beliefs, not all aspects of health decline as we age.

- In Canada, significant inequalities in health exist. Health varies with such factors as socioeconomic position, gender, ethnicity, race, and age.

- Among older adults, the most common forms of health care consist of self-care and informal care, provided primarily by family members. Most people who provide health care are women.

- Recent years have seen increased emphasis placed on privatization and profit-making within Canada's health-care system, particularly when it comes to services that are most important to older adults. As a result, the people who are most in need of care are the least likely to access it and the most likely to have to rely on themselves and their family members for care.

Neena L. Chappell
UNIVERSITY OF VICTORIA
Margaret J. Penning
UNIVERSITY OF VICTORIA

CHALLENGING COMMONSENSE BELIEFS ABOUT HEALTH AND AGING

One of the authors of this chapter scans the birthday cards at the card shop, looking for just the right one to give to a friend who is about to turn 50. It is very difficult. On the front, most offer congratulations but once opened, offer only sympathy. Later in the day, while conducting an online scan of aging-related articles appearing in the nation's major newspapers, she is struck once again by the contradictory messages that seem to recur. One headline asks "Can We Prepare for Life at 100?" (Ibbitson, 2005). It informs us that the global population of centenarians, those aged 100 or more, is about to increase from 250 000 today to about 3.7 million in 2050. Most of these people will live in developed countries, such as Canada, suggesting that these countries have managed to achieve some measure of victory over human mortality. Yet, it is an achievement that the writer suggests people may not want to celebrate:

> Demographics don't lie. Unless younger workers prepare now to delay their retirement. . ., unless they are ready to take care of more of their own retirement costs rather than relying on the state, unless they are braced for a steady increase in taxes to pay for the health and pension costs of an older population . . . then the political shocks that accompany declining economies and bankrupt governments could shake our social foundations. And you won't want to live to see that day. (Ibbitson, 2005)

Although this article suggests that we may not want to live a long life, many others tell us how to live to see that day. One is part of a four-part series with a headline announcing that "It need not be all downhill" (Wister, 2005). It quotes Jeanne Calment, a French woman who lived to be 122 and who holds the record as the world's longest-lived person. When asked how she had managed to live for so long, Calment credited port wine, a Mediterranean diet, and a sense of humour. She also reported that she rode a bicycle until she was 100 and maintained a positive outlook: "I dream, I think, I go over my life. I never get bored." The article does not mention whether Calment was glad to have lived so long but it sounds as if she was. It does quote an expert in the

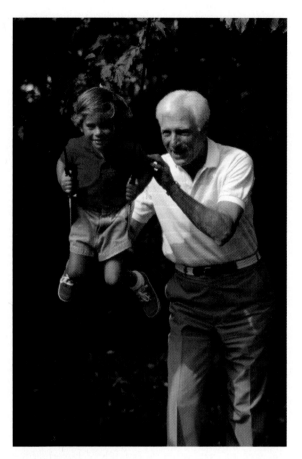

At Confederation, average life expectancy in Canada was 42 years. In 1999, it was 72 years. The number of people aged 65 years and older has increased because of improved hygiene, sanitation, and nutrition, as well as medical advances.
SOURCE: Photos.com.

field of aging as saying that although it is a matter of good luck and good genetics, above all, it is a matter of good lifestyle. Similarly, another article notes that although we can do little to lengthen our lives, we can avoid shortening them "through foolish choices," according to the *Saskatoon Star-Phoenix* (Fayerman, 2005). One story declares that "the fat of the land" is Canada's new burden and labels fat "the new tobacco" (Simpson, 2005).

However, other stories lead us to wonder if everyone is equally able to exercise such choice and access the benefits of a healthy lifestyle. Stories about Hurricane Katrina in New Orleans in August 2005 repeatedly asked why people didn't heed warnings issued before the storm to evacuate the city. Yet we were also told that it was the old, the sick, the poor, and the racial minority groups who did not evacuate and who died. An article reports on the writer's "days of watching the news on-line or on TV with utter disbelief" as she observed "a row of elderly poor people in the New Orleans Superdome waiting to die," or as she watched television coverage showing "the corpse of an old woman in a wheelchair, her feet rotting . . . in the heat" (Mallick, 2005). The articles remind us of similar stories told in relation to heat waves, floods, power outages, and other disasters. Several articles ask whether a similar situation could take place in Canada. Most answer yes. "In Canada, we tell ourselves the situation is much better. . . . But is it really? Or are we fooling ourselves? Canada has its share of poor, neglected and forgotten, and we shouldn't have to wait for a natural disaster to admit it" (Picard, 2005a).

Canadians often take pride in the fact that our health-care system is accessible to everyone who needs care, regardless of age, race, gender, or ability to pay for services. However, other stories paint a very different picture. One reports the results of a study indicating that heart failure patients who are at the greatest risk of death—those who are the oldest and who have the most chronic conditions—are the least likely to be prescribed drugs that could prolong their lives. Yet, they are also the ones who could benefit the most (Picard, 2005b). Another tells us about the lack of care available outside of hospitals for those who are dying. It reports that a city the size of Ottawa has only nine hospice beds (i.e., beds where those with three to six months remaining to live receive specialized end-of-life care). We wonder if Canada is not providing these services because it cannot afford the additional costs. This article notes that the average cost of a hospital bed in Canada is $1000 a day, while end-of-life care at home or in a hospice is much less expensive and better for the dying and their caregivers (Bains, 2005).

If it is too difficult for the public system to provide hospice care, why are private companies eager to make a profit by offering such services? An article discusses the Alberta government's plan to expand private health insurance (Cotter, 2005). In response to concerns that a private system will benefit only the well-connected and the wealthy, it quotes the provincial health minister as saying that private plans would not be allowed to have a negative impact on the public health-care system but instead would focus on private insurance for "continuing care, for supplemental health services not covered under the Canada Health Act and on drugs." Several of these services are particularly important to older adults. Another article published in the *Toronto Star* (Crane, 2005) tells

readers that "demographic shifts leading to population aging . . . create potentially big opportunities for today's innovators."

These stories point to the many contradictions we encounter when thinking about aging, health, and health care. The relationship between health and aging is a matter of both common sense and paradox. Is good health a problem? Is bad health a problem? If so, whose fault is poor health? Is it the individual's fault because of poor lifestyle choices? Alternatively, does it reflect problems of inequality and stratification? Will providing appropriate health care services for an aging population bankrupt our public health-care system? Will it offer opportunities for private interests to make a profit from health care? If so, what implications will this have? In this chapter, we discuss these issues. We begin by focusing on health as people age. Next, we address links among social inequalities, health, and aging. Finally, we examine health-related issues within Canada in the context of international and global trends in health care.

INDIVIDUAL AND POPULATION AGING

Today, most Canadians can expect to live to old age, barring accidents and wars. This was not always the case. In 1921, at birth, men could expect to live to be 58.8 years of age and women 60.6 years of age. In 2002, life expectancy was 79.7 years overall, 77.2 years for men and 82.1 years for women. People can now expect to live more than 20 years longer than if they had been born in 1921. Not only can people expect to live longer when they are born but once they reach age 65, they can expect to live even longer than before. That is, a baby born in 2002 in Canada could expect to live to 79.7 years of age (77.2 if a boy; 82.1 if a girl). However, a person aged 65 in 2002 could expect to live another 19.1 years (17.2 if a man; 20.6 if a woman) or to age 84.1 or an additional 4.4 years than the baby at birth (Belanger, Carrière, and Gilbert, 2001; Statistics Canada, 2004). Not until their 90s do men and women have approximately the same number of years left to live (see Table 17.1).

The fact that almost everyone can expect to live to old age distinguishes our era from other historical periods. Although past historical periods saw some individuals in society live as long as people live today, never before in history did the vast majority of people in a particular country expect to live to old age (see Figure 17.1).

TABLE 17.1 AVERAGE REMAINING YEARS OF LIFE, CANADA, 2001

AGE	MALES	FEMALES	ALL
65	17.0	20.5	18.8
70	13.5	16.6	15.1
75	10.4	12.9	11.8
80	7.8	9.7	8.9
85	5.6	7.0	6.4
90+	4.1	4.9	4.6

SOURCE: Data is adapted from Statistics Canada's "Vital Statistics-Death Database," and from Statistics Canada's Demography Division.

These demographics have profound implications for our lives: We now live much of our lives assuming that we have a considerable future before us so that forward thinking is realistic. In addition, most of us have multigenerational families. Young people today often know their grandparents and even their great-grandparents. As will be discussed later, increased longevity also means that the illnesses and disabilities that accompany old age are more prominent and that the health-care system has different demands on it than it did when fewer people lived to old age. Longer life expectancy results in more health care and service jobs for the younger generation. It affects when people retire and what they do after they retire. In a society with a history of mandatory retirement, but with almost all of its population now living to their late 70s and into their 80s, people can expect 15, 20, and even more years when they are not employed. This has implications for how they spend their time and how society treats them.

Life expectancy, the number of years that the average person can expect to live, increased steadily

FIGURE 17.1 CANADIAN POPULATION AGE STRUCTURE 1851–2001

Note: Numbers are thousands of people; figure scales are constant between years.
SOURCE: Calculated from Statistics Canada data.

during the twentieth century, but that does not mean it will necessarily continue to do so. How much more it will increase is open to debate. Some analysts argue that in the West, we are approaching our maximum biological life span (National Institute on Aging, 1996). It is not known whether this is correct, whether biomedical advances will enable the prolongation of life, or whether improvements in lifestyle factors, such as nutrition and exercise, can extend it further.

With most of us now living to old age, it will not be surprising to you that an increasing proportion of the Canadian population comprises seniors (see Box 17.1). In 1921, just more than 5 percent of the population was age 65 and over; this cohort is projected to constitute 20 percent of the population by 2021 (Desjardin, 1993). **Demography** (a research area that studies the characteristics of populations and the dynamics of population change) considers a country to be old if at least 10 percent of its population is age 65 and over. With 13 percent of its population currently aged 65 and over, Canada is old (Statistics Canada, 2001a). When the baby-boom generation reaches old age, fully one-quarter of Canada's population will be seniors. The baby-boom generation (the large cohort born between 1946 and 1962, now the parents of university-age children) will begin turning 65 in the year 2011. The youngest baby boomers will turn 65 in the year 2027. During this span, the older population will grow substantially. Young university students of today will live a substantial portion of their adult lives in a society with historically high levels of seniors because their parents are part of the baby boom generation.

The main reason for the increasing proportion of seniors in the population is not obvious; it is due to decreases in fertility. With declines in the number and proportion of children in the population, the proportion of older persons necessarily increases. Fertility is the major predictor of population aging until a population reaches a life expectancy at birth of 70 years of age, at which point almost all young persons survive. Further declines in mortality are then concentrated at the older ages (Chappell, Gee, McDonald, and Stones, 2003). Declines in mortality then result in relatively larger, older age groups and thus contribute more to population aging.

Deaths in old age usually result from chronic degenerative diseases. Circulatory diseases, including heart disease and stroke, are the major causes of death, followed by malignant neoplasms (cancers), respiratory diseases, including emphysema and chronic bronchitis, as well as infectious diseases, such as influenza and pneumonia (Statistics Canada, 2006).

GENDER

Not surprisingly, given their greater life expectancy, elderly women have lower mortality rates for all causes of death than do elderly men. This differential is one of the reasons why aging is often considered more of a women's issue. There are more older women than there are older men. This gender imbal-

---

BOX 17.1 DEFINING OLD AGE

The most common way to define old age is to refer to all those age 65 and over. This definition arose in the late nineteenth century. Otto Von Bismarck of Germany chose this age for his military personnel to be eligible to receive pension benefits. The decision was made because he believed offering a pension would increase the loyalty and productivity of his men. In addition, the average life expectancy assured him that most of his men would die before or shortly after that age, thus costing him little money. After Bismarck, private pension schemes and eventually governments adopted the same definition. Neither the characteristics nor the needs of older people were taken into account in setting this definition. As people live longer and live healthier into old age, 65 is becoming questioned as the accepted age of retirement. Several places in the United Sates have raised the age of mandatory retirement, and thus of old age, to age 67. In Canada, provinces that include age in their human rights legislation make it illegal to have a mandatory retirement age (Manitoba and New Brunswick are two examples).

Another measure of old age is median age of the population, referring to the age at which one-half of the population is older and one-half is younger. In Canada, the median age was 36.8 years in 2000 (Statistics Canada, 2001b). If a country's median age is 30 or over then the country is usually considered old.

ance increases the older one becomes. Said another way, there are even more women relative to men among those aged 80 and over compared to those aged 65 and over. For example, in 2001, 57.2 percent of those aged 65 and over in Canada were women whereas the figure for those aged 85 and over was 70 percent (Statistics Canada, 2002a). The reasons that women outlive men are not fully known. It is believed that there is a biological/genetic component, but current gender differences are determined at least in part by social and economic factors. For example, research (Rogers, Hummer, and Nam, 2000) shows there is less of a difference in mortality rates between men and women among more highly educated and economically advantaged segments of the population. Those in the working class in particular tend to engage in more dangerous work, such as construction and mining. This is important because it means that improvements in male mortality rates are possible.

The gender differential has important implications. It means, for example, that women are likely to be widowed, not to remarry, and therefore to live alone or in a nursing home late in their lives. They will also tend to be grandparents for a longer period than men are and will more likely be poor in old age, not only because of their general lower earning power when younger but also because their savings have to cover a longer time. Finally, women are also likely to have more age peers in the same situation as they are and thereby be able to maintain their social support networks into old age. Men, conversely, tend to die before their spouses both because they have a shorter life expectancy and because they tend to marry women younger than they are. Those who do outlive their wives are much more likely to remarry after becoming widowed because they prefer marriage to single life and because there are many unmarried (divorced, widowed) women available as potential partners. The fact that it is more acceptable for men to marry women considerably younger than themselves means there is an even larger pool of potential partners from which they can choose. However, if they do not remarry, they are at greater risk of social isolation because men are less likely to maintain social support networks than are women. Women are often the "kinkeepers" in society, whereas men tend to rely on their wives for social connectedness.

OTHER SOURCES OF DIVERSITY WITHIN AGING

In addition to gender, there are many other important variations within individual and population aging, including ethnocultural variations, rural-urban variations, and socioeconomic and class differences. Just because a person is 65 or older does not mean that person is like all others in that age group. Indeed, the period from age 65 to age 85 spans fully 20 years; that population is as diverse as any other.

There are more foreign-born individuals within Canada's senior population than there are within the younger population. In 2001, 18.4 percent of Canada's population was foreign born compared to 28.4 percent of the senior population. Most foreign-born seniors immigrated to Canada when they were younger and have lived here for many years. Thus, the ethnocultural composition of our senior population is heavily influenced by the immigration policies that were in effect during each period of immigration. For example, when many of today's seniors were immigrating to Canada, it was primarily English- and French-speaking (Canada's official languages) individuals from Europe and other Western countries who were granted permission to enter. Thus, in 1996, only 6 percent of seniors were members of visible minority groups.

The Chinese serve as an extreme example of the type of discriminatory policies that prevented some visible minorities from moving to Canada. In 1923, the Chinese Immigration Act barred Chinese people from entering Canada. Those already in the country, including many who were Canadian citizens, were not allowed to vote (but could be conscripted into the military). Occupational exclusion was legally sanctioned. It was not until 1947 that the Act was rescinded and many of the discriminatory laws removed from the books. By the late 1950s, the provinces and the federal government had rescinded most discriminatory laws. Although immigration rules changed over the years, it was not until 1967 that a universal point system was embraced, applying to persons from all countries, including China (Li, 1998).

Canadian immigration policies now allow various categories of immigrants to be admitted, including independent immigrants with educational and professional skills, close relatives of citizens and permanent residents of Canada, and business immigrants with substantial investment capital. Among those younger than 65 years of age, fully 35 percent of recent immigrants were born in Asia and another 12 percent in Africa or the Caribbean (Citizenship and Immigration Canada, 1999). This means that future generations of Canadian seniors will be much more ethnically and racially diverse than is true today.

Within the seniors' population, ethnic minorities constitute a relatively small but important group. Approximately 6000 seniors immigrate to this country every year, most often as family-class immigrants. Most of them are of non-European origin. Because they are sponsored, their economic resources tend to be limited and they are not eligible for any public pension until after they have resided in Canada for 10 years. Many cannot communicate in English or in French. For example, a seven-city study of Chinese seniors (Victoria, Vancouver, Calgary, Edmonton, Winnipeg, Toronto, and Montreal) reports that 82.5 percent chose to be interviewed in Cantonese (only 3 percent chose to be interviewed in English) and less than 25 percent spoke English well (Chappell, 2005).

Aboriginal seniors compose only 3.5 percent of Canada's total Aboriginal population because of high fertility rates and high mortality rates (and therefore shorter life expectancies). However, Aboriginal seniors are expected to double their percentage by 2016 (Statistics Canada, 1999). These seniors are more likely to live on reserves than younger Aboriginal people, raising questions about the availability of appropriate care. Reserves, like other rural locations across the country, watch young adults leave for educational and employment opportunities in urban settings; most do not return.

Place of residence is especially relevant to aging. Rural areas and small towns often have higher proportions of seniors primarily because of out-migration of the young. Northern areas (reflecting high Aboriginal birth rates) and rural areas that are adjacent to urban centres are exceptions (Bollman, 2000). Although some seniors move to rural areas in retirement as a lifestyle choice, this is not the major factor affecting the rural senior population. Provinces with higher percentages of seniors have older populations for the same reason: Nova Scotia and Saskatchewan experience high levels of emigration of younger people to other provinces, such as Alberta. Because of the influx of younger people, Alberta has a lower percentage of seniors. Notice that internal migration has an effect on the age structure of smaller areas (provinces, towns) even though it does not have a major effect on age structure at the national level.

Rural living presents unique challenges for seniors, particularly when their health begins to decline. Adult children often live at some distance from their parents, making it difficult for them to provide day-to-day care should the need arise. Because of smaller population sizes, it is not often cost-effective to provide many of the formal services found in large urban areas. If rural seniors require these services, they must travel to where the services are located.

APOCALYPTIC DEMOGRAPHY

The belief that a demographic trend, in this instance population aging, has drastic negative consequences for society is sometimes called *apocalyptic demography* (Gee, 2000). Here, the complex issue of an aging population is reduced to the notion that society cannot afford increasing numbers and percentages of older people. Five interrelated themes characterize apocalyptic demography: (1) aging is a social problem, (2) all old people are stereotyped as being the same: well-off "greedy geezers," (3) the increasing number of seniors is the reason for government debts and deficits and for overuse of social programs, (4) seniors are receiving more than their fair share of the country's resources and this will lead to intergenerational conflict, and (5) the negative aspect of aging guides social policy reform; deep cuts are necessary to accommodate the increasing number of seniors—that is, a large and growing senior population will bankrupt our welfare system, which will have to be dismantled or cut back.

Although it is true that the number and proportion of seniors in Canadian society are increasing, Canada's **dependency ratio** is remaining steady. (The dependency ratio is the number of people under the age of 19 or over the age of 64 divided by the number of people between the ages of 19 and 64.) This is because the number and proportion of youth are decreasing at the same time. Furthermore, the view of aging as a social problem does not take the economic productivity of the country into account. The extent to which a country can afford an aging population is not considered. In response to the belief that all seniors are well-off greedy geezers, it must be noted that most older Canadians are not wealthy and nearly one-half of older women without a spouse live in poverty. Although the largest proportion of social spending goes to public pensions and health care, population aging per se accounts only for a small part of future health care costs and will require little increase in public expenditures (Evans, McGrail, Morgan, Barer, and Hertzman, 2001). Costs for Canada's health-care system are increasing (see discussion below), but a major reason is the rising cost of pharmaceuticals and of biotechnology rather than aging. In short, apocalyptic demography does not withstand a careful review of the evidence.

HEALTH IN OLD AGE

The typical stereotype of old age is one of declining health. The image is partially valid with regard to physical health; however, it is not true of psychological and emotional health or of social well-being.

With age, our physical health does decline and most seniors, including those living at home in the community (that is, not in nursing homes), suffer from at least one chronic condition. More senior women than men suffer from chronic conditions (71.5 percent versus 60.6 percent). The most common chronic conditions are arthritis and rheumatism, followed by high blood pressure, and food and other allergies (Statistics Canada, 2001c). Chronic

conditions are not curable; they are not acute illnesses but rather are problems that persist over long periods.

The fact that a person has a chronic condition doesn't necessarily mean that it interferes with day-to-day functioning. Limitations on our activities in old age affect fewer seniors than the prevalence figures for chronic conditions would suggest. For example, many people at all ages wear glasses because of deteriorating eyesight but function well with corrective lenses. Similarly, when people with diabetes take their medication and follow appropriate nutritional and exercise regimens, they generally cope well. Many people with high blood pressure do not even feel any effects; often they do not know they have the disease. The extent to which health problems interfere with day-to-day functioning or limit activities is typically referred to as *functional disability*. Overall, about 30 percent of seniors experience restriction in their daily activities because of health problems (25 percent of males and 33.9 percent of females). This figure rises to 40.2 percent among those aged 75 and over.

Another important area of physical health that is not captured when examining disease, chronic conditions, or functional disability is that of pain. Pain is a problem for many but certainly not all seniors. In Canada, 25.4 percent of those aged 65 and over suffer chronic pain or discomfort. This increases to 28.7 percent among those aged 75 and over. Most (84 percent) take some form of medication, either

The typical societal stereotype of old age is one of health decline, particularly of our physical health.
SOURCE: Ilse Hughes, *In the Corridor.*

prescription or over the counter, for their pain (Statistics Canada, 2004).

Mental or brain disorders are viewed as diseases by the medical profession. Typically, they are viewed as having physical causes. Dementia is an example. The most prevalent form of dementia is Alzheimer's disease. Canada's only national study to date to establish the prevalence of dementia revealed that between 6 percent and 8 percent of seniors have this disease (Canadian Study on Health and Aging, 1994). Seniors are more likely to suffer from dementia than are younger individuals. Most (three-quarters) seniors who have dementia live in long-term care facilities. As is true of other illnesses, the "old old" (variously defined as those aged 75+, 80+, or 85+) are more likely to have this illness—approximately 20 percent of those aged 80 and over have dementia.

Despite the fact that physical health deteriorates as people age, seniors tend to view their general health as good, very good, or excellent (73.3 percent overall, 73.7 percent for men and 72.7 percent for women). For those age 75 and over, the overall figure is 67.8 percent (Statistics Canada, 2004). The same positive picture is evident if we examine measures of psychological well-being. Those aged 75 and over are three times more likely than 18- and 19-year-olds to score high on a sense of coherence (that is, a view that life is meaningful, events are comprehensible, and challenges are manageable). Self-esteem and mastery also seem to improve with age, peaking in middle age, followed by only modest declines in later life (Statistics Canada, 1995). According to a recent national survey, fully 89.4 percent of older adults reported being satisfied with their lives. The figure was 83.7 percent among 15–24 year olds (Statistics Canada, 2005). The reasons that seniors have such good psychological well-being and indeed often exhibit better psychological well-being than younger adults do—even though seniors' physical health is often worse—is unknown. It may be that they compare themselves with the alternative (being dead) or it may be that after living many decades the importance of material and physical matters wane.

The same type of favourable situation is found when examining the social lives of seniors. Their social lives tend to be healthy and characterized primarily by social embeddedness or integration rather than by social isolation. A minority of seniors, particularly the frail, poor, and old old, are vulnerable to social isolation. However, most of them are embedded within **modified extended family** networks (Litwak, 1960) characterized by mutual and close intergenerational ties, responsible filial behaviour, and contact between the generations. Although family forms are becoming increasingly diverse—including gay and lesbian families, single-parent families, and blended families—no evidence suggests that families in all of their varied forms do not support their members. Rather, gerontological research conducted since the 1970s has been debunking the notion that Canadian families abandon their seniors (Chappell, 1992). Most elderly individuals in the Western world have extensive social contacts, live close to at least one of their children, and can name friends and confidantes (Antonucci, 1985, 1990).

Although sociologists of health and aging often focus on the negative aspects or problems of old age, and particularly on how seniors can prevent, delay, and cope with declining physical health, they also study quality of life. They want to know how society can ensure that old age is a stage of life when individuals are valued and consider their lives worthwhile.

This focus has led to an interest in increasing the number of years of life that are free from disability. According to the compression of morbidity hypothesis (Fries, 1983), Western nations are successfully postponing the age of onset of chronic disability so that more and more people experience it later and later in life. It is thought that eventually we will all be able to live relatively healthy lives until very shortly before death when our bodies will deteriorate rapidly. Until recently, evidence was contradictory—some supported the idea that we were increasingly living disability-free lives in old age while other research indicated this was not the case (Hayward, Crimmins, and Saito, 1998; Roos, Havens, and Black, 1993). However, recent figures suggest that although we are far from a dependency-free old age, Canadians nonetheless are experiencing a later age of onset of functional limitations (the same is not necessarily true of chronic illnesses, such as diabetes). This is good news, if the trend continues. To do so, it would probably need to occur in all segments of the population. Unfortunately, the vagaries of old age are not evenly distributed, as you will now learn.

INEQUALITY, HEALTH, AND AGING

In Canada, as elsewhere, whether and how we grow old varies considerably depending on social factors. Inequalities in health and longevity reflect the fact that our society is stratified by such factors as socio-economic position, ethnicity, race, and gender. Although less frequently recognized as such, it can also be said to be stratified by age, insofar as the aging process itself brings with it differential treatment and resources (Krieger, 2000).

Research suggests that not all improvements in health and longevity experienced over the past decades have been equally shared; declines in death rates in the past few decades have been more rapid in some segments of the population, such as higher-income groups, than in others (Schalick, Hadden, Pamuk, Navarro, and Pappas, 2000). This is also found in other countries. In the United States, healthy or disability-free life expectancy has been shown to increase over time but only among those with higher education; the opposite pattern is found among those with lower education. Also, declines in disability have been shown to vary depending on such factors as gender and age (Crimmins, 2004; Laio, McGee, Cao, and Cooper, 2001).

In general, those who are advantaged with regard to such factors as education, occupational status, income, and wealth live longer than those who are disadvantaged on these factors. They also tend to live a greater number of healthy years and spend a greater proportion of their overall lives healthy. As noted previously, as age increases, the likelihood of illness (chronic and acute) also increases. However, those with more education seem to be able to avoid or postpone disability to a greater extent than those with less education, although it has also been suggested that education may be of less benefit once disability is already present (Huisman et al., 2005). People with a university degree often feel healthy and function well late into their 60s, 70s, and 80s, whereas those with less education do not (Ross and Wu, 1996). A recent Canadian study (Buckley, Denton, Robb, and Spencer, 2005) focused on what happened over a three-year period among adults aged 50 and over, all of whom were in good health in the first year. They found that the likelihood of remaining in good health over the next two years was greater among men and women in the highest educational and income groups.

Although education is important to health, it has been estimated that approximately 23 percent of premature mortality (i.e., potential years of life lost) among Canadians can be linked to income-related differences (Raphael, 2005). One report indicates that men with the lowest 5 percent of earnings before retirement are twice as likely to die between 65 and 70 years of age as men with the highest 5 percent of earnings. On average, high-income earners appear to experience about 12 more years of good health than those with lower incomes (see Segall and Chappell, 2000). Among seniors, they also tend to see themselves as being in considerably better health. As well, among seniors with disabilities, those with low income also tend to be more functionally disabled than those with higher income. As a result, even though people with low income are less likely to live to old age, those who do are more likely to be institutionalized in long-term care facilities than those with higher income (Trottier, Martel, Houle, Berthelot, and Légaré, 2000).

Gender also has a significant influence on health and well-being throughout life. As already noted, in Canada, women tend to live longer than men, which might lead you to expect that women will be healthier than men throughout life. However, studies reveal a more complicated pattern. For example, women appear more likely than men to report multiple health problems associated with chronic conditions, such as arthritis and rheumatism, high blood pressure, back problems, and allergies (Chappell et al., 2003; Statistics Canada, 1995). Among older women, 85 percent report one or more chronic conditions, compared with 78 percent of older men. The likelihood of disability increases with age for both men and women. However, women are more likely to report limitations in activities of daily living or disability in later life than men (Statistics Canada, 2001c). Women also tend to report more severe disability than men. As a result, although men have lower life expectancy, they live a greater proportion of their lives without disabling conditions.

Racial, ethnic, and immigrant inequalities in health are also widely reported. Much of the research in this area focuses on racial inequalities evident in the United States, where black, Hispanic-American, and Native-American adults are consistently found to have considerably poorer health and longevity than whites. An exception involves very old African

Americans. It seems that at about the age of 75, African Americans begin to outlive their Caucasian counterparts. Some also report similar findings with regard to differences in disability (Kelley-Moore and Ferraro, 2004). Does this mean that among African Americans, health improves in the last years of life? It appears not. Instead, it is probably the result of selective survival; African Americans are much more likely to die at younger ages and consequently, those who survive to old age are a very select group.

In Canada, major differences exist in the health and well-being of Aboriginal versus non-Aboriginal adults. According to Canada's Royal Commission on Aboriginal Peoples (1996), the life expectancy of registered Indians in Canada is seven to eight years shorter than that of non-Aboriginal Canadians. Variation also exists within the Canadian Aboriginal population. For example, among Aboriginal women, life expectancy is shortest among the Inuit, followed by registered North American Indians, then Métis, and finally, by non-registered North American Indians. Death rates from infectious and parasitic diseases (diseases associated with inadequate housing, unsanitary conditions, and so on) are well above average national levels. Suicide rates are also higher, as are death rates from injuries and accidental deaths (drowning, fire, homicide, motor vehicle accidents; Allard, Wilkins, and Berthelot, 2004). According to Wister and Moore (1998), 66.5 percent of all Aboriginal elders reported disabilities, compared with 37.4 percent of non-Aboriginal people of the same age. Finally, although most older adults in Canada rate their health as excellent or very good, just under one-half (45 percent of women and 44 percent of men) of older (aged 65+) non-reserve Aboriginal adults in Canada reported fair or poor health (see Figure 17.2).

In Canada, health inequities associated with ethnicity and race are not restricted to Aboriginal groups; they are also apparent when we compare other ethnic and racial groups. Less than one-quarter of older Canadians who were born in Canada or in the United States, Europe, Australia, and Asia tend to report fair or poor health. This percentage is considerably higher (about 33 percent) among seniors born in Central and South America and Africa (Chappell et al., 2003). Interestingly, however, research findings also indicate that immigrants, especially recent arrivals, enjoy better health than their Canadian-born counterparts, a pattern observed to varying degrees for such health outcomes as chronic diseases, dis-

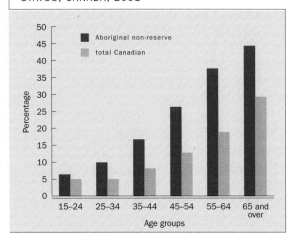

FIGURE 17.2 FAIR OR POOR SELF-RATED HEALTH STATUS, CANADA, 2001

SOURCE: Statistics Canada, Aboriginal Peoples Survey, 2001, and Canadian Community Health Survey, 2000–01.

ability, dependency, life expectancy, and disability-free life expectancy (Chen, Ng, and Wilkins, 1996; see Table 17.2). This may seem surprising at first glance. However, it likely reflects the fact that the Canadian government requires potential immigrants to meet a minimum standard of health before they will be admitted, and consequently, healthier people are more likely to immigrate. What is perhaps more notable is that immigrants who have lived in Canada for a longer period do not have a similar advantage. Does this mean that immigrants' health tends to

The life expectancy of registered Indians in Canada is seven to eight years shorter than that of non-Aboriginal Canadians.
SOURCE: PhotoDisc.

TABLE 17.2 LIFE EXPECTANCY AT BIRTH AND AT AGE 60 FOR SELECTED COUNTRIES, 2000–2005

Country	LIFE EXPECTANCY AT BIRTH		LIFE EXPECTANCY AT AGE 60	
	W	M	W	M
Hong Kong SAR[1]	85	79	26	22
Japan[1]	85	78	27	22
France[2]	83	76	26	20
Spain[2]	83	76	25	20
Australia[3]	83	78	25	21
Canada[4]	**82**	**77**	**25**	**21**
Israel[1]	82	78	24	21
Sweden[2]	82	78	24	21
Germany[2]	81	76	24	19
United Kingdom[2]	81	76	23	20
United States of America[4]	80	75	24	20
Cuba[4]	79	75	23	20
Poland[2]	78	70	22	17
Mexico[4]	77	72	22	21
Venezuela[5]	76	70	22	20
China[1]	73	70	20	17
Egypt[6]	72	67	18	16
Iran (Islamic Republic of)[1]	72	69	18	17
Ukraine[2]	72	60	19	14
Russian Federation[2]	72	59	19	14
Bolivia[5]	66	62	19	17
India[1]	65	62	18	16
Iraq[1]	60	57	16	15
Ghana[6]	57	56	18	17
Papua New Guinea[3]	56	55	14	12
Haiti[4]	52	51	17	16
South Africa[6]	51	47	18	14
Kenya[6]	46	48	18	16
Afghanistan[1]	46	46	15	14
Botswana[6]	37	36	18	16
Swaziland[6]	33	32	17	15

SOURCES: United Nations, *World Population Prospects: The 2004 Revision*, Vol. 1, Comprehensive Tables (United Nations publication, forthcoming), supplemented by Demographic Yearbook 2001 (United Nations publication, Sales No. E/F.03.XIII.1); Demographic Statistics, accessed January 12, 2006, at http://unstats.un.org/unsd/demographic/products/indwm/ww2005/tab3a.htm#src.

Notes: [1]Asia, [2]Europe, [3]Oceania, [4]North America, [5]South America, [6]Africa

decline after immigration? In fact, this seems to be what is taking place (Pérez, 2002).

EXPLAINING SOCIAL INEQUALITIES IN HEALTH

What is it about age, gender, ethnicity, race, social class, and related inequalities that results in poorer health? In brief, higher social status leads to better opportunities, living situations, and access to resources that also lead to better health and well-being. Poor health may well limit opportunities to attain a good education, secure a desirable job, and achieve an adequate income. However, this tends to affect people who encounter illness and disability early in life, a fairly small minority of the population as a whole.

Three types of factors have been linked to structured social inequalities on the one hand and poorer individual physical and mental health on the other: (1) individual health behaviours and lifestyles, (2) material conditions and resources, and (3) social psychological resources.

A recent public opinion survey (Canadian Population Health Initiative [CPHI], 2005) reports that when Canadians were asked what the major determinants of health were, the most common responses referred to individual behaviour and lifestyle factors, including whether a person smokes (80 percent), a person's eating habits (72 percent), whether a person is overweight or obese (71 percent), how much stress a person has (68 percent), and the amount of exercise she or he gets (65 percent). Consistent with these views, it is widely believed that the primary reason that those seniors who experience poor health do so is that, either currently or in the past, they have had poorer health-related lifestyles—that is, they tended to smoke and drink more than those not in poor health, they were generally "couch potatoes" who exercised less than they should, they tended to eat fatty foods, they did not seek or listen to appropriate medical advice, and so on.

Interestingly, research findings do point to a link between social location and individual behaviour and lifestyle factors. Individuals with higher levels of education and income are more likely to engage in health-promoting practices and are less likely to engage in risky health practices than those with lower levels of education and income. Yet, at the same time, studies that have compared the importance of individual behaviours and lifestyle factors with other

When surveyed, Canadians identified a person's smoking, eating, weight, experience of stress, and exercise habits as the major determinants of health.
SOURCE: Shutterstock.

social factors as determinants of health among middle-aged and older adults have found that the impact of health behaviours is minor when compared with other social factors, such as income adequacy (Lantz et al., 1998; Williamson, 2000).

Sociologists have often been highly critical of attempts to explain social inequalities in health primarily with reference to individually chosen lifestyle behaviours. The emphasis on lifestyles allows choice to be considered. Yet, according to many, it ignores the fact that social inequalities themselves (that is, inequalities of socioeconomic position, gender, ethnicity, race, and age) are more important than individual behaviours for an understanding of health outcomes. Also, focusing on individual behaviour tends to ignore the fact that such behaviours are not freely chosen nor chosen from an equally full range of possible options but rather are themselves products of and responses to structured social inequalities. Consequently, such a view encourages us to **blame the victim**—those who do not appear to have made the proper choices—for what are in fact socially produced inequalities in health. It also leads to interventions that are unlikely to be effective in addressing inequalities in health, are also inequitable, and generally ignore older adults in favour of those who are younger.

Based on these criticisms, many sociologists have argued for the need to focus directly on the impact that such factors as age, gender, ethnicity, race, and socioeconomic position have on differences in access to material living conditions and resources and, consequently, on health (Raphael, 2005). For example, a study conducted by Shields and Tremblay (2002) found that income and other social location factors (percentage Aboriginal population, percentage visible minority groups, unemployment rate, population size, percentage aged 65 and over, years of schooling) accounted for about 56 percent of differences in life expectancy, 32 percent of the variation in disability-free life expectancy, and 25 percent of the variation in subjective perceptions of health status within the Canadian population. That is, Canadians who experience inadequate income, dependency on welfare, substandard living conditions, stresses, physical violence, sexual abuse, and substance abuse suffer worse health. Unfortunately, Aboriginal peoples and other ethnic and racial minority groups are more likely to be living in circumstances that are injurious to their health (Segall and Chappell, 2000).

Another explanation for how social location generates health inequalities draws attention to the role of stress in linking the two: Inequality and lack of access to resources generate stress for the individual, which then results in poor health. In addition, some analysts argue that it is not just poverty that is at work here. They note that if poverty was the only problem, then we would expect to find substantial differences in health between the poor and nonpoor, with smaller differences between those who are only moderately well-off versus those who are very wealthy. Yet this is not the case. Instead, we see that each increment in education or income brings with it an additional health advantage. This suggests that it is not just poverty that is bad for health but inequality itself. Accordingly, health inequalities should be seen "as a result of citizens experiencing systematic material, social, cultural, and political exclusion from mainstream society" (Raphael, 2005: 4; see Box 17.2).

But what is it about inequality itself that will affect health? According to proponents of the **hierarchy stress perspective** (Link and Phelan, 2000: 36), the answer lies in psychosocial factors, particularly the stress that may result when people compare their situations with those of others and see their situations in negative terms. From this perspective, the stress associated with lower relative position in the social hierarchy can have a negative impact on health both directly and indirectly. In other words, stress itself can not only cause poorer health, but it can also lead people to smoke, consume too much alcohol, eat too much or too little, or sleep too little, all of which can also have a negative impact on health (Link and Phelan, 2000).

BOX 17.2 WHICH TIPS FOR BETTER HEALTH ARE CONSISTENT WITH RESEARCH EVIDENCE?

The messages given to the public by governments, health associations, and health workers are heavily influenced by the ways in which health issues are understood. Contrast the two sets of messages below. The first is individually oriented and assumes individuals can control the factors that determine their health. The second is societally oriented and assumes the most important determinants of health are beyond the control of most individuals. Which set of tips is most consistent with the available evidence on the determinants of health?

Ten traditional, individualistic tips for better health:

1. Don't smoke. If you can, stop. If you can't, cut down.
2. Eat a balanced diet with plenty of fruit and vegetables.
3. Keep physically active.
4. Manage stress by, for example, talking things through, and making time to relax.
5. If you drink alcohol, do so in moderation.
6. Cover up in the sun, and protect children from sunburn.
7. Practise safe sex.
8. Use cancer-screening opportunities.
9. Be safe on the roads; follow the highway code.
10. Learn the first aid ABCs: airway, breathing, circulation.

Ten nontraditional, social tips for better health:

1. Don't be poor. If you can, stop. If you can't, try not to be poor for long.
2. Don't have poor parents.
3. Don't own a car.
4. Don't work in a stressful, low-paid manual job.
5. Don't live in damp, low-quality housing.
6. Be able to afford to go on a foreign holiday.
7. Practise not losing your job and don't become unemployed.
8. Use all benefits you are entitled to if you are unemployed, retired, or sick or have a disability.
9. Don't live next to a busy major road or near a polluting factory.
10. Learn how to fill in the complex housing benefit/asylum application forms before you become homeless and destitute.

SOURCE: D. Raphael, 2005, "Social Determinants of Health: Canadian Perspectives," Toronto: Canadian Scholars' Press, p. 13. Reprinted by permission of Canadian Scholars' Press Inc.

Debate continues regarding which of these factors—structural inequalities themselves, individual behaviours and lifestyle characteristics, material conditions and resources, or stress and other psychosocial factors—are important for an understanding of inequalities in health in later life. The answer may well be "all of the above." As one study notes, "material conditions are intimately tied to psychological states, health behaviors, and social circumstances that also influence health" and we can see "these psychosocial states and health behaviors . . . as responses to adverse conditions imposed by broader social and economic structures" (Lynch and Kaplan, 2000: 25).

INTERSECTING INEQUALITIES AND HEALTH OVER THE LIFE COURSE

When we think about age or gender or class or ethnic inequalities, we tend to think about each on its own. If we do consider them together, it is often to ask which dimension is the most important. For example, are racial inequalities really about social class or income inequalities rather than race? Also, what about gender differences, given that poverty in later life is often concentrated among women? Alternatively, we may wonder about the implications of adding one type of inequality to another. For example, are the health consequences of being old and poor as well as female worse than those associated with being old and poor but male? What happens when we add ethnic or racial minority group status to the mix?

Some argue that each factor has an impact and that experiencing more than one source of inequality will make the situation that much worse, an idea known as "multiple jeopardy." Others suggest that the factors cannot simply be added together. Instead, such features age and gender intersect so that one cannot be understood apart from the other. As a result, "the 'difference' between a young man and an old woman is greater than that between a young man and an old man" (Chappell et al., 2003: 95). What this means when it comes to health inequalities is that older women may respond differently from older men to economic or other factors that influence health (e.g., health behaviours, stressors). For example, it has often been found that women's health is more adversely affected by living in poverty than is the health of men (Prus and Gee, 2002). As a result, the greatest differences in life expectancy between men and women have been seen in the most deprived areas (DesMeules, Manuel, and Cho, 2004). Providing care to other family members also seems to be more important to the health of older women than men, while there are indications that smoking and alcohol consumption may have a greater impact on the health of older men (Denton and Walters, 1999). According to Popay and Bartley (1993: 31), "we need to ask why the experience of living on a low income . . . would have a different meaning for women than for men and in what ways these differences might explain the higher rates of morbidity that women report."

Intersections of age and other social determinants of health are also important to consider. Some factors seem to become more important in later life (e.g., smoking and other health behaviours) and to result in greater gaps or inequalities in health later in life. According to the Aboriginal Peoples Survey (Statistics Canada, 2003b), the gap in perceived health status of Aboriginal people and the total Canadian population widens in older age groups. Other factors appear to be less important in later life. For example, differences in health across socioeconomic groups become evident at the very beginning of life, contributing to what has been called "the first injustice" (Gortmaker and Wise, 1997; cited in Link and Phelan, 2000: 34). The gap in health between these groups seems to increase in size as people reach their middle years of life (40s–60s), followed by declines in old age (Martel, Bélanger, Berthelot, and Carrière, 2005). Does this mean that socioeconomic inequalities in health diminish with age? Perhaps, but this seems unlikely. Recall that many of those in poorer groups will already have died before they reach old age. Comparing the health status only of survivors ignores this fact.

The social and economic factors that influence health also change over time. Therefore, we need to adopt a **life course perspective** when focusing on health inequalities in later life. According to this per-

spective, what happens to health in later life is influenced by the circumstances evident in later life and by what took place earlier in life. Advantages and disadvantages experienced in early or mid-life may well have long-term health effects. For example, the low-income population can be said to consist of at least two distinct groups: those for whom poverty is a temporary experience (approximately one-half of those counted as poor at any one point in time) and those for whom it is a long-term or chronic experience (Finnie, 2000). Many university students exemplify the former; many older adults who live in low-income apartments exemplify the latter.

LINKING INEQUALITIES IN HEALTH TO HEALTH CARE

The answers we as a society give to questions about what causes health problems and inequalities will influence how we go about dealing with them. For example, if we see the health problems of older adults as the result of what happens only in later life, we will target our interventions to older adults. If we adopt a life course perspective and conclude that many of the health problems evident among older adults have their roots in lifelong experiences with poverty, inequality, and lack of access to social, economic, and other resources, we will want to address what happens earlier in life as well.

Other approaches have similar implications. If we attribute health problems to personal behaviours and see these as freely chosen, we will consider older adults responsible for their own health problems and will likely implement solutions aimed at educating people, hoping they will make different choices in future or demand people deal with the problems they themselves have created. Alternatively, if we attribute health inequalities to perceptions of stress, we may focus our energies on altering how people view their circumstances rather than changing those circumstances directly.

Finally, if we see the main determinants of health as lodged in how a society organizes and distributes economic and social resources, we will be more likely to direct attention to economic and social policies as a means of improving health (Raphael, 2005). As we have seen, most Canadians consider individual behaviours, like smoking, diet, and exercise, to be important determinants of health. Many also consider stress important. However, relatively few recognize the importance of a person's education (22 percent), income (22 percent), or the safety of the community in which they live (25 percent) (CPHI, 2005).

HEALTH CARE AND GLOBALIZATION

So far in this chapter, you have learned about the aging of Canada's population, including the fact that almost all of us can expect to live to old age. Although everyone hopes that they will not experience major health decline in old age, the reality is that physical health will deteriorate at some point. For most, it will do so gradually and they will adjust. In general, however, emotional and psychological health and overall satisfaction with life will not decline and might even improve. You have also learned about some of the tremendous diversity evident among those considered seniors—differences between the genders, differences between any number of subcultural groups, and differences based on socioeconomic status—and some of the consequences of these differences for individuals' health. Not surprisingly, given what we have just learned, our needs for health care vary depending on our problems and these are not homogeneous among all older people. But there is more to the story of health care than this: availability and access to health care also vary depending on your situation in life. This section of the chapter discusses care when health fails, focusing on Canada's health-care system.

SELF-CARE AND INFORMAL CARE

Before beginning the discussion of the health-care system, it is important to note that most people most of the time care for themselves. Sociologists refer to this as **self-care**. Self-care is the primary form of care even when health declines. Even when we require help from others and from the health-care system, we continue to provide care for ourselves in any number of ways, from washing our hands, exercising, and choosing what to eat, to establishing lifestyle practices, having a positive attitude toward life, and choosing health-care providers.

When we do need help from others, we do not turn first to our formal health-care system. Rather, we turn first to family and friends. This is as true in old age as it is when we are younger. Indeed, throughout our history, our network of family and friends, also

referred to as the informal network, has been the first resort for care when we need assistance.

Despite what you may hear about modern, Western societies, such as Canada and the United States, being individualistic, youth-oriented, and dismissive of their older members, Westerners tend to provide care to senior members of their families as they grow older and their needs for care increase. It has been estimated that in virtually all developed countries, irrespective of what type of health-care system they have and whether or not they have universal health care, approximately 75 percent of all care that is provided to seniors comes from the informal network, primarily from family members (Kane, 1990). It is, first of all, the spouse who provides care when the health of the other spouse fails. Typically, it is the wife who is the first to provide care to her husband. This is because men have a shorter life expectancy than women and women tend to marry men a few years older than themselves. As a

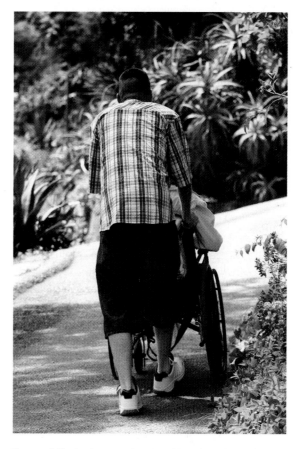

Responsibility for the care of seniors falls to an informal network of family members in virtually all developed countries, regardless of what type of health-care system is available.
SOURCE: Shutterstock.

result, the husband's health often begins to fail before that of his wife and his wife usually is available and able to care for him in his last years.

After the husband's death, the wife may enjoy a few more years of good health and then her health often fails to the point where she needs assistance. In this situation, it tends to be her children, typically daughters, who provide most of the care before her death. You will notice that informal caring comes primarily from women, from wives and daughters. Daughters provide most of the emotional support and the hands-on caring to their mothers. Sons primarily provide financial assistance and advice. However, if there is no daughter available or geographically proximate but there is a son close by, then the son usually steps in and provides the necessary care (Chappell, 1992; Keating, Fast, Frederick, Cranswick, and Perrier, 1999). This is possible because the vast majority of seniors live close to at least one child.

Furthermore, it seems that families want to provide this care. They provide it willingly and they do not want to give it up. The myth that seniors in modern-day Western societies are abandoned by their families has been put to rest over the last two decades by social gerontological research (Montgomery, Borgatta, and Borgatta, 2000). Moreover, despite what we have been hearing for many years about changing family forms, more and more women working in the paid labour force, fewer children being available to provide help, and greater geographic mobility, there is no indication that families are decreasing their involvement in senior care.

FORMAL MEDICAL AND HOME CARE

Sometimes the health of their loved one deteriorates sufficiently that families cannot provide all of the care themselves. Sometimes too much care is needed and sometimes it calls for specialized knowledge and skills or for specialized medicines and equipment that only physicians can prescribe. When this happens, we turn to the health-care system and its many formal services. Canada's health-care system, like those of most other developed countries (the United States is a major exception), offers universal access to physician and acute care hospital services for its citizens based on need. In Canada, this system is known as medicare.

In Canada, health care is a provincial government responsibility. The federal government assists with funding these services, but it is the responsibility of each province to deliver the services. Through medicare, every province offers physician and acute care hospital services at no out-of-pocket costs to its residents. That is, these services are publicly funded. But this does not mean that we have socialized medicine. Rather, a third party, our government, pays for these services on our behalf. Most physicians in Canada operate as private entrepreneurs, paid by the government for the services that they decide are necessary and that they render. The more services they provide, the more they earn. The difference between their jobs and those of other private entrepreneurs is that their incomes are virtually guaranteed. They hold this privileged position because of the importance society attaches to their specialized expertise, an expertise that makes them the gatekeepers to our health-care system. Only physicians can order medical tests, admit us to hospital, and certify that we are sick.

The availability of many other types of health care, such as long-term care institutions (nursing homes), physiotherapy, home nursing, counselling, chiropractic services, podiatry, and massage therapy, varies across provinces. Some provinces provide these services as part of their provincial health-care system at no cost to the user, while others provide them at minimal cost or on a means-tested basis (i.e., your finances are assessed and if you can afford to pay for a service that you are deemed to require for your health needs, you pay for it yourself; otherwise, the government will either partially or totally subsidize the cost of the service). How these services are accessed (for example, whether you need a physician referral or you can self-refer) also differs across provinces. Services can also vary across jurisdictions and regions within a province.

Although any or all health services may be important to different individuals at different times depending on what their health needs are, one type of health service is particularly important for an aging society. It is usually referred to as home care and includes services that are brought into people's homes to help them live there, rather than move to a nursing home. Almost everyone, including seniors, prefers to stay in their own homes in the community rather than move to long-term care facilities.

Typically, home care includes such services as home nursing, home physiotherapy, and homemaking services. Homemaking is considered a health service because as seniors become more and more frail, they are often unable to do heavy housework or to do it only at the risk of causing serious injury to themselves. For some services, such as adult daycare, the person leaves the home temporarily, for a few hours one or two days a week. These services offer socialization and stimulation and, importantly, often provide necessary respite for family members who may be providing around-the-clock care. It is important to note that home care is not primarily about providing medical care. There are some exceptions, such as home nursing care, but important components of home care, notably homemaking, are not medical services. Instead, it provides social care, a type of care that typically we provide for ourselves until we are unable to do so.

Why is it critical that sufficient and adequate home care services are provided for seniors? These services allow seniors to remain independent in their own homes in the community. Importantly, scientific research has demonstrated that maintaining seniors in their own homes is not only their preference but it is also cost effective when compared with maintaining these individuals in nursing homes (Chappell, Havens, Hollander, Miller, and McWilliam, 2004; Hollander and Chappell, 2001). For many seniors, staying in their own homes requires not only home care but also the presence of an informal caregiver. If an informal caregiver (unpaid) is not available, their only option may be to go to a nursing home.

Researchers in British Columbia have had the opportunity to compare health regions within the province that changed their regulations with regard to offering homemaking services. In the mid-1990s, the B.C. government suggested that health regions stop providing this service if it was the only service the client needed. Some regions did so; others did not. Hollander and Chappell (2001) compared the use of health-care services by clients in regions that followed these instructions with those that did not. They reported that clients who had this service cut were more likely to die, and if they survived, they were more likely to be admitted to hospital or to a nursing home and therefore to cost the system more than was true of those who continued with the homemaking service. Importantly, these differences did not begin to show up until two years after the cuts; they were more pronounced three years after the cuts.

Despite its importance historically, home care has received relatively little governmental funding. This continues to be the case. Home care is very much the poor cousin to medical care within the health-care system. The medical focus is entrenched within medicare (physicians and acute care hospitals) whereas home care lies outside medicare. This has important consequences because it means that the availability of home care services (that is, what is actually provided) varies from jurisdiction to jurisdiction (both provincial and regional). It can be, and often is, provided at a cost to the patient by for-profit companies. It can also be provided publicly as part of the public health-care system or as a mix of the two. At the present time, most provinces favour an approximate 50/50 mix of for-profit and nonprofit home care agencies.

HEALTH-CARE SYSTEM CHANGE AND REFORM

It is important to understand the biomedical focus within Western health-care systems. The clearest indicator of this focus is the fact that medicare, our national health-care program, provides universal coverage only of physician and acute care hospital services. Physicians are the gatekeepers to our system and to public health care dollars. They control access to hospitals, medical tests, and prescription drugs. Without denying the importance and value of medical care or of physicians, reviews of the health-care system carried out in the 1990s in Canada (and virtually all other developed countries) concluded that it needed to refocus on a broader conception of health that included more than a biomedical perspective. That is, it should also recognize psychological, emotional, and social aspects of health (World Health Organization, 1948). In Canada, federal and provincial task force reports released during the 1990s recommended broadening the definition of health away from only disease and incorporating a health promotion and disease prevention emphasis. They also argued for the need to deinstitutionalize health services and provide more care outside hospitals, closer to home and to the community. Canada's current health-care system focuses on illness after it has arisen rather than focusing on preventing it from occurring in the first place. It also deals with it in a primarily medical way and in medical settings. Anything that lies outside medicare is not protected—the service may not be offered at all, or if it is, it may not be offered through the public system.

Public spending on health care since the 1990s has not expanded in the directions recommended by health reform. Canadian research does indicate a decreased supply of acute and extended care beds, decreases in hospital admissions and hospital lengths of stay, and shifts of surgical treatment to out-patient settings (Brownell, Roose, and Roos, 2001; Carriere, Roos, and Dover, 2000). In addition, it appears that community-based home care budgets are increasing but the funds are going to short term post-hospital and nursing care rather than to meet the long-term chronic care needs of seniors (Penning, Roos, Chappell, Roos, and Lin, 2002). Increased demand for intensive short-term post-hospital care is a result of the shortened lengths of stays and increases in out-patient surgeries performed by hospitals. A recent federal Commission on the Future of Health Care in Canada (2002; called the Romanow Report) argued that short-term post-hospital care, that is, short-term home care, should be part of Canadian medicare; it provides care that used to be provided in hospitals but now, technologically and pharmaceutically, can be provided in the home.

However, the Romanow Report did not discuss the needs of seniors who, it will be recalled, suffer primarily from degenerative chronic conditions. Medicine does not have cures for chronic conditions. The enhancement of short-term post-hospital home care reinforces a medical focus of care and demonstrates Canada's lack of support for a broader social model of care that acknowledges the needs of those with chronic conditions. The lack of understanding of the need for enhanced long-term home care services for an aging society is tied to the internationalization of capital, often referred to as globalization.

GLOBALIZATION

Globalization has become a shorthand term used to refer to a cluster of related changes occurring throughout the world. Of interest here is economic globalization, referring to the growing power and mobility of capital (wealth, including money or property) in production and financial markets (Helvacioglu, 2000). The globalization of the economy includes the growth of transnational networks of investment, finance, advertising and consumption markets, and sophisticated information and communications technologies. Part of the current trend toward globalization is increased emphasis on *profitization* (i.e., profit-making as distinct from privatization, which can include nonprofit private organizations). The

increased pressure toward a for-profit ideology has been embraced by the health-care sector. For example, Mendelson and Divinsky (2000) note that hospitals in the United States increased their aggregate profits by 25 percent in 1996 alone—hospitals had become big business. By the end of the 1990s private American hospitals were looking to Canada to expand.

Canada is under pressure to be part of the great global economy that is increasingly considered the solution to every country's economic and financial crises. In 1998, the World Health Organization argued that countries resisting globalization "will find themselves marginalized in the world community and in the world economy" (Navarro, 2002). The particular type of global economy that is being promoted favours privatization, deregulation, decreases in welfare programs and public services, and liberalization of trade and monetary policies. State regulation of the labour market is considered bad; social protection guaranteed by the welfare state is considered bad; redistributing wealth from haves to have-nots is considered bad; any state intervention in regulating foreign trade or international financial markets is considered bad. Since this move toward economic globalization has begun, the gap between the rich and poor has widened, unemployment has increased, social expenditures by governments have decreased, working-class rights and unions have been undermined, and new jobs tend to be part-time and home-based, and involve self-employment, temporary work, and contracting out with no job security and few benefits (Coburn, 2002).

The changes that have been taking place in Canada's health-care system (such as shortened hospital lengths of stay, removal of beds from the system, and the decimation of long-term chronic home care) have been occurring within this climate of globalization and the commodification and privatization of health-care services. Armstrong, Armstrong, and Coburn (2001) show that the proportion of private funding financing within Canada's total health-care system is increasing. Increases in out-patient surgeries and the shifting of post-surgical care into the community also provide opportunities for these types of services to be taken over by private for-profit corporations that form part of multinational corporations headquartered outside of Canada (Williams, Dever, Baranek, and Gildiner, 2001). When this happens, profits usually leave the country.

Increased profitization of Canada's health services is especially problematic because, under the North

American Free Trade Agreement (NAFTA), once the Canadian government allows for-profit business to enter into an area that was once within the public sector, returning it to the public sector becomes all but impossible. Under the terms and conditions of NAFTA, we can do so only if we provide compensation to for-profit firms for their lost future profits. This is why the Romanow Report (2002) devoted an entire chapter to this topic, arguing that Canada must, at every opportunity, state publicly that our health-care services are not included in NAFTA. To date, our government has not been making such statements.

As more of our health-care services are privatized, more people with health-care needs are going to be disadvantaged. The inequalities in health and illness noted earlier will be accompanied by similar disadvantages in receiving needed care. That is, access to needed care will vary systematically with class, gender, race, and ethnic inequalities in health. With fewer options available, those without economic resources to purchase health services will do without or will rely on self-care or informal care from family and friends, often within the household

(Arber and Ginn, 1991). Lack of access to formal care services places greater burden on family caregivers who, as you have learned, are disproportionately women. In this way, health reforms of this nature lead to a greater burden being put on the shoulders of family members.

In addition, for-profit health care tends to be more expensive than universal public schemes. For-profit health care costs governments less, but those who use the services pay more. Much of the increased cost comes from administrative "overhead" charges (Marmor and Sullivan, 2000). A for-profit system also leaves many citizens without any insurance. Research has amply demonstrated that Canada's public medicare system provides care to those in need (Broyles, Manga, Binder, Angus, and Charette, 1983). Those with lower incomes, seniors and women, receive more services because their needs are greater.

Ultimately, whether you support privatization of the health-care system or not, it has consequences for Canadians. Current trends toward market-style economic globalization are not supporting a type of health-care system that is appropriate for an aging

SOURCE: Graham Harrop, *Vancouver Sun,* September 20, 2001, and the Simon Fraser University Editorial Cartoons Collection (http://edocs.lib.sfu.ca/projects/Cartoons/). © Graham Harrop.

society—that is, one that includes medical care along with a strong emphasis on an expanded long-term home care program that includes social services for seniors. They are leading to a dismantling of many existing services. By shrinking public involvement in this area and expanding opportunities for profitization, existing differentials in health-care needs are being translated into additional disadvantages in receiving required health-care services. These conse-

quences are being disproportionately felt by disadvantaged seniors and by the families who care for them. Globalization can be allowed to exploit people or it can be used to promote democracy. One indication of a civil society is how it cares for its seniors; this includes its health-care system. That is why Canadian politician Ed Broadbent (2002) argues for "a market economy not a market society," wherein we have both individual liberty and social equality.

SUMMARY

1. The health and longevity of the Canadian population has been increasing in recent decades. Although this could be considered a positive feature of modern society, it is frequently regarded as a social problem. Older adults are seen as overly dependent on health and social services and, consequently, responsible for the crisis in our health-care system and depriving other generations of their fair share of the nation's limited resources. Sociologists have referred to this type of thinking as apocalyptic demography and suggest that we consider whose interests are served by promoting this view of an aging society; the older population is not the primary source of increases in health-care costs. Increase in the number of elderly people who need to access social programs appears to be offset by decline in the proportion of younger people in the population.

2. Health is about more than the presence or absence of disease and, in contrast to generally accepted beliefs, not all aspects of health status decline as we age. Older adults generally assess their health in positive terms and have good mental health and social well-being.

3. Despite the overall picture of good health in old age, in Canada, significant inequalities in health exist. They are associated with socioeconomic position, gender, race, and ethnicity. Past increases in health and longevity have been concentrated in more advantaged social groups. Aboriginal and immigrant seniors, older women, and the poor continue to experience major health inequalities. It is generally believed that tomorrow's older adult population will be better educated and in better health than the older adults of today. In Canada, inequalities are widening, and the situation may not improve in the near future.

4. Health-related inequalities have been attributed to individual health behaviours and lifestyle factors; psychosocial factors, such as stress; and material conditions and resources. Research findings suggest that economic circumstances, living conditions, and other material factors are the most important and that, to a large extent, health-related lifestyles (e.g., diet, exercise, drinking patterns) and stress levels reflect these conditions.

5. We tend to equate health care with medical care generally provided by physicians located in clinics or hospitals. However, the most common forms of health care consist not of medical and hospital care, but rather of self-care and informal care, generally provided by family members. When it comes to formal health-care services, home care is particularly important to the health and well-being of older adults, yet it is not included in Canada's nationally insured health-care system (medicare).

6. Increased emphasis is being placed on privatization and profit-making within Canada's health-care system, particularly when it comes to services that are most important to older adults. The implications are that those most in need of care will be least likely to access it and the most likely to have to rely on themselves and family members for care.

QUESTIONS TO CONSIDER

1. Choose any societal myth about old age and discuss the reality in Canada.
2. What are the arguments against apocalyptic demography?
3. How can we account for inequalities in health among older adults in Canada?
4. How well does Canada's health-care system currently meet the health-care needs of its older population?
5. What are some of the possible consequences of economic globalization for Canada's health-care system?

GLOSSARY

To **blame the victim** is the tendency to hold victims of various negative events or situations (e.g., ill health) completely or partially responsible for what has happened to them.

Demography is the study of human population size, structure, and distribution, and of how populations change over time in association with changes in fertility, mortality, and migration.

The **dependency ratio** is the ratio of the economically dependent portion of the population to the economically productive portion. It is often calculated as the number of people too young to work (<18 years of age) plus the number who are retired (aged 65+) relative to those likely to be in the work force (aged 18–64).

The **hierarchy stress perspective** is an approach to understanding health inequalities that emphasizes the stress associated with occupying a lower position in the social hierarchy and its negative impact on health.

The **life course perspective** is a theoretical perspective within gerontology that draws attention to the interplay between individual life course change and larger societal changes.

Life expectancy is the number of years that the average person can expect to live.

The **modified extended family** is a family type characterized by mutual and close intergenerational ties, responsible behaviour on the part of adult children, and contact between the generations.

Self-care is the range of activities that individuals undertake to enhance health, prevent disease, and restore health. They may be undertaken by individuals acting on their own or in conjunction with professionals.

SUGGESTED READING

Armstrong, Pat, Hugh Armstrong, and David Coburn. (2001). *Unhealthy Times: Political Economy Perspectives on Health and Care in Canada.* Toronto: Oxford University Press. This collection of papers uses a political economy perspective to explore reforms that influence our health and health care.

Bolaria, B. Singh, and Harley Dickinson. (2002). *Health, Illness, and Health Care in Canada* (3rd ed.). Scarborough, ON: Nelson Thomson Learning. This book provides an interesting collection of articles written from a sociological perspective and examining key issues in the areas of health, illness, and health care.

Chappell Neena L., Ellen Gee, Lynn McDonald, and Michael Stones. (2003). *Aging in Contemporary Canada.* Toronto: Pearson Education Canada. This comprehensive introduction to the area of aging covers such topics as demography, theory, and social research methods; issues of health and well-being; the involvement of social institutions in the aging process; and the realities of social policy regarding aging in Canada.

Novak, Mark, and Lori Campbell. (2006). *Aging and Society: A Canadian Perspective* (5th ed). Toronto: Thomson Nelson. This text is a readable introduction to aging within the context of Canadian social institutions.

Segall, Alexander, and Neena L. Chappell. (2000). *Health and Health Care in Canada.* Toronto: Pearson Education Canada. This book provides a sociological examination of health and health care in the Canadian context.

WEB RESOURCES

Companion Web Site for This Book

http://www.newsociety5e.nelson.com

Begin by clicking on the Student Resources section of the website. Next, select the chapter you are studying from the pull-down menu. From the Student Resources page, you have easy access to InfoTrac College Edition® and other resources, such as the Glossary and Flashcards. The website also has many useful tips to aid you in your study of sociology.

InfoTrac College Edition Search Terms

Visit http://www.infotrac-college.com for access to more than 20 million articles from nearly 6000 sources when doing your online research.

ThomsonNOW™

http://hed.nelson.com

This online diagnostic tool identifies each student's unique needs with a Pretest that generates a personalized Study Plan for each chapter, helping students focus on concepts they are having the most difficulty mastering. Students then take a Posttest after reading the chapter to measure their understanding of the material. An Instructor Gradebook is available to track and monitor student progress.

CHAPTER EIGHTEEN

Politics and Social Movements

In this chapter you will learn that

- The level of democracy in a society depends on the capacity of citizens to influence the state through their support of political parties, social movements, and other groups. That capacity increases as power becomes more widely distributed in society.

- The degree to which power is widely distributed influences the success of particular kinds of parties and policies.

- People sometimes riot, strike, and take other forms of collective action to correct perceived injustices. When they do so, they are participating in social movements.

- People are more inclined to rebel against the status quo when they are bound by close social ties to other people who feel similarly wronged and when they have the money and other resources needed to protest.

- For social movements to grow, members must make the activities, ideas, and goals of the movement congruent with the interests, beliefs, and values of potential new recruits.

- The history of democracy is a struggle for the acquisition of constantly broadening citizenship rights.

Robert J. Brym
UNIVERSITY OF TORONTO

INTRODUCTION

I almost caused a small riot once. It happened in Grade 11, shortly after I learned that water combined with sulphur dioxide produces sulphurous acid. The news shocked me. To understand why, you have to know where I lived: in Saint John, New Brunswick, about 100 metres downwind of one of the larger pulp and paper mills in Canada. Acrid waves of sulphur dioxide billowed day and night from the mill's imposing smokestacks. The town's pervasive rotten-egg smell was a longstanding complaint in the area. But, for me, disgust turned to upset when I realized the fumes were toxic. Suddenly it was clear why many people I knew—especially people living near the mill—woke up in the morning with a kind of "smoker's cough." By the simple act of breathing we were causing the gas to mix with the moisture in our bodies and form an acid that our lungs tried to expunge, with only partial success.

Twenty years later, I read the results of a medical research report showing that area residents suffer from rates of lung disease, including emphysema and lung cancer, significantly above the national average.

However, even in 1968 it was evident a serious problem was brewing in my hometown. I therefore hatched a plan. Our high school was about to hold its annual model parliament. The event was notoriously boring, partly because, year in, year out, virtually everyone voted for the same party, the Conservatives. But here was an issue, I thought, that could turn things around. The pulp and paper mill was owned by K.C. Irving, an industrialist so powerful that his companies were said to control 40 percent of New Brunswick's economic output. *Forbes* magazine in the United States annually ranked Irving among the wealthiest men in the world. I figured that once I told my fellow students the political implications of the fact that water combined with sulphur dioxide produces sulphurous acid, they would quickly demand the closure of the mill until Irving guaranteed a clean operation.

Was *I* naïve. As head of the tiny Liberal Party, I had to address the entire student body during assembly on election day to outline the party platform and mobilize votes. When I got to the part of my speech explaining why K.C. Irving was our enemy, the murmuring in the audience, which had been

Nineteen sixty-eight was a year of student rebellion worldwide.
SOURCE: ©Bettmann/Corbis.

growing like the sound of a hungry animal about to pounce on its prey, erupted into loud "boos." A couple of students rushed the stage. The principal suddenly appeared from the wings and commanded the student body to settle down. He then took me by the arm and informed me that, for my own safety, my speech was finished. So, I discovered on election day, was our high school's Liberal Party. And so, it emerged, was my high school political career.

This incident troubled me for many years, less because of the embarrassment it caused me than because of the puzzles it presented. Why did I almost cause a small riot? Why didn't my fellow students rebel in the way I thought they would? Why did they continue to support an arrangement that was enriching one man at the cost of a community's health? Why weren't they enraged? Couldn't they see the injustice? Other people did. Nineteen sixty-eight was not just the year of my political failure at Saint John High School. It was also the year that student riots in France nearly caused the fall of the government of Charles de Gaulle. It was the year in which the suppression of student strikes by the Mexican government left dozens of students dead. It was the year in which American students at Berkeley, Michigan, and other universities fought with unprecedented vigour for free speech on their campuses, an end to American involvement in the war in Vietnam, increased civil rights for American blacks, and an expanded role for women in public affairs.

I didn't know it at the time, but by asking why students in Paris, Mexico City, and Berkeley rebelled while my fellow students did not, I was raising the main question that animates the sociological study of politics

and social movements. Why are some groups more successful than others in formulating their demands and getting them carried out? In other words, who gets what and under what social circumstances? That is the main issue addressed by this chapter.

Power is the ability of an individual or a group to impose its will on others, even if they resist (Weber, 1946 [1922]: 180). In the first section of this chapter, you will learn that the power of a group may be widely recognized as legitimate or valid under some circumstances. If it is, raw power becomes legitimate **authority** (see Box 18.1). The people who occupy the command posts of institutions are then generally seen as **authorities.** Under other circumstances, however, power flows to nonauthorities. This undermines the legitimacy of authority. In this case, nonauthorities form **social movements,** or collective attempts to change part or all of the social order. They may riot, petition, strike, demonstrate, and establish pressure groups, unions, and **political parties** (organizations that seek to control state power) to achieve their aims.

The terms defined above allow us to distinguish between "normal politics" and "politics beyond the rules." Normal politics is politics as it is practised when authorities are firmly in power. Politics beyond the rules is politics as it is practised when the legitimacy of authority grows weak. Sociologists have proposed various theories to explain the two types of politics. In the second and third sections of this chapter, I evaluate these theories using mainly Canadian data.

Finally, in the chapter's concluding section, I place our discussion in historical context. How has politics developed over the past 300 years? What

---

BOX 18.1   THREE BASES OF AUTHORITY

Max Weber (1947) argued that authority can have one of three bases:
1. *Traditional authority:* Particularly in tribal and feudal societies, rulers inherit authority through family or clan ties. In such circumstances, people believe the right of a family or clan to monopolize leadership derives from God's will.
2. *Legal-rational authority:* In modern societies, authority derives from respect for the law. Laws specify how one can achieve office. People generally believe these laws are rational. If someone achieves office by following these laws, their authority is respected.
3. *Charismatic authority:* Sometimes, extraordinary, charismatic individuals challenge traditional or legal-rational authority. They claim to be inspired by God or some higher principle that transcends traditional authority, such as the principle that all people are created equal. Their claim is widely believed. Charismatic figures often emerge during a **political revolution,** a concerted attempt by many people to overthrow political institutions and establish new ones. Political revolutions take place when widespread and successful movements of opposition clash with crumbling traditional or legal-rational authority (Skocpol, 1979).

developments can we reasonably expect in the near future? This section will help you better to understand your political options in coming years.

POWER FROM ABOVE: NORMAL POLITICS

In 1998, the RCMP used pepper spray to disperse Vancouver crowds demonstrating against visiting Indonesian President Suharto. The incident caused a scandal because it was widely seen as excessive use of force sanctioned by the prime minister. The solicitor general, who is responsible for the RCMP, was forced to resign over the incident.

This incident illustrates the use of **force** or coercive power by authorities. Paradoxically, the use of force by authorities is a sign of their weakness: If authorities are truly in a position of strength, their rule will be widely recognized as legitimate. They will not need to use force to impose their will because most people agree with their policies. Here, politics will be routine, nonviolent, or "normal." To be sure, minor outbursts of violence occur even under normal politics. However, such events are unusual in Canada today. They rarely result in fatalities. For the most part, Canadian politics today is normal politics.

Power is exercised in all social settings, from the family to the classroom to the workplace. However, the ultimate seat of power in society is the state. The **state** is a set of institutions that formulate and carry out a country's laws, policies, and binding regulations. Why is the state's power "ultimate?" Because its authority stands above all others, and if the state needs to use force to maintain order or protect its borders, most people will regard its actions as legitimate.

In democratic countries, such as Canada, the government is formed by the elected members of the political party that wins the most seats in a general election (see Figure 18.1). It comprises the head of the party, who becomes prime minister, and the cabinet ministers whom the prime minister selects to advise him or her. It is the job of the government to initiate policies, propose laws, and see that they are enforced. That is why the government is also called the *executive* branch of the state. Proposed laws are turned into operating statutes by the *legislature*, which consists of all the people elected to Parliament. It is the responsibility of the *judiciary* or court system to interpret laws and regulations, that is, to figure out whether and how particular laws and regulations apply in disputed cases. The state's *administrative*

FIGURE 18.1 THE INSTITUTIONS OF STATE AND CIVIL SOCIETY

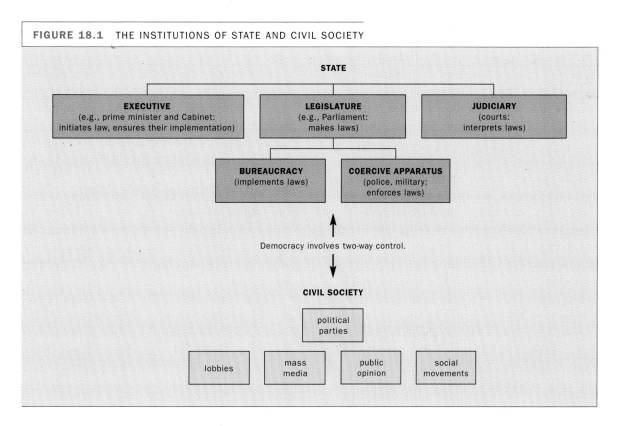

apparatus or *bureaucracy* undertakes enforcement of laws. If laws are broken or the state's security is jeopardized, it is the role of the *coercive apparatus*—the police and military—to enforce the law and protect the state.

The state, then, is a set of institutions that exercise control over society. However, individuals in **civil society,** the private sphere of life, also exercise control over the state through a variety of organizations and institutions. We have already noted how social movements may influence the state. In addition, the mass media are supposed to keep a watchful and critical eye on the state and help keep the public informed about the quality of government. Pressure groups or "lobbies" are formed by trade unions, manufacturers' associations, ethnic groups, and other organizations to advise politicians of their members' desires. Lobbies also remind politicians how much their members' votes and campaign contributions matter. Finally, political parties regularly seek to mobilize voters as they compete for control of government.

How democratic is the Canadian state? Does the interaction between state and civil society ensure that every citizen has a roughly equal say in the determination of laws and policies? Or, as George Orwell asked in *Animal Farm*, are some citizens more equal than others? Do we, as Abraham Lincoln claimed for the Americans, enjoy "government of the people, by the people, for the people?" Or is it more accurate to say, in the words of one wit, that we are subjected to "government of the people, by the lawyers, for the business owners"? These are among the chief questions asked by sociologists who study the state and its operations. It is now time to consider them in greater detail.

PLURALIST THEORY

Pluralist theory is one interpretation of the relationship between state and civil society (Polsby, 1959; Dahl, 1961). According to pluralists, we live in a heterogeneous society with many competing interests and centres of power. For example, the interests of parents with school-age children may differ from the interests of pensioners. Parents may want school budgets to grow. Pensioners may want them to shrink. Because of such heterogeneity, no one group can control politics, according to the pluralists. They argue that, over time, all voters and interest groups influence the political process almost equally. Sometimes one category of voters wins a political battle, some-

times another. Most often, however, politics involves negotiation and compromise among competing groups. According to the pluralists, because no one group of people is always able to control the political agenda or the outcome of political conflict, democracy is guaranteed.

ELITE THEORY

Elite theorists, C. Wright Mills (1956) foremost among them, sharply disagree with the pluralist account. *Elites* are small groups that occupy the command posts of a society's institutions. In the United States, the country that Mills studied, the most powerful elites are the people who run the country's several hundred biggest corporations, the executive branch of government, and the military. Mills wrote that the men who control these institutions (they are almost all men) make the important decisions that profoundly affect members of society. Moreover, they do so without much regard for elections or public opinion.

Mills showed how the corporate, state, and military elites are interconnected. People move from one elite to another over their careers. Their children intermarry. They maintain intimate social contacts on a day-to-day basis. They tend to be recruited from the upper-middle and upper classes. However, Mills denied that these similarities and interconnections turn the three elites into a **ruling class,** that is, a self-conscious and cohesive group of people, led by corporate executives, who act to advance their common interests. The three elites are independent of each other, Mills insisted. They may see eye-to-eye on many issues, but each has its own jealously guarded sphere of influence, and conflict between elite groups is therefore frequent (Mills, 1956: 277).

The Elitist Critique of Pluralism

Most political sociologists today question the pluralist account of democratic politics because research has established the existence of large, persistent, wealth-based inequalities in political influence and political participation.

John Porter's classic, *The Vertical Mosaic* (1965), was the first in a series of Canadian studies that demonstrate the weaknesses of pluralism and corroborate some aspects of elite theory (Brym, 1989; Clement, 1975; Olsen, 1980). These studies show that a disproportionately large number of people in

TABLE 18.1 FEDERAL POLITICAL CONTRIBUTORS PER 10 000 TAX FILERS, BY INCOME AND REGION

ANNUAL INCOME	ATLANTIC	QUEBEC	ONTARIO	WEST	CANADA
Less than $25 000	21	17	34	80	42
$25 000–$50 000	126	73	126	253	150
$50 000–$75 000	429	242	304	467	353
$75 000+	1149	679	790	964	830

SOURCE: Based on Jeffrey Frank, "Voting and Contributing: Political Participation in Canada," *Canadian Social Trends*, Vol. 2, Toronto: Thompson Educational Publishing, Inc., 1994, p. 337.

Canada's political and other elites come from upper- and upper-middle-class families. For example, about 40 percent of Canadian prime ministers, premiers, and Cabinet ministers were born into the richest 10 percent of families in the country (Olsen, 1980: 129). In their youth, members of Canada's elites are likely to have attended expensive private schools. As adults, they tend to marry the offspring of other elite members and belong to exclusive private clubs. In the course of their careers, they often move from one elite to another. Arguably, people with this sort of background cannot act dispassionately on behalf of all Canadians, rich and poor.

Controversy persists over whether Canada's elites form a ruling class. Porter (1965), noting frequent conflict among elites, argued against the view that a ruling class controls Canada. His top students disagreed. They argued that the interests of large corporations dominate Canadian political life (Clement, 1975; Olsen, 1980). However, both Porter and his students did agree on one point: Contrary to pluralist claims, Canada's well-to-do consistently exercise disproportionate influence over political life in this country.

Studies of political participation in Canada add weight to the elitist view (Blais, Gidengil, Nadeau, and Nevitte, 1997; Frank, 1994; Mishler, 1979: 88–97). Many surveys show that political involvement decreases with social class. For example, the likelihood of voting falls with a person's class position. The likelihood of phoning or writing a member of Parliament, helping a candidate in an election campaign, contributing money to a political party, and running for office declines even more steeply as we move down the class hierarchy (see Table 18.1). As intensity of political participation declines, so does political influence. Consequently, although political apathy and cynicism are high among Canadians, the poorest Canadians are

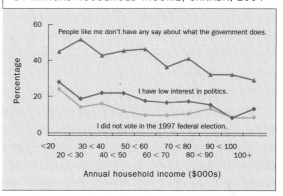

FIGURE 18.2 POLITICAL APATHY AND CYNICISM, BY ANNUAL HOUSEHOLD INCOME, CANADA, 2004

SOURCE: Canada Election Survey, 2004 (2005). Reprinted by permission of Professor Andre Blais.

the most politically apathetic and cynical. They have less interest in politics than do the well-to-do, and they are more likely to think that government does not care what they think (see Figure 18.2). As one of the world's leading political sociologists writes: "The combination of a low vote and a relative lack of organization among the lower-status groups means that they will suffer from neglect by the politicians who will be receptive to the wishes of the more privileged, participating, and organized strata" (Lipset, 1981: 226–27).

The Marxist Critique of Elite Theory

Although compelling in some respects, elite theory has its critics, Marxists foremost among them. Some Marxists, known as "instrumentalists," deny that elites enjoy more or less equal power. Actually, they say, elites form a ruling class dominated by big business. From their point of view, the state is an arm (or "instrument") of the business elite. Big business gains control of the state in three main ways. First, members of wealthy families occupy important state positions in highly disproportionate numbers. Second, government officials rely mainly on the representatives of big business for advice. Third, political parties rely mainly on big business for financial support. According to some Marxists, members of different elites may disagree about specific issues. However, as a result of the three control mechanisms listed above, they always agree about one issue: the need to maintain the health of the capitalist system (Miliband, 1973 [1969]).

A second group of Marxists, known as "structuralists," offers a somewhat different interpretation of why the state in capitalist society is necessarily biased in favour of big business. For the structuralists, it is not so much the social origins of high government officials or the social ties linking them with big business that encourages the state to act with a pro-capitalist bias. Rather, they argue, the capitalist state acts as an arm of big business because it is constrained to do so by the nature of the capitalist system itself. For example, if the Canadian government doubled the corporate tax rate, investment would be redirected to countries with regimes that are kinder to company profits. Such a move would cost Canada jobs and prosperity. It would be highly unpopular. The government could easily fall. Fearing such outcomes, governments in capitalist societies find their field of action restricted to policies that ensure the well-being of big business. According to the structuralists, it is the very fact that the state is embedded in a capitalist system that forces it to act in this way (Poulantzas, 1975 [1968]).

It follows from both the instrumentalist and the structuralist positions that ordinary citizens, and especially members of the working class, rarely have much influence over state policy. According to Marxists, true democracy can emerge only if members of the working class and their supporters overthrow capitalism and establish a socialist system in which economic differences between people are eliminated or at least substantially reduced.

POWER-BALANCE THEORY

Pluralists assume that all major groups in society enjoy approximately equal power. Elitists assume that members of the upper class enjoy most power. Both approaches, however, assume that the distribution of power in society does not change much over time, except in those rare instances when revolutions take place.

Karl Marx predicted that capitalism would drive small business owners into bankruptcy and peasants into cities. Marx thought that in the cities huge masses of workers would become class-conscious and socialism would be born.
SOURCE: Diego M. Rivera, *Parade in Moscow* (1956). 135.2 × 108.3 cm. Collection Banco National de Mexico, Mexico City. Reproduced with permission of the bank.

In contrast, **power-balance theorists** argue that the distribution of power in society changes significantly more frequently. They admit that power is usually concentrated in the hands of the wealthy. However, they also note that other classes sometimes gain power. This has big implications for political life. Among other things, the distribution of power determines how democratic a society is.

To make their case, power-balance theorists first measure variations in the social distribution of power. They then show how those variations are reflected in the successes and failures of different political parties and the rejection and adoption of different state policies. Along with the pluralists, they recognize that society is truly democratic only when power is widely distributed. Along with the elitists, they recognize that society is not very democratic when power is highly concentrated in the hands of a few wealthy citizens. However, by

The peak year of strike activity in Canada was 1919. In that year, 17.3 strikes took place for every 100 000 nonagricultural workers in the country. This photo was taken on "Bloody Saturday," June 21, 1919, during the Winnipeg General Strike. It shows a violent confrontation between rioters and Mounties and special police.

SOURCE: David Miller Collection/National Archives of Canada/C-33392.

treating the distribution of power as a variable, they improve our understanding of the relationship between power and democracy.

We can better understand power-balance theory by examining Canadian politics in comparative perspective. We first note that a group's power is partly determined by the degree to which it forms organizations to further its interests. For example, unionized blue-collar and white-collar workers are more powerful than their nonunionized counterparts. That is because unions allow workers to speak with one voice. Unions enable workers to effectively bargain with employers and governments for improved wages, working conditions, and social policies. Moreover, if bargaining fails, they can go out on strike to force the issue.

If level of unionization increases working-class power, that should be reflected in the political behaviour of citizens and the policies adopted by governments. And, in fact, it is. Compare Sweden and Canada, for example (Casper, McLanahan, and Garfinkle, 1994; Korpi, 1983; Myles, 1989; O'Connor, 1996; O'Connor and Brym, 1988; O'Connor and Olsen, 1998; Olsen, 2002; Olsen and Brym, 1996). In Sweden, more than three-quarters of blue- and white-collar workers are union members. In Canada, only about a third of workers are members of unions. Several consequences follow:

- About 85 percent of Swedish citizens vote in federal elections, compared with about 65 percent in Canada. That is mainly because working-class Swedes are more likely to vote than working-class Canadians.
- The Swedish socialist party has formed the government almost continuously since World War II. In contrast, Canada's socialist party, the NDP, has never formed the federal government or even had a representative in the federal cabinet. The parties that have formed Canada's federal governments (Liberals, Progressive Conservatives, and Conservatives) are those that are most strongly supported by business (see Figure 18.3).
- Swedish governments have acted more vigorously than Canadian governments to eradicate poverty and equalize incomes. Thus, fewer than 4 percent of Swedes are classified as living below the poverty line. The comparable figure for

Canadians is about 15 percent. In Sweden, about 20 percent of all income goes to the top 10 percent of income earners. The comparable figure for Canada is about 30 percent of all income. And in Sweden, a broader range of retired people receive more generous pensions and more frequent cost-of-living adjustments than pensioners in Canada.

- Since women are disproportionately concentrated in low-income, low-status jobs (see Chapter 7, "Gender Inequality"), they benefit more than men when the working class is more powerful. As a result, the ratio of women's to men's earnings is about 80 percent in Sweden and 67 percent in Canada. Moreover, in Sweden, the ratio of women to men who live below the poverty line is just above 90 percent, while in Canada the comparable figure is nearly 130 percent. Finally, parental benefits are superior in Sweden and child-care facilities are more widely available and affordable.

We thus see that elections matter a great deal in the lives of ordinary people. Elections determine the types of parties that get elected. Elected parties, in turn, shape government policies. The outcome of any particular election depends on the appeal of party leaders, their effectiveness in presenting issues to the public, and myriad other short-term factors (Clarke,

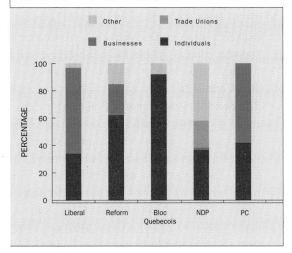

FIGURE 18.3 CONTRIBUTIONS TO FEDERAL POLITICAL PARTIES BY SOURCE

NOTE: Data are for 1997.
SOURCE: Data used to create the above chart was taken from the Web site of Elections Canada, www.elections.ca, 2006. It is used with the permission of the Chief Electoral Officer. Adaptation and analysis are the responsibility of the author.

Jenson, LeDuc, and Pammett, 1996; see Figure 18.4). But considering the types of parties that get elected over several decades, as we did previously, we see that the distribution of power between classes and other groups shapes the character of politics in a country.

The preceding analysis also implies that Sweden is more democratic than Canada. True, citizens of both countries are legally free to vote and influence their governments. But because the working class is more powerful in Sweden, Swedes' legal right to vote and influence governments has been turned into real political influence on a wider scale. In general, only if more citizens wield more clout can society become more democratic (see Box 18.2).

STATE-CENTRED THEORY

Power-balance theory suggests that democratic politics is a contest among various classes and other groups to control the state for their own advantage. When power is substantially redistributed—when, for example, a major class gets better organized while another major class becomes less socially organized—old ruling parties usually fall and new ones take office.

Note, however, that a winner-take-all strategy would be nothing short of foolish. If winning parties monopolized the spoils of office, passing laws that benefit only their supporters, they might cause massive outrage and even violent opposition. Yet allowing opponents to become angry, organized, and resolute would be counterproductive. After all, winners want more than just a moment of glory. They want to be able to enjoy the spoils of office in a stable political environment over the long haul. To achieve such stability, it is crucial that people who *lose* elections are given a say in government. To a degree, the party in power must attend to the wants of losing minorities. That way, even determined opponents are likely to recognize the legitimacy of the government and its right to rule. Pluralists thus make a good point when they say that democratic politics is about accommodation and compromise; they only lose sight of the fact that accommodation and compromise typically give more advantages to some than others, as both elite theorists and power-balance theorists stress.

There is, however, more to the story of politics than conflict between classes and between other groups. Theda Skocpol and other **state-centred theorists** have shown how the state itself can structure political life independently of the way power is distributed

FIGURE 18.4   RESULTS OF 2006 CANADIAN FEDERAL ELECTION

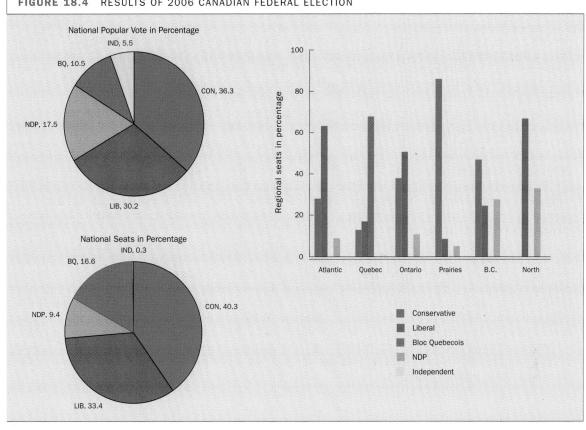

SOURCE: Data used to create the above chart was taken from the Web site of Elections Canada, www.elections.ca, 2006. It is used with the permission of the Chief Electoral Officer. Adaptation and analysis are the responsibility of the author.

among classes and other groups at a given time (Block, 1979; Evans, Rueschemeyer, and Skocpol, 1985; Skocpol, 1979). Their argument is a valuable supplement to power-balance theory.

To illustrate how state structures shape politics, consider the problem of nonvoting in the United States. Fewer than 55 percent of American citizens have voted in recent presidential elections. With the exception of Switzerland, the United States has the lowest voter turnout of any rich democracy in the world (Piven and Cloward, 1989: 5). How can we explain this?

The high rate of nonvoting is largely a product of voter registration law—a feature of the American political structure, not of the current distribution of power. In every democracy, laws specify voter registration procedures. In some countries, such as France, citizens are registered to vote automatically once they receive state-issued identity cards at the age of 18. In other countries, such as Canada, a database of citizens who are eligible to vote was first created by state-employed canvassers who went door-to-door to register voters. The database is updated between elections with information supplied mainly by provincial, territorial, and federal data sources. Only in the United States do individual citizens have to take the initiative to go out and register themselves in voter registration centres. Yet many American citizens are unable or unwilling to register. As a result, the U.S. has a proportionately smaller pool of eligible voters than the other democracies do. Only about 65 percent of American citizens are registered to vote (Piven and Cloward, 1989: 256–59).

Apart from shrinking the pool of eligible voters, American voter registration law has a second important consequence. Because some *types* of people are less able and inclined than others to register, a strong bias is introduced into the political system. Specifically, the poor are less likely to register than the better-off. People without much formal education are less likely to register than the better educated. Members of disadvantaged racial minority groups,

BOX 18.2 ELECTRONIC DEMOCRACY

Recently, some analysts have proposed a technical means for making democracy more widespread. They say that computers linked to the World Wide Web could allow citizens to debate issues and vote on them directly. That would give politicians mass feedback and clear signals on how they should conduct public policy. Accordingly, in an era of low and declining political participation, computers can reinvigorate and even save democracy, making public opinion the law of the land (Westen, 1998).

The evidence does not support these claims. Already by the mid-1980s, more than a dozen experiments had been conducted on electronic public meetings. In a comprehensive review of those experiments, one researcher showed that even in the most successful of them, participation was extremely low. He concluded that, even if the technology needed for such meetings were universally available, citizen interest is so limited that no more than a third of the population would participate (Arterton, 1987).

Subsequent experience with the World Wide Web bears out this conclusion and allows us to qualify it. The people who are most likely to take advantage of electronic democracy are those who have access to large computer networks. Such people form a relatively privileged and politically involved group that is far from representative of the adult population.

Survey results show that, compared with the general population, Web users are younger, better educated, and wealthier, and contain a higher proportion of men, whites, and people in occupations requiring substantial computer use. Thus, if electronic democracy becomes widespread, it will probably reinforce the same inequalities in political participation that plague democracy today. It is less likely to reinvigorate democracy than it is to help form a digital divide. In 2000, 18.2 percent of Canadian Internet were among the top 10 percent of income earners, while 3.5 of Canadian Internet users were among the bottom 10 percent of income earners. Internet use is also concentrated among the most highly educated and urbanized Canadians. Thus, in 2000, 42 percent of Canadians had never used the Internet and another 10 percent used it rarely. Those 52 percent of Canadians tend to be seniors, have low incomes, and lack postsecondary education (Crompton, Ellison, and Stevenson, 2002; Sciadis, n.d.).

especially African Americans, are less likely to register than whites. Thus, American voter registration law is a pathway to democracy for some but a barrier to democracy for others. The American political system is less responsive than other rich democracies to the needs of the disadvantaged. That is partly because, as state-centred theory suggests, the law requires citizen-initiated voter registration. As a result, many disadvantaged people are effectively disenfranchised.[1]

Big shocks sometimes rock state structures. In general, however, they are resistant to change. The foundations of state structures are anchored by constitutions, which can be altered only by large majorities of federally elected representatives and state- or provincial-level legislatures. Their upper stories are girded by laws, regulations, and policies, some of which help to keep potentially disruptive social forces at bay. American voter registration law is a case in point.[2] And then there are the many ideological reinforcements. All states create anthems, flags, ceremonies, celebrations, sporting events, and school curricula that stimulate patriotism and serve in part to justify existing political arrangements.

In sum, each school of thought reviewed above makes a useful contribution to our appreciation of normal democratic politics (see Table 18.2). Pluralists teach us that normal democratic politics is about compromise and the accommodation of all group interests. Elite theorists teach us that, despite compromise and accommodation, power is concentrated in the hands of higher-status groups, whose interests the political system therefore serves best. Power-balance theorists teach us that, despite the concentration of power in society, substantial shifts in the distribution of power often occur, and they have discernible effects on voting patterns and public policies. And state-centred theorists teach us that, despite the influence of the distribution of power on political life, state structures exert an important independent effect on politics too.

POWER FROM BELOW: POLITICS BEYOND THE RULES

RELATIVE-DEPRIVATION THEORY

All five theories of democracy reviewed above focus on normal politics. We know, however, that politics is sometimes anything but normal. Routine political processes can break down. Social movements can

---

TABLE 18.2   FIVE SOCIOLOGICAL THEORIES OF DEMOCRACY COMPARED

	PLURALIST	ELITE	MARXIST	POWER BALANCE	STATE-CENTRED
How is power distributed?	dispersed	concentrated	concentrated	concentrated	concentrated
Who are the main power holders?	various groups	elites	ruling class	upper class	state officials
On what is their power based?	holding political office	controlling major institutions	owning substantial capital	owning substantial capital	holding political office
What is the main basis of public policy?	the will of all citizens	the interests of major elites	capitalist interests	the balance of power between classes, etc.	the influence of state structures
Do lower classes have much influence on politics?	yes	no	rarely	sometimes	sometimes

---

form. Large-scale political violence can erupt. As Vladimir Lenin, the leader of the Russian revolution of 1917, said, people sometimes "vote with their feet."

Until about 1970, many sociologists argued that social movements tend to emerge when people experience **relative deprivation.** People feel relatively deprived when they experience an intolerable gap between the social rewards they think they deserve and the social rewards they expect to receive. Social rewards are widely valued goods, including money, education, security, prestige, and so on. Accordingly, people are most likely to rebel against authority when rising expectations (brought on by, say, rapid economic growth and migration) are met by a sudden decline in social rewards (because of, say, economic recession or war) (Davies, 1969). In addition, until about 1970, many sociologists held that the people who lead and first join social movements are likely to be "outsiders" who lack strong social ties to their communities.

A large body of research has now discredited these ideas. For example, we now know that the leaders and early joiners of social movements are usually well-integrated members of their communities, not socially marginal newcomers. In the 1930s, for example, Saskatchewan farmers and workers formed the Cooperative Commonwealth Federation (CCF) to protest federal government policy toward the West in general and Western agriculture in particular. The movement's leaders and early recruits were not outsiders. The workers were mainly local trade union

activists. The farmers had been involved in the establishment of community-owned retail stores, credit unions, and marketing cooperatives (Lipset, 1971).

Much research also calls into question the idea that relative deprivation leads to the formation of social movements. For example, sociologists have compared measures of relative deprivation with the frequency of demonstrations, strikes, and acts of collective violence in France, Italy, Germany, and England. They have found that, in general, outbreaks of collective unrest do not increase with mounting relative deprivation (Lodhi and Tilly, 1973; Snyder and Tilly, 1972; Tilly, 1979a; Tilly, Tilly, and Tilly, 1975).

RESOURCE-MOBILIZATION THEORY

Because of the inadequacies of relative deprivation theory noted above, an alternative approach to the study of social movements has gained popularity over the past 30 years. **Resource-mobilization theory** is based on the idea that social movements can emerge only when disadvantaged people can marshal the means necessary to challenge authority (Jenkins, 1983; McCarthy and Zald, 1977; Obserschall, 1973; Tilly, 1978). Foremost among the resources they need to challenge authority is the capacity to forge strong social ties among themselves. Other important resources that allow disadvantaged people to challenge authority include jobs, money, arms, and access to means of spreading their ideas.

You can appreciate the significance of resource mobilization theory by considering patterns of strike activity in Canada. When blue-collar and white-collar workers go out on strike, they are withholding their labour to extract concessions from employers or governments in the form of higher wages and improved social welfare benefits. When are workers most inclined to challenge the authority of employers and governments in this way? Research shows that in Canada since World War II, strike activity has been high when (1) unemployment is low, (2) union membership is high, and (3) governments have shown themselves to be generous in their provision of social welfare benefits. Low unemployment indicates a strong economy. Workers are inclined to strike when business activity is robust because they know employers and governments can afford to make concessions. (Employers make bigger profits and governments collect more taxes during economic booms.) A high level of unionization is also conducive to more strike activity because unions provide workers with leadership, strike funds, and coordination. Thus, as resource mobilization theory predicts, strong social ties among workers (as indicated by a high level of unionization) and access to

jobs and money (as indicated by a booming economy) increase challenges to authority (as indicated by strikes).[3]

Figure 18.5 shows the pattern of strike activity in post-World War II Canada. It supports the arguments of resource mobilization theory. Until 1974, the trend in strike activity was upward. (In the 1970s, Canada was, in fact, the most strike-prone country in the world.) This was a period of growing prosperity, low unemployment, expanding state benefits, and increasing unionization. With increasing access to organizational and material resources, workers often challenged authority in the three decades after World War II. In 1973, however, economic crisis struck. Oil prices tripled, and then tripled again at the end of the decade. Inflation increased and unemployment rose. Soon, the government was strapped for funds and had to borrow heavily to maintain social welfare programs. Eventually, the debt burden was so heavy that the government felt obliged to cut various social welfare programs. Unionization reached a peak in 1978, stabilized, and then began to fall (see Figure 18.6). Thus, in the post-1973 climate, the organizational and material resources of workers fell. As a result,

FIGURE 18.5   WEIGHTED FREQUENCY OF STRIKES, CANADA, 1946–2000

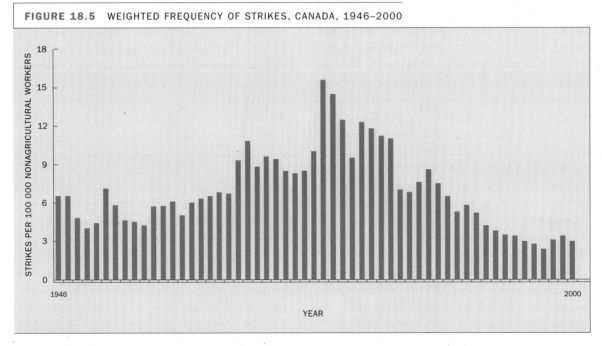

SOURCES: *Strikes and Lockouts in Canada 1968* (1970: 12–13); *Strikes and Lockouts in Canada 1985* (1985: 9); Workplace Information Directorate (1996); *Labour Organizations . . .* (1973: xxii–xxiii); *1994–1995 Directory . . .* (1995: xiii); *1998 Directory . . .* (1998: 15); "Chronological Perspective . . ." (1999; 2001a; 2001b).

FIGURE 18.6 PERCENTAGE OF NONAGRICULTURAL WORKERS UNIONIZED, CANADA, 1945–2000

SOURCES: Calculated from *Labour Organizations* . . . (1973: xxii–xxiii); *1994–1995 Directory* . . . (1995: xiii); *1998 Directory* . . . (1998: 15); "Union Membership In Canada—2000" (2000).

strike activity plummeted. In 1974, nearly 16 strikes took place for every 100 000 Canadian workers. By 2000, that figure had fallen to 3 (Brym, 2003).

FRAMING DISCONTENT

As you have seen, resource mobilization theory is a useful approach to the study of social movements, such as the strike movement in Canada. Even so, the emergence of a social movement sometimes takes sociologists by surprise. In addition, the failure of an aggrieved group to press its claim is sometimes equally unexpected. And movements that do emerge are successful to varying degrees. It seems, therefore, that something lies between (1) the capacity of disadvantaged people to mobilize resources for collective action and (2) the recruitment of a substantial number of movement members. Sociologists call that "something" **frame alignment** (Goffman, 1974; Snow, Rochford, Worden, and Benford, 1986). Frame alignment is the process by which individual interests, beliefs, and values either become congruent and complementary with the activities, ideas, and goals of the movement or fail to do so. Thanks to the efforts of scholars operating mainly in the symbolic interactionist tradition (see Chapters 1 and 3), frame alignment has recently become the subject of sustained sociological investigation.

Frame alignment can be encouraged in several ways. Social movement leaders can reach out to other organizations that, they believe, contain people who may be sympathetic to the social movement's cause. For example, an anti-nuclear movement may use the mass media, telephone campaigns, and direct mail to appeal to feminist, anti-racist, and environmental organizations on the assumption they are likely to have members who would agree at least in general terms with the anti-nuclear platform. In addition, social movements can idealize values that have so far not featured prominently in the thinking of potential recruits. They can also elevate the importance of positive beliefs about the movement and what it stands for. For example, in trying to win new recruits, movement members might emphasize the seriousness of the social movement's purpose. They might analyze in a clear and convincing manner the causes of the problem the movement is trying solve. Or they might stress the likelihood of the movement's success. By doing so they might increase the movement's appeal to the potential recruit and win him or her over to the cause. Social movements can also stretch their objectives and activities to win recruits who are not initially sympathetic to the movement's original aims. This may involve a "watering down" of the movement's ideals. Alternatively, movement leaders may decide to take action calculated to appeal to nonsympathizers on grounds that have little or nothing to do with the movement's purpose. When rock, punk, or reggae bands play at nuclear disarmament rallies or gay liberation festivals, it is not necessarily because the music is relevant to the movement's goals. Nor do bands play just because movement members want to be entertained. The purpose is also to attract nonmembers. Once attracted by the music, nonmembers may make friends and acquaintances in the movement and then be encouraged to attend a more serious-minded meeting.

REFRAIN: BACK TO 1968

Frame alignment theory stresses the face-to-face interaction strategies employed by movement members to recruit nonmembers who are like-minded, apathetic, or even initially opposed to the movement's goals. Resource-mobilization theory focuses on the broad social-structural conditions that facili-

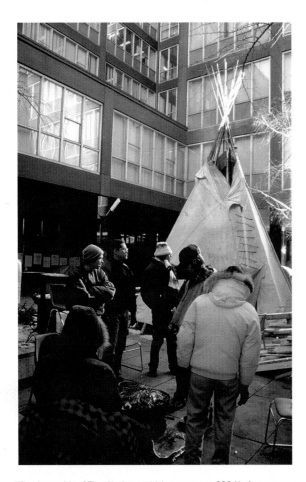

The Assembly of First Nations, which represents 633 Native groups, demands that Aboriginal Canadians have the right to formulate their own laws and reject some Canadian laws. Here, Aboriginal people protest certain taxes outside a government office.
SOURCE: Dick Hemingway.

tate the emergence of social movements. One theory usefully supplements the other.

The two theories certainly help clarify the 1968 high school incident I described at the beginning of this chapter. It now seems clear that two main factors prevented me from influencing my classmates in New Brunswick when I spoke to them about the dangers of industrial pollution:

1. Disadvantaged people in New Brunswick were relatively powerless. They had access to few resources they could mobilize on their own behalf. That is because New Brunswick's economy was underdeveloped. Both per capita income and the level of unionization were among the lowest in the country. The unemployment rate was among the highest. In contrast, K.C. Irving, who owned the pulp and paper mill against which I railed, was so powerful that most New Brunswickers could not even conceive of the need to rebel against the conditions of life that he created for them. He owned most of the industrial establishments in the province—the oil refinery and its network of gas stations, the dry docks, the pulp mills, the mines, and the logging operations. Every daily newspaper, most of the weeklies, all of the TV stations, and most of the radio stations were his too. Little wonder we rarely heard a critical word about his operations. Many people also believed that Irving could make or break provincial governments single-handedly. Should I therefore have been surprised that mere high school students refused to take him on? In their conservatism, my fellow students were only mimicking their parents, who, on the whole, were as powerless as Irving was mighty (Brym, 1979).

2. Many of my classmates did not share my sense of injustice. Most of them regarded K.C. Irving as the great provider. They thought his pulp and paper mill, as well as his myriad other industrial establishments, gave many New Brunswickers jobs. They regarded that fact as more important for their lives and the lives of their families than the pollution problem I raised. Frame-alignment theory suggests I needed to figure out ways of building bridges between their understanding and mine. I did not. I therefore received an unsympathetic hearing.

THE HISTORY AND FUTURE OF SOCIAL MOVEMENTS

I. THE RICH COUNTRIES

Three hundred years ago, social movements were typically small, localized, and violent. In Europe, poor residents of a particular city might riot against public officials in reaction to a rise in bread prices or taxes. Peasants on a particular estate might burn their landowner's barns (or their landowner) in response to his demand for a larger share of the crop. But then the reach of the state grew, soon encompassing most aspects of life. The state taxed nearly all of its citizens at higher and higher rates as government services expanded. It imposed a uniform language and a common curriculum in a compulsory education system. It drafted most young men for army service. It instilled in its citizens all the ideological trappings of modern nationalism, from anthems to flags to historical myths. And in the process, social movements changed. They became national in scope, typically directing themselves against central governments rather than local targets. They grew in size, partly because potential recruits were now literate and could communicate using the printed word, partly because big new social settings—factories, offices, densely populated urban neighbourhoods—could serve as recruitment bases. And, in most cases, social movements became less violent. Their size and organization often allowed them to stabilize, bureaucratize, and become sufficiently powerful to get their way without frequent resort to extreme measures (Tilly, 1978, 1979a, 1979b; Tilly, Tilly, and Tilly, 1975).

Social movements often used their power to expand the rights of citizens. We may identify four stages in this process. In Britain, for example, rich property owners struggled against the king in the eighteenth century for **civil citizenship:** the right to free speech, freedom of religion, and justice before the law. The male middle class and the more prosperous strata of the working class struggled against rich property owners in the nineteenth century for **political citizenship:** the right to vote and run for office. In early-twentieth-century Britain, women and poorer workers succeeded in achieving these same rights despite the opposition of well-to-do men in particular. During the remainder of the century, blue- and white-collar workers struggled against the well-to-do for **social citizenship:** the right to a certain level of economic security and full participation in the social life of the country by means of the creation of the modern welfare state (Marshall, 1965).

In the last third of the twentieth century, the struggle to broaden citizenship rights entered a new phase, which we now examine in greater detail. The broadening of the struggle for citizenship rights was signalled by the emergence of so-called **new social movements** in the 1960s and 1970s (Melucci, 1980, 1995). What is new about new social movements is the breadth of their goals, the kinds of people they attract, and their potential for going global. I will consider each of these issues in turn.

Goals

Some new social movements, such as the peace movement, the environmental movement, and the human rights movement, promote the rights not of specific groups but of humanity as a whole to peace, security, and a clean environment. Other new social movements, such as the women's movement and the gay rights movement, promote the rights of particular groups that have been excluded from full social participation. Accordingly, gay rights groups have fought for laws that eliminate all forms of discrimination based on sexual orientation. They have also fought for the repeal of laws that discriminate on the basis of sexual orientation, such as anti-sodomy laws and laws that negatively affect parental custody of children (Adam, Duyvendak, and Krouwel, 1999).

Since the 1960s, the women's movement has succeeded in getting admission practices altered in professional schools, winning more freedom of reproductive choice for women, and opening up opportunities for women in the political, religious, military, educational, medical, and business systems (Adamson, Briskin, and McPhail, 1988; see Box 18.3). The emergence of the peace, environmental, human rights, gay rights, and women's movements marked the beginning of a fourth stage in the history of social movements. This fourth stage involves the promotion of **universal citizenship,** or the extension of citizenship rights to all adult members of society and to society as a whole (Roche, 1995; Turner, 1986: 85–105).

Membership

New social movements are also novel in that they attract a disproportionately large number of highly educated, well-to-do people from the social, educational, and

BOX 18.3   THE WOMEN'S MOVEMENT

The women's movement was the first new social movement.

A century ago, women began to play a smaller role in domestic and farm work and started to enter the paid labour force in significant numbers. Owning more of their own economic resources, they became more independent-minded. They began to realize they might free themselves of oppressive authority in the home. They also started to understand there was nothing inevitable about their receiving less pay and working in worse conditions than men with comparable jobs (Strong-Boag, 1986: 179).

Formulating a program for social change requires such resources as time, money, and education. Not surprisingly, therefore, the "first wave" of the women's movement comprised highly educated professionals. A group of women with just that social profile established the Canadian Woman Suffrage Association in Toronto in 1883. By demonstrating, petitioning, and gaining the support of influential liberal-minded men, women won the right to vote federally in 1918, in all provinces and territories but Quebec and Northwest Territories by 1925, in Quebec in 1940, and in the Northwest Territories by 1951.

Along with the right to vote, women won the right to run for public office. They immediately exercised that right, running mainly on the CCF and Liberal tickets. A woman was first elected to provincial office in Alberta in 1917 and to the federal Parliament in 1921.

In provincial and territorial legislatures and the federal Parliament, women sought institutional reform through government action. Specifically, they pursued equitable pay for women, easier access to higher education, protection from domestic violence, and a fair share of family assets and child support in case of divorce or desertion. But progress was slow on all these fronts. That was partly because women's representation in the country's legislatures remained meagre. Even as late as the federal election in 2004, women composed just 21 percent of federal MPs (Bashevkin, 1986; "Women," 2005). Moreover, some female MPs were hardly advocates of women's rights.

Because of slow progress, feminists developed a strategy in the 1960s and 1970s that was less oriented toward established political institutions and more oriented toward grassroots action. The new strategy sought to achieve change not just "from above," by means of party politics but also "from below," by creating a whole network of new organizations such as study groups, consciousness-raising circles, women's bookstores, rape crisis centres, abortion clinics, shelters for battered women, and opportunities to publicize the importance of feminist aims, such as International Women's Day marches.

It was not only slow progress on the established political front that led women to create this network of new organizations. Many "second-wave" feminists were deeply involved in the student movement of the 1960s and 1970s. They were appalled to discover that, despite much rhetoric about liberation and equality, men controlled the student movement and often refused to allow feminist issues to become part of their agenda. To pursue their aims they felt it was necessary to create new organizations run by women.

Today, then, the women's movement operates at both the grassroots level and within established political organizations to achieve its aims. It is internally differentiated. *Liberal feminists* believe that women can participate fully in society if they achieve equality of opportunity with men. They therefore advocate policies aimed at pay equity and the elimination of gender discrimination in the workplace. *Radical feminists* hold that male domination is rooted in the family. They champion free and safe contraception and abortion, an equitable division of domestic labour, and the like. *Socialist feminists* maintain that legal equality is not enough to ensure that women can participate fully in society. In addition, they argue, the state should provide affordable and accessible daycare facilities and other services. These services, they say, could alleviate the economic burdens that prevent most women, especially those from the working class, from taking full advantage of available opportunities for education and employment. *Anti-racist* and *postmodernist* feminists have criticized liberal, socialist, and radical feminists for generalizing from the experience of white women and failing to see how women's lives are rooted in particular historical and racial experiences. These new currents have done much to extend the relevance of feminism to previously marginalized groups. Thus, despite their different emphases, the various types of feminism share a strong desire to see members of a previously marginal group expand their citizenship rights and become full participants in society.

cultural fields: teachers, professors, journalists, social workers, artists, actors, writers, and student apprentices to these occupations. Such people are predisposed to participate in new social movements for several reasons.

Their higher education exposes them to radical ideas and makes those ideas appealing. They tend to hold jobs outside the business community, which often opposes their values. And they often get personally involved in the problems of their clients and audiences, sometimes even becoming their advocates (Brint, 1984; Rootes, 1995).

Globalization Potential

Finally, new social movements possess more potential for globalization than old social movements did. In the 1960s, social movements were typically *national* in scope. That is why, for example, the intensity and frequency of urban race riots in the United States in the 1960s did not depend on such local conditions as the degree of black–white inequality in a given city (Spilerman, 1970, 1976). Instead, congressional and presidential action (and lack of action) on civil rights issues, national TV coverage of race issues, and growing black consciousness and solidarity helped to create the view among African Americans that racial problems are nationwide and can be solved only by the federal government.

Many new social movements that gained force in the 1970s increased the scope of protest still further. For example, members of the nuclear disarmament and environmental movements viewed federal legislation as a necessary but insufficient solution to the issues that troubled them. Once they recognized that, say, the condition of the Brazilian rain forest affects climatic conditions worldwide and that the spread of weapons of mass destruction can easily destroy all of humanity, movement activists pressed for international agreements binding all countries to stop environmental destruction and nuclear proliferation. Social movements went global.

The globalization of social movements was facilitated by the ease with which people in various national movements could travel and communicate with like-minded activists from other countries. In the age of CNN, inexpensive jet transportation, fax machines, and e-mail, it was possible not only to see the connection between apparently local problems and their global sources but also to act locally and globally. Greenpeace, for instance, is a highly successful environmental movement that originated in Vancouver in the mid-1970s and now has offices in 41 countries, with its international office in Amsterdam ("Greenpeace," 1999). Among many other initiatives, it has mounted a campaign to eliminate the international transportation and dumping of toxic wastes. Its representatives visited local environmental groups in African and other developing countries, supplied them with organizing kits to help them tie their local concerns to

global political efforts, and published a newsletter to keep activists up to date about legal issues. Thus, Greenpeace coordinated a global campaign that enabled weak environmental organizations in developing countries to act more effectively, and raised the costs of continuing the international trade in toxic waste. Greenpeace is hardly alone on its efforts to go global. In 1953, there were 110 international social movement organizations. Forty years later, there were 631. About a quarter were human rights organizations and about a seventh were environmental organizations, the latter representing by far the fastest-growing organizational type (Smith, 1998: 97).

The globalization of social movements can be further illustrated by coming full circle and returning to the anecdote with which I began this chapter. In 1991, I visited my hometown. I had not been back in years. As I entered the city, I vaguely sensed that something was different. I could not define the change precisely until I reached the Irving pulp and paper mill. Suddenly, it became obvious: the rotten-egg smell was virtually gone. I subsequently discovered that in the 1970s a local woman whose son developed a serious case of asthma took legal action against the mill and eventually won. The mill owner was required by law to install a "scrubber" in the main smokestack to remove most of the sulphur dioxide emissions. Soon, the federal government was putting pressure on the mill owner to purify the polluted water that poured out of the plant and into the local river and bay. Apparently, local citizens and the environmental movement had caused a change in the climate of opinion, influencing the government to force the mill owner to spend many millions of dollars on a cleanup. It took decades, but what was political heresy in 1968 eventually became established practice because environmental concerns had been amplified by the voice of a movement that had grown to global proportions. In general, as this case illustrates, globalization helps to ensure that many new social movements transcend local and national boundaries and that many of them—but, as you will now learn, not all—promote universalistic goals.

II: THE OTHER 85 PERCENT

With variations, the pattern of social movement evolution sketched previously applies to the 20 or so rich countries of North America, Western Europe,

Australia, New Zealand, and Japan. As we have seen, social movements in these rich countries typically sought to broaden democracy through the expansion of citizenship rights. In contrast, social movements in the other 85 percent of the world developed differently. They focused less on broadening the bases of democracy than on ensuring more elemental human rights, notably freedom from colonial rule and freedom to create the conditions for independent economic growth.

The "other 85 percent" of the world is weak economically, politically, and militarily because it began substantial industrialization only after World War I and in some cases after World War II. This circumstance allowed the early industrializers (Britain, France, Japan, Russia, etc.) to carve up most of Asia, Africa, and South America into colonies, protectorates, mandates, spheres of influence, and other administrative forms of subjugation. The nineteenth century was the age of imperialism. The early industrializers used the rest of the world as a captive market for their manufactured goods and a source of inexpensive raw materials and labour. They enriched themselves even as they limited economic growth and welfare in the less developed countries.

Events in the Muslim world were in many respects typical and may therefore illustrate the problem (Hourani, 1991: 265–349). Already by the 1830s the armed forces of France had taken control of part of Algeria, those of Britain had taken control of part of the Arabian peninsula, and those of Russia had taken over the Muslim lands of the Caucasus. A century later, almost the entire Middle East and North Africa were under British and French control. Egyptian cotton fed the looms of Lancashire. Iraqi oil supplied half of France's needs. British and French ships brought European machinery and textiles to the region. British and French financiers profited handsomely from their control of local banking. Some indigenous merchants and landowners benefited from the new economic relations too. However, the growing number of peasants and urban workers remained poor and powerless.

In the world's rich countries, a strong bourgeoisie—an affluent and politically powerful class of merchants, industrialists, and financiers—did much to promote the growth of democracy in its early stages (Moore, 1967). In contrast, in the Muslim countries and the rest of the less economically developed world, the bourgeoisie was small, weak, and dependent on imperial interests. As a result, democratic ideals had

Anti-globalization street protests are now expected at meetings of international trade and finance organizations, such as the World Trade Organization. (This is a scene from 2002 protests in Quebec City.) The anti-globalization movement is a globalized movement too.
SOURCE: Kevin Frayer/CP Picture Archive.

little chance to sink deep roots. Instead, European and (after World War II) American domination of less developed countries bred resentment, resistance, and revolt. Peasants, urban workers, intellectuals, and military officers were increasingly attracted to anti-imperialist independence movements based on various forms and mixes of socialism and nationalism (Brym, 1980: 50–53; Wolf, 1999 [1969]).

In the Muslim world, Islam was an additional source of anti-imperialist sentiment. In 1928, a movement known as the Society of the Muslim Brothers was formed in Egypt ("Muslim Brotherhood Movement," 2002). It served as a prototype for many similar groups. The Muslim Brothers argued against Western values and imperialist domination. They called for a return to the teaching of the Qur'an and demanded that Egypt become an Islamic state based on religious law *(shari'a)*. This type of Islamic fundamentalism became popular in Egypt and throughout the Muslim world in the twentieth century, gaining impetus especially in Iran from the 1960s on and then spreading to Algeria and as far afield as Afghanistan and Sudan by the end of that century. A clear line of intellectual influence and development leads from the early Muslim Brothers to the assassins of Egypt's President Anwar Sadat in 1981 after he made peace with Israel to Osama bin Laden today (Worth, 2001). Bin Laden's chief aims are to remove all Western (especially American) influence from countries and regions with Muslim majorities, create in their place societies based on a fundamentalist interpretation of Islamic law, and destroy Israel as a Jewish state.

It is important to note that, however much al Qaeda is influenced by ideas dating back eight decades, it is every inch a global movement that relies on modern technology for its successes. Al Qaeda has placed operatives in as many as 60 countries. It finances itself through a complex international network of legitimate businesses, charitable and relief organizations, private donors, and opium trafficking operations (Shahar, 2001). Bin Laden communicated with his operatives via satellite telephone until U.S. law enforcement authorities inexplicably revealed they were tapping calls from his base in Afghanistan. Once he learned of these taps, he increased his use of another, more effective means of global communication: sending messages that are easily encrypted but difficult to decode via the Internet (Kelley, 2001; McCullogh, 2000). Some analysts think such messages were used to help plan and coordinate the complex, virtually simultaneous jet hijackings that resulted in the crash of an airliner in Pennsylvania and the destruction of the World Trade Center and part of the Pentagon on September 11, 2001, killing some 3000 people.

Al Qaeda is an extremist movement with few like it. However, it is also one in a whole range of reactions against Western power and influence that grips much of the developing world. In its extreme forms, this anti-Western reaction has little or no respect for minority rights, multiculturalism, elections, relatively open markets, and many of the other freedoms we enjoy and often take for granted in the West. Yet the anti-Western reaction is everywhere, even in its most extreme forms, based on the desire of people to restore the independence and dignity they lost when the industrialized world showed up on their doorstep uninvited. One of the great tasks the West faces in the twenty-first century is to defend itself against violence while doing its utmost to remove the ultimate source of that violence: the gap between rich and poor countries that opened up at the time of the Industrial Revolution and that has widened ever since. Whether we are up to the task is anyone's guess.

SUMMARY

1. Democracy involves a two-way process of control between the state (the set of institutions that formulate and carry out a country's law, policies, and binding regulations) and civil society (the private sphere, consisting of social movements, political parties, etc.).

2. The level of democracy in a society depends on the capacity of civil society to influence the state through citizen support of social movements, political parties, and other groups. That capacity increases as power becomes more widely distributed in society.

3. Although pluralists are correct in noting that democratic politics is about negotiation and compromise, they fail to appreciate how advantaged groups tend to have more political influence than others.

4. Although elite theorists are correct in noting that power is concentrated in the hands of advantaged groups, they fail to appreciate how variations in the distribution of power influence political behaviour and public policy.

5. While power-balance theorists focus on the effect of changes in the distribution of power in society, they fail to appreciate what state-centred theorists emphasize—that state institutions and laws also affect political behaviour and public policy.

6. The degree to which power is widely distributed influences the success of particular kinds of parties and policies. Widely distributed power is associated with the success of labour parties and policies that redistribute wealth.

7. Research does not support the view that social movements emerge when relative deprivation spreads.

8. Research suggests that people are more inclined to rebel against the status quo when they are bound by close social ties to many other people who feel similarly wronged and when they have the money and other resources needed to protest.

9. For social movements to grow, members must engage in frame alignment, making the activities, goals, and ideology of the movement congruent with the interests, beliefs, and values of potential new recruits.

10. The history of democracy is a struggle for the acquisition of constantly broadening citizenship rights—first the right to free speech, freedom of religion, and justice before the law, then the right to vote and run for office, then the right to a certain level of economic security and full participation in the life of society, and finally the right of marginal groups to full citizenship and the right of humanity as a whole to peace and security.

11. In the developing world, social movements have focused less on broadening the bases of democracy than on ensuring more elemental human rights, notably freedom from colonial rule and freedom to create the conditions for independent economic growth. In some cases these movements have taken extreme, antidemocratic forms.

QUESTIONS TO CONSIDER

1. Have you ever participated in a social movement or been actively involved in a political party? If so, explain how your political choices (e.g., which party you joined, your level of participation, the timing of your recruitment) were influenced by the sociological factors discussed in this chapter. If you have never participated in a social movement or been actively involved in a political party, explain how the sociological factors discussed in this chapter influence you to remain politically inactive.

2. How would you achieve a political goal? Map out a detailed strategy for reaching a clearly defined aim, such as a reduction in income tax or an increase in university funding. Who would you try to recruit to help you achieve your goal? Why? What collective actions do you think would be most successful? Why? To whose attention would these actions be directed? Why? Write a manifesto that frames your argument in a way that is culturally appealing to potential recruits.

3. Do you think that social movements will be more or less widespread in the twenty-first century than they were in the twentieth? Why or why not? What kinds of social movements are likely to predominate?

4. Do you think that the twenty-first century will be more or less democratic than the twentieth? Why or why not?

GLOSSARY

Authorities are people who occupy the command posts of legitimized power structures.

Authority is power that is widely viewed as legitimate.

Civil citizenship recognizes the right to free speech, freedom of religion, and justice before the law.

Civil society is the private (nonstate) sphere of social life.

Elite theory maintains that well-to-do people consistently have more political influence than people who are less well-to-do and that society is therefore not as democratic as it is often portrayed.

Force is coercive power.

Frame alignment is the process by which individual interests, beliefs, and values either become congruent and complementary with the activities, goals, and ideology of the movement or fail to do so.

New social movements are post-1950s movements that attract a disproportionately large number of highly educated people in the social, educational, and cultural fields; fight their battles mainly inside established political parties or outside the political system; have an uneasy relationship with older social movements; and universalize the struggle for citizenship.

Pluralist theory holds that society has many competing interests and centres of power and that no one interest or power centre predominates in the long run.

Political citizenship recognizes the right to run for office and vote.

Political parties are organizations that seek to control state power.

A **political revolution** is a concerted attempt on the part of many people to overthrow existing political institutions and establish new ones. Political revolutions take place when widespread and successful movements of opposition clash with crumbling traditional or legal-rational authority.

Power is the ability of an individual or a group to impose its will on others, even if they resist.

Power-balance theory suggests that social movement formation and success depend on how powerful authorities are compared with partisans of change. It also holds that societies with widely distributed power are more democratic and more egalitarian than societies with narrowly held power.

Relative deprivation is an intolerable gap between the social rewards people feel they deserve and the social rewards they expect to receive.

Resource-mobilization theory holds that social movements crystallize and succeed in achieving their goals to the degree that they have access to scarce resources, such as money and effective communication facilities.

A **ruling class** is a self-conscious and cohesive group of people, led by corporate executives, who act to advance their common interests.

Social citizenship recognizes the right to a certain level of economic security and full participation in social life.

Social movements are enduring collective attempts to change part or all of the social order by means of rioting, petitioning, striking, demonstrating, and establishing pressure groups, unions, and political parties.

The **state** is a set of institutions that formulate and implement a country's laws, policies, and binding regulations. It consists of an executive branch (which initiates laws), a legislative branch (which makes laws), a judicial branch (which interprets laws), and an administrative and coercive apparatus (which enforces laws and protects state security).

The **state-centred theory** shows how the state structures political life independently of the way power is distributed among classes and among other groups at a given time.

Universal citizenship recognizes the right of marginal groups and the rights of humanity as a whole to full citizenship.

SUGGESTED READING

Baer, Doug, ed. (2002). *Political Sociology: Canadian Perspectives.* Toronto: Oxford University Press. This useful compendium of Canadian materials covers major issues and debates.

Tarrow, Sidney. (1998). *Power in Movement: Social Movements, Collective Action and Politics,* 2nd ed. Cambridge, UK: Cambridge University Press. This book synthesizes resource-mobilization and framing theories and underlines the importance of political structures in shaping discontent.

Tilly, Charles and Sidney Tarrow. (2007). *Contentious Politics.* Boulder CO: Paradigm Publishers. A new, accessible, and innovative introduction to political sociology by two grand masters.

Wolf, Eric. (1999 [1969]). *Peasant Wars of the 20th Century.* Norman, OK: Oklahoma University Press. The best introduction to Third World social movements.

NOTES

1. In addition, less than 13 percent of the American working class is unionized, making it the least organized working class in any of the world's rich countries.

2. For example, in the 1890s, a coalition of white and black southern farmers threatened the established American political parties. It was precisely for this reason that American electoral laws were made more restrictive.

3. Some of these generalizations do not apply to countries with a long tradition of labour governments. For example, since World War II, Sweden has experienced high levels of unionization and *low* strike rates. That is because Swedish workers and their representatives are involved in government policymaking. Decisions about wages and benefits tend to be made in negotiations between unions, employer associations, and governments rather than on the picket line.

WEB RESOURCES

Companion Web Site for This Book

http://www.newsociety5e.nelson.com

Begin by clicking on the Student Resources section of the website. Next, select the chapter you are studying from the pull-down menu. From the Student Resources page, you have easy access to InfoTrac College Edition® and other resources, such as the Glossary and Flashcards. The website also has many useful tips to aid you in your study of sociology.

InfoTrac College Edition Search Terms

Visit http://www.infotrac-college.com for access to more than 20 million articles from nearly 6000 sources when doing your online research.

ThomsonNOW™

http://hed.nelson.com

This online diagnostic tool identifies each student's unique needs with a Pretest that generates a personalized Study Plan for each chapter, helping students focus on concepts they are having the most difficulty mastering. Students then take a Posttest after reading the chapter to measure their understanding of the material. An Instructor Gradebook is available to track and monitor student progress.

CHAPTER
NINETEEN

Globalization

In this chapter you will learn that

1. Globalization is a term used to describe how the world "shrinks" as capital, ideas, corporations, commodities, and workers rapidly cross vast distances. You will learn about the complexities of globalization, a term much used and abused, and acquire a working definition of it.

2. Globalization is not a distant force but a real-world phenomenon that affects you daily as you eat, drink, work, and go shopping. By the end of the chapter, you will better understand how globalization relates to you as a consumer, a worker, and a citizen.

3. Globalization is dynamic because it is contested by different social forces promoting different kinds of globalization. This chapter will give you a conceptual framework that will allow you to appreciate the "top-down" forces of globalization that promote global capitalism and the "bottom-up" forces demanding greater democracy, social justice, and sustainability in the global system.

Josée Johnston
UNIVERSITY OF TORONTO

INTRODUCTION

THE BURGER AND FRIES GO GLOBAL

Think about your average fast-food meal: a burger, fries, and a soda. This is the food of North America—simple, greasy, fast, and familiar. Maybe fast food has something to do with the sociology of health or the sociology of food, but what does it have to do with the sociology of globalization?

It turns out that globalization has a lot to do with everyday events like eating fast food. The average North American meal travels more than 1600 kilometres to reach your dinner table, so there is a good chance that your burger and fries have been *globalized.*

Let's start with the burger. Although Canadian ranchers pride themselves on their cattle exports, at least 30 percent of the beef eaten in Canada is imported from the United States, Australia, New Zealand, and Uruguay. Even if the beef in your burger did originate in Canada, the process of transforming a cow into hamburger is deeply affected by globalization processes. Because of global market pressures, the meatpacking industry in Canada was restructured in the 1980s and 1990s; the goal was to cut costs by centralizing production and finding cheaper labour supplies. Today, just two slaughterhouse plants (owned by U.S. multinational corporations) account for 80 percent of Canada's slaughtering capacity in heifers and

The Global Hamburger
SOURCE: Reprinted by permission of Steve Crisp.

steers (MacLachlan, 2004: 46). The small town of Brooks, Alberta, is home to one of these plants, Lakeside Packers, which is owned by American meat giant Tyson Fresh Meats, the world's largest beef and pork supplier. Brooks is now a temporary home for hundreds of immigrants from Sudan who come to work at the plant. More than 20 languages are spoken inside the factory, including Arabic, French, Spanish, Tagalog, Chinese, and Cambodian.

Even a vegetarian's fast-food choices are affected by globalization. In 2001, six vegetarians from British Columbia working with an American lawyer moved to sue McDonald's after it was revealed that McDonald's French fries use beef fat for "flavouring." After hearing the announcement, vegetarian activists in India held demonstrations and attacked a McDonald's in Bombay, demanding that McDonald's leave the country (CBC News, 2001). McDonald's settled the lawsuit in 2002 by agreeing to donate $10 million dollars to Hindu and other consumer groups.

If fast food is influenced by global forces, North American fast food also influences global eating. North American markets became saturated with fast-food outlets in the 1980s, so McDonald's made a push in the 1990s for international expansion. The number of countries with a McDonald's more than doubled from 59 in 1991 to 114 in 1998. Today, an estimated 60 percent of McDonald's corporate profits come from its international division (McDonald's, 1999). McDonald's opens a new restaurant every 17 hours and is the world's largest user of beef, and Ronald McDonald himself is the second most recognized figure in the world (after Santa Claus) (Brownell and Horgen, 2004: 58).

It turns out, then, that everyday activities—like eating a hamburger and fries—have a lot to do with globalization. In an obvious way, the resources and labour that make up a fast-food meal originate from locations all around the globe. But even when the ingredients come from close to home, the food itself can be affected by global events, like international trade agreements, European social movements, international labour migration, faraway protests against McDonald's, and global food scares, like mad cow disease.

GLOBALIZATION OR "GLOBALONEY"?

But before going any further, I'll raise perhaps the most difficult question in this chapter: What do we mean by *globalization?* It is one of the most frequently heard buzzwords in the English language, yet there is no consensus on its meaning. The term was coined in the late 1970s, and today there are thousands of globalization books, conferences, university courses, and references in newspapers and magazines, many of which contradict each other. This confusion has led some academics to dismiss the term altogether as a confused mixture of globalization and baloney—what some people crankily refer to as "globaloney."

Although it is hard to find agreement on a definition of globalization, it is easy to find controversy about whether globalization is good or bad. A common tendency on both the left and the right of the political spectrum is to depict globalization in simplistic terms. For right-wing free-marketers, globalization represents the welcome spread of capitalism throughout the world. For many left-wing social activists and politicians, globalization is more like a Death Star. In the words of Barry Lynn, former executive director of *Global Business* magazine:

> Globalization is many things, and much has been written about it and said. But throw all the tomes and studies and placards into a giant try-works, and you'll render two simple arguments: (1) Globalization is good because it spreads what is good in America, such as a liberal approach to business, and McDonald's. (2) Globalization is bad because it spreads what is worst about America, such as a liberal approach to business, and McDonald's. (Lynn, 2002: 34)

A primary objective of this chapter is to get beyond this kind of simplistic thinking and gain a more sophisticated sense of what exactly is meant by globalization. The objective is not to provide the ultimate definition of globalization that will ring true for all people until the end of time, but to understand how different political and economic interests struggle to promote their own brand of globalization.

DEFINING GLOBALIZATION

Although figuring out exactly what is meant by globalization is a primary objective of the chapter, we need a neutral definition to get started: **Globalization** is a social, economic, and political process that makes it easier for people, goods, ideas, and capital to travel around the world at an unprecedented pace (Waters, 1995: 3). Globalization makes the world look and feel smaller.

Of course, the world is not shrinking literally. What is instead occurring is that people, money, corporations, and ideas travel across the globe more quickly and efficiently than ever before. Distance no longer seems as relevant, and time lags that used to characterize our social relations are diminished. It no longer seems crazy to have a romantic relationship with somebody across the country or even across the world. People can now communicate instantly through telephone, e-mail, Instant Messenger, or using a web-camera connection. To see a sweetheart in person, people can take a relatively inexpensive plane trip rather than a week-long journey on an ocean-going vessel. If someone is broke and needs money, we don't have to put a cheque in the mail. Instead anyone can transfer money instantly through electronic banking networks. And single people can systematically search the world for love through the thousands of online dating sites, some of which are devoted just to vegetarians, tattoo artists, and cat-lovers.

One term for this shrinking world phenomenon is **space-time compression,** which suggests that we are no longer slowed down by long distances (Harvey, 1990: 284). Not only do we feel less constrained by distance, but some global phenomena also seem to transcend the idea of physical space altogether. The Internet has facilitated the creation of *virtual communities*, in which people can meet, share ideas, and build relationships across state borders without ever meeting face to face. Use of the Internet has increased dramatically, although it still involves less than 15 percent of the world's population (Table 19.1).

There are many examples of space-time compression but there are also many instances in which time still passes slowly, the limits of geography are still relevant, and people are excluded from virtual communities. Not all people and ideas have access to channels of globalization like the Internet or even the telephone. Inequality of access to means of communication is known as the **digital divide** (see Table 19.2).

There is a lot of academic debate about how recent globalization is. I won't venture far into this hotly contested territory, but it is important to note that the world has been shrinking for a long time. Space-time compression can be traced back at least to the 1500s, with the beginning of transoceanic European exploration. The world became smaller with the invention of the steamship and the locomotive—

TABLE 19.1   WORLD INTERNET USAGE AND POPULATION STATISTICS

WORLD REGIONS	POPULATION (2005 EST.)	POPULATION % OF WORLD	INTERNET USAGE, LATEST DATA	USAGE GROWTH 2000–2005 (%)	% POPULATION (PENETRATION)	WORLD USERS %
Africa	896 721 874	14.0	23 867 500	428.7	2.7	2.5
Asia	3 622 994 130	56.4	327 066 713	186.1	9.0	34.2
Europe	731 018 523	11.4	273 262 955	165.1	37.4	28.5
Middle East	260 814 179	4.1	21 422 500	305.4	8.2	2.2
North America	328 387 059	5.1	223 779 183	107.0	68.1	23.4
Latin America/ Caribbean	546 723 509	8.5	70 699 084	291.31	12.9	7.4
Oceania/Australia	33 443 448	0.5	17 655 737	131.7	52.8	1.8
WORLD TOTAL	6 420 102 722	100.0	957 753 672	165.3	14.9	100.0

SOURCE: Information from this site may be cited, giving due credit and establishing an active link back to www.internetworldstats.com. © Copyright 2005, Miniwatts International, LLC. All rights reserved.
NOTES: (1) Internet Usage and World Population Statistics were updated on September 30, 2005. (2) Demographic (Population) numbers are based on data contained in the world-gazetteer website. (3) Internet usage information comes from data published by Nielsen//NetRatings, by the International Telecommunications Union, by local NICs, and by other reliable sources.

TABLE 19.2   SPACE-TIME COMPRESSION AND THE DIGITAL DIVIDE

EXAMPLE	HOW IT COMPRESSES SPACE AND TIME	LIMITS TO GLOBALIZATION
The telephone	Person-to-person communication is made possible across oceans and most national boundaries.	Many of the world's inhabitants do not have access to a telephone. The executive deputy president of South Africa in 1996, Thabo Mbeki, made a speech at the Information Society and Development Conference, where he informed the delegates that "half of humanity has never made a telephone call."
The Internet	Ideas, images, articles, videos, music, and text forms can be transmitted instantly across vast geographic distances.	On a global scale, access to the Internet is even more limited than access to the telephone. (See Table 19.1.)
Satellite television	Television is no longer restricted to local television stations; satellites allow transmission of programming from multiple points of production around the world.	Television ownership is concentrated in wealthy countries, television production is controlled by a small number of media monopolies centred in the industrialized North, and television content globally is both homogenous and closely linked to consumer capitalism (McKibben, 1993).
Electronic money markets	Capital can flow across national borders almost instantly.	Most of the world's citizens do not have a bank account, let alone access to electronic financial markets.

two technologies that connected distant populations at a rate unimagined by previous generations. Colonial relationships in the eighteenth and nineteenth centuries moved millions of people and shiploads of wealth around the world.

The current phase of space-time compression is not radically different in form, but its pace has grown especially quickly since the 1980s. Jet travel is much faster than by steamship. E-mail is less cumbersome than mail travelling by truck or ship. Ships moving silver, spices, and opium across the ocean can transfer wealth globally, but not as quickly as the enormous and instantaneous flows of capital that move in and out of the stock market in seconds.

THE GLOBAL AND THE ETHICAL

Understanding globalization as a series of processes connecting people, resources, and capital across the globe gets us away from seeing it as either a blessing or an evil. Globalization is inherently neither good nor bad, but the consequences of globalization processes do affect human lives and the environment. These consequences generate strong opinions and ethical positions, particularly as they relate to economic processes and the role of the United States on the global stage.

Ethical debates surrounding globalization became particularly pronounced after the September 11, 2001, terrorist attacks against the United States, symbolically centred on the World Trade Center, the heart of U.S. and global capitalism, and the Pentagon, the planning and coordination centre of the U.S. military. Although the Bush administration explained the attacks as being part of a global war of good against evil, others used the terrorist attacks as an opportunity to raise critical questions about the inequities of global capitalism and the role of the United States in the global system. On the first anniversary of the attacks, then Prime Minister of Canada Jean Chrétien incited a national controversy by suggesting in a CBC television interview that the victims of global capitalism could not be expected to suffer silently and that the wealthy, powerful countries should behave with greater humility in the international arena. In Chrétien's words, the Western world is "looked upon as being arrogant, self-satisfied, greedy and with no limits. The 11th of September is an occasion for me to realize it even more" (CBC News, 2002a). Responding to this controversy, popular Canadian radio and television personality Rex Murphy expressed public anxiety about the widening gap between rich and poor in the global economy:

> Here in the West, a ball player can sign a $100-million contract for playing a game or Britney Spears can yodel and grind for 60 seconds and Pepsi shells out a fortune. The excesses of our way of life must scream like an obscenity. To those parts of the world where children starve and die by the tens of thousands daily, the disproportion between our safety and well being, our nutrition and health compared to so many others does make us arrogant, careless and obnoxious. This is not the germ pile from which Osama and his butcheries were spawned. But it is a situation of grave conscience. It is the theme that leaders should address and it is a subject that Prime Minister Chrétien did well in thinking and talking aloud. (CBC News, 2002b)

TOP-DOWN VERSUS BOTTOM-UP GLOBALIZATION

Questions of equality, security, and social justice are critical in the ongoing debate about globalization and will be explored in the rest of this chapter. These debates can be understood as part of the tension between **top-down** and bottom-up globalization. Top-down globalization involves the actions of groups promoting globalized capitalism and free trade. The term *globalization* was first widely used by the American Express credit card company, which boasted in the 1970s that its card was accepted worldwide (Harvey, 1990: 13). The term was then taken up in financial and business circles, where it came to represent hopes for a world where capital could flow freely around the world, uninhibited by national boundaries or governments insisting on national regulations and taxation.

Top-down globalization has been dominated by **neoliberal** economic policies, which have become prevalent in both rich and poor countries in the past 25 years. Neoliberal policies are associated with a retreat from state spending and regulation, a focus on individual responsibility for our own welfare, less protection for labour and the environment, privatization of state resources, and faith in the power of the market and the profit motive to create wealth (see Chapter 9, Inequality among Nations). Top-down globalization is also strongly associated with the United States because of its role in promoting neoliberal policies globally through institutions like the International Monetary Fund (IMF) and World Bank, headquartered in Washington, D.C. For this reason, top-down globalization has also been referred to as the "Washington consensus." In addition, the United States is often perceived as an exemplar of neoliberal policy domestically, even though it seems to deviate on key matters like balanced budgets (in part because of high levels of U.S. military spending).

Bottom-up globalization describes the actions of groups that criticize the injustices that result from globalization processes. The mass media frequently describe these groups as being opposed to globalization. That is not entirely accurate. Many groups that criticize the injustices resulting from globalization actually support particular types of globalization, such as the spread of international human rights and global labour standards. Moreover, they use technologies, like the Internet, to help them organize and communicate internationally. In general, groups that support globalization from below advocate more democracy, environmental protection, and social justice in the global system. Bottom-up globalizers are against the neoliberal forms of globalization that put capital mobility and profits before people's basic needs, and they criticize the powerful economic, political, and military influence of transnational corporations and the United States government.

Top-down globalization has been targeted by environmentalists, peasant organizations, and farmers unions, but it has also been criticized by capitalist insiders, such as Joseph Stiglitz, Nobel Prize winner and former chief economist and vice-president of the World Bank; international financier George Soros; and world famous economist and policy adviser Jeffrey Sachs (Sachs, 2005; Soros, 1998; Stiglitz, 2003).

Although everyone from rock stars to prime ministers demands greater justice in the global system, it is not clear how to achieve it. There is no consensus on whether moderate capitalist reforms are sufficient, whether trade liberalization will help the poor, or whether the answer lies in partial or total withdrawal from global markets. Because of these differences, globalization from below should be understood less as a cohesive movement and more as a broad framework that encompasses multiple perspectives, including moderate critiques of neoliberalism, radical anti-capitalist positions, various forms of anarchism, armed peasant uprisings, fair-trade coffee projects and so on.

How then do the forces of globalization operate in people's daily lives? People are involved with globalization processes as capitalists, consumer, workers, and citizens (Robbins, 2005: 2–4). In the remainder of this chapter, I explore the profound influence of space-time compression in each of these realms.

CAPITALISTS GO GLOBAL

THE RISE OF FINANCIAL CAPITAL

In economic terms, money used for investment, currency trading, and so forth is *financial capital*. In the globalized economy, financial capital has grown much faster than production and trade. More than US$1.5 trillion flow through electronic financial channels every day, and an estimated 98 percent of these flows are purely speculative, meaning they are unrelated to the buying and selling of physical goods but involve short-term trading of things like foreign currencies. The global trade in goods and services equalled US$6.5 billion in 1998. Although this seems an impressive number, it is equal to only 4.3 days worth of trade on foreign exchange markets (Ellwood, 2001: 72). Using a fully computerized global financial system, traders can move around millions of dollars to profit from minuscule changes in currency rates.

The rise of financial capital has been labelled "casino capitalism" since financial speculators, like casino gamblers, stand to make or lose millions of dollars in short periods (Strange, 1986). The rise of casino capitalism has been facilitated by the financial deregulation that has occurred under neoliberal regimes since the 1980s as governments gave up regulatory powers. The danger with casino capitalism is that investor speculation (a process akin to placing a bet) makes financial systems unstable. Money floods into markets during periods of optimism, creating a financial "bubble" that drives up markets. The bubble bursts when investors realize that the market is overpriced relative to the value of real assets. This causes a period of panic involving an outflow of capital and, in due course, economic recession. This is just what happened during the 1997 Asian financial crisis, which started in Thailand that July and went on to affect the currency, stock markets, and asset prices of Indonesia, South Korea, Hong Kong, Malaysia, Laos, and the Philippines (Bello, 2001).

OVERCAPACITY AND CENTRALIZATION

The growth of casino capitalism is also linked to declining profits and overcapacity in the economy of goods and services. Put simply, global corporations are producing more things than the world's consumers can afford to purchase. China's manufacturing sector has an estimated 40 percent excess capacity and global automotives have 30 percent excess capacity (Bello, 2001: 129). In 1997, the chairman of General Electric, Jack Welch, told the *Financial Times* of London that "[t]here is excess global capacity in almost every industry." In 2000, the automotive industry produced 80 million vehicles for fewer than 60 million buyers. Although financial markets are booming, and wealth appears to be growing exponentially for some, a growing number of economists worry that excess capacity in the productive economy—accompanied by poverty that constrains the worldwide consumption base—means that a global recession is in the works (Bello, 2002).

The creation of a global economy, the rise of financial capital, and the ruthless competition in the economy of goods and services has changed the way corporations look and operate. In short, these conditions have made corporations leaner, meaner, bigger, more diverse in terms of the goods they produce, and more involved in complex financial dealings and investments throughout the world.

To survive overcapacity, corporations have merged to trim operating costs. Volvo and Ford have made an alliance, Renault took over Nissan, and Chrysler teamed up with Daimler-Benz. Chasing the high profits found in the financial sector, traditional corporations have gotten into the money lending business, while banks have become involved in new kinds of businesses, like trading securities. Today, transnational corporations find it hard to survive without diversifying into multiple goods in many countries, and this explains why the last decades have witnessed the greatest rate of mergers and consolidation in history (International Forum on Globalization [IFG], 2001: 6; see Figure 19.1). It also helps explain why the same handful of corporations can be found almost everywhere, offering a similar range of products in the world's shopping malls and airports (Box 19.1). These giant corporations trade with one another, but they also trade goods and services internally. Economists estimate that a third of

FIGURE 19.1   FOREIGN DIRECT INVESTMENT AND CROSS-BORDER MERGERS AND ACQUISITIONS

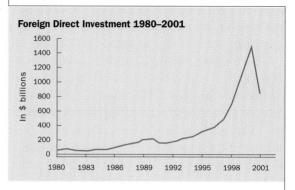

Foreign Direct Investment 1980–2001

SOURCE: World Bank 2003.

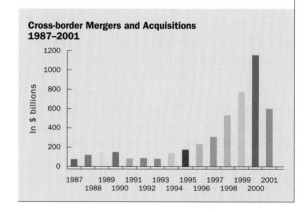

Cross-border Mergers and Acquisitions 1987–2001

SOURCE: UNCTAD 2002:337.

all global trade involves transfers between different branches of the same corporation (Ellwood, 2001:54).

GROWTH OF THE CORPORATE GIANTS

Corporations have become bigger and more powerful than many national governments. Consider just these two facts (IFG, 2001: 6; Karliner and Lewis, 2002):

1. Of the largest 100 economies in the world, 52 are corporations (measured by sales), and 48 are countries (measured by gross domestic product).
2. The world's five biggest corporations in terms of sales (General Motors, Wal-Mart, Mobil, Ford, and DaimlerChrysler) have sales that exceed the gross domestic product of 182 countries combined.

The food brand Kraft demonstrates the complexity and expansiveness of a diversified transnational corporation. Today, it is difficult to go shopping without buying a Kraft product, even if you are a vegan and don't eat cheese! Kraft Foods is the largest food producer in the United States and the second-largest in the world, sells in 145 countries, has more than 200 production facilities, and has a global work force of more than 103 000. Even though Kraft is both large and omnipresent, it can be difficult to keep track of the many corporate structures linked to Kraft products. Kraft's story began simply enough, when it was founded as a wholesale cheese company in Chicago in 1903. Kraft's corporate genealogy quickly became very complicated as it acquired new products, took over other firms, and was in turn acquired by another corporation.

In 1988, Philip Morris—a multinational tobacco company—purchased Kraft Foods for US$12.9 billion. Some analysts speculated that Kraft's family-friendly image might offset the negative associations of Philip Morris being the world's biggest tobacco company. Philip Morris combined Kraft with General Foods a year later to form Kraft General Foods. Like other corporations in the early 1990s, Kraft General Foods experienced merger mania; Kraft gobbled up multiple companies around the world that sold coffee, candy, cheese, chocolate (including Toblerone), and cereals (including Shreddies and Shredded Wheat). In 1995, Kraft General Foods was reorganized and renamed Kraft Foods, while Kraft General Foods International became Kraft Foods International. In 2000, Philip Morris purchased Nabisco Holdings (a giant cracker and snack company), which it also merged into the Philip-Morris Kraft empire. In 2003, after negative publicity about a tobacco giant making food, as well as rising concern about the company's liability in tobacco and obesity class action suits, a company with the vague name of Altria became the parent company to the Kraft and Philip Morris family of food, cigarettes, and beer.

SOURCE: http://www.altria.com/about_altria/01_05_02_kraftstory.asp.

It will perhaps surprise you to learn that big corporations do not necessarily pay big taxes. In fact, corporations are paying less in taxes than they used to in percentage terms. Companies regularly play nation-states against one another, pressuring governments to lower taxes rates by threatening to move production to a more favourable location. The resulting decline in corporate taxes can be observed across all developed countries in the last two decades, as mobile individuals and corporations increasingly take advantage of global tax shelters, forcing governments to rely on taxes paid by less mobile individuals and small businesses (Figure 19.2). Between 1996 and 2000, two-thirds of corporations operating in the United States paid no taxes at all (including Microsoft, which paid no taxes in 1999 even though it reported income of $12.3 billion), while firms like Enron, Colgate-Palmolive, and Goodyear received tax refunds from the government (Burtner, 2004). Canadian corporations have also enjoyed big tax breaks which they justify by their need to compete with low tax rates in the U.S. Reductions in corporate taxes between 2000 and 2010 will decrease the Canadian government's federal revenues by $12.5 billion a year (Jackson, 2005).

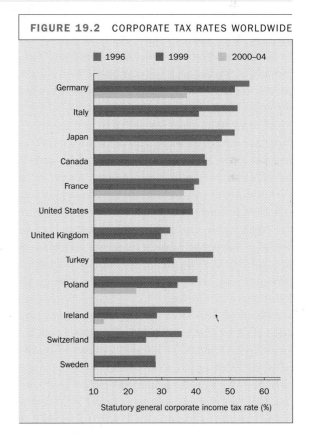

FIGURE 19.2   CORPORATE TAX RATES WORLDWIDE

SOURCE: Canadian Council of Chief Executives, http://www.ceocouncil.ca/en/view/?document_id=133&type_id=6.

CRITICS OF CORPORATE POWER

Bottom-up globalizers have reacted to the growth of global corporations in various ways (Bello, 2002; Starr, 1999). For example, the 1990s saw the emergence of an anti-sweatshop movement in North America after poor working conditions in the garment industry were exposed (Ross, 1997). Of particular importance was the 1996 Kathie Lee Gifford controversy, which revealed that her Wal-Mart clothing line was produced by child labour and involved human rights abuses. In 2000, Naomi Klein's *No Logo* became an international best-seller. She argued that large corporate brands are vulnerable to a backlash against corporate power. "Today," she wrote, "more and more campaigners are treating multinationals, and the policies that give them free reign, as the root cause of political injustices around the globe" (Klein, 2000: 338). AdBusters, a rabble-rousing media organization headquartered in Vancouver, launched multiple campaigns to "un-cool" famous brand names associated with sweatshop labour and environmental degradation (AdBusters, 2005). Corporate Accountability International (formerly Infact) launched a Kraft boycott in 1994 to expose the business practices of its parent company, Philip Morris, such as its alleged promotion of tobacco to children. More recently, Kraft has been targeted by the Sierra Club, which criticizes Kraft for using genetically engineered ingredients in its food products.

Corporations have responded to anti-corporate criticism in various ways. For example, some have changed their name, diverting attention from their infamous brand. Philip Morris became Altria, much to the dismay of anti-smoking groups who argued this was an underhanded public relations move to obscure the company's roots in the tobacco industry. After receiving bad publicity about its genetic engineering, Monsanto became Pharmacia for most of its communications after merging with pharmaceutical giants Pharmacia and UpJohn.

Another way that global corporations are attempting to stem the tide of bad press is through a growing movement for corporate social responsibility, in which corporations voluntarily try to introduce best practices for labour and the environment. The Gap, for example, released a report in 2004 that openly admitted a host of wage, health, and safety violations by its production subcontractors and promised to do better. There is continued controversy over what is certified as responsible corporate behaviour

and who is in control of the certification process. Philip Knight, CEO of Nike, withdrew a $30 million donation to the University of Oregon in May 2000 after the university endorsed a student-run regulatory organization (Workers' Right Consortium) instead of the Fair Labor Association, a labour-rights group backed by the White House with corporate executives on its board of directors.

The growing power of corporations has not emerged in a political vacuum. As corporations have grown in strength, some governments have lost ground, both to corporate power and to international institutions, like the World Trade Organization. This has lead many analysts to wonder if the age of globalization means the end of the state system.

ARE STATES STILL RELEVANT IN A GLOBAL WORLD?

Critics of neoliberal policies have wondered about the extent to which states continue to be the main instrument of democratic governance. Has the state been replaced by a kind of "global governance?" Does real power rest in the hands of unelected officials in the world's three biggest international financial institutions, the International Monetary Fund (IMF), the World Bank, and World Trade Organization (WTO), sometimes called "the three sisters?" Because of pressure to meet the demands of these three powerful international financial institutions, some critics argue that states have become less oriented to meeting the demands of citizens. The result is a **democratic deficit** in which ordinary citizens are disenfranchised from the process of governance. Let's look briefly at how the three sisters challenge the capacity of states to make democratic decisions for average citizens.

THE THREE SISTERS

The IMF was established after World War II. Its official role was to maintain the stability of the international monetary system. Since the 1980s, the IMF has come to serve a different, yet important role as the gatekeeper of the institutional financial system. IMF loans are conditional on the lending government following a package of reforms known as "structural adjustment programmes" (renamed "poverty-reduction strategies" in 1999; Brym et al., 2005; Woodroffe and Ellis-Jones, 2000). IMF

FIGURE 19.3 RESISTANCE TO IMF POLICIES IN POOR COUNTRIES, 1999–2000

SOURCE: Map of IMF protests in poor countries from "World World Development Movement Report" by Jessica Woodroffe and Mark Ellis-Jones, September 2000; cited in Woodroffe and Ellis Jones (2000). Reprinted by permission of World Development Movement.

reforms typically require countries to deregulate capital markets, remove price subsidies, decrease social spending, orient the economy toward exports, and privatize state-run industries. If a country refuses to adopt the reform package, it can find itself shut out of international lending circles and unable to service its debt. Many poor countries have witnessed massive protests against the IMF (see Figure 19.3).

Like the IMF, the World Bank was also established after World War II, and its job was to make loans to help postwar reconstruction. Most World Bank loans were made to poor countries and were often tied to large development projects, such as hydroelectric dams. As a condition of receiving loans, the World Bank required that certain structural adjustment criteria be met. Like the IMF, the World Bank has had its share of critics, both external and internal (see Chapter 9, Inequality among Nations). In response, the World Bank increased its collaboration with local nongovernmental organizations (NGOs). Although some observers applaud these efforts as part of the Bank's self-help approach to

social problems, others argue that the Bank's NGO collaborations do not change its fundamentally undemocratic nature or the severity of its structural adjustment reforms.

The WTO emerged in 1995 out of the postwar trade treaty, the Global Agreement on Tariffs and Trade (GATT). The WTO's job is to lower trade barriers, thereby increasing international trade and, presumably, prosperity. The WTO became known to many North Americans with the famous "Battle of Seattle" in 1999. WTO meetings in that city were met by huge, disruptive street protests. Every major meeting of the WTO since then has elicited protests, often from citizens of poor countries who charge that international trade works only to the benefit of the rich and ignores the unfair protection of corporate agribusiness at the expense of farmers. Although some globalization-from-below organizations argue that trade liberalization will help the poor (e.g., Oxfam and Live 8 organizers), others argue that it will not and that entry to the WTO forces countries to comply to a set of trade rules written by wealthy countries for their own benefit (Bivens and Hirch, 2003).

AN AMERICAN EMPIRE?

Although the IMF, World Bank, and WTO influence state policies throughout the world, not all states are equally affected by these institutions. Some observers note that the age of globalization is also an age of more power for some states, notably the United States, and powerlessness for states at the bottom of the global hierarchy. Critics of the United States accuse it of acting like an empire. Neoconservative thinkers in Washington acknowledge that the United States acts like an empire, although they argue that it uses its power benevolently to promote peace and democracy throughout the world.

Analysts debate whether the United States is actually a modern day empire or a fading superpower (Ferguson, 2004; Wallerstein, 2002). What seems clear, however, is that the United States still possesses a high degree of political, economic, and military power that allows it to make unilateral foreign policy decisions (such as the invasion of Iraq, which took place without the endorsement of the United Nations), adopt unorthodox economic policies (like running huge fiscal deficits), and maintain a substantial military presence globally (see Figure 19.4).

GLOBAL INEQUALITY AND THE "FOURTH WORLD"

Another feature of the global state system is a widening power gap between and within states. In the 1970s, analysts often divided the world into three parts. The "first world" comprised the wealthy capitalist countries. The "second world" comprised the countries of the communist bloc. The "third world" comprised all the rest. This division is now inaccurate. The old third world now comprises a disparate assortment of nations that don't necessarily share common traits, the communist second world has for the most part collapsed, and it has become evident that widespread poverty exists even in the rich first world.

To meaningfully capture asymmetries among the world's countries today, analysts sometimes refer to the division between the "global north" and the

---

FIGURE 19.4 U.S. MILITARY BASES WORLDWIDE

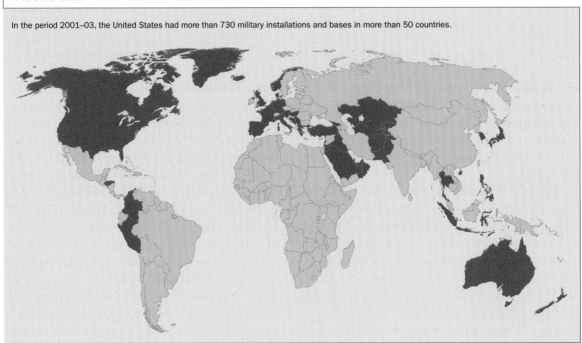

In the period 2001–03, the United States had more than 730 military installations and bases in more than 50 countries.

This map depicts the extent of U.S. military bases worldwide in 2001–03. PBS's news series *Frontline* features interactive maps that allow viewers to compare the U.S. military presence historically and get information about the number of troops stationed in different regions. Visit http://www.pbs.org/wgbh/pages/frontline/shows/pentagon/maps/.
SOURCE: Global Policy Forum, http://www.globalpolicy.org/empire/intervention/.

"global south" or between developed and developing countries. Another useful terminological distinction is between the "majority world," which is generally poor and lacks basic social goods, like housing, food, employment, and education, and the "minority world," which is generally well educated and has access to good jobs and public goods, like health care.

People from the privileged minority world may live in wealthy countries like Canada, but they can also live in Mexico City or Hong Kong. Similarly, people from the majority world can be homeless and searching for adequate food and shelter in downtown Toronto. The majority world/minority world distinction serves as a valuable reminder that state borders do not always indicate who benefits and suffers in a globalized economic system and that the relatively high living standard of the Canadian middle class is a global anomaly (Milanovic, 2005; see Box 19.2).

Although the global economy has made a portion of the world's population wealthy, a large proportion of the world's people (at least 50 percent) are considered poor (and live on less than US$2 a day). The global economy operates independently of large populations and geographical areas, which are seen as irrelevant for its functioning. These marginalized populations and regions are sometimes called the **fourth world** (Cardoso, 1993; Castells, 1998;

Hoogvelt, 1997: 66, 162). The fourth world exists as a result of the new economic and technological paradigm of global competitiveness, where only a portion of the world's states and inhabitants are competitive in the global economy.

Recognizing that time-space compression and the global economy affect people differently allows our understanding of globalization to become more nuanced. Globalization involves intense connections within the core of the global system, as people in the minority world travel more, hold global investments, and integrate the Internet into their daily lives. At the same time, globalization involves a process of *peripheralization* that marginalizes certain groups. Some people in rich countries like Canada—Aboriginal peoples, the homeless—are subject to exclusionary processes like those that affect people in parts of Africa, Asia, and Latin America (Hoogvelt, 1997: 129).

THE GLOBAL CONSUMER

Maybe you have yet to be convinced that globalization has anything to do with you. But have you gone shopping lately? If you consume commodities—goods purchased in the marketplace rather than made from your own labour—then you are inevitably part of globalization. The tags on your clothing are more likely to read, "Made in China" or "Made in Bangladesh" than "Made in Canada."

A **global commodity chain** is "a [worldwide] network of labor and production processes, whose end result is a finished commodity" (Hopkins and Wallerstein, 1986: 159). Global commodity chains are not transparent to the casual consumer. When you eat a tomato on a fast-food hamburger, you usually don't know whether it has been shipped from Mexico or a local greenhouse. When you buy a pair of running shoes, the price tag doesn't tell you much about the workers who made the shoes or the company's environmental track record. In this section you will learn about the critical role consumption plays in the global economy, as well as some of the social and environmental critiques of globalized consumerism.

A GLOBAL GLUT

Although consumers don't always understand the complexity of global commodity chains, consumption plays a critical role, driving growth in the global economy.

BOX 19.2   GLOBAL EXTREMES

The following facts illustrate the extent of economic inequality in the world.

- The wealth of the world's three biggest billionaires in 1999—Bill Gates (US$90 billion), Warren Buffett (US$36 billion), and Paul Allen (US$30 billion)—was greater than the combined income of 600 million people living in 48 of the world's least developed countries.
- In 2004 one family—the Waltons, heirs to the Wal-Mart fortune founded by Sam Walton—controlled US$100 billion. The Waltons are worth more than the GDP of New Zealand and more than the GDP of 123 of the world's nations.
- In 2004 the collective worth of the 100 wealthiest people on the *Forbes* list of the world's elite jumped half a trillion dollars from 2003 to reach US$1.9 trillion.
- About 1.2 billion people lived on less than US$1 per day in 2004.

SOURCES: Bello (2001: 167); Kroll and Goldman (2004).

High consumer spending increases economic growth, while a lack of consumer confidence is associated with economic slowdown and recession. Because North American and European markets are relatively saturated consumer markets, many corporations see expansion into global markets as essential for growth. *Consumerism*—a way of life in which identity and purpose are oriented primarily to the purchase and consumption of material goods—is currently being exported to the world's middle and working classes.

As noted above, the global economy suffers from a problem of overcapacity that makes it essential to find new consumer markets. In particular, many corporations are looking to expand sales to China, the world's most populous country, to solve the problem of overcapacity. So far, Chinese production has been focused primarily on export markets, thereby worsening the problem of global overproduction (Bello, 2002). This might change in the future, however, given that demand for consumer goods is steadily growing. For example, China is now the largest single market for cell phones. Chinese consumerism is fuelling wealth creation; the retail sector grew by 13 percent in 2004 (*Forbes*, 2004).

CULTURE AS COMMODITY?

Another characteristic of globalized consumerism is the tendency to treat culture like any other commodity. The United States has been instrumental in advancing this viewpoint—not surprisingly, given the tremendous size and power of the culture and entertainment industry in the United States. The biggest U.S. export consists of mass-produced products of popular culture (Barlow, 2001).

Although many countries have a tradition of protecting cultural products, like films and magazines, the United States has used the WTO to prohibit states from using subsidies and quotas to protect domestic cultural products, like films, magazines, books, and music. For example, in 1997 the WTO supported a U.S. complaint and ruled that the Canadian government's usage of preferential tax and postal rates to protect domestic magazine industry was unlawful. (American magazines make up 85 percent of the magazines found on Canadian newsstands.)

A growing movement to resist this interpretation of culture as a commodity is centred on a 2005 UN treaty: the United Nations Educational, Scientific and Cultural Organization's (UNESCO) Convention on Cultural Diversity (CCD). The UNESCO Convention was vehemently opposed by the United States, since the treaty will allow states to exclude cultural policies from free trade deals. As with most treaties, the devil will ultimately lie in the legal details, yet the CCD opens up the possibility for states to legally protect domestic cultural industries from the rules of trade.

CULTURAL IMPERIALISM?

The global spread of consumerism has been criticized as a form of *cultural imperialism* (Barlow, 2001). From this viewpoint, global corporations, bolstered by sophisticated advertising tools, media monopolies, and declining trade barriers, are exporting a Western way of life throughout the world (Tomlinson, 1991). Cultural imperialism is often associated with liberal values around sexuality, feminism, and secularism.

Of course, people are not passive recipients of Western cultural products, which can be taken up in unique ways. A Japanese game show like *The Iron Chef*, for instance, represents a unique cultural hybrid that combines an American game-show format with Japanese cultural and culinary mores. The result is unlike any show made by American television producers, yet it has been a huge hit on the U.S.-based cooking network and spawned *Iron Chef America*, an English-language version of the show.

The Iron Chef.
SOURCE: ©TWPhoto/Corbis.

TABLE 19.3 U.S. MARKET SHARE OF FILM INDUSTRY FOR SELECTED COUNTRIES, 2001

COUNTRY OR REGION	PERCENTAGE OF FILM INDUSTRY BELONGING TO U.S. MOVIES
United States	93.1
Canada	85.0
United Kingdom	81.4
Australia	80.6
Spain	67.0
European Union	65.4
Italy	59.7
France	51.0

SOURCES: Global Policy Forum (citing International Networks Archive), http://www.globalpolicy.org/globaliz/charts/movietable.htm. The Canadian statistic was added from data provided by the Media Awareness Network, http://www.media-awareness.ca/english/resources/articles/sovereignty_identity/culture_heritage.cfm.

Western cultural products are transformed as they are consumed by different global cultures. This does not mean that the world's cultural products compete as equals. Free trade favours large economies and big economic actors. Canadians are much more likely to eat in a McDonald's than they are to eat in a Jollibee, the leading fast-food restaurant in the Philippines. Because of the tremendous economic power of Hollywood, filmgoers in Canada are far more likely to watch a movie made in Hollywood than we are to watch a film made in Denmark or even a film made in Canada. French political figures, such as President Jacque Chirac, have been particularly vocal in criticizing the cultural power of Hollywood. He has used the French state to protect and promote the French film industry (see Table 19.3) Chirac warns of a "catastrophe" for global diversity if U.S. cultural dominance goes unchallenged (Agence France-Presse, 2004).

Although tremendous economic and cultural power is centred in the corporate culture of the United States and Europe, there are important exceptions. Arab-language television station al-Jazeera counters the global prevalence of CNN, offering an Arab alternative to U.S.-produced news. An English-language channel of al-Jazeera, featuring such Western journalists as famed British interviewer David Frost, went on the air in 2006, making al-Jazeera's presence felt even more widely. The largest producer of movies in the world is not Hollywood but Bollywood—the film industry based in Mumbai (formerly Bombay), India, which produces more than 1000 films a year and attracts more than 10 million Indians to the cinema every single day. Bollywood films are seen in Russia, the Middle East, Africa, and by Indian immigrant communities around the world. The cultural pervasiveness of Bollywood films is so great that smaller Asian countries, like Bangladesh, have reacted against the perceived domination of Indian movies, which crowd out Bangladeshi films. In addition to Bollywood, a film industry arising out of Nigeria, called Nollywood, produces films with actors and themes that are wildly popular with African viewers, and which some Nigerians believe have "eliminated the cultural stranglehold of Hollywood" (Kennedy, 2004).

GLOBAL BRAND BACKLASH

Although the term "cultural imperialism" may drown out the subtlety of global cultural exchange, visible signs of antagonism toward Western-style consumerism exist. One way that global consumerism is being contested is through a backlash against corporate brand names. Branded goods, like Coke, Barbie, and Nike, have a particular political, social, and cultural importance because of their connections to

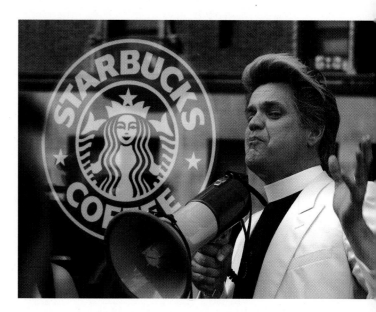

The Church of Stop Shopping, led by "Reverend Billy," promotes "retail interventions" into corporations like Starbucks. To see material on the Reverend's anti-consumer campaign and their intervention scripts see http://www.revbilly.com.

SOURCE: Reprinted by permission of Reverend Billy.

global corporations (Klein, 2000: 5). Just as transnational corporations have spread globally, so have their brands, and now McDonald's, the Gap, and Starbuck's are all frequent targets of street protests around the world.

McDonald's has been the target of protests in more than 50 countries, and Hindu activists have demanded that the prime minister shut down all McDonald's because it offends traditional Indian vegetarian food culture (Brownell and Horgen, 2004: 61). Tens of thousands of Indians protested the opening of the first Kentucky Fried Chicken outlet in 1995, bringing together environmentalists, farmers, health officials, and anti-globalization activists. Eventually, KFC abandoned business in India (Brownell and Horgen, 2004: 61; Schlosser, 2001: 244; Wall, 2000). Anti-American sentiment also affected Coke throughout the world. Consumption has dropped off in favour of domestic soft drinks, leading Coke to retool its sales strategy by focusing on specialized local drinks (Hays, 2000).

The idea that corporate globalization can be effectively fought by protesting against branded products is controversial. Many people argue that global corporations are geniuses at using social dissent to sell

new consumer products (Frank, 1997; Heath and Potter, 2004). Just as 1960s radicals wore tie-dyed T-shirts and drove around in Boogie Vans, today it is also possible to purchase consumer products that express disgust with the global capitalist system. People can wear a Che Guevera T-shirt while reading *AdBusters* and listening to Rage Against the Machine on an iPod. The extent to which anti-consumer activism disrupts global flows of wealth is unclear. Marketing gurus are well aware of them and advise global corporations to advance their brand by using anti-establishment messages to sell products to young people around the world (Lindstrom, 2003: 132).

CONSUMER ALTERNATIVES: FAIR TRADE

Subverting corporate logos is not the only tactic used to disrupt global commodity chains. Bottom-up globalizers also focus on developing consumer products that are environmentally sustainable and produced by well-paid workers. The fair-trade movement is one of the main proponents of this approach, arguing that producers should be paid a fair price rather than the free market price (Figure 19.5).

FIGURE 19.5   COMPARISON OF FAIR TRADE AND FREE TRADE COFFEE PRICES, 1989–2006

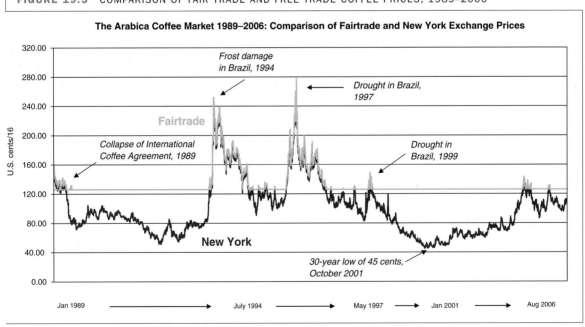

This graph shows a comparison of minimum Fairtrade price and the world market price for coffee, as measured on the New York Stock Exchange.
NOTES: Fairtrade minimum price = 121 cents/lb + 5 cents/lb premium. When the New York price is 121 cents or above, the Fairtrade price = New York price + 5 cents.
SOURCE: UK Fair Trade Foundation Online, http://www.fairtrade.org.uk/about_fairtrade_highlights_2002_fields.htm.

The fair-trade movement has paid special attention to coffee. Around the turn of the twenty-first century, the market for coffee plummeted to a 30-year low, leaving coffee prices below the cost of production for many farmers and causing heightened levels of poverty and debt for 25 million coffee-producing families throughout the world (Oxfam, 2002). According to its proponents, fair-trade coffee is an important solution to the "sweatshops in the field" that characterize contemporary coffee production. Fair-trade coffee allows producers to earn a living wage while protecting the environment since most fair-trade coffee is "shade-grown" (grown alongside trees that support wildlife and biodiversity).

Although the market for fair-trade coffee is growing steadily, it represents only a small fraction of the total coffee market. Although big brands have increasingly agreed to sell certified fair-trade coffee in their retail outlets, it represents a miniscule percentage of their total sales (less than 1 percent of the coffee sold at Starbucks is fair-trade, and less than 1 percent of all the coffee sold in the United States is fair-trade certified; Global Exchange, 2004). Fair-trade coffee organizations must also convince consumers to pay more for their coffee—a choice that goes against the socialization of most consumers to shop around for the best deal.

ECOLOGICAL CONSEQUENCES OF CONSUMERISM

Global consumerism has also been criticized for being based on a Western high-consumption lifestyle that is ecologically unsustainable, particularly if it is adopted by more people around the world. Twenty percent of the world's population (more than 1.2 billion people) living in the industrialized developed world currently consume two-thirds of the world's resources and create 75 percent of all waste and pollution (Speidel, 2003: 5). What would be the implications if even a quarter of the remaining 80 percent of the world's people began to consume at the rate of wealthy Europeans and North Americans?

The size of China's economy alone has increased by two-thirds since 1990, and the Chinese currently consume more grain, meat, fertilizer, steel, and coal than the United States (Speidel, 2003: 5). If China consumed as much oil per capita as the United States, China's total oil demand would be 80 million barrels a day—and currently the world only produces 60 million barrels a day (Speidel, 2003: 5). Although some analysts say the solution to this problem is to find more oil, most experts believe that the world does not have enough reserves to sustain this level of consumption for long. Moreover, current levels of fossil fuel consumption are linked to atmospheric ozone depletion and global climate change. Sustainable consumption probably lies somewhere between the world's two extremes of overconsumers and underconsumers—at levels maintained by the roughly 3.3 billion people who eat moderate amounts of food (especially meat), rely primarily on sustainable modes of transportation, like walking and public transportation, and consume minimal amounts of raw materials in their daily lives (Durning, 1992; see Table 19.4).

Although proponents of top-down globalization hope to turn the global middle-income strata into overconsumers, the ecological challenge is to extend middle-income consumption habits to the world's poor underconsumers and the world's elite overconsumers. This will not be an easy political feat given the push to expand global consumption to address the problem of overcapacity in global production. The global economic system is currently organized

TABLE 19.4 WORLD CONSUMPTION CLASS			
CATEGORY OF CONSUMPTION	**CONSUMER CLASS (TOP 20%)**	**MIDDLE-INCOME CLASS (MIDDLE 60%)**	**POOR (BOTTOM 20%)**
Diet	Meat, packaged food, soft drinks	Grain, clean water	Insufficient grain, unsafe water
Transport	Private cars	Bicycles, buses	Walking
Materials	Throwaways	Durables	Local biomass

SOURCE: Table 2-1, World Consumption Classes, 1992, from "How Much Is Enough? The Consumer Society and the Future of the Earth" by Alan Durning. Copyright © 1992 by Worldwatch Institute. Used by permission of W.W. Norton & Company, Inc.

around, and requires, high levels of consumption. In addition, it seems that the world's consumer class is often more interested in maximizing their individual consumption possibilities than they are in voluntarily curbing their consumption habits. Surveys shows that totally committed ethical shoppers constitute only 5 percent of the shopping population (Bird and Hughes, 1997: 160) and two-thirds of Americans in the US$75 000+ income bracket believe they need 50 percent to 100 percent more income to satisfy their consumption desires (Schor, 1998). It is unclear how to build a more sustainable economy that also provides economic opportunities and good jobs—a topic to which I now turn.

GLOBAL WORKERS

Karl Marx and Friedrich Engels (1972 [1848]) ended the *Manifesto of the Communist Party* with the now famous phrase, "Proletarians [workers] of all countries, unite." The political unification of working people across national borders is, however, relatively rare. Capitalists, in contrast, have proven adept at global planning and organization. Global capitalists have used numerous organizations and venues to formulate economic policy and interact with government policy makers, like the World Economic Forum held annually in Davos, Switzerland.

Global workers are relatively immobile and politically fragmented. Some of them cross international borders, but working abroad is constrained by international travel restrictions and work permits. When workers do move abroad to work, they are not always able to take their families with them and may be separated from loved ones for years at a time. Labour unions are struggling to protect workers in the competitive, footloose business environment of neoliberalism. Although capital can move across borders with relative ease, unions are primarily organized within rather than across states. There have been attempts to increase the level of transnational union organization and solidarity, but most unions are primarily oriented to protect domestic workers and wages against the "threat" of foreign workers. In addition, many workers who travel abroad work in sectors that are relatively un-unionized and underregulated (e.g., nannying, the sex trade, agricultural workers), leaving them vulnerable to exploitation. Although serious obstacles to organizing global workers remain, globalization processes have increased public awareness of

sweatshop exploitation in factories around the world, leading some companies to ban the use of sweatshop labour. This section details some of the opportunities and challenges that globalization processes present for global workers.

WAGE LABOUR AND WAGE INEQUALITY

The world of global labour might seem relatively mundane compared with the branded world of transnational corporations and global consumer goods. Yet without a global labour force, there would be no goods for consumers to consume and no profits for capitalists. For most of human history, people acquired daily necessities through their own work—baking their own bread, making their own clothes, and trading minimally and locally for other daily staples. Today, people in industrialized countries understand the concept of wage labour as both normal and "natural." Most people exchange their labour for a money wage, which they then use to pay their rent, buy groceries, and so forth.

Throughout the world, however, there is still a sizable section of the population for which the concept of wage labour is new. These people gain access to food, water, and shelter directly through their own work rather than receiving a money wage and purchasing needed commodities. Half the world's people still make a living off the land and subsist mainly on what they produce themselves. In South Asia and sub-Saharan Africa, a full 70 percent of the population makes its living off the land, and 80 percent of the Chinese population are peasants (Ainger, 2003; Ross, 2004: 124).

As the use of wage labour spreads across the globe, so does the *segmentation* of labour markets. Women, people of colour, rural workers, and the people from the developing world in general are overrepresented at the bottom of the wage hierarchy. There is a tremendous disparity in global wages, particularly when comparing ordinary workers' pay with the salaries of Chief Executive Officers (CEOs) (see Figure 19.6).

Although American income inequality is the most extreme among the world's rich countries, income and wealth inequality is also a problem in Canada, and one that worsened in the late 1990s (Picot and Myles, 2005). The average Canadian worker earned around $36 200 in 2003, while the average CEO earned $3.2 million (McFarland, 2005). Disparities in the

FIGURE 19.6 CEO SALARIES VERSUS PROFITS, STOCKS, AND WORKERS' PAY, 1990s

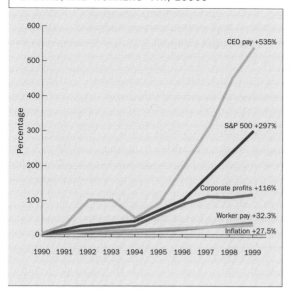

This chart shows the growth of CEO compensation in the 1990s, compared with stock performance, corporate profits, and salary growth for lower-level employees.
SOURCE: "CEO Salaries Under Fire as Stocks Dive," by Bill Catlin, Minnesota Public Radio, March 28, 2001. Available online: http://www.minnesota.publicradio.org/features/200103/28_catlinb_ceo/. Reprinted by permission of The Institute for Policy Studies.

Canadian labour market are based on class, as well as on race and country of birth. Although many Canadians try to avoid minimum-wage work, thousands of migrants from Mexico and the Caribbean travel to Canada each year to work at agricultural jobs for minimum wages seven days a week, with no overtime pay or statutory holidays (Basok, 2002).

Although Mexicans working in Canada are denied the labour rights granted Canadian citizens, minimum wage jobs in Mexico are worse in terms of remuneration. Wages in Mexico remain stubbornly low despite the 1994 North American Free Trade Agreement (NAFTA) that Mexico signed with Canada and the United States. NAFTA was sold as a "rising tide" that would "lift the boats" of workers in the three countries. Yet the Mexican Labour Ministry reported that in 2003 workers earned an average of $360 a month, 16 percent less than they earned a decade earlier (Dussell Peters, 2004: 4; Jordan, 2003). Because 87 percent of Mexicans earn less than half of the minimum wage in the United States, the incentive to migrate (legally or illegally) remains higher than ever before, and cross-border migration remains a serious economic and political issue in both Mexico and the United States (Pickard, 2005).

Are low wages an age-old problem, or are they a unique result of globalization? The historical record shows that the search for cheap labour has been going on for hundreds of years. Indentured workers were brought from China to construct the North American railway system, while impoverished Irish immigrants competed with freed African-American slaves for unskilled work in nineteenth-century North America. Globalization has heightened corporate competition for cheap labour, however. Firms use the threat of relocation as a way of keeping wages low. In effect, workers from different parts of the world compete against one another to attract foreign investment, driving wages down.

Given growing corporate competitiveness to find cheap labour, employment in a solid, blue-collar job can no longer be taken for granted. Millions of North American workers in the manufacturing sector were laid off in the 1980s and 1990s (Beder, 2000: 132) and organized labour suffered serious setbacks, especially in the United States (Nissen, 2000: 3). Not only have the number of North American manufacturing jobs declined since the 1980s, but corporations have also thinned out their management tiers, eliminating white-collar positions, outsourcing service jobs (e.g., call-centre jobs and computer programmers) to South Asia, and making it unclear whether a university degree guarantees middle-class economic status (Anderson, Cavanagh, Lee, and the Institute for Policy Studies, 2005: 33; Ehrenreich, 2005). The solid, blue-collar manufacturing job or white-collar office job that allowed men to financially support a stay-at-home wife and two children in a middle-class lifestyle is now relatively rare, and about two-thirds of Canadian mothers work outside the home. Economists report that a third of Canada's economic growth between 1997 and 2005 was due to the proliferation of two-income households (CBC News, 2005).

Although manufacturing jobs were lost to lower-wage settings in the globalization period, service sectors jobs have mushroomed in the world's rich countries. Certain well-paying job sectors have expanded their ranks (e.g., teachers and nurses), but most new jobs are created in low-wage, temporary sectors of the service sector with median wages that fall near or below the poverty line (e.g., retail salespersons, cashiers, food preparation and serving, janitors, home care workers, and waiters) (Anderson et al., 2005: 43–44). Although unemployment rates are relatively low (hovering around 5 percent in the United States and 7 percent in Canada in 2005), economic analysts have identified the problem of "subemployment" and the "working poor," terms that describe a situation in which workers have work but it is poorly paid, unstable, and un-unionized, and fails to lift workers above the poverty line (CBC Radio One, 2004; Ehrenreich, 2001; Sheak and Morris, 2002; Shipler, 2004).

The growth in service jobs has been partially met by a rising number of migrant labourers who moved from developing countries to Europe and North America. Labour migration has increased the ethnic diversity of the labour force in the world's rich countries and, in turn, fuelled a racist, anti-immigrant backlash in some countries, especially in Western Europe. Despite these political conflicts, international migration is likely to continue to Europe and North America given that the baby-boom generation of workers is aging, birthrates are low, and a potential shortage of skilled workers looms in the future for most advanced industrialized countries. Together, these trends have increased competition between Canadian provinces and between highly industrialized countries to attract highly educated immigrants (Howlett, 2005: A7). The trend of south-to-north labour migration has raised questions in countries like Canada about how to recognize foreign credentials and integrate new immigrants into the economy, particularly since new immigrants experience a disproportionate degree of poverty and lower levels of unionization (Milkman, 2000; Picot and Myles, 2005: 20). Meanwhile, voices from less developed countries speak of a "global brain drain" in which skilled professionals leave their homelands to seek better opportunities in developed countries, a trend thought to cost India US$2 billion a year (United Nations, 2001).

SEARCHING FOR CHEAP LABOUR: "THE RACE TO THE BOTTOM"

Governments have reacted in different ways to the global competition to create jobs and attract corporate investment. In the less developed countries, states have set up **export processing zones (EPZs)** where special financial deals—tax holidays, preferential rates for electricity and telecommunications, special exemptions from national labour laws, and the like—are used to lure corporations to set up shop and provide jobs. The most famous EPZ in North America is the *maquiladora* region in northern Mexico. *Maquiladoras* are factories that allow companies to assemble goods for export by using low-cost Mexican labour and imported high-tech machinery and parts.

Maquiladoras employ low-cost labour compared with the United States and Canada, but since 2001 hundreds of thousands of *maquiladora* workers have been laid off, threatened with layoffs, paid lower wages, and compelled to work in worse conditions. Why? Mexican labour is cheap, but not cheap enough in a global marketplace where transnational firms try to find the world's least expensive, least regulated, and least unionized labour supply. Although Mexican wages are a bargain by Canadian standards, low-cost manufacturing has increasingly moved to Indonesia, Vietnam, and China, where labour is even cheaper (the Chinese legal minimum wage is 31 cents per hour) (Bacon, 2003; Ross, 2004: 8). Wage competition pits workers against one another in a "race to the bottom." Globalization has placed Mexico in a difficult position: Wages are too low to alleviate poverty rates yet too high to continue to attract low-cost manufacturing.

Although working conditions in the factories of the developing countries are often wretched, some members of the world's labour force suffer in conditions that resemble slavery in the literal sense of the word. An estimated 27 million people worldwide are enslaved in economic relationships generating $13 billion of goods and services each year (Bales, 1999). We are connected to this extreme form of labour exploitation through global commodity chains. In the words of Kevin Bales, a sociologist and expert in global slavery:

> Slaves in Pakistan may have made the shoes you are wearing and the carpet you stand on. Slaves in the Caribbean may have put sugar in your kitchen and toys in the hands of your children. In India they may have sewn the shirt on your back and polished the ring on your finger. They are paid nothing. . . . Your investment portfolio and your mutual fund pension own stock in companies using labor in the developing world. Slaves keep your costs low and returns on your investments high. (1999: 3–4)

The injustices of the global labour system have not gone unnoticed or uncontested, even though serious obstacles lie ahead for unions and workers. In Canada, unionized workers as a percentage of nonagricultural workers fell from a high point of 38 percent in 1981 to 32 percent in 2003, while the American unionization rate fell to just 12.5 percent in 2004. Historically, unionism arose in large capitalist factories, yet globalized firms often decentralize and subcontract work to small, independent firms, making unionization and labour regulation more difficult. Unions have responded to these conditions by developing new strategies that include cross-border organization, transnational solidarity campaigns, emphasizing the importance of good wages for all working people (not just union members), and drives to organize service-sector workers, such as janitors, hotel workers, and security guards (Babson, 2000; Frundt, 2000; Milkman, 2000; Nissen, 2000).

The anti-sweatshop movement of the 1990s raised awareness of labour exploitation by transnational firms (Ross, 1997, 2004). Today, prominent retail corporations, like Nike and the Gap, must at least appear to take global labour issues seriously (recent reports suggest that working conditions are still abysmal in Nike's subcontracted operations) (Ross, 2004: 42). Although it was unimaginable to promote a "sweatshop-free" clothing line in the early 1990s, the popular label American Apparel has proven that it is possible to run a successful business without the use of sweatshop labour. Although American Apparel rejects unions, it pays its Los Angeles workers rates above the state's minimum wage and houses all of its workers in one building in Los Angeles (Ross, 2004: 1). Other clothing lines like "No Sweat" use unionized labour in North America *and* developing countries. According to the "No Sweat" website, "We believe that the only viable response to globalization is a global labor movement" (No Sweat, 2005).

GLOBAL ECOLOGY

Capitalists, consumers, workers, citizens, and nations all play critical roles in the globalization processes I have outlined. In turn, all of these actors fit together in a larger global ecology that connects people, resources, and commodities. To better understand these ecological connections, I now examine the globalized food system.

GLOBAL FOOD

Global trade in agriculture allows relatively prosperous consumers to consume a wide variety of exotic fruits, imported bottled water, and distant marine life, like shrimp and fresh tuna. Although the global trade in food products is a boon for discriminating eaters, critics of industrialized global agriculture question its environmental costs. Trade experts and environmental groups warn that agriculture is the largest contributor of greenhouse gas when food production and distribution chains are taken into account, and they suggest that the global food system represents the biggest environmental challenge facing humanity (Clay, 2004; Shrybman, 2000).

One of the major environmental problems with the world's agricultural system is the immense amount of fossil fuel required to produce, package, and transport food. Fossil fuel consumption generates greenhouse gases, such as carbon dioxide, which are linked to the eroding ozone layer and global climate change. But why is food so closely linked with carbon dioxide emissions? The first and simplest answer is transportation. Today, most Europeans and North Americans eat foods that have travelled a long distance to get to their plates. Food's travel time is captured in the concept of "food kilometres," a measure of the distance food travels from production to consumption and an indicator of the amount of fossil fuels burned in the process. A Toronto study compared the food kilometres of conventional agricultural products purchased at a discount supermarket with the same basket of goods purchased at a nearby farmers' market (Bentley, 2004). While the supermarket food travelled 5734 kilometres on average, the same farmers' market produce travelled an average of only 101 kilometres to get to the consumer (Bentley, 2004: 7).

Food transported from far away might add variety to our diet, but it frequently involves an unsustainable and irrational energy tradeoff. For a head of iceberg lettuce transported from California to the United Kingdom, 127 calories of nonrenewable fossil fuel energy are required to produce 1 calorie of food energy (Sustain/Elm Farm Research Centre Report, 2001: 1). The way that most of our foods are produced and packaged also relies heavily on fossil fuels. The food-processing industry uses 10 calories of fossil fuel energy to produce 1 calorie of food energy. Intensive livestock operations are even more wasteful: 1 calorie of beef requires 35 calories of fossil fuel, and 1 calorie of pork requires 68 calories of fossil fuel. Because of these energy-intensive production techniques, food scholars estimate that if the entire world adopted North American food habits, fossil fuel reserves would be gone in just seven years (Manning, 2004: 42, 44).

Soil, Water, and Genetic Engineering

Besides relying heavily on fossil fuel, industrial methods of food production are associated with global environmental problems, like deforestation, soil erosion, and declining water tables. In the past 40 years, soil degradation has caused farmers around the world to abandon about 430 million hectares of arable land. This area amounts to one-third of all cropland (Kindall and Pimentel, 1994; see Figure 19.7). Every year, 130 000 km^2 of forest, an area four times the size of Switzerland, is destroyed to make way for agriculture. By 2020, an estimated 22 million hectares of savannah and forest, an area as large as the United Kingdom, will be cut down in South America to meet global demand for soya, a crop that is used largely for livestock feed and vegetable oil (World Wildlife Fund, 2004).

Even when adequate land can be found to grow crops, water is also needed. Seventy percent of world water usage is for irrigation, and food analysts worry about an emerging "world water deficit" (Brown, 2005: 10). Underground aquifers refill slowly and are currently being pumped at rates that are unsustainable. In Northern China, for instance, groundwater levels are falling by at least one metre a year, while aquifers in the United States are being pumped at a pace that vastly exceeds replacement rates (Pimentel and Wilson, 2004).

Some scientists believe that global agriculture problems can be addressed by switching to genetically engineered (GE) crops that have been designed to be drought- and pest-resistant by reengineering the plant's genetic structure. This technological solution is opposed by many environmentalists, who worry about the long-term health and ecological impact of GE crops, particularly the negative impact on biodiversity, since GE crops tend to out-compete and contaminate related species. GE canola has already infected organic canola in Western Canada to such an extent that it is impossible for organic farmers to grow and market uncontaminated (GE-free) organic canola. A group of Saskatchewan farmers has launched a lawsuit against seed giant Monsanto to sue for damages. Activists in less developed countries are concerned that GE crops will permit large corporations to consolidate their control over agriculture and erode traditions of seed saving and innovation by farmers.

FIGURE 19.7 GLOBAL SOIL DEGRADATION

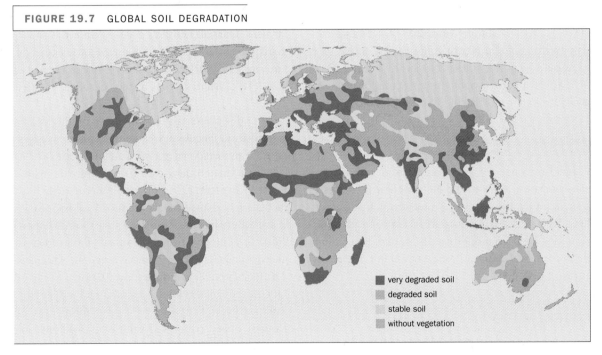

very degraded soil
degraded soil
stable soil
without vegetation

SOURCE: PovertyMapping.Net, http://www.povertymap.net/mapsgraphics/index.cfm?data_id=23360&theme=. Reprinted by permission of UNEP GRID-Arendal.

Because of these controversies over GE technology, most of the world's genetically modified crops are grown in just a handful of countries; 99 percent are from Canada, the United States, Argentina, China, and Brazil. Because of the huge capital investment in these technologies, multinational bioscience companies would like to increase adoption rates globally. One way this is occurring is through food aid, which contains genetically engineered crops. This issue made headlines in 2001–02, when southern Africa experienced a famine and was given genetically modified maize by the United States. African leaders protested, not only for health and safety reasons but also for fear that the GE corn would contaminate their own supplies (assuming that people would save some of the corn to plant in future harvests), and endanger export markets in Europe, where GE foods are banned (African Centre for Biosafety, 2005).

In 2005, scientists discovered that food delivered through the World Food Program (WFP), especially grain supplies from the United States Agency for International Development (USAID), to Central American and Caribbean countries was heavily contaminated with genetically modified corn. Eighty percent of the samples tested included GE corn, including "StarLink," corn that is not authorized for human consumption in the United States (Organic Consumers Association, 2005). The UN Cartagena Protocol on Biosafety stipulates that genetically engineered crops can enter countries only with prior informed consent, but the WFP's heavily reliance on USAID grain supplies means that this right is currently not being enforced and that genetic contamination of the world's global grain supplies seems likely to continue.

Global Hunger amidst Plenty

The world grows enough grain to provide nearly 3000 calories per person per day (Lappé 2005: 13) yet the number of undernourished people in the world has risen since the early 1980s, totalling at least 842 million people today (Wheeler and Thompson, 2004: 212). World grain production is a general measure of global food security. Per capita grain production has been falling since 1984, while overall grain production was flat between 1996 and 2003 (Brown, 2005: 4).

In Europe and North America there is a growing movement to eat foods that are locally grown and produced with organic farming techniques.
SOURCE: Shutterstock.

It is especially troubling to consider these numbers in the context of widespread soil erosion, loss of cropland to urbanization, rising global temperatures, and shrinking water supplies—all of which will have a negative impact on the capacity of global grain production (Brown, 2005: 7). With population rising to an estimated 9 billion people by 2050, and the low likelihood of expanding global grain supplies much further, grain prices will likely rise in the future. For affluent consumers, this would make food supplies, particularly meat, more expensive. For the world's malnourished people—half the global population by some estimates—this situation will make it increasingly difficult to access the basic food staples needed for survival.

Think Globally, Eat Locally

Is there an alternative to the current system of global agriculture? In Europe and North America there is a growing movement to eat foods that are locally grown and produced with organic farming techniques. Researchers in the United Kingdom have estimated that if all farms in the United Kingdom became organic, an estimated $1.1 billion in environmental costs would be saved (Lang and Pretty, 2005; Lappé and Lappé, 2002).

The move to promote organic, locally grown food is not confined to the affluent minority world. The Navdanya movement in India, for instance, aims to promote indigenous agricultural techniques to counter the presence of multinational agribusiness in ways that improve the environment and increase people's food security (Navdanya, 2005). A growing number of Africans believe that organic farming techniques, not genetic engineering or food aid, are the answer to famines and food shortages (Hall, 2005).

The tension between local and global food represents the challenge and the paradox of bottom-up globalization. It is a challenge because most small-scale activists and food producers, like most of the world's workers, are rooted in local places where they grow food and are not nearly as globalized as corporate agribusiness and its CEOs. It is a paradox because peasant and small farmer movements want to encourage *local* food consumption, defend *local* agricultural ecosystems and, at the same time, use *global* networks to fight these battles. Their motto could be "think globally, eat locally."

Cuba: An Island's Isolation and Innovation

What would happen if globalization processes were reversed, and a country suddenly found itself isolated, without the ability to trade for food in global markets? Cuba provides a real-life answer to that question. It is literally an island but is also a metaphorical island in that it is largely isolated from the major ebbs and flows of global food trade. The United States has refused to trade with Cuba ever since the Cuban revolution in 1959. After the collapse of the Soviet Union, Cuba lost access to the food supplies and fossil fuels it received from the Soviet Union. Suddenly, the nation was hungry. Calorie consumption per person per day fell from 3000 calories in 1989 (the year the Soviet Union collapsed) to 1600 calories four years later.

Without fossil fuels or cheap grain supplies, Cuba's agriculture had to change, and change it did. Cuban agronomists began experimenting with more sustainable, low-input agriculture that used crop rotation to provide natural fertilization. They developed large urban gardens to feed and employ thousands of Cubans. Farmers began using oxen instead of tractors, saving fossil fuel. Today, almost completely cut off from global agricultural trade, Havana feeds itself from gardens within city limits. There are still problems ensuring adequate supplies of milk and meat, yet Cuban agriculture is remarkably successful, leading some analysts to suggest that the Cuban model is a possible future scenario for what agriculture could look like when fossil fuel supplies become scarce and the environmental consequences of globalized industrial agriculture become too onerous to ignore (McKibben, 2005: 69).

In an article profiling the costs and benefits of the Cuban agricultural experiment, environmental Bill McKibben concludes with a provocative and difficult question that we would do well to ponder—a question that applies not only to Cuban agriculture but also to globalization more generally:

> Is it also possible . . . that there's something inherently destructive about a globalized free-market society—that the eternal race for efficiency, when raised to a planetary scale, damages the environment, and perhaps the community, and perhaps even the taste of a carrot? Is it possible that markets, at least for food, may work better when they're smaller and more isolated? The next few decades may be about answering that question. (McKibben, 2005: 69)

SUMMARY

1. Globalization effectively shrinks the world; workers, commodities, ideas, and capital cross distances more quickly. Sociologists use the term "space-time compression" to describe this process.

2. Globalization processes have generated contradictory outcomes that benefit some groups but have also been linked with poverty, economic marginalization, democratic deficits, and the digital divide.

3. Developments in information technology have facilitated the economic integration of financial markets. Consequently, global flows of financial capital are much bigger than global flows of tangible goods and productive capital.

4. Corporations in the global era have become much bigger and are under pressure to become more competitive in the global marketplace. Local or even national competitiveness is no longer seen as sufficient for economic survival.

5. Politically, the globalization era has witnessed the creation of new international institutions of governance, such as the IMF, World Bank, and WTO, which have diminished the power and sovereignty of some states.

6. Globalization processes have allowed communities around the world to gain knowledge of the injustice and suffering inflicted by the global economy. Such awareness has inspired efforts to increase social justice in the global system. These efforts are known as "bottom-up globalization."

7. Most of the goods Canadians consume connect them to workers and production processes thousands of kilometres away. The globalization process is almost impossible to escape given the extent of global commodity chains.

8. The period of globalization is associated with a shift in manufacturing employment out of the more developed countries. Competitive pressure is driving corporations to seek the lowest wages possible in the less developed countries (the so-called race to the bottom).

9. Global ecology is not something that exists separately from globalization processes. It is connected to the actions of citizens, consumers, workers, and states.

QUESTIONS TO CONSIDER

1. How do you benefit from globalization processes? What is the negative impact of these processes? Consider you role as a worker, consumer, and citizen.

2. Do you think globalization has caused the Canadian state to lose sovereignty? Do you think Canadians suffer from a democratic deficit?

3. Do you think that consumer activism and social movement campaigns, like the anti-sweatshop campaign, are an effective way to make global commodity chains more equitable? Do you think that the corporate movement for social responsibility offers a more promising avenue for change? Is voluntary corporate action sufficient or are governments needed to make legislation and enforce corporate responsibility?

GLOSSARY

Bottom-up globalization is a short-hand way of describing a diverse range of projects seeking greater democracy, equality, and sustainability in globalization processes. These projects are generally opposed to neoliberal policies and U.S. hegemony in the global system and are also referred to as alternative globalization, the global social justice movement, and "anti-globalization."

A **democratic deficit** involves the disenfranchisement of ordinary citizens from the decisions and process of governments. Democratic deficits are often attributed to the influence of corporate actors and international financial institutions on governments and the transfer of governance to institutions like the International Monetary Fund (IMF) and World Trade Organization (WTO), which do not permit average citizens to vote or influence decisions.

The **digital divide** is the gap between people who are easily able to access communication technologies, like the Internet and cellular phones, and people who lack the material resources, education, or infrastructure to access these technologies.

Export processing zones (EPZs) are manufacturing areas in which government programs providing special incentives to help promote export-oriented manufacturing. Sometimes EPZs are actual territorial "zones" demarcated by fences and borders, while in other cases they indicate programs that apply to all industries within a nation. For instance in 1991, Sri Lanka declared the entire nation an EPZ.

The **fourth world** comprises marginalized populations and regions that are not competitive in the global economy.

A **global commodity chain** is a worldwide network of labour and production processes, the end result of which is a finished commodity.

Globalization is a social, economic, and political process that makes it easier for people, goods, ideas, and capital to travel around the world at an unprecedented pace.

Neoliberalism refers to economic policies that became prominent from the late 1970s onward in both developed and developing countries. Neoliberalism draws from the classical free market economic theory of Adam Smith but is considered new or "neo" because it followed a historical period of vigorous state economic regulation known as Keynesianism (1930s to 1970s). Neoliberalism is associated with a retreat from state intervention and regulation, greater focus on individual responsibility, less protection for labour and the environment, privatization of state resources, and faith in the power of the market and the profit motive to provide the greatest good for the greatest number.

Space-time compression refers to the diminished importance of geography and time lags because of globalization, especially since the late 1970s.

Top-down globalization refers to the extension of capitalism globally, particularly as a result of the neoliberal policies and programs authorized by international financial authorities, such as the IMF and World Bank, and implemented by national governments. Top-down globalization is organized by elites in governments, corporations, and international institutions without much democratic input.

SUGGESTED READING

Brecher, Jeremy, Tim Costello, and Brendan Smith. (2000). *Globalization From Below.* Cambridge, MA: South End Press.

Ehrenreich, Barbara, and Arlie Russell Hoschschild, eds. (2002). *Global Woman: Nannies, Maids, and Sex Workers in the New Economy.* New York, NY: Metropolitan Books.

Ellwood, Wayne. (2001). *The No-Nonsense Guide to Globalization.* London, England: Verso Press.

Sachs, Jeffrey. (2005). *The End of Poverty. Economic Possibilities for Our Time.* New York, NY: Penguin Press.

Scholte, Jan Aart. (2000). *Globalization. A Critical Introduction.* New York, NY: St. Martin's Press.

WEB RESOURCES

Companion Web Site for This Book

http://www.newsociety5e.nelson.com

Begin by clicking on the Student Resources section of the website. Next, select the chapter you are studying from the pull-down menu. From the Student Resources page, you have easy access to InfoTrac College Edition® and other resources, such as the Glossary and Flashcards. The website also has many useful tips to aid you in your study of sociology.

InfoTrac College Edition Search Terms

Visit http://www.infotrac-college.com for access to more than 20 million articles from nearly 6000 sources when doing your online research.

ThomsonNOW™

http://hed.nelson.com

This online diagnostic tool identifies each student's unique needs with a Pretest that generates a personalized Study Plan for each chapter, helping students focus on concepts they are having the most difficulty mastering. Students then take a Posttest after reading the chapter to measure their understanding of the material. An Instructor Gradebook is available to track and monitor student progress.

PART SIX

Methods

CHAPTER TWENTY

Research Methods

In this chapter you will learn that

- Science is one of several sources of knowledge. Like other sources of knowledge, it can be wrong. However, unlike other ways of knowing, science uses methods of gathering theoretically relevant evidence that are designed to minimize error.

- Research methods are used by sociologists to gather evidence in order to test theories about recurring patterns of human activity. Underlying these techniques is a variety of assumptions about the nature of facts, objectivity, and truth.

- In comparison with the evidence available to natural scientists, an added complexity confronts social scientists: Humans assign meaning to their actions, and interpreting meaningful action is complicated.

- Sociologists have devised many useful methods of obtaining evidence about the social world, including experiments, interviews, observational techniques, and surveys.

- Good sociological research adds to our knowledge of the social world, expanding opportunities and options by helping to solve social problems.

SOURCE: Zigny Kalunzny/Stone.

Neil Guppy
UNIVERSITY OF BRITISH COLUMBIA

INTRODUCTION

Social research involves systematic, purposeful study. The systematic nature of sociological research comes, in part, from the methods sociologists use. Fundamental to methods is the careful collection of evidence. However, only evidence relevant to theoretical ideas is useful in social research. The purposeful structuring of sociological inquiry comes from asking theoretically informed questions. Systematic sociological study integrates sound theory with careful methods.

This chapter introduces you to the principles of research methods. I begin by outlining some basic assumptions involved in social science research, including assumptions about personal values or bias, the nature of facts, and the sources of knowledge. Next I explain how the subject matter of the social sciences—people—differs from the objects of inquiry in the natural sciences (e.g., molecules, plants). People studying people adds complexity to social research because social behaviour is meaningful. That is, people interpret their own behaviour and the behaviour of others by trying to understand meanings. This complexity has led to the development of various methods of social research, and I review these techniques of research in the final section of the chapter. Methods of observation and questioning lie at the heart of much research, and I review the strengths and weaknesses of each of these approaches.

PERSPECTIVE

Guy Paul Morin and David Milgaard were convicted of murder. In January 1995, three years after his conviction, but subsequent to new DNA tests, Guy Paul Morin was formally exonerated of all charges against him. David Milgaard had to endure prison longer but in July 1997, after 23 years in prison, he too was exonerated. Again DNA testing was instrumental. Judges, juries, and prosecutors had weighed evidence that they believed demonstrated the guilt of these men. Circumstantial evidence, filtered by expectations and values, had led justice astray. Subjective judgments had seriously compromised these men's lives.

An inquiry into Guy Paul Morin's conviction claimed that science helped both to convict and to exonerate him (Kaufman, 1998). In sharp contrast, Gold (1998) claimed that "good science" exonerated Morin, but it was "not science that helped convict him." But what makes for "good science"?

Wrongful convictions are rare. The criminal justice system minimizes such error through rules of evidence and presumptions of innocence. Likewise

Sociological theories were first proposed in the nineteenth century as secular accounts of rapid social change. By the early twentieth century, systematic methods for empirically testing hypotheses were being introduced.

SOURCE: Carol Wainio, *Untitled* (1985). Acrylic on canvas, 33″ × 50″. Photograph courtesy of the S.L. Simpson Gallery, Toronto. Reproduced with permission of the artist.

science is organized to minimize error. Science is not perfect, however, and it is important not to put scientific practice on a pedestal, somehow immune to human foibles. Like all human activities, the social practice of science is influenced by subjectivity.

SCIENCE AS A SOCIAL PRACTICE

Science needs subjectivity but it cannot be overwhelmed by subjectivity. Subjectivity is important to certain phases in the practice of science while detrimental to others. Understanding the complexities of scientific methods requires distinguishing between times when subjectivity is beneficial and times when it is not. But just what is subjectivity? Most people would agree that our personal values and expectations are a core part of subjectivity. Frequently people separate the world into facts and values; the real and objective versus the personal and subjective.

But what appears to us as reality is filtered or screened. Reality exists, certainly—it is no figment of the imagination. However, our values and expectations filter reality. While the saying "what you see is what you get" has an intuitive appeal, we know the claim is false. It exaggerates. Other things, especially our expectations and values, affect what we see.

Here is an example of filtering. The sun is real. It is no figment of our imagination. We commonly speak about "sunsets" and "sunrises." But these terms deceive. Although we have all watched a "sunset," the sun does not set. Our language conditions us to think of a moving sun, but the earth rotates around the sun. The earth's spin creates the *illusion* of a moving sun.

Being skeptical of my claim about a filtered reality is important. Values and expectations influence our perceptions of reality, but they do not completely determine what we see. This is a critical point. The *extent* to which values and expectations influence what we see is debatable, but that is a secondary point. The key point is that *if* our perceptions of reality can be affected by our values, *then* how can scientists ever know for certain that what they "see" is true? Put another way, if observation cannot be a rock solid foundation of scientific knowledge, then how is the practice of science to be understood?

An important claim of this chapter is that reality does not exist as some neutral scientific judge. Pure observation does not rule supreme. To think of an individual scientist as a detached, arm's-length observer of the physical or social world, making observations to test ideas, is to profoundly misunderstand science. The scientific method is not a mechanical process of collecting facts to prove things. Science is a much more complex activity and the methods of scientists are designed in the face of such complexity. Here is an illustration of how values and expectations may creep into scientific work.

Recall from your high-school biology classes the work of Gregor Mendel. Mendel is the father of genetics. He cross-fertilized varieties of pea plants and noted that inherited traits followed consistent numerical ratios (i.e., the expression of dominant and recessive genes over successive generations). These experiments, demonstrating landmark principles of heredity, remain controversial (see Orel, 1996). R.A. Fisher, while a Cambridge University undergraduate, demonstrated that Mendel's results seemed fabricated. The likelihood that Mendel produced results conforming so closely to his hunches about heredity was, Fisher showed, in the order of 1 in 30 000.

Fisher's contention has itself been hotly disputed. Mendel may have been lucky, producing possible but very unlikely results. Alternatively, Mendel, or his assistant, may have unconsciously misclassified some pea plants. Classifications made by Mendel were not clear-cut, and so his experimental results may have been interpreted as favouring his preconceived ideas. Mendel may not have rigorously checked the experimental results because they proved what he expected. In this vein, Fisher (1966 [1936]: 123) claimed that Mendel's results were a "carefully planned demonstration of his conclusion."

The concept of "observer bias" (making unconscious mistakes in classifying or selecting observations) is now commonly discussed as a danger to good methodological procedure. Mendel did not clearly and publicly describe his procedures. His data are no longer available for re-examination. Although it is impossible to know exactly why his results came out as they did, his ideas about genetics have proven invaluable.

Good research methods are designed to minimize the types of errors that have been attributed to Mendel's experimental evidence. These methods do not eliminate the biasing effect that values and expectations have on scientific research. They do, however, seek to minimize their impact.

MINIMIZING BIAS IN SOCIAL SCIENCE

As a social science, sociology applies scientific practices to the study of human society. These scientific practices incorporate several ways of reducing bias, especially the twin pillars of public (open) scrutiny and skeptical reasoning. Scientific ideas become provisionally accepted only after scrutiny by the scientific community. It is not enough for an individual scientist to proclaim a link between family background and children's school success or between HIV and AIDS; these links must be demonstrated by presenting research findings at scientific conferences, subjecting findings to peer review, and ensuring that research results can be replicated. The scientific community is organized to promote critical scrutiny.

Scrutiny is not enough, however. If the scrutiny is not rigorous and probing, then it is of little value. Scientific practice also encourages skeptical reasoning. New ideas are accepted only after others have critically examined them, only after they have withstood a barrage of questions from doubters. Examples of this doubting come from questions like this: Could something other than HIV cause AIDS? If HIV does cause AIDS, exactly how does the causal process work? Does HIV cause AIDS among all people? This process of doubting is built into the way science is conducted.

Scientists are also trained in methods of research designed to minimize the influence of their personal values and expectations on the results of their research work. They work to root out error both in reasoning and in observation. So, for example, scientists learn to collect and analyze information according to rules that reduce the risk that results will be affected by bias. Much of the latter part of this chapter focuses on these specific research techniques.

Science has prospered because of this healthy skepticism and public scrutiny. Both natural and social science have played a pivotal role in making our world a better place in which to live, by helping to curtail malaria, improving the life chances of children with disabilities, and reducing gender inequity. Scientists are not infallible saints, however. The scientific community is not some sacred haven where only truth and enlightenment reign. Instances of fraud and deceit are part of science (Park, 2000).

It is also important to correct a possible misinterpretation about the role of values and expectations. I have portrayed these as "problems." This is too one-sided. Science would be substantially weaker, if not impotent, without values and expectations. Science is soaked through with individual judgments. Mendel's brilliance came from his expectation that passive and recessive genes played a fundamental role in explaining inheritance. Mendel provided a new way of seeing the world, a new conceptual map for understanding.

Expectations and values are in tension within the scientific enterprise. Without them the spark of creativity and passion would be low, but with them we can be led to false conclusions (as judges and juries are occasionally misled). Put differently, objectivity and subjectivity each play an important role in science, including sociology. **Objectivity,** which is what courtroom judges and jurors strive for, stresses that observations should be free of the distorting effects of a person's values and expectations. Conversely, subjectivity is essential to change and innovation. Without people championing their own visions, we would have little creativity. A hallmark of science is its creativity. Mendel's was a beautiful solution to the mystery of inheritance, even if he may have been overly exuberant in his experimental research.

Science depends on both the creativity of new explanations about how things work and the assessment of whether these explanations are plausible. In sociology this dual character resides in a division between theory (explanations of how the world works) and methods (ways of assessing the veracity of explanations).

Most of this chapter is about assessing evidence. It explores how sociologists work within the rules of scientific method. First, however, I contrast scientific knowledge with other forms of knowledge. The discussion moves next to the steps involved in the sociological research process. I then describe the main methods of gathering sociological data and the decisions that have to be made during the research process. Finally, I return in the conclusion to the role of subjectivity in research.

SCIENTIFIC VERSUS NONSCIENTIFIC THINKING

To differentiate good and bad science, consider what characterizes scientific thinking. Before the 1700s and the rise of science, our ancestors knew many things about how the world worked. Much of this was custom or common sense—when to plant, what to plant, where to plant. Religious knowledge held centre stage in community life. Stories of creation, of how we came to be on Earth, were powerful tales that gave coherence to peoples' lives. Religious doctrine and common sense remain powerful in many societies, but scientific ways of knowing have increasing authority in industrial nations.

What characterizes this scientific way of knowing? A key contribution came from the Scottish philosopher David Hume (1711–76). He disputed the popular argument of his day that science begins with observation. Hume argued that no matter how many observations you make, you cannot infer your next observation. This is known as the *problem of induction*. Put more graphically, no matter how many white swans you see, you cannot infer that all swans are white. However, observing one black swan is sufficient to refute the claim that all swans are white.[1] Hume was railing against Francis Bacon's claim that observation was the bedrock of science. For Hume the collection of "facts" is useless unless you understand how to interpret them.

In Charles Dickens's *Hard Times*, Mr. Gradgrind demands facts: "What I want is Facts. . . . Facts alone are wanted in life." Contrary to the popular saying, though, facts do not speak for themselves. Blue mould growing on spoiling food is a fact of life that many people have observed. It was only in 1928, however, that Alexander Fleming recognized this blue mould as a potent medical tool. Many people had seen blue mould, but only Fleming understood it as penicillin. Mr. Gradgrind could have collected blue mould for a lifetime, but that would have done him little good. Science is not a collection of facts. However, among other things, it is a method of collecting facts.

Facts are bits of evidence, information that you or I can verify by using our senses. Because trillions of bits of human activity might be taken as facts, how do we select what should count as evidence? How do sociologists avoid idiosyncratic fact gathering? Sociological theory provides guidance for the hunting and gathering of facts. Evidence is gathered to test ideas, hunches, or theories. Only selected bits of human activity are used as evidence. Those selected bits are chosen because they relate to a sociologist's theory about how the world works.

In the twentieth century, Sir Karl Popper (1977 [1934]) improved this thinking with his provocative notion of falsification. As he claimed, observations refuting a well-conceived idea are always more important than evidence supporting or proving a theory (e.g., black swans). For Popper, science does not start by gathering raw facts. It starts with a question or hunch, or in his words, a well-conceived conjecture.

Two core ideas about distinguishing scientific thinking from other ways of thinking have been presented earlier: public scrutiny and skeptical reasoning. Popper added the principles of testability and uncertainty. Testability is easy to understand. For an idea to be scientific it must have testable implications; it must be falsifiable.

The concept of uncertainty may be more difficult to accept. Many people misunderstand science as a doctrine of certainty. As Park (2000: 39) puts it, "many people are uneasy standing on . . . loose soil; they seek a certainty that science cannot offer." As Hume argued centuries before, observations cannot be the bedrock of science because of the problem of induction. Equally, however, science cannot proceed, as Popper correctly argued, without the possibility of observations that could refute a scientific claim. Observations based on well-reasoned methods can ferret out error and misunderstanding, although these same observations cannot guarantee universal truth or perfect certainty (see Box 20.1).

NATURAL VERSUS SOCIAL SCIENCE

The scientific practices of chemists and sociologists share many elements. The research methods of both disciplines help in understanding and explaining why certain patterns emerge. Furthermore, values are important in this process because these values underlie the creative imagination so central to scientific puzzle solving. Values also have the potential to bias or distort observations, and both the natural and the social sciences must guard against distortion. If the scientific method is defined as a set of practices or procedures for testing knowledge claims, then both chemists and sociologists are doing science.

There is, however, a profound difference between the subject matter of the natural and the social sciences: Bacteria don't blush. This phrase neatly captures a key distinction between the research methods of chemists and those of sociologists. Human beings are conscious and creative; we can think, act, reason, and decide. We are, as Anthony Giddens (1984) phrases it, "knowledgeable actors." As sociologists, we study "ourselves"—that is, our con-

BOX 20.1   SEEING SCIENCE SOCIOLOGICALLY

One of the most influential academic books of the twentieth century was Thomas Kuhn's (1962) *The Structure of Scientific Revolutions*. Before Kuhn, many people held a "brick-building" conception of scientific progress. They thought that individual scientists contributed to building a structure called scientific knowledge, one brick at a time. As scientific knowledge accumulated, the structure became taller and sturdier.

Kuhn challenged this view on several fronts. First, he held that science developed through contributions from a community of scholars who use "paradigms" as guiding tools about how the world is organized (Mendelian genetics is such a paradigm). Paradigms guide questions and answers. Evidence not fitting a paradigm is ignored. However, if anomalous evidence persists, a "scientific revolution" results. Scholars opt for a new guiding paradigm. The transition from Newton's mechanics to Einstein's relativity illustrates a paradigm shift, or a scientific revolution (Kleppner and Jackiw, 2000).

Second, Kuhn proposed a discontinuous view of scientific progress. The community of scholars did not keep building the Newtonian structure but shifted to a new structure defined by the Einsteinian paradigm. This discontinuous view of scientific progress also influenced debates about truth. The Earth as the "third rock from the sun" we now hold as a fundamental truth. But our ancestor's were equally convinced that Earth was the universe's central rock. In the future, will our "third rock" conception seem equally odd? Kuhn's view suggests that truth is contextual. A new paradigm establishes a new context, showing us that beliefs we once held to be true were naïve or misleading.

Finally, the argument about community was sociologically compelling. In Kuhn's hands the practice of science was not understood as individual scientists ruthlessly questioning all ideas. To the contrary, paradigms provided a set of convictions about how the world was ordered. With faith in a paradigm, a community of scholars searched for what they were convinced existed. Paradigms had a disciplining effect, focusing attention on a delimited set of questions and answers. Notice also that Kuhn's view emphasized that scientific change was not gradual, but sudden (revolutionary) and that the change was organized or predictable (structured). Although not everyone agrees with Kuhn's argument, his book is one of the most influential social science texts of the last century.

temporaries and our ancestors. Bacteria, having no knowledge of social norms, do not blush when exposed to the beam of an electron microscope. Bacteria cannot think, act, reason, and decide; they cannot consciously control their surroundings or reactions in the same way human beings can.[2]

What this difference in subject matter means for sociologists and chemists is a matter of debate. Perhaps the single most important difference is that sociologists study **meaningful action**—that is, activities that are meaningful to the people involved. For example, bacteria may not blush when studied, but people often react self-consciously when they know they are being observed. To study love, friendship, or charm depends on learning something about the meanings people ascribe to their actions. This has advantages and disadvantages for sociologists. Unlike chemists, we can ask questions of the people whom we study (bacteria don't talk either!). But this advantage can also be a disadvantage. Interpreting people's answers is not easy.

Because of this difference in subject matter, sociologists have developed an array of methods to help them understand and explain human activity. Since asking questions has advantages and disadvantages,

good sociological research either employs a variety of ways to ask questions or relies on observational techniques to aid in understanding and explanation.

METHODS OF SOCIAL RESEARCH

EXPLANATION

Sociologists have shown repeatedly that the years of schooling people receive is strongly influenced by family background. Children raised in poverty tend not to go as far in school as do children from upper-class families. Although this research demonstrates a link between family background and educational attainment, this link is, as I have reported it, descriptive, not explanatory. I have offered no reason *why* this relationship between family origin and educational destination exists. It is true that I have noted a potential cause (family background) and an effect (years of schooling), but I have failed to provide any mechanisms through which this implied causal process might operate. An **explanation** would be judged adequate only if it could show how family background actually influences educational outcomes.

The mere association or correlation between social origin and educational destination does not prove causality. The relationship between smoking and lung cancer is a good example of the rule that *correlation does not prove* **causation.** Smoking has long been linked to lung cancer, but only in the past two decades have we learned more about the causal mechanisms underlying this correlation. Cigarette companies, especially, have argued that the presumed connection was **spurious,** meaning that something other than smoking caused lung cancer (see Box 20.2). Accumulated evidence and a more precise notion of the underlying modes of transmission have established that the original correlation is causal.

We might try to explain the link between family and schooling in several ways (Davies and Guppy, 2006). An obvious factor is money. Although public schooling is free, costs are incurred for field trips, tutoring, international tours, postsecondary education, and a host of other events. Children living in poverty may remain in school for fewer years than their upper-class peers because of these costs (and they may seek employment sooner to help with family income).

Money seems to be a partial explanation for the link, but other factors may be at work as well. Many skills and values taught in school may be more readily grasped by children from upper-class families, not because these children are smarter than are children living in poverty, but because the home environments of the children may expose them to different skills and values. The classroom culture may be more like the culture in upper-class homes (e.g., abstract word games are valued, reading and music are prized) and these children may therefore be advantaged.

The first explanation is largely about money and material resources. The policy implications of this explanation point to eliminating or reducing the costs of schooling. This has been accomplished in large measure in Canada. However, even when the costs of postsecondary education have also been reduced (e.g., in Quebec), social-class disparities in educational attainment have remained. The second explanation points to cultural factors in the home (e.g., reading) as a reason for the family-school link. This explanation has influenced policies related to compensatory education, such as Head Start and After Four, educational programs designed to help disadvantaged children by giving them educational enrichment.

The mechanisms by which causes have effects are essential for adequate explanation. Perhaps the cardinal lesson regarding explanation is that there is hardly ever a single cause—*the* cause—for anything. Because multiple causes are involved in social-scientific explanations, a single, unitary cause rarely provides a sufficient explanation. Sociologists search for the multiple factors that can help explain some particular state of affairs. So, in the family-school example, although only two explanations for the link are mentioned here, other explanations may also be tested and refined as sociologists attempt to see how equality of educational opportunity might be attained.

UNDERSTANDING

Sociologists must not be content merely to offer explanations for why a particular relationship exists. These explanations are often sterile unless they also address the meaningfulness of human activity. People make the social world happen, and in doing so they give meaning to their actions and to the actions of others. A failure to address these meanings would leave sociology underdeveloped.

It is no simple matter, however, to understand what someone or some group means by their actions or utterances. One way to think about **understanding** is as follows. The first time I saw a traditional Greek dance, I was unable to follow the patterns of movement or appreciate the symbolism of certain motions. Similarly, the first time I watched a cricket match, I could not fathom what was happening. To the extent that I have come to understand these complex social activities, I have learned *how to proceed with the activity.* To understand a Greek dance or a cricket match means being able to participate fully in the activity, knowing what others mean by their actions and utterances, and knowing how others will interpret our actions and utterances.

A fundamental social process, called "taking the role of the other," nicely captures this idea of understanding. By imagining yourself in another person's role, you come to appreciate someone else's point of view. You come to understand, to reflect on, his or her ideas and issues. I do not mean that you must become Caesar to understand him; that would be impossible. Instead, sociologists focus on the web of relations in which people interact, paying attention to how people

BOX 20.2   CORRELATION AND CAUSATION

Where fires cause much damage, many fire trucks usually gather. This is a correlation; a lot of damage tends to go along with many trucks, while minimal damage tends to draw only a few trucks. But this "truck and damage" correlation does not prove causation. Consider Figure 20.1, below. The curved, double-headed arrow depicts the correlation between the amount of damage and the number of fire trucks. The single-headed, straight arrows show the direction of causation. The size of the fire is a common prior cause of both other variables (number of trucks and amount of damage).

FIGURE 20.1   AN EXAMPLE TO ILLUSTRATE THAT CORRELATION DOES NOT PROVE CAUSATION

Size of the fire

Number of fire trucks present

Damage caused at fire scene

Causality is controversial because it often involves something we cannot observe directly. For example, no one can see lung cancer being caused by smoking. We infer that conclusion from assembled evidence that fits with theoretical conjecture.

Here is another example. Women living in poverty typically eat less nutritious meals and consequently are more likely than better-off women to have premature babies. But not all women living in poverty have premature babies. There is a correlation between poverty levels and the incidence of premature births, and nutrition level has been identified as a key causal stimulus. Notice, however, that living in poverty does not guarantee premature births. Living in poverty only raises the probability that a mother will have a premature baby.

In a causal relationship, a change or variation in one thing produces a change or variation in another. If four basic conditions are met, causality may be established. First, two variables must be associated or correlated. Consider two variables—the likelihood of premature births and poverty. Premature births must be more likely to occur among poor women than among women who are not poor if a causal relationship exists. Second, the cause, or independent variable, (poverty level) must precede the effect, or dependent variable, (premature births) in time. (For more on independent and dependent variables, see p. 524.) Establishing that a woman is poor (or not) while she is pregnant confirms the causal ordering or temporal sequencing of the variables.

Third, the original association must not disappear once the effects of other variables on the dependent variable are examined. We need to verify that we have not made a false inference. Does the causal process really go from poverty to poor diet to premature babies?

Could it be that stress, and not poverty, is the causal agent? It may be that poor women are under more stress and that stress, not poverty, increases the likelihood of premature births. The initial causal relation between poverty and premature births would be spurious if stress was determined to be the operative factor (poverty may be correlated with stress, of course, but stress may still be the real causal agent).

Finally, we must offer a theoretical account of how one variable causes another. We must illustrate the mechanism(s) through which causation operates. This theoretical reasoning also enables us to establish which variables are important to examine when we test to see whether a causal relation might be spurious. In the example, we theorize that poverty affects nutrition, which in turn affects the likelihood of premature birth.

understand and interpret the views of others. They pay attention to "the definition of the situation," to the meanings of the people involved.

Erving Goffman's work in an insane asylum (as it was called then) is a good illustration of sociological understanding (Goffman, 1961). Goffman was not interested in getting inside the heads of the patients to learn what and how they thought about things. Rather, he was interested in how the patterns of social activity in the asylum were organized. He came to see the mental hospital from the patients' point of view. By dispensing with the medical categories and scientific labels assigned to individual patients, Goffman began to understand the ways in which patients worked cooperatively to produce a coherent social structure. He learned to appreciate how the patients defined the routine activities of the asylum and how they coped with institutional procedures that denied them privacy and stripped them of their personal identities (e.g., by issuing institutional clothing and removing personal objects).

Goffman (1961: 129) also learned about what he calls the "careers" of patients with mental illnesses: "Persons who become mental-hospital patients vary widely in the kind and degree of illness that a psychiatrist would impute to them. . . . But once [in treatment] they are confronted by some importantly similar circumstances and respond to these in some importantly similar ways. Since these similarities do not come from mental illness, they would seem to occur in spite of it." Although social life on the "inside" might seem unique or even bizarre at first, Goffman argues that anyone, patient or researcher, would, in time, come to find it much like many other communities in which he or she has participated, possessing an identifiable social organization and rhythm of activity.

Returning to the education example, explanations of high-school dropout rates that ignore the attitudes and values of the people who drop out are one-sided. An appreciation of the experiences of people who drop out is essential to a more complete account of the schooling process. Especially important here is the resistance of students to authority, often expressed through music and clothing. This resistance is not some idiosyncratic expression of random individuals, but represents part of a youth subculture that must be understood by anyone who wants to alter the schooling process to make it a better environment. How young school resisters define the situation of schooling is important to a full appreciation of dropping out.

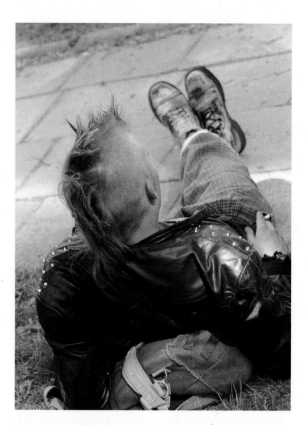

Explanations of high-school dropout rates that ignore the attitudes and values of those who drop out are one-sided. An appreciation of the experiences of student who drop out is essential to a more complete account of the schooling process.
SOURCE: Shutterstock.

Understanding and explanation work together. Although explanations of dropping out that ignore student values are deficient, merely reporting the stories of young resisters would be equally vacuous. A full appreciation of dropping out, or of any other social activity, requires both understanding and explanation. Often these activities are pursued by different researchers and their combined results contribute to fruitful research programs leading to social change.

TECHNIQUES OF SOCIAL RESEARCH

Sociologists have developed a variety of techniques for gathering evidence. I will review three of the most important: experiments, survey research, and observational studies. As you read my accounts of research procedures, keep asking yourself: How do sociologists go about developing insights about, or knowledge of, the social world? How do they come to know what they claim to know? What methods do they use and how believable are the results generated by these methods?

EXPERIMENTS

Experiments are the hallmark of scientific research and are commonly, though inaccurately, equated with science itself. Experiments are useful because they enable researchers to isolate causes and measure their effects. By no other method can researchers determine causation so precisely. An example is the best way to illustrate the point.

In exploring how ethnicity influences social interaction, Martha Foschi and Shari Buchan (1990) assigned people to one of two experimental conditions. Each person was told that he or she would be working with a partner in making judgments about the relative size of images. After seeing two contrasting images, but before finally selecting the larger, people were told of their partner's choice. People often change their mind when they hear what others think. Foschi and Buchan wanted to know whether the ethnicity of a partner would affect people's likelihood of changing their minds.

In one case ("condition one") the partner was described as East Indian, while in the second case ("condition two") the partner was described as English Canadian.[3] Because the experimenters wanted to examine the effects of ethnicity on personal judgments, they had to ensure that the only difference between conditions one and two was the partner's ethnicity. They could not, for example, let the participants meet their partners because that would expose them to more than just the partner's ethnicity (e.g., the partner's demeanour, clothing, height). All of the participants in the experiment were of European ancestry, but their "partners" were either East Indian or English Canadian. How could the experimenters subtly inform people of their partner's ethnicity, without arousing suspicion?

Foschi and Buchan developed a clever solution. First, they asked everyone to complete a questionnaire. Then, under the guise of wanting to let the participants know something about their partners, the experimenters gave everyone their partner's completed questionnaire. In fact, each participant received a questionnaire that Foschi and Buchan had previously completed. By design, only two fictitious partners existed and they differed only by surname (Sidhu or Edwards), country of birth (India or Canada), and language (English/Punjabi or English). Apart from those three attributes (i.e., the difference between conditions one and two),

participants in the experiment received identical descriptions of their partner (e.g., same sex, age, level of schooling).

The experimental results showed men were less likely to be influenced by East-Indian than by English-Canadian partners. Women did not systematically change their judgments according to their partner's ethnicity. The experimenters were confident that ethnicity was the only factor influencing the men since it was the only factor on which their partner's differed—an English-Canadian or an East-Indian partner.

Random assignment or **randomization** lies at the heart of experimental design. Using a random procedure (e.g., flipping a coin, rolling a die), people in an experiment are assigned to an experimental condition on the basis of chance. If the flipped coin comes up heads, a person is automatically placed in experimental condition one; if the coin comes up tails, the person is assigned to condition two. Although individual participants will differ with respect to sex, age, abilities, and so on, the two experimental groups will contain an approximately equal number of women and men; the average age of the two groups will be similar; and so on. This group similarity is accomplished by random assignment. Foschi and Buchan (1990) used random assignment to ensure that the only difference between conditions one and two was the partner's ethnicity.

For women, the partner's ethnicity made no difference. The treatment condition—East-Indian or English-Canadian partner—had no effect on the judgments women made. Exactly why men were influenced by ethnic cues and women were not remains open to debate. Foschi and Buchan (1990) suggest that women might be less prejudiced than men, perhaps because women have more frequently themselves been the victims of discrimination. More recently Foschi, Lai, and Sigerson (1994) have shown men are more likely to use sex as another "cue to competence," a finding that resonates with the results of the experiment just described.

By dissecting the Foschi and Buchan experiment, we can examine more carefully several key design features. The researchers began with a **hypothesis**—an unverified but testable knowledge claim. They hypothesized that ethnicity affects behaviour in social interaction. More formally, Foschi and Buchan (1990: 5) "predicted different perceptions of competence and resulting behaviour for White subjects performing a task with a partner, depending on whether the partner was White or East-Indian."

To test this hypothesis, Foschi and Buchan examined the relationship between two **variables.** A variable is a measurable concept that can have more than one value. Age is a concept we use in referring to how long someone has lived. For newborns, age is measured in weeks or months, but for everyone else it is measured in years. One variable studied by Foschi and Buchan (1990) is ethnicity. They designed the experiment so that ethnicity could have one of two values: East Indian or English Canadian. In this experiment, ethnicity is the **independent variable,** which is presumed to affect other variables. Differences in this variable are hypothesized to affect a second variable, the **dependent variable.** In the experiment by Foschi and Buchan, the dependent variable is the amount of influence a person will accept from his or her partner. It was measured by the frequency with which people changed their initial judgments after learning of their partner's choice.

Nevertheless, how do Foschi and Buchan know that only a partner's ethnicity and not another factor, such as a partner's age or social class, influence judg-ments? They are confident of their conclusion because, by design, they know that only the ethnicity of the fictitious partner differed between conditions one and two. By randomly assigning people to one or the other condition, the experimenters guaranteed ethnicity was the only systematic difference. Because participants cannot choose which treatment condition to enter (i.e., they cannot self-select), the groups can be made alike.

Sociology experiments of the type conducted by Foschi and Buchan are relatively rare, in large part because many social processes that interest sociologists are not amenable to laboratory testing. Ethical and practical problems limit the use of laboratory experiments (see Box 20.3). Furthermore, we must be cautious in generalizing the results of laboratory experiments to non-laboratory situations. The latter problem is technically expressed as the issue of **external validity,** or the degree to which experimental findings remain valid in a nonlaboratory situation. External validity is often low; relationships discovered in sociological experiments do not always hold in

BOX 20.3 ETHICS IN SOCIAL RESEARCH

Three groups share an interest in the conduct of sociological research: the sociological investigator, the people being observed or questioned, and the members larger society who enable such research to occur. Sociologists have a self-interest in their own research but it is imperative that proper weight also be given to the interests of research participants and the public. Although primary responsibility for the rights and welfare of both participants and the public must reside with the sociologist as researcher, the self-interest of the sociologist requires that some arm's-length body review research designs and procedures to ensure the protection of all.

What are the typical risks involved in social research? These are of two broad types: risks to individuals and risks to the communities or social groups. Understanding the first type—individual harm—is fairly straightforward. Social research can cause harm by asking people threatening questions that cause individual trauma (e.g., asking Aboriginal people about their memories of residential schools). Appreciating the second type—collective harm—may be less obvious. The results of social research can harm communities or groups by, for example, reinforcing stigmas and stereotypes (e.g., people living in poverty smoke more) or supporting policies that help some groups at the expense of others. Who sponsors the research of the sociologist is an important issue, especially in this latter context. Here, too, relations between political advocacy and scientific research come to the fore.

Ethically responsible research must minimize threats or risks. Informed consent is one key strategy. Researchers must ensure that people not only consent but that they also consent knowing what the research entails. Very occasionally in sociological research, deception is involved. This occurs in cases where the research requires that people not know exactly what is being studied (on the grounds that such knowledge may lead them to change their behaviour or lead them to respond in certain ways). For example, if you tell respondents your research is about the environment and then ask them what the most important problem is facing their region, many more will respond "environment" than if you did not provide this initial cue (Urmetzer, Blake, and Guppy, 1999).

In discussing a range of research projects in the remainder of the chapter, I will comment further on issues of ethics. An insightful sociological analysis of ethics is also provided by Kevin Haggerty (2004), who discusses "ethics creep" as a form of surveillance. For more details on ethics, see the Statement of Professional Ethics of the Canadian Sociology and Anthropology Association at http://www.csaa.ca/structure/Code.htm.

more "real-life" settings because these settings differ from the laboratory. Still, the relevance of laboratory findings is an empirical question. There is reason to be cautious about generalization, but often findings from the laboratory apply in other real-life contexts.

Field experiments have been used in sociology in an attempt to avoid some of the problems of laboratory experiments, especially problems of external validity. A good example of a field experiment is one undertaken in Toronto by Effie Ginsberg and Frances Henry (1985; Henry, 1999). They investigated the extent of job discrimination faced by people of different ethnic backgrounds. In one study, they sent actors, one black and one white, to apply for advertised job vacancies. The actors had similar credentials and were trained to make their job-search behaviour as identical as possible. The researchers wanted to test the hypothesis that racial discrimination existed in the Toronto labour market. Their independent variable was the race of the job applicant and their dependent variables—their measures of discrimination—included the number of interviews granted and job offers made

One field experiment that investigated the extent of job discrimination faced by people of different ethnic backgrounds found that whites had a 3-to-1 advantage over blacks in job offers.
SOURCE: Photos.com.

to each actor. They found evidence supporting a discrimination hypothesis, with whites having a 3-to-1 advantage over blacks in job offers (for discussion of a similar test of this hypothesis, see Reitz, 1993: 35).

The field experiment, conducted in a natural as opposed to a laboratory setting, reduces problems of artificiality. However, Ginsberg and Henry could explore only a limited range of jobs and were unable to focus on other urban centres, where discrimination may be more or less of a problem.

As I mentioned earlier, when people know they are being studied, they often become self-conscious. The very fact of being studied may influence their behaviour. This was demonstrated in productivity experiments conducted by Roethlisberger and Dickson (1939) at the Western Electric Company's Hawthorne factory. They found that productivity (the dependent variable) increased when they brightened the lighting, but then also increased when they dimmed the lighting. The researchers realized that people worked harder whenever the research team was studying them. Productivity increased in response to the researchers' presence not because of changes they introduced. Social scientists have subsequently used the term **Hawthorne effect** when referring to changes in people's behaviour caused by their awareness of being studied. Sociologists have had to develop other techniques for collecting sociological evidence to avoid some of the problems associated with experiments.

SURVEY RESEARCH

The social survey is the primary means of collecting social science evidence. Researchers collect information using surveys by asking identical questions of a sample of people. Political pollsters, market researchers, labour unions, governments, and university researchers all rely heavily on survey-based knowledge. Survey research is useful because it provides a method of systematically comparing answers to identical questions from a large sample of people, and it allows researchers to generalize the results to the larger population from which the sample was chosen. Questions can be posed either on a **self-administered questionnaire** or through a personal **interview**. Increasingly the Internet is used as a way to conduct surveys (Brym and Lenton, 2001).

Rhonda Lenton (1990) used survey research to investigate parents' aggression toward their children. Because of strong taboos against child abuse, asking questions about abusive behaviour is very difficult. The privacy surrounding child discipline makes observation or experiments inappropriate. Furthermore, asking blunt questions about "smacking your child" is unacceptable. Just as many alcoholics deny they have a drinking problem, many child abusers think of themselves as "strict disciplinarians." Parents use different strategies to influence their children, and Lenton wanted to examine the full range of this behaviour. Therefore, she chose to use a survey in which parents could be questioned by experienced and trained interviewers. She included questions covering an array of child-parent interactions, from praising and positive modelling through withholding privileges and love to spanking, slapping, and hitting.

A key problem facing Lenton was whether her questions about aggression and discipline would really measure child abuse. Child abuse is a theoretical concept. You and I may use the same term to mean different things. What types of maltreatment ought to be considered as child abuse? Lenton (1990: 159) defines child abuse as "any act, excluding sexual mistreatment [which she separated as sexual abuse], carried out by a parent . . . that has the intention of, or is perceived as having the intention of, hurting a child." Lenton wanted to include as "abuse" any act that a parent understands may hurt the child. To measure abuse, she asked parents whether they had done any of the following, ever, and in the past year: yell at a child, ridicule a child, withdraw emotionally from a child, hit a child with an object, withhold food from a child, and 24 other actions. Do these items provide an indication of what Lenton defines as child abuse? That is, are these valid indicators? **Validity** refers to accuracy or relevancy. Lenton's measurement of child abuse is valid to the degree that the items she uses as measures of abuse actually measure abuse as she defines it theoretically.

Lenton interviewed each parent and child separately. Each family member was asked to complete a child-discipline questionnaire, on which each of the 29 abuse items was listed. This sheet was completed privately and handed to the interviewer in a sealed envelope. By comparing the responses of all family members, Lenton could determine the consistency with which abuse was reported by different family members. This gave her confidence in the **reliability** of her measure. **Measurements** are reliable if they are consistent or repeatable. If different measures or indicators of the same concept give similar results, the measurements are reliable or, in other words, internally consistent.

Lenton faced another problem. She needed to find families with children. No publicly available list of such families exists. Lenton selected a random sample of Toronto families from the telephone directory. After first phoning to ensure that children lived in the household, members of the research team visited each eligible address to ask for permission to interview parents and children.

Surveys always involve **sampling.** Lenton's research team could never have interviewed all Toronto families (a complete enumeration of all families would be a *census*), nor would the expenditure of time and money have been efficient. Although the entire population could not be interviewed, it is this larger population about which Lenton wanted to draw conclusions. To use a different example, in doing research on urban household waste, interviewing all city dwellers is both unnecessary and impractical, even though the intention might be to use survey results to help design city policy. Information obtained from a subset of the population, the *sample*, is used to represent the views and characteristics of everyone. Samples selected by using rules of chance or probability provide random samples. These random samples give surveys better external validity than experiments do.

Samples must represent the larger population from which they are drawn. For example, one or even a few kindergarten classes cannot be taken to represent all kindergarten classes, because not all kindergarten classes are alike. Therefore, if we want to generalize about social processes common to all kindergarten classes, we need to select a number of classes for study.

Exactly how many kindergarten classes or, more generally, how many units must be included in a sample is a complex question. How many families should Lenton have selected? The precise answer depends mainly on the amount of variation or heterogeneity in the population and the degree of accuracy required in the study's conclusions. If you need very accurate results, you need a larger sample. Likewise, if the population is very variable, you need a larger sample to reflect that heterogeneity adequately. In studies of the Canadian electorate, very accurate forecasts of voting can be achieved with a random sample of about 1200 voters. The mathematical laws of probability can be used to generate efficient sample sizes.

Selecting samples is not as easy as it might seem. How would you go about selecting a random sample of students in your faculty or school? Distributing

Researchers collect information using surveys by asking people in a representative sample a set of identical questions. People interviewed on a downtown street corner do not constitute a representative sample of a country's adults. That is because the sample does not include people who live outside the urban core, underestimates the number of people with disabilities and seniors, does not take into account regional diversity, and so on.

SOURCE: Dick Hemingway.

questionnaires in classes would be one method, but many students do not attend every class. Students who attend regularly are, by definition, different from those who attend infrequently. A sample of students present in classes would therefore be biased. Using e-mail addresses might seem practical, but many students do not let schools know their working addresses or would filter surveys out as junk mail. Registration lists give an approximation of the student population, but these lists are never perfect. Students drop out as the term progresses, while others change their addresses and phone numbers. If you were studying student retention or student financial needs, the people who might be hardest to find might be the very people to whom it is most important to speak. Even with this severe limitation, however, student lists maintained by the registrar might be the best

alternative available. The list from which a sample is selected is called the sampling frame. This frame must come as close as possible to including everyone in the population.

Recently, market-research firms have been making greater use of telephone interviews in conducting their surveys. These firms usually rely on *random-digit-dialling* procedures to establish random samples. They select "banks" (i.e., lists) of working telephone numbers (e.g., 902-424-79xx), and let the computer randomly dial the last, or the last two, numbers. This method, used by Statistics Canada in some of its surveys, provides a random sample of households, including households with unlisted telephone numbers. Two important refinements are used. First, some households have more than one telephone number, increasing their chances of inclusion.

Statistics Canada asks respondents how many working telephone numbers there are in a house so that it can correct for this small bias. Second, the person who is interviewed in the house must also be randomly selected (because, for example, women are more likely than men to answer the phone even when both are at home). One popular strategy for obtaining a random sample of household members is to interview the person who has had the most recent birthday.

Telephone surveys require that people be interviewed. An alternative to interviewing is the use of self-administered questionnaires, which can be either mailed or delivered to members of the sample. Mailing questionnaires to people and handing them out to groups (e.g., students in a classroom, patients in a clinic) are less expensive than interviewing. However, questionnaires lack the personal touch of interviewing. In an interview, misunderstandings can be clarified and responses can be expanded on. This cannot be done with self-administered questionnaires. Questionnaires work best with what are called close-ended questions, like those on multiple-choice exams, to which there are a limited number of set answers. Interviews, especially face-to-face as opposed to telephone interviews, allow for more open-ended questions, where respondents can be encouraged to elaborate their responses to ensure that they are properly understood. Lenton, for example, chose to use personal interviews because she thought that the subject matter was best handled with face-to-face interaction. Notice, however, that she incorporated a short questionnaire on disciplinary techniques because she thought the questionnaire would be less threatening to people in that it was more anonymous.

Once Lenton had established her sample and pretested her research strategy to ensure that she would obtain usable information, she set out to gather evidence that would allow her to evaluate the merits of three different hypotheses. A "cycle of violence" hypothesis holds that practices of child abuse are handed down from generation to generation. A "social-situational" hypothesis maintains that abusive parents may be reacting to stress and that stress itself may be linked to a family's socioeconomic status. Finally, a "cultural" hypothesis suggests that it is the attitudes of the family toward corporal punishment that best differentiate between the use of aggressive and nonaggressive behaviour in child discipline. Her research was designed to yield evidence that would

help her decide which hypotheses were wrong. After analyzing the data, Lenton (1990: 176) concluded that "parents are inclined to use the disciplinary repertoires they learned when they were children—but only as long as certain current structural conditions are consonant with these repertoires." In particular, she pointed to structural conditions, such as unemployment in the family and low family income. To the extent that these structural conditions can be eliminated or reduced, the "cycle of family violence" can be arrested.

I mentioned earlier that the ability of sociologists to ask questions of people has both advantages and disadvantages. Lenton's work illustrates this. The physical punishment of children in the privacy of the home represents social activity that is not easily studied by any sociological method. Yet, as Lenton argues, child abuse is a public issue, not a private matter. By asking questions of people, she was able, first, to describe the extent of physical aggression used to discipline children and, second, to explain why some families were more likely than others to use physical discipline. The disadvantage of asking questions of people, especially questions that people may find threatening, is that people may distort their responses. For example, Lenton found that in more than 75 percent of all families, children had been spanked or slapped in the previous year. Given current social norms about child abuse, this estimate of physical discipline is more likely to be an underestimate than an overestimate of such activity. If, however, different social classes subscribe to these norms to different degrees, people's responses to the 29 disciplinary measures might have altered. Lenton herself anticipated this criticism and asked people not just about their behaviour but also about their attitudes. She was therefore able to examine whether people from different social classes held different norms about child discipline.

This distinction between attitudes and behaviours, or words and deeds, is important. I always intend to give more money to charity than I do. Most people believe that littering is irresponsible, but most people still litter sometimes. When you read research focusing on people's attitudes, remember that thought is not easily translated into action. This distinction goes beyond the asking of questions to issues of policy as well. Too often, people think that changing attitudes will solve social problems—if only people knew more, they would act more responsibly. A broken New Year's resolution is but one simple reminder of how often good intentions fail to translate into good deeds, no matter how aware we might be of the consequences.

Interpreting the answers that people give to researchers' questions is complicated by more than this behaviour-attitude distinction. In asking people questions, either in interviews or on questionnaires, we must be careful about making assumptions (Gray and Guppy, 2003):

- *Do not assume that people understand what you are asking.* Language is notorious for its ambiguity. How many friends did you see yesterday? This question may look simple at first, but people will differ in their understanding of "friends" and others will take "see" in the most literal way. The same words may mean different things to different people.

- *Do not assume that people know the answer to questions.* Most people do not want to appear ignorant when asked a question. This was illustrated nicely in a study of the prestige of occupations by Peter Pineo and John Porter (1967). They asked people to rate the prestige of two fictitious jobs: archaeopotrist and biologer. Most respondents cooperated and assigned these nonexistent jobs a prestige rating. When asked about their attitude on some issue, many people feel they must respond, even if they have no opinion on the topic or only a weakly formulated view.

- *Do not assume that people will admit the answer to themselves.* Alcoholics frequently claim that they can "quit any time." They refuse to admit that they are addicted. Similarly, child abusers may define themselves as strict disciplinarians. People routinely deceive themselves, sometimes only in minor ways, but "admitting the truth to ourselves" is a problem.

- *Do not assume that people will give valid answers to others.* People feel better about themselves when they are seen in a favourable light. In asking questions of people, researchers face the potential problem of "social desirability," because respondents may only give answers that reflect well on them. "What type of work do you do?" "Oh, I'm in public relations." Such a response could come from people working as telephone receptionists, tour guides, or corporate representatives.

Sociologists use many techniques in asking questions to gather valid and reliable evidence. For example, they will ask several questions rather than relying on only a single question, use supplementary questions to expand on or clarify answers, and test questions before using them to improve any wording that is unclear or misleading (see Houtkoop, 2000).

Survey researchers do not focus only on individuals, although it is individuals who respond to survey questions. For example, it is possible to survey organizations, groups, corporations, electoral ridings, or job vacancies. Although people answer survey questions, the questions may apply to a unit or group of which someone is a member. For example, Janice Aruni (2004) studied private tutoring businesses by using a semi-structured interview survey to gather information about businesses that provide for-profit, supplementary instruction in academic subjects (e.g., K–12 school subjects).

I am making two points here. First, surveys can focus on different units of observation (individuals, businesses, workplaces, etc.). Second, individuals can act as informants to report information that pertains not to themselves but to some group or unit about which they have information. People can, for example, report on individual events (e.g., job vacancies), family composition, or corporate policy. Although each of these represents different units of observation, individuals are still answering the questions.

OBSERVATIONAL STUDIES

Another method commonly used by sociologists to gather information is observation. Sometimes sociologists act as outside observers, at other times as insiders or **participant observers.** The obvious advantage of observation is that sociologists can see what people actually do, rather than relying on reports of what people say they do. One disadvantage is that gaining access to private actions or events can be difficult. For example, Lenton might have tried to observe parents disciplining their children rather than relying on what parents told her they did. But entering people's homes to make such observations would have been difficult. Furthermore, her presence may have influenced the type of discipline parents used (the Hawthorne effect).

In observation studies, examining the intentionality of social action is especially important. Max Weber (1949 [1904]) was one of the first sociologists to address the issue of intention as a focus of social research. Weber argued that in interacting with other people, we draw on meanings. For example, the clothing we choose to wear speaks to others. We attribute meaning to bow ties, jack boots, Laura Ashley scarves, and baseball caps. None of this is done naïvely, because what we wear helps define who we are. Skateboarders, for example, dress in a particular style; they wear a uniform of sorts. Making social life intelligible is part of what Weber thought sociologists must address. To understand skateboarding, it is essential to see how skateboarders "define the situation." It is important to learn about their culture and to understand their systems of meaning. The aim of such research is not to explain the behaviour of skateboarders from an outside point of view, but to investigate their shared values and beliefs—their "worldview."

Weber maintained that causal logic can be used to accomplish some of what sociologists want to explain. He thought, however, that sociology also had to make intelligible the subjective basis of social action. Weber used the German word *Verstehen*, or understanding, to refer to this mode of sociological analysis. To understand the meaning of social action requires being able, at least in principle, to fully engage in the social activity. An example is the best way to illustrate such understanding.

Youth subculture in Canada seems less influential and less prominent than in countries like the United Kingdom or the United States. Sometimes this is expressed in the claim that youth culture in Canada is derivative of trends south of the border or across the Atlantic. However, as skateboarders and squeegee kids have risen in profile, as youth unemployment has grown, and as the plight of young criminal offenders has been debated, understanding Canadian youth subcultures has become increasingly important. For that reason, Brian Wilson (2002) undertook a study of the rave subculture in Southern Ontario.

Locking up all youth considered deviant is an all-too-frequent suggestion for social policy. Banishing squeegee kids or skateboarders to some less visible place, be it jail, another neighbourhood, or "just off the streets," is one reaction. Denouncing ravers as irrational, for amphetamine drug use and social disturbance, is another. What these suggestions mainly reflect is a misunderstanding of youth culture and its social context. Gaining an appreciation of the rave subculture was Wilson's intent. Among the issues he pursued were the reasons for people participating in this subculture—put simply, was it the lure of adven-

In participant observation, it is often necessary to "look" the part. Brian Wilson participated in rave parties in order to study first-hand the rave subculture of Southern Ontario.
SOURCE: Thérèse Joyce-Gagnon, *Génération X*. Courtesy of the artist.

ture and excitement in the rave scene or was it a push from family or school that led to involvement with the rave subculture?

To gain an understanding of this process he chose participant observation as one of his methodological strategies. He attended more than a dozen raves, hung out in rave record stores, sat in on rave radio sessions, and attended public meetings focused on the rave phenomena. He observed the rave subculture by participating in it, by being a part of the party. By participating with ravers in rave parties and in rave settings he was able to learn, first-hand, about their lifestyles, their values, and their aspirations.

However, Wilson did more than just participate in the rave scene. He also interviewed 37 young people who were active participants. He used what he calls "in-depth, open-ended, semi-formal interviews" (Wilson, 2002: 301). An in-depth interview means that he explored specific topics in great detail, often pursuing nuances and tangents. They were open-ended in the sense that he allowed those he interviewed to range widely in the subject matter they discussed. Finally, they were semi-structured in that he had a set of general issues he wanted to discuss, but he did not ask every person he interviewed exactly the same questions in exactly the same order. His goal was to have a meaningful conversation with each person, guided by his interest in the subject but also by their knowledge, willingness, and interest in pursuing specific details.

He also did not interview a representative sample of rave participants. Such a sample would be difficult to define since no one has a list of regular rave members. Instead, Wilson sought to talk with a variety of people and he was careful not to draw all of the people he interviewed from the same place. Diversity was more important to him than was representation.

Finally, Wilson also paid particular attention to written materials that form part of the rave scene. This included magazines (both hard copy and e-zines), flyers promoting specific raves, and rave recordings (complete with commentary by the DJ). These provided another window into how ravers communicated with one another, what they stressed and emphasized.

In essence, he used a cluster of methods, with observation being his primary source of data. The participant observation was critical in giving him personal access to the subculture. He supplemented this by reading material and listening to rave productions. Finally, he also interviewed people to test out his interpretations of the rave subculture. In particular, he used the interviews to assess his own impressions of the rave scene.

Ethnographers study people in their own environment or their own natural setting. Although **ethnography** includes the researcher being immersed in a group or a subculture, it also typically involves a cluster of methods, including both in-depth, unstructured interviewing and the analysis of documents. Speaking with key informants who are central to the group or the subculture is crucial (Cresswell, 1998).

In part, Wilson came to understand the rave subculture in generational terms. Youth rebellion against perceived autocratic organizations (school, family, the justice system) leads to a lifestyle of resistance—to escaping authority, flaunting convention, and disregarding conservative norms. But it is a resistance that is not about political change or efforts to alter organizational forms. It is a resistance focused mainly on creating an autonomous space where social identity can be fostered, nourished, and supported. In this sense the subculture has a "magical" quality where the reality of other worlds can be transcended or bracketed. It is a movement based more on personal identity than on political protest. Contrast this with, for example, the student-led demonstrations in many countries pushing for stronger democratic governance—China, Indonesia, Iran, Korea—or the resistance to globalization seen at WTO settings (Tanner, 2001).

Wilson was able to gain an understanding of the rave lifestyle by participating in the life of the group. By hanging out with them, he gained an in-depth appreciation of their activity. As a participant observer, he was able to ask many questions of many different group members, gradually drawing a sociological portrait of the rave scene. In particular he was able to contrast various interpretations of the rave scene—was it about resistance, simple pleasure-seeking, or simply escapism? As his work progressed, Wilson was able to refine his understanding. He could cross-reference his observations by seeing how other group members reacted to each new insight he gained, thereby increasing both the reliability and the validity of his conclusions. In short, he came to "define the situation" as rave participants themselves define it.

As with experiments, the external validity of ethnography can be problematic. How confident can Wilson be that his conclusions are not dependent on the impressions he formed from a single group of ravers? The intensive, in-depth nature of ethnography makes generalizability problematic. The key tradeoff is between the richly textured, "thick description" of ethnography and the insularity of detailed study of one or a few settings. Unlike survey researchers, ethnographers do not select different sets of random individuals or groups. The groups or settings they investigate are purposively chosen, sometimes because of easy access. For example, Wilson did not randomly choose rave subcultures; he made arrangements to participate with some rave scenes in Southern Ontario, and even then it was only one form of youth subculture. Imagine also, the ethical issues Wilson confronted (see also Haggerty, 2004).

Wilson's research portrays a culture from its members' points of view. There are potential pitfalls of which Wilson had to be aware. First, how much did his presence influence his findings? Did people act differently when he was not around? In principle, there is no way of answering this question, although ethnographers have tried to account for the effect of their presence in various ways. Some researchers conceal their research role; in effect, they try to be known to the other participants as one of them, rather than as a researcher (the ethics of this are dicey). Other researchers report that, with time, participants' awareness of their presence fades and they are treated as a member. Notice that this problem of presence is the Hawthorne effect in another guise. Whether in survey research, experiments, or observation studies, the researcher's presence can distort the domain of investigation. Researcher presence may undermine validity.

Beyond the potential pitfall of mere presence is the second problem: the findings of researchers may be ethnocentric. That is, researchers may impose their own values—their own worldviews—on the subject matter of their study. How do we know, for example, that Wilson depicted the ravers' point of view and not his own? One method of reducing personal bias is known as the "member test of validity" (Douglas, 1970: 21). For example, if the rave participants Wilson spoke with did not recognize themselves in his account—that is, if they saw Wilson's account as inauthentic—then we would worry about bias or distortion. Wilson was careful to "test" his tentative observations and insights on his informants by asking them questions and checking for observations that would falsify his impressions. Again, this is a research problem that extends well beyond ethnography. In fact, ethnography can be seen as the method that takes most seriously the task of understanding the members of a group from the members' point of view, stressing in particular their definition of the situation.

A third problem beyond presence and ethnocentrism is this: How do researchers know that the "tools" of their inquiry (e.g., questions, instructions, requests) did not in fact "create" or "generate" the resulting "findings"? For example, did Wilson create a finding by focusing attention on the ravers' resistance to dominant culture? Alternatively, did Lenton invent a relationship between social class and child discipline by asking questions that might be interpreted in different ways by the members of different classes? Again, this involves issues of reliability and validity. Lenton can be confident that she did not construct or create a pseudo-relationship between class and discipline to the extent that she shows that

the basic pattern of findings is repeated across different questions about the disciplining of children. Wilson distinguished between (1) ravers' comments made in response to his questions and (2) statements his informants volunteered or that he overheard during his fieldwork. In addition, he used information provided to him by others on the margins of the rave scene: DJ's, security guards, and radio station personnel. These alternative sources of information helped him avoid the problem of "creating" meaning. If ravers volunteered information that corroborated Wilson's impressions, and if these impressions were further reinforced by other knowledgeable observers, his faith in the authenticity of his account increased.

Not all observation can involve participation. Rik Scarce (2000) was interested in nature, and especially human domination of nature. His interest was in whether we could still speak of "wild salmon" or whether, like the cow and the dog, salmon were now domesticated. He argues that the very concept of "resource management," a buzz phrase among fishery specialists for several decades, speaks to the idea of humans improving on nature, of scientists enhancing nature.

In studying the "domestication of salmon," Scarce used ethnographic methods. He could not participate as a scientist, but he could observe what scientists did, interview them, read their papers, and listen to their testimony at public inquiries. After doing all these things, he wrote an ethnographic account called *Fishy Business: Salmon, Biology, and the Social Construction of Nature.*

He was especially interested in how salmon on both the Atlantic and the Pacific coasts had been manipulated to serve human ends. In the modern fishery phrases like fish farming, aquaculture, genetic engineering, fish stocking, and fish hatcheries are commonplace. In British Columbia, few natural river systems remain. We have engineered a new breed of salmon, mixing wild stocks and creating farmed salmon (see also Schreiber, Matthews, and Elliott, 2003).

Scarce learned about this in his ethnographic research by hanging around fish hatcheries and asking questions, by visiting fishery research centres and watching what scientists were doing in their experiments, and by talking with scientists at their conventions and at public inquiries. He learned about the controversies and the anxiety that existed among scientists, many of whom worried about how we were increasingly controlling nature, but all too often in ways that were unsophisticated and too superficial. He came to see the fish hatchery as a biological factory and to understand how salmon were increasingly "tooled" and "engineered." Observation was his staple method. He immersed himself in the science of salmon to learn about the social practices of fishery biologists.

The believability of Scarce's research is enhanced by the fact that he observed events in their natural settings. He did not create a situation to see how people reacted (e.g., laboratory experiments) nor did he rely on people reporting on their own attitudes or behaviours (as in survey research). He was not a participant in the activity and so his involvement could not have distorted events (as may occur in participant observation). It is true that his presence as an observer may have influenced how people conducted themselves, but he often was one of many observers (e.g., at scientific conferences and public inquiries).

OTHER METHODS OF RESEARCH

Historical Sociology

Many sociologists study social change. Max Weber, for example, attempted to explain the rise of capitalism by showing how Protestantism invigorated capitalist growth. Émile Durkheim was interested in how moral education helped to socially integrate a rapidly changing society. Both writers sought to answer sociological questions by examining historical change as evidence of significant social processes. Sociologists are more likely than historians to use historical evidence to test theories of social change. Sociologists place less emphasis on history for history's sake.

Gordon Laxer's (1989) work shows how sociologists can also make effective use of comparative, historical methods. Laxer sought to explain why the Canadian economy has remained heavily tied to the production of resources (e.g., wood, oil, grain, minerals) with high levels of capital investment by foreigners. He wanted to test different theories about economic development, such as whether Canada's relatively late industrialization explains our present economic structure. To do this, he systematically compared Canadian economic patterns (e.g., levels of manufacturing activity, levels of foreign investment) with those of other countries, and in particular other late-developing countries, such as Japan and Sweden.

Laxer suggests that we can best understand Canada's relative position in the world economy, and especially our greater reliance on exporting raw mate-

rials as opposed to the sale of manufactured goods, on the internal politics of early Canadian development—principally, a weak farmers' movement around the turn of the twentieth century. In contrast to such countries as Sweden and Japan, Canada did not have a strong, ethnically united farming class that could push for domestic economic policies (such as the creation of banks willing to lend money for long-term investment) that ultimately facilitated strong industrial development.

The logic of Laxer's analysis is not unlike that of other sociological research. His key dependent variable is foreign investment and he measured how this investment changed historically in several different countries. Among his independent variables is the organizational strength of farmers (the agrarian class). By comparing an admittedly small number of cases, he sought to decide what was both similar and different in the cases. By comparing the historical record by using a small number of variables across a set of different countries, he was able to sort out plausible causal factors that influenced Canada's position relative to other countries.

Sociologists like Laxer sometimes rely on other researchers' historical accounts. He relied primarily on economic histories that had already been written about each country he included in his analysis. Other sociologists go back to original sources to reconstruct a historical record pertinent to their focus. For example, Gillian Creese (1988, 1999) examined gender relations in the Vancouver labour force and labour movement early in this century. Her aim was to improve our understanding of the historical dynamics leading to the segregated work of women and men. Included in the archival material that she used were the full proceedings of the Royal Commission on Labour Conditions in British Columbia, documents on strikes and lockouts between 1907 and 1939, the minutes of local labour unions, and press coverage from newspapers. Any single source could give only partial coverage of the events she wanted to examine. By using a variety of sources, she was able to increase the reliability of her findings. Creese also relied on published data from the Canadian censuses for the decades in which she was interested.

Documentary Analysis

Sociologists have also made useful contributions to knowledge through the examination of official documents. Scott Davies (2002) examined how education reformers consciously designed their recommendations about policy change to fit with historically current political priorities and cultural settings. He shows how three successive education commissions in Ontario (1950, 1968, and 1995) each designed messages around "progressive education," while simultaneously making policy recommendations that were diametrically opposed (e.g., some supported and some rejected standardized testing). Most change agents want to do "progressive" things. By carefully analyzing commission reports, Davies shows how the language of progressive education was reshaped by successive commissions to sell their brand of education reform.

Renisa Mawani (2003) examined archival documents including colonial maps to demonstrate a social process whereby geographical spaces were rendered "vacant" and therefore accessible to settlement and development. By showing how Aboriginal land use was made to vanish at some points, only to have later colonial authorities redraw the maps to show their presence, Mawani demonstrates the contested nature of landscape, both then and now. She also draws on legal documents, such as cases and statutes to understand how the rule of law was also used to displace Aboriginal peoples and, again reflecting contestation, how it was used by Aboriginal peoples in resistance. As a third methodological strategy she examines the ways in which an Aboriginal presence has been commemorated (e.g., via totem poles). By a careful comparison of the evidence offered through these documented sources, she argues that Vancouver's civic identity has shifted from a settler society to a postcolonial, multicultural city.

Use of Official Statistics

Governments have a long history of collecting statistical data. Government bureaucracies first began to collect statistics to help rulers determine both the size of their taxation base and the number of men they could put on the battlefield. Since then, the scope of government or official statistics has expanded and now includes information on births and deaths, unemployment rates, imports and exports, and so on. Sociologists have made good use of official statistics (see especially Haggerty, 2001).

For example, Brym (1986) was interested in how support for social-democratic political parties was related to the resources on which different social classes could draw. His dependent variable, electoral support for leftist political parties, was measured as the percentage of voters casting ballots supporting social-democratic or communist parties in ten capitalist democracies, including Canada. He focused on three key independent variables: a measure of the inequality of income in a country, the type of electoral system in a nation, and the percentage of the labour force that was unionized. His measures of these variables (except the type of electoral system) were derived from official statistics. Brym showed that, contrary to earlier research, class-based political activity was still strong in many countries he studied, especially if there were leftist political parties with the resources necessary to run effective campaigns.

McMullan and Swan (1989) used official statistics in their investigation of arson in Nova Scotia. They relied on police-reported arson for the period 1970–85. The data showed a substantial rise in both the actual number and the rate of reported arson (number of arsons per 1000 fires) between 1973 and 1981, with a modest decline in later years. Arson, of course, is difficult to prove, and McMullan and Swan were careful to check with a second source to verify the pattern they had established. When they used fire-marshal data, as opposed to police-report data, they found similar trends. In accounting for the fluctuating arson rate (their dependent variable) they pointed to interest rates and unemployment rates as the variables affecting arson rates. On the basis of official reports, and from interviews that they conducted with enforcement and insurance officials, McMullan and Swan concluded that most arson involves the burning of a person's own property, even though the criminal definition of arson continues to emphasize vandalism.

The arson example illustrates a central problem with official statistics. These statistics are not objective facts on which everyone agrees. The very definition of arson makes it difficult to prove. Furthermore, different interest groups have a great deal at stake over whether a fire is officially reported as arson. Often arsonists are property owners themselves, and their interests are opposed by those of insurance investigators, who do not want to pay settlements for illegal fires. Again, issues of validity are at stake: Do the official definitions used to generate, say, arrest statistics, arson rates, or strike statistics correspond to sociologists' theoretical concepts? In addition, sociologists must be certain that official statistics reflect changes they are examining, rather than changes in the practices of the officials collecting the statistics.

THE ANALYSIS OF NUMERICAL DATA

Sociological evidence frequently comes in numerical form—that is, as quantifiable evidence (e.g., number of disciplinarians, arsons, or voters). Finding and interpreting patterns in numerical data is complex. To help in summarizing numerical information, social scientists routinely rely on statistical techniques. In this section I briefly illustrate some key aspects of the process. I explore the following simple question: Do women and men earn the same income as a result of having the same levels of education? Men and women have, on average, similar levels of schooling. However, as a group, men have higher incomes than do women.

Notice the causal logic here. Education is hypothesized to affect income. However, since women and men earn different wages in the labour market, yet have similar levels of schooling, maybe the causal link between education and income differs by sex. Although I can present only an elementary analysis here, issues of a wage gap between the sexes are part of the continuing debate over pay equity, comparable worth, and employment equity, all important policy questions (Fortin and Huberman, 2002).

To begin, we need to examine the link between education and income. I do this by using data from the 2003 General Social Survey (2004), a survey conducted by Statistics Canada of a nationally representative sample of Canadians (24 951 randomly chosen Canadians, to be precise). Does education have a big effect on income? Table 20.1, called a contingency table or a cross-tabulation, gives us an answer. Education, the independent variable displayed across the top of the table, has three categories (low—high school or less; medium—some postsecondary education; and high—university degree or higher). For ease of presentation, annual personal income, the dependent variable, has two categories (low—personal income below $30 000 annually; and high—annual income at or above $30 000).

Notice first the table's arrangement. The title describes the two variables being related. The independent variable (education) is placed on the top of the table and its values are clearly delineated. Below each value for education is a number. The dependent variable (income) is arrayed on the side of the table, again with the value labels clearly shown. Beside each value of the dependent variable is a row of numbers. To illustrate, Table 20.1 shows that there are 333 people in the top left-hand cell, the cell defined by a

TABLE 20.1 THE RELATIONSHIP BETWEEN LEVEL OF EDUCATION AND INDIVIDUAL INCOME FOR PEOPLE AGED 25–34, 2003

Level of Education

Income	Low	Medium	High	Row Totals
Low	53%	45%	31%	42%
	(333)	(783)	(358)	(1473)
High	47%	55%	69%	58%
	(296)	(939)	(814)	(2049)
Column totals	100%	100%	100%	100%
	(629)	(1722)	(1172)	(3522)

SOURCE: Data is adapted from the Statistics Canada product "SCF Public Use Microdata File: Income of Census Family Units," Catalogue 13M0001XDB, August 19, 1999.

low level of education and a low income. At the intersection of each column and row is a table cell (there are six cells here because row and column totals are ignored in counting the number of cells in a table).

The concept of a contingency table comes from the idea that the category into which a person falls on the dependent variable is contingent on, or depends on, the category that a person occupies on the independent variable. If the hypothesis were true in this case, we would expect that, as we move across the education categories from low to high, the number of people receiving high incomes ought to rise. Do the data reveal this pattern? For people with low education, 296 had high incomes. For people with a high level of education, 814 had high incomes. These figures seem, at first glance, to support our expectation. Notice, however, that because of how education was categorized, 629 people had what I defined as low education, while 1172 had high education. Comparing the actual number of people in each cell is therefore misleading, because there are different numbers of people in each column.

Rather than focusing on the raw numbers, we get a better understanding of the patterns when we standardize the data. We need to ask what *percentage* of people in each education category had high incomes. By expressing the numbers as percentages—that is, by standardizing the data—it is much easier to see the patterns. So, 296 of 629 people in the low-education column had high incomes, or 47 percent (296 divided by 629 and then multiplied by 100). This tells us that for every 100 people with low education, 47 had high incomes. Making the same calculation for the high education column—(814/1172) × 100—we find that 69 percent of highly educated people earned high incomes (or 69 of every 100 people).

If you examine Table 20.1, you will see that the percentages are entered in the table. The actual number of people in each cell appears in parentheses. Notice that the percentages are calculated separately for each column, summing to 100 percent at the bottom of each column.

So, do relatively more people with high education receive high income in comparison to people with low education? Yes. Of every 100 people in the high-education column, 69 receive high income (69 percent), compared with only 47 of every 100 in the low-education column (47 percent). The difference between these two percentages (22 percent) is one measure of the strength of the relationship between education and income; the higher the percentage, the stronger the relationship.

In studying this table, some readers may have taken exception to my definitions of high and low incomes. Why should earning more than $30 000 be considered a high income? What is defined as low and high income is arbitrary. However, when I define the lows and highs of income and education differently and produce several different tables, the basic patterns in the tables do not change. This replication gives me confidence that my decisions about how to categorize the variables do not affect the results.

The evidence in Table 20.1 corroborates the first part of the question about the relationship between education and income. But how does gender figure into the pattern? Table 20.2 contains two contingency tables. Here the question is how the link between education and income varies for women in comparison with men. Table 20.2 can be usefully thought of as Table 20.1 but with women and men separated into their own subtables.

For women, the basic pattern of Table 20.1 is repeated in Table 20.2: 66 percent of women with a high level of education are likely to have high income, whereas only 23 percent of women with a low level of education are likely to have a high income. The difference between these two cell percentages is 43 percent.

For men, although the pattern is similar, the percentage difference is smaller. Of men with a high level of education, 73 percent have a high income, whereas for men with a low level of education, 64 percent have a high income. The percentage difference is only 9 percent. This suggests that for men education level is not as important as it is for women in earning a high income. Contrasting the percentage differences between the two subtables in Table 20.2 gives us a way of comparing the strength of the link between income and education for women versus men. A more complex method of investigating the causal linkages between gender, education, and income relies on multiple regression—see Box 20.4.

So, what do we learn from this analysis? We learn first, from Table 20.1, that people with more education are likely to earn higher incomes. Second, from Table 20.2 we learn that this is especially true for women, in that for men education level has less of an impact on earning high incomes than is the case for women (remember only people between 25 and 34 are included in the tables).

TABLE 20.2 THE RELATIONSHIP BETWEEN LEVEL OF EDUCATION, INDIVIDUAL INCOME, AND GENDER FOR PEOPLE AGED 25–34, 2003

	Women Level of Education				Men Level of Education			
Income	**Low**	**Medium**	**High**	**Total**	**Low**	**Medium**	**High**	**Total**
Low	78%	60%	34%	(893)	37%	32%	27%	(580)
High	23%	40%	66%	(778)	64%	68%	73%	(1270)
Totals	100%	100%	100%			100%	100%	100%
	(252)	(822)	(599)	(1671)	(377)	(900)	(573)	(1851)

SOURCE: Data from Statistics Canada, 2003 General Social Survey.
NOTE: Column and row totals are not equal for women because of rounding.

BOX 20.4 INTRODUCING STATISTICAL IDEAS ABOUT REGRESSION ANALYSIS

In exploring the linkage among gender, education, and income, I introduce a series of alternative explanations. Testing each of these ideas using contingency tables would be extremely difficult because, with so many possible confounding variables, the tables I would generate would quickly become huge and unwieldy. An alternative to contingency-table analysis is regression analysis. The basic idea of regression, in summarizing the linkages between variables, can be explained most easily in graphic form.

Figure 20.2 is a graph with years of schooling arrayed along the horizontal axis (x-axis) and annual income displayed along the vertical axis (y-axis). On this graph I can plot where each person in the sample falls. In other words, I can choose someone from the sample and move along the x-axis until I come to the level of education attained by the selected person. I can then proceed up from there, now using the y-axis as a guide, until I reach the level of the same person's annual income. The point that I reach is the intersection of two perpendicular lines, one drawn vertically from the x-axis (at the person's level of education) and the other drawn horizontally from the y-axis (at that person's annual income). For each person in the sample, I can locate exactly where these two lines fall in the graph and place a mark at the appropriate spot. The result, similar to what I have depicted, is a scatterplot.

A scatterplot can be summarized statistically by using regression techniques. To summarize the relationship between education and income, a straight line can be drawn through the data points in such a way that the distance from each point to the line can be minimized. If all points lie exactly on the line, the fit of the line to the data will be perfect. The farther the points are from the best-fitting line, the poorer is the ability to use a straight line to summarize the information and the weaker is the association between the two variables. The strength of association between two variables in a scatterplot is given by the correlation coefficient (r). The value of r can vary from -1 (a perfectly inverse relationship or negative association) to 0 (no association) to $+1$ (a perfectly proportionate relationship or positive association). The farther r is from 0, the stronger the association. The correlation coefficient is, then, analogous to the percentage difference in tables.

With the education and income scatterplot, I can capture the central characteristics of the best-fitting line with two numbers. One number captures the slope of the line and tells how much vertical increase (or decrease) occurs in the line for every unit of horizontal change along the x-axis. Using my example, for every additional year of schooling, how much does annual income increase? An easy way to remember this is to think of this number as the rise (income increase) over the run (change in years of schooling). A second number tells at what point the line intersects the y-axis. If I have a perfectly fitting line, the equation for a straight line can be expressed as $y = a + bx$, where x and y are values on the two axes of the graph, a is the point at which the line crosses the y-axis, and b is the slope of the line.

What I have described here is a statistical technique known as simple linear regression, for one independent and one dependent variable. To explore the alternative interpretations for the link among gender, education, and income that I offered earlier, you would need to use multiple regression, where one dependent variable can be linked to a series of independent variables. This data analysis approach has been instrumental in shaping social policy related to equal pay for work of equal value.

FIGURE 20.2 HYPOTHETICAL RELATIONSHIP BETWEEN EMPLOYMENT INCOME AND YEARS OF SCHOOLING

$a = \$8500$
$b = \$615$

YEARS OF SCHOOLING

Why is the link between education and income different for women and men? First, men without university education may still earn high pay in resource and manufacturing jobs where education level is less important. That could account for the difference. Second, the labour force is still at least partially differentiated into "male" and "female" jobs, and education level may be more important for finding work in traditional female jobs than in certain male jobs (e.g., welding, oil rigging). Third, women and men could be working different numbers of hours per week, or weeks per year, and these differences could be related to both education and income. Many other possible explanations exist, and further research is essential to sort them out (Fortin and Huberman, 2002; Guppy and Davies, 1998).

THE FUTURE OF SOCIAL RESEARCH

Social research involves systematically studying the social world. The aim of such research activity is to develop explanations and understandings of social patterns so that we may improve the human condition. Today, it is becoming increasingly obvious that we need to find innovative ways of organizing and running our human affairs. Starvation, environmental degradation, terrorism, and social injustice are among the many social problems we must confront. Solutions require adequate explanations and understandings for how these problems arise and persist.

Earlier in the chapter, I outlined several sources of knowledge: common sense, religious faith, and science. Although these forms of knowledge share certain features (e.g., they are all imperfect), scientific reason encourages a set of practices, open review and critical skepticism, which together work to reduce error.

Another way of emphasizing what is distinctive about the scientific method is to compare how social research differs from the work of other professionals who concentrate on similar social issues (e.g., the environment, gender relations). For example, what differentiates the work of documentary filmmakers, novelists, or journalists from that of social researchers?

I have emphasized three features of scientific research that, in combination, separate it from the work of these other professionals:

1. Research results are confronted by the critical skepticism of other scientists.
2. Social theory guides, either directly or indirectly, the evidence gathered.
3. Evidence is systematically collected and analyzed.

Although some of these features are found in the work of other professionals, such as journalists, all three features are found in good social research. Replication and reproducibility have high currency in science as ways of encouraging skepticism. Good research contributes new ideas or evidence to our common stock of social theory. Finally, good research publicly displays the careful collection and analysis of evidence.

These principles are a feature of all good research, but the methods that sociologists use to pursue their goal of explaining and understanding the social world take many forms. This diverse array of methods, including observing, questioning, and experimenting, offers sociologists many ways of inquiring responsibly and ethically about the social world. Each method has different strengths and weaknesses, which makes the choice of research strategy dependent on the sociological question.

Social science research will continue to contribute to our sense of the world around us. Research on the environment, reproductive technology, multiculturalism, violence, and social-support networks all point to practical ways in which our human problems can be influenced by research findings. Effective policy solutions that benefit all people require sound social research.

SUMMARY

1. Research methods are ways of obtaining evidence to test suppositions about the world around us. Behind the various techniques we use to obtain evidence and expand our knowledge of the social world (e.g., experiments, interviews), we must recognize important assumptions about such things as facts, objectivity, and truth.

2. Science is one of several sources of knowledge. Like other kinds of knowledge, scientific knowledge can be wrong. However, unlike other ways of knowing, science incorporates explicit methods designed to reduce error in what is currently accepted as scientific knowledge. Evidence must be systematically collected and rigorously evaluated.

3. Good science integrates both strong theory and robust research. Theories are ideas about how the world works or claims about how to explain or understand the recurring, patterned nature of human activity.

4. Evidence is crucial to developing, revising, or discarding theoretical claims. In comparison with the evidence available in the natural sciences, the evidence available to social scientists presents added complexity because of the meaningful character of human social action. People, unlike molecules, assign meaning to their actions and to the actions of others.

5. Sociologists have devised many useful methods for obtaining evidence about the social world. Observation and questioning are the two principal techniques, although each of them is conducted by using a variety of formats, including experiments, surveys, participant observation, and interviews.

6. Good research adds to our knowledge of the world around us. Such knowledge expands our opportunities and options. Sociological knowledge helps either in solving social problems or by sensitizing us to the human condition, expanding our social horizons.

QUESTIONS TO CONSIDER

1. The teaching of faculty members in university and college departments could be evaluated in various ways. Suggest some different sociological methods of doing such an evaluation and comment on the strengths and weaknesses of each approach.

2. Lenton (1990) chose to examine issues of child abuse by focusing more broadly on child discipline and by surveying parents about their disciplinary techniques. Suggest alternative designs for her study, commenting on the strengths and weaknesses of the various approaches, including important ethical considerations.

3. Policymakers frequently debate raising or lowering age restrictions on activities, such as driving a car, drinking alcoholic beverages, or voting. Suggest how you might design a study that could provide evidence about the possible consequences of either raising or lowering one of these age restrictions.

4. Immigration levels remain a contentious issue in Canada. Construct a short series of interview questions designed to assess people's knowledge of current immigration practices. Ask these questions of your friends or family. Ask how many immigrants enter Canada and from which countries they originate. Compare your findings with official statistics that are available in government publications at your college or university or on the Internet. How might you explain the patterns you discovered?

5. Discuss the claim that "facts speak for themselves." What problems exist in claiming that facts do "speak for themselves"? Conversely, what problems exist in claiming that facts do not "speak for themselves"? Consider especially the claim that we need firm standards against which to evaluate ideas or theoretical claims. Is it possible to establish such standards?

6. At parties, people are expected to be laid back, relaxed. Parties are times for having fun, for stepping outside the routines of school or work. However, phrases like "party pooper" suggest that parties too have rules and that violators of such rules can be ostracized. Others are glorified as "party animals," implying that some people take to partying better than others. How might you engage in a participant observation study to investigate these hunches systematically? Do such categories as "party animal" or "party pooper" exist, and, if so, how are they understood? Do "rules" exist at a party even though parties are in very important ways "escapist"? How might a sociologist seek to understand party life at your college or university?

GLOSSARY

Causation involves a relationship between two variables where change or variation in one variable produces change or variation in a second variable. Four criteria are essential to establishing a causal relation between two variables: association, time ordering, nonspuriousness, and theoretical rationale.

The **dependent variable** is a variable that is assumed to depend on or be caused by one or more other variables (independent variables); it is the variable that is the effect, or outcome, in a cause-effect relationship.

Ethnography is the detailed description of a particular culture or way of life, or the written results of a participant-observation study.

An **experiment** is a controlled test of the causal effects of a particular variable or set of variables on a dependent or outcome variable.

An **explanation** is an account of the causal logic that shows how and why variables influence one another.

External validity is the generalizability of a particular finding from the study group to a larger population; the relevance of conclusions for a larger population; or the ability to infer that the results of a study are representative of processes operating for a broader population.

In the **Hawthorne effect,** people involved in a study may be influenced by the very process of being studied; the study has an impact on the subjects of the study.

A **hypothesis** is a knowledge claim or hunch about how the world works; it is a testable statement, derived from a theory, about the relationship between two variables.

The **independent variable** is a variable that is presumed to affect or influence other variables; it is the causal variable.

An **interview** is a method of collecting information by asking people questions, either in person or over the telephone. Interviews range from highly structured (preset questions in a fixed order) to loosely structured (topic guidelines, but no prescribed question wording).

In **meaningful action,** human action, as distinct from physical behaviour, occurs with specific intentions or reasons in mind. The uncontrollable tic in a person's eye is physical behaviour, which differs from that of a person who is winking at someone, where intention or purpose is central to understanding what is happening. Most human activity is meaningful action, or social action.

Measurement comprises procedures for assigning numbers to observations according to preset rules; it is the act of finding data or information relevant to theoretical concepts.

Objectivity is the attempt to minimize the effect of personal bias on research results or the idea of impartiality, of "fair hearings." Objectivity is an ideal enhanced by the work of any single researcher being open to the critical scrutiny of others. Objectivity as complete impartiality is a myth.

In **participant observation,** the study of social life involves the participation of the researcher, to varying degrees, in the activities of the group under investigation; it attempts to give an "insider's" account of a particular way of life or cultural system.

Randomization is a procedure used in experiments to assign test subjects to experimental conditions on the basis of chance.

Reliability is the consistency of measurements and the ability to reproduce the same measurements on repeated occasions.

Sampling is the process of selecting units from a larger population. Random sampling involves the selection of representative units (e.g., people, organizations) from a population (e.g., all Canadians, voluntary organizations in a city). Samples may be selected by probability (where every unit has a nonzero chance of selection) or nonprobability (where chance does not enter into the selection of sample units).

A **self-administered questionnaire** is a method of collecting information by having people record their own answers to preset questions.

Spuriousness is an incorrect inference about the causal relations between variables.

Understanding is the ability to provide a definition of a situation that members of a culture find authentic and valid.

Validity is the relevance or accuracy of measurement in relation to the theoretical concept that it is supposed to measure.

A **variable** is something that varies or an attribute or event that can take on more than one value (e.g., unemployment rates, age, sex).

SUGGESTED READING

Babbie, Earl, and Lucia Benaquisto. (2002). *Fundamentals of Social Research.* Toronto: Thomson Nelson. Babbie and Benaquisto provide the best general account of research methods available in sociology. This is a Canadian adaptation covering an array of methodologies with many illustrations and examples to emphasize key points.

Becker, Howard. (1998). *Tricks of the Trade: How to Think about Your Research While You're Doing It.* Chicago: University of Chicago Press. Written by one of sociology's best qualitative researchers, Becker's book discusses how to think about research and is valuable to both qualitative and quantitative researchers.

Cresswell, John. (2003) *Research Design: Qualitative, Quantitative, and Mixed Methods Approaches,* 2nd ed. Thousand Oaks, CA: Sage Publications. This text offers an excellent balanced view of the strengths and weaknesses of various research designs and is a useful guide to conducting good research by using multiple methods.

Denzin, Norman. (1997). *Interpretative Ethnography: Ethnographic Practices for the 21st Century.* Thousand Oaks, CA: Sage. Denzin provides a good general introduction to the practices and debates of qualitative research.

Gray, George, and Neil Guppy. (2003). *Successful Surveys: Research Methods and Practice,* 3rd ed. Toronto: Thomson Nelson. This is a practical guidebook to developing research designs and using effective survey research techniques. The authors cover questionnaires and interviews.

NOTES

1. Black swans, native to Tasmania and Australia, were unknown to Europeans before exploration. The idea that all swans are white is thus similar to the idea that Earth is the central body in the solar system—a claim once understood to be true but now thought to be false.

2. Please do not overinterpret this claim. As a community we have frequently treated humans as exceptional. We have distanced ourselves from nature. Our theories and actions often evince a "control of nature" paradigm. Highlighting differences between the subject matter of the natural and the social sciences is extremely complicated. For example, monkeys make friends with zoologists and, when studied, may react in similar ways as humans. It is important to consider in what ways the studying of people by people may add complexity to research, and how this in turn may stimulate us to think differently about how people study non-humans. For example, issues of animal rights and environmental ethics raise questions about our traditionally human-centric view of the world. Perhaps bacteria do blush and we are just too ignorant to notice!

3. Foschi and Buchan (1990) use the term "White" rather than English Canadian.

WEB RESOURCES

Companion Web Site for This Book

http://www.newsociety5e.nelson.com

Begin by clicking on the Student Resources section of the website. Next, select the chapter you are studying from the pull-down menu. From the Student Resources page, you have easy access to InfoTrac College Edition® and other resources, such as the Glossary and Flashcards. The website also has many useful tips to aid you in your study of sociology.

InfoTrac College Edition Search Terms

Visit http://www.infotrac-college.com for access to more than 20 million articles from nearly 6000 sources when doing your online research.

ThomsonNOW™

http://hed.nelson.com

This online diagnostic tool identifies each student's unique needs with a Pretest that generates a personalized Study Plan for each chapter, helping students focus on concepts they are having the most difficulty mastering. Students then take a Posttest after reading the chapter to measure their understanding of the material. An Instructor Gradebook is available to track and monitor student progress.

REFERENCES

CHAPTER 1

Allen, Robert C. (1999). *Education and Technological Revolutions: The Role of the Social Sciences and the Humanities in the Knowledge Based Economy.* Ottawa: Social Sciences and Humanities Research Council of Canada. On the World Wide Web at http://www.sshrc.ca/english/resnews/researchresults/allen99.pdf (8 May 2001).

Babbie, Earl. (2000). *The Practice of Social Research*, 9th ed. Belmont, CA: Wadsworth Publishing.

Bell, Daniel. (1976). *The Coming of Post-industrial Society: A Venture in Social Forecasting.* New York: Basic Books.

Clark, S.D. (1968). *The Developing Canadian Community*, 2nd ed. Toronto: University of Toronto Press.

Coleman, James S. (1961). *The Adolescent Society.* New York: Free Press.

Douglas, Jack D. (1967). *The Social Meanings of Suicide.* Princeton, NJ: Princeton University Press.

Durkheim, Émile. (1951 [1897]). *Suicide: A Study in Sociology.* G. Simpson, ed.; Trans J. Spaulding and G. Simpson. New York: Free Press.

Edel, Abraham. (1965). "Social Science and Value: A study in Interrelations." In Irving Louis Horowitz, ed., *The New Sociology: Essays in Social Science and Social Theory in Honor of C. Wright Mills* (pp. 218–38). New York: Oxford University Press.

Eichler, Margrit. (1987). *Nonsexist Research Methods.* Boston: Allen and Unwin.

Eichler, Margrit. (1988). *Families in Canada Today*, 2nd ed. Toronto: Gage.

Fukuyama, Francis. (1992). *The End of History and the Last Man.* New York: HarperCollins.

Garfinkel, Harold. (1967). *Studies in Ethnomethodology.* Englewood Cliffs, NJ: Prentice-Hall.

Giddens, Anthony. (1982). *Sociology: A Brief but Critical Introduction.* New York: Harcourt, Brace Jovanovich.

Giddens, Anthony. (1990). *The Consequences of Modernity.* Stanford, CA: Stanford University Press.

Goffman, Erving. (1959). *The Presentation of Self in Everyday Life.* Garden City, NY: Anchor.

Granovetter, Mark. (1973). "The Strength of Weak Ties." *American Sociological Review, 78* (6), 1360–80.

Guillén, Mauro F. (2001). "Is Globalization Civilizing, Destructive or Feeble? A Critique of Five Key Debates in the Social Science Literature." *Annual Review of Sociology, 27.* On the World Wide Web at http://knowledge.wharton.upenn.edu/PDFs/938.pdf (6 February 2003).

Guppy, Neil, and R. Alan Hedley. (1993). *Opportunities in Sociology.* Montreal: Canadian Sociology and Anthropology Association.

Hersch, Patricia. (1998). *A Tribe Apart: A Journey into the Heart of American Adolescence.* New York: Ballantine Books.

Hochschild, Arlie, with Anne Machung. (1989). *The Second Shift: Working Parents and the Revolution at Home.* New York: Viking.

Kuhn, Thomas. (1970). *The Structure of Scientific Revolutions*, 2nd ed. Chicago, University of Chicago Press.

Marx, Karl. (1904 [1859]). *A Contribution to the Critique of Political Economy.* Trans. N. Stone. Chicago: Charles H. Kerr.

Marx, Karl, and Friedrich Engels. (1972 [1848]). "Manifesto of the Communist Party." In R. Tucker, ed., *The Marx-Engels Reader* (pp. 331–62). New York: Norton.

Merton, Robert K. (1968 [1949]). *Social Theory and Social Structure.* New York: Free Press.

Mills, C. Wright. (1959). *The Sociological Imagination.* New York: Oxford University Press.

Ornstein, Michael D. (1983). "The Development of Class in Canada." In J. Paul Grayson, ed., *Introduction to Sociology: An Alternate Approach* (pp. 224–66). Toronto: Gage.

Parsons, T. (1951). *The Social System.* Glencoe, IL: Free Press.

Porter, John. (1965). *The Vertical Mosaic: An Analysis of Social Class and Power in Canada.* Toronto: University of Toronto Press.

Robbins, Liz. (2005). "Nash Displays Polished Look: On the Court, of Course." *New York Times* 19 January. On the World Wide Web at http://www.nytimes.com (19 January 2005).

Russett, Cynthia Eagle. (1966). *The Concept of Equilibrium in American Social Thought.* New Haven, CT: Yale University Press.

Statistics Canada. (2004a). "Suicide in Canada's Immigrant Population." *The Daily* 29 March. On the World Wide Web at http://www.statcan.ca/Daily/English/040329/d040329a.htm (6 July 2006).

Statistics Canada. (2004b). "Age and Sex for Population, Canada, Provinces, Territories, Census Metropolitan Areas and Census Agglomerations, 2001 Census—100% Data." On the World Wide Web at http://www.statcan.ca/bsolc/english/bsolc?catno=95F0300X2001001 (22 April 2005).

Statistics Canada. (2004c). *Causes of Death, Chapter XX, 2002.* Ottawa: Minister of Industry. Catalogue No. 84-208-XIE. On the World Wide Web at http://www.statcan.ca/english/freepub/84-208-XIE/2002/tables/table20.pdf (22 April 2005).

Thompson, Kenneth, ed. (1975). *Auguste Comte: The Foundation of Sociology.* New York: Wiley.

Tierney, John. (1997). "Our Oldest Computer, Upgraded." *New York Times Magazine* September 28: 46–49, 97, 100, 104–05.

Tillyard, E.M.W. (1943). *The Elizabethan World Picture.* London: Chatto and Windus.

Toffler, Alvin. (1990). *Powershift: Knowledge, Wealth, and Violence at the Edge of the 21st Century.* New York: Bantam.

United Nations. (2004). *World Development Report 2004.* On the World Wide Web at http://hdr.undp.org/reports/global/2004/ (1 February 2005).

Weber, Max. (1946). *From Max Weber: Essays in Sociology.* Eds. and trans. Hans Gerth and C. Wright Mills. New York: Oxford University Press.

Weber, Max. (1958 [1904–05]). *The Protestant Ethnic and the Spirit of Capitalism.* New York: Scribner.

World Health Organization. (2002). "World Report on Violence and Health." On the World Wide Web at http://www.who.int/violence_injury_prevention/violence/world_report/en/full_en.pdf (22 April 2005).

Yates, Gayle Graham, ed. (1985). *Harriet Martineau on Women.* New Brunswick, NJ: Rutgers University Press.

CHAPTER 2

Adams, Michael. (1997). *Sex in the Snow: Canadian Social Values at the End of the Millennium.* Toronto: Penguin.

Albas, Daniel, and Cheryl Albas. (1989). "Modern Magic: The Case of Examinations." *The Sociological Quarterly, 30,* 603–13.

Baudrillard, Jean. (1988 [1986]). *America.* Trans. Chris Turner. London: Verso.

Beck, Glen. (2002). "Dan Quayle Likes Ozzy." On the World Wide Web at http://www.newsmax.com/showinsidecover. shtml?a=2002/5/9/195211 (1 August 2006).

Bibby, Reginald W. (1987). *Fragmented Gods: The Poverty and Potential of Religion in Canada.* Toronto: Irwin.

Bierstedt, R. (1963). *The Social Order.* New York: McGraw-Hill.

Bissoondath, Neil. (2002). *Selling Illusions: The Cult of Multiculturalism in Canada,* rev. ed. Toronto: Penguin.

Bronowski, J. (1965). *Science and Human Values,* rev. ed. New York: Harper and Row.

Brym, Robert J. (2001). "Hip-Hop from Dissent to Commodity: A Note on Consumer Culture." In R. Brym, ed., *New Society: Sociology for the 21st Century,* 3rd ed. (pp. 78–81). Toronto: Harcourt Brace Canada.

Brym, Robert J., with Bonnie J. Fox. (1989). *From Culture to Power: The Sociology of English Canada.* Toronto: Oxford University Press.

Carpenter, Dave. (2003). "McDonald's High-Tech with Kitchen, Kiosks." KioskCom. On the World Wide Web at http://www.kioskcom.com/articles_detail.php?ident=1856 (23 October 2003).

Clarke, Harold D., Jane Jenson, Lawrence LeDuc, and Jon H. Pammett. (1996). *Absent Mandate: Canadian Electoral Politics In an Era of Restructuring,* 3rd ed. Toronto: Gage.

Delmos, Monika. (2002). "Mangled Words Divide Generations in Japan." *Globe and Mail,* 24 August: A14.

Durkheim, Émile. (1976 [1915]). *The Elementary Forms of the Religious Life.* Trans. Joseph Ward Swain. New York: Free Press.

Fleras, Augie, and Jean Leonard Elliott. (2002). *Engaging Diversity: Multiculturalism in Canada.* Toronto: Nelson.

Frank, Thomas, and Matt Weiland, eds. (1997). *Commodify Your Dissent: Salvos from the Baffler.* New York: W.W. Norton.

Gap.com. (1999). On the World Wide Web at http://www.gap.com/onlinestore/gap/advertising/khakitv.asp (14 September 1999).

Gleick, James. (2000). *Faster: The Acceleration of Just About Everything.* New York: Vintage.

Gunderson, Edna, Bill Keveney, and Ann Oldenburg. (2002). "'The Osbournes' Find a Home in America's Living Rooms." *USA Today* 19 April: 1A–2A.

Hall, Edward, (1959). *The Silent Language.* New York: Doubleday.

Hanke, Robert. (1998). "'Yo Quiero Mi MTV!' Making Music Television for Latin America." In Thomas Swiss, Andrew Herman, and John M. Sloop, eds., *Mapping the Beat: Popular Music and Contemporary Theory* (pp. 219–45). Oxford, UK: Blackwell.

Harris, Marvin. (1974). *Cows, Pigs, Wars and Witches: The Riddles of Culture.* New York, Random House.

Henry, Frances, Carol Tabor, Winston Mattis, and Tim Ress. (1999). "The Victimization of Racial Minorities in Canada." In

Robert J. Brym, ed., *Society in Question: Sociological Readings for the 21st Century,* 3rd ed. (pp. 145–70). Toronto: Harcourt Brace Canada.

Hobsbawm, Eric. (1994). *Age of Extremes: The Short Twentieth Century, 1914–1991.* London: Abacus.

Ignatieff, Michael. (2000). *The Rights Revolution.* Toronto: Anansi.

Kristof, Nicholas D. (1997). "With Stateside Lingo, Valley Girl Goes Japanese." *New York Times,* 19 October: section 1, 3.

Lipset, Seymour Martin. (1963). "Value Differences, Absolute or Relative: The English-Speaking Democracies." In *The First New Nation: The United States in Historical Perspective* (pp. 248–73). New York: Basic Books.

Lowe, Graham S. (2001). "Quality of Work—Quality of Life." Keynote talk at the Work/Life Balance and Employee Wellness Strategies Conference. Edmonton, Alberta, 14 May. On the World Wide Web at http://www.cprn.com/work/files/pzqwq_e.pdf (25 August 2002).

"Mad about Hockey: Superstitions." (2002). On the World Wide Web at http://www.mcg.org/societe/hockey/pages/aasuperstitions_2.html (20 June 2002).

McCrum, Robert, William Cran, and Robert MacNeil. (1992). *The Story of English,* new and rev. ed. London: Faber and Faber.

McLuhan, Marshall. (1964). *Understanding Media: The Extensions of Man.* New York: McGraw-Hill.

Nevitte, Neil. (1996). *The Decline of Deference: Canadian Value Change in Cross-National Perspective.* Peterborough ON: Broadview Press.

Pinker, Steven. (1994). "Apes—Lost for Words." *New Statesman and Society,* 15 April: 30–31.

Pool, Robert. (1997). *Beyond Engineering: How Society Shapes Technology.* New York: Oxford University Press.

Postman, Neil. (1992). *Technopoly: The Surrender of Culture to Technology.* New York: Vintage.

Rifkin, Jeremy. (1998). *The Biotech Century: Harnessing the Gene and Remaking the World.* New York: Jeremy P. Tarcher/Putnam.

Ritzer, George. (1993). *The McDonaldization of Society: An Investigation into the Changing Character of Contemporary Social Life.* Thousand Oaks, CA: Pine Forge Press.

Ritzer, George. (1996). "The McDonaldization Thesis: Is Expansion Inevitable?" *International Sociology, 11,* 291–308.

Rural Advancement Foundation International. (1999). "The Gene Giants: Masters of the Universe?" On the World Wide Web at http://www.rafi.org/communique/fltxt/19992.html (29 June 1999).

Schlosser, Eric. (2002). *Fast Food Nation: The Dark Side of the All-American Meal.* New York: Perennial.

Schor, Juliet B. (1992). *The Overworked American: The Unexpected Decline of Leisure.* New York: Basic Books.

Scott, James C. (1998). *Seeing Like a State: How Certain Schemes to Improve the Human Condition Have Failed.* New Haven CT: Yale University Press.

Statistics Canada. (2000). "Top Ten Places of Birth for Total Immigrants, Immigrants Arriving Before 1961 and Recent Immigrants for Canada, 1996 Census—20% Sample Data." Ottawa: Ministry of Industry. Catalogue No. 93F0023XDB6003. On the World Wide Web at http://www.statcan.ca/english/census96/nov4/table1.htm (13 October 2006).

Statistics Canada. (2002). "Facts and Figures 2002: Immigration Overview." On the World Wide Web at http://www.cic.gc.ca/english/pub/facts2002/immigration/immigration_5.html (29 October 2005).

Statistics Canada. (2005). "Population by Religion, by Provinces and Territories (2001 Census)." On the World Wide Web at http://www40.statcan.ca/l01/cst01/demo30a.htm?sdi=religion (29 October 2005).

Thompson, E.P. (1967). "Time, Work Discipline, and Industrial Capitalism." *Past and Present* 38: 59–67.

United Nations. (1998). "Universal Declaration of Human Rights." On the World Wide Web at http://www.un.org/Overview/rights.html (29 August 2002).

U.S. Department of Commerce. (1998). "Statistical Abstract of the United States: 1998." On the World Wide Web at http://www.census.gov/prod/3/98pubs/98statab/sasec1.pdf (8 October 2000).

"Voter Turnout." (2004). On the World Wide Web at http://www.nodice.ca/election2004/voterturnout.html (29 October 2005).

Weber, Max. (1946 [1922]). "Bureaucracy." In H. Gerth and C. Mills, eds. and trans., *From Max Weber: Essays in Sociology* (pp. 196–264). New York: Oxford University Press.

Woodbury, Anthony. (2003). "Endangered Languages." *Linguistic Society of America*. On the World Wide Web at http://www.lsadc.org/web2/endangeredlgs.htm (19 July 2003).

World Values Survey, 2000. (2001). Machine readable file. Ann Arbor, MI: Inter-University Consortium for Political and Social Research.

CHAPTER 3

Adler, P.A., and P. Adler. (1998). *Peer Power: Preadolescent Culture and Identity.* New Brunswick, NJ: Rutgers University Press.

Albas, Daniel, and Cheryl Albas. (1994). "Studying Students Studying: Perspectives, Identities, and Activities." In Mary Lorenz Dietz, Robert Prus, and William Shaffir, eds., *Doing Everyday Life: Ethnography as Human Lived Experience* (pp. 273–89). Toronto: Copp Clark Longman Ltd.

Ariès, Philippe. (1981). *The Hour of Our Death.* New York: Knopf.

Atchley, R.C. (1994). *Social Forces and Aging,* 7th ed. Belmont, CA: Wadsworth.

Baker, Maureen, ed. (1989). *Families: Changing Trends in Canada,* 2nd ed. Toronto: McGraw-Hill Ryerson.

Baker, Maureen. (1985). *What Will Tomorrow Bring? A Study of the Aspirations of Adolescent Women.* Ottawa: Canadian Advisory Council on the Status of Women.

Ballantine, Jeanne. (1997). *The Sociology of Education: A Systematic Analysis,* 4th ed. Englewood Cliffs, NJ: Prentice-Hall.

Barber, K., and K. Allen. (1992). *Women and Families: Feminist Reconstructions.* New York: Guilford Press.

Begley, S. (1995). "Gray Matters." *Newsweek* November 7: 48–54.

Benokraitis, Nijole V. (1993). *Marriages and Families: Changes, Choices, and Constraints.* Englewood Cliffs, NJ: Prentice-Hall.

Berger, Peter L. (1970). "Identity as a Problem in the Sociology of Knowledge." In J. Curtis and J. Petras, eds., *The Sociology of Knowledge* (pp. 373–84). New York: Praeger.

Best, Raphaela. (1983). *We've All Got Scars: What Boys and Girls Learn in Elementary School.* Bloomington: Indiana University Press.

Bibby, Reginald W. (1992). *The Bibby Report: Social Trends Canadian Style.* Toronto: Stoddart.

Blau, F., and M. Ferber. (1992). *The Economics of Women, Men, and Work.* Englewood Cliffs, NJ: Prentice Hall.

Brim, Orville G., Jr. (1968). "Socialization through the Life Cycle." In Orville G. Brim, Jr., and Stanton Wheeler, eds., *Socialization after Childhood: Two Essays* (pp. 3–49). New York: John Wiley.

Burgess, R.L., and R.A. Richardson. (1984). "Child Abuse during Adolescence." In R.M. Lerner and N.L. Galambos, eds., *Experiencing Adolescents: A Sourcebook for Parents, Teachers and Teens* (pp. 119–52). New York: Garland.

Clausen, John A. (1986). *The Life Course.* Englewood Cliffs, NJ: Prentice Hall.

Coleman, John C., and Leo Hendry. (1990). *The Nature of Adolescence,* 2nd ed. New York: Routledge, Chapman, and Hall.

Cooley, Charles Horton. (1902). *Human Nature and the Social Order.* New York: Scribner's.

Corsaro, William A. (1992). "Interpretive Reproduction in Children's Peer Cultures." *Social Psychology Quarterly, 55,* 160–77.

Davis, Fred. (1961). "Professional Socialization as Subjective Experience: The Process of Doctrinal Conversion Among Student Nurses." In Howard S. Becker, David Riesman, Blanche Geer, and Robert Weiss, eds., *Institutions and the Person* (pp. 235–51). Chicago: Aldine Publishing Company.

Davis, Kingsley. (1947). "Final Note on a Case of Extreme Isolation." *American Journal of Sociology, 52* (March), 232–47.

Duffy, Jim, Kelly Warren, and Margaret Walsh. (2001–02). "Classroom Interactions: Gender of Teacher, Gender of Student, and Classroom Subject." *Sex Roles, 45,* 579.

Erikson, Erik H. (1982). *The Life Cycle Completed.* New York: Norton.

Evans, Donald, and William W. Falk. (1986). *Learning to be Deaf.* New York: Mouton de Gruyter.

Fox, Bonnie, ed. (2001). *Family Patters, Gender Relations,* 2nd ed. Toronto: Oxford University Press.

Fox, Bonnie. (1998). "Motherhood, Changing Relationships and the Reproduction of Gender Inequality." In S. Abbey and A. O'Reilly, eds., *Redefining Motherhood.* Toronto: Second Story Press.

Fussel, James. A. (2003). "Violent Video Game Has Parents, Experts Concerned." *The Hamilton Spectator* March 1: D16.

Garbarino, J. (1999). *Lost Boys: Why Our Sons Turn Violent and How We Can Save Them.* New York: The Free Press.

Giordano, Peggy C., Stephen A. Cernkovich, and Alfred DeMaris. (1993). "The Family and Peer Relations of Black Adolescents." *Journal of Marriage and the Family, 55* (May), 277–87.

Glaser, Barney, and Anselm L. Strauss. (1967). *The Discovery of Grounded Theory: Strategies for Qualitative Research.* Chicago: Aldine.

Goffman, Erving. (1961). *Asylums.* New York: Anchor Books.

Goffman, Erving. (1979). *Gender Advertisements.* New York: Harper.

Gooden, Angela M., and Mark A. Gooden. (2001). "Gender Representation in Notable Children's Picture Books: 1995–1999." *Sex Roles, 45,* 89–101.

Gould, Stephen J. (1996). *The Mismeasure of Man.* New York: Norton.

Haas, J., and W. Shaffir. (1977). "The Cloak of Competence." *Symbolic Interaction, 1,* 1 (Fall), 71–88.

Haas, Jack, and William Shaffir. (1987). *Becoming Doctors: The Adoption of a Cloak of Competence.* Greenwich, CT: JAI Press.

Handel, Gerald. (1990). "Revising Socialization Theory." *American Sociological Review, 55,* 463–66.

Hebdige, Dick. (1979). *Subculture: The Meaning of Style.* London: Methuen.

Hendricks, Jon, and C. Davis Hendricks. (1986). *Aging in Mass Society: Myths and Realities,* 3rd ed. Boston: Little, Brown.

Herrnstein, Richard J., and Charles Murray. (1994). *The Bell Curve.* New York: Free Press.

Hogan, Dennis P., and Nan Marie Astone. (1986). "Transition to Adulthood." *Annual Review of Sociology, 12,* 109–30.

Hooyman, N.R., and H.A. Kiyak. (1993). *Social Gerontology,* 3rd ed. Boston: Allyn and Bacon.

Hopf, D., and C.H. Hatzichristou. (1999). "Teacher Gender-Related Influences in Greek Schools." *British Journal of Educational Psychology, 69,* 1–18.

Huston, A.C. (1983). "Sex-Typing." In Paul H. Mussen, ed., *Handbook of Child Psychology.* Vol. 4, 4th ed. (pp. 387–467). New York: John Wiley.

Jackson, John J., and Michael Rosenberg. (2004). "Recognition and Mis-Recognition: Radio as Interlocutor—A Study of Second Generation Immigrant Use of Radio." Final report submitted to the Multiculturalism Branch of Heritage Canada. Centre for Broadcasting Studies, Concordia University, Montreal, July.

Joanisse, Leanne. (2005). "'This Is Who I Really Am': Obese Women's Conceptions of Self Following Weight Loss Surgery." In Dorothy Pawluch, William Shaffir, and Charlene Miall, eds., *Doing Ethnography: Studying Everyday Life* (pp. 248–59). Toronto: Canadian Scholars' Press.

Kitsuse, John. (1970). "Editor's Preface." *American Behavioral Scientist, 14,* 2 (November/December).

Kohn, Melvin L., Atsushi Naoi, Carmi Schooler, and Kazimiercz M. Slomczynski. (1990). "Position in the Class Structure and Psychological Functioning in the United States, Japan, and Poland." *American Journal of Sociology, 95,* 964–1008.

Kortenhaus, C.M., and J. Demarest. (1993). "Gender Role Stereotyping in Children's Literature: An Update." *Sex Roles, 28,* 219–32.

Lareau, A. (1987). "Social Class Differences in Family-School Relationships." *Sociology of Education, 60,* 63–72.

Lawson, David. (1996). "The Brave New World of Work." *The Silhouette* 7 November.

Leming, M.R., and G.E. Dickinson. (1990). *Understanding Dying, Death, and Bereavement,* 2nd ed. New York: Holt, Rinehart and Winston.

Light, Donald L., Jr. (1980). *Becoming Psychiatrists: The Professional Transformation of Self.* New York: W.W. Norton.

Luster, Tom, Kelly Rhoades, and Bruce Haas. (1989). "The Relation between Parental Values and Parenting Behavior: A Test of the Kohn Hypothesis." *Journal of Marriage and the Family, 51* (February), 139–47.

Lytton, Hugh, and David Romney. 1991. "Parents' Differential Socialization of Boys and Girls: A Meta-analysis." *Psychological Bulletin, 109,* 267–296.

Mackie, Marlene. (1991). *Gender Relations in Canada: Further Explorations.* Toronto: Butterworths Canada.

Mead, George H. (1934). *Mind, Self and Society.* Chicago: University of Chicago Press.

Montemurro, Beth. (2005). "Add Men, Don't Stir: Reproducing Traditional Gender Roles in Modern Wedding Showers." *Journal of Contemporary Ethnography, 34,* 1, 6–35.

Narahara, M. (1998). *Gender Stereotypes in Children's Picture Books.* East Lansing, MI: National Center for Research on Teacher Learning (ERIC Document Reproduction Service No. ED 419248).

Oakes, Jeannie. (1985). *Keeping Track: How Schools Structure Inequality.* New Haven, CT: Yale University Press.

Piaget, Jean. (1950). *The Psychology of Intelligence.* Boston: Routledge and Kegan Paul.

Richer, Stephen. (1988). "Equality to Benefit from Schooling: The Issue of Educational Opportunity." In D. Forcese and S. Richer, eds., *Social Issues: Sociological Views of Canada* (pp. 262–86). Toronto: Prentice Hall.

Rubin, J., F. Provenzano, and Z. Luria. (1974). "The Eye of the Beholder: Parents' Views on Sex of Newborns." *American Journal of Orthopsychiatry, 44,* 512–19.

Russell, Rachael, and Melissa Tyler. (2002). "Thank Heaven for Little Girls: 'Girl Haven' and the Commercial Context of Feminine Childhood." *Sociology, 36,* 619–37.

Scott, Robert A. (1969). *The Making of Blind Men: A Study of Adult Socialization.* New York: Russell Sage Foundation.

Sebald, H. (1992). *Adolescence: A Social Psychological Analysis.* Englewood Cliffs, NJ: Prentice Hall.

Shanas, Ethel, Peter Townsend, Dorothy Wedderburn, Henning Friis, Paul Milhøj, and Jan Stehouwer. (1972). *Old People in Three Industrial Societies.* New York: Atherton.

Shepard, Jon M. (1993). *Sociology,* 5th ed. New York: West.

Skolnick, Arlene. (1991). *Embattled Paradise: The American Family in an Age of Uncertainty.* New York: Basic Books.

Solomon, Yvette, Jo Warin, Charlie Lewis, and Wendy Langford. (2002). "Intimate Talk Between Parents and Their Teenage Children: Democratic Openness or Covert Control?" *Sociology, 36,* 965–83.

South, S., and S. Spitze. (1994). "Housework in Marital and Nonmarital Households." *American Sociological Review, 59,* 327–47.

Spitz, Rene A. (1945). "Hospitalism: An Inquiry into the Genesis of Psychiatric Conditions in Early Childhood." *The Psychoanalytic Study of the Child, 1,* 53–74.

Stebbins, Robert A. (1990). *Sociology: The Study of Society,* 2nd ed. New York: Harper and Row.

Stockard, Jean, and Miriam M. Johnson. (1992). *Sex and Gender in Society,* 2nd ed. Englewood Cliffs, NJ: Prentice-Hall.

Stryker, Sheldon. (1980). *Symbolic Interactionism.* Menlo Park, CA: Benjamin/Cummings.

Thorne, B. (1993). *Gender Play: Girls and Boys in School.* New Brunswick, NJ: Rutgers University Press.

Weitzman, Lenore. (1979). *Sex-Role Socialization: A Focus on Women.* Palo Alta, CA: Mayfield Publishing Co.

White, L., and D. Brinkerhoff. (1981). "The Sexual Division of Labor: Evidence from Childhood." *Social Forces, 60,* 170–81.

Willis, Paul. (1990). *Common Culture: Symbolic Work at Play in the Everyday Cultures of the Young.* Milton Keynes: Open University Press.

Wolff, Michael. (1973). "Notes on the Behavior of Pedestrians." In A. Birenbaum and E. Sagarin eds., *People in Places: The Sociology of the Familiar.* New York: Praeger.

Wuthnow, Robert. (1998). *Loose Connections.* Cambridge, MA: Harvard University Press.

CHAPTER 4

Adherents.com. (2001). "Religion Statistics: Predominant Religions." On the World Wide Web at http://www.adherents.com/adh_predom.html (November 30, 2001).

Averett, Susan, and Sanders Korenman. (1996). "The Economic Reality of the Beauty Myth." *The Journal of Human Resources, 31, 2,* 304–30.

Bagley, Christopher, and Kathleen King. (1990). *Child Sexual Abuse: The Search for Healing.* London: Tavistock/Routledge.

Berch, D.B., and B.G. Bender. (1987). "Margins of Sexuality." *Psychology Today* December: 54–57.

Bergen, D.J., and J.E. Williams. (1991). "Sex Stereotypes in the United States Revisited: 1972–1988." *Sex Roles, 24,* 413–23.

Bibby, Reginald W. (1995). *The Bibby Report: Social Trends Canadian Style.* Toronto: Stoddart.

Bleier, Ruth. (1984). *Science and Gender: A Critique of Biology and Its Theories on Women.* New York: Pergamon.

Blum, Deborah. (1997). *Sex on the Brain: The Biological Differences between Men and Women.* New York: Penguin Books.

Broverman, I.K., S.R. Vogel, D.M. Broverman, F.E. Clarkson, and P.S. Rosenkratz. (1972). "Sex-Role Stereotypes: A Current Appraisal." *Journal of Social Issues, 28,* 59–78.

Buss, D.M. (1994). *The Evolution of Desire.* New York: Basic Books.

Buss, D.M. (1995a). "Evolutionary Psychology: A New Paradigm for Psychological Science." *Psychological Inquiry, 6,* 1–30.

Buss, D.M. (1995b). "Psychological Sex Differences: Origins through Sexual Selection." *American Psychologist, 50,* 164–68.

Buss, D.M. (1998). "The Psychology of Human Mate Selection: Exploring the Complexity of the Strategic Repertoire." In C. Crawford and D.L. Krebs, eds., *Handbook of Evolutionary Psychology: Ideas, Issues, and Applications* (pp. 405–29). Mahwah, NJ: Erlbaum.

Buss, D.M., M. Abbott, A. Angleitner, A. Asherian, A. Biaggio, A. Blanco-Villasenor, et al. (1990). "International Perspectives in Selecting Mates: A Study of 37 Cultures." *Journal of Cross-Cultural Psychology, 21* (1), 5–47.

Caplan, Paula J., and Jeremy B. Caplan. (1999). *Thinking Critically about Research on Sex and Gender,* 2nd ed. New York: Longman.

Colapinto, John. (1997). "The True Story of John/Joan." *Rolling Stone,* December 11, pp. 54–73, 92–97.

Colapinto, John. (2001). *As Nature Made Him: The Boy Who Was Raised as a Girl.* New York: Perennial.

Condry, J., and S. Condry. (1976). "Sex Differences: A Study of the Eye of the Beholder." *Child Development, 47,* 812–19.

Coontz, Stephanie, and Peta Henderson, eds. (1986). *Women's Work, Men's Property: The Origins of Gender and Class.* London: Verso.

Creighton, Sarah, and Catherine Minto. (2001). "Managing Intersex." *British Medical Journal, 323* (7324), 1264–65.

Davis, Simon. (1990). "Men as Success Objects and Women as Sex Objects: A Study of Personal Advertisements." *Sex Roles, 23,* 43–50.

Davis, T., G. Peck, and J. Stormant. (1993). "Acquaintance Rape and the High School Student." *Journal of Adolescent Health, 14,* 220–24.

Dawkins, Richard. (1976). *The Selfish Gene.* London: Oxford University Press.

DeKeseredy, Walter S., and M.D. Schwartz. (1998). *Woman Abuse on Campus: Results from the Canadian National Survey.* Thousand Oaks, CA: Sage Publications.

Duffy, Ann. (1998). "The Feminist Challenge: Knowing and Ending the Violence." In Nancy Mandell, ed., *Feminist Issues: Race, Class and Sexuality* (pp. 132–59). Scarborough, ON: Prentice Hall Allyn and Bacon Canada.

Durex. (2001). "Global Survey 2001: Global Survey into Sexual Attitudes and Behaviour." On the World Wide Web at http://www.durex.com/index.html (5 September 2002).

Durex. (2003). "Global Sex Survey." On the World Wide Web at http://www.durex.com/CA/assets/gss/2003_Global_report_phase_2.pdf (10 December 2005).

Durex. (2005). "Give and Receive: 2005 Global Sex Survey Results." On the World Wide Web at http://www.durex.com/cm/gss2005result.pdf (10 December 2005).

Dworkin, Andrea. (1981). *Pornography: Men Possessing Women.* New York: Penguin.

Eagley, Alice H., and Wendy Wood. (1999). "The Origins of Sex Differences in Human Behaviour. Evolved Dispositions versus Social Roles." *American Psychologist, 54,* 408–23.

Eccles, J.S., J.E. Jacobs, and R.D. Harold. (1990). "Gender-Role Stereotypes, Expectancy Effects and Parents' Socialization of Gender Differences." *Journal of Social Issues, 46,* 183–201.

Eichler, Margrit. (1980). *The Double Standard.* London: Croom Helm.

Eisler, Riane. (1987). *The Chalice and the Blade.* New York: HarperCollins.

Elkin, F., and G. Handel. (1989). *The Child and Society: The Process of Socialization,* 5th ed. New York: Random House.

Feiring, C., and M. Lewis. (1979). "Sex and Age Differences in Young Children's Reactions to Frustration: A Further Look at the Goldberg and Lewis Subjects." *Child Development, 50,* 848–53.

Fitzgerald, Louise F. (1993). "Sexual Harassment against Women in the Workplace." *American Psychologist, 48,* 1070–76.

Freud, Sigmund. (1977 [1905]). *On Sexuality.* Trans. James Strachey; Angela Richards, ed., Vol. 7 of the Pelican Freud Library. Harmondsworth, UK: Penguin Books.

Gadd, Jane. (1997). "More Boys Physically Abused Than Girls." *The Globe and Mail* 9 July: A1, A6.

Garner, David M. (1997). "The 1997 Body Image Survey Results." *Psychology Today, 30* (January–February): 30–44, 74–80, 84.

Goldberg, S., and M. Lewis. (1969). "Play Behaviour in the Year-Old Infant: Early Sex Differences." *Child Development, 40,* 21–31.

Grescoe, P. (1996). *The Merchants of Venus: Inside Harlequin and the Empire of Romance.* Vancouver: Raincoast.

Gruber, J.E. (1997). "An Epidemiology of Sexual Harassment: Evidence from North America and Europe." In W. O'Donohue, ed., *Sexual Harassment: Theory, Research and Treatment* (pp. 84–98). Boston: Allyn and Bacon.

Hamer, D., and P.F. Copeland. (1996). *The Science of Desire: The Search for the Gay Gene and the Biology of Behaviour.* New York: Touchstone Books.

Hatfield, Elaine. (1995). "What Do Women and Men Want from Love and Sex?" In E.D. Nelson and B.W. Robinson, eds., *Gender in the 1990s: Images, Realities, and Issues* (pp. 257–75). Toronto: Nelson Canada.

Hesse-Biber, Sharlene. (1996). *Am I Thin Enough Yet? The Cult of Thinness and the Commercialization of Identity.* New York: Oxford University Press.

Hobart, Charles. (1996). "Intimacy and Family Life: Sexuality, Cohabitation, and Marriage." In Maureen Baker, ed., *Families: Changing Trends in Canada* (pp. 143–73). Toronto: McGraw-Hill Ryerson.

"Homosexuality and Bisexuality." (2000). Report #5 to the *Toronto Sun* in the Third Annual Sun/COMPAS Sex Survey. On the World Wide Web at http://www.compas.ca/html/archivesdocument.asp?compasSection=Sun+Media+Sex+PollandGO=GOandcompasID=61 (9 August 2002).

Hughes, Fergus P. (1995). *Children, Play and Development*, 2nd ed. Boston: Allyn and Bacon.

Human Rights Watch. (1995). *The Human Rights Watch Global Report on Women's Human Rights.* New York: Human Rights Watch.

Jeffreys, Sheila. (1990). "Heterosexuality and the Desire for Gender." In Diane Richardson, ed., *Theorising Heterosexuality* (pp. 75–90). Buckingham, UK: Open University Press.

Jensen, Margaret Ann. (1984). *Love's Sweet Return: The Harlequin Story.* Toronto: Women's Press.

Kerig, Patricia K., Philip A. Cowan, and Carolyn Pape Cowan. (1993). "Marital Quality and Gender Differences in Parent–Child Interaction." *Developmental Psychology, 29,* 931–39.

Kitzinger, Celia, and Sue Wilkinson. (1994). "Problematizing Pleasure: Radical Feminist Deconstructions of Sexuality and Power." In H.L. Radtke and H.J. Stam, eds., *Power/Gender: Social Relations in Theory and Practice.* London: Sage Publications.

Koff, Elissa, and Amy Benavage. (1998). "Breast Size Perception and Satisfaction, Body Image, and Psychological Functioning in Caucasian and Asian American College Women." *Sex Roles, 38* (7/8), 655–73.

Koss, Mary P., L.A. Goodman, A. Browne, L.F. Fitzgerald, G.P. Keita, and N.F. Russo. (1994). *No Safe Haven: Male Violence against Women at Home, at Work, and in the Community.* Washington, DC: American Psychological Association.

Laumann, Edward O., John H. Gagnon, Robert T. Michael, and Stuart Michaels. (1994). *The Social Organization of Sexuality: Sexual Practices in the United States.* Chicago: University of Chicago Press.

Lenton, Rhonda, Michael D. Smith, John Fox, and Norman Morra. (1999). "Sexual Harassment in Public Places: Experiences of Canadian Women." *Canadian Review of Sociology and Anthropology, 36,* 517–40.

Lightfoot-Klein, Hanny, Cheryl Chase, Tim Hammond, and Ronald Goldman. (2000). "Genital Surgery on Children below the Age of Consent." In Lenore T. Szuchman and Frank Muscarella, eds., *Psychological Perspectives on Human Sexuality* (pp. 440–49). New York: John Wiley and Sons.

Lips, H.M. (1993). *Sex and Gender: An Introduction*, 2nd ed. Mountain View, CA: Mayfield.

Lisak, David. (1992). "Sexual Aggression, Masculinity, and Fathers." *Signs, 16,* 238–62.

MacDonald, K., and R.D. Parke. (1986). "Parent–Child Physical Play: The Effects of Sex and Age on Children and Parents." *Sex Roles, 15,* 367–78.

Mackay, Judith. 2000. *The Penguin Atlas of Human Sexual Behaviour.* New York: Penguin.

MacKinnon, C.A. (1987). *Feminism Unmodified: Discourses on Life and Law.* Cambridge, MA: Harvard University Press.

Masters, W.H., and V.E. Johnson. (1966). *Human Sexual Response.* Boston: Little, Brown.

Matrix, C., ed. (1996). *Tales for the Clit.* Edinburgh: AK Press.

Mead, Margaret. (1935). *Sex and Temperament in Three Primitive Societies.* New York: Dell.

Michael, Robert T., John H. Gagnon, Edward O. Laumann, and Gina Kolata. (1994). *Sex in America: A Survey.* Boston: Little, Brown.

Nelson, E.D., and Barrie W. Robinson. (1999). *Gender in Canada.* Scarborough, ON: Prentice Hall Allyn and Bacon Canada.

Nolen, Stephanie. (1999). "Gender: The Third Way." *The Globe and Mail* 25 September: D1, D4.

Peele, Stanton, and Richard De Grandpre. (1995). "My Genes Made Me Do It." *Psychology Today, 28:* 50–68.

Pipher, M. (1994). *Reviving Ophelia: Saving the Selves of Adolescent Girls.* New York: Ballantine.

Pryor, John B., J.L. Giedd, and K.B. Williams. (1995). "A Social Psychological Model for Predicting Sexual Harassment." *Journal of Social Issues, 51,* 69–84.

Raag, Tarja, and Christine L. Rackliff. (1998). "Preschoolers' Awareness of Social Expectations of Gender: Relationships to Toy Choices." *Sex Roles, 38,* 685–700.

Reiss, I. (1986). *Journey into Sexuality: An Exploratory Voyage.* Englewood Cliffs, NJ: Prentice Hall.

Rich, Adrienne. (1996). "Compulsory Heterosexuality and Lesbian Existence." In Stevi Jackson and Sue Scott, eds., *Feminism and Sexuality: A Reader* (pp. 130–43). New York: Columbia University Press.

Rosenkrantz, P., S.R. Vogel, H. Bee, I.K. Broverman, and D.M. Broverman. (1968). "Sex-Role Stereotypes and Self Concepts in College Students." *Journal of Consulting and Clinical Psychology, 32,* 287–95.

Rubin, J.Z., F.J. Provenzano, and Z. Lurra. (1974). "The Eye of the Beholder." *American Journal of Orthopsychiatry, 44,* 512–19.

Ryan, Kathryn M., and Jeanne Kanjorski. (1998). "The Enjoyment of Sexist Humor, Rape Attitudes, and Relationship Aggression in College Students." *Sex Roles, 38,* 743–56.

"Same-Sex Marriage: Canadian Public Opinion Polls: 2005-JAN-01 to the Present." (2005). On the World Wide Web at http://www.religioustolerance.org/homssmpoll05.htm (10 December 2005).

Sanday, Peggy. (1981). *Female Power and Male Dominance.* Cambridge, UK: Cambridge University Press.

Saxton, Lloyd. (1990). *The Individual, Marriage and the Family*, 7th ed. Belmont, CA: Wadsworth.

Shorter, Edward. (1997). *A History of Psychiatry.* New York: John Wiley and Sons.

Statistics Canada. (1994). *Violence against Women Survey.* Microdata File. Ottawa.

Statistics Canada. (2002). *Family Violence in Canada: A Statistical Profile.* Ottawa: Minister of Industry. Catalogue No. 85-224-XIE. On the World Wide Web at http://www.statcan.ca/english/freepub/85-224-XIE/0000285-224-XIE.pdf (8 August 2006).

Steinem, G. (1994). *Moving beyond Words.* New York: Simon and Schuster.

Straus, Murray. (1995). "Trends in Cultural Norms and Rates of Partner Violence." In Sandra M. Stith and Murray A. Straus, eds., *Understanding Partner Violence: Prevalence, Causes, Consequences, and Solutions* (pp. 30–33). Minneapolis, MN: National Council on Family Relations.

Tavris, Carol. (1992). *The Mismeasure of Woman: Why Women Are Not the Better Sex, the Inferior Sex, or the Opposite Sex.* New York: Touchstone.

Thompson, Linda. (1991). "Family Work: Women's Sense of Fairness." *Journal of Family Issues, 12,* 181–96.

Twenge, Jean M. (1997). "Changes in Masculine and Feminine Traits over Time: A Meta-analysis." *Sex Roles, 36,* 305–25.

Udry, J.R. (1971). *The Social Context of Marriage,* 2nd ed. Philadelphia: J.B. Lippincott.

Walters, Vivienne. (1992). "Women's Views of Their Main Health Problems." *Canadian Journal of Public Health, 83* (5), 371–74.

Weeks, Jeffrey. (1986). *Sexuality.* London: Routledge.

Welsh, Sandy. (1999). "Gender and Sexual Harassment." *Annual Review of Sociology, 25,* 169–90.

Welsh, Sandy, and A. Nierobisz. (1997). "How Prevalent Is Sexual Harassment? A Research Note on Measuring Sexual Harassment in Canada." *Canadian Journal of Sociology, 22,* 505–22.

Williams, J.E., and D.L. Best. (1982). *Measuring Sex Stereotypes: A Thirty-Nation Study.* Beverley Hills, CA: Sage Publications.

Williams, J.E., and S.M. Bennett. (1975). "The Definition of Sex Stereotypes via the Adjective Check List." *Sex Roles, 1,* 327–37.

Wilson, Edward. (1975). *Sociobiology.* Cambridge, MA: Harvard University Press.

Wilson, Edward. (1978). *On Human Nature.* Cambridge, MA: Harvard University Press.

Wilson, Margo, and Martin Daly. (1994). "Lethal and Nonlethal Violence against Wives and the Evolutionary Psychology of Male Sexual Proprietariness." In R. Emerson Dobash and Russell P. Dobash, eds., *Rethinking Violence against Women* (pp. 199–230). Thousand Oaks, CA: Sage Publications.

Wolf, Naomi. (1991). *The Beauty Myth.* Toronto: Vintage Books.

CHAPTER 5

AOL Time Warner. (2005). "Time Warner 2004 Financial Information." On the World Wide Web at http://ir.timewarner.com/downloads/4Q04earnings.pdf (8 August 2006).

Attallah, P., and D. Foster. (2006). "Television in Canada." In P. Attallah and L. Regan Shade, eds., *Mediascapes: New Patterns in Canadian Communication,* 2nd ed. Toronto: Thomson.

Attewell, P. (2001). "The First and Second Digital Divides." *Sociology of Education, 74* (July), 252–59.

Baym, N. (2000). *Tune In, Log On: Soaps, Fandom, and Online Community.* Thousand Oaks and London: SAGE Publications.

Bertelsmann. (2006). "Important Key Figures of the Bertelsmann Group." On the World Wide Web at http://investor.bertelsmann.de/bertelsmann_corp/wms41/bm/index.php?ci=255andlanguage=2 (8 August 2006).

Buckingham, D. (1998). "Children and Television: A Critical Overview of Research." In R. Dickinson, R. Harindranath, and O. Linné, eds., *Approaches to Audiences: A Reader* (pp. 131–45). London: Arnold.

Candussi, D. and J. Winters. (1988). "Monopoly and Content in Winnipeg." In R. Picard, J. P. Winter, M. McCombs, and S. Lacy, eds., *Press Concentration and Monopoly: New Perspectives on Newspaper Ownership and Operation* (pp. 139–45). Norwood, NJ: Ablex.

Carroll, W., and R. Ratner. (1999). "Media Strategies and Political Projects: A Comparative Study of Social Movements." *Canadian Journal of Sociology, 24* (1), 1–34.

Carter, C., and M. Durand. (2000). "Market Opportunities: International Trade of Culture Goods and Services." Statistics Canada. *Focus on Culture, 12* (4), 1–15.

Cherny, L. (1999). *Conversation and Community: Chat in a Virtual World.* Stanford: CSLI Publications.

Collins, R. (1990). *Culture, Communication and National Identity: The Case of Canadian Television.* Toronto: University of Toronto Press.

Cultural Access Group. (2001). "Ethnicity in the Electronic Age: Looking at the Internet Through Multicultural Lens." On the World Wide Web at http://www.accesscag.com/internet%20report%20v.pdf (15 September 2003).

Cuneo, C. (2002). "Globalized and Localized Digital Divides Along the Information Highway: A Fragile Synthesis Across Bridges, Ramps, Cloverleaves, and Ladders." Hamilton, ON Institute for Globalization and the Human Condition Working Paper Series.

Dickinson, P., and J. Ellison. (2000). *Plugging In: the Increase of Household Internet Use Continues into 1999.* Ottawa: Ministry of Industry, Connectedness Series. Catalogue No. 56F0004MIE.

DiMaggio, Paul, Eszter Hargittai, W. Russell Neuman, and John P. Robinson. (2001). "Social Implications of the Internet." *Annual Review of Sociology, 27,* 307–36.

Disney. (2006). "Financial Highlights." *The Walt Disney Company 2005 Annual Report.* On the World Wide Web at http://corporate.disney.go.com/investors/annual_reports/2005/introduction/financial_highlights/fh.html (8 August 2006).

Doyle, A., B. Elliott, and D. Tindall. (1997). "Framing the Forests: Corporations, the B.C. Forest Alliance, and the Media." In W. Carroll, ed., *Organizing Dissent: Contemporary Social Movements in Theory and Practice* (pp. 240–68). Toronto: Garamond Press.

Ellis, D. (1992). *Split Screens: Home Entertainment and the New Technologies.* Toronto: Friends of Canadian Broadcasting.

Ericson, R., P. Baranek, and J. Chan. (1989). *Negotiating Control: A Study of News Sources.* Toronto: University of Toronto Press.

Felson, R. (1996). "Mass Media Effects on Violent Behaviour." In R. Hagen and K. Cook, eds., *Annual Review of Sociology, 22,* 103–28.

Fiske, J. (1987). *Television Culture.* London: Methuen.

Ford, T.V., and G. Gil. "Radical Internet Use." In John D.H. Downing with Tamara Ford, Genève Gil, and Laura Stein, eds., *Radical Media: Rebellious Communication and Social*

Movements (pp. 201–34). Thousands Oaks, CA: Sage Publications.

Forman, H. (1933). *Our Movie-Made Children.* New York: Macmillan.

Freedman, J. (1984). "Effect of Television Violence on Aggressiveness." *Psychological Bulletin, 96* (2), 227–46.

Friedrich-Cofer, L., and A. Huston. (1986). "Television Violence and Aggression: The Debate Continues." *Psychological Bulletin, 100* (3), 364–71.

Gauntlett, D. (1998). "Ten Things Wrong with the 'Effects' Model." In R. Dickinson, R. Harindranath, and O. Linné, eds., *Approaches to Audiences: A Reader* (pp. 120–30). London: Arnold.

Geen, R., and S. Thomas. (1986). "The Immediate Effects of Media Violence on Behaviour." *Journal of Social Issues, 42* (3), 7–27.

Gerbner, George, Larry Gross, Michael Morgan, and Nancy Signorielli. (1994). "Growing Up with Television: The Cultivation Perspective." In J. Bryant and D. Zillmann, eds., *Media Effects: Advances in Theory and Research* (pp. 17–41). Hillsdale, NJ: Lawrence Erlbaum Associates.

Gillespie, M. (1995). *Television, Ethnicity and Cultural Change.* London and New York: Routledge.

Gitlin, T. (1980). *The Whole World Is Watching.* Berkeley: University of California Press.

Goffman, E. (1974). *Frame Analysis.* Philadelphia: University of Pennsylvania Press.

Gosselin, A., DeGuise, J., Pacquette, G., and Benoit, L. (1997). "Violence on Canadian Television and Some of Its Cognitive Effects." *Canadian Journal of Communication, 22,* 143–60.

Granovetter, M. (1973). "The Strength of Weak Ties." *American Journal of Sociology, 78* (6), 1360–80.

Greenberg, J. (2006). *The Media and Mental Health: An Analysis of Local News Coverage.* Ottawa: Canadian Mental Health Association.

Gunter, B. (1995). *Television and Gender Representation.* London: John Libbey and Company.

Hackett, R. (1991). *News and Dissent: The Press and the Politics of Peace in Canada.* Norwood, NJ: Ablex.

Hall, S. (1980). "Encoding/Decoding." In S. Hall, D. Hobson, A. Lowe, and P. Willis, eds., *Culture, Media, Language* (pp. 128–38). London: Hutchinson.

Herman, E., and N. Chomsky. (1988). *Manufacturing Consent: The Political Economy of the Mass Media.* New York: Pantheon.

Hobson, D. (1982). *Crossroads: The Drama of a Soap Opera.* London: Methuen.

Hodge, R., and D. Tripp. (1986). *Children and Television: A Semiotic Approach.* Cambridge: Polity Press.

Horkheimer, M., and T. Adorno. (1972 [1947]). *Dialectic of Enlightenment.* Trans. John Cumming. New York: Continuum Books.

Huesmann, L., and N. Malamuth. (1986). "Media Violence and Anti-Social Behaviour: An Overview." *Journal of Social Issues, 42* (3), 1–6.

Innis, H. (1951). *The Bias of Communication.* Toronto: University of Toronto Press.

International Telecommunication Union (ITU). (2004). "Internet Indicators." On the World Wide Web at http://www.itu.int/ITU-D/ict/statistics/at_glance/Internet04.pdf (12 October 2005).

Jupiter Media Metrix. (2001). "In Search of Love Online: Men Outnumber Women on Personals Sites." On the World Wide Web at http://www.jmm.com/xp/jmm/press/2001/pr_020801c.xml (18 April 2003).

Klapper, J. (1960). *The Effects of Mass Communication.* Glencoe: Free Press.

Knight, G. (1982). "News and Ideology." *Canadian Journal of Communication, 8* (4), 15–41.

Knight, G. (1998). "Hegemony, the Media, and New Right Politics: Ontario in the Late 1990s." *Critical Sociology, 24* (1/2), 105–29.

Knight, G., and J. Greenberg. (2002). "Promotionalism and Subpolitics: Nike and Its Labor Critics." *Management Communication Quarterly, 15* (4), 541–70.

Kraut, R., M. Patterson, V. Lundmark, S. Kiesler, T. Mukopadhyay, and W. Scherlis. (1998). "Internet Paradox: A Social Technology that Reduces Social Involvement and Psychological Well-Being?" *American Psychologist, 53* (9), 1017–32.

Kraut, R., S. Kiesler, B. Boneva, J. Cummings, V. Helgeson, and A. Crawford. (2002). "Internet Paradox Revisited." *Journal of Social Issues, 58* (1), 49–74.

Kumar, D. (2006). "Media, War and Propaganda: Strategies of Information Management During the 2003 Iraq War." *Communication and Critical/Cultural Studies, 3* (1), 48–69.

Livingstone, S. (2005). "Assessing the Research Base for the Policy Debate over the Effects of Food Advertising to Children." *International Journal of Advertising, 24* (3), 273–96.

Madden, M. (2003). *America's Online Pursuits: The Changing Picture of Who's Online and What They Do.* Washington: Pew Internet and American Life Project. On the World Wide Web at http://www.pewinternet.org/pdfs/PIP_Online_Pursuits_Final.PDF (12 September 2004).

Mayer, C.E. (2005). "Group Takes Aim at Junk-Food Marketing." *The Washington Post* 7 January: E3.

McChesney, R. (1996). "The Global Struggle for Communication." *The Monthly Review, 48* (2), 1.

McCombs, M. (1988). "Concentration, Monopoly, and Content." In R. Picard, J. Winter, M. McCombs, and S. Lacy, eds., Press Concentration and Monopoly: New Perspectives on *Newspaper Ownership and Operation* (pp. 129–37). Norwood, NJ: Ablex.

McCormack, T. (1994). "Codes, Ratings and Rights." *Institute for Social Research Newsletter, 9* (1).

McLuhan, M. (1964). *Understanding Media: The Extensions of Man.* New York: Mentor Books.

Miljan, L., and B. Cooper. (2003). *Hidden Agendas: How Journalists Influence the News.* Vancouver: UBC Press.

Miller, D. and D. Slater. (2000). *The Internet: An Ethnographic Approach.* Oxford and New York: Berg.

Miller, M.C. (2002). "What's Wrong with This Picture?" *The Nation* 7 January. On the World Wide Wed at http://www.thenation.com/doc/20020107/miller (12 August 2006).

Morley, D. (1986). *Family Television: Cultural Power and Domestic Leisure.* London: Comedia.

Morley, D. (2000). *Home Territories: Media, Mobility and Identity.* London and New York: Routledge.

National Media Archive. (1993). "Immigration I: The Human Interest Story." *On Balance, 6* (3), 1–8. Vancouver: The Fraser Institute.

News Corp. (2005). *News Corporation Annual Report 2004*. On the World Wide Web at http://www.newscorp.com/Report2004/2004_annual_report.pdf (8 August 2006).

Parenti, M. (2004). "Methods of Media Manipulation." In C. Jensen, ed., *20 Years of Censored News* (pp. 27–32). New York: Seven Stories Press.

Perse, E.M. (2001). *Media Effects and Society*. Mahwah, NJ, and London: Lawrence Erlbaum Associates, Publishers.

Postman, N. (1992). *Technopoly: The Surrender of Culture to Technology*. New York: Knopf.

Reid, E. (1999). "Hierarchy and Power: Social Control in Cyberspace." In M.A. Smith and P. Kollock, eds., *Communities in Cyberspace* (pp. 107–33). London and New York: Routledge.

Schutz, A. (1970). *Reflections on the Problem of Relevance*. R.M. Zaner, ed., New Haven, CN: Yale University Press.

Statistics Canada. (2004). "Household Internet Use Survey." *The Daily* 8 July. On the World Wide Web at http://www.statcan.ca/Daily/English/040708/d040708a.htm (8 August 2006).

Statistics Canada. (2005a). "Television Viewing." *The Daily* 31 Thursday. On the World Wide Web http://www.statcan.ca/Daily/English/050331/d050331b.htm (8 August 2006).

Statistics Canada. (2005b). "Newspaper Publishers." *The Daily* 8 December. On the World Wide Web http://www.statcan.ca/Daily/English/051208/d051208c.htm (8 August 2006).

Statistics Canada. (2005c). "Television Viewing, Fall 2003." *The Daily* 31 March, Tables 11 and 12. On the World Wide Web at http://www.statcan.ca/Daily/English/050331/d050331b.htm (8 August 2006).

Statistics Canada. (2005d). "International Trade in Culture Goods: Replacement Data." *The Daily* 17 October. On the World Wide Web at http://www.statcan.ca/Daily/English/051017/d051017c.htm (8 August 2006).

Statistics Canada. (2005e). "Data Tables." *Culture Goods Trade*. Ottawa: Ministry of Industry. Catalogue No. 87-007-XIE. On the World Wide Web at http://www.statcan.ca/english/freepub/87-007-XIE/2005001/data.htm (9 August 2006).

Statistics Canada. (2005f). "Household Internet Use at Home by Internet Activity (All Households)." *Summary Tables*. On the World Wide Web at http://www40.statcan.ca/l01/cst01/comm09a.htm (8 August 2006).

SustainAbility. (2002). "Good News and Bad: The Media, Corporate Social Responsibility and Sustainable Development." On the World Wide Web at http://www.sustainability.com (8 August 2006).

Taras, D. (1990). *The Newsmakers: The Media's Influence on Canadian Politics*. Scarborough, ON: Nelson.

Tekrati. (January 5, 2006). "Worldwide Internet Users Top 1 Billion in 2005, Says eTForecasts." On the World Wide Web http://www.tekrati.com/T2/Analyst_Research/ResearchAnnouncementsDetails.asp?Newsid=6275 (8 August 2006).

The Nation. (2002). "The Big Ten." 7–14 July. On the World Wide Web at http://www.thenation.com/special/bigten.html (12 August 2006).

Tomlinson, J. (1997). "Cultural Globalization and Cultural Imperialism." In A. Mohammadi, ed., *International Communication and Globalization* (pp. 170–90). London: Sage Publications.

Trim, K., with G. Pizante and J. Yaraskavitch. (1983). "The Effect of Monopoly on the News: A Before and After Study of Two Canadian One Newspaper Towns." *Canadian Journal of Communication*, 9 (3), 33–56.

U.S. Department of Commerce. (2004). *A Nation Online: Entering the Broadband Age*. Washington, DC: U.S. Bureau of the Census.

Viacom. (2005). "Viacom Reports Full Year and Fourth Quarter 2004 Results." On the World Wide Web at http://www.cbscorporation.com/media/pdf/qr4q04.pdf (8 August 2006).

Vivendi Universal. (2006). "Annual Report 2005." On the World Wide Web at http://www.vivendiuniversal.com/vu/en/files/20050629_Annual_Report_20-F.cfm (8 August 2006).

Watson, N. (1997). "Why We Argue about Virtual Community: A Case Study of the Phish.Net Fan Community." In S.G. Jones, ed., *Virtual Culture: Identity and Community in Cyberspace* (pp. 102–32). London and Thousand Oaks: Sage Publications.

Wellman, B., and M. Gulia. (1999). "Virtual Communities as Communities: Net Surfers Don't Ride Alone." In M.A. Smith and P. Kollock, eds., *Communities in Cyberspace* (pp. 167–94). London and New York: Routledge.

Williams, T.M. (ed.). (1986). *The Impact of Television: A Natural Experiment in Three Communities*. Orlando: Academic Press.

Wober, J.M. (1998). "Cultural Indicators: European Reflections on a Research Paradigm." In R. Dickinson, R. Harindranath, and O. Linné, eds., *Approaches to Audiences: A Reader* (pp. 61–73). London: Arnold.

Znaimer, M. (1996). "TV Talks Back: A Rebuttal." *Canadian Journal of Communication*, 21 (1), 67–73.

CHAPTER 6

Beauchesne, Eric. (2006). "Canadian Real Wages up 10 Cents an Hour in 15 Years." *Edmonton Journal* 13 February: A3.

Breen, R., and Rottman, D.B. (1995). *Class Stratification: A Comparative Perspective*. Hertfordshire, UK: Harvester Wheatsheaf.

Brym, Robert J. (1979). "Political Conservatism in Atlantic Canada." In Robert J. Brym and R. James Sacouman, eds., *Underdevelopment and Social Movements in Atlantic Canada* (pp. 59–79). Toronto: New Hogtown Press.

Calliste, Agnes. (1987). "Sleeping Car Porters in Canada: An Ethnically Submerged Split Labour Market." *Canadian Ethnic Studies*, 19, 1–20.

Chawla, Raj K. (2004). "Wealth Inequality by Province." *Perspectives on Labour and Income* (Winter), 15–22.

Church, Elizabeth. (2005). "Market Recovery Delivers Executive Payout Bonanza." *The Globe and Mail* 4 May: B1.

Clark, Terry Nichols, and Seymour Martin Lipset. (1991). "Are Social Classes Dying?" *International Sociology*, 6, 397–410.

Davis, Kingsley, and Wilbert E. Moore. (1945). "Some Principles of Stratification." *American Sociological Review*, 10, 242–49.

Derreck, Tom. (2003). "In Bondage." *The Beaver*, 83 (1), 14–19.

Esping-Andersen, Gøsta. (1990). *Three Worlds of Welfare Capitalism*. Princeton, NJ: Princeton University Press.

Galarneau, Diane, and René Morissette. (2004). "Immigrants: Settling for Less?" *Perspectives on Labour and Income* (Autumn), 7–18.

Grabb, Edward G. (2002). *Theories of Social Inequality*, 4th ed. Toronto: Harcourt Canada.

Hall, Karen. (1999). "Hours Polarization at the End of the 1990s." *Perspectives on Labour and Income* (Summer), 28–37.

Krahn, Harvey, Graham S. Lowe, and Karen Hughes. (2006). *Work, Industry and Canadian Society*, 5th ed. Scarborough: Thomson Nelson.

Krahn, Harvey. (2004). "Choose Your Parents Carefully: Social Class, Post-secondary Education, and Occupational Outcomes." In J. Curtis, E. Grabb, and N. Guppy, eds., *Social Inequality in Canada: Patterns, Problems, Policies*, 4th ed. (pp. 187–203). Toronto: Pearson Prentice Hall.

Krugman, Paul. (1994). "Long-Term Riches, Short-Term Pain." *The New York Times* 25 September 25: F9.

Lenski, Gerhard. (1966). *Power and Privilege: A Theory of Social Stratification*. New York: McGraw-Hill.

Li, Peter. (1982). "Chinese Immigrants on the Canadian Prairie, 1919–47." *Canadian Review of Sociology and Anthropology, 19*, 527–40.

Livingstone, David. (1999). *The Education-Jobs Gap: Underemployment or Economic Democracy*. Toronto: Garamond Press.

Longman, Phillip. (1985). "Justice between Generations." *Atlantic Monthly* June: 73–81.

Love, Roger, and Susan Poulin. (1991). "Family Income Inequality in the 1980s." *Perspectives on Labour and Income, 3* (Autumn), 51–57.

McMullin, Julie. (2004). *Understanding Social Inequality: Intersections of Class, Age, Gender, Ethnicity, and Race in Canada*. Toronto: Oxford University Press.

McQuaig, Linda. (2004). "Rich Walk Ever Taller in Canada," *Toronto Star* 12 December: A17

Morissette, René. (2002). "Families on the Financial Edge." *Perspectives on Labour and Income* (Autumn), 9–20.

Morissette, René, and Xuelin Zhang. (2001). "Experiencing Low Income for Several Years." *Perspectives on Labour and Income* (Summer), 25–35.

Morissette, René, Xuelin Zhang, and Marie Drolet. (2002). "Wealth Inequality." *Perspectives on Labour and Income* (Spring), 15–22.

Myles, John, and Adnan Turegun. (1994). "Comparative Studies in Class Structure." *Annual Review of Sociology, 20*, 103–24.

National Council of Welfare. (2001–02). *The Cost of Poverty*. Ottawa: Minister of Public Works and Government Services Canada. Catalogue No. H68-53/2002E.

National Council of Welfare. (2004). *Poverty Profile 2001*. Ottawa: Minister of Public Works and Government Services Canada. Catalogue No. SD25-1/2001E.

National Council of Welfare. (2005). *Welfare Incomes, 2004*. Ottawa: Minister of Public Works and Government Services Canada. Catalogue No. SD25-2/2004E.

O'Malley, Martin, and John Bowman. (2002). "How Do We Measure Poverty?" *CBC News Online*, 7 May. On the World Wide Web at http://cbc.ca/news/features/poverty_line.html (4 November 2002).

O'Neill, Jeff. (1991). "Changing Occupational Structure." *Canadian Social Trends* (Winter), 10.

Palmer, Bryan. (1986). *The Character of Class Struggle: Essays in Canadian Working Class History, 1850–1985*. Toronto: McClelland and Stewart.

Parkin, Frank. (1972). *Class, Inequality and Political Order*. London: Paladin.

Parkin, Frank. (1979). *Marxism and Class Theory: A Bourgeois Critique*. London: Tavistock.

Picot, Garnett, and John Myles. (2005). *Income Inequality and Low Income in Canada: an International Perspective*. Statistics Canada Analytic Studies Branch Research Paper (No. 240). Ottawa: Ministry of Industry. Catalogue No. 11F0019MIE.

Raphael, Dennis, ed. (2004). *Social Determinants of Health*. Toronto: Canadian Scholars Press.

Ryscavage, Paul. (1995). "A Surge in Growing Income Inequality?" *Monthly Labor Review* August: 51–61.

Sauvé, Roger. (2006). *The Current State of Canadian Family Finances: 2005 Report*. Ottawa: Vanier Institute of the Family.

Scoffield, Heather. (2006). "Low-Paying Jobs Behind Employment Boom: CIBC Study." *The Globe and Mail* 31 January: B4.

Simons, Paula. "From Recycling Bin to an Art Gallery." *Edmonton Journal* 28 January: B1.

Statistics Canada. (1984). *Charting Canadian Incomes, 1951–1981*. Ottawa: Supply and Services Canada. Catalogue No. 13-581E.

Statistics Canada. (2001). "2001 Census of Canada". On the World Wide Web at http://www12.statcan.ca/english/census01/home/index.cfm (16 October 2006).

Statistics Canada. (2005). *Income in Canada*. Ottawa: Minister of Industry. Catalogue No. 75-202-XIE.

Steffenhagen, Janet. (2006). "B.C. First Nations to Run Own Schools." *Edmonton Journal* 10 February: A9.

Stewart, Sinclair. (2006). "CIBC, Scotiabank Heads Take Pay Cuts." *The Globe and Mail* 31 January: B6.

Struck, Doug. (2005). "Canada Evacuates Indian Reserve Over Contaminated Water Supply." *Washington Post Foreign Service* 27 October. On the World Wide Web at http://www.washingtonpost.com/wp-dyn/content/article/2005/10/26/AR2005102602173.html (16 October 2006).

Swanson, Jean. (2001). *Poor-Bashing: The Politics of Exclusion*. Toronto. Between the Lines.

"Swimming, Golf, Zoo Free for Poor." *Edmonton Journal* 4 February: B3.

Tanner, Julian, Harvey Krahn, and Timothy F. Hartnagel. (1995). *Fractured Transitions from School to Work: Revisiting the Dropout Problem*. Toronto: Oxford University Press.

"Trump Suing Author Who Questions His Status as Billionaire." (2006). *The Globe and Mail* 25 January: B11.

Vosko, Leah F, Zukewich, Nancy, and Cynthia Crawford. (2003). "Precarious Work: A New Typology of Employment." *Perspectives on Labour and Income* (Winter), 39–49.

Wanner, Richard A. (2004). "Social Mobility in Canada: Concepts, Patterns, and Trends." In J. Curtis, E. Grabb, and N. Guppy, eds., *Social Inequality in Canada: Patterns, Problems, Policies*, 4th ed. (pp. 131–47). Toronto: Pearson Prentice Hall.

Weber, Max. (1948 [1922]). From *Max Weber: Essays in Sociology*. Eds. and trans. H.H. Gerth and C.W. Mills. London: Routledge and Kegan Paul.

Westergaard, John. (1995). *Who Gets What? The Hardening of Class Inequality in the Late Twentieth Century*. Cambridge, UK: Polity Press.

Wilkinson, R.G. (1992). "Income Distributions and Life Expectancy." *British Medical Journal, 304*, 165–68.

Wolff, Edward N. (1991). "The Distribution of Household Wealth: Methodological Issues, Time Trends, and Cross-Sectional Comparisons." In Lars Osberg, ed., *Economic Inequality and Poverty: International Perspectives* (pp. 92–133). Armonk, NY: M.E. Sharpe.

Wright, Erik Olin. (1985). *Classes*. London: Verso.

Wu, Xiaogang, and Yu Xie. (2002) "Does the Market Pay Off? Earnings Returns to Education in Urban China." *American Sociological Review, 68* (June), 425–42.

Yakabuski, Konrad. 2001. "The Extended Family." *Report on Business Magazine* July, 55–56.

Yalnizyan, Armine. (1998). *The Growing Gap: A Report on Growing Inequality between the Rich and Poor in Canada*. Toronto: The Centre for Social Justice.

Zeitlin, Irving M., with Robert J. Brym. (1991). *The Social Condition of Humanity*, Cdn. ed. Toronto: Oxford University Press.

CHAPTER 7

Agocs, Carol, and Monica Boyd. (1993). "The Canadian Ethnic Mosaic Recast for the 1990s." In James Curtis, Edward Grabb, and Neil Guppy, eds., *Social Inequality in Canada: Patterns, Problems and Policies* (pp. 330–52). Scarborough, ON: Prentice Hall.

Agocs, Carol, Catherine Burr, and Felicity Somerset. (1992). *Employment Equity: Cooperative Strategies for Organizational Change*. Toronto: Prentice Hall Canada.

Andersen, L. Margaret. (2005). "Thinking about Women: A Quarter Century's View." *Gender and Society, 19* (4), 437–55.

Armstrong, Pat, and Hugh Armstrong. (1994). *The Double Ghetto: Canadian Women and Their Segregated Work*, 3rd ed. Toronto: McClelland and Stewart.

Arscott, Jane, and Linda Trimble. (1997). "Introduction—In the Presence of Women: Representation and Political Power." In Jane Arscott and Linda Trimble, eds., *In the Presence of Women: Representation in Canadian Governments* (pp. 1–17). Toronto: Harcourt Brace.

Bashevkin, Sylvia B. (1991). "Women's Participation in Political Parties." In Kathy Megyery, ed., *Women in Canadian Politics: Toward Equity in Representation* (pp. 61–79). Toronto: Dundurn Press.

Bashevkin, Sylvia B. (1993). *Toeing the Lines: Women and Party Politics in English Canada*, 2nd ed. Toronto: Oxford University Press.

Berdahl, Jennifer L., and Celia Moore. (2006). "Workplace Harassment: Double Jeopardy for Minority Women." *Journal of Applied Psychology, 91* (2), 426–36.

Best, Pamela. (1995). "Women, Men and Work." *Canadian Social Trends, 36* (1), 30–33.

Black, Jerome H. (2000). "Entering the Political Elite in Canada: The Case of Minority Women as Parliamentary Candidates and MPs." *Canadian Review of Sociology and Anthopology, 37* (2), 143–66.

Boyd, Monica. (1990). "Sex Differences in Occupational Skill: Canada, 1961–1986." *Canadian Review of Sociology and Anthropology, 27*, 285–315.

Boyd, Monica. (1999). "Integrating Gender, Language and Visible Minority Groups." In Shiva S. Halli and Leo Driedger, eds., *Immigrant Canada: Demographic, Economic and Social Challenges* (pp. 282–306). Toronto: University of Toronto Press.

Boyd, Monica, Brenda Hughes, and Jamie Miller. (1997). "Power at Work: Women and Men in Management, Supervision and Workplace Planning." Unpublished paper. Department of Sociology, Florida State University.

Boyd, Monica, Maryann Mulvihill, and John Myles. (1991). "Gender, Power and Postindustrialism." *Canadian Review of Sociology and Anthropology, 28*, 407–36.

Brodie, Janine, ed. (1996). *Women and Canadian Public Policy*. Toronto: Harcourt Brace.

Brodie, Janine. (1991). "Women and the Electoral Process in Canada." In Kathy Megyery, ed., *Women in Canadian Politics: Toward Equity in Representation* (pp. 3–59). Toronto: Dundurn Press.

Broverman, I., S.R. Vogel, S.M. Broverman, F.E. Clarkson, and P.S. Rosenkranz. (1972). "Sex Role Stereotypes: A Current Appraisal." *Journal of Social Issues, 28* (2), 59–78.

Burt, Sandra. (1993). "The Changing Patterns of Public Policy." In Sandra Burt, Lorraine Code, and Lindsay Dorney, eds., *Changing Patterns: Women in Canada*, 2nd ed. (pp. 212–37). Toronto: McClelland and Stewart.

Canada. (1995). *Laws. Statutes of Canada. Employment Equity Act*. 43–44 Elizabeth II, Vol. II, Chapter 44.

Canadian Council on Social Development. (2002). "Free Statistics." On the World Wide Web at http://www.ccsd.ca/facts.html (23 June 2003).

Chafetz, Janet Saltzman. (1999). "The Varieties of Gender Theory in Sociology." In Janet Saltzman Chafetz, ed., *The Handbook of the Sociology of Gender* (pp. 3–23). New York: Kluwer Academic/Plenum Publishers.

Clark, Terry Nichols, and Seymour Martin Lipset. (1991). "Are Social Classes Dying?" *International Sociology, 6*, 397–410.

Collins, Patricia Hill. (1990). *Black Feminist Thought, Knowledge, Consciousness, and the Politics of Empowerment*. Boston: Unwin Hyman.

Connelly, Patricia. (1978). *Last Hired, First Fired: Women and the Canadian Work Force*. Toronto: Women's Press.

Cooke-Reynolds, Melissa, and Nancy Zukewich. 2004. "The Feminization of Work." *Canadian Social Trends, 72* (Spring), 24–29.

Corak, Miles. (1998). "Does Your Parents' Income Count?" *Canadian Social Trends* (Summer), 6–10.

Cranford, Cynthia J., Leah F. Vosko, and Nancy Zukewich. (2003). "The Gender of Precarious Employment in Canada." *Industrial Relations, 58* (3), 454–79.

Cranswick, Kelly. (1997). "Canada's Caregivers." *Canadian Social Trends, 48* (Winter), 2–6.

Creese, Gillian, Neil Guppy, and Martin Meissner. (1991). *Ups and Downs on the Ladder of Success: Social Mobility in Canada*. General Social Survey Analysis Series 5. Ottawa: Statistics Canada. Catalogue No. 11–612E.

Crompton, Susan, and Leslie Geran. (1995). "Women as Main Wage-Earners." *Canadian Perspectives on Labour and Income, 7* (4), 26–29.

Das Gupta, Tania. (1996). *Racism and Paid Work*. Toronto: Garamond Press.

Davis, Kingsley, and Wilbert E. Moore. (1945). "Some Principles of Stratification." *American Sociological Review, 10,* 242–49.

Devereaux, Mary Sue. (1993). "Time Use of Canadians in 1992." *Canadian Social Trends, 8* (3), 13–16.

Duffy, Ann. (1986). "Reformulating Power for Women." *Canadian Review of Sociology and Anthropology, 23,* 22–46.

Duffy, Ann, and Norene Pupo. (1992). *Part-Time Paradox: Connecting Gender, Work and Family.* Toronto: McClelland and Stewart.

Economic Council of Canada. (1991). *Employment in the Service Economy.* Ottawa: Supply and Services Canada.

England, Paula. (1993). *Comparable Worth: Theories and Evidence.* New York: Aldine de Gruyter.

Erickson, Lynda. (1991). "Women Candidates for the House of Commons." In Kathy Megyery, ed., *Women in Canadian Politics: Toward Equity in Representation* (pp. 101–25). Toronto: Dundurn Press.

Erickson, Lynda. (1998). "Entry to the Commons: Parties, Recruitment and the Election of Women in 1993." In Manon Tremblay and Caroline Andrew, eds., *Women and Political Representation in Canada* (pp. 219–58). Ottawa: University of Ottawa Press.

Frederick, Judith A., and Janet E. Fast. (1999). "Eldercare in Canada: Who Does How Much?" *Canadian Social Trends, 54* (Autumn), 26–30.

Gagne, Patricia, and Richard Tewksbury. (1998). "Rethinking Binary Conceptions and Social Constructions: Transgender Experiences of Gender and Sexuality." In Marcia Texler Segal and Vasilikie Demos, series eds. *Advances in Gender Research,* Vol. 3, (pp. 73–102).

Gaskell, Jane. (1986). "Conceptions of Skill and the Work of Women: Some Historical and Political Issues." In Roberta Hamilton and Michele Barrett, eds., *The Politics of Diversity: Feminism, Marxism and Nationalism* (pp. 361–80). London: Verso.

Gaskell, Jane. (1991). "What Counts as Skill? Reflections on Pay Equity." In Judy Fudge and Patricia McDermott, eds., *Just Wages: A Feminist Assessment of Pay Equity* (pp. 141–59). Toronto: University of Toronto Press.

Jackson, Chris. (1996). "Measuring and Valuing Households' Unpaid Work." *Canadian Social Trends, 42* (4), 25–29.

Jaggar, Alison M. (1983). *Feminist Politics and Human Nature.* New York: Rowman and Allanheld Publishers.

Krahn, Harvey. (1995). "Non-standard Work on the Rise." *Perspectives on Labour and Income, 7* (4), 35–42.

Leacy, Frank, H. (1983). *Historical Statistics of Canada* (2nd ed.). Ottawa: Statistics Canada. Catalogue No. 11-516-XIE.

Lengermann, Patricia Madoo, and Niebrugge-Brantley, Jill. (1996). "Contemporary Feminist Theory." In George Ritzer, ed., *Modern Sociological Theory* (pp. 299–305). New York: McGraw.

Looker, E. Dianne, and Victor Thiessen. (1999). "Images of Work: Women's Work, Men's Work, Housework." *Canadian Journal of Sociology, 24,* 2 (Spring), 225–54.

Lorber, Judith. (1998). *Gender Inequality: Feminist Theories and Politics.* Los Angeles: Roxbury Publishing Company.

Lowe, Graham. (1987). *Women in the Administrative Revolution: The Feminization of Clerical Work.* Cambridge, UK: Polity Press.

Luxton, Meg, and Leah F. Vosko. (1998). "Where Women's Efforts Count: The 1996 Census Campaign and 'Family Politics' in Canada." *Studies in Political Economy, 56* (Summer), 49–81.

Mackie, Marlene. (1980). "The Impact of Sex Stereotypes upon Adult Self-Imagery." *Social Psychology Quarterly, 43,* 121–25.

Maille, Chantal. (1990). *Primed for Power: Women in Canadian Politics.* Ottawa: Canadian Advisory Council on the Status of Women.

Martin, Y. Patricia. (2003). "'Said and Done' versus 'Saying and Doing': Gender Practices, Practicing Gender at Work." *Gender and Society, 17* (3), 342–66.

McCormack, Thelma. (1975). "Toward a Nonsexist Perspective on Social and Political Change." In Marcia Millman and Rosabeth Moss Kanter, eds., *Another Voice: Feminist Perspectives on Social Life and Social Science* (pp. 1–33). Garden City, NY: Anchor Books.

Myles, John, and Gail Fawcett. (1990). "Job Skills and the Service Economy." Working Paper no. 4. Ottawa: Economic Council of Canada.

Pal, Leslie. (1989). *Public Policy Analysis.* Toronto: Nelson Canada.

Parliament of Canada. (2006a). "Women—Federal Polical Representation (Current List, June 2006)." On the World Wide Web at http://www.parl.gc.ca/information/about/people/key/StandingsWomen.asp?Language=EandHist=Nandsource=key (11 September 2006).

Parliament of Canada. (2006b). "House of Commons Party Standing, August 2006." On the World Wide Web at http://www.parl.gc.ca/information/about/process/house/partystandings/standings-e.htm (11 September 2006).

Parliament of Canada. (2006c). "Standings in the Senate, June 2006." On the World Wide Web at http://www.parl.gc.ca/common/senmemb/senate/ps-e.htm (11 September 2006).

Pendakur, Krishna, and Ravi Pendakur. (1998). "The Colour of Money: Earnings Differentials among Ethnic Groups in Canada." *Canadian Journal of Economics, 31* (3), 518–47.

Phillips, Paul, and Erin Phillips. (1983). *Women and Work.* Toronto: Lorimer.

Pierson, Ruth. (1977). "Women's Emancipation and the Recruitment of Women into the Labour Force in World War II." In Susan Mann Trofimenkoff and Alison Prentice, eds., *The Neglected Majority* (pp. 125–45). Toronto: McClelland and Stewart.

Prentice, Alison. (1977). "The Feminization of Teaching." In Susan Mann Trofimenkoff and Alison Prentice, eds., *The Neglected Majority* (pp. 49–65). Toronto: McClelland and Stewart.

Robinson, Gertrude J., and Armande Saint-Jean, with the assistance of Christine Rioux. (1991). "Women Politicians and Their Media Coverage: A Generational Analysis." In Kathy Megyery, ed., *Women in Canadian Politics: Toward Equity in Representation* (pp. 127–69). Toronto: Dundurn Press.

Segal, Edwin S. (1998). "Male Genders: Cross Cultural Perspectives." In Marcia Texler Segal and Vasilikie Demos, series eds, *Advances in Gender Research.* Vol. 3 (pp. 37–77).

Séguin, Rhéal. (1996). "Quebec Puts Brakes on Pay Equity." *The Globe and Mail* 8 November: A7.

Ship, Susan Judith. (1998). "Problematizing Ethnicity and 'Race' in Feminist Scholarship on Women and Politics." In Manon

Tremblay and Caroline Andrew, eds., *Women and Political Representation in Canada* (pp. 311–40). Ottawa: University of Ottawa Press.

Statistics Canada. (1998). "1996 Census: Sources of Income, Earnings and Total Income, and Family Income."*The Daily* 12 May. On the World Wide Web at http://www.statcan.ca/Daily/English/980512/d980512.htm (11 September 2006).

Statistics Canada. (1999). "General Social Survey: Time Use." *The Daily* November 9, pp. 2–5.

Statistics Canada. (2001a). "2001 Canadian Census of Population." On the World Wide Web at http://www12.statcan.ca/english/census01/home/index.cfm (11 September 2006).

Statistics Canada. (2001b). *Income in Canada*. Ottawa: Minister of Industry. Catalogue No. 75-202-XPE.

Statistics Canada. (2006a). "Labour Force and Participation Rates by Sex and Age group (2001–2005)." On the World Wide Web at http://www40.statcan.ca/l01/cst01/labor05.htm (11 September 2006).

Statistics Canada. (2006b). *Women in Canada: A Gender Based Statistical Report*, 5th ed. Ottawa: Minister of Industry. Catalogue No. 89-503-XPE.

Steinberg, Ronnie J. (1990). "Social Construction of Skill." *Work and Occupations, 17*, 449–82.

Tremblay, Manon, and Caroline Andrew, eds. (1998). *Women and Political Representation in Canada*. Women's Studies Series. Ottawa: University of Ottawa Press.

Trimble, Linda, and Jane Arscott. (2003). *Still Counting: Women in Politics Across Canada*. Peterborough, ON: Broadview Press.

Ursel, Jane. (1992). *Private Lives, Public Policy: 100 Years of State Intervention in the Family*. Toronto: Women's Press.

Vickers, Jill. (1997). "Toward a Feminist Understanding of Representation." In Jane Arscott and Linda Trimble, eds., *In the Presence of Women: Representation in Canadian Governments* (pp. 20–46). Toronto: Harcourt Brace.

Vosko, Leah, Nancy Zukewich, and Cynthia J. Cransford. (2003). "Precarious Jobs: A New Typology of Employment." *Perspectives on Labour and Income, 4* (10), 16–26.

Weiner, Nan, and Morley Gunderson. (1990). *Pay Equity: Issues, Options and Experiences*. Toronto: Butterworths.

Welsh, Sandy, Jacquie Carr, Barbara MacQuarrie, and Audrey Huntley. (2006). "'I'm Not Thinking of It as Sexual Harassment:' Understanding Harassment across Race and Citizenship." *Gender and Society, 20* (1), 87–107.

West, Candace, and Sarah Fenstermaker. (1993). "Power, Inequality and the Accomplishment of Gender: An Ethnomethodological View." In Paula England, ed., *Theory on Gender/Feminism on Theory* (pp. 151–74). New York: Aldine de Gruyter.

Westergaard, John. (1995). *Who Gets What? The Hardening of Class Inequality in the Late Twentieth Century*. Cambridge, UK: Polity Press.

Wharton, S. Amy. (2000). "Feminism at Work." *The Annals of the American Academy, 571*, 167–82.

Williams, Cara. (2004). "The Sandwich Generation." *Perspectives on Labour and Income, 5* (9), 5–12.

Yanz, Lynda, Deena Ladd, Joan Atlin, and Maquila Solidarity Network. (1999). *Policy Options to Improve Standards for Garment Workers in Canada and Internationally*. Ottawa: Status of Women Canada.

Young, Lisa. (1997). "Fulfilling the Mandate of Difference: Women in the Canadian House of Commons." In Jane Arscott and Linda Trimble, eds., *In the Presence of Women: Representation in Canadian Governments* (pp. 82–103). Toronto: Harcourt Brace.

Young, Lisa. (1998). "The Canadian Women's Movement and Political Parties, 1970–1993." In Manon Tremblay and Caroline Andrew, eds., *Women and Political Representation in Canada* (pp. 195–218). Ottawa: University of Ottawa Press.

Zinn, Maxine Baca, with Bonnie Thorton Dill. (1997). "Theorizing Difference from Multiracial Feminism." In Maxine Baca Zinn, Pierrette Hondagneu-Sotelo, and Michael A. Messner, eds., *Through the Prism of Difference: Readings on Sex and Gender* (pp. 23–29). Boston: Allyn and Bacon.

CHAPTER 8

Abella, Irving, and Harold Troper. (1982). *None Is Too Many: Canada and the Jews of Europe, 1933–1948*. Toronto: Lester and Orpen Dennys.

Alfred, Taiaiake. 1999. *Peace, Power and Righteousness: An Indigenous Manifesto*. Toronto: Oxford University Press.

Anderson, Benedict. (1983). *Imagined Communities: Reflections on the Origin and Spread of Nationalism*. London: Verso.

Angus Reid Group. (1991). *Multiculturalism and Canadians: National Attitude Study 1991*. Ottawa: Multiculturalism and Citizenship Canada.

Appleby, Timothy. (2006). "Harnick Testimony 'Shocked' Harris." *The Globe and Mail* 17 February: A7.

Avery, Donald. (1995). *Reluctant Host: Canada's Response to Immigrant Workers*. Toronto: McClelland and Stewart.

Balthazar, Louis. (1993). "The Faces of Quebec Nationalism." In Alain-G. Gagnon, ed., *Quebec: State and Society*, 2nd ed. (pp. 2–17). Scarborough, ON: Nelson.

Barkan, Elazar. (1992). *The Retreat of Scientific Racism*. Cambridge, UK: Cambridge University Press.

Barker, Martin. (1981). *The New Racism: Conservatives and the Ideology of the Tribe*. London: Junction Books.

Basran, Gurcharn, and Li Zong. (1998). "Devaluation of Foreign Credentials as Perceived by Non-white Professional Immigrants." *Canadian Ethnic Studies, 30*, 6–23.

Bissoondath, Neil. (1994). *Selling Illusions: The Cult of Multiculturalism*. Toronto: Stoddart.

Bolaria, B. Singh, and Peter Li. (1988). *Racial Oppression in Canada*. Toronto: Garamond.

Boldt, Menno. (1993). *Surviving as Indians: The Challenge of Self-Government*. Toronto: University of Toronto Press.

Bonacich, Edna. (1972). "A Theory of Ethnic Antagonism: The Split Labor Market." *American Sociological Review, 37*, 547–59.

Bonacich, Edna. (1979). "The Past, Present and Future of Split Labor Market Theory." *Research in Race and Ethnic Relations, 1*, 17–64.

Bonacich, Edna. (1980). "Class Approaches to Ethnicity and Race." *Insurgent Sociologist, 10*, 9–23.

Bourgeault, Ron. (1988). "The South African Connection." *Canadian Dimension, 21*, 6–10.

Brym, Robert, with Bonnie Fox. (1989). *From Culture to Power: The Sociology of English Canada*. Toronto: Oxford University Press.

Brym, Robert, and Rhonda Lenton. (1993). "The Distribution of Anti-Semitism in Canada in 1984." In Robert Brym, William Shaffir, and Morton Weinfeld, eds., *The Jews in Canada* (pp. 112–19). Toronto: Oxford University Press.

Castles, Stephen, and Godula Kosack. (1984). *Immigrant Workers and Class Structure in Western Europe*. London: Oxford University Press.

Citizenship and Immigration Canada. (1996). *You Asked About . . . Immigration and Citizenship*. Ottawa: Supply and Services Canada.

Citizenship and Immigration Canada. (2002). "Family Class Immigration." On the World Wide Web at http://www.cis.gc.ca/english/sponsor/index.html (10 September 2003).

Citizenship and Immigration Canada. (2004). "Business Immigration Program Statistics, 2002." On the World Wide Web at http://www.cic.gc.ca/english/business/bus-stats2002.html (13 March 2005).

Citizenship and Immigration Canada. (2005a). "Facts and Figures 2004. Immigrant Overview." On the World Wide Web at http://www.cic.gc.ca/english/pub/facts2004/overview/index.html 14 September 2006).

Citizenship and Immigration Canada. (2005b). "Skilled Workers: Will You Qualify as a Skilled Worker?" On the World Wide Web at http://www.cic.gc.ca/English/skilled/qual-5.html (14 September 2006).

Clement, Wallace. (1975). *The Canadian Corporate Elite*. Toronto: McClelland and Stewart.

Cole, Douglas, and Ira Chaikin. (1990). *An Iron Hand upon the People: The Law against the Potlatch on the Northwest Coast*. Vancouver: Douglas and McIntyre.

Collins, Jock. (1988). *Migrant Hands in a Distant Land: Australia's Post-war Immigration*. Sydney: Pluto Press.

Curry, Bill. (2005). "The Government Responds: Indian Affairs Minister Announces Plan to Relocate Settlement, Improve Sanitation." *The Globe and Mail* 28 October: A1.

Daenzer, Pat. (1993). *Regulating Class Privilege*. Toronto: Canadian Scholars Press.

Darroch, Gordon. (1979). "Another Look at Ethnicity, Stratification and Social Mobility in Canada." *Canadian Journal of Sociology, 4*, 1–25.

Department of Indian Affairs and Northern Development (DIAND). (2004). *Basic Departmental Data 2003*. Ottawa: Minister of Public Works and Government Services Canada.

Doob, Christopher. (1996). *Racism: An American Cauldron*. New York: HarperCollins.

Economic Council of Canada. (1991). *Economic and Social Impacts of Immigration*. Ottawa: Supply and Services Canada.

Economist, The. (2005). "A Dream That Does Not Fade (Quebec's Sovereignty)." 3 December: 8.

Edwards, Peter. (2001). *One Dead Indian: The Premier, the Police, and the Ipperwash Crisis*. Toronto: McClelland and Stewart.

Farmer, Nathan. (2005). "Kingston Police Shive Apologies for Forces Systemic Racism." On the World Wide Web at http://friendsofgrassynarrows.com/item.php.?427F (12 November 2005).

Fiske, Jo-Anne. (1996). "The Womb Is to the Nation as the Heart Is to the Body: Ethnopolitical Discourses of the Canadian Indigenous Women's Movement." *Studies in Political Economy, 51*, 65–96.

Fleras, Augie, and Jean Elliot. (1996). *Unequal Relations: An Introduction to Race, Ethnic and Aboriginal Dynamics in Canada*. Scarborough, ON: Prentice Hall.

Fournier, Marcel, Michael Rosenberg, and Deena White. (1997). *Quebec Society: Critical Issues*. Scarborough, ON: Prentice Hall.

Frideres, James, and René Gadacz. (2005). *Aboriginal People in Canada*, 7th ed. Toronto: Pearson Prentice-Hall.

Gerber, Linda. (1990). "Multiple Jeopardy: A Socioeconomic Comparison of Men and Women among the Indian, Métis and Inuit Peoples of Canada." *Canadian Ethnic Studies, 22*, 69–84.

Gibbins, Roger, and J. Rick Ponting. (1986). "Historical Background and Overview." In J. Rick Ponting, ed., *Arduous Journey* (pp. 18–56). Toronto: McClelland and Stewart.

Gray, Jeff. "Officers Make Racist Remarks on Tape. Members of Ontario Provincial Police Slag Natives before Protester Killed in 1995." *The Globe and Mail* 21 January: A7.

GRES. (1997). "Immigration and Ethnic Relations in Quebec: Pluralism in the Making." In Marcel Fournier, Michael Rosenberg, and Deena White, eds., *Quebec Society: Critical Issues* (pp. 95–112). Scarborough, ON: Prentice Hall.

Ha, Tu Thanh. (1995). "The PQ's Narrow Ethnic Vision." *The Globe and Mail* 11 November: D1.

Harries, Kate. (2005). "Harris Uttered Slur, Ipperwash Inquiry Told." *The Globe and Mail* 29 November: A1.

Hawkins, Freda. (1989). *Critical Years in Immigration: Canada and Australia Compared*. Montreal and Kingston, ON: McGill-Queen's University Press.

Henry, Frances. (1989). "Who Gets the Work in 1989?" Background Paper. Ottawa: Economic Council of Canada.

Henry, Frances, and Carol Tator. (2006). *The Colour of Democracy: Racism in Canadian Society*, 3rd ed. Toronto: Thomson Nelson.

Henry, Frances, and Effie Ginsberg. (1985). *Who Gets the Work: A Test of Racial Discrimination in Employment*. Toronto: Urban Alliance on Race Relations and the Social Planning Directorate.

Herberg, Edward. (1990). "The Ethno-racial Socioeconomic Hierarchy in Canada: Theory and Analysis in the New Vertical Mosaic." *International Journal of Comparative Sociology, 31*, 206–21.

Holton, Robert, and Michael Lanphier. (1994). "Public Opinion, Immigration and Refugees." In Howard Adelman, Allan Borowski, Meyer Burstein, and Lois Foster, eds., *Immigration and Refugee Policy: Australia and Canada Compared*, Vol. 1. Toronto: University of Toronto Press.

Howard, Rhoda. (1998). "Being Canadian: Citizenship in Canada." *Citizenship Studies, 2*, 133–52.

Howard-Hassmann, Rhoda. (1999). "Canadian as an Ethnic Category: Implications for Multiculturalism and National Unity." *Canadian Public Policy, 25* (4), 523–37.

Iacovetta, Franca. (1992). *Such Hardworking People: Italian Immigrants in Postwar Toronto*. Montreal and Kingston, ON: McGill-Queen's University Press.

Isajiw, Wsevolod. (1999). *Understanding Diversity: Ethnicity and Race in the Canadian Context*. Toronto: Thompson Educational Publishing.

Jenson, Jane. (1993). "Naming Nations: Making Nationalist Claims in Canadian Public Discourse." *Canadian Review of Sociology and Anthropology, 30*, 337–58.

Kazemipur, Abdolmohammad, and Shiva Halli. (2000). *The New Poverty in Canada*. Toronto: Thompson Educational Publishers.

Krosenbrink-Gelissen, Ernestine. (1994). "The Native Women's Association of Canada." In James Frideres, ed., *Native Peoples in Canada* (pp. 335–64). Scarborough, ON: Prentice Hall.

Laforest, Guy. (2005). "Can Canada Win Back the Children of Bill 101? YES: Canada Can Woo Back Quebeckers—by Admitting Past Insults and Decentralizing, Says a Former ADQ Leader, Guy Laforest." *The Globe and Mail* 20 December: A25.

Latouche, Daniel. (1993). "'Quebec: See Under Canada': Quebec Nationalism in the New Global Age." In Alain-G. Gagnon, ed., *Quebec: State and Society*, 2nd ed. (pp. 40–51). Scarborough, ON: Nelson.

Lautard, Hugh, and Neil Guppy. (2007). "Occupational Inequality among Canadian Ethnic Groups, 1931 to 2001." In Robert J. Brym, ed., *Society in Question*, 5th ed (pp. 124–33). Toronto: Nelson.

Lewis, Oscar. (1961). *The Children of Sanchez*. New York: Random House.

Li, Peter. (1988). *The Chinese in Canada*. Toronto: Oxford University Press.

Li, Peter. (2003). *Destination Canada: Immigration Debates and Issues*. Toronto: Oxford University Press.

Lieberson, Stanley. (1991). "A New Ethnic Group in the United States." In Norman Yetman, ed., *Majority and Minority* (pp. 444–56). New York: Allyn and Bacon.

Macmillan, David. (1985). "Scottish Enterprise and Influences in Canada, 1620–1900." In R.A. Cage, ed., *The Scots Abroad: Labour, Capital and Enterprise, 1750–1914* (pp. 46–79). London: Croom Helm.

Manpower and Immigration. (1967). *Immigration Statistics, 1966*. Ottawa: Queen's Printer.

Marger, Martin. (1997). *Race and Ethnic Relations: American and Global Perspectives*, 4th ed. New York: Wadsworth.

Marx, Karl. (1967 [1867]). *Capital*, Vol. 1. New York: International Publishers.

McMillan, Alan. (1988). *Native Peoples and Cultures of Canada*. Vancouver: Douglas and McIntyre.

Métis National Council. (1983). *A Brief to the Standing Committee on Legal and Constitutional Affairs*. Ottawa: Author.

Miles, Robert. (1982). *Racism and Migrant Labour*. London: Routledge.

Miles, Robert, and Malcolm Brown. (2003). *Racism*, 2nd ed. London: Routledge.

Milner, Henry, and Sheilagh Hodgins Milner. (1973). *The Decolonization of Quebec*. Toronto: McClelland and Stewart.

Mitchell, Marybelle. (1996). *From Talking Chiefs to a Native Corporate Elite*. Montreal and Kingston, ON: McGill-Queen's University Press.

Montagu, Ashley. (1972). *Statement on Race*. London: Oxford University Press.

Nagler, Mark. (1972). "Minority Values and Economic Achievement: The Case of the North American Indian." In Mark Nagler, ed., *Perspectives on the North American Indian* (pp. 131–42). Toronto: McClelland and Stewart.

Nikolinakos, Marios. (1973). "Notes towards an Economic Theory of Racism." *Race, 14*, 365–81.

Omi, Michael, and Howard Winant. (1986). *Racial Formation in the United States: From the 1960s to the 1980s*. New York: Routledge and Kegan Paul.

Parkin, Andrew, and Mattew Mendelsohn. (2003). *A New Canada: An Identity Shaped by Diversity*. Montreal: Centre for Research and Information on Canada.

Pentland, H. Clare. (1981). *Labour and Capital in Canada, 1650–1860*. Toronto: Lorimer.

Pettipas, Katherine. (1995). *Severing the Ties That Bind*. Winnipeg: University of Manitoba Press.

Pineo, Peter, and John Porter. (1985). "Ethnic Origin and Occupational Attainment." In Monica Boyd, John Goyder, Frank Jones, Hugh McRoberts, Peter Pineo, and John Porter, eds., *Ascription and Achievement: Studies in Mobility and Status Attainment in Canada* (pp. 357–93). Ottawa: Carleton University Press.

Porter, John. (1965). *The Vertical Mosaic*. Toronto: University of Toronto Press.

Ramirez, Bruno. (1991). *On the Move: French-Canadian and Italian Migrants in the North Atlantic Economy 1860–1914*. Toronto: McClelland and Stewart.

Reitz, Jeffrey, and Raymond Breton. (1994). *The Illusion of Difference: Realities of Ethnicity in Canada and the United States*. Toronto: C.D. Howe Institute.

Rex, John, and David Mason, eds. (1986). *Theories of Race and Ethnic Relations*. Cambridge: Cambridge University Press.

Roy, Patricia. (1989). *A White Man's Province*. Vancouver: University of British Columbia Press.

Royal Commission on Aboriginal Peoples. (1996). *Report*. Ottawa: Supply and Services Canada.

Satzewich, Vic. (1991). *Racism and the Incorporation of Foreign Labour*. London: Routledge.

Satzewich, Vic, and Linda Mahood. (1994). "Indian Affairs and Band Governance: Deposing Indian Chiefs in Western Canada, 1896–1911." *Canadian Ethnic Studies, 26*, 40–58.

Satzewich, Vic, and Lloyd Wong. (2003). "Immigration, Ethnicity and Race: The Transformation of Transnationalism, Localism and Identities." In Wallace Clement and Leah Vosko, eds., *Changing Canada: Political Economy as Transformation*. Montreal and Kingston: McGill-Queen's University Press.

Satzewich, Vic, and Terry Wotherspoon. (2001). *First Nations: Race, Class and Gender Relations*. Regina: Canadian Plains Research Centre.

Scott, George. (1990). "A Resynthesis of the Primordial and Circumstantial Approaches to Ethnic Group Solidarity: Towards an Explanatory Model." *Ethnic and Racial Studies, 13*, 147–71.

Special Committee on the Participation of Visible Minorities in Canadian Society. (1984). *Equality Now!* Ottawa: Supply and Services Canada.

Statistics Canada. (2001a). "2001 Census (Long form)." On the World Wide Web at http://www12.statcan.ca/english/census01/docs/eng2b.pdf (13 September 2006).

Statistics Canada. (2001b). "2001 Census." On the World Wide Web at http://www12.statcan.ca/english/census01/home/Index.cfm (13 September 2006).

Statistics Canada. (2003). *Ethnic Diversity Survey: Portrait of a Multicultural Society*. Ottawa: Minister of Industry. Catalogue No. 89-593-XIE.

Statistics Canada. (2004). "2001 Community Profiles." On the World Wide Web at http://www12.statcan/english/profil01/Details1pop2.cfm (13 September 2006).

Statistics Canada. (2005). "Ethnocultural Portrait of Canada, Table 1." On the World Wide Web at http://www12.statcan.ca/english/census01/products/highlight/ETO/Table1.cfm?Lang=EandT=501andGV=1andGID=0 (2 April 2006).

Steckley, John. (2003). *Aboriginal Voices and the Politics of Representation in Canadian Introductory Sociology Textbooks.* Toronto: Canadian Scholars Press.

Steinberg, Stephen. (1981). *The Ethnic Myth.* New York: Knopf.

Stoffman, Daniel. (2002). *Who Gets In: What's Wrong with Canada's Immigration Program—and How to Fix It.* Toronto: Macfarlane Walter and Ross.

Thomas, W.I., and Florian Znaniecki. (1918). *The Polish Peasant in Europe and America.* New York: Knopf.

Titley, Brian. (1986). *A Narrow Vision: Duncan Campbell Scott and the Administration of Indian Affairs in Canada.* Vancouver: University of British Columbia Press.

Turp, Daniel. (2005). "Can Canada Win Back the Children of Bill 101? No: Canada Isn't First in the Hearts of Young Quebeckers, Regardless of Their First Language, says PQ MNA Daniel Turp." *The Globe and Mail* 20 December: A25.

van den Berghe, Pierre. (1986). "Ethnicity and the Sociobiology Debate." In John Rex and David Mason, eds., *Theories of Race and Ethnic Relations* (pp. 246–63). Cambridge, UK: Cambridge University Press.

Walcott, William. (2003). "The Toronto Mayor and the Mombassa Natives." *Canadian Ethnic Studies, 35* (2), 100–15.

Whitaker, Reginald. (1987). *Double Standard: The Secret History of Canadian Immigration.* Toronto: Lester and Orpen Dennys.

Whitaker, Reginald. (1993). "From the Quebec Cauldron to the Canadian Cauldron." In Alain-G. Gagnon, ed., *Quebec: State and Society,* 2nd ed. (pp. 18–39). Scarborough, ON: Nelson.

White, Pamela. (1992). "Challenges in Measuring Canada's Ethnic Diversity." In Stella Hryniuk, ed., *20 Years of Multiculturalism: Success and Failure* (pp. 163–82). Winnipeg: St. John's College Press.

Wiley, Norbert. (1967). "Ethnic Mobility and Stratification Theory." *Social Problems, 15,* 147–59.

Williams, Eric. (1964). *Capitalism and Slavery.* London: Andre Deutsch.

Wilson, Edward. (1978). *On Human Nature.* New York: Vintage.

Woodsworth, J.S. (1972). *Strangers within Our Gates.* Toronto: University of Toronto Press.

Wortley, Scot. (2005). *Bias Free Policing: The Kingston Data Collection Project, Preliminary Results.* Toronto: Centre of Criminology, University of Toronto and the Centre of Excellence for Research on Immigration and Settlement (CERIS).

York, Geoffrey. (1989). *The Dispossessed.* Toronto: Lester and Orpen Dennys.

Zong, Li. (1994). "Structural and Psychological Dimensions of Racism: Towards an Alternative Perspective." *Canadian Ethnic Studies, 26,* 122–34.

CHAPTER 9

Adams, Patricia. (1991). *Odious Debts: Loose Lending, Corruption, and the Third World's Environmental Legacy.* Toronto: Earthscan.

Armer, J. Michael, and John Katsillis. (1992). *Encyclopedia of Sociology.* New York: Macmillan.

Arrighi, Giovanni. (1993). "World Income Inequalities and the Future of Socialism." *Socialism of the Future, 1* (2), 195–208.

Asper, Alicia. (2005). "Latin American Debt Relief, Less Than Meets the Eye." *Spectrezine* 18 September. On the World Wide Web at http://www.spectrezine.org/LatinAmerica/Asper.htm (26 March 2006).

Bairoch, Paul. (1982). "International Industrialization Levels from 1750 to 1980." *Journal of European Economic History, 11* (2), 270–71.

Baran, Paul A. (1957). *The Political Economy of Growth.* New York: Monthly Review Press.

Barnet, Richard, and Richard Muller. (1974). *Global Reach: The Power of the Multinational Corporations.* New York: Simon and Schuster.

Bello, Walden. (2002). *Deglobalization: Ideas for a New World Economy.* London: Zed Books.

Block, Fred L. (1977). *The Origins of International Economic Disorder.* Berkeley, CA: University of California Press.

Central Intelligence Agency. (2006). "World Fact Book: Sweden." On the World Wide Web at http://www.cia.gov/cia/publications/factbook/geos/sw.html (31 March 2006).

China Development Research Foundation. (2005). "Development with Equity. United Nations Development Programme." On the World Wide Web at http://www.undp.org.cn/downloads/nhdr2005/NHDR2005_complete.pdf (20 September 2006).

Cobb, Clifford, Ted Halstead, and Jonathan Rowe (1995). "If the GDP Is Up, Why Is America Down?" *Atlantic Monthly* October: 59–78.

Deane, Phyllis. (1979). *The First Industrial Revolution.* Cambridge, UK: Cambridge University Press.

Delage, Denys. (1993). *Bitter Feast: Amerindians and Europeans in Northeastern North America, 1600–64.* Vancouver: University of British Columbia Press.

Esping-Andersen, Gøsta. (1985). *Politics against Markets: The Social Democratic Road to Power.* Princeton, NJ: Princeton University Press.

Evans, Peter. (1985). "After Dependency: Recent Studies of Class, State, and Industrialization." *Latin American Research Review, 20,* 149–60.

Evans, Peter. (1987). "Foreign Capital and the Third World State." In Myron Weiner and Samuel Huntington, eds., *Understanding Political Development* (pp. 319–52). Boston: Little, Brown.

Fishman, Ted C. (2005). *China, Inc. How the Rise of the Next Superpower Challenges America and the World.* New York: Scribner.

Food and Agriculture Organization of the United Nations (FAO). (2006). "Counting the Hungry: Long-term Trends in the Developing World." *Undernourishment around the World.* On the World Wide Web at ftp://ftp.fao.org/docrep/fao/008/a0200e/a0200e01.pdf (20 September 2006).

Forbes. (2002). "World's Richest People." On the World Wide Web at http://www.forbes.com/2002/02/29/billionaires.html (March 26, 2006).

Forbes. (2006). "The World's Richest People 2006." On the World Wide Web at http://www.forbes.com/lists/2006/10/Rank_1.html (19 May 2006).

Gerschenkron, Alexander. (1962). *Economical Backwardness in Historical Perspective.* Cambridge, MA: Harvard University Press.

Goldthorpe, J.E. (1984). *The Sociology of the Third World*, 2nd ed. Cambridge, UK: Cambridge University Press.

Gordon, Gretchen. (2005). "Evo Morales Becomes Bolivia's Next President, Now His Real Challenge Begins." *Znet*. On the World Wide Web at http://www.zmag.org/content/showarticle.cfm?ItemID=9353 (19 December 2005).

Gupta, Surinder Nath. (1979). *British: The Magnificent Exploiters of India*. New Delhi: S. Chand and Co.

Harrison, Paul. (1993). *Inside the Third World: The Anatomy of Poverty*, 3rd ed. Harmondsworth, UK: Penguin.

Herman, Edward S., and Noam Chomsky. (1988). *Manufacturing Consent*. New York: Pantheon.

Hobsbawm, Eric. (1968). *Industry and Empire*. Harmondsworth, UK: Penguin.

Hobsbawm, Eric. (1990). *Nations and Nationalism since 1780: Programme, Myth, Reality*. Cambridge, UK: Cambridge University Press.

Hoogvelt, Ankie M.M. (1982). *The Third World in Global Development*. London: Macmillan.

Hoogvelt, Ankie M.M. (1997). *Globalization and the Postcolonial World. The New Political Economy of Development*. Baltimore: Johns Hopkins University Press.

Hoogvelt, Ankie M.M. (2001). *Globalization and the Postcolonial World. The New Political Economy of Development*, 2nd ed. Baltimore: Johns Hopkins University Press.

Jiang, Wenran. (2006). "The Dynamics of China's Social Crisis." *China Brief: A Journal of Analysis and Information*, 6 (2), 1–3.

Johnston, Josée, and Gordon Laxer. (2003). "Solidarity in the Age of Globalization: Lessons from the Anti-MAI and Zapatista Struggles." *Theory and Society*, 32, 39–91.

Killick, Tony 1999. "Making Adjustment Work for the Poor." On the World Wide Web at http://www.odi.org.uk/publications/briefing/pov5.html (23 March 2006).

Klein, Naomi. (2002). "Revolt of the Wronged," *Guardian Weekly* 4–10 April: 11.

Landes, David. (1969). *The Unbound Prometheus: Technological Change and Industrial Development in Western Europe from 1750 to the Present*. Cambridge, UK: Cambridge University Press.

Love, Joseph L. (1980). "Raúl Prebisch and the Origins of the Doctrine of Unequal Exchange." *Latin American Research Review*, 15 (3), 52–56.

MacLean, Brian, Paul Bowles, and Osvaldo Croci. (1998). "Understanding the Asian Crisis and Its Implications for Regional Economic Integration." In Gavin Boyd and Alan Rugman, eds., *Deepening Integration in the Pacific*. London: Edward Elgar.

Marx, Karl, and Friedrich Engels. (1986 [1848]). *The Communist Manifesto*. Moscow: Progress Publishers.

McCaughan, Michael. (2005). *The Battle of Venezuela*. New York: Seven Stories Press.

Nordlund, Sven. (1989). *Upptäckten Av Sverige [Foreign Investment in Sweden]*. Umea, Sweden: Umea University.

O'Brien, Philip. (1976). "Was the United States Responsible for the Chilean Coup?" In P. O'Brien, ed., *Allende's Chile* (pp. 217–43). New York: Praeger.

Palast, Greg. (2001). "The Globalizer Who Came in from the Cold," *Observer* 10 October.

Palast, Greg. (2003). *The Best Democracy Money Can Buy*. London: Pluto Press.

Palma, Gabriel. (1981). "Dependency and Development: A Critical Overview." In D. Seers, ed., *Dependency Theory: A Critical Reassessment* (pp. 20–78). London: Frances Pinter.

Pastor, Manuel, Jr., and Gary Dymski. (1991). "Debt Crisis and Class Conflict in Latin America." *Capital and Class*, 43, 203–31.

Sampson, Anthony. (1973). *The Sovereign State of ITT*. New York: Stein and Day.

Seers, Dudley, ed. (1981). *Dependency Theory: A Critical Reassessment*. London: Frances Pinter.

Smith, Adam. (1976 [1776]). *An Inquiry into the Nature and Causes of the Wealth of Nations*. Chicago: University of Chicago Press.

Stern, Paul C., Thomas Dietz, Vernon W. Ruttan, Robert H. Socolow, and James L. Sweeney, eds. (1997). *Environmentally Significant Consumption*. Washington, DC: National Academy Press.

Summers, Lawrence. (1996). "America's Role in Global Economic Integration." *Treasury News* 6 January.

United Nations Conference on Trade and Development (UNCTAD). (2004). *Report on the Least Developed Countries 2004*. Geneva: United Nations. On the World Wide Web at http://www.unctad.org/en/docs/ldc2004_en.pdf (28 March 2006).

UNCTAD. (2005). *World Investment Report 2005: Transnational Corporations and the Internationalization of RandD*. New York, Geneva: United Nations. http://www.unctad.org/en/docs/wir2005_en.pdf Retrieved : March 26, 2006.

United Nations Educational, Scientific and Cultural Organization (UNESCO). (2000). *Facts and Figures 2000*. Paris: UNESCO Institute for Statistics. On the World Wide Web at http://www.uis.unesco.org/en/pub/pub0.htm (26 March 2006).

United Nations. (2001). *Human Development Report 2001*. On the World Wide Web at http://www.undp.org/hdr01/ (26 March 2006).

United Nations. (2002). *Human Development Report 2002*. New York: United Nations Development Programme.

United Nations. (2005). *Human Development Report 2005*. New York: United Nations Development Programme. On the World Wide Web at http://hdr.undp.org/reports/global/2005/pdf/HDR05_complete.pdf (26 March 2006).

United States (the President of). (2002). "The National Security Strategy of the United States of America." Washington, DC: Office of the President of the United States.

United States (the President of). (2006). "The National Security Strategy." Washington, DC: Office of the President of the United States. On the Wor;d Wide Web at http://www.whitehouse.gov/nsc/nss/2006 (19 May 2006).

Walker, Stuart. (1993). "This Passing Show." *Alternatives*, 19 (2), 46–49.

Williamson, John. (1994). "In Search of a Manual for Technopols." In John Williamson, ed., *The Political Economy of Policy Reform*. Washington: Institute for Economic Research.

Wolf, Eric R. (1982). *Europe and the People without History*. Berkeley, CA: University of California Press.

Workers' Voice @ WTO. (2006). "Whose Miracle? How China's Workers Are Paying the Price for Its Economic Boom." On the World Wide Web at http://www.workersvoiceatwto.org/www/pdf/WhoseMiracleChinaReport.pdf (4 April 2006).

World Bank. (2000). *Selected World Development Indicators*. On the World Wide Web at http://www.worldbank.org (26 March 2006).

World Hunger Education Service Associates. (2006). "World Hunger Facts 2006." *World Hunger Notes*. On the World Wide Web at http://www.worldhunger.org/articles/Learn/world%20hunger%20facts%202002.htm (26 March 2006).

CHAPTER 10

Anderson, M. (1971). *Family Structure in Nineteenth-Century Lancashire*. Cambridge, UK: Cambridge University Press.

Arat-Koc, S. (1993). "The Politics of Family and Immigration in the Subordination of Domestic Workers in Canada." In B. Fox, ed., *Family Patterns, Gender Relations* (pp. 278–97). Toronto: Oxford University Press.

Baker, M. (1995). *Canadian Family Policies*. Toronto: University of Toronto Press.

Barnett, Rosalind, and Caryl Rivers. (1996). *She Works/He Works*. San Francisco: Harper.

Beach, J., J. Bertrand, and G. Cleveland. (1998). *Our Child Care Workforce: From Recognition to Remuneration*. Main Report for the Child Care Sector Study Steering Committee. Ottawa: HRDC.

Beaujot, R., E.M. Gee, F. Rajulton, and Z.R. Ravanera. (1995). *Family Over the Life Course: Current Demographic Analysis*, cat. no. 91-543. Ottawa: Industry Canada.

Bernard, J. (1972). *The Future of Marriage*. New Haven, CT: Yale University Press.

Bradbury, B. (1982). "The Fragmented Family: Family Strategies in the Face of Death, Illness and Poverty, Montreal, 1860–1885." In J. Parr, ed., *Childhood and Family* (pp. 109–29). Toronto: McClelland and Stewart.

Calliste, A. (2001). "Black Families in Canada: Exploring the Interconnections of Race, Class, and Gender." In B. Fox, ed., *Family Patterns, Gender Relations*, 2nd ed. Toronto: Oxford University Press.

Clarke-Stewart, A. (1982). *Daycare*. Cambridge, MA: Harvard University Press.

Coontz, Stephanie. (1992). *The Way We Never Were: American Families and the Nostalgia Trap*. New York: Basic Books.

Cott, N. (1977). *Bonds of Womanhood: "Women's Sphere" in New England, 1780–1835*. New Haven, CT: Yale University Press.

Davidoff, L., and C. Hall. (1987). *Family Fortunes: Men and Women in the English Middle Class, 1780–1850*. Chicago: University of Chicago Press.

Dunne, Gillian. (2000). "Opting into Motherhood: Lesbians Blurring the Boundaries and Transforming the Meaning of Parenthood and Kinship." *Gender and Society* 14 (1), 11–35.

Edholm, F. (1982). "The Unnatural Family." In E. Whitelegg, M. Arnot, E. Bartels, V. Beechey, L. Birke, S. Himmelweit, D. Leonard, S. Ruehl, and M. Speakman, eds., *The Changing Experience of Women*. London: The Open University.

Eyer, D. (1996). *Motherguilt: How Our Culture Blames Mothers for What's Wrong with Society*. New York: Random House.

Finnie, R. (1993). "Women, Men and the Economic Consequences of Divorce: Evidence from Canadian Longitudinal Data." *Canadian Review of Sociology and Anthropology, 30* (2), 205–41.

Flandrin, J. (1979). *Families in Former Times: Kinship, Household and Sexuality*. Cambridge, UK: Cambridge University Press.

Fox, B. (1997). "Reproducing Difference: Changes in the Lives of Partners Becoming Parents." In M. Luxton, ed., *Feminism and Families* (pp. 142–61). Halifax: Fernwood.

Fox, B., and D. Worts. (1999). "Revisiting the Critique of Medicalized Childbirth." *Gender and Society, 13* (3), 326–47.

Furstenberg, F., and A. Cherlin. (1991). *Divided Families: What Happens to Children When Parents Part*. Cambridge: Harvard University Press.

Gartner, R., M. Dawson, and M. Crawford. (1998–99). "Woman Killing: Intimate Femicide in Ontario, 1974–1994." *Resources for Feminist Research, 3* (4), 151–73.

Gaskell, J. (1983). "The Reproduction of Family Life: Perspectives of Male and Female Adolescents." In J. Veevers, ed., *Continuity and Change in Marriage and Family* (pp. 219–34). Toronto: Holt, Rinehart and Winston.

Gerson, K. (1985). *Hard Choices: How Women Decide about Work, Career and Motherhood*. Berkeley, CA: University of California Press.

Gottlieb, B. (1993). *The Family in the Western World*. New York: Oxford University Press.

Graham, H. (1987). "Being Poor: Perceptions and Coping Strategies of Lone Mothers." In J. Brannen and G. Wilson, eds., *Give and Take in Families: Studies in Resource Distribution* (pp. 56–74) London: Allen and Unwin.

Greven, P. (1973). "Family Structure in Seventeenth-Century Andover, Massachusetts." In M. Gordon, ed., *The American Family in Social-Historical Perspective* (pp. 77–100). New York: St. Martin's Press.

Hanawalt, B. (1986). *The Ties That Bound: Peasant Families in Medieval England*. New York: Oxford University Press.

Hareven, T. (1982). *Family Time and Industrial Time: The Relationship between Family and Work in a New England Industrial Community*. Cambridge, UK: Cambridge University Press.

Hertz, R. (1986). *More Equal than Others: Women and Men in Dual-Career Marriages*. Berkeley, CA: University of California Press.

Hochschild, A. (1989). *The Second Shift: Working Parents and the Revolution at Home*. New York: Viking.

Iacovetta, F. (1992). *Such Hardworking People: Italian Immigrants in Postwar Toronto*. Montreal and Kingston, ON: McGill-Queen's University Press.

Jenson, Jane. (2002). "Against the Current: Child Care and Family Policy in Quebec." In S. Michel and R. Mahon, eds., *Child Care Policy at the Crossroads: Gender and Welfare State Restructuring*. New York: Routledge.

Kibria, N. (1993). *Family Tightrope: The Changing Lives of Vietnamese Americans*. Princeton, NJ: Princeton University Press.

Kurz, D. (1995). *For Richer, For Poorer: Mothers Confront Divorce*. New York: Routledge.

Lasch, C. (1977). *Haven in a Heartless World: The Family Besieged*. New York: Basic Books.

Laslett, B., and J. Brenner. (1989). "Gender and Social Reproduction: Historical Perspectives." *Annual Review of Sociology, 15*, 381–404.

Leacock, E.B. (1981). *Myths of Male Dominance: Collected Articles on Women Cross-Culturally*. New York: Monthly Review Press.

Lee, R.B. (1979). *The !Kung San: Men, Women and Work in a Foraging Society*. Cambridge, UK: Cambridge University Press.

Lewontin, R.C., S. Rose, and L. Kamin. (1984). *Not in Our Genes: Biology, Ideology and Human Nature*. New York: Pantheon.

Luxton, M. (1980). *More Than a Labour of Love: Three Generations of Women's Work in the Home*. Toronto: Women's Press.

Marcil-Gratton, N. (1993). "Growing Up with a Single Parent: A Transitional Experience? Some Demographic Measurements." In J. Hudson and B. Galaway, eds., *Single-Parent Families: Perspectives on Research and Policy* (pp. 73–90). Toronto: Thompson Educational Publishing.

Marshall, C. (1994). "Household Chores." *Canadian Social Trends, 2*, 197–200.

May, E. (1988). *Homeward Bound: American Families in the Cold War Era.* New York: Basic Books.

May, M. (1985). "Bread before Roses: American Workingmen, Labor Unions and the Family Wage." In R. Milkman, ed., *Women, Work and Protest: A Century of U.S. Women's Labor History* (pp. 1–22). Boston: Routledge and Kegan Paul.

McKie, C. (1993). "An Overview of Lone Parenthood in Canada." In J. Hudson and B. Galaway, eds., *Single Parent Families: Perspectives on Research and Policy* (pp. 53–72). Toronto: Thompson Educational Publishing.

McLanahan, S. (1985). "Family Structure and the Reproduction of Poverty." *American Journal of Sociology, 90* (4), 873–901.

McLanahan, S., and L. Bumpass. (1988). "Intergenerational Consequences of Family Disruption." *American Journal of Sociology, 94* (1), 130–52.

McMahon, Martha. (1995). *Engendering Motherhood: Identity and Self-Transformation in Women's Lives.* New York: Guilford Press.

Mitterauer, M., and R. Sieder. (1982). *The European Family: Patriarchy to Partnership from the Middle Ages to the Present.* Oxford: Basil Blackwell.

Morton, M. (1988). "Dividing the Wealth, Sharing the Poverty: The (Re)formation of 'Family' in Law in Ontario." *Canadian Review of Sociology and Anthropology, 25* (2), 254–76.

National Council of Welfare. (1998). *Poverty Profile 1996.* Ottawa: Supply and Services Canada.

Nelson, Fiona. (1999). *Lesbian Motherhood: An Exploration of Canadian Families.* Toronto, Canada: University of Toronto Press.

Parsons, T., and R. Bales. (1955). *Family, Socialization and Interaction Process.* New York: Free Press.

Patterson, C. (1995). "Lesbian Mothers, Gay Fathers, and Their Children." In A.R. D'Augelli and C.J. Patterson, eds., *Lesbian, Gay and Bisexual Identities over the Lifespan: Psychological Perspectives.* New York: Oxford University Press.

Presser, H. (1994). "Employment Schedules, Gender and Household Labor." *American Sociological Review, 59* (3), 348–64.

Rapp, R., and E. Ross. (1986). "The 1920s: Feminism, Consumerism and Political Backlash in the U.S." In J. Friedlander, B. Cook, A. Kessler-Harris, and C. Smith-Rosenberg, eds., *Women in Culture and Politics* (pp. 52–62). Bloomington, IN: Indiana University Press.

Rosenberg, H. (1987). "Motherwork, Stress and Depression: The Costs of Privatized Social Reproduction." In H.J. Maroney and M. Luxton, eds., *Feminism and Political Economy: Women's Work, Women's Struggles* (pp. 181–97). Toronto: Methuen.

Rubin, L. (1990). *Erotic Wards: What Happened to the Sexual Revolution?* New York: Farrar, Straus and Giroux.

Ryan, M. (1981). *Cradle of the Middle Class: The Family in Oneida County, 1790–1865.* Cambridge, MA: Cambridge University Press.

Sayer, Liana C. (2005). "Gender, Time, and Inequality: Trends in Women's and Men's Paid Work, Unpaid Work, and Free Time." *Social Forces, 84* (1), 285–303.

Schwartz, P., and V. Rutter. (1998). *The Gender of Sexuality.* Thousand Oaks, CA: Pine Forge Press.

Singh, S., and J. Lindsay. (1996). "Money in Heterosexual Relationships." *Australia and New Zealand Journal of Sociology, 32* (4), 56–69.

Smith-Rosenberg, C. (1975). "The Female World of Love and Ritual: Relations between Women in Nineteenth-Century America." *Signs, 1* (1), 1–31.

Stacey, J., and T. Biblarz. (2001). " (How) Does the Sexual Orientation of Parents Matter?" *American Sociological Review, 66* (2) 159–83.

Stack, C. (1974). *All Our Kin: Strategies for Survival in a Black Community.* New York: Harper and Row.

Stansell, C. (1987). *City of Women: Sex and Class in New York, 1789–1860.* Urbana, IL: University of Illinois Press.

Statistics Canada. (1992). *Lone Parent Families in Canada.* Ottawa: Industry, Science and Technology Canada. Catalogue No. 89-522E.

Statistics Canada. (2002). "Profile of Canadian Families and Households: Diversification Continues," *The Daily* 22 October.

Statistics Canada. (2005). "Census Families in Private Households by Family Structure and Presence of Children, by Province and Territory (2001 Census)." On the World Wide Web at http://www40.statcan.ca/l01/cst01/famil54a.htm (22 September 2006).

Tarvis, C. (1992). *The Mismeasure of Woman.* New York: A Touchstone Book.

Tilly, L., and J.W. Scott. (1978). *Women, Work and Family.* New York: Holt, Rinehart and Winston.

Turnbull, C. (1961). *The Forest People.* New York: Doubleday.

Weston, K. (1991). *Families We Choose: Lesbians, Gays, Kinship.* New York: Columbia University Press.

CHAPTER 11

Adams, Tracey L. 2000. *A Gentleman and a Dentist: Gender and the Rise of Dentistry in Ontario.* Toronto: University of Toronto Press.

Althauser, Robert. (1989). "Internal Labor Markets." *Annual Review of Sociology, 15*, 143–61.

Andrew, Caroline, Céline Coderre, and Ann Denis. (1994). "Women in Management: The Canadian Experience." In Nancy J. Adler and Dafna N. Izraeli, eds., *Competitive Frontiers: Women Managers in a Global Economy* (pp. 377–87). Cambridge, MA: Oxford University Press.

Becker, Gary S. (1975). *Human Capital: A Theoretical and Empirical Analysis with Special Reference to Education,* 3rd ed. Chicago: University of Chicago Press.

Bell, Daniel. (1973). *The Coming of Post-industrial Society.* New York: Basic Books.

Bendix, Reinhard. (1974). *Work and Authority in Industry.* Berkeley, CA: University of California Press.

Blauner, Robert. (1964). *Alienation and Freedom.* Chicago: University of Chicago Press.

Boase, Sharon. (1998). "Discontented Youth Empower Labour." *Ottawa Citizen* 31 January: J2.

Braverman, Harry. (1974). *Labor and Monopoly Capital: The Degradation of Work in the Twentieth Century.* New York: Monthly Review Press.

Bridges, William. (1994). *Job Shift: How to Prosper in a Workplace without Jobs.* Don Mills, ON: Addison-Wesley.

Burawoy, Michael. (1979). *Manufacturing Consent: Changes in the Labour Process under Monopoly Capitalism.* Chicago: University of Chicago Press.

Calliste, Agnes. (1993). "Sleeping Car Porters in Canada: An Ethnically Submerged Split Labour Market." In Graham S. Lowe and Harvey Krahn, eds., *Work in Canada: Readings in the Sociology of Work and Industry* (pp. 139–53). Scarborough, ON: Nelson.

Campell, Andrew. (1996). "From Shop Floor to Computer Room." *The Globe and Mail* 30 December: A1, A8.

Canadian Labour Congress. (1993). "Two Years under Free Trade: An Assessment." In Graham S. Lowe and Harvey Krahn, eds., *Work in Canada: Readings in the Sociology of Work and Industry* (pp. 115–19). Scarborough, ON: Nelson.

Canadian Policy Research Networks. (2006a). "It's More Than the Money—What Canadians Want in a Job." On the World Wide Web at http://www.jobquality.ca/indicator_e/rew001.stm (9 March 2006).

Canadian Policy Research Networks. (2006b). "Satisfaction Most Common in Social Sciences, Arts/Culture and Management Occupations." On the World Wide Web at http://www.jobquality.ca/indicator_e/rew002_1.stm#2 (9 March 2006).

Canadian Press/Leger Marketing. (2001). *How Much Importance Canadian Place on their Work.* Montreal.

Carey, Alex. (1967). "The Hawthorne Studies: A Radical Criticism." *American Sociological Review, 32,* 403–16.

Catalyst. (2005). *Catalyst 2005 Census of Women Board Directors of the FP500.* Toronto: Catalyst.

Cranford, Cynthia, Leah Vosko, and Nancy Zukewich. (2003). "The Gender of Precarious Employment in Canada." *Relations Industrielles/Industrial Relations, 58* (3), 454–79.

Dassbach, Carl H.A. (1996). "Lean Production, Labor Control, and Post-Fordism in the Japanese Automobile Industry." In William C. Green and Ernest J. Yanarella, eds., *North American Auto Unions in Crisis: Lean Production as Contested Terrain* (pp. 19–40). Albany, NY: SUNY Press.

David, Paul A. (1990). "The Dynamo and the Computer: An Historical Perspective on the Modern Productivity Paradox." *American Economic Review, 80* (May), 355–61.

Eaton, Jonathan. (1998). "Wake up Little Suzy: Women Retail Workers Organize." *Our Times 17* (2), 23–29.

Economic Council of Canada. (1991). *Good Jobs, Bad Jobs: Employment in the Service Economy.* Ottawa: Supply and Services Canada.

Edwards, P.K., and Hugh Scullion. (1982). *The Social Organization of Industrial Conflict.* Oxford: Blackwell.

Edwards, Richard. (1979). *Contested Terrain: The Transformation of the Workplace in the Twentieth Century.* New York: Basic Books.

Friedson, Eliot. (1970). *The Profession of Medicine: A Study in the Sociology of Applied Knowledge.* New York: Harper and Row.

Hall, Marny. (1993). "Private Experiences in the Public Domain: Lesbians in Organizations." In Jeffrey Hearn, Deborah L. Sheppard, Peta Tancred-Sheriff, and Gibson Burrell, eds., *The Sexuality of Organization* (pp. 125–38). Berkeley, CA: Sage Publications.

Henson, Kevin D. (1996). *Just a Temp.* Philadelphia: Temple University Press.

Hodson, Randy. (1991). "The Active Worker: Compliance and Autonomy at the Workplace." *Contemporary Ethnography, 20* (April), 271–90.

Hodson, Randy, and Teresa Sullivan. (1985). "Totem or Tyrant? Monopoly, Regional and Local Sector Effects on Worker Commitment." *Social Forces, 63* (3), 716–31.

Hodson, Randy, and Teresa Sullivan. (1990). *The Social Organization of Work.* Belmont, CA: Wadsworth.

Immen, Wallace. (2006). "Why Executives Quit: Challenge, Not Money." *The Globe and Mail* 3 March. On the World Wide Web at http://globecareers.workopolis.com (9 March 2006).

Jones, Frank E. (1996). *Understanding Organizations: A Sociological Perspective.* Cooksville, ON: Copp Clark.

Kanter, Rosabeth Moss. (1977). *Men and Women of the Corporation.* New York: Basic Books.

Krahn, Harvey J. (1992). *Quality of Work in the Service Economy.* General Social Survey Analysis Series 6. Ottawa: Statistics Canada. Catalogue No. 11-612E.

Krahn, Harvey J., and Graham S. Lowe. (1998). *Work, Industry and Canadian Society,* 3rd ed. Scarborough, ON: ITP Nelson.

Laxer, Gordon. (1989). *Open for Business: The Roots of Foreign Ownership in Canada.* Don Mills, ON: Oxford University Press.

Lehr, Bill, and Frank Lichtenberg. (1999). "Information Technology and Its Impact on Productivity: Firm-Level Evidence from Government and Private Data Sources, 1977–1993." *Canadian Journal of Economics, 32* (2), 335–62.

Livingstone, D.W. (1993). "Conclusion: Aging Dinosaurs or All-Round Workers?" In June Corman, Meg Luxton, D.W. Livingstone, and Wally Secombe, eds., *Recasting Steel Labour: The Stelco Story* (pp. 145–55). Halifax: Fernwood.

Lowe, Graham S. (1987). *Women in the Administrative Revolution: The Feminization of Clerical Work.* Toronto: University of Toronto Press.

Martinsons, Maris G., and Patrick K.C. Chong. (1999). "The Influence of Human Factors and Specialist Involvement on Information Systems Success." *Human Relations 52* (1), 123–52.

McKay, Shona. (1993). "Willing and Able." In Graham S. Lowe and Harvey Krahn, eds., *Work in Canada: Readings in the Sociology of Work and Industry* (pp. 166–71). Scarborough, ON: Nelson.

McKenzie, Donald. (2001). "90% Satisfied with Their Jobs: Poll: 70% Happy with Salary." *Financial Post* 31 December: FP3.

McLaughlin, D.B. (1983). "Electronics and the Future of Work: The Impact on Pink and White Collar Workers." *Annals of the American Academy of Political and Social Science, 470,* 152–62.

Mighty, E. Joy. (1997). "Triple Jeopardy: Immigrant Women of Colour in the Labour Force." In P. Prasad, A.J. Mills, M. Elmes, and A. Prasad, eds., *Managing the Organizational Melting Pot: Dilemmas of Workplace Diversity* (pp. 312–39). Thousand Oaks, CA: Sage Publications.

Mills, Albert J., and Tony Simmons. (1999). *Reading Organization Theory: A Critical Approach to the Study of Organizational Behaviour and Structure.* Toronto: Garamond Press.

Morissette, René. (1991). "Are Jobs in Large Firms Better?" *Perspectives on Labour and Income* (Autumn), 40–50.

Morissette, René, and Anick Johnson. (2005). *Are Good Jobs Disappearing in Canada?* Statistics Canada: Ministry of Industry. Catalogue No. 11F0019MIE.

Myles, John. (1988). "The Expanding Middle: Some Canadian Evidence on the Deskilling Debate." *Canadian Review of Sociology and Anthropology, 25* (3), 335–64.

Myles, John. (1991). "Post-industrialism and the Service Economy." In Graham S. Lowe and Harvey Krahn, eds., *Work in Canada: Readings in the Sociology of Work and Industry* (pp. 124–34). Scarborough, ON: Nelson.

Noreau, N. (1994). "Involuntary Part-Timers." *Perspectives on Labour and Income, 6* (3), 25–30.

Osterman, Paul. (1995). "The Transformation of Work in the United States: What the Evidence Shows." In Bryan Downie and Mary Lou Coates, eds., *Managing Human Resources in the 1990s and Beyond* (pp. 71–92). Kingston, ON: Industrial Relations Centre Press.

"Paradox Lost." (1996). *The Economist* 28 September: S13.

Pescocolido, Bernice, Steven Tuch, and Jack Martin. (2001). "The Profession of Medicine and the Public: Examining Americans' Changing Confidence in Physician Authority from the Beginning of the 'Health Care Crisis' to the Era of Health Care Reform." *Journal of Health and Social Behavior, 42* (March), 1–16.

Polanyi, Karl. (1957). *The Great Transformation*. Boston: Beacon Press.

Pold, Henry. (2004). "Duration of Non-standard Employment" *Perspectives on Labour and Income, 5* (12).

Powell, Gary. (1990). "One More Time: Do Female and Male Managers Differ?" *Academy of Management Executive, 4* (August), 68–75.

Prasad, P., and Albert J. Mills. (1997). "Managing the Organizational Melting Pot: Dilemmas of Diversity at the Workplace." In P. Prasad, A.J. Mills, M. Elmes, and A. Prasad, eds., *Managing the Organizational Melting Pot: Dilemmas of Workplace Diversity* (pp. 3–27). Thousand Oaks, CA: Sage Publications.

"Productivity: Lost in Cyberspace." (1997). *The Economist* 13 September: 72.

Rifkin, Jeremy. (1995). *The End of Work: The Decline of the Global Labor Force and the Dawn of the Post Market Era*. New York: G.P. Putnam.

Rinehart, James. (1978). "Contradictions of Work-Related Attitudes and Behaviour: An Interpretation." *Canadian Review of Sociology and Anthropology, 15*, 1–15.

Rinehart, James. (1996). *The Tyranny of Work: Alienation and the Labour Process*, 3rd ed. Toronto: Harcourt Brace.

Rinehart, James, David Robertson, Chris Huxley, and Jeff Wareham. (1994). "Reunifying Conception and Execution of Work under Japanese Production Management? A Canadian Case Study." In Tony Elger and Chris Smith, eds., *Global Japanization? The Transnational Transformation of the Labour Process* (pp. 152–74). London: Routledge.

Ritzer, George. (1993). *The McDonaldization of Society*. Newbury Park, CA: Pine Forge.

Robertson, David, James Rinehart, Christopher Huxley, Jeff Wareham, Herman Rosenfeld, Alan McGough, and Steve Benedict. (1993). *The CAMI Report: Lean Production in a Unionized Auto Plant*. North York, ON: CAW Research.

Robertson, David, and Jeff Wareham. (1990). *Technological Change: Air Canada Customer Sales and Service*. North York, ON: CAW Research.

Rogers, Jackie Krasas. (1995). "Just a Temp: Experience and Structure of Alienation in Temporary Clerical Employment." *Work and Occupations, 22* (2), 137–66.

Rosener, Judy B. (1990). "Ways Women Lead." *Harvard Business Review* (November/December), 119–25.

Rosenthal, Patricia, Stephen Hill, and Riccardo Peccei. (1997). "Checking out Service: Evaluating Excellence, HRM and TQM in Retailing." *Work, Employment and Society, 11* (3), 481–503.

Schmitt, R., and T.E. Moody. (1994). *Alienation and Social Criticism*. Atlantic Highlands, NJ: Humanities Press.

Shain, Alan. (1995). "Employment of People with Disabilities." *Canadian Social Trends* (Autumn), 8–13.

Sheppard, Deborah L. (1993). "Women Managers' Perceptions of Gender and Organizational Life." In Jeffrey Hearn, Deborah L. Sheppard, Peta Tancred-Sheriff, and Gibson Burrell, eds., *The Sexuality of Organization* (pp. 151–66). Berkeley, CA: Sage Publications.

Smith, Vicki. (2001). *Crossing the Great Divide: Worker Risk and Opportunity in the New Economy*. Ithaca and Cornell: IRL Press.

Solow, Robert. (1987). "We'd Better Watch Out." *New York Times Book Review*, 12 July.

Spenner, Kenneth. (1983). "Deciphering Prometheus: Temporal Change in the Skill Level of Work." *American Sociological Review, 48* (6), 824–37.

Statistics Canada. (1988). "Social Indicators." *Canadian Social Trends* (Winter), 31. Catalogue No. 11-008.

Statistics Canada. (2004a). "Changes in Employment, by Industry." *The Canadian Labour Market at a Glance, 2003*. Ottawa: Minstry of Industry. Catalogue No. 71-222-XIE.

Statistics Canada. (2004b). *Canada E-book*. On the World Wide Web at http://142.206.72.67/r000_e.htm (22 September 2006).

Statistics Canada. (2004c). "Table 282-0088: Labour Force Survey Estimates, Employment by North American Industry Classification System, May 2004." On the World Wide Web at http://cansim2.statcan.ca/cgi-win/CNSMCGI.EXE (6 March 2006).

Statistics Canada. (2005a). "Social Indicators." *Canadian Social Trends* (Summer) 31. Catalogue No. 11-008.

Statistics Canada. (2005b). "Diverging Trends in Unionization." *The Daily* 22 April. On the World Wide Web at http://www.statcan.ca/Daily/English/050422/d050422c.htm (September 22, 2006).

Statistics Canada. (2006). "Latest Release from the Labour Force Survey." *The Daily* 4 August. On the World Wide Web at http://www.statcan.ca/english/Subjects/Labour/LFS/lfs-en.htm (22 September 2006).

Toffler, Alvin. (1980). *The Third Wave*. New York: Bantam.

Triplett, Jack E. (1999). "The Solow Productivity Paradox: What Do Computers Do to Productivity?" *Canadian Journal of Economics, 32* (2) 309–34.

Tyre, Marcie J., and Wanda J. Orlikowski. (1994). "Windows of Opportunity: Temporal Patterns of Technological Adaptation in Organizations." *Organization Science, 5*, 98–118.

Wallace, Michael. (1989). "Brave New Workplace: Technology and Work in the New Economy." *Work and Occupations, 16* (4), 393–415.

White, Julie. (1993). "Patterns of Unionization." In Linda Briskin and Patricia McDermott, eds., *Women Challenging Unions: Feminism, Democracy and Militancy* (pp. 191–206). Toronto: University of Toronto Press.

Womack, J., D. Jones, and D. Roos. (1990). *The Machine That Changed the World.* New York: Rawson and Associates.

Zuboff, Shoshana. (1988). *In the Age of the Smart Machine: The Future of Work and Power.* New York: Basic Books.

CHAPTER 12

Adler, Patricia A., and Peter Adler. (1994). "Reproduction of the Corporate Other: The Institutionalization of After-School Activities." *Sociological Quarterly, 35* (2), pp. 309–28.

American Association of University Women Educational Foundation. (1998). *Gender Gaps: Where Schools Still Fail Our Children.* American Institutes of Research. Washington, DC: AAUW Educational Foundation.

Anisef, P. (1974). *The Critical Juncture.* Toronto: Ministry of Colleges and Universities.

Arai, A. Bruce. (2000). "Changing Motivations for Homeschooling in Canada." *Canadian Journal of Education, 25* (3), 204–17.

Aurini, Janice. (2004). "Educational Entrepreneurialism in the Private Tutoring Industry: Balancing Profitability with the Humanistic Face of Schooling." *Canadian Review of Sociology and Anthropology, 41* (4), 475–91.

Aurini, Janice. (2002). "Fostering the Unique Child: New Trends in Childrearing, A Case Study." Unpublished paper, McMaster University.

Aurini, Janice, and Scott Davies. (2004). "The Transformation of Private Tutoring: Education in a Franchise Form." *Canadian Journal of Sociology, 29* (3), 419–38.

Aurini, Janice, and Scott Davies. (2005). "Choice without Markets: Homeschooling in Context of Private Education." *British Journal of Sociology of Education, 26* (4).

Axelrod, Paul. (1997). *The Promise of Schooling: Education in Canada, 1800–1914.* Toronto: University of Toronto Press.

Becker, Gary. (1964). *Human Capital,* 2nd ed. New York: Columbia University Press.

Bennett DeMarrais, Kathleen, and Margaret D. LeCompte. (1995). *The Way Schools Work: A Sociological Analysis of Education,* 2nd ed. White Plains, NY: Longman.

Blossfeld, H.P., and Y. Shavit. (1993). "Persisting Barriers: Changes in Educational Opportunities in Thirteen Countries." In Y. Shavit and H.P. Blossfeld, eds., *Persistent Inequality: Changing Educational Attainment in Thirteen Countries.* Boulder, CO: Westview.

Borja, Rhea R. (2005). *Education Week, 25* (8), 19 October: 10.

Bosetti, Lynn. (2001). "The Alberta Charter School Experience." In Claudia R. Hepburn, ed. *Can the Market Save Our Schools?* (pp. 101–20). Vancouver: The Fraser Institute.

Bowles, Samuel, and Herbert Gintis. (1976). *Schooling in Capitalist America: Educational Reform and the Contradictions of Economic Life.* New York: Basic Books.

Brint, Steven, M.F. Contreras, and M.T. Matthews. (2001). Socialization Messages in Primary Schools: An Organizational Analysis. *Sociology of Education, 74,* 157–80.

Burkam, David, Douglas Ready, Valerie Lee, and Laura LoGerfo. (2004). "Social Class Differences in Summer Learning between Kindergarten and First Grade: Model Specification and Estimation" *Sociology of Education, 77,* 1–31.

Chubb, John E., and Terry M. Moe. (1990). *Politics, Markets and America's Schools.* Washington, DC: The Brookings Institution.

Cohen, Albert. 1955. *Delinquent Boys: The Culture of the Gang.* Glencoe, IL: Free Press.

Coleman, James. (1961). *The Adolescent Society.* New York: Free Press.

Collins, R. (1979). *The Credential Society.* New York: Academic Press.

Curtis, Bruce, David W. Livingstone, and Harry Smaller. (1992). *Stacking the Deck: The Streaming of Working-Class Kids in Ontario Schools.* Toronto: Our Schools/Our Selves.

Daly, Kerry. (2004). *The Changing Culture of Parenting.* Ottawa: Vanier Institute for the Family.

Davies, Lynn. (1984). *Pupil Power: Deviance and Gender in School.* London: Falmer Press.

Davies, S., and Neil Guppy. (1997). "Fields of Study, College Selectivity, and Student Inequalities." *Social Forces, 73* (4), 131–51.

Davies, Scott. (1992). *In Search of the Culture Clash: Explaining Class Inequalities in Education.* Doctoral Dissertation, Department of Sociology, University of Toronto.

Davies, Scott. (2004). "Stubborn Disparities: Explaining Class Inequalities in Schooling." In James Curtis, Edward Grabb, and Neil Guppy, eds., *Social Inequality in Canada: Patterns, Problems, and Policies,* 4th ed. (pp. 138–150), Toronto: Prentice Hall.

Davies, Scott. (2005). "A Revolution of Expectations? Three Key Trends in the SAEP Data." In Robert Sweet and Paul Anisef, eds., *Preparing for Postsecondary Education: New Roles for Governments and Families* (pp. 149–65). Montreal and Kingston: McGill–Queen's University Press.

Davies, Scott, and Floyd Hammack. (2005). "Channelling Competition in Higher Education: Comparing Canada and the US." *Journal of Higher Education, 76* (1), 89–106.

Davies, Scott, and Linda Quirke. (2005). "Providing for the Priceless Student: Ideologies of Choice in an Emerging Educational Market" *American Journal of Education 111* (4), 596–608.

Davies, Scott, and Neil Guppy. (2006). *The Schooled Society: An Introduction to the Sociology of Education.* Toronto: Oxford University Press.

De Broucker, Patrice, and Laval Lavallée. (1998). "Getting Ahead in Life: Does Your Parents' Education Count?" *Education Quarterly Review, 5* (1), 22–28.

Dei, George. (2005). "The Case for Black Schools." *Toronto Star* 4 February.

Dennison, John D., ed. (1995). *Canada's Community Colleges at the Crossroads.* Vancouver: UBC Press.

Downey, Douglas, and Ainsworth-Darnell, James. (2002). "The Search for Oppositional Culture among Black Students." *American Sociological Review, 67,* 156–64.

Downey, Douglas B., Paul T. von Hippel, and Beckett A. Broh. (2004). "Are Schools the Great Equalizer? Cognitive Inequality During the Summer Months and the School Year." *American Sociological Review, 69* (5), 613–35.

Dreeben, Robert. (1967). *On What Is Learned in School.* Reading, MA: Addison-Wesley.

Durkheim, Émile. (1961 [1925]). *Moral Education: A Study in the Theory and Application of the Sociology of Education.* New York: Free Press.

Entwistle, Doris, and Karl Alexander. (1992). "Summer Setback: Race, Poverty, School Composition and Math Achievement in the First Two Years of School." *American Sociological Review,* 57, 72–84.

Fordham, Signithia, and John Ogbu. (1986). "Black Students' School Success: Coping with the 'Burden' of 'Acting White.'" *The Urban Review,* 18, 176–206.

Frenette, Marc. (2005). "The Impact of Tuition Fees on University Access: Evidence from a Large-Scale Price Deregulation in Professional Programs." Ottawa: Statistics Canada. Catalogue No. 11F00119MIE.

Gamoran, Adam. (2001). "American Schooling and Educational Inequality: A Forecast for the 21st Century." *Sociology of Education* (extra issue), 135–53.

Gardner, Howard. (1998). "A Multiplicity of Intelligences." [Special Issue]. *Scientific American 9* (4), 18–23.

Gardner, Howard. (1999). *Intelligence Reframed: Multiple Intelligences for the 21st Century.* New York: Basic Books.

Gardner, H., and T. Hatch. (1989). "Multiple Intelligences Go to School: Educational Implications of the Theory of Multiple Intelligences." *Educational Researcher, 18* (8), 4–10.

Government of Ontario. (1950). *Aims of Education: Report of the Royal Commission on Education in Ontario (The Hope Report).* Toronto: The King's Printer.

Guppy, Neil, and Bruce Arai. (1994). "Teaching Sociology: Comparing Undergraduate Curricula in the Unted States and Canada." *Teaching Sociology 22,* 217–30.

Guppy, Neil, Robert Crocker, Scott Davies, Claire LaPointe, and Larry Sackney. (2005). *Parent and Teacher Views on Education: A Policymaker's Guide.* Kelowna, BC: Society for the Advancement of Excellence in Education.

Holland, D.C., and M. Eisenhart. (1990). *Educated in Romance: Women, Achievement, and College Culture.* Chicago: University of Chicago Press.

Hurn, C.J. (1993). *The Limits and Possibilities of Schooling: An Introduction to the Sociology of Education.* Boston: Allyn and Bacon.

Jackson, Philip W., Robert E. Boostrom, and David T. Hansen. (1998). *The Moral Life of Schools.* San Francisco: John Wiley and Sons.

Kelly, Gail, and Ann Nihlen, Ann. (1982). "Schooling and the Reproduction of Patriarchy: Unequal Workloads, Unequal Rewards." In Michael Apple, ed., *Cultural and Economic Reproduction in American Education: Essays in Class, Ideology, and the State* (pp. 162–80). London, UK: Routledge.

Kerckhoff, Alan C. (2002). "The Transition from School to Work." In Jeylan Mortimer and Reed W. Larson (eds.), *The Changing Adolescent Experience* (pp. 52–87). New York: Cambridge University Press.

Kingston, P.W., R. Hubbard, B. Lapp, P. Schroeder, and J. Wilson. (2003). "Why Education Matters." *Sociology of Education 76* (1), 53–70.

Knighton, T. (2002). "Postsecondary Participation: The Effects of Parents' Education and Household Income." *Education Quarterly Review, 8* (3), 25–31.

Krahn, Harvey. (2004). "Social Class, Postsecondary Education, and Occupational Outcomes: Choose Your Parents Well." In James E.Curtis, E.E. Grabb, and N. Guppy., eds., *Social Inequality in Canada: Patterns, Problems, Policies,* 4th ed. (pp. 187–203). Scarborough, ON: Pearson Prentice-Hall.

Lewis, Amanada, ed. (2003). *Race in the Schoolyard: Negotiating the Color Line in Classrooms and Communities.* New Brunswick, NJ: Rutgers University Press.

Livingstone, David W. (1998). *The Education-Jobs Gap: Underemployment or Economic Democracy.* Boulder, CO: Westview Press

Livingstone, D.W., D. Hart, and L.E. Davie. (2003). *Public Attitudes toward Education in Ontario: The 14th OISE/UT Survey.* Toronto: OISE.

Looker, Diane, and Victor Thiessen. (1999). "Images of Work: Women's Work, Men's Work, Housework." *Canadian Journal of Sociology, 24* (2), 225–51.

Maclean's. (2005). "Guide to Canadian Universities 05: Your Complete Handbook for Choosing a University."

Milner, Murray Jr. (2004). *Freaks, Geeks, and Cool Kids: American Teenagers, Schools, and the Culture of Consumption.* London, UK: Routledge.

Ontario Department of Education. (1968). *Living and Learning: The Report of the Provincial Committee on the Aims and Objectives of Education in the Schools of Ontario.* Toronto: Author.

Ontario Human Rights Commission. (2003). *The Ontario Safe Schools Act: School Discipline and Discrimination.* Ottawa: Author. On the World Wide Web at http://www.ohrc.on.ca/english/consultations/safe-schools.pdf (20 September 2005).

Ouchi, William. (2003). *Making Schools Work: A Revolutionary Plan to Get Your Children the Education They Need.* New York: Simon and Schuster.

Pallas, A. (2000). "The Effects of Schooling on Individual Lives. In M.T. Hallinan, ed., *Handbook of the Sociology of Education* (pp. 499–525). New York: Kluwer Academic/Plenum Publishers

Porter, J., M. Porter, and B. Blishen. (1982). *Stations and Callings: Making It through the School System.* Toronto: Methuen.

Powell, A.G., E. Farrar, and D.K. Cohen. (1985). *The Shopping Mall High School: Winners and Losers in the Educational Marketplace.* Boston: Houghton Mifflin.

Prentice, A. (1977). *The School Promoters.* Toronto: McClelland and Stewart.

Programme for Internation Student Assessment Canada. (2003). *Measuring Up: The Performance of Canada's Youth in Reading, Mathematics and Science.* Ottawa: Government of Canada. On the World Wide Web at http://www.pisa.gc.ca/pisa/brochure_e.shtml (23 September 2006).

Quirke, Linda. (2003). "When Parenting Becomes a Verb." Paper presented at the annual meetings of the Canadian Sociology and Anthropology Association, Halifax.

Ryan, B.A., and Adams, G.R. (1999). "How do Families Affect Children's Success in School?" *Education Quarterly Review, 6* (1), 30–43.

Sayer, L.C., S.M. Bianchi, and J.P. Robinson. (2004). "Are Parents Investing Less in Children? Trends in Mothers' and Fathers' Time with Children." *American Journal of Sociology, 107,* 1–43.

Solomon, R. Patrick. (1992). *Black Resistance in High School: Forging a Separatist Culture.* Albany, NY: SUNY Press.

Statistics Canada. (2001). *Education in Canada, 2000.* Ottawa: Ministry of Industry.

Statistics Canada. (2005a). "University Enrolment." *The Daily* 11 October. On the World Wide Web at http://www.statcan.ca/Daily/English/051011/d051011b.htm (23 September 2006).

Statistics Canada. (2005b). "University Enrolments, by Registration Status, Program Level, Classification of Instructional Programs, Primary Grouping, and Sex, Annual. CANSIM Table 477-0013." On the World Wide Web at http://cansim2.statcan.ca/cgi-win/CNSMCGI.EXE (23 September 2006).

Stinchcombe, Arthur. (1964). *Rebellion in a High School.* Chicago: Quadrangle Books.

Tanner, Julian. (2001). *Teenage Troubles: Youth and Deviance in Canada,* 2nd ed. Toronto: Nelson Thomson Learning.

Taylor, A., and L. Woollard. (2003). "The Risky Business of Choosing a High School." *Journal of Education Policy* 18 (6), 617–35.

Turner, Ralph H. (1960). "Sponsored and Contest Mobility and School System." *American Sociological Review, 25,* 855–67.

Tyack, David B. (1974). *The One Best System: A History of American Urban Education.* Cambridge, MA: Harvard University Press.

Tyack, David, and Larry Cuban. (1995). *Tinkering toward Utopia: A Century of Public School Reform.* Cambridge, MA: Harvard University Press.

Tyson, Karolyn, William Darity Jr., and Domini Castellino. (2005). "It's Not a Black Thing: Understanding the Burden of Acting White and Other Dilemmas of High Achievement." *American Sociological Review, 70* (4), 582–605.

Walters, David. (2004). "'Recycling': The Economic Implications of Obtaining Additional Postsecondary Credentials at Lower or Equivalent Levels." *Canadian Review of Sociology and Anthropology, 40* (4), 463–77.

Wanner, Richard. (2000). "Expansion and Ascription: Trends in Educational Opportunity in Canada 1920–1994." *Canadian Review of Sociology and Anthropology, 36* (3), 409–43.

Weis, L. (1990). *Working Class without Work: High School Students in a De-industrializing Economy.* New York: Routledge.

Weiten, Wayne, and Doug McCann. (2007). *Psychology: Themes and Variations.* Toronto: Thomson Nelson.

Willis, Paul. (1977). *Learning to Labour: How Working Class Kids Get Working Class Jobs.* Saxon House: Westmead.

Wolf, Alison. (2002). *Does Education Matter? Myths about Education and Economic Growth.* London. Penguin.

CHAPTER 13

Bell, Daniel. (1977). "The Return of the Sacred: The Argument on the Future of Religion." *British Journal of Sociology, 28,* 419–49.

Bellah, Robert. (1967). "Civil Religion in America." *Daedalus, 96,* 1–21.

Berger, Peter L. (1974). "Some Second Thoughts on Substantive Versus Functional Definitions of Religion. *Journal for the Scientific Study of Religion, 13,* 125–33.

Berger, Peter. (1961). *The Noise of Solemn Assemblies.* New York: Doubleday.

Beyer, Peter. (1993). "Roman Catholicism in Contemporary Quebec." In W.E. Hewitt, ed., *The Sociology of Religion: A Canadian Focus* (pp. 133–55). Toronto: Butterworths.

Beyer, Peter. (1997). "Religious Vitality in Canada: The Complementarity of Religious Market and Secularization Perspectives." *Journal for the Scientific Study of Religion, 36,* 272–88.

Bibby, Reginald W. (1987). *Fragmented Gods: The Poverty and Potential of Religion in Canada.* Toronto: Stoddart.

Bibby, Reginald W. (1993). *Unknown Gods: The Ongoing Story of Religion in Canada.* Toronto: Stoddart.

Bibby, Reginald W. (1994). *Unitrends.* Toronto: United Church of Canada, Department of Stewardship Services.

Bibby, Reginald W. (1995). *The Bibby Report: Social Trends Canadian Style.* Toronto: Stoddart.

Bibby, Reginald W. (1999). *The Alliance Future Survey.* Toronto: Christian and Missionary Alliance.

Bibby, Reginald W. (2001). *Canada's Teens: Today, Yesterday, and Tomorrow.* Toronto: Stoddart.

Bibby, Reginald W. (2004a). *Restless Gods: The Renaissance of Religion in Canada.* Ottawa: Novalis.

Bibby, Reginald W. (2004b). *Restless Churches. How Canada's Churches Can Contribute to the Emerging Religious Renaissance.* Ottawa: Novalis.

Bibby, Reginald W. (2005). "The Untold Story of the Role of Women in the Fall and Rise of Religion in Canada." Presented at the annual meeting of the Pacific Sociological Association, Portland, Oregon, April.

Brannon, Robert. (1971). "Organizational Vulnerability in Modern Religious Organizations." *Journal for the Scientific Study of Religion, 10,* 27–32.

Brown, Callum. (2001). *The Death of Christian Britain.* London: Routledge.

Brym, Robert, and Bader Araj. (2006). "Suicide Bombing as Strategy and Interaction: The Case of the Second *Intifada,*" *Social Forces, 84,* 1965–82.

Catto, S. (2003). "Edmonton's Legend: Emery Dosdall." *Time Canada* 13 October: 82.

Catto, Susan. (2003). "In Search of the Spiritual." *Time* 24 November: 72–80.

Clark, S.D. (1948). *Church and Sect in Canada.* Toronto: University of Toronto Press.

Cogley, John. (1968). *Religion in a Secular Age.* New York: New American Library.

Crysdale, Stewart. (1961). *The Industrial Struggle and Protestant Ethics in Canada.* Toronto: Ryerson Press.

Davies, Alan, and Marilyn F. Nefsky. (1997). *How Silent Were the Churches? Canadian Protestantism and the Jewish Plight during the Nazi Era.* Waterloo, ON: Wilfrid Laurier University Press.

Dawson, Lorne L. (2006). *Comprehending Cults: The Sociology of New Religious Movements.* Toronto: Oxford University Press.

Durkheim, Émile. (1965 [1912]). *The Elementary Forms of the Religious Life.* New York: Free Press.

Fallding, Harold. (1978). "Mainline Protestantism in Canada and the United States: An Overview." *Canadian Journal of Sociology, 2,* 141–60.

Finke, Roger, and Rodney Stark. (1992). *The Churching of America, 1776–1990.* New Brunswick, NJ: Rutgers University Press.

Frankel, B., Gail, and W.E. Hewitt. (1994). "Religion and Well-Being among Canadian University Students." *Journal for the Scientific Study of Religion, 33,* 62–73.

Freud, Sigmund. (1962 [1928]). *The Future of an Illusion.* New York: Doubleday.

Gallup. (2006). *Religion.* Poll released January 25.

Gee, Ellen M., and Jean E. Veevers. (1990). "Religious Involvement and Life Satisfaction in Canada." *Sociological Analysis, 51,* 387–94.

Gerth, H., and C. Wright Mills. (1958). *From Max Weber: Essays in Sociology.* New York: Oxford University Press.

Ghafour, Hamida. (2006). "Muslim Fury over Cartoons Hits Britain." *The Globe and Mail* 4 February.

Glock, Charles Y., and Rodney Stark. (1965). *Religion and Society in Tension.* Chicago: Rand-McNally.

Glock, Charles, Benjamin Ringer, and Earl Babbie. (1967). *To Comfort and to Challenge.* Berkeley, CA: University of California Press.

Gorsuch, Richard, and Daniel Aleshire. (1974). "Christian Faith and Ethnic Prejudice: A Review and Interpretation of Research." *Journal for the Scientific Study of Religion, 13,* 281–307.

Graham, Ron. (1990). *God's Dominion: A Sceptic's Quest.* Toronto: McClelland and Stewart.

Herberg, Will. (1960). *Protestant, Catholic, Jew,* rev. ed. New York: Doubleday.

Hobart, Charles. (1974). "Church Involvement and the Comfort Thesis." *Journal for the Scientific Study of Religion, 13,* 463–70.

Johnson, Benton. (1961). "Do Holiness Sects Socialize in Dominant Values?" *Social Forces, 39,* 309–16.

Kiefer, Heather Mason. (2004). "Divine Subjects: Canadians Believe, Britons Skeptical." Washington: The Gallup Poll.

Kirkpatrick, Clifford. (1949). "Religion and Humanitarianism: A Study of Institutional Implications." *Psychological Monographs, 63* (9).

Lee, Gary, and Robert Clyde. (1974). "Religion, Socioeconomic Status, and Anomie." *Journal for the Scientific Study of Religion, 13,* 35–47.

Lewis, David L. (1993). "Canada's Native Peoples and the Churches." In W.E. Hewitt, ed., *The Sociology of Religion: A Canadian Focus* (pp. 235–51). Toronto: Butterworths.

Mann, W.E. (1962). *Sect, Cult, and Church in Alberta.* Toronto: University of Toronto Press.

Marx, Karl. (1970 [1843]). *Critique of Hegel's "Philosophy of Right."* Trans. Annette Jolin and Joseph O'Malley. Cambridge, MA: Harvard University Press.

Marx, Karl, and Friedrich Engels. (1964). *On Religion.* New York: Schocken Books.

Metz, Donald. (1967). *New Congregations: Security and Mission in Conflict.* Philadelphia: Westminster Press.

Monahan, Susanne C. (1999). "Who Controls Church Work? Organizational Effects on Jurisdictional Boundaries and Disputes in Churches." *Journal for the Scientific Study of Religion, 38,* 370–85.

Nason-Clark, N. (1993). "Gender Relations in Contemporary Christian Organizations," in W.E. Hewitt, ed., *The Sociology of Religion* (pp. 215–34). Toronto: Butterworth.

Nesbitt, P.D. (1997). *The Feminization of the Clergy in America.* New York: Oxford University Press.

Niebuhr, H. Richard. (1957 [1929]). *The Social Sources of Denominationalism.* New York: Henry Holt and Co.

O'Toole, Roger, Douglas F. Campbell, John A. Hannigan, Peter Beyer, and John H. Simpson. (1993). "The United Church in Crisis." In W.E. Hewitt, ed., *The Sociology of Religion: A Canadian Focus* (pp. 273–87). Toronto: Butterworths.

Poloma, Margaret M. (1997). "The 'Toronto Blessing': Charisma, Institutionalization and Revival." *Journal for the Scientific Study of Religion, 36,* 257–71.

Poloma, Margaret M., and Lynette F. Hoelter. (1998). "The 'Toronto Blessing': A Holistic Model of Healing." *Journal for the Scientific Study of Religion, 37,* 257–72.

Ray, Julie. (2003). "Worlds Apart: Religion in Canada, Britain, U.S." Washington: The Gallup Poll.

Reimer, Sam. (2003). *Evangelicals and the Continental Divide.* Montreal: McGill–Queen's University Press.

Reimer, Samuel H. (1995). "A Look at Cultural Effects on Religiosity: A Comparison Between the United States and Canada." *Journal for the Scientific Study of Religion, 34,* 445–57.

Rokeach, Milton. (1965). *Paradoxes of Religious Belief.* Information Service, National Council of Churches, 1–2.

Rokeach, Milton. (1969). "Religious Values and Social Compassion." *Review of Religious Research, 11,* 3–23.

Roof, Wade Clark, and Dean R. Hoge. (1980). "Church Involvement in America: Social Factors Affecting Membership and Participation." *Review of Religious Research, 21,* 405–26.

Rouleau, Jean-Paul. (1977). "Religion in Quebec: Present and Future." *Pro Mundi Vita: Dossiers, 3* (November–December).

Shackleton, Eric. (2005). "Pastors and Priests Face Ever More Empty Seats in 2006." Canadian Press Newswire, 20 December.

Smith, Tom W. (1999). "The Religious Right and Anti-Semitism." *Review of Religious Research, 99,* 244–58.

Speaker-Yuan, Margaret, ed. (2005). *Women in Islam.* Detroit: Greenhaven Press/Thomson-Gale.

Stackhouse, John G., Jr. (2005). *Finally Feminist: A Pragmatic Christian Understanding of Gender.* Grand Rapids, MI: Baker Academic.

Stahl, William. (1986). "The Land That God Gave Cain: Nature and Civil Religion in Canada." Presented at the annual meeting of the Society for the Scientific Study of Religion, Washington, DC, November.

Stark, Rodney, and Charles Y. Glock. (1968). *American Piety.* Berkeley, CA: University of California Press.

Stark, Rodney, and Roger Finke. (2000). *Acts of Faith: Explaining the Human Side of Religion.*

Stark, Rodney, and William Sims Bainbridge. (1985). *The Future of Religion.* Berkeley, CA: University of California Press.

Statistics Canada. (1998). "Text of Fatwah Urging Jihad Against Americans." *Al-Quds al-'Arabi,* 23 February.

Statistics Canada. (2003). *2001 Census: Analysis Series—Religions in Canada.* Ottawa: Minister of Industry. Catalogue no. 96F0030XIE2002015.

Statistics Canada. (2004a). "General Social Survey: Social Engagement. *The Daily* 6 July.

Statistics Canada. (2004b). National Survey of Non-profit and Voluntary Organizations. *The Daily* 20 September.

Stiller, Brian. (1997). *From the Tower of Babel to Parliament Hill.* Toronto: HarperCollins.

Thomas, W.I., and Florian Znaniecki. (1918). *The Polish Peasant in Europe and America.* New York: Knopf.

Valpy, Michael. (2006). "Why the Global Rage Hasn't Engulfed Canada: Multiculturalism and Media Likely Muted Protests." *The Globe and Mail* 8 February, A14.

Valpy, Michael. (2004). "Canadians Giving up on Religion, Poll Finds." *The Globe and Mail* 29 November:A8.

Weber, Max. (1958 [1904–05]). *The Protestant Ethic and the Spirit of Capitalism.* New York: Scribner's.

Weber, Max. (1963 [1922]). *The Sociology of Religion.* Trans. Ephraim Fischoff. Boston: Beacon Press.

Whyte, Donald. (1966). "Religion and the Rural Church." In M.A. Tremblay and W.J. Anderson, eds., *Rural Canada in Transition* (pp. 79–92). Ottawa: Agricultural Economics Research Council of Canada.

Wilcox, W. Bradford. (1998). "Conservative Protestant Childrearing: Authoritarian or Authoritative?" *American Sociological Review, 63,* 796–809.

Winseman, Albert L. (2004). *Britons Lack American Cousin's Piety.* Washington, DC: The Gallup Poll.

Winseman, Albert L. (2005). *Who Has Been Born Again?* Washington, DC: The Gallup Poll.

CHAPTER 14

Adam, Barry. (1995). *The Rise of a Gay and Lesbian Movement,* 2nd ed. New York: Twayne.

Anderson, Elijah. (1990). "The Police and the Black Male." In Elijah Anderson, ed., *Streetwise* (pp. 190–206). Chicago, IL: University of Chicago Press.

Beattie, Karen. (2005). "Adult Correctional Services in Canada, 2003/04." *Juristat, 25* (8).

Becker, Howard, ed. (1964). *The Other Side: Perspectives on Deviance.* New York: Free Press.

Becker, Howard. (1973). *Outsiders: Studies in the Sociology of Deviance.* New York: Free Press.

Bergman, Brian. (1999). "Tragedy in Taber." *Maclean's* 10 May: 20–23.

Canadian Centre for Justice Statistics. (1996). *Canadian Crime Statistics: 1995.* Ottawa: Statistics Canada.

Canadian Centre for Justice Statistics. (2005). *Homicide Survey, Policing Services Program.* Ottawa: Statistics Canada.

Cawsey, R.W. (1991). *Report of the Task Force on the Criminal Justice System and Its Impact on the Indian and Métis People of Alberta.* Edmonton: Province of Alberta.

Chambliss, William. (1973). "The Saints and the Roughnecks." *Society, 11,* 24–31.

Chisholm, Patricia. (1999). "The Copycat Syndrome." *Maclean's* 10 May: 23.

Cohen, Albert K. (1955). *Delinquent Boys: The Culture of the Gang.* Glencoe, IL: Free Press.

Cohen, Lawrence E., and Marcus Felson. (1979). "Social Change and Crime Rate Trends: A Routine Activity Approach." *American Sociological Review, 44,* 588–608.

Cohen, Stanley. (1985). *Visions of Social Control.* Cambridge: Polity Press.

Commission on Systemic Racism in the Ontario Criminal Justice System. (1995). *Report of the Commission on Systemic Racism in the Ontario Criminal Justice System.* Toronto: Queen's Printer.

Committee of Concerned Journalists. (1998). "Changing Definitions of News." *Reports and Studies.* On the World Wide Web at http://www.journalism.org (6 March 2000).

Correctional Service Canada. (2005). "Important Facts to Communicate." *Speakers Binder.* http://www.csc-scc.gc.ca/text/pblct/guideorateur/sec7_e.shtml (17 October 2006).

Criminal Intelligence Service Canada. (1996). *Annual Report on Organized Crime in Canada 1996.* Ottawa: Criminal Intelligence Service Canada.

Dauvergne, Mia. (2005). "Homicide in Canada, 2004." *Juristat, 25* (6).

Doob, Anthony N., and Jane B. Sprott. (2004). "Changing Models of Youth Justice in Canada." In M. Tonry, ed., *Youth Justice Systems: A Special Issue of Criminal Justice Review of the Research.* Vol. 31 (pp. 185–242). Chicago: University of Chicago Press.

Doob, Anthony N., Jane B. Sprott, Voula Marinos, and Kimberly N. Varma. (1998). *An Exploration of Ontario Residents' Views of Crime and the Criminal Justice System.* Toronto: Centre of Criminology, University of Toronto.

Doob, Anthony N., Voula Marinos, and Kimberly N. Varma. (1995). *Youth Crime and the Youth Justice System in Canada: A Research Perspective.* Toronto: Centre of Criminology, University of Toronto.

Durkheim, Émile. (1938). *The Rules of Sociological Method.* Trans. S. Solovay and J. Mueller, G.E.G. Catlin, ed. Chicago: University of Chicago Press.

Erickson, Patricia. (1996). "The Selective Control of Drugs." In B. Schissel and L. Mahood, eds., *Social Control in Canada* (pp. 59–77). Don Mills, ON: Oxford University Press.

Eron, L.D. (1986). "Interventions to Mitigate the Psychological Effects of Media Violence on Aggressive Behavior." *Journal of Social Issues, 42,* 155–69.

Federal Bureau of Investigation. (2004). "Crime in the United States, 2004." *Uniform Crime Reports.* On the World Wide Web at http://www.fbi.gov/ucr/cius_04/summary/index.html (25 September 2006).

Findlay, Deborah. (1996). "The Body Perfect: Appearance Norms, Medical Control, and Women." In B. Schissel and L. Mahood, eds., *Social Control in Canada* (pp. 174–200). Don Mills, ON: Oxford University Press.

Findlay, Michael. (1999). *The Globalization of Crime.* Cambridge: Cambridge University Press.

Fine, Sean, and Brian Milner. (1999). "Medical Issue Raised in Law-Firm Affair." *The Globe and Mail* 17 November: A2.

Foster, Cecil. (1996). *A Place Called Heaven: The Meaning of Being Black in Canada.* Toronto: HarperCollins.

Foucault, Michel. (1979). *Discipline and Punish: The Birth of the Prison.* New York: Vintage Books.

Frazier, Charles. (1976). *Theoretical Approaches to Deviance: An Evaluation.* Columbus, Ohio: Charles Merrill.

Frideres, Jim. (1996). "Native Canadian Deviance and the Social Control of Race." In B. Schissel and L. Mahood, eds., *Social Control in Canada* (pp. 288–319). Don Mills: Oxford University Press.

Gannon, Maire. (2005). *General Social Survey on Victimization, Cycle 18: An Overreview of the Findings.* Ottawa: Statistics Canada. Catalogue No. 85-565-XIE.

Gannon, Maire, and Karen Mihorean. (2005). "Criminal Victimization in Canada, 2004." *Juristat, 25* (7).

Gartner, Rosemary, Kathryn Baker, and Fred Pampel. (1990). "Gender Stratification and the Gender Gap in Homicide Victimization." *Social Problems, 37,* 593–612.

Gottfredson, Michael, and Travis Hirschi. (1990). *A General Theory of Crime*. Stanford: Stanford University Press.

Griffiths, Curt T., and Alison Cunningham. (2000). *Canadian Corrections*. Toronto: Nelson Thomson Learning.

Hagan, John, John Simpson, and A.R. Gillis. (1987). "Class in the Household: A Power-Control Theory of Gender and Delinquency." *American Journal of Sociology, 92,* 788–816.

Hamilton, A.C., and C.M. Sinclair. (1991). *Report of the Aboriginal Justice Inquiry of Manitoba*. Winnipeg: Government of Manitoba.

Hermer, Joe, and Janet Mosher. (2002). *Disorderly People: Law and the Politics of Exclusion in Ontario*. Halifax: Fernwood Press.

Hirschi, Travis. (1969). *Causes of Delinquency*. Berkeley: University of California Press.

Irwin, Darrell. (1999). "The Straight Edge Subculture: Examining the Youths' Drug Free Ways." *Journal of Drug Issues, 29,* 365–80.

Lemert, Edwin. (1967). *Human Deviance, Social Problems, and Social Control*. Englewood Cliffs, NJ: Prentice Hall.

Marx, Gary. (1981). "Ironies of Social Control: Authorities as Contributors to Deviance Through Escalation, Nonenforcement, and Covert Facilitation." *Social Problems, 28,* 221–33.

Marx, Gary. (1995). "The Engineering of Social Control: The Search for the Silver Bullet." In J. Hagan and R. Peterson, eds., *Crime and Inequality* (pp. 225–46). Stanford: Stanford University Press.

Merton, Robert. (1938). "Social Structure and Anomie." *American Sociological Review, 3,* 672–82.

Merton, Robert. (1957). *Social Theory and Social Structure*. New York: Free Press.

Ontario Legislature. (1999). *Legislative Debates*. November 2.

Ouimet, Marc. (2002). "Explaining the American and Canadian Crime 'Drop' in the 1990s." *Canadian Journal of Criminology* (January), 33–50.

Phillips, Andrew. (1999). "Lessons of Littleton." *Maclean's* 3 May, 18–21.

Province of Manitoba. (1991). *Report of the Aboriginal Justice Inquiry of Manitoba*. Winnipeg: Public Inquiry into the Administration of Justice and Aboriginal People.

Public Safety and Emergency Preparedness Canada. (2005). *Corrections and Conditional Release Statistical Overview*. On the World Wide Web at http://www.psepc.gc.ca/res/em/_fl/CCRSO11232005-en.pdf (25 September 2006).

Quinney, Richard. (1970). *The Social Reality of Crime*. Boston: Little, Brown.

Rankin, Jim, Jennifer Quinn, Michelle Shephard, Scott Simmie, and John Duncanson. (2002). "Black Crime Rates Highest: 'No One Born Violent . . .' What's Causing These Problems?" *Toronto Star* 26 October: A1, A14–A15.

Richards, James R. (1999). *Transnational Criminal Organizations, Cybercrime, and Money Laundering*. Boca Raton, FL: CRC Press.

Roach, Kent. (1999). *Due Process and Victims' Rights: The New Law and Politics of Criminal Justice*. Toronto: University of Toronto Press.

Roberts, Julian. (2000). "Introduction to Criminal Justice in Canada." In Julian Roberts, ed., *Criminal Justice in Canada: A Reader*. Toronto: Harcourt Brace and Co.

Roberts, Julian V., and Anthony N. Doob. (1997). "Race, Ethnicity, and Criminal Justice in Canada." In Michael Tonry, ed., *Ethnicity, Crime, and Immigration: Comparative and Cross-National Perspectives* (pp. 469–522). Chicago: University of Chicago Press.

Rosoff, Stephen M., Henry N. Pontell, and Robert Tillman. (1998). *Profit Without Honor: White-Collar Crime and the Looting of America*. Upper Saddle River, NJ: Prentice Hall.

Satzewich, Victor. (1998). *Racism and Social Inequality in Canada: Concepts, Controversies, and Strategies of Resistance*. Toronto: Thompson.

Sauvé, Julie. 2005. "Crime Statistics in Canada, 2004." *Juristat, 25* (5).

Schmidt, Lisa. (2001). "Latimer Petition Draws 60 000 Signatures." *Canadian Press*, 13 December.

Scott, Robert A. (1969). *The Making of Blind Men*. New York: Russell Sage.

Statistics Canada. (2005). *Homicide in Canada, 2004*. Catalogue No. 85-002. On the World Wide Web at http://www.statcan.ca/english/freepub/85-002-XIE/0060585-002-XIE.pdf (25 September 2006).

Straight Goods. (2002). "High-Priced Security: Bill C-36, Canada's New Anti-Terrorism Legislation." *Canada and the World Backgrounder, 67* (4), 24–27.

Sutherland, Edwin. (1939). *Principles of Criminology*. Philadelphia: Lippincott.

Sutherland, Edwin. (1949). *White Collar Crime*. New York: Dryden.

Tanner, Julian. (1996). *Teenage Troubles: Youth and Deviance in Canada*. Toronto: Nelson Canada.

Tufts, Jennifer. (2001). "Public Attitudes Toward the Criminal Justice System." *Juristat, 20,* 12.

Turk, Austin. (1969). *Criminality and the Legal Order*. Chicago: Rand McNally.

United Nations. (1999). *Global Studies on Organized Crime*. Vienna: Office for Drug Control and Crime Prevention.

Vold, George. (1958). *Theoretical Criminology*. New York: Oxford University Press.

Wolfgang, Marvin, Robert Figlio, Paul Tracy, and Simon Singer. (1985). *The National Survey of Crime Severity*. Washington DC: U.S. Government Printing Office.

World Health Organization. (1998). *World Health Statistics Annual, 1996*. Geneva: WHO.

Wortley, Scot. (1996). "Justice for All? Race and Perceptions of Bias in the Ontario Criminal Justice System—A Toronto Survey." *Canadian Journal of Criminology, 38,* 439–67.

Wortley, Scot, and Andrea McCalla. (2003). "The Debate Continues: Evidence of Bias against Black People in the Ontario Criminal Justice System?" In J.V. Roberts and M. Grossman, eds., *Criminal Justice in Canada: A Reader*, 2nd ed. Toronto: Thomson Nelson.

CHAPTER 15

Abu-Lughod, Janet L. (1991). *Changing Cities: Urban Sociology*. New York: HarperCollins.

Beaujot, Roderic. (2004) "Population, Aging, and Health." In Robert J. Brym, ed., *New Society: Sociology for the 21st Century*, 4th ed. (pp. 431–64). Toronto: Nelson.

Bélanger, Alain, and Éric Caron Malenfant. (2005). "Ethnocultural Diversity in Canada: Prospects for 2017." *Canadian Social Trends*, 79, 18–21.

Bell, Wendell. (1968). "The City, the Suburbs and a Theory of Social Choice." In Scott Greer, Dennis McElrath, David W. Minar, and Peter Orleans, eds., *The New Urbanization* (pp. 132–68). New York: St. Martin's Press.

Berger, Bennett. (1960). *Working Class Suburb*. Berkeley, CA: University of California Press.

Berry, Brian J.L., and Quentin Gillard. (1977). *The Changing Shape of Metropolitan America*. Cambridge, MA: Ballinger Publishing Co.

Blumenfeld, Hans. (1982). *Have the Secular Trends of Population Distribution Been Reversed?* Research paper 137. Toronto: Centre of Urban and Community Studies.

Blumenfeld, Hans. (1983). "Metropolis Extended." *Journal of the American Planning Association*, 52 (3), 346–48.

Bonner, Kieran. (1997). *A Great Place to Raise Kids: Interpretation, Science, and the Urban-Rural Debate*. Montreal and Kingston: McGill-Queen's University Press.

Bourne, L.S. (1996). "Reinventing the Suburbs: Old Myths and New Realities." *Progress in Planning*, 46, 163–84.

Brym, Robert J. (1986). "An Introduction to the Regional Question in Canada." In Robert J. Brym, ed., *Regionalism in Canada* (pp. 1–45). Toronto: Irwin.

Burgess, Ernest W. (1961). "The Growth of the City: An Introduction to a Research Project." In George A. Theodorson, ed., *Studies in Human Ecology* (pp. 37–44). Evanston, IL: Row, Peterson.

Castells, Manuel. (1989). *The Informational City: Information, Technology, Economic Restructuring and the Urban–Regional Process*. Oxford and Cambridge, MA: Blackwell.

Champion, A.G. (1993) "Urban and Regional Demographic Trends: The Developed World." In Ronan Paddison, Bill Lever, and John Money, eds., *International Perspectives in Urban Studies 1* (pp. 136–59). London and Philadelphia: Jessica Kingsley, Publishers.

Chandler, Tertius, and Gerald Fox. (1974). *3000 Years of Urban Growth*. New York and London: Academic Press.

Clark, David. (1996). *Urban World, Global City*. London and New York: Routledge.

Davis, Judy S., Arthur C. Nelson, and Kenneth J. Dueher. (1994). "The New 'Burbs: The Exurbs and their Implications for Planning Policy." *Journal of the American Planning Association*, 60, 45–59.

Davis, Kingsley. (1955). "The Origin and Growth of Urbanization in the World," *American Journal of Sociology*, 60, 430.

Davis, Mike. (1990). *City of Quartz: Excavating the Future in Los Angeles*. London and New York: Verso.

De Oliviera, Orlandino, and Bryan Roberts. (1996). "Urban Development and Social Inequality in Latin America." In J. Gugler, ed., *The Urban Transformation of the Developing World* (pp. 250–314). Oxford: Oxford University Press.

Drakakis-Smith, David. (1988). "Third World Cities: Sustainable Urban Development II—Population, Labour and Poverty." In R. Paddison and B. Lever, eds., *International Perspectives in Urban Studies 5* (pp. 70–101). London and Bristol, PA: Jessica Kingsley Publishers.

Driedger, Leo. (1991). *The Urban Factor: Sociology of Canadian Cities*. Toronto: Oxford University Press.

Ehrlich, Paul R. (1968). *The Population Bomb*. New York: Ballantine Books.

Epp, Roger, and Dave Whitson. (2001). "Writing Off Rural Communities." In R. Epp and D. Whitson, eds., *Writing Off the Rural West* (pp. xii–xxxv). Edmonton: The University of Alberta Press/Parkland Institute.

Fava, Sylvia Fleis. (1956). "Suburbanism as a Way of Life." *American Sociological Review*, 21, 34–37.

Filion, Pierre. (1991). "The Gentrification–Social Structure Dialectic: A Toronto Case Study." *International Journal of Urban and Regional Research*, 15, 553–74.

Firey, Walter. (1947). *Land Use in Central Boston*. Cambridge, MA: Harvard University Press.

Fishman, Robert. (1987). *Bourgeois Utopias: The Rise and Fall of Suburbia*. New York: Basic Books.

Fishman, Robert. (1990). "Megalopolis Unbound." *The Wilson Quarterly* (Winter), 25–45.

Fishman, Robert. (2005). "Longer View: The Fifth Migration." *Journal of the American Planning Association*, 71, 357–66.

Flanagan, William G. (1995). *Urban Sociology: Images and Structure*. Boston: Allyn and Bacon.

Florence, Elinor. (1997). "A Happy Hoofer Gets On with Life." *The Globe and Mail* 7 January: A18.

Fong, Eric. (1996). "A Comparative Perspective of Racial Residential Segregation: American and Canadian Experiences." *The Sociological Quarterly*, 37, 501–28.

Fong, Eric, and Kumiko Shibuya. (2005). "Multiethnic Cities in North America." *Annual Review of Sociology*, 31, 258–304.

Fong, Eric, and Rima Wilkes. (1999). "The Spatial Assimilation Model Re-examined: An Assessment By Canadian Data." *International Migration Review*, 33, 594–620.

Fowler, Edmund P. (1992). *Building Cities That Work*. Montreal and Kingston, ON: McGill-Queen's University Press.

Frieden, Bernard J., and Lynne B. Sagalyn. (1989). *Downtown, Inc.: How America Rebuilds Cities*. Cambridge, MA: The MIT Press.

Garreau, Joel. (1991). *Edge City: Life on the New Frontier*. New York: Doubleday.

Ginsburg, N., B. Koppel, and T.G. McGee, eds. (1991). *The Extended Metropolis: Settlement Transition in Asia*. Honolulu: University of Hawaii Press.

Goldberger, Paul. (1996). "The Rise of the Private City." In Julia Vitullo Martin, ed., *Breaking Away: The Future of Cities* (pp. 135–47). New York: The Twentieth Century Fund Press.

Golden, Hilda H. (1981). *Urbanization and Cities*. Lexington, MA: D.C. Heath.

Gordon, Ian, and Saskia Sassen. (1992). "Restructuring the Urban Labor Markets." In Susan S. Fainstein, Ian Gordon, and Michael Harloe, eds., *Divided Cities: New York and London in the Contemporary World* (pp. 105–28). Oxford and Cambridge, MA: Blackwell.

Grant, Jill. (2005). "The Function of the Gates: The Social Construction of Security in Gated Developments." *Town Planning Review*, 76, 291–313.

Gugler, Josef. (1996). "Preface." In J. Gugler, ed., *The Urban Transformation of the Developing World*. Oxford: Oxford University Press.

Hannigan, John A. (1995). "The Postmodern City: A New Urbanization?" *Current Sociology, 43* (1), 180.

Harris, Chauncey, and Edward Ullman. (1945). "The Nature of Cities." *Annals of the American Academy of Political and Social Science, 242* (November), 7–17.

Hauser, Philip M. (1965). "Urbanization: An Overview." In Philip M. Hauser and Leo F. Schnore, eds., *The Study of Urbanization.* New York: Wiley.

Heisz, Andrew, and Sébastien LaRochelle-Coté. (2005). "Getting to Work." *Canadian Social Trends, 79* (Winter), 16.

Hou, Feng, and Garnett Picot. (2004). "Visible Minority Neighbourhoods in Toronto, Montréal, and Vancouver." *Canadian Social Trends, 72,* 8–13.

Hoyt, Homer. (1939). *The Structure and Growth of Residential Neighborhoods in American Cities.* Washington, DC: Federal Housing Authority.

Jackson, Kenneth T. (1985). *Crabgrass Frontier: The Suburbanization of the United States.* New York: Oxford University Press.

Kleniewski, Nancy. (1997). *Cities, Change and Conflict: A Political Economy of Urban Life.* Belmont, CA: Wadsworth.

Kremarik, Frances. (2000). "Urban Development." *Canadian Social Trends, 59,* 18–22.

Leinberger, Christopher B., and Charles Lockwood. (1986). "How Business Is Reshaping America." *The Atlantic Monthly* October: 43–52.

Ley, David. (1991). "Gentrification." In Kent Gerecke, ed., *The Canadian City* (pp. 181–96). Montreal: Black Rose Books.

Little, Bruce. (1999). "Tale of Three Canadian Cities: What Makes Them Grow So Big." *The Globe and Mail* 20 September: A20.

Lofchie, Michael F. (1997). "The Rise and Demise of Urban-Biased Developmental Policies in Africa." In Josef Gugler, ed., *Cities in the Developing World: Issues, Theory and Policy* (pp. 23–39). Oxford: Oxford University Press.

Logan, John R., and Harvey L. Molotch. (1987). *Urban Fortunes: The Political Economy of Place.* Berkeley, CA: University of California Press.

Logan, John R., Richard D. Alba, and Wenquan Zhang. (2002). Immigrant Enclaves and Ethnic Communities in New York and Los Angeles." *American Sociological Review, 67,* 299–322.

Lorimer, James. (1978). *The Developers.* Toronto: Lorimer.

Malthus, T.R. (1798). *An Essay on the Principle of Population, as It Affects the Future Improvement of Society. With Remarks on the Speculations of Mr. Godwin, M. Condorcet and Other Writers.* London: J. Johnson.

McGahan, Peter. (1995). *Urban Sociology in Canada,* 3rd ed. Toronto: Harcourt Brace.

McGee, T.G. (1991). "The Emergence of Deschata Regions in Asia." In N. Ginsberg, B. Koppel and T.G. McGee, eds., *The Extended Metropolis* (pp. 3–25). Honolulu: University of Hawaii Press.

McQuillan, Kevin. (1994). "Population." In Robert Hagedorn, ed., *Sociology,* 5th ed. Toronto: Harcourt Brace and Company.

Michelson, William D. (1973). *Environmental Change.* Research Paper No. 60, Centre for Urban and Community Studies, University of Toronto.

Nader, George A. (1975). *Cities of Canada, Volume One: Theoretical, Historical and Planning Perspectives.* Toronto: Macmillan.

Ness, Gayl D., and Michael M. Low. (2000). *Modelling Asian Urban Population—Environment Dynamics.* Singapore: Oxford University Press.

Palen, J. John. (1995). *The Suburbs.* New York: McGraw-Hill.

Reid, Barton. (1991). "A Primer on the Corporate City." In Kent Gerecke, ed., *The Canadian City* (pp. 63–78). Montreal: Black Rose.

Reynolds, Malvina. (1964). *Little Boxes and Other Handmade Songs.* New York: Oak.

Roberts, Lance W., Rodney A. Clifton, Barry Ferguson, Karen Kampen, and Simon Langlois. (2005). *Recent Social Trends in Canada.* Montreal and Kingston: MCGill-Queen's University Press.

Rose, D. (1984). "Rethinking Gentrification: Beyond the Uneven Development of Marxist Urban Theory." *Environment and Planning D: Society and Space, 2* (1), 47–74.

Sanchez, T.W., R.E. Lang, and D.M. Dhavale. (2005). "Security Versus Status? A First Look at the Census's Gated Community Data." *Journal of Planning Education and Research, 24,* 281–91.

Seeley, R.A. Sim, and E.W. Loosley. (1956). *Crestwood Heights: A Study of the Culture of Suburban Life.* New York: Wiley.

Sewell, John. (1993). *The Shape of the City: Toronto Struggles with Modern Planning.* Toronto: University of Toronto Press.

Simmel, Georg. (1950). "The Metropolis and Mental Life." In Kurt H. Wolff, ed. and trans., *The Sociology of Georg Simmel* (pp. 409–24). Glencoe, IL: The Free Press.

Simon, Julian L., and Herman Kahn. (1984) *The Resourceful Earth: A Response to Global 2000.* Oxford: Blackwell.

Smith, David A. (1996). *Third World Cities in Global Perspective: The Political Economy of Uneven Urbanization.* Boulder, CO: Westview Press.

Smith, Neil. (1979). "Towards a Theory of Gentrification." *Journal of the American Planning Association, 45,* 538–48.

Smith, Neil, and Michael LeFaivre. (1984). "A Class Analysis of Gentrification." In John J. Palen and Brian London, eds., *Gentrification, Displacement and Neighborhood Revitalization* (pp. 43–64). Albany, NY: SUNY Press.

Statistics Canada. (2000). "Canada at a Glance, 2000." On the World Wide Web at http://www.statcan.ca/cgi-bin/downpub/listpub.cgi?catno=12-581-XIE2000002 (16 September 2000).

Statistics Canada. (2005). "Deaths." *The Daily* 21 December. On the World Wide Web at http://www.statcan.ca/Daily/English/051221/d051221b.htm (6 October 2006).

Stone, Leroy O. (1967). *Urban Development in Canada.* Ottawa: Dominion Bureau of Statistics.

Stren, R., and M. Halfari. (2001). "The Cities of Sub-Saharan Africa: From Dependency to Marginality." In Ronan Paddison, ed., *Handbook of Urban Studies* (pp. 466–85). London: Sage Publications.

Thomas, William I., and Florian Znaniecki. (1918–20). *The Polish Peasant in Europe and America,* 5 vols. Chicago: University of Chicago Press.

Tönnies, Ferdinand. (1957 [1887]). *Community and Society.* Trans. Charles Loomis. East Lansing, MI: Michigan State University Press.

"Urban Explosion—the Facts." (2006). *New Internationalist, 386* (January/February), 18–19.

Van de Kaa, Dirk. (1987). "Europe's Second Demographic Transition." *Population Bulletin, 42* (1), 1–58.

Warde, Alan. (1991). "Gentrification as Consumption: Issues of Class and Gender." *Environment and Planning D: Society and Space, 9* (2), 223–32.

Weber, A.F. (1963 [1899]). *The Growth of Cities in the Nineteenth Century*. Ithaca, NY: Cornell University Press.

"What Canada Is, Was, and Could Be," *Saturday Night Magazine* (September): 9.

Whyte, William H. (1956). *The Organization Man*. New York: Simon and Schuster.

Wilson, Elizabeth. (1991). *The Sphinx in the City: Urban Life, the Control of Disorder, and Women*. London: Virago Press.

Wirth, Louis. (1938). "Urbanism as a Way of Life." *American Journal of Sociology, 44*, 1–24.

Wittberg, Patricia. (1992). "Perspectives on Gentrification: A Comparative Review of the Literature." *Research in Urban Sociology, 2*, 17–46.

Zorbaugh, Harvey. (1929). *The Gold Coast and the Slum*. Chicago: University of Chicago Press.

CHAPTER 16

Adams, W.M. (1990). *Green Development: Environment and Sustainability in the Third World*. New York: Oxford University Press.

Blowers, A., D. Lowry, and B.D. Solomon. (1991). *The International Politics of Nuclear Waste*. London: Macmillan.

Bullard, R.D. (1990). *Dumping in Dixie: Race, Class and Environmental Quality*. Boulder, CO: Westview Press.

Buttel, F.H. (1975). "The Environmental Movement: Consensus, Conflict and Change." *Journal of Environmental Education, 7*, 53–63.

Buttel, F.H. (1987). "New Directions in Environmental Sociology." *Annual Review of Sociology, 13*, 465–88.

Cable, S., and M. Benson. (1993). "Acting Locally: Environmental Injustice and the Emergence of Grassroots Environmental Organizations." *Social Problems, 40*, 464–77.

Capek, S.M. (1993). "The Environmental Justice Frame: A Conceptual Discussion and an Application." *Social Problems, 40*, 5–24.

Clarke, L., and J.F. Short, Jr. (1993). "Social Organization and Risk: Some Current Controversies." *Annual Review of Sociology, 19*, 375–99.

Cotgrove, S. (1982). *Catastrophe or Cornucopia: The Environment, Politics, and the Future*. Chichester, UK: Wiley.

Cotgrove, S., and A. Duff. (1981). "Environmentalism, Values and Social Change." *British Journal of Sociology, 32*, 92–110.

Cylke, F.K., Jr. (1993). *The Environment*. New York: HarperCollins College.

d'Eaubonne, F. (1974). *La Feminisme ou la Mort*. Paris: P. Horay.

Davidson, Debra J., and Norah A. MacKendrick. (2004). "All Dressed Up and Nowhere to Go: The Discourse of Ecological Modernization in Alberta, Canada." *Canadian Review of Sociology and Anthropology, 41* (1), 47–65.

Denq, F., D.H. Constance, and S. Joung. (2000). "The Role of Class, Status, and Power in the Distribution of Toxic Superfund Sites in Texas and Louisiana." *Journal of Poverty, 4*, 81–100.

Derksen, L., and J. Gartrell. (1993). "The Social Context of Recycling." *American Sociological Review, 58*, 434–42.

Devall, B., and G. Sessions. (1985). *Deep Ecology: Living As If Nature Mattered*. Salt Lake City, UT: Peregrine Smith Books.

Downs, A. (1972). "Up and Down with Ecology: The 'Issue-Attention Cycle.'" *The Public Interest, 28*, 38–55.

Dunlap, R.E., and K.D. Van Liere. (1978). "The New Environmental Paradigm: A Proposed Measuring Instrument and Preliminary Results." *Journal of Environmental Education, 9*, 10–19.

Dunlap, R.E., and W.R. Catton, Jr. (1979). "Environmental Sociology." *Annual Review of Sociology, 5*, 243–73.

Dunlap, R.E., and W.R. Catton, Jr. (1983). "What Environmental Sociologists Have in Common (Whether Concerned with 'Built' or 'Natural' Environments)." *Sociological Inquiry, 53*, 113–35.

Dwyer, A. (1992). "The Trouble at Great Whale." *Equinox* (January/February): 28–41.

"End War in Woods, Poll Says." (2000). *Sustainability Update: A Quarterly Publication of the Forest Alliance of British Columbia* (Spring), 5.

Eyerman, R., and A. Jamison. (1989). "Environmental Knowledge as an Organizational Weapon: The Case of Greenpeace." *Social Science Information, 28*, 99–119.

Fields, D.M. (1993). "We Can't Grow on Like This (Review of Beyond the Limits)." *The Futurist* (January–February), 40–41.

Foster, J. (1978). *Working for Wildlife*. Toronto: University of Toronto Press.

Fowlkes, M., and P. Miller. (1987). "Chemicals and Community at Love Canal." In B.B. Johnson and V.T. Covello, eds., *The Social and Cultural Construction of Risk* (pp. 55–78). Dordrecht, Holland: D. Reidel.

Freudenburg, W.R. (1991). "Rural–Urban Differences in Environmental Concern: A Closer Look." *Sociological Inquiry, 61*, 167–98.

Freudenburg, W.R. (1993). "Risk and Recreancy: Weber, the Division of Labour and the Rationality of Risk Perceptions." *Social Forces, 71*, 909–32.

Gale, R.P. (1983). "The Environmental Movement and the Left: Antagonists or Allies?" *Sociological Inquiry, 53*, 179–99.

Gallopin, G.C., P. Gutman, and H. Maletta. (1989). "Global Impoverishment, Sustainable Development and the Environment: A Conceptual Approach." *International Social Science Journal, 41*, 375–97.

Gerhards, J., and D. Rucht. (1992). "Mesomobilization: Organizing and Framing in Two Protest Campaigns in West Germany." *American Journal of Sociology, 98*, 555–95.

Gidengil, E. (1990). "Centres and Peripheries: The Potential Culture of Dependencies." *Canadian Review of Sociology and Anthropology, 27*, 23–48.

Greenbaum, A. (1995). "Taking Stock of Two Decades of Research on the Social Bases of Environmental Concern." In Michael D. Mehta and Eric Ouellet, eds., *Environmental Sociology: Theory and Practice* (pp. 125–52). North York, ON: Captus Press.

Grossman, G.M., and H.R. Potter. (1977). "A Trend Analysis of Competing Models of Environmental Attitudes." Working Paper no. 127. Department of Sociology and Anthropology, Purdue University, West Lafayette, IN.

Hallman, W.K., and A. Wandersman. (1992). "Attribution of Responsibility and Individual and Collective Coping with Environmental Threats." *Journal of Social Issues, 48*, 101–18.

Hannigan, J.A. (1995). *Environmental Sociology: A Social Constructionist Perspective*. London and New York: Routledge.

Harrison, K., and G. Hoberg. (1991). "Setting the Environmental Agendas in Canada and the United States: The Cases of Dioxin and Radon." *Canadian Journal of Political Science, 24*, 3–27.

Hays, S. (1959). *Conservation and the Gospel of Efficiency: The Progressive Conservation Movement.* Cambridge, MA: Harvard University Press.

Jones, R., and R.E. Dunlap. (1992). "The Social Bases of Environmental Concern: Have They Changed over Time?" *Rural Sociology, 57,* 28–47.

Koppes, C. (1988). "Efficiency, Equity, Esthetics: Shifting Themes in American Conservation." In D. Worster, ed., *The Ends of the Earth: Perspectives on Modern Environmental History* (pp. 230–51). Cambridge, UK: Cambridge University Press.

Kriesi, H. (1989). "New Social Movements and the New Class in the Netherlands." *American Journal of Sociology, 94,* 1078–16.

Ladd, A.E., and S. Laska. (1991). "Opposition to Solid Waste Incineration: Pre-Implementation Anxieties Surrounding a New Environmental Controversy." *Sociological Inquiry, 61,* 299–313.

Lovelock, J. (1987). *Gaia: A New Look at Life on Earth.* Oxford: Oxford University Press.

Macdonald, D. (1991). *The Politics of Pollution: Why Canadians Are Failing Their Environment.* Toronto: McClelland and Stewart.

Maloney, M., and M. Ward. (1973). "Ecology: Let's Hear from the People: An Objective Scale for the Measurement of Ecological Attitudes and Knowledge." *American Psychologist, 28,* 583–86.

McDougall, Dan. (2005). "Pollution Ravages Kerala," *The Observer* (UK) (August 26–September 1), p. 29.

Meadows, D.H., D.L. Meadows, and J. Randers. (1992). *Beyond the Limits: Confronting Global Collapse, Envisioning a Sustainable Future.* Post Mills, VT: Chelsea Green.

Meadows, D.H., D.L. Meadows, J. Randers, and W.W. Behrens. (1972). *The Limits to Growth.* New York: Universe Books.

Milbrath, L.W. (1984). *Environmentalists: Vanguard for a New Society.* Albany, NY: SUNY Press.

Naess, A. (1973). "The Shallow and Deep Long-Range Ecology Movement." *Inquiry, 16,* 95–100.

Perron, B., J.G. Vaillancourt, and C. Durand. (2001). "A Global Problem for a Global Movement? An Exploratory Study of Climate Change Perception by Green Groups' Leaders from Québec (Canada) and Costa Rica." *Society and Natural Resources, 14,* 837–55.

Perrow, C. (1984). *Normal Accidents.* New York: Basic Books.

Robbins, Tom. (2006). "What Is the Real Price of Cheap Air Travel?" *Observer* (UK), January 29.

Roberts, J.T. (2001). "Global Inequality and Climate Change." *Society and Natural Resources, 14,* 501–09.

Saiget, Robert J. (2005). "China Admits Chemical Blast Polluted Major River, City Without Water." *Sino Daily* 23 November.

Schnaiberg, A. (1980). *The Environment: From Surplus to Scarcity.* New York: Oxford University Press.

Schumacher, E.F. (1973). *Small Is Beautiful.* New York: Harper.

Schwartz, John. (2006). "Panel Urges Corps to Study Oversight of Levees." *New York Times* 22 January 22: 1–23.

Séguin, C., L.G. Pelletier, and J. Hunsley. (1998). "Toward a Model of Environmental Activism." *Environment and Behavior, 30* (5), 628–52.

Shrivastava, P. (1987). *Bhopal: Anatomy of a Crisis.* Cambridge, MA: Ballinger.

Silverstone, Martin, and Kendra Toby. (1998). "Pathfinder Talk," *Equinox* (August/September): 90.

Silvertown, J. (1989). "A Silent Spring in China." *New Scientist* (July), 55–58.

Smith, C. (1992). *Media and Apocalypse: News Coverage of the Yellowstone Forest Fires, Exxon Valdez Oil Spill, and Loma Prieta Earthquake.* Westport, CT: Greenwood Press.

Solomon, Lawrence. (2006). "Great Bear Hug: Environmentalists Are Cheering, but Are They the Losers in an Agreement Reached Over B.C.'s Last Rain Forest Area?" *National Post* 10 February.

Stein, I.P. (1988). *Cities under Siege.* Toronto: Atlantic Press.

Theodori, G.L., and A.E. Luloff. (2002). "Position on Environmental Issues and Engagement in Pro-Environmental Behaviors." *Society and Natural Resources, 15,* 471–82.

Tindall, D.B. (1994). "Collective Action in the Rainforest: Personal Networks, Collective Identity, and Participation in the Vancouver Island Wilderness Preservation Movement." Ph.D. thesis, Department of Sociology, University of Toronto.

Turner, J.H. (1981). *Sociology: Studying the Human System,* 2nd ed. Santa Monica, CA: Goodyear.

Ungar, S. (1992). "The Rise and (Relative) Decline of Global Warming as a Social Problem." *Sociological Quarterly, 33,* 483–501.

Uusitalo, L. (1990). "Are Environmental Attitudes and Behavior Inconsistent? Findings from a Finnish Study." *Scandinavian Political Studies, 13,* 211–26.

Van Liere, K.D., and R.E. Dunlap. (1980). "The Social Bases of Environmental Concern: A Review of Hypotheses, Explanations and Empirical Evidence." *Public Opinion Quarterly, 44,* 181–97.

Warren, K.J. (1990). "The Power and Promise of Ecological Feminism." *Environmental Ethics, 12,* 125–46.

Williams, G. (1992). "Greening the New Canadian Political Economy." *Studies in Political Economy, 37,* 5–30.

World Commission on Environment and Development [The Brundtland Commission]. (1987). *Our Common Future: Report to the United Nations General Assembly.* New York: Oxford University Press.

Wynne, B. (1992). "Risk and Social Learning: Reification to Engagement." In S. Krimsky and D. Golding, eds., *Social Theories of Risk* (pp. 275–97). Westport, CT: Praeger.

Yearley, S. (1991). *The Green Case: A Sociology of Environmental Issues, Arguments and Politics.* London: HarperCollins Academic.

CHAPTER 17

Allard, Y.E., Wilkins, R., and Berthelot, J.-M. (2004). Premature Mortality in Health Regions with High Aboriginal Populations. *Health Reports, 15* (1), 51–60.

Antonucci, T.C. (1985). "Personal Characteristics, Social Support and Social Behaviour." In R.H. Binstock and E. Shanas, eds. *Handbook and the Social Sciences,* 2nd ed (pp. 94–128). New York, NY: Van Nostrand Reinhold.

Antonucci, T.C. (1990). "Social Supports and Social Relationships." In R.H. Binstock and L.K. George, eds. *Handbook of Aging and the Social Sciences,* 3rd ed (pp. 205–44). New York, NY: Academic Press.

Arber, S., and Ginn, J. (1991). *Gender and Later Life.* London: Sage Publications.

Armstrong, P., Armstrong, H., and Coburn, D. (2001). *Unhealthy Times. Political Economy Perspectives on Health and Care in Canada*. Don Mills, ON: Oxford University Press.

Bains, Camille. (2005). "Seeking Help for End-of-Life Caregivers." *The Globe and Mail* 3 October: S1.

Bélanger, A., Carrière, Y., and Gilbert S., eds. (2000). *Report on the Demographic Situation in Canada, 2000*. Ottawa: Statistics Canada. Catalogue No. 91-209-XPE.

Bollman, R.D. (2000). *Rural and Small-Town Canada: An Overview*. Ottawa: Statistics Canada. Catalogue No. 21F0018XIE. On the World Wide Web at http://www.statcan.ca/english/freepub/21F0018XIE/21F0018XIE2001001.htm (19 January 2006).

Broadbent, E. (2002). "This Piggy Got Greedy." Comment in *The Globe and Mail* 11 June: A17.

Brownell M.D., N.P. Roose, and L.L. Roos. (2001). Monitoring Health Reform: A Report Card Approach. *Social Science Medicine*, 52, 657–70.

Broyles, R.W., P. Manga, D.E. Binder, D.E. Angus, and A. Charette. (1983). "The Use of Physician Services under a National Health Insurance Scheme." *Medical Care, 21*, 1037–54.

Buckley, N.J., F.T. Denton, A.L. Robb, and B.G. Spencer. (2005). "Healthy Aging at Older Ages: Are Income and Education Important?" *Canadian Journal on Aging*, Supplement, S155–S169.

Canadian Population Health Initiative (CPHI). (2005). *Select Highlights on Public Views of the Determinants of Health*. Ottawa: Canadian Institute for Health Information.

Canadian Study on Health and Aging. (1994). "The Canadian Study of Health and Aging: Study Methods and Prevalence of Dementia." *Canadian Medical Association Journal, 150*, 899–913.

Carriere, K.C., L.L. Roos, and D.C. Dover. (2000). "Across Time and Space: Variations in Hospital Use during Canadian Health Reform." *Health Services Research, 35* (2), 467–87.

Chappell, N.L. (1992). *Social Support and Aging*. Toronto: Butterworths.

Chappell, N.L. (2005). "Perceived Change in Quality of Life among Chinese Canadian Seniors: The Role of Involvement in Chinese Culture." *Journal of Happiness Studies, 6* (1), 69–91.

Chappell, N.L., B. Havens, M.J. Hollander, J. Miller, and C. McWilliam. (2004). "Comparative Costs of Home Care and Residential Care." *The Gerontologist, 44* (3), 389–400.

Chappell, N.L., E. Gee, L. McDonald, and M. Stones. (2003). *Aging in Contemporary Canada*. Toronto: Pearson Education Canada.

Chen J., E. Ng, and R. Wilkins. (1996). "The Health of Canada's Immigrants in 1994–95." *Health Reports, 7* (4), 33–45.

Citizenship and Immigration Canada. (1999). *Facts and Figures, 1998*. Ottawa: Minister of Public Works and Government Services Canada. Catalogue No. MP43-333/1999E.

Coburn, D. (2002). "Beyond the Income Inequality Hypothesis: Globalization, Neo-liberalism, and Health Inequalities." Unpublished manuscript: University of Toronto, Department of Public Health Sciences.

Commission on the Future of Health Care in Canada (The Romanow Report). (2002). *Building on Values: The Future of Health Care in Canada, Final Report*. Ottawa: National Library of Canada. Catalogue No. CP32-85/2002E-IN.

Cotter, John. (2005). "Klein's Private Health Plan Questioned." *The Globe and Mail* 17 September: A15.

Crane, David. (2005). "Future Prosperity Depends on Strategic Innovation." *Toronto Star* 14 January: F2.

Crimmins, E.M. (2004). "Trends in the Health of the Elderly." *Annual Review of Public Health, 25*, 79–98.

Dean, K. (1986). Lay Care in Illness. *Social Science and Medicine, 22*, 275–84.

Denton, M., and Walters, V. (1999). "Gender Differences in Structural and Behavioral Determinants of Health: An Analysis of the Social Production of Health." *Social Science and Medicine, 48* (9), 1221–35.

Desjardins, B. (1993). *Population Ageing and the Elderly*. Ottawa: Statistics Canada. Catalogue No. 91-533E.

DesMeules, M., D. Manuel, and R. Cho. (2004). "Mortality: Life and Health Expectancy of Canadian Women." *BMC Women's Health, 4* (Suppl. 1), S1–S9.

Evans, R.G., K.M. McGrail, S.G. Morgan, M.L. Barer, and C. Hertzman. (2001). "Apocalypse No: Population Aging and the Future of Health Care Systems." *Canadian Journal on Aging, 20* (Suppl. 1), 160–191.

Fayerman, Pamela. (2005). "Growing Old Gracefully." *Saskatoon Star-Phoenix* 5 February: E3.

Finnie, R. (2000). *The Dynamics of Poverty in Canada: What We Know, What We Can Do*. Commentary No. 145. Toronto: CD Howe Institute.

Fries, J.F. (1983). "Compression of Morbidity." *Milbank Memorial Fund Quarterly, 61*, 397–419.

Gee, E.M. (2000). "Living Arrangements and Quality of Life among Chinese Canadian Elders." *Social Indicators Research, 51*, 304–29.

Hayward, M.D., E.M. Crimmins, and Y. Saito. (1998). "Causes of Death and Active Life Expectancy in the Older Population of the United States." *Journal of Aging and Health, 10*, 192–213.

Helvacioglu, B. (2000). "Globalization in the Neighborhood—From the Nation-State to Bilkent Center. *International Sociology, 15* (2), 326–42.

Hollander, M., and Chappell, N. (2001). *Synthesis Report: Final Report of the National Evaluation of the Cost-Effectiveness of Home Care*. A report prepared for the Health Transition Fund, Health Canada. Hollander Analytical Services Ltd., Victoria, B.C., Centre on Aging, University of Victoria, B.C.

Huisman, M., A. Kunst, D. Deeg, F. Grigoletto, W. Nusselder, and J. Mackenbach. (2005). "Educational Inequalities in the Prevalence and Incidence of Disability in Italy and the Netherlands Were Observed." *Journal of Clinical Epidemiology, 58*, 1058–65.

Ibbitson, John. (2005). "Can We Prepare for Life at 100?" *The Globe and Mail* 23 September: A4.

Kane, R.L. (1990). "Introduction." In R.L. Kane, J.G. Evans, and D. Mc Fadyen, eds., *Improving the Health of Older People: A World View* (pp. 15–18). New York: Oxford University Press.

Keating, N., J. Fast, J. Frederick, K. Cranswick, and C. Perrier. (1999). *Eldercare in Canada: Context, Content and Consequences*. Ottawa: Statistics Canada, Housing, Family and Social Statistics Division. Catalogue No. 89-570-XPE.

Kelley-Moore, J.A., and K.F. Ferraro. (2004). "The Black/White Disability Gap: Persistent Inequality in Later Life?" *Journal of Gerontology: Social Sciences, 59B* (1), S34–43.

Krieger, N. (2000). "Discrimination and Health." In L.F. Berkman and I. Kawachi, eds., *Social Epidemiology* (pp. 36–75). New York: Oxford University Press.

Laio, Y., D.L. McGee, G. Cao, and R.S. Cooper. (2001). "Recent Changes in the Health Status of the Older U.S. Population: Findings from the 1984 and 1994 Supplement on Aging." *Journal of the American Geriatrics Society, 49*, 443–49.

Lantz, P.M., J.S. House, J.M. Lepkowski, D.R. Williams, R.P. Mero, and J. Chen. (1998). "Socioeconomic Factors, Health Behaviors and Mortality: Results from a Nationally Representative Prospective Study of U.S. Adults." *Journal of the American Medical Association, 279* (21), 1703–08.

Li, P.S. (1998). *The Chinese in Canada*, 2nd ed. Toronto: Oxford University Press.

Link, B.G., and J.C. Phelan. (2000). "Evaluating the Fundamental Cause Explanation for Social Disparities in Health. In C.E. Bird, P. Conrad, and A.M. Fremont, eds., *Handbook of Medical Sociology*, 5th ed. (pp. 33–46). Upper Saddle River, NJ: Prentice-Hall.

Litwak. E. (1960). "Geographic Mobility and Extended Family Cohesion." *American Sociological Review, 25*, 385–94.

Lynch, J., and G. Kaplan. (2000). "Socioeconomic Position." In L.F. Berkman and I. Kawachi, eds., *Social Epidemiology* (pp. 13–35). New York: Oxford University Press.

Mallick, Heather. "The Brand That Didn't Deliver." *The Globe and Mail* 10 September: F2

Marmor, T.R., and K. Sullivan. (2000). Canada's Burning! Media Myths about Universal Health Coverage." *Washington Monthly* July/August. On the World Wide Web at http://www.washingtonmonthly.com/features/2000/0007.marmorsul.html#byline (21 November 2006).

Martel, L., A. Bélanger, J.-M. Berthelot, and Y. Carrière. (2005). *Health Aging.* Ottawa: Statistics Canada. Catalogue no. 82-618-MWE2005004.

Mendelson, M., and P. Divinsky. (2000). *Canada 2015: Globalization and the Future of Canada's Health and Health Care. Report for the Future of Global and Regional Integration Project, Institute of Intergovernmental Relations.* Toronto: Queen's University.

Montgomery, R.J.V., E.F. Borgatta, and M.L. Borgatta. (2000). "Societal and Family Change in the Burden of Care." In William T. Liu and Hal Kendig, eds., *Who Should Care for the Elderly: An East-West Value Divide* (pp. 27–54). Singapore: Singapore University Press, National University of Singapore and World Scientific Publishing Co. Pte. Ltd.

National Institute on Aging. (1996). *In Search of the Secrets of Aging.* Bethesda: National Institutes of Health.

Navarro, V. (2002). "Neoliberalism, Globalization, Unemployment, Inequalities and the Welfare State." In V. Navarro, ed., *The Political Economy of Social Inequalities: Consequences for Health and Quality of Life* (pp. 33–119). Amityville: Baywood Publishing Co.

Penning, M.J., L.L. Roos, N.L. Chappell, N.P. Roos, and G. Lin. (2002). *Health Care Restructuring and Community-Based Care: A Longitudinal Study.* Project No. 1997-055. Ottawa: Canadian Health Services Research Foundation.

Perez, C. (2002). "Health Status and Health Behaviour among Immigrants." *Health Reports, 13* (Supplement).

Picard, André. (2005a). "Katrina Ripped the Cover off Poverty." *The Globe and Mail* 15 September: A19.

Picard, André. (2005b). "Most Needy Heart Failure Patients Least Likely to Get Drugs." *The Globe and Mail* 15 September.

Popay, J., and M. Bartley. (1993). "Conditions of Formal Domestic Labour." In S. Platt, H. Thomas, S. Scott, and G. Williams, eds., *Locating Health: Sociological and Historical Explanations* (pp. 97–120). Brookfield, VT: Avenury.

Prus, S.G., and E. Gee. (2002). *Gender Differences in the Influence of Economic, Lifestyle and Psychosocial Factors on Later-Life Health.* Hamilton: Program for Research on Social and Economic Dimensions of an Aging Population, McMaster University.

Raphael D. (2005). "Introduction to the Social Determinants of Health." In D. Raphael, ed., *Social Determinants of Health: Canadian Perspectives* (pp. 1–19). Toronto: Canadian Scholars Press.

Rogers, R.G., R.A. Hummer, and C. Nam. (2000). *Living and Dying in the USA.* San Diego, CA: Academic Press.

Roos, N.P., B. Havens, and C. Black. (1993). "Living Longer but Doing Worse: Assessing Health Status in Elderly Persons at Two Points in Time in Manitoba, Canada, 1971 and 1983." *Social Science and Medicine, 36*, 273–82.

Ross, C.E., and C. Wu. (1996). "Education, Age, and the Cumulative Advantage in Health." *Journal of Health and Social Behavior, 37*, 104–20.

Royal Commission on Aboriginal Peoples. (1996). *Looking Forward, Looking Back—Report of the Royal Commission on Aboriginal Peoples*, Vol. 1. Ottawa: Supply and Services Canada.

Schalick, L.M., W.C. Hadden, E. Pamuk, V. Navarro, and G. Pappas. (2000). "The Widening Gap in Death Rates among Income Groups in the United States from 1967 to 1986." *International Journal of Health Services, 30*, 13–26.

Segall, A., and N.L. Chappell. (2000). *Health and Health Care in Canada.* Toronto: Pearson Education Canada.

Shields, M., and S. Tremblay. (2002). "The Health of Canada's Communities, 2000/01." *Health Reports, 13* (Suppl), 9–32.

Simpson, Jeffrey. "The Fat of the Land: Canada's New Burden." *The Globe and Mail* 1 October: A25.

Statistics Canada. (1995). *National Population Health Survey (1994–95).* Ottawa: Statistics Canada.

Statistics Canada. (1999). *Annual Demographic Statistics 1998.* Ottawa: Supply and Services Canada. Catalogue No. 91-213.

Statistics Canada. (2001a). *The Assets and Debts of Canadians: An Overview of the Results of the Survey of Financial Security.* Ottawa: Minister of Industry.

Statistics Canada. (2001b). "Population Projects." *The Daily* 13 March. On the World Wide Web at http://www.statcan.ca/Daily/English/010313/d010313a.htm (10 October 2006).

Statistics Canada. (2001c). "How Healthy Are Canadians? 2001 Annual Report." *Health Reports, 12* (3), 9–52.

Statistics Canada. (2002a). *Profile of the Canadian Population by Age and Sex: Canada Ages.* Ottawa: Ministry of Industry. Catalogue No. 96F0030.

Statistics Canada. (2002b). *Canadian Community Health Survey, 2000–2001.* Ottawa: Ministry of Industry.

Statistics Canada. (2003a). *Canadian Vital Statistics—Death Database and Demography Division.* Ottawa: Ministry of Industry.

Statistics Canada. (2003b). *Aboriginal Peoples Survey 2001—Initial Findings: Well-Being of the Non-reserve Aboriginal Population.* Ottawa: Minister of Industry. Catalogue No. 89-589-XIE.

Statistics Canada. (2004). *Canadian Community Health Survey, 2003.* Ottawa: Ministry of Industry.

Statistics Canada. (2005). *Canadian Community Health Survey, 2004.* Ottawa: Ministry of Industry.

Statistics Canada. (2006). *Causes of Death, 2003.* Ottawa: Ministry of Industry. Catalogue No. 84-208-XIE. On the World Wide Web at http://www.statcan.ca/english/freepub/84-208-XIE/84-208-XIE2005002.htm (10 October 2006).

Trottier, H., L. Martel, C. Houle, J.M. Berthelot, and J. Légaré. (2000). "Living at Home or in an Institution: What Makes the Differences for Seniors?" *Health Reports,* 11, 49–59.

United Nations. (2005a). *World Population Prospects: The 2004 Revision, Vol. I, Comprehensive Tables.* New York: United Nations.

United Nations. (2005b). *Demographic Yearbook 2001.* No. E/F.03.XIII.1. On the World Wide Web at http://unstats.un.org/unsd/demographic/products/indwm/ww2005/tab3a.htm#src (12 January, 2006).

Williams, A.P., R. Dever, P. Baranek, and A. Gildiner. (2001). "From Medicare to Home Care: Globalization, State Retrenchment, and the Profitization of Canada's Health Care System." In P. Armstrong, H. Armstrong, and D. Coburn, eds., *Unhealthy Times: Political Economy Perspectives on Health and Care in Canada* (pp. 7–30). New York: Oxford University Press.

Williamson, D.J. (2000). "Health Behaviours and Health: Evidence That the Relationship Is Not Conditional on Income Adequacy." *Social Science and Medicine,* 51 (12), 1741–54.

Wister, A., and Moore, C. (1998). "First Nations Elders in Canada." In A.V. Wister and G.M. Gutman, eds., *Health Systems and Aging in Selected Pacific Rim Countries: Cultural Diversity and Change* (pp. 103–24). Vancouver: Simon Fraser University Gerontology Research Centre.

Wister, A.V. (2005). "It Need Not Be All Downhill." *Vancouver Sun* 21 January: B2–B3.

World Health Organization. (1948). *Official records of the World Health Organization,* #2. New York: WHO Interim Commission, UN.

CHAPTER 18

Adam, Barry, Jan Willem Duyvendak, and Andre Krouwel. (1999). *The Global Emergence of Gay and Lesbian Politics.* Philadelphia: Temple University Press.

Adamson, Nancy, Linda Briskin, and Margaret McPhail. (1988). *Feminist Organizing for Change: The Contemporary Women's Movement in Canada.* Toronto: Oxford University Press.

Arterton, F. Christopher. (1987). *Teledemocracy: Can Technology Protect Democracy?* Newbury Park, CA: Sage Publications.

Bashevkin, Sylvia. (1986). "Independence versus Partisanship: Dilemmas in the Political History of Women in English Canada." In V. Strong-Boag and A. Fellman, eds., *Rethinking Canada: The Promise of Women's History* (pp. 246–75). Toronto: Copp Clark Pitman.

Blais, André, Elisabeth Gidengil, Richard Nadeau, and Neil Nevitte. (1997). *1997 Canadian Election Survey.* On the World Wide Web at http://prod.library.utoronto.ca/datalib/codebooks/utm/elections/1997/ (20 June 2002).

Block, Fred. (1979). "The Ruling Class Does Not Rule." In R. Quinney, ed. *Capitalist Society* (pp. 128–40). Homewood IL: Dorsey Press.

Brint, Stephen. (1984). "New Class and Cumulative Tend Explanations of the Liberal Political Attitudes of Professionals." *American Journal of Sociology,* 90, 30–71.

Brym, Robert J. (1979). "Political Conservatism in Atlantic Canada." In Robert J. Brym and R. James Sacouman, eds., *Underdevelopment and Social Movements in Atlantic Canada* (pp. 59–79). Toronto: New Hogtown Press.

Brym, Robert J. (1980). *Intellectuals and Politics.* London UK: Allen and Unwin.

Brym, Robert J. (1989). "Canada." In Tom Bottomore and Robert J. Brym, eds., *The Capitalist Class: An International Study* (pp. 177–206). New York: New York University Press.

Brym, Robert J. (2003). "Affluence, Strikes, and Power in Canada, 1973–2000." In James Curtis, Edward Grabb, and Neil Guppy, eds., *Social Inequality in Canada: Patterns, Problems, Policies,* 4th ed. Scarborough, ON: Prentice-Hall Canada.

"Canadian Election Survey, 2004." (2005). On the World Wide Web at http://r1.chass.utoronto.ca.myaccess.library.utoronto.ca/cgi-bin/sda/hsda?harcsda+ces04 (30 October 2005).

Casper, L.M., S.S. McLanahan, and I. Garfinkel. (1994). "The Gender-Poverty Gap: What Can We Learn from Other Countries?" *American Sociological Review,* 59, 594–605.

"Chronological Perspective on Work Stoppages in Canada." (1999). On the World Wide Web at http://labour.hrdc-drhc.gc.ca/doc/wid-dimt/eng/ws-at/table.cfm (30 June 2004).

"Chronological Perspective on Work Stoppages in Canada (Work Stoppages Involving One or More Workers), 1976–2000." (2001). On the World Wide Web at http://labour-travail.hrdc-drhc.gc.ca/doc/wid-dimt/eng/ws-at/table.cfm (27 March 2006).

Clarke, Harold D., Jane Jenson, Lawrence LeDuc, and Jon H. Pammett. (1996). *Absent Mandate: Canadian Electoral Politics In an Era of Restructuring,* 3rd ed. Toronto: Gage.

Clement, Wallace. (1975). *The Canadian Corporate Elite: An Analysis of Economic Power.* Toronto: McClelland and Stewart.

Crompton, Susan, Jonathan Ellison, and Kathryn Stevenson. (2002). "Better Things to Do or Dealt out of the Game? Internet Dropouts and Infrequent Users." *Canadian Social Trends* (Summer), 2–5.

Dahl, Robert A. (1961). *Who Governs?* New Haven, CT: Yale University Press.

Davies, James C. (1969). "Toward a Theory of Revolution." In Barry McLaughlin, ed. *Studies in Social Movements: A Social Psychological Perspective* (pp. 85–108). New York: Free Press.

Elections Canada. (2006). "39th General Election." On the World Wide Web at http://enr.elections.ca/ (24 January 2006).

Elections Canada On-Line. (2000). "Registered Political Parties' Fiscal Period Returns for 1997." On the World Wide Web at http://www.elections.ca/content.asp?section=finanddocument=table03anddir=fisandlang=eandtextonly=false (30 July 2002).

Evans, Peter B., Dietrich Rueschemeyer, and Theda Skocpol. (1985). *Bringing the State Back In.* Cambridge, UK: Cambridge University Press.

Frank, Jeffrey. (1994). "Voting and Contributing: Political Participation in Canada." In *Canadian Social Trends* (pp. 333–37). Toronto: Thompson Educational Publishers.

Goffman, Erving. (1974). *Frame Analysis*. Cambridge, MA: Harvard University Press.

"Greenpeace Contacts Worldwide." (1999). On the World Wide Web at http://adam.greenpeace.org/information.shtml (29 April 2004).

Hourani, Albert. (1991). *A History of the Arab Peoples*. New York: Warner Books.

Jenkins, J. Craig. (1983). "Resource Mobilization Theory and the Study of Social Movements." *Annual Review of Sociology, 9,* 527–53.

Kelley, Jack. (2001). "Terror Groups Hide Behind Web Encryption." *USA Today* 19 June. On the World Wide Web at http://www.usatoday.com/life/cyber/tech/2001-02-05-binladen.htm (13 September 2001).

Korpi, Walter. (1983). *The Democratic Class Struggle*. London UK: Routledge and Kegan Paul.

Labour Organizations in Canada 1972. (1973). Ottawa: Economics and Research Branch, Canada Department of Labour. Catalogue No. L2-2-1972.

Lipset, Seymour Martin. (1981). *Political Man: The Social Bases of Politics*, 2nd ed. Baltimore: Johns Hopkins University Press.

Lipset, Seymour Martin. (1971). *Agrarian Socialism: The Cooperative Commonwealth Federation in Saskatchewan*, rev. ed. Berkeley, CA: University of California Press.

Lodhi, Abdul Qaiyum, and Charles Tilly. (1973). "Urbanization, Crime, and Collective Violence in 19th Century France." *American Journal of Sociology, 79,* 296–318.

Marshall, T.H. (1965). "Citizenship and Social Class." In T.H. Marshall, ed., *Class, Citizenship, and Social Development: Essays by T.H. Marshall* (pp. 71–134). Garden City, NY: Anchor.

McCarthy, John D., and Mayer N. Zald. (1977). "Resource Mobilization and Social Movements: A Partial Theory." *American Journal of Sociology, 82,* 1212–41.

McCullogh, Declan. (2000). "Bin Laden: Steganography Master?" *Wired* 7 February. On the World Wide Web at http://www.wired.com/news/print/0.1294.41658.00.html (13 September 2001).

Melucci, Alberto. (1980). "The New Social Movements: A Theoretical Approach." *Social Science Information, 19,* 199–226.

Melucci, Alberto. (1995). "The New Social Movements Revisited: Reflections on a Sociological Misunderstanding." In Louis Maheu, ed., *Social Classes and Social Movements: The Future of Collective Action* (pp. 107–19). London: Sage Publications.

Miliband, Ralph. (1973 [1969]). *The State in Capitalist Society*. London: Fontana.

Mills, C. Wright. (1956). *The Power Elite*. New York: Oxford University Press.

Mishler, William. (1979). *Political Participation in Canada: Prospects for Democratic Citizenship*. Toronto: Macmillan.

Moore, Barrington, Jr. (1967). *Social Origins of Dictatorship and Democracy: Lord and Peasant in the Making of the Modern World*. Boston: Beacon.

"Muslim Brotherhood Movement Homepage." (2002). On the World Wide Web at http://www.ummah.org.uk/ikhwan/ (7 May 2003).

Myles, John. (1989). *Old Age in the Welfare State: The Political Economy of Public Pensions*, revised ed. Lawrence, KS: University Press of Kansas.

1994–1995 Directory of Labour Organizations in Canada. (1995). Ottawa: Minister of Supply and Services Canada. Catalogue No. L2-2-1995.

1998 Directory of Labour Organizations in Canada. (1998). Ottawa: Workplace Information Directorate.

Oberschall, Anthony. (1973). *Social Conflict and Social Movements*. Englewood Cliffs, NJ: Prentice-Hall.

O'Connor, Julia S. (1996). "From Women in the Welfare State to Gendering Welfare State Regimes." *Current Sociology, 44* (2), 1–130.

O'Connor, Julia S., and Gregg M. Olsen, eds. (1998). *Power Resources Theory and the Welfare State: A Critical Approach*. Toronto: University of Toronto Press.

O'Connor, Julia S., and Robert J. Brym. (1988). "Public Welfare Expenditure in OECD Countries: Towards a Reconciliation of Inconsistent Findings." *British Journal of Sociology, 39,* 47–68.

Olsen, Dennis. (1980). *The State Elite*. Toronto: McClelland and Stewart.

Olsen, Gregg. (2002). *The Politics of the Welfare State: Canada, Sweden, and the United States*. Toronto: Oxford University Press.

Olsen, Gregg, and Robert J. Brym. (1996). "Between American Exceptionalism and Swedish Social Democracy: Public and Private Pensions in Canada." In Michael Shalev, ed., *The Privatization of Social Policy? Occupational Welfare and the Welfare State in America, Scandinavia and Japan* (pp. 261–79). London: Macmillan.

Piven, Frances Fox, and Richard A. Cloward. (1989). *Why Americans Don't Vote*. New York: Pantheon.

Polsby, Nelson W. (1959). "Three Problems in the Analysis of Community Power." *American Sociological Review, 24,* 796–803.

Porter, John. (1965). *The Vertical Mosaic: An Analysis of Social Class and Power in Canada*. Toronto: University of Toronto Press.

Poulantzas, Nicos. (1975 [1968]). *Political Power and Social Classes*. Trans. T. O'Hagan. London: New Left Books.

Roche, Maurice. (1995). "Rethinking Citizenship and Social Movements: Themes in Contemporary Sociology and Neoconservative Ideology." In Louis Maheu, ed. *Social Classes and Social Movements: The Future of Collective Action* (pp. 186–219). London: Sage Publications.

Rootes, Chris. (1995). "A New Class? The Higher Educated and the New Politics." In Louis Maheu, ed., *Social Classes and Social Movements: The Future of Collective Action* (pp. 220–35). London: Sage Publications.

Sciadis, George. (n.d.) *The Digital Divide in Canada*. Research paper. Ottawa: Statistics Canada. Catalogue no. 56F009XIE. On the World Wide Web at http://www.statcan.ca/english/research/56F0009XIE/56F0009XIE.pdf (30 October 2005).

Shahar, Yael. (2001). "Tracing bin Laden's Money: Easier Said than Done." International Policy Institute for Counter-Terrorism. On the World Wide Web at http://www.ict.org.il/ articles/ articledet.cfm?articleid=387 (30 July 2002).

Skocpol, Theda. (1979). *States and Revolutions: A Comparative Analysis of France, Russia, and China*. Cambridge, UK: Cambridge University Press.

Smith, Jackie. (1998). "Global Civil Society? Transnational Social Movement Organizations and Social Capital." *American Behavioral Scientist, 42,* 93–107.

Snow, David A., E. Burke Rochford, Steven K. Worden, and Robert D. Benford. (1986). "Frame Alignment Processes, Micromobilization, and Movement Participation." *American Sociological Review, 51,* 464–81.

Snyder, David, and Charles Tilly. (1972). "Hardship and Collective Violence in France, 1830–1960." *American Sociological Review, 37,* 520–32.

Spilerman, Seymour. (1970). "The Causes of Racial Disturbances: A Comparison of Alternative Explanations." *American Sociological Review, 35,* 627–49.

Spilerman, Seymour. (1976). "Structural Characteristics of Cities and the Severity of Racial Disorders." *American Sociological Review, 41,* 771–93.

Strikes and Lockouts in Canada 1968. (1970). Ottawa: Economic and Research Branch, Department of Labour. Catalogue No. L2-1/1968.

Strikes and Lockouts in Canada 1985. (1985). Ottawa: Minister of Supply and Services Canada. Catalogue No. L160-2999/85B.

Strong-Boag, Veronica. (1986). "Ever a Crusader: Nellie McClung, First-Wave Feminist." In V. Strong-Boag and A. Fellman, eds., *Rethinking Canada: The Promise of Women's History* (pp. 178–90). Toronto: Copp Clark Pitman.

Tilly, Charles. (1978). *From Mobilization to Revolution.* Reading MA: Addison-Wesley.

Tilly, Charles. (1979a). "Collective Violence in European Perspective." In H. Graham and T. Gurr, eds., *Violence in America: Historical and Comparative Perspective,* 2nd ed. (pp. 83–118). Beverly Hills: Sage Publications.

Tilly, Charles. (1979b). "Repertoires of Contention in America and Britain, 1750–1830." In Mayer N. Zald and John D. McCarthy, eds., *The Dynamics of Social Movements: Resource Mobilization, Social Control, and Tactics* (pp. 126–55). Cambridge, MA: Winthrop Publishers.

Tilly, Charles, Louise Tilly, and Richard Tilly. (1975). *The Rebellious Century, 1830–1930.* Cambridge, MA: Harvard University Press.

Turner, Bryan S. (1986). *Citizenship and Capitalism: The Debate over Reformism.* London, UK: Allen and Unwin.

"Union Membership in Canada—2000." (2000). *Workplace Gazette: An Industrial Relations Quarterly, 3* (3) 68–75.

Weber, Max. (1946 [1922]). "Class, Status, Party." In H. H. Gerth and C. Wright Mills, eds. and trans., *From Max Weber: Essays in Sociology* (pp. 180–95). New York: Oxford University Press.

Weber, Max. (1947). *The Theory of Social and Economic Organization.* T. Parsons, ed. Trans. A.M. Henderson and T. Parsons. New York: Free Press.

Westen, Tracy. (1998). "Can Technology Save Democracy?" *National Civic Review, 87,* 47–56.

Wolf, Eric. (1999 [1969]). *Peasant Wars of the 20th Century.* Norman, OK: Oklahoma University Press.

"Women—Party Standings in the House of Commons: Current List." (2005). On the World Wide Web at http://www.parl.gc.ca/information/about/people/house/StandingsHofCwm.asp?lang=E (31 October 2005).

Workplace Information Directorate. (1996). *Special Tabulation of Strikes Statistics for 1986–95.* Ottawa: Human Resources Development Canada.

Worth, Robert. (2001). "The Deep Intellectual Roots of Islamic Terror." *The New York Times on the Web.* On the World Wide Web at http://www.nytimes.com (13 October 2002).

CHAPTER 19

Adbusters. (2005). "Adbusters Homepage." On the World Wide Web at http://www.adbusters.org/home/ (20 March 2005).

African Centre for Biosafety (ACB). (2005). "Organizational Website." On the World Wide Web at http://www.biosafetyafrica.net/index.htm (7 March 2005).

Agence France-Presse. (2004). "Chirac Lashes Out Against US Cultural Domination." *Khaleej Times Online.* On the World Wide Web at http://www.khaleejtimes.com/DisplayArticle.asp?xfile=data/theworld/2004/October/theworld_October196.xmlandsection=theworld (7 October 2004).

Ainger, Katherine. (2003). "The New Peasant's Revolt." *New Internationalist Magazine, 353* (January–February). On the World Wide Web at http://www.newint.org/issue353/keynote.htm (17 March 2005).

Anderson, Sarah, John Cavanagh with Thea Lee and the Institute for Policy Studies. (2005). *Field Guide to the Global Economy.* New York: The New Press.

Babson, Steve. (2000). "Cross-Boarder Trade with Mexico and the Prospect for Worker Solidarity: The Case of Mexico." *Critical Sociology, 26* (1/2), 13–35.

Bacon, David. (2003). "Anti-China Campaign Hides Maquiladora Wage Cut." ZNET. On the World Wide Web at http://www.globalpolicy.org/socecon/inequal/labor/2003/0203maq.htm (3 February 2003).

Bales, Kevin. (1999). *Disposable People: New Slavery in the Global Economy.* Los Angeles, California: University of California Press.

Barlow, Maude. (2001). "The Global Monoculture: 'Free Trade' Versus Culture and Democracy." *Earth Island Journal.* 16, 3. On the World Wide Web at http://www.earthisland.org/eijournal/new_articles.cfm?articleID=270&journalID=48 (22 November 2006).

Basok, Tanya. (2002). *Tortillas and Tomatoes: Transmigrant Mexican Harvesters in Canada.* Montreal: McGill–Queen's University Press.

Beder, Sharon. (2000). *Selling the Work Ethic: From Puritan Pulpit to Corporate PR.* Carlton North, Victoria, Australia: Scribe Publications.

Bello, Walden. (2001). *The Future in the Balance. Essays on Globalization and Resistance.* Oakland, CA: Food First Books.

Bello, Walden. (2002). "Drop Till We Shop?" *The Nation Online.* On the World Wide Web at http://www.thenation.com/doc.mhtml?i=20021021andc=1ands=bello (3 October 2002).

Bentley, Stephen. (2004). "Fighting Global Warming at the Farmers' Market. The Role of Local Food Systems in Reducing Greenhouse Gas Emissions." *A FoodShare Research in Action Report.* On the World Wide Web at http://www.foodshare.net/resource/files/ACF230.pdf (9 January 2004).

Bird, Kate, and David Hughes. (1997). "Ethical Consumerism: The Case of 'Fairly-Trade' Coffee." *Business Ethics. A European Review, 6,* 159–67.

Bivens, Lyle J., and Adam Hersh. (2003). "A Rough Row." *Global Policy Forum.* On the World Wide Web at http://www.globalpolicy.org/socecon/bwi-wto/wto/2003/0909rough.htm (9 September 2003).

Brown, Lester. (2005). *Outgrowing the Earth. The Food Security Challenge in an Age of Falling Water Tables and Rising Temperatures.* Washington, DC: Earth Policy Institute.

Brownell, Kelly, and Katherine Battle Horgen. (2004). *Food Fight. The Insight Story of the Food Industry, America's Obesity Crisis, and What We Can Do About It.* Toronto: Contemporary Books.

Brym, Robert J., et al. (2005). "In Faint Praise of the World Bank's Gender Development Policy." *Canadian Journal of Sociology, 30,* 95–111.

Burtner, Bruno. (2004). "Tax Me If You Can." *Canadian Centre for Policy Alternatives Monitor.* On the World Wide Web at http://www.policyalternatives.ca/index.cfm?act=newsanddo=Articleandcall=954andpA=BB736455andtype=2,3,4,5,6,7 (1 October 2004).

Cardoso, Fernando Henrique. (1993). "The Challenges of Social Democracy in Latin America." In Menno Vellinga, ed., *Social Democracy in Latin America: Prospects for Change.* Boulder, CO: Westview Press.

Castells, Manuel. (1998). *The Information Age: Economy, Society and Culture: Vol. 3, End of the Millennium.* Malden, MA: Blackwell.

Catlin, Bill. (2001). "CEO Salaries under Fire as Stocks Dive." Minnesota Public Radio, March 28. On the World Wide Web at http://news.minnesota.publicradio.org/features/200103/28_catlinb_ceo/ (October 14, 2006).

CBC News. (2001). "McDonald's Apologies for Beefy Fries." On the World Wide Web at http://www.cbc.ca/stories/2001/05/24/Consumers/beefyfries_010524 (25 May 2001).

CBC News. (2002a). "PM says West seen as 'arrogant, greedy.'" On the World Wide Web at http://www.cbc.ca/stories/2002/09/11/chretienjumbo020911 (12 September 2002).

CBC News. (2002b). "Chrétien's Comments on Sept. 11, 2002." On the World Wide Web at http://www.cbc.ca/national/rex/rex20020913.html (13 September 2002).

CBC News. (2005). "Canadians Made Little Economic Headway in Last 15 Years: TD Economists." On the World Wide Web at http://www.cbc.ca/story/business/national/2005/01/18/tdeconomy-050118.html (18 January 2005).

CBC Radio One. (2004). "Paid to be Poor." On the World Wide Web at http://www.cbc.ca/paidtobepoor/index.html (28 March 2004).

Church of Stop Shopping. (n.d.). "Anti-Starbucks/Anti-Brand protest photo from Reverend Billy." *Retail Interventions and Actions: Starbucks Invasion Kit.* New York: Church of Stop Shopping.

Clay, Jason. (2004). *World Agriculture and the Environment: A Commodity-by-Commodity Guide to Impacts and Practices.* Washington, DC: Island Press.

Digital Divide Network. (2004). "Digital Divides Basics Fact Sheet." On the World Wide Web at http://www.digitaldivide.net (14 October 2004).

Durning, Alan. (1992). *How Much Is Enough? The Consumer Society and the Fate of the Earth.* New York: Norton.

Dussell Peters, Enrique. (2004). "Conditions and Evolution of Wages and Employment in Mexico." Occasional Paper published by *The Jus Semper Global Alliance.* On the World Wide Web at http://www.jussemper.org/Resources/Economic%20Data/mexicowagecondit.html (15 April 2004).

Ehrenreich, Barbara. (2001). *Nickel and Dimed. On (Not) Getting by in America.* New York: Henry Holt.

Ehrenreich, Barbara. (2005). *Bait and Switch. The (Futile) Pursuit of the American Dream.* New York: Henry Hold.

Ellwood, Wayne. (2001). *The No-Nonsense Guide to Globalization.* London: Zed Books.

Fairtrade Foundation. (2006). *The Arabica Coffee Market: 1989–2006: Comparison of Fiartrade and New York Exchange Prices.* London, UK: Fairtrade Foundation.

Ferguson, Niall. (2004). *Colossus. The Rise and Fall of the American Empire.* New York: Penguin Books.

Forbes. (2004). "About China's Richest." *Forbes.com.* On the World Wide Web at http://www.forbes.com/lists/2004/11/04/cx_pm_1004crlintro.html (4 November 2004).

Frank, Thomas. (1997). *The Conquest of Cool.* Chicago: University of Chicago Press.

Frundt, Henry. (2000). "Models of Cross-Border Organizing in the Maquila Industry." *Critical Sociology, 26* (1/2), 36–55.

Global Exchange. (2004). "Global Exchange and USFT Respond To Starbucks' Fair Trade Announcement." Press Release. On the World Wide Web at http://www.globalexchange.org/campaigns/fairtrade/coffee/1795.html (29 April 2004).

Global Policy Forum. (n.d.). "U.S. Military Expansion and Intervention." *Empire.* New York: Author. On the World Wide Web at http://www.globalpolicy.org/empire/intervention/ (14 October 2006).

Hall, Sally. (2005). "Hungry for an Alternative." *The Independent* (UK) 28 June.

Harvey, David. (1990). *The Condition of Postmodernity.* Cambridge, MA: Blackwell.

Hays, Constance. (2000). "Learning to Think Smaller at Coke." *New York Times* 6 February: business section.

Heath, Andrew, and Joseph Potter. (2004). *The Rebel Sell: Why the Culture Can't Be Jammed.* Toronto: Harper Collins.

Hoogvelt, Ankie. (1997). *Globalization and the Postcolonial World.* Baltimore, ML: Johns Hopkins University Press.

Hopkins, Terrence, and Immanuel Wallerstein. (1986). "Commodity Chains in the World Economy Prior to 1800." *Review, The Journal of the Fernand Braudel Center, 10* (1), 157–70.

Howlett, Karen. (2005). "Ontario Eyes Brightest Immigrants." *The Globe and Mail* 11 October: A7.

International Forum on Globalization (IFG). (2001). *Does Globalization Help the Poor? A Special Report by The International Forum on Globalization.* San Francisco: IFG.

International Networks Archive. (n.d.). Princeton University. On the World Wide Web at http://www.globalpolicy.org/globaliz/charts/movietable.htm (October 14, 2006).

Jackson, Andrew. (2005). *The Case Against More Corporate Tax Cuts.* Ottawa: Canadian Institute for Policy Alternatives.

Jordan, Mary. (2003). "Workers Falling Behind in Mexico." *Washington Post* 15 July. On the World Wide Web (Global Policy Forum) at http://www.globalpolicy.org/globaliz/special/2003/0716mexico.htm (15 July 2003).

Karliner, Josh, and Ted Lewis. (2002). "World Social Forum Conference on Transnational Corporations," Paper introduced before the Second World Social Forum in Porto Alegre, Brazil, February. On the World Wide Web at http://corpwatch.org/article.php?id51728 (21 July 2005).

Kennedy, Dawn. (2004). "Nollywood Thinks Outside the Box." *Sunday Independent*. On the World Wide Web at http://www.sundayindependent.co.za/index.php?fSectionId=1083andfArticleId=2324573 (28 November 2004).

Kindall, Henry, and David Pimentel. (1994). "Constraints on the Expansion of the Global Food Supply," *Ambio*, 23, 3.

Klein, Naomi. (2000). *No Logo*. Toronto: Knopf Canada.

Kroll, Luisa, and Lea Goldman. (2004). "The World's Richest People." Forbes.com. On the World Wide Web at http://www.forbes.com/2004/02/25/bill04land.html (14 October 2006).

Lang, Tim, and Jules Pretty. (2005). "Farm Costs and Food Miles: An Assessment of the Full Cost of the UK Weekly Food Basket." *Food Policy*, 30 (1).

Lappé, Anna, and Frances Moore Lappé. (2002). *Hope's Edge: The Next Diet for a Small Planet*. New York: Tarcher/Penguin.

Lappé, Frances Moore. (2005). "Diet for a Smaller Planet: Real Sources of Abundance." In Andrew Heintzman and Evan Solomon, eds., *Feeding The Future* (125–54). Toronto: Anansi Press.

Lindstrom, Martin. (2003). *Brandchild. Remarkable Insights into the Minds of Today's Global Kids and Their Relationships with Brands*. Sterling, VA: Millward Brown.

Lynn, Barry. (2002). "Unmade in America. The True Cost of the Global Assembly Line." *Harper's Magazine*, 304 (1825), 34–41.

MacLachlan, Ian. (2004). "Betting the Farm: Food Safety, Risk Society, and the Canadian Cattle and Beef Commodity Chain," In Andrew Heintzman and Evan Solomon, eds., *Feeding The Future—From Fat to Famine: How to Solve the World's Food Crises* (pp. 40–69). Toronto: Anansi Press.

Manning, Richard. (2004). "The Oil We Eat: Following the Food Chain Back To Iraq." *Harper's Magazine* February. On the World Wide Web at http://www.harpers.org/TheOilWeEat.html (15 October 2006).

Marx, Karl, and Friedrich Engels. (1972 [1848])."Manifesto of the Communist Party." In R. Tucker, ed. *The Marx-Engels Reader* (pp. 331–62). New York: W.W. Norton.

Mbeki, Thabo. (1996). "Executive Deputy President Address to the Information Society and Development Conference." Brussels, 24 February.

McDonald's. (1999). Media.McDonald's.com. On the World Wide Web at http://www.media.mcdonalds.com/secured/research/international_news.html (30 April 2004).

McFarland, Janet. (2005). "CEOs Rake It In." *The Globe and Mail* 30 April.

McKibben, Bill. (1993). *The Age of Missing Information*. New York: Plumb.

McKibben, Bill. (2005). "The Cuba Diet. What Will You Be Eating When the Revolution Comes?" *Harper's Magazine* April. On the World Wide Web at http://www.harpers.org/TheCubaDiet.html (15 October 2006).

Media Awareness Network. (2002). On the World Wide Web at http://www.media-awareness.ca/english/resources/articles/sovereignty_identity/culture_heritage.cfm (14 October 2006).

Milanovic, Branko. (2005). *Worlds Apart: Measuring International and Global Inequality*. Princeton, NJ: Princeton University Press.

Milkman, Ruth. (2000). "Immigrant Organizing and the New Labor Movement in Los Angeles." *Critical Sociology*, 26 (1/2), 59–81.

Miniwatts Marketing Group. (2005). "Internet Usage Statistics: The Big Picture." On the World Wide Web at http://www.internetworldstats.com (14 October 2006).

Navdanya. (2005). "Navdanya Homepage." On the World Wide Web at http://www.navdanya.org/ (1 October 2006).

Nissen, Bruce. (2000). "Editor's Introduction: The Labor Movement in a New, Globalized Environment." *Critical Sociology*, 26 (1/2), 3–8.

No Sweat. (2005). "Changing an Industry." Company Website. On the World Wide Web at http://www.nosweatapparel.com/ (1 October 2006).

Organic Consumers Association. (OCA). "Prohibited Gene-Altered Corn Found in Latin American and Caribbean Food Aid Shipments. Source: Environmental News Service." On the World Wide Web at http://www.organicconsumers.org/ge/caribbean21705.cfm (16 February 2005).

Oxfam. (2002). "Mugged: Poverty in your Coffee Cup." Research Paper. On the World Wide Web at http://www.oxfamamerica.org/newsandpublications/publications/research_reports/mugged (7 September 2002).

Pickard, Miguel. (2005). "In the Crossfire: MesoAmerican Migrants Journey North." *IRC Americas*. On the World Wide Web at http://www.yorku.ca/hdrnet/images/uploaded/0503migrants.pdf (18 March 2005).

Picot, Garnett, and John Myles. (2005). "Income Inequality and Low Income in Canada: An International Perspective." Statistics Canada Research Paper. On the World Wide Web at http://www.statcan.ca/english/research/11F0019MIE/11F0019MIE2005240.pdf (10 February 2005).

Pimentel, David, and Anne Wilson. (2004). "World Population, Agriculture, and Nutrition," *World Watch Magazine*: Sept/October. On the World Wide Web (Energy Bulletin Website) at http://www.energybulletin.net/3834.html (5 January 2005).

Rekacewicz, Philippe. (1997). "Overview of the State of Soil Degradation in the World." *Atlas of Desertification in the World*, 2nd ed. London, UK: Arnold Publishers. On the World Wide Web at http://www.povertymap.net/mapsgraphics/index.cfm?data_id=23360andtheme= (14 October 2006).

Robbins, Richard H. (2005). *Global Problems and the Culture of Capitalism*, 3rd ed. Boston: Pearson.

Ross, Andrew. (2004). *Low Pay, High Profile. The Global Push for Fair Labor*. New York: The New Press.

Ross, Andrew, ed. (1997). *No Sweat. Fashion, Free Trade, and the Rights of Garment Workers*. New York: Verso.

Sachs, Jeffrey. (2005). *The End of Poverty: Economic Possibilities for Our Time*. New York, NY: Penguin Press.

Schlosser, Eric. (2001). *Fast Food Nation. The Dark Side of the All-American Meal*. Boston: Houghton Mifflin.

Schor, J.B. (1998). *The Overspent American*. USA: Basic Books.

Sheak, Bob, and Melissa Morris. (2002). "The Limits of the Job Supply in U.S. Capitalism: Subemployment Measures and Trends." *Critical Sociology*, 28 (3), 389–415.

Shipler, David. (2004). *The Working Poor*. New York: Alfred A. Knopf.

Shrybman, Steven. (2000). *Trade, Agriculture, and Climate Change: How Agricultural Trade Policies Fuel Climate Change*. Institute for Agriculture and Trade Policy. On the World Wide Web at http://www.iatp.org (3 November 2000).

Soros, George. (1998). *The Crisis of Global Capitalism. Open Society Endangered.* New York: Perseus Books.

Speidel, Joseph. (2003). "Environment and Health. Population, Consumption, and Human Health." In *Global Environmental Challenges of the 21st Century. Resources, Consumption, and Sustainable Solutions* (pp. 1–13). New York: Scholarly Resources Inc.

Starr, Amory. (1999). *Naming the Enemy: Anti-Corporate Movements Confront Globalization.* London: Zed Books.

Stewart-Patterson, David. (1999). "The Cheap Way to Compete for Jobs." *Fiscal and Tax Policy.* Ottawa: Canadian Council of Chief Executives. On the World Wide Web at http://www.ceocouncil.ca/en/view/?document_id=133andtype_id=6 (14 October 2006).

Stiglitz, Joseph. (2003). *Globalization and its Discontents.* New York: W.W. Norton and Company.

Strange, Susan. (1986). *Casino Capitalism.* London: Blackwell Books.

Sustain/Elm Farm Research Centre Report. (2001). "Eating Oil. Food in a Changing Climate." On the World Wide Web at http://www.sustainweb.org/pdf/eatoil_sumary.pdf (15 December 2001).

Tomlinson, John. (1991). *Cultural Imperialism: A Critical Introduction.* Baltimore: John Hopkins University Press.

United Nations. (2001). *United Nations Human Development Report 2001.* New York: UNDP.

United Nations Development Programme, United Nations Environment Programme, World Bank, World Resources Institute. (2003). "World Resources 2002–2004: Decisions for the Earth: Balance, Voice, and Power." On the World Wide Web at http://governance.wri.org/pubs_content_text.cfm?ContentID=1763 (14 October 2006).

Wall, Melissa. (2000). "KFC into India: A Case Study of Resistance to Globalization Discourse." In Robin Andersen and Lance Strate, eds., *Critical Studies in Media Commercialism* (pp. 291–309). Oxford: Oxford University Press.

Wallerstein, Immanuel. (2002). "The Eagle Has Crash Landed." *Foreign Policy* 131:July/August, 60–68.

Waters, Malcolm. (1995). *Globalisation.* New York: Routledge.

Wheeler, David, and Jane Thompson. (2004). "The Brand Barons and the Business of Food," In A. Heintzman and E. Solomon, eds., *Feeding the Future* (pp. 191–236). Toronto, Canada: Anansi Press.

Woodroffe, Jessica, and Mark Ellis-Jones. (2000). "States of Unrest: Resistance to IMF Policies in Poor Countries," *World Development Movement Report.* On the World Wide Web (Global Policy Forum) at http://www.globalpolicy.org/socecon/bwi-wto/imf/2000/protest.htm (8 September 2000).

World Wildlife Fund (WWF). (2004). "Soy Boom: Doom or Boon for South America's Forests and Savannah." On the World Wide Web at http://www.wwf.org.uk/news/scotland/n_0000001332.asp (2 September 2004).

Yunker, John. (2005). "Going Global: Hooters Goes Global." *Corante* 27 February. On the World Wide Web at http://goingglobal.corante.com/archives/2005/02/27/hooters_goes_global.php (14 October 2006).

CHAPTER 20

Aruni, Janice. (2004). "Educational Entrepreneurialism in the Private Tutoring Industry: Balancing Profitability with the Humanistic Face of Schooling." *Canadian Review of Anthropology and Sociology, 41* (4), 475–91.

Brym, R. (1986). "Incorporation versus Power Models of Working Class Radicalism with Special Reference to North America." *Canadian Journal of Sociology, 11,* 227–51.

Brym, R., and Lenton, R. (2001). *Love Online: A Report on Digital Dating in Canada.* Toronto: MSN.CA

Creese, G. (1988). "The Politics of Dependence: Women, Work, and Unemployment in the Vancouver Labour Movement before World War II." *Canadian Journal of Sociology, 13,* 121–42.

Creese, G. (1999). *Contracting Masculinity: Gender, Class and Race in a White-Collar Union, 1944–1994.* Toronto: Oxford University Press.

Cresswell, J.W. (1998). *Qualitative Inquiry and Research Design: Choosing among Five Traditions.* Thousand Oaks, CA: Sage Publications.

Davies, Scott. (2002). "The Paradox of Progressive Education: A Frame Analysis." *Sociology of Education, 75* (4), 269–86.

Davies, Scott, and Neil Guppy. (2006). *The Schooled Society: An Introduction to the Sociology of Education.* Toronto: Oxford University Press.

Douglas, J. (1970). "Understanding Everyday Life." In J. Douglas, ed., *Understanding Everyday Life* (pp. 3–44). Chicago: Aldine.

Fisher, R.A. (1966 [1936]). "Has Mendel's Work Been Rediscovered?" In C. Stern and E. Sherwood, eds., *Origin of Genetics; A Mendel Sourcebook* (pp. 139–72). San Francisco: W.H. Freeman.

Fortin, N. and M. Huberman. (2002). "Occupational Gender Segregation and Women's Wages in Canada: An Historical Perspective." *Canadian Public Policy, 28* (s1), 11–39.

Foschi, M. and S. Buchan. (1990). "Ethnicity, Gender, and Perceptions of Task Competence." *Canadian Journal of Sociology, 15,* 1–18.

Foschi, M., L. Lai, and K. Sigerson. (1994). "Gender and Double Standards in the Assessment of Job Applicants." *Social Psychological Quarterly, 57* (4), 326–39.

Giddens, A. (1984). *The Constitution of Society.* Berkeley, CA: University of California Press.

Ginsberg, E., and Henry, F. (1985). *Who Gets the Work?* Toronto: Urban Alliance on Race Relations and the Social Planning Council of Toronto.

Goffman, E. (1961). *Asylums: Essays on the Social Situations of Mental Patients and Other Inmates.* New York: Doubleday/Anchor.

Gold, A.D. (1998). "President's Report." *Criminal Lawyers Newsletter, 19* (2). On the World Wide Web at http://www.criminallawyers.ca/newslett/19-2/gold.html (3 November 2000).

Gray, G., and N. Guppy. (2003). *Successful Surveys.* Toronto: Nelson.

Guppy, N., and S. Davies. (1998). *Education in Canada.* Ottawa: Statistics Canada.

Haggerty, K.D. (2001). *Making Crime Count.* Toronto: University of Toronto Press.

Haggerty, K.D. (2004). "Ethics Creep: Governing Social Science Research in the Name of Ethics." *Qualitative Sociology, 24* (4), 391–414.

Henry, F. (1999). *The Colour of Democracy: Racism in Canadian Society.* Toronto: Harcourt Brace.

Hooper, J. (2002). *Of Moths and Men: An Evolutionary Tale.* New York: Norton.

Houtkoop, H. (2000). *Interaction and the Standardized Survey Interview: The Living Questionnaire.* Cambridge, MA: Cambridge University Press.

Kaufman, F.C.M., Q.C. (1998). *Report of the Kaufman Commission on Proceedings Involving Guy Paul Morin* (Morin Inquiry Executive Summary Report) (Conclusion 1). On the World Wide Web at http://www.attorneygeneral.jus.gov.on.ca/html/MORIN/exesumrec/morin_concl.pdf (17 July 2000).

Kleppner, D., and Jackiw, R. (2000, August). "One Hundred Years of Quantum Physics." *Science, 289,* 893–98. On the World Wide Web at http://vega.bac.pku.edu.cn/~rxxu/teach/qp100.htm (21 September 2000).

Kuhn, T.S. (1962). *The Structure of Scientific Revolutions.* Chicago: University of Chicago Press.

Laxer, G. (1989). *Open for Business: The Roots of Foreign Ownership in Canada.* Toronto: Oxford University Press.

Lenton, R. (1990). "Techniques of Child Discipline and Abuse by Parents." *Canadian Review of Sociology and Anthropology, 27,* 157–85.

Mawani, Renisa. (2003). "Imperial Legacies (Post)Colonial Identities: Law, Space, and the Making of Stanley Park, 1859–2001." *Law/Text/Culture, 7,* 98–141.

McMullan, J., and P. Swan. (1989). "Social Economy and Arson in Nova Scotia." *Canadian Journal of Criminology,* 281–308.

Orel, Vitezslav. (1996). *Gregor Mendel: The First Geneticist.* Trans. Stephen Finn. Oxford, UK: Oxford University Press.

Park, R. (2000). *Voodoo Science: The Road from Foolishness to Fraud.* New York: Oxford University Press.

Pineo, P., and J. Porter. (1967). "Occupational Prestige in Canada." *Canadian Review of Anthropology and Sociology, 4,* 24–40.

Popper, Karl. (1977 [1934]). *The Logic of Scientific Discovery,* 14th ed. New York: Harper.

Reitz, J. (1993). "Statistics on Racial Discrimination in Canada." *Policy Options, 14,* 32–36.

Roethlisberger, F.J., and D.W. Dickson. (1939). *Management and the Worker.* Cambridge, MA: Harvard University Press.

Scarce, R. (2000). *Fishy Business: Salmon, Biology, and the Social Construction of Nature.* Philadelphia: Temple University Press.

Schreiber, D., R. Matthews, and B. Elliott (2003). "The Framing of Farmed Fish: Product, Efficiency, and Technology" *Canadian Journal of Sociology, 28* (2), 153–69.

Statistics Canada. (2004). *General Social Survey on Social Engagement, Cycle 17: An Overview of Findings.* Catalogue No. 89-598-XIE. Ottawa: Statistics Canada. On the World Wide Web at http://www.statcan.ca/bsolc/english/bsolc?catno=89-598-XIE (14 October 2006).

Tanner, J. (2001). *Teenage Troubles: Youth and Deviance in Canada,* 2nd ed. Toronto: Nelson Thomson Learning.

Urmetzer, P., D. Blake, and N. Guppy. (1999). "Individualized Solutions to Environmental Problems: The Case of Automobile Pollution." *Canadian Public Policy, 25* (3), 345–59.

Weber, M. (1949 [1904]). *The Methodology of the Social Sciences.* Glencoe, IL: Free Press.

Wilson, B. (2002). "The Canadian Rave Scene and Five Theses on Youth Resistance." *Canadian Journal of Sociology, 27,* 373–412.

NAME INDEX

Page numbers beginning with W refer to Online Chapter 21, Networks, Groups, Bureaucracies, and Societies.

SUBJECT INDEX